THE HISTORY OF MODERN WHALING

J. N. TØNNESSEN
A. O. JOHNSEN

THE HISTORY OF
MODERN
WHALING

TRANSLATED FROM THE NORWEGIAN BY
R. I. CHRISTOPHERSEN

UNIVERSITY OF CALIFORNIA PRESS
BERKELEY AND LOS ANGELES

University of California Press
Berkeley and Los Angeles
ISBN 0-520-03973-4
Library of Congress Catalog Card No. 79-64657

The present edition is a much shortened version of a work
originally published in Norwegian under the title
Den Moderne Hvalfangsts Historie: Opprinnelse og Utvikling,
as follows:
Vol. 1 (by Arne Odd Johnsen), Oslo: H. Aschehoug & Co.
(W. Nygaard), 1959;
Vols. 2, 3 and 4 (by Joh. N. Tønnessen), Sandefjord,
Norway: Norges Hvalfangstforbund, 1967, 1969 and 1970.

Printed in the United Kingdom

CONTENTS

PREFACE TO THE ENGLISH EDITION   xvii

PREFACE TO THE NORWEGIAN EDITION   xvii

I. WHALING OFF THE COAST OF FINNMARK

1. What is Modern Whaling?	3
2. The Emergence of Modern Whaling	16
Endeavours outside Norway	16
Svend Foyn's Norwegian predecessors	23
Svend Foyn and Finnmark whaling 1864-1873	25
Catching monopoly, 1873-1882	32
Species of whales caught before 1883	36
3. The Whaling Industry	37
The whale catcher	37
The shore station	39
Floating factories	41
Whalers and their working life	42
Companies, profits and financial importance	47
Products, markets and prices	50
4. Finnmark Whaling during the Period of Free Competition, 1883-1904	55
5. The Dispute over Whale Conservation in North Norway	61
6. The Importance of Finnmark Whaling	68

II. GLOBAL WHALING

7. The North Atlantic	75
Iceland	75
The Faroes	83
The Shetlands	88
The Hebrides and Ireland	93
Spitsbergen	95
Newfoundland	107
8. The Pacific	111
Northwest coast of North America	111
East Asia	128
9. Towards the South, 1892-1904	147

10. The Start of Antarctic Whaling, 1904-1908   157
   C. A. Larsen and the Compañia Argentina de Pesca S.A.   157
   The first Norwegian companies in the Antarctic   171
   Great Britain, whaling and sovereignty in the Antarctic   178
   Further developments in the Antartic, 1908-1914   182

11. South America and Mexico   202

12. The African Interlude   208

13. Australia and New Zealand, 1911-1916, 1922-1928   220

14. The Basis for the Expansion of 1906-1914   227

15. Technical Developments before 1930   250
   Boiling equipment   250
   The floating factory   263
   Whale catchers   269

16. Whaling Life in the Antarctic   277

17. Whaling during the First World War   292

18. Crisis and Reconstruction, 1920-1923   306

III. PELAGIC WHALING

19. The First Attempts in New and Old Grounds   313
   Africa   315
   Spain and Portugal   321
   The North Atlantic   324
   The Pacific   326

20. Unlicensed Whaling, 1923-1931   329
   Introduction   329
   Britain and the renewal of licences   338
   Pelagic whaling, concessions and licences   346
   —Licensed pelagic whaling   346
   —Non-licensed pelagic whaling; the Lancing *and the slipway* 353
   —Licensed and non-licensed ice-catching   356
   —"Licensees" and "pelagics": the Norwegian whaling act of
      1929   360

21. The Expansion of 1927-1931   367

22. The World Crisis and the Whaling Industry, 1930-1934   386
   The 1931-2 season and the laid-up whaling fleet   386
   The German fat plan and the war on margarine   394
   The British-Norwegian quota agreements, 1932-1934   399

The quota conflict, 1934-1936   407
Germany and the Norwegian sale of whale oil, 1934   410

23. New Nations embarking on Pelagic Whaling   414
    The Soviet Union   414
    Japan   415
    Germany   422

24. The Dispute over Whaling Regulations   433
    The 1935-6 production agreement   433
    Labour unions and whaling, 1935-6   435
    The British-Norwegian conflict, 1936   436
    Norway and Germany in 1936   442

25. The London Agreement of 1937   448

26. Years of Renewed Crisis, 1937-1939   457

27. Whaling during the Second World War   472
    The Whaling Committee   486

28. Rebuilding the Whaling Fleets, 1945-1949   499
    *The Washington Conference of 1946 and the International
       Commission on Whaling (I.W.C.), 1949*   499
    Joint operation of the Norwegian companies, 1945-1948 512
    Rebuilding the whaling fleets of other nations   514

29. The Second Expansion, 1946-1952   521
    The Norwegian crew law   521
    The Netherlands   523
    Great Britain   525
    The fats market   526
    Japan   529
    Germany   532
    Onassis and the Olympic Challenger   534
    Argentina   538
    Other countries' plans   540

30. The International Whaling Commission in the 1950s   545
    Shore-based and pelagic whaling   545
    "A whaling pirate"   552
    *The pelagic whaling nations and the International
       Whaling Commission*   560
    Quota and catching matériel   566

31. The Last Expansion, 1955-1961   573

32. The Dispute over National Quotas, 1958-1962   585

33. The Collapse, 1962-1968   609

34. Antarctic Epilogue   638

35. Whaling outside the Antarctic after 1945   644
     The North Atlantic   644
     North Pacific, East   649
     South Pacific, East   651
     The east coast of South America   653
     Africa   653
     East Asia, North Pacific and Bering Sea   658

36. The Whaling Industry, the Environment and Natural
     Resources, 1972-1978   673

37. Technical Developments after 1930   687

STATISTICAL APPENDIX   731

BIBLIOGRAPHY   756

A FINAL NOTE   774

INDEX   777

PLATES

1. The species of whale of the greatest economic importance to modern whaling   4
2. Comparative table indicating the weight of a big blue whale   5
3. The shrimp, *Euphausia superba*   7
4. Old whaling: outboard flensing in an American sperm whale catcher   8
5. Modern whaling: floating factory with stern slip and aeroplane   10
6. Old whaling: melting blubber in open pan on the deck   11
7. Modern whaling: oil reduction plant in a modern floating factory   12
8. Old whaling: the fo'c'sle of an old whaling ship   13
9. Modern whaling: the crew's mess in a modern floating factory   14
10. The Norwegian town of Tønsberg, 1868   26
11. Svend Foyn   27
12. The whale-gun used by Svend Foyn, 1865   29
13. The small town of Vadsø in North Norway   32
14. Model of *Spes et Fides*   38
15. The shell-harpoon for which Svend Foyn was granted a patent in 1873   44
16. Typical Norwegian shore station on the coast of Finnmark   59
17. Whaling station in the Faroes   87
18. The Norwegian shipowner Christen Christensen   97
19. A group of workers at the whaling station Aquaforte, Newfoundland, 1905   107
20. The whale catcher, *St. Lawrence*   116
21. The *Admiralen* in Seattle, 1912   121
22. Count H. H. Kejzerling   133
23. The *Michail,* the first steam floating factory in modern whaling   134
24. The whaling station at Urusan, Korea   143
25. The *Jason* in Sandefjord, 1893   151
26. C. A. Larsen   152
27. The crew of the *Jason* before leaving Sandefjord, 1892   154
28. The first map of Cumberland Bay, 1905   164

29. The *Fortuna,* the first whale catcher in South Georgia   169
30. Reindeer grazing on tussock-grass in South Georgia   170
31. Grytviken, 1909   171
32. Prince Olav Harbour   177
33. Leith Harbour   179
34. The Norwegian whaling station, Stromness Harbour   184
35. Grytviken, 1913   185
36. Theodore E. Salvesen   188
37. Harold K. Salvesen   188
38. The bay at Deception Island   196
39. The whaling station at Kerguelen   201
40. Lars Christensen   206
41. One of the biggest lumps of ambergris ever found in a
     sperm whale   223
42. Leith Harbour in "the period of barrels", and Stromness
     Harbour with the earliest oil tanks   234
43. William Hesketh Lever, Viscount Leverhulme   239
44. Sigurd Risting   247
45. A whale grossly inflated by autolysis   253
46. Diagram of the open cooker   254
47. Diagram of pressure cooker   256
48. August Sommermeyer's first rough draft of the rotary
     cooker   257
49. Horizontal guano dryer   261
50. Steam driven bone saw   262
51. Sørlle's two patents for the stern slip   266
52. Old type whale catcher with elliptical stern   271
53. Modern type whale catcher with cruiser stern and
     detached rudder   271
54. Modern whale catcher with gunner's bridge   273
55. Old whale gun, muzzle loader without recoil brake   274
56. Modern whale gun, breech loader with glycerine recoil
     brake   275
57. The church at Grytviken   287
58. Parade before the games at Grytviken, 1928   290
59. Burial in Grytviken churchyard, 1926   291
60. The floating factory *Horatio* ablaze in Leith Harbour   298
61. Whalers' homecoming at Sandefjord   302

62. The Whaling Museum in Sandefjord — 307
63. The gun is loaded — 331
64. When chased the whale blows violently — 331
65. The shot — 334
66. *"Fast fisk"* : the whale is hit and is blowing blood — 334
67. The whale is inflated to keep it floating — 335
68. The whale "in flag" — 335
69. Outboard flensing in calm weather — 336
70. The cooker is filled with blubber — 336
71. The meat plant — 337
72. C. A. Larsen on his death bed — 350
73. The *Sir James Clark Ross* in Discovery Inlet — 352
74. The *Lancing,* the first floating factory with a stern slip, 1925 — 355
75. The whale claw — 356
76. Grytviken in the summer, 1925 — 369
77. The White Star liner *Suevic* converted into the floating factory *Skytteren* — 374
78. Anders Jahre, acting manager of Kosmos Co. — 376
79. The *Kosmos,* the first new (not converted) floating factory — 378
80. Grytviken in the 1930s — 388
81. The whaling fleet laid up in Sandefjord, 1931-2 — 390
82. The first Russian floating factory *Aleut* — 415
83. Tosataro Yamaji, Tokusuke Shino, Tatsusaburo Shibuya — 417
84. The *Nisshin Maru,* the first floating factory built in Japan, 1936 — 420
85. The *Walter Rau,* the first floating factory built in Germany, 1937 — 429
86. Scrimshaw on sperm whale teeth — 436
87. Remington Kellogg, Johan T. Ruud, N. A. Mackintosh — 449
88. Antarctic whaling : a catcher in heavy seas — 454-5
89. Francis D'Arcy Cooper, Hjalmar Schacht — 458
90. Margarine : Estimated *per capita* consumption, 1900-38 — 466
91. Chr. Salvesen & Co.'s first post-war floating factory, the *Southern Venturer* — 497
92. The opening of the International Whaling Conference in Washington D.C., 1945 — 500
93. Three stages of the development of the floating factory — 504

94.   A whale carcass half-devoured by killer whales before it
      was brought to the flensing plant   507

95.   Prince Philip visiting Grytviken, 12 January 1957   519

96.   The *Willem Barendsz II,* the new Dutch floating factory,
      built in the Netherlands, 1955   522

97.   The *Olympic Challenger,* Aristotle Onassis's "pirate"
      floating factory   535

98.   Whale catcher at full speed chasing two humpbacks   548

99.   Fifty years of technical developments of whale catchers—
      the *Ørnen* and the *Besstrashnij*   552-3

100. The Russian floating factory *Sovetskaya Ukraina*   583

101. A modern whale catcher—Norway's last effort to
      modernise her whaling fleet   596

102. An 86-foot blue whale on the slip of the whaling station
      in Iceland   607

103. The oil-boring platform *Drillship*   629

104. Union Whaling Co.'s whaling station, Oceanside   655

105. The Japanese partition of the whale for human con-
      sumption   663

106. The first (and only?) Chinese-built whale catcher
      Yanlung   664

107. The shell-harpoon with pointed and flat head   691

108. A dead whale with radio transmitter, colours, and radar
      screen   697

109. Gluewater separators   710

110. The beach of Deception covered with thousands of
      whale carcasses   718

111. The American base at MacMurdo, Ross Sea   725

112. The whaling monument in Sandefjord   728

MAPS

The shore stations in East Finnmark, 1884   56

The whaling stations in Iceland and the years they were operated   79

The whaling stations in Labrador, Newfoundland and Nova Scotia   103

The whaling stations in South Georgia   173

The Falkland Islands and Dependencies   341

Distribution and migration of the humpback whale in the southern hemisphere   474

The Antarctic oceans south of 40°S divided into Areas   562

TABLES

1.	Rorquals caught by modern methods, 1865-72	20
2.	Whalers' monthly wages and bonus, 1901	46
3a.	Catches by species of whale, 1885 and 1886	57
3b.	Catches by species of whale, 1891-6	58
4.	Total catch and whale oil production in Iceland, 1883-1915, and North Norway, 1868-1904	83
5.	Whales caught from the Scottish stations, 1908-14	95
6.	Catch, oil production and barrels of oil per whale in all the grounds of the Norwegian Sea, 1868-1912	101
7.	Catches of fin, sei and Bryde whales in the North Pacific, 1965-75	127
8.	Catch in the Antarctic and northern seas, 1904-10	176
9.	Whales and barrels of oil per catcher in the Antarctic and northern seas, 1905-10	176
10.	Catch matériel, whales and oil production in the North and in the South, 1907-8	185
11.	South Orkney catch, 1911-15	197
12.	Catch and production at Leith Harbour, Husvik Harbour and Grytviken 1912-13	199
13.	World oil production, 1900-14	228
14.	Companies, whaling fleets, catches, production per catcher, 1900-14	241
15.	Profits of four whaling companies in the Antarctic, 1910-15	243
16.	World catch, 1913-24	293
17.	Catch of the most important whaling nations, 1912-24	293
18.	Oil production and catch value of the Norwegian whaling fleet, 1914, 1918 and 1922	305
19.	The Antarctic share of world catching, 1914-38	313
20.	Whales caught from South Africa, 1925-9, by species	317
21.	World catch and pelagic Antarctic catch, 1926-39	330
22.	Catch, production, matériel, whaling days for pelagic Antarctic whaling, 1927-39	333
23.	The Norwegian whaling fleet and its catch 1912-13 and 1917-18	343
24.	Total Antarctic and pelagic Antarctic catch, 1925-9	346

25. Catch in the Ross Sea, 1923-30   353
26. Net profit for some companies per barrel of oil, 1926-7
    and 1927-8   372
27. The expansion of the pelagic Antarctic operations,
    1927-31   385
28. Distribution of matériel and catches by nations, 1930-1   387
29. The Antarctic pelagic whaling fleets and their catch,
    1947-63   488
30. Antarctic seasons with the largest catch, by species,
    1948-65   488
31. Weekly production of whale oil per BWU in the 1953-4
    season   569
32. Total Antarctic oil production and average production
    per floating factory and per catcher, 1952-63   573
33. National quotas, 1962   591
34. Quotas and catch of the pelagic nations, 1961-2 and
    1962-3   611
35. The catch from South Africa, 1946-57   656
36. Antarctic quotas and catch, 1972-3   679
37. World catch 1972-3 and quotas 1977-8   684
38. Oil yield from the different parts of the whale carcass,
    1920-1   711
39. Catch and oil production in North Norway, 1868-1904   731
40. Catch and oil production in Iceland, 1883-1915   731
41. Catch and oil production in the Faroes, 1894-1920; the
    Shetlands, 1903-20; the Hebrides, 1904-20; Ireland,
    1908-20   732
42. Stations, whales and barrels of oil in Newfoundland,
    1898-1939   732
43. Corrected statistics for the catch in the North-east Pacific,
    1903-9   733
44. Catch and oil production in North-east Pacific, 1905-31   733
45. Complete statistics for the catch and oil production in
    Alaska, 1912-29   734
46. Modern catch in Japan, 1899-1910, and revised figures
    for the Japanese catch, 1920-30 by species of whale   735
47. The first season of Antarctic catching from Grytviken,
    1904-5   736
48. Corrected statistics for the world catch of right whales,
    1904-18   736

49. Dividends of the Antarctic whaling companies, 1909-10, 1910-11   737

50. Revised statistics for the catch from Chile, 1908-30   737

51. Production of different qualities of whale oil at Leith Harbour, 1909-14, and Olna, 1905-27   737

52. Catching seasons on all grounds between the two world wars   738

53. Catch, production and dividends of the Norwegian Whaling Company in Spain, 1921-7   738

54. The expansion of the pelagic whaling fleet, 1928-40   739

55. The Antarctic catch, 1931-2, and catches in other grounds, 1932   740

56. Average prices of edible oils, 1929-39   741

57. Price and consumption of margarine and butter in Great Britain, 1924-38   742

58. Nationality of the crews in the Antarctic whaling fleets, 1930-40   742

59. Floating factories lost during the Second World War   743

60. Whaling during the Second World War   745

61. The expansion of the pelagic whaling fleet, 1945-63   746

62. Agreements relevant to the Washington Conference, 1946   748

63. Japanese Antarctic catch, 1946-51   748

64. The Antarctic pelagic whaling fleet, applied catching days, average production per floating factory, and per catcher, 1945-78   749

65. Antarctic pelagic whaling, 1945-78: quotas, seasons, catch, production   750

66. Operative seasons of the shore stations in South Georgia   751

67. Total catch in the Antarctic, 1904-78   751

68. The International Whaling Commission: meetings, chairmen and secretaries, 1948-78   752

69. Average price of whale oil No. 1, 1874-1977, and of sperm oil 1946-77   753

70. Fin whale catch in waters off Korea, 1911-45   754

71. Republic of Korea coastal whale catch by species and year   755

PREFACE TO THE ENGLISH EDITION

The Norwegian edition of *The History of Modern Whaling* ("Den moderne hvalfangsts historie"), Vols 1-4, was published in 1959 (Vol. 1) and 1967-70 (Vols 2-4) by the Norwegian Whaling Association (Norges Hvalfangstforbund). The first of these volumes, *Finnmark Whaling*, was the work of Dr. Arne Odd Johnsen, and Vols 2-4 the work of Dr. Joh. N. Tønnessen, both of Oslo. As this is the first comprehensive account of the commencement and development of modern whaling in all the whaling grounds of the world, regrets have been expressed in a great many quarters that this work, written in Norwegian, should be accessible internationally only to a small number of people. The publishers have therefore come to the conclusion that an abridged edition in a world language, such as English, would prove of interest. The two editions are not identical, in so far as this English edition is a much abridged version of the Norwegian, which covers 2,700 pages. The principle adhered to in the abridgement of the original text is to omit practically everything that is of local or personal interest only to the Norwegian reader. Furthermore, the account has been updated from 1968 to 1978. This work, as well as the work of abridgement, has been entirely carried out by Joh. N. Tønnessen. The English translation is by R. I. Christophersen, of the University of Oslo.

In the English version the comprehensive source references and notes, covering 221 pages, have been omitted. As the chapter division is the same in both editions, the interested reader will find references in the corresponding chapters of the Norwegian version.

The two parts of the work (i.e. Vol. 1 and Vols 2-4) are entirely independent and distinct works, and are not the result of co-operation. For this reason separate extracts of the authors' prefaces which appeared in the Norwegian edition are reproduced here.

Oslo, July 1978   JOH. N. TØNNESSEN

PREFACE TO THE NORWEGIAN EDITION
Volume 1

The preliminary work for the present volume was begun in July 1939 at the request of a number of Norwegian whaling companies. These set up a committee for the purpose of following the progress of the work and assisting the author. In order to clarify important aspects of technical developments in modern whaling I have also found it necessary, in addition to the account presented in this volume, to carry out a number of special investigations that are listed under my name in the bibliography. I have, furthermore, completed two as yet unpublished surveys of a similar nature, one on the development of boiling equipment and the other on radio technique in modern whaling.

During the last years of the German occupation of Norway the work was brought to a halt owing to the evacuation of archives and libraries and on account of various other difficulties.

Now that the work is in print I should like to thank the Book Committee for the large measure of understanding and unfailing interest they have shown throughout these many years. I should also like to express my gratitude to Professor Johan T. Ruud and Dr. Åge Jonsgård, who are partly responsible for the excellent introduction: "What is modern whaling?".

Furthermore, I should like to thank the staff of the Public Record Office in Oslo; the University Library, Oslo; the Board of the Patent Office; the Norwegian Maritime Museum; Commander Chr. Christensen's Whaling Museum, with its library and archives, at Sandefjord; the Royal Library of Copenhagen; the Bibliothèque Nationale of Paris; the British Museum, London; the Library of Congress, Washington; the Firestone Library of the University of Princeton, New Jersey; and the Old Dartmouth Historical Society and Whaling Museum, New Bedford, Mass.; and furthermore various local and private Norwegian archives.

It is likewise both a pleasure and a duty to express my thanks to the many people who have contributed, both by word of mouth and in writing, to assist me in collecting the material.

Oslo, June 1958   ARNE ODD JOHNSEN

Volumes 2-4

The conclusion of my contribution to this book, after eleven years' work, would not have been possible without all the assistance I have received from the various members of the Book Committee, not least from its secretary, the Director of the Norwegian Whaling Association, Einar Vangstein. His detailed criticism of the manuscript and his untiring and copious replies to my countless questions have proved so essential to my account, that to a large extent he may be said to share the responsibility for it with the author.

That the work has taken so long to complete is due in particular to three factors: (1) it has necessitated the study of an overwhelming mass of technical literature and unpublished source material both at home and abroad; (2) apart from the actual history of whaling as such, it has proved necessary to investigate a number of subjects associated with it, such as sovereignty in the polar regions, whale oil in the world fat market, hydrogenation of fat and its revolutionary significance in the application of whale oil, the technical development of reduction methods, designs of floating factories and of whale catchers, etc.; (3) not least, a comprehensive correspondence of an almost global nature. The replies, often in the form of lengthy exposés, that I have received, constitute a very important part of the unpublished source material.

Apart from this, the main sources consisted of the following: (1) the large and very well preserved archives of the Norwegian Whaling Association (from 1912); (2) the archives of the Norwegian State Whaling Council (from 1924); (3) the archives of the Commercial Section of the Royal Norwegian Ministry of Foreign Affairs (from the commencement of Norwegian Antarctic whaling in 1905); (4) the records of Norwegian and foreign whaling companies (not always, unfortunately, well preserved); (5) whaling expedition logbooks; (6) correspondence covering the period 1904-15 between the Governor of the Falkland Islands and the Colonial Office (and the inter-departmental correspondence in association with this) found in thirty-four large tomes in the Public Record Office, London — a principal source for the study of the commencement of Antarctic whaling. These volumes also contain the Colonial Office's correspondence with whaling companies and copies of the Foreign Office's correspondence with the Royal Norwegian Ministry of Foreign Affairs; (7) shorthand minutes of the International Whaling Commission's proceedings at its annual meetings; (8) private letters, diaries and journals, particularly from the Whaling Museum, Sandefjord; (9) several thousands of feet of tape recordings of interviews with old whaling hands.

It would be impossible to record the names of all those who, in addition to the Book Committee, have helped me in my work. However, at the risk of offending anyone who deserves a special mention, I must extend a particular tribute to certain individuals. These include Captain Søren Fagerli, who placed at my disposal his wellnigh inexhaustible store of knowledge on every aspect of whaling. Furthermore, all the directors of previous Norwegian whaling companies have provided me with valuable information.

Two persons abroad deserve a very special mention: these are first and foremost Captain H. K. Salvesen, senior board member of the firm of Christian Salvesen (Managers) Ltd., of Edinburgh, at one time the world's largest whaling company. His contribution involved granting unrestricted access to the firm's comprehensive records, a meticulous and thorough perusal of large portions of my manuscript, and his vast knowledge of the technical aspects of whaling problems. The other is Dr. Hideo Omura, of the Whale Research Institute of Tokyo. Without his help it would have been impossible to give an account of the start and development of modern whaling in Asia. Dr. Omura has made available the necessary literature which had to be translated from

Japanese and Russian. In answer to my questions he has sent me exemplary accounts and statistical tables.

Among others I should like to single out David Geddes, senior board member of the oil brokerage firm of David Geddes & Son Ltd., London; William J. Reader and R. V. Bell of the Information Department of Unilever Ltd., London, who were kind enough to give me access to the minutes of managing directors' conferences, a particularly important source for the place of whale oil in the world fat market. My respectful thanks go to Loftur Bjarnason of Hvalur H/F, of Iceland, to Robert Clarke of the (British) National Institute of Oceanography, to George Ottley of the Library of the British Museum, to the Patent Office, the Colonial Office, the Natural History Museum, the Public Record Office, the Royal Geographical Society, the Universities Federation for Animal Welfare, United Whalers Ltd., all of London; to the Scottish Academic Press and Chr. Salvesen & Co. for permission to reprint plates 33 and 36 from W. Vamplew, *Salvesen of Leith*; to Dr. D. E. Sergeant and Dr. Gordon Pike, both of the Fisheries Research Board of Canada; to Dr. Remington Kellogg of the Smithsonian Institution, Washington D.C.; to Rafael Manrique, director of the Compañía Ballenera del Norte S.A., Peru; to Manuel Labra, director of Compañía Industrial, Chile; and to H. M. Knudsen, director of the Union Whaling Co. Ltd., Durban; and to many, many others.

Despite the considerable amount of ground covered in this work, there are nevertheless bound to be readers who will miss this or that particular aspect of whaling. In this connection it should be pointed out that the authors' task has been to write the economic, commercial, and political history of whaling, international regulations, technical developments, in short, the history of whalers and whaling, not the history of the whale. The views expressed are exclusively those of the authors. Even though the work aims to comprise the history of modern whaling throughout the world, Norwegian whaling has been accorded pride of place, both because it was the Norwegians who initiated modern whaling and exercised a hegemony for seventy years, spreading it throughout the world, and because of the inevitably greater accessibility to the author of the source material in Norway. Writing in similar detail of whaling all over the world would indeed have been the work of a lifetime.

Oslo, June 1967   JOH. N. TØNNESSEN

PART ONE

WHALING OFF THE COAST OF FINNMARK

1

WHAT IS MODERN WHALING?

For a proper understanding of the nature of modern whaling a few brief remarks on the old-fashioned methods of whaling and the species that were hunted in those early days are necessary. The introduction of modern methods of catching in the 1860s, as regards both technique and the species that from then on were the principal quarry, marks such a pronounced watershed in the history of whaling that it has subsequently been divided into two main periods — old and modern whaling. Each of these can in turn be divided into subordinate periods, with their own special features. Whereas modern whaling spans little more than a century, the old dispensation goes back to prehistoric times. The object of this work is to deal with the technical, economic, commercial and political history of modern whaling without, however, touching on any biological problems.

Like the history of whaling itself, the whales whose habitat is the oceans of the world (Cetacea) can be divided into two main groups — whalebone or baleen whales (Mysticeti) and toothed whales (Odontoceti). The former category comprises a mere ten species, the latter approximately sixty-five. The largest of the Odontoceti, the sperm whale (*Physeter macrocephalus*), also known in some countries as the cachalot or pottwal, has been extensively taken by whalers in both periods. In this species, in common with the other toothed whales, the male is larger than the female, attaining at times a length of up to some 65 feet.

There are three families of whalebone whales: the right whales (Balaenidae), the gray whales (Eschrichtidae) and the rorquals (Balaenopteridae). Two species of right whales were hunted before the modern period. The larger of these, the Greenland right whale (*Balaena mysticetus*), was known among British and American whalers as the bowhead. The smaller species (*Eubalaena glacialis*) is also known by a number of common names — right whale, nordcaper, Biscayan right whale — and referred to in the southern hemisphere as the southern right whale (*Eubalaena australis*).

The rorquals most in demand in the modern period are, in order of size, (1) the blue whale (*Balaenoptera musculus*), (2) the fin whale (*Balaenoptera physalus*), (3) the humpback whale (*Megaptera novae-angliae*), (4) the sei whale (*Balaenoptera borealis*) and (5) the closely related Bryde whale (*Balaenoptera edeni*). The female rorqual is larger than the male. The blue whale is the largest mammal that has ever existed on this earth. An unusually large specimen measured 106ft.,

3

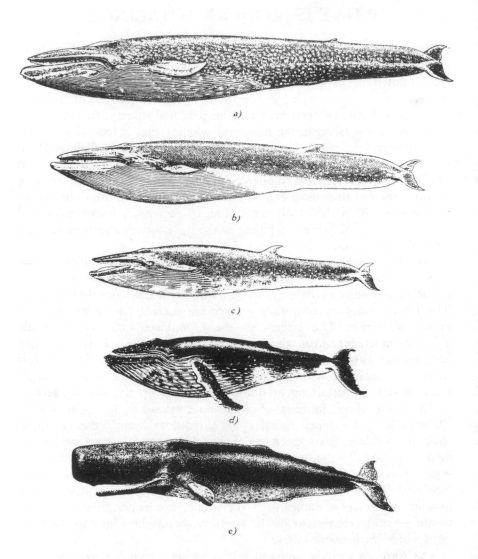

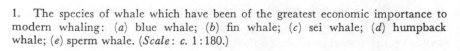

1.   The species of whale which have been of the greatest economic importance to modern whaling: (*a*) blue whale; (*b*) fin whale; (*c*) sei whale; (*d*) humpback whale; (*e*) sperm whale. (*Scale: c.* 1:180.)

2. The weight of a big blue whale is equal to that of twenty-five elephants or 150 big oxen.

weighed approximately 150 tons, and produced some 52 tons of oil. A blue whale weighs as much as twenty-five full-grown elephants or 150 big oxen. On the basis of the quantity of oil produced, the *International Whaling Statistics* estimates that one blue whale, or 1 Blue Whale Unit (BWU), is the equivalent of two fin whales, two and a half humpback whales, and six sei or Bryde whales.

The gray whale is the only species in the family Eschrichtidae. It has never been as numerous or widespread as the other whale species, and although taken by both old and modern whaling, the products from it have only been locally important.

We do not intend to deal with the catching of the many species of small cetaceans, referring to only one of them at the end of this volume, since in recent years it has provided a substitute for the larger and protected baleen whales: this species is the minke whale (*Balaenoptera acutorostrata*), also referred to as the lesser rorqual or the little piked whale.

Old and modern whaling differ biologically, technically and economically. The baleen whales caught in the past were the right whales, first and foremost the nordcaper, and from about A.D. 1600 onwards the Greenland right whale. It should be noted that the term "right whale" has a double meaning, referring as it does both to the family and to the species, as the nordcaper was also called a "right whale".

There were several reasons why only these baleen whales were caught. In the first place, they are relatively slow swimmers with a maximum speed of about 7 knots. This enabled them to be hunted by men operating in land-based rowing boats or, more generally, in long-boats launched from sailing vessels in the open sea. These whales were caught with a hand harpoon thrown by a man standing in the bows of the rowing boat, and killed with a spear or lance. In Japan, as we shall see below, whales were caught in a net. Another particularly important point was that right whales continue to float after being killed, whereas rorquals sink. Right whales are very fat, thus giving a high oil yield, and have an extraordinarily long baleen, extending to more than 4 metres in the Greenland right whale and to 2½ metres in the nordcaper. The baleen plates are flexible and retain their elasticity, and for this reason they can be used in a variety of ways. At certain times the price of baleen was so high that whales were caught merely for its sake; the huge head, comprising one-third of the entire length of the body extending to as much as 16-17 metres in the Greenland right whale, was cut off, and the body, with all its fatty content, discarded. As a rule, however, this was extracted by melting the blubber in open pans. Right whales earned their name simply because they were the "right" whales to catch.

Modern whaling differs from its older counterpart in a number of specific ways (in this connection we shall discount the catching of sperm whales, which is common to both periods). First, it is based on the catching of rorquals. This was imperative if commercial catching of the large baleen whale species was to continue, as stocks of right whales were so decimated in the latter half of the nineteenth century that they were no longer able to provide the basis for profitable operations. Secondly, the rorquals (except the humpback) are highly streamlined, and exceedingly powerful, swift and excellent swimmers, attaining for short periods speeds of 25-30 knots. Thirdly, rorquals sink once they have been killed. Because of the second and third factors, an entirely new method had to be introduced in order to catch this species, and it is primarily this method which we associate with the idea of modern whaling. The solution of the problems which this new method posed is so closely linked with the name of one person, the Norwegian SVEND FOYN, that the modern method of whaling might well be referred to as the Svend Foyn method. The innovations introduced by the new method were a steam-driven (subsequently diesel-driven) whaling boat used for hunting the whale; a harpoon fired from a cannon mounted in the bow of the boat; a grenade, attached to the harpoon, which explodes inside the whale; and a line, fastened to the harpoon, which makes it

3. This shrimp, *Euphausia superba,* is the principal food of the three largest species of rorquals in the southern seas. (Life size.)

possible to haul the whale to the surface and tow it to a shore station or to a floating factory. Commercially, the modern method was almost wholly and exclusively based on the extraction of oil, which was carried out not by melting the blubber in open pans but by cooking the blubber and the highly oleaginous bone and flesh in large pressure boilers. With the introduction of the modern method the Industrial Revolution had made its entry into whaling. In addition to the above, a further factor should be added, namely the many uses to which whale oil could be put. In the old days it was mainly used for lighting, lubrication and softer kinds of soap. While it was still used for these purposes in the modern period, the invention of hydrogenation meant that whale oil was now a highly important raw material in the production of margarine.

Although the term "whale oil" can be used to include the oil both of the baleen whale and of the sperm whale, it is often used to refer to the oil only from baleen whales, the oil from sperm whales being called "sperm oil". It is important to distinguish between these two, as their chemical composition, and hence the uses to which they are put, are quite dissimilar. Whale oil contains genuine fats (glycerides of fatty acids), while sperm oil consists mainly of compounds of wax alcohols and fatty acids.

Modern whaling first saw the light of day off the coast of Finnmark, Norway's most northerly county. From there it spread to all the oceans of the world. The "great adventure" was the conquest of the Antarctic in 1904 and the pelagic operations that subsequently took place there. For this reason our account can conveniently be divided into three main headings: (1) Catching off the coast of Finnmark, 1864-1904; (2) Global catching, 1883-1924; and (3) Pelagic catching (i.e. whaling in the open sea with floating factories, as opposed to shore-based whaling), 1925 to the present day.

In common with fisheries, whaling has raised the question of the right to ownership of the oceans and what they contain. Two contrary views have emerged: on the one hand it has been maintained that

4. Old whaling: outboard flensing in an American sperm whale catcher.

beyond a short distance from a country's coastline — as a rule, until recently, 3 nautical miles — the ocean and its resources were "free for all" or *aqua nullius,* and that anyone could therefore exploit them at will. This was the system on which illegal piracy and legalised privateering were based : beyond the 3-mile limit a vessel was outside the area covered by a country's jurisdiction, and it was consequently "ownerless", and was therefore liable to be seized by anyone powerful enough. The contrary view maintains that beyond the territorial limits the ocean is the common property of all mankind, and that no single nation is entitled to exploit its resources; this must be done in fellowship by all the people of the world, subject to rules and regulations based on international agreements. Fifty years ago any question on property rights to the *water* in the oceans of the world and the immeasurable quantities of raw materials on the ocean bed would have raised a condescending smile, but today this question is the very focus of international discussion, as the many conferences on maritime law eloquently testify. Free whaling and internationally controlled whaling in the "unpropertied" oceans of the world must be considered in the light of these two attitudes.

Growing recognition of the fact that modern whaling might well lead to the extinction of the rorquals, just as older methods decimated the right whales, and the widespread, growing demand from world opinion for conservation of the natural raw materials of the world, have resulted in international agreements on increased restrictions on whaling. Once again, in order to illustrate this, it is possible to divide developments into three sections: (1) free whaling; (2) locally or nationally regulated whaling; and (3) internationally regulated whaling. The Washington Convention of 1946, together with the International Whaling Commission established in 1949 to implement it, are important not only within the context of the history of whaling, but they are of general historical importance as well, because this is the first global agreement in which member-countries have entrusted a commission with the task of establishing how much may be caught in the free and open oceans, a convention subsequently extended to cover the catching of the major species throughout the world, by pelagic whaling (with floating factories) by catching from land stations, and also to some extent by the catching of the minor species. For this reason international regulations play an important part in any account of whaling, and this is true also of the place of whale oil on the world market among other edible fats and oils. Although strictly it has no real place in the history of whaling, it nevertheless goes without saying that whaling would never have been undertaken if there had been no market for the oil obtained from it.

One problem, which will be discussed later, is how it came about that Norway, which initiated modern whaling, introduced it to the world at large and had a 90 per cent stake in the industry, abandoned it completely; why Norway and Great Britain, which right up to the mid-1930s exercised a near-monopoly of Antarctic whaling, should have withdrawn thirty years later; and why two other countries, Japan and the Soviet Union, which were late-comers in the Antarctic, should be the only major whaling nations still operating in both the south and the north.

Why did modern whaling come into being, and why did it do so in the latter half of the nineteenth century? Why were the Norwegians the pioneers and why was a small town on the southeast coast of Norway destined to be the cradle of modern whaling? Problems associated with the answers to these questions are far-reaching and complex, and it is impossible to provide exact and simple answers. Most innovations in this world are promoted by certain factors and retarded by others; and this applies to modern whaling as to other spheres of endeavour. On the one hand industrialisation and the marked growth in population stimulated a demand for the tremendous quantities of fat

5. Modern whaling: floating factory with stern slip and aeroplane.

which the rorquals could supply, while general technical developments made it possible for a method of catching these creatures profitably to be evolved. On the other hand, whale oil was subject to steadily increasing competition from other substances capable of replacing it, as was sperm oil. Whale oils were then used mainly in the manufacture of soap, for lubrication and lighting, and in the tanning and textile industries, as well as for linoleum and paint, for tempering steel, etc. For lubrication and lighting, whale oil was squeezed out of the market by mineral oil, and for various other purposes it could be replaced by vegetable oils, in particular cottonseed and linseed oil. As a result, the price of whale oil slumped considerably after the mid-nineteenth century. Although it rallied somewhat during the years of the 1860s, the general trend was unmistakable. In fact, after 1869, the very year in which modern catching methods were finally put into. practice, there was an almost constant decline in the price, from £60 per ton until finally, in 1904-5, the bottom dropped out of the market with a price of £12 per ton, the lowest price to date. Thirty years were to elapse before the price once again reached rock-bottom, after rallying to £23 per ton before the First World War, with an exceptional rise to £90 during the war, and a stable price of about £32 being attained in the 1920s. Modern

6. Old whaling: melting blubber in open pan on the deck.

whale catching was founded and spread over large areas of the world at a time of declining prices, when there seemed to be no place for whale oil in the world market. What caused the price to rally once again was the entirely new situation that arose after 1905, particularly in connection with the invention of hydrogenation, which gave whale oil its important place in the fat industry.

The Norwegians do not appear to possess any special qualities to mark them out as the pioneers of modern whaling; no whaling was carried out around the middle of the nineteenth century from the shores of Norway, where the technical revolution that was taking place in industry and shipping was still only in its infancy. Around 1850 the Americans were the world's dominant whaling nation, and both they and the British were far ahead of the Norwegians in technical development. Both had invented and applied the use of bombs and grenades, even going so far as to combine the harpoon and the grenade in one single shot. Both in the United States and in Great Britain there was a far greater demand for whale oil and sperm oil, for various technical processes, than there was in Norway. Others before Svend Foyn had suggested the use of steamships in whaling; neither this idea nor the idea of the grenade and the harpoon combined in one shot were original ideas of Foyn's. His great contribution was the ingenious practical application which so many others had failed to perfect. The reasons why

7.   Modern whaling: oil reduction plant in a modern floating factory.

he and not an American solved the problem must be sought on either side of the Atlantic. It was the great value of rorquals, and in particular of blue whales, as a source of raw materials, and the attractive price of whale oil that provided the fillip to this method. Some idea of this may be obtained by comparing a worker's annual wages with the value of an unprocessed whale. In 1868 Foyn sold whale carcasses for as much as Kr.4,000 (then roughly equivalent to £220 or U.S. $1,100), whereas an average Norwegian worker at that time earned an annual wage of about one-eighth of that sum.

In the American economy a tremendous change took place around the middle of the century, which goes a long way towards explaining the decline in whaling and shipping. What took place was a transfer from external to internal expansion. Thanks to the new means of communication and industrialisation, the vast fertile prairies and the tremendous mineral wealth of the nation were now open to investment of labour and capital; and the winning of the West offered far greater profits than did whaling and shipping. The tremendous need for labour on the home market meant that a skilled worker could earn two or three times as much on shore as he could in whaling. The same situation applied to capital, which has always operated wherever the highest profits are to be made. In the United States there was simply no inducement for a regeneration of whaling.

8. Old whaling: the fo'c'sle of an old whaling ship.

Whereas economic factors and population growth brought about a revolution in the American economy away from outward-looking expansion to inward-looking intensification, similar forces in Norway were working in a diametrically opposite direction. Apart from Ireland up till the 1840s, no European country witnessed a greater population growth in relative terms than Norway during the fifty years after 1814. Norwegian agriculture, industry, communications and capital proved unable to absorb or employ the surplus population internally; any expansion that took place was bound to be outwards. Many hundreds of thousands of Norwegians joined the growing stream of immigrants from Europe to America. At the same time, a recession in American shipping and the liberalisation of international trade provided the basis for a phenomenal growth in Norway's merchant fleet, and so when the Americans abandoned whaling, the Norwegians assumed their hegemony.

In Norway, where the hard times in 1815-50 had inured people to austerity and grinding toil to secure the bare necessities of life, whaling was bound to attract any young man on the look-out for a job. In the 1870s and 1880s a manservant earned 60 øre a day, a labourer approximately 110 øre, a sailor about 165 øre, and a sailor on a whaleboat approximately 175 øre, in every case with board and lodging included.

9.   Modern whaling: the crew's mess in a modern floating factory.

When a bonus system in whaling was introduced in the 1880s, there was an opportunity of even higher wages.

The question why a small town in the county of Vestfold, in southeast Norway, should have provided the cradle to modern whaling is difficult to answer. What is beyond dispute, however, is the fact that Svend Foyn's personal contribution was decisive. During the 1840s he had already been a pioneer of Norwegian sealing, an enterprise which had provided an excellent training ground for trapping and catching in the Arctic Ocean, as well as ensuring him the financial basis for the costly work of experimenting with the modern method of whaling. Svend Foyn's native town was in the most populous county in Norway. Archaeological excavation has shown that even in prehistoric times the sea played an important part in providing a livelihood for the inhabitants; moreover, in about 1840 Vestfold was Norway's leading shipping county. There was no lack of skilled crews to man the whaling vessels. But even this does not explain the peculiar fact that modern whaling, which in its earliest period was conducted off the northern coast of Norway, was started by men not from the northern counties but from the county furthest away from the whaling grounds. The same applies to other forms of Arctic catching, the hunting of seals and of medium-sized (i.e. up to 30 feet) bottlenose whales. North Norway's population was sparse, and consisted mainly of poor fishermen, who by tradition were firmly tied to their calling. Nowadays we would have called this part of Norway a developing area, and it is inconceivable that capital could have been found to set up a whaling company there. Any expansion in this region would have to come from within the ancient and naturally-conditioned fisheries, in the form of a revolutionary change away from the primitive methods.

2

THE EMERGENCE OF MODERN WHALING

Endeavours outside Norway

We have indicated some of the differences between the two whaling epochs; but the two epochs can also be shown to have had a certain amount in common. Not everything in the new era was original and previously untried, and in the earlier period inventions had been made and equipment used which were to provide a model for the new. One whaling enterprise in particular provides an interesting link between the old and new eras: this enterprise, mainly operated in Iceland by the Americans THOMAS WELCOME ROYS and GUSTAV ADOLPH LILLIENDAHL, has so far found no place in the history of whaling, and was rescued from oblivion by Dr. Arne Odd Johnsen, one of the authors of this work. The main protagonist was Roys, the Svend Foyn of American whaling. He had had considerable experience in both southern and northern waters before 1856, when he made his first attempt at catching rorquals in the sea between Finnmark, Spitsbergen, and Novaya Zemlya in the Barents Sea. One of his aims was to discover whether there were "polar whales" (i.e. Greenland whales) in these waters. He had carried out a similar investigation in 1848, when he had penetrated through the Bering Strait into the Arctic Ocean, opening up this route for whaling. (It had previously been assumed that he was the first whaler to operate here, but more recent investigations have shown that an American whaler probably passed through the Bering Strait as early as 1819, but we know little of this expedition.)

The subsidiary purpose of Roys' trip in 1856 was, as he himself relates, that if there should prove to be no polar whales, he would "try if a cargo of oil could be obtained from whales previously unavailable to mankind". The expedition found no polar whales, but large quantities of blue, fin and humpback whales. These were fired at with guns of Roys' own design, and he himself describes the results as follows: "We shot twenty-two Leviathans killing one, twenty-six Humpbacks killing four, and four Finbacks killing none. Nine Leviathans were made to spout blood, twelve Humpbacks and two Finbacks which is a proof that our aim was tolerably good and the shells all exploded." Even though the result might appear somewhat meagre, it revealed that there were certain possibilities, and Roys worked intently in the following years to improve his firearms. According to his own account he was at that time using a combined harpoon and shell, whereby a line was attached to the whale. Using this equipment he shot a number of rorquals, but there was always something that seemed to go wrong. However, he was making progress, and in a letter (1858, 1859?) he declared himself highly optimistic with regard to prospects for rorqual catching on a large scale:

I have seen these whales on the voyage at the south end of Greenland, at the South-west, and north East coasts of Iceland, at Jan Mayen, at Bear Island, and along the South Edge of the ice to Nova Zembla, at the mouth of the White Sea and all the bays on the coast of Russia, Sweden and Norway down to St. Kilda rocks near the north Channel and on the coasts of Spain and Portugal and down the African Coast to the Cannairies Islands where they may be found in the Winter season, of the Leviathans 1 sinks out of three killed, of the Finbacks 2 out of 3, of the Humpbacks 1 out of 2. I have now established the fact . . . that every kind of whale that swims the ocean we can get within 100 feet of, I have every reason to suppose. I may entirely prevent all whales from sinking, and it now only wants me well made Weapons and the way to float them prepared for use and ship fitted for one more cruise to make the thing complete to place the whole whaling business upon a broad and sure basis and destroy all chances of the whaling business becoming improfitable, which will soon occur unless some one brings forth the means to make the other whales available to mankind that have never before been so . . .

There is no doubt that Roys was somewhat too sanguine in his hopes for the future : the results he had achieved, for example, hardly gave grounds for such optimism. The above letter was written with a view to obtaining financial support from New Bedford whalers, and Roys for this reason emphasised the promising aspects of this new whaling enterprise. The rocket harpoon with which Roys achieved the results mentioned above is probably the one he patented in 1857.

The idea of a whaling device of this nature can be traced right back to the eighteenth century. After the English South Sea Company had suffered a number of years of poor catches and considerable losses, it despatched in 1737 a whole fleet of twenty-two ships equipped with a freshly invented cannon for discharging harpoons, and, judging by the available sources, that year probably marked the first use of cannon in whaling. This initial attempt, however, was not repeated : it was impossible to get the harpooners to use the cannon, and the net catch of this large fleet was a mere fourteen whales. A fresh attempt was made by another company in 1733, and two whales were successfully shot with the harpoon cannon.

Available sources make no further reference to this gun until the Society for the Encouragement of Arts, Manufactures and Commerce in 1772 presented ABRAHAM STAGHOLT, a smith, with 20 guineas as a reward for a whale gun designed to discharge harpoons. The Society also spent considerable sums in an attempt to ensure the general use of a whale gun for catching purposes, but the results were rather negative. The well-known Scottish polar explorer and whaler WILLIAM SCORESBY, Jr., declared in 1820 that the harpoon-gun had been "highly improved and rendered capable of throwing a harpoon near forty yards with effect but it has not been so generally adopted as might have been expected". Scoresby was accompanied on his voyages to Greenland by GEORGE W. MANBY, who made energetic attempts to work out a better method of catching. Among other things the harpoon was fitted with movable barbs, which only opened once the harpoon had penetrated into the whale. In order to kill the animal more quickly, Manby aimed to shoot a shell as well as a harpoon into the whale's body. Scoresby predicted that this method would make it possible to hunt rorquals as well, and would prove just as good as "Congreve's rocket", a weapon invented by the Englishman WILLIAM CONGREVE in 1804. This had been used, among other things, during the British bombardment of Copenhagen in 1807, when it inflicted great damage and started a number of fires. In the 1820s Congreve planned to use it in whaling. It was his idea that the rocket would not only secure the whale to the boat by means of a line, but that the explosion inside the animal would generate so much gas that the whale would be anaesthetised and remain afloat. In this way the rocket could also be used for the catching of rorquals. He appears, therefore, to have been the first person to pioneer the idea of a shell and a harpoon combined in a single projectile. A British expedition was sent out to test the idea; a great many whales were killed, but they all sank, and further attempts were abandoned.

So far the British had led the way in experimenting with more highly technical methods of catching, but before the middle of the century they were joined by the Americans. Between 1829 and 1860 twenty-two patents were registered, most of them various versions of the so-called "bomb-lances", i.e. a whale shell. Of particular interest was an exploding harpoon, invented in 1851, which combined a shell and a harpoon in a single projectile equipped with a line; it was very different from the one Svend Foyn finally evolved, but it was a step in the right direction. The bomb-lance was as a rule discharged by means of a specially constructed gun or a tube which was rested on the shoulder, and to some extent it replaced the hand-spears that had been used to kill the whale once it had been hit by one or several harpoons.

It has been maintained that the experiments with the new devices involved no decisive change in whaling from about 1830 to 1860. This may be true in relation to the sperm whale, but in the catching of right whales and humpbacks the bomb-lance was widely used around 1860. This is confirmed, *inter alia*, in a note written by Svend Foyn in 1868 stating that he had started amassing information on "the devices that are used in the catching of the ordinary Greenland whale, if we accept the fact that my shells were somewhat stronger than general for that purpose". In this way the types of bomb-lance introduced by the Americans and the British were to provide part of the technical basis for Foyn's first experiments. By discharging bomb-lances and shells separately the Americans achieved good results in the catching of right whales and humpbacks, catching many hundreds of these species between 1830 and 1870. The device proved less successful with rorquals, which tended to sink. None of the Americans made more energetic attempts to catch these whales as well than Thomas Roys and G. A. Lilliendahl, a fireworks manufacturer of New York who had gone into partnership with Roys in 1860. Instead of utilising the bomb-lance, they developed Congreve's idea, and came within an ace of devising a method to solve the problem : catching the powerful and speedy fin whales.

In the early 1860s Roys and Lilliendahl hunted rorquals in the northern Atlantic and in the Norwegian Sea, operating from sailing ships and using their rocket device. In 1865 operations were considerably stepped up thanks to the setting up of a shore station at Seydisfjördur on the east coast of Iceland and by operating with two vessels, a sailing ship and a small steamer. While the sailing boat rode at anchor most of the time near the station, the steamer was constantly scouring the seas in search of whales, towing two rowing boats from which the whales were shot; the steamer then towed the whales to the station. That year forty whales were killed, although it proved possible to retrieve only twenty of them, and the net result was stated to be 900 barrels of oil. In the winter of 1865-6 a greatly extended expedition was planned, using three steamers and a converted schooner. Of the steamers, two were new ironclads (the first of these was lost in September 1865). Each of these two steamers was fitted with costly machinery, consisting of a steam boiling plant, a hydraulic press and a bone-crushing machine. However, almost all this special equipment proved unserviceable.

The rocket harpoon used by the Americans in 1865 and subsequently is undoubtedly identical with the one that was patented in that year. Svend Foyn visited their station, and described their projectile as follows : "The harpoon to which the line is attached is despatched from the shoulder by means of an iron tube which is propelled by a rocket set off by a pistol, and on the forepart of the rocket an explosive arrow (i.e. shell) is mounted, which is ignited when it is burnt out." Roys probably got the idea from the rocket artillery in use around the middle of the nineteenth century, especially in the Crimean War.

Roys' expedition operated approximately as follows. The three steamers set off, towing their rowing boats. As soon as a whale was observed it was pursued by the rowing boats, whose crews endeavoured to get within range. As the shot was fired, the harpoon flew out of the tube, with the line, so that the whale was attached to the boat. If the whale was killed instantly, no difficulty was involved and the carcass was towed off by the steamer to the station; but if the animal was wounded, it might move off, towing the boat, at a tremendous speed. If the whale sank, it would be up to the steamer to endeavour to haul it up to the surface. In 1866 the shooting technique was so far advanced that forty-nine whales were caught, most of them blue whales, while many more were killed. Approximately 2,350 barrels of oil were produced; but even these comparatively good results were meagre compared to the great costs, which resulted in a major loss in 1866, whereupon Roys and his relatives withdrew from the company. Lilliendahl continued as sole proprietor in 1867, when thirty-six whales were caught. That year too produced a loss, with the result that the company went bankrupt, and catching operations were abandoned precisely when success now at last seemed within reach. The entire enterprise appears to have been badly managed, the rocket harpoons were expensive, and just as the company had prospered due to the good price paid for oil during the American Civil War (1861-5), so it collapsed with the marked slump in prices in 1866-7.

The total number of whales caught by Roys' method was not particularly large, but it was significant enough to deserve comparison with Foyn's catches in the same years, as shown in Table 1.

Table 1. RORQUALS CAUGHT BY MODERN METHODS, 1865-1872

Year	Roys' method	Foyn's method	Total
1865	20	—	20
1866	49	—	49
1867	50	1	51
1868	6	30	36
1869	1	17	18
1870	1	36	37
1871	13	20	33
1872	a few	39	39
Total	140	143	283

Roys' and Lilliendahl's large-scale expeditions round Iceland in 1865-7 constitute a highly interesting chapter in the history of whaling during the transition from the old to the new. Although this did not result in a decisive breakthrough for modern methods, it acquired historical significance as their most important predecessor. Others, not least Svend Foyn, learned from the advantages and shortcomings of the American method. Another who tried out Roys' equipment was a Danish naval officer, O. C. HAMMER, who in 1865 founded Det Danske

Fiskeriselskab (Danish Fishing Company), for the purpose of carrying out combined fishing and whaling from Iceland. An agreement was concluded with Roys for the training of Danes and the purchase of his rockets and harpoons, and in his honour the company's first whaling boat was named the *Thomas Roys*. Hammer set up two stations, one on the south-west coast and one on the east coast of Iceland. The proceeds of the first year, 1866, were six whales, while over thirty which were killed were lost. In 1867 fourteen were caught, in 1868 only six, and in 1869 one. Whaling was then abandoned, and the vessel was despatched on a seal-trapping expedition in 1870, but it foundered. The company was dissolved in the following year with losses of £55,000, two-thirds of which were accounted for by whaling. The Danes were quite unqualified for this kind of venture, and it is probable that the Americans sabotaged their agreement.

Perhaps there was an important result of this unsuccessful attempt: namely, the cannon and the shell harpoon for which the Danish fireworks manufacturer GAETANO AMICI obtained a patent in 1867. He had been commissioned by Hammer to produce various types of rocket harpoon, but came to the conclusion that it would be better to launch the grenade harpoon with a cannon instead of with a rocket. A groove running almost the whole length of the gun enabled the projectile, when discharged, to pull a line in its wake. When the grenade exploded inside the whale, three fuses were set off, generating a suffocating gas. Four barbs were attached to the side of the projectile, and these opened when the grenade exploded. As we shall see, there was in principle a similarity between Amici's method and that developed by Foyn: a combined grenade harpoon, pulling a line fastened to a ring and fired from a cannon; yet in many ways they were very different: Amici's method appears never to have been used. Foyn was in Copenhagen, where he conferred with Amici, and although finding his grenades unserviceable, he may in fact have spotted the shortcomings that would have to be eliminated if this device were to be capable of application.

The Dutch, too, attempted to start whaling along American lines. A Captain BOTTEMANNE anchored up at Roys' station in Iceland in 1865 with a cargo of coal, and it is very likely that what he saw there encouraged him to revive the old and venerable Dutch whaling tradition. The attempt, however, was a complete failure. The company was started in 1869, purchased a steamer and two smaller vessels, and with these caught just one whale in 1870. In 1871 twenty-six were killed, but only half of these were saved, and results in the following year were no better. The company had to be dissolved. A fresh Dutch attempt in 1875 also failed, and seventy years were to pass before the Dutch once again launched into modern whaling.

When Foyn visited the American station in Iceland in July 1866, he was shown "an American steamboat which had fished a fin whale". That year forty-nine were caught, and in 1867 fifty, whereas Foyn only secured one whale in 1866 and none in 1867. This might have discouraged another man, but it had completely the opposite effect on Foyn, inspiring him to continue his struggle with the mighty whale until victory was won. With his own eyes he had seen that it was possible.

One predecessor in particular was of decisive importance to Foyn's own design of the grenade harpoon, which he more or less perfected in the 1870s. This was the Englishman GEORGE WELCH, who acquired a British patent for his grenade harpoon in 1867. The similarity between his and Foyn's design is striking, the only essential difference being that Welch's projectile was entirely rigid, while in the case of Foyn's, the head was attached to the shaft by means of a movable joint. Welch's design appears to have been entirely forgotten, but it deserves mention here because it indoubtedly represents the greatest advance before Foyn's patent of 1870, the complete success of which was probably due to Foyn's adoption of Welch's design as a model. We cannot be entirely certain of this; Foyn may well have arrived at his solution quite independently of Welch, but because of the close interest he took in all the experiments being carried out in both America and Europe, it is unlikely that Foyn was ignorant of Welch's patent.

In Scotland, France and Germany as well new methods were being sought and new devices tested. In this connection it should be enough to mention Germany, because this had some significance in the appraisal of Foyn's invention. PHILIPP RECHTEN of Bremen was granted a British patent in 1856 on a harpoon and a gun for firing it. He co-operated with CORDES, a gunsmith in Bremerhaven, who manufactured a double-barrelled gun to Rechten's design. The original idea was to fire a harpoon out of one barrel, and then a bomb-lance out of the other. In the late 1860s Rechten made his way to the United States in an attempt to introduce this idea on the American market, but there is no indication that he succeeded. During the heyday of National Socialism in Germany in the 1930s, a spate of propaganda for German whaling was set afoot, and it was maintained that the true inventor of Foyn's firearms was Cordes, and that he — and Germany — deserved the credit for having created modern whaling. It is true that Foyn ordered a certain amount of material from Cordes, but it proved quite unserviceable. It is incredible that an assertion of this kind could have been made in all seriousness since it is quite clear that Rechten and Cordes did not combine the grenade and the harpoon in a single projectile, as Foyn did in the device he patented in 1870. As we shall see below, when the Nazis boasted that their regime had created modern German whaling in the late 1930s, there was no mention that this had been done almost entirely on the basis of British and Dutch capital, Norwegian know-how, and Norwegian expertise.

Svend Foyn's Norwegian predecessors

There must have been quite a number of people in Norway who at one time or another toyed with plans for making whaling more efficient, but it is possible that only two of them had direct bearing on Foyn's work of perfecting the method. One of these, JACOB NICOLAI WALSØE, was born in North Norway and grew up in a fishing community. Thanks to a grant from public funds he was able to carry out experiments on a device consisting of a projectile, shaped like an arrow, containing an explosive charge, which was set off by a fuse, either on striking the whale or a few seconds later. The projectile was fired by a very sturdy rifle. The grenade harpoon was highly effective, and killed the whale almost instantly if it struck a vital spot. For three reasons, however, it fell short of perfection : it had no line to link the whale with the boat, there was no gun for shooting the projectile, and no steam-driven whaling boat. These were the three problems for which Foyn discovered a practical solution, even though the *ideas* had been launched before. Walsøe was probably the first person to propose the idea of using a small steamboat with a gun mounted in the bows, an innovation which was to prove of revolutionary importance to the development of modern whaling, and which saw the light of day ten years later (1863).

Another of Foyn's Norwegian forerunners was the master mariner ARENT CHRISTIAN DAHL. It is not quite clear whether he used a rocket or a gun for firing the projectile, but the most important feature of his invention was that it combined an explosive and a harpoon in a single projectile, and furthermore it attached the whale to the boat by means of a line. There is no doubt that Foyn was familiar with Dahl's experiments : his and Walsøe's trials were described in Norwegian newspapers. Dahl carried out his experiments (1857-60) in Norway's most north-easterly fjord, the Varanger fjord, which Foyn a few years later selected as his field of operation, continuing where Dahl left off in 1862. The next year he commissioned his first whaleboat and sailed it to Finnmark in 1864. There would therefore be good grounds for assuming that he was familiar with the experiments of his two countrymen, and with the firearms used in the Greenland whaling and the attempts to improve them. In his notes Foyn himself records that he considers 1864 as the decisive initial year. It is not quite clear what shooting methods he used that year and in the following five or six years; in the main he appears to have fired the harpoon and the grenade separately, but at the same time to have worked energetically to improve the grenade harpoon, which he apparently always considered to be the only perfect solution. Nevertheless, Foyn's grenade harpoon patent of 1870 comes as a surprise : it is possible that he preserved such secrecy around his invention that he dared not even reveal it in his own diary. In his application for the patent Foyn describes the grenade harpoon as being more or less the result of his own experiments.

He describes how it happened that, although he fired three of four harpoons and, at the same time, four smaller shells, both the harpoon and a 2¾-inch line would snap like string. Using heavy harpoons and thicker lines and coarser-calibre guns was no use; nor was it any advantage to make the barbs movable. When everything had been made as sturdy as possible, but to no avail, he wrote, "I realised that it was the design of the harpoon that had to be changed. The shaft, instead of being rigid as heretofore, would have to be connected with the head by means of a joint, and free, movable barbs were necessary. I then designed the harpoon on these lines, and it is for this harpoon that I am applying for a patent." Finally, and almost by way of a surprise addition, comes what to us appears to be the main point at issue: "It often happens that the harpoon strikes, whereas the grenade misses its target. In order to remedy this, I have attached a grenade (shell) to the harpoon, which explodes after penetrating into the whale."

There were still two difficulties to overcome : one was the fuse, which was to set off the charge in the grenade a few seconds after striking the whale. In solving this problem Foyn received invaluable aid from H. M. T. ESMARK, the clergyman of a parish not far from Foyn's native town, a man of parts who was well versed in the natural sciences as well as being an outstanding chemist. He had previously invented a primer enabling a bomb to explode on impact, and he was ideally qualified to assist Foyn in developing a grenade which would explode inside the whale. Co-operation between these two men, stretching over several years, resulted in a successful solution. The composition of the powder in the fuse was a secret.

The fuse did not always function as required : its use was always overshadowed by danger, and resulted in accidents on several occasions. It was a glass tube filled with sulphuric acid, placed inside another tube of rubber and surrounded by the special powder. This was placed between the barbs of the harpoon which crushed it when they straightened out as the line was pulled taut upon being embedded in the whale. Occasionally the grenade would explode simultaneously with the firing of the gun, or it might pass through the whale and explode in the water on the other side of the animal. There were cases of people being wounded by shrapnel as a result of both these occurrences. A more serious accident once occurred when a shell exploded during the flensing of a whale on deck.

The other difficulty involved firing the large, heavy shell harpoon, which was no ordinary projectile. After numercus experiments Foyn discovered a method of loading the gun. Being a muzzle-loader, the powder-bag was rammed in first, then "in front of this is placed first of all tow, and then rubber wadding, and between this and the harpoon a certain amount of wool. Only with these simple means has it proved possible to fire the harpoon without destroying it, as making it stronger and heavier would in turn demand a greater charge of powder and larger and stronger guns. I ruined a great many harpoons before I discovered the above simple but effective means, which are an indispensable part of my whole system."

Svend Foyn would never have been the man he was if he had not also solved the problem of the line. Powerful whales demanded foregoers and lines of extraordinary strength and quality. From his diary we can see how Foyn systematically tested the tensile strength of rope from a number of ropewalks. "I have to use 6 in. lines of top-quality hemp, and they must be strong enough to withstand a pull of 32,000-38,000 lb." (i.e. a breaking strength of 16-19 tons). Finally, if we mention that the special gunpowder Foyn required was manufactured in Norway, it may be said that all the material used in catching off the coast of Finnmark was 100 per cent Norwegian, and that the feeble attempts made by other nations at modern whaling prior to 1904 — and for many years thereafter — were entirely dependent on Norwegian material. The production of this, from the whaleboats to the steam boilers, from the gun (cannon) to the gunpowder, harpoons, and lines, provided the basis for a considerable growth in the Norwegian mechanical engineering industry.

Svend Foyn and Finnmark whaling, 1864-1873

In Norway's smallest county, Vestfold, situated in the southeastern corner of the country, three small towns — Larvik, Sandefjord and Tønsberg — are located on a 25-mile stretch of coast. In this county and in these towns, particularly Sandefjord and Tønsberg and in the final phase in Sandefjord alone, the centre of gravity of the world's modern whaling was concentrated, from the time Svend Foyn designed his grenade harpoon and right up to the 1940s. For two generations this little corner of Norway provided recruits not only to practically all the crews of the Norwegian whaling fleet, but also a substantial proportion of the crews on board the whaling fleets of other nations; and for fifty years Sandefjord was the world centre for the conversion, fitting out, and equipping of whaling vessels, floating factories as well as catchers. There are a great many points of similarity between this centre of modern whaling and the small coastal towns of New England which provided the centre of the global American catching of former days. This

10.   The Norwegian town Tønsberg, 1868—the cradle of modern whaling.

similarity applies not only to the material but also to the spiritual : both of these communities practised a Puritan form of Christianity, a God-fearing way of life that went hand-in-hand with frugality. In working and earning money men were obeying God's command : "In the sweat of thy face shalt thou eat bread." The strict discipline maintained both at home and at work was closely bound up with the ascetic attitude of the head of the family and the employer, and the stringent demands they also imposed on themselves. Svend Foyn is a typical representative of this "Puritan Capitalism".

Foyn was born in Tønsberg in 1809. His father was a well-to-do master mariner, and the owner of a large vessel. He was lost at sea in 1813, and during the economic crisis that followed in the wake of the Napoleonic Wars Foyn's mother struggled valiantly to preserve the home. Even as a boy Svend had to help her in this task. The acute shortage of money at home taught him the value of this commodity, inspiring him with a relentless urge to make money, lots of money, not with a view to living a life of luxury, but to ensure that the talent God had given him would multiply many times. In a politico-religious tract entitled *To the Norwegian People* he wrote : "God had let the whale inhabit [those waters] for the benefit and blessing of mankind, and consequently I considered it my vocation to promote these fisheries." It was his hope "to convert the Norwegian people so that they would not engage in politics but fear God". He spent a great deal of money on this, and bequeathed the bulk of his very considerable fortune to the Mission

11. Svend Foyn.

to the Heathen. At the age of twenty-four he became a master mariner, and spent a certain amount of time in England and France in order to learn the languages and so forego the expense of foreign-language-speaking assistants. Apart from the ship's main cargo of timber, most of which he bought and sold on his own account, he carried small quantities of other goods which he sold on a retail basis up and down the Norwegian coast. In this way, bit by bit, he amassed a small private capital, though he realised that this type of business enterprise would never enable him to lay up a considerable fortune. Seal trapping and whaling offered much greater opportunities.

Sealing, in fact, was to provide Foyn with the practical and financial transition to whaling. He acquired his knowledge of sealing in various ways. Scotsmen and Germans at that time trapped seals between Jan Mayen and Greenland (in the so-called western ice). In 1837 a master mariner from Vestfold purchased a small schooner and used it mainly for catching walrus between Spitsbergen and Novaya Zemlya. In 1844, the last year in which he was engaged in this form of catching, Svend Foyn had signed on as an able seaman, and he realised that seal trapping in the western ice, and not this particular type of catching, was bound to be the source of the capital he required in order to realise his great plan. The schooner which was built for him in 1845 was the first vessel specially built in Norway for sealing. In its first season, 1846, Foyn was unlucky, but in the following year he made a handsome profit, and continued to enjoy excellent catches for a great number of years, with the result that his wealth increased with every year, and even after he was well established in whaling, he bought seal-trapping vessels, the last of them in 1871. In the course of these operations Foyn was also in contact with whaling, as it was customary for seal trappers also to try to catch any right whales they came across, and in 1849 Foyn himself caught a Greenland whale, his first whale — as well as 2,500 seals. In the sea to the east of Greenland, however, right whales were so rare that whaling could not be based on this species, but rather on the rorquals, in particular the impressive blue whale, with which, as Foyn observed, the ocean teemed. But as long as seal trapping proved profitable, Foyn bided his time.

Two circumstances in particular proved decisive: the increasing competition in seal trapping in the western ice, undoubtedly involving over-trapping, meant a substantial slump in profits; in 1858 one of Foyn's vessels returned, laden to the gunwhale with 16,000 seal pups, whereas in 1861 and 1862 the catch was only 2,283 and 3,700 respectively. In the second place, Foyn realised that the value of one single blue whale was equivalent to that of 300 to 400 seals, and that whaling operating from a shore station could be carried out with between fifteen and thirty hands, whereas his sealing vessels required a crew of sixty. A third, additional factor was that he had by now acquired sufficient capital to launch out on a large-scale attempt to realise his life's ambition of catching rorquals, on his own account and at his own risk. Armed with a fortune in 1860 of 65,000 specie dollars and an income of 9,000 he was without comparison the most prosperous citizen of his town. In 1863 he contracted from a shipbuilding yard in Oslo the world's first purpose-built steam whale catcher, which he christened *Spes et Fides* (Hope and Faith). This vessel had a length

12. The whale-gun used by Svend Foyn, 1865.

of 94¾ ft. and a beam of just under 15 ft. The main engine, which was of 20 nominal h.p., gave it a speed of 7 knots. Like most steamships at that time she also carried sail, and was schooner-rigged, although sails were only used on the voyage to and from Finnmark: during catching operations she proceeded only on her engines. On 18 (or 19) February 1864, she set sail from Tønsberg with a crew of twelve on board, and completed the voyage in ten days.

With her armament of seven whale guns mounted on the forecastle the vessel had the appearance of a minor man-of-war. The idea, Foyn wrote, was to enable several shots to be fired at any one whale, e.g. two harpoon shots and two grenade shots. These were fired separately, but at the same time he was experimenting with single shots consisting of both harpoon and grenade. The year 1864 proved disappointing; Foyn was made to feel that he was doing battle with the natural elements. Everything seemed to go wrong: there was hardly a whale in the sea, his ship suffered from various shortcomings, his firearms failed to function as they should have done, proving insufficiently powerful to overcome the gigantic strength of the whales, and those that were killed sank to a depth of 120-180 fathoms as soon as they were dead. Several whales were hit; Foyn himself secured three of them, other members of his crew a fourth.

This initial attempt involved Foyn in considerable losses, and in order to redress the balance he set out on a seal-trapping expedition in 1865. Thanks to a record catch he succeeded in straightening out his finances. But the failure of a seal-trapping expedition in the spring of 1866 again produced further losses; shortly after his return he set off in June on board the *Spes et Fides* for Iceland, as already mentioned, to see what he could learn from the Americans. His own catching attempts in these waters were a complete failure, but he learnt a great deal: the fact that the Americans could catch twenty whales in 1865 and forty-nine in 1866 reaffirmed his belief that the catching of rorquals was possible. In mid-July he made his way to North Norway, but as few whales were spotted and some of his guns exploded, wounding a few members of his crew, Foyn abandoned catching attempts that year and returned to Tønsberg without having caught a single whale. The damage to the guns was not the fault of their design, but due to the gunpowder, and with the help of Esmark, the clergyman, Foyn managed to iron out this problem. In every respect he revealed an unflagging energy in testing every stage of whaling: should one experiment miscarry, he would immediately start another one. "It won't work, it won't work, as Svend Foyn said when he lost a whale", became almost a proverb in the county of Vestfold. All this cost a mint of money, but in the spring of 1867 he made yet another record catch of seals, which redressed his finances sufficiently to enable him to try his hand once again at whaling in May. The result was his biggest disappointment to date: three whales were killed but only one was caught! The harpoons in particular proved ineffective, as they failed to hold the whale. Foyn was clearly beginning to doubt whether it really was the will of God that the path he pursued was the right one — it had already cost him three years of substantial loss and great labour. With Roys and Lilliendahl going bankrupt that year, the autumn of 1867 hardly appeared to offer bright prospects for modern whaling.

Foyn resolved to try once again, and in the course of the winter, at great expense, he obtained larger and sturdier equipment, and already on 12 February 1868, he headed north. Delayed by bad weather, the trip took as much as twenty-five days, and not till mid-March could catching commence. After a month and a half only one small whale had been caught, and the prospects seemed forbidding. But just when the situation appeared at its least promising, his luck changed. When catching ended on 24 August, the score stood at thirty whales, of which Foyn was responsible for landing twenty-three and other members of his crew for seven. Some of the whales were sold unprocessed for £820, while others were rendered down to produce oil, some 1,600 barrels in all, which probably netted him the sum of some £13,000. This must have ensured him a small margin of profit. On his return home Foyn was accorded a royal reception: thanks to him, Norway had been launched on a new and profitable industry. It irked him that he had been compelled to sell some of the whale carcasses whole, enabling others to cash in on the processing of the oil. For this reason, for the 1869 season, he not only commissioned the building of a new catcher, but also the apparatus necessary for an oil "try-works" (processing plant).

In the ensuing year the two catchers accounted jointly for only fifteen whales — a big disappointment. The oil they produced was of poor quality, and not very marketable. Foyn must have believed that failure to process the de-blubbered whale carcasses was a waste of God's good gifts, and for this reason he was anxious to build a factory for the production of guano based on whale residues. He contacted a German agent, who promised him a market for his guano in Germany, recommending a German firm as suppliers of the necessary plant. But the whole project proved to be little more than a swindle. Foyn produced sufficient raw material, but the production of guano based on the thirty-six whales caught in 1870 proved so ineffectual that the plant had to be scrapped, at great loss.

By now Foyn had perfected his gun and grenade harpoon. Failure to land more than twenty whales in 1871, therefore, must be ascribed essentially to poor weather. The year 1872, on the other hand, with thirty-nine whales accounted for, was his best season to date. Obtaining the raw materials was one matter: quite another was turning them into a marketable product, and in this field Foyn had considerable difficulties to contend with. Despite the acquisition of new equipment in 1872 and the advice of an English expert in the technique of boiling, the whale oil proved of such poor quality that it was difficult to find purchasers at a remunerative price. Another disadvantage was that in the initial stage sales were based exclusively on the German market, and it was a great shock to Foyn to discover that his German agents were also operating as competitors in whaling. In 1872 a company known as the Deutsche Polar Schiffahrts Gesellschaft in Hamburg was started, based on eleven vessels which were to carry out seal-trapping and whaling between Finnmark, Spitsbergen, and Greenland. The company had acquired a site for a whaling station on the south side of the Varanger fjord, opposite Foyn's own set-up on the north shore. It would have been a disaster for him if Germans were to compete with him for the same whales. He pointed this out in a lengthy letter written direct to the King in 1872: the Germans, he maintained, had engaged the services of his men in order to lay hands on his invention. It would be a simple matter for the Germans to carry out whaling operations if without further ado they could acquire a catching method which it had taken him eight years to develop, and which had involved such considerable

13.   The small town of Vadsø in North Norway with the whaling station of Svend Foyn in the foreground.

financial sacrifices. All his efforts to create a new industry for Norway would be nullified.

At the same time he applied for a ten-year patent on his entire catching system, and this was granted on 14 January 1873. In reality this gave him sole right to carry out modern whaling in Norway for a period of ten years. This patent, in fact, was not an ordinary patent but a charter. The most important effect achieved was that the German attack had been repulsed. Norwegian competitors, too, were kept at arm's length, and now at last Foyn could harvest undisturbed the fruits of his labours and his tremendous expenses. During the ten-year period commencing 1 January 1873, the price of whale oil was on the whole good, and it was during this catching monopoly that Svend Foyn became a multi-millionaire.

Catching monopoly, 1873-1882

It was precisely because he had now acquired the status of a national hero that Foyn had so little difficulty in obtaining his monopoly. He and his whaling activities always provided good newspaper copy, and the leading poets wrote grandiloquent poems in his honour. There was only one discordant note in all this popular acclaim: over the years a state of bitter hostility developed between Foyn and the population of the little town of Vadsø in Finnmark, where he had his whaling station.

The population complained of the disagreeable smell produced by the boiling of oil and the production of guano, and from the de-blubbered and semi-rotten whale carcasses. They were also annoyed that Foyn recruited almost all his hands and obtained all his provisions from Tønsberg, thus depriving Vadsø of any real share in his success. In the third place, there were constant disputes between Foyn and the local authorities on the subject of taxation; for many years Foyn's contribution accounted for about one-third of the town's fiscal income. Lastly, he had hardly started whaling before the local fishermen complained that his activities were a threat to the fisheries. There was no scientific proof of any link between these two factors, but he was a convenient scapegoat for meagre fishing results.

By the mid-1870s, thanks to his intense work to improve them, his shooting and catching tackle were so efficient that the problem was no longer one of obtaining sufficient raw materials, but of evolving a method of boiling which would improve the quality of the oil. This was the most pressing task if the profits from his whaling ventures were to improve, and the one that engaged Foyn's attention most at this time. He was constantly facing production difficulties, but the quality gradually improved, and by 1878 Foyn had won through, both in his catching technique and in his production. This marks a clear watershed, dividing his ten-year monopoly into two five-year periods. From a total of thirty whales in 1877 he more than trebled his catch to ninety-four in 1878. During the first period, 1873-7, the annual average was forty whales (with a maximum of fifty-one in 1874), and in the second period, 1878-82, it was ninety-two (with a maximum of 107 in 1881). During these years — up to 1884 — the price of oil was relatively stable and good, averaging £30-32 a ton. One of the newly established companies returned a dividend of 55 per cent in 1880 and 50 per cent in 1881, while another had a net surplus of 76 per cent, and Foyn, who was sole proprietor, had an annual income of over Kr. 100,000, an enormous amount judged by Norwegian conditions at that time. This made a great impression in his native town, and there were many who were anxious to follow in his footsteps.

Despite his monopoly, a number of local citizens established a whaling company in 1876. In order not to be dependent on his patent, this company had acquired a gun and a grenade harpoon that differed somewhat from Foyn's. He was particularly incensed at the news that the new company had selected the site for its station at the very spot where the Germans had intended to establish themselves the preceding year. In May the new catcher arrived, and whaling commenced. Foyn considered this a breach of his monopoly, and he took the shooter and the station manager to court, but lost his case on formal grounds. Probably because he was sick and tired of the whole case, which had been the cause of annoyance and the loss of much money and time over a whole year, he refrained from appealing to a higher court. Besides, he realised that the new company had enlisted the sympathy of people in Tønsberg : in their opinion Foyn had made enough money, and it was un-Christian and selfish to bar others, especially as on this occasion his own countrymen, and not foreigners, were involved. In the third place it may have weighed with him that in the new company he now had an ally in the struggle against the constant attacks of the fishermen against whaling. However, the new arrivals were — and continued to be — a source of annoyance to Foyn, even though there appeared to be enough whales for both parties. The period from 1878 to 1880 proved excellent years, with Foyn recording catches of ninety-four, eighty-two and eighty-three whales, while the others caught thirty-three, thirty-nine and sixty, with their net profit equalling two-thirds of the share capital.

It was clear to all and sundry that whaling offered tremendous opportunities for rich pickings, at a time, moreover, when shipping, after a number of boom years in 1871-4, entered upon a protracted period of depression. A great many people spoke openly of defying Foyn's monopoly. Faced with this threat he adopted a new line, giving concessions on certain conditions, a pledge not to catch in the Varanger fjord, where his station was situated, and to pay a levy of 10 per cent on net profits, not to himself but to the Heathen Missionary Society. He granted concessions of this kind to as many as four companies that were all established in 1880, three of them in Tønsberg and district. The fourth company is of particular interest, as it marks the debut in modern whaling of Sandefjord, which for half a century was to be the world's whaling centre. This company, furthermore, was the first to make use of a floating factory ship, the barque *Laura,* which had a steam boiler and two cauldrons mounted between decks. There was more than a hint in this that Sandefjord was to prove the pioneer town in the development of the floating factory ship.

The year 1881 proved a rich one for whaling, ensuring financial success to five of the six expeditions, which accounted for a total of 285 whales, of which Foyn, with three catchers, secured 107. This excellent result proved a spur not only to the tremendous expansion of existing companies but also to the establishment of new companies, some of which were started in 1882, others in 1883. The last year of Foyn's monopoly was 1882, and he did his utmost to exploit it to the full, operating with four vessels and seventy-two hands. The proceeds, however, were ninety-six whales — eleven fewer than the year before with three vessels and fifty-seven hands, and an inadequate return for the efforts expended. Others had a relatively better showing, and the year's total catch amounted to 395 whales. Most of the companies paid attractive dividends to their shareholders, and Norway was now in the grip of the whaling fever. In 1883 the number of whaling stations increased from eight to sixteen, and the number of whale catchers from twelve to twenty-three. At the same time modern whaling moved beyond Norwegian waters to Iceland, where Foyn tried his luck, only to withdraw shortly afterwards.

Unrestricted catching, commencing in 1883, lasted for twenty-one years and proved more than the stocks of whales could stand. The best gauge of this was the decrease in the number of whales per catcher. Numbers were actually beginning to slump as far back as 1882, declining to 30.4 from 35.6 in 1881, and in 1883, the first year of unrestricted catching, it reached an all-time low of 23.4. In normal circumstances Finnmark catching in any year never reached the same figures as in 1881. Years in which statistics show higher figures for the number of whales caught were not "normal", for 50 per cent or more of these catches consisted of small sei whales (6 sei whales = 1 blue whale unit, BWU). The slump after 1881 was a warning sign that stocks of whales were being over-taxed; and this was pointed out by scientific whaling research. It has been maintained that unrestricted catching from 1883 was the first disaster that struck Norwegian whaling. A verdict of this kind depends on the angle from which it is considered. It has been said that Norwegians should have regulated catching by means of a licensing or concession system, as the British were wise enough to do from the very start with the whaling based on South Georgia and the other antarctic archipelagoes. In the narrowest sense unrestricted Finnmark catching proved a disaster to the whale stocks off the coast of North Norway, but for modern Norwegian whaling as a whole it was by no means a catastrophe. In the first place, as soon as the stocks off North Norway started to decline and there was no longer sufficient raw material for profitable catching for all concerned, the "superfluous" companies sought other fields in their global search for whales. In the second place Finnmark catching proved a training ground for experts who for a generation ensured Norway the hegemony in world catching. In the third place catching methods, the equipment and the whaling boats, and the boiling technique that set a standard for subsequent development were tested and tried here. Though details have been changed and improvements introduced, the main principles, in every stage of the catching, from the pursuit of the whale to the oil, are the same. One thing has remained unaltered: Sven Foyn's grenade harpoon was such an ingenious invention that to this day, 100 years later, it is still in use, for all practical purposes unaltered.

Species of whales caught before 1883

On closer inspection it will be seen that the ordinary statistical resources of the years prior to 1883 are highly misleading, both with regard to the number of catchers, companies, and the species of whale caught. It has, for example, been said that up to the year 1876 Foyn caught only blue whales. Systematic perusal of a large number of catching logbooks that have been preserved in fact reveals that in the months of June, July, and August, with very few exceptions, only blue whales were caught. However, Foyn's diary reveals that he reached the whaling grounds about the middle of March, and that he secured the bulk of his catch before 1 June (in 1868, for example, eleven out of an annual catch of thirty). Moreover, Foyn himself states that from 1864 to 1889 he secured on an average one-third of his catch prior to 1 June. These can hardly have been blue whales. It is apparent that he pursued such whales as he came across, whether they were fin, humpback, sei, or right whales. It would seem that the almost universally accepted legend that "the sea was teeming in whales" and that Foyn "only took the biggest and fattest blue whales" is little more than a fabrication. Admittedly, on the basis of the material we possess today, it is impossible to provide satisfactory statistics showing the species of whale caught prior to 1883, but it can be stated with confidence that from the very first not only were blue whales caught but also fin whales and others of the species mentioned.

3

THE WHALING INDUSTRY

The whale catcher

Posterity has linked the name of Foyn so closely with the ingenious grenade harpoon that it has been apt to forget that he decisively shaped the development of other aspects of whaling, too, not least the whale catcher. The one Foyn commissioned became the prototype for whale catchers for sixty years. As already mentioned, it was named the *Spes et Fides,* and was supplied by a Norwegian ship-building yard ready for the 1864 season. It might seem surprising that this vessel should have been fitted with such a weak engine — of 20 nominal h.p. (= 50 indicated h.p.) — considering that she was designed to tackle fast-swimming whales. But in those days catching consisted not of pursuing the whale with a fast catcher, until the animal was exhausted, but to sneak up on it with a very quiet-running engine which would not be likely to frighten it. Besides, at that time it had not yet been possible to design a boat and an engine capable of rivalling the speed of the whale. The engine of the *Spes et Fides* was so weak that it could offer little resistance, once the whale set off with the boat in tow; for this reason she was equipped with check boards on both sides, 3–4 ft. wide and situated 6–7 ft. below the waterline. These could be pivoted obliquely forwards, and made it a much harder task for the whale to tow the boat.

"Of essential significance to the success of catching" (to use Foyn's own words) was the winch which was driven by the main engine and made it possible to ease off and haul in the line in time with the whale's movements, and thus help to control them. The winch was equally important for hauling in the whale after it was dead. In order to lessen the jerk on the line, e.g. in a high sea, it was threaded through a block suspended from stout rubber strops, a so-called compensator. This had been invented by Roys, who had patented it in 1866 for five years. After the patent had run out Foyn incorporated it in his winch system. He himself declared that "this elastic strop alone makes it possible in a seaway to haul up the dead whale, as without it, owing to the tremendous jerk, something would be bound to give, and the whale and the tackle would be lost".

As Roys and Lilliendahl made relatively good catches with their rowing boats in 1865 and 1866, Foyn began to doubt whether his *Spes et Fides* was of the right size. Maybe it was too big? For this reason

37

14. Model of *Spes et Fides,* the world's first steam whale-catcher, built to Svend Foyn's design, 1863-4.

he had a considerably smaller steamer built in 1868, only 58½ ft. long (*Spes et Fides* was 94¾ ft.), and the smallest vessel ever built for modern catching. But despite this it had a stronger engine, one developing approximately 100 i.h.p. It must have done yeoman service, as it was in use in Finnmark whaling for twenty years. In 1876 Foyn acquired his third whaling boat, midway in size between the other two, and in 1883 he took the step of contracting the largest whale boat to date, with an engine of 190 i.h.p., which gave it a speed of 10½ knots. This relatively powerful vessel is symptomatic of the development that started that year, and which for three reasons demanded more powerful and sturdy vessels, not necessarily greater tonnage. In the first place, with growing competition and a struggle for whales, the man with the fastest boat would have the greatest chance of winning. A parallel exists in the construction of the top-heavy whale boats of the 1950s, built to ensure the greatest possible share of the 16,000 BWU to be competed for. In the second place, whale boats had to operate further from land in order to find whales, and the return voyage to the station would involve a long tow. The quality of the oil depended to some extent on the length of time from the death of the whale until the raw material was boiled. In the third place, the global expansion was starting, which necessitated larger and sturdier vessels for catching over greater distances and in harsher climatic conditions. When catching started in the Antarctic in 1904 expeditions were operating with vessels of a size of about 150 dead-weight tons, with an engine developing 350 i.h.p. and a speed of 12 knots. Norwegian shipbuilding yards dominated the building of whale catchers for forty-five years after *Spes et Fides* had been launched, supplying boats for catching in all the whaling grounds of the world. It goes without saying that the hull, engine, and equipment of whale catchers were influenced by the general technical development in the construction of ships and engines.

At the end of the 1880s an ordinary whale catcher cost Kr. 60,000-80,000 (£3,300-£4,400), exclusive of catching equipment. Of the latter, the most expensive item was the gun, which cost about £110. It was of cast steel, and was cradled in a pivoting fork. A whale catcher generally carried about fifteen harpoons, which were 1.67 metres long and cost about £4.10 each. The line, made of best-quality hemp, about 300 metres long, was almost as expensive as the gun. Catchers generally carried two lines.

The shore station

With Svend Foyn and whaling, industry made its entry in Finnmark. True enough, close to the little town of Vadsø where he set up his oil-boiling plant and his guano factory there were already seven factories producing train oil from fish liver, but together they employed only seventeen hands for four months of the year. In 1870, for all his operations on sea and on land, Foyn employed forty-six hands for approximately six months, and at times six to eighteen extra casual workers from Vadsø. Fifteen years later there were twenty stations of this kind along the coast of northern Norway and three on the coast of Murmansk. However, the advantages accruing to the province were not as great as might have been expected, because most of the workers came from another part of the country, to which also went most of the profits, because it was there that the capital resided.

Roughly speaking, the processing of a whale at a Finnmark station in the late 1880s proceeded on the following lines. Once a whale had been killed, it was towed into the station and attached at high water on a flat beach as far up as possible. Throughout the entire period of Arctic whaling not a single hauling-up slipway was built, probably because there were no winches strong enough to tackle a load of up to and even over 100 tons. (Even fifty years later the greatest difficulty was experienced in pulling the whale up the stern slipway to the flensing deck on the floating factory.) The whale was flensed at low water, and the job had to be done quickly, before the tide turned. For flensing, slightly curved knives, $1\frac{1}{2}$ ft. long and attached to a $4\frac{1}{2}$ ft. long shaft, were used. The blubber was cut up in parallel strips, about $1\frac{1}{2}$ ft. wide, along the length of the whale. At the end of the strip a hole was cut and a hook was fastened by means of a wire to a winch, which pulled the strip off as it was loosened from the carcass by the flensers. To start with the winch was worked by hand, but in 1895 the first steam-winch is believed to have been used.

After the blubber and whalebone had been removed, what was left of the carcass — i.e. the flesh and the bones — was hauled up into a building where it was cut up. Various chopping and crushing machines were tried out for the bones, but none of them was really entirely satisfactory, and the bones were sawn up by hand, which proved a time-consuming and laborious task. The partitioned pieces were conveyed in waggons running on rails to the try-works. This was a huge shed with a central aisle and sixteen large, cylindrical, upright boilers or "cookers" on both sides. These were variously designed, depending on whether they were to be used for the boiling of blubber, meat, or bone. The blubber boilers were open, and reached right up to the first floor, from where they were filled. Drainage taps were set on the sides of the boilers at various heights, and a steam tube was connected to the bottom of each boiler, continuing in a spiral inside. The largest of these had a capacity of sixty barrels.

When the boiler had been filled, the steam was turned on for eight to ten hours, and most of the oil was then separated from the blubber, as well as a certain amount of gluewater (the liquid remaining in the boiler after the oil had been tapped) which collected at the bottom and run off. Through a tap set higher up on the boiler the oil was run off into large clearing vessels, where it remained standing for a day or two so that the sediment could sink to the bottom and the clear oil could be drawn off into oak vats containing about 160 litres (six vats to a ton). The gluewater which was drawn off from the boilers evaporated, leaving a sticky, viscous mass of glue.

The bone and meat boilers were more or less similar, except that boiling was carried out under a certain pressure, with the lid screwed down over the opening. Near the bottom of each boiler was a hatch, to enable the remains of the raw material to be raked out once the boiling process was completed. At some of the stations this stinking mass (or grax, as it was called) was conveyed to special boilers or re-cookers, in order to separate the oil that was still left. At other stations it was scrapped and shovelled into the sea, where a good deal of it was consumed by sea fowl. Raking up grax was the job whalers loathed most of all: in many cases they had to lower themselves into the still-warm boilers in order to remove the grax. The men who emptied the boilers were the least-respected members of the whaling community, and their wages reflected this. A great many attempts were made to produce guano and whalemeal from the meat residue, and most of these processes were, in fact, capable of producing a serviceable product, but the production costs, not least because of the price of coal, were so great that they left no margin of profit. Only a few of the shore stations had guano factories : one of these was the one Foyn established in 1870 near Vadsø, and subsequently near his other two stations. From his accounts it appears that he found the production of guano not particularly profitable. He probably only continued to produce it because he considered it a sin to waste God's gifts. Though a certain amount of waste took place, the fact is that during the Finnmark whaling an almost total exploitation of raw material was achieved, a very different matter from the old catching methods, not to mention some of the worst examples of waste in the history of whaling, which occurred in the first period of Antarctic and pelagic catching.

Floating factories

We generally associate the term "pelagic catching" with the epoch that was ushered in with the Antarctic whaling of the 1920s. In principle, however, there was nothing new in this, merely a technical change. The old European, the American, and modern catching all reveal three parallel stages of development : from (1) stationary, home-shore whaling via (2) expansive stationary or whale-station coastal catching in distant waters, to (3) catching in the open sea. Finnmark whaling, generally speaking, represents the first stage in this development within modern whaling. It came into being when the old catching of sperm and right whales was mainly carried out on a pelagic basis, and Roys and Lilliendahl reverted to the first stage when they established their modern catching, although they never entirely abandoned the idea of the floating factory. When Roys, after ten years of catching with a vessel in the northern waters, established a shore station in Iceland in 1865, he continued to use a sailing vessel, riding at anchor near the station, as his try-works. An attempt to process the oil on board two newly constructed steamers in the open sea proved a failure, and practically the entire catch in the ensuing year (1866) was processed ashore. It appears from a note in Foyn's diary that he had had word of the boiling equipment on the two steamers, and this may have encouraged him in his plans to experiment with the floating factory, especially as stocks of whale along the coast of Finnmark were declining so noticeably that it was proving difficult to supply the shore station with raw material.

In the summer of 1890 Foyn equipped an expedition for catching around Bjørnøya (Bear Island) and Spitsbergen. It consisted of a whale catcher and a seal-trapping vessel, with equipment to boil some of the

blubber flensed from the whale along the ship's side. After six weeks the
expedition returned with 60 barrels of oil and 200 tons of blubber, as
well as 2-3 tons of baleen (whalebone). When the blubber was processed
ashore the total result was some 970 barrels. This experiment aroused
a certain amount of attention, as it showed that it was possible to operate
without being tied to a permanent shore station. In 1891 bad weather
restricted catching, which was consequently abandoned in this area but
resumed in the waters round Iceland in 1892, when the results were
better — fourteen whales and about 700 barrels of oil. But in 1893,
when only ten whales were caught and the result hardly covered the
outlay, this area, too, was abandoned. Instead, Foyn, now eighty-four
years old, despatched a former sealing vessel to the Ross Sea in the
Antarctic, to search for right whales.

Whalers and their working life

In the 1930s, when the Germans maintained — as we have already
mentioned — that Foyn's grenade harpoon was really a German invention, the assertion was frequently made that he had used German
gunners during the first years of experiment. The latter statement is
just as erroneous as the former. All the crews' lists for Foyn's boats show
that he never signed on a single German. The few "foreigners" to be
found were mainly Swedes, plus a few Danes. The voyage north in
February and March, in heavily laden whale catchers, was often very
hazardous, and it was on such voyages — and not during catching
operations — that the greatest loss of life occurred. In 1887 a catcher
went aground and sank with forty-six hands of whom only two were
saved. In 1892 a vessel foundered in a storm with twenty-eight hands.
On the crossing to Iceland in April 1897 a whale boat, with thirty-two
hands on board, was lost without a trace. Altogether, these three
disasters cost 106 lives, but, as far as we know, very few were killed as a
result of accidents during whaling or working at the factory during these
eleven years.

The pursuit of the whale, however, could be highly dangerous.
During the initial period the gun frequently exploded, killing or seriously
wounding the gunner. This could also happen if the shell exploded
before hitting the whale. On one occasion a shell did not explode until
the whale was being towed along the ship's side. The vessel was badly
holed, and sank. We know of at least five incidents when a wounded
whale in desperation swam at terrific speed straight into the side of the
catcher, sinking it. If a whale was only wounded, it might pull out the
entire length of line, and set off, with the boat in tow, at a good speed,
even though the engine was in reverse. In order to tire the animal, it was
made to "run the loop", as the expression had it, i.e. instead of following

straight behind the whale, the catcher would veer off to one side, running parallel with the whale, with the line in a great curve between them. This could be dangerous, and on two occasions a whale pulled so hard to one side that the boat turned turtle and sank, with the loss of many lives. When the whale was finally quite exhausted and quiet, but not dead, it was killed by a man who rowed across and despatched it with a lance, hence the expression "to lance the whale". This involved a certain risk, as the whale might occasionally suddenly come to life and smash the boat with its tail. On one occasion Svend Foyn nearly lost his life when the line caught round his foot as the whale was pulling it, dragging him with it.

The Swedish natural scientist HERMAN SANDBERG has a vivid description of the sequence of events in catching a whale according to Svend Foyn's method:

The famous whale hunter Svend Foyn had very kindly placed the first of his steamers at my disposal with a view to investigating certain portions of the coast of Murmansk and had allowed me to bring with me the entire equipment for whaling with a view to retaining the catch for zoological use.

As we sailed out there was a stiff nor'wester blowing and a high sea. The way the small vessel rolled made it rather uncomfortable to sit down. I found it most advisable to take to my bunk and get a good nap. But already at the entrance to the Motka fjord, on the south side of Fiskerøya, the captain roused me and said that there were several whales lying around us, spouting, but that the wind was still too strong to try to catch them.

We proceeded up the fjord, past several whales, and shortly afterwards were in more sheltered water. After a while we saw a large and very fat blue whale wallowing and gorging in shoals of small fish, of which huge quantities occur in these waters. Every time the whale surfaced it was surrounded by a number of gulls who were on the alert and secured themselves a meal from the fish. When it submerged again, all the gulls indicated the path the whale had taken.

Whenever the whale came across a shoal of fish, it would open its vast maw and wallow in the shoal, shut its mouth and spurt water high into the air. This manoeuvre was repeated at intervals of a few minutes for about an hour. After watching this meal for a while, I gave orders to shoot the whale.

In the bows of each of Svend Foyn's whale catchers a cannon, 4 ft. long, is mounted on a tenon and can be swung rapidly up and down and to each side. The gun is loaded with ordinary gunpowder and a wadding of gutta percha. On this is placed a harpoon, which Foyn alone succeeded, after costly experiments extending over many years, in developing to a high degree of perfection. The harpoon has a double shaft, made of very tough iron, and at the rear end of it is a ring to which is attached a 5-inch cable of the best quality hemp, plaited in such a way that it will stand twice as much as an ordinary ship's hawser without breaking. The cable runs

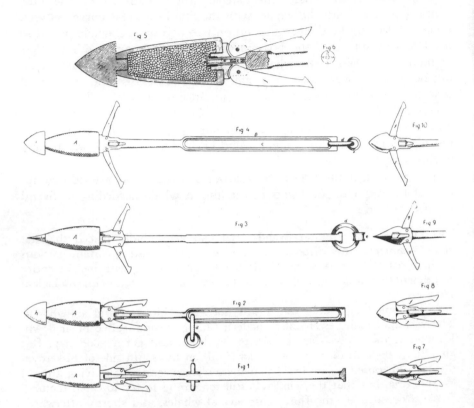

15.　The shell-harpoon for which Svend Foyn was granted a patent
in 1873.

over a winch, which is designed in such a way that the line can be hauled
in or eased off immediately with the whole force of the steam engine,
according to the movements of the whale.

The shooting itself demands such speed and accuracy that a good gunner
is a real treasure. But even the best of them may miss, particularly in a
high sea or when the target is a fin whale, as this animal only appears
for a short moment on the surface of the water, and is much more rapid
in its movements and wilder than the fatter and therefore more sluggish
blue whale. One must be careful not to hit the whale in the tail, because
in such cases, without its strength being diminished, it is merely attached
to the boat, which it tows helplessly at lightning speed through the seething
waves.

The gun is made ready and loaded, the harpoon is inserted, and the
chase is on. Sometimes we came very close to the whale, which was clearly
not the least bit afraid of us. It was almost as long as the boat, and much
wider, and a considerable breadth is regarded as a sign of great strength in

a whale. Finally, we were at a suitable range, and the shot was fired. The
harpoon immediately disappeared inside the body of the whale, and
appeared to have an instantly paralysing effect. At first we all thought
that the animal had been instantly killed, but immediately afterwards it
dived, the line ran taut, and a muffled report told us that the shell had
exploded inside the whale. Once again it stopped, as though struck by
lightning. But now the wild chase began. Maddened with pain, the whale
darted hither and thither, now diving into the sea, now surfacing. Our
boat was pulled along at a brisk pace to one side and the other, so that
the water poured over our bow. Every hand at his post signals his presence
and everyone obeys the smallest gesture from the leader. It was a life-and-
death struggle. The whale stained the sea red in a wide circle around it,
and spouted great columns of blood every time it surfaced.

The struggle lasted for about an hour, until the whale was finally
exhausted. Unconsciously it rolled over on its side, and at times came
straight at us at such a speed that its whole head or about one-third of the
body could be seen above the surface of the water. At this stage the situation could be really dangerous. If the whale with its tremendous force had
struck the boat with its head, it would almost certainly have made a large
hole. For this reason it was important to keep a sharp lookout, and keep
at a respectful distance. A little later it was so weakened with loss of blood
that it could be killed with the thrust of a lance from a boat that was
lowered. By means of a stout halter through the head and a chain round
its huge tail, the whale was lashed to the boat, and towed the six miles
back to port.

In order to keep the whale afloat, and to make it easier to tow it back
to the station, in the 1880s they started pumping up the whale by
thrusting a hollow spear right into the abdominal cavity, and inflating
the animal with air from the ship's pump. As we shall see below, this
lowered the quality of the whale by accelerating the process of spontaneous combustion inside the animal when oxygen from the air was
introduced. As a rule the whale was towed along the ship's side tail first.
Some of the largest blue whales were as long as the boat.

Thanks to ample supplies of fresh whale meat it was possible to vary
the fare on board far more than in ordinary ships, where it was very
monotonous. Plenty of cheap fish was also ready to hand. The diet at the
stations must have been extremely healthy, as accounts agree that there
was not much sickness among the hands despite the unremitting toil and
a seventy- or eighty-hour working week. Once the day was over there
was only enough surplus energy to relax a little before turning in.
Being deeply religious, Foyn was insistent that there should be no work
on Sundays; these were to be real days of rest. At one of the stations he
built a small house where edifying meetings could be held. Otherwise
Sundays were spent reading and writing letters, visiting other stations,
making friends with the local population, etc. As most of the hands

had been recruited from sealing and fishing circles, Foyn insisted that the manager of the shore station should exercise the same discipline, the same legal and patriarchal authority, as the captain on board a ship.

What attracted people to whaling, despite the back-breaking work it often involved, was the prospect of better wages than in comparable employment, e.g. that of a seaman in the merchant service or a manual labourer ashore. Then there was the bonus system, which opened opportunities for still higher wages. This system developed in the 1870s, and more particularly during the growing competition of the 1880s. It was natural that the crews on the whale catchers should be interested in ensuring that the number of whales caught was as great as possible. Foyn was very thrifty and cautious, and to start with paid no bonus, but only monthly wages. But as the other companies paid both a bonus and higher wages in an attempt to attract the best crews, he was forced to follow suit. The bonus, which was originally equally large, irrespective of the species of whale, gradually became more and more differentiated. Wages and bonus varied considerably from one company to another, but in time an adjustment took place, as will be seen from a wages return for 1901 shown in Table 2.

Table 2. WHALERS' MONTHLY WAGES AND BONUS, 1901

	Monthly wage (Kr.)	Bonus per whale (Kr.)
Gunner	120	50, 40, 25, 20
Engineer	130-140	5, 3
Engineer's assistant	55	5, 3
Stoker	25	1
Steward	50	5, 3
Seaman	45	5, 3

Note: Figures for gunners are gradated according to species of whale: Kr. 50 for a blue whale, Kr. 40 for a fin whale, Kr. 25 for a humpback, and Kr. 20 for a sei whale. In the figures given for the other crew members, Kr. 5 was the bonus for a blue whale and Kr. 3 for other species. (£1 = Kr. 18.20.)

The wage returns for the 1887 season for one company lasting five months and twenty-three days, resulting in the catching of twenty-five whales (six blue, twenty-three fin, six sei whales) and 2,000 barrels of oil, show that the total wages were: gunner Kr. 1,541, engineer Kr. 774, bo'sun Kr. 520, stoker Kr. 400, seaman Kr. 358. A total of Kr. 4,709 was paid out to the entire crew for one season. Thirty-five whales was far above the average that year, which was twenty-six and a half whales for all vessels operating in North Norway.

The same return shows that a bonus was also paid to personnel working at the shore station. This was not general in the early years because these hands were not in a position to make a direct contribution to an increase in catching to the same extent as the people on the catchers. But it was soon apparent that thanks to skill, speed, and accuracy in processing the whale and the boiling, both the quantity and not least the quality — and thus the value of the product — could be considerably improved. The entire workforce constituted a team working closely together, and for this reason it would in the long run have been impossible to exclude part of this team from the bonus system. It was just as natural to pay the hands at the station a bonus per barrel of oil as it was to remunerate the catcher crews with a bonus per whale caught. As rates varied a great deal more between companies in this respect, it is difficult to give a general idea of what the bonus amounted to. It varied from Kr. 2.50 per barrel for the manager to a few øre for the hands ($1d = 7\frac{1}{2}$ øre, 1901). The usual trend was for a low bonus whenever monthly wages were high and vice versa. In later wage negotiations, when both employees and employers had set up their trade organisations, it always proved difficult to come to an agreement which coordinated the two types of remuneration. It was a toss-up: in a season with good catches, a high bonus rate and low wages were preferable, but with a poor catch the reverse was the case, as the wages would remain constant.

In whaling, as in all other industries, fluctuations in wages naturally depended on supply and demand. As long as catching was an expanding industry, there was a crying need for specialised workers, which meant that wages achieved a level considerably higher than that in corresponding trades. When other nations embarked on modern whaling they were entirely dependent on Norwegian know-how, and, as we shall see, were prepared to pay prodigious sums to acquire it. There was a hint of this as far back as the 1880s, when the Russians started catching off the coast of Murmansk, and were compelled to a large extent to use Norwegians. In 1886 a whale catcher turned up in these waters with twenty-one Norwegian whalers, some of whom were to act as crew on two catchers, and some as specialists at the shore station. They were paid relatively much higher wages and a more generous bonus than in Norwegian whaling.

Companies, profits, and financial importance

It goes without saying that the chief concern of the companies was not to produce oil, but to sell it. Throughout the period of Finnmark catching they were face to face not only with dwindling stocks of whales and growing competition, but also a declining price of oil. Svend Foyn, who was first off the mark and enjoyed a ten-year monopoly while prices were still favourable, undoubtedly made the handsomest profit. Up to

1883 the price fluctuated between £25 and £35 per ton. In 1878 it slipped to just below £30 for the first time, and then, suddenly, in 1884, it slumped to a maximum of £24 and a minimum of £20, and once again in the following year, when catching results were good, to £24 and £14 respectively. The situation was still worse in 1887, with £20 and £12, and during the subsequent seventeen years, until Finnmark whaling came to an end in 1904, the price never rose above £23 (1890) in any single year, and for nine of these years the maximum price was under £20. This, it should be emphasised, was the rate for Oil no. 1, and in 1885 it was estimated that only 60 per cent came in this category. For Oil no. 4 the price in 1887 reached an all-time low of £10. In years with a market so unfavourable it was difficult for many of the companies to make both ends meet. Right up to 1882, however, whaling was a splendid investment. It was not uncommon for companies to record net profits of 50 to 75 per cent of the share capital. This was all the more remarkable, as shipping suffered a slump after 1874. Whaling was so much more attractive that in 1883 a spate of new companies was started. The result was a decline in the number of whales caught per catcher, and consequently lower profits, a trend that was further accentuated by the drop in prices.

The year 1884 marks a decisive turning-point. It divides Finnmark whaling into two twenty-year periods, the first and formative period from 1864 to 1883, of which the latter ten years proved financially highly advantageous, and produced catches that bore a reasonable relationship to the available stocks of whale. In the second period, from 1884 to 1904, whalers were fighting on four fronts: among themselves in intense competition, a situation that would occur again; against declining stocks of whales; against the vicissitudes of the oil market; and against fishermen and government authorities.

The year 1889 proved particularly poor: the thirty-one vessels operating in the whole of North Norway accounted in all for only about 500 whales, and a great many companies were faced with the choice of closing down or moving to other grounds. They were temporarily saved, however, by relatively good catches during the following four years — 1890-4, particularly 1892 and 1893. In 1893 twenty-seven boats caught 1,225 whales — an average of 45.4 per boat — and as oil prices recorded a temporary rise, the financial results were practically as good as in the record year 1885, with 1,287 whales caught by thirty-three boats belonging to eighteen companies. After a sharp decline in 1885, the next three years, 1896-8, yielded very good catches, with a stable result which varied from 1,198 to 1,063 whales, caught by twenty-five boats. Oil production totalled 29,400, 26,000, and 23,600 barrels respectively.

The nineteenth century drew to its close with poor prospects for

Finnmark catching. It was bad enough that the price in 1899 should slump to £15 (for no. 1), the lowest rate quoted till then, but even worse was the disastrous decline from 1,072 whales in 1898 to 474 in 1899 and 382 in 1900. Admittedly, the price improved somewhat in 1900-2, but the two poor seasons toppled several companies. Some dropped out voluntarily, others went bankrupt, and a few tried their luck in other parts of the Norwegian ocean. It is probable that at that stage catching would have collapsed, had there not been a rise in prices, but improved rates and a surprising catch-increase to 703 whales in 1902 (with five fewer whale catchers) persuaded the remaining ten companies that there was still hope for continued whaling. However, a fresh decline in catch and an absolute all-time low for the price of whale oil (£13 in 1905), made it crystal-clear that if catching had not been forbidden by law, it would nevertheless have been abandoned for financial reasons. It is in point of fact not really correct to speak of Finnmark catching in the narrow sense of the word, as a great deal of the whaling during the last two years (1903-4) took place around Bjørnøya, and the whales caught there were towed all the way — nearly 200 nautical miles — down to Finmark. A considerable number of whales were lost on the way, and many arrived in poor condition.

It is an impossible task to illustrate statistically the economic importance of whaling to Vestfold county and Norway. If an adequate picture of the values involved prior to 1904 is to be given, we should also have to include whaling in other areas, as well as the many subsidiary activities that were associated with whaling, and, first and foremost among these, the engineering industry. Whaling and shipping were closely allied, not only technically but also economically. In most whaling companies we find shipowners on the Board and as major shareholders. After 1874 shipping entered a protracted period of depression which, with the exception of a few brighter years, lasted right up to 1911. This crisis struck with particular severity at the shipping towns of southern Norway, which witnessed stagnation and recession. That the population figures for Tønsberg should have doubled between 1865 and 1910, and those of Sandefjord tripled, and that the merchant shipping of both towns should have undergone a marked expansion, can only be explained by the fact that these towns had whaling to fall back on. At that time it provided a fair amount of the necessary capital, and was to do so to an even larger extent later.

In the course of time several associations of whaling companies have been formed, and on every occasion this has taken place in the face of difficulties, and when a strong need was felt to pull together. There have been two motives at the back of this: to improve the price of whale oil and to defend themselves against attack and criticism. The special reasons that led to the founding of the first association in 1890 were the strained relations with the fishing population of Finnmark and government intervention in the conflict. The companies held several meetings in the 1880s, and agreed on 24 February 1890 to establish the Norwegian Whaling Association. As it had proved a simple matter for purchasers of whale oil to depress the price when they were dealing with a small-time producer, the Association aimed to function as a sales ring. Not much is known about it, and it is uncertain whether it was a reorganisation of this association or an entirely new one that was founded in 1902 under a slightly different Norwegian name. Its most important purpose was to fight the proposed legislation for a ban on whaling from North Norway.

Products, markets and prices

The Norwegian seal trappers, and among them Svend Foyn, had been in the habit of selling the seal oil and pelts in Hamburg. It was therefore natural that they should endeavour, during the first whaling epoch, to find a market in that city for their whale oil. Before long, however, Great Britain, in particular Scotland, became the chief market for Norwegian oil and also for other products. A link was forged between Svend Foyn and CHRISTIAN SALVESEN in Leith, who had emigrated from Norway in 1851 in order to manage the Grangemouth branch of his brother's business. Later, Christian Salvesen established his own business, and became the founder of what, in the inter-war years, was to be the world's largest whaling company. His business was from the very start based on connections between Scotland and Norway, with coal in the main being transported east and timber west.

According to family tradition, it was Christian Salvesen who introduced Foyn to the Scottish market. This is not improbable, as it was Salvesen who supplied Svend Foyn with coal practically from the start of his whaling operations, and who subsequently became a purveyor for most companies in Norway and Iceland. As a Norwegian resident in Scotland it would be natural for Salvesen to be used as an agent for the sale of Norwegian whale oil, and from the start of the 1880s this agency comprised a large share of the firm's business. Whale oil was no new product on the Scottish market: the east coast towns had been used as a base for the catching of Greenland whale, but this finally came to an end, and was superseded eventually by modern whaling. The most important of the Scottish whaling towns, Dundee, had become the centre of the jute trade, on the basis of whale oil, because there was no substitute for whale oil for making jute fibres soft and pliable. For this purpose oil of the poorest quality could, of course, be used. During a hearing undertaken in Dublin 1907 in connection with Norwegian plans for commencing whaling operations from the west coast of Ireland, the

Norwegians' distributor, the firm of Robertsen & Berntsen of Glasgow, stated that it had been established there in about 1870 "as sales representative for Svend Foyn". Subsequently, Glasgow became the centre for the world marketing of whale oil.

Most years, Norway continued exporting oil, with small amounts also consigned to France and Germany, but Great Britain remained the major purchaser, not merely of Norwegian but of world production. Some years there was only one purchaser, and that was the firm of Lever Bros Ltd., from 1930 renamed Unilever Ltd. We shall subsequently see how fatal this dependence on a single purchaser was to be for Norwegian whaling.

Taken all round, Norwegians were dissatisfied with the poor price the Scots paid for their oil because, as they insisted, it was of poor quality. For this reason the Norwegians made considerable efforts to improve the quality, and during the years 1882-1904 a great many patents for processing marine animal oils were taken out. It was said that the Scots tended to buy cheap, poor quality Norwegian oil because they had discovered a method of refining the oil, a method which was a closely guarded business secret. Otherwise the price more or less followed fluctuations in the general state of the British market. We have already mentioned the reasons for the constantly declining prices from about 1870 onwards. One of them was that the price was depressed by competition from other edible oils and fats, both animal and vegetable. In the world market for these commodities whale oil was almost always in the lowest price bracket, even though, after hydrogenisation, it had been made edible for use in margarine. Up till then its functions were restricted to lubrication, the manufacture of soft soaps, of jute, textiles, for tanning, tempering steel, tinning, etc., though in somewhat limited quantities.

Over the years whaling has been arraigned on two counts: in the first place, after the right whales had been practically wiped out, whaling very nearly inflicted the same fate on the rorquals; and secondly, it has been responsible for a fearful waste of raw material, the whale being one of Nature's great sources of fats. As already mentioned, even Svend Foyn realised that the blubber contained only 40-50 per cent of the whale's total fat content, and that the rest, too, should be extracted; and, even when all the oil had been distilled, there still remained other raw materials which could and should be utilised. From as early as 1869 he emphasised the importance of making as good use of the carcass as possible, and established a large guano factory adjoining the Vadsø shore station. Other companies followed his example, and at one time there were six guano factories in Finnmark.

As the residual raw material, after the oil had been extracted, was rich in proteins, attempts were also made to produce *cattle feed,* and two factories were built for this purpose. They did no whaling on their own account, but purchased the whale carcasses from adjacent stations. Some of the stations that produced guano also manufactured cattle feed. Both products found a market in Norway, Sweden, and Great Britain, but the bulk went to Germany, and the price was generally quoted in Marks (c. 20 Marks = £1). In 1883 this was, for guano, 21-22 Marks per 100 kg., plummeting in 1884 to 14 Marks and remaining low for the rest of the century, from 10 to 8 Marks. During the last two years the price of cattle feed was about Kr.13.50. The low price does not appear to have hampered production, but for the companies concerned it was not only a financial but also a technical problem. It was possible to manufacture high-quality cattle feed, but the cost was so great that it was not worth it. Technically speaking the greatest difficulty was to remove all the oil, leaving a dry powder, without any lumps. However well the raw materials were utilised, there was always a certain amount of waste, not least the oil in the gluewater. The problem of extracting this oil was not solved until much later, with the use of gluewater separators.

We have only occasional figures for the production of guano and cattle feed. In 1886 and 1887 it was approximately 14,000 and 11,000 sacks respectively. Figures for 1896-1902 show an annual average of 12,272 sacks, and in the years 1888-95 it may be assumed that production was on about the same level.

During the Finnmark whaling era, *glue* was produced from the gluewater and from the whalebones. In 1889 Foyn was awarded a gold medal for his glue at a Paris exhibition. In the same year another company produced 64,000 kg. of glue, which in its clarity was said to surpass fish glue and bone glue. Some 15,000 kg. were produced from bones and the remains of the blubber.

As early as the start of the 1880s experiments were made for canning *whale meat,* and considerable quantities were produced during the following years. In 1883 one of the companies held a demonstration in Oslo at which canned whale beef and canned meat cakes were served. The papers wrote that it was entirely free from the taste of oil, and had the flavour of beef at one-third the price. In 1893 a Norwegian patriot and whale-meat enthusiast served press representatives in Brussels with a whale-meat dinner. This included Fillet de baleine, Sauce d'anchois, Épigramme de baleine à la Béchamel, and Chaud-froid de baleine, Sauce Groënlandaise. This dinner attracted attention in both Brussels and Norway; one newspaper was full of praise, and declared that whale meat could be of importance to the working class as it only cost 30 centimes a kilo. This, however, is mainly of academic interest. The only country in the world in which whale meat for human consumption has been the chief purpose of whaling is Japan, a fascinating chapter in the history of whaling of which we shall hear more when Japan makes her debut in international catching.

It was the periodically fantastic prices of the long right whale baleens which kept the old whaling alive in its declining years. The shorter rorqual baleens, too, were a valuable by-product. When the hands at the stations had nothing to occupy them, owing to a shortage of whales, they were generally set to work to clean the baleens. The flesh and fat was scraped off them, they were washed in soda lye, dried, and pressed in bundles of about 75 kg. These were exported to Germany, England, and France, where Paris was the most important centre for the marketing of baleens. Their value lay in their lightness, tremendous elasticity, and flexibility, which ensured that they assumed their original form after being subjected to pressure. The longest specimens were used as springs in sofas and mattresses, the shorter ones for a great variety of purposes — for ladies' corsets and frocks, e.g. crinolines, for umbrella and parasol ribs, to preserve the curls in gentlemen's wigs, for brushes (e.g. for chimney sweeps). In France the baleens were split into thin fibres, which were woven into silk fabric in order to preserve its rigidity. In about 1880 it was estimated that on an average a blue whale could provide 250 kg. of baleens, a fin whale 125, a humpback 100, and a sei whale 80. Norwegian exports of baleens, not only from Finnmark but also from other fields, varied very considerably. In 1879 they totalled 27 tons, in 1885-6 130 (all figures are minimum figures), and in the period 1890-1905 exports fluctuated between about 60 and 440 tons annually. The price varied just as much as the quantity. In 1879 an average price of £120 a ton was quoted. A price-list for the years 1885-1900 shows a rate of £45 for blue whale baleen in 1885, a sharp rise to £200 in 1891, and £300 in 1892, after which we plunge to £35 in 1898, only to rise to £78 in 1900. The price of fin whale baleen followed approximately the same pattern, but during the last four years was somewhat higher than that for blue whale baleen, probably because supplies were not so ample. Sei whale baleen was in constant demand, and towards the end of the period the price was considerably above that of the other two. Comparing the prices of baleen with the prices of oil we shall see that the former did not follow fluctuations of the latter, because baleen prices depended on other factors than those that decided market trends in general and those for whale oil in particular. For this reason it sometimes happened that in years with low oil prices sales of baleen constituted a very important source of income, for example in 1892, when the maximum price varied just as much as the quantity. In 1879 an average price of of £300, and the value of baleen exports, some 130 tons, was as much as Kr.650,000. In 1896, on the other hand, the value of exports that were twice this volume, about 260 tons, was only a half of this.

The low price of oil in the last twenty years of Finnmark whaling proved an important spur to the production of all the other commodities based on the whale as raw material. On the whole, good progress was made in this direction during the period we are now dealing with. In this respect the transfer of whaling to the Antarctic, with its tremendous supplies of raw material, proved a major retrograde step, both during the first period, with shore stations, and subsequently on the floating factories, where lack of space made it impossible to install plants for complete processing of the whale. The result was enormous wastage of one of Nature's richest sources of raw material as long as it sufficed to use only the best part of it. When supplies became less plentiful, companies were forced, for financial reasons, to turn every fibre of the whale into a saleable product. In the event this turned out to be technically possible on the floating factories as well, but companies by this time were beginning to feel the pressure of growing world opinion against them, owing to the risk of an extinction of whale stocks on their part.

4

FINNMARK WHALING DURING THE PERIOD OF FREE COMPETITION, 1883-1904

Svend Foyn's monopoly ran out on 1 January 1883, a date impatiently awaited by a great many people, though others had already jumped the gun, either by purchasing the right to catch according to Foyn's method or by paying a levy of 10 per cent of net profits, or by making slight alterations in the catching equipment in order not to infringe the patent. For the right to use his patent Foyn demanded first of all that they should not operate in the Varanger fjord. This, the easternmost of Norwegian fjords, runs east-west into Finnmark, dividing the eastern portion of this county into North Varanger (or the Varanger Peninsula) and South Varanger. Foyn's station was situated almost centrally on the north side of the fjord. According to a Whale Protection Act of 19 June 1880, there was a ban on catching inside a limit of one geographical mile (= 7,420 metres) measured from the outermost islands, during the period 1 January to 1 June. For the Varanger fjord there was a total ban inside a boundary line drawn from the north to the south side of the fjord, at its mouth. Foyn's station was consequently placed in an unfortunate position, as it was situated about 24 nautical miles inside this line, and he had a comparatively long trip to the catching grounds. Apart from this Whaling Act the authorities took no steps to restrict free catching. The result was a mushrooming of new companies, and an excessive concentration of stations immediately north and south of the mouth of the fjord.

As early as 1880-1 five new companies had arrived on the scene, two of them with their stations located in West Finnmark, far from the Varanger fjord. It was here that the pioneer Svend Foyn had started and made his fortune, and most of them were drawn, as though by a magnet, to this part. They established themselves at the very mouth of the fjord, so that they could continue catching during the period when there was a ban on whaling in the fjord itself. Whereas in 1882 there were only two stations in South Varanger, in 1883 there were five, operating with seven vessels; there had also been two in the north in 1882, and in the following year six, operating with eight boats. Thus the number of companies (and stations) increased overall from seven to sixteen, and the number of vessels from thirteen to twenty-three.

With his shore station so far from the open sea, Foyn was at a great disadvantage: his rivals had a much shorter distance to the catching

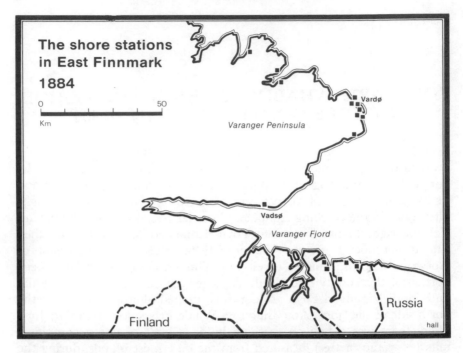

The shore stations
in East Finnmark
1884

0   50
Km

Vardø

Varanger Peninsula

Vadsø

Varanger Fjord

Russia

Finland

hall

grounds, and a shorter return voyage when towing their whales back to their stations, and after 1 June, when the close season came to an end in the fjord, a swarm of whale catchers could hunt the whale before it made its way up the fjord. Foyn suffered the mortification of realising that the large establishment, which had taken him thirteen years to set up, was valueless. But, despite his seventy-four years, he refused to accept defeat. His first thought was to move over to Iceland, and for this purpose he invested three-fifths of the capital in a company established in the little town of Haugesund on the west coast of Norway, with a view to catching from Iceland. But after spending a few months there in the summer of 1883, he abandoned this plan, for reasons which we shall discuss later. Instead, in 1884 he built two new stations, one in the extreme west of Finnmark and one approximately mid-way between this and his old Vadsø station. Using the latter as his base, he operated for the last time in 1884. The increase in the number of whales caught bore no reasonable proportion to the increase in the material used. Records vary considerably : in 1882 a total of some 395 whales was accounted for by all the companies in North Norway; in 1883 the number was somewhere between 506 and 561, and in 1884 between 446 and 465, i.e. a considerable decline in the average number of whales per catcher, from about 20.5 in 1883 to about 17.5 in 1884. For many companies these were years of financial difficulty, and fears were expressed that the expansion had been too great and that stocks of whales would soon be exterminated. It was also pointed out that not only were Norwegians whaling, but that the Russians too, operating from stations on the Murmansk coast, were making inroads in the same stocks.

There was, however, no stopping the whaling fever: it spread to other parts of Norway; three companies were established in the capital, Oslo, and three in other towns. A company known as the Anglo-Norwegian Whaling Company, based in part on British capital, was established in Tromsø, the largest town in North Norway. Tønsberg, however, was still the dominant whaling town, the home of fifteen of the thirty-nine whale catchers, while seven came from the other two Vestfold towns, so that 73 per cent of the Norwegian whaling fleet was registered in this county.

All the gloomy prophesies proved quite unfounded when in 1885 more than twice as many whales were caught as in the two previous years: a total of 1,287. This figure alone, however, provides no realistic reflection of the volume of the catch, as 724 of these were sei whales, and at that time seven sei whales were considered the equivalent of one blue whale in volume of oil and other products. In fact, the 724 sei whales corresponded to only 103 blue whales, of which a mere thirty-four were caught. As far as the total volume of raw materials was concerned, the figure of 1,287 is consequently not very illuminating. In 1886 the catch was 872 whales, but of these 114 were blue whales, corresponding to 800 sei whales, of which only 61 were killed. Thus, despite the fact that 400 fewer whales were caught, oil production was practically just as great — some 24,000 barrels — as in 1885, when it was 25,000 barrels. The tremendous difference in the number of sei whales for these two years confirms the results obtained in other fields, namely that there were typical sei whale years followed by years when this species appears to have disappeared from the sea. It goes without saying that it proved a far more expensive undertaking to catch seven sei whales than one blue whale — seven hunts, seven shots and harpoons, and a longer period spent in flensing and processing. In terms of the scale used by the *International Whaling Statistics,* the catch of blue whale units (BWU) for these two years was as shown in Table 3a.

Table 3a. CATCHES BY SPECIES OF WHALE, 1885-1886

	Blue	Fin	Humpback	Sei	Total	BWU
1885	34	437	92	724	1,287	411
1886	114	609	88	61	872	464

The years 1886-8 mark the absolute maximum use of catching matériel, with 30, 33, and 31 boats respectively, but as far as the volume of the catch was concerned it was not the best period, being surpassed by that of 1892-3 and 1896-8. As catching developed its centre of gravity moved west, and the shore stations in eastern Finnmark either had to be closed down or transferred further west in North Norway or to another area in the Norwegian Sea. In 1888, for example, the twenty-three catchers in East Finnmark accounted for only 341 whales, or 14.8 per boat, while the eight in West Finmark had a score of 286, or 35.75 per boat. Still further west in the neighbouring county two boats caught sixty-seven whales, while four boats on the Murmansk coast accounted for only forty-one, or 10.25 per boat, and when two boats in 1889 together secured only twenty whales, catching in this area was abandoned. Altogether, 1889 proved a turning-point both as far as total activities in the north were concerned and in the flight from East Finnmark. The number of companies never exceeded sixteen or the number of boats twenty-eight. As it turned out, the companies that had not been established in Vestfold were the first to give up, so that the concentration here became stronger than ever. In 1898 there were no stations left in South Varanger, and after two vessels in 1900 had caught only eight whales, this last company also gave up operations on the north side of the fjord.

No official statistics exist for the whale species caught in 1891-5, but various incidental items of information make it probable that a very large proportion of the high figures from 1892-3 — 1,014 and 1,102 — were sei whales. For 1896, on the other hand, we have reliable figures; Table 3b shows catches for the whole of North Norway for those years.

Table 3b. CATCHES BY SPECIES OF WHALE, 1891-1896

	Blue	Fin	Hump-back	Sei	Unknown	Total	Catchers	Whales per catcher
1891	33	248	51	244	128	704	27	26
1892	3	294	49	449	307	1,102	28	39
1893	10	396	30	422	367	1,225	29	42
1894	48	393	95	156	269	959	28	34
1895	15	364	113	93	147	732	29	25
1896	63	800	201	133	15	1,212	27	45

If the "Unknown" animals are assumed to be fin whales, the results in 1896 were 572 BWU, with 50 barrels per BWU. The later were less than one-half of what was achieved in Antarctic catching after the Second World War. (1 barrel = 170 kg., $\frac{1}{6}$ of 1 long ton = 1,016 kg.) The large number of fin whales is remarkable : both with regard to catching and to production, the year 1896 was definitely the best year of the entire Finnmark catching epoch. Both 1897 and 1898 also proved good catching years, but profits for the three years were poor owing to the all-time low price of oil, fluctuating between £15 and £18 a ton.

16. Typical Norwegian shore station, on the coast of Finnmark.

The favourable catching results during these three years provided whalers with a telling argument in the debate on the extinction of stocks of whales. There was, however, a change in attitude when in 1899 less than half the average for the three preceding years was achieved, and catches remained low right up to 1902, when a pronounced improvement engendered fresh optimism, and, as the debate continued, whalers were in a position to point out that it was impossible to establish any decline in stocks of whales. This upswing, however, proved a mere flash in the pan : in 1903 and 1904, the last years of Finnmark whaling, the number of whales caught slumped to the same level as in the three years prior to 1902.

There are two striking features of the three last years of catching, 1902-4. One is a marked increase in the number of blue whales, from 11 in 1901 to 58 in 1902, 126 in 1903, and 235 in 1904. The other is that Finnmark catching was no longer a coastal but a pelagic operation. By all accounts the coastal waters were practically bare of whales and catching took place further and further from the shore. Finally the bulk of the whales were caught right up by Bjørnøya, and it was here that blue whales were to be found. This trend had started in the mid-1890s, and had more or less been completed by 1904, the final year. At that time only one company was operating mainly along the coast, and with very poor returns, while those who used tugs and caught off Bjørnøya did very well. The 235 blue whales caught in 1904 were the absolute record.

How great it really was emerges from the fact that in 1881 221 were caught, otherwise the total in the four years of the Finnmark catch was just over 100. Faced with the inevitable, some companies moved to Bjørnøya and Spitsbergen. These operations, which marked the end of the Finnmark whaling, encouraged experiments with floating factories and boiling plants on board steamships.

Towards the end a change of centre of gravity, from Tønsberg to Sandefjord, occurred in the local basis for the whaling companies. This was in part due to the fact that Svend Foyn died in 1894, at the age of eighty-five. To the very end he was ceaselessly active. He was the first operator to move west from East Finnmark; in 1890-1 he tried operations off Spitsbergen, and in 1892-3 off Iceland once again, for the third time. His last enterprise was to despatch the seal-trapping vessel the *Antarctic* to the south polar regions in 1893 to investigate the possibility of catching right whales in the Ross Sea. This was in fact the first vessel to penetrate into this area since Sir JAMES CLARK ROSS had done so in 1842. Financially, the expedition was a total failure, but it was to have undreamed-of consequences for the exploration of the Antarctic continent and for whaling in these waters. By the time the expedition returned, Foyn was dead: his operations were continued for a number of years, and brought to a complete close in 1899. He bequeathed some Kr. 4 million of his fortune, at that time a tremendous sum by Norwegian standards, to missionary work. That such a large capital sum should have been transferred from productive work to "dead" capital was bound to have unfortunate consequences for whaling and the economy of Tønsberg. This was one of the reasons why Tønsberg's hegemony as a whaling centre passed to Sandefjord.

Tønsberg had developed into one of Norway's leading shipping towns, and the local population apparently preferred to invest in shipping rather than in such a hazardous undertaking as whaling. The town had a more varied economy and a certain amount of industry, which attracted capital and labour. This was not the case with Sandefjord, which was consequently able to concentrate its expansion on whaling and shipping, two closely allied enterprises. Most important of all, perhaps, was the fact that the town possessed among its citizens a number of outstanding personalities, talented businessmen who had confidence in the future of whaling and the courage to gamble on it. A concomitant factor was that, of Tønsberg's seven companies in 1904-5, three were committed to Finnmark, while of Sandefjord companies five operated there and two were engaged in Spitsbergen waters. Here, the number of expeditions in 1905 was so large and competition so keen that returns in every case were small. For this reason Sandefjord was harder hit by the ban in North Norway, and this may be one of the causes of the town's intense interest in opening up new whaling grounds.

5

THE DISPUTE OVER WHALE CONSERVATION IN NORTH NORWAY

The battle waged by the fishing population against whaling, and the dispute that arose in connection with the protection of the whale in North Norway are matters not only of local, Norwegian interest. We shall find the same dispute repeated in a number of other areas, and in every case the fishermen borrowed their arguments from their Norwegian colleagues. Animosity was directed not only against whaling itself, but also against the Norwegians: "After protecting the whale in their own coastal waters, they have the audacity to come and catch it off *our* coasts!"

The Norwegian laws governing the whale and whaling at the time when Foyn established himself in Finnmark were very ancient, and in considerable need of modernisation. The first step in this direction was taken in 1863: two points in particular were important. One was a ban on whaling in "herring fjords" during times when herring fishing was in progress, and this regulation was incorporated unamended in a new Act of 1869. This in no way affected Foyn, since during the period 1869-80, quoting chapter and verse of the law, he could claim the right to free catching everywhere and at all times. The second item involved an old law to the effect that any person finding a whale killed by another person possessed the right to two-thirds of its value. This law was repeated in the Act of 1863, and Foyn considered it highly unfair that he, who had expended a great deal of energy and borne the cost of hunting and killing the whale, should be left with a mere one-third. On one occasion, in fact , a fisherman came across a dead whale which had floated up to the surface; its value was asseessed at £180, and of this, according to the law, the fisherman was to have £120 and Foyn only £60 — or, in other words, he had to pay £120 for the return of a whale he himself had killed. In a new Act of 1869 the finder's remuneration was amended to at least one-quarter. Armed with this Act and his ten-year monopoly Foyn had acquired as large a measure of good will with the authorities as might reasonably have been expected, and for a decade he operated under very favourable conditions.

Not everyone, however, was so amicably disposed towards him. As early as 1872-3 the inhabitants of Vadsø and the fishermen along the Varanger fjord had submitted a concerted demand for the control of whaling. The reason for their dissatisfaction was a marked slump in the cod fisheries in the fjord. Whilst the annual average in 1867-71 had been

2,047,600 cod, in 1872-5 it was only half this amount, plummeting right down to 720,000 in 1876-9. This applied only to the Varanger fjord, and not to the whole of Finnmark, where catches remained relatively stable throughout the period. It is therefore hardly surprising that the fishermen should have blamed the decline in the Varanger fjord on whaling, which, as we have seen, had developed precisely in this part of the country during these years. A great many small steamers darted to and fro across the fjord, firing their cannon and generally dominating the scene. Sometimes a whaleboat or a hunted whale might foul the fishermen's nets, destroying them or in various other ways disturbing the fishermen. The smell from the Vadsø factory befouled the air of the town, while the waste from the factory polluted the water. There was certainly enough cause for irritation, but what weighed most heavily was that the threatened collapse of the economic basis of their existence coincided with a relatively marked increase in the population.

A table showing fishermen's earnings, shares, bonus, etc., gives a rough and ready idea of the whole conflict between whaling and fishing. It shows that during the period 1870-1904 the complaints and demands of the fishermen were generally most insistent in or immediately after years when their earnings were particularly low. The attitude of the fishermen, too, must be considered in the light of the technical revolution that was taking place in fishing from about 1870, from hand lines to expensive long lines, from coastal fishing to fishing off the banks, which needed larger and often superstructured vessels with attendant dories. The tackle and boats were expensive, and the population of Finnmark, with little access to capital, were consequently late starters, garnering relatively more modest returns than the fishermen who came from the south equipped with new tackle and who now constituted a new class of capitalists; and whereas a great many of the fishermen had previously been self-employed, they now worked for others. In every way a change was taking place in catching methods and in economic and social conditions which was bound to create friction between the various vested interests, and stir up discontent among the masses of the people. This dissatisfaction found an outlet in attacks on whaling, which was the major scapegoat.

In the latter half of the nineteenth century Finnmark was in every way the most backward of all the Norwegian counties; today it might be called a developing country. One effect of the whaling conflict was that the attention of the authorities was drawn to the wretched conditions of the population, and during the last decade of the century strenuous efforts were made to make up for lost ground. The impotence and poverty of the fishermen was in striking contrast with whaling interests, which were favoured by the state, and with the earnings of the whalers, which, by the standards of North Norway, were princely.

The whalers were poaching on preserves where, till then, the fishermen had ruled.

In 1873 seventy-three persons submitted an official complaint about whaling. Fishermen's earnings had slumped in 1872; it was maintained that Foyn was exterminating the whale, a senseless exaggeration as he had, up to then, caught some 175 in the course of nine years. Consternation at the prospect of the whale disappearing was based on the old belief, held by the fishermen, that the whale drove the capelin, the favourite food of the cod, in towards the land, and the capelin was, of course, the most important bait used in cod fishing. As there was a marked decrease in shoals of capelin moving in towards the coast during these years, in and just outside the Varanger fjord, and consequently less cod, the fishermen were in no doubt that this was due to whaling. Old superstitions die hard; they remained immune to fact and science, which in this case showed that it was not the whale and the cod that *drove* the capelin towards the coast, but that they *followed* this small fish when, for natural reasons, it sought coastal waters in order to spawn. Nor was it any use proving to the fishermen that no capelin or herring had ever been found in the belly of a blue whale, and that in the initial period this was the species Foyn had hunted most. The fin whale was an entirely different proposition: its most common food species off Finnmark was capelin, and, in other areas, herring. And it was precisely on these two arguments that criticism of a scientific investigation which had been set up by the Norwegian government was based: the investigation only covered blue whale and had not been undertaken during actual fishing, and secondly, a considerable quantity of fin whale had also been caught off the coast of Finnmark.

An unusually poor fishing season in 1878 provided a fresh spur to agitation: the most fanatical demanded a total ban, the more moderate a relatively mild form of protection. A public scientific committee recommended a closed season from 1 January to 31 May, basing their recommendation on the somewhat doubtful premise that it was important to pacify the population. The whalers were highly critical of the fact that they had not been consulted in the drafting of this proposal. In May 1880 the Norwegian Storting (Parliament) held a major debate on the proposal, and the fishermen enlisted the support of such brilliant speakers in favour of their cause that the proposal was adopted with a large majority. One argument that carried a great deal of weight was based on considerations of foreign policy: over a period of many years Russia had cast her eyes on Finnmark, and — as one of the speakers put it — if Russia were to adopt a law of this kind for catching off the coast of Murmansk, and Norway did not do likewise, what would be the feeling of the population in Finnmark? This was a hypothetical, rhetorical question, but its effect was tremendous. The matter became a domestic issue, too, when the Liberals discovered that they could make political capital out of it and win votes for the next general election. As already mentioned, the two most important points in this Act were a ban on catching between 1 January and 31 May less than one geographical mile from the shore, and a total ban during this period on all catching in the Varanger fjord. This Act was to apply for five years as from 1 January 1881. Little more was heard of the whaling dispute until the failure of the fisheries in the spring of 1883 once again prompted a demand for a total ban on catching during the period mentioned (outside the one-mile limit as well). However, whaling had now grown to be such an important industry that the authorities could not simply ignore it. Over twenty stations had been set up, thirty-three boats were in operation, considerably more than 1,000 hands were employed in it, and several hundreds of them were from Finnmark. As Russia failed to introduce any ban, a complete volte-face took place with regard to that country: a unilateral Norwegian ban would favour Russo-Finnish catching, and this might result in Norwegian capital and know-how being transferred to Murmansk. The marine biologists, moreover, expressed themselves in favour of whaling, while those who opposed it merely succeeded in having the Act renewed, in unamended form, for a further five years, from 1886 to 1890.

Once again, however, 1886 and, to a lesser extent, 1887 witnessed poor fishing results and minimal earnings for the fishermen, and it was not long before the whalers were once again in the line of fire. They themselves were dissatisfied with the renewal of the Act: declining oil prices and a decrease in the numbers of blue whales had made the situation precarious for several companies. Catching would have to rely more on the fin whale, a species which on the whole moved with the capelin towards the coast, where there was a ban on catching it during the first five months of the year — whereas catching was unrestricted from the Murmansk shore stations. The mood of the fishermen was whipped up until it almost assumed the character of a mass psychosis, impervious to commonsense and reasonable argument. Four to five hundred fishermen despatched the following telegram to the government: "In the profound conviction of the destructive effect of whaling on the fisheries along the coast of Finnmark, and seriously concerned for the future of themselves and the District, several hundred fishermen appeal to the Government to give the proposal for a Whale Protection Act its full support." In principle a total ban was demanded, alternatively a more effective form of legislation. Yet despite all the gloomy prognostications, 1889 proved a very successful year for the fisheries, with the fishermen earning bonuses more than twice as large as in 1886-7.

This made complete nonsense of the fishermen's argument: they now proved more tractable, and the whalers seized the opportunity for an all-out attack on every restriction, particularly because whaling, as opposed to fishing, had recorded a very poor year in 1889, catching a total of only about 500 whales, some seventeen per boat, while it was estimated that inside the banned zone every boat could have made a catch of a further ten to twelve whales. The companies, including Svend Foyn's, appealed in all earnest to the Government to abolish the close season, as the very existence of Norwegian whaling was at stake. This time, too, the dispute ended with a renewal, the third, of the Act, which was now extended to 1896. It was then not renewed for a fourth time, but replaced by a new whaling law which, however, made few appreciable changes in the old Act, although in some respects it accorded the fishermen a greater measure of protection.

Despite the excellent fishing results of 1899, and in particular 1900, agitation against whaling still persisted, for the simple reason that by now it had become a political issue exploited to the uttermost by the Liberals, who made it one of the most important planks in their programme at the local elections in 1898 and the subsequent general election in 1900. In North Norway the issue and the party were supported by two excellent spokesmen in the guise of a pastor and a postmaster, both talented tub-thumpers. The elections in 1900 proved a victory for the Liberals and the opponents of whaling, with the postmaster elected to represent the urban boroughs of North Norway. In 1903 the pastor, too, was duly elected. Both of them left the Liberals and joined the Labour Party, and as a result the whaling question now entered on a new phase, in which decisions depended not on fact but on the force of political agitation. The whaling conflict developed into a class struggle, fought with increased bitterness when fishing in the Varanger area failed disastrously in 1901-3 : numerous homes suffered hunger and privation in the very area where whaling was most intensively carried on. At the same time seals in inexplicably large numbers descended on this coast, wreaking havoc on the fishing grounds.

Once again relations with Russia were brought into play, *inter alia* in connection with the so-called *Pomor* trade (*pomor* = coastal inhabitant). Every summer, between 15 June and 30 September, Russians from the areas around the White Sea would visit the harbours of North Norway in their small boats, with the right to barter raw and salt fish either for cash or in exchange for grain, flour, groats, hemp, tar, timber, etc. During these weeks the fish was generally maggoty, and for this reason not so easy to sell to Norwegian purchasers and exporters, whereas the Russians bought the fish direct from the fishermen and salted it down on board their boats. Round about the turn of the century this barter trade was very important, providing a vital source of livelihood for the poverty-stricken fishing communities, and as it was exempt from customs duties and the intervention of middlemen it proved highly advantageous to both parties. But it was looked on askance by the Norwegian fish buyers and merchants, who did their best to put an end to it. This more than ever invested the dispute with the features of a class struggle — the fishing proletariat against the capitalists, represented by whalers, fish purchasers, and merchants—and Socialist agitators were not slow to exploit the situation, whipping up tempers to fever pitch. Once again the proximity of the Russian border was emphasised, and the authorities were warned that, should they continue to ignore the vital interests of this part of Norway, the boundary line between the two countries might as well be moved further west. In 1902 a Whale Protection Committee was set up, which received tremendous support throughout North Norway. Its first and most important task was to despatch a major deputation to submit the demands of the population to the authorities in Oslo. It was hinted that the deputation had received financial support from the Russians.

All that was achieved was some indication from the Government that it was prepared to consider the fishermen's demands favourably. At mass meetings thousands and thousands of fishermen demanded a total ban on whaling. The Norwegian Government, with a hard core of Liberals, realised that a great many votes would be lost if the fishermen were not placated, and that these votes would go to the Socialists, who were now winning many adherents in North Norway. But as the Government delayed so the Russians introduced a total ban on the Murmansk coast. When the fisheries failed for the third consecutive year, the fishermen in their desperation took matters into their own hands. On 2 June 1903, 700 fishermen gathered outside one of the whaling stations, and smashed all the doors and windows. Two days later they returned and completely destroyed the station. Troops were despatched to quell the unrest and prevent a similar occurrence at other stations. This incident naturally caused a sensation in Norway, but a still greater sensation, both at home and abroad, was aroused by a statement in one of the papers that supported the cause of the fishermen: "There is no point in arresting eight fishermen when thousands are guilty of the serious crime of drafting cables asking the Russian Government for help, encouraged to do so by their own fanaticism and by prominent Russians who are present [during the riots]. The fishermen are also arming themselves to the teeth, and are determined to declare war in their own country." This smacked of incitement to armed treason.

The Government considered the situation so serious that even before the end of the year a bill was passed which, as from 1 February 1904, forbade all whaling in Norwegian territorial waters in the country's three northernmost counties. Provisionally this law was to apply for ten years; companies were, however, permitted to catch in 1904 in order to give them time to terminate their operations. It was clear to all concerned that this ban had no rational justification, but was based exclusively on consideration for the general discontent with economic and social conditions in Finnmark. Despite the fact that they now had their law, the fishermen were not satisfied, as they considered it quite unreasonable that the whaling companies were to receive compensation for catching operations which in any case would soon have been brought to a halt owing to shortage of whales, a deficiency for which they themselves had been responsible. This was disproved by subsequent results — 459 whales in 1904 as against 383 in 1903. The difference in actual fact was far greater, as in 1904 235 blue whales were caught, as against 126 in 1903, i.e. in terms of BWU, the result was 335 and 229 respectively, an increase in 1904 of 46 per cent. This good catch supported the whalers' claim for compensation, but they only received 41 per cent of what they demanded. It has been said that the fishermen actually did the whalers a great service, by having a law passed for protection of the whale because "the Norwegian State paid the companies Kr.280,000 to abandon a catching ground which they themselves had destroyed". This is undoubtedly correct, calculated not in terms of the number of whales caught but the number per catcher. Four of the eleven companies which received compensation were dissolved, five transferred operations to Spitsbergen, one to Bjørnøya, and one to the Faroes.

The fishermen no longer had a scapegoat on whom to lay the blame in a bad season. It was clear to everyone in 1904 that catches would be good, despite the whaling that had been carried on, and in 1905 particularly good, even though there was hardly a whale to be seen all along the Finnmark coast. The trend in these and subsequent years has confirmed the views of the scientists and the whalers on the relationship between fishing and whaling.

Our purpose in chronicling at such length the dispute that centred around the whale in Finnmark is because it was watched with great interest by fishermen in other areas of the Norwegian Sea, where the development and solution of the dispute were invoked as a precedent for their own local fishing grounds.

6

THE IMPORTANCE OF FINNMARK WHALING

Finnmark whaling was the first phase in the development of a modern industry which for three-quarters of a century assumed global proportions. This was due not to its scope or the size of the profits it brought in, since the achievement in Finnmark was a minor one compared to later pelagic whaling. Statistics are unfortunately not available for the initial phase; accurate figures cannot therefore be given. The somewhat deficient official statistics list a total of 17,745 whales for 1868-1904 for the whole of North Norway (the three northernmost counties). Other, incidental items of information would suggest that a figure of some 20,000 would be nearer the truth. This figure is a modest one compared with the world's total catch in the 1930s, when the annual average was about twice as big, and in the period 1955/6-1965/6 when it was three times as great. In some years, in pelagic catching in the Antarctic alone, twice as many whales have been caught as in the entire North Norwegian whaling epoch. It should be remembered, however, that the latter took place in a thinly stocked, locally restricted area, while the former covered enormous areas.

If, on the other hand, we go further back in history, a comparison will give us an entirely different picture of the quantitive significance of Finnmark whaling. Catching was not really properly organised until 1880, and in 1904 the Norwegians were operating in accordance with modern whaling methods in other areas of the Norwegian Sea, off Iceland, the Faroes, Spitsbergen, the Shetlands, and the Hebrides. If we include these operations, the total catch in the Norwegian Sea between 1864 and 1904 comprised 40,000 whales, i.e. as much as the Dutch catch of Greenland whale in the fifty years between 1670 and 1719. Or, expressed in another way: between 1864 and 1904 some 635 whale catchers operating off Finnmark caught just about the same number of whales as 3,880 Dutch vessels caught between 1660 and 1698. In other words, in the thinly stocked catching grounds off Finnmark small modern steamers accounted for six times as many whales per vessel as each of the Dutch boats, excellent proof of the efficacy of Foyn's method. Even the numerically impressive catches made by the Americans and the British in the eighteenth and nineteenth centuries were relatively modest on the basis of catching units.

The whalers calculated that in 1885 Kr.4.2 million (£230,000), at the time a not inconsiderable sum by Norwegian standards, had been invested. (By way of comparison, a freighter of 1,500 gross tons could at that time be built in England for about £15,000.) Official statistics give the gross value of whales caught in Finnmark between 1871 and 1904 as about Kr.22 million, a sum which judging by other figures must be far too low, but, as only official statistics are available for the entire period, they have to be used. They show a total gross value of all modern Norwegian whaling between 1871 and 1905 of just over Kr.66 million. This sum in itself means very little; we get a clearer picture when we know that the gross earnings of whaling rose from 1 per cent of the value of Norwegian coastal fisheries in 1880 to 9.4 per cent in 1885, dropping to 5.2 per cent in 1888, but fluctuating in all the years 1893-1905 between 11.9 per cent and (the peak, 1898) 18 per cent. Even in its moderate scope, as early as before 1905, whaling began to exercise a certain economic importance, and yet it is neither this nor the number of whales caught that provides the most important basis for assessing its significance, which was that it laid the foundation for a continued development of this industry.

Just before 1905 a number of companies had established themselves which were capable of operating at a profit even on the thinly stocked catching grounds of the Norwegian Sea. These companies possessed the greatest know-how, and when catching in North Norway was banned this could be applied in other fields. A transfer of this kind had little effect on the companies' capital, organisation, or operation; they were able to use the same vessels, matériel, and crews as previously. A ban could be placed on catching in North Norway, but it could not prevent Norwegians from finding other fields, outside the borders of their country, although to start with at no very great distance. In this way the ban worked to stimulate expansion, and during the Finnmark era the Norwegians had developed the means required for this. A staff of Norwegian experts in whaling according to the modern method were to play the part of teachers to other nations in all the oceans of the world, and before the others learnt to construct their own boats and their own equipment, Norway was the sole supplier of this to countries anxious to commence modern catching along Norwegian lines. For half a century, in fact, Norway exercised a world monopoly in this industry. This applied in particular to the whaling crews, and more especially to the gunners. They constituted an exclusive élite, right up to the time when Japan in the 1930s and the Soviet Union after the Second World War succeeded in training their own gunners. This, as we shall subsequently see, created political problems. Of the many factors that influenced catching results, none was as important as the gunner.

In this connection the well-known whaling expert and historian Roy Chapman Andrews wrote as follows in 1928: "Although in various parts of the world I have met two or three gunners who were not Norwegians, there are not many such. From their Viking ancestors the Scandinavians have inherited their love for the sea and since Svend Foyn's time Tønsberg has sent forth her sons to the whaleships much as did New Bedford half a century ago. Thus the present generation has grown up as the industry developed and from boys to men they have seen it in all its phases and learned it afterwards, which is fully as important." This is undoubtedly correct, provided we replace Tønsberg by Vestfold. Andrews also writes that the Norwegian way of flensing the whale was used all over the world except in Japan. The reason for this was that in that country the whale was primarily used for human consumption.

Technical development was based entirely on Norwegian initiative and Norwegian inventions. The chief credit for this goes to persons working for various engineering firms supplying matériel to the catching fleet and the shore stations. A not insignificant spin-off of whaling, despite its modest proportions, was the secondary activity it created in the form of a large number of items which were supplied. There seems, moreover, no doubt that the introduction of the steam engine to whaling in the 1860s familiarised the shipowners of Vestfold, the shipbuilding yards, and seamen generally with steamships, and this was one of the main reasons why Tønsberg and Sandefjord played the role of pioneers in Norway in the transition from sail to steam. It is also interesting to note that for various reasons the principle of shareholding companies was introduced at a very early stage in whaling. This helped to pave the way for the introduction of this form of company which, till then, had been somewhat unusual in Norwegian shipping.

Finnmark whaling and the dispute it engendered proved of fundamental importance to the scientific study of the whale and marine biology in general. The Danish research scientist D. F. ESRICHT devoted a great deal of time and energy to a study of this subject from the 1840s right up to the time of his death in 1863. It was a handicap to his research that he so rarely had an opportunity of studying whales before their carcasses had decayed or been flensed and cut up. The young Norwegian marine biologist G. O. SARS was fortunate enough to come across a small blue whale that had been beached in 1865, which enabled him to give a description of it in the Norwegian Academy of Science. His views on the question of the detrimental influence of whaling on fisheries could not be ignored by the Government, being based on scientific research results, which Sars and a few of his colleagues were commissioned to submit. At the Finnmark stations they enjoyed better conditions for their studies of rorquals than they had ever had previously. The result of the research carried out by these pioneers provided a basis on which subsequent studies could be developed. At a later stage in our account we shall have something to say about Sars's successor as the leading marine biologist, JOHAN HJORT, an outstanding personality in Norwegian whaling policy and in the initial attempts at international regulation and control. In his studies of whales and fishes, which he started off the coast of North Norway in 1900, he was particularly concerned with the relationship of the rorquals with their environment. Among other things he made an interesting discovery of American grenade lances in blue whales captured off the coast of North Norway, thus obtaining proof of the distances covered by whales in their migrations.

In 1814 Norway entered into a period of union with Sweden. A growing nation-wide movement worked to ensure complete freedom and independence. This was finally achieved in 1905. The creation of modern whaling was a Norwegian national triumph, enhancing the Norwegian people's sense of self-reliance and confidence, turning Svend Foyn into a national hero and his enterprise into a victory for Norway. Leading Norwegian writers were inspired by whaling and its protagonists in their struggle with the largest quarry on earth. There was an obvious link between whaling and Norwegian polar exploration, both in the Arctic and in the Antarctic. The newly roused interest in the Antarctic continent at the beginning of our century would have been impossible without whaling.

Summing up, we can say that the supreme importance of Finnmark whaling is that it proved a nursery for the training of the crews and testing of the equipment that made it possible to develop modern catching from a local Norwegian phenomenon to a global industry. With the transfer of whaling to the Antarctic we reach the culmination of this great enterprise. (For catching figures for North Norway, 1868-1904, see Statistical Appendix, Table 39.)

PART TWO

GLOBAL WHALING

7

THE NORTH ATLANTIC

Iceland

The ban on whaling off the coast of North Norway in 1904 was not *per se* directly responsible for the spread of whaling to other areas. Just as Finnmark whaling in 1882-3 reached a temporary maximum, both in the number of whales caught and also in financial returns, operations commenced in the first areas outside Finnmark. Thanks to the excellent results obtained, there was a rush to set up new companies in North Norway, and it was soon obvious that fresh whaling grounds would have to be sought where competition would be less keen. It was no mere accident that Iceland should provide the first solution.

Iceland had been the scene of whaling, as already mentioned, long before modern whaling was established there in 1883. The Americans Roys and Lilliendahl had hunted whales there as far back as 1865-7, using their own special equipment, and Svend Foyn himself had paid them a visit in 1866, with a view to studying their method. The Danish Fisheries Company (Det Danske Fiskeriselskab) had been established in 1866 with a view, *inter alia*, to whaling off Iceland, at that time a Danish dependency. In 1869 and 1875 the Dutch had attempted to resume their whaling activities in these waters, where they had a centuries-old tradition of whaling. These enterprises might have been expected to discourage others to try their hand: company after company went bankrupt, and was forced to go into liquidation. The reason was not a lack of whales, but a lack of technical know-how.

It has generally been assumed that the first step was taken in 1883 by Svend Foyn, but this is hardly correct. The origins are, in fact, somewhat surprising: they cannot be traced to the county of Vestfold, nor have they anything to do with the catching of seals and bottlenose whales, but must be attributed to Haugesund, a small town on the west coast of Norway and a centre of the herring fisheries. In 1879 the inhabitants of Haugesund had started fishing herring off the coast of Iceland (the Icelanders themselves were at that time not involved in the fishing of herring), and they came back with reports of abundant stocks of whales in the mouths of the fjords on the west, north, and east coasts. In his diary Svend Foyn himself reports that he was asked by a herring fisherman, Mons Larsen Kro, a Haugesund man resident in Iceland, for assistance in starting whaling operations from Iceland. A company was established, with Svend Foyn subscribing three-fifths of the capital, and a whale catcher, the *Isafold*, was built, reputedly "the largest to date [built] according to Svend Foyn's patent". It had a burthen of 84 gross tons and an engine developing 180 h.p., ensuring the respectable speed of 11 knots. A shore station was set up on the Alptafjördur, a branch of the Isafjördur in the extreme northwest. At the same time Svend Foyn prepared to set up another station on the Nordfjördur, halfway down the east coast, with a view to making this a second whaling centre.

A few months later Svend Foyn abandoned all plans of whaling in Icelandic waters, not for technical reasons or because of a shortage of whales, but owing to the difficulties he encountered from the local authorities. They demanded that Norwegians should become naturalised Icelandic (i.e. Danish) subjects, that they should build houses and settle in Iceland, that their vessels should be registered there, and that they should sail under the Danish flag. While others submitted to these regulations on a purely formal basis, it went very much against the grain as far as Svend Foyn was concerned: he was such an ardent Norwegian patriot that he rejected out of hand the idea of his boats sailing under a foreign flag. Moreover, the Icelandic fishermen raised precisely the same complaints about whaling as their colleagues in Finnmark. Foyn withdrew from the company and sold his share to the other partners. Of these, the major shareholder was THOMAS AMLIE (1815-97) of Oslo, a relation of Mons Larsen. On the face of it Amlie was the syndicate member least cut out for whaling. The son of a farmer, he had been trained as a teacher, but abandoned this profession and set up as businessman in Oslo. He earned a large sum of money, sold his business, and retired at the age of sixty-eight to spend the evening of his life living on his capital. But when asked by a younger brother in Haugesund whether he was prepared to invest in the whaling company, he felt that he still had so much surplus energy that he not only acceded to this request, but actually assumed the responsibility of acting as expedition manager.

For six years Amlie ruled the roost in Iceland, as whaling operations off the Finnmark coast were enjoying some of their best years. In 1883, his first year as manager, Amlie caught only eight whales, but in the following year he managed to account for twenty-five, twenty-three "big" and two "small". "Big" in this context undoubtedly refers to blue whales. In 1887 another catcher was purchased, and the score for 1888 was twenty-eight whales and 4,000 barrels of oil, ensuring net profits of Kr.77,385, or 34.4 per cent of the share capital, no mean achievement when we consider that the top scorer among the companies operating in North Norway registered 2,700 barrels. In view of this it was not surprising that several companies planned to transfer their operations to Iceland. The year 1889 proved to be the last in which the value of the catch in Finnmark exceeded that of Norwegian catches in other areas. Nevertheless, the years 1889-93 were a disappointment to companies that transferred to Iceland. Not till 1894 did Icelandic whaling enter upon its best period, a period that was to last for seventeen years. In 1894 Amlie acquired a third whale catcher, and in the following year he made a record catch of 128 whales, which yielded 5,000 barrels. Unfortunately the price of oil was so low and operating expenses so high, that the net return was far below the 1888 level.

In 1897, Amlie, by now eighty-two years old, decided to retire. But failing to establish a shareholding company that would take over the business of which he was sole proprietor, he set off in February with a crew of thirty-two in one of his small catchers, determined to lead an expedition for the last time. His ship was lost with all hands in a storm off the Faroes, a tragic conclusion to a career of tremendous variety for the founder of modern whaling in Iceland. Venturing out in small, heavily laden ships, to face the winter storms in one of the world's most hazardous stretches of ocean, was always known to have been a rash and dangerous undertaking. Amlie's company was sold to an Oslo syndicate, which continued to operate with varying success until it was sold in 1904 to the British firm of Chr. Salvesen & Co. of Leith, Scotland. Instead of operating from this station, Salvesen transferred his boats and equipment to his other stations in the Norwegian Sea.

While catches off the Finnmark coast slumped every year between 1886 and 1891 to less than half the figure for 1885, Amlie had demonstrated that there were ample whale stocks along the coast of Iceland. Convinced that Finnmark whaling was coming to an end, a number of operators started casting about for other whaling grounds. In 1889-94 four new companies, all Norwegian, established themselves in Iceland, and their success induced five others to follow suit between 1896 and 1903. Of these, only two were Norwegian firms which had abandoned Finnmark in 1889 and 1890. It would therefore be incorrect to speak of "a mass flight of companies from Finnmark to Iceland". In common with Amlie's company, all the others between 1893 and 1903 had been established with a view to operating from bases in Iceland. The ten companies founded between 1883 and 1915 were based on fourteen different shore stations, eight on the west coast and six on the east coast. An unsuccessful experiment with a floating factory was also carried out.

Two factors in particular made Iceland an attractive base: the season was longer than in Finnmark, and the bulk of the whales caught were blue whales. All in all, hardly any areas in the northern hemisphere have provided such stable catches of blue whales extending over such a long period. Even so, the marked decline in catches during the last decade of this period was undoubtedly due to "over-fishing" in this

area, but at the same time it should be borne in mind that the same
stocks, during their migration to and from the Arctic, were also subject
to catching by whalers based in the Faroes, Shetland, and the Hebrides,
and, after 1908, also from the west coast of Ireland. Next to the blue
whale, the fin whale provided most raw material. In 1898-1902 a
considerable number of humpback whales were caught. Sei whales
proved somewhat erratic : in some years they appeared in large numbers,
in other years they were conspicuous by their absence. The catching of
the first nordcapers in 1890 aroused considerable attention; this right
whale, which ever since the late Middle Ages had been caught in their
hundreds of thousands in the North Atlantic, was now so rare that
Norwegian whalers were even unfamiliar with its name when the first
specimens were caught. In financial terms the three last-mentioned
species were of little importance compared to the blue and fin whale.
At the end of March and beginning of April these would arrive at great
speed along the west coast, continuing on their way towards the Greenland ice in the Denmark Straits. It was possible to commence catching
operations as early as April off the Vestmanna Islands, and then follow
the migrating whales north. In June and July whales caught had to
be towed all the way down to the stations on the Isafjördur; at the end
of August and in September there followed the hectic pursuit of whales
moving south.

The most important company during this period, 1883-1915, was
under the management of HANS ELLEFSEN from the county of Vestfold.
In 1889 he closed down his Finnmark station and transferred it to the
Önundarfjördur, just south of the mouth of the Isafjördur. During the
first four years he operated with two boats, increasing to five from 1893,
seven in the period 1901-7, and as many as nine in 1910. One of his
whale catchers, sold in 1907, had in the course of seventeen years caught
999 whales, an annual average of fifty-nine, an excellent score unmatched
by any whale catcher in the Norwegian Sea. In order to reduce towing
distance, Ellefsen set up a new station on the Mjöafjördur on the east
coast. His intention was to operate from both stations, but when the
one on the west coast was destroyed by fire in 1901, he decided not to
rebuild. Instead, he concentrated on his new station, which was without
a doubt the largest, most efficient, and best organised in the Norwegian
Sea. His best years were 1895, 1902, and 1907, with an annual production of some 11,000 barrels, more than one-quarter of the entire Iceland
production.

Instead of dumping the de-blubbered whale carcass in the sea, Ellefsen
utilised practically 100 per cent of the raw material by setting up a
guano factory. He constantly maintained that the sale of guano played
an important role in the economy, helping to tide the companies over a
critical period when low oil prices obtained, as was the case around

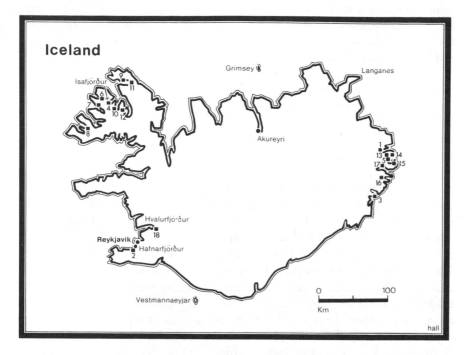

Iceland

1. 1865-7; 2. 1865-71; 3. 1865-71; 4. 1883-1906; 5. 1883; 6. 1889-1901; 7. 1890-9; 8. 1893-1911, 1935-9; 9. 1894-9, 1902-15; 10. 1896-1903; 11. 1897-1903; 12. 1897-1904; 13. 1900-12; 14. 1900-13; 15. 1900-13; 16. 1903-5; 17. 1904-13; 18. 1947- .

The whaling stations in Iceland and the years they were operated.

1905. In 1908 Ellefsen produced 11,400 sacks at a price of Kr.10 per sack. The gross value of the oil was Kr.400,000.

Ellefsen was shrewd enough not to push his luck. After 1907 it was obvious that catching was on the decline, and stocks of whales were dwindling. Whereas in 1907 seven catchers had accounted for 268 whales, enough for 10,900 barrels, in 1910 nine catchers scored a mere 170 whales, producing 6,300 barrels. And so in 1911, with only 2,250 barrels to his credit, Ellefsen sold his station and two catchers and transferred his activities, together with three catchers, to South Africa, where we shall meet him again. After operating here for five years this station, too, was sold to Chr. Salvesen & Co.

We have followed the fortunes of these two companies from their inception to their conclusion because they demonstrate characteristic trends. Amlie was the first person to start catching according to the modern method off the coast of Finnmark, and Ellefsen the first to abandon these grounds and move south. Ellefsen's career, in fact,

symbolises in a way the fate of Norwegian whaling : in three areas — off
the coasts of Finnmark, Iceland, and South Africa — he was responsible
for over-fishing stocks of whale which, given a measure of self-restraint,
might have warranted stable and lasting whaling operations. Warnings
went unheeded : no sooner had one area been exhausted than whalers
hastened to exploit another, where the same process was repeated.

With the takeover by Chr. Salvesen & Co. of these two companies in
Iceland Norwegians for the first time came up against foreign competition.
Salvesen was not the first foreigner to apply modern methods; others
had attempted to do so before him. The founder of the firm, Christian
Salvesen (1827-1911), had for some time hesitated to take an active part
in whaling, as he considered that it would be inconsistent with his
position as agent to other companies to become their competitor. In the
end, however, his son THEODORE EMILE SALVESEN (1863-1942) persuaded his father to invest in whaling.

One of the first companies to attract Salvesen's attention was the
Danish Whaling and Fisheries Company (Dansk Hvalfangst- og Fiskeri
Aktieselskab), which, despite its name, was Norwegian. It had been
started by a Norwegian, operating from 1897 from the Meleyre station
on the Isafjördur. In 1902 Salvesen became the majority shareholder.
A new whale catcher was delivered in 1903, and at the same time
Salvesen took over management, which means that this could rightly
be called the first year in which the firm of Chr. Salvesen & Co. was
actively engaged in whaling. Although the station was managed by
HENRIK N. HENRIKSEN, one of the most capable men in the industry,
the enterprise lost money; the station was closed down in 1904, and all
equipment transferred to the Faroes. This setback did not deter Salvesen
from extending his Icelandic commitments by the purchase of two
additional companies — Amlie's former company in 1904 and, in 1906,
a company established by the Norwegian MARCUS C. BULL, one of the
pioneers of modern whaling and once a trainee of Svend Foyn himself.
Since 1899 this company had operated from the Hellisfjördur on the
east coast, where Bull, who had become a Danish subject, ran the
company on behalf of Salvesen. Bull had patented a number of inventions of importance to whaling, including one for an accumulator
designed to take up the strain on the whale line. Few whalers had a
longer record of service in Iceland at that time; when he quit in 1913,
production was down to a mere 1,360 barrels and was no longer
profitable. His best year, 1909, produced 4,100 barrels.

A visitor to Bull's station in 1901 wrote a description of conditions
which were no doubt typical of every station at that time :

As our ship approached the station the bow wave was red with blood.
An intolerable stench from the cooker rose to meet us, and everything in

the vicinity was covered with a sticky layer of grease. Bull had not yet got the guano factory and the bone mill going, with the result that the flensed carcasses had been tied up in a cove, where about a hundred of these massive beasts lay, polluting the atmosphere. There was slippery, slimy grease everywhere. We inspected the hauling-out slip, which was running with fat and blood. In the cookery, where blubber was boiling in huge vats, we could hardly maintain our footing on the slippery floor. On the beach bits of baleen plates, vertebrae and debris lay drying in the sun.

In the wake of Amlie's success two more companies were set up in Haugesund, one in 1893 and the other in 1902, both operating on the west coast. In 1912 they were merged into one company, the last to operate from Iceland during this period. It thus fell to Haugesund, where whaling had begun in 1883, to close this chapter in 1915. In 1914 and 1915 a total of only eighty-nine whales was caught, producing 3,215 barrels of oil and 3,940 sacks of guano. Despite these low figures, it is probable that catching would have continued, since the price of whale oil rose to £35 in 1915 and £50 in 1916, so that even a modest catch would have guaranteed a good return. Although whaling was to a certain extent hampered by wartime activities, it was the Icelanders themselves who put a stop to it.

If foreigners could make money on whaling from Iceland, then surely the Icelanders themselves should be capable of doing so. This was the argument that lay behind the establishment in 1897 of the Whale Industry Company of Iceland (Hval-Industri Aktieselskabet Island), also referred to as the Icelandic Whaling Company or Asgeirsson's Company, after its promoter and major shareholder, A. ASGEIRSSON, an Icelandic merchant living in Copenhagen. Never was the total dependence on Norway of any foreigner anxious to start whaling more clearly demonstrated: the expedition manager, crews, machinery, catching equipment, whale catchers, even the houses for the factory hands were imported from Norway. The first station was built on a very unfortunate site, deep inside the Isafjördur, and for this reason was moved to the east coast in 1904. The catch never yielded a profit, and shareholders received no dividends. In 1906 the company went bankrupt, and was sold to Asgeirsson for 7½ per cent of the nominal value of its shares. He continued operating, producing fairly good results in the first few years, but from 1910 there was a rapid decline, with only twenty-five whales caught in 1913, and the business was closed down.

Before leaving Iceland we should mention the German attempt to renew whaling after a twenty-year interlude. On the initiative of the German Seafishing Association (Deutsche Seefischerei-Verein), the Germania Whaling and Fishing Industry Ltd. (Germania Walfang- und Fischindustrie A.G.) was set up in Hamburg, and commenced whaling from a station on the east coast in 1903. This was the first company to operate without a Norwegian management: both the chairman of the Board and the expedition manager were Germans without any previous knowledge of the difficult art of whaling. This was probably the reason why the outcome proved so disappointing. As early as 1905 operations were brought to a close, although the company was in receipt of a German government subsidy. The station was sold, nominally to Marcus C. Bull, but in reality to Salvesen, who in 1908 dismantled the very valuable machinery and transferred it to his station in the Falkland Islands, where his firm commenced catching in January 1908. This, the first German attempt at modern whaling, must rank as the greatest economic disaster in the Icelandic whaling industry. In 1913 a fresh attempt was made from German Southwest Africa, and when this was terminated by the war, twenty years were to elapse before Germany once again played a part in modern pelagic catching in the Antarctic.

In Iceland, just as in Finnmark, disputes arose between the fishermen and the whalers. Accounts of the attitude of the local population to whaling, on the other hand, vary considerably : some sources emphasise the welcome extra earnings this new venture provided for the penurious population in the country as a whole, in the form of taxes, duties, and other levies. In 1903 the export duty was raised from only Kr.0.5 to Kr.1 per barrel. Other sources dwell on the fishermen's complaints that whaling, in their opinion, destroyed the herring fishery. The authorities made some concessions to the fishermen's demands by introducing a law on 19 February 1886, banning catching within Icelandic territorial waters from 1 May to 31 October, and in areas where herring fishing was being carried out. The ban hardly affected the whalers, as most catching took place more than three nautical miles from the shore. At no time was there a ban on the towing of whales to a shore station for processing. In 1903, just as agitation in Finnmark was reaching a climax, an attempt was made in Iceland to introduce a total ban on whaling, but a proposal to this effect was thrown out by the Alting. In 1913, however, a ban on all whaling, to run for ten years form 1 October 1915, was imposed, not as the result of pressure on the part of the fishermen, but in order to preserve for the Icelanders themselves the whale stocks still remaining.

The role played by whaling in Iceland's economy can be roughly gauged by comparing the value of whale products exported with the total value of exports : the former was well in excess of 10 per cent of the latter for practically every year between 1894 and 1910, and from 1897 to 1900 the proportion was as high as 19.1 per cent and 25 per cent. The net profits, however, were pocketed by companies abroad, and perhaps the greatest benefit accruing to the population consisted of the paid employment available to 1,200 men in whaling for some fifteen years, and in the good market available for local farm produce.

The country's foreign communications were, furthermore, considerably developed, thanks to transport to and from the whaling stations.

No comparison of catches from Iceland with those from North Norway can claim to be statistically valid, owing to the lack of accurate figures for the early years. Table 4 is based on the best information available.

Table 4. TOTAL CATCH AND WHALE OIL PRODUCTION IN ICELAND, 1883-1915, AND NORTH NORWAY, 1868-1904

		Whales caught	Barrels of oil
Iceland	1883-1915	17,189	618,838
North Norway	1868-1904	17,745	434,259

It is probable that the number of whales listed for North Norway in this table is too low, and should be nearer 20,000. The figure for Iceland, too, should undoubtedly be higher, even though the discrepancy in this case may not be so great. The interesting point that emerges from these figures, however inaccurate they may be, is that the production of oil in Iceland is shown to have yielded some 50 per cent more oil per whale than in North Norway, owing to the far higher proportion of blue whales caught. It should also be noted that the number of whales caught is not identical with the number of whales *killed*. We have numerous accounts of the great loss of whales due to various reasons, the most frequent being the breaking of the whale line. The number of whales that were killed was almost certainly at least 30 per cent greater than the number actually recovered. Thanks to improved equipment and catching techniques, the loss of whales was subsequently almost entirely eliminated.

After the killing of the last whale off the coast of Iceland in the autumn of 1915 the whales enjoyed twenty years of peace. An Icelandic company commenced catching in 1935, but was forced to abandon operations after five years. Not till 1948 did the Icelanders succeed in establishing an industry of reasonable scope, which has been carried on without a break right down to the present, generally showing good returns. (For catching figures for Iceland, 1883-1915, see Statistical Appendix, Table 40.)

The Faroes

It is a striking fact that the dates marking the spread of modern whaling round the Norwegian Sea occur at ten-year intervals: in 1863 the first steam whaler in the world, *Spes et Fides,* was built by Svend Foyn; 1873 witnessed the breakthrough of his methods; 1883 marked the switch to Iceland, and 1894 to the Faroes, while in 1903-4 operations were extended to the Shetlands, the Hebrides, and Spitsbergen, at the same time as the first ship sailed south to the Antarctic. The three dominant whaling towns in Norway, Sandefjord, Tønsberg, and Larvik, seem to have divided the whaling grounds between them by tacit agreement: Sandefjord, never committed to whaling in Iceland, started operations in the Faroes, and subsequently concentrated its efforts there; Larvik played a similar role in the Shetlands, whilst whaling off the Hebrides and Iceland was initiated by Tønsberg, which dominated in this area.

HANS ALBERT GRØN of Sandefjord, who first started whaling in the Faroes, deserves to be remembered, together with Amlie, as one of the leading pioneers in this early phase of modern whaling. He was in personal charge of expeditions based on Finnmark, the Faroes, and Spitsbergen, as well as in the Antarctic. He calculated that whales migrating north to Iceland would be bound to make a landfall off the Faroes before proceeding, and his very first year's catch — forty-six whales in three months, yielding 940 barrels of oil and 5 tons of baleen — confirmed his views. His station at Strømnæs was situated in the narrow sound between the two largest islands, Strømø and Østerø. The logbook of one of his whale catchers throws considerable light on the migration of whales. During the first few years after 1894 a considerable quantity of blue whales were caught, though stocks seem to have been constantly declining, and for this reason the bulk of the catch comprised fin whales. A certain number of humpbacks were caught, and occasionally a sperm whale. Sei whales were found to be as variable as in Iceland and North Norway: in some years they appeared in great numbers, in others they were conspicuous by their absence, and feeding conditions seem to have had no bearing on these fluctuations. In April fin whales would arrive off the west coast of the islands, either spending some time in these waters or proceeding immediately along the submarine ridge between the Faroes and Iceland. On these occasions catching would take place some 10 to 30 miles off shore. Curiously enough, the whales caught were almost all males. In the first half of April a wave of blue whales would arrive, travelling at such speed that the whale catchers could not keep up. Towards the end of June another, larger, wave would pass, making north at full speed. These were very thin; even a large blue whale would provide no more than 50 barrels, whereas migrating south it would be fat enough to make over 100. On their return journey the whales made no stop at the islands, and for this reason the season was brief, hectic, and highly variable, with catches showing considerable fluctuations from one year to another. In terms of the numbers of whales and barrels of oil per vessel the score, for example, was twenty-six whales and 784 barrels in 1893, sixty-two and 1,700 in 1896, forty-eight and 867 in 1899, and sixty-six and 1,703 in 1900. Whaling in Faroese waters was in other words more of a gamble than off Finnmark and Iceland. As in those areas, whales had to be sought further and further from the shore stations as the years went by; as far north as Iceland, as far south as the Shetlands, and even as far as the Hebrides.

Just as Amlie had done in Iceland, so Grøn operated on his own in the Faroes during the first four years. Catches for this period totalled 212 whales and 5,374 barrels, in itself not remarkable, but twice as much as Amlie had scored in his first four years, and to this extent the Faroes proved more attractive. In 1897 a company was set up in Oslo in which Salvesen took a 10,000-Kroner share. This was two years before the Icelandic venture, already mentioned, for which reason 1897 may be regarded as the year in which Salvesen first turned his attention to whaling.

Whaling from the Faroes was regulated by a law of 2 May 1902, modelled on the Icelandic law of 1886, though not so rigorous. Its object was to safeguard Danish and Faroese interests, and whaling was reserved for Danish citizens or companies in which Danes held at least 50 per cent of the share capital. Companies already established, however, were to be allowed to continue operating, but their ships would have to fly the Danish flag, and a levy of Kr.50 was imposed on every whale brought in. The law did not, as in Iceland, establish a close season or prohibit whaling in territorial waters, because, unlike the Shetlands, excellent relations existed between the whalers and the local inhabitants. The Faroese welcomed whaling, as whalemeat had always played an important part in their diet, and they now had plenty of meat for about a farthing a pound (2-3 øre a kilo). The effect of this law was to induce a great many Faroese and Danes to participate in whaling, either personally or as shareholders.

Grøn established his second station in 1901, and subsequently set up a Danish-Norwegian company which operated from 1903 onwards from a station not far from the Faroese capital of Torshavn. The most important company in the islands was A/S Suderø, named after the island on which the station was erected and started in 1901. Originally a Norwegian company based on Sandefjord, it had to be registered as Danish in order to comply with the law of 1902. The capital, Kr.20,000, was part Norwegian, part Faroese, with two leading local businessmen on the Board, and with Salvesen holding a number of shares. The founder of the company was PEDER O. BOGEN, a major figure in whaling, who made his debut as a whaling-ship owner with this company. (At his death in 1914 he controlled seven companies, with five land stations, four floating factories, eighteen whale catchers, and three transport vessels.) In 1908 he built a guano factory at his station, and it was clearly demonstrated that in a year of low oil prices the sale of guano and meat meal would suffice to keep the company solvent.

Four companies should have been more than enough for such a limited field: nevertheless, two more arrived, a lesser one from Tønsberg and the Dansk Hvalfangst- og Fiskeri Aktieselskab, which Salvesen had taken over in Iceland and in 1905 transferred to a new, modern station, complete with a guano factory, at Strømø. Thus in 1906-11 there were six stations operating with as many as seventeen boats, far more than the area could support, and from 1909, the year with a peak production of 13,850 barrels, returns slumped to a quarter, with 3,515 barrels in 1913. One company after another pulled out, Grøn being the first, after a final season in 1911. From his records in 1894-1910 the remarkable fact emerges that even such a small company, with a modest production of 2,800 barrels as an annual average, and with very low oil prices for two-thirds of the time, could nevertheless show a profit on whaling. On the capital of Kr.100,000 an average annual dividend of 28.6 per cent was available (the highest, in 1902, being 56 per cent, the lowest, in 1904, 12 per cent). This success, maintained over so long a period, is probably unique in the history of whaling, even in areas with far more abundant stocks.

Grøn's success in the Faroes was matched by his lack of it when he tried other fields, only to suffer great losses. He was pursued by exceptionally bad luck: three of his whale catchers were sunk with twenty-eight hands, two of them suffering the unusual fate of being sunk by furious, wounded whales. Then his floating factory was also wrecked. In 1914-15 Grøn returned to the Faroes, and enjoyed a good year in 1915, the company making a record catch for the Faroes — 179 whales, producing 4,400 barrels of oil and 5,000 sacks of guano. With prices respectively £24 and £1 the company recorded a net profit of 125 per cent. The year 1916, on the other hand, proved a disappointment, as the whales failed to materialise. Since the war prevented stations from commencing operations in 1917, the whale was left in peace on all the grounds of the Norwegian Sea for the first time in fifty years. In 1920, after a three-year break, it was assumed that the whale stocks would have recovered, and with the oil price now at £90 four companies made tracks for the Faroes with high hopes. Their attempts, however, proved a financial disaster. They had set out at a time of high prices resulting from the boom, in particular for coal, but when the oil was offered for sale in the autumn, the price had slumped to £27. One Norwegian company nevertheless persisted as late as 1930. Subsequently the Faroese themselves have on various occasions, both in the 1930s and after the Second World War, attempted to operate at a profit, but always with considerable losses. The last unsuccessful attempt was made in 1962-4.

The most significant basis for the success of an enterprise is the number

17. Whaling station in the Faroes, operated 1901-16.

of barrels of oil per whale catcher, and in this respect the Faroes on the whole compare with Iceland. The best years were from 1896 to 1906, while in Iceland they lasted a little longer, up till 1909. Catching off the Faroes admittedly reached a peak in 1908-9, but it needed the efforts of as many as seventeen catchers to account for 773 whales, producing 13,850 barrels, an average of 815 barrels per boat. Hardly anywhere in the world was the production of oil per whale so low, the average for the entire period 1894-1920 being 24.4 barrels. The reason was partly that most of the whales were caught on their migrations to the north, when they were in poor condition, and in part that a relatively large proportion consisted of sei whales. One station produced a mere 1,300 barrels from 130 sei whales, 10 barrels per whale, which must be an all-time low. In Iceland the average production was in the region of 40 barrels per whale.

The total yield of whaling from the Faroes between 1894 and 1916 was 6,682 whales and 154,419 barrels of oil, with a value of about Kr.8 million (= £440,000), an almost insignificant amount compared to the results achieved later in the Antarctic. One interesting feature of Faroese whaling with regard to the dispute between whalers and fishermen is that it provided clear proof that whaling has not the slightest damaging effect on fisheries, as the inhabitants of the Shetlands so stubbornly insisted. (For catching figures for the Faroes, 1894-1920, see Statistical Appendix, Table 41.)

The Shetlands

Whaling in Shetland, though its total production between 1903 and 1914 was even less significant than the Faroese, has special points of interest in whaling history : it was the first time whaling had been based on United Kingdom territory; second, the raw materials were probably more fully utilised here than elsewhere; third, a new technique, tried out here for the first time, proved of great significance in the development of whaling; fourth, an attempt was made by the Shetland companies to combine whaling in the Arctic and the Antarctic by means of a rational use of their equipment; fifth, the first non-Norwegian crews used in British whaling were recruited from the Shetlands; and finally, the conflict between fishermen and whalers was nowhere more bitterly contested than here and in Finnmark, and in both cases political capital was made out of the dispute.

Whaling was started simultaneously in 1903 by two Norwegian companies, one from Sandefjord, owned by Peder Bogen, and one from Larvik, owned by CHRISTIAN NIELSEN, one of Norway's leading whaling owners in this early period of modern Norwegian global whaling. At his death in 1914 he owned what at the time was the largest whaling firm in the world, comprising six companies, twenty-one whale catchers, five floating factories, four land stations, and a number of transport ships operating in both the northern and southern hemispheres. In 1913 this firm produced 15 per cent of Norway's total output of whale oil.

These two companies set up their stations on each side of the narrow Ronas Voe on the northwest coast. A certain amount of British capital had been invested in each of these, and an even larger sum in a third firm, Alexandra Whaling (Hvalfangeri Alexandra), established in Oslo in 1904 with half the capital subscribed in Scotland and Shetland. Most of the remaining shares were eventually bought up by British shareholders, including Salvesen, and in 1907 the company was registered as British under the name of the Alexandra Whaling Co. A few years later the management was taken over by Salvesen, who in 1916, as sole owner, liquidated the company. Salvesen's own station at Olna Firth, which commenced operations in 1904, at the same time as Alexandra, was a modern establishment designed to make use of every portion of the whale carcass. Equipment had been brought over from Iceland, and its manager, Henrik N. Henriksen, was intimately connected with the expansion of Salvesen's whaling activities. He has been described as "our principal adviser in whaling matters for many years, one of the most effective individuals in the whaling industry of his time". By 1906 Salvesen had become one of the biggest whaling firms, with stations in Iceland, the Faroes, and the Shetlands, on which ten catchers were based. Operations were co-ordinated, whale catchers and hands being used wherever the catching prospects appeared most promising for the moment. Olna was the main Shetland station, accounting in most years for about a half of the four companies' production. Between 1906 and 1912 these three stations jointly produced some 12,000 barrels of oil on an annual average, far more than any other firm had ever achieved in the Norwegian Sea. In addition, considerable amounts of guano were manufactured. This as a rule appears to have amounted to as many sacks — each of 100 pounds — as the number of barrels of oil produced, accounting for about one-third of the value of the latter. In 1907, for example, 7,457 barrels of oil fetched £23,889, which is equal to £3 4s 1d per barrel (= £19 4s 6d per ton), while 11,747 sacks of guano sold for £7,296 (i.e. 12s 5d per sack).

The prospect of whaling based on Shetland was at first welcomed by the inhabitants, including the herring fishermen. The herring fisheries were of far greater importance to the Shetlands than for any of the other archipelagos. Herring nets were often destroyed by whales, and it was generally believed that shoals of herring, fleeing from the whales, which consumed large quantities of them, were prevented from entering coastal waters in order to spawn. In fact the fewer whales, the more herrings! But after the first season with whaling and herring fishing being carried on simultaneously, public opinion underwent a radical change, as this proved a bad herring year. Once passions had been roused, the Shetland fishermen proved just as unreceptive to fact and reasonable argument as the fishermen of Finnmark, who had clearly inspired this agitation. In 1904, when whale catching from all four stations got into its stride, the herring fishermen reaped an astonishingly rich harvest, but in only thirteen out of 237 whales were traces of herring to be found. The fishermen then complained that blood and offal from the stations and the whale caracasses drifting off to sea attracted sharks, which approached the shore, frightening the herring away. An official committee, set up in 1904, was unable to find any connection between whaling and stocks of herring. The period from 1879 to 1885 had been boom years for the herring industry, but it had then suffered a decline, long before whaling commenced. The fishermen, however, refused to listen to reason when the fisheries failed completely in 1906, and a fresh wave of agitation broke out. A commonly used argument was that "if the Norwegians prohibit catching out of consideration for the fisheries along *their* coasts, why should we allow them, foreigners, to catch off *our* coasts and get all the profits?" "Whale or herring!" was the slogan, and demonstrators even had their own battle hymn, the last verse of which ran as follows:

"Prohibition!" is your watchword.
Be content with nothing less!
Then you may once more be happy,
And success our land may bless.

While the authorities were not prepared to take such drastic steps, certain provisions were nevertheless introduced in order to pour oil on the troubled waters: whales were to be processed within 60 hours after being killed. This struck a particularly hard blow at the Norwegian companies, which did not possess the necessary equipment. All catching was to take place outside the three-mile limit, and from 1 June to 5 July, during herring fishing, at least 40 miles from land. From 1 November to 31 March there was a total ban on catching. The annual levy per boat was £100, and after 1 January 1908, licences could be issued only to British citizens. The fishermen were not satisfied with a ban on catching which only covered a certain period of the year because it merely prohibited catching, and not the landing of whales caught outside the established boundaries. The strange situation arose that, while whale catchers from the Shetlands had to operate beyond the 40-mile limit, there was nothing to prevent boats from the Faroes catching whales only three miles off the Shetland shore. Judging by registered catches, the law appears to have acted as a brake. It had one advantage, however, in that it compelled companies to end needless waste. As a result, the Shetland stations had a higher production of guano and meat meal. As this proved to be a profitable sideline, it can hardly be called a virtue of necessity.

In 1904-14 the numbers of whales caught and of barrels of whale oil produced proved more stable here than in the other areas in the Norwegian Sea (see Statistical Appendix, Table 41). Apart from a slump in about 1912, production attained an annual average of some 12,000 barrels. With the outbreak of the First World War all catching from the Shetlands, the Hebrides and Ireland was stopped. When the companies prepared to start all over again in 1920, the fishermen protested just as vehemently as before. A committee set up by the Fishery Board for Scotland took evidence from, among others, Theodore Salvesen. When asked why the Norwegians were practically the only nation to engage in whaling, he answered that they were the pioneers of this industry, and that all whale catchers, on all the oceans of the world, were manned by Norwegians; it was impossible to induce a Scot to sign on. The committee concluded that all whaling from the Shetlands — but not from the Hebrides — should be banned, even though the committee itself declared that it possessed not a single factual argument in favour of this step, but that "the intense mood that has permeated the whole community has made a deep impression on the committee"; in other words, their reasons for recommending a ban were as ill-founded as had been the case in Finnmark. However, the recommendations of the committee were not adopted, and catching could start once again, though the ever-present threat of a ban was sufficient to deter the Norwegians, with the result that Salvesen operated from his two stations alone. In 1921, however, Colla Firth closed down, and all catching was concentrated on Olna, which continued every year to the end of the 1929 season. The year 1920 was promising — 430 whales, 9,620 barrels of oil, and 12,516 sacks of guano. 1920-6 proved a particularly successful period : with an average price of £35 for oil and low operating costs, profits were most encouraging. The number of blue whales slumped from 1924, as in other areas, and the same was true of the fin whale from 1926. As the 1929 catch produced only eighty-five whales, and 1,695 barrels, operations were terminated, and never, since that day, has there been any commercial whaling based on the Shetlands.

As mentioned in the introduction to this section, whaling in the Shetlands is of very special interest to the development of the industry. In the autumn of 1904 operations had commenced in the Antarctic. The proceeds from the land station in South Georgia in 1904-5 and the first floating factory in 1905-6 were hardly convincing enough to warrant abandoning catching in the northern hemisphere, where a great many stations recorded higher production figures. Another question was whether the costly floating equipment — passive capital for half a year — could be utilised more rationally by operating in the northern hemisphere in summer and in the southern hemisphere in winter (i.e. the Antarctic summer). Salvesen, who had begun catching in the southern hemisphere in 1909, endeavoured for a number of years to use his whale catchers in this way, and a number of companies in the north leased their boats during the winter season to companies operating in the south. The voyage there and back took four months, a great deal of coal was consumed, and the wear and tear on equipment was so great that it is doubtful whether it was worth it. The tremendous expansion of whaling in the southern hemisphere after 1908 created a serious shortage of good gunners in the north. With an opportunity of accounting for a vastly greater number of whales, most gunners preferred to make their way south. In the middle of the 1911 season a company in the Faroes was compelled to dismiss all its gunners for incompetence, and this was one of the main reasons why the year's result proved so poor.

The Scottish author and artist W. G. BURN MURDOCH had spent the 1892-3 season with the famous Dundee fleet in the Antarctic in their search for right whales. We shall return to this a little later. In 1912 he had established a Scottish company, St. Abbs Whaling Co., for which he commissioned the building in Tønsberg of a whale catcher which is of special interest for two reasons. In the first place it was powered by a diesel engine, and in the second it was equipped with tanks sufficient for 120 tons of oil, as well as two blubber cookers on deck. This boat, the *St. Ebba*, was considerably larger than ordinary whale catchers. Murdoch, who has given us an account of the vessel and its voyage, hoped that with this vessel it would be possible to remain at sea for longer periods by obviating the need to make for some harbour at frequent intervals in order to take on coal. Secondly, there would be no need to interrupt catching operations in order to tow the whale to land, now that it could be boiled on board. This was not the only experiment carried out at this time with an eye to combining a whale catcher and a floating factory. The attempt was repeated in the 1960s, once again without success. Murdoch's intention was to operate off the Shetlands in summer and to move south in the winter. On his first voyage, however, he put in at the island of Mahé in the Seychelles and operated from a land station there in 1914-18, when the vessel and the diesel engine proved so ineffective that two ordinary steam-driven whale catchers were acquired.

It has generally been assumed that the *St. Ebba* was the world's first diesel-driven whale catcher. This is not correct: Smith's Dock Co. Ltd. of Middlesbrough, which became one of the world's major suppliers of whale catchers, record that in the spring of 1911 they built two diesel-driven whale catchers for Richard Irvin & Sons of North Shields, who were part-owners in a large whaling company. The engines, however, proved so unreliable that they were dumped ashore after two years and replaced by steam engines. Twenty-five years were to elapse before the next attempt with a diesel engine, and on this occasion it was the Japanese who were the pioneers. The delay in installing diesel engines in whale catchers — they had been in use for several years in floating factories — was due not to technical but to practical reasons: among other things, it was maintained that the noise of the engine scared the whale.

With the Shetlands we also associate another event of major importance to the processing of whale oil, as it was here that the rotary cooker, the so-called "Hartmann's apparatus", with its revolutionary boiling technique, was first tested. It had been designed by the German engineer AUGUST SOMMERMEYER, and was named after the German firm of A. Hartmann, A.G., who manufactured it. We shall describe this innovation in greater detail in the chapter dealing with technical developments.

The Hebrides and Ireland

Whaling met with the same welcome in the Hebrides as in the Faroes. When a ban in Finnmark appeared imminent several operators toyed with the idea of transferring to the Hebrides, as most sites elsewhere were occupied. Nothing came of this, but a Norwegian company made the move from Iceland, setting up the Bunaveneader station in Harris, and commenced catching there in the summer of 1904 with three boats. From 1905 to 1914 the results obtained were very stable, with an annual average of 5,600 barrels, with a drop to 2,570 in 1913 and a record 7,000 in 1909. Apart from the production of companies in Iceland, only in one season had a company shown better results.

What makes the Hebridean venture interesting from a biological point of view is the large number of nordcapers caught. Of the 117 nordcapers which comprised the total catch between 1906 and 1914 in all areas so far mentioned, ninety-one were towed in to Bunaveneader. The long baleens made these animals still very valuable. During the decade prior to 1914 they fetched an average price of £800 a ton. A nordcaper would yield 700 to 800 kg. or even more, and in addition it was generally very fat, one particular specimen in Bunaveneader producing 120 barrels of oil. Together with the baleens this one whale fetched Kr.15,000 (*ca.* £824).

This encouraging yield of nordcapers prompted five expeditions to set out from Norway in 1908-11 to seek out this species in the Atlantic, ranging from Iceland in the north to Gibraltar in the south. As far as is known, not a single animal was caught. The most important outcome of these expeditions was the discovery of such abundant migrations of whales round Gibraltar, that whaling based on Spain and Portugal was started in 1921. The nordcaper's goal on his winter migration is still a matter for speculation.

When the wartime ban on whaling was raised in 1920 the company recommenced catching, with excellent results — 194 whales and 5,450 barrels — but the sudden end of the boom and the state of the whale-oil market proved disastrous. The company was sold in 1922 to the Harris Whaling & Fishing Co., an affiliate of Lever Bros. The real purchaser was Lord Leverhulme, and the deal was part of his celebrated purchase in 1918 of Lewis and Harris. Whaling was part of his plan to transform this ultra-conservative peasant and fishing community into a modern industrial society. He had a strange conception of Norwegian whaling. According to his biographer, "they had been converting the whale-carcasses into guano. Leverhulme had a better idea. He would extract the oil for Port Sunlight and turn the meat into tinned sausages for African natives, where Lever Brothers had extensive plantations. But he was disappointed. 'The meat was hard and tough', he said a year later, 'after some 6,000 tons [there must be at least one nought too many on the end of this figure] had been treated experimentally, 'and I do not think it would really pay to can it even for Africans.' He did not give up the hope of using it in some form, and one of the last installations before his death was a special building for smoking whale-meat, which he intended to export in this form to the Congo." Like most of his plans for the Hebrides, this too proved a failure. Up to the time of his death in 1925 he had spent two million pounds on his totally misconceived Hebridean project.

The name of the station was changed to West Tarbert, and it was run on behalf of Lever Bros. from 1923 to 1928 with a total loss of £50,000, despite relatively good production results. The chief concern of this major undertaking was to carry out experiments which could be applied on a larger scale by its company Southern Whaling & Sealing Co. in the Antarctic. In 1950-1 an entirely unsuccessful attempt to revive catching was made, since when the whale has been allowed to frequent Hebridean waters unmolested.

It was but a step from the Hebrides to Ireland, where it was hoped to catch the whale on its migrations to the north before it fell a prey to any of the other stations. In 1907 the Norwegian-British company of Arranmore Whaling was founded with a capital of £12,000. It was registered in Edinburgh, with three Englishmen on the board, but managed from Norway. The company was named after the island of Arran off the northwest coast of Ireland. The local fishermen had apparently taken their cue from their Shetland colleagues, as the mere rumour that whaling was to be introduced locally was sufficient to provoke the most violent protests. "Down with whaling!" So strong was the pressure exerted on the authorities that the company was refused permission to establish its station there, and this had to be moved to the Inishkea Islands, 90 miles south-west of Arran, where catching commenced so late in the 1908 season that the outcome was a mere 1,800 barrels. On 1 January 1909, a Whaling Act almost identical to the one that applied to Scotland two years previously, came into force.

Norwegian initiative was also responsible for setting up of yet another Norwegian-British company, the Blacksod Whaling Company Ltd., with a capital of £20,000, registered in Dublin. Its name, of course, was taken from that of a far western district of the Irish mainland, close to the Inishkea Islands, where a major and entirely modern station, including a guano factory, was erected in 1910. The high hopes of both companies proved illusory. Arranmore was wound up in 1913. When Blacksod, after the wartime close-down, recommenced operations in 1920, the outcome was surprisingly good — 3,995 barrels — but when the following year yielded 1,000 barrels less and the station burnt down in February 1922, this company was also wound up. And this, for all time, was the end of whaling based in Ireland.

Of special interest is the report from March 1912 to the effect that Blacksod's two whale catchers had been granted a licence, to run for five years from 1 April, to "establish and operate a wireless telegraph station". If this is correct, the vessels acquired this epoch-making novelty many years before whaling is generally assumed to have made use of it.

Statistics for the various species of whale towed into the Scottish stations (the Shetlands and Hebrides) in the period 1908-14 are given in Table 5.

Table 5. WHALES CAUGHT FROM THE SCOTTISH STATIONS, 1908-1914

	Number	Percentage of total
Fin whale	2,418	60.7
Sei whale	1,283	32.5
Blue whale	109	2.7
Nordcaper	66	1.7
Sperm whale	42	1.1
Humpback	31	0.8
Bottlenose	20	0.5
Total	3,969	

If we exclude sperm and bottlenose whales, the result is an average of 27.3 barrels per whale. The large number of sei whales gives a misleading impression of the use to which the Scottish stations put the raw materials: more correctly, this should be expressed in terms of barrels per BWU, which was 68.4.

The bulk of the whales on their migration from the southwest passed between Rockall and St. Kilda, *en route* for the Faroes, where they divided, one trek proceeding northwest towards Iceland, another northeast towards Finnmark and Spitsbergen. The latter consisted almost solely of blue and fin whales. The sperm whale and the nordcaper seldom passed east of the submarine ridge between the Faroes and Iceland. (For catching figures for the Hebrides, 1904-20, and Ireland, 1908-20, see Statistical Appendix, Table 41.)

Spitsbergen

Spitsbergen — incorporated in 1925 into the realm of Norway with the name Svalbard — was discovered by the Dutchman Willem Barendsz in 1596. Apart from Spitsbergen and other islands in the Arctic, he also made another discovery — the incredible number of Greenland whales in these waters. For two hundred years, from about 1615 to the

1820s, the seas between Spitsbergen, Bjørnøya, Jan Mayen, the east coast of Greenland, and the pack-ice to the north became the scene of the richest catches of baleen whale the world has ever witnessed prior to modern catching in the Antarctic. But then never has a species of whale come so close to total extinction as the Greenland whale. (Until recently, it was assumed to be entirely extinct, but a few specimens have been observed and photographed north of Alaska.) It took two hundred years to reduce the Greenland whale to the verge of extinction, but a mere fifty years to do the same to the blue whale in the Antarctic.

The significance of modern whaling in Spitsbergen waters lies in the fact that it constituted a training ground for operations in the Antarctic. It was here that the first serviceable steam boiling plant, a new flensing technique, and a new method of transporting oil were tried out; and, last but not least, catching was carried out in daily contact with the ice under climatic conditions very similar to those that would be met with in the Antarctic.

The leading personality in this significant phase of modern whaling was CHRISTEN CHRISTENSEN of Sandefjord. In the first place he was the creator of Framnæs mekaniske Verksted, one of the world's leading shipbuilding yards engaged in the conversion and equipping of floating factories. Secondly, it was he who developed and tested one of the first two floating steamship factories, which proved highly serviceable and became the prototype for all the subsequent models. Thirdly, he was responsible for setting up Norway's first factory for the refining of whale oil, and fourthly, he patented three techniques which were used in whaling. The most important of these was the transport of oil in fixed tanks in the floating factory instead of in wooden barrels. Filling barrels and stowing them in the hold took a great deal of time, and spillage and leaks were apt to occur as the boat pitched and rolled. Another patent involved incorporating a cooker in the hull instead of installing it on the deck. Fifthly, in the years 1892-3 he sent one, and in 1893-4 four, vessels to the Antarctic to trap seals and search for right whales. Although no traces of this species were to be found, indirectly this expedition triggered off the start of modern whaling in the Antarctic. The expedition manager, CARL ANTON LARSEN (1860-1924), the actual founder of this catching, discovered tremendous quantities of the "modern" whales, and on his intiative the first company was founded for the purpose of operating in the southern hemisphere.

In 1903, as whaling off the coast of Finnmark drew to a close, practically all the catching grounds in the Norwegian Sea were being exploited: only one remained, around Bjornøya and Spitsbergen. It was not entirely *terra incognita,* because in previous years whale catchers from North Norway had had to proceed as much as 200 miles north in search of whales. Inevitably, the idea emerged that the whale

18. The Norwegian shipowner Christen Christensen, a pioneer in modern and Antarctic whaling.

should be processed where it was caught, and if it proved impossible to establish a shore station there, it should be possible to flense the whale from a floating factory. This had been done during the old-time catching of right and sperm whales.

There were several problems associated with outboard flensing from a floating factory and processing the raw material on board. Flensing could not be carried out in bad weather with high seas. There was limited space on board for the cookers, oil barrels, supplies of coal, and water. Some coal was available in Spitsbergen but a more difficult problem was posed by water for boiling and for the steam engines of whale catchers and floating factories. All in all, the capacity of the floating factory was strictly limited, and it proved impossible to sever all contact with the shore or to process any part of the whale except the blubber.

Whaling from Spitsbergen was inaugurated in 1903 by the company A/S Ørnen, established by Christensen for the express purpose of utilising a floating factory. For this purpose he leased a small wooden steamship, the *Telegraf*, of 737 gross tons. It was equipped and fitted out in a highly primitive manner at Christensen's yard. ALEX LANGE, another important personality in the history of modern whaling, was appointed expedition manager. Two important events were to depend on his skill — the success of the first floating steamer factory and the success of the first Norwegian whaling expedition in search of rorquals in the Antarctic.

This expedition, which was to have such important consequences, set off on 18 May 1903. The results were not encouraging : all the fjords on the west coast of Spitsbergen were blocked by ice, which made it impossible to enter and flense the whale in calm water. "As it is impossible to flense the whale and boil in the open sea," Lange writes, seven whales were shot and towed down to the station in Finnmark. Most of them were lost in a gale. On 16 June the floating factory returned, and was now able to enter an ice-free fjord, outside which there were plenty of whales, particularly blue whales. As early as 10 August, however, the ice threatened to close in on the floating factory, operations had to be suspended, and by September the floating factory was back in Sandefjord with 1,960 barrels, produced from fifty-seven whales, of which forty-two were blue whales, i.e. 34.4 barrels per whale or 40 barrels per BWU. This would suggest that only the best blubber was boiled. The result yielded a profit, and shareholders received a dividend of 20 per cent.

As the catch had been limited not by supplies of whale but by the capacity of the floating factory, a secondhand steamer of 1,517 gross tons was purchased in England for £3,750 for use in the ensuing season. It was rechristened *Admiralen* ("The Admiral"), and in the records of the Framnæs shipbuilding yard it is listed as "Kogeri No. 1" (literally : Try-works No. 1). When fully equipped it cost £7,140. The season of 1904 proved a good one from the point of view of both weather and ice. In the course of three months the floating factory was almost fully laden with 5,100 barrels from 154 whales. The try-out was poorer than in the previous year — only 33.1 barrels per whale (38.8 per BWU). This time too shareholders received a 20 per cent dividend.

Inevitably, what had occurred and would recur in other areas took place here as well. The ban on catching from North Norway, the excellent catches made by the first company, and in particular the large numbers of blue whales, resulted in a veritable invasion — one new company in 1904 and as many as six in 1905, one of which directed its attention to Bear Island. At that time Spitsbergen was a no-man's land, and in Norway it would have been unthinkable in those days to regulate catching for Norwegians operating in waters outside the country's jurisdiction; this first took place in the 1930s. Two of the companies built a land station, one on Bjørnøya. One of the companies was owned by THOR DAHL of Sandefjord, a name we shall encounter again in what was to be Norway's largest whaling company.

In 1905 eight companies were engaged in catching, and in 1906-7 seven companies operated with fifteen boats. Little experience was required to forecast the inevitable : there was a slump from 599 whales (337 were blue whales) and 18,660 barrels in 1905 to a quarter of this as early as 1908. After a third successful season in 1905 the A/S Ørnen company closed down, and that autumn *Admiralen* sailed to the Antarctic, one of the very few floating factories to operate in the northern and southern hemisphere in one and the same year. Two of the other floating factories also made their way south, where they provided a base for two of the largest Norwegian companies there. Two companies operating in Spitsbergen closed down in 1907, two in 1908, while three stuck it out till 1912, with such poor catches, however — a total of fifty-eight whales and 2,200 barrels — that they were all forced to retire with very substantial losses. In 1920 and 1926-7 two unsuccessful attempts were made to resume catching, since when no operations have been carried on in these waters, in the narrower sense of the word, although several expeditions operated with floating factories in the waters between Spitsbergen and Greenland. We shall subsequently consider this in connection with the development of pelagic whaling.

The total yield of the Spitsbergen-Bjørnøya venture for the years 1903-12 comprised 2,180 whales and almost 70,000 barrels, a little less than in the Hebridean-Irish period from 1903 to 1914. In view of the tremendous efforts that were made, this proved financially the most disappointing of all the whaling grounds around the Norwegian Sea. Experts have speculated on the reason for this, and the usual argument is that with eight companies involved the area would inevitably be over-fished; but it hardly appears reasonable that a catch of 2,180 whales over a period of ten years — an annual average of 218 — should have been capable of wiping out stocks over an area of this size. The Spitsbergen whalers have been accused of flagrant waste, as they only took the best blubber, owing to the short catching period at their disposal. It is recorded that hundreds of de-blubbered carcasses were floating around, and that the surface of the sea was covered with a thick layer of oil and grax (residue from the boiling process), which attracted swarms of sea-fowl. By boiling only the best of the blubber it was possible to ensure oil of top quality, No. 1, which fetched the highest price.

The question of whale stocks round Spitsbergen is in reality a question of the blue whale. Of the 2,180 whales mentioned above, 973 are known with certainly to have been blue whales, 696 fin whales, and

40 humpbacks. If for the sake of argument one were to assume that the remaining 471 were all blue whales, some 60 per cent of the total of 2,180 would then have been blue whales, and the question then arises: why did such a relatively small catch (at most 973 + 471, i.e. 1,444) over a ten-year period cause the disappearance of the blue whale from the North Atlantic? Åge Jonsgård, an expert in whaling biology, has formulated a theory from the following evidence.

In August 1952 a catcher of small whales in the Barents Sea, operating between Svalbard and Franz Joseph Land, spotted an unusual sight, schools of between three and four and up to eight or ten large blue whales, gorging on krill. This would appear to refute the idea that the blue whale had been practically exterminated in the north, even though there were reasons for believing this. When catching was stopped owing to the outbreak of war and restarted after an interval of several years, it was assumed that stocks had been replenished. These hopes were doomed to disappointment. In Finnmark, where the whale had been protected ever since 1904 until catching was once again allowed in 1918, in order to provide Norway with supplies of fat during the war, two stations, in the period 1918-20, caught 587 whales, of which only two were blue whales. Four stations on the west and south coasts accounted for 1,177 whales, of which only one was a blue whale!

This result aroused widespread astonishment. According to Jonsgård, the explanation must be that the blue whale is highly conservative in its migration in search of food in the north, and there seems to be every indication that the various areas have their own local schools, which return every year to the same pastures. If this were not the case, and the same school visited all the areas in the north in turn, it would be impossible to wipe out the blue whale in one particular area, while it remained numerous in an adjacent area. This conclusion is of prime importance to the protection of the blue whale. Local protection will have little or no influence; only total protection would hold out any hope that stocks would revive. A proposal for total protection in the North Atlantic for a five-year period (1955-9) was adopted by the International Whaling Commission in Tokyo in 1954. Iceland protested, and continued to catch blue whales until 1960, when it accepted the agreement. This has been continuously renewed and, as we shall see, extended to cover all the oceans of the world. Whalers from the station in Iceland have reported since the late 1960s that they have frequently seen blue and humpback whales in the seas between Iceland and Greenland (the Denmark Strait).

A summary of incomplete figures for catching in the European portion of the North Atlantic (the Norwegian Sea) is given in Table 6.

Incomplete figures for the species of whale caught make it impossible to calculate the number of barrels per BWU. The high figure of barrels

Table 6. CATCH, OIL PRODUCTION AND BARRELS OF OIL PER WHALE
IN ALL THE GROUNDS OF THE NORWEGIAN SEA, 1868-1912

	Period	Whales	Oil barrels	Barrels per whale
Finnmark	1868-1904	17,745	434,259	24.5
Iceland	1883-1915	17,189	618,838	36.0
Faroe Islands	1894-1916	6,862	154,419	22.5
Shetlands, Hebrides, Ireland	1903-14	7,157	201,346	28.7
Spitsbergen	1903-12	2,180	69,383	31.8
Total		51,133	1,478,245	28.9

per whale from Iceland may be put down to the large proportion of blue whales, while the low figure for the Faroe Islands can be attributed to the large proportion of sei whales. During the period 1904-14 56,308 whales were caught in the Antarctic, producing 1,775,356 barrels of oil, an average of 31.5 barrels per whale, or about the same as in the northern hemisphere. As Antarctic catching yielded approximately 62 per cent humpback, 24 per cent fin, and 14 per cent blue whale, the try-out came to about 65 barrels per BWU. With the subsequent improved processing of the raw material, twice as much could have been achieved.

In order to maintain as far as possible a correct chronological sequence, we should first consider for a moment the foundation and the initial development of modern coastal catching in other sea areas in the northern hemisphere before Antarctic whaling got into its stride.

Newfoundland

In 1898 modern whaling, in extending its operations to cover New-foundland, was now engaged in an area with centuries-old traditions of fishing and whaling. According to tradition, it was the Biscayans, European past masters in the art of whaling, who first made their way there as far back as one hundred years before Columbus's first voyage in 1492. There is reliable evidence that the Biscayans, from about 1530, crossed the Atlantic every summer to fish and catch whales off Newfound-land. In the latter half of the sixteenth century Dutchmen, Frenchmen, and Englishmen also made their way there. Their quarry was the Greenland whale, the close and somewhat larger relation of the nordcaper, which the Biscayans had been catching in their home waters far back in the Middle Ages. For this reason it was called the *Balaena Biscayensis*. As stocks of whale off Newfoundland had declined markedly around 1600, and vast quantities were discovered off Spitsbergen at about the same time, the interest of the major whaling nations was directed to these waters, while the English colonists commenced whaling on their very own doorstep, an activity which is believed to have started from Nantucket in 1614. By 1850 the right whale had been almost wiped out, but invention of the bomb-lance supposedly made it possible to catch in addition a few fin and humpback whales. Up to about the year 1760 this was a purely coastal form of catching, but from then on the famous catching vessels of Gloucester, Salem, and New Bedford started out on their legendary voyages to distant waters, first and foremost along the east coast of the American continent as far as the Davis Strait and Baffin Bay, and towards the end of the century all the way round Cape Horn up to the Bering Sea, returning to their home ports after an absence of three to four years.

Not till 1890 did Newfoundland whaling finally come to an end. The occasional whale had been caught, and it had been established that large schools of blue and fin whales existed, which could undoubtedly be hunted profitably with the aid of modern equipment. The person to realise this idea was ADOLPH NEILSEN of Tønsberg, who had been active as Fisheries Inspector in Newfoundland since 1889. Before making his way there he had witnessed whaling in Finnmark, and had convinced the people of Newfoundland that modern whaling operating from their shores could prove just as lucrative. At the instigation of a local businessman, Neilsen went to Norway in 1897, and managed to find so many subscribers both in his native country and in Newfoundland that he was in a position to establish the Cabot Steam Whaling Company with a capital of $100,000. The station, also named Cabot, was set up at Notre Dame Bay on the northeast coast. It was completed in August 1898, by which time a great many whales were waiting to be flensed. These had been caught from the whale catcher *Cabot,* which had crossed from Norway in June, shooting the first "modern" whale in the western hemisphere on 25 June. The first year yielded forty-seven whales, 1899 yielded ninety-five, 1900 111, and 1901 258. About one-third were fin whales, one-third humpbacks, and the rest blue and sei whales. The operations were welcomed by the local population, since they provided work for fifty unemployed hands.

In the north, where the station was situated, it was only possible to operate during the summer months. In order to find out whether it was possible to hunt on the south coast in the winter months as well, a station was set up there — Balaena, on Hermitage Bay — and from this base the *Cabot* operated during the winter for three years, and from 1902 throughout the year, while a larger whale catcher was constructed to operate in the inclement seas to the north. Once the teething troubles of the opening years had been overcome, the company showed a very small profit in 1900, when the gross value of the catch was recorded as $36,428. However, it had been proved that there were ample stocks

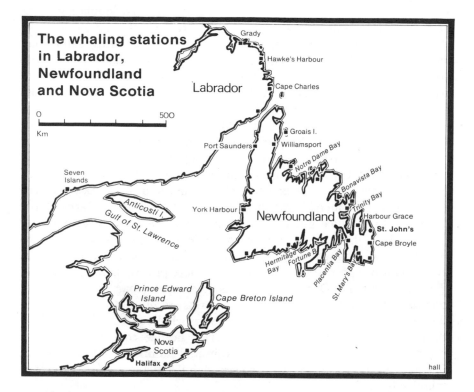

The whaling stations in Labrador, Newfoundland and Nova Scotia

of whales, and the prospects appeared promising. Others, too, were encouraged to start. One of these, the Newfoundland Co., an entirely local venture, was probably one of the first on the North Atlantic seaboard in which Norwegians had no financial interest. It was, however, entirely dependent on Norwegian equipment and Norwegian gunners. In common with the aforementioned company, it established two stations, both on the south coast, and commenced catching in 1901.

As it seemed likely that whaling would have a much larger scope than had been imagined, opposition was encountered from four sources: from previously existing companies, which looked askance at rivals; from fishermen, who held the same conviction as their colleagues in Finnmark, though to a far less pronounced extent, that whaling would ruin their rich fisheries and that the whale, when pursued, destroyed nets; from the population living near the whaling stations, who complained of the stench; and lastly, from the authorities in the Department of Fisheries, who were frightened by the example shown in Norway, "where stocks of whales were exterminated in the course of fourteen years as a result of unrestricted catching". Apart from the fact that the correct figure should be thirty-five years and not fourteen, this shows that the situation in Finnmark was well known, and exerted an influence well beyond Norway's borders. Unfortunately for Newfoundland, the Department did not follow up its good intentions.

The Whaling Industry Act of 22 April 1902, with subsequent amendments added in the following year, laid down that a licence was required, valid for ten years, for which an annual levy of $1,500 was payable. (In the course of three seasons, 1903-5, this brought in a sum of $45,000.) Licences could be issued to foreigners, but employees had to be British subjects, although for the first three years foreign experts could be used to train the natives. Only one whale catcher per station was permitted; whales could not be hunted at a distance of less than one mile from any boat engaged in fishing, and two miles from the coast. The law did not make complete exploitation of the raw material mandatory, but merely specified that a de-blubbered carcass, not processed to produce guano, should be towed at least fifty miles out to sea. There should be a distance of at least fifty miles between each station. A government inspector was to visit all stations every year, and submit a report to the Department. These printed annual reports of the Newfoundland Department of Fisheries, going back to 1903, have proved the most important source for this account. On three points this Act was to set a precedent for later whaling Acts, in particular British regulations in the Antarctic: (1) a licence covering a specified period of time; (2) a licence fee; (3) a limited number of whale catchers. But as a means of restricting Newfoundland catching, the Act proved completely ineffectual.

Despite its English name, the Atlantic Whale Manufacturing Co. was a purely Norwegian undertaking operating from Newfoundland. The bulk of the shares were held by the well-known Norwegian whaling family ELLEFSEN. In 1912 a father, brother, and five sons were active as gunners and expedition managers. In 1901 Anders Ellefsen came to Newfoundland, whose governor was delighted to welcome foreigners willing to set up in business there. He gave Ellefsen "the full rights as to a British subject to establish himself there without a licence". His station was set up at Aquaforte in the extreme southeast, near Cape Race, an area notorious for the many ships that had been wrecked there during the years. On 17 June 1902, catching operations commenced, with Anders Ellefsen's 54-year-old father as a gunner. In the course of six weeks he notched up the brilliant score of eighty-four whales, an average of two a day. After this excellent start his score fell off somewhat, producing an extra twenty-four, or 108 whales for the entire season. The try-out was astonishingly low, only 2,223 barrels, or 20.6 per whale, even though a large proportion consisted of blue whales. This is typical of all Newfoundland whaling, which in this respect had lower figures than any other area: prior to 1915 it never exceeded twenty-eight barrels. In 1907-11 the annual average was a mere 20.8. During the record year of 1904 we know the numbers of the various species of whale: 264 blue, 690 fin, 281 humpback, and 40 unspecified. These produced 35,766 barrels, an average of 28 per whale, or 49 per BWU, a deplorably low figure. The reason was said to be that whales here were leaner than in other areas, because most of them were caught on the migration to the north, and in the second place almost nothing but the blubber was boiled. Furthermore, as the distance the whale had to be towed to land was short, flensing took place a few hours after it was dead, and practically all oil was of Quality No. 1. For 1902 figures for all five stations are given as 331 whales and 9,184 barrels, valued at $112,859, in addition to which baleen to a value of $12,285 was sold.

Newfoundland was beset by a whaling fever, a crazy wave of speculation unequalled in any area in the history of whaling, and the crash, when it came, was a violent one. Between December 1902 and November 1903 twenty-five applications for licences were submitted. Despite the inspectors' insistent warnings, nineteen were granted (including the five already granted); fourteen stations started operating in 1904, and an additional four in 1905, none of them Norwegian, while local, Canadian, and American capital financed the companies involved. The stations were scattered round the entire coast of Newfoundland, most of them on the east coast. On the coast of Labrador there were thirteen stations, from the Straits of Belle Isle and north to Cartwright. The setback in 1905 proved disastrous: the eighteen stations between them processed 892 whales, which produced 25,182 barrels, an average respectively of 50 and 1,400 per station. Four stations closed down, and for the fourteen still in the field 1906 proved even more calamitous — 439 whales and 10,740 barrels, or 31 and 800 per station. Most of them faced total ruin; installations and plant, now worthless, were abandoned, and the whale catchers sold off. Although the licence fee was reduced to $750 in 1906, and abolished in its entirety in 1907, the number of stations and boats dwindled to five in 1910. It was estimated that losses amounted to $2 million. Several of the whale catchers were sold to Japan. For the Norwegian crews this proved an adventurous voyage, two-thirds of the way round the world, a trip of three months. It is indeed astonishing that these tiny vessels should have reached their destination. One of them struck a reef in the Red Sea, and the captain and three hands rowed ashore to get help. That was the last that was ever seen of them. "It is extremely rare," as the Lloyd's agent put it, "for Europeans landing on the coast of Arabia to escape with their lives."

In reports from Newfoundland the name of Dr. L. RISMÜLLER, a German-American engineer, and his method of producing guano and cattle feed from de-blubbered carcasses, constantly recur. Not only did he own two companies, each with its own station, concerned not with the catching of whales but with the purchase of carcasses from other nearby stations, but he also installed his own plant in other stations, and contracted for the purchase of carcasses at a rate of $24 for blue whales, $14 for fin whales and $10 for humpbacks, a very high price compared to what was paid seven or eight years later in the Antarctic — a mere $5 irrespective of species. When modern catching started in 1905 on the northwest coast of North America, Rismüller was asked to install his plant there too. No further details of his method have been unearthed, except that it was an improved boiling technique, with complete exploitation of the carcass of the whale. The method does not appear to have been used outside America.

Although we know little about the technical aspect of Rismüller's inventions, so many favourable accounts of their great significance exist, that they cannot be ignored. The author J. G. MILLAIS, who has provided us with a vivid account of whaling from Newfoundland, writes of Rismüller that "he has done more for whaling and for the use of whale products than any other person". When he came to Newfoundland (in 1900) "the whaling industry was not in a favourable state and was showing no profit, but once Rismüller entered the business, things soon changed. In the end there were twenty-one stations under his management." A newspaper report stated that not until the great advantage of his process had been demonstrated was it possible to persuade moneyed individuals to invest in Newfoundland whaling, and it was also said that the first company on the west coast was only successful in getting production going once "his patented machinery" had been adopted. It is possible that the gradual increase in the production of guano was due to Rismüller's machinery: in 1904 seven stations are reported to have produced 5,000 barrels of meat oil.

Newfoundland whaling is also of some interest as far as the use of a floating factory is concerned, and the attempt by means of this innovation to co-ordinate whaling in the northern and southern hemispheres. In 1903 the Norwegian NOKARD DAVIDSEN, then aged twenty-six, had arrived in Newfoundland as manager of the Newfoundland Steam Whaling Co. With the news that three expeditions had made good catches in the Antarctic in 1906, the company purchased the steamer *Sobraon* and had her equipped as a floating factory in Sandefjord. With Davidsen in charge the floating factory made its way in the autumn of 1907 to uncharted waters round South Shetland, but hardly had catching started when a tragic event struck — Davidsen was washed overboard and drowned. On 9 February 1908, in the presence of 250 whalers, a 22-foot-high column of cast concrete was unveiled on Deception Island in memory of this man, one of the first victims of Antarctic whaling. By May the *Sobraon* was back, operating that summer along the coast of Labrador as far as the Spotted Islands. Her voyage proved a disappointment, yielding a mere 141 whales and

19. A group of workers at the whaling station Aquaforte, Newfoundland, 1905.

4,000 barrels, insufficient to show a profit. In 1909 the results were no better, and in the following year the floating factory was sold. We shall come across it again, operating under other owners, both in the Antarctic and along the west coast of South America.

There were several reasons for the collapse in Newfoundland: running costs were high, and even in the record year of 1904 only three companies declared a dividend, none of more than 6 per cent. The price of oil of the best quality (No. 0/1) had slumped from £21 in 1901 to £16 in 1904, and in 1905 a number of firms were forced to sell out at £14 10s. A rise in price in 1907 to as much as £23 made little difference, since stocks of whales failed to materialise. The annual report claims that food species were not available along the coast; the whale consequently chose an entirely different route, far out to sea. In 1909 feeding conditions for whales were better, and this might have been a good year if the price had not fallen to £17. Both 1910 and 1911 were relatively favourable for the five companies still in the field, who were able to sell their oil for £22. Inevitably, history repeated itself, although no-one appears to have learnt from experience: new companies entered the field, and in 1912 ten of them recorded a smaller total catch than five companies had accounted for in the previous year, too many cooks spoiling the broth. In 1914 seven companies together killed a mere 161 whales, producing 3,000 barrels. "All catching has been run at a loss" was the terse verdict of the annual report. By 1915 there were only three stations left — Rose-au-Rue in the south, Beaverton in the northeast, and Hawke's Harbour in Labrador. The last of these (set up in 1905) was the one which operated for the greatest number of seasons — from the mid-1930s under the management of Salvesen. Of the total catch for 1915 of 141 whales, half had been caught from Hawke's Harbour.

From Newfoundland operations spread to include the Gulf of St. Lawrence, where whales had been observed by seal trappers. In May 1911 the Norwegian-Canadian Whaling Co. was set up for the purpose of catching whales. An old and abandoned plant was purchased on the Seven Islands (Sept Iles), on the north side of the Gulf, from which whaling was carried out in 1912-15 with an annual average yield of 3,450 barrels of oil and an equal number of sacks of guano. After an unsuccessful attempt in the final year to combine whaling with sealing, the station was closed, on suspicion of having traded with the enemy. The entire plant was sold in 1921 for $1,400.

When it became known, after an almost total stoppage in 1916 and 1917, that the Norwegians were prepared to start catching once again from Newfoundland, they were the target of a violent attack from a St. John's newspaper, which declared that once the Norwegians had started, there was every reason to believe that they would carry on as long as there was a whale blowing. If the authorities were anxious for whaling to be ruined for a century, they should allow the Norwegians to start. They had already made a clean sweep along their own coasts, and in a number of other places where previously stocks of whales had been plentiful. In Norwegian quarters it was pointed out by way of reply that the object of whaling was to earn money, that catching was regulated by the price of oil, and that when an area was no longer profitable, they would withdraw. The sole Norwegian company had closed down in 1906, after a return of only eighteen whales and 360 barrels, resulting in a loss so resounding that it wiped out the profits of the four previous years. Losses incurred in Newfoundland involved British-American capital, and not Norwegian. That whaling appeared to be an essentially Norwegian undertaking was naturally due to the substantial Norwegian contribution in the form of matériel and crews used by other companies, and it was in this respect that Norway reaped the greatest benefit. In the course of a few years Norwegian shipbuilding yards supplied fifteen new whale catchers, and several older vessels were sold. All catching equipment — guns, harpoons, and shells, and the bulk of the reduction gear — came from Norway, and all the gunners and crews on the whale catchers and most of the expedition managers were Norwegian. Their wages and all supplies in reality constituted the only financial benefit Norway gained from whaling off Newfoundland.

The years 1918 and 1919 proved so disastrous for the Newfoundland Whaling Co. and another company that operations were at a complete standstill in 1920-2. The Newfoundland Whaling Co. tried for the third time in 1923, and their final success for a number of years in maintaining the most favourable and profitable operations ever carried out in this area proved that stocks of whales had not been exterminated. In 1925-30 the average annual production was 12,500 barrels, while the price of oil was around £31. Wages and the price of coal were low, as were other running expenses. So lucrative was catching compared to previous years that three stations caught 508 whales and produced 20,580 barrels in 1928, or only 5,000 barrels less than eighteen stations had produced in 1905. There was a marked increase in the number of barrels per whale, from twenty-three in 1923 to forty-one in 1929-30. The main reason for this is believed to have been the more efficient boiling technique that had been developed during these years.

The spate of whaling activity all over the world during the latter half of the 1920s once again raised the question of effective protection of the whale. Newfoundland was no exception to this: a new Act, which came into force on 1 January 1928, was to a large extent a confirmation of the Act of 1902, concerning licences and taxes, no whaling where fishing was carried out, etc., but in one or two respects it introduced an innovation. There were to be only six stations in Newfoundland and two in Labrador, but these would be allowed to use two whale catchers each, while the entire whale was to be processed into marketable products. In other respects, however, there was no question of restricting catching: with their sixteen catchers the eight stations were at liberty to catch as many whales as possible all the year round. Licences were not reserved merely for British subjects; theoretically, all eight could be granted to Norwegians. In this respect the Act took no heed of the fears expressed in 1905 and 1918 that the whale would be exterminated once the Norwegians were admitted. That the whale was, in fact, not exterminated was shown not only in the later half of the 1920s, but also in a new peak period of catching in 1937 and 1943-51, the best period in the entire history of Newfoundland whaling.

The total yield in 1898-1915 was about 7,200 whales, 178,000 barrels of oil, and 13,040 tons of guano, a little more than had been produced in the Faroes in 1894 to 1916, and an annual average just over half the figures for Iceland. Hardly anywhere had the large sums invested, involving sixteen companies and eighteen stations, shown such poor returns.

From Newfoundland comes one of the most exciting accounts of a wounded whale towing a whale catcher. In 1903 a blue whale was harpooned on the south coast of Placentia Bay. The animal ran amok, and it proved impossible to approach close enough to fire a second harpoon. It set off, towing 150 fathoms of line as well as the boat, at a speed of 6 knots, with the engine at half-speed astern. In the evening the crew succeeded in making fast a line in the stern of the boat, and the boat now set off with the engine going full speed ahead. Even so, the whale was still so strong that it almost pulled the stern under water. The chase continued throughout the night, and not until early the next day did the whale appear sufficiently exhausted for a boat to be put out and for the *coup-de-grâce* to be administered twenty-eight hours after the first harpoon had found its mark.

Subsequent investigation of whale migration shows that the blue whale generally makes its way across the Gulf of St. Lawrence, through the Strait of Belle Isle, as far north as Hawke's Harbour in June and July. It seldom visits the east coast. Little is known of the fin whale, which after 1905 had accounted for about two-thirds of catches during the first period, about 80 per cent in the 1920s, and about 90 per cent in the 1930s. It was to be found in practically all the months of the year, particularly June and July, and on the great banks to the south-east, where it fed on small spawning fish. From about the middle of July it moved north, spreading over a wide area in the autumn. The migration south took place in October and November, but had been observed as late as January. The humpback, of which considerable quantities existed up to 1906, was speedily decimated and is now rarely seen off Newfoundland. The sei whale has always been a rarity here, only encountered towards the end of the season in the south and the east. Generally speaking, total stocks of whale in this area have varied considerably according to the temperature of the sea, currents, and available feed. (For catching figures for Newfoundland, 1898-1939, see Statistical Appendix, Table 42.)

8

THE PACIFIC

Northwest coast of North America

As we shall see, there is a certain technical and economic link between this area and Newfoundland. Official statistics, furthermore, are guilty of confusing these two areas.

The greater the distance from Norway, the smaller was Norwegian participation in the form of independent companies, and the greater was the contribution of other countries. In Iceland, Norwegians had first encountered the representatives of other nations; in the Shetlands, overseas participation was on a par with that of the Norwegians; in Newfoundland, whaling had been started on the basis of local initiative, and only one purely Norwegian company had operated there, its catches having little bearing on total results. On the northwest coast catching was started by a purely American company, and the subsequent share of the Norwegian companies was of minor importance. In East Asia, not a single station has ever been managed by Norwegians; but everywhere, as has so often been pointed out, it is true to say that beyond Norway's borders no whaling operations could ever have been started without Norwegian personnel, matériel, and know-how.

It was in the waters on either side of the American continent that the old catching methods persisted longest after the modern phase had been initiated. This applies both to catching of the right whale in the Davis Strait and in Baffin Bay on the east side, in the Bering Sea and in the Arctic Ocean to the west, and to sperm whale catching in the open Atlantic and Pacific. A third form of whaling was the catching carried out in coastal waters on both sides of the Pacific. To a certain extent this may be said to have developed almost imperceptibly into modern catching, thanks to the use of the bomb-lance, steam vessels, and steam-operated machinery at the stations. A fourth form was the primitive catching engaged in by the Eskimos from their kayaks. For the sake of continuity one or two features of these highly varied forms of the old catching should be mentioned before discussing the advent of modern whaling in these, the oldest known whaling areas in the world and the richest outside the Antarctic, extending from California to Alaska in the eastern Pacific and from Japan to the Bering Sea in the western Pacific.

The origins of Eskimo whaling are lost in the mists of prehistory. In 1787 the first four catching vessels cruised up and down the coast of Chile, and in 1791 the first vessels from Nantucket and New Bedford rounded Cape Horn and worked their way north. In 1838 the great northwest whaling grounds were discovered, and in order to avoid the long and hazardous voyage round the Horn, San Francisco was adopted as the whaling headquarters. The first Greenland whales are believed to have been discovered off the coast of Alaska in 1848, and the rich catch which the expedition brought home from the Arctic proved a great sensation, ushering in the era of dazzling catches with which the tradition of the old days is so closely associated. The small Herschel Island just west of the mouth of the Mackenzie River, the easternmost point to which the whalers sailed, became a rallying point and the scene of many tragic winterings.

Right up to about 1880 the pursuit of the Greenland whale was carried on just as much for the sake of the oil as for the baleen, but after that time there was such a sharp rise in the price of baleen, that only the head of the whale was kept, and the rest was either abandoned or the meat and the blubber were given to the Eskimos in exchange for baleen.

The whalers were the gold diggers of the sea. The catching vessel *Mary D. Hume,* which left San Francisco on 19 April 1890, returned on 29 September 1892, after spending two winters near Herschel Island, with a catch of thirty-eight Greenland whales, worth $400,000. The price of right whale baleen remained high only up to 1910, but even as late as the 1930s an occasional vessel visited these old hunting grounds. These operations were combined with the last stage of the American sperm whale catching in the latter half of last century, when vessels caught sperm whales in the northern Pacific on their way to and from the Arctic. The last vessel to catch sperm whales according to the old technique was built as late as 1910, remaining active until 1918. The first whale killed by it contained a lump of ambergris that was sold for $30,000.

In considering the changeover to modern-style whaling, the old coastal catching is of major interest, because to a certain extent it was modernised, and as several of the new stations were located on the sites of the old ones not long after these had been closed down, the step from the old to the new on the Pacific coast of the United States was less marked. Coastal whaling in California started in 1854 in Monterey Bay, 80 miles south of San Francisco. In all, there were seventeen stations in California, but this proved a short-lived phase: by 1886 there were only five left, and 1895 marked the last year of catching. The quarry was mainly gray whales, and as these were largely caught in the lagoons of south California, where they took refuge in order to bear their young, stocks were so rapidly and thoroughly depleted that it was eventually believed to be quite extinct. The same had taken place in the case of Japan and Korea. Its re-discovery a couple of years after the turn of the century aroused considerable interest. Locally, the gray whale became the subject of protection in California a few years later and of total protection under the Washington Convention of 1946. This protection is the most promising example of how an almost extinct species of whale can revive when unmolested, and offers the hope that this could also apply to other species of whale. The migration of the gray whale north and south occurs with great regularity, very close to the California coast, where it is now a major tourist attraction.

The great wealth of American literature dealing with whaling ends essentially with the old-style catching around 1900. As in the case of maritime literature generally, that dealing with whaling has likewise invested "the good old days" with a certain aura of romance, tending to ignore the reasons for the decline of the old catching, and likewise omitting to consider it in relation to the start of new-style whaling. Beautiful epitaphs have been written on one of the most dramatic episodes in man's struggle with the forces of nature on the sea and its noblest creature, immortalised in Herman Melville's *Moby Dick*. This has no bearing on the question of why events developed as they did: that is a far more prosaic story. In the nineteenth century the United States dominated world whaling to the same extent as Norway did in the first three decades of this century. Modern whaling, operating from all its stations, was unable to compensate for the decline in American catching. In 1851 this amounted to 428,000 barrels and in 1898 18,000 barrels, while total world production by modern methods, even fifty years after its inception, had by 1909-10 only reached a level of 340,000 barrels. Had the price of right whale baleen not been so favourable, American catching would have suffered a still more rapid and marked decline. In America around the turn of the century confidence in the future of whaling appears to have vanished. In a thesis written by a professor in Philadelphia in 1907 it was categorically stated that whaling was no longer of any commercial interest, and that it would never again revive; it could, in fact, almost be said that whaling was dead. But at the very time this obituary was being written, the deceased woke to fresh life, in the north and the south, in the east and the west, in the Atlantic, the Pacific and the Antarctic — and in America.

The idea of modern-style whaling from the west coast of Canada may have come from Newfoundland in the east, or may have been introduced with the last American catching vessels on the east coast of Asia, where modern whaling was undergoing a rapid development. Ferries and liners operating between the countless islands along the west coast, from Vancouver Island and as far north as Alaska, had observed whales in various sounds and fjords. When the cable between Seattle and Victoria on Vancouver Island was cut in 1905, a dead whale was found enmeshed in it.

In American statistics (reproduced in *International Whaling Statistics II*, pp. 13-14) figures are given for the number of "modern" whales caught in the North Pacific in 1900-2, mainly humpbacks, and a considerable number of blue and fin whales caught in 1903-5 (and corresponding oil production). It is quite inconceivable that this could have been carried out without modern equipment, but no source mentions the use of this prior to an attempt in 1905 and regular catching in 1906. The Americans certainly appear to have caught a considerable number of humpback, gray and sperm whales from as long ago as the 1850s, using the bomb-lance, but this catching was sadly reduced before the end of the century. The entire fleet of twenty vessels operating from San Francisco in 1903 accounted for a total of 169 whales, of which 145 were sperm whales, while the remainder were probably Greenland whales. When a company in Victoria commenced modern whaling in the summer of 1905, it was emphasised that this was something entirely new, and that it was now possible for the first time to catch blue and fin whales. The explanation for the erroneous statistics for the North Pacific, 1903-9, is that they have been confused with the statistics for Newfoundland, which contain the same figures for these years, figures which are correct. This makes a considerable difference to the statistics for world catching 1903-9, and the accounts written on the basis of erroneous figures (see Statistical Appendix, Table 43).

The moving spirit in the establishment of a whaling company was Captain SPROTT BALCOM of Victoria. Mention is also made of Captains RUBE BALCOM and W. BALCOM, probably Sprott Balcom's brothers. Rismüller had encouraged him with accounts of the favourable results achieved in Newfoundland. In 1904 Sprott Balcom founded the Pacific Steam Whaling Co., with a capital of $100,000 and its main office in Victoria. Rismüller was a member of the Board, and supervised the installation of his plant. Sechart, a one-time Indian village on Barkley Sound, on the south side of Vancouver Island, 90 miles west of Victoria, was selected as the site of the station, Bamfield. A whale catcher, the *Orion*, was contracted in Oslo, and Rube Balcom travelled over to fetch it. The entire crew were Norwegian. A local paper in Victoria, which made great capital of this affair, with illustrated articles covering a whole page, declared that on this vessel rested the outcome of the greatest business undertaking ever initiated in Vancouver Island. Balcom, it declared, was the first person to introduce modern methods in the art of killing the most dangerous mammal dwelling in the sea. The newspaper prophesied incredible profits, pointing out that Norwegian companies had issued a dividend of 200 to 300 per cent!

It took four months for the *Orion*, which left Oslo on 10 December 1904, to reach Victoria, on 6 April 1905, a voyage equal to seven-tenths of the world's circumference at the Equator. It was a brilliant achievement sailing this small boat of 108 gross tons in mid-winter, through raging storms, across the North Sea and Atlantic, through the Roaring Forties and all the way up to Victoria. Whaling is often considered more the province of industry than of shipping, and for this reason, in the history of seafaring generally, little mention is made of the fact that some of the finest seamanship has been displayed by crews on board tiny whale catchers operating in the stormiest seas of the world.

The station was complete by the end of August 1905, when the first blue whale was shot nearby. Thus a new area was opened for the expansion of modern whaling. A great many difficulties were encountered: the plant at the station failed to work, it took time to train the native hands, and when production finally started it was discovered that no oak barrels had been made for the oil. These had to be fetched all the way from Ontario, and cost twice as much as elsewhere. No figures are available for the catch in 1905 — it was, at any rate, extremely small — and not till 1906 were some of the great expectations fulfilled, in the shape of 257 whales (3 sperm, 53 fin, 62 blue, and 139 humpback). No gray whales were caught in these waters: the migration passed too far out to sea, as it shaped a course from north California straight across the sea to the Alexander Islands off Alaska. The number of barrels is not listed, but in relation to the preceding season it may have been about 13,000. The price was good — £23 for No. 1 — and operating profits came to $45,522, producing a dividend of 23 per cent on preference shares and 16 per cent on ordinary shares. Even so, the financial prospects warranted no great optimism, and it was even stated that there was no possibility of making catching a financial success unless the equipment could be utilised for catching all the year round. As the weather was too unfavourable on the west coast of Vancouver Island in winter, and there were few whales in those waters, a station, Page's Lagoon, was built on the east, on the Georgia Strait, not far from Nanaimo, where the Canadian Fisheries Research Board subsequently set up a marine-biological station. But as there were so few whales, particularly humpbacks catching proved unprofitable and this station only operated during three winter seasons, 1907-9.

In a whaling regulation couched in approximately the same terms as that for Newfoundland, the company included a provision to the effect that there was to be at least 100 miles between stations, and as at the same time it was granted four concessions for four stations on Vancouver Island; this in reality meant exclusive rights to catching in this area, corresponding to the rights Svend Foyn had enjoyed in North Norway in 1873-82. Another company, the Queen Charlotte Islands Whaling Co., was granted a concession for two stations, Rose Harbour in the extreme south and Naden Harbour in the extreme north on the islands from which the company took its name. It never got

20. This tiny whale catcher, the *St. Lawrence* (111 gross tons), took nearly four months to sail from Oslo round Cape Horn to Vancouver Island, 1906-7.

going as an independent enterprise; instead, a merger of the two companies took place, but the two stations did not become operative until 1911. On the other hand, these were the two that operated for a greater number of years than any other station in this region.

The Pacific Steam Whaling Co. only erected three of the four stations. The third, Kyoquot, was placed on the northwest coast of Vancouver Island and was operative from 16 July 1907. Rismüller wrote with pride that this was "the world's largest whaling station", with a 50 per cent greater capacity than Sechart. It was also situated closer to the whale migration route. A whale catcher, transferred from Newfoundland, covered very nearly as great a distance as the *Orion* had *en route* to Victoria.

The opening of the season in mid-April was highly promising, with as many as nine whales towed in to Sechart alone every day, initially blue and fin whales, subsequently only humpbacks. In October catching slumped markedly, the stations were closed, and the whale catchers transferred to Page's Lagoon, where catching started on about 20 November. Here, too, only humpbacks were caught. The total score for the year is not known, but is believed to have comprised some 500 whales and 22,000 barrels of oil, yielding a profit of $119,657. The company could justly claim to be the largest in the world, while a score of 250 whales and 10,000-12,000 barrels per vessel in one season was in excess of anything hitherto recorded in any area. This was correct, but at the same time it was the last throw of the dice, as the Antarctic adventure, beside which results in the north were to pale, was just beginning.

Despite a larger number of both whales and barrels in 1908, the financial results were considerably poorer. This was due *inter alia* to the heavy operating expenses, of which all the companies on the west coast complained. Annual wages and the price of coal were very high, and the heavy expense in the freight of oil to the market in Glasgow proved a disadvantage in comparison with the stations round the Norwegian Sea. The opening of the Panama Canal in 1914 was a step forward in this respect. At the same time oil was finding an expanding market in America. It is interesting to note that the Pacific Whaling Co. concluded a contract with two Japanese firms in 1908 for delivery of 300 to 500 tons of salted whale meat per month. This was the first time this commodity had been supplied from an overseas market to Japan, where the demand was insatiable. These deliveries provided the company with a not inconsiderable source of extra income, even though special workers had to be brought from Japan to process the meat.

Extending operations to cover four stations had involved the company in an increase of capital to $400,000. What had started so promisingly, and with a little moderation could undoubtedly have developed into a business showing a steady profit, appears to have been subject to pure speculation. At the same time as the Queen Charlotte Islands Whaling Co. was taken over in 1910 and its two stations built, no less than five whaleboats were ordered in Oslo. The company had at its disposal a capital of $5 million, and appears to have had no difficulty in placing a half of this on the stock market in London. Inevitably the crash came. After a violent slump in catches from 1912 to 1913 the company was forced into liquidation, with very heavy losses for shareholders and creditors. The stations and boats were taken over by a new company, Victoria Whaling Co., apparently a subsidiary of Canadian North Pacific Fisheries Ltd.

The slump in 1913 also broke the back of another company, the Tyee Whaling Co., named after the location of the station on Admiralty Island, one of the islands in the Alexander archipelago off the southwest coast of Alaska. Outside Admiralty Island lay Baranof Island, where a Norwegian company established itself in 1912; further inland were two small towns, Juneau and Skagway, famous and notorious as the starting-point for the gold diggers' adventurous trek across the mountain passes to the Klondyke. Tens of thousands of men were drawn there, as by a magnet, and shipping and whaling had their work cut out retaining their crews. The Tyee Whaling Co. was a purely American undertaking, set up by wealthy businessmen from San Francisco, while the expedition manager was an experienced Norwegian from Iceland. The whale catcher *Tyee Junior* is of special interest, as it was the first built in America and one of the first in the world to be built outside Norway. She was of entirely new design, longer in the water and narrower in the beam than the Norwegian boats, had two propellors, was oil-fired, and had electric light. Not surprisingly, she proved very expensive, $65,000, whereas the customary price for Norwegian vessels was $24,000. When catching commenced in the summer of 1907, it was soon discovered that the station was situated too far inshore for the whale catchers to make contract with migrating whales. To overcome this difficulty a remarkable form of floating factory was rigged up, by installing the machinery on two barges, which were towed out and anchored near the town of Sitka on Baranof Island. Commencing in 1911 the barges were towed during the first part of the season to the island of Kodiak, to operate during the whale migration to the north, and in the last part of the season towed back to Baranof Island, in order to catch the whale on its journey south. Despite all this, it proved impossible to operate at a profit, and the company was dissolved in 1913.

One of the company's catchers, *Lizzie S. Sorensson*, earned a place in whaling history on 10 May 1910, when she became the victim in one of the few authenticated cases of a boat being sunk by a whale. A harpoon had found its mark in a large blue whale, but only wounded it. The whale careered off in a wide arc, and returned at full speed, ramming the side of the boat with its head. It repeated this again and again, until the vessel sank. The survivors from among the crew related that the whale seemed to be making a conscious attempt to sink the boat, and that this was not a reflex of the animal's death agony.

Another American company, the American Pacific Whaling Co., commenced catching in 1911 from a station at Grays Harbor on the west coast of the state of Washington, continuing operations until 1925. For this company we have almost complete statistics covering catching and production, showing an annual average in 1911-20 and 1922-5 (operations were called off in 1921) of 193 whales and 5,400 barrels, with 1916 as an exceptional year, when 334 whales and 14,160 barrels were recorded. During all these years a total of 1,933 humpback, 602 fin, 120 sperm, 21 sei and 13 blue whales, one gray whale and 8 bottlenose whales were accounted for.

It would have been remarkable if the Norwegians, in their pursuit of the whale right round the world, had not also made their way to the North Pacific. In 1909 Norwegian whaling faced the following situation : all the whaling grounds around the Norwegian Sea were occupied, Newfoundland was overpopulated by whalers, and had suffered a major setback; access to the Antarctic was in the process of being barred, as the British kept catching within reasonable limits by awarding only a small number of concessions and licences, which the whalers had to have as catching took place in British waters. There were four regions left for Norwegian expansion : Africa, Australia, East Asia, and the North Pacific. The first floating factories had not yet proved their superiority over shore stations. For this reason the Norwegians were primarily interested in whaling grounds which could be operated from land. Even though floating factories were used for these operations, this was to be regarded as shore whaling, as the floating factory was compelled to lie at anchor or moored in a sheltered position. Alaska's 2,000-mile coastline could be expected to provide good harbours. Norwegian whaling companies despatched "explorers", who reconnoitred the entire coast from Queen Charlotte Islands to the Bering Strait, including the Aleutians. The reports they sent back were very optimistic : one went so far as to say that it would be lunacy not to start whaling in these parts, while another considered that there would be employment here for the entire Norwegian whaling fleet for many years to come. Even allowing for a considerable element of exaggeration, the prospects were certainly enough to ensure that, from 1908, Norwegian whaling would make its mark in this area too.

Potential shareholders in the first Norwegian company, the United States Whaling Co., were enticed with the information that in the vicinity of Vancouver Island one single whale catcher had caught 300 whales, producing 12,000 barrels, the best result recorded in the world apart from South Georgia. The company was established in Sandefjord in December 1910, with Peder Bogen, mentioned above, as managing director, and a capital of $400,000, two-thirds of which was subscribed in Scotland by shareholders in his other companies. To save the expense of a three-month voyage for the whale catchers from Norway, three boats were built in Seattle. Until such time as the best site for a station could be found, the intention was to use a floating factory. For this purpose a steamer of 3,850 gross tons, which took precisely three months to make the voyage to Alaska, was leased. The expense incurred during this period when no whales were being caught was a major charge on the budget. As the marine operations were to be regarded as a form of American coastal shipping, the boats had to be registered in the United States and fly the American flag. In order to conform to American law, a cumbrous arrangement had to be established whereby American Customs officials were on hand for clearing whaleboats for entry and exit whenever they were catching outside territorial waters.

Baranof Island was selected as a base for operations, but as the results here were not particularly good, the floating factory moved across to Shumagin Island on the Alaskan peninsula, and worked there for two months. But when the area around Baranof Island proved to be the best one, all catching was concentrated around the shore station there, and the floating factory returned, not only because it had proved somewhat unpractical, but also because it encountered vigorous resistance from the local authorities and the other companies. They argued that a floating factory would destroy the whale stocks, that the employment of foreigners within territorial waters violated the American immigation law, and that the floating factory only made use of the blubber. Dr. Rismüller resorted to the most violent language in his attacks on the Norwegians, whom he described as the pirates of whaling who would soon inundate the coasts of Alaska with their factories and cheap Norwegian labour, persevering until they had exterminated the last whale. No ban put the brake on Norwegian expansion, only the fact that results never came up to expectations. The first year, 1912, produced 314 whales and 8,500 barrels, 2,830 per vessel, only a quarter of the estimated total. Gross earnings were Kr.554,000 (c. £30,000); results for the year showed a loss of Kr.252,000 and liabilities of Kr.420,000.

The other Norwegian company, the Alaska Whaling Co., fared no better. It had been established in October 1911, with a capital of $315,000, a third of which had been subscribed in Norway and two-thirds by leading Norwegian Americans in the United States. The company had been started by — but was not administered by — LARS CHRISTENSEN (1884-1965) of Sandefjord, one of the outstanding personalities in the world of whaling, who made a major contribution to Antarctic research and to Norwegian culture. Before reaching the age of thirty he had played his part in starting a number of whaling companies, and he has personally recounted that he learnt an astonishing amount about whaling from his connections with the Alaska Whaling Co. In common with the previous company, it was intended that this one, too, should operate with both a floating factory and a shore station. For this purpose the little island of Akutan in the Aleutians was chosen, close to the large volcanic island of Unalaska, with Dutch Harbor, well known from the days of old-style whaling. On the east side of the island runs the Unimak Pass, traditionally the most important sea route between the Pacific and the Bering Sea. For a time it appeared that whaling would never get off the ground, as one of President William Taft's last official acts, before his term of office came to an end in 1912, was to sign a decree making the Aleutians a protected reservation for all animal life on land, in the air, and in the sea. By then the ground on which the station was to be erected had been leased, and $100,000 been spent on erection of the station. Under the new president, Woodrow Wilson, an amendment was added to the decree, which made it possible for the company to start. This company, too, was the object of protest; this was directed in particular against the floating factory by the fishermen, who called attention to what had happened in Finnmark, and biologists, who cited the fate of the gray whale and the Greenland whale.

For its floating factory the company purchased the historically most significant vessel, *Admiralen*, which had operated off Spitsbergen in 1904, which had been the first in the field in the Antarctic in 1905, and which was now active in Alaska in 1912. She was one of the first three floating

21. The *Admiralen* in Seattle, 1912 (note the wireless aerial). In 1905 she was the first steam whale factory to operate in the Antarctic.

factories which at this time were fitted with radio telegraphy. Her engine was so underpowered that she took as much as four months to complete the voyage from Sandefjord to Akutan. Her two whale catchers were built in Seattle. Reduction on board *Admiralen* did not start until 3 June, and at the shore station on 24 August, coming to an end in both cases on 21 October. The results were about as disappointing as for the United States Whaling Co. and the large loss of $150,000 was incurred. To some extent because it proved impossible to obtain credit for running operations, and to some extent because there was a possibility that the floating factory would be banned, no catching took place in 1913. In that year the United States Whaling Co. continued with rather better results, though not good enough to prevent a working deficit of £4,700, while liabilities had risen to Kr.572,000. Shares were sold for as little as 15 per cent of face value.

Detailed statistics for 1912 are available for the three Alaska companies (the two above-mentioned Norwegian ones and the Tyee Whaling Co.): 317 humpback, 235 fin, 112 blue, and 23 sperm whales. The further north they operated, the more blue whales they found. These would produce more than 80 barrels per whale. In all, 18,575 barrels of oil were produced, 175 tons of guano, and 35.2 tons of baleen, to a total market value of $311,307, which was just a little more than a quarter of the invested capital of $1,141,000. Catching employed 302 men. As far as the North Pacific was concerned, the results taken all round were out of all proportion to the mass of matériel and plant : sixteen whale catchers, eight shore stations, and two floating factories. At a rate of 3,400 barrels a boat, operations could not pay their way. At that time whalers in South Georgia were trebling this figure with some 10,100 barrels a boat. The lack of success put a stop to several companies that had planned to catch in the North Pacific, and some of them now turned their attention to the south.

In 1912 another unsuccessful attempt to combine a whale catcher and a floating factory in one and the same vessel was tried out in Alaska. A boat equipped on these lines, the *Kit* of Sandefjord, left Seattle on 21 June, called at Nome and took on board sixteen Eskimos who were to serve as whalers, passed through the Bering Strait into the Arctic, and cruised there from 9 July to 14 August in search of walrus, as it was impossible to catch whales. The *Kit* returned to Seattle with 404 animals, and repeated this trip in 1913 and 1914, catching a total of some 1,000 animals each year. The boat was sold to Russia in 1915 without having paid its way. It was the only Norwegian vessel to have passed through the Bering Strait in order to operate in the Arctic Ocean.

The Alaska Whaling Co. was reconstituted in 1913 under the name of the North Pacific Sea Products Co., with an entirely American board. Even with good catches it failed to balance its books. A remarkable number of enormous blue whales, measuring up to 95 ft., were caught, yielding 150 barrels of oil each, while a number of fat sperm whales produced 100 barrels each. Just as both companies were about to call it a day, they were granted a respite, albeit for only a few years, thanks to the tremendous wartime rise in the price of whale oil. The 1915-18 seasons proved brilliant ones, particularly for the North Pacific Co. In 1917 sales of oil netted $600,000 at £41 a ton, while guano accounted for $46,410; expenses totalled $255,400. Shares soared, and good dividends were paid. The general meeting of January 1918 was pervaded by an atmosphere of euphoria. The following day the managing director was visited by a gentleman who expressed a wish to buy the company. The American shareholders, who held a majority, agreed to the sale, whereas not all the Norwegians were of a like mind. They were to regret this, as did the purchaser, the Victoria Whaling Co., which had earlier absorbed the American Pacific Whaling Co. Although 1915-18 provided a nice margin of profit, liabilities and repayments of loans proved such a heavy burden that it was never possible to pay any dividend. The end of the boom period in 1919 not only entailed a disastrous fall in prices, but also made it impossible to market the oil in the United States. In 1921 most of the two previous years' production was still stockpiled, and finally had to be sold at a loss of £46,430. When the company went bankrupt in 1922, shareholders and creditors suffered a loss of £68,680, the biggest disaster to date in the history of Norwegian whaling. This terminated Norwegian westward expansion of whaling in the northern hemisphere, a venture which had ended with a crash on both sides of the American continent. Others, however, continued where the Norwegians had left off.

The high prices paid for whale products during the war witnessed the emergence of a number of companies which made unsuccessful attempts to establish stable catching in Alaska — the Beluga Whaling Co., which, as the name suggests, was based on the catching of beluga (whitefish), the Western Whaling & Trading Co., and the Arctic Whaling & Fishing Co. Of major interest was the schooner *Carolyn Frances,* of 320 gross tons, the first American attempt at a floating factory. It started its voyage in 1921 off the coast of Mexico, and followed the whale migration along the coast of California to Alaska, catching as many as 158 whales on the trip, of which 107 were humpbacks, and 37 gray whales, sufficient for 2,900 barrels. The voyage, however, was not a financial success, and was not repeated.

The history of the companies after the war is so complicated that there is no space here to go into detail. Briefly, we might say that all four companies, the North Pacific Sea Products Co. (Akutan), the Consolidated Whaling Corporation (Rose Harbour, Naden Harbour), the Canadian North Pacific Fisheries Ltd. (Kyoquot, Sechart), and the American Pacific Whaling Co. (Grays Harbor), were under the management of the Victoria Whaling Co. in 1918, with their head office in Toronto and backed by considerable Canadian interests. In 1918, when it ran eighteen whale catchers and six stations, employing 584 hands, it was virtually a whaling trust for the North Pacific and one of the most powerful companies of the age. For a few years after both Norwegian companies had closed down it ruled the roost from California to Alaska, a stretch of 3,000 kilometres. In 1919 it recorded a catch of 1,025 whales and produced 35,000 barrels of oil, as well as a large quantity of guano and frozen whale meat. In 1920 it yielded 32,800 barrels and 23,000 sacks of guano. The production of canned and frozen whale meat was a wartime phenomenon; intense propaganda attempted, albeit in vain, to introduce whale meat for domestic consumption on a par with beef and mutton. An ode was even written in praise of whale meat, the first few lines of which ran as follows:

Welcome, O whale from frigid zones!
This season's greeting I am giving

Because your girth and meaty bones
Will greatly ease the cost of living!

In 1925 operations were radically streamlined. Kyoquot, which had
been running ever since 1907, and Grays Harbor, which had operated
since 1911, were closed down, and plant and equipment transferred to
a new station, Port Hobron, on the little island of Sitkalidak, near
Kodiak. It became the largest and most efficient on the entire west
coast. This meant that as from 1926 catching was concentrated on four
stations, Akutan and Port Hobron in Alaska and Naden Harbour and
Rose Harbour in the Queen Charlotte Islands. The two last-mentioned
continued operating practically without a break right up to 1943, while
those in Alaska kept going up to 1939. All subsequent whaling in these
waters and around the Aleutians has operated with floating factories.

After the reorganisation of 1925 the firm enjoyed four very favourable
seasons from 1925 to 1928, precisely as in the case of Newfoundland.
Annual yields average 40,300 barrels of oil and 2,620 tons of guano.
Thanks to the high, stable prices prevailing, this was the most successful
period in the whole history of whaling in the Northeast Pacific. The
year 1931, however, witnessed the world crisis, hand in hand with
over-production of whale oil, with prices slumping to £9, and for the
first time since 1905 all catching from the west coast of America was
discontinued. In 1932 catching began again, with poor returns in that
and the following year, though later in the 1930s there was some
improvement. We shall return to this and to catching after the Second
World War.

After old-style whaling had come to an end, the whale had been
unmolested off the coast of California for thirty to forty years. This was
no guarantee, however, that stocks had been replenished, because the
whales that were hunted in the north were probably part of the migrant
stream making its way past California. In the old-style catching days
the most famous station was Monterey, 80 miles south of San Francisco.
On 7 December 1914, the California Sea Products Co. was registered
there with $1 million capital. As usual, prospective shareholders were
offered dazzling dividends : 600 whales, each worth $800, and operating
costs of $170,000 would yield a profit of $310,000. This, moreover,
would be the profit of one single station; what might not be expected
once all four stations were operating?

Probably as a result of the war, the Moss Landing station at Monterey
did not start operating until 1918, and the upper station at Trinidad,
240 miles north of San Francisco, not until 1920. They enjoyed a
promising start — 411 whales and 11,835 barrels. With both stations
fully operative, 1922 was the best year in the company's history, with
562 whales, 18,500 barrels of oil, and about 1,000 tons of guano and

meat meal. But once again history repeated itself: after a few years stocks of humpback whale failed to materialise, and production in 1925 was less than a quarter of that in 1922. In the belief that catching had driven the whale further out to sea, a tanker was equipped in 1926 as a floating factory. It operated during the winter of 1926-7 off the Californian coast, proceeded in the summer in the company of four whale catchers to Alaska, and was back in California in the autumn. The first sizeable American floating factory proved a success: the result was 568 whales and 17,100 barrels, a third of all catchings from American and Canadian stations that year. But even with the floating factory catches slumped rapidly, until finally in 1931 operations were discontinued along the entire west coast. At the southernmost boundary for operation off lower California and Mexico the American floating factory encountered the Norwegian ones, which had worked their way north along the west coast of South America in their global search for new whaling grounds. The Norwegians broke off in 1929, while the Americans started up again in 1932, only to experience for the third time the same disappointment, and a rapid decline forced the company to go into liquidation in 1937. Another company which continued in 1938 recorded the smallest catch ever registered by a company in one season: one whale.

Alaska was the uttermost limit of Norwegian expansion in the northern hemisphere. Its failure was due to several reasons: before the Panama Canal was opened in 1914, the voyage to Alaska was twice as far as to the Antarctic. Excessive expenses were incurred before catching could commence, there were difficulties in marketing the oil in America, while high freight rates to and from the European market made competition difficult. It took a long time to train native hands in an attempt to meet the demand to employ as many of these as possible. The labour force was highly mixed and cosmopolitan, comprising Norwegians, Swedes, Finns, Russians, Germans, Newfoundlanders, Americans, Indians, Chinese, and Japanese. The working tempo was slack, while wages were on a higher level than for purely Norwegian crews. Companies were struck a knockout blow in 1920 by totally inadequate whale stocks, enormously high operating expenses from 1915 to 1919, and the end of the wartime boom period. Not until consolidation had been carried out in the mid-1920s by powerful financial forces in America was it possible to achieve stable and profitable catching over a number of years.

Statistics covering the entire west coast are very incomplete prior to 1919, and of doubtful value for the following decade (see Statistical Appendix, Table 44). Only for Alaska do we have reliable figures from the start of catching in 1912 (see Statistical Appendix, Table 45). Random information from before this time appears to confirm the fact that it was primarily the humpback whale which made commercial catching possible during the period we are here concerned with, 1905-30. On the entire west coast of North America some 16,000 whales were caught in 1919-29; of these, 7,301 were humpbacks, 3,839 were fin whales, 1,994 blue, 1,217 sperm, 738 sei, and 234 gray whales. In addition, there were 327 beluga, 17 nordcapers, 2 Greenland whales, 2 beaked and 7 bottlenose whales, and 307 of unknown species. Humpback whales comprised 2,920 BWU, fin whales 1,920 BWU, or almost exactly the same as the number of blue whales. The bulk of the humpbacks were caught either in the extreme north, off the Aleutians (2,200) or in the extreme south off California. In the central area, where the oldest, most numerous, and largest stations were situated, the humpback vanished after ten years, and from 1915 the fin whale dominated. When catching was resumed in 1948 from Vancouver Island, after a break going back to 1925 (catching operated from the Queen Charlotte Islands from 1911 to 1943), not a little surprise was occasioned by the fact that 63 per cent of the catch consisted of humpbacks, which consequently must have been capable of renewal in a limited area, despite the fact that it had been hunted in adjacent areas. This appears to confirm the theory that particular schools consistently make for a particular area of the ocean, and that limited local protection will prove of slight importance in preserving total stocks.

The course of blue whale catching shows a fairly similar picture, as most animals were caught in the extreme north and the extreme south. The largest catch was made by floating factories off the coast of lower California in the latter half of the 1920s. The explanation for this is that the blue whale always migrates far from the shore, whereas the humpback, all over the world, keeps very close to land. The largest catch of blue whale, 239, was recorded on the east side of the Pacific in 1926, while the record on the west side, 242, was set up in 1911. In both areas the whales vanished after a few years. Only to the south of the Aleutians was it possible, with a moderate catch of some 50 animals as an annual average, to maintain the catching of blue whales for any length of time up till about 1930. Catching of blue and humpback whales in the North Pacific was not peculiar to this area, but confirms the general course of events in all areas, most typically in the Antarctic. The number of fin whales, too, declined markedly in the North Pacific, but not to the same extent as the blue whale, and in this area generally the fin whale provided a substantial, though steadily declining proportion of the raw material from the start of new style whaling until it became protected in 1976. Stocks of gray whales were so decimated that pursuit of this species has had no bearing on total yields. Thus the pattern of high exploitation of one species, followed by its decline and the change of emphasis to another species, which in turn declines — as occurred

Table 7. CATCHES OF FIN, SEI AND BRYDE WHALES IN THE
NORTH PACIFIC, 1965-75

| Season | Fin | | Sei | | Bryde | | Sei + Bryde | | Fin as % of total |
	No.	BWU	No.	BWU	No.	BWU	No.	BWU	BWU
1965	3,166	1,583	3,186	531	1	—	3,187	531	75
1966	2,893	1,447	4,458	743	20	3	4,658	746	66
1967	2,273	1,137	6,099	1,017	21	4	6,120	1,121	50
1968	1,884	942	5,744	957	173	29	5,917	986	49
1969	1,245	623	5,148	858	89	15	5,237	873	42
1970	1,012	506	4,505	751	139	23	4,644	774	40
1971	802	401	3,005	501	908	151	3,913	652	38
1972	758	379	2,327	388	201	34	2,528	422	47
1973	460	230	1,856	309	729	122	2,585	431	35
1974	413	207	1,280	213	1,363	227	2,643	440	32
1975	162	81	508	85	1,433	239	1,941	324	20

in the Pacific — is a typical story of whaling in any area and particularly in the Antarctic.

The migrations and living conditions of the whale in the North Pacific have been the subject of intensive research by the Japanese Whale Research Institute. This shows that the blue whale is seldom encountered north of the Aleutians, whereas the fin whale and the humpback undertake the longest migrations, penetrating through the Bering Strait right into the Arctic. The distribution of the sei whale is similar to that of the blue whale : unlike male sperm whales, it is not thought to proceed north of the Aleutians in great numbers. Female sperm whales have never been caught north of the southern tip of Kamchatka, or off the Aleutians. The investigations also appear to confirm that at least two separate stocks of sperm whales, an eastern and western stock, are found in the North Pacific. On either side of the Pacific, those whales surviving one stage of their migration were still a target at another. Whalers reasoned as follows : if we do not catch the whale here, others will catch it somewhere else.

When a new era was ushered in in the North Pacific thanks to the use of the floating factory in the mid-1920s, it encountered offshoots of southern ocean catching off the west coast of Mexico, Japanese pelagic whaling off the Aleutians, and the primitive catching of the Eskimos in Alaska, and it witnessed the last right-whale catchers returning from the Bering Sea. Thus, north and south, east and west, old and new, joined hands.

East Asia

Modern whaling in East Asia has three predecessors: the age-old Japanese coastal catching, the "old" American catching along the entire northeast coast of Asia, and the catching carried out by natives of eastern Siberia (the Chukchi Peninsula). In the last quarter of the previous century all these forms of whaling were still being carried on when modern-style whaling made its debut in this area.

Archaeologists have shown that whaling was practised far back in prehistoric times. A wealth of Japanese literature on old whaling exists, but the language has made this inaccessible to Europeans, and very little of it has been translated. (An attempt to solve this problem was made by the American FRANK HAWLEY in an impressive de-luxe work entitled *Whales and Whaling in Japan*, Kyoto, 1958-60. Unfortunately, the author died after the first volume had been published. We have taken a great deal of our material from the Japanese book *Honpo no Norway-shiki hogeishi* [Whaling in Japan according to Norwegian methods], Tokyo, 1910, which has been specially translated for this study.

Literary sources describe whaling at the end of the sixteenth century on the southeast coast of Honshu, where, in 1606, five companies were established which, for the first time, were engaged in whaling on a commercial basis. From here catching spread all over Japan, first and foremost in the southwest, where whaling was mainly carried on in the Korea Strait (Tsushima). Figures exist, going all the way back to the seventeenth century, which suggest that whaling in Japan must have reached a climax at about the same time as the great era of Spitsbergen catching. A magnificently illustrated Japanese book of 1829 provides a detailed and dramatic account of this. Then, as now, the prime purpose was to provide meat for human consumption. The blubber was also rendered down to provide oil for lighting, and oil was also used in the paddy fields to combat insects. The whale was killed in the usual manner with a hand harpoon, but the use of nets marked a revolution in technique. This is believed to have been invented in about the mid-seventeenth century, and was in use in 1680 at all stations. Briefly, this method involved ten to twelve boats positioning themselves in a semi-circle on the seaward side of the whale, which was then driven towards the shore. Once this had been done an enormous and tremendously strong net was lowered in front of the whale, held in position by stout baulks of timber. Once the whale was enmeshed in it, it was attacked with harpoons, but not killed, as this would mean that it would sink. Three men would then swim across to the whale and climb up on its back, and while it was still alive they cut a hole in its jaw and dorsal fin, threaded a rope through the holes, and fastened this to a huge baulk of timber. The climax was reached when one of the men administered the *coup de grâce* with a long sword. As in bullfighting, these whaling toreadors were celebrated as national heroes. Finally, the whale could be towed ashore and cut up. Catching by means of nets is also known to us from other countries, but nowhere was it reduced to such a fine art as in Japan.

This method of netting was incredibly effective, and it is astonishing how many fin whales were caught. Whaling literature generally states that this species could not be caught before modern catching methods were introduced. From the Yamaguchi prefecture on the Straits of Tsushima alone, 294 right whales, 958 humpbacks, 277 fin whales, 288 gray whales, and 709 of other species were caught between 1698 and 1888. From the five prefectures in the southwest 1,496 whales were caught during the decade from 1882 to 1891; these were sold at an average price of 966 yen (about £200). The meat of the sei whale and young fin whale was of the best quality and fetched the highest price, while the gray whale and sperm whale came at the bottom of the list. The owners of the largest stations are reported to have amassed such large fortunes that "they surpassed the riches of the princes themselves".

It was obvious that modern technique, so superior to the old method in its efficiency, would put an end to net catching. Throughout the century, however, progress was hampered by large-scale American catching along the east coast of Asia, from the Bonin Islands in the south to the Bering Strait in the north. In the south, mainly sperm whales were caught, in the central area humpbacks, and in the north right whales. In the late 1850s 300 American vessels were operating in these waters. A small number of British boats also took part. The Japanese complained that they took the whales before they came within range of Japanese coastal catching. In 1846 two American vessels were wrecked on the coast of Japan and their crews were arrested as criminals and thrown into prison. The Americans protested, and despatched a diplomatic-military mission in 1853, which succeeded in 1854 in concluding a treaty which gave American ships access to Japanese harbours, in the first place to enable whalers to buy food, fuel, and water. "It may be said that the whale was instrumental in promoting friendship between these two countries. The companies should erect one memorial to it, at least", we read in the Japanese history of whaling.

The third form of whaling encountered by the Japanese was the Russian, which had its predecessors *inter alia* in the state-subsidised catching in the Barents Sea off the coast of Murmansk, which commenced in 1883. Profits were low, and for this reason Russian catching in this area came to an end in 1889, to the delight of the Norwegians.

In 1903 Russia introduced a total ban on catching, at the same time as Norway.

In the course of the eighteenth century Russia's eastward expansion reached the sea, Vladivostok being founded in 1860. Thrusting across the Bering Strait, the Russians had penetrated as far as Alaska and annexed it. In 1799 a trading company was given a trade monopoly: this entailed mainly bartering furs and right whale baleen from the Eskimos. In 1850 the company commenced whaling on its own account, but operations were suspended during the Crimean War (1854-5), though they were subsequently continued until the United States in 1867 made its famous purchase of the whole of Alaska, an area of one and a half million square kilometres, for the sum of $7.2 million.

OTTO V. LINDHOLM, the pioneer of Russian coastal whaling in the Far East, was of Finnish extraction, but a Russian subject. He was born in Helsinki in 1831 and for sixteen years, while serving in the above-mentioned company, he was mainly concerned with whaling. He was consequently in possession of a good deal of experience when he and two friends in 1861 established the Helsingfors Whaling Company. In the history of Russian whaling Lindholm's operations in East Asia from 1864 to 1885 have been accorded a place reminiscent of Finnmark catching in Norwegian history, and his struggles and the difficulties he ran up against can be compared with those encountered by Svend Foyn in Finnmark and the pioneers in the Antarctic. Lindholm himself has related the story of his life as a whaler. When he and his friends in 1861 set off on their adventurous voyage with 1,600 roubles they were tackling a stretch of 8,000 kilometres devoid of railways and roads. In the upper reaches of the Amur River they had a boat constructed, which enabled them to navigate the river 2,000 km. down to its mouth in the Sea of Okhotsk near Nikolayevsk. To the west, on the south coast of that sea, they found a good site for their station, in the Bay of Tugur. The bay was shallow, and was visited by whales when the ice had melted. But the season was a short one, as there were only four or five ice-free months every year. They built their houses of driftwood, and not till 20 May 1864 were they finally able to start catching. Behind them lay three years of almost unbearable toil and deprivation, and on this note Russian catching in the Far East commenced.

The three men were richly rewarded for their labours. During the first ten years, 1864 to 1873, results admittedly totalled only sixty-five whales, but this was sufficient to produce 4,710 barrels of oil and 15 tons of baleen, worth 400,000 roubles, ensuring a net profit of 240,000 (c. 10 roubles = £1). In 1872-3 Lindholm also extended his operations southwards in the Sea of Japan, selling salt whale meat and blubber to the Japanese, who paid approximately 5d. per kilogramme, relatively a very favourable price. In 1877 he acquired a small steamer, which he sent out on a voyage along Kamchatka as far as the Chuotka Peninsula in order to barter baleen from the natives. In connection with this Lindholm applied to the Government for a monopoly on this trade and on whaling along the entire Russian coast up as far as the Bering Sea and the Arctic between 60° and 90° N, a stretch of almost 2,500 km. Envious Russians, hostile to Lindholm because he was a Finn, frustrated his plans, whereupon he abandoned all his business ventures and returned to Helsinki.

The person who had most energetically opposed Lindholm's plans to adopt modern-style whaling was the landowner and naval lieutenant AKIM GRIGOREVITCH DYDYMOV. He had served in the Far East, where he had met Lindholm. He exploited his connections among the nobility and in the Government to have Lindholm's application rejected, and to receive a state grant of 50,000 roubles. He sold his estate, persuaded several noblemen to invest major sums, and managed to lay his hands on a sum of 200,000 roubles. Great stress is placed in the older accounts of Russian whaling on the national element involved, that Dydymov "wanted to be the first *Russian* to tackle this profession, still unfamiliar to Russians. It was a patriotic act to exploit on behalf of Russia the sources of wealth which the Americans were drawing on in Russian waters." The latter fact was true, in so far as thirty-one American vessels, in the years 1881-4, operating along the east coast of Siberia, caught 966 whales, which yielded 49,000 barrels of oil and 650 tons of baleen, to a value of £753,000.

In a written account from 1886 Dydymov presented his plan, based on the catching of right whales with a view to selling baleen. In the course of that year, however, he met the Russian consul in Finnmark, who drew his attention to the profitable operations the Norwegians were carrying out there "using Svend Foyn's method". He contracted a whale catcher in Oslo in 1887, which set off as late as 16 July 1889, with two relations of Svend Foyn, in the capacity of captain and mate, on board, both of them also experienced whale gunners. The voyage took three and a half months, terminating at Vladivostok on 31 October. The station of Hajdamak was set up 180 km. east of the town, and on 10 November Dydymov himself shot the first "modern" whale in this part of the world — an honour he reserved for himself — after which the Norwegian gunners took over. In the course of the four winter months twenty-three whales were shot. During the summer, operations moved south along the east coast of Korea, and the catch was sold to Japan. By the end of 1890 seventy-three whales had been accounted for, ensuring a good margin of profit. Despite intense cold and constant storms, Dydymov refused to break off for the winter. On 31 December his vessel sailed off and was lost with all hands. By then he had dismissed the Norwegian crew, as he was convinced that the Russians now had sufficient practice. With Dydymov's tragedy ended the first attempt to establish modern-style whaling in East Asia.

A few unsuccessful attempts were made to get whaling going again, but not until Count HEINRICH HUGOVITCH KEJZERLING appeared on the scene did things really get going. He was a member of a Baltic, German-Russian noble family and, like Dydymov, had been trained as a naval officer. He prepared the setting up of his whaling company with the greatest thoroughness, realising that he would have to go to Norway, "the classic land of whaling", in order to learn the art. "But," he wrote, "the Norwegians, following the example of the well-known Svend Foyn, kept the technical details a close secret". A Norwegian in St. Petersburg, however, helped him to engage the services, as a sailor, of HENRY CARLSSON, serving on a whale catcher with a Norwegian company in Iceland, "and in this way he managed to ferret out of the Norwegians the secret of the new catching technique". He submitted his plans to the Government, and was granted a loan of 125,000 roubles for his company, the Pacific Whale Fishing Company of H. H. Kejzerling, which received a concession for twenty-four years covering five different stretches along the coast of Siberia. In Oslo, two whale catchers were ordered, somewhat larger than the ordinary type, at a price of £5,000 each. In March 1895 they proceeded to Hajdamak, where the abandoned station had been bought. Apart from Kejzerling himself the party included two men who were to exercise a decisive influence on the fate of the company: these were the gunner and expedition manager, the Norwegian HENDRIK G. MELSOM, later to play a leading role in establishing pelagic whaling in the Antarctic; the second was an engineer, AUGUST SOMMERMEYER, the son of German parents, born in St. Petersburg. He had been chosen as technical manager of the whale oil factory. The boats carried a great deal of new machinery, designed by Sommermeyer, including a plant for turning out large tin containers for whale oil, as it proved difficult to procure wooden barrels, which in any case always suffered from leaks.

Melsom relates that summer catching (June-October) was carried on from Hajdamak north as far as Sakhalin, the blubber being reduced to oil. In winter, catching operations moved south in the Sea of Japan and the whales were sold whole in Nagasaki, where the market for meat for human consumption was inexhaustible. A very large whale would fetch £700, though the average was around £165. Melsom's wages amounted to 125 roubles a month, and 20 roubles per whale, irrespective of size and species. The annual average catch in 1895-1903 was 110 whales; he could easily have shot more, but the station capacity was limited. "It was extremely badly managed, had some difficulty in processing the catch, and the entire way in which this enterprise was managed was such a parody that this period spent in Russian service

22. Count H. H. Kejzerling, one of the pioneers of modern whaling off the coasts of East Asia.

was far from encouraging. Absolute chaos reigned." These observations are in marked contrast to Sommermeyer's, who describes how excellently his new plant worked. On board the whale catchers only the gunner was a Norwegian; the captain was a Russian and the crew were Koreans and Chinese.

Conditions at the station may have been bad, but in Melsom's opinion the situation was still worse when Kejzerling acquired a floating factory, an epoch-making step in the history of whaling. This had been suggested by Sommermeyer in 1899, in order to avoid dependence on the shore station. Time would be saved if they could avoid having to tow the whale all that long way; the raw material would be fresher and the quality of the oil improved. In that year a large secondhand steamer, of 3,643 gross tons, was purchased for 156,500 roubles. It was re-christened the *Michail*, and was the first steamer in the world purchased with a view to being used as a floating factory. As it was difficult to find a yard willing to carry out the comprehensive work of conversion, and as freight rates were highly favourable, the ship spent two years as an ordinary freighter, making good money. Conversion and installation of the complicated machinery proceeded entirely according to Sommer-meyer's plans in Danzig in the winter of 1902-3. This proved an expensive business, and when completed the floating factory cost half a million roubles. "The mobile factory *Michail*", as the Russians called it, received its first whale on 27 July 1903, and by 21 October ninety-eight whales had been reduced to oil and guano. It was calculated that the process admitted of a 40 per cent higher utilisation of the raw material than would be the case on shore. The fact that the floating factory

23.   The *Michail*, the first steam floating factory in modern whaling.

nevertheless proved little short of a fiasco, so Melsom relates, was due
not to the use to which the boat itself was put, but to a breakdown
in Sommermeyer's machinery. This had been intended to reduce six
whales a day, but was not robustly enough designed to cope with more
than one. In his account, Sommermeyer is forced to admit that "the
ideal was nothing like achieved".

Figures for the economic results are incomplete, but there appears to
have been a good surplus right up to 1900, while later on a balance was
only just achieved. Revenue accrued mainly from the sale of blubber
and meat in Japan. Administrative expenses were tremendously high, a
common phenomenon in Russian life at that time. The enterprise might
well have proved a good investment, but it collapsed completely with
the outbreak of the Russo-Japanese war in February 1904. The company
enjoyed a secret grant of 50,000 roubles annually from the Russian
state, in return for sounding and charting Korean and Japanese waters,
with a view to naval operations. In the event of war the entire whaling
fleet was to be placed at the disposal of the Russian navy. Consequently,
one of the first steps taken by the Japanese was to capture the floating
factory and the whale catchers, and intern the crews as prisoners of war.
Kejzerling received no form of compensation from the Russian Government, and suffered a loss of some one million roubles. From 1906 he ran
a shipping company in Vladivostok, until he was forced to flee from
the Bolsheviks in 1922. Once again he lost everything. (His whaling
company had gone into formal liquidation in 1909.) He was then active
for a while in business in Japan and China, until the outbreak of war

between these two countries ruined him for the third time. Abandoning the thought of starting again in business in the East, he made his way to Germany, where in 1944 he published a book describing his adventurous life. He survived to witness the collapse of the Third Reich.

Between 1896 and 1912 many Russian companies were started for the purpose of whaling combined with fishing, the trapping of fur-bearing animals, and barter trade with the natives of eastern Siberia. None of them survived for very long, an example of this being the Anglo-Russian Eirojin Kumiai Company in Nagasaki. This had a large whale catcher built in Oslo, and commenced catching in October 1898. Results proved quite favourable during the first year, but so poor during the next two that the whale catcher was first chartered to the Japanese in 1901 and subsequently purchased by them. They bought all the whale catchers they could lay their hands on, just as sixty years later they bought up all the floating factories available.

Only a generation was needed from the start of the Meiji Revolution in 1868 to convert Japan from a medieval feudal community to a modern industrial power. History shows that a social revolution of this kind is followed, almost invariably, by external expansion. Formosa, Korea, and the southern half of Sakhalin became Japanese territory, and the Sea of Japan a Japanese lake. The urge for national self-assertion was strong in the Japanese people; for the men who started modern Japanese whaling national and political motives were just as strong as financial ones. This applied not least to the liberation of whaling from the Russians, the abhorred rivals for leadership in the Far East. A large number of young men were despatched to America and Western Europe in order to learn, and they proved very diligent pupils.

One of those who was sent abroad was JURO OKA, the creator of modern Japanese whaling. The conditions open to Japanese whaling were in two respects different from those in Norway: in the first place, whaling was regarded both by the fishermen and by the Government as an integral part of the fisheries, and secondly the industry later enjoyed the unreserved support of both parties. Ever since the Sino-Japanese War of 1894-5, the Government had systematically protected their fisheries, and as far back as 1897 the country had had a fisheries high school. When Oka made his way to Tokyo with his plan it was immediately recommended by the Government, and he set out on a world-wide tour which, in the long run, was to have fateful consequences, not only for Norway, but for whaling all over the world. He visited Norway first of all, and at various yards in the whaling towns he ordered every conceivable kind of equipment — cannons, harpoons, shells, etc., paying 10 per cent in excess of the usual price in order to ensure delivery one month ahead of schedule. He then made his way to

Finnmark, and familiarised himself with the practical details. From here he travelled to the Azores, in order to take a look at the old sperm whale catching, and then to Newfoundland, where modern-style catching had just started. Oka came to the conclusion that in technique the Norwegian method was superior, but that Japan was not in a position to adopt the system lock, stock, and barrel, as it was based on the production of oil, whereas the basis for Japanese whaling was the marketing of meat.

Oka was not the only Japanese who made his way to Norway in order to learn whaling; several Norwegian newspapers waxed ironical over the naïvety of their compatriots, who parted with the skills of the art, built whale catchers for the Japanese, withdrew boats with their gunners and crew from Norwegian whaling "in order to serve a ruthless and calculating rival". One newspaper made a prophecy the truth of which Norway would one day have to acknowledge all too bitterly: "Once the Japanese have appeared on the scene in any whaling ground, then the Norwegians will soon be banished from it!"

Before Oka had succeeded in organising his own company, a Japanese by the name of T. TAKAHASHI, who had worked on Russian whaling expeditions, had formed a private company of his own, Hogei Gumi, and had the first whale boat in Japan, the *Saikai-maru,* built of wood. (For the translation of a number of Japanese words, see Glossary of Selected Japanese Terms.)

The company was converted to a shareholding company, but even though the services of a competent Norwegian gunner were employed, the yield in 1898 was only three whales. The reason was that the boat was entirely unsuitable for its purpose. The company was dissolved in 1900. Although this first attempt proved a complete failure, Japanese whaling history regards 1898 as the year when its modern-style whaling commenced.

The company Oka had striven to establish, Nihon Enyo Gyogyo K.K., was constituted on 20 July 1899, in Yamaguchi, the headquarters of the old-style catching. Because of the company's trademark, the sign for the figure one (*ichi*) in a ring (*maru*), it was generally referred to as Ichimaru Kaisha (company). After the war with China, Japan entered on a period of economic difficulty, and it was no easy task to acquire a capital of 100,000 yen. Oka was appointed managing director. It was decided to apply for a whaling licence in Korea, to engage the services of an experienced Norwegian gunner, and to build a whale catcher in Japan. Although this last-mentioned decision was considered somewhat rash, for reasons of national prestige the boat was actually built in Japan. It was completed on 30 November 1899, and was christened *Daiichi Choshu-maru* ("No. 1 from Choshu", the old name of the prefecture of Yamaguchi). On 4 February 1900 the Norwegian gunner, MORTEN

PEDERSEN, shot the first whale, a large blue whale. His contract with Oka is of interest because it provided a model for the many subsequent Norwegian gunners in Japanese service. It was valid for three years, regular wages amounted to 200 yen a month (1 yen = 2 shillings), and an additional 30 yen for every whale secured, irrespective of size and species (with the exception that 150 yen was paid for a right whale). Pedersen was entitled to employ three Norwegian seamen at 30 yen a month and an additional 3 yen per whale. With an annual average of about 60 whales, Pedersen's earnings were far in excess of what was usual both in Europe and in Kejzerling's service. It would appear obvious that the Japanese "bought" him at a very high price from the Russians, for whom he had been working ever since 1895.

It was difficult to obtain a licence in Korea. The Russians had great influence at the court in Seoul, and had secured a very favourable twelve-year licence for Kejzerling. The Japanese had to be content with a three-year licence for three very restricted locations on the coast, paying an annual levy of 800 yen for each whale catcher.

The proceeds for the first year, 1900, were not very promising : after winter operations to the north and summer operations along the south coast of Kyushu, the yield was a mere twenty whales. Next season, however, their luck changed : the result was forty-two whales, and as catching generally had been poor "the price was forced up to 5,000 yen for the best whales". The entire loss of the previous year was covered, and shareholders received 5 per cent. For the 1901-2 season a whale catcher, the *Olga,* was leased from an Anglo-Russian company for the very high price of 5,000 yen a month over a period of eight months, practically as much as the boat had cost. But it was worth it : after only forty days the two boats had accounted for thirty-four whales. But disaster struck : on 2 December 1901, the *Choshu-maru* was wrecked in a blizzard on the coast of Korea with the loss of three lives. Her loss, which was regarded as a national catastrophe, almost ruined the company, as no insurance companies had been prepared to insure whale catchers. The shareholders were prepared to give up, but not Oka : he continued catching with the leased whale catcher, with such good results that, after a loss of 90,000 yen had been offset, there was a deficit of only 4,500 yen. Just as the position looked least promising, Oka caught sight of a new, modern Norwegian whale catcher in the harbour of Nagasaki. This was the *Rex,* the property of a Norwegian company. Oka chartered this vessel and her sister ship, the *Regina,* on the spot, and on the same conditions as those mentioned above. This brings us to the remarkable Norwegian participation in Japanese whaling which has been named "charter catching" and which has no known parallel in any other area.

The charter party could be of two different kinds : either a boat was on a time charter for a fixed sum per month, for one or more seasons, or the charterer paid a certain sum per whale, varying according to length and species and the month in which it was caught, as the fat contents and weight varied considerably in the course of a season. For foreign companies chartering was the only possible solution to catching in Japanese and Korean waters, as these states granted concessions to no foreigners but Russians and, in Korea's case, Japanese. For both parties the charter system was a very rational way of using each other's know-how. The Norwegians possessed the matériel and had mastered the catching technique, while the Japanese had from ancient times been experts in the processing and marketing of whale meat. The system worked well, to the satisfaction of both parties, and yielded excellent results. In the case of Japan this was a necessary transitional period, until such time as they themselves could build their own whale catchers and train their own gunners. Chartering commenced in 1901 with the above-mentioned *Olga,* which actually saved Oka's company, thanks to good catches during the three subsequent seasons. With its purchase in 1904 and the chartering of the two Norwegian boats, Oka overcame all difficulties and the crisis threatening his company. The war in 1904-5 produced no real break in catching, which yielded 330 whales, even though only two boats were in operation, an astonishingly good result for Japanese whaling at that time. That this must have been a windfall is obvious when we realise that after the previous season, with a yield of 101 whales, a dividend of 17 per cent had been paid. The company, Nihon Enyo Gyogyo K.K., was reorganised in 1904: the result, a new, larger company, Toyo Gyogyo K.K., had a capital of half a million yen. This was to constitute the core of one of Japan's big whaling companies, Nippon Suisan K.K. The company which sold the *Olga* sent the gunner to Oslo to contract for the building of a new whale catcher. This, the *Togo,* which reached Japan in the autumn of 1906, was the first of the many whale catchers supplied by Norwegian ship-building yards to Japan. It was one of a new, more powerful standard type of 96 ft. length overall, 109 gross tons, and had an engine developing 370 h.p. One shipbuilding yard alone, during the period 1902-13, built forty-one boats of this kind for foreign companies, of which fifteen were supplied to the Japanese, while another supplied respectively thirty-eight and five.

From the Norwegian point of view charter catching opened in 1902-3 with the above-mentioned vessels, the *Rex* and the *Regina.* After two seasons the charter arrangement was altered to a fixed price per whale, varying from 400 yen in the summer to 1,150 yen in winter for fin and humpbacks, while for gray whales ,the meat of which was particularly inedible, the rate varied from 280 to 700 yen. These rates applied to fin whales above 40 ft. and to humpback and gray whales over 30 ft., and for every 5 ft. short of this the rate was reduced by 10 per cent for the former and 20 per cent for the latter. The verdict of the report on this contract was that "it improved the economy of both". When the charterer was in a position to pay up to £115 for a small whale, we realise how lucrative the whale meat trade must have been. A humpback of medium size would at that time hardly have provided more than 30 barrels of oil (or 5 tons). With a price of £20 per ton the whale would not have yielded more than £100, and from this sum the cost of producing the oil would have to be subtracted. So it is not surprising that the owners of the two Norwegian whale catchers were highly satisfied: with an average bonus of 700 yen per whale they had an income in 1905 of £23,600. A whale for which the charterers had paid 600 yen brought in approximately 1,600 yen, and the expense of cutting up and marketing the whale as food was minimal compared to the expense of producing oil.

After Japan had emerged victorious from the war with Russia, her whaling entered a period of expansion and speculation in 1906-9 remarkably similar to that of Norway in 1909-12. Six features of this development can be distinguished: first, the two leading companies tripled their catching capacity; secondly, catching was extended to other fields; thirdly, a large number of new companies were established, the first of which started operating in 1907-8; fourthly, it became more and more usual for companies to own their own boats instead of chartering them, and even to build whale catchers in Japan; fifthly, companies started producing whale oil as well, as the market for whale meat was saturated, and prices for that reason were falling; and sixthly, the expansion — contrary to the case of Norway — terminated with the merger of a number of companies to form a large unit, commanding a great deal of capital, a development which has constantly continued in Japan. By way of a seventh feature it might be added that even at this stage the Japanese Government was intervening in order to control catching.

It is hardly surprising that people should have been gripped by the whaling fever when confronted with Toyo Gyogyo's success: in 1905-6 403 whales and a 50 per cent dividend, in 1906-7 633 whales, net profits of 416,500 yen, and a dividend of 58 per cent. This was not only the best result achieved in the history of this company (prior to the merger in 1909), but it was the largest catch made by any company in the course of one season since the beginning of modern-style whaling. For the original shareholders there was in reality a return of 140 per cent, as an increase in the share capital from 500,000 yen to 1.3 million yen had in essence occurred by writing up the shares without any expense to shareholders. In 1907-8 a 30 per cent dividend was paid on new capital (78 per cent on old) and in 1908-9 27 per cent (70 per cent).

Nagasaki Hogei Goshi K.K. was in a position to submit similar figures; the result was an upsurge of new companies which bore no reasonable relationship to the whale stocks round the coasts of Japan, as no one at the time contemplated any extension of whaling beyond this area. The inevitable happened, as it had done in Newfoundland, and as it would in the North Pacific, in Africa and Australia, and most certainly would have done in the Antarctic, had not Britain during the first twenty years pursued a very prudent restrictive policy. What would have happened there, at a far earlier stage, was dramatically illustrated when unrestricted pelagic catching was begun at the end of the 1920s. As an illustration of the extent to which Japan was gripped by the whaling fever it may be mentioned that when one of the largest new companies closed the subscription of shares in January 1907, the capital had been over-subscribed 230 times! None of the twelve new companies founded in 1906-7 had any difficulty in raising capital amounting to 2 million yen, many times more than was the case with Norwegian companies right up to the First World War. Several of the companies went bankrupt after a few years, but some survived and will be briefly dealt with, as they played a significant role in the development of Japanese whaling and comprised the original core of a few of the five subsequent major companies.

Teikoku Suisan K.K. was established in Kobe on 18 January 1907. It proceeded to purchase two of the many Norwegian-built whale catchers which the bankrupt companies in Newfoundland had been forced to sell, and it built one of the first modern whale catchers in Japan. The company was also a pioneer in the use of Japanese gunners. This was the first company to base its operations mainly on the production of whale oil, for which purpose two large plants were built, one in the north and one in the south on the east coast of Honshu. The company also fished north along the coast of Siberia while its whaling operations joined the large merger in 1909 represented by Dainihon Hogei K.K., established in Tokyo on 10 April 1907, with the largest capital — 3 million yen — of all companies. It was said to have set an example as one of the pioneers in the work to prevent over-fishing of whales. In each of its first three years it paid a 10 per cent dividend, before merging with the others. Nikkan Hogei Goshi K.K. was established in Nagasaki in 1905 with a view to whaling using chartered Norwegian boats. This was also the method used after 1906 by Osaka Kasuga Gumi (from 1907 Naigai Suisan K.K.).

With the merger in 1909 of these four companies, there were, subsequent to 1916, only three companies operating independently. They are often referred to as the Tosa companies, as they were mainly engaged in the Tosa Sea, the large open bay on the southeast coast of Shikoku. For centuries this had been famous for its abundant stocks of whales and for the many stations using the netting method. For twenty to twenty-five years three of these companies recorded substantial catches, but then they amalgamated, took over a few other companies established in the 1930s, and emerged as the large firm of Taiyo Gyogyo K.K.

It will be seen from the above that the expansion had got out of hand, and companies were destroying one another by internecine competition. In one particular area twenty whale catchers were operating. A struggle had developed to secure the best gunners, crews, and factory hands, with high wages as an inducement. "Morale and order in the whaling world were totally destroyed and the effects were catastrophic." For the second time Juro Oka proved himself, rescuing whaling from this chaos. In the face of a very severe threat from the Government he summoned most of the companies to a series of conferences in June, July, and August 1908, and the result was the establishment on 18 December 1908, of Nihon Hogeigyo Suisan Kumiai, the Japanese Whaling Association (actually, the Japanese Whaling [and] Fishing Association. By the terms of a long-standing law they were all obliged to belong to a trade association of this nature. Its head office was in Osaka, and it goes without saying that Oka was its first president. Very detailed and rigorous rules governing the conduct of members and catching were laid down. From the many detailed references to the struggle to recruit gunners and workers it is obvious that one of the main objects was to put an end to this, and it was decided to impose a very severe fine of from 5,000 to 10,000 yen for any breach of the rules for the recruitment and payment of hands. It was decided that whale oil should be divided into three categories and rules were introduced for the setting process, packaging, etc. Of major importance were the powers vested in the Board to restrict the number of whale catchers.

The establishment of the Whaling Association was the first step on the way to consolidation and control of whaling in Japan stricter than in any other country. But it should be noted that it only applied to whaling in home waters; when the Japanese commenced operations in more distant areas they showed little willingness to abide by international rules. Catching in domestic waters was of such vital importance that it *had* to be preserved. The second step involved two provisions of 21 October 1909, which gave the Government practically unrestricted powers to regulate catching. Catching was to be dependent on concessions both for each individual boat and for every station, the relevant department could limit the number of concessions and withdraw them if this proved necessary in order to preserve whale stocks. Provisionally the number of whale catchers was fixed at thirty. In connection with this provision it merely mentioned that two years previously Korea had adopted a Whaling Act on 30 September 1907, which contained two very interesting regulations: a ban on catching between 1 May and 30 September, and on the killing of young whales and a female with young. As far as is known this is the first time we come across the latter provision, which was subsequently adopted in all national and international control regulations.

In 1908 twelve companies were operating, with a total of twenty-eight whale catchers, which caught 1,312 whales during the 1908-9 season. The four largest and two lesser companies merged on 2 May 1910, to form the Toyo Hogei K.K. (Oriental Whaling Co.), with the vast capital of 7 million yen. In 1910 they were joined by a seventh company, and in 1916 by three others. The new company controlled twenty of the twenty-eight boats, or two-thirds of the permissible maximum for the whole of Japan, as well as twenty stations spread all over the country. It owned eighteen auxiliaries, and had under constant charter eleven or twelve small steamers employed in transporting meat to the various markets. Winter catching based on Korea was so important that a licence there was listed at 150,000 yen. From 1 October 1909 to 12 January 1910, a total of 398 whales were caught, including 322 in the Korean Sea (a name used at that time to describe the Sea of Japan). Not only in numbers, but also in price, this catch was of decisive importance to the company's finances. These whales were priced at 3,000-6,000 yen, whereas the average value of 253 whales caught from May to July was only 600 yen. As Oka had been granted a concession by the Korean Government on 11 January 1904, and Russian operations had been halted by the war, his company had a virtual monopoly on catching along the east coast of Korea, a monopoly that was further strengthened when on 1 May 1905 he also obtained a lease for the three Russian stations. In terms of matériel and capital Toyo Hogei was the world's largest whaling company, but not in terms of size of catch. Most years the largest two stations in South Georgia each accounted for a larger number of whales, and four to five times more per whale catcher. Total Japanese coastal catching reached its apex during the First World War, with some 2,100 whales killed annually. Subsequently it maintained an annual average of about 1,500, declining to about 1,000 annually in the early 1930s. This trend might suggest that the regulations had not been stringent enough. Figures in excess of 3,000 a year after the Second World War are due solely to the number of sei whales and sperm whales.

This major expansion resulted in an over-production of meat, and as the price of whale oil rose markedly after 1906, the solution was to produce whale oil as well. This meant that the raw material could be utilised in its entirely all the year round, as the meat was liable to perish in the summer if it failed to find a market in time. The Whaling Association immediately laid down rules for improving the quality of the oil.

24. The whaling station at Urusan, Korea.

After 1906 a number of companies had installed plant for the boiling of meat and blubber and the drying of guano. Oil was graded from No. 1 to No. 3; it was an offence to produce oil of a quality inferior to No. 3, and oil of this category was never exported, being used in Japan mainly for lighting, tanning, and to combat plagues of insects in paddy fields.

The first whale catcher built in Japan had been tragically lost in 1901. Not until six years later did the Japanese venture to try again. Their criticism of the Norwegian vessels was that they were too under-powered to chase the whale. In the course of 1907 four boats were built, which proved so successful that no more orders were placed in Norway. The purchase of secondhand Norwegian boats continued, how-ever; up to 1910 at least eighteen were bought, mainly vessels not under contract once charter catching came to an end around 1910.

Hand in hand with the building of boats in Japan went the training of Japanese gunners. It proved easier to solve technical problems than personal ones. In 1910 80 to 90 per cent of the gunners were still Norwegians, and in 1914 about 60 per cent. The last surviving Nor-wegian was operating there until the 1930s, after spending some thirty-five years in the Far East. For foreign gunners earnings were based on individual contracts. When rivalry to secure their services was at its keenest, they were paid 250 yen monthly and a bonus of 60 yen per whale, enabling some of them to earn as much as 10,000 yen a year. In 1910 average wages were 150-200 yen a month, plus bonus of 30-50 yen per whale. As only half-bonuses were awarded for whales under a certain size (45 ft. for a fin whale, 36 ft. for a sperm, 27 ft. for a humpback and a gray whale), and no rise in bonus existed for whales over a certain size, there appears in Japanese regulations to have been no minimum size for the whales that could be caught. It was said that if a female was encountered with young, the latter was shot first, making it easier to deal with the mother, which was unwilling to abandon its offspring. As already mentioned, only Korea had a ban on the shooting of a mother accompanied by her young.

When the merger of the Japanese companies was completed in 1910 Juro Oka made a speech in which he prophesied a brilliant future for Japanese whaling: "I am firmly convinced that we shall become one of the greatest whaling nations in the world. The whaling grounds round Korea and Japan offer unlimited possibilities, and should stocks of whales, contrary to expectation, fail in these areas, we have the Sea of Okhotsk and the Bering Sea to the north and we are aware of the great treasure houses in the south. The day will come when we shall hear one morning that whales have been caught in the Arctic and in the evening that whales are being hunted in the Antarctic."

As SIGURD RISTING, the author of *Av hvalfangstens historie,* puts it: "Japanese whaling has been of significant interest to whaling as a whole." This is putting it mildly: in the history of European and American whaling Japanese whaling has not been accorded the space which its scope in time, extent, and volume deserves. All the members of the Whaling Association were compelled to submit very detailed figures on every aspect of the company from its inception, and as we also have a particularly copious literature describing the old-style catching, there is no country capable of providing such a comprehensive account of the history of its whaling as Japan.

Japanese shore whaling is the most important of its kind in the whole history of whaling. From the oceans abutting on Japan and Korea larger numbers of whales have in the course of time been caught than have been towed in to the shore stations in any other area. Nor has whaling played a more important role in the economy of any nation. At an earlier stage than in any other country catching was restricted by a monopolistic merger of most companies, by State intervention, and by the existence of a whaling association exercising a wide measure of authority over its members and their operations. It established the first collective wage agreements we know of in whaling. By organised co-operation and government support Japanese whaling succeeded in the course of ten to fifteen years in freeing itself from the Norwegian hegemony and standing on its own feet.

The Japanese divide the sea around their coasts into various areas, in accordance with the predominant species of whale to be found there, and with the season during which most catching operations take place. These are as follows: (1) the Southwestern Sea, comprising the sea off the southeast coast of Kyushu, Shikoku, and Honshu as far north as the Bay of Tokyo; (2) the Colonial Sea, comprises the ocean west of these islands, between them and southern Korea; (3) the Sea of Japan, to the north of the former, between northern Honshu and Korea; (4) the Northwestern Sea, further north still, between Hokkaido, Sakhalin, and Siberia; (5) the Northeastern Sea, on the east side of Honshu, running north from the Bay of Tokyo; (6) the Northern Sea, on the east and north sides of Hokkaido; and, in addition, at a later stage, the Formosa and Bonin grounds.

The *blue whale* was caught mainly in Areas 1 and 2. Catches were substantial right up to 1912 (236), slumped dramatically in 1913 (58), recovered somewhat in the following year (123), but declined steadily, and had practically come to an end when the blue whale was totally protected from 1966. The best area for *rorquals* was along the east coast of Korea. Catching culminated in 1914 with 1,040, and has ever since — and this goes almost without saying — declined so markedly that the fin appears to have suffered the same fate as the blue whale. In the 1920s some 400 were caught annually, in the 1930s just under 300. There appear to be separate schools with different migration treks: one entering the Sea of Japan and then proceeding to the Sea of Okhotsk, another along the east coast of Japan and on to the Aleutians. It was in particular the first school that was hunted right up to the Second World War, while the latter was the subject of pelagic whaling from the mid-1950s. This migration took place for the most part between May and October, while in the Korean area it occurred most frequently between August and September. The real *sei whale* occurred mainly in the northern Areas 5 and 6; the sei whales caught around the Bonin Islands turned out to be Bryde whales (*Balaenoptera brydei* or *edeni*). The gradual decline of blue whales and fin whales was compensated by increased catches of sei whales, which for a time appeared capable of standing almost unlimited inroads; there was, however, no need to be a whaling expert to predict that this species would suffer the same fate. The marked increase in *humpback* after 1924 was due to the opening up of the new whaling grounds near the Bonin Islands. After only a few years, however, a corresponding slump set in. After 1945 humpbacks rarely figure in Japanese catching records. It was long assumed that the *gray whale* — which the Japanese call *koku kujira* (black whale) and the Americans the devil fish — had vanished; it was little less than a sensation when this species was once again caught in winter off the southeast coast of Korea, about 150 being accounted for annually in

1911-15. The figures declined steadily until this species once again vanished after 1933. In summer it migrated all the way up to the Bering Sea, and a considerable number were subsequently caught near Kamchatka.

The *right whale* was the rarest of all; how many were caught before 1911 we do not know. During the following decade a total of 36 were caught; quite a large number were accounted for in the mid-1930s. Although the *sperm whale* was the most numerous whale round the coasts of Japan and throughout the whole of the North Pacific, in ancient times it was not very much sought after, because of its tasteless meat. But because, with the introduction of modern-style whaling, considerable opportunities were created for the use of sperm oil, interest in pursuing this species increased, and numbers rose to some 800 annually prior to the Second World War. After the war whaling based on Japan, as in so many other waters, has increasingly become the pursuit of the sperm whale. In assessing the decline in stocks of the other species around Japan we must take into consideration the tremendous increase in catching in adjacent areas, from shore stations on Kamchatka and the Kurils and pelagic catching in the northern Pacific. The catching of the *small whale* has also been carried on at all times in Japanese coastal waters. This greatly increased during the Second World War, with a view to providing much-needed extra sources of food.

The new phase in East Asiatic whaling, pelagic whaling, was ushered in by a Norwegian expedition in 1925-6. This pioneering effort proved unsuccessful, but it signposted the way for the Russians in 1933 and the Japanese in 1940. The waters that were opened up on that occasion proved to be the richest outside the Antarctic, and were for a time to provide the main arena for whaling.

We have followed the spread of whaling according to Norwegian methods over the entire northern hemisphere. While Norwegians imposed a ban on catching in their own country, they transferred their activities to many other countries, or these countries adopted the Norwegian methods and used Norwegian equipment and the service of Norwegian gunners, until they were competent enough to operate on their own account. This, however, was only one aspect of the expansion; at the same time a far more vigorous expansion was taking place embracing all the oceans of the southern hemisphere. After a few years the returns in the south proved much richer than those in the north, and this was an essential reason why several of the more meagre whaling grounds in the north were abandoned. It was in the north, however, that the method which made the Antarctic adventure possible had been invented and developed. (For catching figures for Japan, 1899-1910, see Statistical Appendix, Table 46.)

9

TOWARDS THE SOUTH, 1892-1904

There is such a wealth of literature on the discovery and exploration of the Antarctic — the sixth continent, 2,000,000 square kilometres larger than Europe — that there is no need to recapitulate. The Antarctic adventure, set on foot by whaling, is one of the most remarkable in the history of mankind. So unknown was this continent that it was not until 1895 that man first set foot upon it. Only fifteen years later, however, the islands and oceans around the South Pole were annually invaded by a few thousand men, who gorged themselves on the indescribable wealth of the ocean. After sixty-five years, during which events developed with well-nigh unbelievable speed, it appears that this great venture is now drawing to a close. The modern floating factory turned the whaler into an industrial worker, enjoying conditions that would have been impossible only a generation earlier. Where Robert Falcon Scott and his men froze to death in the midst of the polar wastes in their tiny tent in 1912, scientists are comfortably ensconced in their atomically heated laboratories, and where Scott and Roald Amundsen struggled and toiled on foot, aircraft now make daily flights to the South Pole. The rivalry of the super-powers has finally reached this continent too.

While it is not the intention to deal in detail here with the story of the Antarctic, a few facts on its prehistory are required if we are to understand its bearing on whaling in 1892-5 and 1904-5.

Both J.-B.-C. Bouvet and James Cook, the two outstanding explorers of the eighteenth century, reported sighting tremendous quantities of whale, and George Forster, a scientist who accompanied Cook on his first circumnavigation of the world, prophesied in 1775 that, should the Arctic Ocean ever run out of whales, whalers would be able to catch as many as they wanted in the Antarctic Ocean. Forty years later this statement was ridiculed: no one could possibly consider anything as crazy as whaling operations conducted so far from their native coasts. One of the aims of the explorers was to discover islands with fur-bearing seals, and these were found, *inter alia* in South Georgia, which had been re-discovered by Cook in 1755. Here, in 1902, were found two large cauldrons for the boiling of seal blubber, used by American seal trappers in the 1780s — hence the name Grytviken (Cauldron Bay), where the first modern whaling station was built in 1904. James Clark Ross relates that, on penetrating the pack-ice and reaching the open sea which bears his name, he observed great numbers of whales, and his notes on these creatures were to prove of decisive importance in the equipping of the first whaling expeditions. Similar importance is attached to the account JAMES WEDDELL wrote of the sea he had discovered, and to which he gave his name in 1823. Years of intense exploration around 1840 were succeeded by a virtual lull lasting some fifty years. Interest focused now more on the north, in an attempt to find the northwest and the northeast passages and to explore Greenland and the archipelago north of Canada, with the dream of the North Pole as a distant goal. The rich sperm whale catching in the Pacific and right whale catching off Alaska proved sufficient for the whalers, as well as covering market needs. With modern Norwegian catching off Finnmark, Norwegian interests focused on the north. The only item of interest after Ross and Weddell was provided by two German expeditions in the 1870s, and the celebrated scientific *Challenger* expedition, which in 1874 visited Kerguelen. The latter reported that American whaling was practically at an end, while the two former came back with news that there were no seals left around South Georgia, but large numbers of whales in the seas between the South Shetlands and Graham Land. There was no doubt that whales abounded round the Antarctic continent, but the great question was: what sort of whale? Was it the much-sought-after right whale or was it the fin whale? The expeditions in the 1890s set out on the basis of a fatal error. In order to understand this, we must retrace our steps.

Reports of large quantities of whales in the south caused a stir in the Scottish whaling towns, where it was realised that whaling in the north was approaching its end. In Peterhead the two brothers DAVID and JOHN GRAY issued a small pamphlet in 1874 entitled *Report on New Whaling Grounds in the Southern Seas* in order to stimulate sufficient interest to start whaling in those parts. This pamphlet, as we shall see, had a decisive effect on subsequent developments. It was reprinted three times — in Aberdeen in 1874, in the periodical of the Royal Society of Victoria in Melbourne in 1887, and once again in Peterhead in 1891. In the rush to organise an expedition the information contained in the pamphlet was cited as authoritative. It reproduced all the statements made by Ross and others who had taken part in his voyage, but although no-one could say with certainty whether the whales observed were fin or right whales, the Gray brothers were in no doubt that the latter species was involved. They based their calculations on this, and declared that fin and humpback whales were of little worth. They do not, in fact, appear to have been familiar with Svend Foyn's blue and fin whale catching. In this way, in the 1870s, new and old came face to face: while in the north a new source of wealth was being discovered in the rorquals, there were dreams of a new golden age of right whale catching in the south. Encouraged by the Grays' pamphlet, which the Scottish Geographical Society sent to the Royal Geographical

Society of Australasia, the latter, in co-operation with the Royal Society of Victoria, set up the Antarctic Exploration Committee. If any one person and any particular point of time were to be selected as marking the newly aroused interest for the Antarctic, it should be the German-born Baron FERDINAND VON MUELLER, who on 18 April 1884, delivered the inaugural speech to the newly established Royal Geographical Society of Australasia in Melbourne. The gist of his speech was an appeal for exploration of the practically unknown continent, and it was a direct cause of the setting up of the committee.

The committee solicited support for its plans in England, where it appeared that similar plans were on foot. In both places it was considered impossible to raise the large amount, £200,000, that a three-year scientific expedition would cost. It was therefore decided to concentrate on a short-term combined research and catching expedition, which could be mounted for between £10,000 and £20,000. The plan was submitted to three persons who might be expected to be interested in a project of this kind, the whaling company owner ROBERT KINNES of Dundee, the shipyard owner Chr. Christensen of Sandefjord, and Svend Foyn of Tønsberg. This appeal started a train of events undreamed of by the committee.

The result in Dundee was that Kinnes set about equipping an entire fleet of four ships, all with auxiliary engines and a total crew of 130 hands. The expenses amounted to £28,000. The Royal Geographical Society and the Meteorological Office and other institutions donated a large number of scientific instruments for observations of land, sea, and air. These were to be carried out by the ships' doctors, one of whom was the subsequently famous polar explorer and science writer WILLIAM S. BRUCE. The adventurous Scottish painter William Burn Murdoch, in a book illustrated by himself, has given us a detailed account of this expedition and the Norwegian one. The destination of the Scottish ships was the western Weddell Sea, where one of the members of the Ross expedition had reported seeing masses of (right?) whales along the east coast of Graham Land. The fleet left Dundee in the first week of September, and reached its destination on 23 December 1892.

The reason Christensen was solicited was because he had constructed in his shipyard a number of very stoutly built vessels for the trapping of seal and bottlenose whales in the ice. He replied that he had four ships for sale or lease. Svend Foyn offered the committee two vessels powered by steam engines. All attempts to finance the expedition, however, failed, as did the hopes of engaging the services of FRIDTJOF NANSEN as leader. The answer given by Nansen was that, much as he would have liked to have taken on the job, the North Pole lay closest and, if this were possible, that would be his first goal. Christensen and Foyn were also kept informed in 1886-9 of plans by Norwegian businessmen in Australia.

It would therefore be wrong to suggest, as has been done, that the expeditions carried out by these two in 1892-5 were the outcome of a sudden flight of fancy: in fact they had had several years in which to consider the matter. Christensen was also in possession of one of the pamphlets issued by the Gray brothers, and was informed of the preparations that had been carried out in Dundee, while Norwegian newspapers were writing that "it would be a pity if others should steal a march on the Norwegians, who possess both the ships and the equipment". National prestige was almost certainly an important motive for both Norwegians, but they were first and foremost lured by the dream of the right whales "with those blessed baleens which literally ooze money". In Norway they were debating whether this catching in the Antarctic Ocean would save them from their crisis.

There is no doubt that the request received by Christensen and Foyn prompted both of them to action: the former decided to despatch his Arctic catching vessel the *Jason*, with its auxiliary, to the Weddell Sea, in direct rivalry, so it appears, with the Dundee expedition. Thirty-year-old Carl Anton Larsen (1860-1924), whom Christensen placed in charge of the *Jason*, was the most capable man available. Despite his youth he could already look back on several highly successful seasons trapping seal and bottlenose in the Arctic. In the course of his life he was responsible for four achievements, each one of which would be sufficient to enshrine him among the leaders in the history of whaling and Antarctic exploration. First of all we have the two *Jason* voyages of 1892-4 to the unknown Weddell Sea; in the second place he skippered the *Antarctic* in 1901-3 on Otto Nordenskjöld's expedition to the same area; thirdly, he was in at the start of whaling in South Georgia in 1904; and fourthly, he opened the Ross Sea in 1923 for whaling. It was here, too, that he met his death. Larsen also had scientific interests, and collected a great deal of valuable material from the islands on which he was the first to set foot.

On 4 September 1892, Larsen sailed from Sandefjord on the voyage which was to have the most significant consequences in the entire history of whaling. South Georgia was passed on 7 November; without a stop-off they shaped a course for the South Orkneys, where seals were caught, though stocks were meagre. The voyage continued to the Trinity Peninsula on the eastern end of Graham Land, and "on our way there blue whale frolicked in countless shoals, as well as humpback, but there was no sign of the characteristic blowing of the right whale". On 4 December he and two of his hands were the first to set foot on volcanic and ice-free Seymour Island, and made the first finds of Antarctic fossils, both of trees and animals, which proved that this country had at some time in the tertiary period enjoyed a climate similar to that of Spitsbergen. But where was the right whale? For a couple of weeks they cruised to and

25. The *Jason* in Sandefjord, 1893.

fro, in fog and storm, in unfamiliar waters, between enormous icebergs. Schools of blue whales, as many as twenty at a time, and several hundred fin and humpback whales would swim right up to the ship's side. But what use were they? Their very presence accentuated the sense of disappointment. The most important point was that Larsen never forgot what he had seen. On 26 December the *Jason* hailed the Dundee ships, and the captains discussed among themselves the problem of the right whale, agreeing to trap seals so as not to return home emptyhanded. Seal abounded, and in next to no time the holds were full. On 20 February sealing was brought to a close, and all the vessels set out for home. Not till 9 June 1893 was the *Jason* back in Sandefjord, having spent six of the nine months on the voyage out and back. The result to the company was a loss of Kr.37,000. The newspapers declared that the trip had been a fiasco.

Despite this, it was decided at Larsen's suggestion to repeat the experiment in the 1893-4 season, on a far bigger scale. Three large sealers were despatched together with an iron barque of 1,100 gross tons as a transport. The intention this time was to trap seals, not to catch whales; indirectly, however, this expedition proved of major importance to subsequent exploration of the Antarctic, and for whaling, by establishing once again the presence of enormous numbers of rorquals. The four Antarctic expeditions in 1892-5 only succeeded in catching one single right whale; a few others were hit, but lost. A negative result is, after all, a result: whaling in the Antarctic could not be

26. C. A. Larsen.

based on the right whale, but only on modern catching of rorquals. Losses that season were still bigger, and Christensen gradually wound up his company, selling off his ships in the course of a few years. The owners of the vessels engaged had lost large sums, but Christensen and C. A. Larsen had been inspired by a vision which they never abandoned, even though the general opinion was that no one would ever grow rich in pursuit of the whale in the southern ocean.

On 27 November 1893, the Royal Geographical Society held a meeting in London after the result of the voyages of the Dundee ships and the *Jason* had become known. An outstanding expert on the Antarctic, JOHN MURRAY, urged that a scientific expedition should be mounted on the basis of the experience gleaned by the two whaling expeditions. He and two professors of marine biology declared that it would be futile to start whaling in the Antarctic: from a commercial point of view, they pointed out, one whale was very different from another. A great many of the largest whales had a thin layer of blubber and short baleens, and it was not worth the whalers' time catching them. The experience of the expeditions would suggest that this ocean was not suitable for whaling. One is astonished to hear sentiments of this kind expressed: were the three authorities not aware of the fact that for twenty years rewarding catching of rorquals had taken place off the coast of Finnmark, and for ten years off the shores of Iceland? So conservative were they in their attitude to whaling that for them it was synonymous with the catching of right whales. Yet the fact remained that the three expeditions referred to above had a total loss of some £13,750. This explains the pessimistic attitude to the commercial potential of catching in the southern ocean, a pessimism which was further increased when the result of the *Antarctic*'s voyage was made known.

It is a tremendous tribute to the vitality of eighty-four-year-old Svend Foyn that he should be experimenting with floating factories in the north and at the same time despatching a whaling expedition to the south, despite the considerable losses incurred by the *Jason* on its first trip. That Foyn should have done so nevertheless was because he believed that C. A. Larsen had been searching for right whales in the wrong area. Ross had brought back accounts of whales in the Ross Sea : that was where the right whale was bound to be, and thither the *Antarctic* was despatched. The leader of the expedition was a relation of Foyn, HENRIK JOHAN BULL, a Melbourne businessman who had returned to Norway in order to inform Svend Foyn of the Australian plans. The captain on board the *Antarctic* was LEONARD KRISTENSEN. Both men have published books describing the voyage, and from these it emerges that a clash of personalities arose, based on differences with regard to the exercise of authority, which made life on board most embarrassing. As far as possible each made strenuous efforts to avoid any mention of the other.

With a crew of thirty-one the *Antarctic* was ready to sail on 20 September 1893. The first point of call was the large island of Kerguelen, where they were forced to land in order to obtain fresh water. The *Antarctic* remained here for longer than intended, as it was now so late in the year that it was too late to penetrate through the pack-ice into the Ross Sea. For this reason the voyage had to be postponed a whole year. At that time Kerguelen, or Desolation Land, as it was called by the British, was uninhabited, but had previously been a frequent port of call for whalers and sealers. We shall hear more about Kerguelen when the Norwegians in 1909 tried to start whaling operations from this island, and when the Germans, during the Second World War, used it as a hiding-place for armed merchantmen which in 1941 seized the Norwegian whaling fleet in the Antarctic whaling grounds. There was no trace of the whale for which the *Antarctic* was searching, but in order to cover part of the expedition's expenses, a great many large, fat sea elephants were killed, so that by 3 February 1894 the vessel was fully laden with pelts, blubber, and oil. The oil was sold in Melbourne for £1,775, but the pelts proved practically valueless. In Melbourne, where the *Antarctic* put in for repairs, remaining from 24 February to 11

27. The crew of the *Jason* before leaving Sandefjord 1892. C. A. Larsen is standing on the left (with bowler hat).

April, Bull was anxious to sell his ship to an Australian syndicate keen to use her for an expedition to Victoria Land, but as the asking price — £10,000 — proved too high, nothing came of the sale. A local paper wrote that Britain should impose restrictions on foreigners whaling from countries under British sovereignty. This was the first time the much-disputed claim of British sovereignty to all territory in the western Antarctic was made in connection with Norwegian whaling, and, what is more, before it had even begun. The paper concluded by expressing its astonishment that fifty years after Ross, no one had as yet followed in his footsteps, until, strangely enough, a Norwegian vessel should one day arrive, despatched by an eighty-four-year-old man. There were clearly many strange things in the world, not least in Tønsberg!

While awaiting the Antarctic summer, a voyage was carried out during the winter to Campbell Island, 350 miles south of New Zealand, where right whales had been reported. And here, at last, they were found — schools of ten to twelve moving through the water, almost grazing the ship's sides, but the catching equipment failed completely. The net result was a small calf worth £170. Repairs due to a breakdown and new equipment cost £2,000. Finally, on 28 September 1894, the *Antarctic* set out on a voyage that had not been undertaken since Ross had done it in 1842. As they approached the ice barrier the propeller worked loose and they had to return a thousand miles back to New Zealand in order to have it repaired. Penetrating the pack-ice proved astonishingly easy, and on 15 January 1895, they enjoyed the alluring sight of the ice-free Ross Sea, twice as large in area as the North Sea. They sailed south along Victoria Land, giving names to many islands and peaks, but as supplies of coal started to run short, they were forced to turn back at 74°S (Ross had reached 78°). The most significant achievement was when, on 24 January, they landed at Cape Adare, the first human beings to have set foot on the Antarctic continent. That it had proved possible to land was regarded by leading geographers such as John Murray and SIR CLEMENTS R. MARKHAM, President of the Royal Geographical Society in London, as highly significant. This more than outweighed the considerable losses Svend Foyn had incurred. But before the *Antarctic* had returned to Tønsberg on 1 August 1895, Foyn was dead; he was never to know that his boldest expedition proved financially a complete disaster. Kristensen returned a profoundly disappointed man. Public opinion merely noted that he had come back with his holds empty, without realising that he had carried out one of the major feats in the history of seamanship. Practically without a hitch he had sailed a small vessel of 226 gross tons across some of the world's most hostile seas, through pack-ice and unfamiliar waters, without charts — he made them himself — and had opened the Antarctic continent for exploration. Kristensen presented a comprehensive report of the voyage, together with charts and excellent photographs and drawings of Victoria Land, to the Australasian Exploration Committee, which in turn submitted them to the 6th International Geographical Congress in London in 1895, where they were studied with the greatest interest and constituted the most significant spur to the many scientific expeditions to the Antarctic from 1897 to 1904 carried out by five different nations. A lecture to the Congress on the voyage of the *Antarctic* was received with enthusiasm, and the following resolution was adopted: "The exploration of the Antarctic regions is the greatest piece of geographical exploration still to be undertaken." Among those who took part in subsequent expeditions were such outstanding personalities as Ernest Henry Shackleton, Robert F. Scott, Roald Amundsen, Adrien de Gerlache, Jean-Baptiste Charcot, Otto Nordenskjöld, and C. A. Larsen.

Four of the seven vessels used in these expeditions were Norwegian; several of them were under the command of Norwegian captains, and yet not a single expedition was sponsored by Norwegians. Norway was reproached for neglecting this opportunity of protecting her interests in the Antarctic. But at this time her polar interests were focused on the north. In the south she could look back on three unsuccessful expeditions and substantial, unfruitful financial sacrifices. From this point of view the Antarctic held no attraction for Norway. In the course of a few years round about the turn of the century tremendous sums were invested in Antarctic exploration. The difference in knowledge about the continent in 1892 on the one hand and in 1904 on the other was vast. Few people were personally better acquainted with its climate and fauna than C. A. Larsen, who further extended his knowledge when, for the third time, he sailed out as captain on board Otto Nordenskjöld's ship the *Antarctic* in 1902. On 12 February 1903, she was crushed by the ice and went to the bottom of the Weddell Sea with a host of valuable collections. The skill and courage shown by Larsen and his nineteen men (one of whom died) in surviving throughout eight months of the Antarctic winter constitute one of the finest achievements in the history of polar exploration. This was the prelude to the chapter in the history of modern whaling which is referred to as catching in the Southern Ocean.

10

THE START OF ANTARCTIC WHALING, 1904-1908

C. A. Larsen and the Compañía Argentina de Pesca S.A.

Practically all the literature dealing with the early days of Antarctic whaling, with its emphasis on two of the pioneers, C. A. Larsen and Chr. Christensen, overlooks the third, ADOLF AMANDUS ANDRESEN, yet another Sandefjord man. The scope of his operations and its significance cannot be compared with that of the two others, but it would be unreasonable to exclude him. After a number of years at sea Andresen had settled in Punta Arenas (now Magallanes), where he was active in coastal traffic in southern Chile. He had noticed that there were stocks of whales — rorquals and right whales — as well as the valuable fur-bearing seals around Tierra del Fuego. In order to acquire skill as a gunner he made his way to Finnmark, where he participated in whaling operations. He returned with a whale gun which he mounted in the bows of a tugboat, and with this he shot a humpback whale on New Year's Eve 1903 in the Straits of Magellan, at a time when C. A. Larsen was still struggling with the ice in the Weddell Sea, and Christensen's first expedition to Spitsbergen was on its way home. Andresen's whale was the first "commercial whale" despatched with modern equipment in the Southern Ocean. In 1905 Andresen acquired a new whale catcher from Norway, and established a whaling station near Magallanes. The results were so promising that he managed to form a Chilean company, the Sociedad Ballenera de Magallanes. Two new whale catchers were purchased and the floating factory *Gobernador Bories* was fitted out, and these operated in 1906 round the South Shetlands, where Andresen discovered a magnificent harbour on Deception Island. This was soon to acquire fame as the centre of whaling operations in the western Antarctic.

While the term "Antarctic Ocean" has gradually fallen out of use, the expression "Arctic Ocean" has come to stay. In the southern hemisphere the various parts of the sea around the continent have acquired their own special names — King Haakon VII's Sea, the Weddell Sea, Roald Amundsen's Sea (also called the Belgica Sea), Bellingshausen Sea, and the Ross Sea. If the northern boundary of the Antarctic Ocean were to be drawn along the Antarctic Circle, most Antarctic whaling would be located to the north of this line. The drift-ice boundary does not run along the parallel of latitude; moreover, South Georgia is situated far south of the drift-ice boundary, whereas Tierra del Fuego is outside it. The criterion for Antarctic whaling will inevitably have to be that it was carried on in practically daily contact with the ice. In our account we shall use the term "Southern Ocean catching" to describe all the whaling in the southern hemisphere, "Antarctic catching" to describe catching in the polar seas — including operations based on shore stations — around the Antarctic continent and adjacent islands, and "ice catching" to describe later pelagic operations from floating factories inside the drift ice. Seamen adopted their own special geographical distinctions in these regions — beyond forty no law, beyond fifty no God!

Of the first three companies in the Antarctic, one was entirely Norwegian; the two others had certainly been started and were managed by Norwegians, with Norwegian crews and equipment, but the capital invested was not wholly Norwegian. As the Norwegian company, after its initial season, was nearly sold to foreign interests, it looked for a moment as if all Antarctic whaling would pass out of the hands of the Norwegians. Negotiations on this sale take us back to the first step that was taken to exploit South Georgia's natural resources. The initiative came from the Governor of the Falkland Islands who, on 2 October 1900, announced that he was prepared to give "a mining and general lease" on South Georgia for twenty-one years. The only reaction to this offer was the establishment on 20 March 1905, in Magallanes, of the South Georgia Exploration Co. The shareholders included a number of people from the Falkland Islands who made a living as shepherds in Patagonia, and its director was an Englishman ERNEST SWINHOE. From 1 July 1905, he leased all South Georgia for two years at a rent of £1 per annum. Some of the shepherds set sail in a small schooner, and despite the fact that the Antarctic winter was not yet over, they made a successful passage to Cumberland Bay, reached on 14 August, where they were astonished to discover an Argentine whaling company hard at work. We shall soon see what came of the meeting between Swinhoe and C. A. Larsen. What Swinhoe saw convinced him that the future of his company lay neither in sheep nor minerals, but in whaling. For this reason he acquired a new concession, lasting twenty-one years, from 1 January 1906, covering the entire island, for a fee of £250 per annum. The 500 acres which the Compañía Argentina de Pesca, referred to by all whalers as "Pesca", had leased in Grytviken (Cauldron Bay) at the same time were not included in the concession.

As far as the history of whaling is concerned the most important aspect of the concession was that it contained the following provision: "The grantees convenant with His Majesty that they *will* erect a suitable oil factory" and will spend £8,000 for this purpose. This admitted only of one interpretation: that there was an obligation to commence whaling. On 8 July 1906, a clause was added to the concession to the effect that no other company should lease an area in excess of 500 acres, and that the number should be limited to seven. As it proved impossible to obtain the capital necessary to build the station or to purchase the first Norwegian expedition with the floating factory *Admiralen,* the concession was sold in 1908 for £1,500 to another company. We have anticipated events in order to show that four years before C.A. Larsen landed at Grytviken, steps had been taken by the Falkland Islands administration to exploit the resources of South Georgia. At the same time this triggered off the dispute, which has not yet been resolved, on the sovereignty over the Antarctic regions. When a second Chilean company, the Tierra del Fuego Sheep Farming Company Ltd., approached the Governor on 13 January 1904, on the chances of obtaining a concession, and in this connection asked in what year Great Britain had annexed the island, the Governor made no reply, as he had no idea when the island had been formally occupied.

It was undoubtedly the many scientific expeditions around the year 1900 that had sharpened Great Britain's interest in the Antarctic, and provided the motive for the Governor's action in 1900. Burn Murdoch and W. S. Bruce, who had accompanied the Dundee fleet in 1892-3, never got over their disappointment that the British had failed to commence whaling operations in their own territory, and expressed their great bitterness at this. They both relate that, on their return in 1893, they were visited by Svend Foyn's agent, Johannes Bull, and that the three of them had together worked out a plan for a modern whaling station in South Georgia. They convoked a representative meeting in the Royal Geographical Society in Edinburgh, which was attended by a number of leading businessmen, including Christian Salvesen. Bruce and Murdoch were unable to convince the assembly of the riches that were to be had for the taking in the Southern Ocean, and that for this reason Norway had been able to earn untold sums. This was doubly annoying, because in Murdoch's opinion the lucrative Antarctic catching had started as a result of the information he and Dr. Bruce had brought home with them in 1893.

This is not correct: Larsen had made no use of the information obtained by these two gentlemen. On his three voyages he had with his own eyes seen all that needed to be seen. In 1903 he had called at South Georgia, and discovered the ideal site for a whaling station — a safe and sheltered harbour, a stretch of flat ground only a few feet above sea-level and — most important of all — with an abundance of fresh water. He never forgot this, and when in the autumn of 1904 he sailed south, he had no need to search for a suitable site, but merely made his way straight to Grytviken, which the British always referred to as King Edward's Cove.

After their enforced wintering Larsen and his men were rescued by an Argentine gunboat and taken to Buenos Aires, where he was fêted for eight days as "the polar hero". At a big banquet in his honour on 5

December 1903, he declared in his highly original English :

I tank youse vary mooch and dees is all vary nice and youse vary kind to mes, bot I ask youse ven I am here vy don't youse take dese vales at your doors — dems vary big vales and I seen dem in houndreds and tousends.

The idea fired the imagination of local business tycoons, most of them immigrants from abroad, including the Norwegian PEDRO CHRISTOPHER-SEN, the Swedish banker ERNESTO TORNQUIST, and the German-born H. H. SCHLIEPER, the last-mentioned a United States citizen resident in Argentina. He became president of the company, while Tornquist was its chief shareholder. Potential shareholders were invited to subscribe a capital of 200,000 gold pesos (1 gold peso = Kr.3.70). Larsen had an option on 2,500 shares at 10 pesos per share, either for himself personally or for interested persons in Norway. As far as the first offer was concerned he was financially not in a position to accept, and as far as the second was concerned, he declared himself that he had no wish to involve Norwegian capital "because this attempt at whaling in the Antarctic regions should involve a risk for foreign capital". His confidence in the success of the venture, in fact, does not appear to have been particularly great, despite the large number of whales he had seen. In order to appreciate this one needs to be familiar with the position of whaling at that time and of whale oil in the world markets.

The ban on whaling from North Norway was to come into force after the 1904 season. The significance of this ban for the transfer of catching to the Antarctic has been misrepresented. The ten companies operating in North Norway in 1903 with seventeen whale catchers accounted for only forty whales and 1,300 barrels per company. About one-half of the oil was of a quality inferior to Category No. 1; the price of this category was £17, and £2 less for each lower category, down to £11 for No. 4. This was hardly enough to ensure that companies made any profit. Admittedly, catches of whales and the number of barrels per boat showed a marked rise in 1904, but this was offset by the steep fall in prices. In Glasgow oil No. 1 was given as low a price quotation as £13. The reason for the slump in price, apart from the general depression, was that the world market had been flooded by a tremendous harvest of oil-bearing vegetable seed. The price of linseed oil slumped to an unprecedented low level, dragging whale oil with it.

In dealing with the crisis of 1903-5, whaling literature has generally attributed the main responsibility to the ban on whaling, for the simple reason that whaling from Finnmark has been considered in isolation, instead of regarding catching throughout the North Atlantic as a whole. As a rule, two errors are constantly cropping up in the available literature : in the first place that, as a result of the ban, "a swarm of companies moved from Finnmark up to Spitsbergen"; and in the second place that whale stocks were so reduced in the north that whalers were compelled to move south. Simple figures suffice to disprove this. Of the nine companies whose operations were terminated by the ban, three moved to Spitsbergen and none south. The number of whales caught in the North Atlantic would appear to prove that stocks had not been exhausted : in the three years 1903-5, they were respectively 3,010, 3,656, and 3,505. If we exclude Newfoundland, the figures for the Norwegian Sea alone were 2,152, 2,380, and 2,613, that is to say, the catches in the other areas more than compensated for the loss of catching off the Finnmark coast. The number of barrels of oil amounted to 64,257, 84,531, and 82,865, reflecting a marked rise from 1903 to 1904-5. A still more important point is that this was not due to the use of increased amounts of catching matériel but to a larger yield per whale catcher, an average of 1,053, 1,281, and 1,275 barrels per boat in each of these years. The results achieved in the Norwegian Sea hardly appear likely to have scared anyone off and sent them packing south. In Iceland, catching reached a peak in 1901-3 with 1,300 barrels per boat, in the Faroes similar conditions obtained, while in 1903 promising operations were started from the Shetlands and Spitsbergen, and round Newfoundland catching appeared to assume substantial dimensions. In 1902-4 fourteen new companies were started in Norway for operations in the north, while six closed down. The Norwegians' need to expand was satisfied in the north. No Norwegian capital was invested in the first two companies in the Antarctic, nor even in C. A. Larsen's company.

Clearly the crisis was caused neither by the ban in Finnmark nor by a decline in the production of whale oil or in the working capacity of whale catchers, but by a slump in the price of whale oil that was almost disastrous. The situation in the world fat market was that up till about 1900 animal (cattle) fat, of which the United States with its tremendous harvest of maize was the greatest producer, was the most important raw material in the manufacture of margarine. This raw material, however, had encountered increasing competition from vegetable fats. For the soap industry linseed oil and cottonseed oil constituted the most important raw materials: and the United States was also the largest producer of the latter, accounting in 1905 for some two million tons. As supplies of animal fat had failed to satisfy demand, owing to a poor maize harvest, prices had been forced up in 1903. In 1904 there was a complete turnabout : an abundant maize harvest resulted in a large production of fat, while linseed and cottonseed too were proving unusually abundant. Whale oil prices reached an all-time low, despite the fact that improved refining methods had enlarged their scope of application. As some 50 per cent of the whale oil was of a quality inferior to No. 1, and exuded an unpleasant smell, its use in the soap industry was, furthermore, limited. Right up until the First World War Lord Leverhulme refused to use whale oil in Sunlight soap, despite the argument that "if it was good enough to eat, it should be good enough for soap".

It was this difficulty of finding uses for whale oil that constituted the most deep-rooted cause of the low prices obtaining in 1892-1905. The whalers' problem was how to make whaling profitable. This could be done by discovering whaling grounds with such ample access to raw material, that this could be utilised to its utmost capacity, even though only the best portion of the blubber was used. This would ensure a higher percentage of oil No. 1, and a better price. This in turn would depend on an extended application of whale oil. The intense research that was initiated in order to solve this problem is shown, *inter alia,* by the fact that the number of whaling patents reached a climax in 1904, coinciding with the transition from catching in the northern hemisphere to global catching with the use of the first floating factories.

Another factor may also have had some bearing on this. The further west Norwegians ventured, the keener was foreign competition. In Iceland, the Faroes, and the Shetlands they had already encountered competition from the British, and to a lesser extent from Danes and Germans, and off Newfoundland in the eastern and western waters of the North Pacific only a small portion of the operations were in Norwegian hands. The potential for further expansion in the north had been exhausted. Buying up shares in an Argentinian company would merely mean giving further support to foreign competition. When C. A. Larsen arrived in Sandefjord in order to purchase matériel for this company, Christen Christensen appealed to "*our* go-ahead whalers to direct their attention to the south".

The Compañía Argentina de Pesca S.A. was constituted in Buenos Aires in February 1904, but has elected to celebrate November 16 of that year as its "birthday", because it was on that day of the same year that the first whale catcher anchored up in Grytviken (Cauldron Bay). Larsen's contract secured him the position of whaling manager for five years (in 1909 this was renewed for a further five years), and an income of 15 per cent of profits after 25 per cent had been placed to reserve. The first season, 1904-5, earned him a mere $474, but in a number of other years he was very handsomely rewarded. In 1901-11 the station produced 56,110 barrels (the highest figure prior to 1926-7) and profits totalled $622,218, or more than three times more than the capital, while Larsen's share was $70,000. After ten years he returned to Norway a highly prosperous man. During the preceding eight seasons shareholders received a total of 243 per cent in dividends. It is hardly surprising that a struggle for concessions and licences ensued. (As the company's records covering these early years have been lost, it proved a difficult task to reconstruct its history before about 1920.)

In the spring of 1904, then, Larsen arrived in Sandefjord, where he ordered all the necessary equipment, as well as a new whale catcher, larger than usual, and two old sailing vessels — a small one for maintaining a link with Buenos Aires and a large one to convey the oil to Europe. All the material was stowed on board, including three prefabricated wooden houses for the factory, the manager, and hands. On 20 September this armada set off, calling in at Buenos Aires on 28 October, where Larsen's nephew FRIDTHJOF JACOBSEN came on board. His career is the history of the company in a nutshell, from its inception in 1904 until his death in 1953, from 1914 as station manager and after 1921 as managing director. In his private life, too, he was very closely associated with South Georgia, as his wife visited the station there in 1912 with their children, one of whom, a daughter, was actually born there and registered as South Georgia No. 1.

It needs little imagination to envisage the difficulties which Larsen faced when he anchored up in Grytviken: in a polar land, with sudden and violent changes of weather, where no quay existed, with boilers, cookers and heavy equipment to be landed, a slipway and a flensing plant to be built, three houses erected, several hundred tons of coal unloaded, etc. At the end of a month everything was in place; on 22 December the first whale, a humpback, was shot, and the process of reduction could start. On 18 February 1905, the smaller of the two sailing ships set off for Buenos Aires with the first 990 barrels of whale oil produced in the Antarctic. Between 15 December 1904, and 31 December 1905, 183 whales were shot — 149 humpback, 16 fin, 11 blue, and 7 right whales. The sale of 5,488 barrels of oil produced $69,886, and of baleen $13,372. Whale stocks were so abundant all the way in to Cumberland Bay that production was merely restricted by the capacity of the boiler and lack of barrels. The figure of 31.5 barrels per whale suggests an astonishing wastage. Had the oil been extracted from every part of the whale, the try-out would have been three times as great. For the following season, 1905-6, an additional whale catcher was purchased, and the number of cookers at the station was increased from twelve to twenty-four.

A hitherto unknown report from C. A. Larsen of 1 February 1906, differs so greatly from previous figures for the first Antarctic catching, that it is reproduced in its entirety in Table 47 (see Appendix): it will be seen that whales were also caught during the Antarctic winter (not only that year, but also in subsequent years), whereas it has always been maintained that it was impossible to catch whales during this period. From this it may be concluded that not all whales migrated north to cross the waters in winter, but that some of them must have remained in the Antarctic for the entire year. The table also shows that catching was based almost entirely on humpback (80 per cent of the total number), the species that kept closest to land and could be most easily caught.

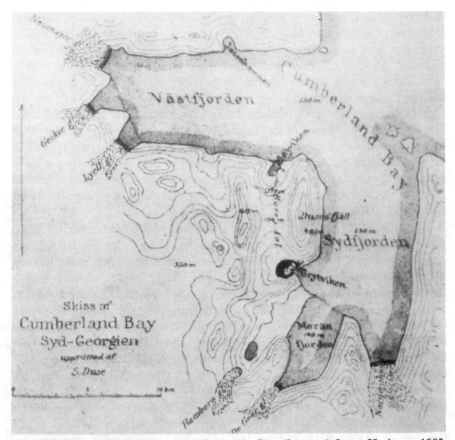

28. The first map of Cumberland Bay with Grytviken and Jason Harbour, 1905, after the whaling had started.

Gunners reported that they could approach right up to the humpback and merely had to drop the harpoon in it. The humpback appears to have been monogamous, for which reason gunners called it the pair whale; if one of the couple was caught, the other would refuse to leave it and would prove an easy prey.

During the ten years, 1904-14, when Larsen was in charge, the humpback accounted for four-fifths of the raw material, catches of this species reaching a peak in 1910-11 with 1,527. Once again, as so often before, we find that the obvious lesson had not been learnt and the same story was repeated as in other whaling grounds : after a few years of intense catching the humpback vanished. From 1916 on it was of subordinate importance. Based on the quantities of predominant species, total Antarctic catching can be divided into the following five periods : the humpback period, from 1904 to c. 1912; the blue whale period, from c. 1913 to c. 1937; the fin whale period from c. 1937 to 1965; the sei

whale period from *c.* 1965 to 1975; and the minke whale period up to
the present. In Grytviken, due to the fin whale alone it was possible to
maintain profitable catching alone until the station was closed down
in 1965. Larsen's dream of shooting right whale came true: in 1905-12
185 were accounted for, and of this number sixty-nine were shot in
1907-8, their baleen realising a sum of $54,334. Catches slumped rapidly,
however: in 1912-13 no right whales were caught, in 1913-21 a total
of twenty-nine, and since then only five specimens have been caught
from Grytviken. The 1905-6 season was very promising, producing twice
as many as in the first season — 399 whales (288 humpback) and 12,000
barrels — but the try-out was still as low as 30 barrels per whale, or 65
per BWU. Profits ran to $35,019, ensuring shareholders a dividend
of $8\frac{1}{2}$ per cent. (For the world catch of right whales, 1904-18, see
Statistical Appendix, Table 48.)

C. A. Larsen had sailed direct from Buenos Aires to South Georgia
without obtaining the permission of the Governor in Port Stanley in the
Falkland Islands, on the assumption that South Georgia was no-man's
land. The company's Board, too, had made no attempt to contact the
British authorities. The main responsibility for this rests on Larsen, and
his excuse was that he was ignorant of the island's history. This was not
the least surprising, as even the British Government was in doubt about
the sovereignty. The basis for the claim to sovereignty was that the
island had been discovered in 1675 by the Englishman ANTHONY DE LA
ROCHE, and rediscovered precisely one hundred years later by James
Cook, who landed on 17 January 1775 at three points and formally
occupied it in the name of George III, in whose honour it was named
South Georgia. But in 1904 the British Minister for the Colonies was
sufficiently uncertain of the situation to write to the Governor at Port
Stanley: "Great Britain does not seem to have formally taken possession
of the island and for some time doubt was expressed as to whether the
island was worth keeping. I think it would be best to say nothing in
answer to the question: by whom and when was the island discovered
and in what year did Great Britain take possession of it?" And the
Colonial Office replied to an enquiry submitted in 1905 by the Foreign
Office in the following terms: "The island of S. Georgia figures as a
dependency of the Falklands but our claim cannot be said to be very
strong in as much as we have never formally taken possession of it."
Whaling removed any doubt as to whether South Georgia was worth
keeping, prompting Great Britain to mobilise every conceivable argument in favour of its sovereignty both to this island and to the other
archipelagos of the western Antarctic: the South Shetland, South Orkney
and South Sandwich islands, and the adjacent continental areas.

When Ernest Swinhoe to his great surprise discovered an Argentinian
whaling station on the best site in South Georgia, he submitted a written

protest to Larsen on 28 September 1905, demanding that he should leave the island, which he personally had leased in its entirety by a contract of 1 July. Swinhoe despatched a copy of his protest to the Governor, insisting that the establishment of the whaling station had taken place with the consent of the Argentinian Government, and as part and parcel of that country's claims to sovereignty. The Governor and the British Minister in Buenos Aires informed their Government of the events that had taken place. At the time the British Government was anxious to avoid at all costs any diplomatic complications with Argentina. The Foreign Office, the Colonial Office, and the Admiralty agreed to send a frigate, the *Sappho,* on a tour of inspection to Grytviken, but the officer in command had strict orders to engage in no action that might provoke Argentina; there was to be no attempt to remove the Argentinian flag, or to hoist the Union Jack, or to engage in any form of negotiations. He was merely to take note of the situation and report back. This contrasts markedly with the traditional Norwegian version, that the officer in command of the frigate gave Larsen fifteen minutes to strike the Norwegian flag, otherwise the station would be blown up. Besides, it was not the Norwegian but the Argentinian flag which flew over the station. The *Sappho* remained in Grytviken from 1 to 5 February 1906, and her commanding officer makes no mention whatever of the flag in his report. He reports that he was very cordially received by Larsen, who supplied him with the above-mentioned detailed figures for catching.

The Pesca's directors were clearly worried that the British Government would accede to Swinhoe's protest and put a stop to whaling. Pedro Christophersen and a representative of the Argentinian Admiralty paid a visit to the British Minister in Buenos Aires and expressed their willingness to pay an acknowledgement rent for the concession they hoped to obtain from the Governor. The issue of sovereignty was never even mentioned; they were interested in one thing alone — to obtain a lease from Britain for the ground on which their station had been set up. In the subsequent dispute with Argentina on sovereignty, this provided the British with a very important argument to the effect that Argentina at that time recognised British sovereignty over the Falkland Islands Dependencies. The Governor was authorised to grant the company a concession for 500 acres, and to inform the South Georgia Exploration Co. that its contract did not ensure it exclusive right to *all* whaling; it could commence whaling operations anywhere else in the island. It was debated whether payment for Pesca's concession should be in the form of a production levy or a ground rent. The first was rejected by the company, and the ground rent was fixed at £250 per annum, corresponding to $\frac{1}{2}$ per cent of the capital or $1\frac{1}{2}$ per cent of the company's presumed earnings. The contract was to be valid for twenty-one years, commencing 1 January 1906. An important argument from the Argentinian point of view was that in not demanding rent for the period prior to 1 January 1906, Great Britain had considered her sovereignty to extend from the time when the frigate visited the island. The contract obliged the company to set up two unwatched lights at the entrance to Cumberland Bay, and to carry out daily meteorological observations.

Both parties were satisfied with the contract. While the Colonial Office sharply rebuked the Governor for behaving in a manner which risked provoking a dispute with Argentina, it recorded that it was very satisfactory and very much better than might have been expected. They were very fortunate to receive £250 annually in rent for a very small portion of the island. (In expressing its satisfaction the Colonial Office uses the word *very* four times!) A time was to come when Britain would be anything but satisfied with this and other similar contracts, which merely yielded a fraction of what a 1½ per cent levy on the companies' profits would have provided. The contract was a whaling *lease* and applied to the companies operating from the shore station. A total of fourteen whaling leases were granted: nine to South Georgia, of which two were granted to the Compañía de Pesca and two to Christian Salvesen, two in South Orkney, one in South Shetland, one in Heard Island, and one in the Falkland Islands. One was also issued for Bouvet Island — but was cancelled when the island was occupied by Norway — and one for Dougherty Island, before it had been established with certainly that the island in fact did not exist. Gradually several problems arose which had not been anticipated when the first whaling lease was granted.

It could, *inter alia,* be interpreted to mean that if no operations were carried out from the station — four were closed down in 1931 — it must revert to the Crown. Companies wishing to operate from a mobile, floating factory in British territorial waters were permitted to do this by virtue of a whaling licence which had to be renewed every year. This was an automatic procedure, once it had been granted. As far as is known, twenty-four licences were granted prior to the First World War — twelve for South Shetland and Graham Land, seven for South Sandwich, and five for South Orkney. When Great Britain attempted to regulate catching by restricting the number of leases and licences, these became a highly valued and attractive security, for which one company would pay another a very high price.

A great deal has been written about South Georgia and the life of the whalers in that part of the world. It would be difficult to find any similar historical example of a country so remote and inhospitable having created such a great deal of wealth. The nearest parallel is probably the Alaskan gold rush of the 1890s. South Georgia is the northernmost of the four Antarctic archipelagos, and the largest island, covering 3,770 square kilometres, 170 kilometres long and 42 kilometres at its widest. Four-fifths of the land area is covered with eternal snow and ice, and from the mountains glaciers drop right down to the fjords where the whaling stations were situated. These were on the northeast side, which is free from ice most of the year, and where there were a number of good harbours, from Allardyce Harbour in the north to New Fortuna Bay in the south. Between them there were, at one time, six stations. Although protected on the seaward side, they would be a prey to sudden and violent winds from the mountains. On a couple of occasions avalanches partly destroyed one station, killing some of the hands. The highest mountain, Mount Paget, 3,180 metres above sea-level, is situated almost in the middle of the island. On the eastern coastal fringe the snow melts in summer, allowing tussock grass to grow, the most important vegetation on the island. Attempts have been made to grow potatoes, but the summer is too short and cold.

South Georgia is a good example of the way in which man has altered the natural fauna. The most important of these were the penguins, millions of which were encountered by the whalers all over the Antarctic. In 1911 Larsen introduced three buck reindeer and eleven does, which were let loose on the extensive Baff peninsula east of Cumberland Bay, where they thrived on the tussock grass. In the course of fifty years they had multiplied, and numbered some 4,000, despite 150 to 200 being killed off each year to provide a highly welcome change of diet. Glaciers extending right the way down to the sea on either side of the peninsula prevented the herd from spreading further afield, but in 1963 they finally succeeded in extending their domain to cover nearby Royal Bay. An air count in 1972 showed that the herd on the Baff Peninsula numbered 1,300 and that in Royal Bay 800. The substantial decrease can probably be ascribed to range degradation, mainly of the tussock grass. In February 1912 Salvesen released five reindeer near his station at Leith Harbour, but in 1918, when the herd had grown to twenty, they were all swept into the sea by an avalanche. In 1925 seven tame reindeer were released near the neighbouring station of Husvik Harbour, and these multiplied until by 1960 they numbered some 200. The above-mentioned air count showed that this herd by 1972 consisted of 800 animals. The increase can probably be ascribed to the cessation of occupancy of the three whaling stations. Between 1972 and 1976 the British Antarctic Survey ran a scientific programme on the reindeer, and a sample of 500 animals was taken from the herds. In 1911 the magistrate in South Georgia brought with him from the Falkland Islands seventeen wild upland geese, which soon made themselves very much at home. These, too, provided a tasty addition to the everyday fare. Every year several hundred live sheep were bought from the Falkland Islands, but the

29. The *Fortuna*, the first whale catcher in South Georgia, built in 1904 in Sandefjord for the Compañía Argentina de Pesca S.A.

attempt to get them to spend the winter in the open proved fruitless, and this was also true of horses and rabbits. The soil is mainly damp and cold. Rats, on the other hand, were very much at home, gorging themselves on the offal from the flensing plant and multiplying at such an ominous rate that they became a major pest. Nature adapted them to the local climate by endowing them with a long-haired thicker coat. A more complete utilisation of the raw material and modern methods have greatly helped to keep their numbers in check.

The following is a brief account, based on that of a whaler, of life in Grytviken during the first three or four years. In 1908 there were a total of seventeen buildings, and 160 men were at work. There was such an abundance of whales in the bay that boats would tow in four to seven every day, but owing to insufficient reduction capacity as many as forty whales would be lying attached to buoys, awaiting their turn. Work in the summer was from six in the morning till six in the evening, and in winter as long as there was daylight to see by. There was a steam-driven electric generator, but it was seldom used, as the precious coal had to be conserved. In between whaling there were always plenty of odd jobs to carry out, such as repair work, building, tidying up. There were no specialised trade unions — these were not started till the 1930s — and the hands had to resign themselves to being put to all sorts of tasks. Every year expeditions brought with them some forty or fifty pigs and 150 to 200 sheep, which were put out to grass during the summer and were

30.   Reindeer grazing on tussock-grass in South Georgia.

slaughtered in the autumn. The manager kept chickens, geese, ducks, and pigeons. Flowers, potatoes, and vegetables refused to grow. There was no form of entertainment for the workers, even if they had had the leisure time to enjoy it. The sea was stocked with an incredible variety of succulent fish, of which there was such abundance that a couple of hands, fishing for two hours or so, could provide dinner for the entire company. Another favourite chore was collecting penguins' eggs, which, when used for baking or in other foods, were as tasty as hens' eggs and as large as goose eggs. The general state of health was excellent. After January 1907 a resident doctor was appointed. The major hazard came with the arrival each spring of the first transport bringing the new workers, an event which was always followed by a violent epidemic of colds and influenza.

Antarctic whaling created a strange pattern of life among hundreds of families in the county of Vestfold, Norway. Every autumn, like migrant birds, thousands of men would travel south, and every spring they would return to their native land. The following winter the fruits of this joyful reunion would appear: the vicar in the parish nearest to Sandefjord holds a Norwegian national record in christenings — thirty-three on a single day, a day which also witnessed eighteen weddings! Many of the whalers never saw their families again; those who died in the Antarctic were laid to rest there. Some never found a grave, vanishing without a trace when a whale catcher went down. British population

31. Grytviken, 1909. The low promontory to the left is King Edward's Point, where the British administration was established.

figures for the Antarctic areas were first started in 1913; they record the fifty-seven deaths in South Georgia during the ten-year period 1913-22, and eight in South Shetland. These figures do not include the thirty-five who disappeared with three whale catchers or the twenty-six who perished when two factory ships went down. It would hardly be an exaggeration to put the number of persons who lost their lives in whaling operations in the Antarctic in the years 1904-22 at not less than 200. We shall return later to the lives of the whalers and the British administration of the Falkland Islands Dependencies.

The first Norwegian companies in the Antarctic

In the spring of 1905 the managers of two whaling companies in the south came to Sandefjord to buy whale catchers and equipment: these were AMANDUS ANDERSEN of the Sociedad Ballenera de Magallanes and C. A. Larsen of the Compañía Argentina de Pesca. In view of the state of whaling in the north and the price of whale oil in the world markets, their optimistic reports must have convinced Christen Christensen that prospects for profitable catching were to be found in the south, provided it could be based on the catching of rorquals. The significance of Christensen's contribution to whaling is not that he conceived the idea of modern catching methods in the Antarctic, but that he was the first to operate in those waters with a floating factory, and that he started *Norwegian* whaling there. It is hardly a coincidence that five days after the optimistic interview appeared in the local paper on 21 August

Christensen should have decided to send the floating factory *Admiralen* south. On 21 October it sailed in company with two whale catchers and a total of sixty-three hands. After calling at Buenos Aires the ships reached Port Stanley on 13 December and remained there for nine days in order to settle catching terms with the Governor. The latter granted permission for whaling round the Falkland Islands, on condition that a customs official was present, at the company's expense, and that a tax of ½ per cent of the value of the catch should be paid. When ALEX LANGE, the Norwegian expedition manager, stated that he also intended to operate off South Shetland, the Governor, to quote Lange's words, declared that he "had nothing to do with that archipelago, as it did not belong to England".

On the morning of Christmas Eve Lange reached New Island, the westernmost of the Falkland Islands. It was by then very late in the season. In the extreme east lies Port Stanley, the seat of the Governor and the Bishop, where half of the inhabitants of the islands live. In 1905 they numbered 2,009. All communication between the scattered settlements had to be carried out on horseback or by boat. The only source of livelihood was sheep breeding and the export of wool. The establishment of whaling in the islands and their dependencies initiated an economic revolution. The arrival of the whalers on New Island on Christmas Eve 1905 was little short of a sensation for the only two isolated families living there — two widows with small children who ran a sheep farm. The *Admiralen* remained at anchor for a month, until 24 January, and the two women provided abundant mutton at the ridiculous price of 8s 6d for a large, fine sheep. The result of catching was forty whales, producing some 1,000 barrels. When Lange realised that he had arrived too late to intercept the whales on their migration to the south, he sailed south and on 28 January anchored up in Admiralty Bay on the south side of King George Island, the largest of the South Shetland group. This harbour was to be one of the two most frequently used by the floating factories; the other was situated on the little island of Deception, 80 miles southwest of Admiralty Bay. Here too operations were carried out for a month, producing fifty-eight whales, twenty-four of them large blue whales, but despite this the outcome was no more than thirty-eight barrels per whale.

Owing to unfavourable weather whaling had to be suspended, and on 27 February Lange was once again back at New Island, where whaling now only brought in sei whales, producing no more than twelve barrels per animal. On 19 April 1906, the *Admiralen* left Port Stanley with a new licence for the coming season, but on different terms: instead of a tax of ½ per cent £10 was to be paid for every right whale, 10s for every sperm whale, and 5s for whales of other species; in other words, least for the rorquals, on which catching was based. Had this

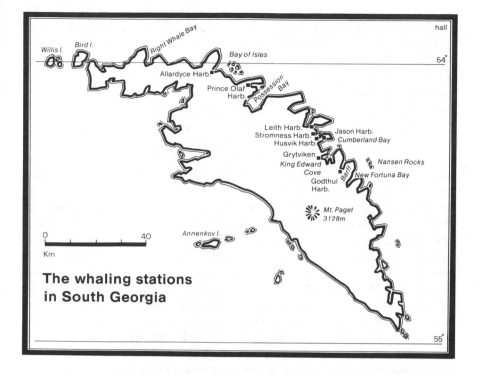

The whaling stations in South Georgia

method of assessment been applied to the year's catch, it would have meant an increase of 50 per cent. But — and this is important for the sovereignty dispute which ensued — the tax was paid and was only to be paid for whales caught in territorial waters, i.e. off the Falkland Islands. This actually amounted to a tacit acknowledgement on the part of the Governor that Great Britain, in his opinion, had no sovereignty over the Dependencies.

On 1 June the first epoch-making Norwegian whaling expedition was back in Sandefjord. Its results were ninety-seven sei, thirty-six fin, twenty-four blue, twenty-three humpback and three sperm whales, amounting to 4,128 barrels of whale oil (23 per whale, 61.6 per BWU) and 109 barrels of sperm oil. As the *Admiralen* had room enough in her hold for 5,600 barrels, full capacity had, in fact, not been achieved. The season produced a deficit of Kr.49,484. Of the whale oil, as much as 3,840 barrels comprised Quality No. 1, as only the best blubber, from whales recently shot, had been used. The company's prospects were not bright : a comparison between results in the north and in the south favoured the former. At a general meeting it was almost unanimously resolved to sell the floating factory and both whale catchers to the Compañía de Pesca or to the South Georgia Exploration Co. The latter were not in a position to raise the necessary capital to purchase, while the former, after the results achieved by the *Admiralen* in her first season, were not convinced that a floating factory had any future. Both, moreover, had been put off by the tragic loss at sea of Norway's second floating factory.

Christensen's determination to get rid of the *Admiralen* was based not on his decision to abandon Antarctic whaling completely, but on the crippling expenses of operating a steam-driven floating factory. On the voyage out and back, when no catching was taking place, it burnt coal for three months, and even though every available space on board was crammed with cheap coal from England (39*s* a ton), supplies had to be supplemented with expensive coal in South America (63*s* a ton). To avoid the latter contingency the *Admiralen* had on this occasion been accompanied by a barque, acting as coal depot as well as carrying flensing and boiling equipment. Christensen's attitude to steam-driven floating factories is also confirmed by the fact that, when a new company was started, he equipped a windjammer of 1,567 gross tons as a floating factory. This vessel was bought in England for £2,700, and the company's entire capital amounted to Kr.102,000, the cheapest company ever started for this kind of whaling. Both attempts with a sailing ship acting as a floating factory were unsuccessful. Thanks, however, to the favourable price for whale oil (£24 for No. 1, the highest price since 1884), a small profit was recorded. Even though the financial results were not encouraging, Christensen had gained valuable experience, which was further confirmed by the 1907-8 season, when the *Admiralen* was forced to abandon catching as early as 12 February, as its holds were bursting at the seams. This convinced Christensen that it was absolutely imperative to concentrate on *large* steamers, with plenty of room for boiling meat and bones. Two vessels of this kind were equipped for the 1909-10 season, and these made a bigger catch than the total recorded for all seasons from 1904 to 1909.

This experience also proved valuable to the next Norwegian company to be established, the Sandefjord Whaling Co. (Sandefjords Hvalfangerselskap A/S), of which Peder Bogen was the managing director. This company purchased the steamer *Fridtjof Nansen,* of 2,563 gross tons, for use as a floating factory. (By contrast the *Admiralen* was of 1,517 gross tons.) Great care and expense were lavished on its fitting out, which marked a considerable step forward in the development of the floating factory. Particular emphasis was placed on the vessel's ability to carry large supplies of coal and water, and in order to make the best use of the short catching season, it was possible to flense three whales simultaneously along the ship's side. The boiling capacity was 300 barrels a day, as against the *Admiralen*'s 110. Officers' and crew's quarters were greatly improved, and she was the first floating factory to carry a ship's doctor. As time went by and Bogen received no reply to his application for a licence, he made his way to London, where the Colonial Office gave him verbal permission to catch, as it would be too late to expect this to arrive in written form from the Governor. The Norwegian Legation in London was obliged to deposit a "moral guarantee" that the company was managed by "trustworthy men". Permission was also given to drop the call at Port Stanley to take on a customs inspector. As we shall see, it was a matter of some interest that this company should have been permitted to carry out whaling operations on the basis of a verbal authorisation direct from the Colonial Office, without a customs supervisor and without any knowledge of the first British Whaling Act of 5 October 1906.

This carefully prepared expedition suffered the first and one of the greatest tragedies in the history of Antarctic whaling. On Saturday, 10 November 1906, the floating factory, together with two whale catchers, was proceeding along the east coast of South Georgia in clear, still weather, looking for the entrance to Cumberland Bay, when she struck an underwater reef and broke in three parts, losing nine hands. Forty-nine survivors were picked up by the whale catchers and brought in to Larsen in Grytviken. After a few days they sailed straight back to Norway. The reef, $2\frac{1}{2}$ miles off shore, which the floating factory had struck, was not marked on any chart. It was subsequently charted and named the Fridtjof Nansen Bank. The company suffered heavy losses, as, although the ship itself was insured, it had proved impossible to obtain cover for the boiling equipment and loss of earnings. For the subsequent season a larger floating factory, with the same name, was purchased and even more effectively equipped.

The fourth of the Antarctic pioneers, and the third to make use of a floating factory, was, as we have said, Amandus Andresen of the Sociedad Ballenera de Magallanes. Together with the factory ship *Gobernador Bories* he deserves to be remembered for two reasons: he was the first person in 1906 to use Deception Bay as a station for a floating factory, a spot where a number of them subsequently operated; in the second place, he caught seventy-nine right whales in the summer of 1907 at the western mouth of the Straits of Magellan. This was the largest number ever caught from a catching vessel in a single season. In the old days of whaling five to ten whales would be considered good going. This would make it possible to send 16 tons of right whale baleen to Paris, where it would fetch £1,500-£1,600 per ton. If we also remember that Andresen was the first person to catch rorquals using modern equipment in the southern hemisphere, it is regrettable that the source material makes it impossible to accord him the place he so justly deserves among the pioneers in the history of modern whaling in the Southern Ocean.

Table 8 illustrates the development of whaling in the Antarctic as compared with the north.

Table 8. CATCH IN THE ANTARCTIC AND NORTHERN SEAS, 1904-1910

	Antarctic				Northern seas (not including East Asia)		
Season	Shore stations/ floating factories	Catchers	Whales	Barrels	Year	Catchers	Whales	Barrels
1904-5	1	1	95	2,870	1905	82	3,536	108,050
1905-6	3	5	712	19,100	1906	79	2,766	81,145
1906-7	4	8	1,112	27,719	1907	80	3,432	100,100
1907-8	7	14	2,312	60,760	1908	81	3,248	95,360
1908-9	10	21	4,125	94,506	1909	78	3,958	120,050
1909-10	13	37	6,099	157,592	1910	83	3,448	112,347

The marked decline in the north in 1906 was due to a failure in operations from Iceland and Newfoundland. In other respects the above figures refute the general assumption that whaling in the north was abandoned in favour of operations in the south. On the contrary, during the vigorous growth in the south over the first six years, whaling in the north was maintained with astonishing stability, even after catching had commenced off the coasts of Africa in 1908. In this respect whaling in the south marks no break with whaling in the north. The most important point in a comparison between the north and the south is provided not by the absolute figures in the above table, but by the relationship between the number of whales and barrels per catcher, as shown in Table 9. (Unfortunately, owing to insufficient statistical returns, it is impossible to convert this into catcher/working days or BWU.)

Table 9. WHALES AND BARRELS OF OIL PER CATCHER IN THE ANTARCTIC AND NORTHERN SEAS, 1905-1910

		Antarctic			Northern seas	
		Whales	Barrels		Whales	Barrels
	1905-6	142	3,820	1906	35	1,027
	1906-7	139	3,465	1907	43	1,251
	1907-8	165	4,340	1908	40	1,177
	1908-9	196	4,500	1909	51	1,539
	1909-10	165	4,259	1910	42	1,354
Average	1905-10	161	4,075	1906-10	42	1,270

In the Antarctic the number of whales per catcher in one season was almost four times greater and the number of barrels of whale oil three times greater than in the north. This is an important explanation of the

32. Prince Olav Harbour—the whaling station of Unilever, operated 1911-31.

explosive development that took place in the south. After two years in the north with rock-bottom whale oil prices (1904 and 1905), whaling grounds were discovered with such abundant stocks that it was possible, using the same matériel, to catch three or four times more, so that, despite low prices, not only could the increased operating expenses be covered, but there was even a margin of profit. Two events occurred which further stimulated this expansion: in 1906 the price of whale oil rose from £15 to £23, and apart from an acute slump to £20 in 1909, maintained this level for ten years. In the second place there is a great deal of evidence that reports of large catches of right whales had all the effects of the news of a gold strike. Apart from the seventy-nine caught by Andresen in 1907, ninety-four were accounted for in 1907-8 off South Georgia, and in June 1908 fourteen off the southeast coast of Africa. This ocean gold appeared to be lavishly spread over a vast area. It seemed obvious that finally the "right" whales everyone had dreamt of since the days of Sir James Clark Ross had finally been located (see Statistical Appendix, Table 48).

In the summer of 1906 five companies, with ten catchers, prepared to operate off the Falkland Islands and their dependencies, while several others planned to follow suit. Only a year and a half had elapsed since the first shot had been fired off South Georgia. This sequence of events drew Britain's attention to possessions she had forgotten, and an activity which could produce revenue. Three foreign states were engaged in whaling — Argentina, Chile, and Norway. While the question of sovereignty and whaling was settled rapidly and easily in dealing with Norway, a new and inexperienced nation in foreign policy, it still remains unsolved with the other two states, which have not even reached agreement between themselves.

Great Britain, whaling, and sovereignty in the Antarctic

No written documents are required to prove that whaling brought to a head the question of sovereignty in the Antarctic. There is a great deal of literature to support this. In the course of a few years whaling completely altered the value of these archipelagos. Yet in the spring of 1906 neither the Governor of the Falkland Islands nor the British Government knew which areas, apart from the Falkland Islands and South Georgia, it could lay claim to on historical grounds and on grounds of international law. When Argentina and Chile rejected Britain's request to submit the question to the International Court of Justice in The Hague, they were undoubtedly prompted by a feeling that the verdict of this court would go in Britain's favour; the two countries preferred a fluid situation to a final decision. Argentina's reasons for this refusal were simply that since these areas have always been Argentinian territory, the question can never be decided by an international court of law. In other respects the most important arguments adduced by these two countries against Britain were that, even though at one time in the distant past the islands might have been occupied by Britain, she had subsequently taken no effective measures to exploit her sovereignty, and had not even notified other powers of her occupation. These were two of the internationally recognised terms for the acquisition of sovereignty. In the third place, a number of British Acts and letters patent in the nineteenth century had admittedly made mention of the Falkland Islands and their dependencies, but apart from the fact that South Georgia was mentioned for the first time in 1883, the others were never referred to until now in 1905 and 1906. Argentina had never recognised Britain's occupation of the Falkland Islands in 1833 nor, for the selfsame reason, that of their dependencies. On the British side a thorough examination of the records relating to the history of the islands was set on foot, and until the results of this investigation were available, it sufficed to state that "they are commonly regarded as an English possession". The principal argument, however, was that the whaling companies' application to the British authorities for the lease of ground involved an Argentinian recognition of British sovereignty. This is the only argument in the British submission to the Tribunal in The Hague that has been asserted *in toto*. The fact

33. Leith Harbour, the whaling station of Chr. Salvesen & Co., Leith, Scotland, operated 1909-32, 1933-42, 1945-61, and by the Japanese 1963-6.

that so much stress had to be placed on this argument shows that the British themselves realised that they were on rather thin ice.

The Argentinian Government regarded the whaling company as an asset in its Antarctic interests. In April 1904 Argentinian scientists had taken over a meteorological station on Laurie Island in the South Orkney Group, and the Government purchased a boat for the sole purpose of maintaining a link between this and any other stations Argentina might establish. As far as South Georgia was concerned Britain considered the matter closed, by virtue of the applications by the Chilean and the Argentinian companies. When the contracts were signed, the Governor wrote to the Colonial Office on 31 March 1906 that "now the sovereignty is indisputably established". The question of the other three archipelagos remained. This, too, came to a head with the Norwegian query as to which areas were under British dominion, a query which proved a welcome support to Britain's claim to sovereignty. That it was tactically unwise of Norway to pose a question of this nature, as this merely drew Britain's attention to these areas and provided her with an opportunity to proclaim her sovereignty, is another matter. The process was repeated again and again, and the Norwegian Foreign Ministry admitted too late its lack of diplomatic experience. A senior member of the Foreign Ministry finally exclaimed: "I am inclined to believe that we should never have asked in London. I believe we could have started whaling around these islands without any risk. There is every reason to believe that Britain, at any rate for a number of years, would have allowed the

whalers to work undisturbed and without any tax, if they themselves
had not drawn attention to the fact that they were there and had asked
for a licence." On 16 May 1906, in answer to a Norwegian enquiry,
the British Foreign Secretary, Sir Edward Grey, replied to Norway's
Minister in London, Fridtjof Nansen, that according to information from
the Admiralty and the Colonial Office, all three archipelagos and
Graham Land were British territory. The Colonial Office wrote to the
Foreign Office to say that the British claim must apply to the whole
archipelago, not to a single island therein, otherwise it would have no
commercial value. By way of reply Norway should therefore be told
that Britain claimed the *whole* group, and the best argument to be used
was that no one had previously claimed it.

The answer raises four points of interest. In the first place, only in
1906 did Britain claim the *entire* archipelago; her reason for so doing
was not historical, but economic; the reply is not positive, in the sense
that Britain has occupied and annexed the islands, but negative, in the
sense that no one else has done so; and in the fourth place, the South
Sandwich Islands archipelago is not mentioned. The Admiralty had been
able to find no evidence to support the British claim; it was the Governor
in Port Stanley who had drawn attention to the fact that these islands
existed, and that they should be incorporated in the Dependencies, as it
was conceivable that whaling would be carried out in that area, too.
The Colonial Office could not conceive of any advantage these islands
might bestow, but if the Governor wanted them, then let him help
himself! In truth, these islands may be said to have been annexed by
Britain for the first time in 1906, and that this was done by a stroke of
the pen in the Colonial Office. In Royal Letters Patent of 21 July 1908,
it was formally established that South Georgia, South Shetland, South
Orkney, South Sandwich, and Graham Land were "a part of the British
dominions as dependencies of our colony of the Falkland Islands". The
Governor was to have the same authority over the Dependencies as over
the colony, *inter alia* "to make laws for the peace, order and good government and to make and execute grants and dispositions of any land in
the Dependencies". In accordance with this the Governor could grant
licences and concessions, and lay down the conditions for whaling. The
discussion on these resulted in an exchange of notes between Britain and
Norway, and to a spate of correspondence between all the interested
parties.

On 5 October 1906, the Governor, WILLIAM LAMOND ALLARDYCE,
issued the first "Ordinance to regulate the Whale Fishery of the Colony
of the Falkland Islands" (The Whale Fishery Ordinance, 1906). This
entitled him to (a) restrict the number of licences; (b) establish the
boundary for the area within which each licence holder had the right
to catch; and (c) settle how many whales each licence holder could

catch. In regulating whaling the British followed the first two of these guidelines, but never the third. In accordance with the Act, Alex Lange on the *Admiralen* was granted a licence from 17 October 1906 to 16 October 1907. All whales, irrespective of where, were to be regarded as caught in colonial waters. The licence fee was £25, and was valid only for a single one of the archipelagos; the expedition, moreover, had to call at Port Stanley in order to take on and maintain a customs inspector. The Norwegians protested vigorously against these last two provisions. In view of the fact that Norway acquiesced over British sovereignty in the areas involved (and has never since protested), Britain was all the more willing to accede to Norwegian demands for reasonable whaling conditions. A new Whale Fishery Ordinance of 8 August 1908 abolished the provision regarding calling at Port Stanley, while the licence was to be valid for all four whaling grounds as a whole. On the other hand, the licence fee was £100. On 6 February 1911, this was once again changed, reverting to the situation prior to 1906, i.e. one special licence for each of the four areas South Shetland and Graham Land, South Orkney, the Falkland Islands and from 22 January 1912 South Sandwich. The fee for the local licence was £100, four times as much as in 1906. Each licence entitled the holder to one floating factory and two catchers (for a further fee of £100 a third catcher was allowed). The question of a general or local licence had no real significance prior to 1911, because up till then whaling had only taken place off South Shetland. The arrangement at that time involving local licences is connected with the fact that in 1911-12 whaling round South Orkney and South Sandwich was tried for the first time. At the same time the number of licences for South Shetland, where prior to 1910 there had never been more than four floating factories, was restricted to ten. Not until the 1910-11 season were there more operating there. In South Georgia, which enjoyed a special status, no new station was established before 1909-10 after Grytviken had been set up in 1904. The others with a concession to operate there used floating factories during the first few years. By then eight concessions had been granted; a final, ninth concession was granted in 1911. Thus the early development in the Antarctic may be divided into two definite periods, 1904-8 and 1910-12.

One incident should suffice to illustrate the way in which Britain used Norwegian whaling to annex Antarctic territory and the Norwegians were simple-minded enough to allow themselves to be used for this purpose. The case in point involves Heard Island (and the small MacDonald Islands), some 250 miles southeast of Kerguelen. It is some 135 square miles in area, volcanic in origin, and almost completely covered by an icecap. It was named after the American John J. Heard, who discovered it as late as 1853. Its inshore waters abounded in seals, stocks of which had almost been exterminated on several occasions by American seal-hunters. No one had formally occupied it or considered whaling in these waters before Peder Bogen in 1908 asked the Norwegian Legation in London to investigate whether the island was British and whether he could be granted a licence to operate a floating factory there. Together, the Foreign Office, the Colonial Office, and the Admiralty concocted a plan for Bogen to acquire exclusive rights to a lease of the islands for three years at £100 per annum, and to be authorised to occupy the island on behalf of His Majesty, hoisting the British flag as a token thereof. Despite the fact that this was a tacit acknowledgement of the idea that the island was not British, and that Bogen could have commenced whaling without a British licence, Norway did not avail herself of the opportunity to do what Bogen had been asked to do for Britain. The Norwegian Foreign Ministry refused most resolutely to allow a Norwegian subject to occupy territory for Britain, but took no steps to secure the island for Norway. Despite the fact that Bogen was asked not to undertake an active occupation on behalf of Britain, the problem was solved in the following manner. The expedition included a British subject who in May 1910 undertook the act of occupation. A feeling that the occupation nevertheless had not been carried out in due and proper form, however, prompted Britain to repeat the act of occupation in 1929, once again making use of the services of Norwegians. A Norwegian whale catcher, with a Norwegian crew on board, left Cape Town, authorised to occupy the island. It appears that the occupations of 1910 and 1929 must have been forgotten, because in 1942, the island was again occupied, this time by Australian troops, and formally annexed by Australia. Norway subsequently had to be content with the somewhat insignificant Bouvet Island and Peter I Island.

Further developments in the Antarctic, 1908-1914

Owing to the loss of the *Fridtjof Nansen*, operations in 1906-7 did not achieve the success that was expected. Compared with Grytviken, the use of a floating factory had not proved encouraging. While the first expedition had registered 5,864 barrels per boat, the last had only managed 2,266. For this reason a concession for the use of a shore station in South Georgia or a licence to anchor there with a floating factory proved the most attractive proposition. Even in a protected fjord it had proved difficult to flense whales alongside in the cold weather, snowstorms, and heavy seas that were so often encountered.

The meagre progress recorded in 1906-7 was more than offset by developments in 1907-8: not only did already established companies expand, but three new ones appeared on the scene. One was the floating factory *Sobraon* of the Newfoundland Whaling Co. already mentioned.

The other two new companies were Norwegian. Tønsbergs Hvalfangeri was established on 1 October 1907. It purchased the floating factory *Bucentaur* and two older catchers from a company in North Norway for Kr.200,000, which was all that was required to equip an Antarctic expedition. The matériel, however, was in such poor condition that an older gunner revealed that the crew never imagined that they would reach their destination. They picked up their lease in Port Stanley on the same terms as the first two companies. They discovered an ideal spot on Stromness Bay, a large flat expanse with a fair amount of sand and stones, abundant fresh water, and no steep mountains capable of starting an avalanche. As most of the hands came from a small place just outside Tønsberg called Husvik, it was not surprising that this station should be named Husvik Harbour. Two miles away lay Stromness Harbour, where the Sandefjord Whaling Co. built its station, and two and a half miles further north lay Leith Harbour, where the South Georgia Company's (Salvesen's) large plant was being established. Of the six stations established in South Georgia, three in fact were situated on the little fjord, and during the years 1910-31 when all three stations were operating simultaneously, whaling operations, surpassing anything ever seen in the history of whaling, were concentrated here in a very small area.

There were incredible numbers of whales right inside the fjord, one whaler reported, but only humpbacks were taken as blue whales were so large and heavy that the available equipment was not strong enough. Of the humpback, which was large and fat, only the dorsal blubber, not the abdominal blubber, was used. There was no time for the latter. The whales' remains drifted into a place known as the Churchyard. During the first few years only the floating factory was used, and profits were greatly restricted by its capacity. Not till 1909-10 had sufficient money been earned for a shore station to be erected, in readiness for the 1911-12 season. Apart from 1913-14, Husvik Harbour had a larger production than Grytviken, and for the shareholders it proved a veritable goldmine.

The Sandefjord Whaling Co. was granted its lease from 1 January 1908, but here, too, in Stromness Harbour, a floating factory was used until 1912. This had nothing like sufficient capacity to deal with all the raw material, and the result was a fearful waste. In order to avoid this a large sailing vessel was purchased in 1910, and equipped as a meat-boiling plant. The extent of the waste was obvious when this plant produced 10,000 barrels out of the carcasses which the steamship floating factory had de-blubbered and would have scrapped. It was general at that time to attach a sailing vessel of this kind to the steam-driven floating factory, and in this way large quantities of oil were saved. Just how much more effective a shore-based station was will be seen from the

34. The Norwegian whaling station, Stromness Harbour, operated 1907-31.

fact that in 1913-14 this company's station produced just as much oil, 26,100 barrels, from 442 whales as the two floating factories had obtained from 921 whales in 1911-12. The company's books show that no dividend was declared for the first two seasons, 1906-8, but in 1909-12 60, 120, and 100 per cent respectively was declared. That a company was in a position to pay such colossal dividends during a depression in shipping could only mean that whaling was the most profitable investment. It is not possible to provide complete statistics for the decisive 1907-8 season, but we are justified in calling it decisive, in the first place because, as already mentioned, the much-sought-after right whale had finally been found, and in the second place because all available reports mentioned the tremendous numbers of whales which made their way to these islands in that year. Great stretches of ocean were discoloured with the plankton, and the whales, particularly humpbacks, were unusually fat. A 15- to 16-inch layer of blubber was not unusual, and towards the end of the season this would often be as much as 18 to 20 inches in thickness. Companies literally wallowed in whales, selecting only the best blubber and allowing the carcass, with 60 per cent of its content, to drift away. A total of 2,300 whales were caught, producing only 61,000 barrels of oil, representing $26\frac{1}{2}$ barrels on an average from a large, fat whale — an all-time low in the utilisation of the raw material and a record in waste. Some 65,000-70,000 barrels of oil, with market value of Kr.$3\frac{1}{2}$ million, were simply thrown away. The history of mankind contains several examples of a

35. Grytviken—1913, operated 1904-62, and by the Japanese 1963-5.

similar senseless destruction of nature's raw materials. In order to put a stop to this waste, and the accumulation of thousands of decaying carcasses around the beaches, one of the conditions for the leases granted to the last four companies in South Georgia in 1909-11 was that the whale should be processed in its entirety, as had already long since been done in the north. In respect of wastage the first twenty years of Antarctic whaling represent a definite retrograde step.

When catches were announced in the spring of 1908, people were seized with a veritable whaling fever. The floating factories had reached full capacity before the season was at an end. Reports from Grytviken were impressive: 846 whales, of which 69 were right whales, 27,360 barrels, gross earnings of Kr.1.5 million, net earnings Kr.0.5 million, a 49 per cent dividend. Compared with results in the north, these figures were overwhelming, as shown in Table 10.

Table 10. CATCH MATERIEL, WHALES AND OIL PRODUCTION IN THE NORTH AND SOUTH, 1907-8

	Shore stations/ floating factories	Catchers	Whales	Barrels	Whales per catcher	Barrels per catcher
North 1907	24	65	2,551	75,545	43	1,200
South 1907-8	7	14	2,321	60,760	165	4,340

The public merely considered bare figures. One of the Grytviken boats had caught more than all the eleven catchers in Spitsbergen together. So blinded were people by these figures, that they failed to consider that the richer yields of the south were to a certain extent counterbalanced by the far higher operational expenses — the three months' voyage to and from the whaling grounds, the expensive freight of coal and other provisions to the whaling grounds, and of oil from the Antarctic to Europe, higher insurance premiums, and the greater wastage of oil during the long voyage. Even so, the adventure in the south resulted in keen rivalry to obtain leases and licences. Of one of the Norwegian expedition managers who had just heard that he would be able to lease a site in South Georgia, the Governor wrote: "You should have seen him plunge his hand into his breast somewhere and produce 250 golden sovereigns at the very thought of getting a station in South Georgia subject to the C.O.'s approval. This just shows what they think of the business."

Just how important the catching of humpbacks was off South Georgia is shown by the fact that of 29,016 whales accounted for between 1904-5 and 1913-14, 69 per cent were humpbacks. This species was preferred not only because it approached closer to shore, but also because it was slower and calmer in its movements, and easier to keel over when flensing. There were probably several separate stocks, each with its highly regular migration pattern, and for this reason whales of this species might be almost exterminated in one whaling ground, as off South Georgia, while they were still numerous in another, off the South Shetland coast. After fattening up and pairing off in the Antarctic summer, they would make the trek north to their breeding grounds which were mainly off the west coasts of Australia and South Africa, and off the east coast of South America. Wholesale killing in these whaling grounds from 1908 on may have been one of the reasons why stocks off South Georgia declined so drastically. As it was feared that the humpback might be entirely exterminated — in 1917-18 only 131 were caught in the Antarctic — the Governor banned humpback catching as from the 1918-19 season. Dispensation from this ban was probably given, because in 1918-21 a couple of hundred were accounted for every season, but when the ban became total in 1921-2, only nine were shot. As the whalers considered that stocks had been replenished during the ban, catching was once again permitted, but results proved a great disappointment. Operations from South Georgia from 1926-7 to 1938-9 accounted for only 360 humpbacks, as compared with 3,986 other whales. One reason also why so few whales of this species were caught in pelagic whaling from 1922 to 1934 was the abundance of blue whales, which gunners preferred, as it ensured them a larger bonus per animal. In the latter half of the 1930s considerable numbers of humpbacks were found at various spots along the ice barrier, and once again a large number were caught (maximum 4,477 in 1936-7). With the London Agreement of 1938 the humpback was protected in the Antarctic. The 883 registered for 1938-9 were all shot by the Japanese, who had not signed this convention.

Favourable reports in 1907-8 resulted not only in increased efforts in the "old" whaling grounds, but also in an intensive search for new ones, and a fourth nation, Great Britain, made her debut in the south. This was in 1908, in the form of the firm of Chr. Salvesen & Co. of Leith, and in 1911 they were joined by Irvin & Johnson of North Shields. Both companies were granted a lease for a shore station in South Georgia. While the latter firm, to which we shall return later, sold its station after eight years to Lever Bros., Salvesen operated their station, with brief interruptions, for fifty years. Formally, the station was owned and operated by Salvesen's affiliate, the South Georgia Co., but all whaling undertaken by the company is known by the name of Salvesen, and for the sake of brevity this is the name we shall use.

Salvesen's share of modern whaling is the largest that has fallen to any single firm. Although in name a public company, it was in reality a purely personal concern owned by four or five members of the family. No other company has operated so widely — off Iceland, the Faroes, the Shetlands, the Falkland Islands, South Georgia, South Africa, and Madagascar. Subsequently the waters off Newfoundland–Labrador, Peru, and in the Norwegian Sea were tried, as well as round the Antarctic continent using floating factories. Christian Salvesen's son, Theodore Emile Salvesen, was the driving force behind this tremendous expansion. From the very start in northern waters Salvesen insisted on complete exploitation of the whale, an outcome, no doubt, of the innate Scottish sense of thrift and dislike of waste, and Leith Harbour from the outset was equipped with machinery which, to the extent contemporary technology made it possible, reduced the *entire* whale to marketable products. He constantly appealed to the British authorities to introduce more stringent regulations to ensure this, and to ensure stricter regulation of catching.

Under his son, Captain HAROLD KEITH SALVESEN, the firm's whaling interests acquired impressive dimensions. Entering the firm in 1928, for twenty years he remained one of the outstanding personalities of international whaling. He was particularly interested in the technical aspect of whaling, always ready to test new apparatus for improving the extraction of oil and the production of by-products, particularly meat meal. No whaling company owner was better acquainted with conditions on the whaling grounds than he, thanks to constant and protracted visits to Leith Harbour and the floating factories. Although the company was British — the owners preferred to call it Scottish — like all other foreign

36. Theodore E. Salvesen.   37. Harold K. Salvesen.

companies it was of great economic importance to Norway, and in particular to the county of Vestfold. The floating factories were generally laid up during the summer, and many hundreds of Norwegians — between about 1925 and 1935 as many as 1,200 — were signed on for the floating factories and whale catchers or sent on board transport vessels to Leith Harbour. We shall subsequently discover the reason why from the latter half of the 1930s more and more British crew were being employed.

Salvesen had his first application in 1907 for a lease in South Georgia rejected; two Norwegian companies had been granted a lease that year, and the Colonial Office declared that it would, at any rate for the present, not issue any more. However, if Salvesen was prepared to start catching from the Falkland Islands, the Colonial Office would consider a fresh application favourably. All the equipment at the station in Iceland was dismantled, and despatched to New Island, where the *Admiralen* had been lying; in 1908 the station was erected, and a slipway was also built for hauling up and repairing catchers. On 16 January 1909, Salvesen's first whale in the southern hemisphere was caught. The result of the first season, which was reckoned to conclude on 30 August, was 226 whales (1 blue, 1 fin, 9 humpback, 215 sei), which produced 3,850 barrels of oil and 3,081 sacks of meat and bone meal. This was hardly enough to yield a profit, and in this respect the firm's debut in Antarctic whaling was a disappointment, although the Governor recorded his satisfaction that "a well-known and prosperous *British* firm" had established a permanent whaling station.

The 1909-10 season was very promising, but 1910-11 witnessed a drastic slump, while the two seasons 1911-13 were disastrous, with 103 and 87 whales respectively accounted for, and as most of these were sei, the result must have been a very considerable deficit. Admittedly, 1914-15 showed an improvement, but obviously there was no basis for permanent and profitable whaling based on the Falkland Islands, and for this reason the station was closed down and the plant transferred to Leith Harbour. Never subsequently have the Falkland Islands provided a base for whaling. In connection with negotiations in 1948 for a renewal of Salvesen's leases in South Georgia, the Colonial Office exercised certain pressure on Salvesen, to persuade them to resume catching from New Island. But on 30 July Salvesen turned down the suggestion : wages, the price of materials, import and export dues had all risen so steeply that profitable operations would have proved impossible.

Despite the fact that the firm was British, it appears to have had certain difficulties in obtaining a lease. But the Colonial Office did not renege on its promise of 1907, granting Salvesen a lease on 25 October 1909, for land on which to build the Leith Harbour station. With the consent of the Colonial Office Salvesen was also allowed to take over a Norwegian lease in Allardyce Harbour. However, as the Colonial Office maintained the principle of not granting more than one concession to any particular company, the South Georgia Company was established on 27 July 1909, with a view to taking over the above-mentioned lease. This was a purely formal arrangement to ensure that Salvesen had legal access to whaling from Leith Harbour, operating as well with the two catchers which the Allardyce Harbour lease entitled him to. The station there was never built. The Compañía de Pesca had also obtained a similar arrangement for a second lease of Jason Harbour, where likewise no station was ever built. The purpose of securing two leases was also to keep potential rivals out.

The site for the Leith Harbour station on the north side of Stromness Bay was not as favourable as for the other two stations. The patch of flat ground was not particularly large, and behind the factory buildings the cliffs rose sheer. In July 1911 the guano factory and the meat meal boiling plant were almost completely destroyed by an avalanche, and several other buildings were swept into the sea. In August 1929 an avalanche crushed several houses, killing three hands. The work of erecting the station was much delayed by a strike of thirty or forty workers, who were sent home after three months. Probably the men considered that they had been employed to catch whales and not build houses. This was one of the very first labour conflicts in the history of whaling, but it was not to be the last. Owing to the strike it took some time before whaling could start, but in view of this the results were nevertheless good — 527 whales and 15,314 barrels of oil. Earnings were £52,680, giving an overall working deficit of £3,342. By the end of 1910 the station had cost £117,656, twice as much as any other station, but then, in addition to pressure boilers for the blubber, it had thirty-six meat and bone boilers, and a guano factory with four driers. Owing to the damage caused in 1911, the production of the latter did not achieve full capacity before 1911-12, with 22,758 sacks, and in each of the two subsequent seasons it reached 30,000. Production at Grytviken was only 3,792 and 6,066 sacks. Theodore Salvesen's insistence on full exploitation of the whale was, in fact, a reality not just empty words, but he doubted whether it was worthwhile. The cost of manufacturing and transporting the product was high; in 1912 the price was some 12s. per sack containing 10-12 per cent nitrogen and 17-23 per cent phosphate.

The next season, 1910-11, proved a brilliant one. The tremendous total of 1,683 whales accounted for, almost all humpbacks, producing 49,000 barrels (Grytviken 55,444), or 72 blue whale units (BWU). Salvesens were now the largest whaling concern in the world, with a catch of 2,350 whales and a production of 66,501 barrels of oil and some 20,000 sacks of meal. The profits for the South Georgia company were £35,142. It was decided to extend the station considerably and seven new whale catchers were ordered in 1912. In all, Salvesen had fifteen new whale catchers built in 1909-12. The improved boiling equipment yielded remarkable results in 1912-13, with 92 barrels per BWU, undoubtedly more than any other station had managed till then. Predictably, the large catches of humpbacks were soon to come to an end : in 1911-12 their numbers slumped to 1,202, in 1913-14 to 89. To make up for this, catches of blue whales during these seasons rose from 29 to 204, and of fin whales from 125 to 329.

Starting with the 1911-12 season, the parent firm of Chr. Salvesen & Co. was granted a licence for two floating factories in South Shetland and Graham Land. This meant, in fact, that the firm had four licences; no other company held so many. With these licences the maximum of ten licences designated for this area had been reached. Two older boats, the *Neko* of 3,576 gross tons and the *Horatio* of 3,239 gross tons, were converted at the Framnæs shipbuilding yard in Sandefjord, the former specially for the boiling of blubber, the latter for the cooking of meat. The idea was that the two floating factories should sail in company, and the latter should take over the whale carcasses from the former. The Governor raised an objection to this, pointing out that it was not permitted to use a special meat-boiling factory ship without a separate licence. At the same time he protested at the use of an extra boat to tow the whale to the floating factory. He also threatened to impose a fine of £300 for every whale that was towed, together with the confiscation of oil and loss of the licence, and the net result was that the tug had to be sent back to New Island.

The floating factories can hardly be said to have got off to a flying start: on board one the coal caught fire, and she had to return to England, while the other encountered so much ice that she did not reach Deception until 11 December. The names Salvesen Cove and Theodore Island in Graham Land recall the geological expeditions Salvesen financed in 1913-14 in a search for coal and minerals. He financed similar expeditions to South Georgia in 1911-12 and to South Shetland in 1913-14. All these investigations proved fruitless. Operations with the floating factory *Horatio* were likewise unsuccessful: an attempt at catching off Madagascar was a total failure, involving the company in such considerable expenses that a deficit was recorded both for 1911-12 and 1912-13. The 1914-15 season, by contrast, marked a decisive change in fortune, with a total of 1,839 whales, 92,459 barrels, and 43,555 sacks, surpassing by far anything till then produced by a single firm in the Southern Ocean. The large number of blue whales in Leith Harbour, 636, was remarkable; this was made possible by using larger and more powerful catchers, capable of hunting large whales further out to sea. The following season, 1915-16, proved still more overwhelming, but this rightly belongs to the history of whaling during the First World War, which in several ways changed the development that might have taken place in peacetime. Ill-luck still pursued the floating factory *Horatio*: as she lay at anchor in Leith Harbour, fire broke out on 11 March 1916, completely destroying the ship and 11,000 barrels of oil.

Bryde & Dahls Hvalfangerselskab, of Sandefjord, had purchased the South Georgia Exploration Company's lease in South Georgia for £1,500. In 1909 they secured a lease on a 114-acre site in Godthul Harbour, seven miles south of Grytviken, for a station. No shore station, however, was ever built by this company: instead, use was made exclusively of floating factories, anchored up in the fjord. Thor Dahl was sole proprietor of the company, a unique phenomenon in Antarctic whaling. A lease in South Georgia was such a valuable asset that although the capital of the company was Kr.400,000, Dahl was compelled in 1911 to pay Kr.132,600 for one-eighth, i.e. at a premium of 265 per cent. No company ever started operations with such a decrepit factory — a thirty-eight-year-old sailing vessel of 1,042 gross tons. On her return home in 1908-9 after her first season, with a cargo of 3,400 barrels, the company's liquidity was so poor that the oil had to be pledged to cover a loan in the bank in order to enable the crew to be paid their wages and bonus. This company, which was to be Norway's largest and one of the biggest in the world, may in all truth be said to have had to a difficult start, but in a country where capital was as hard to come by as it was in Norway, however, this was typical of many shipping and whaling companies. For the 1910-11 season a steamer of 4,356 gross tons was acquired, the largest floating factory till then. It justified its existence with a record catch producing 19,000 barrels, in addition to 2,300 barrels produced by the meat-boiling plant. This, a full load, was acomplished in two months and twenty days.

All the companies, in fact, enjoyed such a good season that year that their earnings aroused considerable attention (see Statistical Appendix, Table 49). Expedition managers and whalers pocketed earnings far in excess of what was usual in shipping and industry. An expedition manager with a fixed annual income of Kr.3,000 and a bonus of Kr.2 per barrel earned during the five years 1910-15 a total income of Kr.250,000. Whaling was certainly a lucrative business! The 1910-11 season was the last big season for humpbacks, with as many as 6,197 being caught from the South Georgia stations alone. The weather that year was quite unusual : while February-April were stormy and catching was impossible, in June, at the height of the Antarctic winter, the weather proved ideal for catching, with whale stocks plentiful. It was obvious that not *all* whales migrated north in winter, as generally assumed.

The last Norwegian company to be granted a lease in South Georgia was Ocean A/S of Larvik. This meant that all three whaling towns in Vestfold were represented in the island. The lease was valid from 1 October 1909, for a site in New Fortuna Bay, four miles south of Godthul Harbour, which was then the southernmost of all stations. As the terms of the licence enjoined processing every part of the whale, it was impossible to operate with a floating factory : a shore station had to be erected immediately, with a blubber, meat, and bone boiling plant and a guano factory. This company's first two seasons proved astonishingly favourable, with a total of 1,281 whales, 43,000 barrels of oil, and 14,400 sacks of guano, which meant that after only two seasons dividends of 30 per cent and 100 per cent respectively could be declared — a unique performance. Almost as remarkable was the very high number of barrels per whale, 43.6, whereas for the Antarctic as a whole the figure was 31.7 and for South Georgia 32.5. The low average of the latter can be accounted for by the fact that Grytviken, with the biggest production, registered as little as 29.7 barrels per whale that year. New Fortuna Bay was the first station in South Georgia to be closed down; after operating for eleven years, the company merged with the Sandefjord Whaling Co., all the equipment was dismantled and transferred to Stromness Harbour, where operations continued for another eleven years. During the eleven years A/S Ocean existed, shareholders received dividends of 450 per cent of the face value of their shares, but even so it was not one of the companies to declare the highest dividends.

When the Colonial Office had granted the three leases in 1909, making a total of eight in South Georgia, it decided that, in order to preserve whale stocks, no more should be granted. Of the eight, six had gone to foreign companies. Nevertheless, despite considerable misgivings, the Colonial Office granted a ninth in 1911; it did so out of national considerations in order to support British whaling. The lease was granted to the fisheries firm of Richard Irvin & Sons of North Shields, one of the largest firms in this business, but one which had never engaged in whaling and which, owing to its lack of experience, was almost totally ruined after three seasons. Like Salvesen, this was a family concern, whose proprietors were Richard Irvin and his four sons. One of them, JOHN H. IRVIN, ran the business in England; another, GEORGE IRVIN, directed it in South Africa, where in 1903 he established the African Fishing & Trading Co. in Cape Town. In 1909 he went into partnership with CHARLES OCEAN JOHNSON, a Swede who had emigrated to Durban in 1897 and started trawl fishing. Together, these two founded the firm of Irvin & Johnson Ltd., which became the most important fisheries enterprise in South Africa. Apart from fishing, Johnson had also engaged in seal trapping round the Prince Edward Islands for his company the Southern Sealing Co. In 1911 this merged with the Southern Whaling & Sealing Co. which Irvin had established in North Shields with a view to adding whaling and sealing to the firm's fishing interests, and it was this company which was granted a licence, valid from 1 July 1911 in South Georgia, for Prince Olav Harbour, 30 miles northwest of Leith Harbour, which was to be the northernmost of the stations in that area.

In 1911-16 a floating factory was used. This incorporated two innovations; firstly, it was equipped for wireless telegraphy, and secondly, as already mentioned, two of its whale catchers were among the first seagoing ships in the world powered with diesel engines. That these engines had to be replaced with steam engines after two seasons is another matter. With the aid of the floating factory one of the many attempts to utilise the matériel all the year round, operating in the Antarctic in summer and off the coast of Africa in winter, was undertaken. The attempt, however, failed to cover the extra running expenses. This company also operated from three shore-based stations in South Africa, but the main base was Prince Olav Harbour, where the station was all set to operate in the autumn of 1916, at about the same time that the floating factory foundered on her way south. In part because of poor administration, catching results and the financial situation were both poor : the number of barrels of oil and sacks of guano was in fact less than half that of the other stations. Every year Irvin would write desperate letters to the Colonial Office pointing out that bankruptcy threatened unless improved lease terms could be granted, as well as permission to use more whale catchers and an extra factory. By 1915 losses amounted to £50,000, the unfortunate experiment with diesel engines had cost £10,000, and the entire capital of £90,000 had been consumed. The Colonial Office was of the opinion that failure was due to concentrating more on whaling off the coast of Africa than round South Georgia. After leasing the Stromness Harbour station and two whale catchers in 1917-19 for £14,000 annually, the company struck its best bargain when Lever Bros., in the autumn of 1919, bought up all the shares in the Southern Whaling & Sealing Co for four times as much (£4) as the face value of the shares (£1). The station in Prince Olav Harbour operated right up to 1930, when it was closed down and subsequently sold to Salvesen, who transferred some of the particularly valuable plant to Leith Harbour. This, however, did not mean the end of Irvin & Johnson's whaling.

The 1909-10 season marks the great leap forward in the history of South Georgia whaling. Whereas in 1908-9 four catching units (shore stations and floating factories) and eight whale catchers were operating, the figures for 1909-10 were seven and seventeen respectively, and for 1910-11 ten and nineteen — three seasons which produced 48,400, 96,200, and 208,500 barrels of oil. As it appeared that after 1909 Britain was not prepared to grant any more leases in South Georgia, an outlet was found in South Shetland, where the great leap forward occurred one season later, catching units increasing from four in 1909-10 to nine in 1910-11, and whale catchers from ten to twenty-two, while comparative figures for 1911-12 were respectively ten and thirty. Whale oil production in 1909-12 came to 41,000, 93,600, and 148,700 barrels. As the quota of licences in this case was reached in 1910, a fresh outlet was once again sought, this time to South Orkney, but to a far larger extent. The first attempt made here was carried out in 1911-12 by a floating factory operating with two catchers, while in the following season three factories operated with six catchers, production for 1911-13 being 7,000, 26,000, and 21,750 barrels. An attempt at operating around South Sandwich in 1911-12 proved a total failure — twenty-eight whales and 1,000 barrels was the meagre result — and the attempt was never repeated. That expansion in the Antarctic should for the time being have come to a halt in 1910-12 with twenty-two catching units was due to the fact that Britain, by prudently restricting catching, put a stop to further development. As it was no longer possible to set up in the Antarctic, interest concentrated on Africa, where whaling reached its zenith in 1912-13. In both these whaling grounds the culmination of the humpback period in 1910-11 has a significant bearing on developments. In the following season blue and fin whale catching started in earnest. This demanded the introduction of more powerful and speedier catchers, extended hunting, longer and heavier towing, and sturdier equipment. This changeover took a certain amount of time and required more capital. The bulk of the old equipment could be transferred to Africa, where almost all whaling involved humpbacks.

Space does not permit an historical account of every single company. (For details the reader is referred to the Norwegian edition, Vol. 2, pp. 380-409.) As the five new companies that arrived on the scene in 1908-10 were all Norwegian, such details belong essentially to Norwegian history. They all appeared at the right moment, and were able to reap the full benefits of the outstanding 1910-11 season, when nothing seemed to go wrong — there was fine weather, plenty of feed, and abundant stocks of whales, while oil fetched good, stable prices. The seven former Norwegian companies declared a dividend ranging from 25 to 120 per cent, the two non-Norwegian 80 and 100 per cent, while the five new companies, after only one season, declared dividends of between 6½ and 50 per cent. For the first time the number of whales caught exceeded 10,000, while production was 310,000 barrels, more than twice as much as in the preceding season. A licence for South Shetland was sold for Kr.225,000, while Kr.65,000 was paid for a one-season licence transfer. Norwegian shipbuilding yards were unable to convert boats to floating factories in time or to supply whale catchers speedily enough. The largest yard turned out a new catcher every five weeks for three years running, and British yards, too, started building whale catchers during these years.

A brief mention should be made of the new Norwegian companies, as they had a bearing on the general development. Hvalfangerselskabet Hektor A/S, of Tønsberg, subsequently operating under the name of Hector Whaling Ltd. of London, was established in 1910 with the relatively large capital sum of Kr.1.75 million. This sum, which proved no problem to raise, was necessary in order to utilise the licence the company had acquired for setting up a shore station on Deception, where otherwise only floating factories were operating. This licence was one of the two awarded outside South Georgia. The other was granted in 1920 for a shore station in South Orkney, a station that was never actually built. Apart from its concession in Deception, the company acquired a licence for South Orkney, and on purchasing another company in 1914 it was also in a position to utilise the latter's concession for South Shetland. The terms for the Deception licence were the same as for South Georgia — twenty-one years (as from 1 October 1911) and £250 annually. Apart from the exclusive right to a shore station, the company was granted a licence to operate a floating factory with two catchers, and the right to utilise, free of charge, the de-blubbered whale carcasses which were strewn about the beachers, decomposing. It was intended that the new factory ship, the *Hektoria,* of 5,003 gross tons,

38. The bay at Deception Island in the South Shetland group. For twenty years
this was the main centre of Antarctic whaling.

the largest in the Antarctic, would boil the blubber, while the shore
station would deal with the meat and bones, as well as producing guano.
Production for the time being, however, never attained any sizeable
proportions, because the shore station never became fully operative
until after the war. For the 1914-15 season another large floating
factory was required, and the company that year had a total production
of 55,830 barrels, a figure only exceeded by Salvesen out of all the
companies in the Antarctic.

The years 1911 and 1912 witnessed the ultimate extension — prior
to pelagic whaling — of the Antarctic area operation to South Orkney
and South Sandwich. South Orkney is a cluster of islands 400 nautical
miles southwest of South Georgia, of which the largest is Coronation
Island, with an area of 340 square kilometres, one-seventh of South
Georgia's. On almost all sides these islands' sheer cliffs rise from the
sea and are mainly covered with permanent ice. Although they are
situated further north than South Shetland, their climate is far more
polar in character, as they are influenced by the annual freeze-up in the
Weddell Sea and can only be reached by ship for three or four months
of the year. It would be impossible to rely on a catching season of more
than two and a half to three months. This island had been discovered
in 1821 by the Englishman GEORGE POWELL and the American
NATHANIEL BROWN, but it was not until the arrival of the first whalers
that the islands were explored and charted. Norwegian names abound
— Norway Fjord, Tønsberg Fjord, Sandefjord, Ellefsen Harbour, Borge

Harbour, Signy Island, Fredriksen Island, Jebsen Rocks, etc. Many of these names are still to be found on British maps and charts, but many have been replaced by English names. Whaling conditions here were the most difficult so far encountered; after two unsuccessful attempts a floating factory eventually succeeded in 1912 in penetrating the pack-ice and reaching the shore. Owing to the brief time available the catch was a small one, but it was established that there were such abundant stocks of large blue and fin whales and such good anchorage, besides access to fresh water, that late in 1912 four floating factories set off for South Orkney. One of them foundered on 4 February 1913; the other three returned in 1913-14, but results were so poor that only one remained in 1914-15, finally achieving the most successful results in these whaling grounds — 381 whales and 14,000 barrels. The dazzling freight rates offered during the First World War proved more tempting than whaling, and all the factory ships that had operated in South Orkney were committed to ordinary cargo transport; one and all were torpedoed. Neither the vessels nor the companies survived the war. The net results of the South Orkney interlude were as shown in Table 11.

Table 11. SOUTH ORKNEY CATCH, 1911-1915

Season	Floating factories	Catchers	Blue	Fin	Humpback	Others	Total	Barrels
1911-12	1	2	67	67	114		248	7,000
1912-13	4	8	199	442	138		779	31,200
1913-14	3	6	29	480	109	3	621	21,750
1914-15	1	3	94	275	10	2	381	14,000
Total			389	1,264	371	5	2,029	73,950

Whaling off South Orkney would have been little more than an episode had it not been of major importance in three particular ways: it proved that it was possible to operate in the pack-ice (pelagic whaling), it put the idea of the slipway into practice, and it provided a great deal of valuable information on the relationship between ice on the one hand and plankton and whale stocks on the other. Two interesting accounts of this have survived. One is that of the gunner PETTER SØRLLE, who invented the slipway. When the floating factory arrived on 20 November 1912, the islands were so blocked by ice that it was impossible to gain the shore before 1 January. To avoid unnecessary waste of time they started catching along the ice barrier, making in effect the first attempt at pelagic catching or ice catching in the Antarctic. They actually succeeded in shooting and flensing a number of whales and producing some 2,000 barrels before the floating factory was able to reach harbour, an event of which the consequences proved so significant that it is surprising that it has received so little attention in the history of whaling.

Masses of whales played along the ship's sides, filling the air with their blowing, but only a few could be caught. "That was when I conceived the idea of building a permanent slipway in the stern of the vessel. I had a model made, but put it aside for several years while I was catching from the shore station in South Georgia and where it was not necessary."

The other account comes from WILLIAM MOYES, the Government representative and customs officer in South Orkney, who spent the entire 1912-13 season there. (His report appears as an appendix to the Governor's letter to the Colonial Office on 11 April 1913.) He relates that the floating factory he was on left Port Stanley on 17 November and reached the pack-ice two days later. However, it proved impossible to go any closer to the islands than 130 miles, whereupon they turned and proceeded to Staten Island (near Cape Horn) in order to water, returning to the ice on 1 December and working their way along the ice for a whole week without finding an opening. As time was running out the Captain decided on 12 December to catch a number of whales to see whether it would be possible to flense them alongside in the open sea, as lying alongside a solid wall of pack-ice was almost the same as lying alongside land. A blue whale and a rorqual were placed by the ship's side, and the blubber was removed just as easily as though the boat had been lying in a sheltered harbour, and it was easy to see that a specially equipped factory ship could reduce the whale just as effectively as an ordinary shore-based station. A factory working in the open sea of course required abundant supplies of coal and water, good condensers, and powerful flensing equipment. Boiling often had to be interrupted for days on end owing to a shortage of water, while huge whales passed close to the ship's sides. On about 1 February twenty-seven enormous, fat blue whales, measuring 93-95 ft., were caught, but these and twenty-nine fin and five humpbacks, when reduced, produced no more than 2,050 barrels. The wastage was enormous, Moyes concludes, worse than in South Shetland. The try-out corresponds to 45 barrels per BWU, about one-third of what was subsequently considered normal. On the basis of big fat blue whales of this kind it was not unusual to extract 150 to 200 barrels, while as far as is known the record stands at 305 barrels.

Conditions in the following season, 1913-14, were the complete opposite: there was no difficulty in approaching land, but less ice meant less feed and fewer and leaner whales, mainly fin. They kept well out at sea, were dry and meagre, and produced very little oil.

While operations in South Orkney had important consequences, the result of whaling in South Sandwich proved an insignificant episode, its only result being to show that weather, ice, and harbour conditions made it impossible to operate there with a floating factory. The seven islands, all of about the same size, are volcanic in origin, and several of them are active volcanoes. C. A. Larsen had visited them on a voyage of exploration from South Georgia in 1908, the first time they had been visited since 1830. The Colonial Office issued seven catching licences for the islands, but six licensees withdrew on hearing of the difficulties encountered by the seventh. The Norwegian Minister in London reported that the impression he had from the Colonial Office was that it knew nothing about the islands, and he thought it was irresponsible to issue licences for whaling grounds where chances of catching whales were unknown. The proceeds of catching in 1911-12 amounted to twenty-eight whales and 1,000 barrels. In the 1920s a great many floating factories operated near the islands.

In 1909-14 a number of "passive" factories were also at work in the Antarctic; these were not themselves engaged in catching whale, but worked at reducing the carcasses discarded by others. It is not possible to produce accurate figures to show how much more oil was extracted from the whole whale than merely from the blubber. Any comparison would presuppose that both kinds of factory had reduced the same species of whale, having the same weight and fat content. Even the ordinary conversion into blue whale units (BWU) — 1 blue whale = 2 fin whales = $2\frac{1}{2}$ humpbacks = 6 sei whales — would only give an approximate result, as the actual boiling technique may also have played some role. Even so, we do get some idea of the relationship by comparing Leith Harbour and Husvik Harbour in 1912-13, where total exploitation of the whale was practised, with Grytviken, which only reduced the blubber (see Table 12).

Table 12. CATCH AND PRODUCTION AT LEITH HARBOUR, HUSVIK HARBOUR AND GRYTVIKEN, 1912-13

	Blue	Fin	Hump-back	Total	Barrels	Barrels per whale	Total BWU	Barrels per BWU
Leith Harbour	58	435	525	1,018	43,781	43	485.5	90.0
Husvik Harbour	46	408	429	886	39,763	45	425.0	93.5
Grytviken	49	324	504	878	23,572	27	413.0	57.0

In the case of four factories in South Shetland in 1909-10, in what was still the humpback period, this was as low as 20.5 barrels per whale, or 51.25 per BWU. In the 1912-14 seasons humpbacks were a mere 20 per cent and blue whales 30 per cent of the catch, and this brought the figures up to 41 barrels per whale for the ten Norwegian floating factories, and in terms of BWU the figure for 1912-13 was 62, and for 1913-14 65 barrels. It is not possible to decide to what extent this increase was the result of the British injunction to reduce the whole carcass. This was incumbent on all who were granted a licence from 1909. On 6 May 1912 there was a ban on the shooting of calves or

females with calves, and on 28 July a minimum size was fixed for the
pressure boiler used for reducing meat and bone. These provisions *per se*
were excellent, but we do not know if they were adhered to. Older
whalers relate that even at the end of the 1920s the provisions were not
taken seriously, and there were no inspectors attached to the floating
factories before the 1930s. Factories which in 1924-9 operated pelagic
whaling without a licence had no need, of course, to abide by British
regulations.

Generally speaking, it may be assumed that about 50 per cent of the
total oil content of the whale is wasted when only the blubber is used.
It was not so much the British order as financial considerations which
led to the utilisation of all the raw material. Cheap raw materials, better
and more stable prices for whale oil, a market capable of absorbing the
entire production of all qualities — these were the factors that led to
the strange form of whaling which consisted of purchasing de-blubbered
carcasses. The idea is said to have come from the Compañía de Pesca's
representative in Norway, who was aware of the tremendous waste in
Grytviken, and realised that good money was being thrown away. In
1909 he established a company based on a sailing ship as a floating
factory for boiling carcasses, and concluded a contract for four years
for £1 for every de-blubbered carcass in Grytviken. This proved good
business: during the four seasons 1909-13 the production amounted
to 21,500 barrels of oil and an unknown quantity of guano. During the
period 1909-16, four sailing vessels and a one-time steam-driven factory
ship were equipped for boiling carcasses, and these extracted 51,350
barrels of oil and some 3,000 tons of guano at South Georgia and South
Shetland. If we calculate nine barrels on an average per carcass, the oil
represents 5,000 to 6,000 carcasses, or about one-half of the number
of whales caught at Grytviken alone. At the start of the 1912 season
the magistrates estimated that there were some 6,000 carcasses lying
around on the beach at Deception. At a conservative estimate one comes
to the conclusion that during the first twelve years of Antarctic whaling
approximately one-fifth of the oil content of discarded carcasses had
been utilised. This means that during this period some 200,000 barrels of
oil had been wasted. How much has subsequently been wasted it is
impossible to calculate. During the First World War the order for full
exploitation was abolished, with an eye to speedy acquisition of oil for
the production of glycerine for explosives. The charge of senseless waste
has been levelled at the Norwegians in particular, but the company
which started Antarctic whaling, discarded the most carcasses, and
waited longest to exploit the whole carcass was not Norwegian but
Argentinian. And it was the Norwegians who took the step of introducing special factory ships to extract the oil from carcasses discarded by
others.

39. The whaling station at Kerguelen, built 1908.

One of the whaling grounds in the Southern Ocean which was explored by Norwegian whalers during this period was Kerguelen (Desolation Land), named after its French discoverer (1772). This island, 5,000 square kilometres in area, was officially annexed by France in 1893. The climate is highly unpleasant, with violent storms, and rain for some 300 days of the year. The coast is heavily indented, and the fjords afford good shelter for ships. The island had been frequently visited by sealers, but no one had plans of starting whaling there before a Norwegian company, A/S Kerguelen, was granted a licence in 1908. The expedition that set out was said to be the best equipped that had ever left Norway's shores. The two new whale catchers were the largest constructed till then. The shore station was an imposing structure, from which whaling could commence in October 1908. The licence gave the right both to whaling and to sealing (sea elephants). While the former proved a disappointment, the latter yielded an excellent harvest. Whaling was therefore abandoned in 1911, while sealing continued until 1914. The best year was 1911, with 10,680 barrels of seal oil, while 1912 recorded 6,480, but the 1913 and 1914 seasons resulted in a major deficit. The licence and the station were then sold off to Irvin & Johnson, who again concentrated on sea elephants, attaining a production of 11,700 barrels in 1920. The result of three years' Norwegian whaling off Kerguelen in 1908-11 was 442 whales (95 per cent humpback) and 13,760 barrels. Financially, this grandly planned enterprise was saved by sealing, but even this failed to turn it into a particularly remunerative business.

11

SOUTH AMERICA AND MEXICO

For practical and natural reasons, whaling off both sides of the South American continent is closely linked with whaling in the Antarctic. During its migration to and from the Antarctic Ocean the whale passed along the coasts of South America, particularly the west coast, and during the winter season it frequented the tropical waters there. The scope of whaling along the Atlantic coast of South America has been minute compared to catching on the other side of the Atlantic Ocean, off the west coast of Africa; and compared with modern whaling on both sides of the North Pacific, whaling along Chile's 4,200-kilometre-long coast and further north, off Peru, Ecuador and Mexico as well, has been at an insignificant level if measured in global terms, but with one important exception : in later years it provided one of the richest fields for the catching of sperm whale.

There were a great many pointers to the existence of whales here, from old American and British whaling expeditions, and from seamen on board windjammers carrying saltpetre from Chile to Europe. Amandus Andresen's sensational catch of right whales encouraged others to try. Christen Christensen, ever searching for new hunting grounds, sent two expeditions in 1907 to investigate. One of these was on board the sailing ship *Vesterlide,* and was skippered by Christensen's twenty-year-old son, without a doubt the youngest expedition manager in the history of whaling. The *Vesterlide* concluded her operations off South Shetland in March 1909, and proceeded via Port Stanley through the Straits of Magellan to the west coast. This passage proved a highly adventurous one, through dangerous waters with strong tidal currents and violent gusts of wind roaring down from the mountains. When Amandus Andresen in 1912 tried to repeat this voyage, using a large transport vessel, the result was one of the greatest catastrophes in the history of modern whaling. In a violent gale the ship was driven ashore and only three out of twenty-three hands were saved. One of the survivors related that most of those who died were clubbed to death and eaten by cannibal Indians. Later, some of their kayaks were found, and on board were Norwegian seaboots filled with human flesh.

The *Vesterlide* put in at San Pedro (Sur) on the southeast coast of the large island of Chiloë, as it had been said that in the Bay of Corcovado there were masses of blue whales. They caught there from 22 May to 14 October 1909, but the result was a mere thirty-seven whales, which produced 1,327 barrels. Christensen, however, was not the pioneer in

Chilean waters; this honour goes to the Norwegian skipper H. C. KORSHOLM, who for eleven years had been in command of vessels operating scheduled services and had noted the existence of whales. In 1906 he established a Chilean company, the Sociedad Ballenera y Pescadora in Valdivia, a town situated on a river some 800 kilometres south of Valparaiso. In 1907 and 1908 Korsholm made some good catches, but he lacked capital to extend his enterprise. He then came into contact with Christensen, who supplied the necessary funds. Operations were carried out both from a shore station and from a floating factory, but the returns in 1909-11 were never sufficient to ensure a profit. A Norwegian syndicate which purchased the company suffered a loss in 1912 of Kr.340,000, precisely when a surplus had been expected. The company then went into liquidation in 1913, a fate which also befell Christensen's own company after suffering a loss in 1912 of almost Kr.200,000. Norwegian whaling on the west coast of South America may therefore be said to have suffered the same fate as on the west coast of North America. Apart from a slump in stocks of whales, the causes were heavy operating expenses in view of the long and costly transport to and from Norway, poor working conditions, and protracted breaks in catching, as it proved impossible to have equipment repaired on the spot.

Amandus Andresen had earned a great deal of money as a manager of his Chilean company, and now, anxious to strike out on his own, he purchased the floating factory *Sobraon* and two whale catchers and set off on a voyage that was, in one particular way, unique: he intended to follow the whales on their outward migratory trek and back again, and to catch them wherever they happened to be at the appropriate moment. At the end of March 1914 he set off from San Pedro, sailing north along the coast of Chile, Peru, Ecuador, and Colombia, catching almost exclusively humpbacks, repeating the process when he turned and followed the migration south until, in September, he was back at his starting point. His total bag, after fourteen months' catching, from April 1914 to May 1915, was 327 whales and 12,100 barrels. The voyage had covered a distance of 8,000 nautical miles, and had provided a great deal of valuable information on stocks of whales in hitherto unknown whaling grounds. Blue, fin, and right whales were seldom encountered north of 35° S; the sperm whale moved further north, and in purely equatorial waters, there was only the humpback, which remained there throughout the summer until, in September, it migrated south. Common to all species of whale was that they were much more cautious and hard to catch while migrating south, when hunger sent them dashing off at great speed towards their pastures in the ice.

The financial collapse in the autumn of 1920 broke Andresen, who was forced to realise all his assets. After overcoming tremendous difficulties he managed to organise an expedition consisting of a small floating factory and two whale catchers in 1933, but it never set sail, and was dissolved in the chaos of world depression and the collapse of the whale oil market. Andresen, an almost forgotten pioneer of whaling in the Southern Ocean, died in Chile on 12 January 1940, in abject poverty. The Chilean state has rescued him from oblivion and raised him to the status of a national hero by erecting a memorial on his grave, on which wreaths are laid every year in memory of the fact that he was the first man to take the Chilean flag to the Antarctic.

In South America the same process was repeated as in all countries where Norwegians had commenced modern-style whaling : in time it was taken over by the local population. Both Norwegian stations were sold in 1913 and 1917 to a new Chilean company, the Sociedad Ballenera Corral S.A., which had a capital of £20,000 and was essentially the property of the Chilean businessman JORJE ANVANDTER of Valdivia (Corral is situated just south of Valdivia). The equipment from both stations was concentrated in Corral. This company succeeded in establishing whaling on a permanently remunerative basis, in some years declaring a dividend of 100 per cent, and there were several reasons for this. In the first place operations could be based on the domestic market, where the oil and guano could be sold in steadily increasing quantities. Coal mines eighty miles north of the station could provide coal at half the price of imported coal and there was an abundance of cheap native labour. In the second place, just after its establishment, the company was greatly favoured by the soaring price of oil during the First World War. Thirdly, the scope of whaling operations was kept within reasonable limits so as not to over-fish stocks of whales, ensuring a smaller but *per contra* regular annual production. This may be paralleled by the operations which have been maintained, along the same lines, around Iceland ever since 1948. During the period 1916-30 whaling from Chile produced an annual yield of 252 whales and 10,357 barrels; it reached a peak in 1926-30, with a maximum of 18,234 barrels in 1929. Four catchers were used. The season extends from November to June, with January, February and March as the best months, particularly for blue whales, which provided most of the raw material, but which showed definite signs of declining stocks. Practically all the oil went to the Chilean mines and the soap industry, and has played an important role in the national economy. During and after the Second World War practically the only species caught off the west coast of South America has been the sperm whale, and for this species these waters are among the richest in the world. There are also known to be large stocks of fin whales in these waters, but they never come close enough to the shore to be a target for coastal whaling. (For revised statistics for the catch from Chile, 1908-30, see Statistical Appendix, Table 50.)

Operations further north along the west coasts of South and Central America belong to a later epoch, apart from one season, 1913-14, when a Norwegian expedition, with a large floating factory, operated there. It left Sandefjord on 6 August 1913, in company with four whale catchers, in order to operate on an extremely expensive licence granted by the Mexican Government. Not till ninety-six days later did the expedition reach Magdalena Bay on the southwest coast of Lower California, where a shore station was built for the production of guano. The expedition carried its own doctor, and he has given an account of all the hardships they encountered — beri-beri and diphtheria, scorching heat, a long way to fresh water, spoiled provisions, smuggling and revolution, drunkenness and brawling. Despite this, by the end of May the floating factory had produced 12,000 barrels. From 20 July to 8 September operations were continued off Colombia in intolerable heat and with poor results. With 14,700 barrels on board, the floating factory passed through the Panama Canal, one of the first vessels to do so, and completed the homeward journey in 44 days, less than half the time taken on the outward journey, and saving about £2,000 for every month. In two seasons the company sustained a loss of Kr.475,000. No more whaling was undertaken, the floating factory was chartered for the transport of oil from South Georgia to Europe, and was torpedoed fully laden off Ireland on 10 August 1917. This was the end of one of the best-equipped expeditions of the age. The company was dissolved in 1920.

Along the east coast of South America old-style whaling had been carried out according to two methods — in the open sea by American and British whalers and also by natives along the coast. In the so-called La Plata area, running in a broad belt between 30° and 40° lat. S extending towards South Africa, the Americans had successfully caught right whales, and at some distance from the coasts of Brazil and Argentina, between 10° and 45° lat. S, large numbers of sperm whales had been caught. Humpback, regarded as inferior, had been left in peace. It was precisely this species, and a certain number of sperm whales, that the natives caught, using small, open boats, boiling the blubber ashore and selling the oil under the name of Bahia oil. This continued side by side with modern whaling, which commenced in 1911, but declined sharply in about 1914 to produce an annual average of about eighty-five whales, whereas ten years previously it had been around 350.

Modern whaling was started not by a Norwegian but by a local company, Deider & Brother, in Bahia (Sao Salvador), who set up a somewhat primitive shore station near the town. Using one boat the returns in the first year (1911) were so favourable that the following year witnessed

40. Lars Christensen.

the arrival of three additional companies — two Norwegian and a third which had a Norwegian management but mainly Brazilian capital. This, the Companhia de Pesca Norte do Brasil, used a floating factory the first few years, but in 1914 likewise set up a shore station. The two Norwegian companies wound up with losses in 1913 and 1914, but the Companhia de Pesca has survived right down to the present. At times, two stations were operated, and a peak was reached in 1961 with 1,083 whales and 16,275 barrels. Since then a marked decline has set in — in 1975 only three sei and fifty-seven sperm whales were caught.

In all areas adjoining the American continents the Norwegians had failed to establish permanently remunerative whaling operations: taken all round, they had lost money, and after 1920 had abandoned all operations there. These were taken over by national companies, while the Norwegians concentrated entirely on the Antarctic. Before this happened, however, they had also tried their luck around Africa and Australia, where their experience proved to be the same as in the other abovementioned whaling grounds.

Practically everywhere around the coasts of America where Norwegians pioneered we meet the name of LARS CHRISTENSEN (1884-1965), who here started his career as a whaling-ship owner, which in the 1920s culminated with his assuming control of A/S Thor Dahl,

Norway's and one of the world's largest whaling companies. He possessed the necessary means to play the part of a munificent patron, financing several expeditions to the Antarctic, in the exploration of which his name is among the greatest. In 1917 he donated to his native Sandefjord the Commander Chr. Christensen Whaling Museum, an institution complete in every respect, whose collections and library he constantly extended and added to, ensuring that it was to become a unique repository of the history of whaling and polar exploration. In 1960 he and his companies erected the magnificent whaling monument which is now one of the attractions of the town of Sandefjord. The firm of A/S Thor Dahl, which abandoned whaling in 1967, lives on today, in common with so many former whaling companies, as one of Norway's most important shipping companies.

12

THE AFRICAN INTERLUDE

In the first Norwegian history of whaling (Sigurd Risting, *Av hvalfang-stens historie*, 1922), when dealing with the years 1904-6 the author writes: "Whaling was in every respect declining, and seemed fated to come to an end in a few years." In 1905 the expansion seems to have come to an end: a measure of this is to be found in the new construction of whale catchers at Norwegian shipbuilding yards, the only ones in the world that at that time provided vessels of this kind. In 1904 twelve were built, in 1905 two, but from 1906, when expansion once again proceeded at a tremendous pace, fourteen boats were supplied, in 1907 twelve, and in 1908 twenty-one. In the three years from 1910 to 1912, when whaling achieved its greatest scope to date, twenty-three, thirty-one, and thirty-one again were built respectively, including vessels which at that time companies had started to build in other countries as well. What occurred after 1905 was in reality not so much a slump as a re-orientation from a west-east direction to a southerly direction. This expansion, which reached its peak in 1911-13, took place mainly in the Antarctic and off the coasts of Africa, with offshoots to Australia and South America. In the Antarctic there were colossal stocks of whales, sufficient to warrant a continued and growing expansion, whereas stocks of whales off the African coast were decimated so rapidly that most countries had to close down with a deficit after four or five years. In 1912 and 1913 whaling in these waters, in terms of barrels of oil, accounted for 29.1 and 31.7 per cent of the world total, but by 1915 had slumped to 11.2 per cent, and in 1917, nine years after its commencement, to 6.5 per cent. As far as Norway was concerned whaling off the coast of Africa proved a short-lived and hectic speculation, for which reason it has been called the "African interlude", putting a brake for a number of years on Antarctic whaling, where the First World War, too, provided a sharp setback. In these waters the great period of expansion dated from the 1923-4 season, when catches were approximately on the 1912-13 level.

In the oceans on both sides of South Africa were to be found the richest whaling grounds outside the Antarctic and the North Pacific. The potential of the latter had not yet been realised. In the period of catching off Africa with which we shall now be dealing — 1908 to 1916 — a total of some 33,200 whales were caught, producing some 962,000 barrels of oil. In the Antarctic, during the same period (1908-9 to 1915-16), 73,550 whales were caught, producing 2,872,000 barrels. The

smaller number of barrels per whale in African waters, as compared with
the Antarctic, was due not to less efficient exploitation of the whale,
but to the fact that African whaling was throughout essentially based on
the humpback, and this species was leaner during its winter sojourn
here than during the summer months it spent in the Antarctic; moreover,
the discrepancy increased the more advanced the season. The season of
1911-12, when whaling off the African coast assumed sizeable proportions, was in fact the last great humpback season in the Antarctic, and
the fact that the number of humpbacks in this area declined at the same
rate as off Africa, makes it obvious that there must have been some
connection. It would in fact hardly be correct to regard Africa as a
separate whaling ground; the distance from the northeasternmost stations
in Mozambique to the northwesternmost ones on the Gulf of Guinea was
6,500 nautical miles. It would be more correct to divide these whaling
grounds into four, in accordance with the positions of the shore stations:
(1) the East Coast (Mozambique); (2) the South Coast (the Cape); (3)
the West Coast (Angola) and (4) the former French Congo.

Reports from the Norwegian consuls in Cape Town and Durban of
whales sighted off the coast awakened the interest of Norwegian
whaling circles. One of those who reacted to the reports was JOHAN
BRYDE of Sandefjord: there were several factors which in his opinion
made the possibility of profitable whaling attractive — a shorter journey
to and from the whaling grounds, a more pleasant climate, cheap native
labour, and cheap coal from local mines, the fact that provisions could
be purchased cheaply on the spot, and that it would not be necessary
to transport from Norway all that was required throughout the season.
The Norwegian consul obtained a licence for him in South Africa, a
company was established, and equipment sent south. African whaling
was not, however, a consequence of the ban imposed in Finnmark;
although Bryde had ceased operating there in 1903, he had started in
the following year in Spitsbergen. He had worked there for five years,
from 1904 to 1908, and it was not until a complete slump set in that he
was forced to look round for fresh fields. The consul's licence was
procured at an opportune moment. Five years had thus elapsed from
the time Bryde terminated his Finnmark whaling until he commenced
operations off the African coast.

The South African Whaling Co. established a modest station at Bluff,
a favourite resort for the population of Durban. Here, on 23 June 1908,
the first "modern" whale off the African shore was shot. By the end of
November 106 had been accounted for, yielding 3,246 barrels. As soon
as whaling commenced, violent protests were raised against it, because
the unpleasant odour emanating from the station severely reduced the
attractions of the locality and because remains of whale carcasses towed
out from the station attracted so many sharks that people were afraid to

bathe. Since by an unlucky coincidence this was a bad fishing year, there were all the signs that the same dispute that had occurred elsewhere would now break out. The authorities ordered the station to be moved from the bay further up the coast, but permitted the slipway to remain. Here whales were loaded on to railway waggons and transported to the factory, a unique occurrence in the history of whaling. The new station was a sizeable establishment with a guano factory, obviating any complaints of carcasses and sharks.

In 1909 Bryde acquired a licence for Saldanha Bay, 50 miles northwest of Cape Town, and at the same time purchased a floating factory which operated at various points off the African coast. With two land stations, a floating factory, and seven whale catchers, this company was one of the largest at that time. Its best years were 1910-13, when an annual average of 22,725 barrels of oil was achieved, and an equal number of sacks of guano, which found a ready market among local farmers. A particularly good yield in 1910 (30,200 barrels) attracted many fresh companies to Africa. The tide turned in 1913, and after the outbreak of war difficulties with the British authorities arose, court cases involving the cancellation of supplies to Germany, an embargo on oil, etc. In 1913 the Durban station was closed down, and the one at Saldanha leased for £10,000 per annum to the Southern Whaling & Sealing Co. (Irvin & Johnson), which in 1920 purchased the entire company and started whaling on a gigantic scale. Since then no Norwegian company has started whaling in these parts of South Africa: all subsequent companies were British.

A few of the companies have a claim to special interest. One of these was A/S Viking, with its floating factory *Ambra* ("ambergris"), the first to be converted in England. This name emphasised that the intention was to catch sperm whale in the open sea; for this reason the stern frame was slightly curved, in the hope that it would be possible to haul the entire whale on board. Both this and sperm whale catching in July and August 1909 off the Azores proved a failure, and the floating factory then proceeded south along the coast of Africa until such abundant quantities of whale were discovered near Porto Alexandre, in the extreme south of Angola, that it decided to stay there, without having any formal permission from the Portuguese authorities. It proved extremely difficult to reach an agreement on licence terms, the Portuguese insisting on excessively high dues. In the end, they moderated their demands, and practically the only due remaining was a 5 per cent export tax. Five licences were granted in Angola to Norwegian companies, and one to a Portuguese company, though this was under Norwegian management.

In common with Bryde's company the *Ambra,* too, had such a successful season in 1910 that a dividend of 100 per cent was declared. The company's books are among the few to reveal the tremendous sums an expedition manager could earn in those days. According to the contract, he was guaranteed 5 per cent of net earnings, Kr.2 per barrel, and shares worth Kr.150,000. The first of these items gave him Kr.22,427, the second Kr.26,600, and the third Kr.150,000, a total of close on Kr.200,000, and in 1911 Kr.134,593, a sum which, in return for two-and-a-half years' employment, was probably the highest — taking into account the relative value of money — ever earned by an expedition manager. Peder Bogen, managing director of the company, had a salary of exactly £10,000. The large dividends declared by these two companies proved their undoing. In whaling circles Africa was now looked upon as El Dorado; while industry and shipping had difficulty in attracting capital, money poured into whaling, and the whalers poured into Africa. This wave of speculation came to an end after a few years in a major crash, a new South Sea Bubble. When the Viking company went into liquidation in 1915, the original shareholders had apparently received an average annual dividend of 20 per cent, but those who bought shares in 1912 at a rate of 200 per cent suffered a considerable loss. Whaling from the Portuguese colonies in Africa was regulated by an Act of 6 July 1913, based on the British regulations for South Georgia — a restriction on the number of catchers, a season extending from 1 May to 31 October, and a compulsion for shore stations to exploit the entire whale.

The foreign competition that the Norwegians encountered was almost entirely restricted to the Union of South Africa, where Norwegian whaling ceased for all time in 1916. When it was resumed in 1922-30, it operated in different areas. Whilst Norwegians had dominated completely during the first period, British operations in the second period were four times as large. The first British company was the Union Whaling & Fishing Co., established in Durban on 9 December 1909, by two local businessmen, the Norwegian consul JACOB J. EGELAND and ABRAHAM E. LARSEN, both of whom had emigrated from Norway. Local capital of £21,000 and a small station near Durban, with two old whale catchers, was a modest start for a company which was to prove the most important and long-lasting in South Africa. Already in its first season, 1910, it recorded a net profit of £14,226, while the next season proved the best of all, as indeed it was to do for all the other companies. Subsequently, however, a decline set in, despite the fact that at one time the company was operating with seven catchers. As whaling declined, so it changed character, the number of sperm whales caught increasing to the same extent that humpbacks declined in numbers. Of the total number of 853 caught off Natal in 1916, 585 were sperm whales. At the conclusion of the 1916 season the company broke off operations, owing to the many difficulties brought on. by war, which made it impossible to muster Norwegian crews, without which it would be impossible to operate the whale catchers. The company was wound up, shareholders receiving their initial stake together with a sizeable surplus, while the six whale catchers were sold to the French Government. In 1921 Egeland and Larsen established a new company, Union Whaling Co., which bought the station, and after a few difficult years succeeded in setting on foot a highly profitable business.

No steps were taken by the South African Government to restrict or regulate catching. All that was demanded was that the entire whale should be used. The new Union of South Africa, victim in 1910 of an economic depression, welcomed this shot in the arm which whaling gave the economy. The excellent results achieved during the first two or three years convinced the authorities that there would be sufficient stocks of whales for all the companies now appearing on the scene. But from the very start voices were raised in protest, prophesying disaster. A Frenchman who travelled right the way up the coast of Natal in 1913 wrote that from the Durban area alone, where seven large factories were situated, twenty-six whale catchers steamed out every morning, and between Durban and Cape Town as many as seventy-five. Excessive competition proved disastrous, and most companies made a very brief appearance. The mention of all of them would merely involve a meaningless enumeration, a catalogue. In 1912 thirteen companies had been registered in Natal, of which only six became operational. Of the twenty-one companies in the Union of South Africa whose names are known to us, only three survived the crisis and the war, and were able to start up again in the 1920s. One of these came to a speedy end, and the Union Whaling Co., continuing till 1975, was the last survivor.

The other two Norwegian companies in Cape Province were not noticeably more successful. One of them was established by the same individuals in Haugesund who promoted the local enterprise that had operated in Iceland and the Faroes, and from the start it was the largest company in the whole of Africa, with an initial capital of Kr.1.3 million. As many as seven new whale catchers were ordered, and a huge station, equipped with every kind of modern machinery, was set up at Plettenberg, just west of Port Elizabeth. Seldom have results failed so dismally to come up to expectations: the first year, 1913, yielded a mere 211 whales and 8,000 barrels of oil, the entire share capital was swallowed up, and there was a debt of Kr.650,000. In 1916 the company was wound up. The disaster that struck this, the best equipped of all enterprises, was due to two assumptions which were unfounded: one was the belief that it would be possible to catch whales both on the northward and southward migration, enabling catching to be carried out all the year round, with November as the peak month. Experience now showed that it was precisely in this month that catching exhibited a downward trend, and that there was no point in starting up again before May.

The other was that it turned out that, in this area and in the nearby Mosselbaai, the migration passed a very considerable distance out to sea. At the latter place another Norwegian company was forced to go into liquidation in 1913, with the loss of its entire share capital of £33,000, after producing a total of only 10,600 barrels over a period of three years.

The South African interlude is of particular interest to British whaling since it was here that Lever Brothers (from 1930 Unilever Ltd.) commenced active participation in whaling. Its keenest rival in the South African fat market was the New Transvaal Chemical Co., which in 1912 had added whaling, based on two stations, to its many and varied enterprises. William Lever (created Lord Leverhulme in 1917) pursued his customary policy as far as this new rival was concerned : if he could not crush the rival, then he would buy him, and this was in fact done in 1914, for a very high price, £135,000 being paid for the whaling company alone. The enterprise was not a financial success, and the company was sold in 1931 to the Union Whaling Co. at a great loss to Unilever. In that year it also closed down its station at Prince Olav Harbour in South Georgia, which had been bought from Irvin & Johnson in 1919. These two companies are the only ones Unilever operated directly, and they both originated in South Africa. Unilever's subsequent pelagic whaling was run through an independent affiliate, the Southern Whaling & Sealing Co.

The word "explosion" aptly describes the expansion in Africa. From four companies with five stations in 1910 it grew to thirteen in 1911, twenty-five in 1912, culminating with twenty-six in 1913, and declining just as rapidly to five in 1917. The peak period lasted a mere six years. After 1916 only one out of eighteen Norwegian companies remained. The expansion increased not only in intensity in the two whaling grounds where it had started, but it also spread to three new areas, to the French Congo (now Gabon), and German South-West Africa (Namibia); to Portuguese East Africa (Mozambique), and in the same year (1912) to Madagascar as well; and in 1914 to the Spanish island of Fernando Poo (now part of Equatorial Guinea).

The Portuguese authorities in Angola, where a Norwegian company had made a start in 1909, must have imagined that there were unlimited whale stocks, as they allowed companies to come pouring in — three in 1911, two in 1912, and one in 1913, one of them British, all the others Norwegian. Most of them operated both with a floating factory and with a shore station for the production of guano. As whales were somewhat lean there was relatively a lot of guano and less oil. In its annual report for 1914 one of the companies states that "the sale of guano has largely been responsible for the good results". Oil totalling Kr.917,355 and guano totalling Kr.210,122 were sold. During this period whaling off the coast of Angola was the enterprise that proved financially most favourable to those who were involved. Of the five Norwegian companies which wound up voluntarily prior to 1916, two were able to do so with excellent results, one with very good results, and two with fair results. Statistical returns for total catching in 1909-16 are of doubtful accuracy: 13,600 whales were probably caught and 315,000 barrels of oil produced. Of this total, 255,000 barrels were accounted for by Norwegian companies, and about 27,500 by the Portuguese and an estimated 32,000 by the British.

The migrations of whales past the coast of Angola might be assumed to suggest that stocks of whales as a basis for catching also existed off the coast of the French Congo to the north. When operations started here the whale proved more stationary, presumably not proceeding further north, but stopping off here for a while before returning south. For this reason there was no break in catching between northbound and southbound migrations. But it was undoubtedly incorrect to believe that whales off the Congo were the same (humpback) stocks as those that proceeded past Angola. Recent research has shown that there are separate stocks of humpback in the Antarctic, each proceeding north to its own particular area. Gunners operating off the Congo and Angola considered it remarkable that they never caught a whale bearing the scars of previous shots — which suggests that the great majority of wounded whales were lost.

Most of the Congo expeditions shared one feature in common : they were originally destined for whaling in more distant fields, off Australia and New Zealand, but switched on hearing of the excellent catches made by the first expedition to the Congo. This meant a two to three months shorter journey, longer catching time, and lower operating expenses. In 1912 the first Norwegian floating factory off the Congo produced 11,300 barrels in the course of two months; a figure of almost 6,000 barrels a month was so outstanding that there is no need to say that this attracted a great many others : not less than four new floating factories worked in the vicinity of the original one in 1913 near Cap Lopez, almost on the Equator, while a fifth was stationed 40 miles further north. All six expeditions were Norwegian. Events in the Congo revealed the haphazard nature of whaling. The two smallest expeditions, operating with a sailing ship as a floating factory, were situated close to one another, and of these one produced 10,650 barrels, the highest figure anywhere outside the Antarctic, whereas the other had to make do with a quarter of this, 2,800 barrels. Although the others employed big steam-driven floating factories and a large number of whale catchers, they failed to register better results than the former of these two companies. These provided shareholders with dividends of 15-25 per cent, whereas one of the larger companies declared a 5 per cent dividend, and the remainder failed to make a profit.

All six companies returned in 1914, with an increase of matériel from six to seven floating factories and 19-20 whale catchers, but despite this, production slumped from 63,240 barrels to 43,100. The two small companies served their shareholders well, while the others registered a loss. The experts were of the opinion that the reason for the decline was not only over-taxation of the whale stocks, but that the many catchers operating scared the whales away from their natural coastal area out to sea where they were more difficult to catch, and where time was wasted sailing to the whaling ground and towing animals back to the factory ships. Thanks to the good price for oil — as much as £23 15s on average for all categories — financial disaster was averted. Despite this, none of the expeditions returned in 1915, as the high freight rates offered in shipping made it more profitable to use floating factories as cargo ships, while the belligerents paid very high prices for whale catchers, which were admirably suited for service as submarine chasers, escort vessels, and mine sweepers. The total yield of the three years' whaling off the Congo from 1912 to 1914 was 4,430 whales (all humpback) and 117,640 barrels, i.e. 68.3 barrels per BWU. We shall return to these figures later on.

There was such keen rivalry to secure licences, that the company which acquired one for Fernando Poo had to pay Kr.72,000 for the privilege, and as the result was a mere 280 whales, the price of the licence worked out at Kr.260 per whale. The company had proved so unsuccessful in another area — twenty-five whales and 480 barrels in two and a half months! — that it needed a licence at any price, in order not to go bankrupt, and catching in 1914 and the excellent freight rates in 1915 and 1916 — until the floating factory was torpedoed in September — not only saved the company from bankruptcy, but, when it was wound up, provided shareholders with a return of 175 per cent on their investment.

Climatic conditions off the Congo were, of course, a complete contrast to what many of the hands, had been used to in the Antarctic : back-breaking work beneath a blazing sun and high humidity. The whalers' opinions varied from "a paradise on earth" to "a roasting hell", with the latter opinion held by a decided majority. In no area were there so many complaints about working conditions : swarms of cockroaches, of bugs and mosquitoes, rotten provisions, deplorable sanitary conditions, dysentery, malaria, and beri-beri. There were constant strikes and disturbances among the hands, followed by court cases and heated debates in the columns of the Socialist and Conservative press. There was unrest among the workers in other areas, too, and in 1912-13 whaling for the first time was brought into touch with the trade union movement and the social struggle — largely the result of conditions in the Congo. Eight years were to elapse before attempts were once again made to operate in this area.

It is in particular whaling off Mozambique that has given the African interlude its reputation. In 1911 Johan Bryde erected a shore station at the mouth of the Inhambane River; he was so confident of the possibilities offered that in 1912 he raised yet another company, which was to operate with one of the largest floating factories of the time and six new whale catchers. The result, however, was a fiasco : the company was wound up and its matériel sold. Bryde's best season was in 1913, which yielded 22,300 barrels of oil and 13,500 sacks of guano. A sharp decline followed : 16,070 barrels in 1914 and 8,000 in 1915. As these two seasons resulted in a deficit of half a million kroner, the company was forced to go into liquidation before it had a chance of transferring the floating factory to profitable freighting. Yet another Norwegian company recorded a deficit in 1912 of Kr.200,000. The greatest disaster befell the Quelimane company, named after the town where it was to operate. Its floating factory was the largest ship engaged in whaling in 1912, and in the course of a seven-month conversion it was equipped with the costliest machinery that could be obtained at the time. It proved one of the greatest disappointments in the history of whaling, as there were few whales, and much of the machinery proved useless. The capacity of the floating factory was 25,000 barrels, but the results obtained were a mere 5,000, and the company went bankrupt. After plans for a British and a Portuguese company had been abandoned, Bryde was once again on his own in 1914 and 1915, when he was again forced out with a sizeable deficit. The entire yield of five years' catching off Mozambique was some 3,360 whales (probably only humpback) and 97,000 barrels, comprising the biggest financial loss that any area to date had inflicted on Norwegian whaling.

Catching off the coast of Africa and particularly the Congo had repercussions far beyond the purely financial. It was one of the reasons why the question of international agreement for the regulation of whaling came to be seriously considered and discussed. Ever since the start of wholesale pursuit of the right whale in about 1600 we come across warnings that whale stocks would be exterminated. And once this species had been exterminated, there was a weighty argument to hand that the same fate would befall the fin whale, if it were pursued by far more effective, modern methods. A certain measure of regulation had been introduced by some countries, but as yet no one had thought of restricting world catching as a whole by means of an international agreement. The world was still living in the age of liberalism, paying homage to free competition on the high seas. Marine-biological scientific research was as yet still in its infancy. The major and fundamental problems — the size of whale stocks, the age of whales, their feeding, reproduction and migration — had not been solved, and any restriction on catching had to be based on the results of research.

In 1913, on the basis of whaling off the Congo, French circles submitted a concrete proposal for an international agreement. Fifteen years were to elapse before this idea was raised again. Whaling was still shore whaling and the conditions of its operation were a national concern. From the mid-1920s whaling became pelagic as well, and operated in seas beyond the sovereignty and jurisdiction of any single country. Every country could, of course, have instituted regulations covering the activities of its own subjects, for example by making whaling dependent on licences for a restricted number of expeditions, but little would have been achieved if other countries caught in unlimited quantities what any separate country might have saved. For this reason an international agreement was a necessity, and the idea was mooted by the French professor A. GRUVEL in 1913. He opened up with a violent attack on Norwegian whaling, which he described as "barbaric and anti-scientific". There were companies, he declared, "which are only interested in guano and bone meal, and completely ignore the blubber". Some of the big profits earned in whaling should accrue to France. The fearful waste could only be stopped by international agreement, but as a great many years would elapse before this could be instituted, France would have to introduce the proposed regulations in her own colonies, of which the salient points were mainly the same as the British ones that applied to South Georgia. One innovation was that the Norwegians were obliged to include three or four French seamen on every boat, with a view to training them, "so that we can fairly soon be in a position to do without foreign aid". An international conference, he insisted, would have to include representatives of France, Britain, Germany, Spain, and Portugal (not Norway!). Gruvel was soon to discover that it was no simple matter to arrive at an agreement.

In Norway attention was drawn to Gruvel's many misleading statements and exaggerations, and the fear was expressed that his campaign might result in very stringent licensing terms. Those that were issued by a decree of 12 April 1914, however, were surprisingly liberal, and even though they regulated whaling in accordance with the British pattern, this was entirely offset by the fact that ten licences were issued, with no restriction on catches stipulated. Six went to the previously operating companies and four to newcomers, one of these being Chr. Salvesen & Co., and three to Norwegian companies, but none of these four were taken up. One of Gruvel's colleagues wrote on this occasion : "France, as always, leads the way with her ideas; by a decree of 12 April she has taken the initiative in establishing regulations our countrymen may be proud of." Either this was sheer jingoism or else he was poorly informed, since many countries had already made catching dependent on a licence and regulated it. Nor was the idea of an international agreement entirely original: in 1911 the Natural History Museum in London had drawn the attention of the Colonial Secretary to this matter, and it had also been mooted in Germany. The World War was hardly conducive to international co-operation, and for the time being the plan was shelved, and reconsidered in the late 1920s.

The reason Germany was mentioned among the potential signatories to an international agreement was that in 1912 whaling had been started from its colony of South-West Africa (Namibia). This colony had a coastal stretch of some 435 miles, along which it might be assumed that the whale would pass on its annual migration. Only two useful harbours were available, in Lüderitz Bay and in Walvis Bay. The latter was a small British enclave, where two companies, one Norwegian and one British, operated a floating factory on a joint fifty-fifty basis, the result being 360 whales and 13,500 barrels in 1913, and 193 and 6,800 respectively in 1914, after which operations were brought to a halt during the best season up to that time, when German troops occupied the enclave. Not till 1923 was whaling resumed here. In Lüderitz Bay the Germans themselves started whaling in 1913 with a semi-national company. A certain amount of capital was also subscribed in Norway, where the management was situated and whence all matériel and whale catchers were supplied. Apart from a floating factory, an impressive shore station was built at a cost of £50,000. Fresh water presented the major problem: it had to be obtained either by condensation or fetched in a small boat which made scheduled runs to Cape Town. Water alone cost £25 a day. Seldom have such meagre results been achieved at such great expense: 1913 registered a mere 2,000 barrels, and 1914 4,000, when British troops, six months after the declaration of war, moved in and occupied the colony. No subsequent attempts at whaling have been made in this area.

During whaling off the African coast a new species of whale was discovered and classified, *Balaenoptera edeni,* popularly referred to as the Bryde whale, after the "African pioneer" who in 1912 financed the first scientific investigation of whale species in those waters. Whalers reported having caught "a sort of sei whale", which on investigation proved to differ so greatly from its close relations that it had to be classified as a separate species. The distinction is to be found primarily in the different shape of the baleen: in the case of the Bryde whale, this is thicker, longer, more rigid, with no curly fringes, and of a deep grey colour (in the case of the sei whale white) reflecting differences in their preferred food species. The Bryde whale differs from the other rorquals in that it makes no annual migrations to the Antarctic. It was previously assumed to be largely confined to the waters off South Africa, but has subsequently been established in practically all the tropical and temperate oceans of the world. It has little significance as an oil producer, tending more to be processed for meat. As it never migrates to the polar seas, the layer of blubber is thin: as a general rule, one whale would provide not more than six to eight barrels, occasionally some of the largest females twenty barrels. The average length is some 40 ft., the largest known specimens measuring 50 ft.

Of all the whaling grounds in the world, those around Africa have been subject to least scientific investigation. *International Whaling Statistics* do not provide specified returns for the various species before 1917, but a large number are simply described under the heading "no specification". When catching culminated in 1913 with 9,300 whales, 4,600 were included in the category "no specification", but it may be assumed that most of these were humpbacks, in addition to the 4,100 registered. The catching of this species then slumped drastically until by the mid-1920s it once again rallied to approximately 1,000, whereupon the process was repeated — a decline to 71 in 1931 and then a recovery to almost 2,000 in 1939. In face of protests by biologists and nature conservationists at the repeated extermination of the humpback in one area, the whalers retorted that catching was self-regulating: it stopped when it was no longer profitable, and the whale was left alone until it had increased sufficiently to provide once again the basis for commercial catching. There was no need for governmental regulation. Every year around Africa a few hundred blue and fin whales were caught, and, after 1922, they were caught in very considerable numbers, reaching a peak in 1926 and 1927 with some 1,750 blue whales and 1,200 fin whales in each of these years. Since the Second World War catching around South Africa has essentially concentrated on the sperm whale.

13

AUSTRALIA AND NEW ZEALAND
1911-1916, 1922-1928

In 1911 Norwegian whaling reached the furthest limits of its global expansion: Alaska and Australia/New Zealand. Old-style whaling in these parts dated back to the 1790s, and was subsequently carried on partly by the local population from shore stations, and partly from British, American, and, somewhat later, French, Dutch, and Portuguese whaling ships. Up to the end of the 1820s the catch consisted mainly of sperm whales, but from c. 1830 the catching of right whales began to play a greater part, as this species was found in abundant quantities in the bays of New Zealand and off the islands to the south. As the whaling ships anchored up in the bays, this period has been given the name bay-whaling. It enjoyed a golden age in the 1830s, culminating in 1840, when several hundred vessels are reported to have operated around the coast of New Zealand and in adjacent whaling grounds in the Pacific. The first shore stations were built in Tasmania in 1804, and in 1841 there were thirty-five stations on this island, as well as many others on the southwest coast of Australia and in New Zealand, where savage clashes occurred between whalers and Maoris, whose extermination was just as cynical as that of the whale. This took place in the course of ten years, and is one of the most glaring examples of the speed at which a species can be brought to the verge of extinction. In the bays there were virtually only females with calves. The whalers would first harpoon the calf, and as the mother refused to abandon her young, she was an easy prey. This right whale catching came to an end in the early 1840s, and was followed by the golden age of sperm whale catching in 1840-60 in the open sea. The Australians themselves took part in this, and Hobart in Tasmania became Australia's New Bedford, with thirty-seven vessels operating from this port in 1848. Australian participation in this off-shore whaling terminated in 1896, when the last Hobart-based vessel returned home practically empty.

Whaling round New Zealand persisted sporadically: now and again a whale or two would be caught, and in 1890 and 1909 two stations were established, one of which operated right up until 1964. It made use of a method which is quite unique in the history of whaling. The 1890 station was established by H. F. COOK, one of the veterans of Australian whaling. This station, Whangamumu, which he ran up until the Second World War, was situated by the Bay of Islands on the northeast coast of North Island, the harbour most in use in the days of old bay-whaling. As was to be expected, Cook caught only humpback, and he was probably alone, apart from the Japanese, in using nets. This method was employed until 1910, when a modern whale catcher, equipped with a gun, was acquired. All the hands at this station, which produced meat meal and guano as well, were Maoris.

The other station, Te Awaiti, established in 1909, was situated near Marlborough Sound, an arm of the Tory Channel, the narrowest portion of the Cook Strait dividing New Zealand into North Island and South Island. Here, too, had been one of the main centres for bay whaling. The last station was closed down shortly after 1840, and the whale had been left to its own devices for seventy years when JOSEPH PERANO appeared on the scene. Only the northern migration passes through here in June, July, and August, and it was almost only males which were caught. The few females caught had, almost without exception, fully developed foetuses of about 14 ft. in length. In these narrow, shallow waters steam-driven whale catchers could not be used; instead, the whale was hunted from 34 ft. flatbottomed motor boats capable of a speed of 35–40 knots. These boats could start, stop, and turn very rapidly. A small 32mm. cannon was mounted in the bows. There was a crew of only two, one operating the engine and one manning the gun, which could fire a light harpoon, together with a shell, weighing a total of some 15 lb. The whale *could* be killed instantly, if the shell destroyed a vital organ, but the prime intention was to anaesthetise the animal. Once this had been done, the boat approached the whale and the gunner stuck a spear in it, to which an explosive shell was attached, linked to a detonator in the motor boat. The boat had to back away from the whale quickly, in order not to risk damage from the explosion. There was a particular risk of this occurring should the grenade explode in any portion of the whale above the water.

Each station had an annual average catch of forty to fifty whales (the record is seventy-four), and production fluctuated in the 1920s and 1930s from 1,000 to 2,200 barrels, fetching a price of from £3,000 to £7,000. Perano has recorded two incidents of interest to the history of whaling. In a humpback he came across part of a harpoon of a type he had given up using eighteen years previously, and in another humpback a splinter from a particular type of shell which he had used for only one season, seven years earlier. Both incidents seem to suggest that the various stocks of humpbacks return to the same breeding grounds. The two small stations in New Zealand confirm what a historian of whaling has said: if you are satisfied with catching a small number of whales, and are prepared to catch cheaply, you will make a profit and your enterprise will not come to an end as a result of a shortage of whales.

WILLIAM JOHN DAKIN, author of the history of Australian whaling, relates that from Norway "hosts of inquiries" poured in to the authorities and the consulates. They were not concerned so much to know whether there were whales — they assumed it was a foregone conclusion — but to know the terms for a licence. Dakin's conclusion was: "A thorough preliminary investigation of Australian seas was lacking. There can be no doubt whatever that whaling came again to Australian waters by reason of its success elsewhere, and through the interest in whaling which now raged like a goldfever in Norway."

When the Norwegian consul in Sydney in 1909 drew the attention of Norwegian whalers to the fact that catching had previously been carried on along the coast of Australia, he hardly expected that the result of his remarks would be such that, two years later, he would have to issue a warning against too many companies. There were good grounds for this. In 1911 no less than ten companies planned commencing operations there. Three of them never got as far as whaling in Australian waters, and a fourth was never constituted. When we consider the tremendous expansion of whaling in the Antarctic that had taken place at the same time from the 1909-10 season to 1910-11, and the many new companies springing up round Africa and off the west coast of America, both in the north and in the south, Australian whaling may be regarded as the final result of the whaling fever that held Norway in its grip, creating the illusion that every ocean teemed with whales and that all that was necessary to ensure shareholders a 100 per cent dividend was a licence and an expedition.

Newspapers and periodicals warned readers against "the Australian gamble", condemning speculation in people's gullibility. This had its effect, because, as already mentioned, four of the expeditions that were planned never reached Australia, two others operated more or less on an experimental basis for a brief period in 1912, one company was active for a mere two years — 1912 to 1913 — while all other catching round Australia and New Zealand in 1912-16 was operated by three companies, all managed by the same firm. The Australian authorities had some difficulty in understanding how it was possible for one firm to "own" three companies, each of which had its own shareholders, and how three companies could co-operate, when competition was to be expected. The object of this tripartite arrangement was to keep competitors at arm's length: one company of the same size as the three jointly would only receive one licence, while three small companies would be granted three of the limited number of licences.

The first phase of modern Australian whaling is almost entirely associated with the little Norwegian town of Larvik. The first Norwegian floating factory reached Tasmania on 10 January 1912, but as it only succeeded in producing 1,500 barrels of mainly sperm oil, it never returned. The fact that another Norwegian floating factory, despite the most miserable catch recorded in the history of whaling — twenty-five

41. One of the biggest lumps of ambergris ever found in a sperm whale, 926 lb., on the floating factory *Southern Harvester*, 1953.

whales and 480 barrels — nevertheless proved an economic success, was due to the largest find of ambergris ever made. The following item is recorded in the company's minutes for 8 January 1913: "It was impossible to continue operations, as it proved difficult to maintain the necessary working capital, even with the company's ships as security." In the minutes for 1 April we read: "This is not an April fool's joke, but the greatest adventure in the history of whaling. The ambergris was sold in London for £23,000. It was decided to redeem the company's debts as they fell due." The find had been made on Christmas Eve! It was one single lump, weighing 1,003 lb., and consequently larger than the one of 926 lb. which is generally quoted as the largest and which was found on Salvesen's floating factory the *Southern Harvester* on 21 December 1953.

The three Larvik companies operated jointly, borrowing each other's factories and whale catchers, the latter towing their whales now to one and now to the other floating factory. The most important discovery they made was that a large number of humpbacks migrated along the entire west coast from Cape Leeuwin in the south to Point Cloates in the north, after which they veered further east. Operations based on these migrating whales, using a floating factory, were largely unsuccessful. Even in the largest bay, Shark Bay, which had one of the very few useful harbours, the swell was so great that flensing along the ship's side and settling the oil proved difficult. Fresh water proved a great problem : on the northwest coast the desert stretches right down to the sea, and wells drilled ashore tended to absorb salt water.

Catching was concentrated on two shore stations, one in Frenchman's Bay near Albany and the other at Point Cloates, where the hitherto unnamed spot was christened Norwegian Bay. The landscape was inhospitable and bleak, with sand dunes as white as snow, and the difficulties encountered here were in a way just as great as those C. A. Larsen faced when he landed at Grytviken in 1904. Besides, he had one tremendous advantage : an abundance of fresh water. In Norwegian Bay a great many of the hands spent all their time digging wells, the water of which was practically always brackish. There were deposits of salt in the cookers, which had to be cleaned at frequent intervals. At this juncture the whalers were rewarded with the same magnificent sight as in Grytviken : a humpback migration close inshore, of an abundance they had hardly dreamed of. The van appeared in early June 1913, consisting of a number of scattered males; then on 24 June the main body turned up, providing a veritable *embarras de richesse*. The two floating factories, which were used before the station became operative, worked at full pressure right round the clock, producing 3,000 barrels a week. On 17 September catching had to be broken off just as the southbound trek was at its most promising. By then all tanks, barrels, and boilers were full to bursting, a total of 23,500 barrels in eleven weeks, in fact quite a record. Had there been sufficient water and space for the oil, production might well have been doubled. One of the company's books shows 28,430 barrels, of which 6,000 were sperm oil, and a net surplus of Kr.167,200. In 1914 1,971 whales were caught in Norwegian Bay, producing 50,800 barrels, which, at a price of £23 a ton, yielded gross earnings of Kr.3.54 million. For the whole of Australia the results were 2,387 whales and 61,200 barrels.

Now that whaling had assumed such sizeable proportions the authorities in Western Australia intervened, introducing catching regulations on the lines of the British regulations for the Falkland Islands Dependencies : (1) catching only in return for a licence, with an annual levy of £50; (2) shore stations to be built, and the entire carcass of the whale to be used; (3) no natives of Africa, Asia, or the South Sea Islands to be employed; (4) a limited number of whale catchers; (5) a ban on the killing of females with calves. So as to restrict catching further, only three licenses were issued for the West Coast, and — interestingly because this was probably unprecedented — a sanctuary was declared eastward from Norwegian Bay, where it was assumed that the females gave birth to their young. As a result of this ban, the companies were compelled to build their stations at Albany in 1914 and at Norwegian Bay in 1915. In the face of great difficulties a factory was erected which was said to be "possibly the best equipped station ever built". It was ready by mid-August, and by the end of the season in October 6,500 barrels of oil and 7,500 sacks of guano had been produced. The floating factory by that time had 16,200 barrels. The floating factory of the other company, operating in the vicinity of Point Cloates, recorded 6,700 barrels, and the station at Albany 7,800 (mainly sperm oil). Total production in 1915 amounted in other words to some 1,430 whales, 37,200 barrels, and 11,000 sacks, a very sharp decline from 1914.

Apart from the three companies from Larvik, a company from Tønsberg operated in 1912-13. As there were no available licences left for the west coast, the floating factory went to Jervis Bay on the east coast, 100 miles south of Sydney. This floating factory was Norway's largest and most fully equipped. With 3,000 barrels as the result of catching in Jervis Bay, it proceeded to Bluff in the south of New Zealand in December, catching sperm whales in those waters till May 1913 when it returned to Jervis Bay. Whaling was the object of so many protests from the population, however, that nothing came of it. Applications were submitted for a licence for the Abrolhos Islands, a number of coral reefs situated halfway up the west coast, and in the so-called sanctuary. In the former place the request met with protests from the companies who claimed that they had exclusive rights to the entire west coast, and as the State Government actually granted licences for the sanctuary, the result was a clash with the Federal Government. The trade union, too, involved itself in the dispute, complaining about wages and at the employment of foreign workers. A commission of enquiry set on foot a series of extensive investigations, and the material submitted has comprised one of the main sources for this account. As the prospects of a licence were so uncertain, the floating factory stayed away in 1914; the carrying trade during the war proved more profitable than whaling — indeed a total of 14,500 barrels for two seasons had produced a large deficit.

In 1916 the stations in Norwegian Bay and Albany were all that was left of Australian whaling, which had held out such apparent promise. For six years all whaling based on the Australian continent was at a standstill, and the large and expensive plant at Norwegian Bay lay there, empty and abandoned, after operating for only one and a half seasons.

In 1922 the station in Norwegian Bay was taken over by a wholly Australian company, the North-West Whaling Co. For several reasons it proved a failure: there was insufficient capital, neither the Board nor the expedition manager had any knowledge of whaling, and it proved impossible to acquire the services of competent Norwegian gunners, "the whole secret of success". There were plenty of whales, but after two seasons the company was forced to wind up with a loss of £24,000.

The Norwegian consul in Perth was convinced that, given the right management, whaling would prove a profitable business. In 1925 he managed to establish a company in Sandefjord, the Norwegian Bay

Whaling Co., an almost purely private undertaking. In return for a certain royalty paid to the previous company the new company was allowed to operate on its licence and use its station. It proved a great success, which showed what could be obtained from whaling, provided it was operated in the right way. During the four years 1925 to 1928 the result was 3,472 whales (nine blue whales, the rest humpbacks), 108,200 barrels of oil, and 1,700 tons of guano. The shareholders received their entire investment plus a dividend of 150 per cent. On the basis of its royalty the old company was in a position to cover all its losses. The average price of oil (No. 1) during these four years was excellent, £33, while wages and the price of coal were low. The company withdrew after the 1928 season, which was the best of all, not so much because a very stringent Whaling Act was being prepared, but because here at last was a company that had learned from the experience of others that exclusive catching of humpbacks had no real future. Furthermore, the price of whale oil was dropping. After 1928 eight years were to elapse before whaling began again in Australian waters, but then with large modern floating factories, and in some years with catches three or four times greater than in 1928.

The Norwegian expedition manager in Norwegian Bay relates that the great southerly migration which arrived at the end of August consisted mainly of large females with calves, moving very close inshore. "We could often go right over to them and drop the harpoon in their backs. It's unfortunate that cows with young should be killed, but there's nothing that can be done about it." That was probably true enough, as there was hardly a single female without a calf; according to the hard laws of whaling there was no other way of doing it than to kill the mother. In doing so one was actually killing two whales, but only capturing one, as the calf was helpless without its mother and soon died, either of starvation or an easy prey to sharks and killer whales. Whalers were not inclined to sentimentality when they had the prospect of extracting 50 to 60 barrels of oil, worth £300, from a large female.

14
THE BASIS FOR THE EXPANSION OF 1906-1914

In the preceding chapters we have given an account of the spread of whaling from shore whaling from Finnmark to all the whaling grounds north and south. Finnmark whaling had become global whaling. Our account has been restricted essentially to companies, their catching, production, and financial results. The production of oil was one aspect of the matter; selling it was another and more important one. It might be useful to establish this truism as a starting point for this chapter. Had there been no market for oil at prices in excess of production expenses, whaling would have stopped of its own accord. The constant opening up of fresh fields, the tremendous increase in whaling matériel, the manifold increase of production, the relatively good and stable prices after 1905, these were all the results of a market capable of absorbing the oil. There was a growing need and demand for it, so much so that at the outbreak of the First World War it was obvious that demand exceeded supply. Why did the conditions for the place of whale oil in the world market for vegetable and animal edible fats and oils undergo such a complete change in the course of a few years?

In order to answer this question we must first establish what quantities of whale oil were involved, and their magnitude in relation to other fats. This poses many difficulties, as far as the period we are to deal with here is concerned. Previous accounts generally take as their starting point the situation in 1910, because in that year for the first time statistics were easily accessible for the world production of whale oil. With regard to the world's total production of oils and fats, the position is somewhat less favourable, as no accurate figures exist even for the 1920s, let alone the preceding years. To a certain extent one must rely on conjecture. An additional difficulty is the regrettable fact that many recent accounts of the history of whaling use figures for global whaling which only relate to "modern" catching. A generation was to elapse before the proceeds, expressed in terms of barrels of whale and sperm oil, of modern catching surpassed that of the old. But that did not mean the end of the old-style whaling. Using estimates where accurate figures are not available, it is possible to calculate catching in terms of barrels for the period 1900-14, as shown in Table 13.

The above calculation is based on a number of uncertain factors, particularly where old-style catching is involved. As East Asia is not included, the figures must be regarded as minimum figures. It is probable that around the turn of the century catching slumped to its lowest level

Table 13. WORLD OIL PRODUCTION, 1900-1914

	Barrels		Barrels		Barrels
1900	87,300	1905	142,600	1910	316,300
1901	91,700	1906	110,300	1911	563,500
1902	115,000	1907	164,200	1912	712,000
1903	111,600	1908	186,400	1913	776,000
1904	149,100	1909	235,700	1914	812,000

for 300 years, ever since the time before Dutchmen and the British started operations round Spitsbergen in the early seventeenth century. American whaling alone during most of the 1840s and 1850s recorded an annual average that was four or five times in excess of the entire global catching in 1900. Not till 1911 did the production of oil reach a volume comparable with the American, and not till then can it be said that modern-style methods had raised whaling to its old level.

The term "whale oil" has often been used indiscriminately for whale oil and sperm oil. This is actually not correct, as the two products, in their chemical composition and for that reason, too, in their practical application, are entirely different. Whale oil, put simply, is a fat, and sperm oil a kind of wax. For certain purposes, e.g. for lighting and lubrication, both could be used, but sperm oil cannot be hydrogenated, and could not be used in the soap or margarine industry. Figures up to about 1910 are so incomplete that it is impossible to show the quantitative relationship between the number of sperm whales and rorquals caught, far less between the production of the two oils. Available returns, however, show that up to about 1910 very few sperm whales were caught by modern methods — in the entire Norwegian Sea from 1870 to 1910 a total of hardly more than a few hundred, probably less. Modern whaling was the outcome of a need to catch rorquals, and consequently for the production of whale oil. Around 1910 a marked increase in the number of sperm whales in modern catching occurred, primarily in the waters off Africa, Australia, and Japan, but even here during the five-year period 1910-14 hardly more than some 2,000 in all were caught. We have therefore used the collective term whale oil because catches of sperm whale and production of sperm oil during the period from about 1900 to 1914 were so low that they were without commercial importance to the whaling industry as a whole.

The most important features revealed by the above table are as follows: the increase from the turn of the century to 1910 is slight compared to the steep rise initiated in the three succeeding years, the very years when the new invention, that of the hydrogenation of fat, commenced on an industrial basis. The relapse in 1906 must be regarded more as a result of a slump in price during the two preceding years rather than a consequence of the abandonment of Finnmark whaling in 1905.

The latter was balanced in that year by an increase in activities from Iceland, Spitsbergen, and operations initiated in the Antarctic. It might come as a surprise that up to and including 1907 the Icelandic whaling grounds were the largest in the world (except for 1904, when they were exceeded by Newfoundland). Comparison between whaling grounds in the northern and southern hemispheres shows that catching in the north reached its peak in 1904; after the marked decline in 1906 catching in the north maintained a steady level during the following three or four years, when whaling in the Southern Ocean was established. In the 1908-9 season the catch in the south for the first time exceeded that in the north, and from then the former surpassed the latter by leaps and bounds. But right up to 1909 purchasers of oil were bound to rely mainly on that available from whaling grounds in the north.

During the decade before and after the turn of the century whale oil seemed destined to disappear from the world market. In its most important uses, lighting and lubrication, it had been replaced by mineral oil; whale oil could not be used in the manufacture of margarine, and in soap it was restricted to the coarser and most fluid kinds. A special application was the production of glycerine. During Svend Foyn's lifetime the Swede Alfred Nobel was carrying out his experiments in the 1860s with the explosive nitroglycerine in the form of dynamite. Glycerine is present in all vegetable and animal fats, particularly in the former. It exists there in the form of glycerides, compounds of fatty acids and glycerine, and in the manufacture of soap the fatty acids combine with alkalis to produce glycerine. This was consequently a by-product of soap manufacture, but there were also factories with glycerine as their main product, and here the quality of whale oil was of lesser importance. To a certain extent the price of glycerine may have had a bearing on the price of whale oil. In Liverpool glycerine had slumped in price from £100 in 1910 to £40 in 1912. During the First World War whale oil was an exceedingly important raw material, and for the soap factories glycerine was no longer a by-product, but a main product.

The place of whale oil among the fat raw materials of the world was limited owing to its fluid form, its poor quality, and its objectionable smell and taste. On the basis of its volume alone, whale oil played practically no role in the world market as compared with the major fats and oils. On the whole, it may be said that right up to the latter half of the nineteenth century world requirements of edible fats were largely covered by cattle fats (butter, lard, milk), apart from a few edible oils, particularly olive oil. As the American prairie was opened up, the United States became the largest producer and exporter of cattle fats, first and foremost in the form of compound lard ("the fat from any and every part of the hog") and tallow. Production of these depended on the maize harvest, an unpredictable factor liable to considerable fluctuations. This twin-stage production and the great demand made American cattle fats a relatively expensive raw material. The West European industrial countries' own production and imports of animal fats was to a lesser and lesser extent capable of covering the needs of the industrial population for fat-containing nourishment that was cheaper and richer in calories than carbohydrates, with their lower calorific content. The deficit was covered by tropical vegetable oils — coconut oil, palm oil, palm kernel oil, and groundnut oil. In this context we are not including the two "biggest" oils, cottonseed oil and linseed oil, which were admittedly edible in their refined state, but less used in the foodstuffs industry. The single-stage oil production of the tropics provided cheaper raw material, which put an end to the United States' fat monopoly.

The deficiency in natural butter was gradually covered by margarine, in the production of which the vegetable oils of the tropics could to a certain extent replace solid animal fat. After a means of production of margarine had been discovered in France in 1869, margarine factories sprang up all over the world from the late 1870s and throughout the 1880s. The Netherlands was an important centre. The raw material for early margarine production was essentially animal fats (compound lard and tallow), mixed with vegetable oils and milk. The firm, solid animal fat was indispensable in giving margarine its consistency. With the tremendous rise in the consumption of margarine this commodity became a keen rival to the soap industry in the purchase of animal fats.

The latter's consumption of fats had increased enormously since the mid-nineteenth century, not only as a natural consequence of an increase in population, but also because of a greater attention to hygiene. Partly because there was a deficiency of animal fats, and partly because it was expensive, the need to replace it with other firm fats became all the greater. The pressure on the raw material market proved a spur to the discovery of a method capable of converting fluid oil into firm fat. This explains the intensive research during the first decade of this century to solve this problem. Side by side with the principal sources of raw material — firm, solid animal fat and vegetable oils — whale oil appeared as a third ingredient. Although the marketed quantity was infinitesimal compared to the other two, it was of considerable financial interest in so far as it was the cheapest raw material available. All fluid oils, generally speaking, were cheaper than firm, solid fats, and they were particularly cheap round about the year 1905, and whale oil was the cheapest of them all. The shortage of raw materials provides part of the explanation for the sudden change in the price of whale oil in 1906, but not the entire explanation.

Without taking into account the low price that whale oil fetched it is difficult to understand the freshly awakened interest in it. This was not due to its quantity. Although exact figures are not available, it would hardly be possible to estimate world production of whale and sperm oil around 1905 at more than, at most, one-thirtieth of world production of edible fats and oils. In terms of its value the percentage is even less, but somewhat greater if we merely take into account the oils and fats included in foreign trade. A few figures will show the amounts involved. The annual average production of whale and sperm oil in 1905-7 was about 23,000 tons. In 1906 340,000 tons of compound lard were marketed; the United States' production of cottonseed in 1905 was 6.4 million tons, from Egypt and India alone Great Britain imported in 1907 687,000 tons of cottonseed, and in that year 1.3 million tons of linseed were imported into Europe; shipments of copra from the East Indies and the Pacific islands in 1908 amounted to 363,000 tons. (The oil contents of cottonseed, linseed and copra are 17, 36 and 62 per cent respectively.)

That whale oil should nevertheless have played a larger role than its actual volume warranted — a role which was constantly growing more important — was because, apart from the fact that it was cheaper, practically the entire production reached the market at the same time, and nearly all the whale oil was on offer in international trade, whereas a large proportion of the other fats was consumed by the producer countries themselves. In one deal major purchasers could cover their needs for any particular length of time at a fixed price, for properly purified whale oil could be stored for years without deteriorating.

Others have maintained that the changed situation as far as whale oil was concerned after 1905 was due to a brilliant invention — the hydrogenation of fluid oils. In the long-term view this is correct, but it does not entirely explain the drastic change in the whaling industry in 1906. The first patents for hydrogenation were granted in 1902, but like all great inventions, it took some time to make the step from laboratory experiment to industrial mass production. This did not occur until 1911-12, and it was applied to other fluid oils before it was tried out on whale oil. When the process was tried on whale oil it proved successful, though producing a far from perfect product.

A detailed technical-chemical description of the hydrogenation process has no place in this work; the interested reader should consult the specialist literature on this subject. Briefly, it can be described as follows: "transforming unsaturated fatty acids and their glycerides to solid fat by binding hydrogen to certain non-saturated carbohydrogen compounds with the aid of a metal catalyst"; or "as a result of the process the highly non-saturated fatty acids contained in the oil, which cause the unpleasant smell and taste, are transformed into saturated fatty acids." Hydrogenation had two notable effects on whale oil: the product became almost entirely white, and it lost most of its unpleasant smell and taste. These qualities could originally only be achieved if whale oil was hydrogenated to a melting point of 40-44°C. As margarine should melt on the tongue at a temperature of 30-32°C, the maximal percentage of hydrogenated whale fat that could be used in margarine was somewhat limited. It was possible to produce a hydrogenated product with a lower melting point, but the unpleasant smell and taste would then reappear. Not till 1929 were methods successfully evolved whereby the two properties were entirely removed from the hydrogenated whale fat with a melting point of 30-32°C, making it possible to use practically 100 per cent whale oil in margarine. The first fifteen to twenty years' production of hydrogenated whale fat were mainly used for the production of soap and artificial lard.

In about 1910-12 world production of animal and vegetable oils and fats consisted of approximately 65 per cent fluid and approximately 35 per cent firm substances. The latter were in short supply for the fat industry. It was here that hydrogenation of whale oil and of other oils proved itself. The transition took place during the years 1911-13. This partly explains the great expansion in the whaling industry during these years, and the keen competition within the fat industry. Whaling and the fat industry became more closely associated. But one, in the guise of vendor, and the other, in the guise of purchaser, clashed in one particular: the price of the commodity. This dependence on the law of supply and demand was not determined by whale oil alone; it was entirely determined by fluctuations in the price of the two "big" oil and fat materials. The expectation that the hydrogenation process would succeed *may,* as early as 1906, have contributed to stimulating a rise in the price of whale oil. As reports were received at the same time of tremendous numbers of whales in the Antarctic and of the prospect of increased supplies of whale oil from this part of the world, this may further have heightened expectations.

The price of whale oil was always "at bottom", depressed by the price of other oils, particularly by the price of linseed oils. "The importance of the linseed oil market to the general oil and fat market can hardly be exaggerated," we read in an annual survey published by a leading brokerage firm in London, "and low prices for linseed will always act as a brake on any rise in the price of whale oil." In 1904 the linseed harvest had been unusually good, and shipments to Europe reached a total of almost one and a half million tons. In Glasgow, Europe's most important centre for sales of oil, the price of linseed oil for most of 1905 was £14 a ton, while that for whale oil fluctuated between £13 10s and £12 for No. 1. For No. 4 it was £9, and because at the time 40 to 50 per cent of the oil was of a quality inferior to No. 1, whaling companies had every reason to complain of completely ruinous prices. The tremendous supplies and low price of linseed oil meant that manufacturers of soft soap made as much use of it as possible, eliminating others as far as they could. In 1905 and 1906 the linseed harvest was smaller, imports to

Europe being two-thirds of the 1904 level, and the price rose to £22 8s in the autumn of 1906, where it remained in 1907. A few years later this was repeated: a poor harvest and reduced imports in 1911 and 1912, with a price in both these years of £41. The year 1913 produced a big harvest, with imports of 1.83 million tons, while the price slumped to £26. But in the same year a whaling company notes with apparent surprise that "it is remarkable that the high price of linseed oil has not resulted in a corresponding drop in the price of whale oil". The reason was "the many new hydrogenation factories and the increased market for whale oil, whose application is constantly being extended to new areas". The explanation of the substantial rise in price from 1912 (right down to £17 at its lowest) to 1913-14 (up to £24) was not only hydrogenation, but also the extraordinarily large sales to Germany.

On the whole it may be said that the price of whale oil had shown a rising, or rather stable, tendency after 1905, the major increase occurring in 1906. Subject to minor fluctuations, the price remained fairly constant there for the next eight or nine years. Two factors were responsible for fixing the price. In the prices noted prior to 1915 barrels are included. This is an important point. Barrels had to be paid for by the manufacturer, and the price of these must be deducted if we are to arrive at a net price for whale oil. Barrels were one of the four major expense items in whaling companies' working budgets: the others were wages, coal, and insurance. The manufacture of oak barrels and sales of both new and old ones constituted a branch of the whaling industry; sometimes barrels were in short supply. The price of new oak ones in Norway in about 1900 was some Kr.4.50 to Kr.5.50 apiece, in 1913 about Kr.7. In Glasgow the price of used, steam-washed oak barrels was about 6s 4d in 1911. From about the turn of the century the use of iron drums, made of $2\frac{1}{2}$mm iron plating, was introduced. They were increasingly used around 1914. They weighed 95 kg. and had a capacity of 88 Imp. gallons (400 litres, = $2\frac{1}{2}$ barrels). Weighing 500 kg. when full, they were huge, clumsy objects. In 1911 the price of used iron drums in Glasgow was about 17s, and for new in 1913 about 20s. They consequently came somewhat more expensive than oak barrels. Generally speaking, it may be said that in about 1910 tare cost manufacturers £2 to £2 10s per ton of oil. To arrive at the net price of whale oil the above-mentioned sales prices will therefore have to be reduced by this amount. As from 1915 prices were noted naked. Without taking this factor into account, the usual price quotations before and after 1915 are consequently not immediately comparable.

The other factor is the expense incurred in refining and hydrogenating the whale oil, which did not arise in the case of oils and fats that could be used untreated. It is difficult to obtain accurate information on the cost of hydrogenation during the first period. In April 1939 the

42. *Above*: Leith Harbour in "the period of barrels". *Below*: Stromness Harbour with the earliest oil tanks, *ca*. 1914.

British oil and fat trade estimated that this was £2 10*s* a ton. Before the First World War it was estimated that hydrogenation cost less than 10 øre per kg. (approximately 2*s* 3*d* a pound).

We cannot here make a detailed analysis of the complicated interplay of well-nigh innumerable factors that influenced the price of raw materials, particularly as these factors have not been clarified. We shall merely single out three factors, or stages, in the fat industry which proved decisive to changes in the price of whale oil and its position among the world's fats. In the first place competition between margarine and soap manufacturers had resulted in a tug-of-war for raw materials. In 1907 the prices of raw materials taken altogether had reached the highest peak for twenty years, and the change that ensued was essentially due to the tremendous rise in the consumption of margarine. The margarine factories had now begun to prefer refined vegetable oils to animal fats, and were able to offer higher prices for these raw materials. "The Soap maker," wrote Lever in 1910, "has no chance against the Butterine maker. The Soap maker gets £24 a ton for soap containing 63 per cent of fatty acids and the margarine maker £60 a ton for 85 per cent fatty acids ... there is practically no good oil or fat but what the margarine maker can make into excellent food." At that time Lever Brothers were not producing any margarine. They started doing so in the autumn of 1914 at the request of the Government, which feared that the war would cut Britain off from supplies of butter from Denmark and margarine from Holland. In 1907-9 Lever Brothers actually suffered big losses in their soap manufacture; other major producers of soap, too, faced difficulties, whereas the Dutch margarine manufacturers were in a very strong position.

The second stage was initiated with the technique of hydrogenation, which initially offered soap manufacturers an opportunity of escaping from their dilemma by affording access to a raw material which was far cheaper than those that had been forced up in price owing to competition between margarine factories. "It might have been expected," writes the author of *The History of Unilever*, "that an invention which promised substantial relief from the shortage of solid fats would bring with it peace and plenty. Any such hopes were disappointed. The discovery of fat hardening was the prelude to a period of intrigue, diplomacy, alliance, counter-alliance and litigation which forms one of the most confused and difficult chapters in the history of the margarine and soap industries." A new cheap raw material meant keener competition : the protagonists were the British fat industry on one side, e.g. Crosfield, Gossage, Lever Brothers and Watson — and the Dutch, German and Austrian industries on the other — van den Bergh, Jurgens, Schicht, and the dominant German oil mill industry — but there was also rivalry between the various firms, particularly in England. Just as the world war eliminated a number of major powers on the political front, so the fat war wiped out a number of firms in the soap and margarine industry. In 1920 this was concentrated mainly in four large groups; by 1927 these had been reduced to three, in 1929 to two, Margarine Unie and Lever Brothers, which from 1 January 1930, merged in the gigantic Unilever Group, the largest single purchaser of oil.

When the tremendous production of whale oil started in the latter half of the 1920s and in the 1930s, it moved into its third phase in the world fat market. In 1939 the Food and Agriculture Organisation's International Institute of Agriculture made available in a number of large volumes the results of an investigation of the world's fat production and needs. Its verdict on the inter-war years was as follows : "The increasing use of marine oils, especially whale-oil, in the foodstuffs industry, particularly in the manufacture of margarine, led to direct competition with the animal fats produced in agriculture. As the crisis developed, and purchasing power declined, the competition became increasingly severe. At last the production of whale-oil became one of the most important factors in the unstable conditions and crises which affected the whole oil and fat market. Compared with this production, the costs of which could be continuously reduced by means of improvements in technique and organisation, even the tropical plantations and the Manchurian soya bean production were in a difficult position."

But it is incorrect, as we shall see, to maintain that "although the production of whale-oil has had a disastrous effect on the prices and markets of the other oils and fats, the fact cannot be overlooked that especially in Europe fat supplies were greatly improved by whale-oil production and that only by the use of whale-oil could there have been so marked a reduction in the price of margarine that it was in fact owing to the cheapness of margarine that a fairly high consumption was maintained even in the years of the great unemployment." It was at this very time that the remarkable and unexpected occurred: Europe's consumption of margarine slumped drastically, while the consumption of butter rose correspondingly. The FAO's statement was made in the light of the breakdown of the whale oil market in 1931-4 during the world depression. In terms of prices the role of whale oil in the world fat market had switched; while its price previously had risen or fallen in accordance with the dominant position of vegetable oils, whale oil had now become an important factor in determining prices.

The big oil buyers appeared to be alarmed at the news of hydrogenation. The struggle that ensued in 1910-14 had a profound importance for whaling, particularly Norwegian whaling. In 1909-10 63.3 per cent of world production of whale oil emanated from Norway, and 22.6 per cent from the British Empire; in 1912-13 the relative figures were 77 and 16.7 per cent. Not only as the biggest whale oil customer, but also as a company with interests in the Norwegian hydrogenation industry, and for a time active in whaling itself, Lever Brothers were in a position to exercise a dominant influence on the whale oil market.

The various patents for hydrogenation were based more or less on experiments carried out by the Austrian GUIDO GOLDSCHMIDT in 1874 and by the Frenchman PAUL SABATIER in 1897. The first, subsequently much disputed patent, was granted to the German chemist Dr. WILHELM NORMANN, who acquired a German patent on 14 August 1902, and an English one on 21 January 1903. The patent proved anything but practicable. England's largest soap manufacturers, apart from Lever Brothers, were Joseph Crosfield & Sons, who were closely linked with the great chemical firm of Brunner, Mond & Co.; Lever Brothers were dependent on the latter firm, as their sole source of caustic soda. In 1905 Crosfield concluded an agreement with Normann to the effect that the latter was to come to England and continue working at the factory there on his experiments, so that the patent could be utilised in industrial production. At first, progress was slow: in December 1905, 20 lb. of cottonseed oil were successfully hydrogenated, throughout 1906 not more than 17 tons of hardened fat were produced, in 1907 100 tons, and in

1908 243 tons. By then the process had proved capable of being put into practice. The first hydrogenation factory was started in the autumn of 1909; in 1910 production was 2,941 tons, in 1911 6,069 tons, and in 1914 just under 20,000 tons.

According to Normann's own account 5 kg. of whale oil were hydrogenated in 1907 for the first time in history; this took place in a small model factory, but in the course of 1908 the process was successfully tried with larger quantities. In the spring of 1909 a small quantity of hydrogenated fat was supplied, admittedly of cottonseed oil, to two German margarine factories, the first attempt to use hydrogenated fat in the foodstuffs industry. For this purpose, in Normann's opinion, it was but a step from vegetable oil to whale oil, and in 1910 Crosfield produced edible fat industrially out of whale oil, and from now events snowballed. The use of whale fat in margarine was kept secret to start with owing to people's deep-rooted antipathy towards it, and officially it was said that whale fat was used only in the soap industry. In recent discussions on the pioneers of hydrogenation it seems that major honours should be equally divided between the German engineer Wilhelm Normann and the English firm of Joseph Crosfield & Sons, which spent millions on experiments and trial production, without reaping corresponding profits.

In 1908, now that the patent had proved viable, Crosfield purchased Normann's rights in most countries. William Lever, self-willed as usual, despite the warnings of his fellow directors, had shown little interest in hydrogenation or in whale oil, which he refused to use in his main product, Sunlight soap. He realised, however, how serious the situation would be if Crosfield were to succeed in having Normann's patent legally established as the only process allowed for hydrogenation in England. The situation appeared fraught with still greater danger when ANTON JURGENS in 1909 bought Normann's patent rights for Germany and (for the manufacture of edible fats) for England. In 1912 he set up a large factory for hydrogenation in Germany, based largely on whale fat. In accordance with an agreement with the leading firm in Austria-Hungary, Georg Schicht A.G., the latter started a hydrogenation plant in Bohemia in 1910.

That its rivals should have failed to close the door on Lever Brothers was due to the fact that other patents had meanwhile cropped up : these had been applied for by the Russian MOSE WILBUSCHEWITZ (1910 and 1912), a former assistant of Wilhelm Normann's, by the Swede NILS TESTRUP (1910) and jointly by the Englishmen F. BEDFORD and C. E. WILLIAMS (1907, 1908, and 1910). The leading German oil-milling firm, Bremen Besigheimer Oelfabriken, acquired the rights to the Wilbuschewitz-Testrup patents, and sold the manufacturing rights for Norway to the recently established company, De Nordiske Fabriker (hereafter referred to by its nickname De-No-Fa). With a hydrogenation factory in Norway, which was a major producer of whale oil, this might easily have become something approaching a monopoly of hardened whale fat. As the U.S.A.'s largest producer of soap, Procter & Gamble, at the same time acquired Crosfield's rights, it seemed as if all Lever Brothers' competitors were arrayed against them. There was no alternative for William Lever to entering into negotiations with the patent-holders, in particular with the Bremen Besigheimer Oelfabriken (B.B.O.), who had a 50 per cent share of De-No-Fa. In Lever Brothers' case it was either-or, and they were forced to pay a high price, £100,000, for B.B.O.'s rights, believed to be the highest sum paid for a patent up till then. These and other large sums paid for hydrogenation patents give an excellent idea of the decisive importance of fat hydrogenation to the soap and margarine industry: it was a question of life or death. The Bremen Besigheimer Oelfabriken paid Wilbuschewitz 1 million francs (c. 25 francs = £1) for his patent, and the factory sold the rights to exploit it to De-No-Fa for Kr. 1 million (c. £55,000).

Lever's acquisition of the patent in February 1913 was the first step on the road to a completely new situation. The second was the outcome of a court case which the proprietors of Normann's rights brought against the proprietors of the Wilbuschewitz-Testrup patents. Levers undertook to conduct the case for the latter. The verdict was awaited with tremendous excitement. It threatened to put an end to De-No-Fa's production, before it had really got going. Thanks mainly to Lever's ruthless method of conducting this case, Crosfield-Normann lost (March 1913) and their patents were declared invalid. The final step was that in September 1913 Levers acquired B.B.O.'s rights in De-No-Fa, thereby acquiring a source of hardened fat which rendered them immune to competition. At the same time Levers bought up a number of other, more advanced patents, and placed them at De-No-Fa's disposal, as well as concluding a highly favourable agreement with Procter & Gamble.

The purchase of a half interest in De-No-Fa was a bitter blow to Anton Jurgens's firm, which was then the largest manufacturer of hardened fat, with a capacity of 500 tons a week, a large proportion of which was bought by Levers at a high price. Levers were now independent of Jurgens, and this was a source of tremendous strength both technically and economically to De-No-Fa, a factory Jurgens had regarded as "a likely failure and one doomed to disappear". As far back as 1911 Anton Jurgens had started buying up shares in a dozen Norwegian whaling companies, without doubt with a view to acquiring a certain measure of control of whale oil producers as a weapon to be used against oil dealers. A handful of these, in Glasgow, Liverpool, London, and Hamburg, had obtained a near-monopoly of the whale oil market by granting whalers credit in return for an option on the purchase of their future production. In Jurgens's opinion they enjoyed an undue advantage of a seller's

43. William Hesketh Lever,
1st Viscount Leverhulme.

market. For this reason he made his way to Norway, in order to establish contact with whaling companies. The oil dealers fought hard in order to retain their position, but in the end they were eliminated and had to be satisfied with the role of brokers.

In yet another way Jurgens, together with van den Bergh, attempted to strike a blow at De-No-Fa and thus indirectly at Levers. The verdict in 1913 in the Testrup case concluded the first phase in this struggle. Hydrogenators Limited was established, based on an idea originally conceived by William Lever, the purpose of which was to form an organisation in which all existing patents for hydrogenation should be pooled and further developed co-operatively. Almost all major firms, including Lever Brothers, agreed to join, but William Lever, who had offered Hydrogenators Limited shares in De-No-Fa, was furious when HENRY VAN DEN BERGH incautiously enquired whether such a large majority of the shares had been secured that one might eventually decide to close down De-No-Fa. William Lever then withdrew his offer of shares as well as his firm's participation in Hydrogenators Limited. Anton Jurgens's motive for getting rid of De-No-Fa was the threat this firm posed to his German market, because, despite a duty of 120 Marks per ton on the factory's products, it was nevertheless able to compete with his German factory. Despite this, Hydrogenators Limited was set up in December 1913, without Lever's participation, and rallied all competitors against their main rival. With his patents and De-No-Fa, however, Lever was strong enough to ride out the storm.

Anton Jurgens's speculation in Norwegian whaling shares produced nothing but losses. The purpose of his visit to Norway was also to submit to whale oil producers a plan that had been discussed by all major purchasers of their products : the formation of a Whale Oil Pool. This was to serve a double purpose : to cut out costly middlemen — the oil dealers — by direct contact between producer and consumer, and secondly, to ensure a reasonable distribution of whale oil among purchasers. The Pool was duly formed, and functioned satisfactorily from the end of 1913. De-No-Fa was also a member.

As there were signs that the whalers would react to the purchasers' ring by establishing a sales ring, in order to maintain price levels, Anton Jurgens came up with a plan for Hydrogenators Limited to start whaling on a large scale. He hoped that William Lever would join in, but the latter replied : "Goldmining or dice-throwing are unexciting occupations compared with whale fishing : this profession should be left to people with lifelong experience." The plan was consequently shelved. Nevertheless, two years before in 1912, Lever Brothers had bought the Premier Whaling Co. in South Africa.

On the buyers' front the situation was this : since 1906 vegetable oils and whale oil had started to supplant American animal fat as the principal raw materials for the soap and margarine makers. Vegetable margarine had become the current demand. Whale oil was already being used to a great extent in the manufacture of soap, and the largest quota from the Whale Oil Pool went to Lever Brothers. Jurgens, always enterprising in the use of raw materials, apparently used whale oil around 1912 as an important ingredient. Van den Bergh was more conservative, advising his German partners not to use whale oil at all : "Whale oil was a delicate matter commercially. To look kindly upon blubber as a source of imitation butter called for a more lively appreciation of the wonders of science than the average housewife could muster."

We should now consider the whaling companies' reaction to this struggle for oil, and the influence it must have had on the development of the whaling industry, which is to some extent reflected in Table 14.

Japan-Korea are included in the first six columns of the table but, as whaling was conducted mainly for meat and very little oil was produced, to include this catching in the last two columns would give a highly misleading picture. Starting with 1905, in accordance with *International Whaling Statistics*, the year's summer catching and the preceding season in the Antarctic are lumped together. Figures for the number of companies and shore stations are the most uncertain and also the least important. A far safer and more important method of illustrating the development is provided by the number of floating factories and whale catchers, particularly the latter. The tremendous increase in the number of companies in 1911 and 1912 was due in particular to the many new expeditions organised for operations off Africa and Australia, while the decline towards the end of the period reflects their demise and an all-

Table 14. COMPANIES, WHALING FLEETS, CATCHES, PRODUCTION
PER CATCHER, 1900-1914

	Companies	Shore-stations	Floating factories	Catchers	Whales	Whales per catcher	Barrels per catcher	Barrels per whale
1900	27	29		54	1,654	30.6	1,746	57.7
1901	25	29		57	2,259	40.0	1,730	43.7
1902	28	32		66	2,837	43.0	1,855	43.4
1903	34	38	2	71	3,414	48.0	1,691	35.0
1904	44	47	2	86	4,546	53.0	1,796	36.2
1905	44	46	6	89	4,315	48.5	1,678	36.9
1906	41	44	6	89	4,028	45.0	1,328	33.5
1907	51	55	9	109	5,705	52.0	1,824	35.5
1908	52	56	10	125	7,071	56.5	1,923	32.4
1909	57	57	12	140	9,526	70.0	2,068	27.1
1910	64	54	14	149	12,298	82.5	2,200	27.9
1911	67	60	25	189	20,408	108.0	3,589	30.5
1912	93	73	42	251	24,767	98.6	3,266	30.9
1913	85	67	39	261	26,134	100.0	3,403	31.8
1914	79	64	39	254	23,409	92.0	3,703	38.1

round consolidation in larger units. The decline is also due to a reduction in activity in the North Atlantic. The number of floating factories shows no marked increase up to 1910, but is tripled in the two subsequent years, particularly with the increase of activity in the Antarctic and round Africa. The number of whale catchers conforms to this increase, and declines with it towards the end of the period.

The number of whales caught is doubled in 1910-12, the great humpback period. The reason why the number of barrels per boat increases in 1913-14, despite the decline in the number of whales, is due to the onset of larger blue and fin whale catches. (Improved exploitation of the raw material — meat-boiling plant — was of minor importance.) This is also reflected in the increasing number of barrels per whale. A more correct relative picture would have emerged for the figures in the last few columns if statistics had been available showing the number of whales of each species. Taken all round, the above table serves to confirm what has previously been said about the crisis around 1905. The number of whales shows a downward trend from 1904 to 1906 and the number of barrels of oil per catcher reaches an all-time low in 1906, after which, in the course of eight years, it almost trebles. As boiling technique in this period made no decisive progress, this factor can be dismissed as an explanation for the increase in the number of barrels per catcher. The most important technical advances occurred in the construction and design of whale catchers. Whaling had reached a stage at which the problem was full utilisation not of the entire raw material, but of as much as possible of its best portions, as long as there were sufficient supplies available. More effective whale catchers and ample access to whales explain the marked increase in the number of barrels per boat and not a particular increase in the try-out of barrels per whale.

With 1,328 barrels per catcher and the price of oil right down to 24 øre per kg. or £13 a ton, rock bottom for economically viable operation had been reached, and it was only a rise in prices from the summer of 1906 that saved whaling from still further stagnation. The number of barrels per boat was decisive to companies' working balance; it was clearly more profitable to market 25,000 barrels of oil extracted from a number of whales caught by five catchers than if the same number of whales had been accounted for by ten catchers. The great increase in the number of whale catchers made it difficult to secure the services of good gunners. Years of experience are necessary to produce good results, and the great difference in the number of whales caught by catchers of the same type, belonging to the same company, in the same whaling grounds, in one and the same season, would appear to show that it was not merely a question of luck or lack of it, but of personal skill. Good gunners were a company's biggest asset.

One factor that would have been of great interest to establish is production costs per barrel as related to market price. A calculation of this kind undertaken on the basis of preserved accounts involves many difficulties. All companies' operating expenses include the cost of production of baleen, guano, bone meal, meat meal, etc., and it is impossible to carry out a calculation for oil alone. On the other hand, proceeds from sales often include earnings accruing from the above-mentioned by-products as well as from occasional finds of ambergris. In the case of companies with a large production of guano the overall picture is greatly distorted when expenses include the cost of its production, whereas sales of guano are not included under earnings. Subject to these reservations, however, an estimate of production and sale price per barrel for a number of leading companies does provide a certain basis for a general conclusion. Accounts reveal such discrepancies between companies, both in production and sales price, that as far as the latter is concerned the figures listed in the ordinary price tables cannot be used to indicate what companies generally were paid for their oil. These tables list the highest and lowest price in the course of the year, and only the price for category No. o/1. Not even the mean figure for highest and lowest would give a correct idea, and because quite 50 per cent of oil production of many companies right up to 1915 comprised lower grades than o/1, the average price per barrel of total production is considerably lower than the price tables mentioned would appear to indicate. In the case of shore stations that extracted oil from every part of the whale, the proportion of lower grades would be relatively larger than for floating factories that merely reduced the blubber (see Statistical Appendix, Table 51).

Production costs per barrel may vary between one company and another in the same whaling grounds by as much as Kr.120 (£6) per ton. This may be due to various circumstances: mechanical or matériel breakdowns, inefficient shooting, coal prices, availability of whales, and, not least, the human factor. In some cases an acute shortage of coal and barrels would compel an expedition to break off before the season was over. The rise in the first two years of the World War was not markedly great; the really great rise did not occur until the last phase of the war, 1917-18, and the sales price curve reached its peak two years later, 1919-20, for reasons that will be explained in the chapter on whaling during the First World War. Sales prices did not fluctuate as much as production costs. The gross profit during this period (1906-15) appears to have been about £12 a ton, Kr.37 (£2) a barrel, 22 øre (3d) a kilogramme for companies in the Southern Ocean. Even with a sales price as low as £13 a surplus was possible. The limit rose somewhat towards the end of the period. With an average sales price in 1910-15 — which includes the poor 1911-12 season — of respectively £19, Kr.57 (£3), 35 øre (5d), there was bound to be a good profit. This is reflected, moreover, in companies' surplus and return on capital. For the four companies on which these calculations are based, these were as shown in Table 15.

Table 15. PROFITS OF FOUR WHALING COMPANIES IN THE
ANTARCTIC, 1910-1915
(Figures in millions of Kroner)

	1910-11	1911-12	1912-13	1913-14	1914-15
Capital	2,400	2,760	4,760	4,760	4,760
Surplus	2,320	727	2,423	1,936	3,654
Percentage of capital	96.6	26.1	50.9	40.6	76.8

Return on capital amounting to nearly 100 per cent was outstanding. In the autumn of 1911 the shares of these companies stood at c. 250 per cent above par. Investing in whaling and whaling shares was a tempting proposition. Capital will always flow wherever there is a prospect of the greatest profit. In 1911 the four companies declared dividends of 50, 60, 60, and 100 per cent respectively, and that at a time when the economy in general was not favourable. Shipping, with which it would be natural to compare whaling, passed through difficult years between 1907 and 1911.

It would, of course, be highly misleading to base our picture of the economic results of whaling on the four most successful companies and one particularly successful season, 1910-11. This, however, has been done intentionally, since the same limited presuppositions provided the basis on which the future of whaling was predicted, resulting in an expansion that burst the bounds of reason, culminating in a series relapse in the autumn of 1912. From the 1910-11 to the 1911-12 season the number of companies rose from sixty-seven to ninety-three, the number of shore stations from sixty to seventy-three, whale catchers from 189 to 251, and capital investment from Kr.22 million to Kr.32 million (in Norwegian expeditions). The increase in production, however, bore no relation to the increase in equipment and capital. Both the number of whales per catcher and barrels per catcher declined. As production costs rose at the same time and prices slumped, the result was as shown above. This relapse was not a peculiarly Norwegian phenomenon : the South Georgia Company (Chr. Salvesen & Co.) considered the 1910-11 season a record, with a profit of £28,484 (on a capital of £20,000), and a dividend of 100 per cent, free of income tax, was declared. The 1911-12 season, on the other hand, produced a loss of £441 10s as a result of lower production and a tremendous slump in selling prices. Some of the blame must be ascribed to "the apparently antiquated whale catchers", which were now replaced by new ones.

It would have been surprising if the relapse had not provoked some criticism. A leading economic historian has described the situation as follows : "1912 saw something of a crash, for production had for once overtaken demand. Prices fell, dividends were passed and share quotations fell sharply. The fact was that the whaling business had lived by the day, squandering its profits by paying grossly inflated dividends and relying on the Norwegian banks for credit with which to fit out its ships. When the banks cut them off in 1912, the whaling companies found themselves unable to pay any dividend at all." To state that companies paid no dividends is an exaggeration, although undeniably there was a drastic slump. Twenty-two Norwegian companies declared a dividend in 1911 and only seven in 1912.

Criticism was countered with the assertion that whaling could not be based on long-term plans. All the whaling grounds had proved that they would only yield a profit for a comparatively short number of years. During this brief period interest had to be paid on capital and plant amortised. A disused whaling station was practically worthless, and if whale catchers and floating factories could not be transferred to other whaling grounds, they were, owing to their special fittings, likewise much reduced in value. The abnormally high running costs were emphasised. "Gunners, managers, and catchers should earn good money, but this has been overdone. This has been aggravated by competition among the companies. All-too-ready capital is also to blame. Gunners have been able to demand a cabinet minister's wages, whilst managers and directors have made fortunes in a short time."

When prices rose in 1913 the crisis was temporarily over. This was due primarily to the steadily growing number of hydrogenation factories.

"The ability to process whale oil has, in fact, to a large extent confirmed the whalers' assumption that whale oil has fetched far too low a price in relation to the actual value of the commodity," we read in a survey of the oil market in 1913. This year is a significant turning-point in many respects — in the price-level of whale oil as compared to other oils, in consolidation on both fronts, of vendors and purchasers. Among the latter this found expression in Hydrogenators Limited, in an attempt to establish a monopoly of the hydrogenation industry, and in the Whale Oil Pool. We shall see how the vendors attempted to counter this.

The first step was the Whalers' Mutual Insurance Association, established in Sandefjord on 10 August 1911. It aroused the greatest resentment among ordinary insurance companies, who now lost a valuable source of revenue. In time the new association was supported by practically all Norwegian whaling companies and also a number of foreign ones, and when companies engaged in ordinary shipping, side by side with whaling, the association also undertook the insurance of cargo ships. Although exact figures are not available, the Whalers' Mutual Insurance Association has saved whaling companies tremendous sums. It was an important step on the road to rendering the whaling industry independent, and to developing the strength that solidarity provided.

The next step was the Association of Norwegian Whaling Companies, founded in Sandefjord on 6 March 1912. The time was ripe for an event of this nature: all categories of seafaring men had during the years immediately preceding established their national organisations. Previously, numerous attempts had been made to organise both shipowners and active seamen, and a campaign in favour of this had been launched when shipping was passing through a depression. When finally, in about 1910, viable organisations were established, shipping was in the throes of a deep depression. The same circumstances attended the establishment of the Association of Norwegian Whaling Companies: the slump in the price of whale oil from the autumn of 1911, extending through the spring and summer of 1912, as well as difficulties in marketing the oil. As long as the big Southern Ocean companies operated separately in the market with their large cargoes, they were a comparatively easy prey to oil buyers. Companies lived from season to season: the sale of the current season's production was necessary to finance the fitting out of the next. This became still more urgent in 1912, when banks limited credit. Conditions of sale, too, were somewhat different from previously, because it was in that very year of 1912 that a change occurred, whereby oil was no longer sold to oil dealers, but direct to soap and margarine manufacturers, and the new customer, the hydrogenation industry. Faced with a tendency on the part of purchasers to team up in a whale oil pool, it was not surprising that whalers should have stood shoulder to shoulder for their common interests, i.e. the highest possible price and a stable price level. But the whaling company owners, in common with the ship-owners, faced another front — the first trade unions of active whalers.

As already mentioned, during an earlier critical period whalers had joined together in a body : this was during the dispute on the ban on whaling in North Norway. From the start the new Association gained widespread support; a month and a half later it had recruited as members companies with a capital of some Kr.28 million, and an estimated annual catch of 500,000 barrels.

Among the aims set out in the statutes was "to endeavour to have the companies' products recommended and introduced to the world market", to keep informed at all times of prices, and "to work for the greatest possible stability in the price of oil". That their attention was directed to the significance of hydrogenation may be seen from the fact that information was to be collected on "chemical and technical means of processing fats". The most important practical object was expressed as "to seek to establish common principles for the prevention of unfavour-able contracts and usages" by preparing standard sales contracts for the union's members. The question of wage agreements and earnings also bulked large in their negotiations. We shall later consider these and other matters taken up by the Association, and the results achieved.

The creation of the Association was immediately noted abroad — and seen as a sales ring. Applications from those seeking appoint-ment as agents poured in. The Association Secretary was sent on a round tour of Europe to champion the use of whale oil and collect information on market conditions. It is difficult to decide to what extent the existence and activities of the Association influenced the price increase that took place in the course of the autumn. A German periodical wrote that the whaling companies' combine had halted the slump in the price of whale oil that had taken place till then, but the most important reason was that the harvest of the more important oleagenous seeds had proved less favourable than expected, and that the new hydrogenation factories were in the market as big buyers.

SIGURD RISTING (1870-1935), who ever since 1903 had compiled his annual reviews of whaling, joined the editorial staff of *The Norwegian Whaling Gazette*, an organ that was entirely independent of the Whaling Association, in June 1913. Its first issue appeared on 15 November 1912. It ceased publication in September 1921, but from April 1922 con-tinued as the Whaling Association's organ, with Risting as editor. In countless articles, he collected and presented a mass of material of inestimable value to the history of whaling, while at the same time making it an indispensable organ of information for members of the Whaling Association and for all those who in some way or another were associated with the industry. Risting became the Association's secretary in 1918, a position he held up to the time of his death. With

44. Sigurd Risting, the founder of the history of modern whaling and of *International Whaling Statistics.*

his eminently sound historical work and as the creator of *International Whaling Statistics,* a unique document of its kind, he has become the founder of the history of modern whaling, an authority who cannot be ignored.

The direct involvement of Norwegian whaling companies with the establishment of a hydrogenation industry in Norway proved of great importance. The initiative for this originated both in Norway and abroad. Norway possessed the raw material and the source of energy, overseas interests owned the patents and the major soap and margarine concerns. Co-operation of advantage to both parties was established. The first contact the Norwegian Whaling Association had with this was in August 1912, when it received a letter from Vienna enquiring whether the Association wished to acquire shares in a factory for the hydrogenation of whale and herring oil. Plans for undertakings of this nature were already being developed in Norway.

The first of these eventually emerged as Vera Fedtrafineri A/S (Vera Fat Refinery Ltd.). At a board meeting of A/S Ornen on 17 October 1913, Lars Christensen, who for this purpose had visited Vienna, was authorised to purchase for a sum of Kr.300,000 a hydrogenation patent from the Hydrier-Patent-Verwertungs Gesellschaft. As this undertaking was more than A/S Ornen could handle alone or was prepared to underwrite on its own, a shareholding company, Vera Fedtrafineri, was established with a capital of Kr.2.5 million. This might be described as a family affair, in which several members of the Christensen family held leading positions. One of the shareholders was Johan Bryde. In 1906 he had started a firm for pressing vegetable oils and linseed, groundnuts, and copra, and for the manufacture of antifoulings for ships, the nucleus of what today has become the large modern paint factory, Jotun Fabrikker A/S.

It was only reasonable that A/S Ornen's floating factory the *Orn* should deliver the first cargo of oil to the factory. The company was constituted on 24 November 1913, and in June 1914 the first pilot production started after the overhanging menace of the outbreak of war had resulted in various delays. As the undertaking got under way later than planned, some of the oil in storage was sold off at a great profit. From the inception of the factory up to 1 April 1915, it was consequently able to record a net profit of as much as Kr.773,000 (£42,500), and to declare a dividend of 10 per cent. Two important reasons why operating results in the following years were likewise so favourable were that capacity, estimated at 12,000-15,000 tons of hydrogenated fat annually, proved to be far greater, and that a particularly advantageous agreement on electric power was obtained.

The factory was in the safe and careful hands of Lars Christensen right up to 1919, when the whole undertaking was toppled by a group of speculators among the shareholders and by the general financial collapse in 1921-2. The company went bankrupt and had to be wound up in 1922. While this undertaking was to have no significant influence on the relations between Norwegian whaling and the great soap and margarine trust, the very reverse would be true of the other fat hydrogenation factory that was not started by the whaling companies, but in which many were major shareholders, and thus, with their support, enabled it to get off the ground. This was De-No-Fa, an important link in the close association between Norwegian whaling and Lever Brothers (Unilever).

The patent to be used by this factory had cost a great deal of money — 2 million Marks — and the only prospects of raising a sum of this size in Norway lay in arousing the interest of the whaling companies. They were successfully persuaded to sign a guarantee for Kr.1½ million. Negotiations with the owners of the patent, Bremer Besigheimer Oelfabriken A.G. (B.B.O.), resulted in the establishment of De-No-Fa (De Nordiske Fabriker) in May 1912. The factory was fully operational on 15 July 1913, an important day for Norwegian industry and whaling. In quality, production, and efficiency the result exceeded expectations. During the second half of 1913 6,800 tons of hardened fat were produced, in 1914 19,000 tons, and in 1915 29,000 tons, nearly all of which was exported overseas. During the war the factory was idle for long periods owing to a shortage of raw material.

Even before the factory had started production, threats to its very existence arose: Anton Jurgens published a warning against the production and sale of fat hydrogenated according to Wilbuschewitz's patent, as it could not be regarded as an independent patent but merely an extension of Normann's. There was no knowing what the verdict of a trial and a confrontation with the powerful Dutch concern would be.

This was the situation when Lever Brothers intervened. In order to escape from the dilemma that this firm was involved in as the result of hydrogenation, it had contracted for a considerable annual quota of production once De-No-Fa was operative. If Levers could obtain control of De-No-Fa, three important advantages would be achieved: the factory, which in its plant and running costs would produce cheaper hydrogenated fat than their corresponding factory in England; secondly, a supply of hydrogenated fat independent of rivals was assured; and thirdly, by increasing De-No-Fa's production beyond their own needs, they could compete on the world market with other manufacturers of hydrogenated fat, and in this way force down the price of raw materials. B.B.O.'s willingness to transfer its interests in De-No-Fa to Levers was undoubtedly so that it would avoid the great risk it was running by guaranteeing De-No-Fa free sales of its products. In September 1913 an agreement was concluded whereby Levers assumed B.B.O.'s shares, and injected Kr.1 million in order to extend the factory's capacity to 45,000 tons annually. The capital was thus increased to Kr.4 million, of which Levers owned 50 per cent.

This agreement caused dismay among Lever's competitors. Negotiations were just being held in order to establish Hydrogenators Limited, and a dramatic showdown occurred on 9 September 1913, between the negotiators. Jurgens threatened to use all means to crush De-No-Fa, not only with a view to eliminating a dangerous rival in the hydrogenated fat market, but also — and this is an indication of how important whale oil had now become as a raw material — in order to exclude it from the whale oil market. De-No-Fa was a member of the Whale Oil Pool and had been allotted its quota. In the game played by the major concerns to establish a monopoly De-No-Fa had now become an important card. We shall later see the important role De-No-Fa played during the First World War in the struggle between Norway and Britain for Norwegian whale oil.

In the course of 1911-13 important events had taken place for the consolidation of the Norwegian whaling industry. It was now in a much stronger position vis-à-vis purchasers, and it had acquired considerable financial interests in the industrial processing of the raw material. But in the course of these years the leading concern, Lever Brothers, had obtained a strong hold on the Norwegian hydrogenation industry, and had become actively engaged in whaling.

15
TECHNICAL DEVELOPMENTS BEFORE 1930

Boiling equipment

At the time with which we are now dealing it was not known with any degree of certainty how large a percentage of the total oil content of the whale was contained in its three main constituents — blubber, meat, and bone. Not till the end of the 1920s was this matter investigated in an entirely satisfactory technical-scientific manner.

At the Stromness station in South Georgia at the start of the 1925-6 season, when the whale was still comparatively lean, the three parts of fourteen whales (eleven blue and three fin) were boiled separately, producing a total of 1,596 barrels (266 tons) of oil, of which the blubber accounted for 620 barrels (38.8 per cent), the meat 515 barrels (32.4 per cent), and the bones 461 barrels (28.8 per cent). In other words, the two last-mentioned constituents together provided 22.4 per cent *more* oil than the blubber. Individual animals would vary enormously : the oil extracted from the meat and the bones would vary from 47 per cent to 73 per cent, and consequently in the blubber from 27 per cent to 53 per cent. The investigation revealed that the average composition of a whale weighing 100 tons was as follows :

	Constituents (%)			Weight in tons		
	Fat	Dry substance	Water	Oil	Dry substance	Water
Blubber and tongue	50	14	36	11.0	3.1	7.9
Meat and entrails	7	23	70	3.8	12.4	37.8
Bone	35	50	15	6.6	9.5	2.9

Theoretically, a whale of this kind contained 21.4 tons of oil, 25 tons of dry material, and 48.6 tons of water. From a large blue whale of 120 tons the following could be extracted :

	Number of barrels	Tons	% of raw material
Blubber oil	89	15.1	59.0
Meat oil	40	6.8	10.5
Bone oil	42	7.1	32.0
Total	171	29.0	24.2

Towards the end of the season there was a clear tendency for blubber to increase its relative share of the total weight and of the total oil content. There are several uncertain factors involved : great variations between the various species, between large and small whales, between males and females, between the various whaling grounds and precise time in the season when the whale was caught, between fresh and old whale, between the various boiling methods. Despite this uncertainty, calculations can be used to show that, once the blubber had been removed, the carcass still retained 40 to 60 per cent of the animal's total oil content. Even though the whalers, until such time as the results of these investigations were available, were not exactly familiar with this, they realised nevertheless that by merely using the blubber they were wasting a very important amount of the total oil contents. There were apparently no technical difficulties in extracting this, but the whalers had to consider the problem from the economic point of view: could it be done in such a way that it would be worth while? In the technique of boiling all improvements had two aims : to extract all the oil and to utilise the residual dry substance, and to carry out both operations in a profitable manner. The latter proved a particularly urgent matter, as injunctions on full utilisation became more and more stringent. As far as the quality of the product was concerned, it was of great importance that the whale should be reduced as rapidly as possible.

During the time between Svend Foyn's brilliant inventions in the 1860s and the invention of the stern slipway, the rotary cooker and the oil separator in the 1920s, no single invention was made comparable to these. If development were to be gauged according to the number of patents, it would have to be regarded as particularly fruitful; but an assessment on this basis alone would prove highly misleading. In the first place, many of the patents were never tested in practice, or else they were abandoned as useless after a short time. In the second place, a great many non-patented improvements were made, which together were of equal importance : a small detail involving the shape of the shell and the harpoon, or the attachment of the forerunner in the harpoon, in the fuse, the line, the whale windlass, the brake accumulator, mooring and towing of the whale, the design of the whale catcher and its manoeuvrability, the gun and its recoil, etc., *ad infinitum*. But even if the technical apparatus was functioning properly, what use was it if the hemp in the line was so poor that it snapped or froze so rigidly that it could not be coiled on the duckboards? Some of the ideas were so far in advance of their time that they were not understood. A great many inventions were not specifically made for whaling, but transferred from other fields : fixed tanks, evaporators, separators, wireless telegraphy, asdic, * etc. The

* Asdic produces bursts of sound that enable diving whales to be echo-located. It can be used in whaling in two different ways: (1) In the case of baleen whales, it frightens the animals, which then swim very fast and near the surface, making

pressure cooker and the rotary cooker had previously been used on terra firma for reducing animal carcasses.

Both by their nature and chronologically, improvements may be said to fall broadly into three categories: around the turn of the century there was a concentration on the flensing and partition of the blubber, and vague dreams of being able to haul the entire carcass on board. A decade later it was a question of improved cookers in order to cope with the large quantity of raw material. In the 1920s the problem of getting the whole carcass of the whale on board was broached once again, in order to make pelagic catching more effective. At the same time companies embark on technical-scientific research with a view to obtaining products of the highest quality and to exploiting the entire raw material. One of those engaged in this research pronounced the following prophecy in 1932, a prophecy which was to come true: "The fact must not be ignored that whaling, with its present production method, with the tremendous strain on the raw material and the poor exploitation of it, will probably stagnate sooner than is believed, and that finally there will only be room for a few of the floating factories that are cheaper to run and most effectively fitted out, unless something is done to increase the processing value of the raw material by means of a complete exploitation of its potential." Wise heads have toyed with the three stages of the problem: the catching technique, the boiling process, and the by-products. The reason why so many of the ingenious patents proved impractical, was that the inventor only considered the technical aspect of the matter, whereas the whaler was compelled first and foremost to assess it from the financial side, and all too often the two did not harmonise.

Before the raw material reached the cooker a certain amount of time had elapsed from the death of the whale. The length of time was important to the quality of the oil, owing to the self-combustion or "autolysis" which sets in after the whale has been killed. The dorsal flesh of a freshly shot whale has a temperature of 37-38°C; after twenty-four hours this may rise to 41° and after two or three days to 48°. Autolysis produces the fermentation process which starts in the food in the digestive organs, and spreads from there. The blubber is affected last of all, but accelerates the process of autolysis by preventing the heat that has been generated from escaping. For this reason autolysis is more pronounced in whales with a thick layer of blubber. The opening of the whale's carcass on the flensing deck would often have the effect of an explosion, accompanied by a repulsive smell. Autolysis splits the neutral fatty acids,

---

them easier to see and tiring them more quickly. (2) With sperm whales its major use is in the tracking of lone animals while they are diving at great depths, enabling the catcher to be in the right place when they eventually surface. It is rarely used with schools of sperm whales as it tends to scatter them and make it difficult to catch a high proportion of animals from one school.

45. A whale grossly inflated by autolysis.

increasing the content of free fatty acids in the oil, at the same time as it turns dark and acquires an unpleasant smell. As the temperature rises, the oleaginous cells burst, and the oil leaks out, and this may greatly reduce the amount of oil yielded. Pumping up the whale, in order to keep it afloat, and thus introducing oxygen into the whale's interior, greatly accelerated the process of autolysis. More recently, autolysis has successfully been greatly reduced by injecting the whale with an antibiotic immediately after it has been killed.

As a rule, a freshly killed whale produces oil from its blubber containing 0.15-0.20 per cent free fatty acid, and oil from the carcass 0.40-0.60 per cent. When boiling takes place more than two days after death, this may rise to 1 per cent in the blubber oil and 20-30 per cent in the carcass oil. Already at an early stage oil was divided into four categories according to quality, which was primarily determined by the percentage of free fatty acids, and the smell and colour accompanying it, according to the following scale: No. 0/1 free fatty acid 0-2 per cent, No. 2 2-6 per cent, No. 3 6-15 per cent, No. 4 15-60 per cent.

After boiling, the oil was never completely pure, but had to stand for a certain time in settling tanks until the oil floated up. This settling process was interrupted when the floating factory was not stationary. Attempts to increase the extraction of the whale's oil content and improve the quality were therefore directed towards all three factors: time, boiling, settling. The relative proportions of the various categories of oil remained fairly constant until the major technical improvements were introduced in the latter part of the 1920s. These resulted in a decisive shift in the

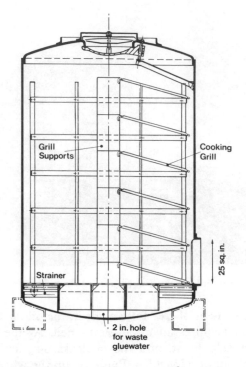

46.   Diagram of the open cooker.

direction of No. 0/1. Nos. 4 and 3 have now disappeared, and No. 0/1 now accounts for approximately 90-95 per cent.

The open pan for melting the blubber was replaced by the open cooker, which has already been described. This was a simple, reliable piece of apparatus, producing relatively large quantities of good, clear quality. The apparatus cost less to buy, but was fairly expensive to run, owing to the considerable consumption of steam, and a great deal of oil was lost in the grax and gluewater. Throughout the first sixty years, 1870-1930, this cooker was practically the only one used for blubber, but because of its shortcomings, especially its size, it was abandoned by most of the floating factories although to a large extent retained in the shore stations. In the open cooker the mass could be subjected to a certain pressure, but it is not the strength of the pressure which constitutes the most essential difference between this apparatus and the pressure cooker, but the fact that there are two different boiling principles. The blubber is mainly boiled in open cookers and meat and bone in pressure cookers, but in the open cooker none of the contents is run off during boiling; everything remains in the cooker until a few hours after boiling has been concluded, when oil has floated up and grax and gluewater have sunk to the bottom.

With the pressure cooker oil and gluewater are each separately blown out of the boiler with the aid of steam pressure immediately after the boiling process has started, a process which then continues almost uninterruptedly. In the pressure cooker, a little way up from the bottom, there is a grid which allows the fluid material to pass out while the solid material is left behind. Also, the steam is introduced into the pressure cooker at many different levels, whereas in the open cooker it enters through a spiral at the bottom.

No one took out a patent on the first pressure cooker, and we have no idea when and where it was first used. It was gradually developed on the model of the pressure cookers used in industry. A Norwegian engineering workshop has provided the information that a huge pressure cooker, with a capacity of 17 cubic metres, was constructed for whaling in 1889. It had eleven shelves or storeys of iron plates, on which meat and bone were placed, a task which took a great deal of time — and so did the boiling, as there was nothing to keep the mass moving. It was nevertheless considered a great advance. MARCUS C. BULL appears to have pioneered use of the pressure cooker. In 1902 he got an engineering workshop to build such a boiler, to take a pressure of 60 lb. per square inch, to be used for both blubber and meat. It was in processing the latter that it proved its superiority, but it was also used for blubber. In the pressure cooker meat had to be boiled for from fourteen to sixteen hours, and the tongue of the whale for as much as twenty-four hours. One shortcoming of pressure cooking was that a high steam pressure had a tendency to increase the acid content and to give the oil a darker colour.

The older type of pressure cooker was a steel cylinder approximately 10 ft. high and 6 ft. in diameter. About $1\frac{1}{2}$ ft. above the slightly curved bottom was a perforated plate, a strainer or sieve, and in the middle of the bottom a tap for running off gluewater, and just above the strainer the tap for running off the oil. On the opposite side, a little higher up, was a steam inlet pipe. After a few hours, when the cooker and the mass had been thoroughly heated, and the separation of the oil started, the oil tap was opened at the same time as the gluewater was run off, so that the level was always lower than the outlet of the oil tap. The pressure cooker had several disadvantages: when it was stacked full of meat, the steam would not impinge with the same strength on all parts of the mass, as it would seek the shortest way to the outlet, and hence the intervening mass would be overcooked and saturated with oil and gluewater from the other parts as the steam reached them. Air and gas would also collect here, and this would set up a counter pressure to the steam. When the boiler was opened after the cooking process was over, practically uncooked (clean) meat could be found in the grax. Drying this for guano was difficult, as it contained as much as 15 per cent fat.

Many attempts were made to overcome these disadvantages in a

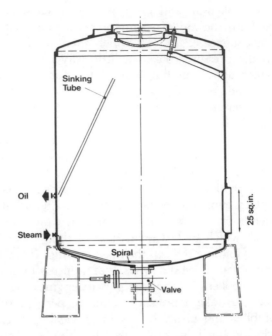

47.   Diagram of pressure cooker.

variety of ways — by introducing steam at various levels, by cutting the meat up into very small portions and placing it on grids in several layers, by allowing the gas to escape through a valve at the top when the boiling process started. In this way it was possible to reduce the boiling time from 18-20 to 10-12 hours, which meant a tremendous saving of coal and water. But despite all these improvements it was almost impossible to produce oil No. o/1. For this reason purchasers preferred oil reduced from blubber in open cookers. No better method for meat and bone, however, existed before the rotary cooker, the most revolutionary invention within this technique.

The idea and design of the first rotary cooker was the work of the German engineer August Sommermeyer. As already mentioned, he had been the technical manager of Kejzerling's East Asian whaling ventures, and had provided plans for most of the boiling equipment. This had been constructed by the firm of R. A. HARTMANN in Berlin. In practice it proved a great disappointment, and in Sommermeyer's opinion the main reason for this was that the mass remained stationary during the boiling process. He was consumed with the idea of solving this problem. Financially a solution depended on the attitude of Norwegian whaling circles, with their dominant position. Sommermeyer produced a sketch

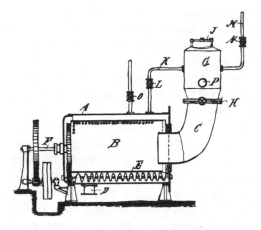

48. The first rough draft (1911) by the German engineer August Sommermeyer of the rotary cooker, the so-called Hartmann apparatus.

and obtained a Norwegian patent for it on 4 April 1911 (No. 23722). It was described as "Process and apparatus for continuous production of meat meal, fat, and glue from animal carcasses, slaughterhouse offal, and the like". Neither in this nor in subsequent patents (1924-9) are whales specifically mentioned, but the whale, of course, is also an animal. An agreement was reached with a Norwegian company in the Shetlands for delivery of one apparatus. Sommermeyer gives an interesting account in his memoirs of the protracted negotiations and of the Norwegians' sceptical approach to anything new. At its first test on 5 September 1911, $2\frac{1}{2}$ tons of grax, which had been boiled in the usual manner, was added, and in an atmosphere of tense expectation the process was started. To everyone's astonishment, not least Sommermeyer's, the result was practically a whole barrel of oil, "a good oil No. 3", as the expedition manager put it. "I would never have believed that anything more could be done with offal of that kind which we had always thrown into the sea."

A detailed description of the apparatus and process would be out of place in this context. In brief, the three main components were: the container for insertion, the rotary and perforated boiling drum, and the screw-like conveyor under the drum. The input container at the top of the horizontal drum had an external lid and a lower internal lid. When the boiling process was started, the lower lid was closed and kept in position by the pressure of steam. Through the upper lid the container was filled, the lid was screwed down, and steam with the same pressure as in the drum was introduced into the container; as a result, the lower lid would open and the mass fall down into the drum. In this way the process could be maintained continuously. The boiled mass fell unseparated through the holes in the drum and was pushed out into a trough by the conveyor, where it separated into three layers, according to specific weight — oil on top, then gluewater, and the solid components, or grax, at the bottom. One obvious weakness in this process was that it gave no indication of the precipitation of the oil. But in four ways the Hartmann apparatus entailed a tremendous improvement, in particular in the floating factories :

(1) It was estimated that one Hartmann apparatus was the equivalent of five pressure boilers, in so far as the boiling time was reduced to $1-1\frac{1}{2}$ hours, according to the nature of the material (blubber and meat), and this meant a tremendous saving in coal and water. The fact that the cooker was not down between each time it was loaded, and did not have to be warmed up again also saved coal. (2) The short time the mass was under the influence of steam pressure ensured a minimum amount of free fatty acid, but this effect was partly offset by the fact that the try-out was left standing at a high temperature for a while in the settling tank. (3) The apparatus was very labour-saving, in so far as the operator was spared the dirty and highly unpopular task of shovelling the grax out of the warm boiler. (4) The apparatus took up little space, a matter of major importance on a floating factory. It could be placed practically anywhere, and not necessarily near the rail, where the pressure cooker was traditionally placed so as to enable grax to be dumped straight into the sea. Space was also saved as there was no longer any need for a machine that cut blubber and meat fine, and the apparatus could be filled by hand with large pieces that could pass through the opening to the charging container.

"Apparatus cooking", as the whalers called it, proved its superiority in particular for boiling meat on floating factories. On the shore stations, where space was not such an important consideration, there was greater freedom in choice of method. This was determined rather by financial considerations than by practical and technical ones, but on the floating factories the choice was not difficult as long as catching was merely based on the production of oil. The verdict on the first apparatuses varies, but is on the whole decidedly favourable. On one floating factory the first attempt to use the apparatus was made off the coast of Africa in 1912, but as operations that year were generally speaking a failure, the first time the apparatus was tried out in earnest was in the same floating factory off South Shetland in 1913-15, when the results were excellent. According to the ship's log, in the 1914-15 season 5,000 barrels of oil and 3,000 sacks of guano were produced on the basis of two apparatuses. The war made it difficult to manufacture the apparatuses, but Sommermeyer spent the time making strenuous efforts to improve them. C. A. Larsen included two apparatuses on his first voyage to the Ross Sea in 1923-4, and they functioned so well that the fourteen large pressure cookers were not used at all. The apparatuses made their final breakthrough in 1925 on board the *Lancing,* the vessel that pioneered the stern slipway, and on the large new floating factories in 1928-31.

Although the rotary cooker was specially designed with a view to boiling meat, the first type was mainly used for blubber, not because the method was not suitable for meat and bone, but because its construction was not sturdy enough. On the whole it may be said that during the first fifteen years the apparatuses only enjoyed a conditional success. Furthermore, they were very expensive, costing 50,000 to 60,000 Marks apiece, although subsequent mass production halved this sum. An ordinary cooker cost no more than the equivalent of 3,000-4,500 Marks. Sommermeyer's new patent was a definite improvement. In the first place the apparatus was larger and more robust, and had two containers for alternative charging, and in the second place it was linked with an oil separator to which the try-out from the drum was transferred by steam pressure, and from which the precipitation of the various parts could take place continuously. However, irrespective of the method of boiling, the three parts could never be entirely separated: after some twelve to twenty-four hours in the settling tank the oil would still contain a small amount of gluewater and solid fibre which could cause fermentation and the generation of acid during transport in the heat in tropical latitudes. This form of settling demanded calm, which was a rarity in floating factories.

On board these the centrifugal method became an epoch-making innovation. The separator was, of course, by no means unknown as a device when it was introduced to whaling; it had been used in dairies ever since the 1880s, but milk and the viscid effluent from a cooker were two entirely different matters, and it was to prove difficult to transfer the method from one substance to the other. Sommermeyer and several others had long worked with the problem before they succeeded in 1924 in making an entirely satisfactory separator for whale oil, and seldom has an innovation been so promptly accepted: by 1930 the separator was in use throughout the whaling industry as a normal part of the production apparatus. It was in particular the Swedish separator marketed under the brand name "Baltic" (from 1929 the "Laval") that was used, but German and British models were also on the market. They all suffered from one drawback: the viscid mass had a tendency to clog the separator. This problem was solved quite simply by heating the oil and mixing it with seawater at a temperature of 90-95°C. This highly fluid mixture made it easier to separate foreign bodies and remove deposits of free fatty acid. The money invested in a set of separators was easily recouped in one season. A test in 1928 showed that separated oil of the same try-out after a month's storage had 1.55 per cent of free fatty acid, whereas oil settled by the old method had 5.7 per cent. A great advantage of the separator was that one saved the large amount of space the settling tanks had occupied on board. Separators worked independent of the ship's movements and could be placed anywhere, the oil being piped from them to the ship's tanks.

The gluewater precipitated in the separators contained 5-15 per cent oil, which was wasted when the gluewater was dumped in the sea. Separating this oil from the gluewater was a far greater problem, not satisfactorily solved until after the Second World War, obviating, as we shall see, considerable losses.

Attempts have been made to extract oil direct without the boiling process in order to avoid the unfortunate effects of high steam pressure and temperature. It was thought that the solution to this was to develop a means to exert mechanical pressure on the blubber, so that the oil would run out in the crude state (it had, however, to undergo a brief boiling period in order to keep). The press that was the fruit of this endeavour was, however, a huge, heavy, and costly machine (approximately Kr.90,000), occupying so much space and consuming so much energy when operated that it hardly paid its way, even though it produced oil of the very best quality. As thirty to forty of these presses were in use in the mid-1920s, it appeared that they would be a standard part of production, but the Hartmann apparatuses made them superfluous.

During this period comparatively few patents were granted for the utilisation of the solids of the whale, the grax. The difficulty was to remove all the oil, in order to produce an entirely dry product which could be ground to meal. In theory, tremendous sums were lost when the solids were scrapped. For the 1937-8 season it was estimated that it would have been possible to have produced 600,000 tons which, with guano fetching a price of Kr.100-150 a ton, would have produced a sum of Kr.60-90 million. This is purely hypothetical: on a floating factory it would only have been possible to produce a small fraction of this, for technical reasons. It is also doubtful whether there would have been a market for it, as guano had three competitors: bird guano from the South Sea Islands, natural saltpetre (Chilean saltpetre), and artificial fertiliser, which was then coming on to the market.

For a while whale meal appeared likely to figure as a form of artificial cattle feed, but interest in it proved limited and production declined, and not till after the Second World War was any large-scale production of a thoroughly satisfactory artificial feed set in motion. When Lord Leverhulme bought the Southern Whaling & Sealing Co. in 1919, and commenced operations from the Hebrides in 1923, he was greatly interested in the production of whale meal as well as herring meal, and in 1924 he started his own company, the Ocean Harvest Co., for the purpose of marketing fresh meat to the natives of Africa as well as all

49. Horizontal guano dryer.

other products of the whale apart from oil. It proved difficult, however, to overcome the conservatism of the farmers. Mixed with other vegetable feed substances, whale meal could be used in particular for feeding pigs and chickens. An investigation of the periods at which major production of the various kinds of whale meal were initiated will reveal that this particular endeavour took place in about 1902-5, i.e. during years when the price of oil was so low that every potential had to be exploited in an attempt to make whaling profitable. But interest in it dropped as soon as the price of oil rose once again. The price of guano rallied slightly from Kr.8-9 in the 1890s to about Kr.11 in 1913-14. Surprisingly, it did not rise as markedly during the war as afterwards: in 1916 it stood at about Kr.14.50, in 1922 at Kr.19, and in 1925 it had risen to Kr.27.50, receding two years later to Kr.19.50, as the result of the general slump in prices.

Several kinds of dryer have been designed: common to all of them was a long, horizontal cylinder, where the mass was dried by the introduction of hot air. From 1911-12 they were used on a number of floating factories with comparatively good results. One of the factories stationed off South Georgia produced in 1913-14 4,750 barrels of oil and 5,200 sacks of guano from de-blubbered carcasses, and in 1914-15 respectively 3,700 and 9,000. The interest in this dropped in the 1920s with stable, good prices for oil, as every available space on board was used to increase the production of oil alone. This was feasible as long as there was no shortage of whales, but after the Second World War, with declining catches, it proved more urgent for companies to utilise all the potential value of their raw material.

50.   Steam driven bone saw introduced about 1921.

Flensing could be carried out in either the so-called "round" way or the "long" way. In "round" flensing, which was most commonly used in floating factories when flensing overboard, the blubber was removed from the whale in strips of a certain width as it rolled round in the sea. In the second case, most commonly in use at shore stations, strips of blubber were removed along the carcass of the whale. Hooks were fastened to holes on the edge of the blubber, and the blubber was pulled off by a steam winch as the flensers worked it loose from the carcass with their flensing knives. The most time-consuming work was cutting up the head and the bones. This was done with 8 to 10 ft. long saws, with a man pulling on either side. It took an hour to saw up a head. The same principle was tried as in a stone crusher, but the bones were tough and flexible, and soft material clogged up the machine.

The introduction of a steam-driven bone saw saved a tremendous amount of time and energy. No one is quite certain who invented it. These saws are believed to have been used for the first time in South Georgia in 1921-2, and were made in the workshop at Grytviken from a drawing from the Framnæs shipyard in Sandefjord. In 1922-3 bone saws made by the firm of John Pickles & Son in England were installed in two floating factories. The first saws were so weak that they often broke, but after a while this was put right. The bone saws had Swedish steel blades, and did excellent work; after a few years they were a standard part of the equipment, as their use removed a technical bar to an easier and more rapid reduction of the entire raw material, and in the course of one season they saved in wages far more than they cost.

The floating factory

In principle, the floating factory and pelagic whaling are not an innovation introduced by modern-style whaling. It was precisely with the use of the floating factory that the old-style whaling reached its peak. It has been calculated that during the years 1835-72 almost 300,000 sperm and right whales were killed. At its height in 1846 the American whaling fleet comprised 735 vessels of a total tonnage of 233,200 tons, with 20,000 hands and an invested capital of more than $21 million. During the record year of 1851 428,000 barrels of oil were produced, almost as much in one year as during the entire period of Finnmark whaling in 1868-1904. This involved a tremendous input of men and material, and losses in both were considerable.

As already mentioned, Roys and Lilliendahl and Svend Foyn had all experimented with a sailing vessel as a floating factory off Iceland, while a whaling company from Sandefjord had done likewise off Finnmark. Neither proved successful, but these attempts kept the idea of the floating factory alive. Apparently Count Kejzerling's *Michail* was the first steamer in modern-style whaling purchased for use as a floating factory, but it was Christen Chistensen's *Admiralen* which was the prototype. An attempt was made in 1903 with a small leased wooden steamer provisionally fitted out (it cost Kr.2,851 !) From the point of view of the catch this was successful, but it was too small. For this reason the *Admiralen* (formerly the *Gibraltar*) of 1,517 gross tons was purchased; she was built of iron in Sunderland in 1869, and had an engine of 800 h.p., producing a speed of 12 knots in ballast. She was converted for permanent use as a floating factory, with four large open cookers and one small pressure cooker, a blubber chopper, settling tanks, evaporators, etc. On the very first trip it was evident that supplies of fresh water would be the major problem for floating factories. Apart from the fact that boiling required large quantities of steam, the cookers on the main deck were exposed to cold winds and sea spray, and neither they nor the pipes were insulated. The floating factory could not continue under way as long as boiling was taking place, because the ship's boilers did not produce enough steam for its own propulsion and boiling at the same time. For this reason, too, the floating factory had to lie at her moorings close to shore. In order to obviate the considerable loss of heat that occurred when cookers were placed on the open main deck, Christensen in 1910 patented cookers built into the hull. These were placed on the 'tween deck with the top lid flush with the main deck. Three advantages were achieved : there was less cooling off of the boilers, they were easier to fill, and more valuable working space was available on deck.

In neither the hunting of the whale, nor the flensing, nor the boiling technique was there a change revolutionary enough to be compared with the slipway (or stern slip). The idea of hauling the whale on board not surprisingly arose at the same time as experiments with floating factories in 1903-6. There was a parallel between these attempts, in the transition from northern whaling to global whaling, and the solution of the problems in the 1920s, with the transition from global whaling to pelagic whaling. In much that has been written about whaling authors make the mistake of assuming that catching in the open sea started at the same time as the first floating factories were introduced, but all modern whaling, with or without floating factories, was shore whaling until the mid-1920s.

Many patents have been granted and the strangest ideas submitted for hauling the whale on board. One of those who, in advance of his time, solved the problem in his own way was the Norwegian whaler MORTEN ANDREAS INGEBRIGTSEN. In 1897 he was operating off Bjørnøya with one whale catcher and a small schooner, the *Herold,* of about 500 gross tons. When a whale had been caught, it was pulled up, with a steam winch, by the tail, over the ship's counter, which was made as low as possible, and the greater the portion of the whale that was pulled in on deck, the lower the stern rode in the water, though not, however, so low that there was a danger of the vessel filling with water. In a way it could be said that the whale was floated on board. In this way ten fin whales could be flensed and the blubber stowed in the hold, transported to Finnmark, and processed there. As it was not processed on board it cannot be said that the *Herold* really fulfils the criteria of a factory ship. The many persons who were granted patents on methods of hauling the whale whole on board did not indicate how to solve the practical problems associated with the following: how to attach a cable to the tail of the whale in a rough sea; how to construct winches capable of a pull of 100-150 tons; how to cut the whale up rapidly enough in the limited space available on deck; how to prevent the whale rolling or sliding on the deck in a rough sea; how to find adequate space for blubber and meat and bone, once the cookers were full. Getting the de-blubbered carcass back into the sea was in itself quite a problem.

Most of these patents for hauling whales on board are of little interest to the history of whaling, as they were so unrealistic that they were never tried. The method suggested can be divided into three main sections: (1) floating the whale through a hatch in the side of the ship into a compartment; (2) hauling the whale on to the deck in a net; (3) hauling the whale up on a slipway, amidships, in the bow, and in the stern. The first and second methods were tried only once, and on both occasions the result was a near catastrophe for the floating factories and had to be abandoned immediately. This was also the case with the slipway set amidships. The third was tried in the bows of a floating factory once only, but this time successfully, many thousands of whales having been pulled up on to the flensing deck in this way, but the huge, heavy port that had to be shut when the ship was moving reduced speed and was one of the reasons why the stern slipway was preferred. However, the reason why the idea of a bow slipway arose and was put into practice was because during the conversion of old conventional ships to floating factories, problems arose in adjusting the stern slipway to the ship's rudder and propellor. A floating factory with a bow port was in operation from 1926 to 1952.

Among the many forerunners who had ideas for solving the problem of the slipway mention must be made of the Norwegian engineer JENS ANDREAS MØRCH (1859-1915). It may sound paradoxical to call him the most ingenious inventor in the history of whaling, since only a few of his patents were actually put into practice. In 1904-6 he obtained not less than fourteen patents, covering every stage of whaling, from the animal itself to the production of margarine. His dream was an interconnected process proceeding from the first to the last stage. Many of his ideas were far in advance of his age, and he suffered the same fate as so many great geniuses : not to be understood by his contemporaries or harvest any of the fruits of his work. We shall meet him again as the pioneer with the basic ideas for the international regulation of whaling. There can be no doubt that many patentees have learnt from his ideas, as set forth in his patent descriptions. Some of his patents were so fantastic that one is tempted to believe that they were not seriously intended, e.g. the idea of floating the whale straight into an enormous cauldron and boiling it whole, or chasing the whale with the aid of an electrically operated soundless submarine, shaped like a whale itself, in order to attract the quarry !

Of the many patents for a slipway Mørch's came closest to a workable solution. The first patent was granted in 1904, and improved by two additions in 1905 and 1906. Above the rounded portion of the counter a crane was placed to assist in lifting the whale up at the same time as it was hauled in. Owing to the rudder stock and the steering mechanism the slip was located too high above the water for the whale to be successfully hauled up. Once the whale's tail was on deck, the rest of its body remained suspended almost vertically, and no crane or winch was strong enough to lift it. His patent failed on one point, in that it provided no information on adjusting the floating factory by means of water ballast, so that the lower end of the slipway was always flush with the surface of the water. This problem was solved by the whale gunner Petter Sørlle (1884-1933) from Sandefjord in his patent of 12 September 1922 (with amendments of 22 May 1928 and 30 May 1929). As already mentioned, he had received his idea when he had operated along the ice barrier in South Orkney but it remained dormant

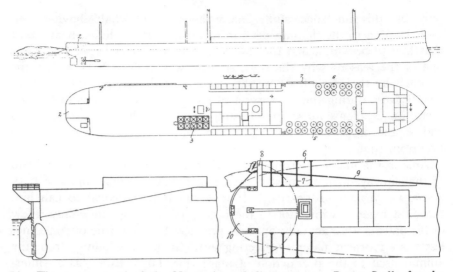

51. The two patents of the Norwegian whaling manager Petter Sørlle for the stern slip: *above*, in a ship with cruiser stern and twin screws; *below*, a slip on each side of a ship with a single screw and elliptical stern.

while for the next eight years he worked from a shore station in South Georgia. The idea was resurrected when the whaling fleet was being rebuilt after the war and the Norwegian companies were in danger of being forced to operate out at sea should Britain refuse to renew concessions and licences.

Sørlle's patent was so-called combined patent: it involved not only the slipway, the lower end of which extended right down to beneath the vessel's load waterline, but also indicated that the slipway, by trimming the vessel, could be lowered sufficiently for its lower extremity to extend beneath the water. The patent also included a broad transport passage running through the entire superstructure of the ship, where the de-blubbered carcass could be drawn from the flensing platform astern to the meat platform forward. The objection to the trimming and the passage was that they were already so well known that they could not be patented, and as they were integrated in the patent this could not be granted in its entirety. The other objection was that several patents had already been granted for a slipway, and in the third place Sørlle did not indicate how the work of building the slip was to be carried out. This was, however, according to the Patent Board, not necessary in order to acquire a patent, which could also be granted for an idea, and Sørlle's patent involved a combination of (*per se* known) factors no one had previously indicated. In a subsequent court case Sørlle was granted sole right to the patent, though the decision was not unanimous. He was also granted an English patent (24 September 1925). It involved so many more details and new additions that it was, in fact, a detailed description of the entire working arrangements on board a floating factory. How the technical problems involving adjusting the position of the slipway to the rudder, rudderstock, propellor, and steering mechanism were solved, we shall see subsequently, when idea, technique, and capital combined to make pelagic ice-whaling a reality (see below, pp. 000000).

In addition to the rotary cooker, the centrifuge, and the slipway, another revolutionary improvement of this era was the installation of tanks in the floating factory for piping the oil. It may seem strange that Christen Christensen should have been granted a patent (16 September 1910) for built-in permanent tanks to contain whale oil in the hull of the floating factory, because by then steam-driven tankers had been transporting mineral oil for over twenty years. What Christensen did, in fact, was nothing more than to apply this principle to whaling. The advantages of carrying whale oil in tanks were so obvious that it was astonishing that no-one had thought of it before. In the first place one was spared the considerable space taken up by oak barrels, and the leaks these often sprung. In the second place time and labour were saved in the manufacture of the barrels, their cleaning, filling, weighing, and on- and off-loading. Despite these advantages, it took some time before the entire transport system was converted, because shore stations, too, and consignees had to have similar tank installations with oil pumps, and this was expensive. The price quoted by the Framnæs shipbuilding yard in 1911 for a complete set of equipment for a medium-sized floating factory was Kr.235,000, the tanks accounting for one-half, corresponding to the price of 30,000 barrels, twice as much as the capacity of the tanks. A number of floating factories had tanks fitted before the First World War, but as far as is known no shore stations, some of which continued to use barrels until well into the 1920s.

The two new floating factories belonging to Christensen's own company, A/S Ornen, were the first to acquire oil tanks for the 1909-10 season. They were in other respects so well equipped that they may be said to represent an attempt to realise the complete floating factory, including a guano factory. The new machinery for this, however, was so useless that it was left behind after only one season. During the tremendous expansion in 1909-12, the number of floating factories increased to forty-nine, representing a total tonnage of almost 150,000 gross tons. The largest of these was of about 6,000 gross tons, an example of how much progress had been made in the fitting out of a floating factory. On the foredeck stood the blubber boiling plant, with eight open cookers, with a total capacity of 200 cubic metres, with the requisite knives for cutting up the blubber. There were also two pressure cookers for parboiling the grax. On the rear deck, for the meat and bone boiling plant, eight pressure cookers were installed with a capacity of

90 cubic metres, as well as two of Sommermeyer's first rotary cookers. Two evaporators, each with a capacity of 20 tons a day, provided fresh water. As this proved quite insufficient, two extra ones, with a capacity of 30 tons each, were installed for the ensuing season. When boiling was going full blast, some 80 tons of fresh water were used daily. The boiling plant had tanks with a capacity of 14,250 barrels. This factory ship, an example of the supreme technical achievements of the time, suffered a tragic fate : after an unsuccessful season off Africa in 1912-13 it operated round South Shetland in 1913-14, accounting for 544 whales, which produced 22,810 barrels — a few smaller factory ships did even better — and when it finally showed what it was capable of doing, it went up in flames in mid-season on 27 January 1915, with its entire catch, 16,615 barrels. The number of cookers on board was not particularly large : Salvesen's significantly smaller *Horatio* carried twenty-eight pressure cookers. A detailed list from November 1924 registers six floating factories (out of seventeen) each with twenty-eight cookers, one with thirty-eight, while the maximum was reached by another in 1925-26 with forty-two pressure cookers. The subsequent tendency was not to increase the number of cookers, but their size.

Up to 1920 all floating factories were converted second-hand ships which before the war could be bought very cheaply in England, for £6,000 to £9,000 according to their size (from 3,000 to 5,000 gross tons) and age. This access to purchases of cheap tonnage is a very important factor in the establishment and economic viability of the companies involved. This applied not only to whaling : the great expansion of the Norwegian merchant navy from about 1900 to 1914 was based essentially on purchases of used ships from abroad, and not on newly constructed tonnage. The first newly built floating factory was A/S Hektor's *Ronald,* which was also up to then the largest, 6,249 gross tons, and had been supplied by the yard in Port Glasgow in 1920. She was fitted with twelve huge open cookers for blubber and six pressure cookers for meat; there were tanks with a capacity of 36,000 barrels, which could be increased to 41,000 by utilising the double bottom. For each season she took on board 8,650 tons of coal. In the course of fifteen years the development had been tremendous : the *Admiralen* of 1,517 gross tons, which could carry 5,100 barrels, had cost Kr.130,000 whereas the *Ronald,* contracted in the peak boom, came to Kr.6,500,000, and even so it did not constitute a complete factory ship; other converted floating factories were larger and more effective. When the largest of all, the *C. A. Larsen,* of 13,246 gross tons, had been fitted out in the autumn of 1926, a paper wrote : "This is the largest ship hitherto employed in the service of whaling, and there is a strong possibility that the limit has been reached." Only a few years were to elapse before it had been exceeded.

Whale catchers

We have previously touched on the development of whale catchers up to the conclusion of Finnmark whaling in 1904. The change that took place during the ensuing twenty years was not so much an increase in the size of the vessels as in their engine power. Between 1914 and 1922 only two catchers were supplied by Norwegian shipyards. When new construction began again in 1923, vessels were constructed just as before the war. There was no reason to alter the design that had been found to be most practical in view of the fact that whaling was operated in the same manner. Not till the arrival of pelagic and ice-whaling, and the subsequent expansion and competition with new whaling nations did the need arise for a new type of whale catcher. Whereas previously the method had been to stalk the whale and to pursue it until it was in range, the idea was now to *hunt* the whale and to pursue it until it was so exhausted that it would fall an easy prey to the gunner.

Right up to 1907 Norway was sole supplier of whale catchers to whaling all over the world. The fact that yards in the North Pacific and in Japan started building whale catchers in 1907 was of minor importance. Norway had a more serious rival when Britain set to work, and when Norwegian companies contracted vessels in that country. The first whale catcher to be built in Great Britain, the *Scapa,* was supplied by Hawthorns of Leith to Chr. Salvesen & Co. The vessel had a fairly powerful engine, developing 400 i.h.p., which on her trials on 8 March 1910, produced a speed of 11½ knots. She was highly manoeuvrable, an important quality when chasing a whale. The firm that has supplied most whale catchers is Smith's Dock Co. of Middlesbrough, which in the course of time turned out some 180, almost as many as Norway's largest shipyard, Akers. Smith's Dock Co.'s first vessel, the *Hananui II,* was supplied in 1910 to H. F. Cook's shore station of Whangamumu in New Zealand. In the following year the company built six boats, three of which went to Christen Christensen's company. These were of the largest type to date, 172 gross tons, with an engine of 420 i.h.p. That Christensen of all people should have been the first Norwegian to contract boats abroad was undoubtedly because, true to his nature, he was keen to try something new. In 1908 his own yard had built two boats that had proved so unsuitable for whaling round South Shetland, that they were sold in 1912. The Norwegian yards had orders for so many boats, that they were unable to supply them quickly enough. Christensen discovered that the English whale catchers were a considerable improvement. They must have been very stoutly built, because the *Scapa*'s sister ship, the *Sonja,* was engaged in active whaling for forty-eight years. Built in 1910, she was sold in 1923 to Den Kongelige grønlandske Handel (The Royal Greenland Trading Com-

pany), which right up to 1958 used it for catching whales for the
Eskimos. When she was successful, they would greet her with a special
song, "Sonja has got a whale".

Three other boats from Smith's Dock Co. in 1911 were built for
Irvin & Johnson for their shore station Prince Olav Harbour in South
Georgia. The diesel engines in two of these boats were, as already
mentioned, an expensive and unfortunate experiment. Although the
diesel engine had garnered laurels in the merchant navy ever since 1912,
practically twenty years were to elapse before it was again tried in
whaling, and on that occasion in two floating factories. The first two
were almost certainly the small Norwegian factory ships the *Haugar*
(2,243 gross tons) and the *Pioner* (1,721 gross tons), which in 1929-30
operated in the Norwegian Sea and later off the Congo. The first of the
large newly constructed floating factories powered with diesel engines
(supplied by Burmeister & Wain of Copenhagen in 1930) was the
Norwegian *Sir James Clark Ross* (14,363 gross tons), whose first season
was 1930-1, with the engine proving a decided success. The use of diesel
engines meant that a floating factory was compelled to include a steam
boiler plant in order to generate steam for boiling. However, a floating
factory powered by diesel was more mobile, for a steam-driven vessel
would generally have to remain at rest when boiling was going full blast
as the main boiler was unable at the same time to produce enough
steam for propulsion and for boiling. With a diesel engine the floating
factory could, as a rule, carry enough bunkers for the entire season.
Economically, this was a saving, as it was calculated that a vessel with
a diesel engine used only 50 per cent of the quantity of oil required by
an oil-burning steam engine developing the same power.

Smith's Dock Co. built sixteen whale catchers in 1912, three of them
for Norwegian firms. Eight of them were considerably larger and more
powerful than the usual type — 203 gross tons and 750 i.h.p. From
1913 to 1920 this yard supplied only one boat, but starting in 1921
it produced an impressive series of eighty-five boats in the course of ten
years, thirty-five in 1929 alone. Of the eighty-five, thirty-five went to
Salvesen. This yard pioneered two important innovations. For the
Southern Whaling & Sealing Co. (Lever Bros) it supplied in 1923 the
first of its whale catchers designed to burn oil, the *Southern Floe*. It was
not, however, the first in the world incorporating this innovation, as the
whale catchers operating from Gray's Harbour, abandoned in 1925,
had already had oil-burning engines for several years, probably from
the end of the First World War. The first Norwegian boat built for oil
burning was supplied in 1923. Oil burning rapidly established itself;
practically all boats after 1926 featured this, and many older ones were
converted to it. Whaling in the open sea and the fact that factory ships
were changing over to oil burning or diesel power were the reasons for

52. Old type whale catcher with elliptical stern.

53. Modern-type whale catcher with cruiser stern and detached rudder.

this. With both floating factory and its whale catchers burning oil, it was considerably easier for catchers to fuel in the open sea, but as it took some time before all whale catchers were oil burning, the expedition's transport vessels also had to carry coal down to the whaling grounds.

The oil-burning floating factory introduced a new problem : cleaning the tanks when they had been emptied of fuel and were to be filled with whale oil. This work had to be done very carefully in order not to allow the whale oil to become polluted. Numerous reports exist describing how detested and almost hopeless this work was: the tanks had to be steamed, boiled out with caustic soda, scrubbed by hand, etc., and even so the consignee might protest. Subsequently use has been made of various chemicals for cleaning purposes.

Smith's Dock Co.'s other innovation was an epoch-making alteration in the design of the whale catcher's hull: cruiser stern and detached rudder. The first two vessels so built, the *Southern Spray* and the *Southern Wave,* were delivered in 1925 to the same firm as the *Southern Floe.* One of the yard's managers has described how he hit on the idea when a gunner complained that ordinary boats, with elliptical counters and a rudderstock, were not easy to manoeuvre when hunting the whale. With the onset of the First World War the whale boats now had a new use, submarine chasing. The British Admiralty argued that chasing a U-boat was not very different from chasing a whale, and immediately commissioned the building of fifteen vessels of an improved type. They were 125 ft. overall and capable of 14 knots, at which speed they were able to turn in a half circle in 27 seconds. After the war efforts were made to improve this type, and the result was the design which the two boats were given in 1925. They proved a great success: with the same fuel consumption they had a speed one knot in excess of a boat of the same size but of an older design. The fact that one of them accounted for 500 whales in a single season was accepted as proof of the superiority of the two new catchers. As the idea of *chasing* the whale gradually came to be more generally adopted, the speed had to be increased. In 1925 Smith's Dock Co. published the following figures for a whale catcher's fuel consumption per day (24 hours): at 8 knots, 7 tons; at 9 knots, 8½ tons; at 10 knots, 10 tons; at 11 knots, 15 tons; at 12 knots, 21 tons. Increasing speed from 10 to 12 knots more than doubled fuel consumption, while a speed of 14 knots required almost four times as much fuel. The larger and more powerful whale catchers were naturally much more expensive than the older ones. Norwegian yards had supplied whale catchers around 1900 for Kr.90,000, in 1913 for Kr.150,000, and the new type in the latter half of the 1920s for some Kr.400,000.

A new feature of whale catchers in the late 1920s was the so-called gunner's bridge. In cold and stormy weather it was impossible for the gunner to remain at his post on the duckboards behind the gun. If the worse came to the worst, he was compelled to seek the shelter of the bridge, but it took some time to scramble down the ladder, across the foredeck, and on to the duckboards, and the chance of a well-aimed shot might easily be missed. Several solutions were tried, but the best was that of the gunner OLE IVERSEN, who in 1925-6 was working for

54. Modern whale catcher with gunner's bridge.

the Salvesen company off South Shetland. On the basis of his drawing a light bridge was constructed running straight from the navigating bridge or from the wheelhouse on one side of the mast and down to the gunner's platform astern of the gun. Gunners were so enthusiastic about this development that one of them said: "If a whale catcher from now on is built without a gunner's bridge, she's only half complete." The gunner could now at his ease follow the chase and reach his platform dry-shod in a matter of seconds. Iversen's gunner's bridge is a good example of how important improvements could be made without any patented invention.

It need hardly be said that the most important piece of equipment was the whale gun. Up till 1885 Svend Foyn's and practically everyone else's guns were manufactured in Norway. In that year the firm of Bofors A/B of Sweden turned out its first whale gun for Norway. All guns were muzzle loaders without any recoil brake. For this reason they had to be made of very tough material in order to withstand the pressure; because of this they appeared clumsy, but they gave excellent service. In 1909-10 Bofors succeeded in producing a good gun with a glycerine recoil brake, and for several years they were the only suppliers of guns of this kind. In Norway large-scale production of a gun of this type was not started until after the First World War. All guns made up to 1925 were muzzle loaders. It took a comparatively long time to load this type of gun, and it was no easy matter in a shower of spray.

55.   Old whale gun; muzzle loader without recoil brake.

In 1924-5 the first breech-loading guns were made in both Norway and Sweden. They had several advantages: the charge could be inserted ready made in cartridge cases, the rate of loading and firing was quicker, and shots had a standard charge compared with when the gunner had to sit in his cabin and weigh the charge in canvas bags. At the same time a more effective smokeless powder was used, which ensured a greater muzzle velocity and a longer range. Practically all the gunners adopted the new gun, although some were so conservative that they refused to abandon the older ones, continuing to use them right up to the Second World War. Bofors supplied some 500 whale guns up till 1950, while Kongsberg of Norway had up till 1963 sold 1,074, some of smaller calibre for use in the catching of small cetaceans. This factory has sold guns to every country engaged in whaling. Thirty-six were supplied to the Japanese when they started operations in the Antarctic in 1936.

No essential changes in Svend Foyn's design occurred with the harpoon and the shell that was screwed fast to the front of it. There could be no better proof of the ingenuity of this construction. Several patents have been granted for other designs of harpoon, but in practice these have all proved inferior to Svend Foyn's. A smaller harpoon with the shell, but without the line, was used for many years in order to finish off the whale if it was still alive after it had been hit and secured by means of a standard harpoon with a line. The fuse, designed to cause the shell to explode inside the whale five or six seconds after it had been fired, became safer. It sometimes happened that the shot passed

56. Modern whale gun, breech-loader with glycerine recoil brake. The man behind the gun is M. A. Ingebretsen, one of Norway's leading whaling managers in the earliest period of modern whaling.

right through the whale with the result that it exploded in the sea, exposing the gunner to the risk of injury from shell splinters.

The value of wireless telegraphy and telephony and radio direction finding to whaling can hardly be overstated. These provided a double function: for communication between whale catchers and the factory, whether this was a ship or on shore, and for communication between the factory and the home country. Pelagic whaling could never have been carried out on such a scale without wireless. In fog and snow whale catchers would not have stood much chance of finding their way back to the factory without wireless, especially as the factory ship was liable to change position. When expeditions left their bunkering harbour on the way to the whaling grounds, they were cut off from the outside world for several months. This imposed great mental strain both on the whalers and their families and on the firm. Occasionally one of the transport ships or a whale catcher would make the trip to Montevideo and Buenos Aires or Cape Town, returning with mail and newspapers. During the first few years of catching in the Southern Ocean companies were often entirely ignorant of the results of catching, or of the fate of the expedition, until the season had been concluded and the first call had been made at a port on the way home, from which the long-awaited cable could be despatched. In whaling, wireless telegraphy made its breakthrough in 1911-12, when we know it was installed in three whale catchers and in a Norwegian floating factory off South Orkney. The first telegrams were sent from here to a station in South America, and relayed by cable to Norway. The other three floating factories had sets with a range of 1,500 miles installed that year. In view of this limited range of transmission, an important event was the inauguration of wireless communication between Port Stanley and Montevideo on 24 September 1912, but not till 1925 was a radio station built by the British authorities at Grytviken. This had regular connections with Port Stanley, and from 1927 was capable of reaching Norway on the short wave. The First World War had temporarily halted the development of radio in the whaling fleet, but when whaling entered a new era in the latter half of the 1920s, it adopted all the latest inventions of radio technology. An account of what this has meant to whaling belongs rightfully to the subsequent chapter on this period.

Finally, around 1920 whaling adopted the aeroplane. A newspaper reported that it was the pursuit of U-boats by planes during the First World War that had inspired the idea of pursuing whales in the same manner, and the paper prophesied a great future for this method. The periodical *Pacific Fisherman* wrote that an engineer in the company operating the Rose Harbour and Naden Harbour stations in the Queen Charlotte Islands had used aircraft to observe whale migrations in 1919. Whilst he was capable of spotting whales twenty miles away, the lookout in the crow's nest on a whale catcher had a visual range of not more than four or five miles. With the aid of wireless telegraphy the airman could direct whale catchers to the whales. In an English book on whaling published in 1927 (F. V. Morley and J. S. Hodgson: *Whaling North and South,* pp. 184-9) a whole chapter is devoted to the possibilities offered by the aeroplane. It describes how in 1920 aircraft were used near Saldanha to track whales. In Antarctic whaling planes were used for the first time on the floating factory *Kosmos,* in 1929-30. This attempt ended tragically, as the plane with its crew of two vanished without trace, and the attempt was never repeated. However, helicopters have shown that they have much greater potential on floating factories. Some time after the Second World War they were in general use, especially among the Japanese, though more for observation of ice conditions than of whale. Helicopters have also been used for marking whales. The role of the aeroplane in Antarctic exploration is not our concern here.

16

WHALING LIFE IN THE ANTARCTIC

The first flights in the Antarctic were undertaken in November and December 1928 by the Australian SIR HUBERT G. WILKINS and the Norwegian-American CARL BEN EIELSON. In an interview with a Norwegian newspaper Eielson paid a tribute to the whalers which as an introduction to this chapter could hardly be bettered.

"Adventure?" said Eielson. "No, neither Wilkins's, nor my, nor any other flights in the Arctic and Antarctic regions are adventure. Adventure, that is whaling in the waters around the Antarctic continent, the greatest and most wonderful adventure of our age. I knew nothing about whaling before I came to Deception Island. Today, I know that there is nothing in the world that impresses me more than the Norwegian whalers in the Antarctic. We can fly for a few hours over the Antarctic regions, maybe no one has done that before, and the newspapers all over the world make a lot of noise and fuss. But just imagine that here a whole whaling fleet of between 5,000 and 6,000 men is lying in these same regions. Down here in the very shadow of the South Pole a livelihood has been created which every year directly and indirectly earns hundreds of millions of kroner. The Norwegians have made the way through the hundred-mile-wide belt of ice into the Ross Sea a thoroughfare. They have taken a gamble and they have won. Whaling in the Antarctic Ocean is undoubtedly the toughest and most hazardous livelihood in the world. People write lengthy articles and voluminous tomes on polar fliers and polar explorers, but where are the books on the whalers in the Antarctic, which should provide reading matter for all the youth of the world?"

Whaling of the old school is no more with us; but there is a tremendous amount of literature on this fascinating subject. The adventure of modern whaling is over too, and the story of the whalers of that epoch can now be written. This still remains to be done, but this is not the place for the complete story. A great many, after spending a season or two in the whaling grounds, have been so overwhelmed by what they have seen that they have given literary expression, with varied success, to their experiences. Few of them have endeavoured to provide a general description of the life of the whalers. (One of the best would appear to be Henry Ferguson: *Harpoon*, London, 1932, which gives an objective description of working conditions on a shore station, a floating factory, and a whale catcher, and a good analysis of the psychology of the whaler.) Only a slight acquaintance with the literature on this subject is sufficient to show that, in this case, personal experience is a highly unreliable source. Accounts are subjectively coloured by the author's social and political viewpoint. There are descriptions from the same time and the same place in South Georgia which, in the opinion of one writer, was an ideal place to work, and in the opinion of others a hell on earth.

The sort of picture people form about whaling becomes open to doubt when we see that both serious and popular literature on the subject is brimful of mistakes and tendentious statements. Some of these fallacies deserve to be quoted. The English weekly, the *New Statesman*, wrote in 1937 that if man had continued to hunt "the Arctic right whales, Nordcaper and Greenland whales" with the harpoon, many would have survived, but Svend Foyn's method "rapidly reduced the *right whale* stocks to insignificant numbers". Svend Foyn's method was, in fact, to catch fin whales, because right whales had been dangerously reduced with the hand harpoon. Foyn caught only one single right whale. In a large scientific work (F. W. Fitzsimmons: *The Natural History of South Africa,* I-IV, London, 1919-20) on the fauna in and around South Africa, we read: "The fin whales (the Rorquals) have their habitat in the seas off the coast of Africa, but do not extend to the Antarctic seas." This after 100,000 fin whales had been caught in the previous fifteen years in the Antarctic waters.

One of the books on the subject that has attracted the largest number of readers is R. B. Robertson's *Of Whales and Men,* New York, 1954. Originally printed in the *New Yorker,* it proved a best seller and has been translated into several languages. The author was employed as a doctor to Salvesen's whalers. A few examples will illustrate the tendency in this book: "Leith Harbour is the foulest place I have seen in a far-travelled life. I have been in Indian and African villages where sanitation is an unknown word, and where the villages raise themselves some inches higher every year on their own excreta; Leith Harbour is filthier than these. I have been in the slums of Glasgow, Cairo, Calcutta and Shanghai; the denizens of these terrifying slums are better cared for by their fellow citizens than are the whalemen living in Leith Harbour cared for by anyone. The whalemen's dwellings are burrows, stinking and sickening. The importation of liquor is not restricted by law but perhaps at the instigation of their ecclesiastical shareholders the whaling companies have declared the island dry. Every whaleman is an expert brewer and an expert distiller too. A South Georgian's brains and ability are estimated by his fellows according to the quality of liquor he can manufacture. There are as many brands of plonk (the local name for liquor) as there are in a well-stocked bar. One product which the whalemen prized highly was distilled from black boot-polish which is imported to South Georgia in vast quantities. Such is the alcoholic life of the Southern Ocean whalemen during their *eighteen*-month isolation" (my italics: "*eight*-month isolation" would be more accurate).

We are told moreover that reports of a floating factory or whale catcher foundering are never printed in the papers! Wages (1950-1) are so meagre that if a full catch is not achieved, the whalers suffer a loss for eight months of ceaseless slaving. (The catching season at that time was three-and-a-half months). Every year "many thousands of whales" are towed into the station. (In 1951-2 the number was 1,050.) *Most* whalers drink whale milk if a nursing whale is brought onto the flensing deck! The British people would go hungry if they got no whale oil! (At the time it comprised 2 to 3 per cent of Britain's total consumption of fats.) A whole book could be filled with such misleading quotations, which in itself would be sufficient to illustrate the great need to tidy up the literature of whaling. It should be added that such was the feeling of resentment in the whaling industry over the false picture of living conditions presented in Robertson's book that the Union of Norwegian Whalers in Chr. Salvesen & Co. were moved to publish an official protest.

What is a whaler? Neither in daily speech in the whalers' home-towns, nor in the crew lists of whaling companies will the word "whaler" be found. And yet everyone talked about "whalers", the generic term for whaling workers. Their work was very varied, and they were employed to carry out a definite and limited function, and were designated and paid in accordance with it. These were first and second flenser, first and second meat cutter, first and second oil cooker, meat cooker, boiler emptier, oil tapper, dryer; there was a foreman, storeman, filer, handyman; there was a cooper, smith, carpenter, bricklayer, repairman; there was a steward, cook, butcher, sausage-maker; there was an electrician, dynamo operator, separator specialist, engine hand; there was a chemist, doctor, male nurse, medical attendant; there was an engineer, stoker, coal heaver. And this covers no more than half. In addition there were gunners and expedition managers, and all the regular crew members from deckhand to captain, from stoker to chief engineer, from cabin boy to steward. Later these categories were streamlined and divided into twelve classes, each with the same earnings for various work within the same category. Of the actual hands, the flensers came highest on the list.

Where did the whalers come from? Not till 1930 do we find statistics for their places of residence. These show that practically 90 per cent came from the county of Vestfold. Before 1930 the proportion was still higher, but after that constantly decreasing, with whalers recruited from every part of Norway. Before the First World War there were at one time so many Swedes in South Georgia that in 1911 the Governor was able to write that "the population of South Georgia consists mainly of Swedes and Norwegians". When some of the companies moved south, a certain number of hands from Iceland, the Faroes, and the Shetlands went with them. In 1918 Salvesen transferred a number of Shetlanders from Olna to Leith Harbour, but they did not return the following season "probably because the Norwegians made it clear that they were far from welcome". The Norwegians realised that foreign companies were entirely dependent on them, and they endeavoured as long as possible to maintain this monopoly. In 1922-5 about half the crew on Salvesen's floating factory the *Sevilla* were British, but this mixture was not a success, and was abandoned. On the whale catchers it was quite impossible to employ other than Norwegians, because the gunners insisted that, while chasing a whale, it was absolutely necessary to have only people who spoke and understood Norwegian.

In whaling, as in seafaring in general, the old argument seems to have applied that the man who proves a failure on land is good enough at sea. When a transport ship arrived at Leith Harbour one autumn with the labour force, the manager, LEGANGER HANSEN, wrote : "I have seen many queer crews on ships in my time down here, but I have never run into anything like the gang who are on board at present. There are supposed to be seventeen nations, and that's counting all negroes as one. When I told the captain that there now seemed to be a fine crew on board, he answered that he had never had more rubbish raked together at once." As late as 1934-5 there were only 2.9 per cent British personnel on Salvesen's floating factories and whale catchers. Why and how in the course of a few years this figure rose to 45.6 per cent by 1930-40 we shall see below. While it might have been difficult during the expansion prior to the First World War to obtain qualified labour, the reverse was the case during the unemployment of the inter-war years. A number of municipalities subscribed to shares in the whaling companies on condition that they engaged the services of a certain number of unemployed. Those who had been taken on in whaling retained their jobs, and the result was a permanent labour force of whalers, for whom this became a life-long occupation. There are men alive today who can look back on fifty years in the whaling grounds; many did not return home between seasons, and South Georgia became their home all the year round. After the Second World War the turnover became more pronounced, a great many hands leaving after a season or two, to be replaced by others.

If today we could simply glance into the quarters of the crew on board the first floating factories and into the barracks on the shore stations, if we could take the flenser's place on the carcass of a whale along the ship's side in biting cold and wind, if we could crawl down into the still hot boilers in order to shovel out the grax, if we could wade on the meat deck in stinking whale carcasses, working from six in the morning till six in the evening, Sundays and weekdays alike, without any overtime pay, in fact if we could experience the backbreaking work that whaling involved, then we should wonder how anyone could voluntarily choose this profession. That so many nevertheless did so was undoubtedly because of the lure of the "bonus".

Right up to 1920 no group of the workers in the whaling industry had a collective wage agreement with their employers: they were all employed on individual contracts. The company's managing director or board of directors engaged the services only of the expedition manager, gunner, and captain, who in turn hired their crews. Collective wage agreements were not possible before the whalers had formed their own organisations. The employees in the whaling industry, however, were such an unhomogeneous group that their organisation was a late starter, as they did not belong in any of the existing trade unions. They were neither seamen, fishermen, nor industrial workers. The only solution was to organise a whaler individually in the union to which, according to the nature of his work, he most nearly belonged. In about 1910 a number of whalers, organised in this way, exerted themselves on the whaling grounds to get their fellow workers to join. The years 1907 to 1912 were a period of breakthrough for the big trade unions in Norway, as they were for employers' organisations. The first strikes among seamen occurred in 1912, and these spread to whalers.

The first strike of whalers, as already mentioned, was in Leith Harbour during the building of the station there in 1909. There were a few strikes of this kind in which workers protested against being put to other work than catching whales. The strike in 1912-13 had other causes: the year 1912 had proved a serious setback to the whaling companies, working costs had to be drastically reduced, to the detriment first and foremost of wages, since other expenses — insurance, coal, equipment, maintenance, etc. — were so fixed that it was difficult to change them. As an average for a number of Antarctic companies, wages accounted for 29 per cent and feeding approximately 7 per cent of working expenses, making a total of about one-third. Apart from wages there were in particular three causes for complaint: the poor sanitary conditions, the food, and the working hours. There can be no doubt that during the tremendous expansion in 1910-12 a great many expeditions were equipped in a great hurry, without paying overmuch attention to the welfare of the labour force. One of the points at issue concerned work on Sundays and holidays. The matter was taken to court and the verdict, which was not unanimous, was that the provision contained in the contact relating to the duty to work on such days must be considered valid, owing to the specific conditions peculiar to whaling. The court decided that big values were at stake, "and it may be necessary to make use of the favourable moment".

In 1913 strikes broke out in several places, among them Grytviken and Leith Harbour. Workers downed tools on 22 March in protest at the poor food. They also complained that the barracks were full of bugs, and that the doctor was "a Scottish quack". An association was formed, with a chairman and secretary. The manager summoned the British magistrate from Grytviken, who had eighteen hands arrested and sent home to Norway. The Colonial Office was clearly embarrassed at the magistrate's high-handed action, declaring that without doubt the arrests were "wholly illegal and we have had a very lucky escape". What would have happened if the eighteen had refused to return home? In Grytviken relations between C. A. Larsen and his Board and their workers had cooled off somewhat during the previous few years, although there can hardly have been any expedition manager who had done as much for them as he had; he had, *inter alia,* even built a church. A number of workers met here on 20 March 1913, and founded Grytviken Workers' Union, with 129 members. Its chairman, committee and a number of members were later dismissed and sent home. Fresh workers were signed on in Buenos Aires and Montevideo, but this did not improve the situation: the Governor blamed later unrest on "this inferior labour". Things were particularly critical in 1920. In a Colonial Report (for the Falkland Islands and Dependencies) we read that of the hands at one station, 200 men, all but three went on strike in January, egged on by thirty-six Russian Bolsheviks who submitted the most outrageous claims, among them that the three who refused to strike should be deported. South Georgia was intended to be the first Bolshevik republic outside Russia. A few days later, by mere chance, a British warship anchored up in the harbour, whereupon the strike immediately collapsed. In the Socialist press the event was blown up out of all proportion, and it was reported that "the revolution in South Georgia has been crushed by British military might".

After C. A. Larsen, on the completion of his ten-year contract, had left South Georgia in 1914, we hear no more about the Workers' Union, but before disappearing from the scene, on the model of the Communist Manifesto of 1848, it issued a challenge "to all workers in whaling stations all over the world to organise". Agitation in the whaling grounds received support from Norway, and pressure for an organisation of the workers grew exceedingly strong after the employers organised themselves by forming the Association of Norwegian Whaling Companies on 6 March 1912. Not everyone considered the conditions as ghastly as the agitators had painted them. A whaler who served on board Salvesen's *Horatio* on her voyage to Madagascar in 1912 relates: "They loved their old ship, with its elegant clipper bow, and a great many of them had spent their pleasantest days there. The ship had her stern moored ashore, with a gangway, and when work was over the hands were given their ration of food, and went ashore. The native women were very beautiful and skilful. A girl or a woman could be acquired for five shillings. She would make a hut out of palm leaves, wash clothes, prepare food, collect fruit and fish, and it is not surprising that they all longed to be there. Now and again missionaries would turn up and make a lot of fuss about weddings and Christian marriage, but apart from that everything was just as in the Garden of Eden."

At intervals during 1913 unions were established in Norway. The first was the Norwegian Whale Gunners' Union (23 July 1913). It was hardly the fruits of Socialist agitation, as Norway has never witnessed a more aristocratic, exclusive, and professionally proud organisation. The date of its establishment indicates that it was composed of the Antarctic gunners who had remained at home — in the other whaling grounds they were right in the middle of a busy season. Anecdotes about gunners and their prima-donna-like whims are legion. The gunner fully realised that the bonus of all the other hands depended on him. While a skilled gunner was hero-worshipped, it was distinctly unpleasant for a poor gunner to bear all the blame for a season's indifferent earnings. Competition to be the highest-scoring gunner of the year was very keen. The gunner's own earnings naturally depended on his skill, but not only on that: hunting and catching a whale was the result of teamwork, of precise co-operation between the gunner, the lookout in the crow's nest, the helmsman, the mate, and the engineer. Misunderstanding a word of command, or even the gesture of a hand, might well mean the loss of many thousands of kroner. Although gunners earned princely salaries, a well-aimed shot represented such tremendous value that the gunner's bonus could not be considered big. If we consider that a blue whale in 1913 produced 80 barrels at Kr.60 a barrel, and that the bonus was Kr.80, this was no more than $1\frac{1}{2}$ per cent. Right up to the First World War the gunner's regular wage was fairly constant at Kr.100 a month, with a bonus of Kr.80 on a blue whale, Kr.50 on a fin whale, Kr.30 on humpback and sei whales, and the same for a sperm whale as for a blue whale. Some gunners could earn Kr.12,000-13,000 in a season, but that was well above normal. In the South Shetlands the average in 1914-15 was Kr.8,090, in the Norwegian Sea about Kr.4,800. Like all the others, the gunner was only paid his fixed salary for about eight months. The princely earnings of the master gunners belong to the pelagic whaling subsequent to 1928. All active organisation work was brought to a halt during the war, and was not started again until the 1920s.

There was little increase in the wages of whalers and ships' crews up to the time when Finnmark whaling came to an end in 1904, but the vast scale of operations in the Southern Ocean led to a tremendous increase. The average earnings of all groups were some five times higher at the big shore stations in South Georgia in 1914-15 than at the shore stations round the Norwegian Sea in 1904, but as this is based on five-and-a-half months' earning time in the north and ten months in the south, the average monthly income was only some three and a half times higher in the south. If we calculate the duration of the season from the day the whaler signed on to the day he signed off, and if we also include the floating factories, we may say that for all groups, in the entire whaling industry in the southern hemisphere as a whole, hands earned approximately 250 per cent more per month in 1914-15 than they had done in the northern whaling grounds in 1904. On the whole, whalers' pay per season was higher than a year's pay in the merchant navy, besides which whalers had an opportunity of increasing their annual earnings by doing casual work between seasons. The prospect of a higher annual income was an important reason why so many preferred the more exhausting work of whaling than signing on as an ordinary sea-man. As the Norwegian Whaling Association was essentially a sales combine and a co-ordinating body *vis-à-vis* the authorities, it took little account of wage matters and crew conditions. These were matters for individual companies to deal with. Only when whalers had combined in one strong organisation, with demands for a joint wage agreement, and were paid the same wages no matter what company employed them, were the whaling companies forced to establish the Whaling Employers' Association in 1936. In order to prevent hands joining a trade union, some of the companies included in the hiring contract — referred to by the Socialist press as the slave contract — the obligation "not to belong to any employees' union in South Georgia or to organise meetings with a view to discussing and seeking by force to carry through anything contrary to this contract and the interests of the company; in which case I shall lose my right to earned wages and bonus". The contract also enjoined the signer to carry out any work whatever and to work on Sundays and holidays and at night at an overtime rate of 40 øre per hour.

During the final war years, and up to the autumn of 1920, all wage earners, including whalers, had enjoyed a tremendous increase in their earnings. It was a nominal rather than a real increase. After the boom came abruptly to an end and inflation set in, employers drastically reduced wages despite strong resistance from the trade unions. The years 1920-3 proved turbulent and restless. In order to strengthen their posi-tion *vis-à-vis* the shipowners a new Whaling Workers Union (Hval-fangerarbeidernes Forening) was founded on 21 August 1920, supported by the Norwegian Seamen's Union, and on 25 August 1921, the first collective wage agreement was concluded with the group of the

Norwegian Whaling Association consisting of the Antarctic companies. A fresh agreement was signed in 1922. These agreements reduced wages to practically half what they had been in 1920, and the 1922 agreement was renewed for 1923-24. A flenser in 1920 had Kr.300 a month plus 10 øre per barrel, in 1922 Kr.190 plus 9 øre; in 1920 a seaman on a whale catcher Kr.275 plus Kr.11 per whale, in 1922 Kr.150 plus Kr.8. Rates were based on operations with three whale catchers. If more boats were engaged, the supplement for increased catches was very small. This system was adopted to ensure that there would not be a major discrepancy between wages in a large and a smaller company where the work involved was the same for the individual hand in both companies. Payment for overtime work from six in the evening to six in the morning was fixed at Kr.1 to Kr.1.40 an hour.

Wages fluctuated in accordance with the price of whale oil. The highest price for No. 1 in 1920 was £93, but in 1921 it dropped to £47, and in 1922 to £33. It then rallied slightly to £34 in 1923 and then more briskly to £40 in 1924. This rise in prices made shipowners amenable to wage increases. After 1924 a steady drop in prices ensued, culminating in the collapse of the whale oil market in 1931-4, when the highest price was £12, and oil was even being sold at £8 10s. The result was increasing pressure to reduce working expenses, including wages. However, the nominal decline was compensated for by deflation, the result of which was a write-up of the Norwegian krone to par in 1928. This meant that in 1928 a Norwegian krone had three times as much purchasing power as in 1920, and whalers received more in return for their nominally reduced wages in 1928 than for the higher rate in 1920. The tremendous expansion in whaling at the end of the 1920s meant keen competition to acquire the best crews, particularly gunners. The board of directors of Unilever's whaling company declared in 1931 that the slump in the price of oil had had a good effect. It had compelled companies to reduce their wages bill and to stop competing for the most successful gunners, whose earnings had soared to ridiculous heights. An agreement was therefore concluded not to engage one another's gunners, but to stick to the agreed scale of wages. In 1925-6 this was Kr.600 a month and Kr.150 for a blue whale and Kr.100 for fin and sperm whales, which in most companies would produce a total profit of about Kr.50,000. The expedition manager, who had a bonus for every barrel, received an extra bonus when production exceeded 50,000 barrels. This alone would amount to Kr.34,000 for a production of 78,000 barrels.

The work of the whaler, with its annual cycle, has often been compared with that of the migrant birds, arriving in spring and departing with autumn. This applies, of course, only to those who worked in the

Antarctic. Right up to the First World War just as many were engaged in other fields, and their life cycle was the reverse of that of the migrant birds. No accurate figures exist for the earlier period to show how many hands were engaged in whaling. Of the years 1885-1905 we have been told that there were from 1,000 to 1,500 men on an annual average; in 1905-26 there were from 2,000 to 6,000. This presumably only includes Norwegians. Gradually, the quota from other nations increased, and if we include the Japanese we shall have to add a couple of thousand.

Not all whalers experienced the joy of homecoming. A whaler returning from South Georgia was asked what sort of season they had had. "Well, as you know, it's hard work, but then we make good money. The only accident we had was when a stoker was killed." The only accident! And "the whaling sickness" which raged when the catch was poor proved worse than typhus and beri-beri. Some were unable to stand the isolation from the outside world, as well as the gruelling pressure of work and the callous male community, and preferred to opt out. A station manager in South Georgia reported that one of his workers asked for a piece of rope to hang himself, as the piece he had was rotten! Statistics could never reveal the anguish suffered in the ice and the loneliness, the absence from home and the longing, in a tough, soulless community in which no sensitive mind could survive. Many, in the course of the years, had to be sent home as mentally deranged. Kid-glove treatment was hardly the order of the day. "X is the laziest devil in the world," a manager wrote, "and apart from this ailment he suffers from epilepsy, so if the chap is found sprawling somewhere there is nothing that can be done about it. The doctor has sent some medicine, but not for laziness."

In the minutes of a board meeting in one of the major companies, we do on one occasion stumble on a human note. This is so unusual as to arouse one's immediate attention. "The floating factory reports that X suffered from melancholia, and was sent home at once. An incident such as this provides some idea of the conditions under which whaling is carried out in the Antarctic." When a clergyman consecrated the church in Grytviken on Christmas Day 1913, and allowed his eyes to wander over the packed hall "of young men in the prime of life, all weather-beaten and hardy, clearly bearing the marks of their toil", he was sadly forced to conclude that "Christian life unfortunately does not wax strong among the whalers". If the catch was plentiful work had to be carried on during church hours, and the chiming of the church bells provided a strangely discordant note to the din of the station machinery. Is it surprising that some of them should grow melancholy, and feel that even a whaler does not live by bread alone? It has been said that the Norwegians have built the northernmost and southernmost churches

57. The church at Grytviken, consecrated on Christmas Day 1913.

in the world, at Longyearbyen in Spitsbergen and Grytviken in South Georgia. (The latter is not quite correct, as the church in the town of Ushuaia on the Argentinian part of Tierra del Fuego is situated some 45 miles further south.) It would have been more natural if the church had been placed somewhere near Stromness Bay, where there were three stations and a far larger temporary population than at Grytviken. There were several reasons why this was not done: Grytviken was situated midway along the east coast of the island, with stations both to the north and the south. In the second place, the British administration was located at Grytviken, which made it the obvious centre of the island. In the third place — and most important — the church was the work of C. A. Larsen. But for him it would never have been built. On several occasions he emphasised that the church was his personal property, and after his death a difficult legal problem arose as to who was the rightful owner. When Larsen left South Georgia in 1914 he had personally come to the conclusion that the church had been built in the wrong place. However, in 1920 operations came to an end in New Fortuna Bay and in 1929 in Godthul Harbour, which meant that four-fifths of the men in South Georgia now lived north of Grytviken.

Out of a sum of Kr.5,600 collected among the whalers for the church, Larsen himself contributed Kr.5,000, and he moreover guaranteed the remaining expenses: it cost Kr.16,000. There was no permanent pastor: clergymen were stationed there 1912-16, 1925-6, 1928-9, and 1930-1. The reason no clergyman served after 1931 was that so many of the stations were closed down that year, leaving only Leith Harbour and Grytviken. As the emphasis was now on pelagic whaling, there was no longer much point in conducting services ashore. The church was subsequently used as an ordinary community centre, and finally as a warehouse.

In most shore stations in South Georgia and on board the big floating factories a doctor was included among the staff fairly early on. The first was on board the *Fridtjof Nansen* when she foundered in 1906. From the 1907-8 season there was a doctor at Grytviken. The three stations at Stromness Bay generally shared the services of a doctor. At Deception, too, there was a doctor in the 1920s on the shore station, which included a small hospital; patients were transported there from the floating factories, and the doctor was brought to the floating factories on board a whale catcher. As time went on floating factories included well-equipped sick bays, and the land stations had operating theatres large enough to enable major operations to be carried out. In such cases the doctor at the nearest station would generally be fetched to assist. As the general state of health was fairly good, common ailments did not keep the doctors as busy as all the vocational accidents. It is surprising that whaling in the Antarctic did not involve a greater loss of human life than was actually the case. However, when ice-whaling started, the number of ships that were wrecked or foundered increased. To some extent this was because the hectic chase, the thought of the possible bonuses, and the gunners' rivalry made them put unnecessary strain on the equipment. Whale catchers appear to have taken unnecessary risks, and yet it was impossible, as the board of one company explained, to prevent crews taking such risks. If a whale catcher was put out of action, this might mean that the company would lose the value of a whole catch, amounting to some £17,000. All in all, nearly thirty whale catchers were wrecked in the Antarctic in 1911-69, two-thirds of them during the first period of ice-catching between 1928 and 1939, with the loss of eighty-six lives.

After a number of temporary measures the administration in South Georgia assumed more permanent form when J. INNES WILSON was appointed Stipendiary Magistrate and Deputy Shipping Master as from 20 November 1909. He took up his residence at King Edward Point, about three-quarters of a mile east of the whaling station. An office building, a house of detention, and a meteorological and biological station were built. A post office was set up, and it was a great event when the first mail, 1,000 letters and 389 postcards, was despatched the day before Christmas Eve in 1909. The amount of mail increased steadily: in 1910 8,346 items were consigned, in 1911 25,325. On that occasion there were fourteen deliveries between South Georgia and Port Stanley, most of them carried out by whale catchers. When Britain imposed an export duty on whale oil, King Edward Cove became a port of entry starting with the 1912-13 season, i.e. a permanently manned customs post. As with the siting of the church, the post was less convenient for the three stations at Stromness Bay that the administration should be situated at Grytviken. For example, they had to fetch the magistrate when his services were required. Although it had been indicated that a portion of the export duty would accrue to the advantage of the whalers, nothing of the kind was done by the British authorities. The duty meant that, starting that season, a magistrate and coroner were annually stationed at Deception. The first of these was EDWARD BINNIE. From 1923 Port Foster on Deception likewise became a port of entry. As a constable had been appointed in 1913 for Grytviken, and the church had been built, the whalers no longer had occasion to feel that "beyond 40° is no law, beyond 50° no God". Binnie was later appointed magistrate in South Georgia.

A regular steamship service was established thanks to a contract between the Governor and a whaling company for a small steamer (the *Fleurus* of 406 gross tons) to undertake five voyages every season from Grytviken to Port Stanley and one from Deception to Port Stanley. The boat made its first trip in December 1924. When the contract lapsed in 1933, it was not renewed and the steamer was sold. Ever since 1907 and right up to the Second World War the Cia de Pesca had maintained regular links between Grytviken and Buenos Aires. As long as Salvesen ran the New Island station they had a contract for carrying mail and passengers between Port Stanley and the western islands of the Falkland Group.

During the first twenty years little was done for the whalers' welfare : in this respect the companies felt no sense of responsibility. In 1912 the Leith Harbour manager received a grant from Salvesen for the purchase of instruments for a band and props for a theatre. In 1918 a large assembly hall was built, as well as a new hospital, and in 1924 a library and a cinema were organised. In 1926-8 cinemas were also introduced to Husvik, Stromness, and Grytviken : Prince Olav Harbour already had one. In many respects the last-mentioned station was the best equipped of all. Here in 1928 the first sports club was founded, and on 23 February the first sports meeting was held, formally opened by the Governor. Grytviken won the football match, thanks to the inclusion in its team of the clergyman, who had been an outstanding football player during his student days. Grytviken had the best football pitch, and for this reason the largest tournament was held there on 14 and 15 February 1931, with teams from five stations. Competitions included one for the Falkland Islands Government Cup. Ski competitions were also arranged, and for Norwegians who wintered there the celebration of Norway's national day, 17 May, was the great event.

58.   Parade before the games at Grytviken, 23 February 1928.

"Seeing all these whalers," writes a manager, "one would have thought that they would be dead tired by evening, but many still had sufficient energy to cultivate their hobby or to make a little extra by making and selling various articles from the whale's organs. One of them collected whales' eyes, which he hollowed out, drying the skin over a round shape to make the most beautiful parchment-like lampshades. When the skin of the heart had been cleaned and dried, it produced a large piece of parchment over one square metre in area. This could be used for making ladies' handbags, tobacco pouches, etc. Some read and tried to learn languages, others carved figures out of whalebone and out of the teeth of the sperm whale; one made violins; some soled boots and patched clothes; one repaired watches and another cut hair. Most of them would foregather in the mess, and discuss politics and solve the problems of this world over a cup of coffee." This was at the shore stations; on the older floating factories there was little opportunity for leisure pursuits. Time was spent working, eating, and sleeping. For the expedition manager, with his responsibility for his hands, the ship and the oil, the mental pressure was considerable. "It is terribly nerve-racking having to manoeuvre among ice and other snags with a ship drawing so much," a manager wrote from the Belgica Strait in 1911. Everyone was possessed by one idea alone: whale, whale, and still more whale. "I think it's strange that the manager on a floating factory and the mates pay no attention to the scenery around them, they're only looking for whale. They don't see the beauty of an iceberg, they don't look at the birds or anything else of interest," notes a whaler confined to his bunk with a broken leg.

59. Burial on Grytviken churchyard, 1926.

The crews of whale catchers had still less opportunity for relaxing:
they had nowhere to stay apart from the confined quarters of the
roundhouse beneath the foredeck. It required only a slight wind for the
seas to wash over the boat, making it impossible to remain on deck.
Preparing food was quite a feat for the cook, and occasionally an
impossibility. Everything on board was designed to make the vessel as
effective for the purpose of catching whales as possible, and there was
little extra space for the crew. With the whale catcher's low freeboard
and water constantly washing over her, hatches had to be battened down,
doors and scuttles closed; as a result, the atmosphere was damp and
stuffy, and there was a smell of mildew from the wet clothes hung up
in the hope that they would dry. The crew only removed their seaboots
and oilskins, keeping all their other clothes on, when they dossed down.
Care had to be taken, and a constant handhold maintained, to prevent
being flung on to the deck, which might well result in a bad injury or
worse. This explains the laconic reference: "We only had a stoker
killed". This was a young lad who was hurled into the engine and ground
to pieces. He now lies in the churchyard in Grytviken, side by side with
many others. Most men on their return swore that they would never
again go a-whaling. But after a couple of months at home, enjoying
the pleasures of home life and the company of wife and children, and
with their money coming to an end, they would dream again of that
great bonus. So why not try once more? This would definitely be the
last time. But it hardly ever was.

17

WHALING DURING THE FIRST WORLD WAR

Four features of this period are of particular interest in the larger history of whaling: (1) the marked falling-off in catching; (2) less satisfactory exploitation of the raw material; (3) the politico-military significance of whale oil; (4) a shift in the relative share of total global whaling on the part of the whaling nations. It would be incorrect to state that the war marked a break in a rapid development; even before its outbreak it was obvious that expansion had culminated. Many whaling grounds had been abandoned as operations there had merely involved a loss, and it was only the high freight rates during the war earned by floating factories that saved many companies from going bankrupt. Rebuilding the whaling fleet took some time; not till 1924-5 was total production of whale oil higher than in 1913-14. Catching was then concentrated in particular on three areas: South Africa, the North Pacific, and the Antarctic. Norway forfeited her dominant position, and never subsequently retrieved it. For several reasons whaling did not reap the financial fruits of the boom period that might have been expected. As the extraordinary conditions for whaling during the First World War provided a reason for the marked lapse, and not changes in the whale stocks or technique, this period is of minor interest to the history of catching itself. A few figures will illustrate its scope (see Table 16).

These figures show that global catching dropped during the war to less than half the pre-war level, both in the number of whales and in the number of barrels. Off Africa it slumped to one-seventh, whereas in the North Pacific and off Japan it maintained the same level. As Japanese coastal whaling was based on the production of meat, figures cannot be stated in barrels of oil. The increase in total production from 1919-20 to 1920-21, despite a decrease in the number of shore stations and whale catchers, was due to the marked rise in the number of barrels per boat, from 2,645 to 4,206 as a total for all whaling grounds, and from 6,200 to 8,311 in the Antarctic. (Seasonal figures in Table 16 indicate the Antarctic season plus the ensuing summer season in other whaling grounds, e.g. 1913-14 plus 1914.)

On the basis of the number of whales, some figures will show how the relationship between the most important whaling nations was readjusted (see Table 17).

At the outbreak of war in the summer of 1914 about two-thirds of global whaling was carried out from territory belonging to the Allied

Table 16. WORLD CATCH, 1913-1924

Season	All grounds Whales	All grounds Barrels	Shore stations	Fl.f.*	Catchers	Antarctic Barrels	Africa Barrels	North Pacific Barrels	Japan Whales
1913-14	22,900	804,118	50	35	254	432,061	183,136	72,100	2,024
1915-16	17,542	699,669	27	12	151	558,806	54,953	61,085	1,803
1916-17	10,088	403,112	12	6	94	363,827	26,311	71,101	1,697
1917-18	9,468	385,855	26	6	130	258,476	26,940	42,000	2,177
1919-20	11,369	407,327	33	6	154	272,817	51,921	5,000	1,276
1920-1	12,147	471,141	14	8	112	390,627	48,453		1,483
1922-3	18,120	817,314	29	16	174	614,547	99,073	34,776	1,435
1923-4	16,839	716,246	30	20	194	464,678	125,732	29,610	1,436

*Floating factories

Table 17. CATCH OF THE MOST IMPORTANT WHALING NATIONS, 1912-1924
(Figures indicate percentage of total world catch)

	Norway	British Empire	Japan	USA	Argentina	Norway & British Empire
1912-13	70.9	13.4	6.3	2.9	3.4	84.3
1917-18	31.9	26.5	23.0	12.0	4.5	58.4
1920-1	51.3	27.1	12.2	1.1	5.3	78.4
1923-4	42.6	34.2	9.1	6.5	3.2	76.8

powers, whereas the Central powers and neutral Holland (which sold a large proportion of its production to Germany) were large buyers of whale oil, a constellation which provides the political background for the struggle for whale oil. In 1912 Norway sold 34 per cent of her production to Germany-Austria, in 1913 32 per cent, and in 1914 26 per cent. As more and more countries were caught up in the war, and whaling operations were called off by many neutral countries, the Norwegian coast in 1918 was finally the only "neutral" whaling ground. In some areas the lull lasted until several years after the end of the war, but only a few less important fields were abandoned for good. The acquisition of new matériel and equipment for the summer season of 1920 and for the Antarctic season of 1920-1 had to be paid for with the soaring prices of the boom period, but when the oil came to be sold, companies only received one-third of the price they had calculated on, as a result of which some of them folded. Others waited for the price level to stabilise before starting up again.

During the war Norwegian whaling was entirely subject to the whims of the British, who had at their disposal very effective ways of imposing their will: there was the threat of refusing to renew licences, floating factories could be refused coal-bunkering facilities, floating factories with oil produced in British waters could be seized on the way home as the whale oil could be used for the production of glycerine and could, for this reason, be considered contraband, or an export ban on whale oil could be imposed. All other considerations were set aside in an effort to prevent Germany having access to whale oil, even if this was produced by a neutral power and was on its way to a neutral country in a neutral ship. A shortage of fats was one of the major problems of the Central powers. Norway's relations with Britain were further complicated by the fact that a British firm, Lever Bros., exercised control over the important Norwegian hydrogenation factory De-No-Fa. In no circumstances would Britain tolerate a British firm supplying the enemy, via a neutral country, with hydrogenated fat produced from whale oil obtained in British waters. De-No-Fa's management had estimated that the demand for hardened fat would increase with the duration of the war. For this reason every effort was made to produce as much edible fat as possible, and this was sent to warehouses in Hamburg and the Netherlands; from the latter large quantities were sold to Germany during the first year of the war at a very high price. And as the fat had been produced from oil supplied on contracts dating back to 1912 at a price of only £20, the company netted a handsome profit.

In other ways, too, Germany obtained whale oil during the first year of the war. At the outbreak of war two Norwegian cargoes of oil were lying in Hamburg, where they were sold. Anton Jurgens controlled 80 per cent of the German margarine industry, supplying large quantities of whale oil and hydrogenated fat to it, the oil being imported via England. Germany was prepared to pay any price, and fortunes could be made by anyone capable of supplying the fat, which found its way, via fictitious sales, *pro forma* contracts, and sales to neutral countries for re-export to Germany. It was maintained that when a Norwegian ship, laden with whale oil, on her way to England was seized and escorted to a German port, this was a ploy arranged between the Norwegian seller, the German purchaser, and the German Navy, and it was said to be the chairman of the Board of De-No-Fa who had revealed the ship's position to the Germans. Whether this story is true or not is of minor consequence : the most important thing was that rumours of this kind and a number of De-No-Fa's transactions resulted in Britain adopting a more severe attitude towards Norway, and in this respect the British Government placed great confidence in the reports received from its Minister in Oslo, Sir MANSFELDT DE CARDONNEL FINDLAY. He was said to be "an Englishman of the most formal and unaccommodating kind". He was extremely suspicious by nature, and at all times very well informed.

The war made whale oil doubly important, not only because supplies of vegetable oils and fats failed, but also because the glycerine in whale oil was at this time a prime necessity for the manufacture of the explosive nitro-glycerine in the armaments industry. Glycerine was a by-product in the production of solid soap (toilet and domestic soap, e.g. Sunlight), from hydrogenated fat of qualities Nos. 1 and 2, which contained about 10 per cent of glycerine. For soft soap No. 3 had to be used; even during the war manufacturers refused to use No. 4, which gave the soap an unpleasant smell.

Before the war Britain had covered the bulk of her margarine needs by imports from the Netherlands. As the Dutch were short of raw materials during the war, they were not in a position to cover Britain's needs. For this reason, as early as the autumn of 1914 the British government requested the country's fat industry to change over production to margarine. The result was a tremendous expansion of the British margarine industry, and as at the same time imports of butter were a problem, in 1916 for the first time the consumption of margarine in Great Britain was greater than that of butter. To achieve this it had proved necessary to multiply many times over the capacity of the fat-hydrogenation industry. In this respect Britain became so self-supporting that there was no longer any need to risk transporting whale oil across the North Sea to be hydrogenated by De-No-Fa, and to have the hardened fat returned the same way.

In order to make the blockade of Germany's fat imports complete, it was necessary for Britain to control Dutch links with the German fat industry. The latter also included the powerful North German oil-milling industry : this had been Europe's largest importer of overseas

vegetable oleaginous materials. After these had been refined the result
was mainly sold to the Netherlands, whose margarine industry in return
had its most important market in Germany and Britain. Most of the
raw material came from British possessions, and one of the two major
Dutch margarine concerns, the van den Bergh Group, was a British-
controlled company. The first effect of the blockade of Germany was
that ships carrying raw materials were directed to the Netherlands and
Britain, where stocks accumulated. This situation changed in the
autumn of 1915, when shortage of tonnage caused a marked decline in
imports. It was here that whale oil came into the picture. The other
Dutch margarine king, Anton Jurgens, was obsessed by the idea that
once the war was over, there would be a tremendous shortage of fats
in Europe, and that the person who controlled the market would make a
tremendous profit. For this reason he had bought and stored — particularly in Britain — vast quantities of whale oil. This was the cheapest
raw material and the best weapon in the struggle against his British
rivals, primarily Lever Bros. When Jurgens rejected the Board of Trade's
offer to buy his whale oil so that soap manufacturers could produce
glycerine, the British Government seized the oil, and paid Jurgens a
price which it had fixed of its own accord. He then started buying large
quantities of raw materials for vegetable oils, storing them in the
producer countries.

   It would be possible to write a large book on the basis of the
tremendous number of available documents dealing with the protracted
negotiations between the Norwegian Foreign Ministry and the Foreign
Office, between the two countries' legations, between oil brokers, whaling
companies, the Whaling Association, De-No-Fa and Lever Bros., the
inter-departmental correspondence in Britain and Norway, the minutes
of numerous conferences, etc. Here we have only space for a mention
of various main issues. Norway's great problem was that she was so
totally dependent on Britain's coal that this could force her to accept
such a one-sided form of trade with the Allies that Germany could rightly
accuse her of having violated her neutrality, and war might well have
ensued. Economically, the problem facing the whaling companies was
that they were anxious to sell to Germany, which paid up to £300 for
the oil, whereas Britain's maximum price, £55 in 1917, left the companies no margin of profit. In Britain it was realised that Norway was
helping the British to "wage cheap war". Up to January 1917 Britain
had purchased 110,000 tons of Norwegian whale oil at an average price
of £38, whereas its market price was quoted at about £100.

   A significant step in this trade war was Britain's declaration on 16
December 1916, that whale oil would be regarded as contraband of
war. It was unnecessary for Britain to take this drastic step of seizing
and condemning as prizes ships laden with whale oil on their way to

Norway, even though there might be a justified suspicion that the oil could eventually reach Germany, because Britain had other means of achieving her object. For the moment the floating factories on their way home to Norway with oil from Africa and Australia were allowed to slip through, but one of these floating factories was to sharpen Britain's suspicion of the Norwegian whaling companies. Despite a Norwegian promise that the cargo would be unloaded in Norway, it ended up in Germany. The British Minister in Oslo was highly incensed, and declared that, as it was no longer possible to trust the Norwegians, other means would have to be used to guarantee that the oil did not go to Germany. And the way to do this would be to cancel Norwegian licences, though these were supposed to run for twenty-one years, and would not lapse until the end of the 1920s. All, however, is fair in love and war.

On 27 January the Governor imposed a ban on the export of whale oil from the Dependencies to all other countries apart from the United Kingdom, and shortly afterwards declared that all licences could be cancelled for as long as the war lasted. Such an act was a two-edged sword. It was not in Britain's interest that Norwegian whaling should come to a complete halt. There was clearly uneasiness at the prospect of so many floating factories being transferred from whaling to the far more lucrative carrying trade. In order to stimulate production, the Governor was authorised on 13 September 1916 to suspend all restrictions on whaling. The threat not to renew licences was almost certainly merely intended to exert pressure, but was taken very seriously by the Norwegian whalers. In the minutes of a Board meeting held on 9 March 1915, we read: "It was resolved to accede to the British Minister's demands in face of the threat of *permanent* cancellation of licences." Findlay's threat was that "the whole future of the whaling industry depends upon the oil not reaching the enemies of Great Britain". One of Britain's main demands was a Norwegian export ban, and the Norwegian Government, much against its will, was forced to accept, introducing the ban on 24 March 1916. This was introduced too late, however, to prevent one cargo being despatched to Germany. The price of this must have been tremendous, as the company issued a dividend for 1916 of 300 per cent. This alone would correspond to £58 a ton, whereas the contemporary forced sales to Britain were on the basis of £32 for No. 1.

In negotiations between Norway and Britain considerations for De-No-Fa played a significant role. In April 1915 an agreement was formally reached between Lever Brothers and De-No-Fa which in fact was dictated by the British Government. The factory was guaranteed a certain quantity of oil, from which the hydrogenated fat was to be re-exported to Britain; if this proved impossible owing to the risk of torpedoing

60. The floating factory *Horatio* ablaze in Leith Harbour with 11,000 barrels of whale oil on board, 11 March 1916.

or seizure by the Germans, the factory was to produce fat for storage on the British Government's account. With this agreement and the export ban, Norway was forced to admit defeat : it now only remained to obtain as good a price as possible, but here, too, Britain was in a position to dictate her own terms, as she was the only purchaser. The first sales in 1915 were a great disappointment, £32, 30, 28, and 26 basic, according to grade, with a supplement of £2 10*s* for oil in barrels. This was actually about £7 or £8 above the preceding season, but in the first place working expenses had risen still more, and in the second place the low rate of exchange of the pound meant a loss to the Norwegian vendors of some Kr.81 per ton. One of the Norwegian companies suffered a loss of Kr.325,000 (£18,000) owing to the unfavourable exchange rate. For this reason sellers preferred to leave their pounds in British banks, in the hope that the rate would improve, and made a very handsome profit. Generally speaking, the erratic market tendencies introduced a new factor of uncertainty to an industry which *per se* was a hazardous undertaking.

In 1915-16 nine floating factories and twenty-nine whale catchers had operated from South Shetland; in 1916-17 there were only four factories and eleven catchers, but these encountered an unprecedented abundance of blue whales, one floating factory registering a full catch, 22,500 barrels, in the course of nine weeks, while another was able to sail home after three months with 27,200 barrels, up to then a record. Gunners who had been active from the very start relate that, thanks to the abolition of all restrictions and the order to produce as much of oil No. 0/1 as possible quickly, the result was waste on a scale never yet witnessed in the Antarctic. Despite the fact that 70 per cent of the catch consisted of large blue whale, only 47½ barrels per whale were produced. As gunners received a bonus for every whale, they blazed away at every whale they came across, without considering whether the floating factory would be in a position to reduce the catch or not. It is said that whales would be left beside the floating factory without being moored, while the whale catcher set off in pursuit of a fresh prey. In order to impose some sort of restraint, the expedition manager issued only one or two harpoons to each whale catcher. The harpoon, however, was merely cut out of the whale and if it was slightly bent it would be straightened out and used once again. It was normal practice for the harpoon to be left stuck in the whale when it was towed to the floating factory.

The result of the negotiations for the sale of all oil produced in 1916-17 proved a still greater disappointment. The British offer was £50 per ton; manufacturers maintained that production expenses in 1915-16 had been Kr.51 per barrel and in 1916-17 Kr.99, an increase from £17 to £33 a ton. But so entirely was Norway in Britain's power in this respect, that the offer had to be accepted, and there was more than a grain of truth in the saying that Norway was forced to produce cheap explosives for Britain. The British Government could wash its hands of the whole affair, since the sale was a private transaction between Norwegian whaling companies and a British firm of oil brokers. In not one document was the British or the Norwegian Government mentioned. In her dealings with Germany it was important to Norway's neutrality to establish that this was a private trade agreement, a procedure which Norway consistently followed in all the many similar agreements.

The 1917-18 season was in many ways the most critical. In order to avoid the risk of being torpedoed in the North Sea, the factories spent the between-season period in England. With a war on, however, setting out was delayed, and therefore the whaling could not start until the beginning of February, with the result that the entire Antarctic catch produced a mere 258,000 barrels, 105,000 less than in 1916-17. In 1918-19 climatic conditions were so exceptionally poor that the catch was still smaller, 245,700 barrels, the lowest result ever recorded in Antarctic whaling between 1909/10 and 1975/6, excepting the war years 1941-5. Conditions were quite abnormal. For carrying oil from South Georgia to the U.K. Kr.270 (£15) per ton was paid, a price that had been paid for the oil alone fifteen years previously, and would be paid thirteen years later. As was to be expected, the price was in dispute in both seasons. On the exchange whale oil was quoted at £165, the price demanded by the companies, but they were paid a little more than one-third of this, £62 10s. As the British restrictions were to apply until six months after the conclusion of hostilities, the 1918-19 production, too, had to be sold to Britain. During negotiations in London to settle the price, there was much bitterness among the Norwegian delegates at the browbeating tactics employed by the British. A representative of the Colonial Office "went so far as to state that if the Norwegians refused to yield, they would lose their licences". We shall see later on what tremendous importance this constantly repeated British threat was to have.

Negotiations ended with an agreement, the main points of which were as follows. Payment for oil in 1917-18 was settled on the basis of £62 10s for No. 0/1, and for 1918-19 oil of £72 10s. The latter sale comprised all oil that might be produced prior to 1 July 1919. All restrictions were to terminate as from 1 October. All current legal proceedings were abandoned, licences renewed, and concessions confirmed. But even for the 1919-20 season, companies did not have a free hand, as Britain (which in reality meant Lever Bros.) had prior right to the purchase of all oil produced after 1 October during the 1919-20 season. The Norwegian companies had every reason to be satisfied with £72 10s, since Salvesen had been compelled to sell two cargoes at £62 10s. Although the Norwegians insisted that £72 10s was a ruinous price, the companies recorded such large profits that they were able to declare dividends of from 30 to 60 per cent. Some of this, however, was the fruit of favourable exchange rates and the carrying trade. At any rate, sale in the open market would have doubled this surplus.

For the 1919-20 season previous catching regulations were once again in force, involving first and foremost complete utilisation of the carcass and the former number of whale catchers. (At one time Salvesen had operated from Leith Harbour with twelve catchers.) On 17 October 1921, new regulations were introduced which to some extent confirmed the main points of the old, and to some extent introduced new ones. One of the latter was that catching should be restricted to the period 16 September-31 May. This was of most significance to the waters around South Georgia, as no catching took place there before or after this period. On the other hand, winter catching round South Georgia from 1 April to 30 September had produced a surprisingly high yield, in 1913-14 an average of 646 whales, 50,600 barrels of oil, and 24,800 sacks of guano. The bulk of the catching took place in April, May, and September, but there was no month entirely devoid of whales. The magistrate in South Georgia, who provided the above-mentioned figures, concluded that there were two categories of whale, one migratory which left the whaling grounds in winter, and the other stationary which spent the winter there. He points out that the relationship between whales and barrels is misleading, because after 1 April a number of whales and a great many carcasses were reduced belonging to whales caught prior to that date. The raw material, furthermore, was better utilised in winter, as there was more time available.

According to the 1921 regulations the licence fee was £200. This entitled the holder to one or two floating factories and two whale catchers, and for a fee of £50 a reserve whale catcher could be used should one of the regular catchers be put out of action. At the shore stations all raw material was, of course, to be exploited on the same lines as previously; on the floating factories, apart from the blubber and the meat, the head, the jaws, the tongue, the tail, and the inside fat were also to be processed.

While Norwegian companies had very good reason to complain at the price of oil during the preceding seasons, the catch recorded in the 1919-20 season proved the greatest bonanza in the history of Norwegian whaling. According to the terms of a contract of 4 March 1920, Lever Bros. purchased the entire Antarctic production at £90, £85, £80, and £72 for Nos. 0/1-4 (plus £3 per ton for oil in barrels). As the exchange rate for the pound had jumped from Kr.13.50 in 1917 to Kr.22.10 in 1920, the seven companies sold for nearly Kr.60 million, recording a net surplus of Kr.22 million (£1 million). Shareholders received fantastic dividends, ranging from 80 to 240 per cent.

The companies considered the licence fees and the regulations reasonable, and posterity has praised Britain for her prudent restrictive whaling policy. However, they felt that the severe increase in the export duty on whale oil was extremely unreasonable. This increase had been introduced on 1 October 1912, chiefly to cover the expenses of administering the Dependencies. At that time it was 3d a barrel (each of 40 Imperial gallons); in 1915 it was raised to $3\frac{1}{2}d$, in 1919 to 1s 6d, and in 1920 to 5s or £1 10s a ton. In 1915 a duty of $1\frac{1}{2}d$ per 100 lb. of guano was imposed, and this remained unchanged. The proposal for radically raising the duty came from the Interdepartmental Committee on Research and Development in the Dependencies of the Falkland Islands, which was set up in 1917 to report on what could be done after the war to preserve whaling and develop other activities in the Dependencies. The Committee considered it entirely reasonable that whaling should pay the expenses of scientific investigation of stocks of whale, in order to preserve these for the benefit of the companies concerned. In view of the enormous profits they had made in 1920-1, the Committee did not consider it unreasonable that the duty should be raised to 5s a barrel, corresponding to $8\frac{1}{2}$ per cent of the value of the oil, whereas $3\frac{1}{2}d$ had represented $\frac{1}{2}$ per cent of the value in 1913-14. But when the price of oil slumped in the spring of 1921 to one-third,

61.   Whalers' homecoming at Sandefjord.

and the bulk of the production was sold for £30 5s, Britain agreed to refund half the duty, which in 1921 totalled £99,832. In order to ensure that the duty bore a constant relation to the market price of oil, a sliding scale was introduced from 5s, when the price was above £50, dropping to 6d for every £5 below this price, which means in fact that the duty has never exceeded 3s 6d (1921-4). This cumbersome system was abolished in 1928, and as from the 1928-9 season a price of 2s a barrel has been levied, irrespective of the price of whale oil.

This duty produced the biggest amount in 1922-31, both because the rate was highest and because licensed catching during those years reached its greatest scope. South Georgia and South Shetland enjoyed some of their best seasons, and licensed catching was also carried on off South Orkney and to some extent in the Ross Sea. The annual average was £106,000, the peak being reached in 1924-5 with £119,000. Altogether, during the thirteen years 1919-31 a little over £1 million was paid. After 1931 revenue slumped, both because four stations in South Georgia and the one at Deception and South Orkney were closed down, and because from now on a large amount of unlicensed pelagic catching was in progress. We shall see below that apart from the wartime threat to cancel licences and concessions, the high export duty was also one of the reasons why whaling companies, by adopting pelagic catching outside

British territory, freed themselves from dependence on Britain.

All amounts in excess of $3\frac{1}{2}d$ produced by the duty were credited to the Dependencies Research and Development Fund, and administered by the "Discovery Committee" — which had replaced the dissolved Interdepartmental Committee — under the Colonial Office. Seldom has a scientific committee had such abundant funds at its disposal. In 1923 this amounted to £300,000, in 1929 £583,105. Of this amount, £70,000 — then a very large sum — was earmarked in 1924 to purchase the famous polar exploration ship *Discovery*. When the results of its first voyage in 1925-9 were published, a storm of criticism met the Discovery Committee for its wanton waste of money. By the summer of 1928 it had expended almost half a million pounds, whereas the administration had received only £11,000, even though it employed a staff of fifty at Port Stanley and 60 per cent of their time and work was involved with whaling matters. It seems unfair that so small a proportion of a revenue from the colony and its Dependencies should have accrued to their advantage. During the debates on this matter it was maintained that, since Norway did most of the whaling, and would derive the greatest benefits from the results of research, then she should cover all the costs, "so much the more because this country makes an enormous profit on the catch without paying anything in return for pursuing it".

This is not the only statement that reveals how poorly informed the public was on the real facts. Admiral Evans, a figure well known from Scott's voyage in 1911-12, gave a lecture in December 1928 on the *Discovery* expedition, and in answer to the question what advantage accrued from Antarctic research, he declared: "Here is one of the answers, that men like Scott, Shackleton, and Amundsen, apart from earlier explorers, have founded the big whaling that brings millions of pounds to a friendly people". It would be difficult to commit a greater historical blunder; without mentioning the real founders of whaling, C. A. Larsen and Christen Christensen, three men are mentioned who had not the slightest connection with it, and whose expeditions (apart from Scott's first expedition of 1901-4) took place *after* whaling had been established. Nor was any mention made of the fact that indirectly the British expeditions were paid for by Norway. One of the minor Norwegian companies alone paid in 1920-30 a little over £50,000 in licence and export duty, and of the £777,144 collected in export duty in 1918-28, as much as £473,221 was contributed by Norway, and in addition to this there were the licence and concession duties, making a total of £525,000.

In 1920 the Interdepartmental Committee concluded that the most important condition for the development of British whaling was that Norwegian labour should gradually be replaced by British, that licences should on no account be granted for more than one year at a time, while the use of floating factories should be limited to a minimum. This, in addition to what has already been mentioned, caused the Norwegian whalers to regard this committee and its successor, the Discovery Committee, with suspicion, auguring a stricter British whaling policy *vis-à-vis* Norway once the twenty-one-year concessions lapsed at the end of the 1920s. The British could hardly have foreseen that this threat would have the opposite effect to that intended.

Britain's claim to all Norwegian whale oil produced in British territory created the paradoxical situation that Norway, the world's major producer of whale oil, with a large hydrogenation industry, would suffer serious shortage of fats. Necessity, as we know, is the mother of invention, and this shortage of fats compelled the Norwegian state to violate both the Whaling Act of 1896 and the ban of 1904. This applied only to the three northernmost counties, and both before and after the ban whaling had been carried out from other places along the Norwegian coast, but with very modest results. The ban of 1904 was valid for ten years, and when it lapsed in 1914 it was renewed for a further ten years. Finally, when the shortage of fats became so precarious that even the fishermen in North Norway, who had been responsible for the ban, pleaded that it might be raised as they needed meat, fats, and lubricating oil, the question was reconsidered in 1916. The dispute with Britain on whale oil, however, had just reached a critical phase. The British Minister, Findlay, looked with considerable misgiving at the possibility of Norwegian whaling outside British control, and in Norway it was feared that this might result in British reprisals, further jeopardising the concessions. For this reason the matter was temporarily shelved. With the growing shortage of fats, the Government decided nevertheless to initiate whaling, at Government expense, from six stations up and down the Norwegian coast, and out of consideration for Britain it was emphasised that this would be carried out under such careful control that it would not entail increased difficulty with the belligerents or jeopardise Norwegian whaling in other waters. The first whale was caught on 18 January 1918, and the result of three years' catching, 1918-20, was 1,874 whales and 46,400 barrels, or 7,734 tons. Some 42,000 sacks of meat meal and guano were produced, and 700,000 kg. of whale meat for human consumption were sold. The operation proved a great disappointment, falling far short of the 15,000 tons annually required if the shortage of fats was to be effectively overcome; besides, only 45 per cent was No. 0/1, capable of being hydrogenated for the production of margarine, the rest going to the soap manufacturers. Norway's shortage of fats was redressed far more effectively when the Norwegian state requisitioned all hydogenated fat, 18,500 tons in all, that De-No-Fa had processed for storage in accordance with the agreement with Britain. The whaling sponsored by the Norwegian Government proved a costly business, the final balance sheet showing a loss of Kr.3,855,000.

The major significance of this catching was that once and for all the "political" superstition that whaling destroyed the fisheries was finally nailed. Convinced of this, the Norwegian Government once again permitted private individuals to carry out whaling from Norway's coast. Concessions were granted for four stations on the west coast, and from these, in 1925-8, an average of 551 fin and sei whales were caught, producing 13,800 barrels of oil. Norwegian coastal whaling, which was entirely abandoned in 1972, subsequently enjoyed a chequered existence. It was mainly based on the sale of whale meat for human consumption and for fox and mink farms.

Whaling in other grounds outside the Antarctic during the war has on several occasions been mentioned above. In many places it came to a complete halt, or was greatly limited. How great were the losses suffered by the whaling fleets as a result of wartime sinkings cannot be accurately assessed, as several of the floating factories were sunk, not while undertaking whaling operations, but as regular merchant ships in the carrying trade. Two whale catchers were casualties of war, and a number were sold to the belligerents. All in all, the whaling fleet by May 1916 had been reduced to seventeen floating factories and eighty-three catchers. As Norway was practically the only nation operating with floating factories, her loss of ships was naturally greatest. Just how reduced Norwegian whaling matériel had become is shown in Table 18.

Table 18. OIL PRODUCTION AND CATCH VALUE OF THE NORWEGIAN WHALING FLEET, 1914, 1918, 1922

	Companies	Shore stations	Fl. f.	Catchers	Whales	Barrels	Catch value (£ million)
1914	50	23	36	149	14,800	575,000	2.00
1918	8	8	5	44	3,300	147,000	1.54
1922	15	9	9	50	6,321	338,000	2.47

Severe reduction had one advantage: a large number of non-viable companies, established on merely speculative grounds, and a great deal of obsolescent matériel, were scrapped, and a marked concentration of companies had taken place, directed increasingly towards the one large whaling ground — the Antarctic — where a new whaling adventure now saw the light of day.

18
CRISIS AND RECONSTRUCTION, 1920-1923

After sales of whale oil from the 1918-19 and 1919-20 seasons at a rate of £72 and £90 respectively, future prospects were optimistic. Whalers estimated that after the war most of Europe would be suffering from a tremendous shortage of edible fats and oils, which would mean a high price for whale oil. An investigation of the market, however, produced the unexpectedly disappointing result that it was extremely difficult to sell whale oil. An offer of £50 from the sellers was turned down, and even £35 failed to find buyers. The agent for the Norwegian companies in Britain advised storing production for 1920-1, and calling off all whaling for 1921-2.

There were several reasons for the failure of the market and the drop in prices. Most European countries were so impoverished by the war that they could not afford to buy. Political and currency conditions were so labile that great risk was involved in the concluding of any deal. In addition, large stocks of vegetable oil had piled up in the producer countries, which it had been impossible to transport to Europe. However, the availability of tonnage and the sharp drop in freight rates in the autumn of 1920 changed the situation completely; in the course of 1921 Europe, and in particular Britain and the Netherlands, received large quantities of vegetable oils at a price that was about one-third of what it had been only a year before, and the price of whale oil joined in the price slide. In the third place, while consumption of margarine had increased markedly in 1915-21, to the amazement of the manufacturers sales slumped from the end of 1920 and in 1921, whereas they had expected that an economic crisis, falling wages, and unemployment would increase the consumption of cheap margarine. In the fourth place, after the purchase of the Southern Whaling & Sealing Co. in 1919, Lever Brothers themselves became major whale oil producers and were no longer entirely dependent on others. In the fifth place, the price of oil was further depressed when the major purchasers banded together in a buyers' syndicate. Faced with this, the Norwegian Antarctic companies united in a sellers' syndicate in February 1921, a move which helped greatly in tiding them over the crisis. An extra source of relief was the fact that the 1920-1 season provided one of the best catches of all time. The weather was superb and there were such ample stocks of whale that operations could be concluded early, and running expenses saved. Using the same plant as in 1919-20, production in the Antarctic amounted to 120,000 barrels more, practically 1,000 barrels more per

62. The Whaling Museum in Sandefjord, a gift to the town by Lars Christensen, 1916.

whale catcher. Furthermore, the currency crisis ensured Norwegian companies a very considerable agio. Without these advantages the prospects would indeed have been sombre.

The whole summer went by without any sale being negotiated, and the date for setting off and starting a new season approached. An offer from buyers of £30 2s inclusive barrels, could not be accepted, as it would not even cover production costs. It was decided to lay up the floating factories, and to store the whale oil. Faced with this ultimatum and the prospect of obtaining no whale oil in the following season, on 19 August ten Norwegian cargoes of 250,000 barrels were sold, and shortly afterwards the cargoes of the British companies, at a rate of £31 5s, to the buying syndicate (Lever Brothers, Jurgens, and van den Bergh). The sellers must have felt a sense of relief on concluding this sale, although the price, one-third of the rate for the previous season, together with the same high operating costs, meant that practically all the companies suffered a loss, in particular the Compañía de Pesca, who went down to the tune of $832,318, having, in a moment of panic and because they were short of liquid assets, sold their entire production two months previously for £25 a ton.

Whaling shares plummeted on the exchange, but with sales in 1921-2 at £33 and much reduced working expenses, the crisis was temporarily over. In 1921 the average rate for Norwegian whaling company shares quoted on the exchange had fallen to 59 per cent of their par value, but by the beginning of 1922 had risen to 116 per cent, and in 1925 to 219 per cent. Confidence in whaling as a lucrative investment had been restored; stable, relatively good prices for whale oil right up to 1929, a reduction in wages and other running expenses, deflation, and the increased purchasing power of money, all these factors together created the economic basis for the tremendous expansion in 1927-31. On both sides, sellers and purchasers, a concentration took place, as contending parties became more powerful and the tug-of-war for whale oil more intense.

With the creation of the buyers' pool the whaling companies now had only one customer. On the one hand this simplified sales, as practically the entire current season's production could be sold on a single contract. But when the producers had no opportunity of marketing their oil out-side the buyers' pool, the latter could more or less determine the price. On many occasions and in many ways the whalers attempted to free themselves from this dependence on the margarine and soap trust.

One such scheme was to set up a hydrogenation factory in the Antarctic, in order to process the oil while it was still fresh, and had not had time to deteriorate during its long transport to Europe. This would ensure that oil of qualities Nos. 2 and 3 would also provide a useful product. As a counter to the fats trust which Lord Leverhulme was trying to set up, the non-committed manufacturers in England worked to persuade the Norwegian whaling companies to contribute a quarter of a million pounds in a syndicate consisting of themselves, one of the oldest and largest soap manufacturers besides Lever Brothers, two major manufacturers of vegetable oils in Africa, and the proprietor of another patent for hydrogenation other than that of the trust. The crisis that set in during the autumn of 1920, however, made it impossible to obtain the necessary capital. Meanwhile, the trust went from strength to strength : its power became plain in January 1920 when Lever Brothers bought up, for a price of £8 million, the Niger Company, possibly the largest plantation company in the whole of Africa, and 1929 obtained control of the powerful United Africa Co., which had a monopoly of practically all trade in the whole of West Africa. It was hopeless trying to fight this all-powerful concern on its own ground, and the only way to achieve independence would be to find other buyers.

For a while this policy had some success, and may well have pre-vented the buyers' pool from forcing prices still further down. Sales to the U.S.A. seemed to offer a solution. In their attempts to penetrate the American market Lever Brothers had met strong opposition from the leading soap manufacturers, Procter & Gamble, who had sole rights to Normann's patent in the United States. Through its agent in Norway a contract was concluded with the Norwegian sales pool in the autumn of 1921 for an advance sale of 100,000 barrels at a price of £32, £29, and £24 for Nos. 0/1-3. This was a slightly higher price than the European buyers' pool had paid in August for the 1920-1 production. The most important point was not the improved price, but the fact that a buyer had been discovered outside the pool. The Norwegian Whaling Association exploited this situation by informing buyers in Britain and the Netherlands that, if they were anxious to obtain any of the oil for the coming season, they would have to pay £35. Though they did not achieve this price, before the season concluded the entire catch had been sold in advance for £33 (for No. 0/1). These sales contracts were of the greatest importance to the companies' credit. One drawback involved in putting Norwegian whale oil on the American market was the high import duty to which it was subject, as a result of pressure from domestic manufacturers of edible fats and oils, i.e. the large slaughterhouses that were sole suppliers of tallow, and the manufacturers of soya beans and cottonseed. The sale to Procter & Gamble amounted to £493,700, and on this sum the duty payable was almost $300,000, i.e. 12 per cent of the purchase price. Neither Britain nor the Netherlands imposed an import duty on whale oil.

Three good seasons, 1920-3, did a lot to tide whaling over the crisis. The 1923-4 season admittedly witnessed a serious setback, with production down by 150,000 barrels and the number of blue whales caught down from 5,600 to 3,300, but the three ensuing seasons, 1924-7, proved so outstanding that they were the best in the entire history of South Georgia, producing an annual average of 410,000 barrels.

PART THREE

PELAGIC WHALING

19
THE FIRST ATTEMPTS ON NEW
AND OLD GROUNDS

From the end of the 1920s whaling concentrated more and more on one particular area, the Antarctic, and this in many ways simplifies the problem of writing the history of whaling. On the other hand, the problems involved become more complicated as new techniques and new catching methods are adopted, as fears are aroused among the whale biologists that stocks will be exterminated, by stricter national and international control of catching, by the availability in the world market of previously undreamed-of quantities of whale oil, by the contrast between concessionary and non-concessionary whaling, and above all by the arrival of new nations in pelagic catching in the Antarctic, an area which could no longer constitute a limited British-Norwegian problem capable of solution by mutual agreement. Whaling now becomes an important factor in the policies of the great powers. (For catching season on all grounds between the two world wars, see Statistical Appendix, Table 52.)

The Antarctic share of world catching, on a percentage basis, varies according to whether one's yardstick is the number of barrels or the number of whales, as Japan's large share is only calculated in numbers of whales (see Table 19).

Table 19. THE ANTARCTIC SHARE OF WORLD CATCHING, 1914-1938

	1914	1922	1925	1930	1931	1934	1937	1938
Percentage of barrels	53.7	70.8	67.0	90.9	97.5	92.6	82.7	91.8
Percentage of whales	40.9	50.4	45.1	79.8	93.2	80.1	67.4	84.0

Catching off the African coast, which in 1913 had accounted for practically one-third of world production (31.7 per cent), slumped to 6.5 per cent in 1917, rose to 17.6 per cent in 1924, and then plummeted to 1.0 per cent in 1931, only to rally somewhat in the 1930s to a peak of 5.3 per cent in 1937.

A highly remarkable feature is the tremendous increase in the number of barrels per whale catcher; in Antarctic waters this was more than quadrupled, from 4,919 barrels in 1918-19 to 21,384 barrels in 1932-3. The annual average was seven times more than in the Arctic and four times higher than in Africa. The other remarkable feature is the improved

313

use made of the raw material, as indicated by the number of barrels per blue whale unit (BWU). (Other whales are reduced to blue-whale equivalents on the following basis: 1 blue whale = 2 fin whales = $2\frac{1}{2}$ humpback whales = 6 sei whales.) This is shown in official figures. In South Georgia in the 1924-5 season this was 87.5 barrels, rising to 110.7 in 1929-30, decreasing in the first half of the 1930s, and reaching a peak in this decade with 117.6 in 1938-9. In pelagic catching it was 85.0 barrels per BWU in 1924-5, rising to 114.6 in 1932-3, and maintaining a high level for the rest of the 1930s, a peak being reached in 1939-40 with 117.2 barrels.

A third feature of the inter-war years is the marked British and Norwegian concentration on catching in the Antarctic, which in Norway's case was entirely pelagic. In South Georgia catching was abandoned in New Fortuna Bay in 1920, in Godthul Harbour in 1929, in Husvik, Stromness, and Prince Olav Harbour in 1931. At Husvik catching was re-started in 1945-57 and 1958-60, but apart from this, all catching from South Georgia after 1931 has been Argentinian and British. (In the 1960s the Japanese leased Grytviken and Leith Harbour for a couple of years, but soon afterwards gave up catching from these bases.)

After the First World War the Norwegians endeavoured to start up again in many of the old whaling grounds outside the Antarctic, but before the end of the 1920s they had withdrawn from practically all of them. Statistics listing Norwegian areas show thirteen names in 1926, only three in 1933, and two in 1938. In some places other nations were engaged in whaling every year during the inter-war period, particularly round Chile, South Africa, Japan-Korea, and (apart from one year) the northwest coast of North America. In other parts there was either a complete stop after a few years or else catching was carried on sporadically for short periods, with intervals in between.

It is generally assumed that since whaling began in the Antarctic the world's largest companies were Norwegian. Of the five largest, only two were Norwegian, and these rated second and fifth in size. Measured in terms of oil production, Chr. Salvesen & Co. was far and away the largest, with about 70 per cent bigger production than its nearest rivals from 1904 to 1929. The strength of Norwegian whaling consisted not of a few large units but of numerous medium-sized ones. If we include Salvesen's operations from Iceland, the Faroes, the Shetlands, and Saldanha, the firm had prior to 1930 produced twice as much whale oil as any other. In 1915 Salvesen ceased operations from New Island in the Falkland Islands, in 1929 from the Shetlands, and in 1930 from Saldanha. Their position in South Georgia, where they purchased the Prince Olav Harbour station in 1935 and the Stromness Harbour station in 1946, became all the more dominant. These stations were not operated, but the plant, including tanks and the floating dock, were utilised in conjunction with Leith Harbour. The purpose of these purchases was without a doubt to exclude other companies. In 1956 negotiations were entered into for the purchase of Grytviken. Apart from a short period of catching after the Second World War from Hawke's Harbour, Labrador, and sporadic attempts in other whaling grounds, all the operations of this firm have since 1930 been concentrated on the Antarctic, pelagic whaling, and Leith Harbour.

In Japan developments took a contrary turn, spreading from home waters to the islands in the south, east, and north, and in 1934 continuing to the Antarctic and in 1940 to the North Pacific. This is a parallel to the spread of Norwegian whaling after 1882, but with one important difference: Japanese catching always preserved a solid foundation in coastal catching based on the home country, whereas whaling of this kind in Norway was almost brought to a complete halt.

Before dealing with the main subject of this section, the development of non-concessionary ice-whaling in the Antarctic, it might be useful to give a short résumé of whaling in other areas during the inter-war years. The reason why an outlet was sought in this direction during the first few years after 1918 was that whaling in the Antarctic was reserved for licensed companies. These could increase production by means of a more effective use of their plant, but access to the richest whaling grounds was barred as long as the problem of unlicensed ice-whaling had not been solved.

Africa

In Africa as a whole whaling during the last war-years had shrunk to three shore stations with twelve whale catchers. Immediately after cessation of hostilities operations were re-started in all the old whaling grounds. In Natal interest focused on the Union Whaling Co. The first four years were very difficult, and this applies also to the Premier Whaling Co., but during the remaining years of the 1920s both recorded good catches, culminating in 1929 with 1,797 whales and 70,804 barrels. During the 1931-2 crisis Unilever suspended operations from its station after the two preceding seasons had resulted in a loss of £31,000. The shares were sold to Union Whaling, which ran both stations from 1933 (in 1954 operating jointly on Premier's site). This is the only company which has subsequently operated from Natal. Catching from Durban has proved one of the most stable in the world; ever since Johan Bryde started up in 1908, catches have been remarkably steady. It has escaped general notice that, as far as the production of whale oil and guano are concerned, Bluff has proved the richest whaling station in the world after the large stations in South Georgia, and in some years production has in fact been bigger than at any of these stations, and every year after 1958 until operations here, too, were provisionally suspended after 1975.

While total catches have been stable, whale stocks have shown great fluctuations, particularly blue and humpback whales. A considerable number of the former were caught in 1923-30, after which it declined gradually, and became a rarity after the war. For brief periods, with intervals of twelve to fifteen years, a fairly large number of humpbacks were caught (approximately 1922, 1934 and 1949), the largest number being recorded in the inter-war years with 514 in 1934. Fin whales probably declined steadily throughout this period, but only in the late 1960s did they reach a level where catches were significantly affected : this area is now, in common with so many others, practically only a sperm whale area (in 1975 twenty-one fin whales and 1,682 sperm whales were caught). Stocks of this species, too, were almost certainly ample in former years, but as long as there were sufficient baleen whales, the sperm whale was disregarded as inferior. Catching of this species was influenced by the special market fluctuations for sperm whale oil, which did not follow the same curve as for baleen whale oil.

Operations from Cape Province during the inter-war years had neither the same scope nor stability as those from Natal. There was a complete break from 1931-5 and 1938-47. There were three stations here — Waaigat, at Cape Hangklip near Whale Bay, just south of Cape Town; Donkergat, at Saldanha Bay, which Johan Bryde had set up in 1909; and the Salamander station, which Salvesen had bought. During the 1921 crisis all three stations were at a standstill; in 1922 both the stations at Saldanha started up again, and in 1925 the one at Cape Hangklip. During the first year of peace, 1919, the results were so meagre that the local magistrate was in favour of banning all whaling for twenty-five years, but when, after the 1921 interlude, whale stocks appeared to have revived, there was no further talk of a ban. The best period was 1926-8 (in Natal, ten years later). The annual average was about 65,000 barrels; large quantities of guano, approximately 80,000 sacks, were also produced, which suggests that the raw material was utilised almost one hundred per cent. Statistics for the three favourable years and the preceding and succeeding years provide an interesting picture of the nature of whale stocks off the South African coast (see Table 20).

There were two striking features of the large number of blue whales in 1926-7 : stocks were far larger on the west coast than on the east coast. On the west coast, the migration path ran past Walvis Bay to Angola, but off the Congo no blue whales were caught. The highest number in any one year off Natal was 265 (1930). In the second place, they were practically all young, not yet sexually mature animals : of the total number from Saldanha in 1920-5 they accounted for 83 per cent,

Table 20. WHALES CAUGHT FROM SOUTH AFRICA, 1925-1929, BY SPECIES

	Blue	Fin	Humpback	Sei	Sperm	Bryde	Right	Total	Barrels
1925	784	698	9	33	60			1,584	52,489
1926	1,000	798	19	258	95	64	1	2,235	62,408
1927	1,020	761	12	65	155	28		2,041	66,253
1928	554	436	21	355	225	47	3	1,641	67,024
1929	316	411	40	193	221	29		1,210	53,661

off Natal in 1918-26 74 per cent. This difference was still more marked for the fin whale — 83 per cent at Saldanha, 49 per cent in Natal. In Angola they accounted for as much as 95.5 per cent of the blue whales and 98 per cent of the fin whales. Everywhere there were slightly more males than females, and they were smaller the further north they were caught. These were not so valuable, and a large number had to be killed to ensure that oil production paid its way. The animals were lean, and suffered grievously from parasites in the warm waters. A whale expert pointed out that this catching of blue and fin whales from Africa made fearful inroads in future stocks of whales. In the warm water the layer of blubber became very thin during the course of the summer as the whale made severe demands on its stores of nourishment. This also meant that the process of autolysis was slower as there was hardly any food in its entrails. The animals were caught when they were at their leanest, and before they had had an opportunity of giving birth to a new generation or growing to be large, fat providers of oil. The whalers also disobeyed the rule of never shooting a female with her young. With the death of the mother, an animal which, some years later, might have replenished the whale stocks, was lost for ever.

In 1930 Irvin & Johnson operated seventeen catchers, and produced 37,000 barrels, 2,172 per boat; Salvesen worked with seven catchers, and recorded 1,963 per boat, as against 13,128 per boat in the Antarctic. Heavy working expenses and declining oil prices made catching unprofitable, and both firms broke off after 1930. In 1936-7 Irvin & Johnson tried again, but with no more success than in 1930. Under different names and owners the Donkergat station was run after the war with greatly varying yields during the first few years, rising however in the 1950s to a maximum of 34,000 barrels in 1960. When this fell to half in 1967 the station was abandoned. Here, too, emphasis changed to the sperm whale, which comprised 630 out of a total of 870 in 1967; of the remainder, 152 were sei.

In 1916 the two last Norwegian companies had left Africa, and after the war they returned to their old grounds. While it was obvious that stocks of whales had been over-taxed before the war, there was an equally strong conviction that these had now revived, as whales had been left in peace for six to eight years. The Portuguese government apparently believed that, with the high prices for whale oil in 1919-20, an unrestricted duty could be levied on whaling. If catching were to get off the ground round Angola, the duty would have to be radically reduced. In expectation of a further reduction, a Norwegian company operated with a floating factory just outside territorial waters in 1923. As we shall subsequently discover, this particular factory, this particular year, and this particular form of catching in many ways marks the birth of pelagic whaling. That Angola should have been chosen for this was because the founder of the company had operated here in 1911-15, and consequently was familiar with local conditions. The results in 1923 proved a disappointment, and for this reason whaling was continued for a short while in the Straits of Gibraltar, but total results were so poor that the company was wound up. Two subsequent attempts, the last in 1926-8, were a complete failure, and since then no whaling has been undertaken from a shore station in Angola.

The establishment in 1925 of a Franco-Norwegian company, with the vast capital of 6 million francs, for the purpose of catching off Capo Blanco (in former French West Africa), illustrates the fantastic dream that existed for a golden age in whaling in African waters. Fortunately for the shareholders, this company never got off the ground. A floating factory, on its way home from Angola, tried its luck off Capo Blanco, but found whale stocks in that part of the ocean virtually non-existent.

On the basis of the number of whales of various species caught we may conclude that blue, fin, Bryde and right whales migrated no further north than Angola, and that the bulk of the sei and sperm whales went no further, either. In addition, the humpback, which in 1910-16 had practically been exterminated off Angola, appears to have avoided these waters later on, and made its way further north to the coast of the Congo. Never in the history of whaling were so few barrels produced per whale as off Angola in the 1920s. In terms of BWU we get 32.5 barrels for the entire period, out of a catch, what is more, consisting mainly of blue whales. The nadir was reached off Angola in 1926, when 76.5 per cent of the catch was blue whales, and the try-out 17 barrels per BWU! One-seventh, in fact, of what the animal would yield in the Antarctic a few years later. It was impossible to operate at a profit on the basis of whale stocks that produced so little oil. Fortunately, this put an end to this miserably irrational exploitation of one of nature's major sources of raw materials.

Catching from the French Congo (Gabon) was not resumed by older companies but by an entirely new Franco-Norwegian concern. This secured all the three licences which France issued for these waters, and as it also obtained a concession for the Spanish island of Annobon, it assumed that it exercised a sort of monopoly on all catching in the Gulf of Guinea. Furthermore, it seemed to come up to expectations.

During the first three years, 1922-4, that the company operated on its own, there was an annual average of 21,000 barrels and a satisfactory surplus. It was precisely this that proved its undoing. In 1925 three new expeditions arrived, operating with floating factories just outside the territorial limits. Little experience was necessary to foresee what would happen when one shore station, four floating factories, and eighteen whale catchers started competing, with no holds barred, in such meagre whaling grounds. "It does little credit to Norwegian whaling. Bearing in mind the results of 1913-14 it should have been realised that this makes everyone a loser," is the bitter comment contained in the annual report for 1925 of the first company. A good margin of profit was turned into a deficit, whereupon this and the other companies abandoned operations after 1926. After leaving the humpback in peace for three years, the concessionary company once again worked from the shore station in 1930, achieving fairly good results, but an obvious decline in the whale stocks towards the end of the season, and the 1931 crisis, persuaded them to give up after one year, whereupon the company went into liquidation. Once again whales were left in peace for three years, until one company started again in 1934 and three in 1935, all of them operating with floating factories outside territorial limits. In the course of a few years their efforts resulted in history repeating itself for the third time. Total yields for all three companies in 1935 were 51,000 barrels, the second highest recorded up till then off the Congo, but it was sufficient to decimate stocks so radically that the last floating factory gave up in 1937, and these waters were left in peace for ten years.

When catching off the Congo was restarted in 1922, Professor Gruvel returned to the attack, that is to say against the whaling that took place just outside territorial limits. For the first time he propounded the interesting idea that whaling should be subject to a special and more extended territorial limit of 15 to 20 miles. In the second place, conditions off the Congo revealed that the conflict between the old licensed shore whaling and the new unlicensed pelagic whaling was not a local problem peculiar to the Antarctic, but a universal one. We shall later consider the dramatic conflict on this subject in Peru. In the third place, after unrestricted catching had once again ruined the Congo area, Gruvel renewed his appeal for international regulation. He persuaded the French Fisheries Congress in Bordeaux in September 1925 to appeal to the Government to establish an international agreement clearly aimed at the Norwegians, "the pirates of whaling". However, the Norwegians themselves were also working to ensure stricter regulation of catching, not only out of considerations of nature conservation, but also to maintain whaling on a permanently profitable basis. These were two aspects of the same problem; without the first, the second would be impossible.

It is surprising that Walvis Bay should have been the area on the west coast of Africa which produced the highest overall yield in the 1920s, and witnessed the longest continuous period of operation, 1923 to 1930. The real reason for this was that operations here were confined to one company, which was spared the detrimental effects of competition. Catching was initiated from a shore station in July 1923 by a Norwegian-British company, but with such poor results that it withdrew, leaving a Norwegian company to continue in 1924. Catching had to be based entirely on the migration of the blue whale from approximately 1 June to approximately 15 September. These dates varied somewhat from year to year, but August was always the best month. The blue whales caught early in the season, which came straight from their feeding grounds in the Antarctic, were as a rule very fat, and also very frequently unusually large. A female blue whale of 91 ft. produced 305 barrels of oil, which at the 1924 rate represented over Kr. 50,000. This how-ever, is not a record: on 21 March 1931, a whale catcher in the Antarctic shot a female of 101 ft. which produced 354 barrels of oil, or 56,640 kilogrammes!

This company, too, failed to establish profitable operations on a lasting basis. Running expenses were very high, owing to the large item of coal, as practically all fresh water had to be obtained by the distillation of salt water. In order to extend the use of plant, whale catchers were sent with a floating factory to the Antarctic, but despite two relatively good seasons off Africa (1928 and 1929) and three in the Antarctic (1928-31), the company failed to survive the crisis of 1931-2. There was such a slump in prices that the floating factory, four whale catchers, and a one-fifth share in the whaling stations were sold off for no more than one-third of what the floating factory alone had cost in 1928. Once again Africa had inflicted on Norwegian whaling one of its greatest losses. In 1930 the station was sold to a group of six Norwegian whaling companies, not for use as a whaling base but for storage and repair workshops for whale catchers in between seasons in the Antarctic, to obviate the need to despatch them all the way back to Norway. The workshop was burnt to the ground on 31 May 1950, and never rebuilt.

Attempts to re-start whaling off Mozambique proved, if anything, an even greater disappointment. A Norwegian company which leased the station and the whale catchers for five months in 1923 recorded a mere eighty-one whales and 2,385 barrels, withdrawing after suffering considerable losses.

A comparison between catching results at Mossamedes (Angola), Walvis Bay (Namibia) and Saldanha (Cape Province) during the years (1926-8) when catching comprised mainly blue whales in all three localities, shows that in the first of these 14.6 barrels per whale was achieved, and in the last approximately 35, and at Walvis Bay 70. The last-mentioned, in fact, appears to have been an area to which particularly large, fat blue whales — above all, females — resorted.

The resumption of whaling off the African coast in the inter-war years had in most cases ended with the same economic crash as before the war. Eleven companies had attempted it, two of them had succeeded in establishing operations which from time to time yielded a modest revenue, the others had been forced to retire with losses, and of these, seven were dissolved or went bankrupt. Not all those who invested in whaling found it as lucrative a business as was generally imagined.

Spain and Portugal

The idea of operating in these waters is believed to have been the inspiration of the manager of the Norwegian station in the Hebrides. In the winter of 1910-11 he set off in search of whales in the seas between the Azores, Portugal, and North West Africa. While bunkering in Gibraltar he noticed that quite a number of whales were passing in and out of the Straits of Gibraltar. After protracted and difficult negotiations with the Spanish authorities, the company Compañía Ballenera Española S.A. was finally established on 11 June 1914. Officially, this was a Spanish company, with its head office in Madrid, and with a Spanish count as chairman of the board of directors, which also included three other Spaniards, an Englishman, and the two Norwegians on whose initiative the company had been started. Actual management was exercised by the last-mentioned, through their office in Tønsberg. A fraction of the share capital, 1.9 million pesetas, was Spanish, the rest was English and Norwegian. Because of the war, catching could not commence before April 1921. The station had been set up at Getares, on the west side of the Bay of Gibraltar. As it turned out, stocks of whales were so plentiful that only one whale catcher could be used, as the station was unable to reduce the raw material quickly enough to keep up with the catching. From its inception and to the end of the year 356 whales (33 sperm and 323 fin) were caught, producing 10,500 barrels of oil. The venture had been based on the assumption that the oil could be marketed in Spain, but as this proved difficult and the price of oil slumped, the year ended with a slight deficit.

As there were far more whales than had been assumed, and since operations could be carried on practically right through the year, the station was greatly expanded in 1923, and two whale catchers were used. The results were outstanding — 38,472 barrels. The figure of 19,236 barrels per catcher, in fact, is one of the highest ever achieved in one whaling ground in one season. It has only been surpassed by pelagic catching in the Antarctic in 1931-4, where the figure of 21,384 barrels per boat is recorded, though this is under-estimated, as it was achieved in the course of 142 days, whereas in Spain catching took place practically every day of the year. Nothing is known of the economic results, but they must have been highly satisfactory, further assisted by the rate of exchange of the pound, which at the end of 1924 was Kr.32, and the high price of whale oil, £34. During the five years 1922-6, a total dividend of 194 per cent was issued. A good price was also obtained for the guano, of which some 400,000 sacks were produced annually (see Statistical Appendix, Table 53).

There is hardly any need to state that history once again repeated itself. A high price for whale oil is the whale's most dangerous enemy. Seven companies, most of them Norwegian, applied for concessions: two were granted, but even this proved too much, especially as catching based on Portugal was also started. The two concessions were given to Norwegian companies, both operating with floating factories. One was established in 1924 at Huelva, 110 miles north-west of Getares; the other had no permanent shore station, but was the first to operate in the Straits of Gibraltar. That the Spanish government in 1924 tried to regulate catching, on the model of the Falkland Islands Dependencies, was of little use, seeing that it had allowed three companies with nine catchers to make inroads in the same trek of whales. The results were not long in coming. One of the new companies folded after producing a mere 4,000 barrels in 1923; the other, operating with a very large and technically very well equipped factory, made 13,000 barrels in 1924 but only 6,100 in 1925. An obvious victim was the station at Getares, which recorded 11,000 barrels less in 1924 than in the preceding year. In order to make good this loss, both companies received a concession for operations off the northwest coast of Spain as well, in the vicinity of Cape Finisterre. But here, too, two companies proved too much, and when the Getares station produced a mere 7,058 barrels in 1927, the Spanish venture was for the time being at an end. Like all fairy stories, however, there was a happy ending of sorts : in a sperm whale a lump of ambergris weighing 304 lb. was discovered, and this is said to have been sold for Kr.400,000, undoubtedly an excessive amount.

As there were whales along the Spanish Atlantic coast, both in the north and in the south, there would be every reason to conclude that stocks were to be found off the intermediate coast of Portugal. A Norwegian company with a Portuguese name, the Sociedade Portuguesa da Pesca de Cetaceas Lda. da Lisboa, registered in Portugal but with Norwegian capital and under Norwegian management, erected a very expensive station at Setubal (just south of Lisbon), but the result of three years' catching, 616 whales and 14,000 barrels in 1925-7, was one of the great disasters of whaling, and the company was dissolved in 1928 with severe losses. If we add 3,160 barrels which a floating factory had produced near Setubal in the spring of 1925, the entire catching from Portugal amounted to 749 whales and 17,000 barrels, and from Spain respectively 6,250 and 202,000, and 173,000 sacks of guano. About 93 per cent were fin whales, the rest mostly sperm, with 66 sei and two blue. During the Spanish civil war in 1936-9, whaling was out of the question, for which reason figures quoted in joint statistics for the two countries indicate catching from Portugal by "different whaling companies" in 1933-45. These small-scale operations came to a halt in 1951, but catching started again from Spain in 1950 from one, and later three stations, continuing right up to the present. For a while the average annual yield was some 5,000 to 6,000 barrels, reaching a peak in the 1960s with 11,300 barrels in 1970. When the catching of the largest species from Norway and Newfoundland, Labrador, and Nova Scotia came to an end in 1972, whaling has subsequently been carried on in the North Atlantic only from shore stations in Iceland and Spain. In both these areas the lesson has finally been learnt of arriving at the correct balance between catching and stocks of whale.

On a couple of occasions, in 1939 and 1948-9, disastrous attempts were made to operate from Spanish Morocco. When a Norwegian company applied for a concession in 1939, the State Whaling Board observed : "This venture is hardly very viable; but the State cannot act as a nurse to all nationals who wish to risk their money in dubious undertakings." And this was probably the most dubious form of whaling on which Norwegians have ever embarked, the result with two whale catchers being three whales! Moreover, the whole venture ended in an acrimonious quarrel.

In the Azores (and in Madeira) old-style whaling can still be studied. It is actually not all that old, having been introduced to the Azores by whaling vessels from Nantucket in 1765, which operated until the local inhabitants started on their own in 1832. Since 1909 motorboats have admittedly been used for towing the whales, while a floating factory installed in a steamer was introduced in 1934, but three typical features of the old-style whaling have been retained : the whale is caught with hand weapons from open rowing boats, flensing is carried out with blubber picks and not with flensing knives, and the oil is still extracted by melting blubber in open cauldrons. In 1941 similar operations were started from Madeira. Only the sperm whale is caught, which at times has comprised a significant share of world catching, in 1910 72.3 per cent, in the 1920s and 1930s approximately 23 per cent, and in 1945 26.5 per cent. Anyone who appreciates this old-world and still surviving method of catching would agree with ROBERT CLARKE, who has made a detailed study of Azores open boat whaling : "But should steam whale-catchers ever be introduced, the stock is unlikely to withstand such exploitation for long unless the catches are rigorously controlled. Open boat whaling survives in the islands today as an economical and efficient industry, and I very much hope that this courageous and adventurous way of living may never disappear from the North Atlantic."

The North Atlantic

We have already described the shore whaling that took place around the Norwegian Sea in the inter-war years. The innovation in these waters after the First World War was that of pelagic whaling. To some extent it may be described as ice-whaling, as it extended to the pack ice and drift ice of the Arctic Ocean. There has been a tendency to associate pelagic catching and ice-whaling only with the Antarctic, and yet this type of operation has also been carried on — though on a small scale — in sub-Arctic seas and to some extent also at an earlier date than in the Antarctic. Two of the first expeditions were assumed not to need any links with terra firma, "as they are both equipped to manage on their own". This catching falls into two periods, 1919-24, when small vessels and older matériel were used, and 1929-37, with larger and more modern floating factories and whale catchers. Just as catching in the north was important to the development of the steam-driven floating factory, so, despite its modest scope, it has also influenced the first attempts at pelagic whaling *before* this method made its breakthrough in the Southern Ocean. Pelagic whaling can be defined in several ways, of which the best is probably this: in modern pelagic whaling catching is carried out by mechanically propelled (steam or motor) whale catchers in the open sea in combination with a floating factory which has no links with the shore, and where the whale is reduced on board to oil or other products. According to this definition, the catching operations carried out by a number of vessels in the North Atlantic prior to 1922 were not pelagic. The captain of the first floating factory in the waters off Spitsbergen in 1904 maintained that he had in fact commenced pelagic whaling, as the whale was reduced in the open sea. But according to reliable sources the factory ship lay at anchor in two fjords in Spitsbergen, and the blubber was not boiled on board, but transported to a plant in Norway. In other words, in two important aspects it did not fulfil the conditions for pelagic catching.

The 1922-4 expeditions, on the other hand, satisfy the criteria for pelagic catching. There were three of these, all Norwegian, and they operated mainly off West Greenland. In order to preserve the whaling that was such a vital necessity for the Eskimos, the Danes consistently refused to grant a licence for a shore station; floating factories were not permitted to lie at anchor inside the territorial limits, and they were not even allowed to take on fresh water ashore, and were therefore compelled to operate in the open sea. All three caught in the Davis Straits and Baffin Bay, but the whale stocks proved far less plentiful than expected, and they all returned with a loss, but with important information on the problems associated with unlicensed catching in the open sea. Considered from this point of view, these initial expeditions in the north have a certain bearing on the development of pelagic catching.

Four years were to elapse after this unsuccessful attempt before anyone again ventured to invest money in whaling in the north. After an interlude of several years, the whale stocks had apparently increased; the whaling grounds were less remote than the Antarctic, and running expenses consequently lower. The years 1929-34 were the real period of pelagic catching in the north. A total of six expeditions operated, catching 2,800 whales and producing 112,300 barrels of oil, but even this was not sufficient to ensure a profit, except for one of the smallest floating factories that has ever operated. For two reasons it lived to its name *Pioner* (Pioneer), 1,721 gross tons. It was Norway's — and probably the world's — first floating factory driven by a diesel engine, and it was the first to be accompanied by a refrigerator ship for whale meat. In addition, during the four-year period 1930-3, it produced 7,837 barrels of oil as an annual average, considerably more than the larger factories. In 1934-5 the company committed the fatal error of despatching the small floating factory to the Congo and the Antarctic; in these difficult climatic conditions the little vessel proved almost useless, and lagged far behind in competition with all the big new floating factories. The very poor price paid for whale oil also ensured that a venture that had started so promisingly ended with a loss of the entire share capital and much besides.

Now that attempts to establish remunerative pelagic catching in the north had failed for the second time, no expedition set out in 1935 or 1936. The only catching in these years was that undertaken by the Danish Government for the Eskimos in the Davis Strait, as well as one shore station in Iceland, one in the Faroes, and three on the coast of Norway. In 1937, however, the Sevilla Whaling Co. (Salvesen) despatched its large floating factory, the *New Sevilla* (13,801 gross tons), north with seven catchers. In so far as the *New Sevilla* had a stern slipway, this may be said to have been the only entirely modern pelagic expedition ever to operate in the Norwegian Sea, and the yield proved to be the highest that any company had ever recorded in the course of one season throughout the entire history of whaling. In precisely three months 552 whales were caught (of these, 184 sperm) and 22,513 barrels produced (of which 11,173 barrels of sperm oil). As was the case with all other expeditions, fin whales proved lean and small, producing not more than 30.7 barrels. The sperm whales were larger, yielding 61.7 barrels. It should, however, be borne in mind that a great deal of the meat was used for the production of meat meal, 235 tons in all. A contemporary Norwegian attempt in 1937 resulted in a large deficit. The total result of this catching in 1929-37 was 3,600 whales and 145,000 barrels of oil.

The Pacific

Norwegian catching in the Pacific during the inter-war years fared no better : in the unshakably optimistic belief that all the oceans of the world teemed with whales, people were persuaded to invest money in enterprises which experience should have taught them were doomed to failure. Three of the four expeditions were despatched from Sandefjord, and one from Tønsberg. The largest of these ventures was prepared with meticulous care. The floating factory *Kommandøren I*, 6,546 gross tons, was one of the largest in the world, and her conversion the most complete ever carried out by the Sandefjord yard. The factory was equipped with tanks for 40,000 barrels, and comprised, together with five whale catchers, the largest whaling fleet that so far had been sent to any whaling ground outside the Antarctic. The Soviet Government had granted a concession lasting for fifteen years for catching along the coast, from the south point of Kamchatka to the Bering Strait, a distance of nearly 1,800 miles. Only with good catching results would the expenses for bunkers, provisions, and wages for 130 hands, on the fifty-nine-day voyage out, be justified. To be on the safe side the company had also secured, at very considerable expense, a concession to catch in Magdalena Bay in Lower California, and it was here that most of the catching was done, commencing in November 1924. Between seasons, in the summer and autumn of 1925 and 1926, the floating factory made its way to Kamchatka, where catching conditions were very difficult, with constant fog and storm. During the two-and-a-half years the factory operated, it actually covered five seasons, with a total yield of 1,645 whales and 60,346 barrels, but the deficit incurred on the protracted voyages out and back, and the intensive catching, were considerable, and the company went bankrupt. The factory ship was sold to the Compañía de Pesca, and rechristened the *Ernesto Tornquist*, in honour of one of the founders of the company. For a number of years it was used as a floating factory, and subsequently as a transport vessel, until it went down off South Georgia on 16 October 1950. The other company, which operated only round Magdalena Bay, incurred losses the first two years, 1924-6, but returned a good surplus in the next two. In 1929 there was an almost total lack of whales, and it was decided to move to the Antarctic. During these five years this small company had paid Kr.492,000 in licence dues to Mexico, while the outward-bound voyage, before catching could commence, had cost Kr.240,000. With the collapse of the oil market the company folded;

shareholders lost their entire investment (Kr.1.5 million), while creditors suffered grievous losses.

Off Mexico, catching of southbound migrations of gray and humpback whales started in December. Most were females in the last stages of pregnancy, author example of the cynical and irrational destruction of whale stocks. Catches declined swiftly: in 1927 472 humpbacks were taken, in 1929 sixteen, in 1925 100 gray whales, in 1929 two. Catches of pregnant blue whales, too, revealed the same tendency, dropping from 235 in 1926 to 115 in 1929. When catching of gray and humpback whales ebbed out at the end of February, blue whales would arrive from the south, following the coast north. The best season for this catching was March-May. This was the species that yielded most oil: the total result of catching by two floating factories off the west coast of Mexico in 1924-9 came to 2,745 whales and 107,000 barrels of oil. A total of 1,568 humpback, 870 blue, 182 gray, 74 sei, 34 Bryde, 8 fin, and 8 sperm whales were caught. Hardly any fin whales were to be found.

The collapse of the two companies was not sufficient to deter a Norwegian expedition manager from trying his luck once again in 1935 with a Norwegian-Mexican company and a floating factory that carried the hopeful name of *Esperanza*. Despite this, the result was meagre — 3,821 barrels — and the floating factory ended on the scrap-heap.

The attempt to revive catching off the west coast of South America likewise for a short period, 1926-7, proved disastrous to those who had been trusting enough to invest their money in this gamble. One of the pioneers from South Georgia, the Tønsbergs Hvalfangeri, acquired two licences for catching off the coast of Ecuador and Peru, and set up two companies, one for each whaling ground. It was intended that the larger of the two, operating off Peru, was to operate both as a floating factory and a shore station, of which it was said that "it could be the finest whaling station in the world". The chairman of the Board made the interesting observation that "the reason why this company was formed was the possibility of losing the concession for South Georgia in 1928 and the need in this event of having another whaling ground to fall back on". This was not the only observation of this nature. The resounding economic failure of the Peruvian venture was due not to poor catches — from July 1925 to April 1927 55,000 barrels — but trickery on the part of the Peruvian authorities and their agents, and a slump in the price of oil. This disaster involved Tønsbergs Hvalfangeri in very considerable losses, while the Board were subject to severe criticism for their recklessness. Shareholders, however, had no real grounds for complaint: on an original share capital of Kr.600,000, they had in the course of twenty years received Kr.20 million in dividends.

The results of the two companies' catching during these two years amounted to 541 blue, 726 fin, 280 humpback, 161 sperm and 32 sei whales, all young animals which yielded little oil.

Large-scale catching of sperm whales off the coasts of Chile and Peru in 1936-8 was not an independent venture; it was undertaken not by companies specially established for this purpose, but by Antarctic companies between seasons, mainly Salvesen. This also applied to the catching of sei whales, which a few companies indulged in off the coast of Patagonia in 1927-9.

From the above it will be seen that in the 1920s a large number of companies were started with a view to operating in old and new whaling grounds, as well as pelagic whaling. What were the results? Records show that between 1922 and 1937 there were thirty-six Norwegian companies which were either voluntarily dissolved after suffering considerable losses or which went bankrupt — ten were older companies, twenty-six were new enterprises. This second phase in Norway's expansion of its global whaling had in fact proved disastrous. Large sums had been lost. This is one side of Norwegian whaling that has not been generally known; it was by no means the gold mine depicted by posterity. It was not of major importance to the world production of oil; its total production during the fifteen years 1923-37 hardly exceeded production in the Antarctic in the single season of 1930-1. On two occasions Norwegian whaling had set out to conquer the oceans of the world, but after the second attempt this approach was abandoned for all time, and interest concentrated entirely on the Antarctic, where unlicensed ice-whaling offered far more promise.

20
UNLICENSED WHALING, 1923-1931

Introduction

The history of whaling from the mid-1920s to the end of the 1930s poses a great many problems, some of which will emerge from the figures shown in the table below. These reveal that the production of whale oil tripled in the course of four seasons, 1926/7-1930/1, that in the ensuing season it was only one-quarter, and that it achieved the same level in 1937-8 as in 1930-1. During the period covered by the table below, Norway's share of world production slumped by about half, whereas Germany's rose from 0 to 12.4 per cent and Japan's from 0.5 to 16.5 per cent. The relationship between the number of shore stations and floating factories revealed by these figures, and also between the number of whale catchers and production, also provides grounds for certain reflections (see Table 21).

If we only consider Antarctic production, Norway's decline is seen to be still greater, from a peak of 71.4 per cent in 1928-9 to 29.9 per cent in 1938-9. In the latter season the German share was 13.2 per cent and the Japanese 17.1 per cent. Not only relatively, but absolutely, too, Norway's setback in the Antarctic was very considerable, from a peak of 2,291,694 barrels in 1930-1 to 842,712 barrels in 1938-9. In terms of personnel, too, Norway was now losing her monopoly. As late as 1933-4 this was nearly complete; in 1938-9 her personnel comprised 60 per cent. Norway's whaling activities became exclusively Antarctic; in 1925-6 27.4 per cent of Norway's catch came from other grounds, ten years later only 4 per cent, and in 1938-9 a little under 2 per cent.

Table 21 is highly revealing in a great many ways: for the moment we shall concentrate on one aspect of it: that the same production which in the entire sphere of global whaling in 1930-1 was achieved by 285 whale catchers, required 357 whale catchers in 1937-8, despite the fact that their efficiency had been greatly increased. It would be a mistake, however, to consider these figures in isolation. For example, the fact that in the Antarctic 112 whale catchers achieved practically as large a catch in 1932-3 as 270 whale catchers managed in 1938-9, cannot be correctly interpreted unless we consider that the average number of catching days per vessel had decreased from 144 to 96. The relationship between matériel and yield is best expressed in the number of whales caught and/or the number of barrels of whale oil per "catcher's day work", even though this yardstick is subject to considerable shortcomings. Expressed

Table 21. WORLD CATCH AND PELAGIC ANTARCTIC CATCH, 1926-1939

	World catch		Pelagic Antarctic catch	Shore stations	Fl. f.	Catchers	Percentage of world catch		
	Whales	Barrels					Norway	Germany	Japan
1926-7	24,215	1,191,922	30,270	34	22	233	57.8	0	0.4
1927-8	23,593	1,321,313	733,912	31	20	222	60.5	0	0.4
1930-1	43,210	3,701,668	3,385,189	13	43	285	62.6	0	0.4
1931-2	13,171	925,293	686,355	11	8	103	3.1	0	2.2
1932-3	28,928	2,606,421	2,401,879	12	22	189	50.5	0	0.8
1937-8	54,902	3,641,314	3,250,064	37	35	357	32.1	10.2	11.6
1938-9	45,783	3,011,813	2,709,281	16	37	362	28.4	12.4	16.5

Note: The figures for the numbers of shore stations may be subject to correction, as the Japanese are included in some years, but not in others.

63. The gun is loaded.

64. When chased, the whale blows violently.

in the number of baleen whales the highest figure achieved in terms of catcher's day work was 1.81 in 1936-7, dropping to 1.32 in 1938-9. In the number of barrels of whale oil the catcher's day work reached its peak in 1933-4 with 162, slumping to 99 in 1938-9. Both figures apply to pelagic Antarctic whaling. In these waters the last-mentioned season witnessed a rapid decline, with 270 whale catchers, operating for a total of 25,954 catching days, catching 34,213 baleen whales whereas in the previous season 244 whale catchers, active for 24,897 days, had accounted for 43,328 whales.

The relationship between equipment, catches, production, and operating time will be seen from Table 22, which illustrates pelagic Antarctic catching, as well as including operations in the Ross Sea, from South Shetland, and from South Orkney.

What does not emerge from Table 22 is that in 1927-8 the average tonnage of floating factories was 6,510 gross tons, in 1930-1 8,736, and in 1938-9 13,751, or that the thirty-four floating factories in 1938 exceeded by 111,000 gross tons the forty-one floating factories operating in 1930. The reduction in the number of catching days was outweighed by an increase in the capacity of floating factories, by the number of whale catchers, and by their efficiency. The average tonnage of whale catchers rose from 226 gross tons in 1930 to 298 in 1938, and the amount of horsepower per engine from 755 to 1,139. Just as important as the quantitative increase was the role played by the qualitative improvement in the technical equipment: the Hartmann cooker, oil separators, direction-finding devices, wireless telegraphy and telephony, the gunner's bridge, the breech-loading gun, etc. All these improvements, however, did not produce a corresponding constant increase in catches (or oil production) per catcher's day work. This rose from 0.85 BWU in 1929-30 to a peak of 1.45 in 1933-4, after which it dropped to 0.92 in 1938-9. Catcher's day work has been introduced in order to express the inflow of whales, but it will only reflect an absolute value if catching in all seasons has taken place under similar weather conditions, with the same matériel, and with the same skill exercised by the gunners. The objection has been raised that this yardstick gives far too optimistic a view of the situation. If, for example, the same whale catchers had been used in 1946-7 as in 1932-3, the number of barrels of oil per boat per day would have dropped still more drastically. These factors must be borne in mind when this yardstick is used without reservations as a diagnosis of changes in the size of whale stocks.

Numbers for "caught" whales and "killed" whales are not the same. For the decimation of stocks of whales the latter is the more important, but where this cannot be calculated with real accuracy, probability will have to suffice. In the discussion on a new Whaling Act in Norway in 1935 it was estimated that 18 to 20 per cent of whales harpooned were

Table 22. CATCH, PRODUCTION MATERIEL, WHALING DAYS FOR PELAGIC ANTARCTIC WHALING, 1927-1939

(a) FLOATING FACTORIES

	Whales	Barrels	Fl.f.	Catchings days Total	Catchings days Per fl.f.	Barrels per fl.f.	Whales per fl.f.	Total	Barrels per day per fl.f.	Whales per day per fl.f.
1927-8	10,126	733,312	17	2,580	152	43,136	596	4,824	284	3.92
1930-1	37,438	3,384,048	41	6,940	169	82,538	913	20,024	488	5.39
1933-4	23,065	2,225,663	19	2,298	121	117,140	1,214	18,394	969	10.04
1936-7	31,965	2,527,026	30	2,881	96	84,234	1,066	26,323	877	11.10
1937-8	43,328	3,201,153	31	3,157	102	103,263	1,398	31,384	1,014	13.72
1938-9	34,213	2,564,506	34	3,273	96	75,427	1,006	26,714	784	10.45

(b) WHALE CATCHERS

	Catchers per fl.f	Catchers total	Catching days Total	Catching days per catcher	Barrels per catcher	Whales per catcher	Barrels per day per catcher	Whales per day per catcher
1927-8	3.6	61	8,824	145	12,022	166	83	1.15
1930-1	4.9	200	33,690	168	16,920	187	100	1.11
1933-4	6.0	114	13,725	120	19,523	202	168	1.68
1936-7	6.1	184	17,656	96	13,734	174	143	1.81
1937-8	7.9	244	24,897	102	13,119	178	129	1.74
1938-9	7.9	270	25,954	96	9,498	127	99	1.32

Note: Both tables include only baleen whales and baleen whale oil.

65.   The shot.

66.   "*Fast Fisk*": the whale is hit and is blowing blood.

67. The whale is inflated to keep it floating.

68. The whale "in flag".

69. Outboard flensing in calm weather.

70. The cooker is filled with blubber.

71. The meat plant.

lost owing to the line breaking, and it was the largest and heaviest blue whales that got away. During the first sixty years of Antarctic whaling, the catch was approximately one-and-a-quarter million whales. If we estimate a loss of 10 per cent, and an oil content of 100 barrels per whale, this would come to approximately 125,000 whales and some 12 million barrels (2 million tons). However, as it was impossible for technical reasons to extract more than about two-thirds of the whale's gross oil content, the net loss may be estimated at some 8 million barrels. In more recent years technique and matériel have improved to the extent that numbers for caught and killed whales approximate very closely, whereas in the period we are now going to deal with the difference is more marked.

Up to the end of the 1930s the problem was not so much the ability to keep the floating factory supplied with raw material, but the ability to reduce the material at a rate that kept pace with catching. A division of patents according to category shows that during this period (1923-40) far more patents were granted for "plant for the extraction of oil" than in any other categories. With ample access to whales, expeditions had shown a tendency to include more whale catchers than the capacity of the floating factory warranted. To put it simply, from the 1930s on the problem may be said to have been transferred from the floating factory to the whale catcher. The increasingly hard battle to secure enough raw material for the floating factory had begun. It was the tremendous expansion of unlicensed pelagic whaling after 1927 that resulted in the present situation of whaling and whale stocks. For this reason it is of the greatest interest to the history of whaling to clarify the factors affecting this whaling. We shall find them in Great Britain's policy of licences and concessions, in whaling conditions in the old grounds, in the general technical development of the age, and in the place of whale oil as a raw material on the world fat market. As we shall see, it is no mere coincidence that the great change in catching took place in the latter half of the 1920s, when the twenty-year British concessions in the Antarctic were lapsing.

Britain and renewal of licences

Only a few years after the Antarctic début the British authorities were subjected to strong pressure to show preference for national interests at the expense of Norwegian. During the first four or five years the British had played a waiting game, but the results of catching from South Georgia in 1910-11, 6,529 whales, as the Governor wrote, aroused the greatest excitement, and applications for leases and licences poured in from Great Britain, South Africa, the Falkland Islands, Norway, Denmark, Sweden, Germany, and other countries. One or two endeavoured to entice the Colonial Office with promises of gratuitous services, free mail and passenger transport, a certain percentage of the surplus for scientific research, etc. Common to all the British applications was the urge to "wave the British flag". Salvesen, not least, did this so energetically that the Colonial Office finally observed : "If it were not tactless, Salvesen might be reminded of their Norwegian origins." Already in their first application (13 May 1908) Salvesen submitted a wholly unacceptable proposal : a monopoly for themselves for catching both from South Georgia and from South Shetland. The proposal appears a remarkable one, as the firm could hardly have failed to realise that by then four twenty-year concessions had been granted, and in referring to this the Colonial Office could merely answer that a monopoly was impossible : they could only be granted a concession for South Georgia on the same terms as the others, or a licence for South Shetland. At that stage this apparently was of no interest to Salvesen, as they considered that too many stations — they expressly requested that there should not be more than five — would result in over-production and spoil the market. As mentioned, the outcome for the moment was that Salvesen were granted a licence for the Falkland Islands, but as operations here, in their own words, resulted in "an enormous loss', they turned their attention once again to South Georgia, where, as we have seen, they were given two concessions, and at the same time invoked British patriotism in order to obtain a licence for the South Shetlands : "We think all Britishers will be proud to hear of British enterprise being revived also at the South Shetlands." But when they applied for yet another licence for the South Shetlands and an additional concession for South Georgia (and were extremely disappointed that Irvin & Johnson should have obtained it), both the Governor and the Colonial Office cried halt. The former, without mincing matters, wrote that he was not convinced that money had been lost in the Falkland Islands, while the appeal for a support to British industry could hardly be taken seriously when they were trying to prevent another British firm being admitted. Their entire approach was dictated by a desire to keep competitors away. The Colonial Office observed, when one of Salvesen's many letters arrived : "We expected this sort of protest — and Salvesens are always first and will probably squeal the loudest as usual."

Time and again the Colonial Office had to remind all British applicants of the way in which whaling in the Antarctic had come into being : it had been started by foreigners in 1904, and no concession could be given to a British firm before an application was received from one five years later. The Colonial Office had only been able to act according to the principle of first come, first served. Several proposals not to renew the Norwegians' annual licences, and to transfer them to Englishmen, were resolutely rejected. After all, what would people then think of Britain abroad?

In 1911 the Colonial Office commissioned a Dr. WISEMAN to draft a report on the entire concession problem. The result was a long and interesting thesis, and, as we shall subsequently see, it touches on some of the most important points in the international agreement on regulation of whaling. Dr. Wiseman's conclusion was that no change whatever could be undertaken in the concessions before the lapse of the twenty-one years. To refuse a licence to floating factories would, in reality, involve a ban on all whaling outside South Georgia. The only step that could be taken was to give no further concessions and licences. In support of this a circular was sent in 1911 to all the new applicants, informing them that no more concessions would be granted. As we shall see, this was not observed.

Now that access to the main whaling grounds was barred, applications were submitted for licences covering all other conceivable areas in the Antarctic, in complete ignorance of whether it was possible to operate in them or indeed if there were whale stocks. The Colonial Office was able to answer conveniently that all licences had, in fact, been granted, as in fact they had no idea how to reply, not knowing who exercised sovereignty over the areas involved. Hardly had the "old" customers received their licences, before applications poured in for leave to extend their catching matériel, to operate with more whale catchers, tugs, an extra floating factory for carcasses, etc. One particular problem was posed by the floating factories which purchased carcasses from other expeditions. On the one hand, there was a hesitation to extend the fleet, but on the other hand it was desirable to utilise all the raw material —

both aspects of a problem on which volumes might be written. Various regulations were amended, and by the outbreak of the First World War the rules had been more or less stabilised to the satisfaction of both parties.

The Governor, WILLIAM LAMOND ALLARDYCE, had every reason to be satisfied when, in April 1915, after eleven years in the Falkland Islands, he was transferred to a "warmer" gubernatorial post. He left behind a colony which was well on its way to becoming a rich source of revenue, whereas previously it had merely been a source of great expense for the mother-country. He had shouldered the main responsibility for the administration of this development, which had imposed a tremendous burden of work to which he had not entirely been equal. According to the report of his successor, W. DOUGLAS YOUNG, Allardyce left his office in a state of near chaos: a large number of decisions had been made orally, without reference to the Colonial Board or without being duly recorded. He had gradually adopted an attitude of opposition to the Colonial Office, and felt that he had not been given due credit for his services. The first whaling regulations had been drafted by him, but the decision on actual details was gradually transferred to the Colonial Office. He failed to understand that whaling also had political consequences, and that regulation of it and the question of sovereignty in the Antarctic were bound to become international problems. For Britain, whaling was not so much a colonial as a foreign political matter, the forum of which was rightly the Foreign Office. Allardyce himself invested in whaling, and at his death in 1930 was a member of the Board of a British-Norwegian company.

During the First World War the Norwegians realised that, in a critical situation, cancellation of concessions would have to be reckoned with, and that a threat not to renew them could be used as a lever against Norway in a trade policy. This was constantly borne in mind in Norway, and there was a general belief that the concessions were in jeopardy, as the date of their expiration approached. This view was given added credence after the war with the renewed British demand for national protectionism, on the grounds of economic depression and unemployment. If Norwegian whaling was not only to survive but also to expand, it had the choice of two approaches: new whaling grounds could be sought, or the problem could be solved by unlicensed catching. Any further restriction or increase in the licence fee would act as a spur to breaking free from concessions and licences, would debase their value, lead to uncontrolled catching, and in this way have the very opposite effect from that envisaged in the work of the Discovery Committee and Britain's whaling policy. Salvesen clearly realised what the problem involved, and pointed this out to the Colonial Office in a letter of 21 May 1928: "It is clear that the development and probable extension

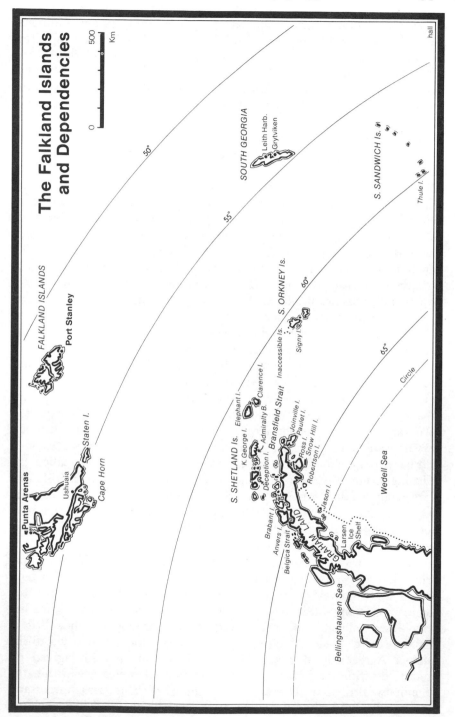

The Falkland Islands and Dependencies

of pelagic whaling cannot be ignored, and in our opinion, any additional restriction imposed upon lease and licence holders will be of direct assistance to pelagic undertakings. Moreover, in the case of the holders of certain licences there will be a stronger inducement to abandon licensed in favour of non-licensed operations, and the reduction in the value placed upon the licences will tend to diminish respect for existing regulations."

An address by Sir SIDNEY F. HARMER to the Association of Economic Biologists on 10 November 1922, created a considerable stir. Sir Sidney, an authority on marine biology, and Director of the Natural History Department of the British Museum, had been a member of the Inter-departmental Committee. In his lecture he expressed himself with considerable feeling, particularly on Norwegian whaling, which he described as "insensate slaughter arousing feelings of horror and disgust". There was only one thing, he maintained, for Britain to do: impose strict catching regulations, reduce the number of whale catchers, and forbid the use of floating factories. The lecture was quoted in Norwegian papers under banner headlines. In Norway the British agitation had two immediate consequences: one was that the ban on catching along the coast of Norway was converted to licensed catching, "as this undoubtedly will make it easier for Norwegian whalers when applying for concessions in foreign countries during the coming negotiations with Britain, where Norwegian whalers are not looked on with much favour". Tactical considerations, in fact, motivated the authorities once again to permit whaling along the coast of Norway. Norway could hardly expect a favourable response to her requests for concessions abroad when she herself granted none on her own territory. In the second place, on 8 February 1924, Norway set up an expert committee, often called the Whaling Committee, whose prime task was to co-ordinate British and Norwegian whaling research and to prepare negotiations between the two countries for a regulation on catching, with a view to preserving stocks of whales in the Southern Ocean and to work out the terms for a renewal of Norwegian concessions.

The extra pressure exerted at precisely this time on behalf of national British interests must be considered on the basis of the situation in both Britain and Norway. It was imperative for Great Britain to put the country's economy on its feet again after the war and find work for her demobilised soldiers and unemployed. In her economic policy Britain abandoned free trade, adopting a protectionist approach that led to the Ottawa Agreement of 1932. The British Commonwealth agreed on protective tariffs for foreign imports and mutual preference within the Commonwealth. For Norway the timing of this was important. Norwegian whaling had dwindled drastically. Table 23, which includes Norwegian coastal whaling, shows the extent of this decline.

Table 23. THE NORWEGIAN WHALING FLEET AND ITS CATCH,
1912-13 and 1917-18

	Whales	Barrels	Shore stations	Fl. f.	Catches
1912-13 + summer 1913	18,186	590,062	24	32	149
1917-18 + summer 1918	3,023	150,525	10	5	46

Norway's share of world catches, at one time a good three-quarters, had shrunk to approximately one-third, and recovery appeared to be a slow process. Admittedly, in terms of barrels, Norwegian whaling had doubled its capacity from 1917-18 to 1920-1, but not till 1924-5 was it on the same scale as in 1912-13, and growth had not been constant, 1923-4 showing a marked recession from the preceding season. This, as a matter of fact, was true of world catching as a whole. Norwegian whaling would appear highly vulnerable to British demands for national preference.

As the time for the expiration of concessions approached, pressure on the British Government increased. Salvesen wrote quite bluntly in a letter to the Colonial Office: "As all the South Georgia leases will shortly expire we think it is indisputable that it is to the interest of this country that whaling concessions should be in the hands of British rather than of foreign companies." The French, too, launched sharp attacks on Norwegian pelagic catching off the Congo in 1925, while in Australia the well-known polar explorer DOUGLAS MAWSON declared that the slaughter perpetrated by the Norwegian whalers would mean that not a single whale would be left in twenty years' time. The assembly he addressed adopted a resolution to the effect that licences granted to foreign companies should be cancelled, and that catching in the Southern Ocean would have to be controlled. Mawson's speech was quoted in a number of newspapers right round the globe: one of them reproduced it with a picture of a station in South Georgia, and the following caption: "A Whaling Station in the Southern Seas — a feature that will soon lapse into the limbo of forgotten days".

The success of pelagic whaling methods created problems of considerable scope biologically, technically, economically, and politically. Although it was asserted in official British quarters that the intention was to preserve the whale stocks from humanitarian motives, there is no doubt that the real motive was to halt pelagic catching, not for the sake of the whale, but to secure to Britain the large sums accruing from licensed whaling based on British territory. This, the Norwegians insisted, was the real aim of the Discovery Committee, and the fact that they had provided the bulk of the finance for this purpose made them particularly bitter.

It has so far not been generally known that it was a Norwegian who initiated the chain reaction resulting in the first Interdepartmental Committee in 1914, continuing with the second in 1917 and its report in 1920, and concluding with the Discovery Committee and its expeditions. The person concerned was the engineer JENS ANDREAS MØRCH, whose fertile brain encompassed not only the fundamental ideas for a solution to the technical problems of whaling, but also how to ensure a constant supply of whales and improved exploitation of the raw material. In 1908 he published in an American periodical an article on "Improvements in Whaling Methods". His conclusion was that the reason waste had reached such horrific proportions was because the British Government was not properly informed of conditions. No licence, he wrote, should be granted to any company without a pledge to reduce the entire carcass of the whale. This obligation was introduced by Britain in the concessions granted from 1 October 1909. According to Mørch, no one could make any definite assertion about the relations between catching and whale stocks before a scientific expedition had been sent out. In an article in the periodical of the Zoological Society of London Mørch revealed that he was well versed in the theories of whale migrations, and he raised the question of whether the waters off Africa did not, in fact, harbour the bulk of the humpbacks that migrated from South Georgia.

Mørch's decisive step was a direct appeal to the Natural History Museum in London, contained in two lengthy memoranda of 7 June and 28 July 1910, in which he ventilated two ideas which have become fundamental to whale research. One was that every catching vessel under British licence should record in a logbook every single whale killed, noting place, species, sex and in the case of females whether the animal was pregnant. The occurrence of plankton, fry, the temperature of the water and of the air, air pressure, etc., should also be recorded. On the basis of these logs, using variously coloured dots, the position where whales of different species had been caught should be charted, and these charts should then be sent to a scientific institution which in this way would have a picture of the state of the whaling grounds every year. As far as we know, this was the first time the idea of a catching log of this kind had been submitted, and it is in principle the one that was followed by Sigurd Risting as the basis for his outstanding *International Whaling Statistics*. The idea of whale charts was used by CHARLES H. TOWNSEND when, in 1915, he prepared his unique charts of the old American whaling on the basis of the logbooks of American whalers. Another of Mørch's ideas was that a certain proportion of the whaling dues should be set aside for scientific research, an idea that was realised with the setting up of the Discovery Fund and the "barrel tax" that was levied by Norway on Norwegian whaling from 1929.

We are able to trace the effects of Mørch's memoranda. The Natural

History Museum sent a copy of both to the Colonial Office on 3 May 1911. In answer to the latter's request for more specific details, the Museum furnished detailed material on 27 October. This included the above-mentioned interesting report by Dr. Wiseman, in which he drew attention to the successful results of the International Fur Seal Conference in Washington, which on 7 July 1911, had signed two treaties on the preservation of stocks of seal in the Bering Sea. A proposal had also been submitted to the Conference for a ten-year period of protection for the right whale and the Greenland whale, as well as a motion to the effect that floating factories should not be permitted in whaling. No agreement on this matter, however, had been concluded by the participating nations, the United States, Great Britain, Russia, and Japan, which had merely discussed seal trapping. In January 1912 the Natural History Museum wrote the Colonial Office that the reports received from the Antarctic confirmed in every way Mørch's assertions. At the request of the Colonial Office the Foreign Office issued a circular on 30 July 1912, to all its diplomatic representatives throughout the world, requesting information on whaling in the country concerned. The gist of the letter was that, on account of the decline in stocks of whales in the South Atlantic, the Colonial Secretary believed an international conference should be convoked in order to discuss a limitation of whaling throughout the entire world on the basis of an international agreement. Consequently when, in January 1913, Britain received an enquiry from Germany as to whether she were willing to take part in an international whaling conference, the Foreign Office was able to reply that it was engaged in collecting material for this very purpose, but as all the answers had not yet been received, Britain was not yet ready for the conference.

As a result of the Natural History Museum's action, Major G. E. H. BARRETT-HAMILTON was sent to South Georgia to study whaling and whales in Leith Harbour during the 1913-14 season. He was unable to complete his studies, as he died there on 17 January 1914. The papers he left behind were later published, and constitute the first scientific report on whales around South Georgia. They refer both to Mørch's memoranda and to the Natural History Museum's detailed report of 27 October 1911. His papers were made available to the Interdepartmental Committee on Whaling and the Protection of Whales which was set up in February 1914, with a mandate "to consider the question of the protection of whales and the regulation of the whaling industry". When the Colonial Secretary reported to the House of Commons, he stated that it was the Natural History Museum which in 1911 had drawn his attention to the slaughter that was going on, and that if the necessary precautions were not taken in time, total extermination would be the inevitable result. The Committee requested the Norwegian

Whaling Association to assist in the collection of material, and this resulted in Professor JOHAN HJORT making his way to London in order to co-operate with the Natural History Museum.

The work of this committee and co-operation with Norway were interrupted by the outbreak of war, but it was resumed with the new Interdepartmental Committee of 1917, from which the Discovery Committee emanated, as well as a recommendation on the way in which its expenses were to be covered. We have already noted the suspicion with which Norwegians regarded this matter, the inspiration for which had come from the Norwegian Jens Andreas Mørch.

Pelagic whaling, concessions and licences

The changeover to new methods of catching was completed with great rapidity; just how quickly will emerge from figures for the pelagic share of total Antarctic catching as shown in Table 24.

Table 24. TOTAL ANTARCTIC AND PELAGIC ANTARCTIC CATCH, 1925-1929

| Season | Total | | Pelagic | | |
	Whales	Barrels	Whales	Barrels	% pelagic
1925-6	14,219	783,307	1,710	83,864	10.71
1926-7	12,665	872,362	2,614	182,340	20.90
1927-8	13,775	1,037,392	10,138	733,912	70.75
1928-9	20,341	1,631,340	15,209	1,282,711	78.63

An added reason why the breakthrough was so marked in 1927-8 may have been that catches had slumped disastrously in 1926-7 in the customary harbours of South Shetland. A great many people believed that these whaling grounds had now been exhausted, and looked around for other fields of operation, particularly the Weddell Sea and further east. After 1927-8, few whales, in fact, have been caught by floating factories in the harbours of South Shetland and South Orkney.

In order to facilitate a general survey we have chosen to deal with the subject under four headings: (a) licensed pelagic whaling; (b) non-licensed pelagic whaling; (c) licensed and non-licensed ice-catching; (d) "licensees" and pelagic whalers.

(a) Licensed pelagic whaling. Apart from the brief interlude off South Orkney in December 1912, all attempts at pelagic whaling up to 1923 had taken place outside the Antarctic. The first person to practise it in these waters was C. A. Larsen, operating in the Ross Sea in 1923-4. His expedition was also significant in so far as his application to Britain for a concession prompted the setting up of a Ross Dependency. Moreover, the floating factory was the largest in the world, and carried new technical equipment of considerable interest.

Among the many applications submitted in 1911-15 to the Colonial Office for licences, there were several for the Ross Sea. A Norwegian expedition planned in 1912 had to be called off because no insurance company would underwrite such a hazardous enterprise. After C. A. Larsen had left Grytviken in 1914, he always dreamed of returning. As there were no licences or concessions available for the West Antarctic, his thoughts turned to the Ross Sea. In the opinion of the Norwegian Ministry of Foreign Affairs, all the territory around this sea was no man's land, and for this reason no concession was necessary, but the Norwegian Minister in London, referring to Ross's voyage there, opined that without any doubt it was subject to British sovereignty, and consequently advised applying for a concession. Protracted negotiations in London resulted in a licence for catching "from the Balleny Islands in the Antarctic Ocean and over and along the waters adjacent to Victoria Land" being granted on 21 December 1922. Britain was not in a position to grant a licence of this kind without a basis in international law for her sovereignty, and this was established by an Order-in-Council of 30 July 1923, dealing with the establishment of the Ross Dependency under British sovereignty. It comprised "the coast of the Ross Sea, with the islands and territories adjacent thereto", i.e. the so-called Ross Sector, including all the area south of 60° latitude S between 160° longitude E and 150° longitude W. Just how far south the boundary ran was not explicitly stated, but with the sector principle it followed *ipso facto* that it extended to the geographical South Pole, and thus included the territory Roald Amundsen had discovered on his journey to the Pole.

The Ross Dependency embraced vast areas: the Ross Sea itself is twice as large as the North Sea, while to the south the Ross Shelf Ice covers a sea that is just as big. The distance from the east side of the Ross Sea (Victoria Land) to the west side (Marie Byrd Land) is as long as from the west coast of Norway to Iceland.

Britain's action aroused a storm of fury among the general public in Norway. The Ministry of Foreign Affairs was ridiculed for failing to learn from its previous folly, that an application for a concession was tantamount to Norwegian recognition of British sovereignty. The idea of lodging a vigorous protest was very much in the air, but the Norwegian Minister in London advised against this. He recalled what had happened in 1906-7 : by refraining from a protest and accepting British licences, the Norwegians had achieved a considerable measure of British goodwill. And this, in fact, is what happened : the licence which the company A/S Rosshavet was granted for whaling along Victoria Land applied to indisputably British territory, and offered more favourable conditions than any other company had received. The licence was valid for twenty-one years, and entitled the holder to use two floating factories, each accompanied by five whale catchers; there was a £200 duty to be paid annually for each floating factory, and 2s 6d in export duty for each barrel over 20,000. During the first five seasons right whales could be caught, and the provision introduced for South Shetland — that floating factories were obliged to produce at least one barrel of oil from meat and bone for every two-and-a-half barrels of blubber oil — did not apply. On one point C. A. Larsen did not achieve what he had hoped for : exclusive rights for the first five years. Several licences, in fact, could be issued, and he had to be prepared to face competition.

Several open questions, which had provoked a fairly voluminous literature of international law, remained : Could Britain regard the Ross Ice Shelf as part of its territory, or was it restricted to terra firma? Was the Ross Sea to be regarded as a British inland sea or as an open sea where anyone was at liberty to catch? Were there in the Ross Sea as yet undiscovered islands which could be occupied by others? The Norwegian Whaling Association in its contemporary form represented the interests of licence-holding companies and in their concern at the prospect that their concessions might be forfeited, they were anxious that Norway should go a long way towards accepting Britain's claims. The conflicting interests between the concessionaires and the "pelagics", as the two parties were called, split the Whaling Association, which was dissolved : in its place, a new international organisation was established capable of reconciling the interests of both parties. By then the concessions of the Norwegian companies had been renewed and pelagic catching was dominant. But before this juncture had been reached in 1928, a great deal had occurred on the whaling front.

On 26 October 1923, on her way south, the *Sir James Clark Ross* had spoken with the Norwegian floating factory *Bas II*, which was operating off the Congo and Angola. It was a truly historic encounter. Both ships represented the dawn of a new era in whaling : one was about to embark upon a season of non-licensed pelagic catching, the other was about to open a new, large area to modern whaling. If we add that a third floating factory in January-March 1923 operated along the ice barrier near South Orkney, this year can be regarded as actually marking the birth of pelagic whaling.

Hvalfangeraktieselskapet Rosshavet (The Ross Sea Whaling Company) purchased an older vessel in England of 8,223 gross tons for £30,550, and conversion amounted to £110,000. She had fourteen pressure boilers, ten open cookers, and two Hartmann cookers, tanks with a capacity of 58,000 barrels, accommodation for a total crew of 170, a fairly powerful wireless telegraphy station capable of maintaining communication with New Zealand, but as only one of the whale catchers carried a small wireless transmitter, contact between whale catchers and the floating factory was out of the question. For this reason Larsen's list of desiderata for the ensuing season gave priority to a direction finder. By the 1924-5 season all whale catchers had been equipped with these, and they proved invaluable. In this respect, too, the expedition pioneered.

Some 9,200 tons of coal were taken on board in England: this proved sufficient, as the scope of catching turned out to be less comprehensive than expected. Supplies of water, too, were sufficient, whereas the third problem, flensing, was almost a disaster. The floating factory met the whale catchers in Hobart, Tasmania, and set off from there on 30 November, arriving in front of the pack ice on 15 December. That year it was particularly thick and extensive, and in the opinion of a great many people it was folly to try to force a passage through with an ordinary freighter towing five whale catchers. From Larsen's diary we can follow from hour to hour the strain imposed by the tremendous responsibility he felt for the many hands and the valuable equipment in his charge. After five days they were safely through, and they now made for Hvalbukten (Whale Bay) in the Ross Ice Shelf, where Roald Amundsen had set up his base, and where there were said to be "masses of whales". The floating factory entered the Discovery Inlet just east of Hvalbukten, and here most of the catching took place in February. The mercury dropped to $-30°C$, and an icy wind blew from the south. Blubber froze hard as bone as soon as it was pulled out of the water, the flensing knives were useless, and the blubber had to be prised loose with axes. Flensing along the ship's side in such conditions was more than could be expected of a human being, and again and again the flensers refused to work. "The whales are as hard as wood", Larsen wrote. "It is deplorable that nothing can be accomplished with this tremendously valuable equipment . . . If we had only had a floating factory to hoist the whale on deck, we certainly need not have despaired."

On 7 March operations had to be abandoned with the following disappointing outcome: 10 fin and 211 blue whales and 17,300 barrels. Although all the oil was blubber oil, it was not of top quality. Apart from technical difficulties, the reason for this was that the large and very fat animals were full of plankton, and the layer of blubber was so thick that autolysis set in very rapidly and very intensely. A blue whale measuring 106 ft. was probably the largest whale ever caught. On 2 April the expedition reached Stewart Island (off the south coast of New Zealand), where the whale catchers were laid up. The floating factory returned home via Cape Horn, and on 2 June, off the coast of Africa, it completed the circumnavigation of the world. The shorter route through the Panama Canal was avoided owing to the high duty, approximately Kr.100,000 return. When the cargo was discharged in Amsterdam on 13 June it was discovered that the percentage of free fatty acid had risen sharply during the three months' homeward voyage. Despite

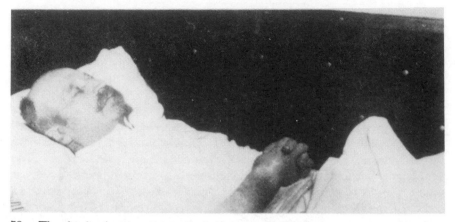

72. The death of a great man. C. A. Larsen on his deathbed, in his cabin on the floating factory, Ross Sea, 8 December 1924.

disappointing catching results, the economic outcome was better than had been feared, with a net surplus of Kr.44,776. This included on the debit side an item of Kr.49,500 for a licence off Lower California, which the company had secured for a period of ten years as a reserve, should it prove impossible to operate in the Ross Sea.

In 1924 the expedition had already penetrated the ice belt by 3 December. It shaped a course for Victoria Land, but hardly had catching commenced before a tragic but not entirely unexpected event occurred: on 8 December C. A. Larsen died in his cabin of angina pectoris. Resigning himself to the inevitable, he had entrusted the management of the expedition to his mate, and had written in his diary: "I no longer expect a long life, but may God's will be done: I have toiled long enough down here." His body was taken back to Sandefjord and buried there on 15 May 1925 at a funeral that was attended by a larger number of persons than at any before in that town. With the death a year previously of Christen Christensen, both the creators of Antarctic whaling had gone just as the most momentous chapter in the history of this industry was about to open.

Nor had Larsen the satisfaction of witnessing the great adventure he had so confidently predicted. This took place between 1 December and 22 January (1925) in the ice off Victoria Land, between Coulman Island and Possession Island. An unnamed island was christened C. A. Larsen Island. Conditions were ideal, with calm water between the ice floes, a light breeze, mild temperature and a mass of whales including huge blue whales. The record was set on 28 December with twenty-eight huge whales and 757 barrels. "I well remember these days," wrote the mate, "Whales, huge, fat fishes, far too many of them. The whale catchers were ordered to remain stationary for certain periods. There was no point in killing without being able to utilise the catch. Masses of meat and bone were wasted in favour of boiling blubber. And a lot of blubber, too, was wasted." The whale fermented quickly, he relates, and this reduced the quality of the oil. On 23 January the floating factory moved to the old site in Discovery Inlet, and enjoyed the same fabulous catches, the record being beaten with 787 barrels in one day; but when the temperature in mid-February dropped to − 30°C, there was nothing for it but to pack up. Already by 12 May, a month earlier than the previous occasion, the floating factory was back in Sandefjord with 31,500 barrels, 75 per BWU — an indication of how large and fat the whales (408 blue and 19 fin) must have been, especially as not all the blubber was utilised in producing this vast quantity. Had there been 100 per cent utilisation, the result would have been 150-200 barrels per BWU. The company's books recorded a surplus of nearly Kr.2 million, enough to ensure shareholders a 15 per cent dividend.

This successful catch was in actual fact the first ice catching on a large scale in the Antarctic, revealing all the necessary criteria: the floating factory was not anchored up or moored to the shore, and catching operations were not carried out in the ice-free Ross Sea, but in the open water between the ice floes. This type of catching was so new and unaccustomed to the gunners, that to start with they felt somewhat uneasy, but the wireless direction finders proved invaluable for finding their way back to the floating factory. C. A. Larsen's idea had triumphed.

The third season, 1925-6, proceeded more or less on the same lines as the foregoing, and 40,000 barrels in nine weeks was, in fact, a record. The excellent results encouraged the company to take advantage of the terms of the licence, which permitted the use of two floating factories. A comparatively new tanker of 13,246 gross tons was purchased in England. It was naturally christened the *C. A. Larsen*. Apart from being the largest floating factory in the whaling industry — very nearly the largest ever converted — the ship incorporated two technical innovations: she was probably the first to be oil-fired, and she had a slipway in the bows, most whales being hauled up through it on deck, where they were flensed. After initially operating inside the Ross Sea, from 7 to 19 March both floating factories caught around the Balleny Islands. It was the first time this area, which was to prove so rich in whales, had been tried. A third large Norwegian floating factory also operated here, as well as inside the Ross Sea, but without a licence. Owing to difficult weather conditions this season, 1926-7, proved a disappointment to all three, production jointly totalling 101,000 barrels. By contrast, the 1927-8 season proved a sensation. The belt of pack ice was very narrow, and easily negotiated, and owing to these favourable ice conditions a large number of big blue whales had entered the Ross

73. A unique photograph of the *Sir James Clark Ross* in Discovery Inlet. This was the first floating factory in the Ross Sea, 1923-4. The inflated blue whale alongside the ship is 106 ft. long, probably the biggest ever caught.

Sea. After little more than two months all the floating factories had to abandon operations, as they were fully laden. The return of all three to Hobart and New Zealand fifteen weeks after they had sailed aroused considerable international attention, not least in Australia and New Zealand. The *C. A. Larsen's* 78,400 barrels was till then the largest cargo of whale oil ever carried in a single hull. Curiously enough, it was precisely twice as much as was produced during the best year by all the stations in Iceland together. This time the degree of exploitation was not much better, at 85 barrels per BWU.

The 1928-9 season proved just as successful for all three, but on this occasion a still larger proportion of the catch was made outside the belt of pack ice off the Balleny Islands. This season really marked the end of catching in the Ross Sea: subsequently, only seventy whales have been shot there. The reason it was abandoned so soon was not because whale stocks were exhausted more rapidly than in any other areas in the Antarctic, but because the voyage into and out of the Ross Sea was highly hazardous, owing to shifting ice conditions. Whereas in 1927 two floating factories penetrated the pack ice in two days, in 1926 a factory took twenty-one days, while in 1929 the ice presented such a formidable barrier that one of the floating factories was precluded from catching from 12 December to 25 January. This risk was avoided by catching outside the pack ice to the northeast of the Balleny Islands, an area which proved far richer — at any rate for a while — than the interior of the Ross Sea. In 1950 a couple of floating factories once again endeavoured to catch there between 74° and 76° latitude S, but they quickly left.

In *International Whaling Statistics* the figures for catching in the

Ross Sea show a steady rise, culminating in the last and best season of 1930-1, when three expeditions jointly accounted for 5,223 whales and 428,211 barrels. These figures, however, show catching in the Ross Sector, and include catching outside the pack ice. Neither of the two new expeditions in 1929-31 which are listed in the statistics under the Ross Sea operated inside the pack ice. The catch of the three floating factories inside it was as shown in Table 25.

Table 25. CATCH IN THE ROSS SEA, 1923-30

Season	Whales	Barrels		Season	Whales	Barrels
1923-4	221	17,299		1927-8	2,012	171,311
1924-5	427	31,850		1928-9	1,742	160,010
1925-6	531	39,630		1929-30	61	5,300
1926-7	1,117	100,838	*Total*:	1923-30	6,111	526,238

Seldom has an area been a more exclusively blue whale catching ground than this: of the 6,111 whales, only 270 were fin, all the others being blue whales. The reason for this, of course, may be that as long as blue whales were plentiful, they were preferred by the gunners, as this ensured them a larger bonus. Few details are available on the sizes of the animals, but it appears obvious that in the main they must have been large animals, since as much 90 barrels per BWU was achieved, despite indifferent exploitation of the raw material. In 1926-7 one floating factory recorded the lengths of 405 animals: this averaged as much as $85\frac{1}{2}$ ft.; 52.1 per cent were over 85 ft., fifty-six were 90 to 99 ft., two were 100 ft., while the largest was 102, possibly 106 ft.

The administration of the Ross Sector had been set up in New Zealand, which in principle maintained sovereignty over the whole of the Ross Sea, asserting that catching there should be licensed, with a penalty of £1,000 a day for unlicensed catching, although no claims to this effect were ever put forward. Non-licensed pelagic catching, in fact, was now a reality.

(b) Non-licensed pelagic whaling; the Lancing *and the slipway.* In several areas it had proved possible to operate entirely independently of a shore station: off the Congo and Angola in 1923, in the Ross Sea in 1923-4, along the edge of the ice around South Orkney in 1924, and in the same year off the west coast of Greenland. Continuous operations, however, had proved impossible, as the whale could not be flensed alongside in a rough sea. Would it be possible to transfer to a floating factory the same technique of hauling the whale on to the flensing deck ("plan") as in the shore stations? In theory it would be a simple matter, but a floating factory in motion was quite a different proposition from a stable shore station.

The two men who put Petter Sørlle's patent into practice were H. G. Melsom, who had worked for Kejzerling and the Japanese in 1897-1915, and his cousin MAGNUS E. MELSOM. They sought the technical assistance of CHRISTEN FREDERIK CHRISTENSEN (son of Chr. Christensen), whose firm became the leading floating factory designers. He solved the very difficult problem of the reconstruction of the sternpost, the rudder, the rudder stock, and the steering mechanism that was necessary with the deeper indentation required to accommodate the slipway, which must not be too steep. The problem was solved without necessitating an unduly expensive reconstruction of the entire stern. It was Christensen, too, who designed the bow slipway on the *C. A. Larsen* in 1926. In doing so he avoided payment of patent dues, but reconstruction in this case proved particularly expensive owing to the large, heavy port which had to be winched up during catching and lowered and closed when the ship was under way.

When the *Lancing*, with the first stern slipway, left Sandefjord on 5 June 1925, both H. G. Melsom and Petter Sørlle were on board. They cannot have been entirely convinced of the success of their invention, as all the necessary equipment for flensing alongside was included. In order to train the hands in the new form of catching, before it was actually tried out in the Antarctic, whaling was carried out that summer off the Congo, and the occasion when the first humpback was hauled on to the deck on 14 July 1925 marked a milestone in the history of whaling. Everything proceeded smoothly, except for one thing: fastening the cable round the whale's tail in a choppy sea. From 14 July to 1 September 294 humpbacks were caught, nearly all of them flensed on deck. Catching commenced off South Orkney on 11 December. A blue whale weighed twice as much as a humpback, and only with the greatest difficulty was it hauled on deck. The friction of its carcass against the slipway was so great that it stuck, a problem that was solved by fixing semi-circular wales at half-inch intervals (an invention patented by Sørlle) and sprinkling the slipway with water. The other difficulty was failure of the winches. During a transition period after the war, winches were used that had been made for the Royal Navy for launching and recovering torpedo nets, until 1929, when an English firm designed winches specially for whaling and powerful enough to haul up the largest specimens. The third difficulty, attaching the cable to the whale's tail in a rough sea, was solved, as we shall see, by the invention of the whale claw.

The report on the *Lancing*'s first season off South Orkney includes expressions such as "when the expedition entered the ice", "caught in the ice", "calmer sea in the ice", and, in the ensuing season, the new term "ice-whaling". By combining non-licensed whaling with ice-whaling and the stern slipway, the *Lancing*'s operations in 1925-6 were to prove

74. The *Lancing*, the first floating factory with a stern slip, 1925.

of decisive importance in the transition to the new epoch of whaling. The expedition is also remarkable because in the course of one year operations took place in three different areas — off the Congo, in the Antarctic, and on the voyage home off Patagonia. The total result was 26,500 barrels, far less than expected. The board of directors, however, had such faith in the new technique that it had no difficulty in establishing another company in 1925, and in a few years both proved a success.

Non-licensed catching can hardly have come as a complete surprise to the Colonial Office. As far back as 1914 it must have been aware of this possibility. When a company was granted a concession at South Georgia it proffered the information that it had operated successfully for seven years without a concession in the vicinity of the South Shetlands. The Colonial Office's reaction is interesting in this connection: "We fear they may have found out a vulnerable point in our whaling policy. We have been aware of the danger, but we can't condict [*sic*] whaling on the high seas and we have not heard of any poaching in the territorial waters." The Colonial Office can hardly have forgotten this incident, as the department dealing with whaling had the same head, C. R. DARNLEY, right from the start of Antarctic catching and for practically thirty years beyond. He had been a member of the Interdepartmental Committee of 1917, and was chairman of the Discovery Committee. In the view of the Norwegian Minister in London, Darnley was "so to speak the British Government in whaling matters, the only person who knows these matters. If we agree with Mr Darnley, we shall certainly get as far as we possibly can in these questions." For a solution of the many disputes between Britain and Norway it was

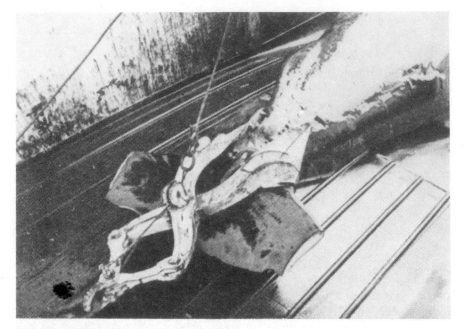

75.   The whale claw.

of great importance that he was a very firm friend of Norway's greatest whaling expert, Professor Johan Hjort.

(c) *Licensed and non-licensed ice-catching.* If old whaling people are asked when ice-whaling started, and who was the pioneer, the answer generally received is that it was in 1925-6, and that the pioneer was LARS ANDERSEN, possibly the most skilled and the best known of Norwegian gunners and whaling managers. He was at that time in charge of Lever Brothers' floating factory, the *Southern Queen.* As usual, operations started from a harbour in the South Shetlands, but as he was dissatisfied with the result, he proceeded east with one of the whale catchers, and gave the floating factory and the other whale catchers orders to follow. Off the Weddell Sea, between South Orkney and South Sandwich, a great many whales were shot over a period of fourteen days inside the ice. When supplies of fresh water ran out, the floating factory was forced to return to her base and refill her tanks. This was repeated on several occasions.

With few exceptions, all Antarctic whaling, apart from off South Georgia, had up till then taken place round South Shetland, where the most important bases for floating factories were Deception and Admiralty Bay. Here, year after year, they had their permanent base, the "Old People's Home", as the whalers called it. A certain amount of extension, however, had taken place, both in a southwesterly direction along Graham Land and northeast towards South Orkney. Here the Tønsberg Hvalfangeri had been granted a concession for 500 acres in 1920, for the purpose of setting up a shore station on Signy Island. But as climatic conditions made it impossible to maintain this station, permission was given for the use of a floating factory.

Gradually, the floating factories moved further and further southwest, right down to Adelaide Island, where a great many useful harbours were discovered between Palmer Archipelago, Biscoe Island, and Graham Land. This was about as far as whale stocks appeared to extend. A whale catcher which made a voyage across the Bellingshausen Sea to Peter I Island found absolutely no trace of ice, plankton, or whales. The whalers gave all these harbours and islands their own particular names, and some of them are still to be found on maps, recalling this period of whaling, although a great many have been replaced by other names applied to them by explorers and scientists ignorant of the fact that they had already been named.

The 1926-7 season at South Shetland was of decisive importance to the transfer to ice-catching. All gunners and expedition managers agreed that they had never experienced such exceptional conditions. There were continuous and violent changes of weather, with periods of protracted fog, the whalers' worst enemy. The whale migrations, which always proceeded southwest on either side of the islands, now moved mainly east, while the blue whale migration, which with great regularity usually passed this way on about 1 December, was entirely missing. As time passed, practically without any whales being caught, the hands grew increasingly nervous, as the situation threatened to develop into a catastrophe. The expedition was continually on the move, while whale catchers were sent in every direction in search of whales, burning coal needlessly. When whales were finally caught, many of them were lost during the long tow in stormy weather. The tempers of the expedition managers were hardly improved by the fact that the *Discovery* expedition was in the area exerting an unwelcome control over the operations. Most floating factories made their way east, some as far as the ice fringing the Weddell Sea.

In March, the floating factories foregathered again in the harbours of South Shetland, and though the season ended on a more promising note, the overall catch was poor. For the companies operating from South Georgia, on the other hand, this proved an outstanding season, with a record of 417,300 barrels. The period 1924-7 was the best in the history of the island, the only three seasons when over 400,000 barrels were registered. Licensed companies saw in this a weighty argument to the effect that shore stations were not finished after all. To this the pelagics retorted that their poor results were not due to a shortage of whales but defects in their equipment, which was not designed for the great strains imposed by ice-catching. What was needed was increased capacity in every respect : larger and sturdier floating factories with slipways, more abundant supplies of fresh water and coal, a larger number of boilers, more steam for boiling and at the same time propelling the floating factory at speed inside the ice. Their views, moreover, were borne out by the 1927-8 season, the most sensational in the history of Antarctic whaling.

Already by the end of September the first floating factories had arrived. They split up into two main groups, one working southwest in the Bransfield Strait towards the old anchorages, and one operating in the ice further and further east past South Sandwich to about 26° W. The main blue whale migration passed this way, but previously no one had been able — or dared — to pursue it at the start of the season further than to the edge of the ice, whereas the whales would continue as far as the large open spaces, between the ice floes, where they would gorge themselves on krill. On this occasion two floating factories ventured to follow the blue whale, the *Lancing* and the *Anglo-Norse,* and both made sensational catches. The *Lancing* entered the ice on 4 October, and on 4 January, after precisely three months, was forced to abandon operations, with a full load of 45,800 barrels. On 8 March, two months earlier than on previous occasions, it was back in Larvik, after discharging its cargo in Rotterdam. The *Anglo-Norse,* catching one week longer, also recorded a full cargo of 44,000 barrels. This result had never been surpassed before : the figures for catcher's day work being respectively 124.5 and 148 barrels, whereas the average for the entire pelagic catching was 83 barrels.

Ice-catching claimed its victims. The *Sevilla* (Salvesen), after a record catch, was forced to break off with serious damage, caused by the ice, to its rudder and propeller. At the beginning of the season a Norwegian floating factory was so badly damaged that she had to lie at anchor in the South Shetlands. The *Southern Queen* (Lever Bros.), which appeared to have the best prospects of all, was so badly holed by an ice floe that she went to the bottom on 24 February 1928, with 22,700 barrels of oil (22,000 barrels had been transferred to a tanker). The *Professor Gruvel,* a one-time floating factory now used as a transport ship, collided with the ice on 10 October 1927, and went down with a cargo of coal which was earmarked for two floating factories which as a result lost a whole month's catching. One of the most tragic accidents — followed by several similar ones — occurred when the whale catcher *Scapa* (Salvesen) capsized in 1928 when making an excessively sharp turn as she pursued a whale. Thirteen hands were lost and four saved in desperate straits after spending five days on an ice floe. When the whale catcher *Southern Sky* foundered in the following year, thirteen hands were lost. On the whole, the marked increase in the number of fatal accidents, sinkings, and wrecks in the period 1926-31 showed that a very high price had to be paid if ice-catching were to be mastered. In 1931 Salvesen was compelled to warn its gunners not to drive their catchers too hard. The repair bill had grown by leaps and bounds since the start of ice-catching. If this kind of operation were to be extended in time, space, and technique, the most stringent demands would have to be made on the boats and their equipment, and not least on the human factor.

We have already seen that the time for ice-catching could be extended. We shall deal with the technique in a separate chapter. Extending operations from the immediate vicinity of the islands had started in 1927-8. Further development and the discovery of new whaling grounds were to a large extent Lars Christensen's achievement. Starting in 1926, for a period of ten years he despatched a number of expeditions at his own expense, with two objects in view: to discover new land or re-discover old land, and occupy it for Norway; and secondly, to search for whales. These voyages of discovery proceeded southwest through the Amundsen Sea as far as the ice barrier outside the Ross Sea, but no whales were to be found. For these expeditions Christensen made use of a former sealing vessel, the *Norvegia*.

The report from the *Norvegia* gave rise to the belief that in the area of Bouvet Island (which it had occupied on Norway's behalf on 1 December 1927) the richest whaling grounds in the Antarctic had been discovered. For this reason Christensen moved his entire whaling fleet, three floating factories and ten catchers, to this area, where an excellent start was made. In a violent storm, however, the ice and the whales disappeared. The largest floating factory continued east in search of fresh ice and fresh whales. Thirty large blue whales lying alongside had to be cast adrift as the ship had no slipway, and it proved impossible to flense alongside in the rough sea. The manager of the expedition was advised to make his way into the ice off Enderby Land at 60-70°E, but at approximately 15°E-68°S, off the part of the continent named Princess Ragnhild Land, such abundant whale stocks were discovered that he had a full cargo, 70,600 barrels, in the course of seven weeks. By then the season was so far advanced (4 April) that the hands were concerned that they might be frozen in. This fear was not unfounded, as on 31 March 1931, a whale catcher was stuck fast in the ice and screwed down. In 1939 three Japanese whale catchers had to be abandoned in the ice, one of them being found and rescued the following year.

The voyage of the floating factory in 1929 broke new ground, not so much by confirming what had been suspected — that whales were to be found in the waters round most of the continent — but by showing that whaling could be extended both in time and space far beyond what had previously been considered possible. In the next season, 1929-30, floating factories operated as far east as 45°E (Prince Harald Land and Queen Maud Land), and in 1930-1 they worked so far east that off the Balleny Islands, at about 155°E, they encountered floating factories from the Ross Sea. Only the stretch between 70 and 60°W, from South Shetland to the Ross Sea (King Edward VII Land) has remained comparatively untouched till its discontinuation in 1954, being a protected area under the name of The Sanctuary. In 1926 Lars Christensen had maintained that everything must be done to ensure that the concessions were renewed, but after seeing the potential for ice-catching he declared: "Experience shows that the floating factories that have entered the ice and carried out pelagic catching have made very good catches, whereas those that have operated off South Shetland made poor catches. Today I should not acquire a new floating factory without equipping it for pelagic catching." After the successful seasons off South Georgia in 1924-7, not everyone was as convinced as Christensen, but when catching here, using the same equipment, slumped from 417,300 barrels in 1926-7 to 303,500 barrels in 1927-8, more and more people lost faith in the future of licensed shore-based whaling.

Britain's original standpoint was to make a renewal of concessions conditional on cessation of pelagic whaling. This view had been supported by Norwegian and British licensees, by the Discovery Committee, and by whale biologists. The great preparations that were made for pelagic catching in 1928-9, however, showed that no threat could stop them, but as long as Britain and Norway were the only pelagic whaling nations, there was a chance of regulating it by means of a bilateral agreement. This could be circumvented by transferring companies to a third country's flag, a possibility that loomed large in the discussions on this subject.

(d) *"Licensees" and "pelagics"; the Norwegian Whaling Act of 1929.* When the Colonial Office expressed its great concern for the consequences of pelagic whaling, the Norwegian licensed companies turned to their Government for help in rescuing their licences: this could best be done by making *all* Norwegian whaling, not only from the Norwegian coast but also in the open sea, conditional on a licence. This would strengthen Norway's position in negotiations with Britain for renewal of *British* licences, as well as the country's position in the international efforts to preserve whale stocks. C. R. Darnley made it quite clear to Johan Hjort that Britain would have to consider seriously not renewing licences, unless pelagic whaling were stopped, because this had completely upset the balance established between whale stocks and catching. What provoked misgivings in Norwegian quarters was that interference in whaling in the international sphere was a violation of the principle of freedom of the seas, and this might have serious consequences for Norway's far-ranging economic interests in shipping, fishing, and catching in the open sea. In the second place, abortive negotiations had just been carried on between Norway and Britain on trawling off the coast of Norway, and as Britain had shown so little willingness to accept an arrangement which would preserve fish stocks of Norway, why should Norway help to save whale stocks for Britain? In the third place, it was better to wait and see what would emerge from the League of Nations' deliberations on the question of an international whaling agreement.

While no official negotiations were initiated, discussions of a more private nature took place between Darnley and Hjort. The latter submitted a lengthy dissertation in which he put the case for the licensees: it was of very great economic importance to Norway to salvage the large capital sums invested in her shore stations, and there were prospects for a renewal of licences if the pelagic expeditions stayed away from the sea areas where the shore-based expeditions caught. For this reason, with the support of the Norwegian Whaling Association, he proposed that non-licensed whaling should be banned in an area between 70°W and 25°E south of 50°S, i.e. within the entire Bouvet area, not only within the Falklands Sector, which extended no further east than 20°W. This suggestion was vigorously attacked by representatives of the "pelagics": the proposed ban would, in fact, mean a ban on pelagic whaling, and this might result in Norwegian companies being transferred to foreign flags. Norwegian whaling was not dependent on retaining its licences: on the contrary, once it was rid of dependence on licences, it would come to full fruition. The transfer of Norwegian companies to foreign flags was no empty threat: several companies were investigating in London the possibility of raising capital for a transfer, and, as we shall see, a few of the oldest and most prosperous companies were taken over by British interests.

Of the four Norwegian concessions, two lapsed on 1 January 1929, the others on 16 September 1929 and 1 October 1930, and in the spring of 1928 the companies were uncertain whether they would be renewed. The situation was now precarious, and as the Norwegian Government appeared unwilling to take any action, the concessionaires took this into their own hands and initiated direct negotiations with the Colonial Office, but the new terms, on which agreement was reached after negotiating for almost a year, were hardly on any point such as the Association had hoped for. Without official support from their Government, with the Norwegian companies split into two groups, and under tremendous pressure from Unilever and Salvesen, and public opinion on the British Government to take over the Norwegian concessions, the Colonial Office had things more or less its own way. Darnley subsequently declared that during the negotiations he was aware of the great risk Britain was running in that Norway might easily counter with a law forbidding Norwegian whalers to serve in foreign expeditions. This would completely paralyse all non-Norwegian whaling. But in view of the split between the Norwegian companies and the Government's reserved attitude, no law of this kind could be expected at that time. It was to be adopted some years later, when Norway employed it in an unsuccessful attempt to exert pressure on Britain and the new whaling nations.

The main points of the new agreement were as follows : (1) All leases and licences were renewed for five years as from 1 October 1928. (2) The export duty was to be 2s per barrel from 1928-9 and during the five-year period never in excess of 2s 6d. (3) Companies holding a licence for one whaling ground were not permitted to operate within one hundred miles of South Georgia and fifty miles of the other archipelagos. (4) At regular intervals the floating factories were to be inspected by a medical officer. (5) Combining the functions of gunner and manager was not allowed. (6) The gunner's bonus was to be gradated in accordance with the size of the whale. (7) Catching in the open sea was in other respects to adhere to the provisions valid for the Dependencies; these terms were also to apply to British companies.

Both the British and the Norwegian companies raised very definite objections to several of the items in the agreement. Everyone had hoped for a ten-year period, but Darnley declared that the future was so uncertain that Britain was unwilling to bind herself for a longer period. As all concessions were to apply from the same date, this meant that those that terminated in 1930-1 were only renewed for one to three years. On the other hand, companies were pleased that licences were to run for five years and not for one year at a time. Energetic protests were raised against the zone principle because non-licensed floating factories would then be able to operate right up to the three-mile limit, and could, in addition, employ as many whale catchers as they wanted to, and pay no export duty; the licensed floating factories would thus be severely handicapped. They were prepared to accept a barrier zone around South Georgia, but the Colonial Office was adamant about all the proposed protected zones insisting that this was on the advice of the Discovery Committee and was designed to ensure that not too many floating factories gathered in the same area. The most energetic protest was raised against point 5, which according to the Colonial Office had been included with a view to ensuring the safety of floating factories. If the expedition manager was at the same time a gunner, the floating factory would not always have on board the person exercising supreme authority. The licensed companies maintained that this once again favoured the non-licensed ones. An expedition's greatest asset was a skilled gunner, and the non-licensed companies would attract the services of the most skilled by offering them the combined position which would ensure them a double income.

The expansion after 1923 had led to companies poaching the best gunners from one another, by outbidding competitors in the wages they offered. One company even went so far as to "buy" a gunner by constructing a new whaler according to his wishes. There were rumours of the most fantastic annual earnings: some Kr.60,000-70,000 at the end of the 1920s was not unusual, and a gunner who combined this with expedition manager would have an income for one season amounting to as much as Kr.100,000 (£5,500), an amount which, in view of the purchasing power of money in those days, would have to be multiplied by ten to correspond to current prices. The situation finally became so untenable that after some difficulty companies came to an agreement not to poach one another's gunners, and to maintain a single wage level. Point 6 was linked to the preceding one, proceeding from the contention that a gunner who was paid a bonus merely on the basis of the number of whales, would shoot anything, irrespective of size. The companies and the whalers protested, declaring that once the chase was on and the whale was swimming at full speed, it was impossible to decide how big it was, and it was even impossible to measure it exactly when flensing was carried out alongside.

Even after the leases had been renewed, the concessionaires endeavoured to place obstacles in the way of the pelagics. Attempts were made to persuade gunners to pledge themselves only to work for licensed companies, and to get the patent holders to grant them sole rights to their patents. The Norwegian Whaling Association urged the Colonial Office to forbid non-licensed floating factories to call at harbours in the Falkland Islands Dependencies (for bunkering and watering), and a similar ban was also mooted by Australia and New Zealand. The Colonial Office disapproved very strongly of a company with a concession, such as Salvesen, also indulging in pelagic whaling. However, it was futile trying to stop it. For the 1929-30 season Salvesen invested vast sums in preparations for pelagic whaling, involving two new floating factories, the *Salvestria* of 9,426 gross tons and the *Sourabaya* of 10,110 gross tons, as well as thirteen new whale catchers. The head of the firm maintained that there was now "no equal to our expeditions". These two floating factories were among the last conversions from older vessels. Licences soon lost so much of their value that the licensees did not renew them, adopting the form of whaling they themselves had opposed. The four licensees in South Georgia followed suit, and in the course of fourteen years — 1932-45 — Salvesen and the Compañía de Pesca were left in sole possession.

As mattters now stood, the distinction between the two whaling categories disappeared, and the Whaling Association, which had only represented one party, was unable to continue in its old form. On 11 May 1929, it was dissolved, and the same day a new organisation, the Association of Whaling Companies (Hvalfangerforeningen) was set up. It was intended to be an in international organisation and at its inception it had thirty-two members, twenty-five Norwegian, four British, two Danish, and one Argentinian. The British members included Irvin & Johnson and Unilever's companies, but none of Salvesen's five. Up to the mid-1930s about 80 per cent of the world production of whale oil came from the members of the association, whose offices were in Sandefjord.

The first resolution adopted by the new organisation on the day of its establishment revealed its main purpose: to act as a sellers' pool. Membership of the latter was not compulsory for members of the Association, and the fact that four Norwegian companies remained outside it weakened the pool. The establishment of the pool was particularly important, because in that very year two events of far-reaching significance to whaling occurred. One was the merger on 2 September 1929 (to come into force on 1 January 1930) of the British and Dutch margarine trust in the all-powerful concern of Unilever Ltd. To a far greater extent than before whaling now had to face a single purchaser. The other event was the Wall Street crash of 29 October, which precipitated a world financial crisis and a depression without a parallel in modern times. The four years that followed have been described as years with the lowest prices till then obtaining on the world market, the greatest unemployment, the smallest production, and the largest number of ships laid up. At the height of this crisis Norwegian-British whaling was faced with the problem of having to sell the largest quantity of whale oil ever produced. Several of the leading personalities in Norwegian whaling were now beginning to have doubts about its future.

The Norwegian Act relating to the catching of baleen whales of 21 June 1929, was a concomitant of the renewal of concessions, but it did *not* make Norwegian whaling in the open sea dependent on concessions, as the holders of British concessions had demanded in order to prevent, among other things, mass establishment of companies. This Act was by no means the first law aimed at regulating whaling, but the new and important principle it represented was that it was the first law controlling whaling in the open sea. In this respect it constituted a norm and a precedent for subsequent legislation in all other countries and for international regulations, first and foremost the Geneva Convention of 24 September 1931. The preamble to the Norwegian law mentioned the three factors that had prompted its adoption: the renewal of concessions; regulation by other countries of local whaling, particularly the British of 17 October 1921; and the fact that the problem was being tackled on an international basis, by the League of Nations and the Comité international pour la protection de la baleine.

The main points of the Act were as follows. Any person or persons desirous of undertaking whaling should inform the relevant Ministry thereof. Oil should be extracted at the minimum from all blubber, from the head with the jaws, from the flanks, and from the tongue, and from the tail. The number of whales caught should not exceed what could be reduced shortly after the whale was dead. All details relating to every single whale, to catching and production, were to be entered in a log-book. It was forbidden to catch right whales, females with calves or calves accompanying the mother, blue whales less than 60 ft. long and fin whales less than 50 ft. long. Every floating factory should carry an inspector. A duty of 20 øre per barrel should be paid to cover the expenses connected with the Act. An important provision was that the bonus to be paid to the gunner and the crew of the whale catcher should not be calculated merely on the basis of the number of whales, but also on their size and the number of barrels of oil extracted. Under no circumstances should a bonus be paid for whales below the stipulated size. The last-mentioned clause was hardly calculated to make the inspector's life on board a pleasant one; considerable moral courage was required, in face of the all-powerful gunner, to declare a whale not long enough and to deprive him of his bonus. One expedition manager welcomed an inspector on board with the following words: "You won't have a very pleasant time on board!" In order not to make life too intolerable, the inspector no doubt occasionally closed his eyes to things that were not permitted, and his records did not always tally with actual fact.

The barrel tax covered the expenses of three Norwegian institutions: the State Whaling Board, which was to administer the provisions of the Whaling Act; the State Institute for Whale Research, which has published a whole series of scientific research findings, a parallel to the British Discovery Reports; and, thirdly, the Committee for Whaling Statistics, which has published *International Whaling Statistics* since 1930. Sigurd Risting made this publication an outstanding medium for scientific whaling research and the history of whaling. The very first two numbers, 1930-1, contained complete statistics for modern whaling throughout the entire world from 1868 to 1930.

With her Whaling Act of 1929 Norway had gone further than any other country in controlling whaling in the open sea. This Act had come into existence as the result of pressure from Britain, and there was considerable bitterness in Norway that Britain should have failed to adopt a similar act for control of her own pelagic catching or to have ratified the Geneva Convention. British eagerness to protect the whale stocks was inevitably regarded as hypocrisy, since Britain did not show in practice that she meant what she said. It was particularly aggravating that no pressure was brought to bear on British companies to call off whaling in 1931-2, as Norway had done. Proof was available that no one over-fished that season to the extent that Unilever's expeditions did. The Norwegian Whaling Council expressed the opinion current in Norway with regard to British whaling policy: "Britain's interest in preserving stocks of whale is undoubtedly considerable, but when her own interests are concerned, she withdraws. Britain is not prepared to sacrifice a penny of her own interests."

The primary aim of the Norwegian Whaling Act was to control catching and exploitation of raw materials, not to restrict it. The Act may be said to have contained one weakness: unhampered by its provisions, expansion could continue, until the world crisis called a provisional halt, and Norwegian whaling finally faced the threat of disaster.

21
THE EXPANSION OF 1927-1931

The penultimate and largest expansion in the history of whaling occurs in two separate periods, the Norwegian-British in 1927-31 and the Japanese-German in 1934-9. Between these two comes the world crisis, as well as the collapse of the whale oil market, and parallel with the latter we have the first attempts at an agreement on international control. For this reason any account of this golden age of pelagic whaling, "warts and all", will fall naturally into four sections: the expansion 1927 to 1931, the crisis in 1931-4, the Norwegian-British agreement of 1932-6, and the new pelagic whaling nations and international agreements in 1937-9.

The main reason for the expansion that started in 1927 was the general improvement of world markets starting in 1926 and lasting right up to the autumn of 1929. For the time being, at any rate, it appeared that the world would enjoy an era of political and economic stability: it was generally believed that the League of Nations and the numerous international agreements would ensure world peace and a peaceful development. After years of chaos in international exchange and currency, countries started once again to return to the gold standard and a stable exchange rate. Living standards and purchasing power were on the upgrade, and on world markets there was increased demand for raw materials for the consumer industry, not least an increasing need for fats. In order to cover this, the production of vegetable and animal raw materials was greatly intensified: output of the former rose 50 to 60 per cent in the 1920s, while that of whale oil was trebled between 1926-7 and 1930-1, the great bulk of it being absorbed by the European market. In 1934, when it was calculated that 84 per cent of the whale oil supplied to Europe was earmarked for margarine, the consumption of this commodity was a decisive factor for whale oil in the European fats market. The successful discovery in 1928-9 of a method for hydrogenation of whale oil, to produce an excellent edible fat, with a melting point of about 30°C, as opposed to 38 to 40°C previously, was a fact of the greatest importance in this connection, as it was now technically possible to manufacture margarine with a whale oil content of close to 100 per cent. Whale oil was also the cheapest of all edible fats and oils, and less expensive to hydrogenate than other oils. If, for example, the price of copra, from which oil had to be extracted by pressure, was £23 a ton and that of whale oil £24, after hydrogenation coconut oil for use in margarine came to £36 a ton, whereas whale fat cost only £29. Whale oil had the additional advantage that, when properly purified, it could be stored for longer periods.

World production of edible fats and oils round about 1930 is estimated at approximately 21 million tons. Of this, some 5.2 million tons was traded on the world markets, the rest being consumed by producer countries. Europe had an annual import need of some 4 million tons net (imports minus re-exports). It was estimated that whale oil could cover about 10 per cent of this, i.e. 400,000 tons or 2.4 million barrels, precisely the amount produced under the agreements between Great Britain and Norway of 1932-6.

Europe's ability to absorb this large amount of whale oil was due not only to the increase in the share of whale oil in the production of margarine, but also the marked increase in consumption of margarine. In Britain, among the raw materials required for margarine, the share accounted for by whale oil rose from 16.8 per cent in 1927 to 37.1 per cent in 1933. In compound lard the increase was even more marked, from 5.1 per cent to 13.4 per cent. The consumption of margarine per head of population reached a peak during the years 1929 and 1930. In Germany, the percentage of whale oil in margarine rose from 9.8 per cent in 1924 to 39.1 per cent in 1933 (and 54.4 per cent in 1935). The annual consumption of margarine per head of population was 6.49 kg. in 1925 and 7.93 kg. in 1930. A rise of 1.44 kg. may not seem very considerable, but for a nation of close on 70 million, this meant nearly 100,000 tons. To cover this increase alone, imports of approximately 35,000 tons of whale oil were required, and to cover a consumption of 7.9 kg., with a 39 per cent content of whale oil, Germany required imports in the region of 216,000 tons of whale oil.

In four different ways Germany played a dominant role in the European fat market. In the first place, there was her considerable production of margarine, of which 98 per cent was based on imports of raw materials. In the whole of Europe, this production amounted in about 1930 to some 1.2 million tons annually, of which Germany accounted for just over one-third. In 1928, for example, Germany's production was 496,000 tons, in 1931 450,000 tons. Britain held second place, followed by Holland. Secondly, after the United States, Germany was the world's largest producer of butter, these two countries accounting in 1931 respectively for 420,000 and 976,000 tons. Denmark ranked third, with 195,000 tons. Thirdly, Germany, in spite of her very large production of butter, was not capable of covering her own needs, but had to import considerable quantities, in 1930 131,000 tons (Britain 341,000 tons). Fourthly, Germany imported practically twice as much solid, oleaginous vegetable raw material as any other European country. On the basis of this raw material, the great North German oil-milling industry produced more vegetable oils than the country itself required,

76. Grytviken in the summer, 1925. In the foreground the British administration (to the left), the wireless masts, and (to the right) the Discovery Committee's marine-biology station. In the background, the whaling station.

considerable quantities being exported. In a way this "superfluous" oil was a by-product, because at the same time large quantities of feed were produced which were of decisive importance to ensure that German agriculture could maintain its tremendous production of butter. If we are to understand Germany's fat problem and currency policy in the 1930s, it is imperative to remember that 98 per cent of the margarine production and 48 per cent of butter production was based on imports of raw materials, and that any change in this relationship would directly or indirectly have a bearing on Germany's imports of whale oil and on its whaling policy.

Right up to 1934 German imports of fats are in reality identical with what Unilever supplied to its German fat industry. Because Unilever bought up practically the entire Norwegian production of whale oil, the impression appears to have gained ground that Britain was the major purchaser, whereas in actual fact the bulk went to Unilever's German factories, and it was the fat situation in Germany which was of the greatest importance to Norwegian whaling. Prior to 1934 Britain, Holland, and Germany accounted for three-quarters of Europe's production of margarine, but whichever of these countries might be the importer, the purchaser was always the same one : Unilever (formally its affiliate, Unilever Raw Materials Ltd.).

In 1929-30, when the big trust was established, the Unilever Group had record sales and profits from margarine. It needed all the whale oil it could lay its hands on, and was anxious to buy up in advance, at a

relatively good price, the whole 1929-30 and 1930-1 production. A few
figures will illustrate the dominant position of the German (and Central
European) market to this concern. In 1929 it sold some 900,000 tons of
edible fats in Europe, an amount three and a half times larger than the
entire Antarctic whale oil production of 1928-9. In addition, it sold
450,000 tons of soap. The German market absorbed approximately 43
per cent, the British 31, and the Dutch 10 per cent. Of German imports
of whale oil, amounting to 234,000 tons in 1932, 169,000 tons went to
Unilever's German factories and only 42,000 tons to independent
factories. In Holland, very nearly 100 per cent of margarine sales were
in the hands of Unilever, in Great Britain about 70 per cent, and in
Germany about 65 per cent. In addition, in 1929 the trust controlled
71 per cent of the German oil-milling industry's imports and sales of
vegetable oils and cattle feed, through which a certain measure of
control with German butter production could be maintained. The
experience of the First World War had shown that in a situation of
crisis, supplies of fats were the German domestic economy's Achilles heel.
After their assumption of power in January 1933, one of the first blows
struck by the Nazis was directed at Unilever, to ensure that German
supplies of fats would be independent of a foreign power and that the
German fats market would sever its links with the world market. We
shall see later what fatal consequences this was to have for whaling,
particularly Norwegian.

Strangely enough, the question why practically all whale oil has been
absorbed by the Germanic peoples of Europe has never been raised in
the relevant literature. Undoubtedly this is due to climate, tradition, and
taste. For natural reasons, life in the Nordic countries has perforce been
based on animal sources of food : fish, meat, bacon, milk, and butter,
and — in more recent times — its substitute, margarine. In the more
southerly countries it has to a larger extent been based on vegetable foods
— fruit, vegetables, and olive oil. In 1931 France, Spain, and Italy
jointly produced as much olive oil as the quantities of whale oil produced
in the Antarctic during the record 1930-1 season.

With whale oil assured of advance sales at prices which in 1924-9
averaged £32 a ton, and production costs varying from £15 to £18 a
ton, whaling was inevitably an attractive investment. In this respect whale
oil during the latter half of the 1920s had a parallel in another oil,
mineral oil. This was the great period of expansion for tanker tonnage.
In the summer and autumn of 1929 it was fashionable to subscribe to
shares in tanker companies, and it was just as easy to obtain capital
for the establishment of tanker companies as it was to set up whaling
companies.

The expansion in whaling took place with explosive effect during the
three years 1928-30, to be followed by a complete standstill, and an

almost equally violent expansion in 1936-8. In 1928-30 110 new whale catchers were built, twenty-four floating factories became operative, and twenty-three new whaling companies started. In 1933-4 only one whale catcher was launched, and no new floating factories, while five companies were started. In 1936-8 134 whale catchers were built and ten new floating factories. During the first period of expansion all twenty-three companies, with the exception of two, were British or Norwegian, but during the last period of expansion only one, whereas ten were German or Japanese. The expansion comes to an end in 1938, and in 1939 the only fresh additions comprised seven whale catchers.

A salient feature of the first phase of this expansion was not only the setting up of new companies, but also a considerable enlargement of old ones, while at the same time the first purpose-built floating factories made their appearance. The scope of this expansion was greater in Britain than in Norway, partly as a result of the transfer of Norwegian firms to British ownership and by Norwegian participation in the establishment of British companies. Norwegians also assisted Denmark and the U.S.A. to launch their first pelagic ventures. In South Africa, Australia, and New Zealand ambitious schemes were being devised, while in Germany in 1929 a move was on foot for the revival of whaling. This time it was not Norway alone but half the world that was in the grip of the whaling fever. Most of the plans were laid in 1927-8, during a boom period, but when the time came to put them into practice, the bottom had dropped out of the market.

The expansion took place entirely within the sphere of pelagic whaling, side by side with a marked decline in shore whaling, particularly in the Antarctic, where three stations in South Georgia and the one on Deception were closed down in 1931. It was the same story at several stations in South Africa, as well as on the west coast of North America, in the Shetlands, the Hebrides, in Spain, Australia, and West Africa. Only along the coast of Japan did shore whaling continue as before, declining somewhat during the early 1930s but rallying sharply towards the end of that decade.

The spate of new companies in the spring and summer was set off by the successful results of the 1927-8 season, which surpassed every expectation. And when the rich whaling grounds around Bouvet Island were discovered, at the very time that operations from South Georgia were on the decline, all the sceptics must have been convinced that the future lay in unlicensed pelagic catching. Facts spoke for themselves: more than two-thirds of all Antarctic whaling was pelagic. A comparison of net earnings per barrel (in kroner) for the two South Georgia companies, five licensed companies in the South Shetlands, and three pelagics in 1926-7 and 1927-8 was little less than sensational (see Table 26).

Admittedly, the figures in Table 26 reflect the poor season in the

Table 26. NET PROFIT FOR SOME COMPANIES PER BARREL OF OIL,
1926-7 and 1927-8

Companies	Net profit per barrel	
	1926-7	1927-8
5 South Shetland	1.97	31.55
3 pelagic	8.10	37.22
2 South Georgia	28.25	27.55

South Shetlands 1926-7, but it was remarkable that while the two companies in South Georgia showed a slight decline, the others recorded a tremendous increase in their surplus. One important factor was that successful ice-catching had been achieved with equipment not specifically designed for this type of whaling. Inevitably, the idea arose of constructing a ship which could be designed on the lines of a floating factory and not a floating factory that had to be designed on the lines of a ship.

Of the world's thirty-two floating factories in 1929, the smallest group, 4,000 to 6,000 gross tons, comprised nine; there were twelve of 6,000 to 8,000 gross tons, and two of about 9,500 gross tons, and from these in turn it was a considerable jump to the nine largest, of 12,000 to 13,000 gross tons, which was the extreme limit for converted floating factories. Seven of the nine were operational in the 1928-9 season, one was completed in the following year, and subsequently twelve older ships were converted; all other subsequent floating factories were specially designed and built for the purpose. All conversions after 1929 were undertaken for non-Norwegian companies.

Before 1929 not a single new floating factory was built with a slipway; between 1929 and 1938 fifteen were built. During the few years prior to 1929 when shipping had enjoyed relatively good times it had been difficult to purchase secondhand ships suitable for reconversion of the desired size of 12,000 to 13,000 gross tons. Owing to the specially good tanker freight rates it was particularly difficult to buy tankers, and these were the vessels most easily adapted to floating factories. The only vessels available in the 14,000 to 16,000 gross ton categories were older passenger ships or liners; eight of the nine largest converted floating factories in 1931 belonged to this category, or were sister ships belonging to the White Star Line, built around the turn of the century and now ready for replacement. They were sold for from £33,000 to £40,000, about twice as much as they would have commanded as scrap. Converting ships of this kind was a very expensive business. One of these converted liners of 12,279 gross tons with a load capacity of 80,000 barrels cost Kr.4.1 million, whereas the first new specially built floating factory, the *Kosmos,* of 17,801 gross tons and with tanks for 120,000 barrels, came to Kr.6 million in 1929.

It seemed, in fact, to be beyond doubt that it was worth investing in large, newly constructed floating factories. While the Norwegians were pioneers in this field, it was one they soon abandoned. All six floating factories contracted for at Norwegian expense were built between 1929 and 1931, but of these, three were transferred to British ownership, leaving only three in Norwegian hands. Of the fifteen floating factories built in 1929-38, two were the property of German companies, three Norwegian, five British, and five Japanese. Neither Salvesen nor Unilever commissioned the building of any new floating factory prior to the Second World War. It was both for technical and financial reasons that all the new Norwegian floating factories were contracted in Britain: the British shipbuilding yards were in a position to offer fairly favourable credit terms, while British banks did not entertain the same misgivings as their Norwegian counterparts for the expansion of whaling. The Oslo Exchange, in fact, was not particularly keen to quote the shares of the new companies, a difficulty not encountered on the London Stock Exchange.

When the Norwegian occupation of Bouvet and the discovery of the rich whaling grounds there were known in England, the event aroused considerable interest in the City for investment in Norwegian pelagic whaling, an interest stimulated by the success of ice-catching, the rise in the price of whale oil in the spring of 1928, and the security represented by advance sales. The Norwegian company A/S Pelagos was established on 30 June 1928, but already a month previously, when the building of the floating factory had only just started, and invitations to subscribe had not yet been issued, the expected production had already been sold at £31 a ton. Considerable profits could safely be predicted, and this proved to be the case: the results of the first season enabled a dividend of 30 per cent to be declared, after considerable sums had been written off and placed in the reserve fund. After three seasons the company had cleared its debts and presented shareholders with a handsome return of 115 per cent. "The whaling world is in the grip of senseless optimism," a Norwegian newspaper wrote in autumn of 1928, "and this will undoubtedly result in other, skilled nations intervening, and if they cannot buy our matériel, they will set off on pelagic whaling with their own." A typical feature of Norwegian-British co-operation was the creation of British holding companies, who, by holding a majority of the shares, could control the company but had no influence on actual whaling operations, which continued unchanged as a wholly Norwegian enterprise.

The complex financial transactions that attended the establishment of holding companies and their registration in other countries for fiscal reasons cannot be dealt with here in detail. This was a procedure which was not peculiar to whaling, and was a quite common occurrence in international finance. The transfer from Norway to Britain started

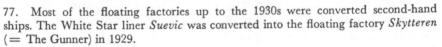

77. Most of the floating factories up to the 1930s were converted second-hand ships. The White Star liner *Suevic* was converted into the floating factory *Skytteren* (= The Gunner) in 1929.

in March 1929 with the principal Norwegian shareholder in Tønsbergs Hvalfangeri selling his shares (1,500 out of a total of 3,840) to a new company, the Anglo-Norwegian Holding Co., at a rate of 300 per cent, although the Stock Exchange quotation was only 252.5 per cent. When the holding company had secured a number of shares by means of other purchases, it controlled this old, well-established company, which had now passed out of Norwegian hands. For tax reasons the new company was registered in Montreal, where a local paper welcomed the event in the following words: "British interests have obtained virtual control of Toensberg Hvalfangers Company, Norway's biggest whaling firm in Antarctica." The periodical *Fishing News* in England insinuated that the reason Norwegians were now so keen to attract British capital was because whale stocks would be exterminated within ten to fifteen years. "Therefore, the managers are looking for foreign capital in order that their own countrymen shall not suffer the consequences, a lot of old iron laid up in a number of ports, but no buyers." About 70 per cent of the shares of yet another of the older and well-established Norwegian companies, A/S Hektor, were sold to a holding company in England, Hector Whaling Ltd. The Board's reason for selling was fear that concessions would not be renewed, but an international agreement restricting catches would bear particularly hard on Norway, and the Norwegian Whaling Act would place Norwegian companies in an unfavourable position in their competition with foreign ones. The new company issued shares for the tremendous sum of £600,000, as well as borrowing £300,000 to finance large-scale expansion for the 1929-30 season.

There was considerable regret in Norway that these two companies in particular should come under foreign control: they had been involved in the Antarctic practically from the very start, they were the source of considerable national pride, and during the period 1922-9 shareholders had received some 300 per cent in dividends. What was now happening was that Norway's national pride, an industry at one time dominated by Norwegians, was slipping out of their hands. Ironically, it was observed that by purchasing Norwegian companies Britain was achieving precisely the same as she would have done by depriving them of their licences and granting them to British companies. It was some consolation and an advantage to Norway that daily practical management of whaling remained within the company : crews were Norwegian, and a great deal of the equipment was bought in Norway, where the floating factories, too, lay at anchor between seasons. It was said that in actual fact the real purchaser of the Norwegian companies was Unilever, acting through intermediaries. To what extent this was true is not known, but there is no doubt that in one company it had a holding of £30,000. The date for this sale, favourable as it was to the Norwegian owners, was equally disadvantageous to the purchasers. The crisis in 1931-2 very nearly toppled both companies, and throughout the 1930s they struggled with great economic difficulties, eventually selling off their equipment and abandoning active whaling.

It has been said that in the winter of 1927-8 Norwegian company directors were queueing up in London to have their projects financed. It was not always as easy as had been supposed. The invitation to take up shares for £350,000 in the British Whaling Co., published in the City on 3 January 1929, was indifferently received and had to be abandoned. The same was the fate of an attempt to obtain £500,000 for the International Whaling Co. for the purchase of two Norwegian companies with shore stations in Spain and Labrador, and the building of two floating factories. Attempts were made to attract shareholders by pointing out that the company in Spain had in 1924-6 declared annual dividends of 57 per cent, and it was estimated that the net annual surplus would continue at £16,000 for the two land-stations and £220,000 for the two floating factories. As we have already seen, the Spanish venture fared quite differently, and luckily for the shareholders, the company never got off the ground.

As attempts to raise capital in the City made little headway, one of the directors suggested that they should return to Norway and start companies there. This person was ANDERS JAHRE, with whose name the

78. Anders Jahre, acting manager
of Kosmos Co.

expansion of whaling and its subsequent development are indissolubly
associated. A lawyer by training, from the early 1920s his interest in
in whaling had been promoted by his work as legal adviser and board
member of a number of companies. With admirable clarity, initiative,
and personal ambition, he realised the opportunities open to the future
of whaling and the furtherance of his own career. These qualities enabled
him to establish Norway's largest concerns in whaling, shipping, and
industry, as well as providing him with the means of becoming Norway's
biggest patron of scientific, humanitarian, and cultural undertakings.

In the spring of 1928 he was one of the promoters of two companies,
Antarctic A/S and Pelagos A/S, for which the capital was immediately
over-subscribed. One of the reasons for this was that production had
been sold in advance at a good price, and shareholders were consequently
guaranteed a dividend. In fact, as things turned out, for the first three
seasons, 1928-31, dividends of 110 and 115 per cent respectively were
declared.

Even before these companies had been established Anders Jahre had
conceived an idea which took shape in 'Kosmos', the name of a company
and of its floating factory. Christen F. Christensen had the surprise
of his life when, in a cable from Jahre consisting of a few lines, he was
asked to acquire as soon as possible a combined tanker and floating
factory of some 22,000 tons dead-weight, with a capacity of 2,500 barrels
a day, and — almost as an afterthought — seven to eight whale catchers

with engines developing 800 to 900 h.p. The problem of finding a yard capable of constructing so unusual a ship, as well as granting the necessary credit, found its solution in Workman Clark (1928) Ltd. in Belfast. One-third of the purchase sum was to be paid on delivery, the remainder over six years. The contract for seven whale catchers was placed with Smith's Dock Co. When complete, the expedition came to Kr.8.96 million, of which each whale catcher accounted for £20,000, a very reasonable sum. Hvalfangerselskapet Kosmos A/S (The Kosmos Whaling Co. Ltd.) was established on 9 November 1928, with a capital of Kr.6 million (£330,000). It proved impossible to raise the entire capital sum in Norway, for which reason one-third was subscribed abroad, mainly in England, and a certain amount in Denmark and Sweden. In the summer of 1929 attempts were made to form a holding company in London, the Antarctic Whaling Investments Co., with a capital of £500,000, in order to take over control of Jahre's three companies. This move proved unsuccessful; instead, in the course of the succeeding years, practically all the foreign shares were repurchased by Norwegian interests.

The floating factory was delivered from the yard on 31 July 1929. Getting this unusual and complicated construction ready in time for the season was in itself a notable feat. The ship was of 17,801 gross tons, 22,500 dead-weight, with tanks for 120,000 barrels. She was not diesel driven but had an oil-fired steam engine of 5,000 h.p. For her first season 21,200 tons of fuel-oil were taken on board, sufficient for five months' catching, and for the outward and homeward voyages. The ship's hull was similar to that of an ordinary tanker, and in this respect the largest in the world. On top of the tanks a deck had been laid for the boilers — twenty-four pressure cookers, twelve rotary cookers, and twelve separators — and above this was the deck with the blubber and meat platform. Between seasons the boat could, if necessary, be used as an ordinary tanker, carrying mineral oil. It goes without saying that the expedition carried the most up-to-date equipment: among other things, it was the first to include an aircraft. The *Kosmos* was not the only innovation in the whaling grounds in 1929-30: she was accompanied by the *Vikingen,* of 12,639 gross tons, to which we shall presently return. Neither of them could be said to be epoch-making; that, however, would be true of the *Lancing,* without which neither the *Kosmos* nor the *Vikingen* would ever have been constructed. In one respect, however, the *Kosmos* does mark the start of a new epoch: its size, 5,000 gross tons larger than the next largest, with extra capacity for 26,500 barrels. The sister ship, *Kosmos II,* was a little smaller, and the other five floating factories built in England were 3,000 to 5,000 tons smaller. The belief appears to have been held that with the *Kosmos* a rational order of magnitude had been exceeded, and eight years were to elapse before floating factories

79.   The *Kosmos*, the first new (not converted) floating factory, built in 1928 by Workman Clark of Belfast for Kosmos Co., Sandefjord, Norway.

of a similar size were built, and then in Germany and Japan. Those who had prophesied that the floating factory would prove *too* large to achieve a full load in the short Antarctic season were proved wrong. In the second season, 1930-1, the floating factory was actually too small. A new design of this kind naturally permitted far more rational installation and fitting out, without the disadvantages of a conversion. Even so, highly profitable catching did not necessarily require a new and specially built floating factory: neither Unilever's nor Salvesen's floating factories prior to the Second World War were constructed as such. If we include the operations from Leith Harbour, Salvesen's whaling company, the South Georgia Co., recorded in every season from 1928-9 to 1936-7 (with the exception of 1931-2) large surpluses — some of them very large — and declared an annual average dividend from 1928 to 1940 of 56.25 per cent, as well as writing off large sums.

The results of the *Kosmos'* first season were awaited with the greatest eagerness by the whaling world. Practically the entire catch was made in the new grounds to the northeast of the Balleny Islands, and with 120 effective catching days 1,822 whales were caught, producing 119,400 barrels. These came to Kr.48.82 per barrel, as compared to an average of Kr.69.90 for the Norwegian expeditions in 1928-30. Operations next season, too, started off the Balleny Islands, but as there were fewer whales this time (1930-1), the bulk of the catches was made between 86° and 102°E in the ice off Wilkes Land. The result proved more fantastic than even Anders Jahre had dreamed off: 199,190 barrels from 2,431 whales (1,986 BWU), all the oil of quality No. 0/1. Two-hundred and seventy whales (221 BWU) had been caught per boat, and production costs were a mere Kr.33.53 per barrel, whereas the average for the Antarctic was 173 whales and Kr.60.23. Jahre had every reason to triumph over the pessimists: after two seasons shareholders had received dividends of 40 per cent, shares were being sold at a rate of 150 per cent, the company had cleared its debts, and large reserves had been laid up which tided them over during the crisis of the next few years.

It was not only amazement at these astonishing results that silenced criticism of Anders Jahre, but also the fact that his four companies remained Norwegian. And that the participation of Norwegian financiers in starting British companies should have provoked no major criticism was because in this case new ventures were involved, and not the sale of old and well-founded Norwegian companies. The floating factory *Vikingen* and the Viking Whaling Co. were the first fruits of Norwegian-British co-operation, Norwegian know-how, and British capital. This was initiated by Johan Rasmussen, whose plan was to establish a company for catching near Bouvet. In the belief that the island was British territory, he had applied for an exclusive licence and had provisionally received an affirmative answer from the Colonial Office. At the time he was ignorant of Lars Christensen's plan of occupying the island, and nor was Christensen apprised of Rasmussen's application for a licence. This was a regrettable clash of conflicting Norwegian interests, and Rasmussen was severely criticised for thwarting Norwegian plans. To ensure that his British licence should not prove a bar to Norwegian sovereignty over the island, he renounced the licence and altered the name of the company from the Bouvet Whaling Co. to the Viking Whaling Co.

Although the *Vikingen* was 5,000 gross tons smaller than the *Kosmos*, with her five whale catchers she cost just as much as the latter with seven whale catchers. The group of four companies controlled by Johan Rasmussen & Co. was not only engaged in active whaling, but was also a holding company for shares in other undertakings. This prompted Salvesen to write to the Colonial Office, pointing out that it was now impossible to make any hard and fast distinction between licensed and non-licensed companies. The Rasmussen Group had twenty-one whale catchers with licences, but a large amount of the share capital was owned by the Viking Whaling Co., which carried on pelagic whaling. The *Vikingen*'s first two seasons were favourable, ensuring shareholders 13 and 12 per cent respectively. This whaling company was the first British one to be founded after Salvesen and Unilever; it was established on Norwegian initiative, and was the first to have its shares quoted on the London Stock Exchange.

Each of the other three companies in the Rasmussen group contracted a new floating factory in England with the Furness Shipbuilding Co. These were sister ships of 14,500 gross tons, equipped with tanks for 14,000 barrels. One of them, the *Sir James Clarke Ross II,* was completed in such good time that it was able to catch in the 1930-1 season, which proved the salvation of the company, whereas the other two, the *Svend Foyn* and the *Vestfold,* had to proceed straight from the shipbuilding yard in 1931 to their laying-up buoys in Sandefjord. As this meant that they were unable to make any contribution to repayment of loans and interest, the companies were soon in financial straits. They subsequently established close co-operation with the Viking Whaling Co. Without going into details of these complicated transactions, it might be mentioned in passing that in 1935 the *Vikingen* was registered under the Panamanian flag for tax reasons for the Viking Corporation, and in 1938 sold to Germany. After the war she was made over to the Soviet Union, and operated under the name of the *Slava* right up to 1965 in the Antarctic, and during the succeeding three years in the North Pacific. The *Vestfold,* with seven whale catchers and a shore station in Stromness Harbour, was sold in 1934 for £325,000 to a new company, the Vestfold Whaling Co. of London, of which the Norwegian Vestfold Company owned about one-third of the share capital. In 1936 this floating factory, too, was placed under the Panamanian flag for the Vestfold Corporation. In 1946 Salvesen purchased the South Georgia station from this company for £30,000. A/S Vestfold has continued to operate as a shipping company right down to the present, but the new floating factory and the 1931-2 set-up meant the end of independent whaling for a Norwegian company that had been among the pioneers in the Faroes, Shetland, and South Georgia.

After being laid up, the *Svend Foyn,* too, was sold in 1932 for £240,000 (she had cost £303,000) to the Star Whaling Co., Guernsey. Formally, she was sold to the St. Helier Shipowners Ltd., of Jersey, a company which was established in order to purchase the floating factory, but all the shares of which, except for six, were owned by the former.

Of a capital of £170,000 in the Star Whaling Co., Tønsbergs Hvalfangeri owned £80,000, which was taken over by Star Holdings Ltd., Jersey. If we recall that the majority of the shares in Tønsbergs Hvalfangeri were owned by the Anglo-Norwegian Holding Co., London, we might well ask who the actual owner of the floating factory and the company was. Another Norwegian company, Sydhavet, sold all its remaining equipment and was dissolved in 1936. A piece of highly traditional Norwegian whaling was at an end, and was continued under foreign auspices.

The last of the Norwegian companies in this period to end its days in British ownership was the A/S Sevilla, founded in Tønsberg in 1929 when the floating factory *Sevilla* and four whale catchers were purchased from Salvesen. In 1930 the company acquired the large floating factory *New Sevilla*, which, with her 13,801 gross tons, was the largest vessel ever converted for this purpose. After her first season she was laid up and involved in financial difficulties, the net result of which was that Salvesen bought all the shares at a very low price, both in A/S Sevilla and in its two British affiliates, the Sevilla Whaling Co. and the Polar Whaling Co. The *New Sevilla* proved an excellent investment for Salvesen, whose shareholders received a 100 per cent tax-free dividend in 1936-7. A few years later, in September 1940, this floating factory was sunk by enemy action. The *Sevilla*, after doing duty as a transport vessel, was broken up in 1946. Through the Polar Whaling Co. Salvesen operated the Hawke's Harbour station in Labrador in 1938-51, though not during the war years; it was sold in 1956. With the A/S Sevilla yet another large Norwegian-inspired undertaking became 100 per cent British.

It was thanks to Norwegian initiative that the United States and Denmark got their first pelagic whaling companies. In 1930 Lars Christensen had acquired a majority of the shares in A/S Frango (established 1928), which owned a small floating factory (6,331 gross tons) of the same name, with the intention of re-selling her to the American Whaling Co., which he had persuaded two American banks to form in order to ensure that whale oil, as an American product, could be imported free of duty into the United States. The reason this particular floating factory was chosen was that an American law laid down that only ships built in the United States could be registered there, and the *Frango* was the only ship in the entire whaling fleet to satisfy these requirements. With the transfer to the American company, the seller retained 51 per cent of the shares, thus ensuring that control and management remained in Norwegian hands. On 1 September 1930, the first American pelagic expedition left New York for the Antarctic. Though catches were excellent, the economic crisis in the U.S.A. made it impossible to sell the oil there, and consequently the floating factory was laid up, with her cargo of oil on board, and not till 1935 was it eventually sold to European buyers. The company suffered severe losses from 1930 to 1935, and had to be re-established with fresh capital. The commencement of American pelagic whaling was, in other words, not particularly encouraging, but, as we shall see, the situation improved later.

The Danish Fraternitas company was set up by A. P. MØLLER, Denmark's leading shipowner, and Anders Jahre, with the latter as managing director. For their floating factory they purchased the *Sir James Clarke Ross*, from A/S Rosshavet, renaming her the *Fraternitas*. Good catches were recorded in the opening season of 1930-1, but the *Fraternitas* was forced to lay up in 1931-2, and remained in that state till 1936, without ever again catching in the Antarctic. In the following year she was sold to the Union Whaling Co. (Irvin & Johnson) of Cape Town.

With the success of his *Kosmos* Jahre had little difficulty in raising in Norway practically all the capital for A/S Kosmos II, which was to take over his contract for a floating factory of the same name and nine whale catchers, built at the same yard that had built the *Kosmos*. After the unpromising start to American pelagic whaling, in its first season (1932-3) the floating factory clearly demonstrated what a technical marvel it was. In 123 days, from 20 October to 20 February, eight whale catchers accounted for 1,979 whales, and production came to 222,224 barrels, the all-time unbeaten record for a Norwegian expedition throughout the entire history of Antarctic whaling. In view of the low price of whale oil it was of tremendous importance that production costs per barrel should have been reduced to Kr.21.55. This figure reveals not only the technical superiority of the new equipment and the outstanding skill of the expedition manager, but also that the slump in prices had compelled a drastic reduction of working expenses.

One of the new companies is unique in that it was set up by a number of gunners who, in their own words, were unwilling to enrich others but themselves. One of the liners of the White Star Line was converted and named *Skytteren* (The Gunner), and five whale catchers were contracted. Despite the number of boats laid up in 1931-2, the crisis, and the low price of oil, the gunners came out on top. When they decided in 1936 to dissolve the company, they recouped the share capital of Kr.3.6 million, which was precisely the same amount as company profits from 1933 to 1936. The reason why assets were sold off in 1936, just after the company had enjoyed its best season and was in a position to declare a 50 per cent dividend, was closely connected with the Norwegian-German whaling dispute.

The special feature of the third of these floating factories was that it was the only one from Haugesund, and with its 7,562 gross tons it was one of the smallest of the new floating factories. This was a privately owned company, whose owner was not a member of the whalers' organisations, refusing to participate in voluntary quota agreements and in the large-scale joint sales of oil. The floating factory survived the war, and was sold for scrap in 1959. The fourth and last of the floating factories, the *Solglimt,* of 12,279 gross tons, was taken over in 1930 by the Lars Christensen group, which carried out an expansion in matériel on an unprecedented scale. Four old floating factories, totalling 17,621 gross tons, were replaced by four new ships, all converted, totalling 44,852 gross tons, and fourteen new whale catchers were acquired. Christensen was the butt of a great deal of caustic criticism for this large-scale expansion, seeing that at the same time he was always expressing his doubts about the general expansion of whaling. His reply was that his share of it was entirely Norwegian, that he had been offered foreign capital in order to start new companies, but had turned these offers down, which unfortunately not all Norwegians had done. They were the people who should be criticised.

The old British companies, too, were faced with the choice either of selling their obsolete equipment and abandoning pelagic whaling or participating with a completely new whaling fleet. All of them chose the latter, though Salvesen did so with a certain amount of hesitation, as they were not convinced that this kind of whaling would last for long. In an interview with a Norwegian paper in 1930 H. K. Salvesen (the company's chairman) gave his opinion that if one could count on another twenty years of catching, it might be feasible to train their own people, but since intense whaling could hardly be expected to last for more than four or five years, they would, as hitherto, use Norwegians for their expeditions. He can hardly have had much confidence in the advantages of the slipway; his new floating factories were only equipped with them some years later. In 1929 two large converted floating factories were acquired and thirteen new whale catchers. The last of the old floating factories was destroyed by fire in 1932, but at the same time the big *New Sevilla* was taken over. In 1936 yet another floating factory, an older one, was completely re-equipped and provided with a slipway. It should be remembered that Salvesen purchased or leased a few of the abandoned shore stations in South Georgia, but as only matériel from these was used and no active whaling undertaken, the result was a dispute with the Colonial Office, which maintained that according to the licensing terms failure to use the station for active whaling would entail its reversion to the Crown after a certain number of years.

Again and again at Unilever's board meetings the question of whether the concern should actively participate in whaling or merely purchase oil from others was constantly debated. Faced with the start of pelagic whaling, the question came to a head: either a complete break or radical renewal. Lord Leverhulme's successor, FRANCIS D'ARCY COOPER, chose the latter course: "It would be a risky proceeding, owing to our great interest in all that relates to animal oils and fats, if we were not in the whaling industry." He phased out the unprofitable sections of its whaling, the Harris Whaling Co. in the Hebrides, the Premier Whaling Co. with its shore stations near Durban, and Prince Olav Harbour in South Georgia. When operations there came to a close in 1931, over a million pounds were said to have been invested in it, and Salvesens acquired the large and costly plant almost free of charge. Even after the effects had been sold off, Unilever stepped up its interests in whaling in three different ways: by purchasing shares in Norwegian-British companies, by complete renewal of pelagic catching equipment, and by partial financing of the German whaling fleet in the latter half of the 1930s.

The *Southern Queen*, the floating factory which had been lost in 1928, was replaced by the large converted *Southern Empress* (12,028 gross tons), and in the following year by her sister ship, the *Southern Princess*, while practically all the whale catchers were replaced by new ones. Both these two vessels were equipped for catching in the Ross Sea, but never operated there. If we include the loss incurred by the sales mentioned above, Unilever's modernisation and rationalisation programme of its whaling fleet cost the company some £2 million. But it was estimated that, with a production price of £12, there would be a saving of a quarter of a million pounds as compared with the purchase of oil from others at the current price (1929), approximately £30. Profits in 1928-31 were estimated at £848,000, but the loss on oil purchased in advance in 1929-31 was more than twice as much. Unilever's own whaling operations, in fact, had the effect of levelling the price of its raw materials.

The third of the older British companies, Irvin & Johnson of Cape Town, contracted for the building of one of the seven new floating factories in England. She was named the *Tafelberg,* and was of 13,640 gross tons.

Expansion had proceeded far enough : luckily for whalers and share-holders alike, a great many other projects never got off the ground. From all over the world came reports of attempts to start pelagic whaling — from Germany, the United States, Canada, Chile, and Argentina. In 1930 the Russians explored the possibilities of having whale catchers built and floating factories fitted out at Norwegian yards, while the Japanese turned their attention to pelagic catching in the Bering Sea. Most ambitious of all were the plans hatched in Australia and New Zealand for harvesting the riches which others were garnering in their waters. Sir Douglas Mawson made this stirring appeal to Australian patriotism : "Almost at the doors of Australia lie mighty stretches of sea teeming with wealth. It is for Australians to develop this heritage for Australians yet to be. Too long has Australia neglected the wealth that lies in whaling !" The public were invited to subscribe to a large number of companies, with capitals ranging from £300,000 to £750,000. The world crisis and the slump in the price of whale oil, however, proved a rude awakening to this pipe dream.

In considering the main results of this phase of whaling, one inevitably comes to the conclusion that to speak of a huge *Norwegian* expansion is by no means justified. Admittedly, the initiative in most cases was Norwegian, but so much long-established Norwegian whaling had come under foreign control that this was hardly outweighed by the new companies remaining in Norwegian hands. Whaling and whaling shares had become an object of international speculation, and after 1930 it was hard to decide in which country the catch processed by a floating factory was to be registered. If the flag principle was to be followed, the Vestfold and Viking corporations would, for example, have had to register their catching as Panamanian, as was done in the *International Whaling Statistics,* even though hardly a single cent of Panamanian capital was invested in these companies. The subsequent catching carried out by the Norwegian floating factories *C. A. Larsen* and *Skytteren* on behalf of the Germans should not be registered as Norwegian, even though these ships flew the Norwegian flag. They were processing, at the risk and on the account of another government, a product that was entirely German property. Moreover, the German charters owned 40 per cent of the capital. One thing is at any rate certain : Norway had embarked on a course of action which resulted in the loss of her hegemony.

Finally, a few figures will show the scope of the expansion of pelagic whaling between 1927 and 1931 in the Antarctic (see Table 27).

Table 27. THE EXPANSION OF PELAGIC ANTARCTIC OPERATIONS, 1927-1931

Total

Season	Whales	Barrels	Shore stations	Fl. f.	Catchers
1927-8	13,775	1,037,392	6	18	84
1930-1	40,201	3,608,348	6	41	238

Pelagic

Season	Whales	Barrels	Fl. f.	Catchers
1927-8	10,138	733,912	17	61
1930-1	37,438	3,384,048	41	200

The rise in the total gross tonnage of floating factories from 117,178 to 358,168, and of whale catchers from 13,568 to 45,200, and their total number of horsepower from 45,148 to 151,000, provides an equally eloquent expression of the scope of this expansion. We can sum up by saying that pelagic Antarctic whaling was quadrupled in the course of three seasons. But when over-expansion and over-production coincided with the world crisis and the abnormal slump in the price of all raw materials, the result was inevitably the collapse of excessive whaling capacity. (For the expansion of the pelagic whaling fleet in the periods 1928-40 and 1945-63 see Statistical Appendix, Tables 54 and 61.)

22

THE WORLD CRISIS AND THE WHALING INDUSTRY, 1930-1934

The 1931-2 season and the laid-up whaling fleet

The greatest increase in matériel for pelagic whaling in the Antarctic took place from 1928-9 to 1929-30, with fifteen floating factories and seventy-five whale catchers. The build-up continued over the next season, with three large floating factories and thirty-seven whale catchers, while three new floating factories were contracted. The armada that sailed south in the summer of 1930 was not the largest that had ever operated in the Antarctic : in its total gross tonnage, tank capacity, and catching potential it was surpassed by the fleet of 1936-9. The 1930-1 fleet, however, caught the largest number of BWUs and produced the largest number of barrels of whale oil ever chalked up in a single season. A total of 28,325 blue whales were caught, almost 10,000 more than in any other season. Thirty-five years later, the catch amounted to twenty! The total number of baleen whales in 1930-1, 37,438, is the second-highest for any one season, only surpassed by the 1937-8 season, with 43,328, though this included only half as many blue whales as in 1930-1. If we calculate a loss of 10 per cent, it may be estimated that in the whole of the Antarctic approximately 31,500 blue whales were killed in that season.

In 1930-1 the floating factories had a total tank capacity of 2.44 million barrels, but so favourable were catching conditions that a great many floating factories had full tanks before half the season had elapsed. A fleet of transporters ferried coal and fuel oil out to the whaling grounds, returning with whale oil, enabling catching to be continued well beyond load capacity, in some cases almost 100 per cent beyond, the average for all floating factories being 40 per cent. Among many subsequent proposals for restricting catches, one involved breaking off once a full load had been achieved and a ban on transporters. The use of the latter was to some extent abandoned during the period of subsequent quota agreements. While five nations participated in Antarctic whaling, they all had one common feature: with the exception of 142, the 10,691 hands were Norwegian, and of these almost 8,000 were resident in the county of Vestfold. Only seven seasons later, not more than 60 per cent were Norwegians.

The figures in Table 28 relate to the nation under whose flag the floating factory was sailing, but, as already mentioned, the "flag prin-

Table 28. DISTRIBUTION OF MATERIEL AND CATCHES BY NATIONS, 1930-1

	Shore stations	Fl. f.	Catchers	Barrels	% of barrels
Norway	3	27	147	2,291,694	63.5
Great Britain	2	11	68	1,094,145	30.3
Argentina	1	1	9	88,154	2.4
Denmark		1	5	84,995	2.4
U.S.A.		1	3	49,360	1.4
Total	6	41	232	3,608,348	100.0

ciple" will not necessarily present a correct picture of a nation's actual interests in whaling, particularly after 1929.

Would the season of 1931-2 fulfil the great expectations? Would the world market be able to absorb the tremendous production, and what would the price of oil be? Already during advance sales in the autumn of 1929 considerable pressure had been exerted by the Buyers' Pool to reduce prices, and this sale had been the most important reason for the reorganisation of the Norwegian Hvalfangerforening on 11 May 1929, which now assumed the name of the Association of Whaling Companies, thus enabling non-Norwegian companies too to become members. All sales were to be carried out for a joint account by the Sales Pool, and were it to prove impossible to achieve a satisfactory price, two-thirds of the members could decide to store production. But one weak point in the Sales Pool was that it did not include four Norwegian companies or Salvesen. The concluding sales negotiations with the Buyers' Pool (i.e. Margarine Unie, Lever Bros. and De-No-Fa) in London on 29 November 1929 proved an exciting and dramatic showdown. What was involved was the biggest single sale that had till then taken place in the history of Norway, that of some 265,000 tons of whale oil. Every pound sterling per ton would mean Kr.5 million. The average price for the previous season had been £29, and the Sales Pool was under no circumstances prepared to go below £27. Similarly, the buyers had definitely bound their members not to offer more than £25, as well as guaranteeing members oil at that price. Wherever sellers sought to make contact with buyers, they were offered precisely that price. Several circumstances ensured that, as far as the sellers were concerned, the battle was lost before it started. These were as follows:

1. One month before the sale, the financial world was shaken by the Wall Street crash. The prices of all commodities plummeted, and the price of whale oil followed suit.

2. Buyers had reason to believe that they would be able to acquire the oil at £25, because three companies had already sold at that rate.

3. When the whalers insisted that the price gave them no margin of

80.   Grytviken in the 1930s. On the far right the church, on the far left the hydroelectric power station and above it the magazine.

profit, Unilever was in a position to answer that, with a rate of £23, their company had a surplus of £87,000.

4. The margarine and soap trust had consolidated its position so strongly that other buyers were excluded, and in this process of consolidation whale oil had played an important role. This was shown by the integration of the firm Hartog, the only large uncommitted firm in the Netherlands in this business apart from Jurgens and van den Bergh, and their major competitor. On 24 September 1927 these two had joined forces in the Margarine Unie concern, and were now set to crush Hartog, because this firm, apart from its great economic strength, possessed, as one of its formidable armoury of business weapons, special skill in the use of materials; it had brought the use of hardened whale oil in particular to a high state of efficiency and economy. "The implication was clear that in some quarters there was a disposition to squeeze Hartog out of the whale oil market. But such a policy could achieve nothing except an inflation of raw material prices. The only solution was another amalgamation" (*History of Unilever*, Vol. II, p. 285). The merger took place in January 1929, and an extremely high price had to be paid for it. The sale of whale oil in April 1929 to Hartog at £25 was thus in actual fact a sale to the trust. In the course of 1928 the latter had also acquired control over the leading French firm in this field, Calvé, and the two co-operating concerns of Schicht and Centra, which controlled the bulk of the fat industry in southeast Europe. The structuring of Margarine

Unie, in other words, was almost complete, and during the boom years of 1925-9 turnover and profits had soared. When the keystone to this empire was finally fitted into position on 2 September 1929 with a merger between Margarine Unie and Lever Bros. to form Unilever Ltd., practically all other buyers were shut out from the whale oil market with negotiations due to commence two months later. The struggle for whale oil had been an important motive for the amalgamation that produced Unilever Ltd.

5. In these negotiations Unilever was not bargaining from a position of weakness: the firm was in a position to cover practically all needs outside the Sellers' Pool. By means of the purchases mentioned in point 2 above, as well as other purchases, they had secured 650,000 barrels. To this could be added their own production of 250,000 barrels, and outside the Sellers' Pool Salvesen was in a position to offer approximately 300,000 barrels.

Faced with this situation, the Sellers' Pool was forced to accept £25, but as things turned out, by advance sales of production in 1929-30 and to an even greater extent by sales in the following season, members struck an excellent bargain, whereas Unilever, having failed to appreciate the price development correctly, had to pay dearly for this. The quantity purchased by the Pool in the autumn of 1929 totalled 386,000 tons at a price of £9.5 million, 83 per cent of total world production. Now that the warehouses were full, factories were ordered to step up the use of whale oil in soap and margarine, particularly the latter, and as a result only some 75,000 tons was earmarked for other products. Even in Sunlight soap, the recipe for which no one had dared to alter, 20 per cent of hydrogenated whale oil was now used without consumers noting any change of quality. In short, as D'Arcy Cooper declared in July 1930, "The interests of the Family as a whole might require more whale oil to be used."

No fresh sales pool was set up for 1930-1, and in harmony with D'Arcy Cooper's remarks on the use of whale oil, Unilever continued their tremendous purchases through separate contracts with twenty-nine companies for their 1930-1 production at a rate of £25, totalling the enormous amount of 470,000 tons for £11.75 million. Some 58,000 tons, likewise at £25, had been sold to Procter & Gamble, but by the start of the 1931-2 season 150,000 tons still remained unsold, and it proved impossible to find a purchaser even for as low a rate as £12. There had been ominous signs that a situation of this kind might arise, and to the whalers the only solution appeared to be to limit production. In this connection two considerations were of importance: what would Salvesen's attitude be, and how much of the 1931-2 production would Unilever be willing to purchase in advance? When Lars Christensen asked Jacob Hartog how much whale oil he needed, the latter answered:

81.   The whaling fleet laid up in Sandefjord during the 1931-2 Antarctic season.

"Do not use that word, we *need* nothing." Salvesen's answer was discouraging: the Norwegians and not he were responsible for over-production, which could be reduced if the contract for three new floating factories (with whale catchers) was cancelled. Unilever's reply was that there were 150,000 tons of unsold oil on the market, that production in 1930-1 would be far above normal, that the price of raw materials was falling, and that its stocks were so large that only a minor part of the 1931-2 production would be required.

The companies received a still less unequivocal answer during the introductory negotiations in March 1931, when they submitted demands which they were bound to know Unilever would not accept: purchase of the 150,000 tons at the price of £25, as agreed for the other purchases; purchase too of all the oil produced by the floating factories beyond their tanker capacity; purchase by joint contract of the entire 1931-2 production; if sales did not materialise and companies suspended catching, Unilever were to do the same. All four propositions were turned down out of hand. All that was achieved was that Unilever promised to give companies from which they had made advance purchases of oil preference in the event of subsequent purchases, provided they suspended catching immediately. Only six companies did so.

In two ways Unilever endeavoured to ward off the detrimental effects of being saddled with a stockpile at twice the price for which oil could be purchased when the contracted oil was supplied: by having operations suspended before the end of the season and by refusing to buy the oil produced by floating factories *beyond* their tanker capacity. Both these methods resulted in interesting lawsuits. Unilever calculated that suspending catching before the close of the season would mean a saving of 55,000 tons at a price of £25. Even without this amount the firm had stocks sufficient for eighty-eight weeks, and it was assumed that sooner or later the 150,000 tons would be available at a cheap rate.

When one of the Norwegian companies in January 1931 informed Unilever that some of the oil would be despatched from the whaling grounds by transporter, while the floating factories continued catching, Unilever refused to buy not only that oil but also the floating factories', as this was a breach of contract. They offered, however, to purchase all available oil at £12, provided that catching was immediately suspended. The company rejected this, and took the matter to court, demanding compensation at £14 a ton (£25, the contractual price, minus £11 for the current market price). The entire case turned on the interpretation of the phrase "the entire production of the whale oil for the season 1930-1" in the contract. Both in the King's Bench Division and in the Court of Appeal the Norwegian company's plea was rejected. Somewhat hesitantly, the company then took the case to the House of Lords, where on 18 May 1933 the Lords of Appeal in Ordinary (the law lords) unanimously ordered Unilever to pay compensation amounting to £447,160 (plus costs). The case had been followed with the greatest interest in financial and legal circles in the City and in Norway. The verdict laid down for the future that by "the entire production" was meant everything a floating factory was capable of *producing*, irrespective of how the oil was brought back from the whaling grounds.

On 21 March 1931, all the Norwegian companies agreed to Uunilever's request not to catch in 1931-2 — a black day in the history of Norwegian whaling. The first to suffer were the whalers: in 1930-1, 10,549 Norwegians had been engaged in whaling; in 1931-2 1,884. Wages paid were respectively Kr. 58 million and Kr. 8.5 million. Norwegian production in 1930-1 had been sold for Kr. 158 million (£8.7 million); now the so-called "whaling pounds", which had been one of the Bank of Norway's steadiest sources of foreign currency, were not longer available. This occurred, moreover, during a terrible economic crisis.

Resentment against Unilever was further increased when they decided to allow their own Southern Whaling & Sealing Co. to catch despite the large quantities of unsold oil still on the market; what was more, while inveighing against the use of transporters, they increased the number of whale catchers from five to eight, enabling their two floating factories to produce more than twice (360,000 barrels) their tank capacity (160,000 barrels), and made no attempt to refute accusations of gross over-catching. Unilever's reason was that, through their own production, they would increase their stocks to correspond to two years' consumption; for this reason, if necessary, they would likewise not require to buy any of the 1932-3 production, especially after purchasing in March 1932 150,000 tons at £13 10s, and had fully covered requirements to the end of 1933. Unilever were convinced that, if their expeditions had not been despatched, the Norwegian ones would have been. They were prepared for floating factories being laid up in 1932-3 as well, in which case the situation would be so desperate for the companies concerned that they would be prepared to produce at any price.

In Norway it has been the accepted thing to sit in judgment on Unilever. Several theories have been aired on the purpose of their whaling policy. One of these was that Unilever hoped for a collapse, in order to be able to buy up bankrupt companies and set up a whaling trust, in line with their margarine and soap trust. Another theory was that since the concern's main interest was in vegetable oils, of which they were not only major manufacturers and purchasers, but also sellers, they regarded whale oil as an invidious rival in the world markets for edible fats and oils, as it tended to depress the price of other oils. None of these — nor indeed, any other theories — can be considered as correct. In their consumption of whale oil they were bound to consider their affiliates which produced vegetable oils. The largest producer of these, the United Africa Co., exerted considerable pressure on Unilever in order to get them to reduce the consumption of whale oil; that they nevertheless should have purchased such large quantities was because the price had never been as low, compared to other oils, as in 1931-4.

In order to understand Unilever's action it should be remembered that they were hard hit by the world crisis : large stocks of raw materials, bought at high prices, involved them in losses of £5 million; in whale oil alone a sum of £1.47 million was written off; their losses in De-No-Fa amounted to £792,000, in the United Africa Co. to £527,000, in the sale of their whaling companies, including Prince Olav Harbour, approximately £1 million, while the lawsuit cost them half a million pounds, for which they received not a drop of oil in return. Advance purchases of whale oil in 1930-1 had provided a very costly experience and shown that this type of purchase was a pure gamble. Sales of the finished consumer goods and their price showed a downward trend, and these had to be produced from expensive raw materials. The concern needed all its resources in order to survive the crisis; they were in business to make money, not out of sentimental considerations for Norwegian whaling. For the first time for many years the Norwegians went to the whaling grounds without an assured market for the oil they would produce. The situation was so critical that D'Arcy Cooper, at a board meeting on 17 November, declared: "Christensen would like to sell us his fleet and manage it in conjunction with our own. This is a sign of Christensen losing confidence in the future of the industry."

Though Unilever's unwillingness to suspend catching provoked considerable disappointment, even more resentment was felt at the fact that Salvesen was intending to operate with all his three expeditions, and from Leith Harbour too. (The Union Whaling Co. also did, but not Irvin & Johnson.) Salvesen intended to make full use of the situation by providing each floating factory with an extra whale catcher. And the catch amounted to 402,000 barrels, 100,000 more than in 1930-1. The latter sold at £25, the former at £12, and inevitably this season produced a small deficit. Salvesen's professed reason for catching was that employers should avoid restrictions in times of depression out of consideration for their employees; moreover, preparations had been made for departure so far in advance that it could not be put off, despite the considerable risk that advance sales would be impossible. In the opinion of both Unilever and Salvesen the object of the Norwegian set-up was to maintain such a high price for whale oil that older, smaller, and obsolete floating factories would also have a chance of making a profit. The entire industry would be best served if future price levels were such that expeditions of that kind would be unable to compete, and would have to throw in the towel.

The Compañía de Pesca had made their catches conditional on Salvesen's, and operated from Grytviken. Two shore stations and five floating factories recorded a total Antarctic catch in 1931-2 of 9,572 whales and 808,560 barrels, 94 per cent of this being British. It is estimated that some 25,000 whales were spared. Total world catches were only 13,000 whales and 925,000 barrels, approximately one-quarter of Antarctic catches in 1930-1. Only in three other areas was there any whaling of importance — South Africa, Japan, and Norway — in all of them from shore stations, including two small floating factories in the Norwegian Sea. (For the world catch for 1931-2, see Statistical Appendix, Table 55.)

The Association of Whaling Companies took advantage of this interlude to investigate the possibility of sales to other concerns than Unilever. There were two potential markets, the United States and Germany. A considerable sum was earmarked for a campaign against an import duty on whale oil in the United States, which was 6 cents a gallon, corresponding to £3 10s a ton, the same amount as the cost of hydrogenation. On a cargo of 3.74 million gallons supplied from a Norwegian floating factory in 1930 there was a duty of $224,000. The farmers of the United States protested loudly against imports of fats: 30,000 tons of whale oil was the equivalent of cottonseed from 850,000 acres or tallow from a million head of cattle. Imports of whale oil from Norway had from 1921 to 1930 been approximately 20,000 tons annually, but in 1931 they soared to 65,000 tons, or 18.6 per cent of Norwegian exports. In view of this large import, pressure on the part of the farmers was so strong that on 10 May 1934 an excise tax was levied of 3 cents a pound, approximately £14 a ton, making the total duty £17 a ton. Norwegian exports then practically came to a halt, and instead attempts were made to introduce the oil tax free to the American market by the medium of American companies managed in Norway. The grotesque situation then arose that while one group of Norwegian whalers, supported by the Ministry of Foreign Affairs, endeavoured to have the duty lowered, another worked to have it maintained.

Before the German plans could be put into practice, the fat situation in Germany had changed completely, presenting Unilever with an increasingly urgent problem. When on 1 December 1932 they decided to purchase, at a rate of £13, the 1932-3 production, limited to a fixed maximum, they believed they had achieved four advantages: they were secured against over-production, as the companies would hardly produce more than they had a guaranteed market for; their requirements of whale oil were covered up to June 1934 at a reasonable price; this had been fixed for at least a year; and there was no chance that the oil would fall into the hands of any other concern. Nevertheless, as D'Arcy Cooper put it, there was one reason for uncertainty as to whether the the contract should be concluded: Germany's attitude to whale oil. This uncertainty was not unfounded; it was confirmed four months after the great purchase, when Hitler, a mere two months after assuming power, issued his order on the consumption of domestic fats. This had the most far-reaching consequences for Norwegian whaling, for the development of whaling generally, for Unilever, and for whale oil on the world market. If we are looking for the primary reason for the whaling crisis of the 1930s, we shall surprisingly enough discover it in the European and the American agricultural crisis. There is no space here to describe this in detail: we can only point to its two most significant consequences for whaling: the German fat plan and the war on margarine. It is, however, necessary to add that the former, and as far as Germany was concerned the latter too, was not only a result of the agricultural crisis but an important part of the preparations for a wartime economy.

The German fat plan and the war on margarine

Any alteration in the composition of the raw materials for margarine and in its consumption would inevitably influence the whale oil market. Thanks to the great difference in price of butter and margarine, consumption of the latter had reached its peak both in Germany and in the other European countries in 1929 and 1930. For the trust these had been two outstanding years, but commencing with 1931 sales of margarine showed a steady decline. In his speech to the general meeting of Unilever's shareholders in 1932 D'Arcy Cooper indicated the reasons for this : the collapse of the raw materials market, the import duty on certain raw materials, devaluation and currency restrictions, and state intervention in the production of margarine in support of butter. The collapse in the prices of raw materials was on a greater scale than the world had hitherto witnessed. Roughly speaking, it may be said that the price for the most important edible fats and oils slumped to about one-third of its previous level in 1929-34 (see Table 56). The fall in prices was greatest for coconut oil and whale oil, the two most important raw materials for margarine. One example should suffice to show what this meant for a major fat importer such as Germany, with her minimal resources of foreign currency. Compared to 1928, it was possible in 1932 for the same amount to buy two or three times more whale oil, and for one Mark a consumer in the two years referred to could purchase respectively 5,500 and 15,400 calories in the form of margarine, but only 1,900 and 2,800 in the form of butter. This explains Germany's large-scale imports of raw materials for margarine, but also the difficulties facing the country's butter producers, and why the German farmers regarded whale oil as an enemy. It is this German fats problem that exercises such a decisive influence on the whaling market in the 1930s.

After the economic crisis had burst on the world in the autumn of 1929 Germany came under tremendous pressure from foreign creditors, who drained the country of foreign currency. The Reichsbank fought desperately to save the Mark from fresh collapse. From 1930 various import restrictions had been introduced, and these were further intensi-fied in 1932 with import quotas and high tariffs. In about 1930 Germany had an annual fat consumption of approximately 2.1 million tons, of which only about 39 per cent was covered by domestic production, the remainder deriving either from direct imports or being obtained in-directly from domestic production of edible fats from imported raw materials and from artificial feed for farming. In 1932 the number of unemployed had risen to 6 million. They were compelled to buy margarine of the cheapest quality, of which, for the same price, they could buy five times as much as they could butter. This meant that German agriculture was faced with serious difficulties in marketing its products. This resulted as early as 1930 in a marked switch in German fat consumption from vegetable to animal, primarily by increasing the country's own production of milk, butter, lard, tallow, and bacon. Hand in hand with this the Germans started agitating in favour of a whal-ing industry of their own. This, too, would comprise a form of domestic production of animal fat, and would save foreign currency, the two arguments that were used in this campaign.

Hitler's decree of 23 March 1933 provided a dramatic conclusion to the measures initiated, clearly aimed at preparing for a wartime economy. It was a declaration of war against the trust's margarine and a blow struck in favour of domestic butter. A fat monopoly — the Reichsstelle für Milcherzeugnisse, Öle und Fette — was set up, armed with full powers to control all imports, marketing, and production of fats, to lay down quotas, customs rates, maximum prices, sales tax, etc. From 1 April of that year a three-month period for reducing margarine production to 50 per cent (subsequently 60 per cent) was ordered. It was decided that margarine should contain an admixture of 5 per cent domestic fats (subsequently increased to $12\frac{1}{2}$ per cent). All bakeries and restaurants were compelled to display notices clearly informing the public that whale oil was used in the margarine. The customs duty on imported fats was drastically raised: on tallow, for example, it was 40 times higher than previously. This meant that American tallow, of which Germany had imported 108,000 tons in 1932, was shut out from the German market. Imports of butter were cut to less than half, and the import duty was raised. To aid farmers, the price for home-produced butter was fixed at a rate well above that on the world market. In 1934 butter in Berlin cost wholesale 251.34 Marks for 100 kg., in Copenhagen 90.70 Marks; in Berlin, lard cost 191.94 Marks, in New York 46.67 Marks.

The war on margarine was in a fair way to succeeding: production slumped from 526,000 tons in 1932 to 360,000 tons in 1934, while production of butter rose from 489,000 tons to 523,000 tons. Two objects had been achieved: the German fat market had been relieved of pressure from the world fat market, and Germany's agriculture had been rescued from economic collapse.

"Eating margarine now is not thrift but a waste of national resources," was how the propaganda put it. The position would have been quite different if Germany had been able to make margarine from whale oil she herself had produced. This was part of a plan which aimed at financing imports necessary for the country's rearmament, stockpiling the necessary war reserves and assuring Germany immunity against a blockade, the effects of which she had felt during the First World War. "Had Germany in 1914 had 300,000 tons of whale oil, the shortage of fats would never have been so menacing." The well-known slogan "guns before butter" was not coined by the Nazis, and did not have the misinterpreted sense of either guns or butter, but without (eating) butter — no guns. Ever since Bismarck's time the farmer had been protected for strategic reasons. "A cow in the field is worth more to the General Staff than one ton of groundnuts."

Actually, the Nazis were merely doing what all European governments were doing in face of the pressure exerted by agriculture against margarine. Various methods were used — sales, production, equalisation tax on margarine, compulsory mixing of butter in margarine, direct restriction of production. Italy even went so far as to forbid the production of margarine, and in the Netherlands a similar ban very nearly received a majority in the National Assembly in June 1933. While Norway had only used 418 tons of butter in margarine, in 1935 3,059 tons were used and in 1939 12,139 tons. Britain alone took no steps to protect domestic production of butter or to restrict the consumption of margarine. When the Government broached the idea in 1933, Unilever made it clear that this would contravene the Ottawa agreements, as it would adversely affect the imports of raw materials from the colonies and Dominions. As the cattle-breeding industry was essentially based on the production of meat and milk, the competition offered by margarine was of minor importance to the country's own production of butter. Nevertheless, statistics from Great Britain throw a great deal of light on the margarine-butter relationship in the 1930s (see Statistical Appendix, Table 57). All in all, these figures reveal the successful struggle waged by butter against margarine. Most surprisingly, the figures show that during the Depression in the 1930s, consumption of fat *per capita* rose, and this rise was entirely covered by butter. One of the reasons was that the price of butter dropped more markedly than that of margarine. Britain was inundated by foreign butter, and in March 1934 it could be bought in London for 8*d* a pound. The figures for 1938 indicate another surprising fact, that as the economic climate improved towards the end of the decade, the consumption of butter decreased while that of margarine rose, and the increase in total consumption was now entirely covered by margarine. This also applied to most countries in Europe from 1936 to 1937.

The German fat plan and war on margarine had serious consequences for Unilever. At the general meeting in 1932 D'Arcy Cooper was forced to concede that the previous year had for the first time registered a drop in sales of margarine both at home and in Germany. He predicted that 1932 would prove a still more difficult year, as indeed it was, the slump continuing for the next four years. Not till 1938 was there a decided rise. Total sales of edible fats declined from 881,256 tons in 1929 to 628,706 tons in 1934.

In the face of Nazi intransigence Unilever had to admit defeat. Apart from setting a ceiling on production, favouritism was shown to prominent manufacturers friendly to the Nazis, while Unilever, as a foreign concern, was under constant threat. Its earnings, some £2 million annually, on its German subsidiaries were blocked and had to be re-invested in Germany. Thus it came about that Unilever became the biggest customer of German shipbuilding yards. In 1935 32 per cent of all ships at German yards were being built on Unilever's account, formally for its Dutch subsidiary, Unilever N.V. All in all, from 15 November 1934 to 31 October 1936, sixty-eight ships were contracted, totalling 460,000 tons. At a board meeting on 28 May 1936, D'Arcy Cooper stated that till then 214 million Marks had been spent on the building of ships in Germany alone. Unilever themselves had no use for all these ships, and most of them were sold — several to Norway, particularly to whaling companies, who paid partially in whale oil. The net result was that Germany acquired whale oil without spending any foreign currency; Unilever managed to extract their frozen Marks from Germany; Norway added to her merchant navy a number of ships that proved of enormous importance to the Allied war effort; Norway and Britain made a contribution to the setting up of the German war economy; and German shipbuilding yards were fully employed while the British yards were empty. It was not surprising that D'Arcy Cooper should have ordered "that all reference to the newly purchased ships in Germany should be avoided".

When Unilever in 1936 refused to commission the building of more ships, the director of the German Reichsbank and Economics Minister HJALMAR SCHACHT compelled Unilever to finance the building of a German whaling fleet by the device of threatening a drastic reduction of its margarine quota. Much against his will, P. D. H. HENRIKS, head of Unilever's German section, had to comply. In their exultation at having acquired a new whaling fleet under the German flag, the Nazis naturally concealed the fact that this was being done with Dutch-British capital. At the general meeting in 1938 D'Arcy Cooper pointed out that of the four German expeditions operating in 1937-8 (not including the two chartered from Norway), one, the *Unitas*, was entirely owned by Unilever, while in the others it had interests of 50 per cent or more. Foreign capital and Norwegian whalers "offer the possibility of supporting the supply of fats to our people, and thereby contributing to the attainment of the great goal of freedom in raw materials and food", to quote Goering on the importance of German whaling. In other words: they were helping Germany to set up her wartime economy. We shall return to this point later.

In this introductory survey the attempt has been made to provide some of the background for the most dramatic epoch in the history of modern whaling, when it was no longer a purely private business undertaking, but had attained the status of an international political problem. It is more difficult to understand why Norwegians transferred a number of companies to foreign flags and ownership, why Norwegians should set up and manage companies for other nations, and why Britain and Norway should have made it possible for Japan and Germany to develop their whaling, although it must have been obvious that they would prove dangerous competitors, and that the more nations that participated, the more difficult it would be to conclude an agreement on a reduction of catches before it was too late to call a halt to the extermination of whale stocks. It would be hypocritical for Norwegians to complain about this, as Norway herself had contributed to it. Was there any possibility of halting this development? This is one of the problems with which we shall deal in the ensuing chapter.

Several important factors must be taken into account if we are to obtain a correct picture. The expansion of Norwegian whaling without foreign capital would have been just as inconceivable as in shipping or industry. The very start of the Antarctic venture had been financed entirely by foreign capital. Secondly, Norwegian companies transferred to foreign flags always retained strong links with Norway. Companies started abroad with Norwegian assistance, too, remained to a very large extent under Norwegian control, operating with Norwegian crews, and they were mainly fitted out in Norway. In this development the mid-1930s mark a parting of the ways. In the first half of this decade the initiative was essentially Norwegian, but in the latter half foreign nations make their appearance on the scene, depriving Norway of her influence on the scope and direction of the development. There will never be any gainsaying the fact that Norway herself, in order to finance an expansion that was highly speculative, had involved foreign nations in it. It is one thing to persuade foreigners to invest capital in Norwegian whaling, another thing — and this was beyond the comprehension of the age — to start companies abroad in direct competition with Norwegian ones.

The British-Norwegian quota agreements, 1932-1934

At its first meeting in Copenhagen in September 1926 'Le conseil international pour l'exploration de la mer' had set up a committee to draft principles for an international agreement on the regulation of whaling. This committee, Le comité international pour la protection de la baleine, held its first meeting in Paris from 7 to 9 April 1927 and at its request the League of Nations summoned a meeting of experts in April 1930, with representatives from France, Germany, Great Britain, Japan, Norway, Portugal, and the United States. The proposal for an agreement submitted at this meeting followed in essence the principles of the Norwegian Whaling Act of 21 June 1929. This proposal and the comments on it were examined by a new expert committee which met in Geneva on 9 September 1931, and on 24 September its report was adopted by twenty-six delegate nations. This so-called Geneva Convention provided the basis for all subsequent agreements. Its most important articles were : No. 4, ban on the catching of right whales; No. 5, a ban on the catching of calves, sexually immature whales, and lactating mothers; No. 6, full utilisation of the carcass; No. 7, the whalers' bonus to be fixed essentially according to the size, species, and oil yield of the whale, and not according to numbers; No. 8, no catching to be undertaken without a licence from the Government or at least informing such Government of the intention to carry out whaling; No. 10, an accurate catching log to be maintained; No. 12, statistics to be submitted to the Bureau international de statistiques baleinières (the Committee for Whaling Statistics) in Norway; No. 17, the convention to come into force when ratified by at least eight signatory powers, which must include Norway and Great Britain; No. 19, the convention to run for three years from the date of its coming into force (16 January 1935); No. 20, after a lapse of the three years specified it may be terminated at six months' notice.

Three of the articles encountered criticism in Norway, and are of interest to the British-Norwegian quota agreements of 1932-4. One of these was Article 7, which was based on the belief that whale stocks would be spared, as the gunner, in his own interest, would concentrate on large adult animals. Although there were doubts in Norway whether this object would be achieved, the Wage Agreement of 1932 embodied the principle of a barrel bonus instead of a whale bonus, although admittedly more out of consideration for the whaler than for the whale.

The insistence in Article 8 on a concession (for pelagic expeditions) had been rejected by Norway during negotiations for renewing in 1927-8 Norwegian concessions in the Antarctic, and not included in the Norwegian Whaling Act of 1929. It was British whaling under Norwegian management in 1931-2 and particularly Unilever's operations 1931-3 which disinclined Norway to accommodate Britain on this point (and others). Again and again Norway called attention to "British hypocrisy". It could be shown that at a time when Unilever increased the number of whale catchers from five to eight for each expedition, there were so many more whales than the floating factories could reduce, that the try-out amounted to a mere 94.4 barrels per BWU, whereas, for example, Salvesen achieved 113.4. The same sort of thing occurred in 1932-3. In the second place, Unilever had insisted that the Norwegian floating factories should not catch more than their tank capacity, whereas their own floating factories caught more than twice their tank capacity. Norway made powerful representations to persuade England to introduce the same restrictions as in the Norwegian Whaling Act and to ratify the Geneva Convention. Britain, however, delayed doing so until 18 October 1934 (Norway had ratified on 18 June 1932), a delay which meant that the Convention could not come into force until four and a half years after it had been adopted. Eighteen nations had ratified before Britain. In Norwegian quarters it was stated that Norway might be forced to abolish all restrictions, because unrestrained British catching had created so much bitterness among Norwegian whalers that the situation was untenable.

In 1929-31, particularly in the United States, a very strong movement was on foot among scientists to introduce an international agreement on the protection of stocks of whales. Six leading zoological organisations set up a council for the preservation of whales in 1929, and this body paid unreserved tribute to Norway for leading the way with her Whaling Act of 1929, which was described as "the most constructive legislation ever drawn up to save the waning animal life. Norway, by the royal decree, has accomplished more than all the nations of the world." The United States, among the first countries to ratify the Geneva Convention, on 7 July 1932, waited impatiently for Britain to follow suit. Norway did so, and Britain's hesitation was the reason why Norway rejected the British invitation, in a note of 15 April 1931, to start official negotiations. As the entire Norwegian whaling fleet had been laid up in 1931-2, and as catching would be markedly restricted by private agreement in the following season, decimation of stocks of whales would not increase along the lines presupposed in the British note. For this reason there was no basis for official negotiations. Norway was willing to negotiate once she had received an answer to the following questions : When would Britain ratify the Geneva Convention? Would she enforce the use of whaling logs and make them available for inclusion in joint statistics? Would Britain — and this was the crux of the Norwegian reply — make the same stringent provisions as in a voluntary agreement applicable to *all* British companies, in particular Unilever? In other words: Norway could not negotiate with a nation unwilling to ratify the Geneva Convention and which did nothing to prevent its nationals from over-fishing. Thus clearly Norway's point of view was not a matter of restriction for the sake of restriction, but aimed at compelling Britain to regulate her catching in the same way as Norway.

Ever since the autumn of 1931 a so-called "Restriction Committee" had been at work, and after overcoming enormous difficulties of a formal and practical nature, it succeeded in having the agreement adopted. It had the support of all Norwegian and foreign companies, with one almost obvious exception, Unilever, who perceived the advantage of remaining uncommitted, with a view to being able to use their own production as a trump card during sales negotiations. Without restrictions, their expeditions could produce as much oil as they were capable of, using only the best parts of the whale, and therefore at lower cost. This advantage would be forfeited if they were to adhere to the agreement. The most Unilever was prepared to do was to promise to start the season a little later, to reduce the number of whale catchers from eight to seven, and to make better use of the carcasses. The price of whale oil on the world market was in the opinion of Unilever the best regulator of catches. When the price was so low that production was uneconomical, the number of expeditions would be reduced, and this they considered was the most important and most effective factor in preventing extermination of the whale. The market should be allowed to regulate itself.

The production agreement that was signed on 9 June 1932 marks a milestone, introducing for the first time the term 'quota', both barrel quota and whale quota, and the idea of limiting the duration of the season. As far as the latter was concerned, signatories pledged themselves not to start catching before October 20, and not to continue after 30 April. The latter date was of no importance, as in 1931 the last floating factories had left the whaling grounds on 29 April, but of the forty-one floating factories, thirty-six had started before 20 October. The establishment of maximum catches, both in terms of barrels and in terms of whales, was a combination of the Committee's proposals and those of H. K. Salvesen. As over-production was the cause of the slump in price, the Committee's proposal merely aimed to reduce production, whereas Salvesen's proposal also reduced the number of whales killed and ensured a minimum of waste of the raw material. The agreement laid down the following proportion: whale quota = barrel quota divided by 110. As it was not allowed under any circumstances to exceed the whale quota, this would force floating factories to produce at least 110 barrels per BWU in order to fulfil their barrel quota. Up to 10 per cent in excess of the barrel quota could be produced, should anyone be capable of doing so. Quotas could be transferred, but no rate was fixed for this. Salvesen claims to have purchased quotas for £8,443, thus helping to keep three floating factories away from catching. In 1933 he purchased quotas for £16,675 in order to keep two floating factories at home.

Out of the matériel that had operated in 1930-1 thirty-five floating factories and four shore stations were committed to the agreement, and in addition there were three new floating factories catching for the first time. However, only fifteen floating factories and one shore station were anxious to take part in active catching. The idea was that production should be reduced to less than two-thirds of that for 1930-1. Quotas were established as follows: 2,031,455 barrels ÷ 110 = 18,584 BWU. The result for the sixteen units surpassed all expectations: 2,090,825 barrels from 16,985 BWU, or 116.4 barrels per BWU, well above the 110 barrels expected. Average production per day per floating factory rose from 488 to 970 barrels and per whale catcher from 100 to 140, as compared with 1930-1. The private agreement had achieved its two objects: to limit production to two-thirds of the 1930-1 season, and to spare some 2,500 blue, fin, and humpback whales by improved utilisation of the raw material. As it turned out, it was not the new specially designed floating factories that had the highest try-out, but the converted ones, particularly Christensen's three factories, which topped the list with 126.6, 123.1, and 122.7. They did not even need to use up their whole quota of whales in order to complete their barrel quota.

It was not the agreement alone that was responsible for the excellent results: now that there were fewer expeditions it had been possible to select the best-qualified expedition managers, gunners, and crews. This was particularly important as far as gunners were concerned. There are examples of a poor gunner, with indifferent crew, under otherwise equal conditions, scoring only one-fifth of the number achieved by the champion. In 1932-3 differences were not so pronounced: the best catcher accounted for 299 whales (289 BWU) and the least successful 162 (122½ BWU). Only the most effective whale catchers were used, and, with the exception of one, all the floating factories had been built or converted between 1929 and 1931. In order to reduce the permissible maximum, the cooking equipment had been considerably increased. Several new technical improvements were utilised; *inter alia*, this was the first season during which the whale claw was tried out — with great success. The seventeen floating factories (including Unilever's two) could now spread over the whole of the enormous whaling grounds, without having to compete for the same whales. Much of the old matériel was scrapped once for all. Of forty-eight floating factories operating in 1930-1 (six in other whaling grounds than the Antarctic), eleven were not used for whaling after 1932, five were used for one season, four for two seasons, while one was destroyed by fire in 1932. In all, twenty-one older factories were weeded out. To make up for this, eleven newly built and two newly converted ones were introduced between 1932 and 1938, and the capacity of these thirteen was about three times that of the twenty-one.

It was not entirely clear whether the agreement had had a favourable influence on whale stocks. The number of whales had admittedly been established in terms of BWU (i.e. 1 blue whale = 2 fin whales = 2½ humpback = 6 sei whales), but a blue whale was a blue whale, whether it was 70 or 90 ft. long, and yielded twice as much oil. Now that the barrel quota (number of barrels) was to be fulfilled on the basis of a whale quota (a limited number of BWU), which must not be exceeded, and the bonus was based on the number of barrels and not on the number of whales, the gunners would obviously concentrate on the largest animals, the ones that yielded the greatest number of barrels, and these would be female blue whales, and the pregnant ones as a rule produced the largest amount of oil in proportion to their size. The increase in the killing of this category was alarming: in 1932-3, for every

100 bulls killed, there were 422 blue whale cows of a length exceeding 85 ft. Sigurd Risting considered it ominous to the future of stocks of whales that there was such a concentration on large females, most of which had foetuses. His conclusion was that for this reason the whale quota should be abolished. If gunners agreed not to receive any bonus for lactating whales, they would be careful not to kill them, but in practice it was almost impossible to avoid this during the chase. On the other hand, to ensure that an excessive number of small whales were not killed, the minimum size laid down by the Act had to be increased to 65 ft. for the blue and 55 ft. for fin whales, an amendment that was adopted in the 1933-4 agreement and enforced by a supplement to the Whaling Act in 1934.

Up to 1931-2 gunners had earned a bonus per whale according to size, Kr.110 for a blue, Kr.60 for a fin, and Kr.40 for a humpback, provided they were above the permitted minimum, and a half-bonus if they were below. Gunners were very dissatisfied at an arrangement whereby a mere foot might reduce the bonus by 50 per cent. In the 1932-3 agreement the bonus was based exclusively on barrels, a more satisfactory arrangement. The agreement also contained three other new provisions: there was the same wage rate in all companies, and the expedition manager could "ration" catches if he considered this necessary. To sum up we may say that the 1932-3 agreement was an important step in the direction of a better use of the raw material, a regulation of catching aimed to prevent over-production and over-fishing of whale stocks, and a more uniform system of wages for crews. In view of subsequent events in the regulation of the 1930s, the British-Norwegian agreement on a catching quota in 1932-4 seems to be the best and most successful form.

Did the agreement live up to its intention of providing a better market for whale oil? To a certain extent this question too can be answered in the affirmative. The sales agreement between the participants in the production agreement was an answer to Unilever's statement that they were not prepared to give more than £10 for oil in 1932-3, and it was at this rate that, in August 1932, they had bought 23,000 tons of oil stored from 1930-1. All but two of the whaling companies agreed not to sell before 17 October. This appears to have helped, as Unilever were obviously scared that they would not have any oil unless they raised their price bid to £12 10s for the entire quantity of the Sales Pool, some 280,000 tons. This was turned down, and in order to exert pressure on sellers D'Arcy Cooper advised the British banks against granting the companies credit for fitting out for the ensuing season. When companies, despite this, were promised credit, Unilever raised their bid to £13. As a counter to the companies' insistence that this price would leave them no margin of profit, Unilever once again trotted out the results obtained by their own company, which, so they said, at that price had netted a profit in 1931-2 of £169,000 and in 1932-3 of £216,000. With several companies pressing for a sale, including Salvesen, this tug-of-war came to an end with Unilever purchasing the 280,000 tons at a rate of £13, £3.64 million in all. Two years previously, this sum would only have bought 141,000 tons.

Great though the difficulties were in producing an agreement in 1932-3, they were far greater for 1933-4, while for 1934-5 they proved insuperable. There was disagreement both between the Norwegian companies and Salvesen and internally among the Norwegians. The greatest difficulty involved the older and less competitive companies, whose floating factories were often referred to as "corpses", and these also included the shore stations in South Georgia (and three in Africa), which had not operated since 1931. The agreement covered a total of forty floating factories, eight shore stations, and 228 whale catchers, but only sixteen, two, and 106 respectively were used for active catching of their own and purchased quotas. In other words, a great deal of matériel which would not have been used for whaling even as partners of an agreement, continued to exist as "quotas". This had now become a valuable saleable perquisite, and there was always the risk that outsiders or new whaling nations would buy them up. We shall see how tremendously valuable a quota was to become when, after the Second World War, a total quota was fixed for pelagic catching in the Antarctic.

The 1933-4 agreement on which unanimity was finally achieved after a great deal of dispute, differed in a number of points from the previous one. It raised the compulsory try-out level from 110 barrels per BWU to 115, thus enabling the whale quota to be lowered to 17,074. Minimum measurements for blue whales were raised to 65 ft. and for fin whales to 55 ft. The bonus for the latter was increased in relation to the former, in order to spare as many as possible of this species. This had little effect that season, as the number of fin whales was 23.8 per cent of the total number of whales caught, but in 1934-5 it rose to 39.3 per cent.

The start of the season was postponed from 20 to 25 October. As might have been expected, this time too Uniliver refused to join in. They had refused to believe that there was sufficient unity among the companies for an agreement to be concluded, and were not a little surprised when this did, in fact, take place and a rigidly binding sales agreement was concluded. When Unilever's two floating factories recorded a try-out of nearly 96.8 and 85.6 barrels per BWU, whereas the sixteen covered by the agreement had 115.7, there were good grounds for complaining that "while British scientists and press put the blame on the Norwegians, British businessmen cynically exploit their matériel and their strong political position". One of Unilever's floating factories was so badly damaged that it had to abandon catching for the rest of the season, after producing 66,500 barrels, but to make up for this the other factory ship, the *Southern Empress*, achieved 226,000 barrels, an unbeaten record in the whole history of Antarctic whaling. This record was nevertheless not as impressive as might appear, as 153 days were required for this catch, whereas e.g. the *Kosmos II* completed its quota in ninety-seven days.

The quota and time limitation incorporated in the private agreements of 1932-4 are two principles which subsequent international agreements have retained as the most practical. In five of the seasons during the 1930s, 1932-7, catches were successfully limited to two-thirds of the scope they had had in 1930-1, the utilisation of the raw material was considerably increased, and taxing of whale stocks was kept at a level which at that time a great many people believed would be sufficient to preserve them. Private agreements, however, would not have been concluded if their intention had not also been to improve the price of whale oil by limiting production to the quantity the market was capable of absorbing. That stocks of whales in this way were spared was not so much a motive as a consequence of the original intention. It is not the task of the historian to speculate on "ifs", but nevertheless it is tempting to observe that the development of whaling after 1934 would have been a very different one if every nation and every company had adhered to the system of private quota agreements. The outstanding Norwegian marine biologist Professor JOHAN T. RUUD sums it up as follows: "It must be admitted that no subsequent agreements have been in a position to show more successful results than those achieved by voluntary agreements. Under extremely unfavourable price conditions companies succeeded in creating a balance, because the agreements facilitated rational exploitation of both the raw material and the matériel." The withdrawal of a number of Norwegian companies, Unilever's reluctance, and insufficient Norwegian-British co-operation in the face of new whaling nations were the reasons why this approach was not continued. When catches once again went beyond defensible limits, this was due not to an extension on the part of the old whaling nations, but of the new.

The agreement had failed to halt the price reduction, which had continued after the sales in the autumn of 1932 at £13. A very abundant harvest of vegetable fats, Germany's policy of self-sufficiency, the United States' prohibitive customs, import, and currency restrictions, and the slump in the consumption of margarine, all these made the marketing of whale oil difficult. For this reason the Sales Pool decided to store the oil until further notice. Time went by, and a new season approached without any sale having been effected.

For Norwegian whaling this summer was one of the most critical. The lowest price for whale oil in the history of modern and possibly also old whaling, the breakdown of production and sales agreements, a plea — entered by Unilever too — for laying up the fleet (but not its own), Unilever's rejection of a final request to participate in a restriction on production, the start of Japanese whaling in the Antarctic, Germany's politico-commercial pressure on Norway for a free hand in her whaling policy, all these factors seemed to conspire to give Norwegian whaling the *coup de grâce*.

The quota conflict, 1934-1936

The years 1934-6 were filled with an uneasiness hitherto unknown in whaling. Skirmishing now gave way to open warfare, the prelude to which was the shock registered by the other companies when they received the news of Lars Christensen's contract with Unilever. "A stab in the back for Norwegian whaling, the most disloyal act ever perpetrated in the history of whaling", was the universal judgment. Posterity can assess this more dispassionately, and for this purpose it is necessary to revert to the situation in the spring of 1931, and to the agreement then in force between Lars Christensen and Unilever, and his offer in 1932 to transfer his fleet to them, an offer that was almost certainly unknown to the other companies. The most significant consequence of this conflict was that it provided the immediate occasion for the Norwegian Whaling Acts of 26 June 1934, and 14 June 1935, which for the first time in the history of whaling restricted catching in the open sea in space, time, and volume.

On the basis of personal research on whale stocks throughout the entire Antarctic continent, Lars Christensen submitted a proposal for a total set-up which also included Unilever's fleets, for the 1934-5 season. His concern was not only to spare whale stocks, which in his opinion were greatly diminished, but also the fact that there were over 300,000 tons of whale oil on the market still unsold. His proposal was not accepted by the other companies, and Unilever dealt with it at the same time as they considered his offer to catch on their behalf during the two seasons 1934-6, without any quota restrictions, up to an amount of 110,000 tons a season, in return for Unilever's covering production costs on the basis of £6 10s a ton plus a supplementary £2, totalling £8 10s. It was an absolute precondition that the price should remain secret; should it be known, it would be impossible for the Sales Pool to obtain the rate of £13 that had been demanded. On 3 May Christensen informed Unilever that he accepted the contract, and two days later he wrote to the Whaling Association that as his plan had been rejected, he intended to catch during the following season. He argued that the quota distribution had favoured the new companies, whereas the entire reduction had been to the disadvantage of the old ones. This was unfair, because it was the new companies who had placed whaling in its present situation. Under cover of the agreement the share allotted to the foreign companies had increased markedly by transfers to their flags and by the purchase of quotas allotted to Norwegian floating factories, and by extorting excessively large quotas as a condition for joining the agreement. The result was that Norway's share of Antarctic whaling was now 43.4 per cent and that of foreign concerns 56.6 per cent, whereas prior to the agreements the relationship had been 67.9 per cent and 32.1 per cent.

The 660,000 barrels Christensen was to produce every season for Unilever were more than twice what he would have received on a quota basis; it was therefore impossible to join in a quota agreement which would prevent him from fulfilling his contracts. But what he was unwilling to agree to voluntarily, the Norwegian Government was forced to compel him to do, under pressure of the other companies, in the form of the new Whaling Act of 26 June 1934, embodying these three points : (1) a ban on the sale of matériel to overseas countries; (2) catching time to run from 1 December to 31 March; (3) total exploitation of the raw material. Everyone realised that point (2) constituted a counterblast to Christensen, but the Act was also inspired by the hope that Britain would introduce the same time limit in the Whaling Act which she was drafting. In this respect Norway was disappointed, and once again Unilever proved the stumbling-block. When the British Minister of Fisheries asked the British companies to accept a law of the same nature as the Norwegian, Unilever retorted that this law was exclusively aimed at their contract with Christensen, and was not intended to establish a general limitation. Unilever would never be able to agree to postpone catching till 1 December or to catch a limited quota. A year later a spokesman for the British Government declared that a quota would mean limiting British whaling so that it could not expand. Should the British Government intervene in whaling, Norwegian companies anxious to transfer their flags would not be in a position to do so. For this reason the Government would never lend itself to a step of this nature.

Faced with this rebuttal the Norwegian Government informed the Foreign Office that if Britain did not immediately ratify the Geneva Convention, Norway might be compelled to renounce it, abolishing all restrictions in order to place Norwegian whaling on equal terms with British. Should Norway abide by the Convention and maintain her Whaling Act, she would have to make it known to the entire world that Norwegian whaling was subject to restrictions from which British whaling was exempt. The possibility was also mentioned of forbidding Norwegians from accepting employment in foreign expeditions, the so-called "Crew Clause". Possibly, this Norwegian threat expedited Britain's adoption of the Whaling Act on 31 July 1934, and her ratification of the Convention on 18 October. During the debate on the latter in Parliament, several speakers criticised the fact that a single firm had endeavoured to put the brake on every sort of regulation, and had persuaded a Norwegian company to join forces.

While Britain had undoubtedly been compelled to adopt a whaling law, as far as regulation was concerned this was an empty gesture, mere lip service. It neither made catching dependent on a concession nor did it set a time limit to the season. Admittedly, the law stated that a company intending to engage in whaling was required to obtain a licence from the Board of Trade, but this was nothing more than a certificate of sea-worthiness, and all persons fulfilling the provisions of the law were entitled to a licence. While practically all companies, including Salvesen, maintained the "Norwegian" season, Unilever's two floating factories and Irvin & Johnson's operated without any such limitation. It seems obvious that Unilever's purpose in concluding a contract with Christensen was to ensure independence of the other companies and to control the whale oil market. Together, the two contracting parties could produce a million barrels, and from the two British companies mentioned they could bank on being able to purchase half a million barrels, plus a little extra from a number of outsiders. This would approximate to the 1.8 million barrels that Unilever regarded as their minimum annual requirement. As there were few sales outside Unilever, there was no need for the other whaling companies, and in that sense they were able to maintain that in their way they, too, were working for a restriction. But if the remaining companies were to be in a position to cover Unilever's requirements, they would have to catch without any restrictions, and the British Whaling Act in no way prevented this. Unilever's object, "to get rid of the Norwegian tyranny", had almost been achieved.

As it was impossible for Christensen to fulfil the contract during the short period available, he endeavoured to transfer his matériel — three floating factories and twenty-one whale catchers — overseas, but this was turned down. In 1934-5 production was a mere half of what had been contracted for. For this reason production costs were far higher than had been foreseen, and the company faced a loss of £154,000. Unilever then agreed to pay a supplementary £45,000 to cover some of the increased expenses. When a quota of 285,000 barrels was imposed in 1935-6 by the Norwegian Government, he informed Unilever that this was a *force majeure* which rendered their contract invalid. Unilever was not prepared to accept this, and the lawsuit to decide this point was followed with just as much interest as the case against Unilever two years previously. A tremendous amount of documentary evidence was submitted in court to clarify the relationship between catches and markets, material which has proved highly useful in writing this account. The legal aspects were rather obscure, but there was little difficulty in arriving at a settlement, whereby Unilever paid £13 15s (instead of the contractual £8 10s). While Christensen, as a result of this settlement, received £250,000 more than the contractual price, Unilever obtained 50,000 tons at a rate £7 cheaper per ton than the market price at the time (January 1936).

We are, however, anticipating the course of events. A great deal had occurred since 1934 to frustrate Unilever's plans for complete control of the whale oil market, and to make this year a decisive turning-point in the history of whaling. The 1934-5 season was the first (apart from the laying-up season of 1931-2) when Norwegian production in the Antarctic accounted for less than half — 47.9 per cent — of total production, which in the case of the British Empire was 49.7 per cent. On this basis one might well pose the question : who had done most to limit catching? In the second place, this was the time when a new nation, Japan, made its Antarctic debut. This complicated the work of setting up an international agreement, and the situation became still more complicated when Nazi Germany joined in in 1936. Thirdly, this was the first time the German state operated on the whale oil market as a direct competitor to Unilever. Fourthly, it resulted in such a steep rise in the price of whale oil that Unilever's plans were blown sky-high, and a feeling of optimism was created that gave rise to fresh expansion. Fifthly, the organisation of whalers in trade unions achieved its breakthrough in the 1934-5 season, and we shall see what a direct bearing this had on development. But above all, Germany's new political system created an entirely changed situation.

Germany and the Norwegian sale of whale oil, 1934

When it proved impossible for the Sales Pool to find buyers at £13, the price had to be lowered to £12, £11, £10 10s, and finally to £10, without any sales being achieved. The situation was saved when the German Government bought 151,317 tons at a net price of £10 3s 1d, and the remainder of the Sales Pool's stocks, 152,196 tons, was sold off at £9 9s 7d. With production costs marginally below £10, companies just broke even.

This big sale to Germany was the prelude to a Norwegian-German whaling war, often bitterly contested and reaching its menacing climax in the spring of 1939. That the German state should have been the purchaser tallied with the German fat plan of 1933, and, as far as Norway was concerned, with the search for a purchaser outside the trust, and this again tallied with the Nazi desire to be free from any restrictions imposed by a trust. The newly aroused German interest in whaling went back as far as 1928. Three alternatives were discussed : the building of a German fleet or the chartering or purchasing of

Norwegian expeditions. For the time being the first of these alternatives was abandoned, at it demanded a larger capital investment than could be raised during the Depression. The two last-mentioned alternatives appeared easier, as there were enough Norwegian expeditions laid up. Home production of whale oil was a threat Germany used to induce Norway to sell at the lowest possible price. German traditions in whaling and the high standard of German mechanical skills were also adduced. But at the same time the Germans realised that they would not be able to start their catching without Norwegian crews. For this reason the matter was not pressed until this had been secured. But once this had been done, they made good their threat.

The fat plan aroused such alarm in Norway that several prominent Norwegians immediately made their way to Berlin to contact the German authorities on future imports of fats. The price and method of payment were decisive to sales. The former was in reality decided by Unilever, who were clearly anxious that the Germans would pay more for their whale oil than they themselves were paying in accordance with the Christensen contract, and for which, in time, they hoped to acquire the rest of the whale oil, i.e. £8 10s. PAUL RYKENS (shortly afterwards appointed managing director of Unilever N.V.) had negotiated with the German Government and persuaded it to promise not to buy from the Norwegian purchasers, but to let Unilever do it for them. They would then offer £8 instead of the £11 that the German Government had expected to pay. Admittedly, Rykens reported back that the negotiations had been broken off, though without proving unsatisfactory to Unilever N.V. They were alarmed at the idea that the German Government would pay £11, which Unilever's intervention had prevented.

The reason why the price paid by the Germans was so much higher than Unilever had hoped for is due in part to the fact that Germany was unable to pay in sterling or in cash but only on a long-term basis via clearing and in Reichsmarks (the price quoted in pounds was merely nominal). The sale on 31 August 1934 was concluded on the German side with the new Fats Directorate, and the man the Norwegians encountered on this occasion, and subsequently dealt most with in all their negotiations on sales of whale oil, clearing, and German whaling, was the so-called Ministerialdirektor in the Reich Economics Ministry, HELMUTH C. H. WOHLTHAT. He was a youngish and very energetic man, and impressed the Norwegians as the person who, more than any other, stood up for Germany's wishes in Norwegian-German whaling matters. In the course of negotiations with him in March 1935 for a change in the payment of whale oil via clearing, he declared that if the Norwegian Government's intention was to exempt whale oil from clearing, Germany would immediately implement her threat to start whaling on her own account in order to cover her requirements, a threat Norway was often to hear repeated.

The other interesting aspect of the sale to Germany was the exchange of goods that started with ships, ship repairs, and whale oil plant. After the sales had been concluded the Sales Pool was left with 131,000 tons; of this, 90,500 tons was purchased by Unilever at £10. Two floating factories were overhauled in Germany, and machinery for meat meal was installed against payment in whale oil. Anders Jahre had four ships built, which were partly paid for in the same way. In 1935 Lars Christensen acquired two tankers for transportation to and from the whaling grounds on the basis of Unilever paying for the boats with their blocked Marks as part-payment for the oil Christensen was to produce for Unilever. The oil acquired by the German yards was resold by them, mainly to Unilever's German factories, amounting in all to about 35,000 tons. Whale oil had become a form of international currency in a three-cornered transaction : the whaling companies sold their oil, the German shipbuilding yards obtained contracts, and the German state obtained the whale oil it needed to carry out its fat plan, and this it managed to do without dipping into its scant reserves of foreign currency, which had to be reserved for raw materials essential to a war economy. Indirectly, Norwegian whale oil was assisting Germany's rearmament.

Documents submitted at the War Crimes Tribunal in Nuremberg reveal that the German economy, from as far back as the summer of 1933, was based on war. In May of that year Hitler appointed a highly secret Reich Defence Council, in which Hjalmar Schacht was the supreme authority and Wohlthat his right hand. It was entrusted with the seemingly impossible task of covering, with the national coffers stripped of foreign currency and gold, the raw material imports of a wartime industry and the tremendous demands made by the Ministry of Food. This could only be done by increased German exports and by ensuring that payment for exchange of goods was arranged by clearing agree-ments, as foreign countries showed increasing unwillingness to discount German Government bonds. In the Defence Council Wohlthat was active, on the highest level, in fitting whale oil into the German war economy.

Immediately after the German-Norwegian clearing agreement had been set up, an interesting plan for an exchange of goods was submitted by the Norwegian JOHAN O. NYGAARD, the inventor of a method for the production of meat meal. It had proved technically feasible, but the low price of meat meal and the fact that the new machinery would involve scrapping practically all the old boiling plant, made the Nor-wegian companies somewhat reserved. Disappointed that the expected support was not forthcoming in Norway, Nygaard enquired at a German shipbuilding yard about the possibility of building a floating factory equipped with his apparatus. The cost would be some £400,000, and would be paid for by advance sales of the 1935-6 production, the value of which was calculated at £600,000. This would help to satisfy Germany's whale oil requirements as well as providing artificial feed for agriculture. When he applied to the Bank of Norway for this transaction to be included in the clearing arrangement, his request was rejected, as it would have meant far exceeding its limits, while at the same time the political situation in Europe was so unstable that it was difficult to predict how the situation would be in 1936. It was realised in Norway that a rejection of this plan might well involve the risk that it might be carried out entirely under German aegis.

Reviewing developments in 1934, it may be said that Unilever now had a rival buyer in the German state, and that Norway could sell whale oil direct to Germany and not through Unilever. At their general meeting in April 1935 D'Arcy Cooper was forced to admit that in Germany the task of supplying the necessary raw materials for their factories had now slipped out of their hands. At the end of the year plans for independent German or, rather, German-English whaling began to take shape, and the main interest in 1935-6 focuses on the dispute with Norway this provoked, and on the new nations involved in Antarctic and pelagic whaling.

23
NEW NATIONS EMBARKING ON PELAGIC WHALING

The Soviet Union

An *Izvestiya* article dealing with Russian resumption of whaling after it had been halted by the Russo-Japanese war opens as follows: "The *Commander I* left the Bering Sea in 1926. The practised Norwegian whale gunners puffed their smelly pipes and pondered the problem of the decline of stocks of whales in the Arctic regions. The Norwegians left the Soviet Arctic waters convinced that whaling along the coasts of Kamchatka and Chukotka was coming to an end. But that time the world's best whalers were mistaken." It was indeed this Norwegian expedition that prompted the Russians to resume whaling a few years later in the same waters. In September 1930 a Russian trade delegation visited Norway, and contracted for the building of three whale catchers for the State-run Souzmorzverprom company. In August 1932 these vessels sailed for Kiel, to join the floating factory *Aleut* of 5,106 gross tons, a one-time American ship that had been converted in Leningrad but had acquired most of its boiling plant in Norway. The captain on board was named SCHMIDT and the expedition manager A. J. DUDNIK. After 206 days this fleet reached Vladivostok via the Panama Canal, and caught twenty-two whales, mainly to train Russian whalers before catching started in earnest in the Bering Sea at the end of June 1933. According to the Norwegian papers thirty Norwegians had been engaged at a rate of 190 roubles a month. The gunner received 450 roubles, and a bonus of 75 roubles for a blue whale and 50 roubles for a fin whale, with a supplementary 50 per cent for the period during which operations took place to the north of 48° N. After the first three seasons the expedition manager would have earned 30,000 to 40,000 roubles, and the other hands 10,000 to 12,000 roubles. On the London Exchange the pound was quoted at 6.9 roubles. The Norwegians were only allowed to take 40 per cent of their wages out of the Soviet Union in pounds or dollars; the remainder had to be spent there. The intention was probably to induce whalers to settle with their families in Russia. In 1939 the Norwegian Legation in Moscow reported that during the first few years only Norwegian gunners were employed, but now only one was left, and the previous season one of the new Russian gunners had beaten his score by twenty whales.

In 1933, between 22 June and 6 November 199 whales were caught,

82. The first Russian floating factory *Aleut* at Chukotka peninsula in the middle of the 1930s.

of which 105 were fin whales, 57 sperm, 26 humpback, and a few sei and blue whales, and 6,705 barrels of oil were produced. In 1934, when operations started as early as 29 April, almost half of the catch, as in most later years, consisted of fin whales. The number of gray whales caught varied tremendously — 102, 9, 54, and 29 in the seasons 1936-9. Production reached a peak in 1935 with 19,398 barrels, slumping to 9,102 in 1938, rallying again to 18,854 in 1939. Every year the same matériel was used. In 1936 there were rumours that the Russians were about to have a 25,000-ton floating factory built in Hamburg for pelagic catching in the Antarctic, but in fact they did not start pelagic catching until 1946-7. Off Kamchatka the *Aleut* continued catching during most of the Second World War, and operations here were greatly expanded after the war when the Soviet Union annexed the Kurils and operated from the five one-time Japanese shore stations that had been established there in 1913.

Japan

In pelagic catching the Japanese reversed the Russian process, in so far as they started in the Antarctic in 1934 and subsequently in the Bering Sea in 1940, even though originally the idea had been the opposite. It may seem surprising that such an energetic nation as the Japanese,

so eager to try anything new, did not start using floating factories before
the 1930s. But from the Bonin Islands in the south to the Kurils in the
north it was possible to operate from land stations so close to the whaling
grounds that there was no need for floating factories. It was the Toyo
Gyogyo K.K. (subsequently the Toyo Hogei K.K.) which in 1929
planned to start pelagic whaling in the Bering Sea. One of the directors
of this company, T. SHIBUYA, came across a suitable ship in England,
but its conversion was abandoned owing to the collapse of the whale oil
market, and after being laid up for a few years the vessel was sold for
scrap in 1933, as a possibility arose of buying a complete Norwegian
expedition among the many that had been laid up. Through a Norwegian
firm in Kobe, Shibuya had an offer for the purchase of the *Antarctic*
with five whale catchers for a sum of £56,000. In 1930 the London
Exchange quoted the pound at 17 yen. Two snags threatened to
frustrate the deal. In Japan, as in Norway, there was a law banning
the import of old ships, while the Norwegian Whaling Act of 26 June
1934 forbade the sale of floating matériel to foreign countries. There
was considerable astonishment in the Japanese Foreign Ministry when
they were informed of this law. A request for dispensation was sent to
Oslo, and this was granted, even though the purchase contract was
not signed until 1 August. The Japanese Government then granted
an import licence on 11 August. The *Antarctic* was twenty-eight years
old, and for a ship of this age an import duty of 27.50 yen per gross
ton had to be paid. In order to cover this large sum, according to
Shibuya, the company would, at any rate in its initial season, endeavour
to catch in the Antarctic, and sell the oil in Europe.

Previously, ships had been sold by Norway to countries abroad, the
Frango to the United States, the *Sir James Clark Ross* to Denmark,
while Britain had bought or acquired control over several Norwegian
companies. The reason why the sale of the *Antarctic* caused such a
tremendous stir and aroused so much criticism was that this did not
involve a transfer to a foreign flag with the retention of Norwegian
management and crews, but was a sale of matériel over the use of
which Norway would exercise no influence whatever in the future. It was
also considered regrettable that Norwegian personnel were to some extent
involved. The argument submitted by those in favour of the sale was
that if we did not sell, foreign countries would organise new expeditions,
and there would be an extension of the total whaling matériel in the
world, instead of a reduction in already extant matériel. Sale could be
conditional to a pledge on the part of the purchaser or adhere to
Norwegian regulations. This argument augured an optimistic confidence
in the purchaser for which, as we shall see, there was no basis.

This sale also caused a considerable stir abroad. One of its sharpest
critics was H. K. Salvesen. He had been an ardent champion of total

83. Three prominent men in the start of Japanese Antarctic whaling: Tosataro Yamaji, Tokusuke Shino, Tatsusaburo Shibuya.

scrapping of matériel not required to fulfil the quotas laid down in the 1932-4 agreements. What so many had feared now became a reality : that moribund companies would be kept alive by selling quotas which they did not catch, while the sale of matériel enabled them to wind up without a loss. Salvesen was very pessimistic at the thought of the Japanese expanding without being subject to any regulation. One way of preventing this, he claimed, would be to allow their rivals, for one season at least, to catch on the same conditions. In the long run it would be better for a large number of whales to be killed in one season than to have the Japanese placing orders for fresh vessels.

The *Antarctic*, rechristened the *Tonan Maru* (rendered in translation by Dr. Hideo Omura as "Aspiration towards the South"), left Tønsberg on 25 October 1934, with Captain Seizo Kobayashi and a crew of fifty Japanese and seven Norwegians. In the ensuing season no Norwegians went; in 1936-7 there was one; in 1937-8 there were two Norwegian gunners. In Walvis Bay the floating factory met up with the whale catchers, taking on board the expedition manager K. Baba and 160 hands who had arrived on board a transport vessel. With a total crew of 223 and three whale catchers, operations commenced in the Antarctic on 23 December and were completed already by 17 February with a score of 213 whales (of which 125 were blue whales), yielding 12,955 barrels or only 77 barrels per BWU. The expedition returned to Japan via Fremantle in Australia, where the Norwegians signed off and returned to Norway, and by 21 March 1935, the first Japanese pelagic expedition to the Antarctic was safely back in Kobe. A chapter in the history of whaling had begun which even before the outbreak of the Second World War threatened to put other whaling nations out of business, and after the war actually succeeded in doing this.

There were rumours in Norway that the Japanese had bought Norwegian gunners for dazzling sums. This is hardly correct : owing to the considerable reduction in the number of whale catchers operating after 1931, gunners were in plentiful supply, and there was no difficulty in finding men who were unemployed. To start with they were paid a fixed wage of 200 yen a month and 50-60 yen per whale as a bonus. The position was a very different one after 1937, when the Japanese and German expansion meant a considerable increase in the number of whale catchers, and there was great competition to acquire gunners. Japan was then compelled to adopt the customary Norwegian wage rates. Two gunners engaged in 1937 on a two-year contract were guaranteed a minimum income of 30,000 yen a year, and in 1938 five gunners were secured on a three-year contract at 40,000 to 50,000 yen a season. The bonus was particularly high, some 200 yen per whale. In a highly confidential report the Norwegian Legation in Tokyo wrote that "even though Japan to a certain extent can manage with her own nationals, they would very much like in the first few years to have the services of experienced Norwegians to start the whole thing off on the right lines. This entails a serious danger to Norwegian whaling. In view of their ruthless and uncontrolled method of working it is to be feared that the Japanese will in a few years' time wipe out all the whales in the Southern Ocean." Everything had to be done to prevent this. Barring the Japanese from using Norwegian gunners and expedition managers would admittedly not be a vital blow, but it would be felt. However, nothing was done by the Norwegians — or, rather, nothing effective could be done.

That the Japanese were capable of managing on their own was shown by the *Antarctic* in her second season, 1935-6, when, without a single Norwegian on board, she produced 44,145 barrels, and by the time the oil was available on the European market prices were rising, while the Japanese home market was supplied with large quantities of whale meat, salted during the first few seasons, subsequently deep frozen. The first deep-freezing experiments were undertaken in 1937-8, and the first large refrigerated ship was despatched to the Antarctic in 1939-40. Both these events created tremendous optimism with regard to the future of Japanese whaling in the Antarctic. A third factor was that the sale of oil procured foreign currency for the import of raw materials for the armaments industry and for the stockpiling of fuel for the navy and air force. Furthermore, the floating factories were to prove their worth in wartime transport.

In December 1935 a delegation representing a new company, Taiyo Hogei K.K., made its way to Europe to investigate the possibilities of having a floating factory built or for buying design drawings and plans. On hearing this, H. K. Salvesen implored the Ministry of Agriculture and Fisheries to instruct all shipbuilding yards which had built floating factories not to sell drawings, because the Japanese carried out unrestricted whaling. The Furness Shipbuilding Co., however, sold the plans for the *Sir James Clark Ross* for £7,000. This was to provide Japan with the key to her tremendous expansion, and the Japanese had every reason to crow. The *Japan Chronicle* expressed this with ill-concealed delight: the British shipyard required eighteen months to complete the job, but the Japanese yard could deliver in four and a half months; Britain had no grounds to complain for not having received the contract, but rather should be satisfied with £7,000 for the plans. Japan was now well and truly launched on her programme of new construction, based entirely on these plans, and this would make the country a highly formidable rival to Great Britain, Norway, and Germany in the Antarctic. Most of the whale oil would be sold in Europe, providing the final proof to Britain's shortsightedness. Japan was within her rights; she caught whales in the open sea, and would conclude no agreement restricting her operations before she was in a position to negotiate on an equal footing with the other three nations. It was a matter of business pure and simple, and although the complicated nature of this matter might cause bitterness in certain quarters, the fact that Japan was a latecomer in the Antarctic was not sufficient reason for keeping her out. The whaling problem could be seen to be a warning to Britain as to what she might expect in her competition with Japan.

The Kobe shipyard broke all records in completing a ship of this size, when on 1 August 1936, after 157 days, the *Nishin Maru* (*nisshin* = always new) was launched. She was powered by diesel engines powerful enough to give her a speed of 15 knots, approximately 3 knots more than the European floating factories. The twenty-three pressure boilers were made in Japan, but six Hartmann cookers had been ordered in Germany. At the same time eight whale catchers were built in Japan, each of 267 gross tons, and with engines developing 795 h.p. With TOKUSUKE SHINO as expedition manager and three Norwegian gunners the expedition left Kobe on 7 October and called at Fremantle on 19 October. Here Shino died quite unexpectedly, just as he was about to realise the dream of his life: he had started life as a gunner as far back as 1907, had been one of the most ardent champions of whaling in the Antarctic, and become a joint founder of Taiyo Nogei K.K. Management of the expedition was now entrusted to RISABURO NAKABE, son of the company's president, and on 3 November they set off for the whaling grounds. Here, during a period from 13 November 1936 to 17 March 1937, 1,116 whales were caught, producing 91,368 barrels, 95.3 per BWU. On 15 May the oil was discharged in Rotterdam, and from here the floating factory proceeded via the Panama Canal to California,

84.   The *Nisshin Maru,* the first floating factory built in Japan 1936.

loading 19,600 tons of fuel oil for Japan. Formally, the whale oil was purchased by Unilever, almost certainly operating on behalf of the German state, just as the price reached its peak of £20 10s. The profit was stated to be 5 million yen — very useful when Japan was in very considerable difficulties with her foreign balance of payments. Practically all the meat had been scrapped, only a small amount being salted. Foreign whalers were seized with panic at Japan's rapid progress : that the whale oil should have ended up in Germany was part and parcel of the extensive trade connections between the two countries, ushering in the military-political alliance of the Tokyo-Berlin Axis.

The rate of expansion was disturbing : for the 1937-8 season Taiyo Hogei K.K. and Nishon Hogei K.K. each ordered a new floating factory, the *Nisshin Maru II* and the *Tonan Maru II.* The former was practically a sister ship to the *Nisshin Maru,* though a little larger, 17,553 gross tons, while the *Tonan Maru II* was built according to the plans for the *Svend Foyn,* which were also sold by the Furness Shipbuilding Company. She was of 19,262 gross tons, and had storage space for 2,000 tons of salted whale meat. For each of the floating factories eight whale catchers were built. One of these, the *Seki Maru,* was the world's first diesel-powered whale catcher, apart from the unsuccessful attempt in 1911-12, with an engine developing 790 h.p. During the 1937-8 season four Japanese expeditions in the Antarctic, with thirty whale catchers, caught a total of 5,582 whales and produced 388,683 barrels. After three seasons Japanese pelagic whaling in the Antarctic, starting from scratch, had risen to 11.6 per cent of the world total, whereas the Norwegian capacity during the same period had been reduced from 48.2 per cent to 34.7 per cent and the British from 49.1 per cent to 34.5 per cent. This in itself was alarming enough, but the full scale of this menace was obvious when keels were laid for another three floating factories for the following season, with plans complete for another two. Furthermore, the Japanese were interested in purchasing three Norwegian floating factories and one British one.

Japanese whaling appeared to assume such proportions that, with its low operating costs, it threatened to put Norway and Britain out of business, disrupt the whale oil market once again, and exterminate stocks of whales. When Japan refused to sign an agreement for regulation, and proof was adduced that the Japanese, among other things, hunted lactating blue whales, the Norwegian and British Ministers in Tokyo made repeated representations to the Foreign Ministry. After preliminary discussions they were left with the impression that the Japanese, with their low operating costs, were bent on knocking out their European rivals, so that they could have the Southern Ocean to themselves. The Japanese press agency issued an official statement to the effect that two nations (Britain and Norway) were anxious to halt the growth of Japanese whaling with a view to securing their own dominant position. For this reason the Japanese companies had opposed Japan's adherence to the agreement. Japan would not be prepared to negotiate with others until she had completed the building of her own whaling fleet, i.e. until it comprised eight expeditions.

Of the seven new floating factories that were planned, only two were ready for catching before the war, each with nine whale catchers. These were the *Tonan Maru III*, a sister ship of the *Tonan Maru II*, and the *Kyokuyo Maru* (*Kyokuyo* = Arctic Ocean) of 17,459 gross tons, built for the newly established Kyokuyo Hogei K.K., an affiliate of the Sumatra Takoshuko K.K. (Sumatra Rubber Co.). The latter engaged the services of six and the former of eight Norwegian gunners. All the guns for forty-nine whale catchers built in Japan 1936-9 were supplied by a Norwegian armaments factory. Much of the other equipment, too, was Norwegian.

For a number of reasons the large-scale planned construction project was not carried through: the war in China and the preparations for Japan's war to obtain "living space" in Southeast Asia absorbed more and more of the country's resources. From 1939 the war party in Japan adopted a policy that led to its alliance with the Axis powers in September 1940. World-wide rearmament had caused a sharp rise in the cost of shipbuilding, while the price of whale oil had fallen so low in the spring of 1938 that the entire Japanese production was sold at £12 16s, far below the estimated rate, while operating expenses had risen 20 per cent. On an average, companies can hardly have had a surplus of more than about 100,000 yen. The company directors were nervous, and between seasons employed their floating factories in transporting oil from the U.S.A. The price in the 1938-9 season was admittedly some £3 higher for oil, but expenses continued to rise. As a business undertaking whaling had not provided the dazzling profits envisaged up to 1937, but from a politico-military point of view it was successful.

In the 1938-9 season Japan's share of Antarctic whale oil production rose to 17.1 per cent; however, the Norwegian share sank to 29.9 per cent, and the British to 31.6 per cent, while at the same time another new nation, Germany, was responsible for 13.3 per cent. "The commercial and political rapprochement between Japan and Germany represents the greatest danger to Norwegian whaling," wrote the Norwegian Legation in Tokyo. "Owing to her present great difficulties Japan may one fine day turn up in Berlin and offer her whale oil production as payment for her purchases of German goods." On 28 July 1939 a Japanese-German trade treaty was signed in Berlin, one of the clauses of which pledged Germany to increase her purchases of fish and whale oil. The ominous growth that the catching of the new nations represented both to stocks of whales and to the "old" nations was the main reason for the London Agreement of 1937 and 1938.

Germany

The disputes between Norway on the one hand and Germany and Britain on the other, and later of Norway and Britain versus Germany and Japan, sprang from Norway's attempts to compel the other countries to regulate their whaling, to restrict the total quota and to prevent the establishment of new companies. In Germany this was closely bound up with Unilever's efforts to provide raw materials for their German margarine industry and to make the best possible use of their blocked accumulated capital. The entire pressure on the whaling front, however, was due to German and Japanese preparations for war, an acute lack of fats, and a rise in prices. When prices rocketed in the course of 1935 from £8 10s to £20, here was proof once more that a high price is the whale's worst enemy.

Before the First World War Germany had made three attempts to enter the field of modern whaling — in Iceland in 1903-7, in Chile in 1907-8, and in South West Africa in 1912-14. In September 1918 there were rumours of a plan for German operations in the Norwegian Sea, but this plan never materialised. Thanks especially to two persons, Captain OTTO KRAUL and Captain CARL KIRCHEISS, the idea was revived after 1927. The former was the only German with personal experience of modern whaling; he had even worked both as a gunner and expedition manager. At the start of the war he was in Argentina, and as it was difficult for him to return to Germany, he managed to find employment with the Compañía de Pesca, and spent the entire war in Grytviken. After a short period in Germany he returned to South America and became gunner and manager of a German-

Argentinian company in Buenos Aires. In 1930 this company went bankrupt, and Kraul returned home and attempted to find support for an independent German whaling industry. When this proved unsuccessful he obtained employment with the Russian whaling company, until he was called home to manage the first German expedition to the Antarctic in 1936.

That this should have seen the light of day was due in large measure to Carl Kircheiss, an adventurer and tireless champion of his idea. He had made a name for himself as one of the officers on board the famous German auxiliary cruiser *Seeadler* on her forages in the Southern Ocean during the First World War. After the war he completed a circumnavigation of the globe in a small fishing smack, and on his return set about clamouring for the establishment of German whaling. In order to gather more information he undertook a two-year voyage to the Antarctic, and along the west coast of America, right the way up to Alaska. He worked for a while on board a Norwegian whale catcher, recording his experiences in a book. In lectures up and down the country, illustrated with films taken on his voyages, he made propaganda for his cause.

As far back as 1927 both these two men had been in contact with the third of the pioneers, the president of the Deutscher Seefischerei-Verein, Baron JASPAR von MALTZAHN, who for three years had worked intensely to raise capital for a German company. Plans were sufficiently advanced for a search to be made in Norway for an expedition manager, preferably "a Mussolini type". Maltzahn died in 1930, and with Kraul and Kircheiss abroad at the time, plans were placed in abeyance until 1933, when fresh endeavours were made. There were four arguments in favour of German whaling: it would mean a saving of 50 to 80 million Marks in foreign currency; whale meat would provide excellent cattle feed; it would absorb a great many unemployed hands; and, from the point of view of national defence, whale oil was a very important fat because it is exceptionally durable and could be stored without much expense for an unlimited period of time. These were arguments that fitted in excellently with the fat plan launched by the Nazis. After the latter had taken over power in 1933, Government support was no longer a question of a guarantee to a private firm on a commercial basis, but of the realisation of a programme for a wartime economy under the aegis of the Government.

On 25 March 1935 the Erste Deutsche Walfang-Gesellschaft m.b.H. was established, with Kircheiss as a member of the board. When, after a year, it proved impossible to raise the necessary capital, the company was transferred to the soap manufacturing firm of Henkel & Cie. of Düsseldorf. The latter required fats for its manufacture of soap, but according to the fat plan the soap industry was allotted no oil quota, as this was entirely reserved for the foodstuffs industry. As there was a ban on the sale of expeditions from Norway, and there was no time available to have a new floating factory built in time for the 1936-7 season, as Henkel had hoped for, a boat called the *Württemberg* was bought and converted in Hamburg, where she was re-christened the *Jan Wellem*. After her conversion, she measured 11,776 gross tons, and was fitted with tanks for 66,000 barrels. She was in fact as well equipped as German thoroughness allowed. Apart from rotary cookers there was a plant for whale meat meal and 350 cubic metres of refrigerator space for whale meat, a plant for whale meat extract, and a machine for the production of synthetic wool from blubber fibres after the blubber had been reduced. In addition, this was probably the first floating factory whose technical machinery was entirely driven by electricity. Eight new whale catchers, some of them with engines of as much as 1,700 h.p., and christened *Treff I* to *VIII*, accompanied the floating factory. The managing director was DIETRICH MENKE, whom we shall encounter later on as the most ardent champion after the Second World War of a scheme for the renewal of German whaling. At that time the company still existed, though only in name.

One difficulty remained — the crew. Owing to the crew clause in the Norwegian Whaling Act of 1935 and the boycott instituted by the seamen's organisations in the summer of 1936, it looked for a moment as though the expedition would never set off. The reason for this will soon be apparent. The boycott had to be called off, nor could the demand for a 100 per cent Norwegian crew be maintained. The result was an almost exclusively German crew : of 272 hands, only seventeen were Norwegian, but — very important — the latter included all the gunners. In mid-September the expedition set off for the Weddell Sea, accounting in its first season for 920 whales and 62,000 barrels. The *Jan Wellem,* however, was not the only floating factory operating on behalf of the Germans; there were also two Norwegian floating factories and the *Terje Viken*, the first floating factory built in Germany and till then the largest.

The reason for the rise in price and increased demand for whale oil was due to a decline in the quantity of other edible fats and oils coming on to the market. This was due in part to a poor harvest, and in part to increased consumption in the producer countries, as well as Roosevelt's New Deal, which among other things offered a Government bonus for the slaughter of cattle and hogs in order to reduce stocks, and a limit on the area of land under cotton. In its review for 1935 one of the leading British oil-broking firms noted that for the first time for several years the market no longer suffered from the glut of previous seasons, which had not only depressed the whale oil market, but also most other markets for oil and fats. The rise in prices was not a steady one, fluctuations being entirely determined by Germany's whaling policy. In February 1935, with the prospect of the Germans having to pay what the Norwegians demanded, £14 10s, Unilever Raw Materials was authorised to buy for £16 for immediate delivery and for £17 for future delivery. The announcement on 14 March that the German Government, owing to a breakdown of negotiations with Norway, had decided to build a German whaling fleet and was anxious for Unilever's co-operation, had an immediate effect on the price, and by the end of March Unilever bought the whole of Salvesen's production for 1934-5 for £13 10s. In April, 63,400 tons were sold to Germany for £15 10s, and later that month Unilever bought 30,000 tons at a rate of £14 10s on behalf of the German Government. All the oil for 1934-5 was thus accounted for.

When twenty-one companies agreed to limit catching time in the 1935-6 season to 1 December to 15 March, and the Norwegian Government fixed a quota for the other Norwegian companies, while at the same time there was much talk of compelling the foreign companies to accept a quota as well, D'Arcy Cooper declared that this would mean a shortage of whale oil and a rise in price not only for that community but for other fats. Unilever informed the German Government that they could not accept the idea of a German whaling company before the services of Norwegian crews had been secured. If a company of this kind was not established, there would be a serious shortage of whale oil for the German factories; in the circumstances it would therefore be highly satisfactory if 100,000 tons of the 1935-6 production could be bought, even at a rate of £20. Unilever moreover had such large stocks of cheap whale oil that even with the high price that might have to be paid for that amount, there would still be enough for two years' consumption at an average rate of £13 11s. A rumour that the Norwegian-German problem had been settled was all that was required for the price to drop to £16. But as Unilever would not obtain as much oil as they had reckoned on in their contract with Lars Christensen, they were compelled in October 1935 to purchase 55,000 tons at £18. The price remained high throughout 1936, and during the first part of 1937. In December 1936 D'Arcy Cooper admitted that it was getting more and more difficult to obtain whale oil, with the result that Unilever was compelled to break off sales to third parties. In February the remainder of the season's production was sold, 66,000 tons to Germany and 96,000 tons to Unilever, both at £21. Japanese oil was likewise bought at this price, the highest price in the inter-war years after 1931.

In the early summer of 1937 the price showed a downward trend, continuing to fall throughout the rest of that year. One reason was the excellent harvest of vegetable raw materials, another the large production of whale oil anticipated for 1937-8, and the ability of German whaling to cover so much of national requirements that outside purchases would be greatly reduced. Buyers bided their time; the news that the Japanese, fearing a drastic slump in prices and in order to steal a march on their rivals, had sold 24,000 tons in February 1938 for £13 to Unilever and 42,000 tons for £12 5s, came as a great shock. Norwegian and British companies were now forced to sell at the same rate. When D'Arcy Cooper was asked whether he believed that the Norwegians would now give up the idea of whaling next season, he replied that the Norwegians no longer controlled whaling, and whether or not they operated was not of much importance, as Germany, Japan, and Britain would in any case do so. In Norway, the Japanese sales were regarded as downright dumping, to overcome a shortage of foreign currency, but this is hardly correct. The banks that had financed the expeditions were frightened of a complete collapse of the market, and demanded immediate and advance sales in order to secure coverage for their credit. When D'Arcy Cooper, with a certain air of triumph, declared that Britain was now about "to get rid of Norwegian tyranny", he was at the same time forced to admit that this "tyranny" was a necessity for the German whaling fleet which Unilever had been compelled to finance.

The idea of the *Terje Viken* expedition is said to have originated with a Norwegian expedition manager. A German yard had given him an option on a large floating factory and nine whale catchers, provided that he could obtain the necessary capital. The plan aroused the interest of the Hector Whaling Company in London, and through them the Svenska Handelsbank, who realised that this gave them an opportunity, in common with Unilever, of getting their frozen assets out of Germany. When attempts were made in Norway to prevent the building of the floating factory, the German Government retorted that it could not accede to Norway's desire not to support the building of this ship unless compensation was available in the form of other contracts for construction, not paid for under the clearing system. The Norwegian Legation in Berlin reported that permission to build the floating factory was given with unexpected alacrity; there was no reason for showing deference to Norway "on account of the passive attitude of the Norwegian Government to anti-German articles in certain papers". This statement was made on 22 June and it became plain that negotiations on this subject, which were carried on at the same time as the sales negotiations, were mere humbug on the part of the Germans when one of Schacht's assistants declared on 3 July that even before Easter the building permit had been "an established fact".

The Svenska Handelsbank transferred the matériel to United Whalers Ltd., a new company registered in London on 4 October 1935. This was in reality an affiliate of the Hector Whaling Company, in which Unilever owned 20,000 shares. The salient point in this complicated owner relationship was that the company was managed in London and could consequently be regarded as British. Payment to the shipbuilding yard was in the form of a guaranteed sale to the yard of 3,333 tons at a rate of £15, the rest being sold for £21. The company acquired a quota in a manner which once again revealed how difficult it was to limit catching as long as the passive "quota factories" existed. In return for a mortgage bond of £40,000 on the matériel, the quota was purchased from two laid-up Norwegian floating factories, as well as the shore station on Deception, plant which had not been used for whaling since 1931. This placed the matter outside the scope of the German interests of Svenska Handelsbank, the original motive for starting the company. The new floating factory, it was said, was not an extension but merely a replacement of old plant that was now being withdrawn from catching. In actual fact it had already been withdrawn four years previously, and it was quite inconceivable that it would ever again have been used for whaling.

In Norway, a storm of protest greeted the acting manager, who was also chairman of the Association of Whaling Companies, for placing his services at the disposal of a rival company. The papers used terms such as "traitor", and declared that the only way to stop Unilever and Germany would now be for Norway to abolish all restrictions and use all the matériel at her disposal. Such a threat of the total extinction of whales would make other nations reflect. Lars Chistensen asked Unilever not to buy now or later any of the oil produced by the *Terje Viken*. He received a discouraging reply to the effect that any purchase would be assessed on the basis of the market situation, and that it would be unnatural for Germany as the major consumer of whale oil not to participate in whaling.

That Unilever had nothing against a floating factory being built in Germany is revealed by an enquiry addressed to Smith's Dock Co. asking them if they were prepared to sell the plans for the last whale catcher they had built for use by an expedition for one of the German associated companies. The yard expressed considerable astonishment that a British company was prepared to support a venture of this nature, when British and Norwegian authorities were working for restrictions. Was there not a law in Norway forbidding Norwegians taking employment with foreign expeditions? If so, how would Unilever be able to man their floating factory in Germany? Nothing, however, could prevent the building of the *Terje Viken*, which sailed under the British flag, and, with her 20,638 gross tons, was up till then the world's largest floating factory. Thanks to the good price for whale oil the first season was successful, producing 17,384 tons of oil which, together with profitable freight carrying between seasons, yielded a net surplus of £106,182 and a dividend of $7\frac{1}{2}$ per cent. Next season's fall in price, however, despite an extra 2,500 tons produced, resulted in a deficit of £58,819. In time, Hector Whaling bought up so many of the shares that by the end of the 1940s they owned practically all the ordinary share capital in United Whalers Ltd. The *Terje Viken* was torpedoed on 7 March 1941, and was replaced in 1946 by the *Balaena*.

A contemporary German account states that "in Norway the idea of a German whaling fleet encountered tremendous resistance. Any Norwegian prepared to help Germany would be regarded as a traitor." On 28 August 1935 the Association of Whaling Companies had unanimously resolved "neither directly nor indirectly to contribute to the establishment of German-Norwegian or German or any other foreign companies". In Germany, too, the opinion was generally held that whaling was so specifically Norwegian that it would be unwise to interfere and upset the balance of trade between the two countries. But, it was said, "English capital, Japan, Russia, and the U.S.A. had long since broken the Norwegian monopoly". And why shouldn't Germany do the same?

Along with Otto Kraul, Carl Kircheiss and von Maltzahn, the Germans regarded WALTER RAU (1874-1940) as the outstanding pioneer of their pelagic whaling. He was head of a major concern operating oil mills, producing margarine, hydrogenated fat, vegetable oils, and cattle feed. He had long planned a German fat industry independent of foreign imports, which would be replaced by an independent German whaling industry. On 5 March 1935, three weeks before the Erste Deutsche Walfang G.m.b.H., he established the firm of Walter Rau Walfang A.G. He tried, unsuccessfully at first, to obtain financial support from the German fats industry and subsequently co-operation with Norway, before the German Government promised to assist him in contracting for a new floating factory, the *Walter Rau*, and eight whale catchers, *Rau I-VIII*. The floating factory, renamed the *Kosmos IV* after the war, was of 14,869 gross tons. As German shipyards had their hands full, and owing to the uncertainty of securing Norwegian crews, the floating factory was not completed before the 1937-8 season. In answer to an application for a concession the German Government replied on 26 June that for the time being they had no intention of making whaling subject to a concession.

"With the *Walter Rau* — a technical marvel — the Germans aim to revolutionise whaling", a Norwegian paper wrote. She was without a doubt the most completely equipped floating factory to date. There was a plant for meat meal, a pilot plant for blood meal, whale meat extract and vitamin preparations, a refrigeration plant for whale meat, and a canning factory. As it turned out, not all these devices functioned as expected, even though production of the various items during the first season was impressive. On the basis of 1,700 whales 18,246 tons of whale

85. The *Walter Rau*, the first floating factory built in Germany, 1937.

oil, 240 tons of sperm oil, 1,024 tons of meat meal, 104 tons of canned meat, 114 tons of frozen meat, 18 tons of meat extract (apparently the first to be produced from whale meat), 5 tons of liver meal, and 21½ tons of blubber fibre were produced. In addition, the expedition brought back 11 tons of glands for medical experiments. The expedition mustered 363 hands all told, of whom only forty-two were Norwegians. Out of a total of 1,434 hands manning the four German expeditions, 38.5 per cent were Norwegian; in the following season, 1938-9, this slumped to 26.5 per cent. Norwegian action to bar Norwegian labour from German whaling had failed completely.

That so many Norwegian whalers should have worked for the Germans was without a doubt a blow to Norwegian public opinion; this could, however, to a certain extent be excused on the grounds of unemployment caused by a reduction of the Norwegian whaling fleet, but that Norwegian marine engineers, Norwegian gunners, and Norway's most skilful expedition manager, Lars Andersen, should have terminated their Norwegian appointments or broken their Norwegian contracts because they were bought by the Germans for high wages, raised a storm of resentment. The newspapers wrote that Andersen was guaranteed Kr. 300,000 (*c.* £16,500) blood money, and that gunners would earn two or three times as much as in Norwegian service. Andersen's excuse was that the industry had been ruined by Norwegian whaling company executives, and that anyone was entitled to protect his own interests if there was a risk of finding no employment in Norwegian whaling. "Whether foreign countries take over now or later is in my opinion a matter of supreme indifference."

Norwegian anxiety reached almost panic proportions with the news in the summer of 1935 that Unilever contemplated building three floating factories in Germany. When the Ministry of Trade wrote to Unilever and to Berlin that the Norwegian Government would do everything in its power to prevent the new floating factories from operating, Unilever replied that Norway should try to understand the situation, whereas Wohlthat declared that no one had been compelled or induced to commence whaling under the German flag. But at the same time he pointed out that as the whale oil reaching Germany was quite insufficient for Unilever, "the company was forced by the currency situation to start whaling under the German flag, so that they could obtain the raw material they required. Moreover, Unilever's tremendous currency deposits could not be spent outside the country's borders." In other words, Unilever had a choice between suspending their production in Germany or whaling under the German flag. They could hardly be blamed for choosing the latter, in order to save their vast German investments.

Unilever were driven from pillar to post by Schacht, and finally had to capitulate completely: the freezing of their assets had started as far back as 1931, when they amounted to £7½ million. They then contracted for the building of ships, and when these were sold it was seen that 25 Marks to the £ had been paid in on the building contract, whereas the clearing rate was only 16.50 Marks. This transaction involved such tremendous losses that it was terminated despite an overtly expressed threat for a drastic reduction of Unilever's import and margarine quota and the expropriation of one or several of their factories.

This was the situation when Schacht in May 1935 proposed to Unilever that they should build a whaling fleet. Unilever protested, pointing out that Norwegian personnel would be necessary in order to operate, and the Norwegian Government was unwilling to allow Norwegian whalers to sail under the German flag. At the beginning of 1936, however, it became known that Schacht had invoked the aid of Henkel and Rau, and that these had agreed, on condition that they were given state aid and that the difficulties with Norway were overcome. Unilever was then forced to give in, and in May 1936 the floating factory and the nine whale catchers were contracted.

In the minutes of Unilever's managing directors' meetings the matter appears in a somewhat different light. After the breakdown of the Norwegian-German sales negotiations on 14 March 1934, the German Government had decided that a whaling fleet was to be built, and had asked Unilever to participate; and as D'Arcy Cooper put it, the most satisfactory solution for Unilever would be to be given priority in supplying Germany with whale oil, and an opportunity of spending their German Marks. The crewing problem would be solved, because in the ensuing summer, when the German expedition was ready, Unilever would be able to distribute their Norwegian crews among several ships, and gradually shake themselves free of dependence on Norwegians. In the light of this it looks undeniably as though the German proposal for a whaling fleet, on Unilever's account, came at a convenient moment.

The *Unitas* (after the war re-named the *Empire Victory*, the *Abraham Larsen* and, after 1957, the *Nisshin Maru II*) was built in 1936-7 as a sister ship to the *Terje Viken*, but as she was given an extra shelter-deck her tonnage was greater, 21,845 gross tons. The eight whale catchers were copies of the Smith's Dock Co.'s *Southern Star*. As the prices at German yards for ships built on a compensation trade basis were exceedingly high, the whole expedition cost 14.44 million Marks (£1.17 million). Of this sum the German state subsidy came to 3.5 million Marks. Clearly, Germany took advantage of Unilever's dilemma to exact a good price. When the British Government sold the *Unitas* as a prize after the war to the Union Whaling Co. in Durban for £1.05 million — whereas it was entered in Unilever's books at £375,000 — the latter could note with some regret that the Government had concluded a very profitable deal. When the Taiyo Gyogyo K.K. in 1957 paid £3,275,000 for the floating factory and its whale catchers, the high price reveals not only the inflation but also the value of the quota that went with it. In the *Unitas'* first season, 1937-8, a Norwegian was employed as expedition manager, and of the 420 hands, 197 were Norwegian. A total of 1,715 whales were caught, producing 20,054 tons of oil and 2,000 tons of meat meal.

The question of the ownership of the *Unitas* was a very complicated one, reflecting the structure of the concern. The floating factory and the whale catchers were in their entirety owned by the Jurgens–van den Bergh Margarine Verkaufs Union G.m.b.H., the company's German sales organisation. This in turn chartered the ships to the Unitas Deutsche Walfang G.m.b.H., Hamburg, a company established on 23 September 1937, with a capital of 1 million Marks, of which the above-mentioned Margarine Verkaufs Union owned 486,000 Marks and two representatives of the independent companies the remainder — in other words a shareholding majority. One of these was the chairman of the board of directors, of whose seven members Unilever had three and consequently were not in a position of decisive influence on the final stage, an arrangement which they were forced to accept. According to its terms, the charter was to be paid for with 54.2 tons of whale oil for every 100,000 Marks the owners had paid for the matériel, i.e. 10.94 million Marks.

As a result, Unilever's share of the first season's yield was 6,000 tons of oil (109.4 x 54.2). At a rate of £13 Unilever purchased the oil for £78,000, i.e. 8.76 per cent of its share of the capital. As all expenses, in accordance with custom, were paid for by the charterers and the production costs for their own expedition came to £18, Unilever, through the *Unitas*, acquired cheap whale oil for their German factories. As from 1939-40, the charter payment was changed to a fixed sum of 1.65 million Marks a season, but owing to the outbreak of war the floating factory did not catch that season. As the German company was unfamiliar with whaling, supervision of the building and most of the practical arrangements were carried out by the Southern Whaling & Sealing Co. (whose technical manager received £10,000 for his pains).

The *Völkischer Beobachter,* mouthpiece of the National Socialist Party, had announced that Germany would construct ten whaling expeditions. The reason why an ambitious programme of this nature was not realised was that Norway gave way to German pressure and transferred three expeditions to Germany, two by means of a charter and one by sale, and that a British expedition was sold. This in actual fact meant an extension of the total matériel, as two of the expeditions had been inoperative for several years. But in order to understand why, we shall have to retrace our steps by a few years.

24

THE DISPUTE OVER
WHALING REGULATIONS

The 1935-6 production agreement

The dispute on the 1932-4 agreements developed into a struggle for quotas in 1935 and 1936. Volumes could be written on this subject, particularly on the dramatic conclusion to this struggle in 1936. No agreement had been reached for 1934-5, the only limitation being that for most floating factories catching time extended from 1 December 1934 to 31 March 1935. This was not observed by Unilever's and Irvin & Johnson's floating factories, which produced 101,157 barrels prior to 1 December. Total Antarctic production amounted to 2,418,837 barrels. While the fact that this was only 60,000 barrels more than the previous occasion gave no cause for concern, a number of other factors nevertheless did so: production was about the same although there had been no limitation imposed either on the whale or barrel quota, and despite the fact that four floating factories and seven whale catchers more than in 1933-4 had participated. New British, Japanese, and German floating factories were being built, and improved prospects in the oil market would prove a temptation for re-introducing laid-up floating factories and abandoned shore stations. To prevent this was an important purpose of the work of establishing an agreement in 1935-6, while another was to prevent Lars Christensen achieving a large catch for Unilever. When members of the Association of Whaling Companies, despite endless and difficult negotiations and countless proposals, failed to reach agreement on a total quota lower than the catch of the preceding season, or on the distribution of quotas among themselves, both the Norwegian Government and the British Government intervened, though in entirely different ways.

On 10 May 1935, Salvesen wrote to the Ministry of Agriculture and Fisheries that he feared that, should he refuse to participate in an agreement, negotiations would break down. In response, the British Government decided three days later that the period of whaling should run from 1 December to 15 March. As the Association of Whaling Companies was not prepared to agree on the reduction of the quota bringing it down to the level demanded by the Norwegian Government, the latter set a quota on 21 June of 1,887,000 barrels of whale oil (sperm whale catching was unrestricted) and divided the quota among the seven factories on the following basis — 118,750 barrels for the large, newly built ones, 95,000 for the large converted ones, and so on down to 57,000 for the smallest. The Norwegian Government was naturally not in a position to impose a quota on a foreign floating factory, but Unilever promised to limit the catch of the two floating factories to 260,000 barrels (they actually produced 262,415). The *Svend Foyn* was in a special position, being granted 161,500 barrels, since this quota comprised all the companies in the group whose ships were not operating. In addition, the group received £45,000 from the other participants to the agreement in return for laying up a floating factory. A total of £145,000 was paid for the laying up of four floating factories, which were used for transport purposes. In Salvesen's opinion it was absurd to pay them, not for abandoning active catching, but for preventing them from resuming whaling operations which they had not carried out since 1931. This would have prevented a situation in which all four floating factories once again commenced catching in 1936-7, and on this occasion for foreign companies.

The total Antarctic catch for 1935-6 was almost the same as for 1934-5. The companies which, voluntarily or compulsorily, had joined the agreement caught 77.7 per cent. All in all, the agreements for 1932-4, despite their obvious weaknesses, had succeeded in stabilising production at 2.4 million barrels (400,000 tons), an amount the market appeared to have no difficulty in absorbing. The innovation in 1935-6 was that for the first time all floating factories reduced their catching times, none of them operating for more than 106 days (the Japanese only for 57 days), the shortest season up till then. This was a source of gratification for all who were fighting to preserve stocks of whales. Nevertheless, insufficient attention was paid to one particular factor: a shorter season could be compensated for by employing a larger number of whale catchers. For this reason the supporters of a stricter limitation in catching demanded that the regulation should also cover the number of whale catchers. This in turn could be compensated for by the various companies by increasing their efficiency.

The purpose of the late seasonal opening was to spare stocks of blue whales, which, as a rule, did not arrive in the whaling grounds of the Antarctic as early as the fin whales, and it was therefore poor policy to catch blue whales in the "lean" part of the season. This question was much discussed among the experts. A comparison between the average try-out per BWU in March and in November showed that in the first case the yield would be approximately 20,000 barrels more from the same number of BWU than in the latter. This was met with the objection that it pre-supposed the same catching conditions in both parts of the season, and as these varied greatly it was impossible to draw the conclusion mentioned. It should also be taken into consideration that when there were ample supplies of whales, the raw material would be less efficiently utilised than in a period with few whales.

Labour unions and whaling, 1935-6

The reason why the labour unions became so involved in the dispute on regulation was that for them this was a struggle for a livelihood. The 1934-5 season marked the breakthrough for organised labour. When the fleet returned home in the spring of 1935, most of the whalers were organised in a union affiliated to the Norwegian Federation of Trade Unions (L.O.). Here, as in all labour unions, the object was to improve wages and working conditions. In this particular case the demand put forward was compensation for a decline in fixed wages due to the shorter season and, partly, to the reduced catch caused by the introduction of quotas. The whalers succeeded in exacting most of their demands. One of these was that a greater proportion of the total earnings (wages plus bonus) should be included in their wage, the argument being that whale stocks and production, and consequently bonuses, would decline with every year. In the second place, they managed to get the bonus raised for floating factories with a small quota and lowered for those with a larger quota, thus ensuring that this part of the wage packet was just as big for a hand serving on board a factory with a quota of 60,000 barrels as for one with a quota of 120,000 barrels. Thirdly, the bonuses of the crews of the catchers were evened out. On one with a skilled gunner the bonus might be twice as high as on a catcher with a poor gunner. From now on half of the bonus was based on the catch of a single boat and half on the average for each one of the boats in an expedition. Fourthly, a bonus was not to be calculated according to the customary proportion between species of whale (1 - 2 - 2½ - 5), but according to the number of feet per calculated whale (1 calculated whale = 75 blue whale feet = 110 fin whale feet = 125 humpback feet = 110 sperm whale feet).

The result was an increase of about 15 per cent in average wages. Even so, this fell far short of earnings in 1930-1, the highest in the inter-war period. But in order to obtain a correct picture of this the time during which these wages were earned must be taken into account — 260 and 193 days respectively — and on this basis the increase in 1935-6 comes to 26.5 per cent, and monthly earnings during this season were only about 12 per cent lower than in 1930-1. It was pointed out, however, that whalers (and their families) also had to live during the remaining 172 days of the year on what had been earned in 193 days. Some obtained casual employment between seasons, but by no means all. What companies saved in running expenses as a result of shorter catching times was more than made up for by increased matériel in order

86.   Scrimshaw on sperm whale teeth was very popular.

to ensure full catching capacity during the shorter period. In 1935-6 there were one floating factory, twenty whale catchers, and 725 hands more than in 1934-5, but the result was some 80,000 barrels less. This can also be expressed as follows : in 1934-5, for 213 days, Kr.19.7 million (£1.1 million) was paid to 6,198 Norwegians, and in 1935-6, for a period of 193 days, Kr.25 million (£1.4 million) was paid to 6,865 hands to produce approximately the same quantity.

Organised labour had recorded a victory. It should be remembered that over 90 per cent of the whalers were Norwegian. Secure in the knowledge that foreign countries were entirely dependent on them, and conscious of the strength inherent in their organisation, they endeavoured to exploit this during the following season, not only in their wage struggle but also in order to compel foreign nations to accept the Norwegian form of regulation. As we shall see, this led to a very grave conflict with Britain, and to some extent with Germany too.

The British-Norwegian conflict, 1936

The Norwegian Government had made known its willingness to co-operate with the British on a joint regulation in 1936-7. At an exploratory meeting the British representative, HENRY G. MAURICE of the Department of Fisheries, and C. R. Darnley's successor in whaling matters, declared categorically that the British Government would never prevent its country's whaling from expanding, and that it was inconceivable that it would compel companies to accept a quota which they were not prepared to accept voluntarily. Astonishment was caused when he declared on behalf of his government that he was not against the use of the Norwegian crew clause, but, of course, not with the intention of enforcing regulations by means of quotas, but only against nations which were not prepared to abide by any regulations that Britain and Norway might agree on jointly.

No less than twenty-three different proposals were submitted for an agreement for 1936-7, i.e. almost as many as there were companies, all of whom were dissatisfied with the quota others had proposed for them. They were all anxious to exploit the rise in prices with as large a quota as possible, using all the matériel at their disposal. The average price for the season almost doubled from £12 in 1934 to £23 in 1936. One of the proposals was that floating factories not equipped with a slipway should be excluded : faced with this threat, work was immediately set on foot to construct slipways on three floating factories which had not operated for several years and which were practically ready for the scrapheap.

One of the proposals which appeared to have the greatest chance of being successful was submitted by Anders Jahre. It presupposed that the Norwegian Government and the seamen's unions would lend their support to press foreign companies to accept the proposal. The former could only do this by applying the crew clause, the latter by means of a boycott. For the moment the Government held back, fearing complications on the foreign policy front, but the labour unions prepared to make good their threat. They declared that they would refuse to commence wage negotiations for the coming season until a limitation of catching by means of quotas and time restrictions had been adopted. They also insisted on 100 per cent Norwegian crews in the expeditions of every country. In order to back the official Norwegian request to Britain and Germany to accept a total quota (for the Antarctic) of 2,265,000 barrels, the unions declared that it was forbidden to seek employment before the question of quotas, catching time, and crewing had been solved, and those who had already signed on with the German floating factory *Jan Wellem* were given eight days in which to cancel their contracts. They wrote to Unilever that they would use every means to prevent the building of a new floating factory in Germany. Unilever's board of directors discussed whether it would be possible to replace Norwegians with Britons and Germans; D'Arcy Cooper considered it encouraging that the Japanese were able to operate without Norwegians. Accordingly, the unions were told that it would be worse for themselves if their campaign were to result in others being trained to replace them. Unilever and Germany bought 85 per cent of the world's whale oil production, and were thus the largest purchasers of the unions' labour. The unions' task was to ensure that their members had work and wages, not to interfere in the management of a business.

Salvesen, too, took the same view of this conflict, and had special reasons for doing so when the blockade was directed against intended operations by the *Sourabaya* off Peru, between the Antarctic seasons. The unions blacklisted this expedition, until such time as Salvesen accepted the Norwegian proposal for a distribution of quotas and the demand for 100 per cent Norwegian crews. Salvesen accepted in part, pledging themselves to impose a limitation by means of quotas and to re-employ all the organised hands. The expedition was now able to set off.

This dispute was important for two reasons: in the first place it was regarded by the unions as a victory for the quota system, by implementing the threat of blacklisting a foreign company. In the second place, it transferred the dispute to government level, in so far as it occasioned the first diplomatic intervention on the part of the British Government. Salvesen reported the matter to the Foreign Office, which instructed its representative in Oslo to ask the Norwegian Government what it intended to do in the event of blacklisting. Although this was not expressed in so many words, it clearly emerged from its reply that the Norwegian Government looked with sympathy on the action of the unions, even though this was not concerned with wage and working conditions. The Government neither could nor wished to interfere with the unions' unrestricted right to negotiate and lay down certain conditions for their employment. Reading between the lines in this reply, it emerged that the accord existing between Government and unions was not the result of mere coincidence, as both supported the political party (Labour) then in power in Norway.

In answer to Norway's proposal for a total quota of 2,265,000 barrels, Britain replied in a note on 13 August by raising this to 2,529,000 barrels, which, together with the Japanese catch, would result in 250,000 barrels more than in 1935-6. This alone made the proposal unacceptable to Norway, but what aroused a storm of resentment was the division of quotas between the British and the Norwegian groups — in the first group 900,000 barrels to fourteen expeditions and in the latter 1,499,000 barrels to twenty-eight expeditions. Nor was this all: the Norwegian group also included South African, Panamanian, American, Argentinian, and Danish floating factories, and even the German *Jan Wellem*, which the Germans, moreover, declared would undertake unrestricted catching. A floating factory which had gone to the breaker's yard two years earlier, and eight without a stern slipway, which would never be sent to the Antarctic, were even included. Salvesen transferred his floating factory to the Irish Free State, as he said, to avoid British control. The general verdict in Norway was that the British proposal was a cynical attempt to make capital at the expense of others, and the note, a document which would for all time constitute a stain on the history of whaling, was not one that could be taken seriously. The situation was hardly improved when the British press published an official communiqué which repeated the monstrous assertion that the *British* companies would be restricted to a mere 900,000 barrels, while the *Norwegian* would have as many as 1,499,000. British official circles must have realised that the proposal was so unreasonable that it could not even provide the basis for a discussion. In order to support the Norwegian refusal, the trade unions informed the foreign companies on 15 August that if wage negotiations on the basis of the Norwegian quota proposals had not been initiated by 18 August, blacklisting would ensue on the next day.

The British Government expressed its surprise that the unions had anticipated the Norwegian Government's answer. It could be in no doubt as to the real connection. An answer was requested within forty-eight hours to the question of whether Norwegians would be forbidden to take employment on British ships, and if this answer proved unsatisfactory, the British expeditions would immediately be granted catching licences "with a minimum of regulation". The British Government had been forced to suspend the limited catching time because it was impossible to obtain profitable catches within this period with all the unskilled hands the companies had been forced to employ. A new set of regulations would be issued unless blacklisting was suspended within twenty-four hours, and this was an absolute condition for continued negotiations. Faced with this ultimatum, the Norwegian Government was forced to back down, and in response to its most urgent request the unions agreed to suspend blacklisting on 2 September. One weakness in using this as a lever was that the gunners, the key personnel in all whaling, were not involved. When asked by the unions they answered shortly that blacklisting was no concern of theirs.

With the suspension of blacklisting the last British condition for negotiations was retracted and — with two important exceptions — the Norwegian proposal was adopted in principle : catching time from 8 December to 7 March, the division of floating factories into four classes, A to D, with quotas ranging from 95,000 to 47,000 barrels and respectively seven, six, five, and five catchers; but there was no total quota, so that there was nothing to prevent all available floating factories being engaged. The other major source of resentment in Norway was that exceptions had been made of Unilever's two floating factories and Salvesen's *New Sevilla,* which had been placed in a special category with far higher quotas. The explanation was that they should be given the opportunity of making good the financial loss suffered because of blacklisting. This was interpreted as the British Government's way of retaliating against the intervention of the unions in the official negotiations, and in her final answer, on 12 September, Norway expressed this view in the usual diplomatic phraseology. In the Norwegian view there were no plausible grounds for placing the three floating factories in a special category, but Norway was prepared to give in to prevent whaling coming to a chaotic conclusion. The final word in this matter was exchanged between the Norwegian Foreign Minister, Professor HALVDAN KOHT, and the British Minister in Oslo, Sir CECIL DORMER, who said that it would be best not to stir up more mud, because the dispute would soon be forgotten. In British quarters, however, it was certainly not forgotten: during the negotiations in 1937 it was once again referred to by Britain in collusion with Germany, and in a very serious form.

The British-Norwegian whaling dispute of 1936 aroused considerable attention, not least in Germany, where it was followed with the greatest interest, as a solution to the conflict would have considerable bearing on the crewing of the German whaling fleet. A German professor of international law discussed the conflict in a couple of articles, and his conclusion, as might be expected in those quarters, went against the Norwegians. Intervention of the kind undertaken by the Norwegian labour unions was inconceivable in the Third Reich, which was not prepared to submit to catch limitations imposed by other states, but was *compelled* to obtain whale oil, irrespective of the state of the whale stocks. With the price at £21 a ton, Germany was not in a position to buy oil, owing to her shortage of foreign currency, so had to produce it herself; but once the price sank to £9 or £10 it could be considered worth buying.

The outcome of this dispute was a clear defeat for Norway. She had been compelled to abandon any idea of inducing Britain to submit to a limitation based on a total quota; she had to accept the granting of special advantages to British floating factories; and she had had to abandon the idea of blacklisting. Some gains had, however, been made: Britain had in principle accepted the Norwegian proposal, and the three exceptions merely confirmed the rule. The number of whale catchers had also been limited. The most important point was that the reaction of the labour unions had broken the deadlock and raised negotiations on to the international plane; without this dispute, the international conferences and agreements of 1937 and 1938 could hardly have taken place. The tragic aspect of the matter may be said to be that on the first and only occasion blacklisting was used in an international dispute on the regulation of whaling, this weapon was aimed at Britain, a country with which for thirty years Norway had shared whaling in the Antarctic, and with which there was every reason to continue co-operation, in order to ensure that the new nations would limit *their* catches.

What was the success of the other demand made by the labour unions, that of 100 per cent Norwegian crews in international expeditions? When Unilever announced that they were only going to employ half the Norwegians used in the previous season, it was decided to blacklist the company till all of them were assured of re-employment. The threat made little impression on Unilever, as they had Government assurance that they could catch without restriction, should the Norwegians create any further difficulties. Even though, during the initial seasons, production would be less with a mixed crew, in the long run it would be an advantage to be released from total dependence on Norwegian labour. Some 450 of their Norwegian crew were presented with the ultimatum to accept that one-third of the crew engaged were to be British, otherwise all the Norwegians would be dismissed. Two-hundred and sixty-six of them voted to accept this condition, with the result that the expedition set off with 75 per cent Norwegians and 25 per cent Britons, i.e. some 160 Norwegians lost their jobs. According to the agreement British gunners would also have an opportunity of "having a go" that season.

Statistics kept by Salvesen show that the number of Norwegians fell from 95.9 per cent in 1935-6 to 64.9 per cent in 1938-9, and in the latter season 296 one-time Norwegian crew members were made redundant. This was particularly the case with the floating factories and the shore stations. Most of the whale catchers clung on as long as possible to an entirely homogeneous Norwegian crew, as it was most important, when the chase was on, that no linguistic misunderstandings should occur. In the entire Antarctic fleet the 1936-7 season marks a decisive turning-point in the relative relationship between Norwegians and other nations. The decrease was mainly due to the fact that there were no Norwegians serving with the Japanese, apart from a few gunners, but very soon the Japanese were in a position to dispense with these too. In the second place, in the German expeditions the number of Germans rose from 61.5 per cent in 1937-8 to 73.5 per cent in 1938-9; on board the *Jan Wellem* it was 86.8 per cent and the remainder were not all Norwegians. Off the Faroes the Germans carried out exercises with two whale catchers to train their gunners.

In Norway, the real connection between Unilever and German whaling was only faintly understood. It was humiliating to the Nazi régime to be dependent on Unilever's German fat industry and on the amount of whale oil and the price Norway offered. It was an economic, national, and military aim to shake off dependence on these two countries.

The crewing development during the 1930s can best be illustrated by the increase of 2,200 up to 1938-9, but by then 3,000 fewer Norwegians were engaged than in 1930-1. As gunners the Norwegians maintained their eminence : in the entire world fleet of about 350 whale catchers at the end of the 1930s, Norwegians still accounted for about 80 per cent of the crew, and in the Antarctic for almost 90 per cent. In the latter the remaining 10 per cent were already Japanese. (For the nationality of crews in the Antarctic whaling fleet, see Statistical Appendix, Table 58.) Even the application by the Norwegians of the crewing clause and blacklisting could never have altered the trend, but merely slowed it down for a while. Antarctic whaling had in the course of a few years, changed from a Norwegian-British business enterprise to an international political problem, which consequently could only be solved on an international basis. It has been said that Norway, by banning the use of gunners in foreign expeditions, could have paralysed the whole whaling industry, but there were so many ways of evading this ban that it could never have been made entirely effective. During the dispute it was suggested that, should no other approach prove effective, Norway should despatch to the Antarctic all the ships and crews at her disposal, and without any restrictions "knock the novices and inexperienced out, so that there would be no whales or oil prices for writing off the new floating factories". Thanks to Norwegian-British co-operation a chaotic situation of this nature was avoided, and the basis laid for international control. Norway's relations with Japanese and German whaling would have been simpler if the competition could have been carried out on a business basis, but for both these countries catching was a state-subsidised preparation for war: in Japan's case by the sale of oil in order to procure foreign currency for rearming, in Germany's case to save foreign currency and, without having to spend it, lay up stocks of fat for use in wartime.

Norway and Germany in 1936

The whaling dispute between Norway and Germany in 1936 was a complicated one. It involved not only the sale of whale oil but also the sale and/or lease of Norwegian expeditions, Norwegian crews in these expeditions and in purely German expeditions and the Norwegian whaling tax levied on them, Germany's acceptance of the Norwegian-British system of regulation, the Norwegian-German clearing system, and the share of whale oil in it as well as wages paid to Norwegians employed in German whaling. There is no space to go into details. The main problem was as follows: was Norway to co-operate with Germany, and could she in this way prevent the building of new floating factories? Already in the summer of 1935 Germany had expressed a wish to buy one or several of the laid-up Norwegian factories, but as in accordance with the Norwegian Whaling Act there was a ban on the sale of matériel to foreign countries, Henkel & Cie purchased the vessel which was to be converted to the *Jan Wellem*. In October 1935 they were still willing to cancel the contract, if they were allowed to buy a corresponding floating factory in Norway, operated with a Norwegian crew and with a Norwegian manager. Exemption could be granted according to the law from the ban on sales, nor was there any ban on chartering to foreign countries. Later on protracted argument developed as to whether the term "floating factory" within the meaning of the Act meant "floating factory with whale catchers" or simply "floating factory" alone.

In Norway there were some who believed that their country could stop German whaling by selling at a reasonable price the quantity of oil Germany needed. Others were of the opinion that it would be better to sell two or three of the laid-up expeditions, as this would not involve any increase in total catching matériel. Sales would have to be carried out on the condition that Germany built no new floating factories, that 100 per cent of the crew were Norwegian, and that catching took place according to Norwegian rules. According to the production agreement between the companies for 1935-6 it was not permitted prior to 1 May 1936 to sell or lease matériel to companies outside the agreement, to build new floating factories for the 1936-7 season, or to assist others in doing so. When companies were asked whether the regulation should be suspended it was obvious that opinions were very divided. The majority were in favour of suspending them, but those who were against this pointed out that by then as much as $56\frac{1}{2}$ per cent of whaling was under the control of other nations than Norway, and every effort should be made to prevent this figure increasing still further; that new competitors would appear in the whaling grounds, and that Norway would lose her biggest customer. German national economic pressure, however, proved too powerful, Germany's politico-commercial hold on Norway too strong, and Unilever's economic interests in Germany too large for Norway to be able to prevent Germany developing her whaling. In this matter Norway stood alone : she not only had Germany against her, but also Britain and Japan. In answer to Norwegian terms for sale or chartering, the Germans replied that German whaling could not be dependent on 100 per cent Norwegian crewing, and for this reason, as expeditions during the initial seasons would have to make use of a great deal of unskilled labour, it would be impossible to place a time limit on whaling or to join in a quota agreement.

On 9 May 1936 two Norwegian companies applied for permission to sell or lease their expeditions (the *C. A. Larsen* and the *Skytteren*), and two days later the Margarine-Verband (the German Association of Margarine Manufacturers, which included Unilever) made the same request with regard to three expeditions. Norway answered that a sale was out of the question, and a lease only in accordance with Norway's two main demands : that 100 per cent Norwegian personnel should be employed and that a new floating factory should not be built in Germany during the charter period. When negotiations with the Margarine-Verband produced no results, the German Government gave Unilever permission provisionally to build one floating factory. The message spelt out by "provisionally one" was clear : permission would be extended if Norway would not come to heel. A statement to the effect that the German authorities could not prevent private companies from building could hardly be taken seriously in Norway. The German dictatorship could hardly be *so* powerless to control the interests of private industry. As things turned out, permission had already been given two months previously. The Margarine-Verband declared that it was willing to issue a statement to the effect that it would undertake no extension (by new construction), but a statement of this kind was never issued, despite the fact that Norway on several occasions reminded them of it. As the Norwegian Government was not in a position to demand a similar guarantee from the German Government in a private time-charter contract, Norway gave permission for the lease of up to four expeditions. Apart from the two mentioned above there was talk of the *Kosmos* and the *Kosmos II,* but chartering of these two failed to materialise, as the parties involved could not agree on the contract.

The Germans appear to have been willing to pay any price to charter the two expeditions, each of six boats, judging by the highly favourable terms obtained by their owners. The *C. A. Larsen* and the *Skytteren* were, pro forma, sold for Kr.3 million and Kr.3.5 million respectively to two new companies with 60 per cent and 40 per cent German capital. By contracts signed on 4 November 1936, they were chartered for four years by the Margarine-Rohstoff Beschaffungsgesellschaft m.b.H., an affiliate of the Margarine-Verband. The charterer was to pay £3 10s per ton of whale oil on an estimated production of 12,700 tons per floating factory. This calculated rental was for all four years paid in advance when the contract was negotiated. As the charterers — as usual in the case of time charters — paid practically all the running expenses, and the companies were able to enter in the books a 25 per cent depreciation per annum, this meant that after four years the entire matériel had been paid off and they were even left with a surplus. In addition to this the former managing directors were appointed as agents of the companies, at a salary of £5,000 annually plus £1,000 for office expenses, and the £24,000 this represented was also paid in advance ! Financing was organised through Hambros Bank, London, the Germans supplying the bank with four new 10,000-ton freighters which the bank in turn sold to Norwegian shipowners. The charters were just as unfavourable to the German charterers as they were favourable to the Norwegian owners. The former faced production costs in 1936-7 of £19 a ton, only £1 lower than if the oil had been purchased at the current market price. While expenses in 1937-8 were just as high, oil could then be purchased for £12 10s. The important point for Germany, however, was not to obtain *cheap* whale oil but to procure it without having to spend any foreign currency. At the negotiations in 1939 for an extension of the contract the Germans insisted on a drastic reduction in the rental to about £20,000 per annum, but the outbreak of war intervened.

Norway had suffered a still greater defeat at the hands of Germany in her whaling policy than at the hands of Britain. Despite a crewing clause and a ban on the sale of matériel, three Norwegian (and one British) expeditions operated in 1938-9 on behalf of the Germans, with several hundred Norwegians on board. Furthermore, a total of six expeditions produced for Germany almost as much whale oil as she had imported in 1935. Did this mean an end to sales of oil by Norway to Germany?

The quota dispute had only involved Antarctic whaling, particularly pelagic. Any restriction here could be made good by catching in other areas between Antarctic seasons (summer whaling). This was attempted in two places, off Australia and off the coast of Peru. In 1936 there were plans for sending four expeditions to Australia, but as it was obvious from previous experience that this would destroy stocks of whales in a short time, successful efforts were made to limit operations to the two smallest floating factories, one of which was the *Frango*, belonging to the American Whaling Co. Catching proved very successful. Both had voluntarily agreed to set a limit of 60,000 barrels, and this they achieved in ten and thirteen weeks respectively, and with a price of £19 10s this gave a large surplus, particularly in the case of the *Frango*, as the oil, being American-produced, could be imported free of duty to the United States. It was purchased by Procter & Gamble for £36, i.e. the market price of £19 plus £17 which it would have had to pay in duty, had the oil been produced by a foreign company. As might be expected, these prodigious results unleashed a spate of American whaling fever. The *Frango* also made good catches in 1937-8, though with a reduction to 42,550 barrels in the latter year, and as the price of oil had slumped to £12-£13, this venture was abandoned.

The other floating factory, the *Anglo-Norse*, after a season round Australia, operated off the coast of Peru with a view to catching sperm whales, undoubtedly attracted to that area by reports of the good catches made by two Salvesen floating factories there in 1936 between the Antarctic seasons. Within two months, the two floating factories had a total of 12,000 barrels of whale oil and 48,000 barrels of sperm oil. The *Anglo-Norse* reported 42,700 barrels in four months, not enough, however, to ensure a surplus. Salvesen repeated the operation in 1937, this time, too, with good results, but did not return in 1938. In that year the only floating factory in these waters was the *Jan Wellem,* when pelagic catching was carried out in this area for the last time before the war.

The above-mentioned whaling operations brought to a head a question which had always existed regarding a ban on whaling between the Antarctic seasons with matériel that had been used there; or *vice versa,* a ban on catching in the Antarctic with matériel which in the preceding summer had operated in other whaling grounds. The final agreement between Norway and Britain in 1936 included a provision to the effect that matériel that had operated to the south of 40°S should not be allowed to catch between 40°S and the Equator after 8 March (the concluding day for pelagic Antarctic whaling). The agreement, however, was never ratified, and even if it had been it would not have applied to Salvesen's factories, which were registered in Ireland, or to the others registered outside Norway and Britain. Uncertainty on this point resulted in a bitter conflict in 1937, mainly because of the extended and resumed American whaling operations, which were to take place in Australian waters. The only rule adopted at the Conference in London in 1937 was ˙that the catching time for shore stations should be six months per annum, and that outside this period it was forbidden to use whale catchers in any other whaling grounds. This resulted in a complicated argument as to whether a moored floating factory was a floating factory or a shore station, or a floating shore station. All of these definitions involved special advantages for particular people, and the important thing was to discover the one which at the opportune moment proved most advantageous.

Now that whaling had become an international problem, national authorities had had to intervene in the negotiations and conduct them at government level. The whaling organisations were forced to restrict themselves to economic, commercial, and technical problems. Pressure on the part of the employees to obtain a collective wage agreement resulted in the Association of Whaling Companies being compelled to set up an Employers' Association in 1936. Its first task was to deal with the wage negotiations for 1936-7. The good price commanded by whale oil made it easy to agree on a wage rise of about 20 per cent. The 40 or 50 different grades that existed previously were now slimmed down to twelve groups. The principle of equal wages, irrespective of the size of the floating factory, i.e. a larger bonus the smaller the floating factory, was also adopted. The working day was twelve hours minus two hours for meals. All hands were obliged to work overtime night and day, Sundays and holidays. The companies in other countries accepted the Norwegian wage scale without much demur. In 1937, too, whalers received a considerable raise in wages, but when the price of oil in 1938 dropped to practically half, approaching the 1932 level, the result was a marked slump in wages for 1938-9.

The pelagic Antarctic catch for 1936-7 amounted to 2,527,000 barrels, 257,000 barrels more than in 1935-6, accounted for by thirty floating factories and 184 whale catchers compared with 24 floating factories and 165 whale catchers the previous year. The gratifying feature was that this increase was not the result of a larger catch, in so far as the BWU number was exactly the same in both seasons, but of a considerable increase in the number of barrels per BWU from 101.6 to 111.7.

Difficulties in arriving at agreements between the Norwegian and foreign companies resulted in the Norwegian ones establishing their own organisation in 1939, the Association of the Norwegian Whaling Companies (in 1953 this became the Norwegian Whaling Association). Reviewing the development in the 1930s, the leading personalities in Norwegian whaling had every reason to be pessimistic. Norwegian production in the Antarctic had fallen to practically one-third, while Germany's and Japan's was together greater than Norway's. Norwegian crewing of the world's whaling fleet had dropped from 100 per cent to 60 per cent. Many statements by leading executives are on record which indicate that they were losing confidence in the future of Norwegian whaling, particularly on account of the indiscriminate catching of the Japanese, who applied no restrictions whatever. Lars Christensen regarded whaling as a declining branch of his firm, and when his son joined the firm, he was told not to waste time familiarising himself with the problems of whaling. As the end was in sight, he had switched over to shipping, and already had ten vessels active in the carrying trade. Who was responsible for the way things had gone? Among members of the Norwegian Labour Government there was no doubt that it was the greedy desire for profit of the whaling company directors that had brought about the dilemma of Norwegian whaling. In an attempt to stave off a final catastrophe, the Association of Whaling Companies was excluded from the coming negotiations; the Government even wished to have control of the purely commercial sales negotiations, out of consideration for Norwegian trade relations with other countries. The State Whaling Board, which represented the whaling industry, was dissolved in 1937 and replaced by a new one, which represented the State. We shall encounter its chairman, Professor BIRGER BERGERSEN, again and again in international negotiations, for the drafting of which he was mainly responsible. He was the obvious representative at international congresses, and the first chairman of the International Whaling Commission.

25

THE LONDON AGREEMENT OF 1937

During the period from 1904 to 1925, when Antarctic whaling was based on British territory, Great Britain alone was in a position to regulate catching. As catching during the ensuing ten years was confined essentially to Norwegian and British expeditions, a bilateral agreement between these countries was sufficient to cover practically all operations. Argentina and the Union of South Africa had partially supported these agreements. A great many nations, however, held off : not only Japan, Germany, and the United States, but also, in a formal sense, non-whaling nations such as Denmark, France, the Irish Free State, Canada, Panama, and New Zealand. On the basis of the flag flown, twelve countries participated in Antarctic pelagic whaling in the course of the 1930s; if regulation of this catching was to be effective, an agreement on the subject had to be ratified by all these countries, and an agreement covering global whaling had to involve a number of other countries, too. This was the purpose of the London Conference of 24 May to 7 June 1937.

The Conference was organised at the initiative of the Norwegian Foreign Ministry, and the head of this department, Halvdan Koht, soon discovered that organising international conferences was no easy matter. He had originally hoped to convene the conference in Oslo, or alternatively in Berlin, as this would hold out more hope of persuading Japan to participate owing to the political rapprochement between Japan and Germany. If it were held in London, it would appear in the eyes of the world that Norway had handed over to Britain her leadership in whaling policy. All requests from Britain and Norway to Japan to attend the meeting were rejected on the grounds that Japanese whaling was of such recent origin that as yet they were not sufficiently informed of the problems. Japan therefore preferred to wait until she could negotiate on equal terms. The other disappointment was that Britain, on 27 January 1937, replied that "for practical reasons" it would be best to hold the conference in London. This was the diplomatic reason: the real one was undoubtedly an unwillingness to send a delegation to Norway after the 1936 dispute. The third disappointment was the German reply, to the effect that they were unable to attend as early as March, as they would have to await the report from the first German expedition. Much against his will, and greatly disappointed, Koht was forced to announce on 2 March that Norway would entrust Britain with the task of convening the conference.

87. R. Kellogg (U.S.A.), Johan T. Ruud (Norway), N. A. Mackintosh (U.K.)—
three leading marine biologists and advocates of stricter catching regulations.

The Norwegian whaling companies represented the fourth difficulty. They had taken it for granted that they would not only be represented in the Norwegian delegation, but that they would also conduct negotiations on Norway's behalf. They nominated their representative, who initiated preliminary negotiations with Unilever, but Koht refused to allow the whaling companies to have anything to do with a conference which was to deal with an important international political question, and nominated as Norway's representative the chairman of the new Whaling Council. There were two other reasons why the whaling companies represented such a stumbling-block that the Government excluded them. One was the sales negotiations with Germany. On 14 January 1937, a sales pool consisting of Norwegian companies had offered Germany 100,000 tons at £25, making the transaction conditional on two points: (1) that any further lease of Norwegian expeditions should be made from among those already operating and not from among those that had been laid up since 1932; (2) that Germany should accept the same restrictions that might be imposed on the Norwegian and British expeditions in 1937-8. The offer was interpreted as an insult in Germany, and rejected out of hand; it was felt that the sellers' offer should be ignored, and that every effort should be made for Germany to produce the oil herself. Koht greatly resented the fact that the companies should have made the transaction conditional on terms of a politico-commercial nature; the Norwegian Government was unwilling to give a Government guarantee for the sum involved, unless an official Norwegian representative took part in the sales negotiations with authority to accept or reject the conditions of sale. This meant that the companies, who on 20 February were forced to sell unconditionally 66,000 tons for £21 10s, were stripped of all authority.

This by no means meant that the difficulties with Germany had been swept away. On 25 February 1937 a highly confidential meeting took place between H. G. Maurice and Birger Bergersen on the principles for regulation it might be hoped that the conference would adopt, and whether Britain and Norway, by joint action, could prevent German and Japanese expansion. A Norwegian plan aroused great interest with the British: the companies of the two countries should guarantee to cover Germany's whale oil requirements for four or five years at a price regulated in accordance with the price of vegetable seed. This would re-establish good relations between Britain and Norway, and stop German and Japanese expansion by satisfying the former's need for whale oil and depriving the latter of its major customer. In its very simplicity the plan was too ingenious to be put into practice. Moreover, it was frustrated because Germany was unwilling to accept a proportionate price for whale oil as against oleaginous seed. A meeting on this subject in Berlin from 10 to 16 April concluded with Wohlthat launching a violent attack on Norwegian whaling policy vis-à-vis Germany: if Germany encountered the same resistance in Norwegian quarters as in 1936, "nothing could prevent Germany from extending her whaling so that in addition to covering the country's needs, she would produce whale oil for sale on the world market in competition with Norway, and then buy oil seed instead".

Koht was very concerned at this German threat, and was willing to make considerable concessions in order to maintain friendly relations, but it cost him a great deal to agree to a dispensation allowing the sale of a Norwegian expedition, on condition that for three years mainly Norwegian crews were used. At the same time Wohlthat was made to realise that the Japanese had offered Kr.1.5 million more for the expedition, "and if we get nothing in return in the form of a promise from Germany, no one in Norway will understand why we should now turn down an offer of Kr.1.5 million". In diplomatic language it would have been difficult to state more clearly that Kr.1.5 million was the price Norway was willing to pay for German participation in the conference, but even at that price Germany would give no pledge that she would not further extend her whaling operations.

The floating factory Sydis — re-christened the Südmeer — which was sold with five whale catchers, was one of the oldest (built 1902) and smallest (8,118 gross tons) in the Antarctic whaling fleet. The whale catchers, too, were old and out of date. The purchaser was the Deutsche Oelmühlen-Roshstoff G.m.b.H. and the price Kr.2.55 million £140,000). The somewhat high price was due to the keenness shown by the Germans in the boiling plant on board the floating factory. That the Germans did not fully implement their threats against Norway was because in March 1938 they also purchased the floating factory Vikingen (re-christened Wikinger) with five whale catchers for £225,000.

On paper, these were sold by the Viking Corporation of Panama, but in reality by the Johan Rasmussen group of Sandefjord. Both Lars Christensen and Anders Jahre applied for permission to sell one of their floating factories, with whale catchers attached, but the application was turned down. An offer was also made for purchase of the *Tafelberg*. By applying economic pressure to Britain and Norway, Germany had succeeded, with a minimum outlay of foreign currency, in acquiring seven floating factories and fifty whale catchers to register a catch in 1938-9 of 77,982 tons of whale oil, 5,280 tons of sperm oil, 8,639 tons of whale meat meal, and various other products. Of the total crew of 1,886, Germans accounted for 1,386 (73.5 per cent). With a few exceptions, all the expedition managers and gunners were Norwegian. In 1936-7 and 1937-8 Captain Kraul on the *Jan Wellem* was also expedition manager, while a German combined both positions on the *Südmeer* in 1938-9.

Norway's position at the conference was undermined by one episode. In January 1937 many newspapers carried the news that Anders Jahre had visited the U.S.A. and taken part in the establishment of an American whaling company, the Western Operating Corporation Ltd., registered on 6 December 1936 with a Danish-born New York shipping executive, HANS J. ISBRANDTSEN, as its president. The latter was a cousin of the Danish shipowner A. P. Møller of Copenhagen, together with whom Jahre had started the Fraternitas whaling company in 1929. Isbrandtsen was then running a shipping office in New York, which was one of Møller's subsidiaries. There hardly seemed to be any doubt as to how the whaling company had come into being. The news was received with dismay in Norway by the Government, the Whaling Council, and the whaling companies, and all sorts of possible devices were attempted in order to prevent it, but in vain. A tanker, the *Ulysses*, of 10,780 gross tons, converted in Gothenburg, set off with eight chartered Norwegian whale catchers to catch off the coast of Western Australia on 11 June 1937, four days after the London Conference was at an end. Of the capital, one-sixth was American, the remainder British, Danish, and Norwegian. The captain and chief engineer were American citizens, and this sufficed to enable the oil to be imported duty free into the U.S.A. In addition, 331 Norwegians accompanied the expedition.

In Australian waters 2,036 humpbacks were shot, producing 78,750 barrels. The company was accused of ordering its gunners to shoot humpbacks as little as 30 ft. in length, whereas the London Agreement of 1937 specified a minimum of 35 ft. After discharging the oil into a tanker, the expedition proceeded to the Antarctic, and procured 114,015 barrels, thus using in these waters matériel which the previous summer had been used elsewhere. The plan of catching with the same matériel once again in Australian waters, however, aroused so much resistance that it had to be abandoned. With the two floating factories the *Anglo-Norse* and the *Frango,* the *Ulysses* signed an agreement to the effect that they would alternate in laying up for one season in return for receiving remuneration from the two engaged in whaling. No quota was agreed on, but catching was to last for 105 days. The *Ulysses* affair proved a great disappointment to Foreign Minister Halvdan Koht, who had expected that the conference might be started off with a declaration to the effect that Norwegian whalers would not contribute to any domestic or foreign extension of whaling tonnage; Norway was thus deprived of an initial position of advantage during the international negotiations. The American authorities, too, looked askance at the expedition, which once again reawakened the domestic fat producers' dislike of whale oil, and in a protracted hearing before the Congress Shipping Committee doubts were expressed whether the expedition was genuinely American : the conversion of the floating factory had taken place abroad, the whale catchers were chartered abroad, all personnel with the exception of two were foreigners, and the oil was transported to the United States in a foreign tanker. This vessel was forced to lie off for fourteen days beyond the territorial limit before being allowed to discharge the oil, while a bond was deposited in the event of duty being payable. The incident led to a law which stated that only whale catchers built in the United States, crewed by American citizens, could shoot "tax-free" whales. As Procter & Gamble, the only purchasers of the oil, were not prepared to guarantee that they would buy future production, and the price of oil slumped, the company's very existence was undermined. The floating factory was placed in regular tanker service, and sold in 1942.

The conference could now begin, a conference which hardly went the way the Norwegian Government had imagined, and at which the fight was lost in advance. Delegates of Argentina, Australia, Ireland, Germany, Great Britain, Norway, South Africa, and the United States participated, while Canada and Portugal sent observers. Two episodes occurred in the opening phase that struck a jarring note in the assembly. H. K. Salvesen drew the attention of the British delegation to the presence of the chairman of the Norwegian Seamen's Union in the role of expert adviser. This hardly augured well for an agreement with the Norwegians. Only the permanent delegates, and not the experts, had access to the conference room, because regulations were to be discussed that governments but not private organisations could enforce. The Argentinian delegate reminded the conference of his country's claims to sovereignty over the islands in the Falklands Sector, and declared that he could not agree to anything that would prejudice this claim.

The main lecture on stocks of whales was delivered by the Norwegian delegate Birger Bergersen, who dwelt in particular on the very marked decline in stocks of blue whales, of which there were numerous indications. Little or nothing, however, was done to prevent further decimation. Although on the basis of the available material it could be said with a degree of certainty that the minimum length for sexual maturity in the blue whale was 74 ft. for males and 78 ft. for females, and in the fin whale 64 and 66 ft. respectively, the Conference resolved that it was permissible to catch blue whales down to 70 ft. and fin whales down to 55 ft. So there were ample opportunities for catching immature animals. In the case of the humpbacks there was a greater measure of agreement: the agreement with the gunners of 1936-7 had set the limit as low as 30 ft., and this was now raised once again to 35 ft., which represented the estimated minimum length for sexually mature animals.

A proposal to restrict the pelagic Antarctic season to three months, from 8 December to 7 March, was frustrated by German opposition. It was extended by one week to 15 March. A proposal to reduce the time taken from the killing of a whale to the reduction of its carcass from thirty-six to twenty-four hours was also rejected at the insistence of Wohlthat, who also resolutely opposed any restriction on the number of whale catchers. The agreement which was signed by the nine delegate states on 8 June 1937, after sixteen days of negotiating, was a meagre document, and, with the exception of Article 1, contained nothing new. This article laid down that large areas of the oceans of the world were to be barred for pelagic catching of baleen whales. Approximately, this comprised all the ocean between the latitudes 40°S and 20°N, and the sea on both sides of Greenland. In other words, pelagic catching could now not take place in the Norwegian Sea or off the coast of Australia, Africa, and practically the whole of South America. The entire North Pacific and the Bering Sea, which were to prove the richest after the Antarctic, were open to pelagic catching. It seems strange that it should have been so easy for the conference to agree on a step of such significance, which has been maintained in all subsequent agreements, but the explanation is extremely simple: is was easy to bar pelagic whaling from oceans where hardly any pelagic whaling took place. Indeed 90 per cent of world catches in 1937-8 were recorded in the Antarctic, and of the remaining 10 per cent, nine-tenths was based on shore stations.

The primary object of the conference, to restrict catches in order to preserve the whale stocks, proved a total fiasco. It was unable to prevent 11,519 *more* baleen whales and 683,815 *more* barrels of oil being produced than in the previous season. It is probable that in the 1930s so much in excess of the maximum sustainable yield of Antarctic whale stocks was taken that even at that time they were dealt a blow from which they never recovered. The large yield of 1937-8 was made possible by a substantial increase in the number of whale catchers.

88a. Antarctic whaling: a catcher in heavy seas.

Although only one floating factory more than in 1936-7 took part, there were sixty more whale catchers, nearly all of them working with the Japanese and German floating factories. These two countries accounted for 84 per cent of the production increase in 1937-8, and only 16 per cent fell to the "old" whaling nations. The considerable increase in catches in whaling grounds outside the Antarctic in 1935-7, from about 239,000 barrels to 556,000 barrels, seems to have escaped notice. If this is taken into account, for the second time world production in 1936-7 plus the summer of 1937 totalled 3 million barrels. The third occasion was the following season of 1937-8 plus the summer of 1938.

Provisionally, the agreement was to apply up to 30 June 1938 but it was not to come into force before it had been ratified by five signatory powers. The last of these ratified on 7 May 1938 and not till then could Britain announce that the agreement had come into force. It had thus *de jure* not been in force before the 1937-8 season, merely between 7 May and 30 June 1938, when it was extended for the 1938-9 season with amendments adopted at the London Conference of 24 June 1938.

While the prelude to the London concert of 1937 had produced one or two jarring notes, its aftermath produced a very real sense of disharmony. On 9 July the British and German Ministers in Oslo presented themselves simultaneously at the Foreign Ministry, and handed over identical memoranda in which they demanded a written guarantee that the Norwegian Government would prevent a ban on Norwegian crews signing on with foreign expeditions. If a guarantee of this nature were not given before 8 August neither of the two countries would ratify the

88b. Moments later. Note the gunner on the gunner's bridge.

agreement. Foreign Minister Halvdan Koht was greatly incensed, not so much at the content of the memoranda as at the fact that they were presented in the form of an ultimatum, and at the idea that a Great Power should presume to issue commands to the Government of a small country. The Norwegian Government had demonstrated its goodwill by intervening in the blockade, and preventing it in 1936, and at the conference in London the Norwegian seamen's organisation had declared that it would not apply a ban in questions involving regulation. In Berlin and London, Norway expressed her profound disappointment at the lack of confidence the two countries placed in the Norwegian Government. In both capitals a certain measure of astonishment was evident at Koht's violent reaction. The Foreign Office asked that the memorandum should be regarded as never having been sent, while the German Minister even went so far as to request Koht to help him out of this embarrassing situation.

Though the seamen's organisations had forborne applying a blockade in the question of regulation, they were in a position to use it in a wage dispute, without the intervention of the Norwegian Government. This occurred during the wage negotiations in the summer of 1937, when the situation was so grave that the companies began to make preparations for laying up the fleet. On 13 September, the last possible date on which it could be despatched, both parties came to a new wage agreement, which produced an average rise of 11 per cent.

Much of the effect of the London Agreement was ruined by the un-successful attempt to restrict the number of whale catchers. In 1936 and 1937 the companies had undertaken the building of an unprecedented number of whale catchers, in order to make up for the reduced catching in other ways that the Conference would come to adopt. During these two years nineteen catchers were built in Norway, twenty in England, forty in Germany, and twenty-eight in Japan, a total of 107, of which twenty-three were for Norwegian companies, thirty for British, twenty-four for German, twenty-eight for Japanese, and two for a Panamanian company. This development was precipitated by a restriction merely in time, and had to be exploited to the maximum. The tremendous investment this involved imposed a great financial strain on the companies, and was the reason why they themselves raised the question of restricting the number of whale catchers. In negotiations with the Norwegian companies, Unilever, and Salvesen in connection with the London Conference, agreement had been reached on a maximum of seven catchers per floating factory. When Germany refused to agree, Unilever withdrew, and in Norwegian circles there was no doubt that collusion existed between the two in order to provide Unilever with an excuse for avoiding the agreement. The Norwegian Government took it much amiss that the whaling companies should have blamed them for the breakdown of the agreement, and when in the winter of 1937-8 the companies formed a sales pool and resolved to lay up six floating factories without informing the Government in advance, a serious clash occurred between the two. The mood of bitterness was occasioned by the very gloomy prospects for the economic result of the 1937-8 season.

26

YEARS OF RENEWED CRISIS, 1937-1939

The situation during the 1937-8 season was as follows. In Antarctic pelagic whaling the number of whale catchers was the largest to date, only subsequently surpassed in three seasons. The number of whales killed was an all-time record, and there were also signs that the production of oil would beat all previous records. The number of blue whales out of the total of whales caught fell from 43.2 per cent to 33.5 per cent, and of humpbacks from 13.6 per cent to 4.6 per cent. The result was a fearful slaughter of fin whales, twice as many of which (28,000) were killed as in the previous season. There was only one conclusion to be drawn: the blue and humpback whales had been over-fished, and fin whales would suffer a similar fate, a prediction confirmed in 1938-9, when 7,200 fewer fin whales were caught, despite the fact that three more floating factories and twenty-five more whale catchers participated. Though the London Agreement limited catching to ninety-eight days, the four Japanese expeditions caught for 125 days. Any new international conference would have to set itself three goals: first, a reduction of pelagic Antarctic catching; secondly — one of the means of doing this — a reduction in the number of whale catchers and in the entire catching matériel, and finally Japanese adherence to the agreement. Neither a minimum length, a shorter season, prohibited whaling grounds nor other provisions had been able to prevent the catching in the Antarctic 1937-8 of 11,500 more baleen whales than in 1936-7. How many more, one might ask, had been *killed* but not recovered?

In addition to the above-mentioned problems the oil market collapsed in the course of the season. This was a matter of minor importance to Germany and Japan. The year 1937 had opened with sales at £22 10s, had then shown a slight decline, until suddenly in October contracts were being concluded at £17 for the next season's production. Apart from the tremendous quantity anticipated, the fat market in the United States as usual was one of the reasons for the slump in price: harvests of oleaginous seed, particularly of soya bean, broke all records. In the course of the 1930s, production of the latter rose twelvefold, from 200,000 to 2.34 million tons. At the beginning of 1938 the United States was landed with enormous stocks of fats and oil, which turned it from an importing into an exporting country. The news that the Japanese had sold 67,850 tons in February and March at £12 10s, and that Hector Whaling had sold its entire production to Unilever at £12, came as a bolt from the blue for the whaling companies which had refrained from

89.   Francis D'Arcy Cooper. Hjalmar Schacht.

selling oil in advance at £17. Unilever did not view the slump in price with unmixed delight: they had paid practically twice as much for a large proportion of their stocks as the current price, which in effect meant a loss of £185,000. Some of their rivals had been able to cover their entire requirements at the lower rate. Unilever was forced to supply De-No-Fa with Japanese whale oil, as the Norwegian oil had been sold to other customers, primarily to Germany, to whom Norway had been compelled to sell 107,000 tons on 9 April 1938 for £12 15s.

Of world production in 1937-8 Germany acquired 197,000 tons (including the catches made by the two chartered Norwegian expeditions) and Britain 215,600 tons. If we include Unilever's own production, 47.6 per cent was accounted for by the British and 32.5 per cent by the Germans. The experience of the First World War had shown that in a new war supplies of fat would prove Germany's Achilles heel. Chamberlain had stated that it was less important for Britain to secure whale oil than to prevent Germany getting it. In this respect a large measure of success was achieved. In April 1937 Wohlthat declared that Germany would require 200,000 tons of the 1937-8 production, and she acquired almost exactly this amount in 1938, one-half from her own production and one-half by purchases, but in 1939 only 110,200 tons (including 20,000 tons which Wohlthat calculated that Unilever would supply for their German factories). In May 1940 Germany's reserves of whale oil were estimated at 114,310 tons, whereas Britain had four times as much, some 468,000 tons. Germany, in fact, started the war with a deficit in her calculated reserves of whale oil. What this led to, and how Germany during the war supplemented her meagre stocks, constitute two dramatic events.

On 8 October 1937 twelve companies, with an equal number of

floating factories — seven Norwegian, three British, and two under the Panamanian flag, which in reality were Norwegian-British — formed a Sales Pool (the agreement was renewed on 7 November 1938). The agreement also stipulated that six floating factories were to be withdrawn from whaling and employed in the carrying trade, the earnings to be divided pro rata among the companies whaling. The Sales Pool secured storage space for 165,000 tons, most of the quantity at its disposal. The Norwegians' first offer to Germany was 110,000 tons at £13 via the clearing account, i.e. payment over a year on the basis of twelve monthly bills of exchange. In any comparison with the subsequent British offer it is important to note that 10s was always deducted from the German price to cover clearing expenses. For this reason, £13 in Germany would correspond to £12 10s net in Britain, where payment was also cash. A difference in price of 10s may appear insignificant, but as we shall see, it was to prove of the very greatest importance in the final phase of the struggle between the two great powers for Norwegian whale oil. Norwegian sellers also suffered a certain loss of interest on sales via clearing. The Germans were willing to purchase the 100,000 tons for £13 (via clearing), but were annoyed that the Norwegians introduced matters that had no bearing on the sale: Norwegian state guarantees and at the same time a sale to Unilever of 50,000 tons. They were also surprised that Norwegian companies failed to appreciate significantly the fact that they were dealing with a *government* and not with an oil broker in the City or any other private firm. This is an argument constantly cropping up in German quarters, and one that involved a great deal of prestige. The sellers' attitude was an insult to the Third Reich. When the German offer was finally rejected, because Unilever was unwilling to buy at the same time, the German negotiators declared that 24 February 1938 was a day that would not be forgotten. Maybe the Germans remembered this when they invaded Norway two years later?

Under pressure from the Norwegian Government, the Sales Pool repeated its offer on 18 March without insisting that Unilever should buy at the same time, and the deal went through. The demand could be more easily weighed, as the British Government bought the 50,000 tons for emergency stores. The purchase was undertaken in the greatest secrecy by an oil broker, and very few knew that he was acting on behalf of the Government. The Sales Pool had no need to store any of the oil, because in May the whole lot was sold at an average price of £13 2s. This was a little lower than working costs, and all the companies involved therefore showed a deficit, while the prospects for 1938-9 were very gloomy. The attempt to form a new international sales pool failed because the Norwegian Government was against foreign companies participating in sales via the Norwegian-German clearing system, and the companies refused to participate if they had no opportunity of doing this. What saved the sale in 1937-8 was the British Government's unexpected purchase of 130,000 tons. When Chamberlain returned from Munich waving a scrap of paper mortgaged for "peace in our time", Unilever thanked him cordially for saving the peace. It was therefore probable that the British Government would release its emergency stores on to the market, and this would mean a complete collapse. It had proved impossible to arrive at an agreement on a restriction in the number of whale catchers. When the balance sheet for 1937-8 was published, shares dropped catastrophically. The situation for Norwegian whaling was desperate. On 21 November a general meeting in both Kosmos companies voted almost unanimously either to lay up the floating factories or sell them and invest the money in anything but whaling. Salvesen, too, warned his personnel that they must be prepared for floating factories to be laid up. That the new conference in London should have made so little progress in the question of regulation, and in fact on one important point even have taken a step backwards, was a further reason for the prevailing pessimism.

A preparatory meeting was held in Oslo on 19-21 May 1938 which was, in fact, more important than the London Conference of 14-24 June because at the meeting the course that the Conference would take emerged quite clearly. Although the head of the Norwegian State Whaling Board chaired the meeting, it was entirely dominated by Helmuth Wohlthat of Germany, H. G. Maurice of England, and Remington Kellogg of the U.S.A. The discussion developed into futile hair-splitting on entirely peripheral matters, which had little or no bearing on the preservation of the whale stocks, until finally Kellogg, taking the bull by the horns, came straight to the point: why had the 1937 agreement failed? With reference to the brilliant results achieved by international agreements on sealing and halibut fishing in the North Pacific and the Bering Sea, he submitted a revolutionary proposal which after the war was to constitute a pivotal item in regulation: that the sea around the Antarctic continent should be divided into areas, some of which should be closed, while for others a maximum quota should be laid down, and expeditions should submit a weekly report on their catch to the International Whaling Statistics, which, on the basis of these reports, would work out the estimated date when the quota would be achieved and order a cessation of whaling on that particular date, irrespective of whether the season had come to an end. Maurice agreed in principle, but was in favour of a global quota, which would be shared out among the various nations, and these in turn would share their quotas out among their floating factories. This was how the system was organised after the war. Wohlthat was not interested; he failed to understand how the system would work. Questions such as the number of whale catchers, a ban on the sale of matériel to countries not included in the agreement, and against the purchase of oil from such countries, were matters the assembly dared not even consider for submission to the Conference. All in all, the Oslo meeting reflected the greatest caution, in the hope of persuading the Japanese to turn up in London — which they did.

The most important amendments to the London protocol of 24 June 1938 were :

1. A total ban on the catching of humpback whales south of 40°S during the period 1 October 1938 to 30 September 1939.

2. A total ban on the catching of baleen whales for two years from 8 December 1938, to the south of 40°S in the so-called Area I (the Sanctuary), i.e. the waters between South Shetland and the eastern borders of the Ross Sea. (There was no difficulty in reaching agreement on this point, as very few whales were known to be found in this area, and no expedition would consider catching there.)

3. No floating factory which had operated in the Antarctic could catch baleen whales in any other grounds within twelve months of conclusion of the Antarctic season.

4. Only the floating factory which in 1937 had operated in the territorial waters of a signatory power could continue to operate as such and be regarded as a shore-based station with an allocation of six months' catching annually. This was important to the floating factories operating in Australian waters and off Madagascar.

5. The back-down involved, in order to placate the Japanese, was that, for catching from a land station, minimum lengths were lowered (from 70) to 65 ft. for blue whales and (from 55) to 50 ft. for fin whales and (from 35) to 30 ft. for sperm whales.

6. As some doubt had existed on the interpretation of the Greenland Sea and whether the Mediterranean was included in the ban on pelagic catching of baleen whales, a ban of this nature was adopted for "the Atlantic and adjacent areas north of 40° latitude south". As in the case of Area I in the Antarctic, it was easy to agree on a ban of this kind, because, apart from brief periods off the west coast of Africa, pelagic whaling in these waters had never been successfully undertaken.

7. There was considerable discussion on lowering the time allowed for reduction of the whale from 36 hours after killing to 32 or 30 hours. This ended in a compromise of 33 hours from the time the whale was killed until it was hauled on deck.

The final minutes are actually of the greatest interest to the history of whaling, because they set out the reasons why the conference failed to achieve more important results, and the concessions that had to be made in order to ensure the support of countries that had not as yet ratified the main agreement of 1937, in particular Japan and France.

An important point was that the Japanese declared that they would adhere to the agreement in one year's time, a piece of information that was received with spontaneous delight on the last day of the conference. The Japanese would as far as possible abide by the declaration during the coming season too. This statement was on the whole considered as the most favourable result of the conference, and well worth the trouble of convening it, but, to conclude with Bergersen's own words, "it might have been nice to return home with a little bit more in the way of results". It was of great importance that the main problems of regulation had been raised, and that the various nations had been made to realise that with every passing season a solution was becoming more and more urgent.

The 1937 and 1938 agreements were the work of marine biologists and diplomats. The agreements provided the whaling companies in their precarious situation with no relief; in order to improve matters they had organised the agreement of 1936 on the reduction in the number of whale catchers and of 1937 on the laying up of expeditions, and now in 1938 they tried once again to set a limit on the number of whale catchers, both to prevent over-production and also to put an end to a ruinous competition. But since Germany resolutely opposed this, and it proved impossible to enlist the support of Japan and Unilever, an agreement between the other countries would have had a very limited effect. One factor that made agreement difficult was that the proposals were linked to a ban on the sale or lease of whale catchers to companies not participating in the agreement, and a great many were precisely at that moment negotiating on this point. On 28 July the Association of Whaling Companies declared that this issue had now definitely lapsed, and that anyone was now free to sell or lease whale catchers.

Apart from this proposal, the Association of Whaling Companies submitted a number of others with a view to preventing a collapse of Norwegian whaling. Among other things the Norwegian Government was asked to summon an international conference, and if agreement was not arrived at between all whaling nations on a reduction, Norway should declare that she would abolish all regulations, as it was confidently hoped that in a free-for-all Norway would prove superior to her rivals. A proposal was sent to companies all over the world for a maximum of seven whale catchers per expedition and the laying up of at least three expeditions, of which one was to be Japanese. Negotiations, which also included Japanese representatives, were initiated for a total co-operation on production and sales. The position of Norwegian whaling appeared desperate.

Abroad, too, it was considered that the days of Norwegian whaling were numbered. On 13 January 1939 a German periodical carried a lengthy article on future prospects. It is of considerable interest because, by comparison with Nazi distortions, it is factual and based on precise statistics. After describing the relative decline in the share of the world catch enjoyed by the old whaling nations (i.e. Norway and Britain), the author points out that two factors more than any others have ruined Norwegian whaling: Germany, with her own large production had largely dictated the price, and for this reason could not participate in an international production cartel. The second reason was that Japan had largely exploded the myth that no whaling was possible without the co-operation of Norwegian whalers, and the possibility of a repetition of the dispute of 1936. Does Norway have any chance of despatching expeditions this season? No: it is difficult to reduce production costs still further, there are no new whaling grounds, the number of whales and oil production per catcher's day work is decreasing, and, technically, no major increase in the quantity of oil per BWU or in quality could be expected. Finally, the author predicts the following outcome: "There is every sign that England and Norway will lose just as much as Japan has won. The rapid expansion of the German fleet intensifies this tendency. Finally, after a shorter or longer transitional period, a new balance will be created, the results of which will probably be technically perfected whaling under German and Japanese supervision." But even for these nations "stocks of whale will one day be so decimated that the question of whether the whale can be exploited to economic advantage will involve the very existence of whaling". The article naturally presumes that German-Japanese expansion would have continued as planned, uninterrupted by war, and there are grounds for believing that the course of events would have been as predicted. As already mentioned, in 1938-9 leading Norwegian whaling directors were inclined to abandon the struggle on the whaling front.

As all attempts on an international basis had to be given up, the Norwegian companies formed the "Norwegian Sales Pool for Whale Oil 1938-9" on 7 November 1938, and on 23 October 1939, its successor, the "Association of Norwegian Whaling Companies". A proposal from the Association of Whaling Companies on 29 October 1938 to continue the old sales pool of 1937 with foreign participation for the 1938-9 season attracted a great deal of support, but was wrecked partly by the demand that all previous participants should join the new pool, and partly by the fact that a number of foreign companies refused to join as long as they were not allowed to participate in sales to Germany via the Norwegian-German clearing system. At this stage the result of pelagic catching in the Antarctic changed the situation, and the companies glimpsed a ray of light in the gloomy prospects ahead. It almost looked as though the whale itself regulated catching in a way mankind had failed to. With an increase in the matériel a catch of up to 3.5 million barrels had been expected, and the result turned out to be only just over 2.5 million barrels, in other words 636,647 barrels, or 106,525 tons less in the market than in 1938, with an expected price rise as a result. It was a striking decline, which provided champions of stricter regulation with a welcome argument : the consequences of the tremendous over-fishing of whale stocks in 1937-8 could hardly be demonstrated more clearly. As usual, when times were bad, the whaling managers blamed the weather, and that particular season they appeared to have good grounds for doing so. The number of man-days lost on account of weather conditions rose from 14.9 per cent to 18.9 per cent of the total number of days spent in the whaling grounds, and the number of days with zero production increased 47 per cent. Another factor, it was said, was that the whales were spread over larger areas than usual; this meant that the floating factories were constantly on the move. During catching days the distance covered per day by each floating factory was 22.2 nautical miles in 1937-8 and 27.8 in 1938-9. This represents an increase of as much as 66 per cent over the 1935-6 season. As far as complaints of poor weather are concerned, however, there is more than a grain of truth in Bergersen's remark at the Whaling Conference in London in 1939 : "We should, perhaps, remember that bad weather undoubtedly makes a greater impression when stocks of whales are small than when catching is exceptionally good."

Not all had a poor season, but in relative terms the Japanese recorded the poorest results. Although they had two large newly built floating factories, with a total of an extra eighteen whale catchers, and although they operated without any restrictions whatever, they only produced 59,000 barrels of whale oil more than in 1937-8. It is calculated, however, that if they had observed the same season 8 December to 7 March as the others, they would have produced something like 20,000 barrels less in 1938-9, despite the two new expeditions. This explains to some extent the Japanese unwillingness to abide by the London Agreement. Producing no more than 95.4 barrels per BWU, they were far behind the others. Norway had 112.2, Great Britain 110, and Germany 106.7. Once again, we must remember that in assessing the Japanese quantitative production of oil, it should be taken into account that a considerable portion of the whale meat, from which others would extract oil, was used by the Japanese for human consumption.

The average number of barrels per day per whale catcher (catcher's day work) was 99, not as low as 1929-30 (90), but in 1933-4 it had been as high as 162, and in 1937-8 it was 129. A slump of 30 barrels, 5 tons, would at a price of, for example, £14 a ton, mean whale oil valued at £77 *less* per day per whale catcher. As there were so few baleen whales, a far larger number of sperm whales were caught, and the production of sperm oil was exceptionally heavy, some 150,000 barrels, three times more than in the previous season. For this reason the price of this oil, too, was relatively low, and the market difficult, but even though companies failed to make big profits, it was important for the bonuses earned by the crews. The low production of whale oil and the consequent high costs would have involved companies in tremendous losses, had this not to some extent been compensated by the rise in price, approximately £2 15s, and a marked reduction in wages, approximately 22 per cent.

Reviewing its seven seasons, the managers of the Kosmos company faced the following facts: 1932-3, 222,244 barrels; 1937-8, 148,320 barrels; 1938-9, 66,294 — the last two seasons without any restriction by way of voluntary or compulsory quotas. The annual surpluses for 1935-7 of about Kr.4 million had been changed into a deficit. The company's shares were falling. It is hardly surprising that the managing director should have carried out the threat of implementing the powers conferred on him by the general meeting to sell the *Kosmos II*, just as the previous year he had been anxious to sell the *Kosmos* in order to invest the proceeds in a less risky form of business venture. At a meeting of Unilever's board of directors on 12 January 1939, D'Arcy Cooper presented a plan which appeared to have every prospect of success: to exchange the *Southern Empress* for the *Kosmos* plus a balance of £70,000. The attraction of this plan was to acquire not only a floating factory which could be operated economically, but also a ship built as a tanker, which the *Southern Empress* was not. This plan must have been changed because on 2 February the chairman of the board stated that for five weeks they had a firm option on the sale of *Kosmos II* and eight whale catchers for £272,000, adding: "It will now be possible to negotiate with the Germans for the sale of the *Southern Empress*." The advantage of the plan for Unilever was that it would satisfy Germany's demand for more whaling tonnage without having to participate in a new construction. Rumours of the sale made big news in the press, which maintained that in order to avoid the difficulties of a concession for a sale to a foreign country, De-No-Fa was to act formally as the purchaser; the *Southern Empress* would be sold to Germany, and would be paid for in terms of tankers which Unilever would transfer to Kosmos II A/S to pay for the expedition. The transaction was an interesting operation: had it succeeded, it would seriously have undermined Norway's position as a whaling nation and strengthened Britain's and Germany's.

Companies endeavoured to balance an expected large production, and consequently a drop in prices, by cutting down on operating costs, i.e. on wages, as other items were less flexible. Companies demanded a reduction of either 20 per cent in wages and 48 per cent in the bonus, or alternatively 32 per cent and 40 per cent. An innovation was a sliding

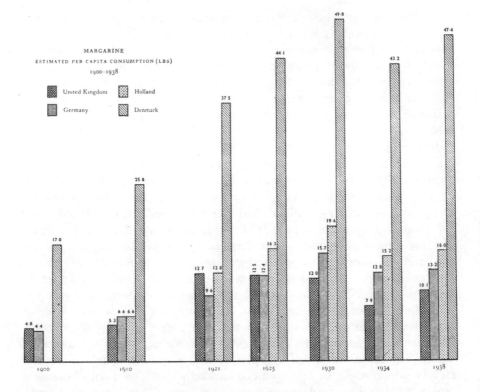

MARGARINE
ESTIMATED PER CAPITA CONSUMPTION (LBS)
1900-1938

United Kingdom   Holland

Germany   Denmark

90. Margarine: estimated *per capita* consumption (lb.) 1900-38 (from Charles Wilson, *The History of Unilever*).

scale with a reduction in the bonus of 5 per cent for every 10*s* the price of oil dropped below £13, and a corresponding supplement over £13. The proposal was rejected on 21 July 1938 by the unions, and companies now prepared to lay up their floating factories. The new season approached, and on 30 August a joint meeting was held in London by Norwegian and British trade unions and employers. A majority recommended a proposal for a reduction of 22 per cent, 5 per cent of which was to be a reduction in wages and the remainder a reduction in the bonus. This proposal was rejected by the Norwegian trade unions, which declared a blockade on all companies, including foreign ones, but when the British accepted the proposal, the Norwegians were forced to toe the line. They tried to explain away the defeat they had suffered in the wage question in this first attempt at joint negotiations with their British colleagues by pointing out that the engineers had withdrawn from the joint negotiations and concluded their own agreement. In 1939 the British unions concluded separate agreements with their companies, and in Norway the dispute had to be settled by arbitration. In 1938 gunners had accepted a 28 per cent reduction. Reduced wages and lower production resulted in a very considerable decline in whalers' earnings in 1938-9, despite the fact that the rise in the price of oil ensured an extra 6 per cent in the bonus, on the basis of the sliding scale.

The price rise was not so much a result of the Sales Pool as of intensified international political relations and, maybe first and foremost, because production was less than expected, in fact 637,000 barrels less, although an extra three expeditions and twenty-six whale catchers were involved. It was expected that this would make up for the reduction in catching time by six days. The decrease was clearest in the amount of catcher's day work registered, which fell from 1,014 to 784. Some surprise was caused by the fact that a rise in prices did not automatically follow, and particularly that Germany was not interested in buying and on 26 January rejected an offer from Norway of 100,000 tons. The Sales Pool secured storage space for this amount. When the Germans declared that they had stored 220,000 tons, which, together with a German catch of 80,000 tons, sufficed for one and a half years' consumption, this was interpreted as bluff, intended to depress the price. Unilever estimated German stocks at 130,000 tons. Another reason for Germany's diminished interest in whale oil was the tremendous purchases undertaken in the winter of 1938-9 of vegetable raw materials at extremely low prices. Of Manchuria's export of 1.37 million tons of soya beans, from the 1938 harvest, 790,00 tons went to Germany. In the third place, Germany assumed that Norway had no other purchasers, and if Norwegian oil was not available, Japanese oil could be obtained.

This was the situation in January and February, at a time when it was still expected that production would rise markedly in the last "fat" part of the season, but when final results were available in March, prices reacted instantly. On 11 March Salvesen sold 6,000 tons at £15. With some dismay Unilever noted that they only had stocks for twenty-six weeks, half of what was usual. The Sales Pool was approached with a view to purchases at £15, but held out for £17. The Germans were evidently afraid that they would be on the market too late and would have to pay a high price. They offered to purchase the entire holdings of the Sales Pool for £14 15s, but were turned down and told that the price was £16 10s (inclusive of clearing, thus £16 net). The companies informed the Government that they could sell to Britain for cash but were afraid of doing so for fear of German reprisals in the form of further extension of whaling, in which case Norwegian whaling would be doomed. The Germans were furious at the Norwegian refusal, and threatened the direst consequences : they would expand their whaling to such an extent that Norway would have no more oil to sell, they would use the clearing quota for whale oil to purchase other oils, and they would withdraw from the London Agreement.

As the Germans consistently refused to go any higher than £15 10*s*
via clearing, the Sales Pool offered the Norwegian Government 25,000
tons at £16 as an emergency reserve, but the Government was so
anxious not to do anything that might prejudice Norway's friendly
relations with Germany, that it practically asked Germany's permission
to buy this oil, and expressed its willingness to forgo purchase, should
this jeopardise sales. So far was Norway prepared to go in deferring
to Germany that her Government was willing to waive its right to
purchase reserves of 25,000 tons of fat at a time so critical that, already
four months before the outbreak of war, it referred to Germany and
Britain as "the two *belligerent* powers". After their offer had been turned
down by the Government, the Sales Pool was free to sell wherever it
could. An offer was forthcoming from London at £15 10*s* cash, and in
order to comply with the Government's earnest request to do everything
possible to maintain good relations with Germany, the Sales Pool made
a new offer, at 10*s* less, so that the price was £16 via clearing or £15 10*s*
net, the same price as in London. A time limit for a final answer was
set for 4 p.m. on 24 April. The Chairman of the Sales Pool has described
how he remained glued to his desk, a telephone in each hand, one on
the line to Berlin, the other to London. When a call came through from
Berlin at 8 p.m. which suggested that the Germans, despite everything,
were willing to pay £16, he was able to tell them that the oil had been
sold in London at ten past four. Thus ended the dramatic day which
the Germans swore would never be forgotten, on a par with 24 February
1938.

It is hard to understand why the Germans, shortly before the outbreak
of a war which was already a foregone conclusion, failed, mainly
because of a difference in price of 10*s*, to secure 80,000 tons of whale
oil, the most important raw materal for 160 million kg. of margerine,
which they could have had if they had been willing to pay £40,000
more than they offered. Many theories have been submitted and
Wohlthat himself has an explanation, which was that the German
negotiators were under such strict orders from their Government
not to go beyond £15 10*s*, that they dared not do so. The probable
explanation is that the Germans, after successive acquisitions — the
Rhineland, Austria, Czechoslovakia, Memel — were so convinced that
they were able to browbeat others, that they hardly imagined that such
a small country would dare to thwart their wishes. At the time Germany
possessed such large stocks of vegetable oils that it was difficult to find
sufficient storage space. The Germans were furious at their failure to
secure the whale oil, not so much because they failed to get it, but
because Britain succeeded in doing so.

Unilever considered the most important event in the whale oil market
that spring was that the British Government, in competition with the

German, had purchased the bulk of Norway's whale oil for £15 10*s*, that Germany had only acquired 13,352 tons, and would have to base herself mainly on her own production, which was not more than two-thirds of what had been expected. Whereas the Ministry of Food, in its own words, had "whale oil running out of its ears", Germany had "because of our buying of the Norwegian whale oil, started buying copra, palm oil, and soya beans steadily and continued doing so during the summer".

Simultaneously with the tug-of-war for the whale oil, another tussle was going on between politicians and biologists over the whale. The result in Norway was the new Act of 16 June 1939, which in the main was merely a résumé of all current legislation together with amendments required to bring this into line with the London protocols. The Act had been drafted on the assumption that so many nations would ratify the agreements in London that they would really apply to all signatory powers, and that Japan would support them. Meanwhile, the situation had become so complicated, with numerous agreements, protocols, supplementary protocols and recommendations, and who had ratified what, and what at the moment was a binding agreement, that it was difficult to decide what was the internationally applicable regulation for each individual country. The result was a hair-splitting discussion on the difference from the point of view of international law of the obligations inherent in an "accession", "agreement", and "ratification". Even before the London Conference of 17-20 July 1939 the problem had become so complicated that clarification on this point appeared as the first item on the agenda.

On this occasion it was Germany who had asked for the conference, because German expeditions in particular had suffered from a decline in catches. None of the other whaling nations was in any doubt that the real reason for declining stocks was the ruthless catching undertaken by the Japanese, starting as they did four to five weeks before the others, ignoring the ban on the catching of humpbacks or minimum size limits. Germany, Britain, and Norway despatched notes on this to Japan at the same time. The Japanese answer was so diplomatically non-committal and insipid that it could hardly be taken seriously.

Delegations from Germany, Great Britain, Japan, Norway, and the U.S.A. took part in the conference and Canada, Ireland, New Zealand, and South Africa sent observers. More than anyone else, Helmuth Wohlthat tended to dominate the conference. Hacking his way through diplomatic verbiage, he called a spade a spade. When the Japanese delegate declared that his Government would first have to adjust national legislation on whaling to the international agreement, Wohlthat replied that all the other nations had gone the other way about it, i.e. first adhering to the agreement and then adjusting their legislation in accordance with it. Japan had ample time to do so before the beginning of the next season. He stressed this point, with a threat that if an unconditional declaration of Japan's adherence was not available before the start of the season, the other whaling nations would come together for a separate conference of their own, to discuss what steps would necessarily have to be taken *vis-à-vis* Japan. Despite all the pressure, however, Japan went no further than to promise "as soon as possible" to take the necessary steps for formal adherence. When war broke out in September the Japanese Government informed the Foreign Office in a note of 11 December that the totally changed circumstances "will inevitably result in a decline in catching and occasion considerable price fluctuations"; for this reason the conditions for Japan's adherence no longer existed, and she was not in a position to implement her promise. However, "with a view to protecting the whale" the Government had instructed companies to observe the conditions "in line with" international agreement and hoped that the companies would comply with this request.

It is not difficult to see through the diplomatic hypocrisy of the Japanese note. At the same time the *Japanese Advertiser* announced that the price quoted for whale oil had risen to between £30 and £40, but owing to the war a great many expeditions would not be operating, and for this reason there would be less whale oil on the European market. Another newspaper wrote that each of the expeditions estimated profits of 7.5 million yen. There is hardly any doubt that this was the real motive for Japan's refusal to adhere; the Japanese now saw their chance of making up for the poor catches the two previous years. This, however, was not to be : owing to the war it was impossible to transport the oil to Europe, and instead it was stored in Manchuria, from where attempts were made to despatch small consignments by rail to Europe.

The same excuses were put forward for the 1940-1 season. Japan had actually increased its Antarctic production to a very considerable extent during the first two pre-war seasons, producing 483,476 barrels of whale and sperm oil in 1938-9, 538,862 in 1939-40, and 622,413 in 1940-1, using the same matériel in all these seasons: six floating factories and fifty-one whale catchers. In the last season the ban on the catching of humpbacks was not in force, and six Japanese expeditions accounted for 2,394 of this species, while the three Norwegian, two of which were seized by the Germans on 14 January, only accounted for 281, and the British caught none. In that season Japan actually accounted for 59 per cent of the pelagic Antarctic production. The usual accounts give the impression that Japan adhered to the international agreement on the regulation of whaling in 1939, but this did not happen until 1951, after the Japanese had resumed catching in the Antarctic in 1946. Generally speaking, the Japanese argument was that the more restrictions there were, the more difficult it would be for them to appear, and the Conference considered Japanese adherence so important that it was inclined to give way on the first point.

As far as more extensive international reduction of whaling was concerned the London Conference of 1939 was not only a disappointment but also in some respects a step in the wrong direction: the humpback was protected for only one more year, the area open to pelagic catching was extended, and an exception was made from the principle of a ban on pelagic summer catching using "Antarctic" matériel — each one of them concessions to meet Japanese conditions for adhering to the main agreement of 1937. Even so, the Conference did not succeed in extracting an entirely binding promise to this effect for the 1939-40 season. The final act of the Conference was to reject a proposal to convene in Oslo in 1940. When the delegates broke up on 20 July 1939 the Germans had already concentrated troops for the invasion of Poland, and six weeks later the Second World War was a fact.

How difficult whaling conditions were in 1938-9 emerges from comparison with 1939-40, when conditions were not particularly good either. Although, in the latter season, six fewer floating factories and forty-two fewer whale catchers were involved, production of whale oil only decreased by 187,745 barrels. In other words, on an average each expedition produced 9,457 barrels more than in 1938-9. Total pelagic Antarctic production amounted to 2,376,761 barrels of whale oil, approximately what it had been in 1932-7, and which it had been calculated could be absorbed by the market.

Finally we should mention that the excellent results of the 1935-7 seasons evoked certain plans for an extension of Norwegian whaling which it had been intended to put into practice in 1938-9, just as efforts were being made in international conferences to limit catches. Fortunately, none of these plans was realised.

27

WHALING DURING THE
SECOND WORLD WAR

The situation at the outbreak of war on 3 September 1939 was that Germany was precluded from whaling with her own fleet and that Britain was in a position to control all supplies of oil to Europe. Both in Germany and in Britain great importance was attached to the question of whale oil. In principle now, as during the First World War, the British were out to stop all Norwegian exports to Germany and they were particularly stubborn over the question of whale oil, which was definitely contraband. They demanded the right to check Norwegian stocks, and even wanted to decide where these were to be placed; they should be moved further inland in order to be safe from German attack. They would go no further than allowing an import to Norway of 50,000 tons in order to cover the country's own needs. In principle the German view was that completely impartial neutrality must be based on the principle of *normal trade,* i.e. an exchange of goods just as in peacetime, and in the case of whale oil this would mean an average of the import from Norway during the period 1936 to 1938 (86,266 tons). As oil was a Norwegian-produced item, the Norwegians should be allowed to decide exactly what to do with it. The Germans attached so much importance to whale oil that they submitted a proposal to allow the Norwegian and British whaling fleets to operate in peace, provided they themselves obtained a major share. In return for the oil and hydrogenated fat from De-No-Fa they offered to supply Norway with armaments, *inter alia* forty anti-aircraft guns.

The question of Norwegian whale oil was settled in two trade treaties, one with Britain on 22 February 1940, and one with Germany on the following day. The chronology in itself is interesting : Norway could not conclude a trade agreement with Germany before she knew what Britain was prepared to allow. On certain points Britain was very liberal in her concessions with regard to Norwegian exports to Germany. This applied in particular to fish, of which an export many times more than the normal quantity was allowed, and this is still more remarkable in view of the fact that this concession was made in return for Germany supplying the aforementioned forty pieces of anti-aircraft artillery, complete with ammunition. Britain's liberal approach on this point was undoubtedly intended to balance the rigid restriction on whale oil. The most Britain would concede was that Norway should be allowed to export 18,000 tons to Germany, inclusive of herring oil, hydrogenated fat, and other oil (only 12,360 tons of whale oil). This, it should be noted, was to be supplied from the quantity — 53,000 tons — which Britain allowed Norway to set aside for use in Scandinavia, or of the 55,000 tons which was the maximum Britain allowed Norway to stockpile. Even though this was totally unacceptable to the Germans, there was no getting round it.

The German negotiators had vowed that 24 February 1938 would not be forgotten, and on 24 April 1939 Britain deprived Germany of much-needed whale oil. In 1938 Germany had obtained 107,053 tons of Norwegian-produced whale oil (plus 29,223 tons from the two chartered Norwegian expeditions), in 1939 13,352 tons (plus 18,441 tons), while in 1940 they would obtain at best 12,360 tons. From this point of view Norway *vis-à-vis* Germany was supposed to be a neutral ally, as during the First World War. As far as whale oil was concerned it may be said that the invasion of Norway on 9 April 1940 took place too early for the Germans: at that time the entire Norwegian whaling fleet was on its way north from the Antarctic, and had the Germans waited a couple of weeks there would have been 55,000 tons in Norway.

It goes without saying that the bulk of Antarctic whale oil, 71 per cent, found its way to Britain, where the Ministry of Food purchased approximately 273,000 tons (of which amount Norwegian production accounted for 143,248 tons), together with Unilever's own production of just under 28,000 tons. By June the Ministry of Food had so much stockpiled that further imports had to be stopped and some of the oil stored in America. Owing to special freight considerations and because operating expenses had rocketed, Britain was prepared to pay a much higher price (£37 10s) to Norway than for oil produced by British companies. Thanks to the high price, whalers enjoyed excellent earnings, since the agreement had established a sliding scale for the bonus based on the sales price. Total excess earnings amounted to 96.2 per cent. Companies announced that they were in considerable doubt as to whether they should operate: crewing costs had risen so steeply that under normal conditions no whaling would have taken place at all.

During the war most of the world's floating whaling matériel was used for other purposes. Mineral oil was now more important than whale oil for the waging of war. Most of the floating factories were used as tankers, as well as carrying bulky war matériel on their extensive flensing plans. All the Japanese floating factories were incorporated in marine operations as transport ships, *inter alia* for the miniature submarines used in the attack on Pearl Harbor on 7 December 1941. These were said to have been launched and hauled up the slipway just like whales. The belligerents requisitioned practically all whale catchers for service with their navies, where they proved very useful as patrol and escort vessels, submarine chasers, and minesweepers. The slow-moving floating

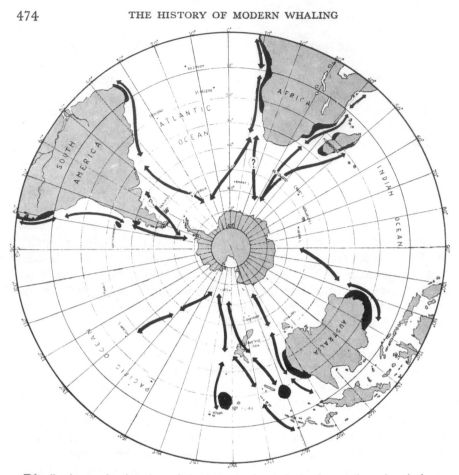

Distribution and migration of the humpback whale in the southern hemisphere.
(From E. J. Slijper, *Whales*.)

factories, with their considerable superstructure, proved an easy target
for U-boats, and there were heavy losses. Japanese and British floating
factories were hardest hit: every one of these serving under the Japanese
or British flag was lost, including the two South African ones. The
United States' two floating factories, which had been sold at the outbreak of the war to Japan and Argentina, and which were operating
as tankers, were also lost. Norway escaped comparatively lightly: five
of the previous floating factories survived to operate again. Relatively
speaking, German floating factories came off best: two out of the five
were sunk by enemy action, and three were found after the war
more or less undamaged. However, these were handed over as reparations to Britain, the Soviet Union, and Norway, so that Germany too
lost all her floating factories as a result of the war.

It has been calculated that about 40 per cent of the world's merchant fleet in existence at the outbreak of war were casualties. But at the same time so many ships were built in the course of hostilities that world tonnage was 8 million gross tons more in 1946 than in 1940. This was not the case with the whaling fleet. Of the forty-three floating factories in existence in the autumn of 1939, some of which had for several years been used only as freighters, sixteen sailed again after the war, twelve engaged in whaling and four in transport. If we include all of them, both the floating factories active when war began and older vessels no longer engaged in whaling, 63 per cent were lost, and only 37 per cent could be used again after the war. During the last season of peacetime (1938-9 plus the summer of 1939), thirty-seven floating factories had been engaged in pelagic whaling. During the first post-war season (1945-6), seven pre-war floating factories and two new ones were put into operation. But in the very next season, 1946-7, seven more joined in, two of which had caught before the war. (See Statistical Appendix, Tables 54, 59, 61 and 64.)

It is difficult to find entirely accurate figures for whale catchers. In the autumn of 1939 there were probably close on 400 throughout the world, but some had been laid up, a number were used for other purposes, while approximately 350 had been engaged in whaling during the previous season. The four major whaling nations, Germany, Great Britain, Japan, and Norway, had about 314 catchers; of these, about 112 were lost, leaving about 200. To these should be added fifty-six of the boats built during the war. Japan's losses were considerable: she lost fifty-one of the seventy-eight catchers she had had when she entered the war in December 1941. In addition to the twenty-seven that survived into the peace, there were eight built of wood during the war, designed apparently mainly for catching small cetaceans. The whaling countries apart from the "Big Four" lost few of their vessels as a result of acts of war. If we include the whale catchers of these countries, the total number of "survivors" and new whale catchers built during the war would come to about 300 at the conclusion of hostilities. Only a limited number, however, could be re-employed for whaling. Common to most of them was the fact that they had been used for war service, and their typical whaling equipment had been removed. Furthermore, they were so run down or damaged that it was not worth restoring them for their original purpose. A large number were also so obsolete that it was necessary to replace them with new ones. Despite the quite large number still in existence, the question of whale catchers proved a bottleneck for whaling during the first post-war seasons.

Total world production of whale and sperm oil was 343,057 barrels less during the first wartime season, 1939-40, than in 1938-9. All the German expeditions, as well as the two chartered from Norway, were absent from the Antarctic. Apart from these, the same expeditions took part as on the previous occasion, as well as a newcomer, *Uniwaleco* (ex *Fraternitas*) of South Africa. The same two shore stations, Grytviken and Leith Harbour, were also in operation in 1939-40. Although six fewer floating factories and forty-one fewer whale catchers participated in the Antarctic, the decrease in catches was not as marked as had been expected, only 276,518 barrels less. During the ensuing season, 1940-1, Japan, still neutral, operated to the full extent of her capacity with all her six expeditions, but only three Norwegian and two British expeditions did so. Of the land stations, only Grytviken was operational. Production amounted to 1.1 million barrels, 56.6 per cent of which was accounted for by Japan. Apart from Leith Harbour for a short period in 1941-2, the only whaling in the Antarctic during the 1941-3 seasons was based on Grytviken. In addition, one pelagic (Norwegian) expedition caught in each of the seasons 1943-5. During the four seasons 1941-5 a total of some 7,000 whales were killed in the Antarctic, less than a fifth of the last peacetime season, 1938-9. The effect this might have had on whale stocks was awaited with some excitement, and it was a great disappointment to discover that they had apparently not recovered as much as expected.

Not only in the Antarctic but also in most other whaling grounds catching decreased so markedly that for the entire world 1941-5 produced an average annual yield of only 238,700 barrels. Not since the years previous to 1909 had such low figures been recorded, and the number of whales killed throughout the world was probably the lowest since 1908. Average production of baleen whale oil during the same four seasons was 154,600 barrels, approximately a third of what it had been during the First World War. Neither politically, militarily, nor commercially, in fact, did whaling during the Second World War have anything like the importance it had had during the First World War (see Statistical Appendix, Table 60).

A striking feature of catches in all the whaling grounds of the world during the war was the relatively large yield of sperm whales. Only on one occasion, 1937-8, had numbers exceeded those for 1940-1, and in 1941-3 this species comprised 61.8 and 65.7 per cent respectively of the total number of whales caught. During the same two seasons the production of sperm oil was 49.9 per cent and 57.8 per cent of total world production of whale and sperm oil, whereas in 1938-9 it had been merely 6.8 per cent. The reason for this relatively large production was not only the poor catches of baleen whales in the Antarctic, but also the extraordinarily large catches of sperm whales off the coast of Peru, undertaken by the Norwegian Government in 1941-3 in order to meet a crying need for sperm oil for special technical uses in the American armaments industry. The war years proved a golden age for the "old" catching of sperm whales from the Azores; during the last two years the number of sperm whales caught in these waters accounted for 22.6 and 26.5 per cent of world catches respectively.

In the two largest whaling grounds outside the Antarctic, the waters off South Africa and Japan, catching was maintained without serious restriction. Japan was only affected in the last year of the war, when Allied action, closing in on the Japanese coasts, disrupted whaling, and all Antarctic whale catchers and half the vessels engaged in coastal whaling were commandeered by the Navy. The failure to obtain any whale meat either in the Antarctic or in the North Pacific after 1941 and the slump in coastal whaling in 1945 to one-quarter of normal proved a serious blow to Japan's food supplies, and prompted the United States to permit Japan to recommence whaling in the Antarctic and off the Bonin Islands in 1946. When the Russians brought their pelagic whaling off Kamchatka to a close after 1943, and at the same time whaling came to a halt along the west coast of North America and off Peru, the whale was left in peace throughout the entire North and South Pacific, apart from coastal operations off Japan and Chile and a little sperm whale catching round Peru. Throughout the war in all oceans around the Norwegian Sea (apart from an inconsiderable amount based on Norway), round West Greenland, Alaska, Brazil, and off Madagascar, all whaling was brought to a halt (off the Australian coast after 1938). Around the Bonin Islands, too, 1943 witnessed a cessation of whaling.

Except for the waters round the Azores, whaling underwent a relatively marked expansion towards the end of the war in two other fields: off Newfoundland (including Labrador), where one shore station and one boat were active up to 1942, the Hawke's Harbour station (Chr. Salvesen & Co.) was re-opened in 1943, and during the last three years of the war (1943-5) both stations operated with a total of two, four, and six whale catchers. Whale stocks proved surprisingly abundant, and in the latter half of the 1940s Newfoundland enjoyed the third and best period in its whaling history. Something of the same sort occurred in Chile where in addition to a small station, a new one, Quintay, was in operation from 1 December 1943, ushering in a period of considerable activity.

War is a *force majeure,* and in times of dire necessity the law will be broken, including the international agreement on whaling. In 1940 practically all whaling, including small cetacean catching based on Norway, came to a halt. Owing to the increasing shortage of meat and fats, the authorities received a great many applications from small cetacean catchers for permission to catch the larger cetaceans. A number of concessions for this purpose were granted, but at the same time a number of larger cetaceans were caught illegally and in violation of the London Agreement. In September 1939 Norway had asked the governments in Berlin and London whether, despite the outbreak of war, they still considered the London Agreement to be in force as far as their countries were concerned. The question was occasioned by a statement to the effect that the Department of Fisheries would propose that the season be extended to 31 March 1940, because the British expeditions could not be despatched in time to start catching on 8 December. The ban on the catching of humpbacks would also be raised. Norway could not signify her approval of this unless Germany did so too. The German envoy in Oslo, however, entered a strong protest on behalf of his Government against this breach of the agreement. The British Government countered this criticism apparently by allowing catching after 8 March, but not for longer than three months from the day it began, "thus in principle observing the provision of the Convention". Japanese postponement of adherence to the London Agreement was mentioned as an additional reason. The Norwegian Whaling Commission in New York was of the opinion that "in times with production problems simplified and reduced to one thing alone, viz. producing as much oil as possible in the shortest possible time without consideration for the source of raw materials, all pre-war agreements involving restrictions on production should be allowed to rest in peace". The minimum size for blue whales was lowered to 65 ft., for sperm whales to 25, catching of humpbacks was permitted, and the insistence on reduction of the carcass within thirty-three hours was dropped. During Norwegian operations off the coast of Peru so many small sperm whales were caught and the try-out was so low that the result was a mere 20 barrels per whale, whereas on a global scale it had in 1939-40 been 35.5. Of the total number of sperm whales caught in 1941-3, 53 per cent were under 35 ft. (of the females 81 per cent). In the Azores, furthermore, the try-out throughout the war was only 15.4 barrels. During the war, whale oil production per BWU in the Antarctic remained at a high level.

Apart from Germany, the other whaling countries do not seem to have had any great hesitation in sending expeditions south in the autumn of 1939. Theoretically, Norway would run less risk than Britain, which was a belligerent nation; but the First World War had ended with no distinction of this kind being made during the waging of war against an enemy's overseas lines of communication. And in this respect the Second World War commenced where the First had ended. From the very start it was clear that this time even less distinction would be made, as the Germans realised that a large proportion of the Norwegian merchant marine was operating under British control, and in this way had forfeited its neutrality. There was a certain amount of warranty for this in international law. Article 46, section 3, of the London Declaration of 1909 — which admittedly had never been ratified — states that a neutral ship will be confiscated or generally regarded as an enemy merchant ship when it has been entirely chartered by the enemy government. Even before 9 April 1940, fifty-five Norwegian ships had become casualties of war, with a loss of 373 lives, a far more drastic prelude than on the previous occasion.

On 4 September 1939, the day after Britain's declaration of war, the Association of Whaling Companies wrote to the Norweigan State Whaling Council to ask if it might be possible to arm a number of whale catchers, and place them under naval command in order to escort the floating factories to the West Indies; this, it was stated, would hardly violate Norwegian neutrality, and with an escort of this kind there should be no risk of being torpedoed. The idea that, once the West Indies had been reached, one would be safe was to prove highly optimistic. The enemy could reach right down to the Antarctic. However, unarmed and without an escort all the expeditions reached the whaling grounds unmolested in the autumn of 1939. The Germans could easily have wrought havoc in their ranks as they left Norway, but undoubtedly they assumed that they would have an opportunity of buying a large proportion of their production.

The risk run by Japanese expeditions was the least, both in this and in the following season, at any rate as far as the Germans were concerned, owing to the *entente cordiale* between the two countries. Furthermore, Germany was interested in securing Japanese whale oil, and negotiations were on foot for advance sales or for an exchange of whale oil for vital armaments. The Allies, who would undoubtedly have made every effort to prevent Japanese whale oil reaching Germany, constituted the real danger.

Of the ten British expeditions, four floating factories and thirty-three whale catchers were lying in Bergen in September. As many of the British crew had been called up for military service, Norwegians had signed on in their place. The ships were armed and went in convoy across the North Sea. In 1941 Salvesen purchased both Unilever's floating factories, together with fifteen whale catchers, probably with a view to taking over the Southern Whaling & Sealing Company after the war. During the war Salvesen managed a total of eight floating factories, of which three admittedly had done no whaling for several years. Six of the floating factories were lost, and the whale catchers were commandeered by the Royal Navy, except for those that were allowed to operate in Leith Harbour from 1939 to 1942 and Hawke's Harbour from 1943.

Whaling in the Antarctic 1939-40 season proceeded without any complications, but a number of the whalers were careless enough on the return voyage to transmit telegrams which invited German interception. An immediate halt was called to this. On 9 April 1940, when Germany invaded Norway, all the expeditions were on their way north.

The Japanese sailed home, and most British expeditions reached home safe, but all links were severed for five years between the home country and 6,270 Norwegians engaged in Norwegian expeditions and those of other countries. Back in Norway the most important task was to ensure the welfare of whalers' families, and for the Norwegian exile Government in London it was to administer the large Norwegian merchant navy and the whaling fleet. Both were requisitioned by the State and managed by the Norwegian Shipping and Trade Mission (Nortraship), which opened its offices in London as early as 25 April, and later a branch office in New York, of which the Whaling Commission mentioned above, with Lars Christensen as its chairman, was established as a sub-section. As its name implies, the task of this Commission was to administer whaling to the very limited extent that it was still being carried on.

While the British floating factories returned to home waters without mishap in the spring of 1940, the Norwegian floating factories were ordered to make for the nearest Allied or neutral port. From here they were directed to America, where the oil was discharged in Curaçao and New Orleans, with a view to subsequent transport in small consignments to Britain. Of the oil the Ministry of Food had purchased from Norway, by 9 April, 40,451 tons had been delivered by freighter to Britain, 17,010 tons had been lost as a result of enemy action, and 86,091 tons were stored at the two ports mentioned, after which they were successfully conveyed to England without loss.

One by one the Norwegian floating factories assembled in Halifax, Nova Scotia, one of the main bases for the Atlantic convoys. They were accompanied by only thirty whale catchers, which were kept back in the event of some whaling expeditions being sent out. Most of the catchers were laid up in South Africa and South America, from whence they were requisitioned for wartime service. Only one of the floating factories did not arrive in Halifax, the *Kosmos*: at Dakar she received orders to sail for Curaçao to discharge her oil, and off the northeast coast of Brazil she was intercepted by a German raider on 26 September, which took the Norwegian crew on board. The intention had been to sail the prize with her valuable cargo to France, but as she did not carry enough fuel, she was sunk, with 17,010 tons of whale oil. Not till 21 December was the crew landed in France, together with several hundred men from other captured ships, and after four-and-a-half months in internment camps in France and Germany they reached Norway on 3 May 1941. The *Kosmos* was the first Norwegian floating factory to be lost. By then two British floating factories, both belonging to Salvesen, had been lost as a result of enemy action. The *Salvestria* had almost reached home with a cargo of mineral oil from the United States when she struck a mine in the Firth of Forth, in Scotland, only two miles from land, and sank on 27 July 1940. The next victim was the *New Sevilla,* which on 20 September, on her way from Liverpool to Leith Harbour in South Georgia with provisions and 285 whalers, was torpedoed off the coast of Northern Ireland. The *Strombus,* sent to replace her, fared no better : only an hour's voyage out of Swansea she struck a mine and sank on 26 October. She was sailing under the Norwegian flag and had been chartered by Salvesen, who in this way lost three floating factories in three months. An early casualty was the *Jan Wellem,* used as a transporter carrying fuel oil for the German Navy during the invasion of Norway. During the battle for the town of Narvik in North Norway between British and German naval units she was hit and set on fire.

A tug-of-war for the floating factories ensued between Nortraship and the British whaling companies on the one hand and the Ministry of War Transport on the other. The latter argued that the aim was to win the war; for this purpose every sacrifice must be made, and whaling brought the Allies no nearer to their goal. The counter-argument was that it was highly irrational to use valuable and specially designed vessels on operations which would make them an easy target for German torpedoes. Owing to the space occupied by the boiling equipment, these vessels were not capable of carrying very much oil, in proportion to their tonnage. They should be spared till after the war, in order to cover the tremendous shortage of fats that would then ensue. The Ministry of War Transport maintained that since the British floating factories were ferrying cargo across the Atlantic, the Norwegian ones would also have to follow suit. "The transport of war materials to Great Britain is just as much in Norway's interest." The result was that three of the smaller, older converted floating factories were released for whaling, and three others of the same kind made available for freight carrying. The Whaling Committee had hoped to despatch the three largest and most modern floating factories, partly to save them from being casualties of war, partly because they had such large tank capacity for their own bunkers and those of their whale catchers, that they required no transporters. In addition to these Norwegian expeditions the Ministry of Food decided to catch with the British floating factories the *Svend Foyn* and the *Southern Express* entirely on their own account. As the intention was to obtain as much oil as possible in the shortest possible time, most restrictions were suspended.

Besides these five, six Japanese floating factories were caught in the Antarctic in 1940-1. Of the shore stations only Grytviken operated after two unsuccessful attempts to despatch personnel and matériel to Leith Harbour. Most of the floating factories started catching around 20 October. After three months the Norwegian floating factories had accounted for about half of the expected catch, when on 14 and 15 January 1941 disaster struck. The floating factory *Solglimt,* used as a transporter, had a few days previously taken on board 20,400 barrels from the *Thorshammer,* and was lying alongside the *Ole Wegger* in order to take oil on board when the German raider *Pinguin* ("HK 33") suddenly appeared and put prize crews on board both the ships and four whale catchers. Three succeeded in escaping, two made off at full speed towards the *Thorshammer* and managed to sound the alarm, enabling her with all her seven whale catchers to make her way into Grytviken. Unfortunately attempts to contact the *Pelagos* proved unsuccessful, and she was captured next day with her seven whale catchers. The two Norwegian transporters on their way to the whaling grounds were recalled. The haul of the German raid was three floating factories, eleven whale catchers, and 23,626 tons of oil, the most valuable ever acquired by any German raider. It was a brilliantly planned and executed manoeuvre, but bringing these vessels with their valuable cargo all the way to Bordeaux was a still greater feat. The 700 or so whalers reached Norway on 3 May 1941, together with the crew of the *Kosmos.*

The Germans had sent three raiders to the Antarctic. The smallest of these, the *Komet,* had been given the Ross Sector as its field of operation, where it cruised to and fro without any action resulting. She had reached the Antarctic by an extraordinary route. On 9 July 1940 she left Bergen, on the west coast of Norway, and in accordance with the terms of the German-Russian non-aggression pact was assisted through the North East Passage by Russian icebreakers, as far as the Bering Straits. The third and largest of the raiders, the *Atlantis,* used Kerguelen as a base for her destructive operations against Allied shipping in the Indian Ocean. After conveying her prizes to Bordeaux the *Pinguin,* too, made her way to Kerguelen, and was shortly afterwards sent to the bottom with practically all her crew by a British cruiser.

The disaster raised a storm of criticism against the administration of whaling: in the first place, the departure of the expeditions had not been kept secret, but had been announced, to the dismay of the whaling managers, in a Norwegian news broadcast on the American radio. In the second place the expeditions were neither armed nor escorted by naval units. The British counter-argument was that, after the collapse of France, Britain stood alone against Germany and needed every single gun she possessed to meet the threat of invasion. If Norway preferred to commit her floating factories to whaling, rather than submitting them to the risks of freight carrying in the Atlantic, she would have to do so on her own responsibility. In the third place, owing to an oversight, the oil had not been insured against acts of war, with the result that Nortraship suffered a loss of £900,000. To this must be added the loss of a season's catch and of any possible earnings throughout the rest of the war. For the defence of Grytviken a 4-inch gun was positioned at the harbour entrance, but it was never used. For Norwegians expeditions of 1940-1 the results of pelagic whaling amounted to 2,387 whales and 203,317 barrels, for the British, who operated without any interference, 3,116 whales and 229,780 barrels, and for the six Japanese expeditions 622,413 barrels from 9,992 whales. In addition, Grytviken accounted for 868 whales and 44,498 barrels, a total of 16,363 whales and 1.1 million barrels, 56.6 per cent of which fell to the Japanese.

After what had happened in 1941 it was considered too risky to despatch any expedition to the Antarctic in 1941-2 or 1942-3. On 7 December 1941 the U.S.A., too, had entered the war, and in the desperate struggle to preserve the Atlantic lifeline every single vessel afloat was urgently required. Leith Harbour operated for a short while in 1941-2, but otherwise whaling based on Grytviken was the only activity of this nature in the Antarctic from 1941 until January 1944, when a Norwegian expedition was despatched.

One of the grounds where whaling could be carried out without any danger of acts of war was the west coast of South America. An American firm which for several years before the war had been a major purchaser of sperm oil drew Nortraship's attention to this area, and to the fact that the American armaments industry required sperm oil for the lubrication of precision instruments. A contract was concluded with Nortraship for the purchase of the 1941-2 production at a rate of $120 a ton. Once again a dispute arose between Nortraship and the British authorities for permission to use the Norwegian floating factory *Thorshammer* (which had evaded the German raider in the Antarctic) for whaling. An official declaration to the effect that sperm oil was vital to the conduct of the war settled the matter. The floating factory operated off the coasts of Ecuador and Peru from 27 October until catching was brought to a close on 11 January 1942, by which time the outbreak of war between the United States and Japan in the Pacific made the situation insecure. By then 1,914 whales had been shot and 41,359 barrels produced, i.e. only 21.6 barrels per whale. This suggests that a great many whales far below the minimum permitted size had been shot, and this is confirmed by pictures of whales on the slipway which appear to have been not many months old. Owing to premature termination of catching operations and a resultant lawsuit, Nortraship suffered a major loss. By contrast, the two ensuing seasons, the summer of 1942 and the autumn of 1943, proved all the more favourable. They were the result of an urgent request by the American Government, since the need for sperm oil had greatly increased. Both seasons proved highly profitable to Nortraship. A total of 6,645 whales were caught and 136,500 barrels produced. This time, too, a great many under-sized whales must have been included, but necessity knows no law.

By the end of 1943 all the German raiders had been put out of action, and the Allies had obtained such superiority at sea, both in the Atlantic and in the Pacific, that no risk would have been involved in despatching a floating factory once again to the Antarctic. The only specially designed floating factory at Norway's disposal was the *Sir James Clark Ross,* which was then employed in carrying mineral oil. The Whaling Commission made strenuous efforts to have this floating factory released, as Norway's access to fats would be disastrously undermined after the war should this factory ship be lost. The British, who had lost all their floating factories, were accused of deliberately jeopardising its safety so as to ensure that after the war Norway, once whaling was resumed, should not enjoy a more favourable initial position than Britain. Norway had to accept the Ministry of Food's demand that the oil produced by the Norwegian floating factories before the end of hostilities should not be earmarked for Norway alone, but be allocated to a pool which would be distributed to the countries most sorely in need. Since the *Sir James Clark Ross* was not ready, after a protracted refit, the *Thorshammer* was despatched and operated from 18 January to 3 April 1944, catching 837 whales and producing 82,600 barrels. In 1944-5 only the *Sir James Clark Ross* operated, because Britain was not prepared to release whale catchers for both expeditions, "despite all the talk of the pressing need to procure whale oil for a world desperately short of fats". The result was excellent — 148,000 barrels and 12,000 sacks of meat meal.

Space will not permit an account of the fate suffered by every individual floating factory during the war. A glance at the chronological list of sinkings during the war reveals certain striking features: (1) The first and last wartime sinking involved the two German floating factories the *Jan Wellem* and the *Südmeer,* both serving with the Germany Navy in Norway. (2) One of them was the only floating factory to be sunk by aircraft (details of Japanese floating factories are uncertain). (3) Although it was said that the slow floating factories, with their large open decks, would be an easy target for aircraft, not a single one was sunk by German planes. (4) The German sinking of Norwegian and British floating factories is not evenly distributed throughout the war period. With one exception, they were all sunk in the course of two-and-a-half years, from the summer of 1940 to the spring of 1943, more especially from March 1942 to March 1943, when the Battle of the Atlantic had reached its peak of intensity. (5) To a certain extent it might appear as though the Germans expressly allowed floating factories to proceed unmolested on their way west in ballast, so that they could strike a still shrewder blow at the Allied war effort by sinking ships on the return journey to England, when they were laden with oil and munitions of war. (6) The reason why certain sinkings occasioned such a considerable loss of human life was that the floating factory, with crew quarters capable of accommodating a couple of hundred whalers, generally had a number of passengers on board, as a rule survivors from torpedoed ships or discharged crew.

The first floating factory to feel the full effect of war was, as already mentioned, the *Jan Wellem*. A good while before 9 April 1940 she had been despatched north and was lying in the port of Polarnoje on the coast of Murmansk, awaiting orders. On the afternoon of 8 April she anchored up in the harbour of Narvik with 8,500 tons of fuel oil, intended to fuel German destroyers for their return voyage to Germany, after landing troops. When the Royal Naval squadron arrived on the scene the *Jan Wellem* was hit and set on fire, and scuttled by the Germans themselves, as they effected a temporary withdrawal from the town. She was subsequently raised, sailed to Germany and, handed over to Britain after the war, was broken up in 1948. As the Battle of the Atlantic increased in intensity, so the number of sinkings increased, and the winter of 1942-3 was the worst of the war, with eight floating factories sunk. The protection and armament they were given do not appear to have made much difference — possibly against aircraft, but hardly against U-boats. After completing twenty-two voyages from the West Indies to New York with cargoes of oil the *Kosmos II* was armed with two heavy guns and eight anti-aircraft guns for protection in the New York-Glasgow run, carrying oil and armaments. Her first two voyages were successfully completed; on the third, she carried 24,000 tons of oil, as well as a deck cargo of nine assault vessels and twelve planes. There were 150 men on board all told. On 27 October 1942 she was struck by a torpedo, but not sufficiently damaged to prevent her continuing on her course. The next day she was struck by another torpedo, but still remained afloat, after which a third torpedo sent her to the bottom in a matter of a minute and a half, with some of her crew, including the captain. Many of the crew were picked up by an escort vessel, but worse was to follow when the overcrowded ship was torpedoed two days later, with the loss of forty lives.

Using vulnerable floating factories for the transport of vital war supplies as deck cargo appears irrational. The greatest loss of this kind was undoubtedly the sinking of the *Tafelberg* on 8 September 1944. She had been taken over by the Ministry of War Transport under the name of the *Empire Heritage*. She left New York on 25 August and was struck by a torpedo when only half a day's voyage out from Malin Head, on the northwest corner of Ireland. She sank in two minutes. Her deck cargo included sixty heavy Sherman tanks. In terms of human lives lost this, the last sinking of a Norwegian or British floating factory, was the most tragic: forty-seven crew members, fifty-two passengers, and nine gunners, a total of 108, perished.

Not all the floating factories listed as casualties of war could, in the strictest sense, be regarded as losses due to direct enemy action. This applies *inter alia* to the *Svend Foyn.* On her way to England with 20,000 tons of oil in October 1941 she ran into a violent storm in the North Atlantic, in the course of which she was hit by a torpedo, which blew a tremendous hole in her side. Several of the boilers worked loose, and crashed through the gap. The U-boat was engaged with cannon fire and disappeared. Thanks to magnificent efforts on the part of the crew the floating factory limped into port in Iceland, where she was repaired. Later on, when proceeding in a convoy that followed the northern route, she lost contact with their escort, and on 19 March 1943, collided with an iceberg off Cape Farewell, on the southern point of Greenland, and went down with fifty-nine of the 180 on board.

Of the nine Norwegian floating factories reported as sunk during the war, it is surprising to note that five were captured — this was not the case with a single one of the floating factories belonging to other countries; of the remaining four, *Skytteren* was scuttled by her own crew, and "only" three, the *Kosmos II,* the *Lancing,* and the *N. T. Nielsen-Alonso,* were torpedoed. Of floating factories seized by the enemy, one (*Solglimt*) was sent to the bottom by Allied planes in the autumn of 1942 in the harbour of Cherbourg, where she was blown up after the war, as it proved impossible to salvage her. Another (the *Ole Wegger*) was sunk by the Germans in the Seine near Rouen to block the channel. After the war she was raised, and while being towed to England went aground and sank once more. Once again she was raised, but was so badly damaged that she was condemned and ended her days on the scrapheap.

The Whaling Committee

Members of the Norwegian Whaling Commission had given the impression that Norway should take the opportunity of monopolising pelagic whaling now that the other countries had lost their floating factories. This view, however, was so radical that it had no chance of being accepted by the responsible authorities. Their point of view was that Norway and Britain should co-operate both in rebuilding and in preventing other countries joining in. This view was based on two assumptions: that the Allies would not allow Germany and Japan to renew pelagic whaling, and that a ban on Norwegians being employed in expeditions from countries that had not participated in pre-war pelagic whaling would render such expeditions impossible. Both these assumptions, however, proved groundless.

Communications between whaling people at home and abroad and with the Norwegian authorities in London were after a while so good that even a few years before conclusion of hostilities it was possible to co-operate on plans for the rebuilding of the whaling fleet once peace had come. These practical and economic preparations went hand in hand with the work of hammering out an international regulation of whaling, and both were closely linked. We shall consider the latter point first, since the scope of rehabilitation necessarily presupposed preparing for the maximum extent of pelagic whaling that an international convention would allow. There seemed no point in building and operating with a whaling fleet with a greater capacity than would be required to achieve the total quota. But for several reasons this proved illusory : although the capacity of the matériel was already sufficient to cope with a maximum quota of 16,000 BWU by 1947-8, it continued to expand, not so much in the *number* of floating factories, as in their size, and above all in the number of whale catchers and their tonnage and mechanical power. As it proved impossible once again to prevent Japan as well as other, new, nations from participating in pelagic catching in the Antarctic, or to restrict their expansion once they had joined in, this type of whaling now entered its last and decisive era, the *struggle for quotas*. It was a struggle not only among whaling nations, but also between whalers and biologists.

With the conclusion of the Second World War there appeared to be a chance to call a halt to the development that threatened, for the simple reason that it was now necessary to start from scratch. It might appear a simpler matter to halt the reconstruction of the whaling fleet when it had reached an acceptable maximum, than to scrap matériel that could still be used. But it would be wrong to attribute the present situation to an increase in catching equipment and efficiency. Once total pelagic catches in the Antarctic were reduced to 16,000 BWU, it was a matter of minor importance to the stocks of whales how much equipment was employed for the purpose of killing this number, or what country's expeditions made the catch. The increase in matériel aimed at obtaining the greatest possible share of the total quota during the short period to which the season was restricted. The fact that, after fifteen post-war seasons, catching matériel which was roughly twice as effective as earlier matériel, failed by a long way to achieve the total quota, suggests, or even proves, that the quota was too high for the whale stocks to sustain over a period of years. Statistics would appear to confirm this (see Table 29).

The figures in Table 29 clearly show how much greater efforts were required to reach the 1961-2 quota than was the case in 1951-2. In 1961-2 total national quotas amounted to 17,780 BWU, and the actual catch to 15,152.6; in 1962-3 respectively 15,000 and 11,306.1, a decline of 2,527.4 and 3,694.9 BWU. Clearly a quota of 15-16,000 units had

Table 29. THE ANTARCTIC PELAGIC WHALING FLEETS AND THEIR
CATCH, 1947 and 1963

	Floating factories		Catchers				
	Number	Gross tons	Number	Gross tons	H.p. per catcher	Total catch (BWU)	Quota
1947-8	17	234,759	162	56,156	1,302	16,364	16,000
1962-3	17	354,581	201	141,327	2,957	11,306	15,000

Another set of figures which illustrate the same tendency may be obtained by
comparing matériel and catches for 1951-2 and 1961-2:

	Floating factories				Catchers			
	Number	Gross tons average	Catching days average	Barrels per day average	Number	Gross tons average	H.p. average	Catcher's day work average
1951-2	19	15,217	64	1,690	263	473	1,774	122
1961-2	21	19,352	115	744	261	657	2,732	60

been excessive. The slump was sudden, for total catches as well as for
the various species. In the period 1962/3-1965/6 the number of BWUs
caught fell to about one-third. This could by no means be attributed
to a lowering of the quota, because in none of the seasons was this
successfully reached. Nor was it due to a shorter catching period, as this
remained constant during all these seasons.

Another point of interest is that the quota was fixed in terms of blue
whale units. Theoretically, this would mean that the quota could be
filled by either 16,000 blue whales, 32,000 fin whales, 40,000 humpbacks or 96,000 sei whales. In practice this has meant, since the humpback period before the First World War, that the fewer that could be
caught of a larger species, the more catches were made of smaller species,
in order to achieve a full quota. This is illustrated in Table 30 in which
the largest number of each species caught in pelagic catching in the
Antarctic is shown underlined. In this connection it should be noted
that in 1948-9 total protection of the humpback was in force, in 1958-9
and 1960-1 it was protected in certain areas, and in 1964-5 there was
total protection both for the blue whale and for the humpback.

Table 30. ANTARCTIC SEASONS WITH THE LARGEST CATCH,
BY SPECIES, 1948-1965

	Blue	Fin	Humpback	Sei	Total	BWU catch	quota
1948-9	7,399	17,201	13	16	24,629	16,007	16,000
1958-9	1,191	25,837	2,394	1,402	30,824	15,301	15,000
1960-1	1,740	27,374	718	4,310	34,142	16,434	—
1964-5	20	7,308	—	19,874	27,202	6,986	8,000

If the intervening seasons had been included in Table 30 they would have shown that for each individual species, too, there was a certain decline after catches of it had reached a climax. After four seasons catches of blue whale had been reduced by half, of fin whale by about a quarter, and in 1967-8 2,155 fin whales and 10,000 sei whales were caught.

Setting total pelagic catches of baleen whales in the Antarctic at a maximum quota of 16,000 BWU was considered, along with reductions in the catching seasons, a great advance in international regulation; Dr. N. A. MACKINTOSH thought it more significant than the 1937-8 agreements. A few years later Bergersen wrote that "this was such a decisively important decision that the little conference of 1944 may be regarded as one of the most significant events in the history of whaling regulation". Later he wrote that "much of the blame for the unsatisfactory state of stocks of whale" (in 1947) must probably be attributed to the huge catches in 1936-40 "when they showed a marked tendency to decline". In the last three of these four seasons throughout the entire Antarctic 30,000, 25,000, and 21,000 units respectively were caught. When the quota was fixed at 16,000 after the war, it was in fact not reduced by more than the annual decline during the last pre-war seasons, or by the amount of the "trend". The reduction tended rather to *follow* this trend than to *retard* it. No representative of active whaling took part in the 1944 conference. The total quota was the work of three scientists, Bergersen, Kellogg, and Mackintosh. Four circumstances prompted them to fix the quota at 16,000: (1) in relation to the "big" season of 1937-8 it meant a reduction to about one-half; (2) together with a curtailment of the season it was assumed that stocks, of the exact size of which little was known, would stand inroads of this nature; (3) there appeared to have been an exaggerated idea of the increase in stocks during the war; (4) an important aim was to spare the blue whale. They did not realise that this might systematically result in over-taxation of other species. Sensing that, despite everything, the quota *might* be too big, Bergersen viewed the future in the following terms: "It remains to be seen whether the limitation adopted in 1944, 1945, and 1946 can be maintained — if this is *not* the case, whaling will soon be a thing of the past." The three men had taken a chance, and when things went wrong later on it was too easy to say that it was because they had set too high a quota.

Although the convention on 16,000 BWU presupposed that the number could be altered, as things turned out it was very difficult to lower the quota, and every time this was done it was not until it was proved impossible to fill it entirely. It is therefore of great interest to the history of whaling after the war to examine when, how and why the number was fixed at 16,000 and why these were BWUs. If the principle suggested at the pre-war conferences had been adhered to, that of national quotas, the present situation might well have been different. The convention also suffered from the weakness that any member could renounce it and operate unrestrictedly.

The first conference convened to prepare post-war regulation held four meetings in London in January 1944 and the minutes were signed on 7 February. These have subsequently been referred to as the Protocol of 1944. The signatory powers were Australia, Canada, Great Britain, New Zealand, Norway, South Africa, and the United States. The purpose of the conference was to adopt amendments to the 1937 and 1938 London agreements to apply to the first post-war season. It was decided that 1945-6 should be regarded as the first post-war season, and that the protocol should apply only to this, and not be regarded as setting a precedent for subsequent seasons. It was important to ensure that the reduced whaling fleet would be able to produce as much oil as possible for a fat-hungry world without impairing whale stocks. The former London Agreement was amended on two points: catching time was extended to four months, from 24 November to 24 March, but the number of baleen whales caught was not to exceed 16,000 BWU. This was the first international agreement in which mention is made of this figure.

The limitation of Antarctic catching by means of a maximum quota of whales and/or barrels was no new idea in 1944. A combination of both had been agreed between the British and Norwegian companies for 1932-4, and had been imposed on the Norwegian companies by the Government for 1935-6. But a proposal for national quotas and quotas for every area and for every species was at the time considered so utopian that the 1937 and 1938 conferences did not even discuss them. At the Washington Conference in 1946 these proposals ran into determined opposition, not least from Norway. Nearly twenty-five years elapsed before the International Whaling Commission, in a last attempt to save the remaining whale stocks, managed to get a regulation adopted for quotas for each area and for each individual species of whale, and the setting up of a total quota in BWUs was abolished.

The agreement on national quotas concluded on 6 June 1962 was the result of four years' negotiations between the pelagic whaling nations, and not the work of the International Whaling Commission. The reason why, at the London Conference of 1945 and that in Washington in 1946, there was no discussion of sharing out the total quota among the various countries, but only of a total quota of 16,000 BWU, was also because making whaling available to all nations tied in with the principles of free trade. It was all the easier to accept this point of view as it was assumed that after the war it would in practice be Norway and Great Britain that would share the quota among them, and that it would not be difficult for these two to agree on the share. The losers, Germany and Japan, would no longer have access to pelagic whaling and in the peace treaties signed with these two countries a provision to this effect would be included. Limiting catching by means of a total quota would in itself deter others from starting, once they realised that they would have to compete with Britain and Norway for a share.

How did they arrive at the exact figure of 16,000? At the 1944 conference it was stated that even though this amount could not be caught during the first season, the intention was "to prevent the present situation being exploited for unchecked building of new floating factories", and secondly, "because there is a desire to create a precedent for total limitation in the future". The first intention was expressly published as a counter to Swedish plans for new companies which were said to be backed by Norwegian and British interests. The Norwegian delegate gave an account of these plans at the conference: "We proposed therefore that for this season a total limitation of catching should be established. A total catch of 16,000 BWU was agreed on, i.e. 1.6 to 1.7 million barrels, which it was calculated could be extracted from about 20,000 whales, about half the yield immediately before the war". He relates that he proposed 16,000, instead of 15,000 or 20,000 as proposed by Kellogg and Mackintosh, as "it seemed to be rather more reassuring". In this fortuitous fashion was this fatal figure for a total catch arrived at! This impression of chance was further confirmed by the fact that the three gentlemen in question agreed that "the figure for the total quota was of minor importance", the principle of total limitation being the most important. It appears that at an early stage Bergersen realised that the decision was a step in the wrong direction. In a lecture in 1952 he declared that 16,000 "is just a bit too much". And the reason for this was *inter alia* "increasing catches of Antarctic stocks of whale from shore stations [outside the Antarctic], a circumstance not foreseen in 1944". He hoped that in the not too distant future it might be possible to reduce the quota. This did not take place to any major extent till 1963-4. In whaling, the general biological principle of establishing for each species the number that could be safely killed without depleting the species was not followed. The whaling nations were not yet ready to accept this, either in 1944, or in 1952.

There was certainly not agreement in every quarter on the figure arrived at, on the procedure in the agreement, or on the agreement as a whole. In September 1942 H. K. Salvesen had urged the Department of Fisheries to pull out of the agreement as an international convention of this kind was unnecessary with only Great Britain and Norway engaged in pelagic whaling. As the important thing in the first season was to ensure that the world had as much oil as possible, the international agreement should be entirely suspended; it would in any case not be possible to catch as much as the quota permitted. As the whaling fleet increased, regulations to preserve whale stocks could gradually be applied. The Department was not prepared to go so far, but was not averse to extending catching time in the first season to seven months, and to suspending Article 8 of the 1937 Agreement (on full exploitation of the carcass). On the other hand it would propose a limitation of 20,000 *animals* (not BWU). But this would undoubtedly have resulted in a mass slaughter of blue whales.

The reason why the figure was somewhat arbitrarily fixed was because there was uncertainty not only about the size of stocks, but also about the extent to which they had increased during the war. There seemed to be no doubt that blue whale stocks had been over-fished in the 1930s. Figures for stocks of fin whales were apparently somewhat exaggerated. A number of 400,000 was suggested, which would stand a killing of 10 per cent, viz. 40,000 a year, corresponding to 20,000 blue whale units. In relation to this a total quota of that number of units appears somewhat moderate, and even this was a reduction on pre-war figures. In the last five pre-war seasons, 1934-9, an average per season of *c.* 33,400 whales had been caught pelagically in the Antarctic (blue, fin, and humpback), or about 24,000 units. It was therefore considered that with a reduction to 16,000, i.e. two-thirds of the figure for the pre-war seasons, there would be a good margin of safety. Furthermore, it was assumed that stocks must have increased considerably during the war. Assuming that 20,000 whales could be killed annually without reducing stocks, then these must have increased by 80,000, and if young were included, to 90,000. With a quota of 20,000, stocks would therefore continue to be preserved. But as the Norwegian and British companies were clearly going to insist on the same catch as before the war, it would have been prudent to start at a figure of 25,000, to ensure that regulation would not run up against too much opposition. On the other hand, the whale had not been left in peace in the Antarctic during the period 1940-4, as 20,585 (of which 1,038 were sperm whales) had been killed.

Attempts have been made to calculate the probable increase in stocks of whales in the Antarctic from the autumn of 1941 to 1946. This presupposes that catches of blue and fin whales were "modest", and consequently does not take into consideration the fact that during these years over 20,000 whales were caught. Depending upon the extent to which various uncertain factors may have operated, the estimate comes to the conclusion that there was at best an increase of 71.9 per cent, at worst 38.5 per cent. This tells us nothing, however, about the absolute size of stocks; this has more or less to be guessed at. Among whaling people some believed that notions of an increase during the war were far too optimistic. The Whaler Section of the British Chamber of

Shipping, of which H. K. Salvesen was chairman, declared in August 1945 in its plan for post-war whaling that stocks of whales during the seasons immediately prior to the war had been so greatly over-fished that the holiday enjoyed by the whale during the war was not sufficient to "heal its scars". The report quoted the manager of the *Sir James Clark Ross,* who on the basis of observations 1944-5 did not consider that there appeared to be more whales than previously. Total quotas were fixed in terms of blue whale *units* in the hope of sparing stocks of this species, on the assumption that as far as the quota was concerned it was just as well to take two fin whales as one blue whale. In any case this might be an advantage; two large fin whales could produce more oil than a blue whale of minimal length. No one paused to think that this might endanger stocks of fin whales. The great surprise for those who expected an increase in whale numbers during the war was the decline in stocks of blue whales, as revealed in post-war whaling. During the last peacetime season, 1938-9, 14,081 blue whales were caught in the Antarctic. After the war the largest catches were 9,192 in 1946-7, 7,625 in 1948-9, and 7,048 in 1950-1. Between the laying-up season of 1931-2 and the first wartime season of 1939-40 an annual average of 16,254 blue whales were caught, while in the seven post-war seasons 1946-53, the annual average was 6,565, only 40 per cent of the pre-war average.

The change in the species of whale caught might appear to result of necessity in an increase in operating costs. It is obviously a more expensive business to pursue and catch two fin whales than one blue whale, and six sei whales would involve greater operating costs than two fin whales: six pursuits, six shots, six harpoons, etc., cost more than one of each. However, the extra costs are so trivial compared to other operating conditions, that they are of little importance. Later on *inter alia* the production of meat was to play an important part, and six sei whales provided more and better meat than one blue whale or two fin whales.

At the conference in 1944 Remington Kellogg announced that after the war the United States would convene a comprehensive international whaling conference in Washington with a view to complete regulation of catching in future. Partly by way of preparation for this, and partly in order to establish provisional rules for the 1946-7 season, Britain invited delegates in April 1945 to a conference to be held in London the following autumn. It convened from 21 to 23 November, and the minutes are dated 26 November. Apart from the same powers that had participated on the previous occasion there were Denmark, France, and the Netherlands. The last-mentioned had originally not been invited, not having ratified the London Agreement of 1937. The Netherlands now hastened to do so on 29 October, as its whaling plans were already far advanced, and requested an invitation to the conference. That Britain should have agreed without discussing the matter with

Norway was a matter of considerable concern to the Norwegian Government, as it was bound to be interpreted as British recognition of a new participant in pelagic catching in the Antarctic. It was said that Unilever, with the connivance of the British Government, was at the back of the Dutch plans.

With forty-six delegates from twelve countries this conference was far more representative than the 1944 one. The conference was under pressure from three sides: the demand for a control system that would preserve whale stocks, starving Europe's crying need for fat, and new nations anxious to start whaling. Demands for freer whaling, at any rate for a few seasons, were not only motivated by a desire to provide undernourished Europe with fat: it could be taken for granted that demand would result in a steep rise in prices, which could be exploited. The buyers supported the demands for an easing of restrictions in order that greater production would keep prices down. Unilever was of the opinion that owing to the shortage of fats the risk should be taken of raising the quota to 20,000: this would give 80,000 tons more whale oil, and help to bring "down to more reasonable levels the present high prices of oils and fats". There was anticipation of the same trends in world trade as after the First World War, but instead of a collapse of the market after a few years the world entered a boom period.

The final minutes of the conference open with the three abovementioned points. The British Minister of Food summed up the fats situation in the world in the nearest future, and expressed the opinion that this justified somewhat freer whaling. But world production of edible fats and oils in 1935-9 on an annual average had been 21.6 million short tons (1 short ton = 907.2 kg.), whereas in 1945 it was estimated at only 17.3 million. The proportion of these items reaching the world market had fallen from 6.5 to 2.5 million tons. For 1946 there would be a need for imports, mainly to Europe, of 6 million tons, but only 3 million tons were available. The Minister feared that it would take some time to increase production. He was to prove right. In 1946 it rose no higher than 17 million tons and in 1947 18 million tons. World exports of these items in 1947 were 4 million tons, i.e. more than 40 per cent below the pre-war level. In that year Europe would only be able to cover 55 per cent of the consumption of fats it had had in 1939, and it was estimated that not till 1952 would Europe reach the same level of fat consumption as before the war. While it would take a great many years to resurrect war-ravaged Europe's agriculture and stocks of cattle and South East Asia's ruined plantations, whaling, it was maintained, was an area where only a couple of years were required to set on foot a whaling fleet large enough to make a substantial contribution to Europe's fat requirements.

The conference was willing to make certain concessions in this direction, but on two essential conditions: in the first place, continued preservation of stocks of whales, and in the second place, any temporary relaxation of control must not encourage countries which had previously not been engaged in whaling "to embark on it only to discover in the end that their expeditions proved economically unprofitable". The warning, however, proved ineffective, as prices rose and rose, culminating in 1951 with £172 10s (for a single sale of a small consignment). With an average price in 1947-52 of £110 there was money to be made in whaling, even though this would be done in a struggle for a share of the 16,000 units. Only on less significant points did the conference relax previous agreements. The first was that if the expeditions failed to reach the whaling grounds before 24 November 1945 they should be allowed to catch for four months as from the day of arrival, but not beyond a date two months after 24 March, and during this period they should not be allowed to use more than ten whale catchers. For 1946-7 the season was altered to 8 December to 7 April, but without leave to exceed this last date. The other point was the amendment to Article 3 of the 1938 protocol, which laid down that only floating factories that had operated in 1937 on a stationary basis (i.e. as shore stations) in territorial waters should be allowed to operate as such after signing of the protocol of 24 June 1938, and were then to remain moored at one and the same spot throughout the catching period (six consecutive months). This rule was now entirely suspended for the period from 1 May to 31 October 1947. During this period, in fact, "mobile" catching was allowed in territorial waters with any number of floating factories.

The most important innovation for future regulation was the conference's adoption of Article 4, Kellogg's proposal from 1938, that within two days from the end of each week expeditions were to submit a report to the International Bureau of Whaling Statistics, stating the number of units caught. Should the Bureau then come to the conclusion that the total quota fixed would probably be achieved before the last date of the open season, it was to set a date for bringing operations to a halt, and advise contracting governments to this effect at least two weeks prior to the termination of whaling. After this date it was forbidden to catch baleen whales. This rather complicated set-up was simplified in 1953 by cutting out the governments. When the Bureau, on the basis of weekly reports, had established that 85 per cent of the quota had been caught, expeditions would be ordered to send daily reports. The Bureau would then inform whaling managers four days in advance when operations were to be concluded, and all operations would have to cease by midnight on that particular day. It was exciting and a matter of some concern for the management of the Bureau to see how its predictions fared. During this period 1947-59 when the system was in use it proved possible to predict the closing date with astonishing accuracy. With the exception of a single season, 1952-3, the deviation from the total quota of the actual catch varied between +2.60; −1.14 per cent; for the whole period the total deviation was only +0.15 per cent. In other words, in the course of twelve seasons expeditions have only caught 275.4 units more than the quota allowed. All in all, the system as such appears to have worked satisfactorily. When national quotas were introduced as from 1959-60, the system of a closing date was abolished. In two seasons, 1960-2, the total quota was in abeyance. As from 1962-3 a total quota was once again adopted, which the sum of national quotas was not to exceed. In this way the struggle for the greatest possible share of the common quota was transferred to the political plane. Quotas were linked to floating factories, and could not be bartered. Finally, this floating factory quota became such a valuable asset that expeditions were bought and laid up merely with a view to acquiring their quotas.

With the adoption of an open season for a certain number of days, a total or global quota, and the right to terminate catching once the quota had been achieved, the main principles in post-war international regulation of pelagic catching in the Antarctic that were followed from 1947 to 1959 were established. At no time during these years was the open season exploited in its entirety in order to ensure a full quota. In 1947-8 catching was terminated after 115 out of 122 days; in 1955-6 after only 58 out of 92 days, and on an average for the entire period 78 out of 99 days. This can only suggest that the matériel used had attained a size and efficiency that far exceeded what was necessary to catch the quota in the course of the open season.

The extent to which whaling could be carried out in the first post-war seasons depended on three circumstances: regulation, stocks of whales, and production possibilities. The first had been decided by the London Conference of November 1945. Stocks of whales proved a great unknown factor, about which nothing could be done. The matériel available included the surviving Norwegian floating factories and the German and Japanese floating factories that had been preserved. It was almost considered a foregone conclusion that the latter would be transferred to Norway and Britain as spoils of war. There were also the new vessels completed by the end of the war. As it was uncertain how many floating factories would survive the war, the last-mentioned point had to be taken care of in reconstruction plans. It was probable that Norway would be left with four or five floating factories, while all the British and Japanese had been lost. For this reason, even before the end of hostilities, Britain was even more anxious than Norway to build floating factories that would be ready to operate once the war was over.

At that stage only two countries were capable of building, Britain and Sweden, but in Norway there was a distinct aversion to building

91. Chr. Salvesen & Co.'s first post-war floating factory, the *Southern Venturer*, built in England in 1945, and sold to Japan in 1962.

in Sweden, owing to Swedish plans to commence whaling. This feeling was so strong likewise on the political and diplomatic plane that nothing ever came of the Swedish company. In principle, Britain and Norway were of the opinion that all pelagic whaling after the war should be reserved to themselves. To this extent there was agreement, but how was the quota to be divided between them? Norway considered that 60 per cent for herself and 40 per cent for Britain would be reasonable, but in British quarters a division was proposed on the basis of production capacity — H. K. Salvesen's oft-repeated idea — which would give Britain a more favourable percentage, 47, leaving Norway with 53 per cent.

In order to co-ordinate the two countries' reconstruction of their whaling fleets, the British-Norwegian Joint Committee was formed, and this held its first meeting on 29 June 1943. There was considerable disagreement here on the lines along which the whaling fleet should be rebuilt. The British view was that initially she should build or convert a number of tankers as "emergency floating factories" in order to help make good the world's acute lack of fats, and then wait to build special floating factories when these requirements had been filled. This view was based on the reluctance of Britain — i.e. Salvesen — to allow Norway to operate alone during the first few seasons, because she had maintained four or five floating factories, whereas all the British vessels had been lost. The Norwegian viewpoint won the day, and two floating factories were contracted for in England, one on Norway's account, the *Norhval*, and its sister ship the *Southern Venturer*, of 14,500 gross tons, for Salvesen. Both were ready for the first post-war season of 1945-6.

In Norway there were many different opinions on the future of whaling. Some believed that it was far too risky to invest Kr.40 million in a new floating factory when the world's leading economists predicted that the history of the years immediately following the First World War would be repeated, i.e. that after a few years' hectic boom a violent crash would occur. Others were less pessimistic in their views: Norway, they believed, should as soon as possible rebuild her whaling fleet before her rivals had done so, in order to cash in on the favourable prices that whale oil would fetch. The floating factories that could definitely be relied on were the three Norwegian ones assisting the Allied war effort in the carrying trade and the two new ones. It was not known what had happened to the two Norwegian floating factories seized by the Germans or the German and Japanese ones. As it turned out, as many as nine expeditions managed to set off, and two shore stations in South Georgia were to be opened, apart from Grytviken. It proved a difficult task to obtain the ninety or so catchers, which were spread all over the world and presented the further problem of identifying ownership. One of the stations and six of the floating factories were Norwegian, which assured a dominant position in the struggle for the 16,000 units the first season. But already the next season Norway's position was somewhat undermined by the fact that of the seven other floating factories that arrived, only one was Norwegian. It is, moreover, a misunderstanding to assume that all the floating factories after the war had been newly built, specially designed vessels. Since 1945 there have been forty floating factories (of which only thirty-four were actively engaged in whaling), and of these sixteen were pre-war while twenty-four were built subsequently, and of these twenty-four, nine had been converted and fifteen were new, and two of these fifteen were never used for whaling. (For the expansion of the pelagic whaling fleet, 1945-63, see Statistical Appendix, Table 61.)

28
REBUILDING THE WHALING FLEETS, 1945-1949

For convenience we have divided this work into three main sections, Finnmark whaling, global whaling, and pelagic whaling. However, the period after the Second World War differs in so many ways and so markedly from the pre-war period that it might well have provided the material for a fourth section, entitled "Quota whaling" or "Internationally regulated whaling". This could most conveniently be divided into four: (1) Revival, 1945-9; (2) The struggle for global quotas (or the "open season"), 1946-59; (3) National quotas, 1959 to the present; (4) The return from the south to the north. In the first period interest is concentrated mainly on three events: (1) the Washington Conference of 1946 and the establishment of the International Commission on Whaling (now the International Whaling Commission); (2) the joint ventures of Norwegian companies, 1945-8; (3) the third and penultimate expansion, 1946-52.

The Washington Conference of 1946 and the International Commission on Whaling, 1949

As far back as 1944 Dr. Remington Kellogg had announced that immediately after the war the United States would convene a comprehensive international conference to revise the previous agreements and establish the main guidelines for future regulation. Except for one point, the establishment of the Commission, the motions adopted by the Conference consisted mainly of codifying previous agreements. This was necessary because considerable confusion existed as to who had ratified what (see Statistical Appendix, Table 62).

Invitations to the Conference were accepted by nineteen countries, fourteen sending delegations and five observers, and only one, Mexico, of the countries invited did not attend. In response to a request the Food and Agriculture Organisation (F.A.O.) also sent three observers. There were seventy-two persons present; the largest delegations were from Norway (8), Great Britain (12), and the United States (9). The father of this conference, Kellogg, was naturally elected chairman. Anxiety was expressed that such large participation might mean that a great many countries were thinking of taking up whaling. It was, however, more the result of the need for general international co-operation, which found expression in so many ways after the war. The actual work of the Conference was carried out by its ten sub-committees. The result was

92. The opening of the International Whaling Conference in Washington, D.C., 20 November 1945.

primarily the work of the United States, and this may seem surprising, as the United States was no longer the whaling country it had once been, but was now the real victor of the war, with a feeling of power and a duty to resurrect a war-torn world and consequently it supported all international co-operation. The United States acted as host and sponsor to the Conference, had taken the first steps to convene an international commission, was now submitting a complete draft for its organisation, and was in a position to point to favourable results of similar agreements for fishing and sealing. In his opening speech the Secretary of State DEAN ACHESON emphasised that codification of the agreements then in force was one of the aims of the conference, the other being to establish a permanent and effective organ for supervising and modifying the regulation of whaling in accordance with developments. On the first point he encountered no opposition, but with regard to the latter a major debate arose on four items that were just as much political as technical and biological in nature.

The International Whaling Convention or the Washington Convention, as it is called, consists in essence of five parts: (1) the *Final Act,* containing formulas and recommendations; (2) as an *Addendum,* the Dutch proposal aimed at the Norwegian crewing law; (3) the *International Convention for the Regulation of Whaling,* which consists of the eleven articles of the main agreement; (4) the *Schedule,* containing all actual regulating provisions, what and where whaling will be carried out, and where it is banned. These rules might be subject to amendment by the Commission, and it was particularly important to lay down the boundaries for the areas of the regulation where the Commission had the authority to undertake such amendments; (5) the *Protocol for the*

Regulation of Whaling. This was to apply only for 1947-8, and merely lays down that for that particular season the London Agreement of 26 November 1945 was to apply. These five parts were supplemented by an annex on the *Nomenclature of Whales,* giving the scientific (Greek-Latin) names for species of whales and their corresponding names in English, French, Dutch, Russian, Spanish, and Scandinavian (not Norwegian!). As Part 2 was not strictly part of the Convention and Part 5 was only temporarily applicable, we need only concern ourselves below with Parts 1, 3 and 4.

Nevertheless, Part 2 was one of the four semi-political items that gave rise to the most acrimonious discussion. This opened with the Dutch chief delegate, Fisheries Director D. J. van Dijk, launching a sharp attack in a long speech on Norway, whose crewing law made it difficult for the Dutch to start whaling and prevented them contributing to world fats supplies, not least their own. The Netherlands *had* to start whaling, needing 30,000 tons of edible fats, but did not possess the necessary currency to buy. When he was told that catches were limited to 16,000 units, and that however many floating factories the Netherlands built, this would not produce a drop more oil, van Dijk replied that it was by no means out of the question for the Conference to suspend the total quota.

The Norwegian delegation countered these attacks by stating that this was an entirely Norwegian domestic matter, and that the ban merely aimed to preserve the whale stocks. The Dutch, however, declared that the ban was discriminatory, because Norwegians were allowed to serve with the expeditions of other countries, and there were rumours that dispensation would be granted in the case of the *Slava.* Norway was supported by Britain, whereas the Soviet Union, France, and Argentina supported the Netherlands, as all these three countries were preparing to embark on pelagic whaling, and would depend on Norwegian crews, or at least on Norwegian gunners. The United States and Denmark were anxious to dismiss this matter as irrelevant to the business of the Commission, and one that should be settled mutually between Norway and the Netherlands. The Dutch motion that a statement in their favour should be included in the Final Act was defeated by nine to three votes. Instead, an amendment was included consisting of a statement that governments of nations participating in the Conference should refrain from preventing a nation from adhering to or ratifying an international agreement on the preservation of stocks of whales. The minutes also recorded that a number of countries voted against because they disagreed with the facts of the matter, others because they considered that it lay outside the jurisdiction of the Conference.

The other item that was the subject of debate was the American proposal that the Commission should be an organ under the United

Nations, comprising a section of the F.A.O., the reasons given being that whaling was one of the activities belonging to the F.A.O.'s field, that costly duplicate administration would be avoided, that this would ensure stronger pressure from world opinion, that countries besides those signing the convention would be eligible, and the F.A.O. would make available offices with qualified personnel, and also finance the Commission. By and large, the Americans opted for centralisation under the United Nations, in order to strengthen the power and position of this organisation. The proposal was rejected, particularly by the Norwegian delegation, which pointed out that the F.A.O. was mainly concerned with agriculture, and to a very small extent with fisheries, and that the organisation had fifty-one members, most of which had not the remotest connection with whaling. Norway was also afraid that this would be the end of the *International Whaling Statistics.* No actual vote was take on this point, as it was decided that the contracting governments should decide within a period of two years whether the Commission was to work within the framework of the United Nations or not. At the Commission's second meeting in Oslo in 1950 the attempt to make the Commission subordinate to the United Nations was finally abandoned. The reason for this was in part that in 1946 Britain was assigned the task of convening the first meeting of the Commission, while the Commission itself was to decide the time and venue of subsequent meetings. At the meeting in 1949 it was decided to accept Britain's offer to make premises and a trained administrative staff available. When the idea of integration within the United Nations Organisation was turned down in 1950, the reason given was that the British offer would be the most practical solution, and it has been maintained. By way of a gesture "the Commission decided to maintain its present close connection with the F.A.O. The first secretary of the Commission in 1949-58 was the British fisheries director A. T. A. DOBSON. He had headed the British delegation in Washington, and taken part in most previous conferences, and had wide experience of international whaling negotiations.

The third item with a certain political flavouring was the ban on the transfer of floating matériel from a contracting government's flag to that of a non-contracting one. Norway had championed this idea since 1937, and a ban of this kind had been incorporated in the Norwegian Whaling Act. In 1937 she had not succeeded in having it embodied in the agreement, but merely as a recommendation in the Final Act, and this was also the case in 1945. The British and Norwegian delegations had been instructed to press both for this ban and for the ban on the import of oil from a non-contracting state. To their great astonishment the United States on this occasion was definitely against, whereas in 1945 it had been decisively in favour of the first point. The reason was undoubtedly of a constitutional nature : according to the American Constitution ratification of the protocol by the Senate would automatically make it valid American law, and with a ban of this kind in the Convention, in view of the then political composition of the Senate, there would be very little prospect of having the Convention ratified. The proposal was supported only by Britain and Norway, whereas countries, including the Netherlands, Sweden, and the Soviet Union, which intended to start pelagic whaling, took the same standpoint as the United States. In this respect it may be said that 1946 marks a setback from 1945.

This can also be said of the fourth point, where national, political, and economic interests were involved. It involved the argument whether the definition of a "land station" also included "floating factory in territorial waters". The French in particular were in favour of this, and urged that it should be included in the Convention and not in the Schedule. This would mean that the Commission would be unable to amend it in future. France was supported by Australia, which expected to be allotted one of the two Japanese floating factories operating in the Antarctic in 1946-7. Norway, supported by Britain and Chile, was strongly opposed, on the grounds that experience had shown that catching the leaner whale it its breeding grounds in tropical waters was economically irrational and destructive of whale stocks. Though this went very much against the grain, these three countries were forced to accept a compromise; thus, according to the regulation, within the definition of a land station also lie floating factories operating in territorial waters off Madagascar, the coast of French West Africa, and certain areas off the east and west coasts of Australia. This provision, however, was incorporated in the Schedule, and the Commission was instructed to keep a particularly close watch on this catching. The reason why the French were so committed in this matter was that they hoped to realise the plan for the Norwegian-French Sopecoba company.

As far as regulation was concerned this 1946 rule was in some respects an advantage over the 1945 rule, but if we trace regulation back to the main agreement of 1937 it is a step in the wrong direction. The minutes of the latter state that "land station means a factory on the land, or in the territorial waters adjacent thereto". As this last-mentioned phrase could be misinterpreted to mean that in *territorial waters* it was only possible to use a floating factory, the 1938 conference made it clear that, although it was in no doubt that "land station" could not be a "floating factory", it would nevertheless make an exception for those floating factories that had operated in territorial waters in 1937. These would be allowed to continue, but it stated expressly that they would have to "remain *moored* in territorial waters in *one* position". In 1945 France succeeded in making this possibility general for all contracting powers' territorial waters, and when the phrase "the movements and anchorage"

93.   From the left, three stages of the development of the floating factory, the
1920s, 1930s and 1940s.

was included, it permitted the floating factory to operate as a mobile
unit. In relation to this the territorial limitation of 1945 was a step
forward; but in the first place the interpretation of land station appears
to be contrary to natural common sense, in the second it was a violation
of the main principle in all agreements from 1937 to 1946, that it was
forbidden to use a floating factory for the catching of baleen whales in
the Atlantic and the Indian Ocean and certain areas of the Pacific north
of 40°S, and thirdly it was an unfortunate precedent that an international agreement should grant special national rights, in this case
France and Australia.

This was one of the most important items on the agenda of the first
ordinary meeting of the Commission in 1949. This was occasioned by the
great catch of humpbacks that summer off the coast of Madagascar
and the French Congo. In the former of these grounds, the *Anglo-
Norse* had operated under the British flag, though chartered by the
Norwegian-American Spermacet Whaling Co., and in the latter the
Jarama, belonging to an affiliate of the Spermacet Whaling Co. in
Panama, had operated. She was transferred to the Norwegian-French
Sopecoba Company. Both companies were mainly Norwegian-owned
and were managed from Norway. Schedule 17 of 1946 describes floating
factories in territorial waters as factory ships under the jurisdiction of a
Contracting Government, but — clearly with the two floating factories
flying the British and Panamanian flags in mind — a rider was added to
this in 1946 with the view to preventing the two floating factories from
operating in French territorial waters. Furthermore, an addition was
made to the effect that a floating factory that operated in one of the

permitted territorial waters could not, within one year of the termination of the season, operate in one of the others, nor could it catch baleen whales south of 40°S.

The penalties for unlawful catching also aroused a certain amount of discussion. The United States proposed confiscation of the total value of illegally caught whales in accordance with American law and practice. As the statistics on which this proposal was based also included Japanese catches, which produced meat for human consumption and applied a minimum length that differed from the one that was valid for pelagic catching, statistics showed fearfully high figures. When this point was clarified, and it was shown how low the percentage of illegally caught whales really was (for Norwegian expeditions : 1945-6 2.33 per cent for blue whales and 0.33 per cent for fin whales), the proposed was dropped. It was agreed that all illegal catching should be reported to the Commission, which in turn would request the contracting countries to take steps of as uniform a nature as possible.

With regard to the minimum lengths both an American proposal to raise the length to 40 ft. for sperm whales and a British one, put up by H. K. Salvesen, to lower it to 30 ft., were voted down. For the first time a minimum length of 40 ft. was fixed for sei whales. Salvesen also spoke at some length on the unreasonableness of a ban on pelagic catching of humpbacks when land stations could kill unlimited numbers in their breeding grounds. As the 1946-7 rules were also to apply for 1947-8, humpbacks were actually protected to the south of 40°S for another two seasons. The Commission was to decide, on the basis of available biological data, whether it was advisable to recommence humpback catching in 1948-9. The ban was retained for that season, too, but for 1949-50, in accordance with Norway's proposal, permission was given for pelagic catching of 1,250 humpbacks (= 500 BWU).

The question of the length of the season — three or four months — developed into a Norwegian-British issue. Here, too, a compromise was arrived at: the season was to be three and a half months from 15 December to 1 April in 1948-9, fourteen days less than 1947-8. Fears that the quota could not be filled in this short period of 108 days proved groundless, as it was completed in 102 days.

The rule governing the two areas in which pelagic catching of baleen whales was allowed was reinstated precisely as in the 1938 Agreement, i.e. the concessions made to the Japanese in 1939 were suspended. It was agreed to maintain protection of the so-called Southern Pacific Sector (the Sanctuary, the most important part of the former Area I) between 40°W and as far west as 160°W (from South Shetland to the Ross Sea). A proposal by Mackintosh for alternating protection of the five areas had to be abandoned, as this would have required intense scientific research, on which any changes in Schedule, in accordance with the

Convention, would have to be based, but the I.W.C. was authorised to organise investigations of this nature.

It may appear remarkable that the two main issues at the Conference, a total quota of 16,000 BWU for pelagic catching in the Antarctic and the establishment of an international commission, should have occasioned the least discussion and been unanimously adopted. The only cause for concern was that, on the basis of the statistical material, "the quota might possibly prove to be rather high". In Salvesen's opinion it was a compromise "between the certainty that it would result in a reduction of the whale stocks and the conviction that the future ought to be sacrificed to some degree to meet the immediate shortage of oils". The latter consideration suggested that the quota should be as high as possible. The F.A.O. had resolved to ask all whaling countries adhering to the Convention to increase the number of floating factories as rapidly as possible, and "to modify the agreement in order to facilitate more abundant catches". That no one at the conference should have mooted the idea of a higher quota was due to the effects of the disappointing catches of 1945-6. With a catching season of four months and an estimated increase of whale stocks during the war, the outcome had been eagerly awaited by whalers, by governments in countries suffering from a shortage of fats, by whale biologists, and by whale oil dealers. After 154,000 fewer whales had been caught in the five preceding seasons, 1940-5, than in the five seasons immediately preceding them (1935-40) there were well-founded hopes that stocks had increased to such an extent that one would have an idea of what quota to set, in order to ensure complete restoration of stocks. As yet, terms such as "optimum stocks" and "maximum sustainable yield" were not in common use.

Surprise at the results was considerable: these amounted, for the entire Antarctic, to 13,114 baleen whales (8,308 BWU) and 804,907 barrels of whale oil (plus 273 sperm whales and 13,745 barrels of sperm oil). For pelagic catching results were 11,474 whales and 739,775 barrels, an average of 82,197 barrels per expedition, and for South Georgia — the great surprise — 1,913 whales and 78,877 barrels, not appreciably more for three stations than for one station in 1944-5. Apart from the other war years and 1932-3, when only one station was likewise operating, it would be necessary to go right the way back to 1908-9 (four stations) to find lower production. The relative number of blue whales, 30.7 per cent, was the lowest in pelagic Antarctic catching, as was the number of blue whales per whale catcher (including land stations), only 45.8. Only in the 1920s are lower figures found for the number of barrels per BWU pelagic, a mere 98.6. It was remarkable that, while the percentage of sexually mature blue and fin whales showed an increase, the number of lactating females showed a tremendous decline, in the case of blue whale from 43.8 per cent in 1938-9 to 20.7 per cent

94. A whale carcass half-devoured by killer whales before it was brought to the flensing plant.

in 1945-6, and for fin whale from 43.7 to 23.2 per cent. As was always the case after a poor season, excuses were soon in evidence : many floating factories had set off too late, the world catches were poor, weather and ice conditions were exceptionally difficult, there was little krill and whales were lean, while poor lines resulted in unusually high losses of whales after harpooning. On this occasion the excuses were to some extent justified, as the percentage loss was, in fact, particularly high as a result of defective lines. One inspector reported that for a single whale catcher a breakage of lines up to 40 or 50 per cent was not a rarity, while the average for all whale catchers was probably 20 to 25 per cent. The weather was wretched and there were tremendous numbers of killer whales. (The latter hunt whales and other marine animals, generally confining themselves to calves or to ill or wounded adults. Their method of attack is to tear lumps of flesh off their prey and in particular the large tongues of exhausted animals. Dead whales which were waiting to be hauled on to the flensing deck were obviously easy prey, and in this season particularly it was rare for a whale to be hauled on deck with its tongue intact.) Reports from the South Georgia stations also told of large numbers of whales being lost because of broken lines. In 1945 the Setubal station in Portugal reported that thirty-two out of seventy-five harpooned whales were lost owing to the poor quality of the lines.

The establishment of the International Commission on Whaling (I.C.W. or International Whaling Commission, I.W.C., as it was more generally known) was the most significant achievement not only of the Washington Conference but in the whole history of whaling as far as regulation was concerned. It was also of interest to international co-operation in that almost all nations that had some connection or other with the exploitation of one of the earth's natural sources of raw material, delegated their authority to control this exploitation to a permanent commission. Similar treaties had been concluded for fisheries and sealing, but these were restricted both locally and with regard to the number of members. The immediate post-war period was a fruitful one for international co-operation. This was headed by the United Nations which included such subdivisions as the F.A.O., Unesco, the World Health Organisation, and many others. In an atmosphere of this kind it would have appeared a simple matter to solve the problems of whaling as well on an international basis. That the conference should have agreed to the setting up of the Commission does not necessarily mean that it unconditionally accepted the draft submitted by Remington Kellogg. The most important administrative change was that the Commission was to be an independent organ, not a subdivision of the United Nations Organisation. Other changes were that a three-quarters and not a two-thirds majority of votes was required to amend the Schedule. The proposal that the Convention should come into force once it had been ratified by *three* powers was amended to require *six* signatories, to include the Netherlands, Norway, the United Kingdom, the United States and the Soviet Union.

Each contracting government of the Commission nominates a Commissioner who is entitled to one vote. He may be assisted by experts and advisers, although these have no vote. Meetings of the Commission may be attended by observers from non-member-states, intergovernmental organisations such as the F.A.O. and I.C.E.S. (International Council for the Exploration of the Sea) and non-governmental international organisations such as Friends of the Earth and the Royal Society for the Prevention of Cruelty to Animals (R.S.P.C.A.). At the Annual Meeting of the Commission in June 1979, seven non-member-states, seven intergovernmental organisations and twenty-seven non-governmental international organisations were represented by observers.

Altogether twenty-three nations have adhered to the Convention: Argentina, Australia, Brazil, Canada, Chile, Denmark, France, Iceland, the Republic of Korea, Japan, Mexico, the Netherlands, New Zealand, Norway, Panama, Peru, the Seychelles, South Africa, Spain, Sweden, the United Kingdom, the Soviet Union and the United States. Of these only Mexico, the Seychelles (joined 1979) and Sweden have never been active whaling countries. Commercial whaling is currently carried on at varying levels by ten member-nations: Brazil, Chile (joined 1979), Denmark (Greenland), Iceland, Japan, Republic of

Korea (joined 1979), Norway, Peru (joined 1979), Spain (joined 1979) and the Soviet Union. (Until 1979 Chile and Peru had remained outside the Commission as they were unwilling to accept the provision that a shore station was only allowed to catch baleen whales for six months in one year. They also wanted a lower minimum size limit for the sperm whale and maintained a 200-mile territorial limit for whaling. They had therefore established their own whaling commission in co-operation with Ecuador.) Several countries have resigned from the Commission and later rejoined: Brazil (resigned 1966, rejoined 1974), the Netherlands (resigned 1959, rejoined 1962, resigned 1970, rejoined 1977), New Zealand (resigned 1969, rejoined 1976), Norway (resigned 1959, rejoined 1960) and Sweden (resigned 1946, rejoined 1979). The situation fluctuates continuously. For the situation at the time of going to press in mid-1981, see "A Final Note" (p. 774).

In common with other international organisations, the Commission had to be based on full equality between sovereign states. This has produced the grotesque situation that, whereas during the first twenty years it was concerned almost exclusively with pelagic catching in the Antarctic, a majority of its members who were not active in this or, indeed, any form of whaling, or operated from shore stations on a limited scale, were in a position to outvote a minority of pelagic nations. The composition of the Commission was not an adequate expression of the national scope and significance of whaling. As things turned out, however, eight nations emerged as the most active: Australia, Canada, Japan, the Netherlands, Norway, the United Kingdom, the United States and the Soviet Union. Of these, the two first-mentioned and the United States have never engaged in pelagic whaling, and to a very large extent the Commission became a forum for the common and conflicting interests of the five pelagic nations. They share common interests *vis-à-vis* the non-pelagic nations, and wherever they conflict several lines of division may be noted : e.g. the old whaling nations, Great Britain and Norway, and the new, Japan, the Netherlands, and the Soviet Union; the state-subsidised and state-run whaling of the two last-mentioned countries as opposed to the entirely private companies that are a feature of the others. With its main emphasis on meat production, Japan occupies a special position. The pelagic countries have settled a number of questions among themselves outside the Commission.

As well as covering widely differing and divergent interests, the rules of procedure of the Commission contain another weakness, as they lay down *inter alia* that any amendment to the Schedule shall be effective ninety days after the contracting powers have been informed thereof. If a government lodges a protest against the amendment before the lapse of the ninety days, the amendment shall not be valid for any party during a fresh ninety-day period. Before the lapse of this the other governments may also protest, and the amendment will then still not apply to them until they have withdrawn their protest. In practice, this means that every member has virtually a right of veto, on the same lines as the United Nations Security Council, and thus the Commission cannot make any amendment to the Schedule without a unanimous vote. Furthermore, any member may resign from the Commission on 30 June every year, provided notice to this effect has been issued prior to 1 January of the same year. Any other country may then, within one month after receiving notice thereof, likewise renounce the Convention as from 30 June. Already at the constituent meeting of the Commission in 1949 it was clear that a member would make use of the right of protest to evade a decision taken with a valid vote. Within a period of ninety days France protested against the amendment, already mentioned, of the provision with regard to floating factories in territorial waters, and as none of the others protested before the period had terminated, the resolution applied to them but not to France.

The Commission's own rules of procedure, in fact, not only provided a reason but also a necessary condition for arriving at a unanimous acceptance of the Convention : the fact that any member knew that, by lodging a protest, it could legitimately evade the obligation to observe a decision which the Commission had adopted with a sufficient number of votes. Without this loophole it is inconceivable that some states would have supported the Convention.

Another weakness was the Commission's very limited powers to amend the regulations once they have been adopted. Amendments must not involve "restrictions on the number or nationality of factory ships or land stations, nor allocate specific quotas to any factory or ship or land station or to any group of factory ships or land stations, and shall take into consideration the interests of the consumers of whale products and the whaling industry". This is evident in the preamble to the Convention, which starts off by recognising the interest of all nations to preserve for coming generations the great natural source of raw materials that stocks of whales represent. It continues by deploring the fact that over-fishing has jeopardised this source. In the next section, however, it is "recognised that it is the common interest to achieve the optimum level of whale stocks as rapidly as possible without causing widespread economic and nutritional distress", and it concludes by stating that there is agreement "to conclude a convention to provide for the proper conservation of whale stocks and thus make possible the orderly development of the whaling industry". It is the impossibility of reconciling these two aspects, conservation of whale stocks and the economic interests of whaling, that constitutes the real reason why the Commission has not been in a position to carry out its task. It has not possessed the necessary powers to implement its decisions.

Despite these weaknesses it would be wrong to say that the Commission has been unimportant, but it has still not been successful in preventing the whale stocks from being heavily reduced. Every year the major dispute involved the size of the total quota. Everyone agreed that whale stocks were in jeopardy, but there was no agreement on the magnitude of this danger, nor on the extent to which the quota should be reduced. Such large economic interests were associated with whaling that it was difficult to accept the idea of scrapping precious special matériel. The Convention stated that regulation should be based on scientific research, but the commercial interests cast doubts on the results of science. The Commission established three permanent committees: the Scientific Committee, which was to investigate the biological and scientific material and submit its findings; the Technical Committee, dealing with the whaling laws and regulations of various countries, reporting violations of the Convention, catching methods, etc., although its most important task was to propose figures for the global quota and other restrictive measures, on the basis of other considerations apart from purely scientific ones (the meetings of this committee for this reason turned out in practice to be plenary sessions, where the most important decisions were made); and the Finance and Administrative Committee dealing with budgets, subscriptions of member countries, and staff matters.

What effects have the first thirty years of the I.W.C.'s activities had on stocks of whale? In order to save what is left, the world quota for 1977/8-78 (i.e. the 1977/8 Antarctic season and the 1978 season elsewhere) as follows: 459 fin whales (essentially off Iceland), 1,379 sei/Bryde, 8,645 minke, 13,037 sperm. If one BWU is equal to 30 minke whales, the total quota of baleen whales south of the Equator (including the Antarctic) is 317 BWU, not more than a single floating factory in the "olden days" could catch in the course of a couple of weeks. On these grounds the thirty years of work undertaken by the I.W.C. have proved a fiasco.

This is not the fault of the Commission as such, but is because a number of members have refused to recognise facts and have argued that they should be allowed to catch as long as there is anything to be caught. Perhaps the most positive result of the Commission's work or mere existence has been that developments in the Antarctic, despite the Commission, have reflected the most blatant example of the extermination of one of nature's major sources of raw materials, and that under the growing pressure of world opinion to preserve natural resources, it has been possible to allow the larger species of whale to live in peace long enough to ensure restoring them to the "optimum level" that will provide the "maximum sustainable yield". It will, however, take a generation or two, or even longer, before that goal is reached.

If we compare the Schedule of 1946 with today's we shall find that only a few unamended rules are left, and yet an amendment as important as national quotas was arranged among the whaling nations themselves, because the Convention was not empowered to do so. How and why these amendments have been carried out is one of the principal themes in the history of whaling after the Second World War. When the Commission was constituted in 1949 the expansion of pelagic Antarctic catching appeared to have stabilised at around some eighteen expeditions. This number admittedly rose to nineteen in 1950-2, but when it dropped to sixteen the following season and it proved possible in 1953 to conclude an agreement between practically all the companies for limitation of the number of whale catchers, developments appeared to be heading in the right direction.

Before the 1949 meeting there had been a tug-of-war between Norway and Britain over the chairmanship and the location of the Secretariat. In London the argument ran that Britain had convoked previous conferences, and that meetings had been held in London, where the necessary staff qualified to deal with international matters was to be found. The Norwegians maintained that it would be natural to locate the Secretariat in Norway, because Norway was the oldest and biggest whaling nation, and had already taken over *International Whaling Statistics*. On grounds of prestige, however, Britain was so insistent on this point that she got her way. By way of compensation Norway was to fill the chairmanship, and as an added gesture she was to have the honour of organising the I.W.C.'s first ordinary meeting in Oslo from 17 to 21 July 1950, with Birger Bergersen as chairman and A. T. A. Dobson as secretary.

By the time the Commission was constituted in 1949, the rebuilding of the British and Norwegian whaling fleets had been completed, the joint operation of the Norwegian companies had ceased, and Japan, the Netherlands, and the Soviet Union were participants in pelagic catching in the Antarctic.

Joint operations of the Norwegian companies, 1945-1948

Although the joint operation of the Norwegian companies in 1945-8 is entirely a Norwegian phenomenon, and consequently of minor interest internationally, it proved nevertheless of such decisive importance to the rehabilitation of the Norwegian whaling fleet, and in this way to Norway's place in international catching and competition for the 16,000 units, that it deserves a brief mention in this context. Companies were compelled to operate jointly by the Norwegian Government, which made this a condition for releasing requisitioned floating factories. The principle was that companies that had retained their floating factories should pay to those that had lost theirs a part of the building sum for new vessels. All in all, the State paid the companies Kr.213 million by way of paid-up insurance, freight earnings, and compensation for the use of their ships. This sum did not even cover half of the value of the vessels lost, the loss of five seasons' catches, the sale of 1939-40 production, and the price of new matériel, which was three times higher than the insurance payments for what had been lost. Companies were also forced to sell a large amount of the oil on the home market at a very low maximum price, in order to ensure that the Norwegian people would have cheap margarine. This deprived the companies of Kr.244 million, which was the extra amount they could have obtained for the oil had it been sold without restriction at market prices. None of Norway's rivals was subject to a similar obligation, and this was one of the reasons adduced by Norwegian companies to explain why the matériel was not modernised sufficiently to stand comparison with that of their rivals. For the Kr.244 million gross (or Kr.120 million net) the smaller, less effective pre-war floating factories could have been replaced by three of the largest and most modern expeditions, which would have placed the Norwegian whaling fleet in a better position to compete.

The idea of joint operation was naturally enthusiastically welcomed by those who had lost their ships and now had an opportunity of financing expensive new constructions. As it was generally assumed that after a short boom period prices would drop to normal pre-war levels, a number of companies dared not risk building expensive ships except on the basis of joint operation. For those who had retained their ships the joint operation entailed a considerable sacrifice, as they had to forgo most of their earnings in order to supply rivals with modern floating factories and reduce their own chances of an improved catch. In order to force their hand, the State made it an absolute condition that all companies that had caught in 1939-40 should take part in this joint venture.

Faced with the market trend that had been predicted, several companies hesitated to resume operations under any conditions. The floating factories that had been casualties of war had been insured for Kr.7-8 million each, while the whale catchers had been insured for some Kr.800,000 each; replacements would cost respectively Kr.22-24 million and Kr.1.75 million. Production costs were calculated at £35 a ton, and the market price in the autumn of 1945 at £40, too small a margin to ensure any profit. If Great Britain and Norway had entirely replaced their twenty expeditions, and could have produced 1.8 million barrels from 16,000 units, there would only be 90,000 for each expedition. If other countries joined in, there would be still less. Norwegian whaling was saved from these gloomy predictions by joint operation, and its success was ensured by the rise in price, a rise that no one could possibly have foretold in 1945. It set in during the late autumn of 1946, and was particularly marked the following winter. It applied to all edible fats and oils. In the course of a year and a half the price of palm kernel oil rose from £48 10s to £115 10s a ton, copra from £31 to £83, soya oil from £58 to £114, and American lard from 13.27 cents a pound to 31.50 cents (all prices c.i.f. U.K. port). The price of whale oil followed suit: the average price for the three seasons of joint operation 1945-8 was £67 10s, £100, and £110, and the operating profits Kr.28.8 million, Kr.166.5 million, and Kr.137.5 million, a total of Kr.333 million.

The companies were not free to dispose of their oil as they wished: world production of all edible fats and oils was allocated to the various countries by the Combined Food Board (from July 1946 known as the International Emergency Food Council, I.E.F.C.) during and after the war in order to ensure distribution to countries most in need, and in order to prevent it being bought up by economically well-placed countries or speculators. Norway, for example, was allowed to retain 110,000 tons out of a production of 411,400 tons for her own needs. The remainder had to be sold according to allocations made by the I.E.F.C.

What significance did joint operation have for the rehabilitation of Norwegian whaling? In all, the three seasons netted Kr.800 million gross, or Kr.334 million net, of which companies which had no floating factory received Kr.94.5 million to pay off the five new floating factories, which together cost Kr.135 million. The results of the joint operation far surpassed all expectation, thanks to three splendid boom years, which ensured that Norwegian whaling, at the end of this three-year period, was economically in a far stronger position than anyone had dared to hope. But once it had recovered so strongly, one is tempted to ask: why did the history of the 1930s repeat itself, why after a decade was there a threat not only to Norway's leadership but to her very existence as a whaling nation?

Rebuilding the whaling fleets of other nations

To say that Norway was edged out in the competition for the 16,000 units is no satisfactory answer, unless at the same time the reason for this can be indicated. Maybe rehabilitation itself bore the seeds of decline?

Just how rapidly and to what extent global whaling could be resumed depended on three factors: the number and effectiveness of the surviving floating factories and whale catchers; the distribution of German and Japanese matériel; the contracting of new floating factories. When the war came to an end the only floating factories which were known to be able to operate in 1945-6 were the four in Norway. Two more were discovered, which the Germans had used as depot ships for their Navy;

they were severely damaged, but were repaired in time to participate in the first season, though one was not ready until 12 January. In Britain, Salvesen's new *Southern Venturer* would be ready in time. In the autumn it was obvious that Japan had lost all her floating factories. There were four floating factories in German harbours, the *Unitas,* the *Wikinger,* the *Walter Rau,* and the *Jan Wellem.* The last-mentioned was such a wreck that it was broken up; the others were towed to British ports in the hope that they might be repaired in time for the first season; the two first-mentioned were patched up in time, but the *Walter Rau* was so badly damaged that she had to be built up practically from scratch.

A violent dispute arose on the distribution of these three floating factories as German war reparations The principles had been set up in the Potsdam Agreement, and their realisation entrusted to the Inter-Allied Reparations Agency (I.A.R.A.). Several countries had their eye on these floating factories — the Soviet Union, Norway, the Netherlands, Great Britain, and the United States. The upshot of it was the Soviet Union was given the *Wikinger* re-christened the *Slava*), while Norway acquired the *Walter Rau* (rechristened the *Kosmos IV*), which was sold by the Government to Anders Jahre's Kosmos company. In 1951 she was almost completely rebuilt, and extended an extra 26 ft. No one had ever imagined that the symbol of Nazi Germany's pride as a whaling nation would in 1968 be the last Norwegian floating factory active in pelagic Antarctic whaling, or that the Norwegian floating factory *Kosmos III,* renamed the *Nisshin Maru III,* was to be the last Japanese floating factory in pelagic Antarctic whaling. Before the war the *Unitas* had actually been owned by Unilever N.V., and for this reason the Netherlands demanded that she should be a Dutch vessel again. Unilever's right of ownership, however, was rejected by the prize court because the floating factory had been captured in a German harbour by a British warship, and would therefore have to be awarded to the British Government by the Admiralty, on the basis of the principle of international law that a ship has the nationality of the flag she is flying at the moment she is captured; since the *Unitas* was flying the German flag, she was "a good, lawful prize". After operating, together with the *Wikinger,* for the Ministry of Food in 1945-6 under the name of *Empire Victory,* she was sold to the Union Whaling Company of Durban for £1.05 million.

This purchase must have been one of the best bargains in the history of whaling. The 1946-7 production was sold for £1.8 million, so that after one season the floating factory had paid for itself, the operating expenses had been covered, and shareholders were left with £420,000 out of a capital of £1.5 million. How magnificent the following seasons must have been, with prices of £110, no debts to pay on floating factories, and no extra expenses, as in Norway. In 1950 the name was changed to the *Abraham Larsen*; in 1957 the ship was sold, together with eight whale catchers, for £2,715,000 to Taiyo Gyogyo K.K. of Japan, and re-christened the *Nisshin Maru II*. She caught for the last time in the Antarctic in 1964-5 and in 1967 was converted to a floating fish-processing factory. This floating factory has in other words operated under four different names, and for as many different countries, a typical example of the varying fortunes of whaling.

Altogether, nine floating factories operated in 1945-6, while two shore stations were re-opened in South Georgia : Husvik Harbour, closed since 1931, and Leith Harbour, where operations had been suspended after 1942. This was altogether more than had been foreseen. Apart from the Germans, the companies that did not resume whaling after the war included the Vestfold Corporation, of Panama, and Unilever.

One big problem remained to be solved : whale catchers. Forty-two of the Norwegian catchers had been lost, and seventy-nine were available, but even if all of them were released from requisitioning and equipped for catching, they were in very poor condition. 1,200 h.p. was considered a minimum power output. Fifty-two of the seventy-nine were below this limit, forty-nine as low as 900 h.p. and even less, fifty-one were old and worn out. The Norwegian fleet would require a complete replacement for these boats, with eighty-five new vessels ranging in power from 1,800 to 2,400 h.p.

Of the British vessels, only fourteen had been lost, and 140 were still afloat. Qualitatively they were far superior to the Norwegian; only fifty-five of the 140 were below the 1,200 h.p. limit and nine were 2,000 h.p. or above, while Norway had no boats in this category. Even if no new vessels were constructed, the British fleet possessed a very effective fleet of whale catchers, and could employ eleven for each of the three floating factories in 1945-6, whereas Norway had only seven available for each. The right to possession of the fifty-five whale catchers the Germans had had built in Norway in 1941-5, with whale catcher hulls but provisionally equipped for naval service, proved an international problem. The idea had been that Germany would in this way possess a fleet of powerful whale catchers, capable of whaling after the war once the expected German victory had been won. The I.A.R.A., however, would not recognise these boats as Norwegian. Norway lodged a vigorous protest, and after protracted negotiations and thanks mainly to the goodwill of the United States, the net result was that Norway was handed eighteen of the boats that she herself had built and paid for with Norwegian money taken by the Germans from the Bank of Norway. A demand from the Allies for Japanese boats to be handed over was rejected by the Combined Food Board on the grounds that the few boats available must be used for catching near the coast in order to provide the Japanese people with food, and if the European nations required boats, these could be built in Japan. As things turned out, the United States, with the support of the Combined Food Board, had far more ambitious plans for the Japanese whale catchers.

An unexpected source of whale catchers was made available by British sales of the many corvettes built during the war as submarine chasers and escort vessels, some of them on the basis of the Smith's Dock Company's whale catcher designs. In Canada alone sixty-four were built in 1940-1. Although the sale price was so low (approximately one-tenth to one-fifteenth of the building price) that these might almost have been regarded as gifts, conversion was necessary on such a scale that they turned out to be almost as expensive as new whale catchers. Owing to their size (700-750 gross tons) and powerful engines (2,750 h.p.) they were also expensive to run, but the most important point was that they could be handed over quickly in a converted condition, whereas there was a long waiting-list for new boats. Yards lacked materials, and for the moment had their hands full overhauling a much run-down merchant fleet. Once the building of whale catchers, however, got into its stride, the result was almost a new armaments race. Before the end of 1951 126 new boats had been delivered, sixty-eight for the Norwegians, thirty-four for the British, twenty-three for the Japanese, and one for the Argentinians. Exactly one-half were built in England, and of the remainder, an equal number in Norway and Japan. Altogether, a total of £24 million was invested in whale catchers alone during these years, half of it by Norwegian companies. Despite this the Norwegian whale catcher fleet was inferior to the British both in number and in efficiency. This was reflected in the results of catching, even though other factors, too, were involved. In 1947-8 the Norwegian floating factories operated with an average of 10.1 whale catchers per floating factory, while the British had 13.3; in 1948-9 it was 12 and 16 respectively; and the average horsepower for the British was 1,722, for the Norwegians 1,484. In 1947-8 the four British floating factories had, by 28 February, accounted for 4,356 BWU, whereas the five Norwegian ones, of the same size, had only managed 3,960, and in 1948-9 the British boats had an average day work of 115.5 barrels, the Norwegian 97.1. With a price of £110 a ton the former provided sufficient raw material for the production of oil amounting to £2,200 a day, and the latter £1,750.

The whale catcher fleet showed a tendency that was still more to the disadvantage of Norway after 1952, when that part of the fleet was considered to have been rebuilt, this being the last year a comparatively large number of catchers (ten) had been built for Norwegian account, while other countries (apart from Britain) built 103 new ones, with increasingly powerful engines, the Japanese up to 3,500 h.p., the Russians 3,600 h.p. Is this one of the reasons why Norway, despite the

fact that in 1948 she had rebuilt her whaling fleet, which in size was
superior to the others, only fifteen years later was almost left trailing
behind her rivals? By then, incidentally, Britain, South Africa, and the
Netherlands had thrown in their hands. Do the floating factories provide
yet another answer?

In 1946-8 Norway received another four floating factories, the
repaired *Walter Rau* (*Kosmos IV*) and three new ones. Rebuilding was
thus at an end, at the same time as joint operation. Norway then had
ten floating factories, the same number as in 1939-40. One more had
been completed, the *Kosmos V*, but the Norwegian Government refused
to grant it a concession, in accordance with the principle that had at one
time been adopted that Norway would not increase *her* whaling fleet
after the war, despite the fact that this floating factory would undoubtedly have proved the most effective of all. The *Kosmos V* was now
compelled to operate as an ordinary tanker right up to 1966, when she
was sold to South Africa and fitted out as a fish-oil and fish-meal factory.
Britain's rebuilding programme was restricted to four floating factories,
Union Whaling's *Abraham Larsen* (ex *Unitas*), United Whalers' new
Balaena, and Salvesen's two new vessels, the *Southern Venturer* in 1945
and the *Southern Harvester* in 1946. Subsequently, no floating factory
has been built or converted for Norwegian or British account, while other
nations have introduced thirteen new ones — Japan five, the Soviet
Union five, the Netherlands two, and Panama one. Three of these have
only operated in the North Pacific. Furthermore, Japan has purchased
eight floating factories from other countries, all four British, both Dutch,
one Norwegian, and one Panamanian. Three of them were purchased in
order to acquire their quotas, and they have never been used for whaling.
We shall return to this below.

A serious drawback for the Norwegian fleet was that it included four
older converted pre-war floating factories. Norway was the only nation
with floating factories of this category, and it seriously reduced production. In 1946-52 the average price of whale oil was £100, a price never
previously nor subsequently recorded over such a long period of time.
The average catch of the ten Norwegian floating factories was 102,000
barrels, the British 146,000, a surplus margin over the Norwegian of
44,000 barrels which would give an extra annual income of £790,000.
In this comparison the four old Norwegian floating factories are included.
If we compare the six new Norwegian with the four British, the latter
produced 30,000 more barrels, to a value of £500,000. The objection
may of course be raised that whaling was a gamble, with the result
depending on so many uncertain factors, not least the human, which
cannot be expressed in statistics. A few examples will illustrate how
fortunes could change. The *Southern Venturer*, which in 1947-8 was
responsible that season for the record, with 203,198 barrels, secured only

95. Prince Philip (fourth from right) visiting Grytviken, 12 January 1957, the only royal visit to South Georgia.

117,323 in 1951-2, whereas the *Kosmos IV* during the same seasons had 105,000 and 141,000 barrels, the *Norhval* in 1946-7 accounted for 170,000 barrels, in 1950-1 89,000. While the Norwegian-British floating factories recorded a total decline during these years, the Russian floating factory the *Slava* increased her production from 35,000 to 140,000 barrels, the Dutch rose from 77,000 to 93,000, and the two Japanese doubled their production from 73,000 to 148,000 in 1950-1, and almost tripled it to 207,047 barrels in 1951-2. Even if all allowances are made for incalculable factors, the trend appears quite obvious.

In Norway's case three reasons for her poor showing can be found. The authorities did not allow the two oldest floating factories to be replaced by the large new *Kosmos V,* and secondly the Norwegian companies, as the result of compulsory sale at reduced price, were deprived of Kr.244 million, which could have been invested in modernisation of their floating matériel. In the third place the Norwegian floating factories do not appear to have been as practical and efficient as the British. A sign of this is that in 1951-6 four of them underwent a considerable amount of conversion, being lengthened by from 26 to 66 ft. For the sum this involved twelve of the largest and most powerful whale catchers could have been built. Just what significance a fourth factor, the boiling equipment, may have had, is impossible to calculate. A great deal too depended on chance events. Two large fat fin whales ($=$ 1 BWU) at the end of the season would produce far more oil than one lean blue whale (= 1 BWU) of almost minimum size at the beginning of the season. The try-out per BWU bore no relation to the size of the floating factory and its boiling equipment. One of the smallest and oldest floating factories succeeded in 1950-1 in producing 136.1 barrels per BWU out of its 387 BWU, whereas one with the largest catch, 1,313 BWU, only recorded 105 barrels. Perhaps the most important reason for Norway's inferiority has not yet been mentioned. The companies realised that, with so many nations engaging in a free-for-all for the 16,000 units, whaling would be a dying industry before many years had elapsed. For this reason the companies preferred to invest a considerable portion of their earnings in shipping — and to some extent industry — rather than ploughing it back into whaling. After the boom years of 1946-52 the price of whale oil clearly revealed a downward trend. In short, whaling had seen its best days, shipping was more attractive, and capital has always sought an outlet where the prospects of profits are greatest. In British whaling the same factors may have operated. We should remember also that Dutch whaling was subsidised by the state and Russian whaling was state-operated, and that therefore neither of them was responsible for the economic results of their catch, as was the case with companies based on private capital.

29

THE SECOND EXPANSION, 1946-52

The Norwegian crew law

In 1945-50 it looked as if the whole world wanted to go whaling — Americans, Argentinians, Australians, Austrians, Brazilians, Canadians, Chileans, Danes, Dutch, Finns, Germans, Italians, Japanese, Russians, Swedes, all had whaling plans, and practically everyone was thinking in terms of pelagic catching in the Antarctic. There was also talk of operating from shore stations in a number of places. On this occasion expansion ran into three obstacles that had not been encountered before: the Norwegian crew law, the I.W.C.'s 16,000 units, and the fact that the losers of the Second World War depended on the good grace of the victors. Two new countries, which had not previously taken part in whaling in the Southern Ocean, secured a place for themselves. Of the other whaling countries, Japan was admitted, but Germany was excluded, while Panamanian plans were only put into practice for a brief period.

The Dutch plans, which have been mentioned several times already, were hatched out in the underground movement during the war by a number of businessmen. They assumed that the Dutch East Indies (Indonesia) had suffered so much damage that it would take several years to restore production of vegetable oils, and whaling would be able to cover immediate needs for fats after the war. The plan was supported by the Government, by Prince Bernhard personally, and by a syndicate of banks and shipbuilding yards. The founders realised that without Norwegian experts it would be impossible to realise this plan. A delegation, which came to Norway with a proposal for crews consisting of 90 per cent Norwegians the first year, 80 per cent the second, and 70 per cent the third, were met with the Norwegian "crew law" of 21 December 1945. This highly controversial piece of legislation, which was passed primarily with a view to halting the Dutch plans, but which also had a bearing on other countries, ran as follows: "It is forbidden for Norwegian companies, nationals, or residents of the realm directly or indirectly to participate in or to assist in promoting whaling with floating factories under a foreign flag. Exceptions to this provision may be made in cases of a foreigner or foreign company whaling in the last season in the Southern Ocean prior to 3 September 1939, or to a foreign floating factory which prior to this date was used for whaling." An important addition stated that "this ban shall apply irrespective of contractual or service relationships established before the law came into force".

96.   The *Willem Barendsz II*, the new Dutch floating factory, built in Holland 1955.

The motive behind this proposed law was that the restoration of the whaling fleet to its previous level was based on the presumption that Japan and Germany would be excluded. The size of the Norwegian and British whaling fleets was considered suitable for rational exploitation of stocks of whale. In the second place it was believed that the boom would soon be over and that prices would fall. The appearance on the scene of even one minor new competitor would mean that the catch would be reduced below the profit margin or else that stocks would be over-fished. As Norway could not count on recognition, using diplomatic channels, for her "natural right" to whaling on the same scale as before, the only alternative was to prevent other nations participating by forbidding Norwegians to assist them. The breakdown of whaling would be a national catastrophe for Norway, which for this reason had a moral right and duty to protect its interests. Allowing Norwegians to participate in expeditions operating the last season prior to 3 September 1939 would not mean joining new whaling ventures. An exception, for example, could be made for all Japanese and German floating factories, including the two chartered from Norway, and for the American company, the Western Operating Corporation (the *Ulysses*), and naturally for the British. As all the Japanese floating factories had been lost, and Unilever and the American company had no intention of resuming whaling, an exception to the rule would at the moment only involve the three German floating factories, and all three were granted dispensation. This was a necessary provision in the law, in order not to prevent serviceable floating factories being used to assist in redressing the world fats shortage, and they would be used not by Germany but by the Allies. One of these Allied nations was the Soviet Union, which had not been active in pelagic catching in the Southern Ocean before 1939, but the floating factory, the *Wikinger,* which they acquired had done so, and could consequently be granted a dispensation. This would have been given, too, had the ship been granted to the Netherlands. This point was not realised in Holland, where the fact that the Norwegians were allowed to serve with the Russians, but not with the Dutch, was regarded as discriminatory. The Russians applied for leave to employ thirty Norwegian specialists, including gunners, and dispensation was granted on two conditions: that the Soviet Union would ratify all international agreements and that dispensation was only valid for 1946-7 and would not be regarded as a precedent for subsequent seasons. The latter point was intended as a warning against further extension of pelagic whaling.

The Netherlands

In Norway, too, there was dissatisfaction among whalers with the law. It was regarded as a grave encroachment on personal liberty, and the result would be that the new expeditions would set sail with crews recruited from other nations, while Norwegians were out of work. The gunners in particular were bitter, because foreign companies held out tempting offers. They discovered many loopholes in the law, involving Norway in a great deal of foreign-political unpleasantness. Norway could not prevent new expeditions, even foreign ones with Norwegian crews, from setting out. The first to do so was the Dutch expedition.

The Nederlandsche Maatschappij voor de Valvischvaart N.V. was constituted on 22 February 1946, with a share capital of Fl. 7.5 million. A Norwegian shipowner in Gothenburg managed to get hold of a tanker of 10,409 gross tons which was suitable for conversion. The work of conversion took place in Amsterdam, and the boat was called the *Willem Barendsz* after the famous Dutch polar explorer who gave his name to the Barents Sea. He it was who, in 1596, discovered Bjørn-øya and Spitsbergen with their tremendous quantities of Greenland whale. The next problem was the boiling plant and catching equipment, which was also subject to the Norwegian ban. This was evaded by having the rotary cooker supplied by a firm in England, which produced it on licence from the Norwegian patentholder. Harpoons were obtained in Sweden. The problem of whale catchers was solved by the purchase of eight from the Vestfold Corporation in Panama (in reality Norway), which had lost its floating factory during the war and had no intention of resuming whaling. The company now obtained a very good price for twenty-year-old vessels.

It now remained to enrol a crew, in defiance of the Norwegian crew law. All Norwegian consuls abroad were instructed by the Norwegian

Government not to sign on any Norwegians. This was openly sabotaged by the consul in Amsterdam, who was a director in the company and signed on about fifty Norwegians. It was particularly difficult to stop the gunners, who went wherever there was a chance of earning most money and where they would be able to retain most of their earnings. It is hardly an exaggeration to say that the Norwegian gunners' evasion of Norwegian law made Dutch whaling possible, and there was no nation destined to create so many difficulties for the I.W.C. and regulation as the Netherlands. Not being able to sign on gunners in Amsterdam meant very little, seeing that they could join the expedition in Cape Town, where this became the general practice, and where they could be put ashore beyond the reach of Norwegian law. They usually signed a five-year contract with a guaranteed minimum income of Kr.50,000 a season. The second best (No. 2) of the gunners made Kr.80,000 in 1947-8. It was worth paying a skilled gunner good money, as the catch for which he was responsible *in excess of* No. 3 represented in 1946-7 a value of Kr.1.04 million and the value of what the best gunner caught over and above the catch of the least successful amounted in that season to Kr.4.8 million, and in 1947-8 to Kr.6.4 million.

The departure of the *Willem Barendsz* with her eight whale catchers from Amsterdam on 27 October 1946 was celebrated as a national event, and as a triumph over Norway. There were 200 Dutchmen on board the floating factory, sixty-eight Faroese, fifty Norwegians, and a few Britons, Swedes, and South Africans, but on board the whale catchers all the gunners and practically the entire crew were Norwegian. The expedition leader was also a Norwegian. Many of the crew on board the floating factory had never set eyes on a whale, and were completely inexperienced. This was the main reason why the first season, for which a catch of 120,000 barrels had been calculated, only produced 76,000. Not unexpectedly, the Netherlands placed the blame for this on Norway, which was subjected to considerable diplomatic pressure. It was pointed out that the law contained a ban on participation in whaling on board a foreign *floating factory,* in other words the ban could not apply to whale catchers. To this Norway replied that the law had been expressly framed in this way, since Norway would not have any objection to a foreign country using Norwegians for catching from shore stations.

The company received state support in the form of generous credits and a guarantee of purchase of the entire production at the current market price. As this was £93 10s, the result was satisfactory, despite the disappointing catch. For the seasons 1946-50 dividends of 3, 5, 7, and 6 per cent respectively were declared. In 1950-2 results were also very favourable, and by then the cost of matériel had been almost written off. In 1950 the Russians offered to buy the entire expedition for a very large sum, and since catching had not proved as lucrative as expected, and a sale would yield three times as much as the face value of the shares, shareholders were anxious to sell, but the Government refused, anxious that the country should not be deprived of such a rich source of fats. Instead, it concluded an entirely unique contract with the company : this was to run for eight years, from 1 July 1951. Fl.46.6 million were to be invested in a new floating factory of 26,500 dead-weight tons, and eight new whale catchers would be ready in time for the 1955-6 season. The state guaranteed that as much as Fl.38 million would be written off during the contractual period, and it annually advanced the necessary funds for operating, as well as guaranteeing shareholders a dividend of from 6 to 3 per cent, according to the size of the catch. The state likewise guaranteed loans and interest. In actual fact this was not very far removed from being state-run whaling, on the same lines as the Russian.

Great Britain

There was a certain measure of irritation in Britain because, although dispensation from the Norwegian crew law would automatically be given, an application had to be submitted every year. The problem became more complicated when the dispensation was requested for the catching of sperm whales in Peruvian waters between Antarctic seasons, with matériel that had been used there. Norway had no hesitation in granting this request, as "it was a small floating factory with little capacity and with whale catchers that cannot be used in the whaling grounds of the Southern Ocean". As things turned out, its capacity was by no means so small, and the result proved one of the great bonanzas in the history of whaling. Almost 92,000 barrels were produced, and the price rose from $180 per ton in the autumn of 1945 to $520 in February 1947. Others, too, were naturally anxious to try their luck, and Salvesen was granted a dispensation for one of his floating factories in 1947, and applied on behalf of both in 1948, as did the Union Whaling Company for the *Empire Victory*.

The Norwegian authorities were in considerable doubt as what to do. Britain protested, saying that refusal would be a serious act of discrimination against Salvesen. Besides, catching meant a great deal to Britain's foreign currency earnings, and Norway could not on her own regulate a foreign nation's catching in international waters. Relations with Britain regarding the whaling question were at that time strained; while Norwegian gunners were making it possible for new, foreign nations to enjoy a share of the 16,000 units, Norway was appealing to Britain for support in preventing the restoration of Japanese and German whaling. Salvesen was exasperated that Norwegian dispensation had made it possible for the Spermacet Whaling Company and for the French Sopecoba Company — both of which were largely Norwegian owned and were managed from Norway — to catch large numbers of humpbacks in tropical waters in the breeding grounds, while catching of these whales was strictly regulated in the Antarctic.

The problem was solved with the aid of the seamen's organisations in response to a direct appeal from the Norwegian Government. With reference to the fact that the wage agreement only applied to the Antarctic season of 1947-8, the principle that no one should sign on for whaling in two areas in the same season was adopted by the gunners as well. Salvesen then declared, after being officially informed by Norway of the situation and the decision of the organisations, that he would be unlikely to despatch his expeditions to Peru. This episode had shown how difficult — or impossible — it was for Norway to implement the crew law without running into diplomatic problems. This was further emphasised by the operations of the *Anglo-Norse*. Whaling off the coast of Peru in 1947, 1948, and 1951 proved a tremendous success : 103,834 barrels of sperm oil during the last of these years was a record for a single expedition in one season. In all three seasons a total of 283,821 barrels were sold at top prices. Great were the rewards for an expedition that operated alone.

Catching humpbacks off Madagascar in 1949 and 1950 and off the French Congo in 1952 yielded less brilliant results. Neither the crew law, the seamen's organisations, nor the I.W.C. could put a stop to these operations. The reason was that France had not accepted Article 17 of the Convention, because, according to the French, whaling could only be undertaken in French territorial waters with a French floating factory. For this reason the *Anglo-Norse* sailed under the French flag. Hostility towards this company was directed against the Norwegian tycoon Anders Jahre, since it was entirely thanks to his assistance that it had been possible to form this company. He had personally helped to finance, and obtain whale catchers and crews. He was most severely criticised because he was destroying whale stocks in tropical waters, regardless of past experience. The notably declining catches made, from 60,600 barrels in 1949 to 16,500 in 1952, were an indication of this. The floating factory was then taken out of whaling, spent a few years in the tanker trade, and foundered in 1957. Despite this, the expedition had been a veritable goldmine for the owners, but at the same time it had greatly complicated Norway's position in discussions on international regulation.

The fats market

The crew law faced its real test when confronted with the many plans of 1947-50. These projects had all sprung to life owing to the high price paid for whale oil, although the noble aim of redressing the global shortage of fats was invoked. Just how hollow this argument really was emerged clearly from the simple fact that, however many expeditions were involved, they could jointly only account for 16,000 units. Nor would the argument hold water that the Norwegian and British unwillingness to admit new companies was an inhuman gesture to a world short of fats, for the simple reason that the fleets of these two countries on their own were capable of catching and reducing all these units. Europe would not receive as much as an extra drop of oil if others were allowed to join in. In 1950, when there were prospects of several new large floating factories being engaged, even the Dutch had to admit that they too benefited from the Norwegian crew law, which at one time they had so furiously condemned. The only way in which production could be increased was to improve exploitation of the raw material or to catch in violation of the Convention, and without an international system of inspection it was impossible to prevent this happening.

The universal shortage of fats was caused by not only the upheavals of war, but a poor harvest in 1947 and increased consumption on the part of the producer countries of their own production. The International Emergency Food Council had estimated that the world's minimum requirements would be covered by 1947 production. Meanwhile, grain harvests in Europe failed owing to a period of drought, and the same happened in the United States, with the result that much of the grain that otherwise would have been earmarked for animal feed had to be allocated for human consumption. A maize harvest in the United States that produced 250 million hectolitres less than expected, and the consequent drop in the production of animal fats were significant factors. In the Far East the rice harvest was poor, and for this reason, for example, India — the world's largest producer and exporter of groundnuts — was practically eliminated from the market, since the bulk of this harvest was consumed by the native population. World exports of groundnuts declined from 1.1 million tons in 1938 to 0.52 million tons in 1948, and meanwhile Manchuria was out of the picture as an exporter of soya beans. As 60 per cent of the world's population had an annual fat consumption of less than 10 kg., an increase of only a few per cent of their consumption of domestic production would have a bearing on exports. In Indonesia as a result of the war the entire transport system for the collection of copra from the thousands of islands had broken down. The level world food production was expected to have reached in 1947 could at the earliest be achieved in 1951, but even if by then production were to reach the pre-war level there would still be a considerable gap, owing to increased population and a rise in the standard of living for many of them. In 1947 a deficit of 3 million tons of fats was calculated, and it was predicted that this would be reduced to 1 million tons by 1951.

In view of this it is not surprising that prices rose, despite every attempt at national and international price control. From 1939 to 1947 the price of groundnuts c.i.f. U.K./Continent rose 352 per cent, copra 388 per cent, palm kernels 411 per cent, whale oil 270 per cent; nor was there any prospect of prices falling before the balance of supply and demand had stabilised sometime in the 1950s, a forecast which on the whole proved correct. In 1934-8 it was estimated that the annual average production of vegetable oils was 10 million tons and of animal fats 10.4 million tons, of which whale oil accounted for 500,000 tons or 2.5 per cent of the total. Of this amount, only a quarter — 5 to 6 million tons — came on to the market (in 1938 5.83 million tons), of which whale oil accounted for 9 per cent. (Approximately 7 million tons of butter fat in consumer milk is not included in total production.) It would be difficult to state with certainty how large production was in 1947; as far as whale oil was concerned, the most important point was that the quantity of edible fats and oils reaching the market had dropped to 3.1 million tons, and of this total global production of whale oil in 1946-7 accounted for 11 per cent, or 340,000 tons. This and the fats market in Europe, where 95 per cent of the whale oil was consumed, constituted the most important factor in determining the price level of whale oil, and encouraging new projects. Another factor, which cannot be discussed here in detail, was the currency situation. It should be recalled, however, that Western Europe's shortage of dollars made it impossible to purchase larger quantities of fats in the United States — or in other countries that demanded payment in dollars — than what was included in Marshall Aid.

In 1938 net imports of fats and oils to nine of Europe's leading importing countries had been 3.57 million tons; in 1947 they were only 1.95 million tons. The F.A.O. estimated an import deficit of about 55 per cent for the whole of Europe. Added to this, domestic production of fats had declined markedly during the war, from 4.2 million tons annually in 1934-8 to 2.77 million tons in 1947 and 3.2 million tons in 1949, while population and living standards were once again showing an upward trend. These figures give a good idea of the shortage of fats during the post-war period. For this reason whale oil, constituting 12 per cent of imports in 1947, made a not insignificant contribution to covering this deficit. Gradually, however, the picture changed, due to a shift in the relationship between the raw materials used in margarine. While production in 1951 was 100 per cent more than in the 1930s, the use of hard vegetable oils (coconut, palm, and palm kernel oils) as the raw material had rocketed to 400 per cent, while the use of hydrogenated whale and fish oils had dropped from 38 per cent of the total raw material consumption in 1938 to 13 per cent in 1951. The same tendency was even more in evidence in the soap industry, where the share of whale oil dropped from 13 to 1 per cent. This trend was clear not only in Great Britain, but also in the Netherlands, West Germany, and the United States, a development by no means welcome to Unilever since whale oil was still the cheapest raw material. For this reason Unilever constantly raised the question of easing restrictions on whaling, and declared in favour of a resumption of German whaling in order to obtain whale oil for their restored German fat industry, and they noted with satisfaction that Japan was once again a vendor of whale oil. The extent to which the soap industry to a large extent abandoned the use of "soft oils" — linseed, cottonseed and soya oil — was due to a steady increase in the use of synthetic detergents. It almost seemed that the world fats industry, realising that one fine day there would be no whale oil left, was on the lookout for substitutes.

In short, although there were factors at work which in the long run would prove unfavourable to whale oil, during the first six or seven post-war years pressure on the whale oil market in Europe was so considerable that the price rocketed, and whaling offered an attractive investment. Apart from the Soviet Union and the Netherlands, four countries in particular were prepared to play for high stakes in order to join in — Japan, Germany, the United States, and Argentina, here mentioned in chronological order. Norway made every effort to oppose their entry, and was not always supported in this by Britain.

Japan

The first announcement of fresh Japanese whaling in the Antarctic reached Norway on 13 August 1946. This caused the Association of Norwegian Whaling Companies to write to its Government: "It is naturally a shock if the Japanese have been allowed by the U.S.A. [to resume whaling in the Antarctic] without informing the other whaling nations, Britain and Norway. This is the most serious blow aimed at the whaling of these countries since the war." In order to anticipate the expected criticism, the United States War Department issued a press release a week later to the effect that "this limited expedition cannot in any way be regarded as a Japanese enterprise as it is entirely under the control and management of the Occupying Power, is only intended for one season, and will not set a precedent for future Japanese whaling". The whale oil was to be allocated by the I.E.F.C. and the whale meat to be used for human consumption in Japan. It was the United States War Department that had authorised General MacArthur, Supreme Allied Commander of the Japanese Occupation, to permit whaling, if he considered this advisable and in accordance with the Occupation statutes.

In May the Japanese Government submitted an application for catching in the Antarctic "in a desperate attempt to rescue the country from a serious shortage of food". Permission was given on the following conditions : catching was only to be carried out south of 55°S between 90°E and 170°W, and in accordance with international rules. Catching was permitted with two floating factories (and twelve whale catchers), and two tankers, out of the very few that had survived the war, were hastily converted : the *Hashidate Maru* and the *Nisshin Maru,* both of about 11,000 gross tons. It goes without saying that permission was greeted with the greatest delight throughout Japan. Dr. Hideo Omura relates that one day in August 1946, as he sat in a department with a budget for a projected expedition, the telephone rang with the news that the application had been granted. "The news created so much joy and delight that no one would listen to my report on the economic problems."

Norway immediately contacted Britain with a view to a joint démarche *vis-à-vis* the United States, but the two countries failed to agree on the conditions they should insist on in accepting, however reluctantly, the fact that the Japanese should be allowed to catch for one season. At the time the British Ambassador in Washington declared that this inability to reach agreement would weaken their case so much that Japanese catching would start as planned. The Whaler Section of the British Chamber of Shipping — which in reality meant H. K. Salvesen — despatched a sharp protest to its Government, pointing out that the Japanese before the war had indulged in such "ruthless slaughter" of whales that there was far less reason to allow them to start whaling than to permit the Germans to do so. The sharpest protests came from Australia and New Zealand. None of this, however, carried really any weight. Nor did the United States keep its suggested promise that the permission was purely temporary, and applied only to 1946-7. Permission was also granted for the following season, on the grounds that the American Government could recognise only security reasons in refusing the Japanese permission to continue whaling.

That economic and political grounds were at the back of the American willingness to allow Japanese whaling was directly stated in an answer of 9 June 1947, to one of Norway's many protests. The meat that Japan acquired from whaling in 1946 corresponded to 34 per cent of meat from cattle. The protein content of whale meat was a vital necessity in order to replace the protein which the country previously obtained from soya beans from Manchuria. From the Norwegian point of view it was disturbing to note that the Japanese were to be regarded as disqualified from future whaling owing to their many violations of international agreements of a politico-commercial or other nature; this would merely postpone the day when Japan would be able to take her place once again among the peace-loving and law-abiding nations. To adduce the low Japanese try-out per BWU against them was an entirely untenable argument. According to reports from Norwegian inspectors, the raw material was utilised to the last ounce; in 1946-7 4,424 tons of blubber was shipped to Japan for human consumption. Had this been reduced it would have produced 12,000–13,000 barrels, and the try-out would have been every bit as high as that of other nations. The Japanese set about punctiliously observing the international agreement on total utilisation of the raw material, with a view to rehabilitating themselves and depriving their opponents of any argument about Japanese wastefulness. "When the Japanese realised," writes the inspector, "that the Americans were the only ones who were interested in allowing them to operate Antarctic whaling, they were as patient as sheep and as servile as slaves. With lower Japanese running costs whaling is clearly a splendid business, and I am in no doubt that the Americans at the moment are reaping the profits."

Year after year Norway lodged her protests, but these were politely and patiently countered in the same terms, until the last note was received on 8 January 1951. When Britain declared that there was no longer any point in protesting, Norway, too, gave up. She had intended to raise the matter at the Peace Conference with Japan in San Francisco in 1951, but on that occasion the question was not even mentioned, and the Occupying Power no longer exercised any authority over Japanese whaling, which from now on was free to expand.

The first step was to replace two smaller floating factories in 1951 with the *Tonan Maru* of 19,209 gross tons, belonging to the Nippon Suisan K.K. (Japan Sea Products Co. Ltd.). This was the former *Tonan Maru III,* which had been sent to the bottom in February 1944, and now raised and practically rebuilt from scratch. The other was the new *Nisshin Maru* of 16,811 gross tons, belonging to the Taiyo Gyogyo K.K. (Taiyo Fishing Co. Ltd.). Strangely enough, this is the only new floating factory the Japanese have built since the war; the entire expansion of Japanese whaling has been carried out by means of purchases of floating factories from other nations. Of the first two floating factories one was scrapped while the other operated both in the Antarctic and the North Pacific until she was broken up in 1965. The next step in the process of expansion was taken in 1956, with the rebuilt *Matsushima Maru* of 13,815 gross tons, re-christened in 1957 the *Tonan Maru II,* of the Nippon Suisan K.K., the purchase the same year of the *Olympic Challenger* (re-christened the *Kyokuyo Maru II*) of the Kyokuyo Hogei K.K. (Polar Whaling Co. Ltd.), and in 1957 of the *Abraham Larsen,* re-christened the *Nisshin Maru II,* of the Taiyo Gyogyo K.K. The final step was the purchase in 1960-3 of five expeditions. We shall revert later to Japanese expansion in the North Pacific.

The campaign against the Japanese was based on the fear that, with their superior skill and low operating costs, they would outmanoeuvre all rivals in the competition to obtain the 16,000 units, as they were well on the way to doing before the war. In the long run it would have been impossible to exclude Japan. She was in many ways the oldest whaling nation in the world, with a long and unbroken tradition. At the peace settlement she lost territory from which she had carried out whaling based on shore stations, and for this reason it was all the more urgent that she should be allowed to exploit the resources of the open sea. At the Washington Conference in 1946 Dean Acheson had greeted delegates in a speech which included the following words: "The world's whale stocks are a truly international resource in that they belong to no single nation nor to a group of nations, but rather they are the wards of the entire world." This was clearly aimed at Britain and Norway; the United States would not recognise their sole right to catch in the open sea as a privilege. When Japan became a member of the I.W.C. on 21 April 1951 the last argument against her participation was removed. That she should be allowed to do so created a precedent for similar claims on the part of other countries, not least Germany, which occupied a much more favourable position because before the war she had adhered to and maintained the international regulations (the London Agreement). Already before the war Japan had freed herself from dependence on Norwegian crews; Germany had not yet done so, and for this reason Norway would exert greater pressure on her through the crew law. This stated that the Crown *may* grant dispensation, not that the Crown *shall*. (For the Japanese Antarctic catch, 1946-51, see Statistical Appendix, Table 63.)

Germany

As might have been expected, the first German requests to be allowed to engage in whaling referred to Japan, indicating that it would be discriminatory not to allow Germany the same rights. In other respects the same arguments were used as by the Japanese. Admittedly, the Potsdam Agreement of 2 August 1945 forbade the building of German ships in excess of 1,500 gross tons, but floating factories could be acquired merely by converting a few large passenger vessels. It was even maintained that Germany had a right to the whale catchers she had had built in Norway during the war "at German expense"! German claims, too, could count on similar support from the United States as shown to the Japanese, and on the same grounds. Well-known persons such as former President HERBERT C. HOOVER and Professor KARL BRANDT, an expert on the economic history of whale oil, supported the German claims.

These were raised in various quarters, among trade unions, politicians, humanitarian organisations, former whaling companies, and a great many others. In the spring of 1946 an intense campaign was conducted in various organs of the German press, quoting Dean Acheson's remarks already referred to and stating that in accordance with the principle he supported Germany might expect the return of both the *Unitas* and of the *Walter Rau*. One of the most active champions of this line was DIETRICH MENKE, director of the Erste Deutsche Walfang-Gesellschaft, the only one of the German companies that had not gone into liquidation during the war. On 2 July 1947, however, the German papers carried a short statement to the effect that the Allies had decided that the ban on German whaling should be maintained. This merely gave the German campaign fresh impetus. In the course of July, August, and September a number of papers contained unusually virulent attacks on Norway for allowing her standpoint to be dictated by narrow economic interests. A representative of the Walter Rau Group pointed out that the Germans could rely on the support of Unilever, and this assumption was not unfounded. At Unilever's board meeting on 27 May 1948, it was announced that the British authorities had inquired in confidence what the attitude of the company would be if Germany was allowed to resume whaling. The answer had been that the company would be in favour of a development of this nature. Both the British and the Allied Control Commission appeared to share these views. Unilever were engaged in rebuilding their German fats industry — by 1951 this process had almost been completed — and with the high price of raw materials and the shortage of these commodities it was obvious that they considered it a great advantage to have German whaling financed and controlled by their concern. Minutes of board meetings constantly stress the fact that, despite the high price, we *must* have whale oil — the Continent needs it.

There was intense propaganda in the autumn of 1947 and throughout 1948 when a deputation was sent from West Germany to the United States, in the hope that their requests would be as sympathetically considered as those of Japan. As the Cold War developed, and Germany was promoted from the status of a defeated enemy to an ally, hope rose that German whaling would no longer encounter resistance. On 2 April 1951, restrictions on German shipbuilding were lifted, and from then on there was nothing to prevent Germany building her own floating factories. For several reasons, despite the fact that the campaign continued for a few more years, this was not done: building and equipping a German expedition would have cost some 55 million Marks. With Onassis's *Olympic Challenger*, the 1950 expedition, the two new Japanese floating factories in 1951, and an Argentinian giant floating factory ready for action, competition would have been so keen that it would have been difficult to ensure a dividend on such a large capital investment. The decisive factor, however, was the drop in the price of oil, with sales down to £67 10s in 1952. The mood changed so radically that even the newspapers advised against this hazard.

The reason why German whaling was thwarted so long was that in this question Norway and Britain shared a larger measure of agreement than vis-à-vis Japan. Furthermore, the United States was the sole occupying power in Japan, whereas in any question relating to Germany there were Allied partners to consider. German whaling found a certain outlet through Onassis. Dietrich Menke, who had been German "commissar" during the war for the Norwegian whaling companies in Norway, was appointed agent for Onassis's company in Germany, where the floating factory and corvettes were converted, and furthermore, apart from the expedition manager and the gunners, practically the entire crew were German whalers who had survived the war. In Germany this enterprise was hailed as a triumph. "Germans will again go whaling" was a typical newspaper headline, and it was pointed out that had Norway not introduced her crew law, 500 Norwegians would have had highly paid employment.

Onassis and the Olympic Challenger

The reason why this section is not headed by the name of a country is that it would be difficult to know which country to choose. The company, the Olympic Whaling Co., was financed by the Argentinian citizen (born an Anatolian Greek) ARISTOTLE ONASSIS and was an affiliate of his American company Pacific Tankers Inc. of New York. A T-2 tanker, which the Olympic Whaling Co. in turn transferred to the Olympic Whaling Co. S.A. in Montevideo, was purchased to serve as a floating factory. The board of directors, consisting almost entirely of American citizens, had its head offices in New York. The floating factory and some of the whale catchers flew the Panamanian flag, others the Honduran. With a German captain on board the floating factory, a Norwegian expedition manager, and the fact that daily management of the expedition was in the hands of a former German whaling company suggests a somewhat cosmopolitan set-up. Formally it was under Panamanian jurisdiction, but in actual fact it was an American company entirely managed and largely owned by an Argentinian national. One of the board members was CLIFFORD N. CARVER, who before the war had participated in the American Whaling Co. (the Frango) and the Western Operating Corporation (the Ulysses). He appears to have provided one of the many links leading to the Olympic Whaling Co. When Anders Jahre resolutely opposed a resumption of catching by the Western Operating Corporation, Carver contacted Onassis. The latter

97. The *Olympic Challenger*, Aristotle Onassis' "pirate" floating factory, converted in Germany 1950, sold to Japan 1956 and renamed *Kyokuyo Maru II*.

was a gambler in the international business world whose sporting instincts were aroused by the excitement and risk that whaling represented, while a price of £110 to £120 for whale oil was an added incentive. Since the floating factory was registered in Panama and the company in Uruguay, nations which had not ratified the Washington Convention, they were not subject to regulation. All attempts to reach agreement with Norway on the question of crews proved abortive. The plan, by contrast, found a ready response in Germany, which was capable of offering all that was required — a yard for converting the floating factory and whale catchers, Hartmann cookers, a company to provide the executives, and — best of all — experienced whalers. There were, however, items Germany was not in a position to offer, namely an expedition manager and gunners.

Onassis is said to have declared that he would never have embarked on whaling if he had not been fortunate enough to have had Lars Andersen as his expedition manager. After facing a charge of collaboration with the Nazis and subsequently endeavouring in vain to rejoin his organisation, Lars Andersen had made his way to Buenos Aires, apparently with a view to taking employment with the Compañía de Pesca as manager of their new floating factory, the *Juan Peron*. It is possible that Onassis, as an Argentinian national, had come into contact with Andersen there, though it is more probable that Onassis's German agent brought them together, as Andersen had been in German service before the war. Strenuous efforts were made in Norwegian quarters to induce him to withdraw from service with Onassis, but the conditions he demanded were so unreasonable that the attempt had to be abandoned. Fifteen corvettes were converted to whale catchers, and these required gunners. The problem was solved by hiring gunners who had assumed foreign nationality or who were living abroad. Gunners resident in Norway were lured with the prospects of handsome incomes and payment in dollars, but only a few fell for the temptation and broke the Norwegian law. A German paper stated that the expedition counted 504 Germans, three of whom were gunners, and fifteen Norwegians.

Onassis's entry into whaling caused, if possible, still greater dismay in Norway than Japanese and Dutch whaling, and every effort was made to thwart it. What would it mean to Norwegian whaling to have to share the 16,000 units with yet another expedition, in addition to the eighteen operating in 1949-50? Assuming that the *Olympic Challenger* was awarded one-nineteenth of the total quota, in theory the Norwegian share would be 64,620 barrels, a reduction of 10,812 tons, which at a price of £115 a ton would mean nearly £1.37 million. In four or five seasons this might rise to £5.5 million. It would therefore be well worthwhile spending a considerable amount in buying out Onassis, provided he was for sale. Negotiations for this purpose were initiated. Onassis calculated what it would cost to cancel the expedition — twelve corvettes would come to $384,000, $150,000 would have to be paid for towing them and the tanker to Kiel, and $130,000 on other expenses, a total of $664,000, in addition to which the yard would demand $100,000 for cancellation of the contract. The Norwegian companies offered to pay $730,000, but an application for the necessary currency was turned down by the Bank of Norway, as the price appeared much too high. A fresh offer from Onassis, involving payment in pounds, was acceptable to the Norwegian companies, even though the price had risen considerably, but this time too the currency application was rejected. A third and last bid involved the Norwegian and British companies jointly making over 4,000 tons of whale oil to Onassis annually for four years, in return for which he was to pledge himself not to convert the tanker and to prevent the Argentinian floating factory *Juan Peron* embarking on whaling. If we take the average of the highest and lowest price operating during the four seasons 1950-4, this would have ensured Onassis oil to the value of £1.5 million, half of which would have been a net gain after all expenses in connection with cancellation of the expedition had been covered. On the other hand, it might be argued that during the four seasons other companies would have produced an extra 40,000 tons, provided Onassis stayed away, or 24,000 tons net after he had been given his agreed 16,000 tons, in other words an extra £2.25 million. Onassis's lengthy cable to the Norwegian companies on this point is an interesting document, revealing how the Norwegian-

British attempt to create a whaling monopoly was regarded abroad, and how whaling had become an object of speculation in the world of international finance and how — in the Norwegian view — the right to undertake pelagic whaling in the Antarctic had become such a highly esteemed privilege that the Norwegian companies were willing to pay £330,000 to one individual and — as we shall see — £550,000 to another for refraining from undermining this privilege. Onassis's dealings may be described as little short of blackmail, the more so as he had previously declared his desire to withdraw from his involvement.

With the departure of the *Olympic Challenger* under the command of the German WILHELM REICHERT from Kiel with her twelve whale catchers on 28 October 1950, the first act in this highly remarkable drama of whaling came to an end. The second act was played out in the whaling grounds, where the crews soon discovered that they had been fooled. As the floating factory flew the Panamanian flag they assumed that their taxes would be deducted in accordance with the laws of that country, but as they had been hired by German agents in Germany, German law had to be observed. The first whale was shot on 6 December. Once again the crew sensed that they had been cheated, as they were well aware that the open season did not begin before 22 December, and they were unwilling to aid and abet a breach of the Convention which might be used as an argument to prevent German whaling from being restarted. They protested to the Captain and to Andersen, but their protests were brushed aside on the grounds that the expedition flew the flag of Panama, a nation which had not ratified the Convention and therefore was in a position to operate without restriction. Humpbacks were shot without any regard for the total quota of 1,250, including females with young. The 1950-1 season extended till 7 April, but was halted on 9 March, as the total quota had been fulfilled. By then the *Olympic Challenger* only had 86,000 barrels. When it was observed that other expeditions were preparing to leave the whaling grounds, the crew asked to be allowed to obtain permission from Sandefjord, by radio, to continue catching, but when they were refused access to the radio, the names and funnel-marks of the ships were camouflaged, and catching continued until a full cargo of 126,522 barrels had been achieved on 26 March, whereupon the expedition headed north. The oil was transferred to a tanker *en route*.

The crew now received another shock when they discovered that they were not homeward bound, but were making for the coast of Peru, to catch sperm whales. Though not in violation of the Convention, this was not in accordance with the crews' contracts. They all protested, and demanded overtime pay. The Captain was willing to grant this, but Andersen refused to transmit their demands to Onassis. The latter suddenly appeared one day, fetched from Peru in one of the whale catchers. He offered the crew 50 per cent over their agreed pay if they were prepared to continue catching until 25 June. This was almost unanimously rejected, and was followed by a sit-down strike, without a single whale being hauled on board. By way of a compromise it was agreed to continue whaling until 10 May, but hardly had Onassis left the floating factory before he issued orders by radio to continue until 25 June : this was absolutely necessary owing to the contracts he had concluded for supplies of a definite quantity of oil. It must have been a matter of considerable urgency for him, as he offered double rates of pay and free air fares home. This was rejected out of hand. Even with all his money Onassis failed to get his way. With approximately 24,500 barrels of sperm oil, catching was brought to a close on 10 May, and by 8 June the floating factory was back in Germany, where 25 per cent of the crew's pay was frozen in order to cover tax demands, while the two managers, directly employed by the Panamanian company, got off with 2 per cent payable to Panama.

The third and most dramatic act, played out in 1954, finally put a stop to Onassis's irregular whaling, but by then a great many others had launched plans which were thwarted by the Norwegian crew law. Had they been realised, whaling would have ended in complete chaos. The most menancing was the Argentinian plan.

Argentina

Juan Peron, dictator of Argentina from 1946 to 1955, had dreams of turning his country into the Germany of South America. Everything that could contribute to this end received his support and sympathy. On the diplomatic plane he worked to secure recognition for Argentinian sovereignty over the entire Falklands Sector. This was supported to a certain extent by the Compañía Argentina de Pesca's shore station in South Georgia, and the Argentinian bases, allegedly "meteorological", in the Antarctic region. He considered that his country's position internationally would be considerably enhanced if it could fly its flag in pelagic whaling as well. With the promise of state aid, the chairman of the board of directors of the Compañía de Pesca, who owned approximately 70 per cent of its shares, ALFREDO R. L. RYAN, had contracted with Harland and Wolff of Belfast for a floating factory, which was to be the largest in the world — 24,570 gross tons. The contract was signed on 22 November 1947 but the yard required three whole years to carry it out, and promised to deliver the vessel at the latest on 7 September 1950. However, owing to financial difficulties on the part of the contractor and delays in supplying the boiling equipment, the floating factory was not ready until October 1951, by which time the price stood at £2,125,000.

Ryan was a British subject, born in Gibraltar and trained as a ship repairer and ship's engineer. In 1924 he settled in Buenos Aires, started a shipbuilding yard, and made so much money during the Second World War, as well as successfully playing the stock market, that he was in a position to buy up little by little enough shares in the Compañía de Pesca to enable him to wrest control from the so-called Tornquist Group. In 1944 he was elected president of the company, whereupon he nominated an entirely new board and proceeded to a wholesale extension of the share capital. As a result, there was heavy trading in the company's shares on the exchange. Ten whale catchers were contracted in Japan, and five from Smith's Dock Co. The entire expedition was estimated to cost £4.2 million, or twice as much as the new Norwegian expeditions. The reason why Ryan committed himself to this expensive venture was that he had exaggerated ideas about the quantities of whale in the Antarctic: he certainly expressed an opinion to this effect, though this may have been propaganda with a view to boosting shares. He believed that the price of whale oil would continue to rise steadily, until it reached the £200 level, where it would remain. Crewing was a matter of no concern, as he was convinced that a sufficient number of Argentinians would soon acquire the necessary skills.

At the beginning of 1949 Ryan ran into financial difficulties, shares began to slide, and he was forced to deposit every stock and share he owned as security for a loan. It was at this juncture that the Norwegian companies hit on the idea of buying Ryan out of whaling in the same way as they had attempted with Onassis. Through him and in part through Lars Christensen these two deals were connected. In Buenos Aires lived a small clique of Norwegian Nazis who had escaped from Norway and who, thanks to their contacts in Government circles, had arranged for an entry visa for Lars Andersen in 1949, with a view to employing him in Argentinian whaling. But as the managing director of the Compañía de Pesca, the Norwegian Fridthjof Jacobsen, refused to have anything to do with him, and Ryan was anxious not to employ him, as this might prejudice any hopes of obtaining dispensation from the Norwegian crew law, and, moreover, since the floating factory would not be ready before 1951, Andersen preferred to accept the offer tended by the *Olympic Challenger*.

Norway attempted initially through diplomatic channels to persuade Britain to prevent the building of the floating factory, but was told that there were no grounds for this, as Argentina had operated in the Antarctic every year before the war and had been a signatory to the 1946 Agreement, and that therefore it would be an act of discrimination to intervene. Moreover, Britain was anxious not to do anything that might damage the important trade connections between her and Argentina. Ryan visited Norway and presented all his arguments, but was forced to return empty handed, even though he tried blandishments and threats by turns, aided and abetted by the Argentinian Minister in Oslo.

This was the situation when Ryan found himself unable to pay an instalment on the floating factory of £300,000 which fell due on 9 March 1950. According to the terms of the contract the yard was then entitled to sell the vessel. The Norwegian companies immediately agreed to take advantage of this situation, purchase the ship, and employ her as a tanker. The Norwegian Government was favourably inclined towards this plan, which involved eliminating, for a price of £330,000, a floating factory and acquiring instead a tanker at a highly reasonable price. Negotiations for the sale had almost been concluded when, on 3 April, came the news that the instalment that had fallen due had been paid in dollars "from United States sources". No one was in any doubt that this was Onassis. When a fresh instalment, due to be paid on 4 May, was also paid in the same way, work on the floating factory continued, and by the summer of 1951 approached conclusion. Two essential items, however, were still missing — whale catchers and crews. The contract for the ten whale catchers in Japan had had to be cancelled, while the five boats from Smith's Dock Co. had been sold to Salvesen. Ryan negotiated for the building of sixteen boats in Germany, in return for payment in whale oil, but nothing came of this.

Ryan thus failed to realise his avowed dream — to see the world's largest floating factory flying the Argentinian flag, but Norway succeeded in preventing it being used as a floating factory. On her maiden voyage the *Juan Peron* called in the Persian Gulf and took on a cargo of oil for Buenos Aires, where the vessel was confiscated by the Government because of alleged currency frauds, and incorporated in the state-run merchant navy. After being laid up for a year she was offered to other countries anxious to start whaling, but the price, £5.3 million, was much too high. She was then re-named the *Cruz del Sur,* and operated for the state-run oil company, for which she has sailed ever since. She has frequently been offered for sale, but without finding a purchaser. The entire affair proved a blow to Peron's prestige and proud ambitions. The mistake that was made was that the entire project was too grandiose and expensive in its design, lacking sufficient capital, and failing to secure the requisite crew. In this case the Norwegian crew law contributed to put an end to a speculative endeavour which might have created great difficulties for international regulation.

Other countries' plans

From all over the world came reports of plans for pelagic catching in the Antarctic. These are of minor interest in this context, as none of them saw the light of day, but they all reveal how tremendously important it was that a total quota should have been established for post-war whaling, and that the Norwegian crew law acted as a sort of deterrent. One is left with the impression that no one — with the exception of a virtually stateless person such as Onassis — was prepared to expose his country to the pressure of world opinion by violating the international agreement, but also that an agreement of this kind could not be effectively enforced without a system of international inspection. All those who toyed with plans of whaling came to Norway to sound out opinion there, and were always presented with the same two arguments: legally, not a single extra whale would be killed, however many expeditions were engaged; on the contrary, the more expeditions, the fewer whales for each of them. And in the second place, the *law* forbade Norwegians to take part in new post-war expeditions. It was an unpleasant task for the Norwegian Foreign Ministry to maintain at all times this discouraging attitude, and to be told that Norway's motives were purely selfish, aimed at maintaining a Norwegian-British whaling monopoly on the high seas at a time when the world was moving in the direction of a greater measure of free trade and economic co-operation between groups of nations. Time and again threats were made to submit the matter to the O.E.E.C. An account of the crew law might suitably conclude with Bergersen's letter to A. T. A. Dobson of 31 January 1950: "None of the Norwegian authorities liked the crew law but I hope that all our friends now understand that it was necessary. It has been a brake to new enterprises. Without it Norway would only have been a training school for all sorts of new firms. What would have been today the international whaling if we had not got this law?"

In Sweden the Kooperative Förbundet (Co-operative Association) submitted plans after the war for whaling, not in order to compete with the Norwegians, it was said, but in order to be independent of the Fats Trust. With this in view a hydrogenation factory had been built during the war, but it was never used because Norway had signed a trade agreement which ensured supplies of whale oil to Sweden in hydrogenated form. The plan failed to gain the support of the authorities, and after 1950 no more is heard of it.

One of Britain's leading shipowners addressed an enquiry to the Norwegian Foreign Ministry on the future prospects of whaling. He had been asked by a firm of ship brokers to participate with them. It was said at the time that the idea really originated with the large oil broking firm of Frank Fehr & Co. A Norwegian was also mentioned as an interested party; he had started a factory in Britain for the production of equipment for the whaling fleet. His name is also mentioned in American and Canadian papers in the latter half of 1945, in connection with a plan to build two floating factories in Canada. There is no further information on this matter.

In 1946 a Norwegian shipbuilding yard received an enquiry from Spain on the delivery of two floating factories with whale catchers, and from Austria came a request for permission to allow sixty seamen to be trained by Norwegians in whaling "until they gain sufficient experience to be able to man a ship capable of participating in whaling. Desperate shortage of food compels us to seek entirely new ways."

In Denmark, too, interest in whaling was largely prompted by a desire to save foreign currency in the country's large production of margarine. In 1946 whaling was re-started from two shore stations in the Faroes, the result being 101 whales and 3,215 barrels. The Danish oil industry financed the stations' modernisation and extension, and with five whale catchers the yield rose to 11,251 barrels in 1950. Denmark would have preferred to have a floating factory stationed in Faroese territorial waters, not only for local catching, but to train crews for pelagic catching in the Southern Ocean "where the Norwegians are now making a fortune". But this would have been in violation of the ban in the Convention against floating factories in the Atlantic north of 40°S. At the I.W.C. meeting in 1949 Denmark was granted permission to use the floating factory, as it would have to be considered as a shore station when it was permanently aground and the propellor had been removed in order to ensure that it did not move, despite the self-contradiction in "a floating factory which did not float". This illustrates in one way what was to be one of the I.W.C.'s great problems — reconciling the interests of pelagic whalers with those of the shore stations. The problem became acute with Australia's large-scale catching of humpbacks in the 1950s, and for that reason the "pelagics" exerted pressure in order to extend catching of this species in the Antarctic.

Reports from other countries were vague. Only in one country were plans for pelagic catching in the Antarctic sufficiently advanced to warrant strenuous efforts to prevent them, and this, strangely, was in Italy, which already before the war had been inspired by Germany in a similar direction during their close political co-operation. The idea was revived after the war by HANS HEINRICH RAU (son of Walter Rau), who together with a successful Italian firm of ship's brokers established the Società Antartide (Compagnia Generale per la Grande Pesca Oceania) in 1949. Rau apparently subscribed 50 per cent of the capital and Austria 10 per cent in return for corresponding shares of the oil. The state promised its support, and it was even suggested that funds from Marshall Aid (E.C.A.) should be channelled into the project. Norway protested against this.

The keel for a floating factory, the *Trinacria*, of 24,000 dead-weight tons, was laid at a yard in Trieste in July 1951. The matter was considered serious enough in Norway for two individuals to be sent to Italy in an attempt to prevent the building of the ship by offering 10,000 tons of whale oil annually for five years at a reasonable price, and to purchase the boat if it was completed as a conventional tanker. Great stress, too, was also placed on all the difficulties the project would run into. This appears to have made a certain impression, because in December 1953 ideas of Italian whaling were finally shelved owing to the slump in the price of whale oil, and protests from producers of olive oil and butter. Rau withdrew his support, while the state was only willing to back the project if the vessel were built as a tanker.

Several abandoned shore stations were also reopened. In South Georgia the Tønsberg Whaling Company (Tønsbergs Hvalfangeri) had recommenced whaling in 1945 from Husvik Harbour, which had been closed since 1931. The catch proved surprisingly good. During the eleven seasons from 1920 to 1931 the annual average was 44,867 barrels, and during the eleven seasons from 1946 to 1957 54,677 barrels, although the station was closed for one season. A large quantity of whale meal was also produced, amounting annually to some 46,500 sacks. It fetched such a good price that in the mid-1950s it accounted for about one-third of earnings.

Starting in 1948, Salvesen was involved for a number of years in a conflict with the Colonial Office on the concession tax for Leith, Allardyce, Prince Olav and Stromness Harbours, the concessions of which had terminated on 30 September 1948. The dispute involved the duration of the new concession, the tax levied on non-operational stations, export tax on pelagic oil stored at shore stations, etc. The Colonial Office proposed a reasonable solution provided Salvesen would resume catching from the Falkland Islands, where it had been suspended since 1915. In 1948 Salvesen announced that this would have to be finally abandoned, as it would be impossible to operate at a profit. From 1 October 1951, Salvesen was granted an eighteen-year joint lease for Leith and Stromness Harbours, at an annual rental of £1,000, and for Prince Olav Harbour at £50, while the lease of Allardyce Harbour lapsed. In 1956, when Ryan declared that he would not renew the concession for Grytviken, Salvesen considered taking it over, but nothing came of this. As we shall see, it was taken over by another company, and in the 1960s leased for two years to the Japanese.

The station on Deception which A/S Hektor had abandoned in 1931 had not been maintained, and finally had to be rebuilt from scratch. In May 1950 United Whalers requested permission to employ Norwegians, a request to which Norway had to accede, as the ban did not apply to shore stations. At the same time dismay was expressed at the fact that, apart from this station, two were reopened in South Georgia, three in South Africa, and three new ones installed in Australia, all of which would make inroads on the same whale stocks as pelagic catching in the Antarctic. The 16,000 units were based on the assumption that this (plus catching from South Georgia) was to be the total take from these stocks; but now it would exceed 20,000 BWU. All agreed that this would have to be reduced, and that the reduction would inevitably affect both parties. This could, for instance, be done by raising the minimum length of fin whales from 55 to 60 ft. This was unanimously adopted at the I.W.C.'s meeting at Cape Town in 1951. It struck a particularly hard blow at the shore stations, which protested, and in 1954 the minimum measurement was lowered to 57 ft.

Three ships, the *Kosmos V*, *Juan Peron*, and *Trinacria*, and Germany had, in various ways, been prevented from starting whaling in the Antarctic, partly as a result of the Norwegian crew law. This, however, had failed to halt the *Willem Barendsz* and the *Olympic Challenger*. Stabilisation of the world fats market and a lower price for whale oil had once again shown that this was one of the best ways of preventing a complete disruption of international regulation. But it was nothing like sufficient. The I.W.C. welcomed the decline in the number of expeditions from nineteen in 1951-2 to sixteen in the following year, but this was rather an effect of the slump in prices (from £83 to £72 and finally down to £68 in 1954), than of the work of the Commission. Furthermore, the decline in the number of expeditions was entirely temporary: already in 1956 there were as many as twenty (while the price of oil rose to £86) and in 1960 twenty-one, at the same time as operations from shore stations showed a marked increase. The Commission faced two problems: the clash between shore stations and pelagic catching, and secondly, reducing the Antarctic quota in the face of a growing whaling fleet. Later, two fresh problems arose: the tremendous increase in the killing of sperm whales and an increased volume of whaling in the North Pacific, two large areas in global whaling on which for the moment the Commission had no influence whatever.

30

THE INTERNATIONAL WHALING
COMMISSION IN THE NINETEEN-FIFTIES

Shore-based and pelagic whaling

The conflict between pelagic catching in the Antarctic and coastal whaling in the southern hemisphere was essentially one concerning humpbacks. This problem arose when Australia started catching humpbacks from several shore stations. Already during the war enquiries for Norwegian crews and matériel had been made, both for pelagic whaling and for two or three shore stations. After the war the Federal Government in Canberra entertained big plans for Australian whaling. In January 1946 it was decided to contract a floating factory in Britain of 20,000 tons, and to start state-run whaling off the west coast and possibly from Tasmania as well. Two thousand men were required, and of these 500 would, it was hoped, be skilled Norwegian hands. A press campaign for Antarctic whaling, to support an Australian demand for "2½ million square miles of the richest whaling grounds in the world", was mounted. The Australian Fisheries Director F. F. ANDERSON visited Norway in order to submit his wishes. He proffered the information that a bid for the purchase of the *Juan Peron* was in the offing, and that Anders Jahre would be prepared to sell the *Kosmos V,* which would only be used for catching humpbacks in Australian territorial waters. He assumed that permission would still be available to undertake whaling of this nature, on a par with operations off Madagascar and the Congo. Along with this, Australia wished that the ban on whaling of this kind in the Antarctic might be maintained. In reply he was told that the sale of equipment that could be used in pelagic whaling would hardly be permitted, but there was no law forbidding Norwegian participation in whaling based on foreign shore stations. The Australian Government was all the more concerned that whaling from shore stations should be developed. As a preliminary step it was decided to ratify the Whaling Convention, and in accordance with this a new whale law was adopted in November 1948, while a special law governing state-run whaling saw the light of day on 12 July 1949.

The most remarkable feature of these laws is that they also regulated land-based whaling by means of a total quota (for humpbacks); this was divided among the stations on the basis of a quota which, it was assumed, stocks would stand. By the end of the 1940s no sure and scientifically based knowledge of the actual size of stocks was available, but it was established that there were two separate stocks of humpbacks which migrated from the Antarctic along the east and west coasts of Australia. Those approaching the west coast came from Area IV, between 70°E and 130°E, and those that made their way to the east coast from Area V between 130°E and 170°W. For this reason regulation of these two stocks had to be carried out separately. By allotting a definite quota to each station it was hoped to avoid competition between them for the total quota, as in the Antarctic. Another provision was for gunners to receive a special bonus for taking the largest animals. However, the main purpose of the laws was naturally to restrict catching to a level that would ensure continued operation.

The basis on which the total quota was established was supplied by experience from previous whaling off the coast of Australia and in the above-mentioned areas of the Antarctic. In accordance with this it was assumed that the quota in the west could be fixed at 1,200 and that in the east at approximately 900, and that in doing so one would be on the safe side, especially as humpbacks had been almost entirely protected in the Antarctic between 1939 and 1949. This assumption, however, proved groundless when the catching of humpbacks in the Antarctic was permitted once again in 1949 : the estimate of available stocks had proved far too optimistic. After the collapse some ten years later biologists concluded that in a completely regenerated state the maximum sustainable yield of Group IV had been 390 annually, and of Group V 330, making a total of 720. When, in 1949, the quota was fixed at 2,000, the same mistake was being made as so frequently in the past when similar efforts had been made in many whaling grounds to limit the catch. The good results of the first few years led people to believe that *this* time all would be well. Four years' catching off Point Cloates and the three years' pelagic whaling off the west coast in 1936-8 did not provide sufficient information to confirm the fact that stocks of humpback whales can only stand intensive catching over a limited period of time, and so allow a rational quota to be set.

Before state-run whaling started in 1950, three private companies had been granted a concession, two of them round Albany. One of these dropped out as early as 1952, while the other succeeded in catching nearly all its yearly quota of 120, until forced by the lack of whales to cease operating in 1962. The third, a major concern, was the Nor' West Whaling Company, which was granted a quota of 600 for operating from the abandoned station at Point Cloates (Norwegian Bay). After an indifferent start in 1949 the high price of oil ensured a considerable surplus in 1950-1, but from 1952 there was a distinct reverse of fortune.

The Norwegian consultant recommended that the State's station should be located on a small island at the entrance of Shark Bay in

Western Australia, where over a million pounds was invested. Thanks to the good market prices, the result was a large surplus in 1950-1, but partly as a result of a slump in price and partly because this station was situated so close to Point Cloates that both were pursuing the same quarry, the State sold its station to the private company; this then abandoned its station at Point Cloates and concentrated on the new one, which was granted a quota of 1,000. However, 1,000 soon proved to be excessively high. A decline set in as from 1954; in 1959 only half the quota was caught, and 1963 witnessed one of the greatest disasters in the catching of humpbacks, a yield of sixty-eight whales and 2,920 barrels — compared with about 500 whales and 22,000 barrels the year before! There appeared to be some truth in the saying that the humpback protected itself until it once again proved profitable to pursue it.

On the east coast, where Norwegians had made an unsuccessful attempt in 1912, Whales Products Pty Ltd. set up a station at Tangalooma on Moreton Island, off the coast near Brisbane, and commenced operations in 1952 with a quota of 600. On this side of the Australian continent the humpback had been left in peace for forty years; it had also been relatively seldom caught in the Antarctic. The yield was highly successful, the quota being fulfilled in two months, with a very high try-out, practically sixty barrels per whale, corresponding to 150 barrels per BWU. For ten years shareholders received excellent dividends, but, just as on the west coast, the year 1961 marked a definite decline : despite a prolonged season, the yield was sixty-nine short of the full quota, and in the following year the collapse was complete — here too only sixty-eight whales and 2,780 barrels. After the favourable results of the first two years a concession was granted here for 120 whales to the Byron Bay Whaling Co., named after the station just south of Brisbane. In 1956 it was transferred to an affiliate of the Pacific Sea Products Inc., of San Francisco, which was less interested in the oil than in imports of frozen whale meat to the United States. After eight years stocks of whales were exhausted in this area, too. In 1958 the same company started whaling from the Norfolk Islands (800 miles east of Brisbane). As it proved an easy matter to catch the quota of 120, this was increased in 1960 to 170, apparently with disastrous results — 170 humpbacks and 2,548 barrels in 1961, four humpbacks and 79 barrels in 1962, twenty barrels per whale!

In New Zealand waters whaling followed almost precisely the same pattern as in Australia, culminating in 1959-60, the two best years in the modern period, with a total of 681 whales and 31,522 barrels, half this accruing to J. A. Perano, who continued to operate in his very special way from Te-Awaiti in the Cook Strait. But with only nine whales caught in 1963 and none at all in 1964, he, too, had to call it a day, after the station had functioned without a break since 1909. An interest-

98.   Whale catcher at full speed chasing two humpbacks.

ing chapter in the history of whaling was thus at an end. A company
which attempted to continue H. F. Cook's catching from Whangamumu
proved a complete failure. Both stations tried to make up for declining
yields of humpbacks by catching sperm whales, but as the price of sperm
whale oil dropped from £85 to £40 in 1964, this venture too had to
close down.

This changeover to catching sperm whale is typical of the main
trends in whaling in the 1960s: since 1966 the world production of
sperm oil has exceeded that of whale oil. We need to go a hundred
years back in time to find a similar situation. The other characteristic
feature was that, as from 1966, for the first time since 1909 the catch
(i.e. total production of whale and sperm oil) in the north was again
greater than in the south, and in 1967 pelagic catching in the North
Pacific was almost as big as in the Antarctic. In this development of
global whaling, operations off the coasts of Australia and New Zealand
in 1949 to 1962 are interesting in many ways. Here we find the last
major catching of baleen whales from shore stations in the southern
hemisphere, apart from South Georgia; it is one of the biggest consecutive catches of humpbacks that has ever taken place, and it provoked
the sharpest conflict between pelagic whaling and shore-based whaling.
In this connection its bearing on the Australian economy is of minor

interest: it can hardly have been particularly great. After operations had ceased the shore stations were valueless, and the total loss of investments in them and in other plant and equipment must have greatly outweighed the profits on the sale of oil and by-products. Most of the oil had been exported to Europe, whereas the meat meal, bone meal, and guano had found a ready market in Australian agriculture.

In 1949-62, 22,799 baleen whales were caught in Australian and New Zealand waters, exceeded only (in respect of catching from shore stations in one area) by South Georgia with 36,919 (nearly 10,000 being the smaller sei whales). Second to Australia we have the shore stations of the North Pacific, with about 18,000 (of which almost 12,000 sei). As only fifty-eight other whales were caught in this period in Australian and New Zealand waters, this was humpback catching pure and simple. Other big humpback periods were the Antarctic in 1904-16 with approximately 38,000, and off the coast of Africa in 1908-14 with approximately 25,000. (Statistics for both areas during these years are somewhat unreliable.) In 1945-63, all in all, 46,800 humpbacks were caught in the southern hemisphere, and of these, 23,256 — or almost exactly 50 per cent — were accounted for in Australian and New Zealand waters. These figures include the illegal catch made by the *Olympic Challenger* in 1954-5, but as there is strong evidence that some 5,000 others were caught illegally, the total figure comes to about 52,000 humpbacks, and the Australian and New Zealand share thus accounts for 44 per cent. Any question regarding regulation of humpback catching would therefore affect Australia to a far greater extent than it would nations operating pelagically in the Antarctic. For the latter, 1958-9 provided the largest catch of humpbacks since the war: 2,394. This yield, however, was a mere 6.26 per cent of total catch in terms of BWU, and in the rest of the 1950s it was less than half of this. For pelagic whaling, in fact, cessation of humpback catching meant very little, whereas in the case of Australian whaling it was entirely vital. For the pelagics it was more a question of the principle of equal right to whaling for all and the need to spare the blue whale.

Up to the time when Australia started whaling in 1949 the humpback had been totally protected in pelagic whaling ever since 1938, except for the 883 caught by the Japanese in 1938-9 and 2,675 during a temporary easing of the ban in 1940-1. Protection had been imposed as a result of the large catches made in the immediately preceding years (from 1934 till 1938 there was an annual average of 5,420 whales). During the eight years before Australian catching started in 1949, the number was only 270, the lowest figure since catching began in the Antarctic in 1904. Experience from other whaling grounds suggested therefore that stocks had made a good recovery. On the basis of this assumption and on the most recent scientific whale research, as well as favourable reports from the whaling grounds on humpback stocks, Norway submitted a proposal at the I.W.C.'s first meeting in 1949 consisting of three items which all aimed at sparing in particular the blue whale and the fin whale : (a) an annual pelagic catch of 1,250 humpbacks, a somewhat arbitrarily chosen number; (b) the opening of the season to be postponed till 26 December (previously 15 December), with a corresponding extension in April, and (c) a reduction of the total quota from 16,000 to 15,600 units. It was hoped that this would probably reduce the kill of blue and fin whales to 15,100 units (15,600 minus 1,250 humpbacks) and have a substantially favourable influence on whale stocks in the years ahead. The first item was approved, with — as expected — Australia voting against. It was more surprising that Australia should have been supported by the Netherlands, undoubtedly on emotional and tactical grounds vis-à-vis Norway, whose crew law had queered the pitch for Dutch whaling. With regard to the second item, a compromise was reached with 22 December, while the third item was rejected.

Expeditions were to submit a weekly report direct to the International Whaling Statistics Office, which at four days' notice was to terminate catching of humpbacks from the day the figure of 1,250 could be assumed to have been reached. In accordance with this a warning was sent out that the last day of fishing would be 3 January 1950. Operations must apparently have been intensified, because during the four-day period of grace so many humpbacks were caught that the final result was 2,117, 867 above the set figure. But even with a changeover in the following season to daily reporting and a postponement of the seasonal opening to 1 February to avoid catching whales during the "lean" season, it proved difficult to achieve the correct figure. This attempt at imposing a special quota for humpbacks was therefore abandoned, and from 1953-4 to 1962-3, permission to pursue this species was granted for only four days each season. Yields proved tremendously variable — 1,432 in 1955-6, 396 in 1957-8, and a sudden rise to 2,394 in 1958-9, the highest figure achieved since 1940-1. After that, catches declined 50 per cent every season, right down to 270 in 1962-3, the last year prior to total protection. In the South Georgia area the pursuit of humpbacks ceased in 1955, and after 1946 only 136 were caught.

This tremendous fluctuation in catches may be partly explained by the transfer of catching from one area to another, as certain areas were at times protected, mainly I and II. As the annual average after 1951-2 was well under 1,250, Norway raised the question at the I.W.C. meeting in 1957 of extending catching time from four to eight days, as it was probably the brief period allowed which prevented the quota being reached. However, it proved impossible to obtain the necessary number of votes in favour of this, and not even for an alternative proposal to extend catching by a mere two days. Australia naturally opposed any extension. The same situation arose again in 1958, when Australia received the support of all the countries — New Zealand, South Africa, Brazil, and France (the Congo) — which pursued humpbacks in non-Antarctic waters, whereas the five pelagic countries voted in favour.

The sudden and tremendous decline in catches round Australia appeared quite incomprehensible to the Scientific Committee. Catches from these stocks in their Antarctic feeding grounds were not sufficiently large to provide the sole explanation for the mortality that must have taken place, particularly in Area V. The only explanation must be that a very considerable measure of illegal catching had taken place, approximately 4,000 in 1960-1, about 1,000 in 1961-2, in this area alone. The decline off the west coast of Australia could to some extent be explained by the large catches (1,796) in Area IV in 1958-9. This, however, was not sufficient for Australia to lay the entire blame for this on the pelagic nations. During the entire period 1949-63, 59 per cent were caught in Australian and New Zealand waters and 41 per cent in the Antarctic (including the "illegal" 5,000), and the 59 per cent — it should be noted — were caught in the breeding grounds and at a time when the whale was at its leanest. In the second place, although catching in west coast waters showed a considerable decline as compared to the quota in 1958 and 1959, the quota was not only maintained but even increased.

The preamble to the Washington Convention states that "the history of whaling has seen over-fishing of one area after another and of one species after another to such a degree that it is essential to protect all species of whales from further over-fishing" and the Convention had therefore been concluded "in the common interest to achieve the optimum level of whale stocks as rapidly as possible without causing widespread economic and nutritional distress". The course of humpback catching that we have considered — and we shall see the same happening in the case of the blue and fin whales — showed how impotent the I.W.C. was in fulfilling the aims of the Convention. The total protection that was finally accorded the humpback — and shortly afterwards the other species — was a statement of a deplorable fact, a virtue of necessity, not the fruit of the work of the I.W.C. Its Scientific Committee considered that it would take sixteen years before it would again be possible to catch 100 humpbacks annually from the stocks in Area V, twenty-six years for 200, and thirty-two years for 300. What had happened? Just as large-scale whaling in Australian waters started, protection in the Antarctic was suspended, and although already after the mid-1950s it was obvious that stocks in Australian waters were on the decline, a demand for doubling the figures for the Antarctic was

99a Fifty years of technical developments of whale catchers: the *Ørnen* (Norwegian) built 1902, 103 gross tons, 300 h.p. steam engine.

submitted. Both accorded ill with the aims of the Convention, and the result was as might have been expected. Considering that the catch of humpbacks in the Antarctic played such an unimportant role in the economic results of whaling as a whole, from Australia's point of view it would have been reasonable for the pursuit of this species to have been their special preserve. The pelagics riposted, with good reason, that it was poor policy to kill the leaner whales in the breeding grounds instead of securing the fatter beast in its pastures in the ice, where catching of humpbacks would spare a corresponding BWU number of blue and fin whales. Illegal catching of 5,000 humpbacks might have influenced the result: in this case there were only uncertain clues to go by, but in another case it was possible to document illegal catching.

"A whaling pirate"

The fact that it took such a long time to implement an agreement on neutral inspectors raises certain questions. Reports of national observers had to be relied on and statistics based on them. Onassis's notorious expeditions are an outstanding example of the sort of thing that could happen. In 1951-3 he once again despatched the *Olympic Challenger,* and the same sort of incidents occurred as during the first season. In 1953-4 the floating factory operated as a tanker, owing to the slump in the price of oil. In the hope of a rise in price he kept back 40,000 tons of his former production, possessing as he did sufficient capital to be able to do so. Unilever considered him a disturbing element in the market: they badly needed 30,000 tons for their factories in Germany, the

99b. The *Besstrashnij* (Soviet Union), built 1952, 843 gross tons, 3600 h.p. diesel engine.

Netherlands, and Belgium, and were anxious to purchase Onassis's holdings, for which they offered £70 per ton; Onassis demanded £72, a price he received for 5,000 tons from other purchasers. Of the Norwegian production, expected to amount to 160,000 tons, 140,000 tons was pledged in advance by various contracts, and the Norwegians were anxious to delay sales of the rest until they knew whether Onassis would be despatching an expedition. When it was obvious that he would not do so, the Norwegians sold the consignment for £70, whereas Onassis received £72 for 22,000 tons. By then there was hardly any whale oil left on the market, while the bulk of the coming season's production had been sold in advance.

Onassis was one of the few who still had oil to sell, and, as Unilever put it, he just sat back and waited. The price rose: at the beginning of December £74 was paid and by the middle of the month £80, whereupon Onassis offered his oil for sale at £84. No one was prepared to pay this price, and he was forced to sell at £75. A further rise in price was curbed by the British Ministry of Food, which still had large stocks and offered 50,000 tons at £75. At this price Unilever purchased 130,000 tons of the Norwegian-British production, but were prepared to have to pay £80 for the remaining 70,000 tons. At that price, Onassis declared, he, too, would despatch his expedition: he had read the market correctly, the rise in price took place, and every effort was made to achieve maximum production in 1954-5.

With sixteen converted corvettes and 600 hands all told, the *Olympic Challenger* left Kiel on 25 August 1954 and made her way through the Panama Canal to the west coast of South America for the purpose of catching sperm whales before the Antarctic season from 7 January to 7 April. At the I.W.C. meeting in Tokyo on 19 to 23 July the announcement of his plans had the effect of a bombshell. Apart from the fact that there would bc onc more competitor in the field for the 15,500 units, no one doubted that he had operated and would continue to operate in violation of the Convention. Panama had ratified this on 1 December 1953, and was therefore responsible for ensuring that it was observed. But no one had any confidence in the two Panamanian inspectors, who had no qualification whatever for their posts.

When the *Olympic Challenger* reached the whaling grounds off the coast of Peru in the beginning of October 1954 it ran into a new political situation. At the instigation of Chile a conference was held from 11 to 19 August 1954 in Santiago attended by delegates from Chile, Peru, and Ecuador (The Conference on the Exploitation and Conservation of the Maritime Species in the South Pacific). The Conference had been prompted by the fact that at the I.W.C. meeting in Oslo in 1950 Chile had received no support for her three special demands: (1) 30 ft. as a minimum size limit for sperm whales; (2) the suspension of the six-month consecutive catching time annually for baleen whales from shore stations; (3) suspension of the rule for a minimum distance of 1,000 km. between such stations whose seasons did not coincide in time, and an eight-month season for sperm whales. The Conference now resolved that the rules proposed by Chile should apply to whaling in the territorial waters of the three countries. Just as the Santiago Conference was a counterpart to the Washington Conference, so in turn it had its counterpart to the I.W.C. in the Permanent Commission for the Exploitation and Conservation of the Marine Resources of the South Pacific (generally referred to as the Permanent Commission), with a corresponding authority to supervise and regulate the Convention. In this connection what was most important was that the Conference resolved that "every single state shall have the right to establish a protection, control, and exploitation zone a distance of 200 nautical miles from such countries' coasts and islands, within which area they can individually exercise military, administrative, and physical jurisdiction" (Article 2). This was the first time that what was subsequently called an economic zone was established, and as from 1 January 1977 such zones were created *inter alia* by Norway and the Soviet Union. As a reason for the three countries' claim to sovereignty over their continental shelves the British proclamation of sovereignty over the continental shelf and adjacent ocean areas of the Falkland Sector was quoted as a precedent. As far as Norwegian whaling was concerned, the resolution adopted by these three countries was of minor importance, though it did result in the Spermacet Whaling Company suspending catching of sperm whales off the coast of Peru in 1954. It was a matter for greater concern that Chile and Argentina should wish to apply the same 200-mile zone to the areas in the Antarctic, the sovereignty of which they disputed with Great Britain. To some extent the whaling companies considered this a threat, and some of them ordered their expedition managers not to approach within 200 miles of South Shetland and Graham Land, in part because it was difficult to obtain full insurance cover for seizure within this limit. At that time Chile and Argentina were intensely active in the Antarctic, constantly establishing new bases (which went by the name of meteorological stations) and patrolling these waters with naval units, occasionally hailing Norwegian floating factories. For the time being everything passed off amicably, as the commander of a British naval vessel explained to the Norwegian Minister in Buenos Aires: "We bow, deliver the note of protest, they bow and hand over their note of protest, and then we shake hands and have a drink together." For Norway there was nothing for it but to join with the other countries in their protests against the 200-mile zone. But as *The Economist* wrote: "Onassis sailed in where the Norwegian Government feared to tread."

After a number of skirmishes with tunny fishers from the United States off the coast of Peru, Onassis's whaling provided the serious test for how far the country was prepared to go in maintaining the Santiago Convention. When the attack on his whaling fleet had taken place, Norway found herself in the strange position — while she waited for an opportunity to expose his illegal whaling — of being forced to side with him, together with all the nations that condemned Peru's action as a violation of the freedom of the seas. After the *Olympic Challenger* had left Kiel, the Peruvian newspapers carried the most blatant attacks on Onassis's business morals, and warned him of what he might expect "if the whaling pirate dared to violate Peru's territory".

On 15 November 1954 Peru acted. Four of the whale catchers were apprehended by Peruvian destroyers and escorted in to Paita. The following day a plane flew low over the floating factory and ordered her to sail towards the coast immediately. Captain Reichert ordered full speed ahead in the opposite direction. The result was a shower of warning bombs around the ship, while several salvoes of machine-gun fire raked the deck. "We're being bombed and fired at by a Peruvian plane," was the last radio message the ship managed to transmit, and her position was then given as 380 miles off the coast. Together with the floating factory two whale catchers were apprehended, while the rest ran for the Panamanian town of Balboa. A maritime court in Paita established that 2,500 to 3,000 whales had been caught inside the territorial limit, and on 29 November imposed a fine of $3 million on the company, to be paid within five days, otherwise the ships and the cargo would be sold by auction. Panama's diplomatic protest naturally proved ineffective. There were rumours that Onassis would endeavour to transfer his ships to the Argentinian flag, as he expected that this would give him better protection than Panama could afford. Norway appealed to the United States to prevent this transfer, since Argentina had not ratified the Convention, and unrestricted catching in the Antarctic areas over which Argentina claimed sovereignty threatened to blow the entire system of international regulation sky-high. It was still not realised that Onassis, operating under the Panamanian flag, operated as though that country, too, had not yet ratified the Convention.

The affair was a world sensation : the person who appeared to accept the turn of events with the greatest calm was Onassis himself, and the reason was that the bill would have to be footed not by himself but by Britain and the United States. Through Lloyds in London Onassis had covered himself with a network of policies against all hazards for a sum of up to £5 million in the event of total loss. He had also insured against interruption in catching to the tune of $30,000 a day for up to thirty days, should operations be prevented by confiscation, while another policy insured him against loss should his fleet fail to reach the Antarctic before the opening of the season. The outcome was that the fine of $3 million was paid under protest, the ships were released, and promised a month's extra wages if the expedition reached the Antarctic before 7 January 1955, they steamed south at full speed.

In the world of international insurance and shipping, as well as in political circles, there has been a great deal of speculation about this affair. On the one hand it has been said that Lloyds accepted this risk, in the belief that the United States would tolerate no action against its protégé Panama, and would maintain its traditional policy of unrestricted freedom of the seas. On the other hand, it is said that influential financial circles, which in many areas considered their interests threatened by Onassis's manipulations, were delighted at the sight of the United States tacitly allowing Peru to strike a blow at him.

Onassis's departure from whaling proved as inglorious as his opponents had hoped, but he would not have been the man he was had he not emerged from whaling with just as big a profit as he did from the Peruvian affair. When his ruthless catching methods were exposed by Norway, he very conveniently received an offer from Japan for his entire whaling fleet, and he succeeded in forcing the price up to $8.5 million. Under the name of the *Kyokuyo Maru II* the floating factory operated in the Antarctic until 1965, in the North Pacific from 1966 to 1968 and again in the Antarctic from 1968 to 1970.

"The floating factory the *Olympic Challenger* will take its place in the history of whaling as one of its blackest chapters." With these words a newspaper commenced its account of what had occurred. The first warning of Onassis's irregular whaling was submitted at the I.W.C. meeting in Moscow 18-23 July 1955. The Japanese submitted a report, together with photographs purporting to show that humpbacks had been caught outside the permitted period. Panama replied that the two inspectors were public servants, competent and reliable men. The great sensation of the meeting was Norway's protest to Panama to the effect that for several seasons there had been a total violation of the regulations of the Washington Convention. For the time being the matter remained within the I.W.C., but it proved a world sensation on a par with the Peru affair when the *Norwegian Whaling Gazette* in November 1955 published the entire findings submitted to the Foreign Ministry by the Association of Norwegian Whaling Companies. It was a complete surprise that it was able to reveal with the aid of documents and statistics, to the smallest and most exact detail, how the *Olympic Challenger,* season after season, had on every conceivable point violated the Convention which Panama had ratified. The most important charges were:

1. For catching off the coast of Peru in the autumn of 1954 the inspectors had made returns of 2,348 sperm whales and 73,000 barrels of sperm oil. The actual catch was 580 baleen whales (285 were blue whales), 4,068 sperm whales, 22,390 barrels of whale oil, and 50,620 barrels of sperm oil. Of the blue whales 51.2 per cent and of the sperm whales 96.4 per cent were under the permitted minimum lengths, while the try-out amounted to a mere 54 barrels per BWU and 12.4 barrels per sperm whale. As pelagic catching of baleen whales was forbidden in this area, they had all been caught illegally. The total irregular catch was 67,210 barrels.

2. During the following season's whaling in the Antarctic (1954-5), catching had taken place both before and after the open season, while blue, fin, and humpback whales below minimum length had been caught.

3. As it would in the long run prove impossible to conceal the amount of the production — this would be revealed when it was discharged — the inspectors had fiddled the catching returns in order to ensure that they bore some sort of relationship to production. Seven hundred fin whales which had, in fact, never been caught, were recorded, together with specification of sex, length, and position of capture.

Similar breaches of the Convention had taken place in the Antarctic in 1950-1 and 1952-3, and off Peru in 1951; no figures were available for 1951-2, and in 1953-4 the *Olympic Challenger* had operated as a tanker. For the seasons registered, illegal catching amounted to 216,555 barrels, of an estimated value of £3.1 million. Adding illegal catches in 1951-2, when oil fetched top prices, it would hardly be wrong to assume that Onassis pocketed gross earnings of at least £4 million thanks to his sovereign contempt for an international agreement which the company's home country had ratified. The total value of Onassis's catch (in 1955-6 the floating factory recorded the tremendous production of

160,960 barrels) can be estimated at £13.7 million gross and £5.5 million net This was the sum Onassis earned from his whaling venture. He maintained that the Norwegian action directed against him "was not only an attempt to maintain as long as possible the Norwegian whaling monopoly" but also that "many of the Norwegian whaling companies, which at the same time are owners of tankers, have felt their interests threatened by the agreement entered into between Onassis's companies and the Government of Saudi Arabia". In Panama the accusations were dismissed as figments of the imagination, while Onassis, instead of refuting them, preferred to make serious counter-charges against Norwegian whaling: that, for example, the Norwegian companies had threatened the Kiel yards, tried to prevent his whale catchers from obtaining fuel oil, tried to keep his fleet at home by bribery, and sold their oil below the mutually agreed price.

The inspectors and Onassis would hardly have reacted as they did, had they known that Norway possessed further documentary proof. This was published in the *Norwegian Whaling Gazette* in January 1956, and proved a second great sensation. There were reports from the floating factory's chemist and chief engineer, which confirmed the charges that had been made, but this, too, was refuted by Panama on the formal grounds that the charges were made by a private association "which was not even connected with the Norwegian Government". Norway then dealt Panama and Onassis a decisive blow, by publishing affidavits sworn before the Norwegian Consul-General in Hamburg, a logbook kept on the whaling grounds, and photographs taken during reduction of the whales. All this material was sent to the Panamanian Government from Norway in a note of 3 February, a note to which Norway never received any reply. Nor, for the moment, did Onassis comment, though in a newspaper interview he made light of the whole affair, referring to the Norwegian Whaling Council as the most ridiculous thing he had ever come across. In Germany, a country which was highly committed to his ventures, the press at first tried to defend Onassis against "Norwegian competitive envy", but when the facts of the case emerged headlines such as "World Scandal involving Onassis", "Norway harpoons Onassis's Whaling Fleet", and the like appeared.

One question repeatedly cropped up in the world press: how had Norway managed to get hold of the compromising documents? This is still to a certain extent a well-kept secret. It can at least be said of the fantastic story presented by JOACHIM JOESTEN in his biography of Onassis that *se non è vero, è ben trovato*. Briefly, his account is as follows: when Lars Andersen's five-year contract ran out in 1955, it was not renewed. He then settled in Argentina, where he had no difficulty in acquiring citizenship. One day he was visited by an emissary from Norway, who presented an interesting proposition: would he like to return home? Lars was cautious, knowing full well what he might risk if he set foot on Norwegian soil. His visitor reassured him; he would be unmolested, all his travelling expenses would be paid, and there would be a good job waiting for him. In short, all that had taken place would be forgiven and forgotten, on one condition. Andersen accepted. In August 1955 he was back in his native town of Sandefjord. The prodigal son encountered no unpleasantness. There was even an attractive house waiting for him. This was the way, according to Joesten's account, in which Onassis was exposed! The story is hardly credible: it contains a gross insinuation against public morals in Norway, and presupposes that the Norwegian Government would be capable of reversing the verdict passed on Andersen for his collaboration with the enemy during the German occupation of Norway, a step which neither Government nor Parliament could take in accordance with the Norwegian Constitution.

The solution is a very different one, and has nothing whatever to do with Lars Andersen. The explanation is quite simply that the Association of Norwegian Whaling Companies gained possession of papers from German members of the crew. The German weekly *Der Spiegel* maintained that the latter had offered the Norwegian Consul-General in Hamburg these papers in return for a sizeable sum, and that a representative from Norway turned up almost immediately afterwards with Kr.20,000. Be that as it may, the most important point was that Onassis's whaling activities were halted. The damage he had inflicted, however, was considerable, both on stocks of whales and on the companies, and the latter now felt that they had a legal right to compensation.

In the summer of 1954 the possibility was discussed in Norway of persuading Onassis to refrain from resuming whaling in return for payment of £400,000. The offer was turned down. This is probably what Onassis refers to in his charges against Norwegian companies that they "had offered to pay ridiculous sums of money to persuade us to refrain from participating in the whaling season". When he rejected the Norwegian documentary evidence out of hand, the Norwegian companies took action, and on 24 March received the approval of the *Landesgericht* in Hamburg to seize 6,300 tons of whale oil discharged in that port from one of Onassis's tankers, and shortly afterwards the District Court in Rotterdam authorised the seizure of the *Olympic Challenger* and her cargo. The next day Onassis countered by seizing the *Kosmos III* and her cargo, likewise in Rotterdam, while deploring that this would affect "his good friend Anders Jahre" and not one of the other companies. Onassis endeavoured to evade the entire issue by a proforma transfer of the floating factory to another of his companies but this was not accepted by the court as a proper sale. After a week the *Kosmos III* was released, on deposit of Fl.230,000 as security, while the seizure of the *Olympic Challenger* was upheld, as the security deposit demanded, Fl.1.6 million, was not paid. The question also arose whether the Japanese purchasers were the legal owners of the boat. All in all the matter threatened to be so complicated, and a court case so expensive, that the Norwegians sought to effect a compromise with Onassis. After difficult negotiations this was achieved on 31 May 1956, on the following conditions: both sides were to drop all mutual court proceedings, the sureties would be remitted, and the sequestration suspended, and a "pelagic fund" of Kr.4 million (£220,000) would be established, to which Onassis would make the largest contribution, and the Norwegian companies the remainder. The agreement described Onassis's contribution as "an expression of goodwill and recognition of the experience he had gained from Norwegian whaling".

The pelagic whaling nations and the International Whaling Commission

The *Olympic Challenger* affair had shown that, without impartial inspectors, there was no guarantee against illegal whaling. It was doubtful whether the I.W.C. would ever be capable of establishing and maintaining control of this kind. According to the Schedule the inspectors were responsible only to their own governments, but amendments could be made to the Schedule "such as are necessary to carry out the objectives and purposes of this Convention and to provide for the conservation, development, and optimum utilisation of the whale resources". It augured ill for the fate of regulation that no issue encountered greater opposition than the carrying out of this system of control. A more practical solution than working through the formal approaches of the Commission appeared to be for the pelagic nations to arrive at agreement among themselves, but implicit in the proposal itself was a distrust of national inspectors which an acceptance of the proposal would recognise as justified.

At the height of the dispute in April 1956 Onassis declared that it was a terrible principle to have to catch in forty-five days the number of whales which, "in accordance with nature's own development and laws", it would be more reasonable to catch in 125 days. In his opinion this could be solved in two ways: quotas for the various expeditions and a restriction in the number of whale catchers. Four points in this statement are worth noting: in the first place, were the words "nature's own development and laws" really anything more than a phrase? In the second place, the permitted period of whaling has never been as much as 125 days nor the time spent in catching as little as forty-five days (see Statistical Appendix, Table 64). Thirdly, a restriction in the number of whale catchers, and whale quotas, were far from being an original conception, having been practised in the 1930s. Fourthly, there was a contradiction between theory and practice that was hardly surprising, coming from those quarters : Onassis refused to accept the restriction in the number of whale catchers which the other pelagic nations (apart from the Soviet Union) agreed on for 1953-5, and he resumed catching with the biggest number of whale catchers of any expedition. The two proposals made by Onassis — a restriction of catching matériel and national quotas — are interesting in that they involved the two items which the pelagic nations and the companies themselves had raised outside the Commission. They affected the economy of whaling, and this was a matter beyond the scope of the I.W.C.

In establishing the total quota it had not been anticipated that competition for this would result in a tremendous expansion of the whale catcher fleet, both in numbers and in the efficiency of the vessels. From the point of view of operational results it was better to fill the quota in ninety-six days with ten whale catchers than in seventy-six days with fifteen whale catchers. In the mid-1950s it was calculated that the cost of running a whale catcher per season amounted to about £40,000. However short the catching season, wages were paid for seven months, and the bonus was the same, no matter how long or short the time required to earn it. The result of competition was that, if an expedition had been fortunate enough to catch a relatively large share of the 16,000 BWU early in the season, operations would be called off at an earlier point of time, and this would deprive a less successful floating factory of the opportunity of completing its catching during the remaining part of the open season. In 1955-6, for example, the open season extended from 7 January to 7 April, ninety-two days (for blue whales from 1 February to 4 March), but operations were called off as early as 4 March, after fifty-eight days, when the total catch was 0.84 per cent short of the permitted quota. This was the shortest period in the history of pelagic whaling, but the average daily production per floating factory was the second highest ever recorded. This may have been the reason why catches varied so much even for floating factories with the same number of whale catchers and the same reduction capacity — this ranged from 155,000 barrels to a mere 55,000 barrels when operations were called off.

This may have been because the protected sector, which covered parts of Areas I and VI and had been closed to pelagic whaling ever since 1937, had been reopened in 1955, provisionally for three years. Investigations in this sector in the 1930s seemed to show that it was almost entirely devoid of whales, and several expedition managers doubted whether there was any point in operating there, whereas those who did found surprisingly rich stocks. Of the season's total catch of

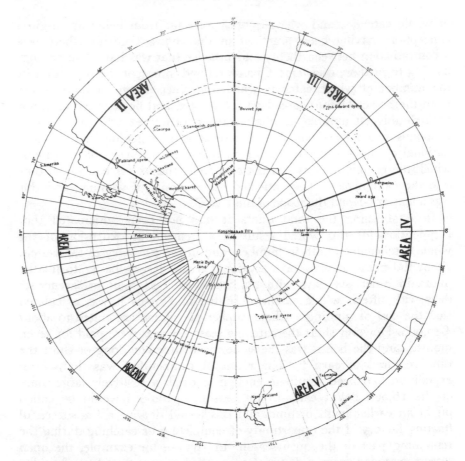

The Antarctic oceans were divided south of 40°S into Areas where the pelagic catching of baleen whales was allowed in the open season. In the hatched Area, called the Sanctuary, this whaling was forbidden between 1937 and 1955.

14,874 units, approximately 25 per cent was caught in this area, thus preserving the other overfished areas from a corresponding catch. The average catcher's day work in Area I was 1.16 BWU as against 0.95 in the other areas. Area I, too, had the highest try-out, 135.8 barrels per BWU, as against an average of 121.6 for the entire Antarctic. This was because twice as many units were caught in Area I in the latter half of the season as in the first half; the later in the season they are caught, the fatter they are, because they have had a longer time in which to feed. In 1955 the I.W.C. Scientific Committee had concluded that the catch should as soon as possible be reduced to 11,000 units. In one way this might be said to have been done in 1955-6, as only 11,000 units were caught in the areas where practically all the catching had taken place since 1938. The problem then was whether Area I could continue to relieve some of the pressure on the other areas, without depleting its own stocks. The favourable results obtained induced others to transfer their catching in 1956-7 to Area I, which provided practically 40 per cent of the catch, whereas in the two eastern areas, IV and V, it slumped from 22.9 per cent to 2.4 per cent, all in all a shift in whaling from east to west. The decline to 25 per cent of the total catch in 1957-8 showed that stocks in Area I had been heavily overfished, and in 1958-9 no whaling took place in the new Area I (120°W-60°W), where in the last season 7.9 per cent of the total catch had been taken, while in the new Area VI 9.1 per cent of the total catch was caught, as against 18.4 per cent in 1957-8.

The Scientific Committee was in a quandary with regard to the protected sector. At a meeting in London, influenced by the decline in catching in 1957-8, it stated: "It was recalled that the original purpose of the Sanctuary was to safeguard a reserve supply of whales, but that it had been thought desirable to open it to whaling and spread the hunting as widely as possible, so long as the limit to the total catch was not increased. Nevertheless, a sanctuary can be regarded as probably the last defence of the southern stock against disastrous depletion." Actually, it was by no means certain that stocks of whales in the new Area VI were separate from the others: there were grounds for believing that they were part of the group of whales in Area V. If marking of whales confirmed this, Area VI should be incorporated in V, and regulation should apply as far east as the limit of Area VI, i.e. to 120°W. From a purely biological point of view the Committee was of the opinion that the Sanctuary should not be reopened, but at the I.W.C. meeting in 1957 it was decided to keep it open in 1958-9 as well, and when it was stated that it would be an advantage for the companies, in planning their season, to know in plenty of time whether whaling would be permitted in the whole of Area I or not, it was resolved in 1959 to keep it open for an additional three years. At the end of this period, in 1962, the I.W.C. decided to keep this sector open until such time as was otherwise decided, as in fact Japan had proposed in 1958. Since then the sector has never been closed. Nor has this been necessary, seeing that there is a total ban in the Antarctic on the killing of all the large whales, except minke whales, from factory ships. Thus the five largest species (blue, fin, humpback, sperm and sei whales) are now protected in the Antarctic.

The opening of the Sanctuary was a sacrifice made by science to whaling in the (feeble) hope that this would correspondingly ease pressure on stocks in other sectors. No consideration was taken of the fact that this would reduce whaling from shore stations on the west coast of South America, to which whales migrated from Area I, because catches here were quite insignificant compared to those of humpbacks in Australian waters from Areas IV and V. The opening of the Sanctuary was used by several members of the I.W.C. as an argument against lowering the global quota, since whaling was now spread over larger areas, and not concentrated in those whaling grounds where it had operated since 1938. This argument found insufficient support in the I.W.C. To offset the fact that the whale no longer had a sanctuary, the quota was lowered to 15,000 in 1955-6, with the proviso that in the ensuing season it would also be reduced by 500 (Japan, the Netherlands, and Panama voted against). The quota was, in fact, reduced to 14,500 for the two seasons 1956-8. This would appear to be the correct approach for the I.W.C., i.e. by means of a gradual reduction of 500 every year or every other season, to reduce catches until the ideal level was reached, which would constantly ensure the maximum sustainable yield, provided that it was not already too late. A continuation of this approach was deadlocked in 1958 when the Netherlands maintained that it would not be possible to trust calculations of the size of fin whale stocks. This point of view had always been maintained by the Netherlands delegate to the I.W.C. and its chairman in 1957-8, Professor G. J. LIENESCH, ever since the idea of lowering the quota had first been mooted. The Netherlands consistently refused to accept the necessity of the proposed reduction every season. In opposition to the unanimous views of all the other ten members of the Scientific Committee, that a catch of 25,000 fin whales a year would rapidly result in the extermination of stocks, the Netherlands asserted that there were equally good grounds for maintaining that stocks of fin whales were twice as large as biologists calculated, and were therefore capable of sustaining the yield desired by the Netherlands. For this reason they wanted the quota to be raised to at least 16,000, and took not the slightest heed of what the New Zealand representative said : "I hope that the Netherlands Government will be influenced by the great weight of opinion expressed in this Commission in favour of adequate measures of conservation. There is a great evidence that a crisis caused by over-killing faces the whale industry, and if that crisis were to eventuate it would surely lie heavily on the conscience of any nation which, by its single action taken in opposition to all its partners in an international body, caused the dissipation of a mighty store of wealth."

The Scientific Committee considered that the 11,000 units which it believed necessary to ensure continued whaling, could be filled by approximately 19,000 fin whales (i.e. 9,500 units), instead of 26,000 fin whales taken in 1954-5, while the remaining units could be made up essentially by blue and a certain number of humpback and sei whales. But out of tactical consideration for companies that would find it difficult to readjust at such short notice from an expected competition for 15,000 to 11,000 units, it was anxious to introduce a lesser reduction at this juncture and a larger one during the ensuing two seasons. That the Committee in this way should have acted contrary to its conviction, and not proposed the entire reduction at once, occasioned a very vigorous attack from New Zealand on the chairman of the Committee, Professor N. A. Mackintosh, at the I.W.C. meeting in 1956. From one meeting to another, he asserted, one gained a stronger and stronger impression that the Committee took into consideration factors that were anything but purely scientific, and in particular the effect of a reduction on whaling operations or the fact that governments would not accept the restrictions that conformed with the Committee's optimal wishes. He put a direct question to Mackintosh: What was the *scientific* reason why the Committee proposed such a small reduction now and a larger one later? Mackintosh was openly forced to admit that the Committee had allowed itself to be influenced by factors that were irrelevant to it. On the other hand, the Committee had felt that it should take into consideration what was feasible, and not what it considered *should* be done on the basis of a biological view of what might be desirable.

As early as 1956 the Netherlands, which had high hopes of the performance of its new large floating factory, protested against a lowering of the quota, but withdrew the protest at the request of the other nations. When it was proposed in 1958 to maintain the 14,500 units for a third season, 1958-9, as well, the Netherlands was the only country to protest. All the other nations thereupon lodged a protest, in order to ensure that the Netherlands did not enjoy a special advantage. The effective quota thus was fixed at 15,000, an increase and a retrogressive step as far as regulation was concerned, for which the Netherlands alone must bear the responsibility. This was the source of one of the disputes that almost tore the Commission apart, and resulted in the pelagic nations taking matters into their own hands.

The tug-of-war between science and whaling, which became increasingly acute after 1955, culminated in the victory of the latter, though it proved a Pyrrhic victory that sealed its own fate. Instead of lowering the quota, the only weapon in the armoury of science, the quota was increased by 500 in 1958-9, and in 1959-62 suspended (see Chapter 32). It benefited the companies' nationwide competition that there were national quotas during these seasons, but it had the opposite effect on whale stocks. In 1959-60 the sum of national quotas amounted to 17,800 units, while the catch was greater than at any time since 1951-2. The season of 1960-1 recorded the largest catch of baleen whale since the war, while the catch in 1961-2 was unmatched since the 1959-60 and 1954-5 seasons. In actual fact the three seasons when whalers had things practically their own way constituted a complete breakdown of the Convention, and struck a serious blow at stocks of fin whales and the small number of blue whales still surviving. In 1962-3, when the quota was once again 15,000, the companies, despite a period of 111 days at their disposal, failed to kill more than 11,306, a deficit of almost 25 per cent. The drastic reduction that had to be imposed for the five ensuing seasons came too late. Even when the 1967-8 quota was reduced to as little as 3,200, not more than 87½ per cent of this was caught. One is inclined to believe that if the 1955 quota had been lowered to 11,000, and if national quotas had been established as far back as the London Agreement of 1937-8, then it is quite possible that today and well into the future an annual catch of 9,000 to 10,000 units would have been possible, and this would have supplied the world with 200,000 tons of fat, the main raw material for 300 million kg. of margarine, and 300,000 to 400,000 tons of meat to a hungry world.

It now remains to discover why this in fact was not done. This is all the more unexpected, as the 1950s had been ushered in with signs that developments would take a more favourable turn, both for the whale and for the companies.

Quota and catching matériel

In time, the practice of operating with 16,000 units showed that the Convention was by no means the ideal that had been envisaged. Admittedly, it had restricted the total number to what was considered sufficient to sustain whale stocks, but in accordance with the principle of free competition it had left it to the companies themselves to determine the amount of matériel they wished to use in this competition. Here, in fact, lay the seeds for the failure of the Convention. Just how changed the situation had become as compared with its original intentions can perhaps best be illustrated by the fact that the chairman of the Norwegian delegation to the Washington Conference in 1946 considered that it would be a catastrophe for Norwegian whaling if national quotas were adopted, and refused to include in the Norwegian delegation persons whose loyalty to the Norwegian point of view could not be relied on. In 1959 Norway resigned from the Commission in order to enforce national quotas. In short, the problem was that more and more nations and expeditions were competing for fewer and fewer whales. This situation could persist as long as the value of the product covered the expense of catching a certain share of the quota. Competition, however, could result in the development of matériel of such capacity that operating it would prove unprofitable. On an economic basis there was no question of equal opportunities: not only did the Japanese pay wages which were approximately half of those paid by Norwegian-British expeditions, but they had a domestic market for whale meat at prices which in most seasons made this more lucrative than the production of oil. The Dutch company enjoyed large Government subsidies, while the Russian expeditions were entirely state-run, independent of the economic results. It was openly alleged that Russian whaling did not obey the rules of the game; for example, as if to demonstrate its efficiency, the *Slava* expedition reported a catch which was technically impossible in view of its capacity. Compared with the British expeditions, the Norwegians suffered the handicap in 1945-52 of having to hand over to the state a large proportion of the operating surplus that could have been ploughed back into the companies and improved their competitive ability.

The disadvantages of "super-capacity" catching matériel were obvious. The results of more matériel were greater operating costs, a shorter season, and a smaller oil production for each catcher's day work. The situation had reached the paradoxical stage that less matériel would ensure a longer whaling season and a greater yield of oil per catching unit. The constantly reiterated theme of expedition managers and gunners in the 1950s was that whaling conditions were approaching the untenable. Competition resulted in an intense, hectic pursuit, nerves were on edge when the season had reached the stage when whaling might be called off any day. There was no time then for gunners to select the most favourable animals; it was a question of aiming at the first whale that appeared to satisfy the minimum length requirements. Nor was there time to reduce the raw material as thoroughly as it could have been. This is not the place for a scientific discussion of the importance of a minimum length for stocks of whales, or of the relative merits of hunting sexually mature or immature animals, old or young animals. The case of whaling, however, should be a warning to those inclined to express themselves categorically that they cannot be in possession of sufficient knowledge to resolve the entire complex of problems involved. The more one knows, the more one realises one does not know.

During the debate on revision of the Convention an idea was mooted in several quarters that had been considered when the Commission was established : to make it an organisation under the jurisdiction of the United Nations, to "internationalise" whaling by auctioning it in a manner of speaking to interested parties in return for a royalty payable to the developing countries, so that one nation or private individuals would no longer be able to exploit and destroy a source of raw material that was the common property of mankind. Instead of utopian ideas of this nature, the whaling companies endeavoured themselves to arrive at a more realistic and practical solution.

The purpose of deferring the opening of the catching season to a later and later date was not of a biological so much as of an economic nature. The bulk of the quota would be caught in the latter half of the season, when whales were fatter and consequently yielded more oil. The opening, which in 1945 and 1946 was on 24 November, was gradually put back to 7 January between 1954-5 and 1958-9. After that, the reverse approach was tried, as we shall see. The purpose of the later opening was also to spare the blue whale, which appeared on the scene earlier in the season than the other species. For this whale the same opening dates applied up till 1953. In the 1953-4 season it was 16 January, in 1954-5 21 January, in 1955-60 1 February, and from 1960-1 14 February. The special period set aside for the catching of humpbacks has already been mentioned. Fin and sei whales could be caught throughout the open season. It is difficult to say precisely what influence the postponement of the season generally, and for blue whales in particular, may have had on the try-out per BWU. Statistically, it is impossible to trace any relationship between the opening date and the try-out. Admittedly, the try-out rose from 117.3 to 129.4 barrels per unit when the opening in 1951-2 was put back from 22 December to 2 January, but it dropped from 128.6 to 117.3 barrels in 1954-5, when the opening was put back from 2 to 7 January. For that particular season the decline was undoubtedly due to the extraordinarily poor weather conditions, with small quantities of krill and meagre whales. There were 133 fewer units caught in 1953-4, but production was 185,000 barrels less. Better production methods, an amendment in minimum size limits for fin whales, the opening of Area I, the whale's varying degrees of fatness from season to season, as well as other factors, have played an important role in the variations in try-out in the 1950s, and at other times. It would appear difficult, in fact, to trace any connection between the duration of the season and the oil try-out, as there are two great deviations from what nevertheless appears to be a tendency indicating that the longer the season, the greater the try-out. The 1954-5 season, with seventy-two catching days, and 1958-9, with sixty-nine days, had a considerably lower try-out than 1955-6, with only fifty-eight days, and this does not confirm the assertion of whaling managers that the greater the degree of urgency, the worse the exploitation of the whale.

As the catching period was never utilised in its entirety in any of the seasons in the 1950s, no evidence was available to show how much the yield of oil could be increased if, using fewer whale catchers, hunting had been extended to cover the entire open season. In 1953-4, the first season when a reduction in the number of whale catchers was introduced, weekly production of whale oil per BWU rose as shown in Table 31.

The figures in Table 31 should be treated with considerable caution, and can merely be said to indicate a tendency — an increase in the try-out towards the end of the season. A theoretical estimate of the probable loss of production suffered owing to competition for the 16,000 units would of necessity be based on many uncertain factors, whilst in "real life" an entirely different result might well have occurred.

Table 31. WEEKLY PRODUCTION OF WHALE OIL PER BWU IN THE 1953-4 SEASON

	Barrels		Barrels		Barrels
3-9 Jan.	113.4	31 Jan.-6 Feb.	117.5	21-27 Feb.	126.8
10-16 Jan.	113.9	7-13 Feb.	138.8	28 Feb.-6 March	137.6
17-23 Jan.	119.7	14-20 Feb.	143.6	7-13 March	163.1
24-30 Jan.	117.4				

The other factor that a reduction in the number of whale catchers would affect was the operating expenses, and this applies not only to their number, but also to their size and engine power. From 1945 to 1953 they increased in size from 316 to 398 gross tons, and from 1,190 to 1,874 h.p. on an average. The largest catchers required more fuel merely to maintain the same speed as the smaller ones, and twice as much fuel consumption was required to increase the speed of the same boat from e.g. 13 to 15 knots. After the outbreak of the Korean War in 1950 the price of fuel rose sharply. The increase in the number and efficiency of whale catchers was not only a result of competition, but also because whaling became much more a matter of pursuit for a prey that in time was spread over larger areas and was much more "thin on the ground". But although there were fewer whales, a smaller number of boats could have covered the floating factory's field of operation, and even if whales had been plentiful, it would not have been necessary to employ a large number of catchers. Catching was limited by the floating factory's capacity to reduce the raw material within the period of time established by the Convention. The result of this might be that whale catchers would have to ration their catch and hunt less than they were capable of. With the depletion of stocks, however, this became less and less common.

From the annual reports of several companies it emerges that deploying fewer whale catchers meant a saving in operational costs, as this obviated the need for a transport vessel to bring fuel oil to the whaling grounds. Even though the operating expenses of a whale catcher increased with a longer season, this was insignificant compared to the great savings achieved by deploying a smaller number, provided the same production was achieved. For the 1955-6 season it was estimated that using one whale catcher less would have involved a saving worth approximately as much as 3,500 barrels, and this at a price of £90 a ton meant £52,500. The great increase in the expeditions' operating expenses incurred by using "unnecessary" whale catchers could not be outweighed by a corresponding increase in production under the whaling regulations in force.

The initiative for a limitation in the number of whale catchers came from the Association of Norwegian Whaling Companies. The first time this was mentioned was on 18 February 1952, when it was decided to invite all foreign and domestic companies to conclude an agreement, whose efficacy would be determined by the number of adherents. The reaction of Onassis and the Russians was negative, and a number of companies posed special demands that the Norwegian companies were unable to accept. For this reason it proved impossible to come to any agreement for 1952-3. But when the "arms race" continued, and the number of catchers per expedition rose to a record level, 14.4, and there were prospects of a further increase for the ensuing season, the Association raised the matter afresh, and after complicated negotiations a form of agreement was arrived at on 30 June 1953, to which all adhered with the exception of the *Slava* (the *Olympic Challenger* was not operating in 1953-4). The agreement was very simple and brief. The thirteen floating factories were to be allowed to use up to thirteen catchers, two could use twelve, another two could use ten, and one, the *Suderøy,* could use eight. Owing to her production of meat the *Balaena* was allowed to use one extra catcher, making a total of fourteen. Not all of them made use of the permitted maximum. The number for seventeen pelagic expeditions amounted to 206, as against 230 for sixteen expeditions in 1952-3, while the average dropped from 14.4 to 12.1, a considerable reduction, but not as big as the Norwegian companies, who wanted a maximum of 10, had hoped. (For the Antarctic pelagic whaling fleet, catching days, production, etc., 1945-78, see Statistical Appendix, Table 64.)

It is difficult to find any actual result of this reduction in whaling as compared with the preceding season, partly because the same expeditions did not participate, partly because the 1953-4 quota was set at 500 BWU less, partly because catching in 1952-3, for reasons it was impossible to predict, was called off so early that only 14,867 out of the possible 16,000 units were accounted for, i.e. a deficit for the companies of 7.08 per cent. With the same margin as in 1953-4, −0.28 per cent, the catch in 1952-3 would have been 15,945 units, and the period of hunting presumably longer. The seasons 1954-6, which were considered operationally extraordinarily difficult, would have produced a deficit, had they not been saved by the rise in price. After seven fat years came four lean years. In the course of 1951-2 production of vegetable oils satisfied the demand: there was no longer any need for emergency stores, and the British Food Ministry sold its whale oil stocks, some of which helped Unilever to cover the bulk of its needs. The slump in price came in the first half of 1952. In January the Sales Pool sold 15,000 tons for £120, in February 20,000 tons for £100, and 55,000 tons in May-June for £72 10*s.* The low catch in 1954-5 came as a surprise, as noted by the oil brokers Frank Fehr & Co., and proved a disappointment to the margarine manufacturers. It could be regarded as a warning on the profits of intending expeditions. Prices rallied slightly when the entire Antarctic production the following season proved equally low.

Considerable difficulties were encountered in obtaining a renewal of the agreement for 1954-5 with the same participants as on the previous occasion. While Norway operated with the same matériel (minus one whale catcher), there were two new expeditions, though they had both operated previously. They were the *Olympic Challenger* and the *Kinjyo Maru* (which had operated under the name of *Nisshin Maru I* from 1946 to 1951). This meant an increase of twenty-seven on the total number of whale catchers. The attempt to renew the agreement for 1955-6 failed, *inter alia* because of the Netherlands company, which refused to participate, as it maintained that eighteen whale catchers were necessary in order to utilise the capacity of their new floating factory. The result proved a great disappointment, as eight other expeditions, employing ten to fifteen boats, caught far more than the Dutch factory. The total number of whale catchers amounted to 257, exceeded only by 1951-2 with 263, and 1961-2 with 261. In 1956-9 there was a fresh reaction against this expansion.

In the 1950s it appeared that not only the number of whale catchers but also the number of floating factories would be reduced. In 1952 the oldest of the Norwegian floating factories was withdrawn from whaling and broken up. Its history reflects the fluctuations before and after the war. From 1926 to 1931 it produced 383,889 barrels (whale and sperm oil) to a value of £1.75 million; in 1936-9, operating for Germany, 200,696 barrels to a value of £580,000; and in 1945-52, 594,564 barrels to a value of £9.14 million, a mean average during the three periods of £4 10s, £2 16s, and £15 8s per barrel. One other Norwegian floating factory was not operative in 1952-3, owing to the state of the market, and a third owing to damage, but in 1953-4 both were once again in the whaling grounds. What the Norwegian fleet lost in capacity by one floating factory was more than outweighed by considerable conversion and re-equipping in 1951-6 of three other floating factories. With three fewer Norwegian expeditions operating in 1952-3, the result was a decline in the total amount of matériel used of three floating factories and thirty-three whale catchers, but it also meant that 1,355 fewer whalers were employed in the Norwegian fleet, whereas the number in the foreign fleets was the same as in the previous season.

The reduction in 1952-3 from nineteen to sixteen floating factories was only a passing phenomenon. Plans were already being hatched which, when realised, led to the last expansion in pelagic Antarctic whaling, supported by economic and political interests against which the Norwegian-British whaling companies and the I.W.C. waged a hopeless struggle. Step by step the old whaling nations trailed behind in a competition which paid no regard to whale stocks. In the latter part of the 1950s we encounter once again various features of the struggle that took place in the latter half of the 1930s, *inter alia* the dubious practice of stopping other nations building new expeditions by selling them existing ones. It is interesting to trace the cycle through which regulation passed. It commenced with a private agreement between companies on quotas, continued with an agreement between the pelagic nations, was extended to an international agreement, to which even nations which had never been engaged in whaling were admitted, and came full circle with an agreement among only the pelagic nations and quotas for individual expeditions, subject to buying and selling between companies. In other words, the first attempt at an international convention to preserve the rich fats resources of the Antarctic had proved a failure, and ended with the parties involved coming to terms with one another as best they could. Why did events take this turn? (For pelagic Antarctic quotas, catch, catching days, seasons, daily production, etc., 1945-78, see Statistical Appendix, Table 65.)

31
THE LAST EXPANSION 1955-1961

The seasons 1960-2, particularly the last of these, proved decisive in ushering in the final phase of Antarctic whaling for Argentina, Britain, the Netherlands, and Norway, and a marked reduction for the two remaining countries, Japan and the Soviet Union. After a decline in 1952-3, the number of expeditions increased, reaching a peak in 1960-2. The number of floating factories and whale catchers, however, do not tell the whole story. The average tonnage of floating factories rose from 14,903 to 19,352 gross tons, and that of whale catchers from 494 to 657 gross tons, and their horsepower from 1,862 to 2,723 h.p. In its catching and production capacity the fleet operating in 1961-2 was the most effective that had ever been seen in the whaling grounds. A few figures will show how intense was the competition for whales, and how depleted stocks had become (see Table 32). The paradoxical situation had emerged with whaling growing in inverse proportion to the whale stocks.

Table 32. TOTAL ANTARCTIC OIL PRODUCTION AND AVERAGE PRODUCTION PER FLOATING FACTORY AND PER CATCHER, 1952-1963

| | Total oil production | Average per floating factory | | | Average catcher's day work | |
| | | Catching | Barrels | | | |
	barrels	days	total	per day	barrels	BWU
1952-3	1,884,207	74	117,763	1,591	110	0.86
1961-2	1,797,178	115	85,580	744	60	0.51
1962-3	1,293,491	110	76,088	689	57	0.50

It was hardly surprising that the production in 1961-2 should have slumped to 1.8 million barrels: this was about the level it had maintained for several post-war seasons. Most significant is the fact that, while the number of catching days rose 55.4 per cent, production per floating factory was 27.3 per cent less, and that daily factory production sank to less than one-half. The marked increase in production costs that this involved coincided with one of the sharpest falls in the price of whale oil from one season to the next ever recorded during the post-war period, from £70 9s 4d in 1960-1 to £44 2s in 1961-2 (in terms of average prices for Norwegian production). The price of sperm oil, on the other hand, was good: £78 11s 6d. It is in fact striking how often during a year with a high price for whale oil the price of sperm oil has been low or vice versa. Rarely have the prices of these two commodities been comparable. Their very different consistency and use have not conformed to the same market fluctuations. The price of whale oil rallied considerably in 1962-3, though the average of both seasons (1961-3) was the lowest since the war, and some £25 lower than the average for the preceding and succeeding seasons. It is estimated that some £100 million had been invested in the whaling fleet in 1961-2; it produced commodities with a market value of approximately £34 million, i.e. about 34 per cent of the invested capital. This could hardly cover more than production costs, at any rate for companies based mainly on the production of whale oil and not of whale meat, or on a relatively large production of sperm oil. For the owners of the state-subsidised Dutch company catching results played a minor role since dividends were guaranteed; in 1961-2 there was a deficit of Fl.2.3 million (c. £230,000). The company continued to operate for another two seasons, recording a deficit on each occasion, and finally closed down. It reaped what it had sown. The purely state-run Soviet whaling fleet had no need to consider prices: with their tremendous and costly matériel the Soviets must have paid a high price for their whale oil; it was even said that they could have purchased it in the open market for half their production costs.

For the purely private Norwegian and British companies, with operations based mainly on the production of whale oil, the 1961-2 season, with its poor economic results, proved a turning-point. The number of Norwegian and British expeditions dropped in 1962-3 from seven to four and from two to one respectively, and their shares of pelagic production in the Antarctic from 27.7 per cent to 15 per cent and from 10.4 per cent to 5.3 per cent respectively. The South African company had bowed out as far back as 1957. What the other nations relinquished, the Japanese took over. One tends to forget that the Japanese, since they had started to use the new and converted *Matsushima Maru* in 1956, have not extended their total Antarctic whaling fleet by the addition of new expeditions. Subsequent Japanese expansion has been based entirely on the purchase of existing expeditions. The only expansion of the total world fleet by the accretion of new expeditions after 1956 was caused by the Soviet Union, with its 3 huge expeditions in 1959-61, the largest ever to have operated in the Antarctic. That the Soviet Union should have taken this step at a time when it was obvious to all and sundry that whale stocks were rapidly declining is difficult to understand, unless we also take into account matters of prestige, political and military aims, which were all part of the tremendous naval expansion in every field, in fishing and whaling, in the merchant marine and in the navy. Ever since 1955, when it was decided to build an Antarctic whaling fleet, the Soviet Union has also been highly active in Antarctic exploration and research. There is an important difference between the Soviet and Japanese expansions: the Russians increased the Antarctic whaling fleet *per se,* whilst the Japanese increased their fleet by taking over floating factories from others.

The 1961-2 season also marked a decisive turning-point in whale stocks. There was now a huge whaling fleet making inroads on stocks of whales which were being rapidly reduced. After this season this fact would be obvious to all who till then had been unwilling to acknowledge it. This was the last season when catches of blue whales only just exceeded 1,000, and when only 309 humpbacks were caught. In 1962-3 catches of fin whales, which then accounted for about 70 per cent of pelagic baleen whaling, and since 1953-4 had remained at a steady level of about 26,000 annually, slumped to 18,000. Although the global quota was 15,000 units and the open season 117 days, only 11,306 whales were caught, a deficit of 24.62 per cent. The decline in the number of fin whales caught continued at a rate of 5,000-6,000 with every season. Then, and not till then, were the whaling nations able to agree to reduce the quota to the level which the scientists had considered necessary ever since the mid-1950s. Hardly had Norwegian-British whaling enjoyed a short breathing space in the early 1950s in their struggle against all the new whaling nations, than they were involved in a new and still more bitter struggle for their existence. The first phase in the struggle was partly won, the last was lost, and Norwegian-British Antarctic whaling thus passed over into history.

Hopes for a brighter future, for which there appeared to be good grounds during the early 1950s, were frustrated in various ways in 1955-6. In 1955 the new large Dutch floating factory and in 1956 Japan's new one first operated. The Soviet Union announced that her sixth five-year plan, 1956-60, included the building of five new large expeditions, and in addition it proved impossible to extend the agreement on the limitation in the number of whale catchers to cover 1955-6. The decline from nineteen to sixteen expeditions was entirely at the expense of the Norwegian whaling fleet; the motive for laying up, however, was not in order to reduce the amount of matériel *per se,* but because of the slack whale oil market. The limitation in the number of whale catchers was the result of Norwegian initiative.

Events in and around 1955-6 constituted such a threat to Norwegian and British whaling that they tended to obscure the only ray of light: a new agreement for a restriction in the number of whale catchers for the 1956-7 season, which was also successfully renewed for the two following seasons, 1957-9. All three agreements stated in their preamble that the express reason for concluding them was "to improve the profitability of Antarctic expeditions". During the 1955-6 season, when there was no agreement in force, the average number of whale catchers had increased for the Norwegian expeditions from 11.2 to 12.2, and for the foreign expeditions from 12.6 to 15. A reduction in this number, and consequently in operating expenses, was a matter of urgency. In principle the Norwegian standpoint, as on the last occasion, was that there should be a maximum of ten whale catchers per expedition, and a somewhat lower number for smaller floating factories. In order to include the new *Willem Barendsz II,* an exception had to be made, permitting it to use fourteen; the *Slava,* not covered by the agreement, increased its number from fifteen to eighteen. A note to the Soviet Ministry of Fisheries remained unanswered. The difference between the previous agreement and the ones for 1956-9 was that the latter did not allocate a definite number to each expedition, but to each nation, which then in turn re-allocated it to its companies. The result of the agreement was that in 1956-7 there was a total of thirty-two fewer whale catchers in pelagic expeditions, despite the fact that there was one additional expedition. The agreement was the best that could be achieved, and in the circumstances at any rate better than no agreement at all.

Although there was no rise in price, there was no fall, either; for production in 1956-7 the price remained at about the same relatively high level, £85 10s, as for 1955-6. Thanks to the excellent catch the operational results for the Norwegian expeditions were good; with sixteen fewer whale catchers and the same number of expeditions (nine), Norwegian pelagic production in 1956-7 amounted to 167,000 barrels (whale and sperm oil) more than the preceding season. This alone accounted for some 18,750 tons or £1.6 million. In addition to increased yield, Kr.15 million to Kr.16 million was saved by reducing the number of whale catchers. While this was not such an urgent matter in that season, it became all the more urgent the following season, when the price dropped £13 and production amounted to 17,000 tons less. In 1958-9 it dropped a further 9,500 tons, while the production apparatus for all three seasons remained the same.

A comparison between the number of whale catchers per expedition and the Norwegian and foreign whaling fleets which subscribed to the regulations for a reduction in whale catchers shows that the average number of Norwegian whale catchers was always lower than foreign ones. As in the 1930s it was once again maintained that Norway was always the loser in any agreement; it was always the Norwegians who had to make concessions in order to have an agreement adopted. To a certain extent this could be done as long as Norway was the dominant whaling country, but in the long run it weakened her ability to compete. Just how a tug-of-war would usually end with Norwegian compliance was demonstrated by the negotiations for renewal of the Whale Catcher Agreement for 1957-9. The final result was that the Japanese expeditions were able to increase their number of whale-catchers from nine to eleven per floating factory, one of the British was allowed thirteen, while the *Willem Barendsz* was able to continue whaling with fourteen. A couple of the largest Norwegian floating factories operated with ten catchers, one had nine, and one only seven.

The agreement included one interesting clause. Japan requested and and was given permission, in return for a duty of Kr.300,000, to use one of the Norwegian-British whale catchers, so that in actual fact Japan operated with one whale catcher more than the agreement entitled her to. On the one hand this was a concession that had to be made in order to induce Japan to adhere to the agreement; on the other hand, it was calculated that there would be an average of 63 BWU per whale catcher and the extra earnings of one boat would far exceed the payment of the rent. This ushered in a period of purchase and sale of matériel (of which more below), not for the sake of the matériel but in order to acquire the quota belonging to it.

Statements to the press by leading Japanese whalers show that the agreement was regarded as something of a triumph over Norway. Japan, it was said, had "shown a considerable degree of self-control [by not demanding thirteen or fourteen whale catchers] in order to save Norway's face, as Norway had made great efforts to bring the conflict to a peaceful conclusion". The price for the right to use the whale catcher was considered very reasonable — "they had expected Norway to demand an exorbitant price" — and if the other two companies had known that it was so cheap, they would have asked for the same.

In Japan the situation was that the two smaller floating factories converted in 1946 had in 1951 been replaced by the two larger ones, the *Tonan Maru* and the *Nisshin Maru*. For three seasons Japan operated with these two alone, but in 1954 a third was in use. For the 1955-6 season a company, the Kyokuyo Hogei K.K., worked with a smaller floating factory in the North Pacific, and in 1956-7 in the Antarctic with the *Olympic Challenger,* which had been purchased and rechristened the *Kyokuyo Maru II.* That the Japanese should be operating with this floating factory was, in the opinion of the Norwegian companies, the lesser of two evils: the Japanese had, after all, shown a reasonable willingness to co-operate over the regulations, and this was better than to have the vessel in the hands of a company that did not observe international agreements. From the Norwegian and the British point of view the appearance of four Japanese expeditions in 1956-7 was sufficient cause for dismay, but complete consternation was created by the report from the Norwegian Legation in Tokyo in the spring of 1956 that the Nippon Suisan K.K. had been granted permission to convert a tanker, the *Matsushima Maru,* into a floating factory. The Japanese aim was to restore all the six expeditions she had had before the war. Norway's counter argument was that she, Norway, at that time had had twelve expeditions, as well as managing three operating under other flags. Of these fifteen, only ten had been replaced, and after a few years one had been withdrawn. The Norwegian companies requested the Foreign Ministry to make it quite clear to Japan that Norway was not willing to agree to a restriction in the number of whale catchers if the increase in the Japanese fleet went beyond the purchase of the *Olympic Challenger*; Norway would otherwise have to review her attitude to the Convention. As might be expected, the effect of the Norwegian protest proved a negative one, particularly because it was not supported by Britain and the United States. Britain was doubtful of the efficacy of this approach, while the United States replied that whaling was a vital necessity for the Japanese people, more than ever now that the Soviet Union had placed such considerable difficulties in the way of the Japanese fisheries, and major political considerations suggested that America should take no step that would involve the risk of losing Japan to the free world. The main argument in the Japanese reply was that the more limited the catching, the more important was it to make full use of the raw material, and no one did this more thoroughly than Japan, in itself an irrefutable argument. As the crew law allowed for a dispensation to the Japanese companies — a dispensation which had to be given, as they had operated in the season prior to 3 September 1939 — the Norwegian Government informed the companies that it would take no further steps against the Japanese expansion. The question of dispensation for the Norwegians who had served on board the *Olympic Challenger* before she was sold to Japan never arose, as the Japanese had a sufficient number of whaling crews and practically all the Norwegian gunners on the expedition had taken out foreign citizenship or were resident abroad.

The reaction of the Norwegian companies to the Government's announcement was a unanimous demand that Norway should resign from the Commission, not only owing to relations with Japan but also because the Soviet Union had openly declared that its avowed aim was to put Norway out of competition. No attempt was being made to disguise the fact that not only the *Olympic Challenger* but also the *Slava* had perpetrated quite blatant breaches of the Convention. The matter was very thoroughly discussed by all interested parties in Norway, and as the discussion developed Japanese whaling tended to fade into the background, whereas the Soviet operations loomed more ominously, as their expansion was on a much greater scale than had been anticipated, and involved the use of newly-built floating factories, whereas Japan purchased those that were being sold by other countries.

In Japan the possibility of Norwegian resignation from the Commission was received with some dismay, because in that event the other pelagic nations, too, would obviously resign. It was assumed that the reason for Norway's action was the poor results achieved by a number of companies in 1955-6, the fact that Norway had not been backed by other nations in restricting the number of whale catchers and that she had led the way in proposing regulations that led to the Washington Convention, but had not been able to prevent certain other countries from perfidiously acting on their own counter to the Norwegian endeavours. The impression in Japan was that whaling was not the main interest of the Norwegian companies; they were heavily committed to the tanker trade, and it would be no catastrophe if whaling came to an end in a few years' time. The reason for the Japanese superiority was that, unlike the Norwegians, they were not exclusively concerned with the production of oil, but much more with frozen whale meat. Three technical advances apparently contributed to this superiority: one was the flat-headed harpoon grenade (to which we shall return later), which marked a milestone in whaling and was the reason why the floating factory *Nisshin Maru,* whose whale catchers used this grenade, recorded the season's largest catch — and the biggest after the war — in 1955-6. Another was the powerful diesel-driven whale catchers of 650 to 750 gross tons, with engines developing 3,000 to 3,300 h.p. and a speed of 17 knots, of which in 1956 Japan had fifteen, while other nations had only one. The third was said to have been the use of Asdic. It seems highly improbable, however, that this should have given the Japanese an advantage in the 1950s, as some of Salvesen's whale catchers used it as long ago as 1945-6, and some of the Norwegians in 1946-7. At that time the Japanese were using a British device, and not till 1958-9 did they produce their own, which they claimed was much better than the British and capable of showing both the distance of the whale from the boat, the direction in which it was swimming, and the depth below the surface. What was more, this device only cost half (£11,000) the price of the British one.

There were other reasons, too, why the Norwegian companies were anxious for Norway to withdraw from the I.W.C. One, apparently trivial, typifies the way in which certain member countries tried to find loopholes in the Convention. According to its Article VIII a country could be permitted to catch a small number of whales outside the open season, for scientific purposes, with a view to carrying out biological research. The Russians took it greatly amiss when the Norwegians accused them, under cover of Article VIII, of carrying out regular whaling on a far larger scale than was necessary for research. At the I.W.C. meeting in 1957 it was resolved that permission for whaling of this kind should only be given to a very limited extent.

This matter was connected with the question of international (neutral) observers. The proposal for the so-called Observer Scheme was the one that appeared longest on the agenda of the I.W.C. meetings, before finally, and then too late, it was resolved. Article V of the Convention authorised the Commission to amend the Schedule on eight carefully specified points, one of which was the setting up of a control system. An amendment of this nature could be carried out either by being adopted and ratified by all the powers that had ratified the Washington Convention, or by the pelagic whaling nations concluding an agreement on the matter outside the Commission. When Norway raised the subject at the 1955 I.W.C. meeting, this body was only in a position to declare discussion of the supervision of observation to be outside its jurisdiction. Both approaches were to prove long and difficult, and ran into interminable objections of a formal, practical, and political nature, full details of which have no place in this account.

A solution appeared to be in the offing when, on 26 September 1956, the United States submitted a proposal that a supplementary protocol to the main agreement should come into force as and when ten of the member countries had notified their adherence. The proposal, however, fell through, as the Soviet Union would not accept it, nor were the Russians prepared to take part in a meeting of the pelagic nations to discuss an agreement between them. For this reason the United States submitted a fresh proposal on 19 November of the same year, to the effect that the protocol should be ratified by all nineteen member countries. At the 1957 I.W.C. meeting ratification fell short by nine states, and in 1958 by three — Brazil, Mexico and Panama. Thus the Commission was unable to deal with Norway's proposal, because Article V did not contain the three words "methods of inspection". The weakness of the Convention is graphically illustrated by the fact that three countries with no whaling (Mexico and Panama) or only a little (Brazil) were in a position to thwart a measure that was important to the aims of the Convention. When the last of the members, Brazil, finally ratified it on 4 May 1959, the protocol came into force the same day. Everything now appeared to be set for carrying out inspection; it only remained to agree on its form, but before this stage had been reached the proposers — Norway and the Netherlands — had resigned and withdrawn from the Commission. Volumes could be written on the disputes revolving round international control; suffice it to say that it strikingly reveals the uneasy conscience of a number of whaling nations, and their fear that illegal catching would be exposed.

British whaling, too, felt that calling a halt to Russian and Japanese expansion was a question of its own continued existence. Failing to receive the support it had expected from the British Government, the British Whaling Association, too, resigned, abandoning the unequal struggle more rapidly than the Norwegian companies had done. Just before the opening of the 1956-7 season Salvesen despatched a message to his three expeditions informing them that he had been forced to enter into negotiations with Japan for the sale of the *Southern Venturer,* together with seven whale catchers, because the policy of the I.W.C. had made it impossible to set up a system of national quotas and to ensure economic operation, as well as directly encouraging the establishment of new Panamanian, Japanese, and Russian expeditions. All overtures to the Government to intervene had proved futile. At the same time negotiations were on foot for the sale of the *Abraham Larsen* (ex *Unitas*), which was purchased in 1957, together with eight whale catchers, by the Taiyo Gyogyo K.K. for £3,275,000. The high price the Japanese were prepared to pay for a twenty-year-old floating factory, which in 1947 had been sold for £1,050,000, reflects not only the rise in prices or inflation, but also how vitally important it was for Japan — and profitable as well — to invest in her own particular form of whaling. This is also shown by the fact that the Japanese were willing to pay a still higher price, £3.6 million, for the *Southern Venturer* and its whale catchers. This sale was never concluded, as the Japanese Government refused a licence for the purchase of more than one expedition per season.

This was not the only Japanese offer to purchase matériel, and in Norway the authorities were in considerable doubt as to what attitude they were to adopt to sales of this kind. The high price offered for a floating factory which would soon no longer be capable of operating in the Antarctic was a strong inducement to sell, but the inconsistency involved in Norway increasing Japan's capacity, while at the same time endeavouring to restrict its expansion, was an argument against sale. Finally, the Norwegian Government issued an export permit, on condition that the purchasers guaranteed that the floating factory would never be used in the Antarctic. This was at first rejected but subsequently accepted, provided that the vendor did not operate there (with other matériel) for a period of three years subsequent to the sale. The vendors of the *Abraham Larsen* (Union Whaling Company) had been compelled to accept the same condition for a period of five years.

One Norwegian attempt to put the brake on Japanese expansion involved the Dutch floating factory *Willem Barendsz II.* We shall later return to this complicated matter and its tie-up with the agreement on national quotas. As already mentioned, the Dutch Government had guaranteed operations and a reasonable dividend. After six years (in 1957) this guarantee had cost the Dutch state Fl.29 million, and continued Government support was hotly contested by the political opposition. The company explained that the disappointing result was due to the international agreement on a reduction of catching. This explains why the Netherlands was always opposed to a lowering of the total quota and why it demanded an unreasonably high national quota, thereby almost torpedoing the quota agreement. In order to ensure its acceptance the Norwegian companies offered to buy the *Willem Barendsz* for £3 million, with a view to withdrawing it from whaling. But when the Netherlands, after exerting very considerable pressure on the I.W.C., was awarded the quota she demanded, nothing came of the sale. The floating factory continued to operate with a constant deficit until in 1964 she was sold to Japan exclusively for the sake of her quota, because the year after, without the appurtenant quota, she was resold to the Netherlands, and ended up in 1966 as a floating fish-oil factory in South Africa. The *Willem Barendsz I* had been sold to Japan in 1962 and operated in the North Pacific until she was broken up in 1966.

The reason why the Japanese companies were prepared to make such sizeable investments in whaling which, to all and sundry, was obviously becoming more and more reduced in scope, was that they had a sound economic basis in the sale of whale meat, at fairly stable prices, on the domestic market, and were not in any way dependent solely on the highly variable prices of whale oil. In 1957-8 the Japanese produced 522,104 barrels (87,016 tons) of whale oil, 108,199 barrels (18,033 tons) of sperm oil, 80,373 tons of whale meat, and 12,254 tons of various by-products. The average price of whale oil that year was £73, of sperm oil £65, of meat 80,000 yen (£90 a ton). This was the outcome of 4,628 BWU. Norwegian oil production based on 5,558 BWU was 744,100 barrels of whale and sperm oil to a value of £12.1 million (including approximately £1 million for by-products), whereas the total value of Japanese production based on 930 *fewer* units was £13.1 million; in other words, each Japanese unit provided £3,000 and each Norwegian unit £2,200. In addition to this, some of the Japanese expeditions operated in the North Pacific between Antarctic seasons. We are speaking here of gross value, net profits being an entirely different matter : the production of meat, transport to the home market, and marketing entailed considerable costs. During the season in question the Japanese were using forty-five refrigerator and deep-freeze ships, and tremendous deep-freeze storage plants in Japan, from which sales took place all the year round. For this reason a number of companies ran into financial difficulties in the early 1960s. The Japanese were, of course, in a position to vary production in the economically most favourable manner, according to the fluctuating price of meat and oil, which did not always follow the same curve. In time, as the quantitative yield of whaling became smaller, its value tended definitely to swing in favour of the Japanese, and the difference between Japanese double production of meat and oil on the one hand and oil production on the other became far greater than mentioned above. One might be tempted to ask : from the point of view of the world economy, is it not true that

100. The Soviet floating factory *Sovetskaya Ukraina*, built 1959 and at 32,024 gross tons the biggest in the world (along with her sister ship the *Sovetskaya Rossiya*).

the nation capable of transforming a given raw material into the most valuable product has the greatest moral right to such a raw material? In Japan the market for whale meat was so insatiable that the Japanese even concluded agreements for the purchase of whale meat from other expeditions in the whaling grounds.

At the end of the 1950s the interest of the whaling world was diverted more and more from Japanese to Russian expansion. There is plenty of evidence that it was in this quarter that the Japanese anticipated the keenest competition, not only in the Antarctic but even more in the North Pacific, where Japanese territorial possessions, so conveniently sited for whaling, had been considerably amputated after the war. The other whaling countries became increasingly apprehensive as the Soviet programme of new construction proceeded and it became clear that the Soviet Union was unwilling to participate in an agreement on a limitation of matériel, while it was doubtful whether the Russians would accept an agreement on national quotas. In addition to the two she already possessed, the *Aleut* and the *Slava* (ex *Wikinger*), the Russians were building or planning to build five large floating factories. The *Sovetskaya Ukraina* was completed in 1959 and the *Sovetskaya Rossiya* in 1961, sister ships of 33,000 gross tons (45,000 dead-weight tons) built at the Nosensko yard at Nikolayev on the Black Sea. In 1960 the *Yuri Dolgorukij* of 25,376 gross tons, a converted one-time German vessel, was completed. The last was the *Dalnij Vostok* of 16,974 gross tons, completed in 1963, and designed for catching in the North Pacific. Plans were well advanced for building a sister ship, the *Sovetskij Soyuz*, and in West Germany two floating factories of about 18,000 gross tons had been contracted. Still more impressive was the armada of enormously powerful whale catchers, sixty-seven in all in 1956-64, a serially built standard type of 843 gross tons, with diesel-electric engines developing 3,600 h.p., which were said to be capable of giving a speed of 19 knots or even more. Inevitably, the other nations awaited with trepidation the results of three or four expeditions of this kind, each accompanied by almost twenty whale catchers.

As Japan did not despatch more new expeditions after 1956 or increase the total number in the Antarctic, and as she was indisputably the nation that processed the raw material most completely and to the maximum degree of refinement, arguments against Japanese whaling inevitably lapsed. All the greater was the hostility directed against the Soviet Union, and it became increasingly urgent to divide the total quota up into national quotas before the Russians had scooped the jackpot and there was nothing left to share out. National quotas would enable each and every whaling nation to make free use of the matériel desired in order to catch as much of the national quota as possible during the permitted season. That whale stocks nevertheless were rapidly being exterminated was due not to the amount of matériel used or the distribution of national quotas, but to the fact that the total quota that was shared out was excessive.

32
THE DISPUTE OVER NATIONAL QUOTAS, 1958-1962

The idea of a separate quota for each nation or each expedition was not a new one when it was launched at the end of the 1950s. It had actually been practised, though in a different form, during the Norwegian-British agreements of the 1930s; it had been debated at conferences before the war and during the preparatory work for the Washington Conference in 1946, even though it was then not included in the agenda. It was in particular the biologists who had favoured this idea. For practical and political reasons the plan was not considered feasible: it violated the doctrine of the freedom of the seas to grant privileges to certain nations, and, should new ones join in, they would have a claim to their share, and it would be difficult to persuade the older nations to concede this. Trusting in their historical right to whaling, their favourable starting-point after the war and their superior expertise, the old whaling nations had been confident that they would preserve their hegemony. The Convention signatories felt that there would not be more participants in pelagic whaling in the Antarctic in 1946-7, and it was taken for granted that companies would adapt the quantity of their matériel to ensure the best operational results. No one had considered the possibility that it might be necessary to allow the Convention to exercise any control in this matter. As far as the older nations were concerned, the very presupposition on which they had based their whaling proved groundless. The only way in which they could still hope to carry on with an economic margin would be for a certain share of the global quota, which they could catch at their leisure with the most practical matériel, to be reserved for them. It was consequently for this reason that the old whaling nations once again raised the question of national quotas, if necessary by resigning from a Convention which had not lived up to its aims. The situation might possibly have been a different one if as far back as 1946 national quotas had been established; those who had proposed this at the time now had every reason to exult.

The idea had been discussed among the Norwegian and British companies since 1956. In Norwegian quarters it was considered that a system of national quotas would make it possible to preserve as much as possible for Norwegian whaling before the Japanese and Soviet expansion became excessive, and in Norway's case withdrawal from the Convention would be the best way of enforcing this system. From July

1956 to July 1958 the Association of Norwegian Whaling Companies submitted a number of requests to this effect to its Government, and at the I.W.C. meeting in 1956 the Chairman of the Association had made it clear that Norway might be compelled to take this drastic step. At the meeting in the following year it was Remington Kellogg's turn to warn the I.W.C., by pointing out how tremendously difficult it had proved to reconcile science and morals. He was profoundly shocked that commercial considerations had influenced negotiations to such an extent that a continuation of this trend might lead to the break-up of the Convention. The I.W.C.'s obligations to future generations were of far greater significance than obligations to shareholders. If whaling came to an end the I.W.C. would have failed in its duty towards its governments and, what was more, it would have gambled away the rightful heritage of coming generations which it had been appointed to guard by its governments. This might be called sentimental and melodramatic, but there were good grounds for hearkening to these words, and they certainly did not paint the situation in too sombre colours. They were also in a way the deepfelt words of the father of the Convention faced with the tragedy that an important part of his life's work had failed. He may possibly have felt a joint responsibility in that, in drafting the Convention, he had failed to ensure that it embodied a sufficient number of safeguards against a development which, as he now realised, was possible within its framework.

Kellogg's assessment of the situation provided no clue to the practical solution of the problem. This was provided by the speech of the British representative in the I.W.C., Fisheries Director R. G. WALL, at the conclusion of the meeting at The Hague from 23 to 27 June 1958. He was elected chairman for the ensuing three years, the most critical in the history of the I.W.C. At the last plenary session the Dutch representative opened a discussion on the size of the global quota by proposing that it should be raised to 16,500 or 16,000 units from its present 14,500, partly because a portion of this could now be filled by catching humpbacks, which could not be caught when the quota in 1946 was set at 16,000, but primarily because sufficient sound scientific proof had not been submitted that a reduction was necessary. In answer to this Wall maintained that practically all scientists agreed that since stocks of blue whales could no longer support the bulk of catching, and the catching of humpbacks only covered a small proportion of the quota (in 1957-8 158 units), fin whale catching had reached proportions that stocks of this species could not support, and would therefore have to be reduced. How could this be done without infringing the demands of the Convention for consideration of the interests of the industry? The tremendous amount of equipment used prevented a reduction in the quota. It was useless trying to reduce the latter without at the same time making a corresponding reduction in the former. He proposed a conference of the pelagic countries in order to arrive at a better balance between catching capacity and the quota, and suggested that the best way might be to share this out. This could not be done within the framework of the Convention, but the Commission could issue a declaration of sympathy to support the work of the pelagic nations in finding a solution to the problem. If they failed to do this, Great Britain would regard the future of the Convention with considerable trepidation.

Wall was supported only by Norway, but the Netherlands' proposal for a quota of 16,000 only received its own vote; the Dutch were likewise alone in voting against 14,500, which was adopted by twelve votes, with one abstention. This was New Zealand, which, in agreement with the majority of the Scientific Committee, considered that the quota should not exceed 10,000, but as a proposal of this kind would have been thought ridiculous, 14,000 was proposed. This received no support, and was consequently not discussed. As mentioned above, the Netherlands first protested against 14,500, and was followed by the others, with the result that the 1958-9 quota was set at 15,000.

For three years running the I.W.C. had received a timely warning, from Norway, the United States, and Great Britain. For the time being the Soviet Union and Japan had remained silent, while the Netherlands was opposed to any reduction. When a proposal was submitted that the Commission should express support for the conclusion arrived at by the Scientific Committee that the present catching limit, namely 14,500 units, was too high, this was passed by eight votes, with four abstentions, including Norway, while Japan voted against. These five, however, acted on formal grounds; in principle they were agreed, which meant that the Netherlands alone voted against the actual substance of the proposal. The Commission, however, was not capable of acting upon the conviction of the majority alone.

During the period prior to the next meeting, in 1959, which everyone realised would be critical for the future of the Convention, intense activity took place on both governmental and private levels to arrive at a distribution of national quotas, while an *ad hoc* scientific committee endeavoured to amass so much data on the ominous decline in stocks of whales, particularly the females, that even the Netherlands would be convinced. It was the Dutch who had proposed a committee of this kind, on the assumption that they would abide by its verdict if it could submit tenable arguments to show that stocks of fin whales were overfished at a maximum limit of 15,000 BWU. The first step on the private level involved negotiations for the laying up of floating factories — a familiar scenario — to facilitate the acceptance of an agreement for national quotas once there were fewer nations sharing the global quota. The Norwegians declared themselves willing to lay up four or five expeditions in return for suitable compensation, totalling approximately half a million pounds. As all companies, irrespective of nationality, would benefit from the withdrawal of Norwegian floating factories from the scene, it was only right and proper that they should all pay their relative share of the compensation. The Soviet Union could not be counted on, and the Dutch refused, leaving Japan. The chief Japanese objection was that its whaling was based on free competition, and that it was consequently against any system which involved paying to eliminate a competitor. Negotiations also broke down owing to insufficient agreement on the basis for calculating compensation before the countries involved had decided to despatch their expeditions.

At a meeting on 2 July 1958 between representatives of the Norwegian Government and the whaling companies the latter requested that it should be made known to the other members of the I.W.C. that Norway might be forced to repudiate the Convention, as it was not in the interests of Norwegian whaling. At the same time it should be expressly stated that Norway would observe all the provisions of the Convention and fix a national quota which bore reasonable relationship to that of other countries. Before this could be done Britain, with the connivance of Norway, invited the pelagic nations to a conference in London on 19 November. Before this convened it was thought to be of major interest to discover the attitude to be adopted by the Russians. For this purpose a Norwegian delegation was sent to Moscow, where it was received by the Minister of Fisheries, A. ISHKOV. While he expressed his willingness to attend a meeting in London, it boded ill when he declared that a sharing out of the number of units would have to take into consideration the fact that the Soviet Union's whaling fleet would be increased in the immediate future, because its proposed share of the catch was not reasonable and did not conform with its interests.

Before official negotiations between the delegations began, representatives of the four "private" whaling nations met to discuss the problem. It was immediately obvious that a formal difficulty had arisen: since members of the I.W.C. were unable to amend the Schedule to limit the number of floating factories or to give them special quotas, could members do this outside the Convention? If the answer was in the affirmative, the question was bound to be asked: what then is the point of the Convention? If the answer was in the negative, there were three possible approaches. Either the Convention would have to be amended by means of a supplementary protocol, ratified by all members, which would enable the Commission to allot special quotas, or the members would have to resign from the Commission in order to do what, as members, they were unable to do; or an agreement could be concluded on a private basis between companies, without governments being involved. But even the last-mentioned alternative was an evasion of the Convention if the private company concerned resided in a member nation, since its government was responsible for ensuring that the company observed the Convention. Furthermore, national quotas violated the Convention's spirit and principle of free competition for a common quota. The argument could also be adduced that the Convention mentioned *special* quotas for a floating factory or a group of floating factories, not *national* quotas. This point, however, appears unduly subtle.

The Netherlands and Japan, in particular, emphasised the formal aspect of the matter. In Norway the Government was in doubt. It admitted that on a formal basis it might reasonably be maintained that national quotas violated the Convention, but a quota agreement was the only salvation for Norwegian whaling, and if an agreement of this kind could not be established within the framework of the Convention, Norway would have to renounce it. The Government was aware of the serious consequences: other member countries might do the same if they were dissatisfied with some point or other, while the extreme consequence seemed to be that all seventeen member countries could, by means of agreements outside the Convention, establish an entirely different system of catching.

Discussion at the meeting revolved mainly round what could be done in order to get the Russians to accept the agreement. The Norwegian proposal involved offering them the use of two new floating factories, in addition to the *Slava,* and allocating 2,400 units, 16 per cent of the 15,000. Britain proposed that the four countries should make known their resignation before 1 January 1959 and conclude an agreement for three years for the catching of 12,000 units during a season of 105 days. The Dutch, who consistently opposed any reduction in the quota and always voted in favour of raising it, submitted a radical proposal which aimed to show that, with 15,000 units shared among all, the yield would be so small that it would not be worth pursuing. The only way out would be to leave the Commission and operate freely for three months. It was calculated that the catch would come to about 24,000 units. The scientists of every country — except the Dutch — agreed that within a very few years this would utterly decimate the whale stocks. It is not hard to imagine what the result of 24,000 units spread over five years would have been. In 1964-5 fifteen expeditions could only account for 7,000 in three and a half months.

Official negotiations between government delegations were opened by the British Minister of Fisheries, J. B. GODBER, who posed two questions: did catching exceed what stocks could support, and was the matériel used in excess of what was economically defensible? The answer to both questions was bound to be in the affirmative, and the purpose of the conference was to indicate a system agreed on among the pelagic nations which would re-establish the balance. The discussion, which commenced on the 19 November, was not concluded until 27 November, and briefly this was the gist of it : Norway and Britain were decidedly in favour of a quota agreement, and Norway was prepared to resign if a system had not been established before 1 June 1959. The Netherlands and Japan adopted a sceptical attitude, and they reverted again and again to the formal aspect of the matter : that their Governments could not compel them to carry out anything that violated the Convention (which, as was also the case with the United States, automatically became valid law in the country). Any agreement could therefore only be a private matter between companies. None of the others entered into any discussion on this formal question. Ishkov rejected the Norwegian proposal of 16 per cent, and proffered the information that the Soviet Union would increase its whaling fleet not with two but with three large new expeditions. This was a shock. Norway then raised the offer to 20 per cent, which was considered generous by the others, and which they reluctantly agreed to in order not to deadlock the negotiations. The Netherlands made it an absolute condition for its participation that it would under no circumstances be allocated less than 8 per cent. If all countries were given a corresponding share, the result would amount to 184 per cent of the current quota.

The first question on which agreement was reached was the number of expeditions. This was not to exceed twenty-three. All delegations declared that they would not expand their fleets with new floating factories; the Soviet Union would not do so after acquiring four. The Japanese emphasised that the agreement should recognise the right to buy expeditions, together with their quotas, from other parties to the agreement. In connection with the other item, the share-out of the remaining 80 per cent, Norway submitted a proposal based on the average of each expedition's catch in 1947-58. This allocated 3.73 per cent per expedition to Norway, 4.39 per cent to Japan, 4.60 per cent to the Netherlands, and 5.06 per cent to the United Kingdom, practically the same as the 5 per cent that the Soviet Union was allotted. Norway was willing to adjust the Dutch quota to equal that of the Soviet Union, and as the Netherlands had herself declared that the offer made to the Soviet Union was a generous one, the same would have to apply to the Netherlands. In a last attempt to arrive at an agreement Norway was also prepared to transfer from her quota the bulk of the increase allowed to the Netherlands. This was rejected out of hand by the Netherlands. The attempt at sharing out the quota broke down on this point already at this particular meeting, which concluded by recommending to the governments concerned an agreement, dated 27 November 1958. It was set out in six points :

1. A plan shall be negotiated for a distribution among the five present

pelagic whaling nations of the total quota which shall be established every year by the Commission.

2. The plan shall remain in force for a seven-year period from and including 1959-60.

3. In the course of this period the Soviet Union shall not increase her whaling fleet with more than three expeditions, over and above the one she now has. The other nations shall not increase their whaling fleets otherwise than by the purchase of expeditions which, at the time of purchase, are engaged in pelagic Antarctic whaling.

4. A transfer of this kind — of a floating factory from one party to the agreement to another — shall not be allowed unless a relative share of the vendor's quota or a guarantee not to use the vessel in Antarctic catching during a seven-year period, is also transferred.

5. Of the annual total quota 20 per cent shall be allotted to the Soviet Union, and the remaining 80 per cent shall be divided among the other four nations *"in a manner satisfactory to them"*.

6. If a floating factory under another flag commences catching in the Antarctic (otherwise than as set out under 4) and the government of the "flag country" is or becomes a member of the Convention, the agreement shall be null and void.

Negotiations on the distribution between the four countries shall be concluded in time for the agreement to come into force before 1 June 1959.

The italicised words in 5 were responsible for deadlocked negotiations for several years. Anyone could claim that this condition had not been fulfilled.

It is interesting to see what Norway's revised proposal for distribution would have produced, and then compare it with the final result (see Table 33).

Table 33. NATIONAL QUOTAS, 1962

	1947-58 catch	Norway's proposal		1962 agreement
	%	%	BWU	%
Norway	39.45	33.63	5,045	32
Japan	30.94	26.37	3,955	33
United Kingdom	17.32	15.00	2,250	9
The Netherlands	5.44	5.00	750	6
Total	93.15	80.00	12,000	80
Soviet Union	6.85	20.00	3,000	20
Total	100.00	100.00	15,000	100

For the twenty expeditions in 1959-60 the Soviet Union, the United Kingdom, and the Netherlands were allotted the exact average, i.e. 750 BWU, Japan was given 659, and Norway 631 per expedition. That the United Kingdom should apparently hand over so much was due to the sale of the *Balaena* with her quota to Japan. As the Soviet Union with her two expeditions was hardly in a position to catch 3,000, the idea had been that the units short of the catching of her full quota "should accrue to the benefit of whaling". If the agreement had come into force as and from the 1959-60 season and the Soviet Union already then had the right to 3,000 units, then the Russians would have had the special advantage of being able to catch up to 1,500 units per expedition up to 1959-60 and 1,000 in 1960-1. Not till 1961-2, with four expeditions, would the Soviet Union have been down to "normal" with 750 per expedition. The *Slava* had in fact recorded 1,600.5 processed units in 1958-9, a figure which a great many people considered tactical rather than actual, as it exceeded by 622 units the highest achieved by any floating factory, and was considerably more than twice the average. The recorded production of whale oil was 200,540 barrels, 65,000 more than the second best, and only three times throughout the history of Antarctic whaling has a higher production been recorded by one floating factory in the course of one season. The *Slava* admittedly operated with twenty-four whale catchers, but there were limits to what its boiler capacity could achieve in the course of sixty-nine days. In view of this Ishkov was in a position to state that the 20 per cent allotted to the Soviet Union was very modest; this would give the three new Soviet expeditions only a half of what the *Slava* had shown it was capable of, and, moreover, the new expeditions had a still bigger capacity. Basically, the Soviet Union was the only one of the five powers that was satisfied with the proposed agreement. The Japanese attitude was highly reserved; when the agreement was signed, the leader of the Japanese delegation, H. OKUHARA, sent a circular to the other delegations to the effect that signing could in no way be regarded as binding on his Government or the companies. He considered the Convention to be the best means of protecting stocks of whales and utilising the raw material. Japan was in no hurry to adhere to the quota agreement; as long as she was a member of the Convention it would be difficult for the Government to conclude an agreement "on a quota system which was a violation of the Convention's prescript". If this system was of vital importance to the economy of whaling, the companies would have to conclude an agreement on their own responsibility.

The Association of Norwegian Whaling Companies, with the support of all the seamen's organisations, requested its Government to notify Norway's resignation before 1 January 1959. This was the only way in which Norway could bring pressure to bear, and it was imperative to set up the quota agreement while the Russians were still prepared to accept 20 per cent. Resignation on the part of Norway would exercise pressure on Japan, which would prefer the agreement postponed, knowing that her position would be strengthened to the same extent as Norway's was weakened. At every stage where the matter was dealt with, before the Government made its decision, it was pointed out that the Netherlands constituted the greatest stumbling-block; if the Dutch insisted on their 8 per cent, the appointment of quotas would break down and Norway's resignation, with its serious consequences, would come into force. The Dutch Minister of Fisheries, VONDLING, was adamant; there was great dissatisfaction with the large subsidies to whaling, and to put an end to this, whaling would either have to be suspended or made profitable, and the latter condition could only be fulfilled with a quota of 1,200 units. As it was impossible to obtain this by means of an agreement, and it was impossible to operate at a profit within the framework of the Convention, the Dutch would consider renouncing it "in order to test the scientists' analysis of the catching basis". On 29 December the Government notified Norway's resignation, with effect from 1 July 1959. It would be withdrawn if, prior to that date, a satisfactory agreement could be reached between the five states. On 30 December the Dutch resignation followed. As Japan would find herself in an unfavourable position if the Norwegian and Dutch resignations took effect, she, too, renounced the Convention on 6 February.

Before the I.W.C. meeting in London on 22 June intense negotiations took place in the hope of coming to some agreement prior to that date, with a view to preventing resignations from taking effect. As the Soviet Union's quota of 20 per cent was fixed, the dispute revolved round the apportionment of the remaining 80 per cent among the other four, and as the Netherlands stubbornly insisted on 8 per cent (or 1,200 BWU) and Britain was on the whole satisfied with the proposed 5 per cent, negotiations in the main involved Japan and Norway, and the apportionment of the quotas between them. The first unofficial meeting between the companies of these two countries took place in Tokyo in February 1959. An important point was a potential purchase of the *Willem Barendsz* in order to secure the quota agreement. The Dutch Government was anxious to sell in order to remove the political taint of subsidies. The vessel's owners were definitely against the sale, as they were confident of profitable whaling provided the floating factory was allotted a large quota or, after resigning from the Convention, was in a position to operate freely, and they were incensed that the Government should have conducted secret negotiations with Norway regarding the sale. Admittedly, the company was not in a position to sell without Government agreement, but the latter could not force the company to sell. The Norwegian companies were willing to pay £2.75 million for the floating factory alone, despite the fact that it would not be used as such; the price, too, was more than a new floating factory with all its equipment would cost. This was the price Norway was willing to sacrifice for the quota agreement. The Dutch claim to 1,200 units was so high that, if everyone had been allotted the same, there would have been room for only ten floating factories, as against eighteen now. An equal apportionment of the total quota between these would give each of them 750. The reason why the Norwegian Government supported the purchase was because this would solve the whole international crisis in which whaling was involved and it would then willingly cancel its resignation. Time was pressing, too, since the Soviet Union had made it an absolute condition for accepting 20 per cent that the others would agree on their share of the remaining 80 per cent before 1 July.

An endless number of proposals were discussed with a view to solving the problem. One of them was to put the *Willem Barendsz* to work and lay up three Norwegian expeditions. Norway would then have seven expeditions for 5,250 units (on the basis of an average of 750), but was willing to make do with 5,200, and to allow Japan to have the remaining fifty presuming this would make it easier for her to consent to the quota agreement. Another plan was joint purchase by the Norwegian, Japanese, and British companies, which would operate the *Willem Barendsz* through a separate company. A third plan was a joint Norwegian-Japanese purchase, the laying up of the floating factory, and a distribution of its 750 units between the two countries. All this hectic work, however, proved in vain: on 18 March the offer to purchase was finally rejected.

The meeting in Tokyo in February produced no results; nor did a fresh meeting in Oslo in April, nor a third meeting in Tokyo in May. On this occasion Norway was willing to reduce her claim to 4,850, but even this was rejected by the others. When Britain demanded 2,250, the Netherlands 1,200, and Japan 4,900, Norway was left with a mere 3,650, or an average of 456 for its expeditions, as against respectively 750, 1,200, and 817 for the others. This was so unreasonable that Norway could only interpret it as indicating that the others had never wanted a quota agreement in the first place. Their reason for allocating such a small amount to Norway was that they insisted that the sum of the floating factories' *capacity* should decide the national quota, and in this respect Norway was definitely at a disadvantage. The unfortunate consequences of Norway failing to weed out the old, small floating factories during the period of rebuilding and failing to get the permission of the authorities to replace them with entirely new ones, were now apparent. The others knew this, and bided their time until Norway was forced to withdraw some of her floating factories from operations. The exorbitant demands made by the Dutch were openly said to be a form of revenge for the Norwegian crew act, while Britain demanded that the production of by-products should also be taken into account, a point of view always championed by H. K. Salvesen and naturally supported by Japan. The tussle for quotas became a war of attrition which Norway may be said to have lost. When the agreement on national quotas was finally signed on 6 June 1962 it was too late to save Norwegian whaling. Its effect now was merely to postpone for a few years the withdrawal of all the Norwegian expeditions. A fourth meeting in London in June proved just as abortive as the others, and when the Commission convened on 22 June it faced the prospects of three member countries, one of which, Norway, edited *International Whaling Statistics,* resigning on 1 June. This naturally made its mark on negotiations.

The I.W.C.'s eleventh meeting, 22 June to 1 July, proved the longest and most critical in its history, and probably the most dramatic and at the same time somewhat chaotic. The discussion revolved mainly round formalities; occasionally the assembly was uncertain what item on the agenda was being discussed, or whether, in accordance with the Convention, it was in order to discuss what was being discussed.

After the introductory statements the discussion was opened by New Zealand, with a violent attack on the five pelagic nations for ruining the Convention and exterminating whale stocks. Kellogg proposed that everything should remain as before for one more year, in order to give the five more time to agree. So as to facilitate this, Canada proposed that for that year the quota should be 16,000. The British representative referred to a Government statement made in Parliament to the effect that if the agreement were not concluded and the Commission failed to save the whale stocks, it was doubtful whether Britain should continue as a member. But — and this boded ill for the agreement — Britain could not accept a lower quota than she had demanded, as this was a minimum for profitable catching. The statement failed to reveal any really profound understanding of the situation; "a profitable quota" could hardly be a British privilege. It seemed to presuppose that there were still sufficient whales available; the problem was merely to put the national quota so high that whaling would show a profit. Naturally, this was what everyone wanted, and for this reason it was impossible to conclude the agreement, as no one was willing to lower his sights. The Dutch expressed unwillingness to participate within the framework of the Convention in a discussion on the apportionment of quotas, as this was no concern of the Commission. A sharp distinction had to be made between a discussion "on the industrial level" and "on the governmental level". As the Dutch on previous occasions had not been able to acquire a satisfactory share of 16,500 units, the prospects of this on the basis of 16,000 units were even smaller, and for this reason the Dutch were not in a position to withdraw their resignation. They were determined to operate without any restrictions on the number of whales and the duration of the season, but *vis-à-vis* their

101. This modern and very powerful whale catcher, built in Japan in 1964, was Norway's last effort to modernise her whaling fleet. After a few years she was resold to Japan.

Government they had declared that they would not catch *more than* 1,200 units annually for seven years! This was in truth the height of magnanimity and optimism! Not in any season, not even with un-restricted catching, did the floating factory succeed in catching the 1,200 units; after only three seasons only just over half that amount was caught. Norway declared that she would cancel her resignation if the total quota was set at 15,000, of which she was allotted 4,850, "and if this is not settled today, we shall have resigned from the Convention by midnight". It now only remained for the two countries to bid adieu and for the I.W.C. to conclude its negotiations on 1 July without these two members.

The only positive measure achieved was that the blue whale was to continue to enjoy protection in the North Atlantic for another five years. Regulation suffered a reverse, however, when the opening of the season was put forward from 7 January to 28 December, with the same concluding date, 7 April. The major reverse, however, was that the conclusion of the blue whale season, which commenced on 1 February, was postponed till 7 April (from 16 March), with the result that catches of blue whales, the species most sorely needing to be spared, rose from 1,191 in 1958-9 to 1,740 in 1960-1.

The year 1959 marks a collapse of international attempts to save whale stocks in the Antarctic. In order to try to prevent the breaking-up of the Commission a competent majority, against its better judgment, was prepared to increase the total quota and in the following year even to suspend it. Henceforth I.W.C. meetings became get-togethers of pelagic nations, with the others as mere supernumeraries. While the Commission retained its right to fix the total quota, it was in reality the pelagic nations which decided how big it was to be. Norway's step was originally directed against Japanese and Russian expansion. But what was the result? Three seasons without a total quota, but with an average catch greater than at any time since 1951-2. When a quota was once again adopted in 1962-3, four Norwegian expeditions had abandoned catching, while the Japanese-Russian whaling fleet had increased by the same number. The latter's total share of the catch had risen from 43.4 per cent in 1958-9 to 79.3 per cent in 1962-3, while the Norwegian had slumped from 37.4 per cent to 12.2 per cent, and the last of the one-time six Norwegian stations in the Antarctic had closed down for good.

Without a quota agreement and with two members uncommitted to the Convention, the result might have been anarchy in the whaling grounds. That this was not the case was because Norway, Japan, and Britain voluntarily accepted quotas. During the autumn intense negotiations were carried on, developing into a struggle for prestige to see who could exact the highest figure without any regard for the whales. Finally, Norway settled for 5,800, Japan for 5,000, and Britain for 2,500. The Dutch replied magnanimously that "despite the country's considerably reduced wishes, it was prepared to settle for 1,200", and to cap it all they were prepared to abstain from voting on Canada's proposal for 16,500 units! It was not particularly difficult to do this, seeing that they had got what they wanted. This was not the end of the struggle for quotas; it continued with the apportionment of quotas between companies. The dispute was at its most hectic in Japan. Norway withdrew the oldest and smallest of her floating factories, so that a larger share of the national quota was allocated to the other eight floating factories. This confirmed Japan's assertion that Norway had raised the question of national quotas in order to rationalise her whaling under cover of them.

Already in the first season, 1959-60, there was an indication of the way things would go. Japan alone managed to fill her quota, and even exceed it (5,217) with a catching time of ninety days. In the course of 122 days the Netherlands only managed 86.5 per cent of the 1,200 units that had deadlocked the entire quota agreement. In Norway's case a deficit of 1,233 units, or 21.4 per cent, came as a shock, but relatively speaking the British expeditions registered the greatest deficit with 24 per cent. The total catch of 15,512 was 12.7 per cent lower than the countries had set themselves, but 3.14 per cent higher than a total quota of 15,000.

Two members no longer in the Commission; a rise in catches of blue and fin whales (but only 212 BWU more in 1959-60 than in 1958-9, despite a thirty-day extension of catching time); a tremendous decline in catcher's day work from 0.94 to 0.73, the most marked in the post-war period; grave warnings from two scientific committees that only drastic reductions would save the whale stocks — these were the facts the I.W.C. faced at its twelfth meeting from 20 to 24 July 1960 in London. Britain and the United States exerted very considerable pressure on Norway to get her to rejoin the Commission, but Norway maintained her standpoint : first negotiations and a solution of the quota question, then possibly re-admission. From the Netherlands it was reported that there was no chance of the Government then in power renewing its whaling contract when this lapsed in 1961.

In order to strengthen its economic position once the subsidies were withdrawn, the *Willem Barendsz I* was sold for £420,000 to a Japanese company which operated with it in the North Pacific from 1962 to 1966, when she was broken up. The sum she fetched was invested in a few new and powerful whale catchers and in an extension of the refrigerator plant for whale meat on board the *Willem Barendsz II*. Apart from her own production of frozen whale meat, a contract was concluded with a Japanese company for refrigeration, for Dutch account, of very considerable quantities of meat. This had been sold in advance to Petfood Ltd. at £75 a ton, and proved an excellent deal for the Dutch. Annual production in 1960-4 was approximately 8,500 tons. Proceeds from the floating factory's production of meat meal were also good. With the prospect of losing the subsidies, with the favourable Japanese contract included, with new whale catchers, and with two quite good seasons, 1959-61, the *Willem Barendsz II*'s owners considered that not only would it be possible to catch the 1,200 units, but these *had* to be caught in order to enable the company to survive once the subsidies had come to an end.

Another event of importance to future quota negotiations was the upset in the relationship between the countries' number of expeditions brought about by the sale (28 July 1960) of the *Balæna* together with the refrigerator ship the *Enderby* and seven whale catchers, for £3.4 million to Kyokuyo Hogei K.K. It was to be expected that Japan would not maintain her 1959-60 quota, but demand an increase of e.g. 850 units, and corresponding reduction for the British companies. This would involve a new tug-of-war between the nations, and presumably, too, between the Japanese companies themselves. Before this stage was reached, however, the Commission met for a stormy meeting at which Norway, though absent, was subject to very considerable pressure. In his speech of welcome the chairman, R. G. R. Wall, appealed to the Netherlands and Norway not only to regard themselves as observers, but to take part in the discussion on any item on the agenda. In the debate on acceptance of the Secretary's draft minutes of the last year's meeting, which were to be printed and published, it emerged how tremendously sensitive the five pelagic nations were to the representation of their negotiations and the establishment of their quotas. If we compare the draft with the final edition (produced after members' objections had been raised), one is struck by the fact that words such as "quota", "unsuccessful attempts", "claims", "unilaterally fixed quotas", had been deleted, and an expression such as "the U.S.S.R. indicated that she would be satisfied with 20 per cent" was erased. At the same time the Soviet representative expressed the opinion that it would be more correct to retain the words "individual claims" than "national quotas" as more appropriate to the actual facts. In Point 12 of the minutes, in their new version, all stumbling-blocks were removed. As amended it now stated that all countries would either set a "ceiling" for their catch or this would be approximately as in the preceding season, and the criticism which some delegations considered inherent in the phase "unsuccessful attempt" was removed simply by stating that "agreement could not be reached". The reason the word "quota" was avoided was because the Commission was not entitled to deal with this matter, and it was important to emphasise that negotiations on this point had been conducted outside the Commission.

The head of the British delegation, Director of Fisheries Basil C. Engholm, made a very long speech and suggested that, in order to secure the re-admission of the two countries concerned, the issue that had been responsible — the maximum limit for the total quota — could be removed for two seasons. By way of a security precaution the I.W.C. would ensure that the five countries voluntarily accepted quotas which did not exceed those of the preceding season. Finally, Engholm recommended that a third independent scientific committee be set up, on the basis of whose finding the I.W.C., after the two seasons, would take the measures necessary to preserve stocks of whale capable of providing "the sustainable yield". The proposal was supported by the United States, which was anxious to give it extra bite by including an obligation on the part of the I.W.C. to abide by the control measures this committee might consider necessary in order to fulfil the aims of the Convention.

The British proposal was based on the erroneous idea that Norway's resignation was due to a reduction of the quota to 15,000 units. This was in no way the case, as the Canadian representative rightly pointed out. Norway had always been in favour of as low a quota as possible. It was in order to arrive at an apportionment of the quota that Norway had resigned. The Netherlands, on the other hand, had insisted in principle on free catching for three years, or alternatively a considerable increase in the quota. In the course of the debate the Netherlands also had to admit that it "had exercised a certain amount of pressure in order to increase the total quota, to make it possible for it to remain a member of the Commission".

As might have been expected, a long debate ensued, mainly on the formal aspects of the matter, degenerating into a discussion on such hairsplitting niceties as, for example, whether "shall", "will", or "should" should be used and on the obligation of the Commission to abide by the instructions of the "Three Wise Men" — a special committee of three outstanding marine biologists appointed by the I.W.C. It is not surprising that the Russian interpreter should have found it difficult to convey the fine shades of meaning to his delegation. Obviously, everyone wished the resolution to be as vague and non-commital as possible. A neutral observer would find the shorthand notes of the discussion most depressing. No country was more consistently opposed to the suspension of the maximum limit than the Soviet Union, and no one spoke more eloquently of the noble task of the Commission to preserve whale stocks for humanity, but the Russians made no mention of the fact that at the same time they were about to despatch the three largest expeditions that had ever pursued the whale. A few delegates managed to address a few home truths to the Commission, but, as the British delegate remarked, it was like preaching in an empty church. One strange feature was the almost complete silence of the Japanese during the debate. Japan was, moreover, the only one of the pelagic nations to abstain from voting on the proposals, on the grounds that she had not had time to study the matter properly.

The proposals the Commission finally submitted to the vote were:

1. Three specialists in the field of population dynamics were to be appointed, and these within a year after their appointment should submit findings on what is "a sustainable yield" at that particular point of time and what controls must be set on foot to increase it. It was the aim of the Commission that Antarctic catching should be brought into line with these findings not later than 31 July 1964. Unanimously adopted.

2. The maximum limit for Antarctic pelagic catching was to be lifted for two seasons, 1960-1 and 1961-2. New Zealand and the Soviet Union voted against, four countries (Argentina, Canada, Japan, and Sweden) abstained, and seven (Australia, Denmark, France, Iceland, South Africa, the United Kingdom and the United States) voted in favour. Thus there was a sufficient three-quarters (77.8 per cent) majority for the proposal to be adopted. The United Kingdom was thus the only one of the pelagic nations voting in favour, and it was with the support of six non-pelagic whaling nations that the proposal was adopted.

3. A proposal submitted by the United States consisting of three points — (a) that none of the pelagic nations should catch more than in 1959-60, and that (b) the Netherlands and (c) Norway were to be requested to conform to the amendments in the Schedule adopted for the catching of blue whales and humpbacks — was unanimously adopted

with regard to the last two points. The first point received eight votes in favour, four abstentions, and one nation, the Soviet Union, voted against on principle and on formal grounds, i.e. that it was the duty of the Commission to set a total quota and "not to consider special, voluntary limits".

4. A proposal submitted by the United Kingdom involved an appeal to the Netherlands and Norway to rejoin the Convention so that all the pelagic nations (and naturally the Commission) could co-operate on measures which would also include a system of apportioning the total catch and introducing an international system of inspection. Ten voted in favour and three (Japan, New Zealand, and Sweden) abstained.

In Norway a whole series of conferences between the whaling companies and the authorities took place. The Government, compelled to consider the matter in the context of Norway's other international agreements and her trade policy, was anxious to rescind the resignation. The companies, too, could consider Norway rejoining, on the following four conditions: (1) that the Netherlands joined; (2) that the Soviet Union would never demand more than 20 per cent; (3) that agreement was reached on the apportionment of the 80 per cent; and (4) that a satisfactory system of control was established. The companies emphasised the threat posed by the Russians, who, with their four powerful expeditions, scooped so much of the 15,000 units that there would only be 8,000-9,000 left for all the others, and Norwegian whaling would be impossible. The serious charge was directed against the Russians that, when they voted against all proposals for extending catching and the catching period, and against a suspension of the maximum limit, "the reason must be that the Russians do not adhere to the Convention and that this is merely regarded by the Russians as imposing restrictions on their competitors".

On 23 September the Norwegian Government resolved to adhere to the Convention, but continued membership depended on the first three of the four above-mentioned conditions being fulfilled: the fourth was not included as a *conditio sine qua non,* but recommended as a vital point. As Britain and the Soviet Union had insisted that all pelagic nations be members in order to settle the quotas, it was important to get the Netherlands to join, and both Norway and the I.W.C. appealed earnestly to the Dutch to do so, but both appeals were rejected on the grounds that the Netherlands would only rejoin if, before the two-year suspension of the total quota had lapsed, an agreement were reached on the size of the total quota and its apportionment. The result was a state of deadlock, due to two contrary points of view: first of all, membership of all nations, then an agreement on quotas, and first an agreement on quotas and then membership.

The Dutch were pleased with the step Norway had taken, as the

Willem Barendsz was now the only floating factory that could catch without restriction. On the other hand, there was considerable astonishment at Norwegian whaling policy : Norway had excused her resignation on the grounds that an agreement had not been reached, and had declared that she would not rejoin before this had taken place, and she now rejoined without negotiations on quotas having made any progress whatsoever. With reference to this, and the fact that none of the three conditions had been fulfilled, the Norwegian companies launched a violent attack on the Government in order to persuade it to rescind its decision before 1 January 1961. It is emphasised that the decision had been taken for other reasons than the interests of whaling: this, too, was admitted by the Government, which was compelled to consider whaling within the context of Norway's foreign policy, including the problems of Norway's larger merchant navy, conferences on fishing limits, the confidence of other nations in Norway's willingness and ability to abide by international agreements, etc. As the Government clearly ignored the interests and the advice of the companies, the latter withdrew their representatives in the State Whaling Council and refused to participate in any future quota negotiations.

In order to get these going the British Government convened a meeting in London on 20 February 1961. The eighteen months that followed will stand as the most tragic, or possibly tragi-comic, in the entire history of whaling control. All in all, quota negotiations between 1958 and 1962 accounted for eleven international conferences in London, Oslo, Moscow, Tokyo, and Vancouver, in addition to taking up most of the I.W.C.'s four annual meetings. Every time a solution was round the corner, it was postponed in the face of new demands. In the end, the dispute revolved around a mere 70 units, for the sake of which the Netherlands was prepared to jeopardise the entire agreement. Not till it was proven that the Dutch would not be capable of catching more than half the quota, were they prepared to go down to 900 (plus 70 on certain conditions), and when in 1962-3 not even half (458) of the 970 were caught, the company blamed poor weather. In this way the Netherlands demonstrated to the entire world that her assertions on the size of whale stocks were completely erroneous. What would the result — for the Netherlands too — have been if her proposal for free catching over a period of three years or of 24,000 units had been adopted?

Briefly, the negotiations proceeded as follows. At the meeting in London on 20-23 February 1961 delegates submitted the following minimum claims : the Netherlands 1,200, Britain 2,400, the Soviet Union 3,000, Japan 4,850, and Norway 4,850, totalling 16,300, 1,300 more than the last total quota. At the meeting the last four countries mentioned agreed on a reduction: Britain 1,350 and Japan 4,950 (after the sale of the *Balaena* and the *Kinyo Maru* had been withdrawn), the Soviet Union 3,000, and Norway 4,800, totalling 14,100. With a ceiling of 15,000 that left 900, or 6 per cent, for the Dutch expedition, more than anyone else, but it was rejected. When the Netherlands was offered a "bonus" of 80 units, which it would have to catch within the season fixed by the I.W.C., this, too, was turned down, with a demand for 90 units. and on this difference of 10 units the Conference was deadlocked! There is no doubt that as far as the Netherlands was concerned the size of the quota was not the most important matter: the important thing was to ensure that no agreement was reached, so that the company could carry on with unrestricted catching for as many seasons as possible. At the meeting a system of inspection was also broached, and Ishkov is said to have declared that the observers on the Soviet floating factories would have to come from communist countries, as the Soviet Union could not allow anyone from a capitalist country to inspect its catch.

The tragi-comedy continued with two conferences, in Vancouver in April and in London in May (after a meeting in Tokyo had been cancelled), where the entire set-up was staged once again in order to discuss — incredible as this may sound — whether the Netherlands should be allowed to catch a "bonus" of 60 or 70 units in addition to the 900, after a fixed date. When the Dutch had had their demand for 70 accepted and when all seemed set for a final agreement, they refused to sign it unless the opening of the season was put forward to 12 December. After this, too, had been granted and the return of the Netherlands to the fold seemed to be a *fait accompli,* fresh conferences had to be convened owing to a hairsplitting detail revolving round the date after which it would be permissible to start catching the "bonus".

The next conference, scheduled for Tokyo in August, was cancelled as the Soviet Union had not even answered the invitation. Before a new meeting could be called an event occurred which had considerable bearing on the apportionment of quotas. This was the Norwegian sale to Japan of the *Kosmos III*, together with five whale catchers, for £2,775,000, including 700 units. (Under the name of the *Nisshin Maru III* she appears to be the latest Japanese floating factory whaling in the Antarctic, where she and two Russians were operating in 1977-8.) The Japanese also made a bid for two older converted Norwegian floating factories, each with 400 units, of £700,000 and £1 million respectively. They also wanted to buy *Norhval* for £2½ million. Instead of selling, the owners of the two first-mentioned vessels were prepared to withdraw them from whaling after 1961-2, in return for compensation corresponding to the value of the quota, compensation which had to be paid in its entirety by the Kosmos company to the tune of Kr.7.5 million per company. Kr.15 million (£825,000) may appear to be a very large sum for the whaling rights of two floating factories, vessels which in any case would soon probably have to be withdrawn, but it should be taken into account that, when the quotas of the two floating factories were shared out among the others, the company's other floating factory, the *Kosmos IV*, would also benefit. On the other hand, the quota attached to the *Kosmos III* had a value of between Kr.15 million and Kr.18 million, according to the price of oil. It was transferred on 4 August 1961 to the Taiyo Gyogyo K.K. and operated in the Antarctic. Both the laid-up floating factories were sold for scrap, aged forty-eight and sixty-one years respectively.

The laying up of the Norwegian floating factory *Suderøy* in 1959, the sale of the *Kosmos III* in 1961, and the scrapping of two floating factories in 1962 were steps in the direction of the final winding up of Norwegian Antarctic whaling. All the signs indicating a marked and rapid decline in whale stocks supported this move: the slump in catcher's day work from 0.94 BWU in 1958-9 to 0.68 in 1960-1 had a very marked bearing on the economy of operating results. This meant higher production costs, while at the same time the price of whale oil in 1962 dropped to £44, the lowest ever recorded after the war. In view of this trend it was essential to undertake a reduction, and this appeared an opportune moment, when a very favourable price could be obtained for the floating factories. As these had been completely written off when sold, and the companies had sound shipping interests to fall back on, whaling could be wound up without the companies, the county of Vestfold, or Norway suffering any crisis. Nor was there any difficulty in finding other employment for whalers. But all this provides no answer to the question of why Norway in 1961-3 only managed to achieve less than her quota, while Japan and Russia more than filled theirs. Convinced that the end was in sight for Antarctic whaling generally, and Norwegian in particular, it was not difficult for Norway to show a small measure of compliance in quota negotiations.

At a meeting in London in October 1961 the *four* countries agreed on a proposal which would give Japan 33 per cent, Norway 32, the United Kingdom 9, the Netherlands 6, and the Soviet Union 20. But when the Netherlands insisted that they would not adhere to the Convention before a binding agreement existed between all *five* countries, the draft had to be approved by the Russians, and if they rejected it as long as the Netherlands stood aloof, "it would be obvious to all and sundry that it was the Soviet Union and not the Netherlands that made an arrangement impossible". But when the Soviet Union just as emphatically refused to participate in the negotiations before all five were members, deadlock once again ensued. Consequently, when Norway's conditions for continued membership of the Commission after

31 December 1961 had not been fulfilled, the companies took it for granted that the Government was bound to announce Norway's resignation once again. They had the full support of the State Whaling Council and of the seamen's organisations, and the Government followed their advice and notified Norway's withdrawal on 29 December. However, it added a rider to the effect that the resignation would be cancelled if agreement were reached between *all five* nations prior to 1 July 1962.

The Japanese attitude to the quota agreement is of great interest. An account of this appeared in the leading Japanese economic periodical, *Nihon Keisai Shimbun*, on 10 January 1962. Norway's resignation had been a shock, because it now looked as if each country would fix its own quota for 1962-3 as well. In order to secure a Japanese basis for as high a quota as possible, all three companies had jointly purchased from Salvesen the *Southern Venturer*, together with two whale catchers, for £2.15 million, before the Commission had fixed the total quota. This purchase had also been carried out in order to ease the tremendous pressure on the other Japanese expeditions in fulfilling the quota before the season was called off. It was also said that the economic position of Japanese whaling was under pressure, owing to the slump in the price both of whale oil in Europe and of meat in Japan, and on account of the substantial instalments and high interest that had to be paid on the equipment, purchased at a high price, and rising wages as well as other operating expenses. In 1961-2 Japanese production of oil was close to 1 million barrels and of meat 200,000 tons. In Japan the price of meat was approximately 100,000 yen a ton (approximately 2s 4d per kg.). The total gross value of Japanese whaling was approximately £30 million, about four or five times more than the Norwegian.

Before the meeting of the Commission in London from 2 to 6 June 1962, the result of the 1961-2 season was available. The Russians had not only fulfilled but even exceeded their quota; the Japanese had almost filled theirs, while the Norwegians had managed only 75 per cent and the British 60 per cent, while the Dutch recorded a catastrophic 51 per cent. The result was bound to make the Netherlands more willing to accept an agreement that would secure 900 units, at best 970, and to rejoin the Convention, and all the more so since the Soviet Union on 9 April declared that she would accept the quota agreement as it now was once the Netherlands rejoined. This occurred in a note of 4 May, and on 6 June the ambassadors of the five countries were finally able to sign the agreement in London. Norway then withdrew her resignation. The agreement was to run up to and to include the 1965-6 season, and the percentage of the total quota established at all times for the five countries was to be as follows: Japan 33,

Norway 32, the Soviet Union 20, the United Kingdom 9, and the Netherlands 6. As the sale of the *Kosmos III* and the *Southern Venturer* involved a transfer of quotas, the 1962-3 distribution was: Japan 41, Norway 28, the Netherlands 6 per cent (plus 70 BWU), the United Kingdom 5, whereas the Soviet Union as a matter of course retained her 20 per cent.

In Norway it had always been the definite impression that the quota agreement should be followed immediately by an agreement on observers. But on various pretexts the Russians always managed to postpone negotiations. In answer to an invitation to a meeting in London on 28-29 June the Russians replied that they "were not in a position to send negotiators". Although Article 7 of the Quota Agreement did not expressly state that, in order to be valid, it had to be *ratified* by the five countries, but it would become valid when their governments had *notified* acceptance of it, the Russians insisted that discussions were useless before the Quota Agreement had been ratified. The others had to accept this. Negotiations were also delayed as the Soviet Union, the last of the five countries to do so, did not ratify before 4 April 1963. Norway had already done so on 5 October 1962, and the other three countries before the end of January 1963. Consequently, although the agreement formally could not be said to have come into force before the 1963-4 season, the five countries adhered to the quotas which, according to the agreement, they had the right to catch — Japan 6,150, Norway 4,200, the Soviet Union 3,000, the Netherlands 900, and the United Kingdom 750.

With the Soviet Union's ratification in April 1963, the curtain had been brought down on the last act of what one might be tempted to label the tragi-comic period in the history of regulation which goes by the name of the Quota Agreement. Seven years had elapsed since Norway had mooted the plan, and five years from the time Britain had submitted a proposal on this to the Commission in 1958. So drawn out and difficult had this plan been in its conception and birth, that it was practically stillborn. When it was finally enforced it failed in every way to accomplish what had been its objects. It may possibly have prolonged catching for a few seasons, but failed to prevent the collapse which took place in the very first season, 1962-3, in which the agreement was followed. Norway laid up three expeditions, apart from sending off the *Kosmos III,* which also marked the demise of the Norwegian towns of Tønsberg and Larvik as whaling towns. Britain despatched only the *Southern Harvester.* The result was remarkably poor : Britain only managed two-thirds of her quota, the Netherlands one-half, and Norway one-third, whereas Japan wholly filled hers and the Soviet Union all but. A concomitant reason for Norway's poor result was that one of the floating factories suffered such considerable damage at the

102. An illustration of the enormous size of an 86-foot blue whale on the slip of the whaling station in Iceland.

start of the season that it was debarred from catching for most of the time.

The actual Quota Agreement was undermined by the system that was initiated with the sale of the *Southern Venturer* to the Japanese in 1962 and continued with the *Southern Harvester* in 1963 and the *Willem Barendsz* in 1964. The Japanese purchasers were not interested in the floating factories, but in their quotas, which could be transferred together with the vessels. The three floating factories mentioned were not used for whaling by their purchasers. The first-mentioned was a genuine sale, but the vessel was laid up; the two last-mentioned were mere formalities, as the floating factories after a while were re-transferred to their vendors as tankers. This system emerged most clearly with the *Willem Barendsz*. The sales contract expressly laid down that after a few years the floating factory was to be re-sold to the Netherlands company, but no price was agreed on for the floating factory, nor did any money pass back and forth. The sum of £425,000 was paid for the right to catch, or £800 per BWU if the right had been limited to only this one season, but the right was "for all time". From 1961 to 1964, by her four purchases of floating factories together with their quotas, Japan increased her percentage of the global quota from 33 to 52 and, as far as could be calculated, the right to an extra catch of 7,500 units in 1961/2-1968/9. If we make the necessary deduction for the seasons when the entire quota was not accomplished, the figure comes to about 7,000. At an average value of £5,500 a unit, in terms of oil, meat, and other by-products, the result is a gross amount for 7,000 units of £38.5 million. £3.3 million, or about 8.5 per cent, was paid for the *right* to produce this, if we calculate with the same price per unit for the quotas of the other floating factories as for the Dutch. This 8.5 per cent may not seem unnecessarily expensive for this luxury, but it was an extra burden on the operating expenses of the Japanese companies which the others did not have to face. In spite of this the Japanese could operate more profitably. Today we may say that without the Quota Agreement the Japanese would have acquired this "quota right" for nothing, and could probably have bought the floating factories at the price of scrap iron.

Even before this season opened there were many signs that the Norwegians realised that the battle was lost. Doubts were expressed whether it was worth making so much fuss about an agreement which in any case came too late, and whether there was any point in adhering to a convention whose form of control had outlived its day, but first of all it might be as well to see what would come of the agreement on observers. Ishkov declared that there was no urgency involved. Whaling, *inter alia* through the sale of expeditions, had reached a transitional period. The best course would be to wait until the situation was clarified. The long-term quota negotiations had not proved favourable to co-operation. The Norwegian Whaling Council also debated whether the time were not now ripe for a suspension of the crewing clause, since, despite the ban in principle included in the law, dispensation was granted for the sale of complete expeditions. One Norwegian had described this clause as "a breach of human rights and one of the most reactionary laws ever passed". When the Bill relating to Norway's resignation from the Convention was submitted to the Storting on 12 February 1963, the assembled House listened in silence to the epitaph pronounced on Norwegian whaling. The Scientific Committee in a comprehensive report submitted to the Commission in 1963 pointed out the way in which the natural basis for whaling was being undermined. Finally, in 1963, on the basis of its recommendations and the marked slump in catches, the Commission managed to enforce the drastic reduction in the global quota which should have been introduced many years previously, had the Convention fulfilled its object, i.e. "to achieve the optimum level of whale stocks as rapidly as possible without causing widespread economic and nutritional distress" or "to provide for the proper conservation of whale stocks and thus make possible the orderly development of the whaling industry".

33

THE COLLAPSE, 1962-1968

Although the original idea had apparently been that the location of meetings of the International Whaling Commission should rotate between member countries, for practical reasons it had been customary to hold meetings in London, where the Secretariat was situated. The fourteenth meeting, held in London on 2-6 July 1962, was probably one of the most representative, with seventy-one delegates attending, including the Secretariat, advisers and observers, and also perhaps the most peaceful, as no amendments to the Schedule were made. A return to normality was made with a global quota of 15,000 units; it was noted with satisfaction that the Netherlands had returned after an absence of three years, that Norway had cancelled her resignation, and that in 1962-3 four floating factories and sixty whale catchers less than in 1961-2 had operated. After a long and harrowing dispute the Quota Agreement was home and dry. Negotiations were conducted smoothly and effortlessly. This might be regarded as a tribute to the Commission's new chairman, the Russian M. N. SUKHORUCHENKO, the first Russian to hold this office, which he retained until the end of 1966. In 1967 the office was once again held by a Briton; however, in 1968 the vice-chairman, the Japanese I. FUJITA, presided, and was elected chairman for the ensuing season. He was the director of the Japanese Whaling Association and the first chairman directly associated with the whaling industry. The others had been biologists and/or civil servants (e.g. Fisheries Directors). For this reason they may not have had the proper understanding or insight into the practical problems of whaling. It seems to be more than a coincidence that precisely when the Russians started full-scale whaling, they should have taken over the post of chairman in the Commission, but that after an interlude with Britain in 1967 a Japanese should have presided. This harmonised with developments in the whaling grounds.

The reason why nothing of note was accomplished by the Commission at the 1962 meeting was that the delegates awaited the final report on whale stocks before any amendment in global quotas was proposed, and it was desirable to see how the first season with the Quota Agreement worked out. Despite the fact that a provisional report painted a very gloomy picture of whale stocks, the Commission made absolutely no move to comply with its warnings. The discussion on a figure of 15,000 for the global quota was the shortest (half a page of minutes) of all the items on the agenda. New Zealand was the only country to oppose this move: "We regret that the Commission has not yet found the courage to grasp the nettle of taking the action which is required in this connection, but note the action which the majority of the Commission wishes to take." A proposal on behalf of the Commission for a further reduction in the catching of blue whales was not even tabled; this was allowed to continue for one more season, with a figure of nearly 1,000 blue whales, before any action took place. The reaction of the meeting was: wait and see. Only on one item was there some slight measure of disagreement: this was the seventh item on the agenda, the agreement on observers, when Sukhoruchenko refused to admit any general debate before the agreement had been drafted in detail and discussed at conferences between the five countries. He failed to explain, however, how it was possible to hold conferences of this kind when the Russians refused to participate in them before the Quota Agreement had been ratified. They themselves constantly postponed ratification. This was clearly a tactical move aimed at putting off a system to which they were opposed.

A tremendous change occurred from 1961-2 to 1962-3 in the relative participation of nations in Antarctic whaling. In 1961-2 Britain, the Netherlands, and Norway had been numerically equal to the total number of Japanese and Russian expeditions, i.e. eleven in each group. In 1962-3 these three countries had only six, whereas the other two were still operating with eleven. This was the first season Norway had fewer expeditions (four) than Japan (seven), while the Soviet Union had just as many as Norway and, furthermore, twice as many whale catchers. In 1961 Salvesen abandoned operations from Leith Harbour, and in the following year Grytviken closed down after functioning without a stop for fifty-eight seasons. Both stations were leased for a few years after 1963 by the Japanese. 1962-3 was the last season of British Antarctic whaling. The 1961-3 seasons produced a marked change in the relationship between the proportion of the quota which the two groups managed to catch. This is shown in Table 34.

Table 34 shows several striking features. Whereas the Netherlands, Norway and the United Kingdom fell considerably short of their quotas, Japan and the Soviet Union achieved almost full quotas. Secondly, the decline in Norwegian catching was striking. Thirdly, assuming that a global quota of 15,000 had been in force in 1961-2, as in 1962-3, then the latter was the first season after the war in which the global quota had not been achieved in its entirety. The reason this had not been the case in a number of previous seasons was that operations had been called off too early. Two circumstances may help to explain why two-thirds of the total deficit was recorded by Norway: in the first place, that one of the floating factories, owing to severe damage, was unable to catch for most of the season, and in the second

Table 34. QUOTAS AND CATCH OF THE PELAGIC NATIONS

(a) 1961-2

	Quota BWU	Quota %	Catch BWU	Catch % of national quota	Catch % of global quota
Norway	5,100	28.7	3,702	72.6	20.8
Japan	6,680	37.6	6,574	98.4	37.0
U.K.	1,800	10.1	1,070	59.4	6.0
Netherlands	1,200	6.8	615	51.3	3.5
U.S.S.R.	3,000	16.8	3,292	109.7	18.5
Total	17,780	100.00	15,253		85.8
Quota catch			−2,527		−14.2

(b) 1962-3

	Quota BWU	Quota %	Catch BWU	Catch % of national quota	Catch % of global quota
Norway	4,200	28	1,381.5	32.9	9.2
Japan	6,150	41	6,149.6	100.0	41.0
U.K.	750	5	502.4	67.0	3.4
Netherlands	900	6	457.4	50.8	3.0
U.S.S.R.	3,000	20	2,816.0	94.0	18.8
Total	15,000	100	11,306.9		75.4
Quota catch			−3,693.1		−24.6

place, that only eight whale catchers per expedition were used, as against ten the previous season. Other reasons for the poor showing include unpredictable factors such as weather and unfortunate choice of whaling ground, but also, of course, the fact that the more numerous and more powerful whale catchers of the Japanese and Russians were superior to those of the Norwegians, whose total horsepower was 73,300, while the others had at their disposal respectively 224,690 and 243,950, an average of 2,291, 2,844, and 3,485.

The Japanese and Russians were to some extent right in maintaining that the decline in whale stocks, which operations in 1962-3 appeared to show, was merely apparent, as it affected only the other three nations, and must be put down to their lack of catching efficiency. It was to be expected, owing to reduced participation, that the yield in 1962-3 would not be as great as in 1961-2. The smaller number of

BWUs was not in itself a sure indication of a decline in stocks of whales; a surer indication, despite fewer and more powerful whale catchers, was that the catcher's day work was slightly lower, 0.50 BWU as against 0.51 in 1961-2. This was a factor to which the Commission attached more weight than the total decline in catches, which would have to be considered in relation to the size of the matériel used; at its fifteenth meeting in London on 1-5 July 1963, it was to pronounce on the global quota for the coming season. However, the future prospects envisaged by the Scientific Committees weighed most heavily.

In one way this meeting was the most important one in the history of the Commission, and the most positive as far as regulation was concerned. It marks the decisive turning-point in the lowering of the global quota, in an attempt to bring it more into line with what whale stocks could stand. Never before had the Commission had at its disposal such an overwhelming mass of scientific data on the condition of the whale stocks. Reports had been submitted by the special committee of "Three Wise Men", by the scientific *ad hoc* committee which had co-operated with it, and by the Commission's Scientific Committee. This material was studied by the Technical Committee, which submitted its findings. According to their mandate the "Three Wise Men" were to submit the results of their analysis not later than 31 June 1964, but as they considered that continued whaling in 1963-4 on the same scale as before would have the most serious effects on whale stocks, they were anxious to submit a provisional report at this early stage. As this was the first time the Commission was confronted with as broad and meticulously documented a picture of the state of whale stocks and their reproduction, in relation to catching, as scientific whale research at that time was capable of giving, it might be useful to consider this a little more closely. What is important is not so much the details of these results, but the general picture on which the recommendations are based, to quote the Committee itself.

By way of preamble the report provides the definition of the effect of catching on stocks of whale which is necessary for a layman, if he is to understand what follows:

In the early years of most fisheries the catch is small in relation to the total number in the stock. This was true in Antarctic Whaling. As the exploitation continues and intensifies, this proportion rises and the effect of exploitation in reducing the stock numbers becomes evident in a change in the catch per unit effort. This decline in stock is not in itself evidence of over-exploitation, though it does indicate that catching (i.e. whaling) is becoming a major factor determining natural stock size. Whales in a stock of particular size and composition have a certain capacity for reproduction and a certain rate of mortality. The difference between these, that is, the excess of reproduction and subsequent recruitment to the exploitable stock, over the natural deaths is the measure of the "surplus" population, or in other words, the catch which could be taken from that stock without either causing it to decline or allowing it to grow. This is what in this respect we term *the sustainable yield* at any given time. The sustainable yield is zero in an unexploited stable stock. In such a stock, which is neither growing nor decreasing, effective reproduction and natural deaths must be balancing each other. As the stock is reduced by whaling the rate of recruitment (defined as the ratio of effective reproduction to stock size) must increase or the natural mortality (the ratio of natural deaths to stock size) must decrease or both; this process results in an excess of recruitment over natural mortality which can be taken as sustainable catch.

Everyone realised that stocks of every species were less in 1963 than when catching began, and for many years more than the sustainable yield had been caught. If from then on only the sustainable yield were to be caught, thus ensuring that stocks retained their level, then obviously catches would be less than the sustainable yield that could be achieved if stocks were allowed to build up to the *optimum stock size,* capable of providing the *maximum* sustainable yield. The fin whale, the species with which the Committee was naturally most concerned, as it constituted three-quarters of the yield, provides a good example : in 1963 stocks were assessed at approximately 40,000, and this, with a net accretion of 10 per cent, would ensure a sustainable yield of about 4,000, i.e. this amount could be killed without a further decline in stocks. But if less than this amount were caught and stocks were thus given an opportunity of achieving the optimum stock size of about 200,000, this would give a maximum sustainable yield of 20,000.

Stocks capable of providing this were not identical in size with stocks before they were fished. Stocks would not continue to increase *ad infinitum,* but would stop at a level determined by the natural basis, where natural accretion and decretion would balance one another.

One of the Committee's main tasks was to indicate at what level the sustainable yield could be fixed, if stocks were to be retained at their present level. An equally important task was to calculate how long it would take for stocks to be restored to the level where they could provide the maximum sustainable yield. There were two alternatives : either a short period of complete suspension or a longer period with continued catching. A necessary condition for the latter was that this was less than the sustainable yield, and the further below this level catching was permitted, the shorter would be the time required to restore stocks. It was possible to calculate what whaling, in the long run, would lose by continuing to show moderation, and by waiting until such time as the maximum sustainable yield could be taken for all time. But the Committee was also in a position to point out that there was a danger of blue whale stocks and possibly also humpback stocks being reduced to such an extent that they would no longer be capable of regeneration. Experience of other species of animal appeared to show that they became extinct once their numbers fell below a certain minimum.

The results on size of stocks arrived at by the Committee, and the forecast they posed for future catching were as follows:

Blue whale. Natural stocks were estimated to have been about 150,000; by the late 1930s this had been reduced to an estimated 40,000, and at the beginning of the 1950s to about 10,000. Prior to the 1961-2 season there were probably something between 930 and 2,790; there were still fewer in 1962-3, when the sustainable yield was 0-200, but 250 were killed, or approximately one-third of 1961-2 total. This confirmed that the species was rapidly approaching extinction. If this were to be prevented and stocks built up again, it would have to be totally protected for a great many years. With a growth rate of 10 per cent it would take fifty to sixty years before it could provide a maximum sustainable yield of approximately 6,000 to 8,000 from stocks of 100,000 to 125,000.

The question of the blue whale was somewhat obscured by the problem of the so-called "pygmy blue whale", a Japanese "invention". The Japanese maintained that in the whaling grounds round Kerguelen they had found and caught a species of blue whale with such divergent features from the ordinary blue whale that it would have to be classified as a separate species and could therefore not be included in the provisions for the protection of the blue whale. This whale was not unknown to previous Norwegian expeditions. As far back as 1929 it was reported that catches had been made of a number of "this semi-adult whale which is a blue whale under 65 ft., but the gunner earns only half a bonus for a whale of this kind. This is something the companies have introduced to ensure that as few of this species as possible are killed." (The pygmy blue whale is now recognised as a sub-species of blue whale, and it has been described in detail by several biologists.)

Both in the Technical Committee and in the plenary session of the Commission there was general agreement to grant the blue whale total protection south of 40°S. Japan opposed this, demanding that, in view of their catching of pygmy blue whales, an exception should be made for the grounds north of 55°S between 0° and 80°E. The Scientific Committee was in doubt; little was known of the size of this stock and how much fishing it could support, but the danger was that it was impossible during the pursuit to spot the difference between a pygmy blue whale and an ordinary blue whale, and for this reason there was no doubt that some of the latter would be killed during migration across these whaling grounds, probably as many as about seventy, if in 1963-4 a total of 400 were caught in the open field. If this were to continue for another two seasons (the Japanese wanted the field open for three seasons), the blue whale would fall below the critical low point, from which it would not be able to regenerate. The choice facing the Commission, in the opinion of the Committee, would then have to be a potential catch of 6,000 blue whales a year some time in the future or a yield of a few hundred pygmy blue whales less over a very short period. As a closure of the whaling grounds mentioned would inevitably evoke a protest from Japan, and later from others, and as it would be possible to catch blue whales on the same lines as in 1962-3, the Commission chose the lesser of two evils and decided that the area should be exempt from total protection. Eight voted in favour, none against, while there were five abstentions. The open field actually had little bearing on the catching of blue whales. In 1963-4 112 were caught. However, as this was more than the Scientific Committee considered defensible, and the marked decline in catches indicated that stocks of pygmy blue whales must be less and over-fishing greater than they could tolerate, the Commission resolved in 1964 on total protection. Protests were raised against this, first by Japan, subsequently by the other pelagic nations, and for this reason these whaling grounds were opened to them in 1964-5. The yield was a mere twenty blue whales. Faced with this, the protests were retracted before the 1965-6 season, and from then on the blue whale enjoyed total protection south of 40°S, and yet it required this yield of as little as twenty animals before the Japanese could be made to realise that protection was necessary. The statistically recorded decline in catches of pygmy blue whales may also be due to the fact that the Japanese found it unprofitable to pursue it. In the quota it was assessed as 1 BWU, but provided much less oil and meat than two fin or six sei whales. Some of them have also been registered as fin whale, i.e. $\frac{1}{2}$ BWU.

Humpback. The picture the Committee presented of stocks of this species was a depressing one. In "Group IV" there were estimated to have been about 10,000 when catching started in 1940, and the Committee was of the opinion that this would give the maximum sustainable yield. If catching were immediately suspended, it would probably take eighty years to restore stocks, and every year of continued catching on present lines would postpone by twenty-three years the date when the 1949 level would be reached. The situation in "Group V" was a little brighter : it would take sixteen, twenty-six, and thirty-two years to restore stocks to the level where they could support an annual and continued catch of respectively 100, 200, and 300 animals. The only objection which the proposal for total protection of the humpback "south of the Equator" encountered was one for "south of 40°S" submitted by New Zealand, as this would make possible operations from the northernmost part of the country. This proposal, however, received only the one New Zealand vote.

Sei whale. This was the species about which least reliable information was available. The catch rose from (pelagic) 4,749 in 1961-2 to 5,503 in 1962-3, but these figures were insufficient to provide a definite clue. In its supplementary report in June 1964 the Committee felt it was on slightly safer ground. The catch had increased in 1963-4 to 8,286; this increase, however, numerically speaking did not equal half the decrease in the numbers of the other three species, not even the decline in the number of fin whales (4,798). In terms of BWU the extra yield of sei whales amounted to 464, but the decline in the other three species was 3,341. This, the Committee declared, supported the view that stocks of sei whales were not sufficiently large to sustain a catch of the same scope as previously, because it must be assumed that if there had been plenty of them, expeditions would have caught so many that this would have outweighed the shortage of other species required to complete their quotas. It would thus be all the more urgent, if the Commission complied with the Committee's recommendation to suspend the limitation of catching in terms of BWU and to set special quotas for each species. On the basis of the somewhat inadequate material available the Committee assessed sei whale stocks at a maximum of 70,000 and the upper limit for a sustainable yield at 8,400, and was of the opinion that with an annual yield in excess of this stocks would rapidly decline. In this the Committee has been proved right. When the catch of fin whales slumped as much as 6,500 from 1963-4 to 1964-5, expeditions attempted to make up for it by intensified catching of sei whales, resulting in an increase during these same seasons from 8,286 to 19,874. That this was more than the sustainable yield appears quite clear in the light of the marked decrease in the following seasons (to 10,357 in 1967-8). This was not due to the fact that catching stopped because the global quota had been achieved; this was 3,200, but in 1967-8 only 2,804 were caught, i.e. a deficit of 12.5 per cent.

Sperm whale. The Committee also discussed this species, although it was of minor importance in Antarctic whaling. Three features of sperm whale catching gave cause for alarm. One was the general increase in world catches, and of catching from pelagic expeditions in tropical and semi-tropical seas on the way to and from the Antarctic in particular. The second was the growing percentage of females taken in this sector and the third was that the minimum size of 38 ft. was not adhered to. That 70 to 80 per cent and more of the whales caught were recorded as being exactly 38 ft. or very close, could hardly be due to the gunners' unerring eye measurement. In order to put a stop to this catching the Committee mooted the idea of a ban on pelagic catching of sperm whales north of 47° or between 40°S and 40°N. It would also be an advantage if the minimum measurement in the case of shore-based whaling was raised from 35 to 38 ft. But as there was not the slightest chance of these proposals being adopted, they were not put forward. Instead, it was recommended that more stringent measures should be introduced to ensure that the minimum length was observed and that a thorough investigation of the sperm whale should be continued.

Fin whale. As expected, the Committee had concentrated on investigating this species, as at the time it was responsible for four-fifths of the pelagic Antarctic yield of baleen whales. In terms of BWU the 1961-2 catch consisted of 86.7 per cent fin, 7.3 per cent blue, 5.2 per cent sei, and 0.8 per cent humpback. On the one hand the fin whale was the only one of the three major species of which there were sufficiently large stocks to enable catches to be increased by means of reasonable regulation in the course of a comparatively short period, to ensure a maximum sustainable yield. On the other hand it was feared that if the catching of blue and humpback whales was subject to a complete ban, and the sei whale was unable to replace the portion of the global quota it had previously provided, catches of fin whales would be so intensified that this species would be in grave danger of extermination. The natural stocks were assumed to have been more than 250,000, but in the mid-1950s they comprised only about 110,000, and by 1960 this had been halved. The sustainable yield was fixed at 9,000, but in 1960 twice as many were caught. In 1963-4 the estimated stock was 48,000 and the yield 13,870. The Committee considered it quite a triumph for its methods that it had forecast a yield of approximately 14,000. This method, however, must have failed completely for the 1963-4 season, as a yield of 12,000 had been forecast but only 7,308 were caught. The fact that seven whale catchers less were employed was not sufficient to explain this. The reason was bound to be that stocks were less than estimated. On the basis of the many reports submitted by the Committee, the situation facing the Commission in 1963 was as follows: to maintain a sustainable yield from the present stocks demanded an annual catch of not more than between 6,000 and 7,000. In order to regenerate stocks so as to ensure the presumed maximum sustainable yield of 20,000, catches must be well below 7,000. If whaling was unrestricted in 1963-4, and thereafter brought to a complete halt, it would take eleven years to achieve the desired maximum, but if expeditions continued to kill over 7,000, stocks would be practically exhausted in the course of ten to twenty years, according to the size of the yield.

A table issued by the Committee showed the effects of the alternatives for restriction of catching, and what would be gained or lost in the course of twenty years from and including 1963. The most favourable alternative was a complete halt for eight years, when stocks would reach a level giving the maximum sustainable yield; in the next 12 years a total of 239,000 could then be killed. If from 1963 4,000 were caught annually, it would take thirteen years to achieve the maximum, and the total catch in the twenty years would be 199,000, in other words a loss of 40,000. The least favourable alternative was a catch of 6,000 annually, with nineteen years to achieve the maximum, i.e. a total catch of 138,000, and consequently a loss of 101,000. Even though these and other calculations were by necessity somewhat hypothetical there could at any rate be no doubt on *one* point : they showed an ominous tendency which called for drastic measures, if the fin whale were not to suffer the fate of the blue whale.

As one of the ways of preventing this the Committee discussed the possibility of changing the limitation of the joint quota in terms of BWU to a special quota for each particular species. In its day the BWU had been administratively the simplest method, but it had also revealed certain difficulties; and it was easier to fix special quotas for each separate species, now that blue and humpback whales were protected, and only the fin and sei whale were involved. The experience harvested in the use of special quotas for these species would prove useful when catching the other species was once again allowed. In the Scientific Committee eight voted in favour of this, while one, the Soviet Union, abstained, but the Commission, which in principle was in agreement, came to the conclusion that a limit in terms of BWU was for the time being the only practical one. It was a contradiction *per se* to regulate catching by means of blue whale units when blue whales no longer existed, but ten years were to elapse before the whaling nations were forced to accept the inevitable and admit that the Committee's proposal was the only right one, and from 1972-3 special quotas for each species were set. A maximum quota was also fixed for the sperm whale.

One result of the Scientific Committee's support for the proposal of special quotas for each species was that it recommended to the Commission a reduction of Antarctic catching to the extent this was possible at a level of less than 4,000 fin whales and 5,000 sei whales. When the Commission found it impossible to put this system into practice, it discussed instead a global quota of either 4,000 or 10,000 units. The latter was proposed by Japan, with the support of the Soviet Union, and was carried by seven votes, with 1 against and 5 abstaining. Some of these, including Norway, who would have voted for 4,000, omitted to do so as three countries maintained that it would be economically impossible to operate with such a low quota. It was therefore to be expected that they would protest, and there would be a return to the 15,000 of the last season. If the Convention had not contained a protest clause, which could have prevented any favourable resolution, the Commission in all probability would now have had an opportunity of establishing the quota at 4,000, which could have been made up with e.g. 4,000 fin whales and 12,000 sei whales, bringing catches into line with what all scientific experts maintained was the maximum to ensure that stocks could have a chance of regeneration. With 4,000 fin whales annually this could be done in the course of thirteen years.

The decision to adopt a ceiling of 10,000 proved a considerable disappointment to all who felt responsible for preserving whale stocks in accordance with the recommendations of the scientists. For two or three years the experts had carried out a great deal of time-consuming and expensive work, and now the whole operation was shown to be almost pointless. One of those who was keenly aware of his responsibility and was profoundly disappointed was the Secretary General of the Food and Agriculture Organisation, B. R. SEN, who voiced his feelings on this matter in a letter to the Commission on 3 September 1963. He feared that all the work that had been carried out was to be wasted, in view of the fact that the findings were being entirely ignored for the coming season. He furthermore emphasised the duty of all nations to take care of natural resources; a violation of this principle would have far-reaching repercussions. His letter can hardly have made much impact.

Despite these disappointments, in view of the many previous abortive meetings of the Commission, a number of important events occurred at the 1963 meeting. The assembly appeared profoundly affected by the gloomy prospects. South of 40°S — apart from a small restricted area and during the period 1 February to 7 April — there was a ban on the catching of blue whales; south of the Equator, humpbacks were protected; the global quota was reduced by a third, and a draft agreement on observers had been signed and accepted by the Commission. The latter decided to entrust the agreement's implementation to the five pelagic nations. It had almost been taken for granted that the agreement was to come into force for 1963-4, but the degree of inventiveness in evading this issue was remarkable. New negotiations ensued, and not till 28 October 1963 was the final agreement signed in London. Fresh difficulties, fresh negotiations from 5 to 20 November led to the conclusion that by then it was too late to despatch observers with all the floating factories! This procedure was repeated from year to year.

"There is a world of difference between catching just over and just under the sustainable yield" is the final conclusion of Mackintosh's book (1965) on whale stocks. A hundred more — even one whale more — and stocks will inevitably be exterminated, slowly at first and then at an increasing rate. And, he continues, it is worth noting that a greater effort is required to kill a certain number of whales belonging to an over-fished than of an optimum-sized species. It has been calculated that while catching on the level of the previous two years had demanded 20,000 or more catcher's day work units, using 16 or more expeditions, the yield per catching unit would have been much higher with stocks at their optimum level, and it would have been possible to achieve the maximum permanent yield of 20,000 fin whales with 5,000 catcher's day work units, using only three or four expeditions. Mackintosh might also have added that in this way whaling was not only uneconomic exploitation : the many hundreds of thousands of whales that could not be caught during the next fifty years had also to be taken into account. To give some idea of the values involved, the following purely theoretical sum can be calculated. According to the forecast of the Scientific Committee a permanent maximum catch of 17,800 units (6,000 blue whales, 20,000 fin whales, 1,000 humpbacks and 8,400 sei whales) could be caught from the optimal stocks of the four species mentioned. If we estimate that only 3,000 units can be caught annually during the first twenty of the fifty years required to restore total stocks to their optimum level, and 10,000 units annually during the remaining thirty years, we shall find that there is a loss on an average of 9,400 units annually, or a total of 890,000 minus 420,000 : a net loss of 470,000 units. Assuming a value of £5,500 a unit, the loss amounts to £260 million. This is the price the next generation will have to pay.

A serious objection can be raised to the above sum : that whaling, among other things, had given the world a great deal of short-term wealth by the very process of tapping this "non-interest-bearing capital", i.e. the difference between natural stocks and the optimum that would produce the maximum sustainable yield.

In 1963 our Antarctic chapter properly ends; what followed mainly continued earlier development. But our account might be extended to cover another two seasons up to 1965, when the second major pull-out took place and five floating factories and forty-four whale catchers withdrew from Antarctic catching; or up to 1968, when Japan and the Soviet Union operated alone in the whaling grounds, both in the south and in the north, and were the only ones active in pelagic whaling.

At its last meeting in 1963 the Norwegian State Whaling Council dealt for the fourth time with a request from the Norwegian companies to withdraw Norway from the International Whaling Convention. For eight years work had proceeded on a system of observers which had not as yet been put into force and which quite obviously the Soviet Union opposed — and Japan too. There is little doubt that the

Soviet expeditions did not observe whaling seasons, protected species and minimum measurements, while the Japanese failed to observe the last-mentioned. Information was available that in the foregoing season each of their expeditions, operating outside the Antarctic, had produced 9,500 barrels of sperm oil. The Norwegians had tried their luck in the same whaling grounds, but had been forced to abandon catching, as only a small number of the whales came up to minimum measurements. If the Norwegian expeditions were to have any chance of competing, they would have to have the same conditions as those enjoyed by the others, and this could only be done outside the framework of the Convention. The proposal received little support : the general opinion was that if Norway had not been able to introduce the Observer Scheme before, it would be quite impossible now if she resigned. The Soviet Union would never negotiate under pressure, and least of all if Norway accused the Russians of blatant violations of the Convention. It is highly probable that Norwegian resignation at this juncture would have been merely an empty gesture, and one hardly calculated to add much to the life-span of Norwegian whaling. Whaling did not end with Norway : Japan and the Soviet Union continued, and as long as they are to be found in the whaling grounds, Antarctic whaling is not an entirely closed chapter capable of overall assessment. Our task from now on is to give a brief account of essential events during the years after 1963.

It might seem ironical that Norway should have been given the honour of arranging the sixteenth I.W.C. meeting on 22-26 June 1964 — at Sandefjord. It was the first to be held outside Britain, and the last with the Netherlands as an active whaling nation. The final phase would be played out between Japan, Norway, and the Soviet Union, and no one could be in any doubt as to who would be the first of these three to drop out. In an interview in January 1964 Dr. Hideo Omura of the Japanese Whale Research Institute declared that in Japan it was considered that Dutch and Norwegian whaling would soon be a thing of the past. On the subject of whale stocks he believed that from a scientific point of view it would be an advantage to introduce a total ban on catches for ten years, but that it was impossible to persuade the companies to agree to this, as it would result in serious economic and industrial difficulties in Japan. The same opinions were expressed by the two leading personalities in the Japanese Fisheries Administration shortly before the Sandefjord meeting : they were in favour of preserving whale stocks, so that the seven expeditions could continue to operate, but they were against such a drastic reduction in the quota that it would force several of these expeditions to abandon whaling. But they gave no indication of how this impossibility was to be made into a possibility. They seemed to expect a tough battle for quotas, as the Japanese were represented in Sandefjord with a delegation of eighteen, including the director of the whaling companies, and it transpired that the reduction they were prepared to accept would involve drastically cutting down the Norwegian quota, which the Norwegians anyway were unable to fill.

The Japanese attitude to the size of the global quota was furthermore influenced by negotiations for the purchase of the *Willem Barendsz*. These had been broken off by the Japanese in anticipation of the size of the 1964-5 quota. If this were drastically reduced, the Japanese were not interested in buying, and the Netherlands would stand little chance of selling the floating factory or its quota. No one could be in any doubt that this was the reason why the Netherlands voted in favour of Japan's high quota proposal. It was, furthermore, right up to the very last, entirely in line with the consistent Dutch resistance to any lowering of the quota. In their own interests they placed an economically advantageous winding-up of their company above preservation of whale stocks. Once the Japanese had been given the desired global quota, the purchase of the *Willem Barendsz*'s quota followed almost automatically.

One of the Japanese arguments was that in terms of world economy the most rational procedure would be to leave whaling in the hands of the nation that made most complete use of the raw material, and there was no doubt whatever that this was Japan. Annually, Japan received some 130,000 tons of meat from the Antarctic, corresponding to approximately 1 million head of cattle. A counter-argument to this was that a Norwegian floating factory, as well as the Dutch one, also had refrigeration plant for meat on board, that in the case of the *Kosmos IV*, for example, 40 per cent of the value of her production in 1963-4 consisted of meat. From the Japanese point of view, however, this was of minor significance, as the meat produced on the *Kosmos IV* was not for human consumption, but for feeding animals (dogs and cats). We have previously mentioned the inferiority of the Norwegian whale catchers. In order to obtain concrete proof of the fact that Japanese whaling efficiency was based on their catchers, Anders Jahre commissioned the building of a whale catcher of the largest and most powerful type — of 735 gross tons and with an engine developing 3,600 h.p., the *Kos 55*, with a top speed of 18.5 knots — at the Hayashikane shipyard in Japan. Its performance was not *so* superior to that of the other whale catchers that a total replacement of Norwegian whale catching matériel with this type of vessel should be expected to raise the Norwegian catch to the level of its quota. Of Norway's thirty-six whale catchers in the 1964-5 season, only one other had an engine developing more than 3,000 h.p., whereas forty-five of Japan's seventy-one were of this size.

In 1964 four proposals on global quotas were submitted to the Commission. The most far-reaching was that of the United States. Referring to the resolution in 1960 to bring catches into line with the recommendations of the Scientific Committee by 31 July 1964, the American delegation proposed 4,000 units for 1964-5, 3,000 for 1965-6, and 2,000 for 1966-7. Norway proposed 6,000 and Japan 8,500 for 1964-5. The United States' proposal only just failed to gain the required three-quarters majority, ten voting in favour and four against. With eleven to three the proposal would have been adopted. As none of the proposals obtained a three-quarters majority, the situation was that not only had the Commission failed to reduce the quota, but no ceiling had been set at all, and to this extent there was now a free-for-all. In order to prevent this, negotiations took place outside the Commission between the four pelagic nations, and at the conclusion of their meeting they announced that they had agreed to recommend to their governments that their joint quota should not exceed 8,000. As all responsible bodies agreed that the catch would have to be reduced to less than half, in order to allow stocks to regenerate, it was of relatively minor importance whether 8,000 or 8,500 were killed, and the latter would have been preferable if done under the aegis of the Commission. Now, however, the quota was fixed without the co-operation of the Commission, and this was significant. On the other hand, it was now exempt from the responsibility of a quota being set that was twice as high as a large majority of the members considered feasible. Responsibility rested now primarily on Japan, thereafter on the Netherlands and the Soviet Union.

During the discussion that followed Norway was also made to share responsibility, as the Norwegian delegation had voted against the United States' proposal of 4,000 which, with Norway's vote, would have been adopted by eleven votes to three. The charge can more justly be directed against the Netherlands, because in giving her vote she was entirely uncommitted, not being actively engaged in 1964-5. In Norway's case the situation was that Japan and the Soviet Union had told Norway in advance that they would protest against 4,000 (and their protests would undoubtedly have been followed by that of the Netherlands), and these countries could then, without contravening the Convention, have caught without any quota limitation whatsoever because — and this is important — the resolution on 10,000 units had been expressly adopted only for the 1963-4 season. Norway in reality had a choice of two evils: either a quota of 8,000 or unrestricted whaling. It should be recalled that in 1963 Norway had endeavoured to submit a proposal for 4,000 units, without receiving any support. It was unfair to put the blame on Norway for the highly regrettable fact that the Commission failed in 1964 to follow up the necessary conditions for the nomination of "The Committee of the Three Wise Men". It was all the more unfair in view of the fact that Norway had pioneered international regulation, that its fundamental ideas had emanated from Norway, that seasonal and quota limitations were Norwegian "inventions", as well as the system of inspectors, and that she had always supported the minimum possible global quota. Her attitude in 1964 was tactical and realistic. It might also be adduced in Norway's favour that ever since voluntary limitation of catches had been started in 1959, and during the continued quota agreement, she had caught 7,364 units less than her quotas, and consequently "saved them up". Whatever the reason may have been, it was an indisputable fact that Norway had "saved" more units than the combined Japanese and Soviet Union catch in 1963-4. By the time Norway dropped out in 1968, she had "saved" 9,106 units, and it was this "saving" that made Japanese and Soviet catching possible.

On a more sentimental note it might justifiably be said that there was something deeply tragic in the fact that, on the only occasion Sandefjord was to have an opportunity of organising the meeting of the Commission, Norway should be forced to abandon the line she had always followed and vote in favour of a quota twice as large as she was convinced was the only correct one. There were some who maintained that, in order to be consistent, and as she would sooner or later have to give up whaling anyway, Norway should have voted in accordance with her convictions, irrespective of the consequences. It was also doubted whether Japan and the Soviet Union, in the full glare of world opinion, would have protested; but there were equally no indications in their previous relationship to the measures introduced by the Commission that suggested that they would have taken any notice of this.

The 1964 meeting proved the parting of the ways — where science and whaling met and parted. For the next meeting the scientists made far-reaching preparations, with no less than five committees involved. New difficulties, however, cropped up, and the tragi-comedy continued. The voluntary quota limitation of 8,000 had been accepted by the Japanese and Norwegian Governments, but the Soviet Government declared that, owing to the change that had taken place in the allocation of national quotas since the 1962 agreement, it considered a revision necessary, and this would have to be carried out before it could accept voluntary limitation in 1964-5 and introduce the Observer Scheme. Delaying the latter was probably behind the Soviet intransigence, which had its way in this season too. As expeditions were by this time about to sail to the Antarctic, it would only have been possible to embark observers in Spain or South Africa. This was turned down by the Soviet Union as a Soviet ship, for political reasons, would be unable to call at ports in either of these two countries. The other participants to the agreement of 1962 declared their willingness to discuss a revision, but Japan made it an absolute condition that *first of all* the Soviet Union would have her two conditions for revision fulfilled. The problem was thus deadlocked, precisely as before 1962. All attempts to persuade Japan to attend a conference were rejected; a conference in Oslo between the Soviet Union and Norway on 20 October 1964 had to be held without Japanese participation. After the purchase of the *Willem Barendsz*'s quota Japan's share of the quota was 52 per cent (4,160 units), Norway's 28 per cent (2,240), and the Soviet Union's 20 per cent (1,600). To a certain extent, from the Soviet point of view, a revision might appear justified. The basis for a quota of 20 per cent had been a share-out of the total quota among five nations; now there were only three. In 1964-5 an average of 7.43 per cent would fall to the lot of each Japanese expedition, 7 per cent to the Norwegian and 5 per cent to the Soviet. That Japan by (partial) pro forma purchase of expeditions for the sake of their quotas had been able to increase her share of the quota from 33 to 52 per cent was, in the opinion of the Russians, if not a formal at any rate a virtual breach of the basis for the quota agreement. It would undoubtedly have been right — although this was not said — that if a country abandoned whaling, its quota should be distributed among the "survivors". The Japanese approach to this problem was that, if they were to hand some of their quota over to the Soviet Union, this would in reality be tantamount to handing over gratuitously units for which Japan had paid dearly.

For a majority of the member countries the situation appeared so precarious that at their earnest request the Commission was convened for an extraordinary meeting (called the Special Meeting) in London from 3 to 6 May 1965. Its task was to consider the size of the quota on the basis of the Committees' analyses. A whole series of proposals was submitted, all of which appeared to offer the hope that now at last catching could be reduced to the level that should have been fixed from 1963 and onwards. The Soviet Union's proposal was the most surprising — a reduction in the number of expeditions of 50 per cent and a quota of 4,000. The least sweeping — but even so surprisingly moderate — proposal was the Japanese: 4,500, 4,000, and 3,500 for the next three seasons, but on condition that the quota agreement of 1962 was followed and that the Observer Scheme was in operation. As might have been expected, the United States' proposal was the lowest, with respectively 3,000, 2,000, and 2,000 for the three seasons involved. The many proposals were collated to produce a final one which involved 4,500 in 1965-6, with the important rider that the Commission realised that this was not below the sustainable yield. This quota, however, was to be considered as a transitional one, in order to give whaling companies sufficient time to adapt themselves to the reductions which would also be necessary in 1966-7 and 1967-8. This was *unanimously* adopted, and at the seventeenth ordinary meeting in London from 28 June to 2 July 1965 it received all the twelve votes of the members of the Commission.

This drastic reduction in the quota made a great deal of matériel superfluous. In addition to forty-four whale catchers, five floating factories were withdrawn from Antarctic catching — two Norwegian and two Japanese and the Russian *Slava*. For 1965-6 the Japanese quota was 2,340 units, all of which were killed, the Norwegian 1,260, of which 829 were killed, the Russian 900, which was exceeded by 22. Relatively, the season was a successful one for Norway, with 415 units per expedition, 468 for Japan and 307 for the Soviet Union; the Soviet expeditions, however, registered a very high production of sperm oil. In the production of whale oil the single Norwegian floating factory came third out of all ten expeditions. Norway, in fact, still seemed capable of holding her own. A notable feature in the total catching picture was the marked increase in the yield of sperm whales *en route* to and from the Antarctic, from 3,600 in 1963-4 to 6,104 in 1965-6. Of the latter total, 4,954 were killed by the Soviet expeditions: their try-out was merely 37.3 barrels, for the Norwegians 46.4, and for the Japanese as low as 31.5. Who, one may ask, killed sperm whales below minimum length? This was not merely a Norwegian charge directed against the others; the Commission itself stated in its report from the 1965 meeting that "while the minimum size limit — 38 ft. — should be enough to save the great majority of females, massive evidence was available to the Commission to show that this regulation was being broken on a large scale". Of other measures one can mention that blue whales were totally protected for five years from 1966 in the Pacific north of the Equator, and when the protests against the closing of the pygmy blue whale field round Kerguelen were withdrawn, the blue whale was totally protected in all the oceans of the world, and has been ever since. This was also the case with humpback, but in the North Pacific for the time being only for the one season, 1966-7.

The Observer Scheme suffered the same fate in 1965 as before. Norway submitted a proposal that adherents to the agreement should undertake in writing to enforce the agreement not later than the 1965-6 season. The reason for this proposal was that when the agreement terminated after the 1965-6 season, it was to be feared that it would never be enforced, unless it were done in this season. While Japan and Norway made the desired declaration, the Soviet Union declared that its declaration depended on both the quota agreement and the Observer Scheme being extended to include as well all shore stations pursuing Antarctic stocks of whale, and that in addition to this a reappraisal of the allocation of national quotas should be undertaken. Soviet inventiveness in dreaming up new arguments against the agreement is truly remarkable. The Russians managed to stave off the agreement until it terminated; by that time ten years would have elapsed since negotiations on this point commenced, and little imagination is required to guess what would have happened to a new agreement, especially when we consider the complications involved in adapting this to shore stations, and the fact that the two most important countries involved in this aspect of whaling, Chile and Peru, were not members of the I.W.C.

Two circumstances were shrewdly exploited by the Soviet Union in support of its attitude. In the first place, the Commission decided to appeal to Chile and Peru to join the Washington Convention. In the second place, the I.W.C. laid down that, in the light of the state of whale stocks in the Antarctic, catching from land stations that fished the same stocks was now increasingly important. It was decided that a special group should make a total assessment of fishing and regulation of all whales migrating to and from the Antarctic, and that in establishing the quota for pelagic whaling, operations from land stations should also be taken into consideration. Formally, the Soviet Union could quote this agreement in support of its attitude both to the Observer Scheme and to the quota agreement.

The Special Group submitted its findings at the eighteenth meeting of the Commission in London, 27 June to 1 July 1966. As in accordance with the Convention it was not possible to allot special quotas to shore stations, two alternatives were available: (1) combined limitations of pelagic catching and land-based catching, which it was left to the countries involved to share among themselves, or (2) a voluntary agreement between countries that operated shore stations; this agreement should be taken into consideration when the pelagic quota was fixed. Without the adherence of Chile and Peru, however, it was impossible to ensure whale stocks in the southern hemisphere effective protection. Total protection of blue and humpback whales had no bearing on these two countries, as they were not members of the I.W.C. That it was urgent to solve this problem as quickly as possible was shown by statistics of baleen whale catching from shore stations in the southern hemisphere: 1963/4 and 1964 2,866 whales (1,044.5 BWU), 1964/5 and 1965 4,398 whales (1,581.7 BWU). The large blue whale catch, 119 and 458, nearly all of them killed by Chileans, was a particular eye-opener. There was therefore less point in protecting them in the Antarctic if they were killed elsewhere. A combined F.A.O./I.W.C. committee of six also pointed out in its report that catches made from shore stations must be included in the establishment of the total quota designed to prevent a decline in stocks. It was estimated that catching from shore stations would comprise approximately 30 per cent of the sustainable yield at the time, which was then assumed to be 2,500 BWU. For the Antarctic this would then have to be lowered to 1,600, if shore-based catching was to continue on the same scale as previously. If the quota for pelagic catching was 2,200, it could not exceed 300 from shore stations if stocks were to be allowed to grow.

On the whole, this and subsequent meetings were characterised by a growing interest in land-based operations, and in pelagic catching in the North Pacific, the importance of which grew with the declining catch in the Antarctic. The fact that practically all the Commission's measures dealing with this catching were adopted unanimously, and without any subsequent protests, should be considered in the light of this. In accordance with the agreement that in the course of three seasons catching should be brought below the sustainable yield, the quota for 1966-7 was set at 3,500 without any opposition (Japan, 1,633, the Soviet Union 1,067, Norway 800), and for the first time since 1958-9 Norway filled her entire quota. As the Committee had concluded that the sustainable yield for the *entire* Antarctic was 4,500 fin and 4,500 to 7,000 sei whales, or 3,000-3,500 BWU, there being no catching from South Georgia, this harmonised with a pelagic quota of 3,500, and this was the first time a balance of this kind — so it was believed — had been established. The Japanese withdrew one floating factory with eight whale catchers, but in other respects there was no change in the amount of matériel used. On this point the 1966 meeting was one of the most peaceful and united, but this was not true of the Observer Scheme and the quota agreement. With regard to the former a commission was to submit in 1967 a plan embodying pelagic catching and shore-based stations. With regard to the latter, abortive negotiations had been carried on in London: these were to continue in Tokyo. In principle, the Soviet Union was in favour of dividing the quota into three equal parts, a proposal which it could be expected that Japan would turn down flat. Moreover, as the Russians were also anxious to include catches from shore stations in the total quota, the Japanese quota would have to include their catches from shore stations in South Georgia. In 1963-4 these came to 552 fin and 409 sei whales, in 1964-5 503 and 506 respectively, and in 1965-6, when they only leased Leith Harbour, 218 and 4 (plus a number of sperm whales during all these seasons). Partly for the reason mentioned, partly because yields were so small, the Japanese preferred to cancel their contract with Salvesen for 1966-7 in return for a fee of £150,000.

A week-long tug-of-war ensued at the meeting in Tokyo, which commenced on 31 August 1966 with the former chairman of the I.W.C., R. G. R. Wall, presiding. The result was a compromise, Japan and Norway agreeing to cede part of their quotas to the Soviet Union, Norway receiving 22.85 per cent (800 units), Japan 46.67 per cent (1,633 units), and the Soviet Union 30.48 per cent (1,067 units) of the

103. After the decline of pelagic whaling some of the floating factories were broken up, some converted to floating fish factories, and that shown above, the last to be built for a Norwegian company (1948), was converted to the oil-boring platform *Drillship* in 1964-5.

total of 3,500 units for the 1966-7 season. This meant that Japan had contributed 5.33 per cent and Norway 5.15 per cent. Great Britain continued to preserve the right to resume catching. In Norway there was general satisfaction with the quota, which was the minimum the Norwegians felt they needed to have in order to be able to despatch two expeditions, as on the last occasion. Both expeditions had signed contracts with the Japanese for the supply of meat to their refrigerator ships in the whaling grounds, and for both this contract was a necessary condition if operations were to show a profit.

The year 1966 was a milestone in the history of Norwegian whaling. The last of the floating factories from the golden age of the 1930s, the *Sir James Clark Ross,* slipped out of Sandefjord harbour, one-time whaling capital of the world, on her long voyage to Taiwan to be broken up. Her very name recalled the first attempts in 1893-5 to catch whales in the Antarctic. In the course of thirty seasons this floating factory had accounted for 42,161 whales and produced nearly 3 million barrels of whale oil and 160,000 barrels of sperm oil. Shortly afterwards, in January 1966, the *Norhval* was towed to Spain to end her days in the breaker's yard, while the *Thorshøvdi* was converted into an oil rig. In that year, too, Johan Rasmussen and Lars Christensen died. They had been involved in the Antarctic from the first, and with them an era of Norwegian enterprise lasting nearly a hundred years came to an end. Norway had only two floating factories left. Just how long they could continue to operate depended on the outcome of the 1966-7 season, and on the size of the quota they would be allotted in the ensuing season, and also if they would be capable of filling it.

As all the three nations — Japan, Norway, and the Soviet Union — completed their quotas in 1966-7, Norway proposed that the same total ceiling, 3,500, should also apply to 1967-8. The I.W.C. Technical Committee, however, considered that it should be set at 3,100. A proposal for 3,200 was adopted, and for the third time it was believed that the quota was below the limit which would permit stocks to recuperate. The result, only 2,804 BWU, however, appeared to show that even 3,200 was too much. This became still more evident when only 2,473 out of the same quota were caught in 1968-9. For the three countries involved a quota of 3,200 was so low that each of them had to withdraw an expedition. After five days of negotiation they agreed in August 1967 to share out the quota by giving 1,493 to Japan, 976 to the Soviet Union, and 731 to Norway. The absolute minimum was considered to be 400 if an expedition was to pay its way, and this figure was even more vital in view of the tremendous fall in the price of whale oil — from £84 in 1965-6 to £55 in 1966-7, and as low as £40 in 1968. There was a similar slump in the price for sperm oil. The Norwegian floating factory *Kosmos IV* had supplied 6,900 tons of meat to the Japanese, and in view of the low oil price the meat contract had been of vital importance to operational results. In order to squeeze Norway out of whaling altogether the Japanese now terminated the contract. The Kosmos company promptly installed refrigeration plant and concluded a contract with Petfood for the supply of 6,000 tons of whale meat at the favourable price of £100 a ton. As there would only be room for one Norwegian floating factory in 1967-8 this would without question have to be the *Kosmos IV*, while the Ørnen company's *Thorshavet* would have to withdraw, the more so because during the last two seasons this floating factory had run at a considerable loss. This company's withdrawal was a momentous event: it had pioneered in the Antarctic and operated without a break from 1903 to 1967, killing 66,792 whales and producing 4,095,711 barrels of oil to a value of Kr.0.75 milliard (£41.6 million). For ten years shareholders had received no dividends, but on an average over the sixty-four years they had netted 14.4 per cent. There were few companies that could look back on a similar record, especially if we remember that some of these years included the Depression of the inter-war period.

A crew of 384 Norwegians signed on for the *Kosmos IV*. Ten years previously 7,299 Norwegians had made a living from whaling. The season produced 34,240 barrels and 7,752 tons of meat. The expedition manager, who had spent thirty-five seasons in the whaling grounds, declared that the weather was the worst he had ever experienced. Of her quota of 731 BWU, Norway registered 292, thus saving 439 units, her last contribution to the preservation of stocks. It was for this reason that only 2,804 units out of a total quota of 3,200 were killed. As the *Kosmos IV* only operated with five whale catchers, the catcher's day work rate was relatively high at 0.49 BWU. In Japan's case it was 0.37 and for the Russians only 0.19. That the Soviet figures were only 39 per cent of the Norwegian suggests how expensive Soviet production must have been. Whale oil only accounted for 20 per cent of the earnings of the *Kosmos IV*'s catch, and meat 80 per cent. The entire operation produced a small surplus of £27,500. (Devaluation of the pound sterling involved the company in a loss of Kr.1.8 million.) As prospects of a surplus in the following season were not very great, and as the price of oil continued to fall, while wages and other operating expenses would rise, the company notified all its employees on 27 June 1968 that they would be redundant.

The news that Norwegian Antarctic whaling had come to a close made a considerable stir throughout the world. Tremendous pressure was exerted in many quarters on the company to persuade it to try one more season. Since the Second World War it had produced a surplus of some Kr.320 million after depreciation, with no deficit in any season, and possessed sufficient reserves to stand the risk of a minor loss without any difficulty. It was pointed out that cessation of activities occurred at a particularly unfortunate point of time as far as the I.W.C. was concerned. The latter had agreed to fix the quota as high as 3,200, allotting Norway a large share because it calculated that Norway would only despatch one floating factory, which would be incapable of filling its quota and would save some 400 units, a valuable contribution to regeneration of stocks. If Japan and the Soviet Union ruled the roost alone, they would catch the full quota. All appeals and arguments, however, were in vain; on 12 September 1968 the company made an irrevocable and final decision. With the 1968-9 season, apart from an unsuccessful attempt by Norway to resume whaling using a combined whale catcher and floating factory installed in a smaller vessel, the field had been left to Japan and the Soviet Union.

A review of the history of Antarctic whaling from 1904 to 1968 raises three questions. How much did Norway earn from Antarctic whaling? Why did Norway and other countries have to give up? Why have Japan and the Soviet Union considered it practicable to continue, even with a catch in 1977/8 + 1978 in the southern hemisphere of a mere 295 BWU (of the lesser cetaceans, i.e. sei and minke whales, plus a number of sperm whales)? It is difficult to give an entirely exact answer to these questions, because we are not familiar with all the factors involved, nor do we know how forcefully each of them operated. Owing to the fact that, relatively speaking, whaling played a much more important role in the Norwegian economy than in that of any of the other whaling nations, and because Norway started modern whaling and spread it all over the world, the answers to these questions are of great interest to the history of whaling generally speaking and to the history of Norway in particular.

1. Norway's earnings consisted mainly of the following elements : (a) the sale of whale and sperm oil and by-products, amounting to Kr.6.4 milliard; (b) wages paid by foreign firms to Norwegian whalers, amounting to Kr.570 million; (c) Norwegian equipment, etc., supplied to foreign whaling ventures, approximately Kr.115 million, making a gross total of about Kr.7,000 million. The major items to be deducted include : purchase of equipment and matériel from abroad; operating expenses abroad, in particular bunkers; concession, lease, licence, and export duty, etc. At a conservative estimate it appears that approximately Kr.1,400 million was spent abroad, giving a net revenue during the period 1904-68 of Kr.5,600 million, or, if we omit the five years of the Second World War (which have not been included in our calculation), an annual average of about Kr.95 million. The most lasting gain accruing to Norway consists of the capital which, thanks to whaling, has been made available for shipping and industry.

2. The second question has been answered : in short, the quota of 16,000 units was excessive. At the Washington Conference, the outcome of which was mainly decided by the United States, Britain, and Norway, 12,000 units would, for example, have had little difficulty in being accepted. There was no supervision to ensure that the provisions of the scheme were being observed; there were a great many clear indications that the quota was exceeded and that "forbidden" species were killed. The Convention had failed to co-ordinate the catching of the same whale stocks from shore stations with catching in the Antarctic, where only pelagic catching had been subject to regulation. In the second place, doubts were cast on the results of scientific whale research, as this was based on uncertain material. Whaling operations themselves — and too late at that — provided the practical proof of the decline of stocks. In the third place, it was impossible to bring biological interests into line with commercial interests. The rise in the price of whale oil after the war resulted in an over-investment out of all proportion to what was necessary to catch the limited quota. Amortisation of the expensive and over-sized production apparatus made production so expensive that companies were not in a position fully to enjoy the benefits of a rise in price. When world production of other edible fats and oils satisfied demand, whale oil was no longer so attractive, and when prices slumped, other objects for investment appeared to offer better prospects.

The Norwegian and British decision to restore their whaling after the war was based on the assumption that, in accordance with established tradition, they had the sole right to catch a quota that bore a reasonable relationship to the matériel used. Just as this provided the basis for regulation, it was tacitly assumed by the international Convention that on the whole this state of affairs should be allowed to continue. This principle could not be maintained in violation of the doctrine of the freedom of the seas and access for all to free competition in exploiting its riches. Unrestricted access to unrestricted exploitation of stocks of whales, however, led to cut-throat competition, with the nation that stood to gain most having the greatest chance of survival. The protracted opposition to national quotas was not only due to the individual countries' dissatisfaction with their shares; they would also put an end to free competition for those who believed they had an opportunity of coming out on top in the competition. When it was obvious that the Netherlands, Norway, and Great Britain were being left behind, as they were incapable of catching their voluntary quotas, or unwilling to make the necessary effort to achieve them, Japan and the Soviet Union decided that they could accept the compulsory quota system.

It has also been argued that Norwegian whaling was handicapped, in its competition with other countries, because the Government actually confiscated a large part of the surplus earnings during the boom period in the first six post-war seasons, thereby undermining the companies' ability to keep their matériel sufficiently up-to-date to make them competitive. It is doubtful, however, whether a re-investment of this kind would have produced a different result. After all, British whaling, which was not as severely taxed as Norwegian, considered it an advantage to close down, and even the state-subsidised Dutch whaling, with matériel technically on a par with the best, failed to hold its own. After Japan, the Netherlands, and the Soviet Union had joined in, and Onassis's behaviour had made it obvious that the Convention could not provide much protection, it was undoubtedly more sensible, from the point of view of national economy, for Norway to invest in shipping than in an industry with such an uncertain future as whaling. This is not a matter of hindsight, but a development which whaling people realised in time to initiate a gradual withdrawal and redeployment, which would avoid the acute economic crisis and large-scale employment problems that a sudden and total cessation of whaling would have caused.

The question of why the International Whaling Commission failed in its attempt to maintain whaling at a level of maximum sustainable yield was put to two foreign experts, who explained it, in a word, by distrust. First, the whaling world was unwilling to place any confidence in the forecasts of science, and secondly, without neutral observers there was no guarantee that one country's self denial would not prove to be someone else's advantage.

3. Why should the Soviet Union and Japan continue when the others had been forced to stop? This question has often been posed, and will be the last to be answered. To take Soviet whaling first, in so far as it is state-run it is in a very special position. When, for example, one sees that during the 1965-8 whaling seasons three Soviet expeditions comprising a total of fifty-five (in 1967-8 forty-eight) of the most powerful whale catchers with which any nation has operated in the Antarctic, and three floating factories each with a capacity of about 40,000 tons, produced *jointly* on an average per season just under 20,000 tons of whale oil and 30,000 tons of sperm oil, one might wonder what the purpose of the exercise was. The three expeditions, had they been built and run on the basis of private capital, would have cost Kr.800 million, and operating expenses would have come to Kr.120 million a year. If the oil had been sold at the same rate as the Norwegian, it would have fetched Kr.53 million a season, and if we include Kr.48 million for by-products (meal, meat, liver), a total of some Kr.100 million. If we calculate 15 per cent annually for interest and repayment, production would cost Kr.240 million per season. In other words: for Kr.100 million the Russians could have bought what it cost them Kr.240 million to produce. Economic considerations or pressing needs can therefore not have been the reason why a country with such ample natural resources as theirs should have felt compelled to carry out their exceedingly expensive Antarctic whaling.

In the case of Japan, on the other hand, whaling, for several reasons, answers urgent needs; thus the Japanese have invested heavily in it, and the gradual development has imposed a greater strain on them than on anyone else. It has involved serious problems in the transfer of personnel to other industries and professions, for food supplies, and for the economy of the two companies based on whaling. Whale meat and blubber are not only eaten on their own, but to a large extent as "fish-sausage", a mixture of fish (mostly tunny) and whale meat, and producers are constantly complaining of a shortage of the latter. Japan has always been one of the major fishing nations of the world and had been in a position to export fish right up to 1966. Imports, however, have been on the increase, and 1966 marks the moment when Japan ceased to be a fish-exporting country, partly owing to a decline in supplies of whale meat. Japanese Antarctic production for human consumption dropped from 136,018 tons in 1961-2 to 79,526 tons in 1967-8. The reason why this decline did not reflect the slump in the number of units caught — from 6,574 to 1,493 — was due to a much greater degree of processing. During the quota seasons daily catches were regulated in order to ensure the maximum production of by-products of optimum quality. While the average production of these was 18.9

tons per unit in 1958-9, in the two seasons 1966-8 it exceeded 60 tons, and quality is said to have been substantially improved. This can also be ascribed to a shift to the catching mainly of sei whales, as six sei whales provide more and better meat than one blue whale or two fine whales. We shall see below how the drop in the catching of sei whales has been made good by increased catches of minke whales.

Trebling the production of by-products per unit could partly compensate for the slump in the national quota, and meant a very great deal to companies' operating results. By-products were also produced from sperm whales. Of these, 114 were caught in 1967-8, and if we equate two sperm whales with one unit, the total catch amounted to 1,550 units, out of which 28,972 tons of oil were produced and 94,701 tons of by-products, of which meat (and blubber) accounted for 79,526 tons, or 18.69 tons of oil and 51.3 tons of meat per unit. As the price of oil was £45 a ton (after sterling had been devalued in 1967) and of meat £160 a ton, the value of production represented per unit £800 in oil and £8,000 in meat. The value of the remaining 9.8 tons of by-products is not known, but it would probably be right to assess the value of one unit in Japanese whaling at £11,000, or a total of £16.4 million for its quota of 1,493 units. In 1969 the price of meat rose £200 a ton, i.e. £10,000 per unit. This rise in price alone meant more than a doubling of the oil price would have meant. If the Japanese were capable of pressing the exploitable value of the sei whale as high as £2,000, it was impossible for others to compete, and the Japanese were morally justified in maintaining that whaling should be reserved for the nations capable of extracting the greatest value from their catch.

The high exploitable value was a necessary factor for the amortisation of Japan's considerable investments in the Antarctic after the war. As the decline set in more quickly and more strongly than anticipated, it was only possible to use some of the floating factories purchased for a few seasons, and the purchasers have hardly made much of a profit. Some of the matériel could be used for pelagic catching in the North Pacific, and attempts have been made to compensate for the decline in the Antarctic by operating from shore stations in other areas as well. Even so, there is no doubt that some of the matériel proved superfluous, and the Japanese, unlike the others, have never been in a position to execute a favourable withdrawal by selling off their matériel. Information is available that only two of the four Japanese expeditions in 1967-8 showed a surplus. In 1968-9 only three expeditions were despatched, but the number of whale catchers was increased by two for each expedition.

An Englishman, Dr. HARRY D. LILLIE, who had been with a pelagic expedition in 1946-7 and visited South Georgia in 1954, and had published a book about his visit (*The Path through Penguin City*), went to Moscow in 1965, where he had an interview with Prime Minister Kosygin, and to Tokyo, where he met the leaders of the Japanese whaling companies. His idea was that the Soviet Union and Japan in collaboration with Norway should demonstrate to the world that they were able to achieve what had eluded the I.W.C.: a total ban on Antarctic whaling for twenty to twenty-five years, the dissolution of the I.W.C. and the transfer of its functions to the United Nations.

In a report to the Norwegian Embassy in London Lillie later described how he had told Kosygin of the accusations against the Russians of irregular catching and how Kosygin had promised to look into the matter. The Russians, for their part, were annoyed that the Japanese had acquired such a large quota by buying up expeditions from other countries. In certain whaling circles in Japan Lillie had found some sympathy for his campaign; they had admitted that Japan had been wrong in exacting larger quotas for the sake of short-term gains, instead of thinking in terms of preserving future catches. They had turned up at the meeting of the Commission in 1965 with a demand for 4,500 units as a feeler; but the Commission, believing that they "had a gun levelled at their heads", granted the 4,500 merely to prevent a breakdown of the Commission. Lillie placed the greatest responsibility on the Commission's Scientific Committee, which year in, year out, had merely talked of more research and more statistics in order to prove what was obvious to the most inexperienced whaler. In explaining the large sei whale catch by declaring that the population preferred this meat, the Japanese were simply explaining away the fact that there were no longer any fin whales to be caught. What the Commission had failed to do Japan, in co-operation with the Soviet Union and Norway, would have to show the world that they could accomplish : total protection of Antarctic whales for twenty to twenty-five years, and the transfer to the aegis of the United Nations of a task the Commission had proved incapable of fulfilling.

A plan on these lines had been submitted by Dr. J. A. GULLAND, one of the "Three Wise Men", through the Fauna Preservation Society in October 1965. The plan was patterned on the system practised for sealing in the North Pacific, where operations were entrusted to a single country, the United States, with compensation paid to other countries with sealing interests (the Soviet Union, Canada, and Japan). In the case of whaling it would be natural for the United Nations to assume the place of the United States. A body under the aegis of the United Nations would issue licences for as high a fee as possible, for five years at a time; the licence would entitle the holder to catch a specific number of whales of each species, and no more than would ensure that stocks were always maintained at a level capable of producing the maximum sustainable yield. The amount of money produced by this tax would be divided into four parts, one of which would be allocated for scientific research, one to the United Nations, one to member countries in proportion to their U.N. subscription, while one would be shared among the countries taking part in whaling. The nations at that time engaged in whaling would be pressed to abandon it in return for compensation at the rate of between £1 million and £2 million per expedition, in addition possibly to a small annual amount, until such time as they could once again recommence whaling. Until this were possible, small catches of species able to sustain catching would be allowed, and the tax for this could cover the interest on the lump sum compensation. Gulland was probably right in assuming that the four Norwegian companies whaling at the time would be willing to withdraw in return for compensation on those lines, but it is very doubtful whether the Russians would have done so, and it is certain that the Japanese would not. Putting the suggestion into practice entailed so many problems — for example, who would be granted a licence? — that its realisation appeared an impossibility. Why should whaling and not all other sealing and fishing in the oceans of the world be subject to a pool under the aegis of the United Nations?

Lillie's and Gulland's suggestions have a certain interest in that they show the sort of work that was taking place outside the Commission in planning to save whale stocks.

In 1968-9 three expeditions in the Antarctic apparently had no difficulty in filling their quotas. The borderline appeared to have been found which would permit stocks to recuperate, until they once again could provide the highest sustainable yield. This, however, was not to be the case.

34

ANTARCTIC EPILOGUE

For the first thirty years — 1904 to 1934 — two countries, Norway and Great Britain, had been almost entirely on their own in Antarctic whaling, as well as completely dominant in global whaling. After 1968, two different countries once again occupied the same position, Japan and the Soviet Union, but with one great difference: that they are entirely alone not only in the Antarctic but also in the North Pacific. In 1977 almost 90 per cent of world whaling was divided between these two countries, Japan with 44 per cent and the Soviet Union with 56 per cent (including small cetaceans). Growing world opinion against every kind of whaling has conveniently forgotten that several other countries, too, had played their part in destroying stocks in the Antarctic during the intervening years, 1934-64, and has concentrated the entire weight of its disapproval on the two countries still left, all the more so because, from the very start of modern whaling in the North Pacific, these two have been mainly responsible for decimating whale stocks in an area where, for practical purposes, they have been on their own for the last fifty years.

Faced with the demands of opponents of whaling for a ten-year moratorium on commercial whaling, the Japanese delegate to the meetings of the Commission and its chairman in 1968-71, Dr. IWAO FUJITA, emphasised the very serious economic consequences a moratorium would have for Japan: 50,000 people were dependent for employment on whaling, annually 150,000 tons of whale meat were consumed, and this, together with a number of by-products, had a value of $110 million; it corresponded to half the domestic meat production or 10 per cent of the country's total consumption of meat. Whale meat was one of the most important sources of protein. The Japanese had used whale for food from prehistoric times, and not till a hundred years ago had they started eating the meat of quadrupeds. The decline in the production of whale meat from 203,000 tons in 1965 to 122,700 tons in 1973 had already created considerable difficulty.

In 1973 nature conservationists organised a protest demonstration in front of the building where the I.W.C. was holding its meetings, and speakers vied with one another in their violent attacks on Japan and the Soviet Union, appealing for a boycott of the products of these countries: "It may not matter right now to your business, but, believe me, Datsun and Sony, and the vodka producers in Russia will soon be feeling the effect." Signatures were collected as part of a campaign in favour of the moratorium, and even in Japan the names of over a hundred leading personalities had been obtained.

In 1968 the situation in the Antarctic was as follows. After the Japanese had given up the lease of Grytviken in 1965 and of Leith Harbour in 1966, no more catching was carried on from shore stations. Pelagic whaling was in the hands of Japan and the Soviet Union alone, involving three floating factories each and a total of eighty-four whale catchers, in other words, an average of fourteen whale catchers per floating factory, the highest number throughout the entire post-war period. In a season extending from 12 December to 7 April this fleet was set the task of catching a total quota of 3,200 BWU — 1,493 for Japan, 976 for the Soviet Union, while Norway's quota of 731 would remain untouched. The quota covered not only Antarctic waters in the narrow sense of the word, but all pelagic catching of baleen whales south of 40°S. It was forbidden to catch blue and humpback whales, and hence the quota could only be filled by catching fin whales (of at least 57 ft.) and sei whales (40 ft.) The *number* of sperm whales was not limited, but the *season* was of eight months' duration and the minimum length permitted was 38 ft. Without Norwegian competition the two countries required not more than ninety-nine days of the 117 days of the open season in order to achieve their quotas. As the considerable discrepancy in catch, 22.7 per cent, as compared with the total quota, was due exclusively to the fact that Norway was not catching her quota, there was no justification for using this apparently large discrepancy as an argument against a tremendous decline in whale stocks. The way in which the quotas had been covered gave more cause for concern : in 1967-8, when Norway was involved, 2,155 fin and 10,357 sei whales had been caught, and in 1968-9 3,020 fin and 5,776 sei whales. There was, in fact, a disturbing increase in the number of fin whales and an equally disturbing decline in the number of sei whales.

As will be seen from Table 64 (see Statistical Appendix) only on one previous occasion had there been a greater deficiency in yield, and that had occurred during the first season with a fixed total quota, after three seasons of unrestricted catching (1962-3) with an *actual* deficiency of 24.6 per cent. In view of the fact that during the four seasons 1962-6 there was a deficiency of 24.6, 15.7, 12.7 and 9.1 per cent respectively, even though the quota had been reduced from 15,000 BWU to 4,500, it seems possible to show on a purely statistical basis that it was during the three seasons of unrestricted catching that so many more whales were killed in excess of the sustainable yield that stocks rapidly approached extermination point. In *each single one* of the three seasons 1,313 *more* BWU were caught than in all the nine seasons 1968-77 *together*. Attacks on nations whaling in the 1970s came too late : responsibility for the situation today falls on those answerable for the situation in 1959-62. Scientific investigations suggest that stocks of whale today are once more on the way up, and a new and exciting chapter in the history of whaling has thus been ushered in.

In the regulation of Antarctic whaling 1968-72 can be regarded as peaceful years, almost without any changes. The reason why it was possible to lower the quota from 3,200 to 2,300, without any protest from Japan and the Soviet Union, was that their national quotas were not reduced. Reduction was purely fictitious, in so far as it involved decreasing the Norwegian quota from 731 to 50, an amount that was not fished anyway. Only during the last season, 1971-2, did the two countries have to accept minor reductions — Japan from 1,493 BWU to 1,346 and the Soviet Union from 974 to 904, i.e. an actual reduction of the total quota by 217. This excludes the entirely insignificant catch of 6.2 BWU over two seasons (1969-70, 1971-2) by the Norwegian factory catcher *Peder Huse* (787 gross tons), an unsuccessful attempt to combine both operations in one and the same vessel. This was the third time this was attempted, every time with the same result. During all these seasons Japan and the Soviet Union filled their quotas without any difficulty, using the same matériel — six floating factories and eighty-four whale catchers, requiring a much shorter time than the open season allowed. One sign, however, that it was gradually becoming more difficult to fill the quota was a decline in catcher's day work in BWU from 0.30 during the three foregoing seasons to 0.27 in 1971-2. All the above figures apply only to baleen whales: all the expeditions, particularly the Soviet, also caught sperm whales in the Antarctic, i.e. south of 40°S, and north of this latitude on their way to and from the Antarctic.

One of the new features of whaling from the end of the 1960s is the appearance of the minke whale (*Balaenoptera acutorostrata*). This is one of the small baleen species, measuring when fully grown approximately 24 to 27 ft. In Norwegian it is generally called the *våge* whale and in English the lesser rorqual or the little piked whale. In appearance it resembles most the fin whale, and looks like a dwarf species of it. The name minke is said to have derived from one of Svend Foyn's crew by the name of Meincke, who mistook a school of these whales for blue whales. Whalers all over the world considered this incident so amusing that they used his name as a household word to describe this species. It is to be found in most oceans, and has been the object of pursuit, not least from Norway, owing to its tasty meat. A minke whale will hardly provide more than about two barrels of oil, and in this respect 50 or 60 would be required to equal one BWU. The "big" whalers had scorned the pursuit of such a small animal, until it became a welcome supplement to a dwindling quota of the large species.

As might be expected, it was the Japanese in particular who were interested in catching minke whales, owing to its good meat and the price this fetched — in 1977 it was reported to be as high as $2 per lb., and as a minke can provide 3,000 kg. of meat, its production value is around $13,500. In "the good old days" the meat and oil value of the fin whale was between $3,000 and $4,000. An occasional minke had been caught in the past, but the 1967-8 season was the first time a Japanese expedition bagged a large number (597). Special equipment was required for this species, including guns of lesser calibre and harpoons without shells. In addition to the three ordinary expeditions the Japanese equipped a fourth specially for catching minke whales (the floating factory *Jinjo Maru* of 9,000 gross tons and four whale catchers) and chalked up 3,000 in 1971-2 in the course of eighty-five days. The I.W.C. had laid down that the open season for catching minke whales was to extend over six months. As the Soviet Union meant to start catching them in 1972-3, the I.W.C. intervened with surprising speed, having learnt from experience. For the first time a quota was fixed for a species, practically before catching had started, which, it was assumed, would ensure the maximum sustainable yield. It is interesting to note that at any rate on one occasion in its history the Commission has done so. Actually, the results were not as successful as intended. The quota was set at 5,000, and following the provision in the Schedule the Bureau of International Whaling Statistics, on the basis of daily catching reports, was to lay down the date when the quota could be assumed to have been reached. When it was reported on 2 January that 4,250 had been caught, averaging 110 a day, it could be expected that the remaining 750 would be caught in seven days, and the closing date was therefore set at 9 January; but, as had happened before when this system was in use, catching during these seven days was so intensified that it rose to 214 a day, and the quota was exceeded by 745. This was the last time this system was in use.

For 1973-4 the quota was once again set at 5,000, but Japan and the Soviet Union protested, maintaining that this previously unmolested species would stand far greater inroads without falling below the level that would ensure a maximum sustainable yield. They agreed to catch 4,000 each. The result was 7,713, and that the quota for the ensuing season was set at 7,000, all of which were caught. The regulation, quotas, and catches this season of this and other species must be considered in conjunction with the reorganisation of all global catching, the co-ordination of rules for shore-based and pelagic catching, and the new system for the Commission and its administration which was introduced between 1972 and 1976.

The appearance of the minke whale is one of the new features of Antarctic whaling in recent years; another is that the last of the "Big Three", the fin whale, disappeared after 1975-6. This too is linked up with the above-mentioned new regulations. A third feature was the rising share of sperm whales in the total Antarctic catch. This was 15,207 whales in all in 1975-6, of which 7,046, or 49.5 per cent, were sperm whales, and of the 8,161 baleen whales it should be noted that 6,034 were minke whales. Ten years previously, 1965-6, the total number was 26,007 whales, of which 6,104, or 23.5 per cent, were sperm, and of the 19,903 baleen whales, not one was a minke. Of the total oil production of the same expeditions, 30 per cent in 1965-6 was sperm oil, in 1975-6 65 per cent. The production of whale meat had slumped from 136,499 to 66,308 tons, and for Japan alone there was a reduction from 107,130 to 31,090 tons. As large numbers of sperm whales were to be found in all the oceans of the world, it had previously not been considered necessary to regulate the catching of this species, but the tremendous catches in the 1960s — reaching a peak in 1963-4 of nearly 30,000 — gave the scientists food for thought, and commencing with the 1972-3 season the catch was limited — in the Antarctic as well. This regulation, too, was an integral part of the new system, and before we look more closely at this, we must consider the development of whaling after 1945 in areas outside the Antarctic.

On 8 February 1977 the *Japan Economic Journal* of Tokyo published an article entitled: "The U.S.S.R. proposes tie-up on Antarctic whaling". It went on to say: "The Soviet Union lately has proposed a complete tie-up with Japan on whaling in the Antarctic centering on setting up a joint venture, industry informants revealed last week. They said that the Russians had made such an offer to Nippon Kyodo Hogei Kaisha Ltd., a whaling company set up last year to unify the activities of six Japanese fishery firms at that time which had been seriously hit by successive Antarctic catch quota cuts. The informants said that the Soviet proposal was made by the Soviet Fishery Ministry. Collaboration between them can work as a big deterrent against further reducing the international quota.

"From this standpoint the Soviet bid is being welcomed by Japanese whaling interests, and it is also received favourably as a foothold for other bilateral co-operation with the advent of the 200-mile offshore zone era.

"A 'two-stage type' seemed most probable at the present time. The first stage could take the form of mutual exchange of information or pooling quotas of both nations and dividing the catches between them on the basis of a given formula. In the second stage the two nations would go on to establishing a joint Japan-U.S.S.R. whaling company."

(For Antarctic pelagic quotas, catches, seasons, catching days, average production etc., 1945-78, see Statistical Appendix, Table 65. For the operative seasons of the stations in South Georgia, see Statistical Appendix, Table 66.)

35
WHALING OUTSIDE THE ANTARCTIC
AFTER 1945

By way of introduction it should be pointed out that in the following account a date (e.g. 1912) indicates the sum of the previous Antarctic season (1911-12, winter) and the indicated year's catch in other fields (1912, summer).

Throughout the Second World War whaling continued uninterrupted in seven areas — Japan, New Zealand, South Africa, Chile, and Newfoundland, from Grytviken, and in the Azores (old-style whaling). Either during or immediately after the war whaling recommenced in all the grounds where it had been suspended, and in a few new ones. In 1951 the largest number of shore stations since 1912 were in operation. Owing to the marked increase of shore whaling, total world operations in 1951 made use of 100 more whale catchers than at any previous time, while world production of oil was the largest since 1938-9. Of the total number of whales, twice as many were sperm whales as ever before, an indication of things to come. Another notable feature is that after 1965 the centre of gravity of whaling moved from the Antarctic to the North Pacific, where it became more pelagic than shore whaling. (The North Pacific is taken to include Japan-Korea, Kamchatka, the Kurils, and pelagic catching in the North Pacific Ocean and the Bering Sea. For certain other areas, in particular Australia, post-war whaling is dealt with in another section, to which the reader is referred, as it will not be dealt with here.)

The North Atlantic

In global terms whaling here has been on a small scale: only in the case of Iceland has it had any significant bearing on the national economy, and provided one of the more fruitful sources of foreign currency. The most striking feature of whaling in this ocean has been that, unlike global whaling in general, it has not concentrated mainly on the sperm whale, and has been mainly involved in the catching of fin. While operations in pursuit of this species showed a clear downward trend from its peak in 1952 (374), and declined markedly from the Faroes after 1950 (377), a similar tendency has not occurred in the case of Iceland. Here, over a period of thirty years a more stable yield and production of oil, meat, and meat meal than in any other whaling grounds in the world has been maintained. It seems as if here the dream of the I.W.C. Scientific Committee has come true: a balance has been achieved between stocks and catch that has ensured the maximum sustainable yield of stocks in these waters since 1945. Steady catches of sei whales have also been maintained in Icelandic waters, but they disappeared almost entirely around Norway and the Faroes after the mid-1950s. In the post-war period until they were protected in the North Atlantic after 1959, 430 blue whales were caught, 163 round Iceland, 54 in Norwegian waters, 40 round the Faroes, 6 from the Hebrides, 15 off West Greenland, 152 in the Newfoundland-Labrador area.

After the war, three stations were established on the west coast of Norway, and results were so favourable in 1946 — seventeen blue and 392 fin whales — that it seemed as if stocks had benefited from being left in peace for six years. It was assumed that this would be the case to an even greater extent in North Norway, where practically no whaling had taken place since 1904. For this reason a concession was granted for a station here in 1948. Both in catches and economic results the Norwegian stations had their best years in 1950-2, but subsequently catches of fin whales declined steadily, while those of sperm whales showed a certain increase. There were not sufficient whales to provide a basis for profitable operations for three stations situated so close to one another in the west of Norway: one after the other they closed down, the last to do so being in 1967, while the station in North Norway held out until the 1971 season. The production of whale oil as far as Norwegian whaling was concerned was always relatively small, as operations were based mainly on the production and sale of meat for human and animal consumption. In this respect competition was provided by catchers of small cetaceans, who protested that the market was so glutted with meat that occasionally it collapsed altogether.

There is scarcely any doubt why the catching of fin whales in Norwegian waters came to an end. Four stations proved too much. With one station and a moderate catch it would probably have been possible to keep going, as in the case of Iceland. Recent research has shown that it is probably one and the same stock that has been subject to catching from the Faroes and West Norway, and that this is the same stock that is also pursued off the coasts of Spain and Portugal. Fluctuations in catches in one place must therefore be assessed in connection with catches of the same stock in one or several other areas.

The good catches in Norwegian, Icelandic, and Faroese waters encouraged attempts at operating from the old Bunaveneader station in the Hebrides, but the poor results in the 1950-1 season proved that there was no basis here for operating at a profit.

Round the Faroes, on the other hand, results during the first few years were so promising that there were prospects of the best period in the whaling history of the islands: 377 fin whales in 1950 was about the highest number registered in any area in the North Atlantic after the war. No area, however, has produced such marked fluctuations: as early as 1952 figures slumped to twenty, recovering in 1957 to 141. As the following year produced a mere sixteen, whaling was suspended for three years, 1959-61, and two subsequent attempts have proved a total failure, the last occasion being in 1968, when the total yield was six fin and six sperm whales.

Of major interest is whaling from Iceland, started in 1948 by the Hvalur H/F company, which purchased at a bargain price an American naval base at the head of the 18-mile-long Hval fjord, 35 miles northeast of Reykjavik. At very little expense this was converted into an ideal shore station. Its position is convenient for operating in the Denmark Strait, between Iceland and Greenland, where most of the whaling takes place. Whale catchers generally do a three-day stint of duty, one day *en route* to the whaling grounds, one on the spot, and one for towing whales back to the station. The six months' continuous catching period permitted by the Convention for shore stations usually runs from 15 May to 15 October, but is seldom fully utilised. Catching starts in the southwest and follows the migration of the whales north towards the Greenland ice. The number of fin whales caught has proved surprisingly stable, with an annual average of about 250, whereas catches of sei whales show tremendous fluctuation, just as was the case before the First World War in all the whaling grounds of the Norwegian Sea. In 1950 two sei whales were caught, in 1955 134, in 1968 three, in 1971 240, and in 1974 nine. From 1948 to 1975 a total of 163 blue, six humpback, 6,916 fin, 1,839 sei, and 2,198 sperm whales were caught. The baleen whale production has been based rather on frozen meat and meat meal than on oil. The bulk of the meat is sold to Petfood in England, while the meal, which is very rich in protein, goes mainly for cattle feed to the domestic market. The total world quota for fin whales for 1978 was set by the I.W.C. at 459, of which 304 was allocated to Iceland, but the total catch in these waters during the six years 1977-82 may not together exceed 1,524, i.e. an average of 254 per annum. The sei whale quota for 1978 is 84.

The whaling run by the Danish state using one whale catcher from a station in West Greenland, mainly with a view to providing meat for the Greenlanders, had come to a halt in 1958, since when a small number of whales, mainly humpbacks, have occasionally been caught by the Eskimos using their ancient methods. The general protection of certain species did not apply to whaling undertaken by the original inhabitants with a view to obtaining food. The halt in the catching of major cetaceans has been compensated for by catches of white whales (beluga).

Operations from the shore station in Portugal were halted in 1951, when the entire yield was no more than twenty-two whales. Catches subsequently credited to Portugal in the *International Whaling Statistics* involve the catching of sperm whales using the ancient hand-harpoon method from rowing boats, round the Azores and Madeira. The yield in 1951 was particularly good, not least economically, producing 1,658 whales and 41,346 barrels; apart from this, only four years have registered just over 20,000 barrels, the last occasion being 1957. In recent years catches have declined markedly: in 1975 the result was 150 whales and 2,915 barrels. The animals caught must have been mainly small whales, as the average try-out was only just over 20 barrels, and in some years as little as 18.5.

There had been no whaling from the stations in Spain since the Norwegians gave up there in 1927, until two Spanish companies started up from the old shore stations at Getares in the south and Corcubion in the north in 1950 and 1952, and from a new station near Vigo in 1956. Ever since, whaling, sometimes with two, sometimes with three stations, has been carried on, using as many as six boats. As records of the catches in recent years are very incomplete, it is not certain what species have been pursued, but there can hardly be any doubt that, as in the 1920s, these have mainly comprised fin whales, a certain number of sei and sperm whales, with a marked tendency towards a relative increase of the last-mentioned. Figures available for 1970-4 show that the first of these seasons must have been an exceptionally good one, with a yield of 152 fin and 261 sperm whales, and an estimated production of 11,300 barrels, considerably more than in any other year after the war. From the Benzu station near Tetuan in one-time Spanish Morocco, where a Norwegian company tried its luck in 1948, a Spanish concern operated from 1949 to 1954, when it closed down, after registering only sixty-five whales (forty-one sperm) and 983 barrels. In 1954 five blue whales, a species seldom seen in the Mediterranean, were caught.

In hardly any other area in the world does whaling appear to have been such a gamble as off Newfoundland (including Labrador). A successful year may be followed by one in which the seas appear to be completely empty of whales, even though this cannot be due to over-fishing of stocks in foregoing years. This must be due to substantial changes in ocean currents, temperature, and feeding conditions. The seven-year period starting with the last year of the war proved the best in the entire history of this area, with an annual average of 464 fin, 23 blue, 13 humpback, 13 sei, and 23 sperm whales, and 22,000 barrels of oil (1948 providing a peak with 57 blue, 669 fin, and 30,500 barrels). The most important station was Hawke's Harbour, Labrador, from which the Polar Whaling Co. (Chr. Salvesen & Co.) operated between 1943 and 1951, after a break in 1941-2. With the price of oil dropping and with rising operational costs, operations were suspended after 1951, despite relatively good results. In 1956 another company made a highly unsuccessful attempt to re-start catching, and a third company, starting in 1966, had a successful run of six years with an average of 355 whales, almost all fin, and 11,147 barrels. In 1967 a new area was opened up from a station in Nova Scotia, where catching culminated in 1967 with 309 fin whales, 50 sei whales, and 11,051 barrels. It was remarkable that so many sei whales should have been caught here every year, whereas this species was rarely encountered in the nearby grounds off Newfoundland.

When the I.W.C. at its 1973 meeting debated the proposal for a ten-year general moratorium, the Canadian representative declared, not without a certain amount of pride, that his country, not merely on economic grounds but primarily in order to make *its* contribution to saving world whale stocks, had closed down all three stations on the east coast at the conclusion of the 1972 season. On the west coast operations came to a halt in 1967. "The government has taken this action to ensure that the stocks will rebuild as rapidly as possible, so that there will be no doubt of the survival of these species [fin and sei] and that the stocks will reach high levels of productivity in as short time as possible." There are two striking points in his statement. In the first place he said : "Our operations on the east coast have only been in existence for about ten years." True, they had only been restarted here on a large scale in the mid-1960s after fourteen years of very limited catching, but whaling had been carried out from Newfoundland-Labrador since 1898. In the second place, catching in these waters and from Nova Scotia had shown such a marked decline, from 576 fin whales in 1970 to 360 in 1972, that it would have probably been terminated as it no longer paid its way. This was also the reason why catching was terminated on the west coast (British Columbia) in 1967, where the yield of fin whales had slumped from 573 in 1958 to 102 and of sei whales from 604 in 1965 to 89. Together with the ban on the catching of large cetaceans, it is also forbidden to catch white whales (beluga) in Hudson Bay, where this had become a popular sport. After the war a considerable amount of small cetacean catching has also been carried out, particularly of potheads, in order to supply local fur breeders with meat.

North Pacific, East

There are three whaling grounds off the west coast of North America — Alaska, British Columbia, and California. Operations in the first-mentioned have been suspended since 1939. In the second area whaling was closed in 1943, and the old shore stations were closed. In 1948 the Western Whaling Corporation Ltd. started up again from an entirely new station, Coal Harbour, on the northwest coast of Vancouver Island. Using six whale catchers, these operations showed a steady increase right up to 1959, and numerous species were killed every year — in 1959 28 blue, 369 fin, 27 humpback, 185 sei, and 260 sperm whales, producing almost 23,000 barrels. Owing to difficulties in finding a market for this production, operations were closed down in 1960-1. They had mainly been based on frozen meat, after the company had been taken over in 1949 by the large fisheries firm of British Columbia Packers Ltd., for which reason the try-out of oil was relatively low. The large catch of sei whales from 1955 to 1966, averaging annually 375, was remarkable. This was the reason why the Japanese, in their global search for every possible source of whale meat, became interested in Coal Harbour. Together with the British Columbia Packers Ltd., Taiyo Gyogyo K.K. founded the Western Canada Whaling Co., which after the two-year break started up again in 1962, after the refrigeration plant had been greatly extended. The Japanese operated with two catchers and special workers for processing the meat. When the number of fin and sei whales declined sharply, and the catch comprised mainly sperm whales, the meat of which was of no interest to the Japanese, operations closed down at the end of 1967, and have subsequently not been restarted. A company known as Bioproducts Inc. caught a total of thirteen whales between 1961 and 1965; the small number, as well as the name of the company, suggests that the intention was to carry out scientific investigations. In California after the war several companies attempted to establish permanently profitable operations from shore stations. The best period was the latter half of the 1950s, when a large number of humpbacks were taken, reaching a peak of 199 in 1957. Apart from this, the great range of species is a feature of these whaling grounds. There are are blue, fin, humpback, sei, Bryde, gray, and sperm whales. Blue and humpback whales had been totally protected in 1965, and the gray whale, in common with the right whale, had been ever since the Washington Convention of 1946. In 1964, however, stocks appeared to have increased so greatly that they appeared capable of sustaining a limited yield, and between 1966 and 1969 an annual average of seventy-three were caught. Catching on this side of the North Pacific was then suspended; we shall consider below operations on the other side of the ocean. In 1976 original stocks were estimated to be approximately 15,000, and were by then approximately 11,000. The protection of the gray whale is one of the most tangible signs that stocks of a species assumed to have been entirely exterminated have been rebuilt to give a maximum sustainable yield. The migration of the gray whale along the coast of California has, in fact, become a major tourist attraction.

The ban on the catching of totally protected species was subject to the rider that they could be caught, "but only when the meat and products are to be used exclusively for local consumption by the aborigines". This involved in particular the Eskimo catching of bowheads off Alaska. When this, too, was banned by the I.W.C. in 1977, it was owing to the increased catches of recent years. Reports from the U.S. National Marine Fisheries Service for 1972 (see *International Whaling Statistics* LXXI, pp. 27-8) listed Eskimo catching of this whale off Alaska from 1850 to date. In most years this was less than ten, but between 1968 and 1972 the annual average was twenty-four. What gave particular cause for concern was that in 1976, apart from the twenty-eight whales captured, seventy-seven were lost and probably so badly injured that they are unlikely to have survived. The United States was anxious for the ban on Eskimo whaling to be suspended owing to the whales' great importance for the diet of the native population. As stocks may be assumed to number at least 1,000 animals, it should be permitted to kill at least five animals annually, a number which the Eskimos themselves consider far too low. That stocks of bowheads proved to be so ample was a great surprise, because whaling literature over a hundred years had constantly preached that they were totally exterminated, and this was one of the main arguments used by opponents of whaling. At the earnest request of the United States a total ban on the killing of bowheads by the aboriginal population was suspended by the I.W.C. at its special meeting in Tokyo on 6-7 December 1977. It was resolved that "a harvest, limited to the striking of eighteen whales or the landing of twelve, should be permitted from this stock for 1978 ... exclusively by persons under the jurisdiction of the Government of the United States".

The Eskimos' catch of Greenland whales (bowheads) was one of the main items on the agenda of the I.W.C.'s June 1978 meeting. Based on the number of whales seen and estimates of the number missed during bad weather, at night, etc., the American biologists estimated that the number of bowhead whales that had migrated northward off Barrow, Alaska, in April and May was between 1,783 and 2,865 — i.e. a mean of 2,264. The United States therefore proposed a catch of 2 per cent (forty-four animals), but this was turned down and a proposal of twenty animals passed. The Eskimos of the American delegation protested by leaving the meeting with the declaration that they never more would set foot in an I.W.C. meeting. They intended to go on with the catching of what they needed for their living in an Arctic climate. It would be a hard blow to the authority of the I.W.C. if one of the member nations deliberately breaks the rules even if it is on a small scale.

The problem is complex. Apart from the low stock size (2,264 represents about 9-16 per cent of the original population size), one of the major worries of the Scientific Committee is the apparently very low gross recruitment rate (2.5-3.5 per cent). Over the years 1973-8 (assuming 50 per cent of the animals struck and lost subsequently die) the average number of removals from the stock was 45 per annum of which 90 per cent were immature. Thus a very high proportion of the recruitment to the adult stock has been removed. If one assumes natural mortality lies in the range of 4-8.5 per cent which is found for other baleen whales, then it appears that the stock might decline even if *no* whales were taken.

South Pacific, East

Over the years the largest numbers of whales, outside the Antarctic and the North Pacific, have been caught in the sea off Peru and Chile. Here, sperm whale catching has dominated, particularly in Peruvian waters. In 1951 one-third of the entire world production of sperm oil came from this area, almost 200,000 barrels (from 6,414 whales), almost all from foreign pelagic expeditions. After 1955 operations were conducted from shore stations, and this reached its peak in 1959-61, with approximately 3,500 whales and 75,000 barrels annually. In Chilean waters, too, sperm whale catching dominated from 1957 to 1964, but in these waters throughout all the post-war years, and in Peruvian waters in the 1960s, a considerable catch of baleen whales has taken place. In particular the number of blue whales has been strikingly large — 449 in 1965. This culminated in 1965-6 with respectively 787 and 508 BWU, while at the same time the catch of sperm whales declined markedly. Towards the end of the 1960s a considerable number of sei whales were also caught.

The relatively large catch of baleen whales drew the attention of the I.W.C. to the fact that this accounted for so many of the animals spared by the lowering of the quota in the Antarctic, and the protection of blue whales, as to reduce the effect of these measures. In fact the members of the Commission were protecting whaling operations that benefited non-members, but as long as the two countries — and also Ecuador — remained outside the Commission, the I.W.C. was powerless. All subsequent attempts to persuade the three countries to join the Commission proved in vain till Peru and Chile joined before the 1979 Annual Meeting. The protests directed against the I.W.C. and the operations of its members could far more justifiably be directed against members of the Santiago Convention, which permitted operations from shore stations all the year round, not only for six months, and permitted the killing of whales protected by the I.W.C., as well as setting a lower minimum size limit. The whaling conducted from the shores of these two countries was additional to the quotas laid down for I.W.C. members. The large catch of baleen whales in Chilean waters came to a somewhat abrupt end in 1964, and the catching of sperm whales also slumped: in 1975 the total yield was fifty-eight sei and forty-eight sperm whales.

Owing to political unrest and shortage of capital it proved difficult to recommence whaling in Peruvian waters after the war. It only got into its stride in 1953 when a German-Peruvian company, the Consorcio Ballenero S.A., built a modern shore station at Pisco, 150 miles south of Lima, and the firm of Archer, Daniels, Midland Co., of Minneapolis, one of the world's largest consumers of sperm oil, established the Compañía Ballenera del Norte S.A., with American and Peruvian capital on a fifty-fifty basis, and built near the town of Paita in the extreme north of Peru "the American continent's most modern whaling plant", completed in July 1957. Based exclusively on the processing of sperm oil, this was the largest plant of its kind in the world. The reason why operations from Peru's three stations declined so markedly in 1964, and even more in 1965, was hardly because of reduced stocks of whales, but because of the price of sperm oil. The two companies then closed down, while the Compañía Ballenera del Norte continued, though concentrating now for a number of years more on the catching of baleen whales. Catches and the production of the two kinds of oil were varied in accordance with market prices, and in 1965-8 the prices of sperm oil fell drastically. When it rose again in 1969, and then rocketed to more than double the price in 1970 (from £84 to £177), the catching of sperm whales was once again intensified. The price of whale oil, too, showed similar, thought not as violent, fluctuations. The main reason for the fall in price was Peru's own tremendous production of fish oil and fish meal. Her total catch of fish in 1971-2 was 10,225,000 tons, and her production of meal 1,746,200 tons. Chr. Salvesen & Co. had a major interest in these fisheries, through their firm Propesca Peruaná from 1963, which in 1971-2 produced 79,200 tons of fish meal and 14,000 tons of fish oil. In April 1973 the Peruvian Government nationalised the entire fish meal industry, with the result that Salvesen lost their three factories. The following account occurs in the firm's annual report: "This has brought to an end a venture which lasted almost exactly ten years and which absorbed much of our energies after the end of whaling. It provided a useful and interesting bridge in the company's transition from whaling to more modern industries." With fish oil available in the market for £37, whale oil was not in a position to compete.

In their hunt for whale meat all round the world the Japanese eventually reached Chile, where the Taiyo Gyogyo K.K. hoped to establish a shore station in co-operation with a Chilean company. No concession, however, for this project was granted, partly because it was too close to the station of another company, and partly because the Japanese workers who were required for processing the meat ran up against a ban on the use of foreign labour.

The east coast of South America

The highly restricted whaling in these waters is confined to operations off the coast of Brazil. Hardly any information on this is available prior to 1948, when the country joined the Washington Convention. There was a small station, Imbituba, in the south, and a larger one, Costinha, near Recife (Pernambuco) in the north. Operations were clearly intensified after 1960, when it was taken over by the Japanese-Brazilian Sociedad de Pesca Taiyo. Catching was concentrated on the sei whale, in which the Japanese were particularly interested owing to its meat. These operations culminated in 1960-2 with approximately 775 animals annually, producing 3,000 to 4,000 tons of meat. In 1963 the yield slumped considerably, while at the same time catching of small numbers of fin and humpback whales ended. Since 1970 the sei whale, too, has almost entirely disappeared from these waters. As in the Antarctic, attempts have been made to compensate this by catching minke whales, some 700-1,000 a year. Brazil, which notified its withdrawal from the I.W.C. in 1966, rejoined in 1974, and was compelled from then on to operate in accordance with the accepted regulations, which co-ordinated pelagic with shore-based catching. This also applied to sperm whales, of which a certain number had been caught from Brazil every year from 1959.

Africa

We must crave the reader's indulgence in recording that the course of whaling off the African coast after the last war reflects the same picture as in all other whaling grounds — more shore stations and floating factories in the 1950s, rich catches of fin and humpback whales and a few blue whales, then sei and sperm whale catching in the 1960s, terminating in the 1970s with catching of sperm whales alone from one single shore station. This, in rough outline, is all that can be said, and yet at one time the scope of these operations was such that a few details are necessary to fill out the picture.

At about the same latitude as Recife in Brazil is the Republic of Gabon, once part of French Equatorial Africa. Since humpbacks had been allowed to frequent these waters in peace ever since 1937, whalers assumed that stocks were now restored and could be fished anew, whereas the biologists prophesied that history would repeat itself. They proved right: this time it took three years to destroy stocks, but the boom in whale oil was exploited, yielding large profits. As already mentioned, operations were started by the French-Norwegian company Sopecoba (Société des Pêcheries Cotières à la Baleine), registered in Port Gentil, Gabon, which was active in 1949-51, both from a shore station, Cap Lopez, and with a floating factory, the *Jarama* (the last one without a slipway). It will be recalled that France, by her protest at the I.W.C. meeting in 1949, despite the ban on use of floating factories north of 40°S, had forced through their use in French territorial waters round Gabon and Madagascar, with the express intention of allowing the *Jarama* to operate. This was an ominous undermining of the Convention at its very inception. On this occasion responsibility for decimating humpback stocks must be placed fair and square on France. In the French account of these operations the use of the floating factory is not mentioned. "As the use of a floating factory north of 40°S was not permitted", we read, "a station was set up at Cap Lopez."

Stocks of humpback whales were under still greater pressure when the Portuguese Government granted a Norwegian company a concession to operate from the island of Sao Tomé only 130 miles from Cap Lopez. The I.W.C.'s Scientific Committee declared that "this competition constitutes a threat to local stocks of humpback". The result was as might have been anticipated: Sopecoba made a killing in 1949 and 1950 with peak prices for oil, registering 1,400 humpbacks and 60,000 barrels every season, and approximately 1,900 tons of meat meal from the shore-based station. Already in 1951 there were signs of a slump, both companies totalling a mere 1,105 whales, which they tried to eke out with sei and sperm whale catches. The Norwegian company at Sao Tomé was forced to suspend operations with a deficit after this one season. Sopecoba then brought in a large floating factory (with slipway), which in 1949 and 1950 had made a rich haul of humpbacks round Madagascar. Despite using seven whale catchers, however, the result was only 16,500 barrels, and there can hardly have been a surplus. Since it was assumed, as usual, that stocks had built up after a few years, Sopecoba was granted a licence in 1959 for the catching of 600 humpbacks from a shore station, but the rèsult was a mere 160. From then on this species was protected in these waters, and after 1963 throughout Africa.

104. The Union Whaling Co.'s whaling station, Oceanside, near Durban, operated every year, 1909-76.

Apart from the Antarctic and Japan, South Africa has been the scene of the most constant operations in the history of modern whaling. During the Second World War, too, whaling was continued on a relatively large scale, only surpassed in the last years of the war by the Antarctic. Two-thirds of the whaling in South Africa was based on Natal and one-third was based on Cape Province. In Natal, operations were based on the Oceanside station at Bluff, outside Durban, operated throughout by the Union Whaling Co., which, established in 1909, is one of the oldest whaling companies in the world. Between 1947 and 1953 it also operated the station of its affiliate company, the Premier Whaling Co., but this, too, was closed down and operations and matériel transferred to Bluff, where in 1954-5 a large sum was spent on radical modernisation. It should be borne in mind that this station also operated pelagically between 1946 and 1957 in the Antarctic, using the former *Unitas*, and during this period was one of the major producers of whale and sperm oil. Economically, this company was highly successful between 1949 and 1952; from the point of view of production, the decade from 1957 to 1966 was the best, with an annual average of some 65,000 barrels. In the following year a marked decline occurred in the catching of both baleen and sperm whales, and while catching of the former almost reached vanishing-point (in 1975 twenty-one fin, one sei, and three Bryde whales), it picked up somewhat in the late 1970s (in 1975 1,682 sperm whales). At the conclusion of the 1976 season operations were provisionally suspended.

The Union Whaling Co. was the one to make most methodical use of aircraft for whaling from 1954 onwards. In local waters the whale is not stationary, but moves on its migration from day to day. For this reason the gunner is constantly on the lookout for his quarry. Aircraft can patrol large areas in a short time and direct the whale catchers. The pilot is accompanied by an experienced whaler, who from a height of 400 to 500 ft. can recognise the various species by the way in which they swim and blow. Since the early 1960s aerial reconnaissance and pursuit have taken place further and further out to sea. The whales are still hauled up the slip inside the mole in Durban harbour, and from there transported a mile and a half on specially built railway flats to the station. The processing of raw material is almost complete, most of the oil, meat, and meal being marketed in the country. All the workers were blacks, who generally had their own smallholdings up-country, where they worked during the summer, spending the winter at the station.

After the war, all whaling in Cape Province was carried out from the one station of Donkergat near Saldanha Bay by the Donkergat Whaling Co., of Cape Town. In order to exploit the boom, twelve boats were put into operation in 1952, but, even though production doubled, the tremendous apparatus involved failed to show a profit. Nor was the next season, with six boats, lower prices, and less than a half of the preceding year's production, any better. For this reason whaling was brought to a close in 1954-6, but renewed in 1957 by a reorganised company, Saldanha Whaling Ltd., which enjoyed a number of good years. By 1962 the fin whale had almost completely disappeared, and to make up for this great emphasis was placed on the catching of sei whales and its close relation, the Bryde whale, but when they, too, vanished, and the catch of sperm whales in 1967 produced only one-third (630) of the catch at Bluff (1,822), Donkergat station was closed down, presumably for good.

Table 35. CATCH FROM SOUTH AFRICA, 1946-1975

	Blue	Fin	Hump-back	Sei	Right	Bryde	Sperm	Total
Bluff, 1946-67	176	10,319	1,378	4,388	2	13	22,939	39,215
Donkergat, 1947-53, 1957-67	53	2,695	106	6,842	–	1,240	9,131	20,067
Bluff, 1968-75	–	457	1	95	–	30	13,699	14,282

Statistics for Bluff for 1946-67 and for Donkergat for 1947-53 and 1957-67, the years both stations were operating, show that the whale migration was different on the east and west coasts of Africa. Table 35 indicates that blue, fin, and humpback whales generally made for the east coast, while the sei whale and the Bryde whale made for the southwest coast. In this area the humpback continued on its route, making a landfall further north off Angola and the Congo. The Bryde whale appears to be much more markedly located round the west coast, and only occasionally has one proceeded east. As already mentioned, thorough investigations have been carried out on the relationship between the catching of the humpback in Australian and Antarctic waters. No similar investigation has been made as far as Africa is concerned, and for this reason it cannot be said with the same certainty as in Australia which Area in the Antarctic humpbacks make for in summer. It is, however, highly probable that they reach the east coast from Area III (0-70°E) and the west coast from Area II (0-60°W). Within these two Areas the catch of humpbacks was small compared to Area IV and V, from which the whales made their way up to Australia. As humpback catching in South African waters between 1946 and 1967 in terms of BWU only comprised 6.3 per cent of the total baleen whale catch, humpback catching there did not involve the same conflict with pelagic catching as in Australian waters.

In October 1975 Norway's leading national daily prominently displayed the news that the International Society for the Protection of Animals (I.S.P.A.) had accused the Norwegians of engaging in large-scale catching of threatened stocks of sei whales and fin whales off the coast of West Africa, in contravention of international quota agreements. The case in point involved the *Sierra,* a vessel which had reported to *International Whaling Statistics* that in 1974 it had caught 449 sei whales and two fin whales off West Africa. The company ran no risk in reporting this catch over and above the catch regulated by quota by the I.W.C., as it was registered in Somalia, a country that was not a member of the I.W.C. This boat had been built in Holland in 1960, as a fishing boat of 654 gross tons; in 1967 she was sold under the name of the *Run* to the Run Fishing Co., which was backed by Norwegian interests. She was converted to a combined catcher-factory ship, and caught off Angola from 1968. Her catch was quite considerable: in that first year she caught 366 sei and Bryde, 46 sperm and 3 minke whales, and produced 1,739 tons of meat and 62 tons of liver, which was supplied to the Japanese. In 1970 catch and production were almost double. The reason for this may be that the *Run* was operating in company with a small floating factory, the *Sao Nicolau,* of 1,957 gross tons, owned by a company registered in Monrovia (Liberia), and which operated along the west coast of Africa with two catchers. According to information supplied by the owners the floating factory was mainly used as a refrigeration and transport ship for the *Run,* apart from catching a few humpbacks.

In 1972 the Run Fishing Co. went bankrupt, the most important reason for this being that Britain intervened to ban its catching, a step that could be taken for the simple reason that the company was registered in Nassau in the Bahamas. The company was found guilty of catching forbidden species without a licence, and fined a sum of 13,516 Bahamas dollars. As it was no longer possible to continue operations in this way, the vessel was sold to the Sierra Fishing Agency in Somalia, and resumed catching off the Ivory Coast. The I.S.P.A. maintained that the boat had a Norwegian captain, and used indefensible whaling methods. Between 1968 and 1975, according to the company's returns, the boat caught a total of 4 fin, 2,876 sei and Bryde, 7 minke, and 780 sperm whales — considerably in excess of the strictly quota-regulated catch.

In the opinion of the I.S.P.A. 10 per cent of world catching was in contravention of regulations. Among the many important resolutions passed at the 1972 I.W.C. meeting was one to increase pressure on whaling nations outside the Convention in order to persuade them to join. This motion had the support of the United Nations, but came to nothing.

East Asia, North Pacific and Bering Sea

This includes operations from shore stations in Japan and the Kuril Islands, pelagic catching round Kamchatka, in the North Pacific and in the Bering Sea, i.e. in the ocean on both sides of the Aleutians. This does not include the brief period of pelagic Japanese whaling round the Bonin Islands in 1946-52 and Japanese operations from the shore station on the Ryukyu Islands (Okinawa) 1957-63, or the shore-based catching that started from Korea in 1965.

Even though the Convention of 1945 states that it "applies to all waters in which whaling is prosecuted", the entire prehistory from the 1930s and the first twenty years in which the Convention was in force show that its primary aim was to regulate pelagic catching in the Antarctic, and so overwhelmingly had the attention of the world been directed towards this kind of whaling and so one-sided was the work of the Commission in regulating, that it failed to concern itself to any great extent with the North Pacific until the mid-1960s, when it became obvious that there was a risk that developments in that area would follow the same pattern as in the Antarctic. The only two countries operating in the North Pacific, Japan and the Soviet Union, had therefore been able to proceed fairly freely, but as Antarctic catches declined and whaling in the North Pacific was intensified, the attention of the I.W.C. was turned in this direction too, and it became at the same time more and more obvious that effective regulation would have to be entire and global, and comprise both pelagic and shore-based whaling.

It may seem strange that the Japanese and Russians should not have run into any competition. Anyone attempting it, however, would have been doomed to failure. In the first place, catching takes place in the home waters of the two countries concerned, with only a short distance to and from the whaling grounds, and with resultant low costs as compared with a voyage to and from Europe. In the second place, production had to be based mainly on meat supplied to the Japanese market, and there were limits to what could be absorbed. In the third place, there would have been consternation if an outsider had tried to push his way into an area where the Japanese and Russians, by tacit agreement, had established a traditional right to be alone, the same right that Norway and Great Britain had believed they had in the Antarctic. That the Norwegians should not have succeeded between 1912 and 1922 in establishing lasting operations was because they only operated within the limited range from the shore station in Akutan, and not with a floating factory.

The decisive change in balance between the Antarctic and the North Pacific occurred in 1967. In terms of whales caught the Antarctic catch represented 38.7 per cent of world catches, in oil 40.3 per cent; comparable figures for the North Pacific were 45.9 per cent and 44.2 per cent. There was, however, one important difference : of the total number of whales in the Antarctic, 24.5 per cent were sperm whales, but in the North Pacific it was 63.3 per cent, and of total oil production in these two whaling grounds, sperm oil comprised respectively 36 per cent and 73 per cent.

After the war Japan lost several of her old whaling grounds, round Taiwan (started in 1919), the Bonin Islands (1923), Korea (1904), Sakhalin, Kamchatka (1940) and the Kurils (1913). Whaling thereafter had to be based on coastal operations round Japan and pelagic catching in the Antarctic and North Pacific. Around the Bonin Islands, a rich area for sei whales producing 200-300 animals annually, whaling was kept up till 1942. Although it represented no more than about 10 per cent of total Japanese coastal whaling, it was important because it took place during winter when there were few whales in Japanese waters and a shortage of whale meat. This was consequently the first area where the Japanese requested American permission to resume whaling. After their occupation of the islands, they were not allowed to rebuild their shore stations, but had to fish pelagically with two converted military transports of about 1,500 tons. Whaling was carried out from 1946-8 with one or more of these, with the somewhat larger *Kaiko Maru* (3,000 gross tons) in 1948-9 and the *Baikal Maru* (4,800 gross tons) in 1950-2. Although the catch rose to 411 sei whales in 1952, operations were not profitable, as it proved more expensive to operate with the floating factory than from a shore station. By April 1951 Japan had joined the International Whaling Convention, and as catching round the Bonin Islands took place so close to land that it was regarded as coastal catching, it was subject to the same rules as Japanese coastal fisheries, i.e. six continuous months from 1 May to 31 October. This made it impossible to carry on winter operations at a profit.

At Okinawa in the Ryukyu Islands, famous as the scene of bitter fighting during the last war, the Japanese had operated from a shore station as far back as several years before the First World War. The catch comprised almost entirely humpbacks, between fifty and seventy per annum, and although this was not very much, there was also a certain amount of profitable winter catching. In December 1957 the two Japanese companies Taiyo Gyogyo K.K. and Nitto Hogei K.K. were able to start up from a couple of shore stations, using three whale catchers in all. Now, too, only humpbacks were caught (plus a very few sperm whales), with a quota of 120 allotted to each company. But even with this rationing this subtropical humpback area suffered the fate that time and again had befallen all the others. In 1962 six catchers operating from three stations had a combined catch of only twenty-four humpbacks, and that was the end of that.

During the last year of the war Japan-based catching had slumped to 531 whales, but already in 1946 it had reached almost pre-war figures, 1,750, but so much was used for human consumption that only 5,719 barrels of oil were produced, or 3.3 barrels per whale. Up to 1947 catching was allowed all the year round, but from 1947 onwards, in accordance with the Washington Convention, it had to be restricted to six months. This meant that whaling from the southernmost island, Kyushu, which was essentially a winter occupation, had to be almost entirely abandoned, and many stations were closed down. Operations have to a large extent shifted north towards the northernmost portion of Honshu, and particularly to the northernmost island of Hokkaido. They have also shifted from west to east, as practically all catching in the Sea of Japan has closed down after the loss of the shore stations in Korea. It was from these that a great deal of the fin whale catching had taken place, and their loss was a hard blow.

There are assumed to be two distinct stocks of fin whales, one migrating through the Sea of Japan along Korea's east coast and one along Japan's Pacific coast. The catching of fin whales from Japan remained steady, with occasional fluctuations, at around 200 to 300 up to 1958, after which it showed a downward trend. Up to 1920 the southwestern waters were the main blue whale grounds: subsequently, this species disappeared from the catch. In the northeast, in the first post-war decade, twenty to forty were caught annually, and this appears to have been too much for stocks: after 1956 only a few were taken (between one and seven), until total protection for this species in 1965 put an end to these operations. Up to that year, from the Japanese shore stations (apart from the Bonin Islands), a few were caught every year. In the pursuit of whales for human consumption the sei whale played an increasingly important part. As already mentioned, the pursuit of this species from the shore stations in Japan, too, was subject to great fluctuations, from as many as 1,340 in 1959 and 1,229 in 1962 to 785 in 1960-1 and 291 in 1966. The decline in the catches of sei whales after 1970 has to some extent been made good by the catch of Bryde whale. From the Bonin Islands, where the sei whale is now allowed to proceed in peace, it migrates due north to the northeastern part of Japan, where practically all the catching takes place. Till recent years Bryde whale were included in sei whale catching. In 1968 the Commission resolved that the Bryde whale should be regarded biologically and statistically as a separate species.

Even though sperm whale meat is used to some extent for human consumption in Japan, it is the least sought after. For this reason most of the sperm whale is reduced to oil. During all the post-war years the number of sperm whales in Japanese coastal whaling has been greater than the total number of baleen whales, and in recent years this tendency has been accentuated, as the number of baleen whales has dropped. Of the total number, sperm whales represented 57 per cent in 1962, 80 per cent in 1966 and 1967, and 93 per cent in 1975. The profitability of Japanese coastal whaling has therefore increasingly depended on the price of sperm oil. When this dropped drastically after 1963, and as there was a glut of the less easily marketable sperm meat, a maximum quota for coastal catching of 1,800 was set for 1964 and 1965. When this limit was suspended, catches rose far above 3,000 in 1968-72.

Loss of territory after the war deprived Japan of many stations. In the first post-war period the number remained steady at ten, nine of them on the northeast coast, and only one, Oshima, on the south coast of Honshu. The number of whale catchers was limited to twenty-five in active operations, some of them being used for pelagic catching in the North Pacific. Nippon Suisan K.K. attempted in 1952 to revive catching in the Sea of Japan from Senzaki, in the southwest corner of Honshu, where modern Japanese whaling had seen the light of day in 1896. After very poor seasons in 1952 and 1953, however, the station was finally closed down : it was probably situated too far from the whale migration. In order to intercept this as it passed into the Tsushima Straits from the East China Sea, Taiyo Gyogyo K.K. initiated catching in 1955 from the station (Arakawa) on the southern tip of the Goto Islands (Fukushima), immediately west of Nagasaki on Kyushu. The result was remarkable : 225 fin whales with two catchers, whereas all the other stations, operating with twenty-five, only managed to kill 129. In 1956 Nippon Suisan K.K., too, commenced whaling from another station (Tomie) on the same island, and a total of 277 fin whales were caught from these two stations using three boats, whereas all the others registered a mere seventy. In order to preserve whale stocks, a maximum quota of 300 was set for the Goto area. The reason why the fin whale stopped here on its migration north was the abundance of plankton, as the warmer northgoing Kuroshio current met colder water from the north. The whaling grounds were situated as much as 150 km. from the station, halfway between Kyushu and the coast of China, and this involved a long tow of the whale. In order to keep the animal as fresh as possible, it was not inflated with air but allowed to sink to the bottom, where the water temperature was about 14°C, compared to 24-27°C on the surface. The towline was cut, and a balloon or radio buoy was fastened to the other end. It was possible to employ this method here as these waters are comparatively shallow, approximately 50 fathoms at the deepest. After the whale had been "parked" in this way, the whale catcher could set off in pursuit of fresh prey, without having to tow it alongside, as was done round Iceland.

We shall deal below with the production of by-products; at this stage mention, however, should be made of two Japanese special products in the use of whale for human consumption. This is the use of the tail fin and the belly blubber (see diagram). The tail fin (*oba*) is cut off at line A when the whale is secured alongside the whale catcher; these pieces are discarded. At the station the rest of the tail fin is cut off at B, and the pieces cut in slices of a thickness of about 3 cm. and salted down. Retailers would then cut these into extremely thin slivers (under 1 mm.) called *obake*, and these are then cooked in the traditional way in the home. The belly blubber consists of an outer layer, called *une*, and the inner meat, called *sunoko*, together referred to as *unesu*. During flensing this is cut into blocks of about 35 cm. square, and this again is cut into thinner slices and used as whale bacon, or the two layers are separated and the *une* cooked in thin slices like whale fin. *Sunoko* is very tough, and is mainly canned. The thin slices of tail fin are also eaten raw; they are considered a great delicacy, and fetch the highest price. The belly blubber is often cooked in order to extract some of the oil and sold in the dried state. The price of whale meat goes according to season: it drops when large supplies arrive from the Antarctic during the spring, and in the summer, when there are ample supplies of fresh meat from the shore stations and from pelagic catching in the North Pacific. The price of whale meat is about one-third the price of beef. During the war one of the few successful attempts to produce efficient leather from whale skin was made in Japan. The skin of the sperm whale's head proved suitable for shoes, and at that time large numbers of Japanese wore shoes of whale (and shark) leather. In 1938, the Japanese whaling companies jointly set up a factory (Kyoritsu Suisan Kogyo K.K.) for the manufacture of whale leather. It operated success-

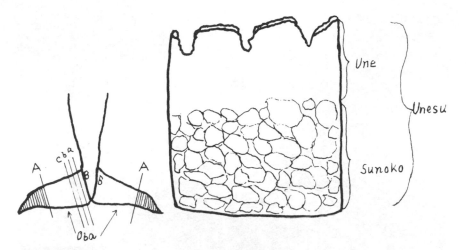

105. The Japanese partition of the whale for human consumption. On the left, the division of the tail fin, *oba*; on the right, the division of the belly blubber and meat, *unesu*. (Drawing by Dr. Hideo Omura.)

fully during the war, but was closed down shortly afterwards.

Encouraged no doubt by Japanese whaling in the East China Sea, the Chinese People's Republic decided to try its hand at whaling. In April 1956 the catching of small cetaceans in the Yellow Sea was started under the auspices of the state-owned company Talien Marine Products Co. using a converted fishing boat of 30 tons. The captain had served for eighteen years with Japanese whaling expeditions, where, despite racial discrimination, he had managed to attain the rank of gunner. On the island of Haiyang outside Dairen (Port Arthur) a modern whale station was erected. "We need more powerful guns and more experienced personnel", said the captain. "It will take time, but we shall then not only catch large whales here, but we shall be able to organise a fleet for Antarctic operations." It certainly took time: not till 1964 could the Chinese Information Service proudly display the picture of the first modern Chinese whale catcher, the *Yanlung* ("Big Dragon"), built at the Chuishin Shipyards in Shanghai. It had a diesel engine of 1,200 h.p., a speed of 13 knots, and a crew of twenty-four. On 22 April 1964, the first whale was killed in the northern Yellow Sea. This was a 61 ft. fin whale. It was pursued from 8 a.m. until the first shot found its mark at 5 p.m., but not until 9 p.m. was it killed by a second shot. "It was by far the biggest whale China had ever caught." The only other information available was that "a large number of big whales were caught". The Chinese must have lowered their sights somewhat, because after their first whale they declared: "We will sail far out into the East China Sea for even bigger whales." During the early 1970s the Japanese, too,

106.   The first (and only ?) Chinese-built whale catcher *Yanlung* ("Big Dragon"),
built in Shanghai 1963-4.

caught a number of fin whales in these waters.

For the catch of the Republic of Korea, see Statistical Appendix,
Tables 70 and 71. Till 1979 Korea was not a member of the I.W.C.,
and for this reason its catch is supplementary to the quotas laid down
for members (Japan and the Soviet Union). This also applies to Japan's
catches in the East China Sea.

The Japanese appear to have kept up the catching they had started
from shore stations in the Kurils in 1913 right up to 1942. This was
then discontinued, until the Russians, after annexation of the islands,
renewed catching in 1948 from five stations, continuing until 1955,
subsequently restricting operations in 1962 to two stations, and halting
all shore-based catching after 1964. Baleen whaling was mainly for fin
and sei whales, reaching a peak in 1958 with respectively 328 and 336.
In that year, too, sperm whale catching reached a peak, with 2,184,
production culminating in 62,478 barrels. A certain number of blue
whales were also caught (forty-five and forty-four in 1956 and 1957)
and a few humpbacks, but in no whaling ground did the number of
sperm whales represent such a large percentage of the total number of
whales from 1948 to 1964 as in this: 82 per cent. After the peak year,
1958, catching of all species declined drastically, and when the total
number in 1964 amounted to only 563 (452 sperm), operations in this
area were closed down in favour of a more intensive pelagic effort.

This whaling in the North Pacific was started by the Russian factory ship *Aleut* in 1932, six years after the last Norwegian attempt at whaling in these waters. The *Aleut* operated mainly along the east coast of Kamchatka, and as far as is known throughout all the war years, even though no figures are available for 1944 and 1945. Baleen whales exceeded sperm whales in number. A certain number of gray whales were also killed, 340 between 1938 and 1943, while on the east side of the Pacific every effort was being made to preserve stocks. In common with the Greenland whale, the gray whale, too, was accorded total protection by the Washington Convention as from 1947, with the proviso, however, that it could be caught by the aborigines for human consumption. From the northeast coast of Siberia a considerable number were caught between 1969 and 1975, producing an annual average of 166. The Commission set a quota for 1980 of 179, the average of the previous ten seasons' catches.

The *Aleut* operated alone in this area up to 1940, when the Japanese for the first time started here with a factory ship, proceeding north as far as the Arctic pack ice and returning after eighty days with 681 whales. In 1941 they operated round Kamchatka, killing 590. Half the total catch these two years consisted of fin whales, of which very ample stocks were discovered. In 1950-1 the Japanese operated with a factory ship round the Bonin Islands and in 1952 both there and along the east coast of Kamchatka, and the south coast of the Western Aleutians. The expedition was a success, recording 749 whales, eighteen of them sperm. In 1953 the expedition proceeded northwards only, killing 701 baleen whales, of which 470 were fin and ninety-one blue. There was no doubt that this was a particularly rich whaling ground. Plentiful stocks of sperm whales were also observed.

For convenience's sake the Japanese divided this part of the North Pacific into three areas: the A area, bounded to the west by southern Kamchatka, to the north by the Commander Islands, to the east by one of the Western Aleutians, and to the south by 50° latitude N; the B area, running along its northern side; and the C area, along the south side of the Eastern Aleutians. As for the migration paths of the various species, it was observed that while the blue whale in the Antarctic migrated all the way to the continental ice, it was seldom observed north of the Aleutians. This was also true of the sei whale. The sperm whale made its way some distance up the Bering Sea, while the fin and humpbacks passed through the Bering Strait into the Arctic Ocean.

In 1954 a new factory ship was given permission to catch 350 BWU by way of an experiment in the B and C areas. This was the first time a Japanese factory ship had operated so far to the east as Akutan, where with a few intervals, operations had taken place from a shore station between 1912 and 1939. The factory had no difficulty in filling its quota in three months. With both Japanese factory ships operating in the Antarctic, they could not, in accordance with the international Convention, be used till at least a year had passed for catching baleen whales in any other area, a rule which at Japan's request was suspended for the North Pacific by the I.W.C. in 1970. With the marked reduction in catches in both areas, it was increasingly incumbent economically on Japanese whaling to operate with two sets of floating factories, one for each area. Until this change was made, the "Antarctic" factory ships were licensed to catch sperm whales in the North Pacific.

There was no binding agreement between Russians and Japanese to divide the whaling grounds between them, but they respected one another's preserves strictly, as though bound by agreement. While the Japanese took over the whole of Areas B and C off the Aleutians, the Russians ruled the roost in Area A round Kamchatka. Consequently, the catches registered in the statistics for the Bering Sea are entirely Japanese, and those under Kamchatka entirely Soviet.

In Aleutian catching the number of blue whales allowed to be killed was set at seventy in 1955, an amount that was caught right up to 1961, when there was a slight downward trend. Catches of fin whales remained very constant — around 1,000–1,400 between 1954 and 1966 — but after 1967 showed a more marked decline. Every year an occasional humpback was also killed. The catching of sei whales was greatly intensified, as in the Antarctic, and for the same reason. Numbers rose from 260 in 1962 to 3,474 in 1967, and remained above the 3,000 level right up to 1970. In this area, too, as round Japan, the catching of sperm whales has at times been limited, to 1,700 in 1957, 1,500 in 1958, 1,800 in 1959-61, 2,700 in 1963, and 3,000 in 1966-9. In 1961-3 a licence was granted for the catching of three right whales annually for scientific purposes. For baleen whales a maximum quota was set, as we shall see, in order to preserve stocks in this area, which were of increasingly vital importance to Japan's supplies of food as the Antarctic quota declined, and whaling in the other Pacific areas came to an end (after 1964), and as baleen whale catches based on Japan were of little importance. In 1967 the Japanese catch in terms of BWU in the Bering Sea was two-thirds that of the catch in the Antarctic.

Soviet whaling expansion also started slowly in the North Pacific. Just as the *Slava* operated alone in the Antarctic between 1946 and 1958, so did the *Aleut* off Kamchatka between 1932 and 1961. Expansion then took place here just as suddenly and on as big a scale as in the Antarctic. Between Antarctic seasons the *Sovetskaya Rossiya* caught sperm whales off Kamchatka between 1962 and 1965. In 1963 the new factory ships *Dalnij Vostok* and *Vladivostok*, sister ships of 17,000 tons, went into service. These were specially built for whaling in these areas by the Howaldtswerke A.G. in Kiel, which, apart from these ships, has also supplied a large number of trawlers and factory ships to the Soviet Union. The two vessels were equipped both as floating whale factories and fish processing factories. Up to 1968 they appear to have been used mainly for whaling. During the five seasons 1963-7 the *Dalnij Vostok* had an annual average catch of 3,515 whales and a production of 107,933 barrels and the *Vladivostok* of 3,829 and 111,930. More than 80 per cent of the oil was sperm oil. Off Kamchatka, the richest annual catch of sperm whales ever harvested in any one area was made, averaging annually between 1963 and 1971 7,500, over one-third of the entire world catch of sperm whale. The production of sperm oil was well over 300,000 barrels annually, and the large quantities on offer in the world market were largely responsible for forcing the price down. The catching of baleen whales showed the same trend as in the other areas; there was a decline in the case of fin whales after 1964, and a rise in the number of sei whales right up to 1969. In 1963 stocks of humpbacks received a marked setback with the killing of 2,242 animals; the following year only 10 per cent of this number was recorded. As from 1966 this species and the blue whale were totally protected. In that year the *Slava* was transferred from the Antarctic to the North Pacific. When the *Aleut* completed her last season in 1967 she was the factory ship with the largest number of seasons behind her (thirty-four), covering a span from 1932 to 1967 (less 1944 and 1945). Second in the world ranking list come the Norwegian factory ships *Thorshammer* with thirty-three, *Sir James Clark Ross* with thirty, and the *Pelagos* with twenty-eight. The *Slava* also completed twenty-eight seasons.

Initially, the I.W.C. was not concerned with whaling in the North Pacific, which was of such limited scope that it could not constitute a danger to stocks. The pelagic catching of baleen whales was permitted between the coasts of North America and Asia, from 20°N to 66°N, and from 66°N to 72°N between 150°E and 140°W, i.e. the Arctic Ocean between the New Siberian Islands and the Canadian-Alaskan border. Off the west coast of Mexico and Lower California there was a forbidden zone between 20°N and 35°N as far as 150°W. The first time the attention of the Commission was drawn to pelagic whaling in the Pacific was in 1953, when Canada considered it advisable to prohibit the use of factory ships in this area. When the Scientific Committee was set up in 1954, with N. A. Mackintosh as chairman, its working area was to include pelagic whaling in the North Pacific. This now assumed a larger dimension, with the arrival on the scene of two Japanese expeditions in addition to the Soviet one. In its first report the Committee merely stated that continued investigation was necessary in order to obtain more certain information on the size of whale stocks. The resolution at the Tokyo meeting in 1954 to protect the blue whale for five years from 1 January 1955 encountered a protest first from Japan and the Soviet Union, subsequently from others, and proved ineffective. The Japanese declared that as stocks had been allowed to rest for fifteen years, they had probably increased. In spite of this the Japanese set a quota, as from 1955, of seventy for the Bering Sea, and the Commission appealed to others to follow Japan's example if a limitation in some other way proved impossible. The question was to be left in abeyance until the 1957 investigations had produced more concrete results. Apart from the Japanese restriction on blue whale catches, the Scientific Committee declared in its findings of March 1958 that there was no need for further regulation, as the Soviet Union appeared particularly interested in the catching of sperm whale. The Committee drew attention, however, to the increasing importance of whaling throughout the North Pacific, amounting in 1957 to approximately 11,000 whales, almost one-third of the total Antarctic catch. There seemed no sign of decline in sperm whale stocks, and provided the minimum size limit was observed, a continuation of the state of things could be anticipated with satisfaction, although it was striking that a large number of sperm whales were only just over the minimum length. "This looks unnatural" — a statement that was subsequently to recur again and again. A certain limitation took place in 1959, when Japan announced that 400 fewer whales would be caught, and that larger animals would be pursued; meanwhile, the Soviet Union reduced its number round the Kurils by 300.

Not till 1962, owing to intensified whaling, were more effective measures taken by the Commission in setting up a special committee to study whale stocks in the North Pacific. It included representatives of Canada, Japan, the United States, and the Soviet Union. The question was, in fact, left to national interests, not as in the Antarctic. The above-mentioned *ad hoc* committee agreed to the Japanese request to lower the minimum measurement for sperm from 35 to 33 ft., but only on the condition that this applied to shore stations and that Japan was given a quota of 1,800 for her land-based operations. This was repeated from 1962 to 1965, although in 1962 the Commission refused to agree to lowering of the minimum measurement before the economic and biological effects were known. In the first report of the special Pacific Committee (June 1963) Canada maintained that the very opposite course should be adopted and the minimum measurement raised to 38 ft. (as for pelagic catching), in order to lower the increasing proportion of sperm whales in the world catch. On the question of stocks of baleen whales, the Committee declared that it had not yet sufficient material to prove over-fishing, "but it was imperative to provide data in order to discover signs of a decline". This statement is typical not only of this Committee, but of the approach of the entire Commission, which was incapable of preventing a decline in stocks of whales before it was proved that there *was* a decline, nor could it reduce the decline before it had been established with a reasonable degree of certainty *how great* this decline was. At its June 1964 meeting the Scientific Committee of the Commission concluded that there was no objection to suspending the minimum length for sperm whales if the countries in whose whaling grounds catching took place introduced such a strict limitation of catching that the continued maintenance of stocks would be ensured. Until that time, the minimum length would have to be observed, "but it is unfortunately all too clear that it is not observed".

At its meeting held at the same time the Pacific Committee emphasised the disturbing increase in catching in 1961-3, an increase accounted for almost entirely by the Soviet Union, of blue whales from 92 to 457, of fin whales from 1,876 to 2,569, of humpbacks from 500 to 2,353, and of sperm whales from 7,283 to 11,165. The number of expeditions had increased from three to seven, and their whale catchers from thirty to sixty-seven. The catching of baleen whales had shifted east, and in 1963 most of this species were taken in the Gulf of Alaska. No concrete proposal for regulation was submitted by the Committee, nor was one dealt with by the Commission, however urgent it considered the need for this. It merely proposed that a committee of the same four countries as the foregoing should meet every year at the conclusion of the season and go through catching results. For regulation in the North Pacific of pelagic catching the Commission's resolutions, in fact, proved even more of a sham than was the case for the Antarctic. Japan and the Soviet Union were the only nations who would be affected, and they were in a position to veto any proposal, and in fact to decide on any regulation as they might desire. The only step taken at the Commission's meeting in 1964 was a recommendation from the Scientific Committee for complete protection of blue and humpback whales for 1966 — and a request not to catch more in 1965 than in 1964, which was partly agreed on. A New Zealand proposal to ban the catching of sperm whales from factory ships within 500 miles of a shore station was almost adopted, nine voting for and four against. Not unexpectedly, Japan and the Soviet Union protested most vigorously.

The most important step taken by the Commission at the 1965 meeting was a unanimous resolution to protect blue whales for five years and humpbacks for one year, starting in 1966, until more detailed investigations had been made. This, however, did not mean any decline in the total exploitation of baleen whales. A request not to exceed 1,800 BWU was not agreed to. During the first half of 1966 a number of meetings were held (in Honolulu and London) by various committees, particularly the one dealing with the North Pacific. Japan and the

Soviet Union had no objection to total protection of blue and hump-back whales, and both agreed to set a BWU limit for catching of baleen whales, but whereas Japan was only prepared to accept this for pelagic whaling, the Soviet Union, in common with its standpoint in the south, insisted that it should also include shore stations. The Russians had, they declared, unilaterally reduced their catching of baleen whales to about one-half in the course of three years, from 1,911 BWU in 1963 to 1,030 in 1965. In the case of shore stations Japan was not prepared to go further than to set a limit corresponding to the 1962-4 average (when there had been a particularly good catch of sei). The Soviet Union protested against this, as it would mean that the catch in 1966 would be double that in 1965. The Scientific Committee supported the Soviet proposal. In 1966 the Commission resolved that countries operating in the North Pacific should arrive at an agreement which in 1969 would ensure that the catch of fin whales was below the sustainable yield. The regulation in force for the catching of sei and sperm whales appeared suitable and would not be changed until the size of stocks had been more closely investigated.

This is remarkable, as it is not known that any limit was set for sei whales; on the contrary, the catching of this species had grown markedly and steadily from 1961, even after 1966, the number caught rising to over 2,000 in 1967. The only regulations known were those of Japan which, after 1954, had fixed a quota of 800 BWU for the Bering Sea, increased to 1,000 in 1965, and the above-mentioned quota for sperm whales in certain years in Japanese waters and in the Bering Sea. At a meeting of the Pacific nations in February 1967 a sharp clash occurred. In 1965 a gentleman's agreement had been concluded to keep the catching of fin whales in 1966 10 per cent below that for 1965. The Soviet Union emphasised that they had done this by lowering the number round Kamchatka from 1,492 to 1,347, and castigated the Japanese who, from their shore stations, had increased their catch from 71 to 104; Canada (British Columbia) had done the same from 83 to 134. On the basis of the bare figures, the Soviet Union was in the right, but Japan emphasised that she had reduced her pelagic catch just as much, from 1,406 to 1,266, and that shore-based catching played a less important role in the total exploitation of the whale. At a fresh meeting in November 1967 there was another sharp conflict between the Soviet Union, which at that time only operated pelagically, and the other three countries operating from shore stations, on the exploitation of the same species of whale, an exact parallel to the conflict between Australia and the pelagic nations on the humpback. Faced with the Soviet Union's demand for equal regulation for both methods, Canada pointed out that it was beyond doubt that it was the Soviet Union's own over-fishing of blue whales in 1963 (347) and of humpbacks in 1964 (2,500) from which the others were now suffering. "When that sort of thing happens, the desired principle of equality goes by the board, since one nation enjoys the advantage of over-exploitation, whereas all nations are forced to adopt precautions for the rebuilding of stocks without regard for their share in their decimation." The Soviet answer was that the others had shown themselves unwilling to reduce catches of fin and sei whales, in spite of the fact that the Scientific Committee declared that stocks were endangered, and both the Japanese and Russians vastly increased their catch of sei whales in 1967 (all in all, from 4,044 to 6,007), while from stations on the east coast it declined from 414 to ninety-two. A proposal from the United States and Canada to forbid pelagic whaling east of 140°W was turned down outright by Japan and the Soviet Union as violating the freedom of the seas.

All in all, there was such a conflict of ideas that it was surprising when, at the I.W.C. meeting in 1968, the Commission for the North Pacific announced that there had been a voluntary limit on fin and sei whale catching for 1968, and a proposal had been agreed on for 1969 for a quota of 1,600 fin whales (exclusive of the East China Sea), and that the catch of sei whales would not exceed that of 1967 (6,153), while the catch of fin whale was 2,273. The final result was a total quota for 1970 of 1,332 fin, 4,924 sei, and 11,273 sperm whales. In the case of the first two species this meant a reduction of 10 per cent of the 1969 quota and for the last-mentioned 10 per cent reduction on 1968. Fin whales could be converted into sei whales or vice versa, calculated in terms of BWU, provided the number of each species did not exceed the 1969 quota. This agreement applied to pelagic whaling. For land-based catching Japan, the Soviet Union and the United States agreed not to exceed the 1969 catch. At the same time the I.W.C. agreed to extend by three years total protection of blue and humpback whales. It is, in other words, worth noting that the main difference from regulations in the Antarctic was that in the case of pelagic catching of baleen whales in the North Pacific no open season was fixed. Japan mentioned this at the Commission's meeting in 1966, but no proposal on it was put forward. There was also this difference: that the maximum quota was set, not in terms of BWU but for each single species, as had often been proposed for the Antarctic but not introduced there before 1972-3.

At the Commission's twenty-first meeting in 1969 delegates were congratulated in the opening address on the important agreement to limit catching of fin and sei whales in the North Pacific. This augured success maybe for the coming twenty-one years. But in the opening address the speaker, a representative of the British Government, was forced to admit that, in comparing the high ideals and aspirations of 1946 with the fact that three nations had been forced to withdraw from Antarctic catching, he was not sure on what grounds he could congratulate the Commission on the past twenty-one years. "But although this flame that was started in 1946 has perhaps been flickering and burning rather low, it still burns. On looking back, the Commission can, I think, legitimately congratulate itself on the fact that but for its work the whole stocks in some areas might well have been extinct altogether, and that through the deliberations of the Commission there has been a greater readiness among member countries to recognise the danger signals and to take action in time."

The Commission stood to pay silent homage to its father, Dr. Remington Kellogg, who had died the previous year.

36

THE WHALING INDUSTRY, ENVIRONMENT AND NATURAL RESOURCES, 1972-1978

The interest in environmental conservation and the preservation of natural resources has been reflected in the setting up of a number of international organisations, which have launched attacks on whaling and the International Whaling Commission. They were given an opportunity of participating in I.W.C. meetings as observers, and submitting their views. At the meeting in Canberra in 1977, the following organisations were represented: the United Nations Food and Agriculture Organisation (F.A.O.), the International Union for Conservation of Nature and Natural Resources, the Fauna Preservation Society, the Friends of the Earth, Greenpeace, the International Society for the Protection of Animals, and the World Wildlife Fund. Together, they presented a formidable opposition to whaling, though only too often using arguments based on emotional rather than factual grounds. At the 1974 meeting of the I.W.C., the Mexican delegate concluded his speech with words that sum up the attacks on the Commission: "This Commission will be known to history as a small body of men who failed to act responsibly in terms of their very large commitment to the world, and who protected the interests of the few whalers and not the future of thousands of whales."

It was unfair to attack the Commission as such, and to mock it for ineffectiveness. A majority of members had long sought a drastic reduction of catching, but they ran up against the Commission's own Rules of Procedure, which made it impossible, despite a rule for a three-fourths majority, to prevent a member getting his way. In time, however, the pressure of world opinion became so strong that in the 1970s no member was prepared to defy it. The two big surviving whaling nations, Japan and the Soviet Union, opposed a reduction of quotas for as long as possible. It was difficult to take the Soviet delegate seriously when he thundered against a proposal to lower the quota for sei whales in the Pacific from 3,000 to 2,000, insisting on 2,400 which would be divided approximately on the basis of two-thirds to Japan and one-third to the Soviet Union. In other words, with a quota of 3,000 the Soviet Union would have 1,000, and with a quota of 2,000 it would have 655. What would be the effect of forfeiting these 345 sei whales (= 57.5 BWU)? "The proposed sharp drop in the sei whale catch by over 30 per cent poses a problem to our industry, a problem which essentially is impossible to solve. It would damage the economy to an extent to which we could not agree." The quota was set at 2,000, which the Soviet Union accepted without protest, and even Japan voted in favour.

The I.W.C. also realised how ineffective this measure was. At its 1972 meeting the United Kingdom delegate admitted "We are in danger of making ourselves ridiculous", when an interminable debate was carried on to decide whether the quota for fin whales was to be 2,000, 1,960, 1,950, 1,900, 1,800 or 1,600. The Chairman's remark, after a figure of 1,950 had finally been adopted, was certainly not ironical in its intention. "I want to thank you", he said, "for working out a solution to what was a very difficult problem. I think this is another great victory for this meeting — at least it is from the Chairman's point of view."

The main reason why the attacks on whaling in the I.W.C. were so greatly intensified, and the working methods of the Commission were so radically changed after 1972, is to be found in the three-part resolution on whaling adopted by the U.N. Conference on the Human Environment at Stockholm in that year. The resolution's three points were : an increase in international research efforts on whales, a strengthening of the I.W.C., and a ten-year moratorium on commercial whaling. We shall see how the I.W.C. reacted to these demands.

We shall take last item first. The United States was the country most strongly in favour of the principle of a total ban for an indefinite period on all catching, or alternatively "a ten-year moratorium on commercial whaling". (The word "commercial", as we shall see, is important.) The United States submitted proposals to this effect at the I.W.C. meetings in 1971, 1972 and 1973. In 1971 the I.W.C. Scientific Committee stated that it could not recommend the proposal, and this for two reasons. In the first place, it aimed to regulate catching of all species of whales as though these comprised one group, whereas it was necessary to regulate catching on an individual basis. Secondly, it was precisely through whaling that scientific research obtained its most important information. In both 1972 and 1973 the proposal was turned down. As expected, almost all passive whaling countries voted in favour of the moratorium, whereas the active ones (Iceland, Japan, South Africa and the Soviet Union) opposed it. That Norway should have been the only passive country to vote against caused some surprise, but on the whole this was on formal grounds : the I.W.C. had seldom achieved positive results in decisions that ran counter to the interests of its members. All the passive members had to realise that adoption of the proposal would mean a complete breakdown of the I.W.C. The Soviet Union's arguments were also of a formal nature. Its delegate observed sarcastically to the American proposer, Dr. R. M. WHITE : "Regardless of his background or experience, he is a newcomer to our Commission. As for the agreements on the allocation of quota and on the international observer scheme, Dr. White does not appear to know the sad history of our Commission." He bluntly declared that the Soviet Union would not respect a ten-year moratorium, and was supported by Japan.

At the 1974 meeting, the United States declared that, even after the sharp drop which there had been in the previous season's catch, it would once again propose a ten-year moratorium. But this proposal too failed to obtain the necessary majority. The United States then proposed that a ten-year period of intensive whaling research, called the International Decade of Cetacean Research, be established. Canada declared that it had contributed to the moratorium by halting all catching along the west coast in 1967 and along the east coast (two stations in Newfoundland and one in Nova Scotia) in 1972, not only for economic reasons but also to preserve stocks. As there seemed no prospect of getting the moratorium adopted, pressure for a reduction of quotas increased, while on the opposite side Japan, most of all, fought a bitter fight to preserve the little that was still left. Clearly, world opinion against whaling — and sealing — was having its effect; it was easier for the I.W.C. to have strict regulations adopted without protest, and the active whaling nations did not dare to use their protests to evade the quota that had been adopted. However, they did not give in without a struggle. For example, in 1976 ten rounds of voting were needed before the quota for male sperm whales in one particular area could be established. One has the definite impression that the Japanese were very anxious lest the I.W.C. or the United Nations would adopt a moratorium or even a total and indefinite ban, and that of the two possible evils the lesser was preferable: "It was a serious blow to our fishery industry", said Japan's delegate, "and for this reason our industry watches the outcome of the meeting with vital concern." He had the last word at this meeting: "My delegation is really disappointed with the results of this conference."

When New Zealand rejoined the I.W.C. in 1976 after an absence of eight years, the event was greeted with great satisfaction, and the New Zealand delegate said that his country's principal reason for resuming work with the I.W.C. was consideration for world opinion: "When New Zealand left the Commission in 1968 the international community was perhaps less sensitive than today to environment and conversation issues. Much has changed in the world since 1968. The past few years have seen a new spirit in the Commission and new measures which demonstrate a determination to make it a more effective body. . . . Like it or not, the whale is now a symbol of mankind's failure to manage the world's resources responsibly. The attention of concerned people throughout the world now focuses on the decisions of this Commission with an intensity none of us would have thought possible when the Commission was established." The I.W.C. could be excused on the ground that there were no similar international organs on whose experience it could base itself, and this might explain some of the mistakes that had been committed.

Within the I.W.C., opinion was sharply divided over the extent to which the Commission should go in taking public opinion into account. Essentially, discussion at the 1973 meeting revolved around this point. As might have been expected, the extremes were represented by the United States and the Soviet Union, in accordance with the political systems of those countries. In a long speech, the American delegate maintained that the "I.W.C. cannot emerge from this Conference without committing itself firmly to end fin whaling if it is to maintain the credibility of the Organisation before the world. . . . I do not believe that my Government will run the risk of affronting world opinion by continuing to take fin whales. . . . Are we here to serve the whaling industry or to serve the world?" The Soviet delegate replied very sharply: "At the present meeting there was a tendency which suggested that the basis of the decisions of the Commission should not be formed out of the recommendations of science but out of so-called public opinion. What will happen if each Commissioner addresses himself not to well-grounded scientific data but to public opinion when seeking support for his position . . . ? The Soviet delegation hopes that the agenda of the next meeting will be relieved of this ballast." The Japanese delegate feared that a suspension of fin whaling would merely be a step in the direction of a total ban on the catching of one species after another.

The United States should have been warned not to throw stones while occupying such a sensitive glasshouse. One of the mistakes for which the I.W.C. was criticised was that it had merely concerned itself with the larger cetaceans. It had been quite natural for it to do so, since as long as there were enough of these species, the catching of minor cetaceans had been insignificant, although interest in them increased in proportion as catches of the larger species declined. In 1972 the Scientific Committee declared *inter alia* of its "research needs" that it felt its priority to be large whales and whaling, "but where smaller cetaceans, including dolphins and porpoises, are taken, these should also be a main concern of the Committee. Catches of certain dolphins taken by aboriginals or incidentally in purse-seine fisheries have now reached considerable proportions, and the opinion has been expressed by some members that the Scientific Committee should take some action on these problems." It was proposed to set up a "Sub-committee on Small Cetaceans", entrusted with the collection of data on them; "this would supplement the tables in *International Whaling Statistics* on small whales." It might thus appear that the *I.W.S.* had not previously provided such figures, but they had in fact been published since 1953, and were comprehensive and detailed even in the 1960s, and more so in the 1970s.

The above statement was occasioned by the Committee's "concern over the large incidental kill of porpoises and dolphins in the U.S. tuna fishery, reported to be about 250,000 per year". These animals were killed when they were caught in fishermen's nets and drowned. They were not processed in any way at all, and there was worldwide dismay when the incredible extent of this wastage became generally known, the more so as the United States had exerted the strongest pressure to have a ten-year moratorium on commercial whaling introduced. They excused themselves by stating that mass killings of small cetaceans were not "commercial" but merely "incidental killing". Tremendous quantities were involved : according to the United States' own figures, more than 300,000 in each year from 1970 to 1972. Certain measures reduced this figure somewhat in 1973-5, but even then it amounted to some 136,000 annually. Altogether, in the course of six years 1.34 million had been killed in this, the world's greatest example of waste, so total because nothing whatever was processed or utilised.

Among members themselves the feeling grew that the organisation was not sufficiently up-to-date and that the Commission, the Convention and the Schedule required revision. In this respect 1972 proved a significant year. The meeting was probably the most representative of all, comprising 102 participants, of whom fourteen were Commissioners, sixty-five consultants, seventeen observers, and six members of the Secretariat. The United States, which most strongly championed a total cessation of all whaling, arrived with as many as nineteen consultants; Japan, which defended its position most stoutly, had fifteen, and the United Kingdom, which supported the United States, had eight. The most important resolutions were the following :

1. The Observer Scheme was finally put into operation. As already mentioned, it had had a long pre-history before the agreement was signed in 1963. It lapsed at the conclusion of the 1965-6 season, without having been practised. A new agreement adopted in 1968 was extended to include "any place in the world oceans", and in this form the agreement was adopted in 1971. Member-countries agreed to exchange observers, in such a way that an Australian was stationed in South Africa and a South African in Australia, an Icelander in Norway, a Canadian in Iceland, and a Norwegian in Canada; in the North Pacific Russians were stationed on the three Japanese factory ships and Japanese on the two Soviet ships, and there were two United States observers at the Japanese shore stations. In the case of the Antarctic the two whaling nations sought to delay as much as possible — "owing to practical difficulties", they said, it was impossible to introduce the scheme during the 1971-2 season. At the I.W.C. meeting in 1972, Japan, Norway and the Soviet Union committed themselves to implementing the agreement in 1972-3, and this was accordingly

done. It lapsed, however, at the end of that season, for which reason the I.W.C. requested the contracting parties at its meeting in 1973 to renew the agreement. However, they expressed doubt whether this could be done "in view of the situation that has arisen as a result of differences on quotas and subdivision of areas". But as things turned out, it was quite feasible.

2. Ever since 1963, the I.W.C. Scientific Committee had recommended that the setting of quotas in terms of BWU should be discontinued. This had been the most practical arrangement, and administratively the simplest, but it gradually revealed various weaknesses. The effect of the system was that not all species had been caught in the right proportion, as catching concentrated on a single species, and it had proved impossible to limit the killing of that species. As long ago as 1963 it had been emphasised that it would be easier to fix a quota for each species when killing of humpback and blue whales had come to an end. It was expected that an upper limit would gradually result in an increase in stocks of fin whales and prevent over-killing of sei whales, which on the whole would prove a more effective form of control. At the 1971 meeting, the Committee pointed out that in the North Pacific a system of special quotas for the various species had been successfully practised for two seasons; for this reason it earnestly recommended that the same system should be adopted in the Antarctic, particularly in order to enable stocks of fin whales to regenerate. The Committee's resolution was adopted by the Commission, but for practical reasons the scheme could not be put into operation before the 1972-3 season. This was considered one of the I.W.C.'s greatest triumphs, and an answer to the attacks to which it had been subjected.

The quotas for 1972-3, after much dispute, were fixed at 1,950 fin whales, 5,000 sei and Bryde whales and 5,000 minke whales. The first two categories comprised a total of 1,808 BWU, a considerable decline from 2,300 in 1971-2. On the basis of voluntary agreement the quotas were divided between Japan, the Soviet Union and Norway, as shown in Table 36. Japan and the Soviet Union agreed to limit the number of sperm whales as shown. There was no allocation of minke quotas: it was a matter of competition to see who could kill most.

Even if we do not include the Norwegian quota (40 BWU), which was not filled, there was nevertheless a deficiency of 244 BWU, i.e. 14 per cent of the Japanese and Soviet catches of baleen whales, the deficiency falling in its entirety on the Russians, who only managed to catch 66 per cent of their quota. The explanation is partly to be found in the other figures, which show that the Russians must have been more interested in catching sperm whales, of which species they caught nine times more than the Japanese. As ever, the prime consideration for the Japanese was to obtain as much food as possible for human con-

Table 36. ANTARCTIC QUOTAS AND CATCH, 1972-3

	Japan	U.S.S.R.	Norway	Total
Fin whales				
Quotas	1,142	768	40	1,950
Catch	1,142	619	—	1,761
Sei/Bryde whales				
Quotas	2,919	1,961	120	5,000
Catch	2,919	945	—	3,864
Minke whales				
Quotas				5,000
Catch	2,092	3,653		5,745
Sperm whales				
Quotas	1,890	7,900		9,790
Catch	843	7,898		8,741

sumption. The low catch was probably also a consequence of the effect
of international inspection.

Arguments of this kind failed to impress the opponents of whaling:
they considered only the bare figures — that there was a catch of 1,325
fewer fin and sei whales than the quota permitted. They were certain
of one thing only, namely that stocks were continuing to show a marked
decline. Hence at the 1973 meeting they attacked the I.W.C. with
renewed vigour because it had failed to adopt a ten-year moratorium
for all whaling. An alternative proposal for a zero quota for fin whales
in the Antarctic received a majority in the Technical Committee, but
was voted down in the plenary session with seven in favour, five against,
and two abstentions. The United States then proposed 1,450 for the
coming season, with the important proviso that catching should be
successively reduced to nil in a period of not less than three years. This
was adopted by seven votes, only two voting against (Japan and the
Soviet Union), while five abstained. The result of this voting revealed
one aspect of the Commission's rules of procedure which its opponents
criticised severely: while it was true that three-quarters of the *votes cast*
had to be obtained if a resolution were to be adopted, this was also
possible with a number of votes representing less than half the number
of members of the Commission. The voting on the proposal from Japan,
backed by the Soviet Union, to raise the minke whale quota from 5,000
to 8,000 revealed another aspect of the Rules of Procedure which was still
more severely criticised: when the proposal only received the votes of
two nations and was consequently rejected, they protested, and agreed
to catch 4,000 each. This was the last time a member-country imposed
its will in this way: opponents now had reason to attack the I.W.C.
anew, on the grounds that its decisions were null and void, seeing that a

member of the Commission could, according to the Rules of Procedure, catch quite legally, should it so desire, what it wanted, even if all the other members had reached a different decision. This was one of the motives for a revision of the Convention and the Schedule.

3. Of the major cetaceans, the one that yielded the largest catches anywhere after the Second World War was the sperm whale. Of a catch of 1.46 million between 1946 and 1975 the sperm whale accounts for 564,000, or nearly 40 per cent. This reached a peak in 1963-4, with about 30,000, and dropped to about 25,000 during the next seven years. All the oceans of the world seemed so plentifully stocked with sperm whales that, despite the heavy catches, stocks did not appear to recede as in the case of other species. In 1966-7, for the first time, sperm whales comprised more than half the global catch, and their proportion continued to rise, reaching 58 per cent in 1970-1 and 70 per cent in 1972-3; it has remained around this level ever since. As old-style whaling came to a close in the late nineteenth century, its final form being sperm whale catching, it appears that the sperm whale will prove the last redoubt of modern whaling. When the opponents of whaling protested that in 1970-1 39,000 whales had been killed, they did not mention that nearly 60 per cent of these were sperm whales. A drastic drop in the total number could best be achieved with the exclusion of the sperm whale. Catches of this species did in time become strictly regulated.

The 1972 meeting resolved that "the number of sperm whales taken in the southern hemisphere in the 1972-3 pelagic season and the coastal season shall not exceed 8,000 males and 5,000 females". There were three important amendments. First, an "Antarctic" limit at 40°S was not established; with a view to regulation, the entire southern hemisphere was regarded as one whaling ground, and pelagic and shore-based catching were regulated jointly. Secondly, a quota was fixed for sperm whales. And thirdly, the quota was divided into males and females. From 1974-5 the quotas were divided into Areas or Divisions and within each of these they were divided by the participating countries into national quotas. For this reason the total quota could not be caught wherever this was desired. Japan and the Soviet Union agreed in 1972 to limit their catching of sperm whales to respectively 1,890 and 7,900, making a total of 9,790; the remaining 3,210 were reserved for others, i.e. Australia and South Africa. By the terms of an agreement the four countries divided the quota among themselves for the 1973-4 season, on the following lines: the Soviet Union 7,900, Japan 1,415, South Africa 1,783, and Australia 1,079. Of this quantity, the respective yields were actually 7,898, 843, 1,606, and 971. In the following season Brazil also joined in, for which purpose the others chipped in a quota of 75. For 1975-6 the quota was set at 10,740, which the five countries shared on a pro rata basis. The 1972 meeting resolved to lower the minimum length of the sperm whale (in shore whaling) from 35 to 30 ft., except in the North Atlantic, in response to a statement from the Scientific Committee that "since the stock assessments suggest that proper management of sperm whale stocks calls for a higher proportion of catches of females, reduction of minimum size limits be considered". In pelagic whaling the minimum length was still 38 ft.

4. For the North Pacific, too, the 1972 meeting resolved to set a limit to the number of sperm whales, particularly for males and females. In this respect, in fact, the whaling nations themselves had voluntarily taken steps in 1969 and in 1970 to preserve stocks. For pelagic whaling, where two Russian and three Japanese factory ships operated, the 1970 quotas were 1,332 fin, 4,924 sei/Bryde, and 11,285 sperm whales. Catching from shore stations was not to exceed the 1969 level. In the first year the I.W.C. intervened, setting quotas for the next year somewhat lower than the above, but as catches of all species showed great deficiencies, the 1972 meeting introduced a considerable reduction in quotas.

Finally, we should recall that at the 1972 meeting a quota for minke whales was set for the first time, and that in this year there was the satisfaction of having the Observer Scheme in operation. The ten-year moratorium was rejected, but an alternative proposal was adopted to strengthen the Commission and the Secretariat in order to carry out the International Decade of Cetacean Research more efficiently. An *ad hoc* committee was set up to submit proposals for this purpose. The eighth meeting adopted three recommendations: that there should be more detailed returns, respectively, of catches of smaller cetaceans and of the whaling of aborigines, particularly bowhead whale in Alaska and gray whales in North-east Siberia, and considerable pressure was exerted on non-member countries to persuade them to accept the Convention. Here it was pointed out that it would be easier if the Convention were revised, as it had originally been drafted with the special (pelagic) form of catching that developed in the 1930s in mind. Since then a great deal had changed, but a new Convention proved to be a matter for discussion at Government level, whereas the Commission could amend the Schedule, which very definitely needed to be modernised: in the course of time so many amendments had been incorporated that it was almost impossible to discover which provisions had applied in any particular year.

An unsuccessful attempt to revise the Convention was made at an international conference at government level in Copenhagen on 4-7 July 1978. The shore whaling nations vigorously opposed the interference of the Commission in their sovereign rights within the 200-mile zone. It was impossible to arrive at a decisive conclusion, and a second inconclusive conference was held in the spring of 1979.

At the 1973 meeting the *ad hoc* Committee made proposals for re-organising the structure and functions of the Secretariat, including the establishment of an office for the Commission and the appointment of full-time staff including a scientist as its chief officer, and submitted for consideration alternative methods of funding the new organisation. There would be a considerable increase in expenses, from approximately £6,000 annually to about £36,500. Even though the proposal for the moratorium was again rejected after a fresh and protracted debate, its very existence posed such a serious threat that it made it difficult to finance the new Secretariat. In the words of the report: "This agreement was reached on the assumption that whaling by member nations on a proper management basis would be maintained, but some delegations were unable to support a recommendation to adopt a method of funding at this time because of the uncertainties created in the consideration of the moratorium proposals. The report was adopted by the Commission but no progress was made on the question of providing the necessary funds. The Japanese and Soviet Union Commissioners said that they fully supported the idea of strengthening the Commission through its Secretariat but in view of the uncertain future of whaling, particularly having regard to certain decisions reached at this meeting, they were unable to agree at the present time to the increased contribution that the adoption of the re-organisation proposals would require." A method of sharing out expenses among members, however, was arrived at and this was adopted in 1974. Expenses were to be covered by a flat subscription rate paid by all members, i.e. approximately 50 per cent, while the next 25 per cent was to be paid by countries who had been engaged in whaling between 1954 and 1973, in proportion to the number of units they had caught, while the remaining 25 per cent was to be paid in proportion to their catch by countries who had operated in the immediately preceding season. Naturally, the bulk of the expenses had to be covered by Japan and the Soviet Union. The United States proposed the removal of the Secretariat to U.S. territory, but as this would have increased expenses it was not adopted.

The new Secretariat, established in Cambridge, became operative from 1 May 1976 when the new secretary, Dr. RAY GAMBELL, took up his appointment. The work of previous secretaries had been purely administrative, and consisted mainly of preparing the meetings of the Commission and issuing its publications. It had not been a full-time job, and the Ministry of Agriculture, Fisheries and Food had placed premises and personnel at the Commission's disposal for its meetings. The new Secretariat had a staff of four full-time officials (secretary, assistant, executive officer, clerk/typist), who, apart from administration, were to co-ordinate all scientific whale research in the member countries, as well as work closely with the Bureau of International Whaling

Statistics, the F.A.O., and other relevant organisations. The Secretariat would not carry out independent investigations, but would endeavour to provide the necessary funds for research projects.

Apart from the purely general declarations in the Preamble, there is little similarity between the 1945 Schedule and the latest editions of 1975 and 1977. It is naturally impossible to reproduce the Schedule in this context. One is, however, particularly struck by two features: in the first place with what tremendous precision it specifies the number of whales of the various species that can be caught within specifically delimited areas in all the whaling grounds of the earth, particularly in the south. For catching of baleen whales the southern hemisphere is divided into Areas I-VI from the Ice Barrier to 40°S, but for sei, Bryde and minke whales the area stretches as far north as the Equator. The same ocean is divided similarly for catching of sperm whales into Divisions 1-9 and, within each of these, further divisions specifically delineating catches of males and females. In the North Atlantic catching was regulated by means of a specific number of baleen whales for the various areas, in some of which no whaling was carried out. A special provision applied to Iceland (East Greenland-Iceland stock), where the number of fin whales between 1977 and 1982 was not to exceed 1,524, and not in any single year during this period to exceed 304. It should be noted that, except in this area, fin whales were not to be caught anywhere else in the world. Equally, it was not permitted to catch sei whales in the North Pacific, only sperm, Bryde and minke. In short, there was no free catching of any single species. Apart from the catching of fin whale in Icelandic waters, and the Soviet catching of a small number of gray whale for the aborigines on the northeast coast of Siberia, the four largest whales — blue, fin, gray, and humpback — were totally protected, and for the fifth largest, the sei whale, the number had been forced right down to one-twelfth of what it had been in the mid-1960s. All in all, quotas were so small that they approximated to the minimum limits for commercial operations. There can be no doubt that world opinion had had its effect.

An entirely new classification of whales was introduced into the Schedule in relation to the catch which, it was assumed, stocks could stand:

1. *Protection Stocks* (P.S.) are those which are more than 10 per cent below the level giving their maximum sustainable yield (M.S.Y.). For these stocks there is a complete and automatic protection and the species may not be hunted. All blue, humpback, grey, right, bowhead whales and nearly all fin and some sei and sperm whales are protected stocks.

2. *Sustained Management Stocks* (S.M.S.) are those whose stock levels are between 10 per cent below the level of the M.S.Y. and 20 per cent above it, and for these whale catches are permitted in carefully con-

trolled numbers. Nearly half of the stocks of sperm whales fall into this category as well as some individual stocks of fin, sei, and minke whales. As a safeguard, catches are limited to only 90 per cent of the M.S.Y. for these stocks.

3. *Initial Management Stocks* (I.M.S.) are those whose abundance is more than 20 per cent above the M.S.Y. level. Commercial whaling is permitted on these stocks, again in strict accordance with the quotas set by the I.W.C. Most minke and Bryde whales and the remainder of the sperm whale stocks fall into this category.

The new management procedure represents a significant step forward in the protection and conservation of the world's whale stocks. Under these arrangements the number of species of great whales caught commercially has been reduced to five, sub-divided into twenty-nine geographical management units which approximate to biologically independent stocks. The I.W.C. sets separate annual quotas for all these species in each whaling area based on scientific assessments of each of the component stocks concerned.

What had the Commission achieved during these six years, 1972-7? This will be seen from a comparison of the 1972/3-1973 *catches* with the drastic reduction of *quotas* which, without any protest, were adopted at the 29th Annual Meeting of the I.W.C. in Canberra, Australia, in June 1977 (see Table 37).

Table 37. WORLD CATCH 1972-3, AND QUOTAS 1977-8

		Fin	Sei/Bryde	Minke*	BWU	Sperm
Catches	1972/3-1973	2,616	7,425	10,438	2,893	22,073
Quotas	1977/8-1978	459	1,379	8,645	748	13,037

* 30 minke = 1 BWU

In Table 37 figures for 1972-3 include the catching carried out by the then non-members (Spain, Portugal, Peru). Their catch is supplementary to the 1977-8 quotas. 317 BWU were allocated to the southern hemisphere, and of the 459 fin whales it was unlikely that more than Iceland's quota of 304 would be caught, or that the entire sperm whale quota of 685 for the North Atlantic would be filled. The reduction that the I.W.C. had been forced by world opinion to accept in the six seasons was so great that to a certain extent it satisfied the champions of a total ban or a ten-year moratorium. For the 1976 meeting the United Nations Environment Programme stated its "satisfaction with the recent advances in stock management". It was also emphasised that further regulation must harmonise with the results arrived at by the conferences on the law of the sea.

At the meeting of the I.W.C. in London in June 1978 there was a further reduction of the quotas for the Atlantic in 1978-9 and for the other grounds in 1979. The global quota of baleen whales was set at fin whales 304, sei/Bryde whales 538, minke whales 6,221, a total of 448 BWU. In addition there was a quota of ninety fin whales for the Newfoundland stock and sixty-one for the Norwegian stock, but neither of these could be caught.

For the shore station in Iceland the quota of fin whales was set at 304 and that of sei whales at 84 (a total of 166 BWU). Nothing gives a better picture of the centennial circulation of modern whaling round the world: Iceland, the first country to which modern whaling was transferred from Norway, ends up as the biggest baleen whale catching nation in the world, and yet its quota is a mere 166 BWU.

It goes without saying that the tremendous decline in supplies of whale products to the world market resulted in a corresponding increase in prices. (The figures listed below show the highest prices quoted in the course of the year.) In the mid-1960s the price of whale oil was around £85, dropping in 1968 to £49. This low price was one of the reasons why Norway at that stage abandoned whaling. During the next two years the price rose sharply, reaching £114 in 1970. There was a slight fall down to 1972, when the price was quoted in dollars at $210, after which a record price of $550 was recorded in 1974. After a sharp drop during the next few years the price rallied to $460 in 1977. Sperm whale oil has shown an incredible rise in price. From an all-time low of £60 in 1967 it was quoted in 1975 at $400, a price that almost doubled to $780 in 1976 and to $850 in 1977. The prices registered are those paid to whaling companies per long ton (2,240 lb. or 1,016 kg.). Asked whether the Russians were responsible for dumping sperm oil, one of the major British oil broker firms stated that "the Russian production of sperm oil from the Antarctic was exported to Western Europe from November 1960 until November 1972. It was negotiated at world prices and never dumped on the market. The quantities were normally about 10-15,000 tons per annum but went as high as 40,000 tons in about 1965, ending with 4,000 tons in 1972. From 1973 the production was consumed within the Soviet bloc but now the satellite countries are excluded and the Soviet Union keeps the entire production."

The price of whale meat shows a similar curve to that of oil. For human consumption the price in 1972 was $1,053 per (metric) ton, and in 1976 $2,395, for pet food in 1973 $236, and in 1977 $368. The halt in the catching of the largest cetaceans has made the minke whale particularly valuable. On the Japanese market the meat of this species is said to have fetched a price of $4 a kilogramme, and as one animal will provide some 3,000 kg., its production value is around $12,000. When the price of whale products was at its lowest in the 1960s, the oil and meat value of the fin whale together amounted to some $3,000.

(See Statistical Appendix, Table 68 : The International Whaling Commission : meetings, chairmen and secretaries, 1949-78; and Table 69 : Average price of whale oil No. 1, 1874-1977, and of sperm oil, 1946-77.)

37

TECHNICAL DEVELOPMENTS AFTER 1930

The many patents granted in the whaling sector, as well as the applications for patents that were turned down, provide a very good picture of the technical development and the problems that needed to be solved in order to ensure more effective catching. It is a more difficult matter, however, to get a good idea of the many practical changes that were never patented. When the manager of a factory ship was asked in 1934 about the effect of the improvements introduced on his vessel during the last few years, he answered: "The whale claw is excellent, and so are the ventilator fans for fresh air down to the boiling plant; it's made a tremendous difference. The bulkhead aft, for'ard of the cabins, is also very convenient in preventing heat and fumes from penetrating. Then we have the exhaust tubes for the Hartmann cookers on the ship's side, which we managed to place lower down and which work excellently. Above the Hartmann intake we have a tight lid, and in this way we avoid a lot of fumes and steam getting into the boiling plant, as there are drainage tubes running out to the ship's side."

The whale claw was not invented for the convenience of the hands, so much as to make the job of hauling up the whale more efficient and secure. The other items mentioned by the manager were merely improvements, but taken altogether they helped to make working conditions on board far more pleasant. We cannot accurately measure the effects of these and similar improvements on the human factor in the same way as we can measure the results of the purely technical advances. With keener and keener competition to acquire steadily declining supplies of raw material, attention was mainly directed towards more accurate methods of shooting, and a more complete processing of the raw material. The two largest groups of patents concentrate on these two points, particularly the former. Great efforts were made to develop an electric harpoon, stimulated by pressing demands for a less painful method of despatching the whale. Similarly, attempts at fuller exploitation of the raw material were dictated not just by the need to avoid waste, but also by the critical necessity of extracting full value from the dwindling catches. A notable feature of the latest phase of whaling is the increasing importance of by-products for the working economy. This in turn encouraged new inventions. The aim of whaling was no longer identical with the production of oil. (In this context by-products are any other products apart from oil and sperm oil.)

If we compare the whaling equipment of the 1930s with that in use

687

at the time of Svend Foyn and the *Admiralen*, we shall find that, except on one particular point, great changes had taken place in the whale catchers, the factory ship, the boiling apparatus, and in communications between the owners at home and the expeditions in the whaling grounds. But with regard to the shape of the whale catcher, the prototype of the newly constructed factory ship introduced with the *Kosmos* and the rotary boilers and oil separators, subsequent technical advances were not so revolutionary, however significant they might have been. The breech-loading gun with its glycerine recoil brake was a very great advance. The technical improvements, the new apparatus, the new instruments, the increased emphasis on by-products, the growing demand for job satisfaction — all these helped to change working conditions and the rhythm of life on board, to such an extent that in 1960 the lives of whalers were very different from what they had been in 1930. Although a large number of new inventions were utilised, they only constituted a small number of the many that were patented. A great many of them involved changes in the one aspect of whaling that has remained practically unchanged: the shooting of the whale. So ingenious was the harpoon, with its cleft shaft and the shell screwed on to its head, that despite the expenditure of vast sums of money, energy, and scientific know-how, practically every whale caught today is shot with the grenade harpoon.

The most striking change in the hull of the whale catcher was the raised bow with a platform; this gave the gunner a wider range of vision, and made it easier for him to follow the movements of the whale. The greatest technical innovation in the whale catcher was the diesel engine. After the first unsuccessful attempts in 1911-12, the Japanese in 1937 designed the successful diesel-driven whale catcher *Seki Maru* for Taiyo Hogei K.K. It was of 297 gross tons, with an engine of 824 h.p. It was built at the insistence of one the company's directors, KANEICHI NAKABE. All the gunners, however, refused to use it, as they insisted that it was impossible to catch a single whale with a boat that made such a tremendous amount of noise. Finally, one gunner, KINJIRO YOSHIDA, was persuaded to have a try, and to everyone's surprise he succeeded in making a catch which was almost equal to the average for all Japanese whale catchers. For the ensuing season the company had two more diesel-driven boats.

For the Japanese gunners the diesel engine brought about a change in the pursuit phase. With a silent steam engine it was possible to creep up on the whale, but a diesel-driven whale catcher frightened the whale and was compelled to race it in order to tire it out by the time it was within range, a method which the Norwegians called "Prussian pursuit". Yoshida is believed to have been the first Japanese gunner to use this method in the 1937-8 season, although Norwegian gunners had used the Prussian pursuit method many years previously, particularly after they had started using more powerful whale catchers. In 1928 the manager at Leith Harbour reported that gunners were using these new tactics. In the gunners' opinion, no whale was safe against a boat capable of 14 knots. While the Japanese switched entirely to diesel-driven engines for their Antarctic fleet after the war, the British and Norwegians were more conservative. In all, Norwegian companies have only commissioned the building of two diesel-driven whale catchers. However, a number of corvettes were converted to diesel. Previously they had had very heavy steam engines and a high fuel consumption; after conversion the fuel consumption was reduced to manageable proportions, while the boats were lighter and just as fast.

One obvious advantage of the steam engine was that it offered greater scope for changing speed and made less noise, but these advantages were outweighed by the diesel-driven vessels' use of variable-pitch propellors and the adoption of Prussian pursuit tactics. A steam-driven factory ship had to carry two kinds of fuel oil, while the building of a whale catcher was rendered more expensive as it had to carry a steam boiler in order to provide steam for the whale winch, for the thawing out of frozen lines, and the like. The main advantage of diesel-driven boats was that they were more economical to operate with lower fuel consumption, and had a larger radius of action and thus needed fewer breaks for bunkering. The whale catcher race had started in the mid-1930s, producing a type of approximately 600 gross tons with an engine of 2,700 h.p. A great many people had seriously doubted the wisdom of boats of these dimensions, so expensive to build, run, and maintain, but they were necessary if one was to stay in business. Since the whale catcher with a cruiser stern and detached rudder was designed and the diesel engine adopted, no correspondingly epoch-making innovations have seen the light of day. The type that had been evolved by around 1935 proved to be the most convenient.

The further development of the gun produced nothing new of importance that could be compared with the breech loader and the recoil brake. Any subsequent changes in gun design were merely detailed improvements of the mechanism.

The number of patents in the various categories more or less conforms to the situation in the whaling grounds. In the 1930s the dominant group of patents involved the reduction of the carcass, extraction, and the refining of oil. While this category admittedly bulked large after the war as well, there was a marked, steadily rising tendency in the 1930s in the number of patents involving the actual catching of the whale. With rising competition and more and more effort required to obtain raw materials for the boiler, interest concentrated more on a sure and efficient method of killing the whale. All the many patents in this field aimed to prevent the most common ways in which a whale might be lost: by missing, as a result of the grenade harpoon bouncing off the surface of the water or off the whale; by transpiercing the whale with the shell going off in the water, as a result of the harpoon failing to grip; or by the line breaking. Even though very few of these patents were ever actually used, they are interesting in that they reveal weaknesses in the ordinary method of shooting. Some of them have been applied for by active whalers, who in their daily work at sea realised that everything was not entirely as it should be. These inventions involve primarily the shape of the shell and the harpoon, but they also involve the fuse and its location, timing the detonation, an arrangement to prevent the harpoon passing through the whale, securing a grenade that fails to detonate, flukes (claws), the forerunner attachment, methods of absorbing the shock in the line when the harpoon has run out, sealing the wound inflicted by the shot, and so forth. We cannot go into details of the many proposals and improvements; two, however, deserve to be considered a little more closely: the shape of the harpoon and the shape of the shell.

The ordinary cleft harpoon stock had one weakness in that it was apt to bend if it struck any bone structure in the whale or when the carcass was hauled in. A harpoon with a whole, tubular stock would have been much stronger, but the difficulty would then have been how to attach it to the forerunner. In order to be more sure of hitting the target, the ordinary artillery principle was adopted of giving the harpoon a rotary movement, but the difficulty was that the harpoon was not free, like a projectile, but pulled a line, which was not designed to rotate. In short, the technicians did not succeed in solving the problems connected with the use of a whole harpoon stock, and the smiths on board the factory ships continued to have a great deal of work to do straightening bent harpoons.

Several attempts were made to solve the problems of preventing the harpoon passing right through the whale. The best solution was the one hit on by the engineers CARL and ERLING CORNELIUSSEN, owners of an engineering workshop in Sandefjord which was a major supplier of whaling equipment. Together, they had a record number of patents for whaling, amounting to some forty from 1923 to 1960. One of these patents aimed to prevent the shot passing through the whale by means of an automatic stopping device which was soon in general use, and which in the opinion of the inventors "helps to explain why gunners can register such a large number of whales caught per day".

The decisive changes to the shape of the shell were discovered quite independently in Norway and in Japan. Experience in the use of pointed shells showed that when they struck the surface of the water a few yards away from the whale, instead of continuing on down into the

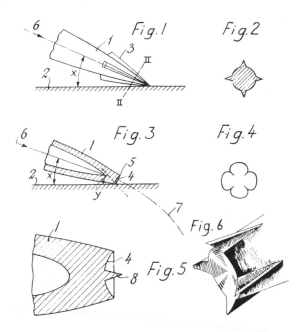

107. The shell-harpoon with pointed (1) and flat (3, 5, 6) head.

water, they bounced over the whale and exploded in the air. A great many whales were lost in this way. In order to get a proper strike, the pointed shell would have to strike the whale head-on, and as much at right-angles as possible. Using this grenade, the gunner's target was restricted to the small portion of the tail that emerged above the surface of the water when it came up to blow. Experiments had shown that the larger the surface of a truncated shell head, the straighter it would continue on its course once it was in the water. After several inventors had come close to finding a solution to the problem, it was finally solved in 1938 by a Norwegian shipowner. It is said that he hit on the idea when, in the whaling grounds in 1936, he took the top off a boiled egg. In his design the shell was given a saucer-shaped depression and four small flukes on the edge, placed around the sides of a square. This shape has not changed since. It was tried out with great success for the first time in 1937-8, and also proved to have the advantage that, owing to the greater resistance inside the whale offered by the flat head, it seldom passed through the body of the animal, even if the shot was fired at close range. This saucer-shaped shell was soon in common use in all European expeditions.

The Japanese never adopted it, because they evolved their own shape, which they considered superior to the Norwegian. This completed flat-headed shell, without any saucer-shaped impression or flukes, was invented by a professor of physics at the University of Tokyo, Dr. MORISO HIRATA, and was in use in the winter of 1949. When a ring was fastened round the pointed head of the harpoon, it pursued a more shallow curve and could strike the whale under the water too. An application for a Norwegian patent was rejected, reference being made to the Norwegian patent of 1938.

The well-known Japanese paper *Asahi Shimbun* wrote in 1956 that one of the main reasons for the superiority of Japanese whalers was "the original Japanese shell with the straight head, which has completely destroyed the ordinary Norwegian whaling theory". Be that as it may, neither of the two countries has at any time used the other's shell, even after both patents lapsed in the early 1960s. Confronted with this, Dr. Omura has cautiously expressed the opinion that the shell with a flat head *may* have been the reason for Japanese superiority. He also relates that he has a photograph of a Soviet whale catcher with a similar shell. The Japanese considered that their shell improved the gunner's ability to hit the target by 50 per cent, and that the chance of an instantaneous killing was 80 per cent against 50 per cent for the pointed shell. In other words, the new shell was more humane in its effects, and for this reason there was less urgency for solving the problem by electric killing.

Once the harpoon had been driven home, the whale had to be pulled in, pumped up, and marked with a flag. No essential changes were made in the whale line winch and the line brake, although the line was subject to a great many improvements. The Norwegian ropeworks had to a large extent depended on supplies to the whaling industry. In the 1930s some 90 km. of fibre rope and 15 km. of wire were required for the initial fitting-out of an expedition with six whale catchers. The line was generally 4 inches and the forerunner, connecting it to the harpoon, 7 inches in circumference. A 600-fathom length of line (inches and fathoms were standard measurements for the Norwegians as well as the Anglo-Saxons) was kept coiled up and ready, and, unless the gunner missed, the entire length might have had to be paid out.

The whale might be allowed to tire by "running a loop"; instead of pursuing the whale the catcher sheered off to one side and set off on a course parallel to the whale, with the result that the latter had a tremendous length of line to pull. The ordinary hemp line had certain weaknesses; although it was impregnated, it absorbed water, became heavy, and was stiff if the temperature dropped below zero. A machine was patented which squeezed the water out of the line as it was hauled in. The forerunner was 60-70 fathoms long, and the gunners insisted on thinner and lighter forerunners in order to ensure greater accuracy of aim at long range. A distance of 40 fathoms was long considered the extreme limit for getting a shot home; there were gunners, however, who could hit a target at 50-60 fathoms. The commonest reason for losing a whale was that the line broke, and this happened most often when the line, running out in a spiral, formed a kink when it was pulled taut, producing a weak spot, so that the forerunner snapped like twine when the whale made a sudden movement. In about 1930 an "un-kinkable" forerunner was produced, which soon became world famous. While the forerunner was coiled up on the line basket under the cannon, the line was "shot" down below deck into a line bin.

Probably because of a shortage of foreign currency the Japanese had started to make forerunners of silk in the 1930s. They were pliant and strong, but not very compact. By mixing the silk with other materials, however, a firmer line was produced, but these were much more expensive, and so heavy that the Norwegian gunners disliked them. The great innovation after the war was the nylon forerunner. The first ones were made towards the end of the war out of parachute line, owing to a shortage of manilla fibre, and proved very successful. Nylon forerunners made out of new material were produced for the 1945-6 expeditions. They had obvious advantages: their tremendous strength as compared to manilla rope made it possible to use line with less weight per unit of length, thereby increasing both the range and the accuracy of the harpoon. They absorbed less water and did not freeze in low temperatures, and for that reason were less liable to snap when fired. Their great elasticity absorbed the strain of any sudden movement made by the whale, and this obviated the use of the system of springs necessary for manilla forerunners. Through a special process a nylon forerunner was developed which had the quality of returning to its original shape after being subjected to a tremendous strain and sudden release. They also lasted much longer: it was estimated that each nylon forerunner could be used for between fourteen and sixteen whales, as against eight or nine with a manilla one. Although the price of nylon during the first few years was about ten times higher than that of manilla, it was nevertheless considered to be worth the extra expense, as the loss of a whale represented just as large a value as the whale catcher's supply of rope for a whole season. The price of nylon yard dropped in the 1950s to less than half of its 1947 price.

Inflating the whale not only took time, but accelerated the process of autolysis, as the oxygen in the air increased the rate of combustion. A great many attempts have been made to solve this problem. The only woman who is known to have taken out a whaling patent suggested that instead of air a carbide container should be introduced into the carcass of the whale, and the acetylene gas produced, which was both germ-free and antiseptic, would prevent autolysis and possibly keep the whale afloat. Subsequently, a great many proposals have been made to introduce preservative fluids into the whale, but they generally had side-effects like making the meat unfit for consumption. Because the putrefaction of the whale's internal organs was produced by bacteria, an attempt was made to use antibiotics, which after the war had revolutionised the struggle against infectious diseases. In about 1950 experiments were started with antibiotics for the preservation of fish, and shortly afterwards of whales as well. Tests produced astonishing results, particularly in the use of CTC (aureomycin hydrochloride). The number of bacteria per gramme of meat in various parts of a whale treated with antibiotics was only a tiny fraction of what it was in untreated whales. The animal did not swell up, and the oil had a much lower percentage of free fatty acid. In 1960 it was reported that the Russians had started to use antibiotics at the shore stations in the Pacific, and that "they had to a considerable degree extended the period for transport of the whale to a shore station, which had also conceivably extended their field of operation for whaling". At the whaling station in Iceland use of an antibiotic (Biostat) was started in 1953. The quality of the meat became better, and the offal, which according to the regulations had to be boiled, was also better preserved. Previously, the offal had given the oil a larger acid content and a darker colour, with the result that it had been dumped in the sea. The use of antibiotics was comparatively expensive — approximately 275 g. at a price of about £9 a whale had to be paid, but this was considered worth it. The last whaling patent taken out in Norway was granted to Nitto Hogei K.K. and involved "conservation of the freshness of whale meat by introducing into the whale a condensed gas which expands adiabatically, so that the temperature of the carcass of the whale is lowered". Two Japanese patents had been granted for this in 1964. All in all, the many patents aimed at preventing autolysis were due to concern for whale meat; as far as the whale oil was concerned it was of minor importance, as the highly developed system of separating produced practically only best-quality oil, No. 0/1.

A great many whales were lost because the buoying boat failed to find them in poor visibility. For a long time there was no solution to this. In 1927 two whalers with a certain amount of technical knowledge were granted a patent for an electric signal horn, fastened to the whale with the aid of four long claws, and driven by a battery with a clockwork mechanism which regulated periodical emission of signals, in fact a whale foghorn. Early on, the use of radio was considered: wireless in all its forms, the telegraph, the telephone, direction finding, radar, and asdic are inventions which whalers have adopted to track down and pursue a whale, and to find their way back to it once it has been "flagged". The last-mentioned was the subject of tests and experiments, extending over many years, conducted by the Norwegian affiliates of two major manufacturers of wireless equipment. Experiments were initiated in 1927 : the first step was to make a small transmitter, which omitted a series of dots and dashes, placed in a box, with an aerial mounted on a pole. This solution, however, proved impracticable. The attempt in 1928 to place the transmitter in a buoy beside the whale was more successful. This principle, which is in use today, was abandoned at the time. Instead, the whale transmitter was built into a stainless steel transmitter fastened to the flagged spear and attached to the carcass of the whale by two spikes. It emitted bearing signals every minute in the special code of each expedition. Before the war this transmitter was used by a great many companies and appeared to have every prospect of establishing itself as an invaluable aid to whaling. It has, in fact, done so, with this difference; the transmitter is now placed in a container which floats in the sea beside the whale and has its own aerial mast. Whale catchers can home on it from a distance of 40 to 50 miles. In the course of time the whale transmitter has kept pace with the progress of radio technology, and is now more reliable, lighter in weight, and has a bigger range.

In 1947 a British whaling company wrote that the most recently constructed catchers were equipped with asdic, which, it was stated, could well revolutionise whaling and make it possible for British companies to employ British crews, thus making them independent of the whims of the Norwegian Government and the Norwegian trade unions. The real skill of the gunner, it went on to say, involved guessing where the whale would surface and getting his boat as close as possible to the spot. With the aid of asdic he would now know with a fair degree of certainty, and it should be fairly simple to learn how to fire a shot. While radar was already known before the Second World War, asdic was developed by the Allies during the war.

As long ago as the London Conference in 1944 it was suggested that the device used to locate U-boats might well have a major bearing on whaling. The possibility that this would mean that whalers would possess one more weapon for the depletion of whale stocks, which it was the desire of the Conference to preserve, was probably not even considered at that time. During the first post-war season two of Salvesen's whale catchers were equipped with devices on loan from the Admiralty. With the use of asdic it was possible to follow the track of the whale under the surface; the first devices, on the other hand, suffered from one weakness : they failed to register if the whale surfaced too near the whale catcher. This has subsequently been corrected. In the report from the *Southern Harvester* in 1949-50 the manager wrote that asdic was not much use in locating whales, but excellent for the pursuit. As soon as the asdic was switched on, the whale came to the surface and set off at speed in order to escape. The sound waves must have disturbed the whale's ear. The pursuit of a whale in this way required catchers capable of speeds in excess of 15 knots. It was difficult to maintain contact with a whale when it submerged to great depths and when it was close to the catcher; it was easiest when it surfaced some distance from the boat, but on such occasions it could generally be seen. After the 1952-3 season more experience in the use of this device was gained. An efficient operator was a necessity; a poor one was a handicap to the gunner who was forced to rely on him.

The fact that the whale was frightened by the sound waves and compelled to surface gave a Norwegian gunner the idea of producing a "whale scarer" by transmitting ultrasonic waves. In the 1951-2 season he tried it out in a combined apparatus which made it possible to "see" the whale under the water and frighten it up to the surface. But as the wake of the whale made it difficult to "see" it, he abandoned asdic and improved the sound apparatus. This was so effective that the very next season, 1952-3, twenty-five Norwegian boats were equipped with this "whale scarer". Like ordinary asdic it was accommodated in a dome under the whale catcher's bottom and could be pulled in and submerged as required. This apparatus was manufactured by the German firm of Elektroacustic G.m.b.H. of Kiel. That season thirteen of Salvesen's whale catchers had a similar British-made apparatus, the Kelvin-Hughes Echo Whale Finder, installed. The asdic operator in his cubby-hole on the bridge and the asdic apparatus are now just as regular adjuncts to whaling as the gunner and his harpoon, but not everyone has been equally enthusiastic about its use. In the annual report of the Tønsberg Whaling Company (Husvik Harbour) for 1958-9 we read that the Governor at Port Stanley had forbidden further use of asdic "after our company, with the support of leading scientists, showed that continued use of such apparatus could have serious con-sequences for catching at South Georgia". A decree in 1960 valid for the Dependencies declared that the Governor could give special permis-sion for the use of "detection devices in whaling" for experimental and scientific research.

Radar was used in whaling immediately after the end of the war. When the factory ship *Norhval* underwent trials on 24 November 1945, she carried "this fabulous system, with the help of which in fog as well as in darkness one can locate everything on the surface of the water within the area that was being scanned". From the very first radar was used as a navigation aid, but, just as asdic could be used to assist in catching the whale, so radar could be used to find flagged whales. As the flagged whale was so low in the water that it could hardly be picked out on the whale catcher's radar screen, a special mast was placed on the whale with a many-sided container of metal, reflecting radio waves from the whale catcher's radar. A flagged whale came to look like a

108. A dead whale with (*from the left*) the radio transmitter, the colours of the company and the radar screen.

three-masted schooner, a proof of the extent to which technology had influenced whaling, to such an extent that the whale had very small chances of escaping its fate. From about 1950 radar was standard equipment on whale catchers and buoy boats. It served both to track a flagged whale and to find the way back to the factory ship. So absolutely dependent on modern techniques is the present-day whaler that were he deprived of them and supplied with the tools that were in existence during the first years of Antarctic whaling, and particularly pelagic whaling, hardly a whale would be caught. Catching a whale in 1910 required a far greater measure of human skill, and was a much more difficult art than in 1960. The entry of technology into whaling increased step by step with the decline in stocks of whales.

As already mentioned, aircraft and helicopters have also been pressed into service in order to track whales. There was no limit to what was expected from these by people outside the circle of whalers, not only in finding the whale, but also catching it direct from aircraft. There is a story from the United States that an Air Force lieutenant was the first person to kill a large whale with a burst of machine-gun fire off Los Angeles in 1919. A motor launch towed the whale to land, and the lieutenant received a good price for the meat and the oil. The idea of using aircraft to spot whales blowing is attributed to Lars Christensen, who was the first to include aircraft on his Antarctic expeditions.

After the first attempts with aircraft in Antarctic whaling on the *Kosmos* in 1929 had ended in disaster, no one attempted to use them again until the *Balaena* expedition of 1946-7. Two full accounts are available, written by the pilot. It was the director of United Whalers Ltd. who insisted on using aircraft, and as this was decided while the factory ship was being built, the necessary adaptation could be made. Above the slipway a hangar was constructed, with enough room for two Walrus aircraft (high-wing seaplanes) and a crane for swinging them over the side. On the way to the Antarctic the aircraft located two schools of sperm whales, of which twenty-seven were caught on one day and twenty-two on the next. When the baleen whaling season opened, there were so many whales that whale catchers had to be rationed; for this reason the aircraft were not greatly in demand for their task. They were mainly used for reporting ice conditions, to direct the factory ship to a spot where there would be shelter during bunkering of oil from a tanker, and to follow the operations of rival factory ships. "On several occasions we shadowed the *Norhval* and reported her movements. One day we discovered her 61 miles away without a whale. On that day we ourselves caught fifty." The manager of the *Balaena* declared that the aircraft had proved a disappointment, and despite the enthusiasm for all that was accomplished the author and pilot was forced to admit that the expedition would have fared better with a helicopter. The *Willem Barendsz* had two planes of the same type, but they were never used, and the factory ship had neither a hangar nor a special crane for launching planes. The *Empire Victory*, too, does not appear to have used her aircraft. On her next season, 1947-8, the *Balaena* did not take aircraft, and the hangar was converted to cabins for 100 hands, as it had proved necessary to increase the crew owing to the production of meat and other by-products.

Experience showed that, as far as catches were concerned, the aeroplane was no advantage. It was never subsequently known to have been used in pelagic whaling. Its greatest limitations were those of weather; it could only be launched and take off in practically calm seas. In this respect the helicopter was more independent: it was able to take off from and land on the deck in almost any sort of weather. Helicopters were first used for the marking of whales, and for counting gray whales off the coast of Lower California in 1947. The *Olympic Challenger* was probably the first factory ship to use a helicopter for whaling. One of the officers told a German paper: "Our helicopter, with its American crew, has proved excellent. It hovered in the air like a hawk and kept the whale catchers informed by radio of where some whales had been seen." Whalers declared that helicopters had also been very useful for investigating ice conditions. A helicopter of the Sikorsky 51 type was purchased for the 1952-3 season in Britain for the *Norhval*. With spare parts and training of the pilot it cost £57,000. It was a big expense item, but the price of oil was good, and the company expected so much advantage from it that "already in the course of one season it would have earned this outlay in foreign currency many times over". Lars Christensen, too, acquired a helicopter for his expeditions in 1952-3. In 1956-7 each of Salvesen's two factory ships had two helicopters, while the *Nisshin Maru* had one for a number of seasons, starting in 1953-4. The reason why the *Norhval* gave up using helicopters after 1961 was that whaling shifted further and further north, encountering more stormy weather, which was less favourable for operating with a helicopter than along the ice barrier. This is also why the Japanese gave up their use. The shift in catching from blue to fin and sei whales may also have made some difference.

Radio-technical aids adopted by the whaling fleets around 1930 were unable to prevent the number of losses of ships and human lives increasing sharply at that particular time, a trend that continued well into the 1930s. Between 1928 and 1939 twenty-one whale catchers went down, with the loss of eighty-six lives. Fourteen of these whale catchers went down in the Antarctic with fifty-four hands. It is interesting to note that fifty of these fifty-four were on board British ships and only four were from the five Norwegian whale catchers that were lost. Of the remaining seven, four went down off the African coast with seven hands and three off the Chilean-Peruvian coasts with twenty-five hands. Just as striking as the large number of sinkings during the twelve years 1928-39 is the small number during the twenty-four years after the Second World War, when only four whale catchers are known to have gone down, three of them in the Antarctic — one Panamanian and two British. One of these was Salvesen's *Simbra,* which in 1947 turned turtle when in pursuit of a whale with the loss of fifteen men, the largest number in a single sinking. If this first period of polar catching, from 1928-39, is compared with the entire period from 1911 to 1969, the number of casualties is disproportionately large, twenty-one whale catchers with eighty-six hands out of forty-five whale catchers with 149 hands, which, as far as is known, foundered in all whaling grounds together, between 1911 and 1969; and of these twenty-eight whale catchers with eighty-one hands went down in the Antarctic. The large losses of the 1930s may be ascribed to catching along the ice barrier, the hectic pursuit and the ruthless competition. The gunners undoubtedly exceeded the limits of what the matériel, which was not designed for such tremendous stresses, could stand. The reason why casualties dropped so markedly after the Second World War must be due to sturdier matériel, new radio-technical navigating instruments, and the fact that whaling shifted further and further north — admittedly to stormier waters, but away from the ice. British statistics for the

Falkland Islands Dependencies show a large number of fatalities around 1930, forty between 1928 and 1931 but only eight in the rest of the 1930s and forty altogether from 1947 to 1962. From then on (3 March 1962), as already mentioned, the territory was divided into the Falkland Islands Dependencies, comprising the Falkland Islands and South Sandwich, and the British Antarctic Territory, comprising everything south of 60°S, as a separate colony.

In the foregoing account of whaling it has been assumed that the whale was killed by a shell harpoon. The idea of using other methods of killing has a long history: the main ones have been poison, gas, and electricity. All those who worked to promote these methods maintained that in this way it would be possible to avoid the disadvantages resulting from the use of a shell: the explosion caused such havoc inside the whale that some of the meat was destroyed and the intestines burst, with the result that the release of their contents accelerated the process of autolysis; and shell splinters were liable to damage tools and machines during the processing. If at the same time it were possible to kill the whale in such a manner that it remained floating, without being inflated, time, work, and money would be saved. Another factor was the urgent and constant demands of the big international organisations for the protection of animals to cut short the suffering the shell harpoon often inflicted on the whale. This factor was exploited on a greatly exaggerated scale by a manufacturer of electric whaling equipment in a letter to the Washington Conference in 1946. If all the cruelty were known "the whole civilised world would rise in protest against it". Now that technology had made such notable advances, the cruelty could be avoided, as "it would be easy to produce the ideal harpoon". This was, in fact, not the case, and was the reason why the shell harpoon was not abandoned.

The idea of using the ancient method of killing the whale with poison has been renewed in recent times. In 1831 a whaling firm in Leith appealed to a doctor to assist it in finding a practical method for the use of a cyanide compound which would be fired in small glass tubes into the whale, where it would be crushed when the flukes of the harpoon were straightened out. This would not kill the whale, but paralyse it, enabling the whalers to despatch it at their leisure. A vessel with equipment of this sort on board was sent to Greenland, where it was crushed in the pack ice. When the experiment was repeated in 1834, it proved partially successful, but had to be abandoned as the hands refused to strip the whale, fearing that they might be poisoned. The last occasion this was tried was in the 1950s, this time using curare, which paralysed the motor nerves and killed by suffocation. Experiments were carried out both in Sweden and in Norway, but these showed that the method was useless. It had been discussed by British scientists as far back as

October 1947 at a meeting organised by the Universities' Federation for Animal Welfare. They considered the use of curare impossible : a large enough dose would cost £100, the entire world production of curare would be needed, and the meat would be useless for human consumption. In 1959 the I.W.C. set up a subcommittee under pressure from the animal protection societies to study catching methods and the possibility of more humane killing. It concluded that poison would have to be rejected for three reasons : it was unreliable in its effect and as a more humane device; there was danger that the meat and persons processing the whale might be poisoned; and it was automatically excluded owing to the tremendous expense that would accrue to the whaling companies.

The other method, which was taken more seriously and appeared more promising, was the use of compressed carbonic acid or some other form of gas or air. The idea was not only to kill the whale more swiftly and painlessly, but also to keep it afloat without inflation. The gas was also intended to have an antiseptic effect. Experiments were carried out with various kinds of gas, but one inventor came to the conclusion that the simplest method was to use compressed air, which could easily be produced on board. Despite all the advantages on paper, this invention too has shared the fate of so many other vain efforts. It is possible that this is the one that was tried in Prince Olav Harbour in 1924-5; out of four shots, three hits were secured on blue whales, but all three were lost. For one of its first seasons the Netherlands whaling company obtained a container of compressed carbonic acid to be screwed on to the head of the harpoon, but the whalers were so afraid that it would explode in their hands, that they dared not use it. For the 1959-60 season a Netherlands armaments factory made harpoons with compressed carbonic acid. Six of these were tried, but were a complete failure.

The Norwegian engineer CARL U. WETLESEN worked assiduously at perfecting carbonic acid shells, and in 1943-51 took out five patents for his carbonic acid harpoons, which he tried again and again to improve, after tests with the previous type had failed. It was tried year after year, but as soon as one feature had been put right, another went wrong. It turned out that if the whale appeared to be dead after the shot had been fired, it would soon come to life again and would have to be killed with an ordinary harpoon shell. Wetlesen himself was forced to admit that "the tests with the new gas harpoon were a failure". The report from the above-mentioned subcommittee of the I.W.C. declared that it envisaged "no possibility of a speedy solution of the problem of a more humane killing of the whale with carbonic acid". After 1961 the matter appears to have been dropped entirely. The subcommittee's report, however, does not agree with that of the *Balaena* from 1946-7, according to which two whales were shot with the carbonic acid shell, that it killed whales very speedily, and that the meat was of much better quality than usual. But it proved impossible to persuade the gunner to use more than these two shells.

The proposal to torpedo the whale was even less realistic, although the method was patented. However, the most fantastic and original invention in the history of whaling was made by no less a person than J. A. Mørch. His idea was to use an electrically propelled, unmanned submarine, which received its current through electric wires from the mother ship, by which it was manoeuvred through regulating the revolutions of the whale catcher's two propellers. The submarine was to be built in the shape of a whale, in order to deceive the quarry into believing that this was a colleague. Owing to its noiseless approach, the whale catcher would be able to get close to the whale, and ram it unerringly with the harpoon from the gun in the bow. The explosive charge would be set off by an electric impulse. This invention was apparently just as seriously intended as Mørch's other ideas, but one is tempted to wonder whether, in this particular case, Mørch perhaps was not pulling the leg of whalers and the Patents Board.

The I.W.C. subcommittee investigated electric killing in great detail, as this was the only method which appeared capable of replacing the shell harpoon. In 1929-39 *fifty-one* inventions were patented in Norway in connection with the electric killing of whales. The story of this, however, goes right back to man's first practical application of electricity. As far as is known the first patent for an "electric whale apparatus" was granted to two Germans on 30 March 1852. The line carrying the electric cable would be fastened to the whale with a hand harpoon, and a hand-operated induction machine would produce "such a terrible current that no living creature could survive". The electrical circuit would pass through the water back to the ship, which for this reason was copper-sheathed. This theoretical invention contains within it the main principle for all subsequent apparatuses. In 1868 two Englishmen, F. BENNETT and R. WARD, were granted a patent for a somewhat different method.

In about 1880 several practical attempts were made by Norwegians. Several shots were fired at whales, but on each occasion the cable broke, as it was not as elastic as the forerunner. This exposed what was frequently to prove one of the greatest problems of electric whale catching. The Norwegian physicist KRISTIAN BIRKELAND, inventor of the method for extracting nitrogen from the air, took out five patents for the hydrogenation of oil, and he also designed an electric gun. Tests, however, were not successful, and they were abandoned at Birkeland's death in 1917. Subsequent efforts to solve the problem occurred in two periods, interrupted by the Second World War, i.e.

mainly in the 1930s and 1950s. In the first period they were principally Norwegian efforts and to some extent German, in the latter period they were a continuation of the Norwegian efforts, but mainly British. In the opinion of the I.W.C. subcommittee, a combination of the two last-mentioned had a prospect of success. The Japanese, too, experimented with electric killing, but abandoned it. We know nothing of Soviet attempts. In Norwegian quarters work was intensified with the expansion of whaling at the end of the 1920s. The slump in the price of whale oil could to a certain extent be outweighed by more effective and consequently cheaper catching methods.

After intense preliminary work in the mid-1920s, the patents came thick and fast — thirteen in 1929 and twenty-eight in the succeeding six years. In 1929 three companies in Norway were working on the problem, and one of them succeeded in coming very close to a solution. Between 1929 and 1938 this company alone took out twenty-nine patents on its method, and in addition had to use those of a great many others. It was tried out for the first time in 1929 on the coast of Norway, when three whales were killed, and in 1930-1 in the Antarctic, where it proved quite a triumph, accounting for twenty-one blue and ten fin whales. The conclusive proof that the method was the equal of the shell harpoon came in 1934-5. A Norwegian whale catcher shot 212 whales, of which 198 were killed and caught. In the following season two other whale catchers were fitted with this apparatus, and in the six seasons from 1934 to 1940 a total of 2,348 were killed electrically, an average of 200 per whale catcher per season, whereas the average for the entire pelagic catch was 170. In terms of BWU, however, the electrically equipped catchers registered below the average, as they had a much larger percentage of fin whales, experience showing that these whales were far more susceptible to electric shock than blue whales.

Why did the company abandon the system, when it was so close to success? The company itself declared that this was for financial reasons. The equipment for the electric method cost Kr.40,442 per catcher and the shell method Kr.16,219. Furthermore, the electric method was more expensive to maintain. On the other hand it was stated that the percentage of whales lost was smaller, *inter alia* because the animal was so instantaneously paralysed that the air was not squeezed out of its lungs and it therefore remained afloat. Other advantages mentioned were that there was hardly any use for lines, that there were no shell splinters to damage machinery during processing, that the method saved time, and that it was more humane. Reports, however, differ so markedly that it is most probable that the success of the method was entirely dependent on the gunner's skill. How many whales were killed electrically can only be stated with certainty as far as Norwegian whalers are concerned: a total of 2,658 before the war. In addition a smaller, unknown number were killed by the Germans.

After the war experiments were continued both by Norwegian companies and particularly by the British company United Whalers. Their aims, however, clearly differed: while the Norwegians were concerned with discovering more effective catching methods, the British were out to find more humane ones. This was primarily due to insistent lobbying by Dr. Harry Lillie. As ship's doctor on board the *Southern Harvester* on her maiden voyage in 1946-7, he had been so shocked at the cruelty to whales involved in the use of the shell harpoon — on one occasion it had taken five hours and nine harpoons to kill a female — that he tirelessly championed electric killing, which in his opinion was more humane. He persuaded the major animal protection societies, first and foremost the Universities Federation for Animal Welfare (U.F.A.W.) to campaign vigorously against the shell harpoon. They in turn persuaded Sir VYVYAN BOARD, chairman of United Whalers, to start wide-ranging experiments on the *Balaena* expedition. All in all, United Whalers are believed to have spent £118,000 on these experiments. Together with the General Electric Company and Westly Richards Ltd., arms manufacturers of Birmingham, a company was formed, Electric Whaling Ltd. Two hundred different types of forerunner, with an electric lead woven in, were tried, but all of them suffered from some weakness or other. The special cannon proved so inefficient that they reverted to the ordinary kind.

The system was not entirely useless: during the first season, 1949-50, thirty-eight whales were killed by the electric method. The I.W.C. subcommittee concluded its assessment of the electric method by stating that it had shown such considerable possibilities that the experiments should continue. It deplored the fact that Norwegians and Englishmen were experimenting separately and recommended co-operation, where "the special advantage of British equipment and the superior Norwegian forerunners and harpoons should be combined". A meeting for this purpose was also arranged, and its unanimous conclusion provides a final judgment on electric whale shooting: "For the moment there does not appear to be a basis for starting new experiments. The electric method involves so many uncertain factors, both technically and biologically, that it cannot today be said to offer definite advantages over the shell harpoon method." However, at the time of going to press, the Commission is still investigating humane killing, and has funded a study of the problem.

In 1956 three Japanese companies jointly despatched a whale catcher to the Antarctic with electric catching equipment. The whales, however, were not killed instantaneously and — most significant of all for Japanese whaling — the electric current prevented circulation of the blood, thus lowering the quality of the whale meat. As the Japanese paper *Asahi Shimbun* put it: "At that time the harpoon with a flat head had already proved its superior strength, and the electric harpoon and the harpoon with the pointed head became obsolescent and useless." The Norwegian engineer who was responsible for the United Whalers experiments in the whaling grounds was of the opinion that the nylon forerunner had played an important role in the abandonment of electric shooting. Its great elasticity and tremendous strength, combined with the improved shells, provided a safe and superior method. The problem of a cable capable of stretching and contracting in tune with the fore-harpoon and shell had again resisted innovation.

In February 1958 the United Nations held a conference in Geneva on rules at sea. On this occasion the World Federation for the Protection of Animals, with Dr. Lillie as its energetic spokesman, supported a proposal to incorporate in the laws a provision on cruelty to animals, but the resolution adopted restricted itself to requesting states to "prescribe such methods for the catching of living creatures in the sea, particularly seal and whale, as to spare them as much suffering as possible". Both this result and the defeat of a Bill introduced in the British House of Lords to provide £10,000 government aid to United Whalers for its electric catching experiments discouraged the champions of a "project where disappointment has followed disappointment".

We have previously followed the development of wireless in communication between the ships of an expedition, and between these and the home country, up to the mid-1920s. We have also mentioned C. A. Larsen's profound regret that he had no direction finding apparatus in the Ross Sea in 1923-4, when one of his boats had only an ordinary transmitter. For the next season, 1924-5, all five whale catchers had regular direction finding apparatus, and these were of inestimable value to enable them to find their way back to the factory ship from a distance of up to 100 miles. From then on direction finding apparatus was standard equipment on all whale catchers.

The work of further developing wireless in whaling was resumed just after the war. The radio telephone was also adopted almost at the same time as the wireless telegraph. The latter was installed on one of the *Sir James Clark Ross*'s whale catchers in 1923-4, and the first complete set-up for $\frac{1}{4}$ kW spark transmitter was fitted up in the whale catcher *Nebb* (A/S Ørnen) in 1924. During the 1924-5 season the wireless operators on the whale catchers in the Ross Sea had contrived a provisional radio telephone, which did good service and was also used in the following season. In 1926-7 regular telephone systems were installed in both factory ships, the *C. A. Larsen* and the *Sir James Clark Ross*, and in all their whale catchers. The apparatus was so effective that in favourable atmospheric conditions they could hear one another at a distance of 2,000 miles. In that season Unilever's two expeditions were both equipped with direction finding and telephone stations. These have been considered the first of their kind in whaling, but at the Stromness station radio telephone communication with whale catchers was in use as far back as 1925-6. In 1929 the British Marconi Co. supplied direction finding apparatus and radio telephones to all Salvesen's boats. It goes without saying that the introduction of the radio telephone caused a veritable revolution : the factory ship was at all times informed of the whale catchers' positions and catch, of quantities of whales, etc., while the catchers could be directed to areas where catching prospects were most favourable. But rivals, too, could listen in on conversations and draw useful conclusions. This lesson was soon learnt, and conversations were carried on in code, each company having its own.

What the radio telephone meant to intercommunication, the short wave transmitter meant to the expeditions' links with the outside world. The powerful long wave transmitter which the *Sir James Clark Ross* had been equipped with in 1923 enabled it to maintain a connection with Norway via New Zealand at all times. It would otherwise have been difficult to make contact with the floating factory. A few years later these complications were done away with, thanks to the short wave transmitter, and in 1925 the *Sir James Clark Ross* succeeded in establishing direct communication with San Francisco, a distance of 5,000 miles, an event which caused a sensation. Thanks to further progress on 11 February 1927 the factory ship was able to contact Bergen Radio in Norway with the first message by short wave that this station had ever received from a Norwegian vessel. The very next season a number of factory ships, with the aid of their short wave transmitters, were able to maintain daily contact with the home country.

The company was kept informed constantly of the situation in the whaling grounds, and the contact whalers had with their families was of inestimable psychological value.

Among the many inventions that constitute milestones in the technical development of whaling should be mentioned the whale claw, for which ANTON GJELSTAD, of Sandefjord, was awarded a patent in 1931. The whale claw was first tried out in 1932-3, and from the outset achieved success. It weighed *c.* 1½ tons, but stout equipment was needed to hoist a weight of over 100 tons. The heavier the whale, the firmer was the grip of the claw. It meant that the hands no longer had to undertake the highly risky work of making their way down the slipway and adjusting the rump strap in a heavy sea. The importance attached to the claw was shown when the *Kosmos II*'s claw broke at the very start of the 1934 season; one of the whale catchers was immediately despatched to fetch a reserve claw 850 miles away. In the meantime, work was considerably slowed down as it was necessary to revert to the old method.

No innovations were made in flensing or lemming (cutting up the meat) on deck. The curved flensing knife and the bone saw were and still are the tools used by the hands, despite many attempts to replace them by mechanised equipment.

For reducing the raw material and extracting as much oil as possible two new apparatuses have proved exceptionally important. These are the Kværner cooker and the gluewater separators. As the name indicates, the former of these was made by the firm of Kværner Brug of Oslo, on the firm's own patents. The Kværner cookers were based on the same principle as the Hartmann cooker: an internal rotating perforated drum (draining drum) and an attached reception tank and oil separator. The reason why a patent could be given to the former without violating the latter was that it differed from it in two respects: the Hartmann cooker had a transverse axle and was filled continuously, whereas the Kværner cooker had a shaft journal at each end and was filled completely prior to every try-out. Subsequent Hartmann cookers were made on a smaller scale, and intended for the boiling of blubber, with a larger one for meat and bone. The largest Kværner cooker had 50 per cent greater capacity than any previous apparatus. The numbers of the three types — 19, 29, and 34 — indicate the metric cubic capacity and the approximate weight in tons. From the very first (1930-1) these cookers, with their sturdy design, reliability and their large capacity, successfully competed with the Hartmann apparatus. Of the latter, 164 had already been delivered before the first Kværner cooker reached the market. Three-quarters of them were designed for boiling blubber, for which they were still preferred, while the Kværner cooker appeared to be unrivalled for meat and particularly for the more fatty bones. Both factories produced approximately 350 apparatuses each. The last Kværner cooker was supplied to the Barrier Whaling Co., New Zealand, in 1960. Kværner Brug supplied much other equipment for the whaling fleet, *inter alia* very large evaporators capable of producing as much as 350 tons of fresh water a day.

Both the Hartmann and the Kværner apparatuses worked quickly and effectively in dealing with the raw material, but opinions differ as to their ability to extract oil, and a number of whalers still swore by the open cookers for processing blubber and the pressure boilers for meat and bone. The rotary apparatuses were primarily intended for the factory ships, where they were economical in terms of both space and efficiency. On the *Salvestria* in 1930-1 there were fourteen Hartmann cookers and nineteen pressure boilers, and on the *Saragossa* respectively two and twenty, as well as eight open cookers. It was consequently possible to make a comparison, and it turned out that a Hartmann bone boiler could be filled eleven times in the course of two days and the pressure boiler three times. In 1929 Hartmann had started making the larger, special bone boilers, which were not intended for continuous filling, as the other boilers had such a small opening that it took a disproportionately long time to divide up the bones (jawbones had to be cut up into forty pieces). A main objection to both types of rotary boilers was that, with their tremendous capacity, although they processed the raw material quickly, enormous wastage was involved, with as much as 20 per cent of the oil being dumped in the sea with the gluewater.

How was the raw material utilised in the 1930s? According to the Norwegian Whaling Act "the *oil* of all whales shall be extracted by the boiling or other method of all blubber, meat, and bone, except for the internal organs, baleen, and fins". The law, in fact, is concerned only with the oil, clearly indicating that as far as the legislative authorities at the time were concerned whaling meant the extraction of oil. Subsequently this provision has been amended to run "all parts of such whales shall be processed by boiling or in some other way", and the word oil is not mentioned. The material prior to 1936-7 does not provide a very reliable picture of the extent to which the whale was processed. Not until after that time do we have technical-scientific research results on which to base ourselves. These show that boiling could mean a great many different things, and that it was bound to vary very considerably according to the nature of the raw material (lean or fat, blubber, meat, bone), and that there was still a long way to go to the perfect result in terms of both quality and quantity. In the season mentioned there were two inspectors with each expedition, and there is probably a connection between this and a rise in the try-out of meat oil and bone oil. The increase, however, varied enormously, from 3 to 68 per cent for seven Norwegian factory ships, while a few recorded a decline. Whilst one factory ship had 40 per cent *more* meat and bone oil than blubber oil, on another the processed quantity of meat and bone oil only constituted 22 per cent of the blubber oil. The difference may be due to two factors: that blubber was also processed in the meat and bone apparatuses, and in the second place that, given good catches, the carcasses were either wholly or partly thrown overboard, only the blubber being used.

On the basis of five years' research, scientists concluded that in whales with normal fat content it could on an average be calculated that the proportion between blubber oil and meat and bone oil (carcass oil) was as 100:127 (44:56 per cent), but returns from ten Norwegian factory ships in 1935-6 showed a proportion of 100:86 and from twelve factory ships in 1936-7 100:102. Despite this discrepancy it was not considered that any charges could be raised for violation of the statutory injunction of full processing (since calculations were based on so many uncertain factors). Only in two cases between 1930 and 1939 was a whaling manager fined for a poor try-out.

The most difficult task of the observer was to ensure complete extraction of the oil. The greatest loss did not occur when unprocessed raw material was dumped into the sea, but when oil was blown out to sea or thrown overboard with the grax. Both these losses were avoided with the use of the gluewater separator and by processing the grax and turning it into meal on the factory ships. At the shore stations the bulk of the oil was skimmed off in clearing troughs and most of the stations produced meal, but the motion of the ship and lack of space made this a difficult problem on board the factory ships.

A distinction must be made between two kinds of separator, oil separators and gluewater separators. To put it quite simply, the former separated gluewater (and foreign bodies) from the oil, the latter the oil from the gluewater. To these can be added the American Super-D-Canters, which separated solid bodies (fibrous remains) from the gluewater. The three types most in use were the Swedish "De Laval", the German "Westfalia", and the British "Sharples". About 90 per cent of the separators in Norwegian whaling were of Swedish manufacture; the other two naturally were most used in their respective home countries. The first attempts to extract oil from the water from pressure boilers by means of separators were initiated in Stromness Harbour in 1924. Since the 1870s separators had been made for dairies, and in 1916 the first models for the purifying of ordinary oil, but separating whale oil posed special problems, which it took several years to solve. Not till the 1927-8 season can it be said that the various types of separators were in general use in the Antarctic. The very different results achieved appear to show that in the case of separators, as with all other apparatus, the yield depended upon how they were used and not on the apparatus *per se*. Be that as it may, the innovation was quickly adopted and prior to the 1928-9 season we find four brands competing keenly with one another.

Initially, all these exhibited one weakness: the viscous oil, containing fibrous remains, tended to block the separator. This problem was solved by warming up the oil and mixing it with sea water at a temperature of 90-95°C; this made it easier to get rid of foreign bodies, probably because their specific weight in relation to the thinly flowing mass was different from that in relation to the viscous oil. The great advantage of separators was that they obviated the use of clearing tanks and recookers, thus making available much needed space in the factory ship. The separators worked independent of the ship's motion: they could be placed anywhere on board, and the oil conveyed direct from them to the tanks. The tendency for the free fatty acid to increase during storage and transport was almost entirely removed as a result of purification, and this meant better quality and price. Samples taken in 1928 showed, for example, that separated oil from the same try-out, after

109. Gluewater separators.

a month's storage, had 1.55 per cent free fatty acid, whereas oil clarified in the old manner had 5.7 per cent. With the slipway, the whale claw, and the separator, pelagic catching in the 1930s had acquired three invaluable aids to save time, labour, and money. During the years when the whale oil market was slack this was of tremendous importance to operating results.

These separators improved the quality of the oil, but failed to save any of the oil that was wasted. Everyone realised that this took place, and attempts to avoid loss have been made ever since modern whaling started. Two methods were in general use: the clearing troughs, where the oil that floated up was skimmed off, and re-cookers. Some oil was obtained, but by no means all, and it was of poor quality. One of the first and most comprehensive attempts to calculate how much oil was wasted was carried out at Prince Olav Harbour in 1920-1 by Unilever experts. Like so many other calculations of a similar kind, this one, too, of necessity is based on several uncertain factors. It is obvious that entirely accurate figures could only be obtained if all the oil could have been extracted. But by precise analysis of the fat content of the various parts of the whale and in the gluewater and the residues, it was possible to get approximate figures. The result was as shown in Table 38.

Of the blubber there was a wastage of 2,300 barrels, of the meat 2,202 barrels, and of the bone 1,818 barrels of oil, a total loss of 6,320 barrels or 16.3 per cent of the total estimated oil content of the raw material. In addition to this, a wastage of 300 to 500 barrels had to be

Table 38. OIL YIELD FROM DIFFERENT PARTS OF THE WHALE
CARCASS, 1920-1

376 BWU reduced to 31,387 barrels, 83.5 per BWU.
Of the blubber oil 13,193 barrels of No. 1; 2,280 barrels of No. 2; all meat and
bone oil: 16,914 barrels of No. 3.
The grax (the residues) had the following composition:

	Water	Oil	Dry Substance
Blubber	51.7%	30.0%	18.2%
Meat	54.0%	9.6%	35.8%
Bone	23.0%	10.5%	66.3%

reckoned with during storage and transport. With a price of £40 a ton,
the 6,320 barrels represented a gross sum of £42,000. Experiments had
shown that oil could be separated from blubber residue in three ways:
by centrifugal force, by evaporation of the water in a vacuum, or by
filtering. Centrifugal force showed the most promising results. References
to gluewater, however, only mention all the glue material that could be
extracted, and say nothing about the extraction of oil from it, a problem
which at the time offered no solution. As far as the drying of meat and
bone residues for production of guano was concerned, all the managers
in South Georgia agreed that it was unprofitable. In Prince Olav
Harbour it would have been possible to obtain 6,031 tons of guano
from the residues, once all the oil had been removed from it by the
petrol extraction method; with a price of £12 a ton this would have
amounted to £73,200. Since the guano factory had not yet been
completed in 1920-1, it was impossible to say what production would
have cost. Of the 3,735 tons of coal used throughout the season,
exactly one-half had been used for boiling and the other half for
heating and propulsion machinery. Given that about 15 per cent of the
oil was being wasted, it is no surprise that there was a proposal to obtain
two kinds of separator for the ensuing season, one for purifying the
blubber oil so that all of it was Quality No. 1, and one to separate
the oil from the blubber residues. The latter indicated the way in which
the problem was finally solved. In September 1924 Lord Leverhulme
wrote that he would be disappointed if in 1925 "centrifuges for the
extraction of oil" were not installed in all stations, in the Hebrides,
in South Africa, in South Georgia, and on the factory ship. The fact
that it should have taken fifteen years to devise a satisfactory gluewater
separator may be ascribed to increasing use of rotary cookers. Separating
gluewater from these cookers posed the problem that, owing to the
thoroughness of the boiling, the raw material was broken down into
such fine particles that it was difficult to extract it.

Strenuous efforts were made to solve the problem in the 1930s, partly
for economic reasons, partly in order to observe the demand for full

utilisation of the raw material. When separation of gluewater is mentioned on several occasions, this is a reference to separation of the oil from the clearing tanks. This was, in fact, how it was done on the *Skytteren* in 1934-5. On that occasion no oil was obtained because the separators simply seized up, but in the autumn of 1935 472 barrels were obtained, an amount that could have been doubled if all the gluewater had been treated. Separation was carried out in connection with a meal plant. Briefly, the process involved passing the residues in the hot residue and gluewater mix from the rotary cookers through a strainer so that the oily gluewater was piped into an emulsion tank. In a press as much oil and gluewater as possible was pressed out of the residues and piped to the same tank, from which it was conveyed to the separators. The oil from these was pumped into the tanks, and the separated gluewater was dumped overboard. From the press the residues passed through a drying section to the mill and strainer, and were then ready to be placed in sacks. The extracted oil was a little darker than usual, but even so "good, merchantable oil", as the station manager said.

It was not until after 1938, following a great many unsuccessful tests, that the De Laval gluewater separators had been perfected and proved sufficiently reliable and simple for the first four to be installed on board the *Unitas* in 1938-9 and four on the *Terje Viken* the following season. On the latter, 4,000 barrels of oil were extracted from the meat- and bone-gluewater; if everything had been separated, the result would have been 6,000 barrels. The reason this was not used for blubber was because the whalers insisted that the loss of oil here was so small that it was not worth it But the above-mentioned tests had shown that this was precisely where the wastage in oil was greatest. The factory manager relates that when he tried to sell the separators to a whaling director, the latter took umbrage and interpreted this as an accusation of not extracting properly; but when he saw how much more oil the others obtained, an order was soon placed for a large number. It is true to say of these gluewater separators that they were unable to take the gluewater direct from the boil-up, but only after it had passed through the vibration strainers, or had remained in the clearing troughs to separate the solid elements.

De Laval (later Alfa-Laval) used the war years to improve separators further, and they were ready after the war to supply the whole of the restored whaling fleet. The first experiments were an unconditional success: on one factory ship 6,900 barrels were extracted, and on another 4,700. In 1948 Salvesen's two factory ships had eight oil and sixteen gluewater separators each; the *Balaena* had a total of thirty-two, the *Thorshøvdi* eight of each kind, and so on. How much of the high-quality oil that previously had been lost was saved in this way is given in the records of the various floating factories: in 1948-9 for the *Balaena* 20,000 barrels, for Salvesen's two factory ships together 21,000, and for the *Kosmos III* 10,200 and in 1949-50 14,000. In that season the *Empire Victory* had 13,500, the *Balaena* 12,000, etc., all the way down to 6,000. For the seven Norwegian and British factory ships for which figures exist the gluewater oil comprised 7.4 per cent of total production. If this percentage is used for all the floating factories of the two countries, the result is 20,366 tons in 1949-50, which with a market price of £82 provided a sales value of £1.67 million. In 1950-1 the price was £112, and as it may be assumed that all the factory ships mentioned were at that time extracting gluewater oil, the total value was in the region of £2.6 million. If we include the factory ships of other countries and the shore stations, even larger sums are involved. There is hardly any investment in direct increase of oil production that has proved more profitable than this. To this must be added the extra value of the improved quality of the ordinary oil, thanks to purification by the separators.

The De Laval separators were not the only kind available: before the gluewater passed into these separators, the solid mass had been separated from it by means of vibratory strainers. On the one hand a great deal of oil was lost in this, and on the other hand the oil content made it unserviceable for drying out as meal. As a replacement for these vibratory strainers the American Super-D-Canters were tested. The first was installed in 1948, and proved so successful that three more were bought for the 1949-50 season. The oil content in the residues dropped from 15 to 5 per cent, while at the same time the unseparated gluewater was clarified and had no difficulty in passing through the gluewater separators. A Super-D-Canter had a capacity of 6,800 litres of gluewater residue per hour, i.e. with a sludge content of 15 per cent, of which 45 per cent was dry substance, it would be possible every day to obtain approximately 9 tons of feed meal, and, through the separators, about 20 tons of oil. Ten of these at a time were purchased for another factory ship, costing Kr.100,000 (*c.* £5,500) each, but all had paid their way by the end of the first season. They revealed the following advantages over the vibratory strainers: (1) The dry substance content of the unseparated residues amounted to about 50 per cent, in the vibratory sieves (strainers) to about 31 per cent. (2) The oil content using this was twice to three times higher, and with the Super-D-Canter less than 2 per cent, i.e. the dried residue meal contained about 4 per cent of oil. (3) The gluewater was purer, so that it could be separated more frequently without an addition of heated sea water. (4) Using the Super-D-Canter approximately 90 per cent of the oil passed into the gluewater, with the vibratory strainers only 50 per cent, while the remainder was lost with the residue that was dumped overboard. (5) The same result as with the Super-D-Canter could be achieved with the screw presses used in the herring industry, and they would have a far greater capacity, but in the factory ship they would occupy too much space. In short, the Super-D-Canter was much simpler to operate, occupied little space, and replaced both the vibratory strainer and the press, and there was no need to tear the residue up into small pieces, as it emerged in the form of a fine meal once it had passed through the apparatus.

In 1953 a new method for recovering dry material was adopted in Iceland. This consisted of evaporation of gluewater in a plant that had been used in the herring industry as well as on a shore station in Norway and in South Georgia since the end of the war. The evaporated concentrate, containing 45 to 50 per cent dry substance, was then, after being mixed with residual meal, conveyed through a flame dryer to the mill and poured into sacks. This process increased meal production by 50 per cent. However, as the evaporated gluewater was highly hygroscopic, there was a tendency for whale meal mixed with it to clog.

These experiments show the interest that was being devoted to the utilisation of the dry substance content of the whale carcass. This is the reason why so much space has been devoted to this subject: it was one of the main problems with which practical and scientific whaling research had long been concerned. If a process could be discovered using such simplified apparatus that there was room for it on a factory ship, a process combining increased oil extraction with grax that had such a low oil content that it could immediately be dried to produce meal, considerable sums could be saved.

By following the development of the separators we have anticipated the course of events and need to revert to the first attempts at commercial exploitation on board the factory ships of the dry substance of the whale. In the course of time so many methods have been invented for this purpose, that there is no room here to describe them all: we need only mention the main principles of three or four of the most generally used methods. This aspect of whaling research became a technical-chemical science of which no one had dreamed twenty or thirty years earlier, when boiling was a straightforward matter. Now detailed investigations were made of the importance of the various methods for the protein content of whale meal, for the consistency of the vitamins during the production process, and for the digestibility of the various types of feed meal in feeding experiments with cattle.

We can distinguish between two kinds of whale meal: whale meat meal, which was produced from pure meat, mainly the lean dorsal meat, and whale meal, which was produced from the grax. Both kinds were commonly designated (whale) feed meal. (Pure whale bone meal was also produced: its content of organic substances and protein was very low, and of alkali very high, so that in its pure state it was only suitable as guano.) In the former successful attempts were made to raise the protein content to over 65 per cent when it was made of raw material with a low fat content, i.e. below 2 per cent. In the other, the fat content was higher, 10 to 20 per cent, and the protein content 60 to 75 per cent. As whale meal was to be used as a source of albumen, its value depended on its protein content, and this declined as the fat content increased. To ensure that whale meal should be capable of being used and of competing with other artificial cattle feed rich in albumen, the fat content should be as far below 10 per cent as possible. As it proved possible, using various methods, to reduce the fat content to an absolute minimum, in the late 1930s whale meal with a low fat content became the artificial feed richest in albumen of all artificial feeds on the market, and by fully exploiting the raw material it was possible to supply practically unlimited amounts of it, but, as one group of experts declared, protein can mean a lot of very different things. It consists of twenty-two different amino acids, of which ten are of vital importance to animals and human beings. For this reason it was very important to establish the contents of these in pure whale meal, in order to assess its value as feed, and the influence of the various production methods on the relative composition of the different amino acids.

The above should indicate that the problem was not as simple as suggested by those who criticised whalers for throwing overboard so much nourishing raw material, and for failing to show more consideration for the F.A.O.'s earnest appeal to assist in remedying the most serious problem facing the undernourished portion of the world's population — the shortage of albuminous substances. In the case of whaling two problems were involved, one of a practical-technical nature and the other of an economic nature, which critics likewise failed to take into proper account. The first involved the question of space in the factory ship. The apparatus for the production of feed meal took up so much room that it was difficult to accommodate it in the most convenient places without displacing the boiling equipment; and also the finished product required storage space on board, which inevitably would mean less space for oil. There was little point in solving the problem technically if it could not be solved economically, and this depended entirely on the market needs, which in turn determined the price. The apparatus and its installation had to be amortised, the product stored and transported to market and sold, production on board required an increased labour force which had to be accommodated and paid, the energy for production required increased supplies of fuel oil, and so forth. Shore stations all over the world had for a great many years been turning out feed meal, but as a rule it had proved difficult to market it at a profit, and it could be assumed that it would prove still more difficult, and further depress prices, if the market were flooded with the large quantities which the factory ships could, in theory, produce. Briefly, the problem was as follows: would it be more profitable to restrict production merely to whale oil or to supplement it with feed meal? The nature of the problem, however, changed somewhat in more recent years, as there were not sufficient supplies of raw material to engage the entire capacity of the factory ship in the production of whale oil, and there was now time, place, and sufficient labour available for other forms of production. Other by-products were also introduced which paid off better than whale meal. In conclusion we might say that its production never really established itself as an integral part of whaling from a factory ship: a great many factory ships never had the necessary apparatus, and on those that had, it was essentially more experimental than a question of regular commercial production. Although large quantities of high-grade feed meal have been produced in pelagic whaling, attempts to make it just as important a product as oil have proved a failure.

In the 1930s there were two main methods for the production of whale meat meal competing with one another, the "Fauth" method and the "Nygaard" method, the first the invention of the German business-man PHILIPP L. FAUTH, the second the brainchild of Johan O. Nygaard of Oslo. After an agreement had been made with Fauth an experimental plant was installed in 1932-3 on board the *Sir James Clark Ross*. Although it revealed many weaknesses, the tests that season and the following season were so promising that a new, larger plant was purchased for regular operations. This new plant failed to come up to expectations: 40 tons of feed meal a day and 30 to 40 kg. of oil per ton of meat. The entire production in 1934-5 was 186 tons and no oil.

After £55,000 had been spent during the first three seasons on these experiments, starting with the 1935-6 season, there was some return: 1,163 tons of meal, which was sold to Germany at £10 a ton, a price that covered reasonable depreciation. In 1936-7 937 tons of meal were produced, and this sold for £12 10s; also sold were 470 barrels of oil No. 1 from the lean dorsal meat. The season of 1937-8 proved more successful, with 1,250 tons of meal and 170 tons of oil, but the bulk of this had to be stored, only 219 tons being sold. When war broke out 1,567 tons were in storage, which, incidentally, proved a much-needed standby after Norway had been occupied. As so often in the past in the case of shore stations, feed meal proved a difficult item to market, as Norwegian production of herring meal more than covered the require-ments for albuminous animal feed stuffs. Owing to its very special taste, the meal was not used in its pure state, but with other vegetable feed material added. In 1939-40 the Ross Sea Co. suspended production, as the company had operated at a loss in every season, but the plant was retained, and in 1944-6 approximately 1,100 tons a season were produced. Although the price was as high as about £30 a ton, at the very most this could only ensure a profit of £5 a ton. A complete Fauth plant cost at that time approximately £38,000. Fauth's method was also in use on the German factory ships *Jan Wellem, Walter Rau, Unitas,* and *Wikinger,* and on the *C. A. Larsen* after she was chartered to Germany in 1936. The factory ships operating for the Germans produced in 1937-8 7,100 tons of feed meal and in 1938-9 approximately 11,400 tons, three times more than any of the other whaling nations.

A method which in its main principle approximated closely to Fauth's, but which has been less used, goes by the name of "Rose Down", after its manufacturers, Rose, Down & Thompson Ltd. of Hull, who produced machinery for the oil industry. Here, too, the meat was cut up into small pieces and carefully preheated. Attempts were then made first of all to dry the mass in a vacuum, but either very large masses were involved, requiring such a large consumption of energy that production could not take place on board a ship, or else the fat could not be dehydrated, as so much of it contained about the same fat percentage as the meat. If the meal had a high fat content, it was indigestible. Vacuum drying was tried in Leith Harbour; it apparently proved possible to obtain a meal with over 60 per cent protein, while retaining all the nutritive substances, including the oil, which made it difficult to market it. Towards the end of the season, when the whale was fatter, production had to be suspended. Unilever, whose engineers carried out extensive laboratory studies of the whale oil and the dry substance, also tried a so-called *Schlotterhose* apparatus on the *Southern Empress,* but after a few seasons it was taken ashore in order to make room for larger cooking apparatuses for oil.

While the method of the German Philipp L. Fauth was the one most generally used in Norwegian whaling, the apparatus invented by the Norwegian Johan O. Nygaard was the one most used in British whaling. As noted elsewhere, Nygaard, embittered when he failed to get the support he had expected in Norway, tried his luck abroad, "with the result that this, I am convinced, will mean a marked decline in the Norwegian whaling industry, while a new whaling industry flourishes" (abroad). Briefly, his process was as follows. The meat was boiled at a low temperature in an oil bath in a vacuum. While in the vacuum, the water was expelled and — this was the most important feature of the process — all the other component parts of the raw material were retained. In other words, this involved a 100 per cent use of the dry substance content of the raw material. One of the objections to the method was that it demanded somewhat complicated apparatus: first of all a machine which cut the meat into pieces of 15 to 20 kg., then a

110. This picture shows the enormous waste of raw material in the blubber and left to putrefy with 60-70% of the total oil contents earliest period of Antarctic whaling. The beach of Deception is (c. 1914). covered with thousands of whale carcasses stripped of only the belly

scavenging container to rinse out the blood, then a meat grinder converting it into mincemeat. After boiling the mincemeat, mixed with oil, was conveyed to a horizontal boiler with a system of tubes (pipes) and indirectly heated by steam in the tubes, so that the steam made no contact with the meat and the oil. This boiler was connected to a vacuum pump, with a condenser, where the water forced out of the meat was condensed, and together with the condensed steam in the heated tubes, conveyed back to the boiler, so that no fresh water was wasted. When as much of this as possible had been removed, reducing the water content to about 7 per cent, the oil had to be removed. The first stage of this process was done in a clearing tank, where the dry substance sank to the bottom and the oil was run off, and then in the ordinary way in a screw press, which theoretically would reduce the oil content to 6 per cent.

Among the advantages claimed for this method were that it used no fresh water, that oil of the poorest quality could be used for the oil cooking, and that it could be used again and again, and that the quantitative utilisation of dry substance was almost complete, whereas using other methods there was a loss of 10 to 12 per cent. Among the objections to this method one was that the apparatus required thirty hands to operate it, that when lean meat was used more oil was added than was recovered, and that the oil content in the finished meal was as much as 12 per cent. As in the case of all these inventions theory was one thing, practice something quite different, especially when it came down to the costs of installation and operation. A complete Nygaard plant would come to about £36,000, whereas a Kværner cooker, for the extraction of oil from the same raw material, cost £7,000, and it could be serviced by one hand. The price of the meal would then determine whether the larger investment was worth it. Salvesen would not install it on more than one factory ship, as he had been forced to sell (1933) 631 tons at £9 18s, and this left no margin for profit. According to Salvesen's records the price fluctuated between 1934 and 1939 from (at its lowest) £8 10s in 1936 to (at its highest) £12 1s 6d in 1938, giving an average of £10 3s 7d.

Nygaard's method was tried out from the 1932-3 season onwards. Reports issued from year to year enable us to follow the constant improvements that were made in this apparatus. Finally, in 1935-6 comes the announcement that the plant functioned well, with a daily production of 16 tons (whereas the Rose-Down apparatus yielded six tons) and in 1937-8 there is a report that the plant functioned completely as planned. A very detailed estimate of production expenses in 1932-3 (including insurance, loss of interest, amortisation, freight, loading and discharging, fuel, wages, etc.) produced a result of £4 16s a ton. With a sales price of £10 this would leave a good margin of profit. However, expenses rose sharply up to 1939. Despite the relatively high fat content, 10-12 per cent, Unilever declared themselves satisfied with the meal, especially in experimental feeding of pigs.

Large-scale production of meal created the problem of finding storage space on board and of transferring sacks to a transport ship in the open sea. In 1936-7 the factory ship with the largest production, 2,115 tons, was the *Sydis*; in 1937-8 it was the *Unitas* with 2,852 tons. When Rosshavet suspended production of meat meal in 1939-40, the following three reasons were given: the difficulty of finding storage space on board, expensive transport over long distances, and the impossibility of finding a market for the production of the two last seasons, which had resulted in a deficit of £70,000. For 3,288 tons, sold to Germany, a price of between only £10 and £12 had been obtained. On the basis of a thorough analysis of the various methods two experts concluded that Fauth's method gave the most favourable operational results, and Nygaard's the best utilisation of the raw material, but neither had succeeded in discovering a rational way of utilising the dry substance of the whale on a factory ship. The *theoretical* solution of the problem doubled the value of production, and preserved huge quantities of nourishing material for the world, but the *practical* solution was somewhat different, and this was not understood by those who categorically demanded full utilisation of raw material, and levelled the most violent charges of waste against the whaling industry.

The production of whale meal showed a very sharp rise in the 1950s, amounting to double between 1950-1 and 1960-1 in the Antarctic. During the same period the production of whale meat increased sixfold, and there was also a sharp rise in the production of other by-products. This may have been because the drop in the production of whale oil meant that there was more storage space on board, and that the labour force was not fully occupied in the production of oil alone. For economic reasons the interest in production of whale meal slumped markedly in the 1960s, while whale meat retained its position : it was difficult to get the production of whale meal to show a profit, while the price of whale meat was relatively stable and favourable.

In the Antarctic production of whale meat for human consumption Japan has been predominant. Up to 1958 Britain was the only country apart from Japan with any sizeable production : she was then joined by Norway and in the following year by the Netherlands, but Britain then dropped out after 1961. For centuries the Japanese had been experts in the treatment of whale meat, and other nations learnt from them. A distinction must be made between two kinds of meat : that for human consumption and that for petfood, according to quality. While, naturally, putrefied meat could not be used for the latter purpose, the standard of quality was not so strict. Generally other substances were added, it was canned and sold as cat and dog food. The largest producer of this was the British firm of Petfoods Ltd. Meat from the Japanese shore stations could be marketed raw in neighbouring areas, meat from further afield could be salted, and to a certain extent air-dried (like pemmican from seal meat). In pelagic catching, too, there was initially no other method of preservation, before it became possible to deep-freeze meat. This could either be done in separate freezer plants in the factory ship or in special refrigerator vessels accompanying it. Transferring meat from one ship to another posed another problem.

In 1937 Taiyo Hogei K.K. despatched, initially by way of experiment, a refrigerator ship of 1,000 tons with the *Nisshin Maru* expedition. Some of the meat was transferred simply by allowing it to drift in the water just as it was, or inside a net fastened to a buoy, to be picked up by the refrigerator ship. Whale catchers, too, were used, but none of these methods was satisfactory, and only 167 tons were deep-frozen, while 184 tons were salted. In the following season, 1938-9, they started using small powered boats, which could carry a load of 4-5 tons, but this was often made impossible by rough seas. During that season the production of frozen whale meat in the Antarctic enjoyed a breakthrough. In 1939-40 Nippon Suisan K.K. sent the large refrigerator ship *Kosei Maru* of 8,223 gross tons with the *Tonan Maru II*. Production then rose to 2,547 tons of frozen and 4,436 tons of salted meat. The former was only one-third of the vessel's refrigerator capacity, as there was still difficulty in transferring and processing the meat at the speed the quality control demanded in the case of food for human consumption. In 1940-1 4,650 tons out of a total production of 13,560 tons of foodstuffs were deep-frozen from the six Japanese expeditions. The production of meat at the Japanese shore stations was far greater — in 1941 25,745 tons.

The other Japanese companies, instead of using large refrigerator ships, made use of a number of smaller vessels of around 1,000 tons. The Japanese Government fixed the following maximum prices in 1942 : for frozen whale meat 732 yen per long ton, frozen meat from the flukes 1,220 yen, and salted 407 yen. With frozen meat fetching almost twice the price of salted meat, it was not surprising that after the war every effort was made to deep-freeze all the meat and not to salt any. The Norwegian observer on board the *Hashidate Maru* in 1947-8 reported that apart from this factory ship with its 388 hands, the expedition included a refrigerator ship of 9,977 gross tons, an equally large vessel for salted products with 236 hands, a tanker of the same size for the transport of fuel to the whaling ground and of whale oil from the whaling grounds, two refrigerator ships of about 1,000 tons to transport rapidly frozen material from the refrigerator ships to Japan, and sixteen so-called Kawasaki boats, 12 metres long and with a beam of 3 metres, powered with 25 h.p. diesel engines, for transferring meat from the factory ship to the refrigerator ship.

Enough has already been said about Japanese meat production in the previous chapter : here we need merely mention that in the Antarctic production in the year 1956-7 exceeded 50,000 tons, in 1960-1 100,000 tons, culminating in 1964-5 with 147,721 tons out of a total production of 171,622 tons, the highest in this catch. It should also be pointed out that the bulk of the meat production in 1960s, recorded in statistics compiled in Norway, was sold to Japan. It is remarkable, and the clearest indication of the development, that as from and including 1960-1 up to and including 1964-5 meat production increases in inverse proportion to the production of whale oil. While 8 tons of meat per BWU were produced during the first season, in the last season the figure was 24.5 tons, and in 1967-8 nearly 40 tons. At that time the price of oil was £45, and if, at a conservative estimate, we put the price of meat at £125, the value of the total meat production in the Antarctic in 1967-8, 103,982 tons, was more than five times as much as the value of the whale oil (53,639 tons). Compared to the tremendous Japanese production in the Antarctic, in the North Pacific, in home waters, and in other areas, the production of other countries is insignificant.

The first non-Japanese expedition after the war to commence production of frozen whale meat was the *Balaena* of United Whalers Ltd. The meat was transferred from the floating factory to the refrigerator ship *Bransfield* as from the season 1947-8. The result that year was 4,062 tons. In 1948 Salvesen purchased and equipped the *Southern Raven* as a refrigerator ship, in answer to an appeal to assist in overcoming the acute shortage of meat in Great Britain. After two seasons, however, the demand for whale meat proved so small that production was suspended in 1950-1, for all time by Salvesens — the firm concentrated instead on a substantial production of whale meal — while the *Balaena* recommenced in 1951-2, continuing until both factory ship and refrigerator ship were sold to Japan in 1960. The first Norwegian meat production in the Antarctic was started by the Tønsberg Hvalfangeri in Husvik Harbour in 1957-8 and 1959-60 (for the 1958-9 season the station was closed). Norwegian meat production did not attain sizeable proportions until 1960-1, when the *Kosmos IV* was equipped with a refrigeration plant and concluded a three-year contract with Petfood Ltd. for the supply of its entire production. In 1965-7 production, approximately 7,000 tons, was doubled, because, in addition to this contract, one was also concluded with the Japanese for the supply of meat in the whaling grounds. During the seasons 1961-4 two other Norwegian factory ships concluded similar agreements with the Japanese and one factory ship did the same in 1966-7. Apart from the *Kosmos IV,* the *Willem Barendsz II* was the only European factory ship (apart from the Soviet ones) equipped with a refrigeration plant. Production commenced in 1959-60, and averaged 7,750 tons annually between 1960 and 1964. Finally, mention should be made of the relatively large amounts of frozen whale meat regularly produced by the station in Iceland. The value of sales of meat here between 1952 and 1968 varied between 56.7 and 31.1 per cent of the total production value, for oil from 57 to 24.9 per cent, and for feed meal from 25.8 to 7.2 per cent.

In 1948-9 careful investigations were carried out by a veterinary surgeon of the factors determining the quality of the meat. This turned out to depend not only on such an obvious factor as the time elapsing from the death of the whale to freezing, but also on the duration of the pusuit and the death agony, where the shot hit the whale, treatment (sanitary conditions) on the flensing deck, etc. It was an advantage if the whale, from which the meat was to be deep-frozen, had its belly split immediately after catching, so that the intestines fell out, and one of the main arteries severed so that heavy bleeding could ensue. As it was not always easy to do this at sea, one of the conclusions was that the meat of a whale whose belly had not been split and which had been towed for eight to ten hours, was not suitable for food.

Of the other by-products that have played a role both in the economy of whaling and as raw materials for other industries, mention may be made of various liver products and meat extract. It has long been known that the liver of marine animals is rich in vitamins. In the whale, and especially in the sperm and blue whale, Vitamin A is particularly prevalent, and Vitamin B also, including the important B12. The tremendous progress made by pharmaceutical research in the use of the endocrine glands of the major mammals had directed attention to the rich sources that are to be found in the whale's large internal organs. The liver in a blue whale of about 80 ft. weighs about 800 kg. The vitamin content was to be found in the liver oil, which was extracted, and a number of factory ships and shore stations had special plant for this purpose. Most of the liver was transported back home salted, frozen, or in the form of liver meal (liver flakes). As far back as the mid 1920s factory ships had brought home considerable quantities of salted liver. The extracted vitamins were either used alone, or they were added to other preparations, in particular to cod-liver oil, in order to increase the vitamin content. On the menu in the whaling grounds the liver of young, smaller animals was served as beef and is said to have been very tasty. There are no figures for the production of liver preparations in various forms prior to the Second World War, but we know that in the 1930s a great many experiments were carried out. Unilever were greatly interested in vitamin production, and, besides making use of their own two factory ships they rented space on four others for liver presses. In these presses the liver emerged rather like oatmeal: this was lightly dried and preserved under pressure in barrels without salting. In 1938-9, 1,893 tons of "liver cake" were imported into Britain, from which the vitamins were extracted and used mainly as a margarine additive. The *Unitas* produced approximately 350 tons of liver flakes every season between 1937 and 1939. In Norway we hear mention in the 1930s of two companies interested in whale liver.

As the whale liver required no complicated mechanical treatment before being transported home, every factory ship was capable of handling it. The total quantity in various forms varied from 1,000 to 2,000 tons annually from the Antarctic in the latter half of the 1940s and 1950s. While Norwegian and British production showed a marked decline during this period, Russian production increased, and rose even more in the 1960s, to over 2,500 tons in 1964-5. From then on the production of vitamins was also carried out on board Russian factory ships. Judging by statistics Japan appears to have shown less interest in this aspect of Antarctic whaling, probably because the liver as such was used as a foodstuff and because there was enough raw material in whaling grounds nearer home. Even though one source of raw material disappeared with the blue whale, there was no lack of this thanks to the tremendous increase in catches of sperm whales.

The famous German chemist JUSTUS VON LIEBIG, the founder of modern agricultural chemistry, discovered a method of producing meat extract at the end of the 1850s, and from the mid-1860s factories were set up in a great many of the major cattle-breeding countries of the world, particularly in South America. First to apply this method to major marine animals was the Swede, CARL ADOLPH SAHLSTRÖM, who in 1882 acquired American and British patents for the production of meat extract from sharks, whales and seals. A factory was built in Aberdeen in 1885, and it was said to have produced considerable quantities of a substance which in every way resembled beef extract. The process patented in 1933 by two Germans, Dr. H. SCHMALFUSS and Dr. H. WERNER, has been widely used since that time. There is no space here to deal with all the niceties of the various processes: common to all of them was that meat as free as possible from bone and fat was ground up fine, mixed with water, and carefully heated to a temperature of about 70°C. After a while the water was drained away from the meat mass, which was then pressed. The extracted "broth" was filtered and evaporated to the consistency of the extract — a thick, almost solid, dark-brown fluid, readily soluble in water. The components of the extract vary according to the nature of the raw material and the method of production. In the sales contract of the whaling companies the water content was not to exceed 24 per cent, the alkali 20 per cent, and the salt 5 per cent. The rest consists of other organic substances. The extract is in itself practically without nutritional value, but excellent

111. Seventy years after the first human footsteps on the Antarctic continent, the United States established its base at MacMurdo, Ross Sea.

as a full-bodied and tasty additive for sauces, dressings, beef cubes, etc. The major purchaser has been the Nestlé company in Switzerland.

Before the war experiments in the production of meat extract had made considerable progress on German factory ships: the Germans, after all, had discovered the best method, and yet comparatively small amounts were produced. In 1937-8 the *Walter Rau* produced 18 tons, though of such poor quality that the price was only 2 Marks per kilo. In 1938-9 production was 80 tons, and the *Jan Wellem* produced 1.2 tons of improved quality. After the war United Whalers introduced meat extract on the market. At times, however, it proved difficult to sell profitably. In the 1946-7 season the *Balaena* had a production of 101 tons of meat extract, in 1947-8 123.3 tons. Operating expenses for oil production at that time amounted to £1.1 million, and for by-products to £900,000. The latter provided a return of £2.9 million, whereas in the summer of 1948 none of the meat extract was sold, as the price was so poor. The balance between oil and by-products, on the other hand, fluctuated rapidly: in 1952-3 the *Balaena* earned £770,000 less on oil, but £550,000 more on by-products than in 1947-8. This, the manager declared, was an indication of how important it was to be able to vary production according to the market situation.

As demand rose, and with it the price, a great expansion ensued in 1958-9, when seven, and in 1959-60 eight, factory ships and Leith

Harbour had large plants. Production doubled to 1,101 tons in 1958-9, reaching a peak of 2,147 tons in 1959-60 and 2,768 tons in 1960-1. There was now a glut on the market, and prices dropped to an unprofitable level, and companies entered into an agreement to restrict production to two Norwegian and two British factory ships. As a result, production dropped to 923 tons in 1961-2 and to 518 tons in 1962-3. As the market improved, production rose sharply once again on the Norwegian factory ships from 1963-4, when the *Kosmos IV* had a large plant installed. The process on board was such that the best and leanest meat was frozen for pet food, gristly or fat meat was made into extract, and blubber and bone were cooked in order to extract oil. In this way a rational and total exploitation of the raw material was achieved. Apart from a very small quantity on board the *Willem Barendsz* and somewhat more on the Japanese factory ships, the Norwegians were practically the only ones to produce extract between 1963 and 1967. Whether the Soviet factory ships did so is not known. Norwegian production varied, according to whether the factory ship made contact with the Japanese for supplies of meat or not. When the *Sir James Clark Ross* was broken up, her extract plant was sold to Iceland, where the shore station, after 1967, introduced meat extract as a fourth product in addition to oil, meat, and meal. Produce has often had to be stored for long periods, but there seems to be no limit to the length of storage.

Of the endocrine glands in the whale, medical science has found the hypophysis the most important. That this small gland, set beneath the rear brain, was of vital importance *inter alia* for growth, had long been realised, but the discovery in the 1930s that it also contained the substance known as ACTH (adrenocorticotropic hormone) was a great advance. In 1949 an American doctor made the important discovery that ACTH was an excellent medical aid in the battle against rheumatic ailments, particularly arthritis. The main source for factory production was the swine hypophysis, weighing between 0.20 and 0.25 g. Countries such as Denmark and the United States, with their large pig-meat industries, were in this respect favourably placed compared to Norway. The director of a pharmaceutical factory then hit on the idea that Norway, as a whaling country, would have access to a very rich source, as a whale hypophysis weighs on an average some 20 g., i.e. a hundred times more than that of a pig. Furthermore, in the whale it was placed in such a way that it was much easier to extract. As a result of an agreement with whaling companies the collection of whale hypophyses on Norwegian and British factory ships was initiated. The first season, 1950-1, proved a great success, with 9,250 hypophyses, weighing a total of some 185 kg., corresponding to the hypophyses of almost a million pigs. These were given free by the whaling companies and the manufacturers for medical research. The companies earned considerable praise for the understanding shown in this matter. In 1951-7 some 4,000-8,000 hypophyses were collected every season, after which the number dropped to about 2,000 in 1960-1, and appears subsequently to have come to an end. In the statistics this item will be included under "other products". A manufacturer has explained that the collection of whale hypophyses stopped because the medical importance of ACTH declined, and it would be risky to base future production on such an uncertain source as whaling.

The collection of pancreases for the production of insulin and of thymus glands for the production of *inter alia* growth hormones was less successful. A small plant was installed in the *Thorshavet* for the production of insulin on board. On the *Kosmos* expedition a large number of pancreases were also collected in 1947-8, and these provided the basis for a considerable quantity of insulin. It was, however, a disappointment to discover that the insulin content in the whale's pancreas was less than expected. Nor did the collection of adrenal glands for the production of cortisone prove a success.

It need hardly be emphasised that for some of the whalers the technical changes and the production of new substances involved a new working rhythm on board. New personnel were now employed in whaling — radio telegraphists, radar and asdic operators, special workers for the manufacture of feed and meat extract, and several others. There is no need either to give details of wages, bonuses, working hours, holidays, etc., areas in which whaling largely followed developments elsewhere without any disruptive strikes or lockouts. The reason why relations were relatively free of strain is clearly linked with the fact that the whalers gradually had most of their demands met. Without doubt, too, the great efforts made to ensure improved welfare and wellbeing on the job were of some importance. In this connection the most effective innovation was the organised welfare work, most notably planned use of leisure time on board. Free time became longer and longer, as catches declined and the so-called "whale sickness" was at its most rampant. There were three main forms of leisure occupations: entertainment pure and simple, with films undoubtedly as the most popular item, as well as "home-made" attractions such as revues, sketches, singing, music, bridge tournaments, and the like. Then there were lectures and language teaching by qualified instructors. The third and most time-consuming category involved hobbies such as rug-making, building model ships, and "scrimshaw", in particular the carving of sperm whale teeth. On the voyage out and back sports meetings were organised, and in Norway a popular item was the Whalers' Cup, a football tournament held at home in the summer between teams from factory ships and shore stations, first

112. The whaling monument in Sandefjord, unveiled
23 June 1960.

held in 1937 and last in 1963. In short, the new apparatus, production
of the new by-products, the closer radio links with home, the new
technical aids for pursuit and catching, the transfer of operations ever
further north away from daily contact with the ice, and the organised
welfare work on board — all these elements drastically changed the
whaler's daily life from what it had been before the Second World War.

Thus in Norway, the country which pioneered it in its modern
form, whaling departed from the scene with honour. Finding new
jobs for unemployed whalers did not seem to present major
problems; there was a great need for ordinary deck and engine room
personnel in the merchant navy, and as all the one-time whaling companies also ran ordinary shipping lines, many could be absorbed by these.
For specialist workers there was room in the engineering industry.
Those who found themselves least favourably placed were the older
"real" whalers — the flensers, the lemmers, and others. Many of them
had small farms to which they could retire and enjoy their leisure.
Thanks to the gradual run-down and restructuring of the industry;
neither Norway nor the county of Vestfold was shaken to its
foundations when whaling came to an end. As for the boats, many
whale catchers are in service as herring drifters, and some of the factory
ships are now floating fish factories. In agriculture, industry and

shipping, the fruits of a century of whaling enterprise have been rich and varied. Norway has not relinquished her claims to her Antarctic quota. Perhaps the enterprise may one day become a reality again.

STATISTICAL APPENDIX

In this shortened English version of the Norwegian work *Den moderne hvalfangsts historie,* the quantity and the content of statistical tables have both been reduced, giving only some selected years with maximum and minimum catches and oil production. At the bottom of some of the tables there is a reference to the complete table in the Norwegian edition (abbreviated to *D.m.h.h.*).

Table 39. CATCH AND OIL PRODUCTION IN NORTH NORWAY, 1868-1904

Year	Blue	Fin	Humpback	Sei	Total	Oil (barrels)
1868					30	
1868-77					345	
1878	26	40			127	
1881	221	52	9		283	
1885	24	437	92	724	1,287	25,800
1889	14	188	5	22	500	15,570
1893					1,225	
1895					732	
1898	24	488	53	547	1,072	23,600
1900	12	263	68	39	382	11,200
1902	58	456	151	34	699	22,000
1904	235	161	39	24	459	17,900

Table 40. CATCH AND OIL PRODUCTION IN ICELAND, 1883-1915

Year	Total whales	Oil (barrels)
1833	8	320
1886	25	1,000
1890	199	7,000
1894	523	21,585
1895-1909	912	32,822*
1911	428	14,800
1912	152	6,100
1915	54	1,715

*on average. Max.: 1902, 1,305 and 40,000

Note: See *D.m.h.h.*, vol. 2, pp. 539, 540

Table 41. CATCH AND OIL PRODUCTION IN THE FAROES, 1894-1920;
THE SHETLANDS, 1903-20; THE HEBRIDES, 1904-20; IRELAND, 1908-20

The Faroes			The Shetland Isles		
Year	Whales	Oil (barrels)	Year	Whales	Oil (barrels)
1894	46	940	1903	127	3,392
1898	118	3,300	1904	415	12,171
1901	235	6,700	1904-10	481	12,617
1904-11	503	11,009	1912	238	7,829
1913	143	3,515	1914	432	10,281
1915	302	7,230	1920	430	9,615
1920	341	8,954			
Annual average 1902-11	479	10,653	1905-10	491	12,692
Maximum 1909	773	13,850	1907	566	15,100
Total 1894-1916	6,682	154,419	1903-14	4,917	128,242

Note: See D.m.h.h., vol. 2, pp. 541, 543

The Hebrides			Ireland		
Year	Whales	Oil (barrels)	Year	Whales	Oil (barrels)
1904	95	2,600	1908	76	1,800
1906	145	5,100	1911	131	4,300
1908	124	3,900	1912	60	2,357
1909	192	7,000	1913	114	4,405
1911	146	5,600	1914	89	3,300
1913	83	2,570	1920	125	3,995
1920	194	5,450			
Maximum 1909			1913		
Total 1904-14	1,550	50,642	1908-14	690	22,462

Note: See D.m.h.h., vol. 2, p. 543

Table 42. STATIONS, WHALES AND BARRELS OF OIL IN
NEWFOUNDLAND, 1898-1939

Year	Stations	Whales	Oil (barrels)
1898	1	91	2,500
1902	5	331	9,184
1904	14	1,275	35,766
1908	9	396	8,417
1914	7	161	3,003
1925	2	331	8,400
1928	3	508	20,580
1935	2	198	7,165
1937	2	483	19,075
1939	1	144	5,980

Note: See D.m.h.h., vol. 2, pp. 547-8. However, attention is called to these errors:
1902 stations: for 6 read 5, for 1920 read 1923; 1925 stations: for 3 read 2.

Table 43. CORRECTED STATISTICS FOR THE CATCH IN THE NORTH-EAST PACIFIC, 1903-1909

According to the *International Whaling Statistics*, II, p. 17, the catch from Newfoundland and North Pacific (east) was:

Year	Newfoundland	N. Pacific	Difference
1903	858	857	1
1904	1,276	1,275	1
1905	892	892	0
1906	439	429	10
1907	481	481	0
1908	396	395	1
1909	518	518	0

The figures from Newfoundland, being in accordance with the Annual Reports of the superintendent, must be the right ones. Nothing indicates that modern whaling had started from the Northwest coast before 1905. The errors in 1903 and especially 1904 are of great consequence, 1,275 whales being 26 per cent of the total world catch. All conclusions in the history of whaling based on these erroneous figures are subsequently wrong. How wrong will become evident by comparing the wrong figures with the right ones:

Year	Wrong	Right	Year	Wrong	Right
1902	3,065	2,873	1906	3,519	4,028
1903	3,867	3,414	1907	4,490	5,705
1904	4,931	4,546	1908	5,509	7,071
1905	4,592	4,315	1909	8,490	9,526

Table 44. CATCH AND OIL PRODUCTION IN THE NORTH-EAST PACIFIC, 1905-1931

Year	Whales	Oil (barrels)	Year	Whales	Oil (barrels)
1905	—	—	1921	208	5,328
1906	c. 500	c. 22,000	1922	1,356	47,845
1910	1,131		1926	988	34,104
1912	1,860	c. 55,000	1929	1,107	47,194
1915	1,164	26,452	1930	975	41,181
1916	1,060	3,411*	1931	No catch	
1920	1,527	54,459			

* only sperm oil.

Note: See *D.m.h.h.*, vol. 2, pp. 553-4. Due to lack of exact returns, the figures for the earliest years are estimated.

Table 45. COMPLETE STATISTICS FOR THE CATCH AND WHALE OIL PRODUCTION IN ALASKA, 1912-1929

	Whales Total	Oil (barrels)	Blue	Fin	Humpback	Sei	Sperm	Gray	Right	Others
1912	685	18,575	112	235	315		23			
1913	186	9,335	58	29	21	3	73	1		1
1914	482	15,903	35	259	131		43			14
1915	470	19,566	53	239	153		25			
1916	367	16,160	64	161	121		30		1	
1917	414	21,971	138	153	44		51			26
1918	406	20,238	82	170	58	4	92		2	
1919	539	25,048	68	242	132	2	95			
1920	429	22,178	81	179	75	4	90			
1921	79	1,140		2	75		1	1		
1922	445	18,087	77	204	95	1	69			
1923	355	13,105	29	151	155		16		3	
1924	283	12,664	46	148	71		17		1	
1925	512	19,265	36	234	208		33		1	
1926	584	20,142	16	177	388		1		2	
1927	718	22,326	35	122	554	3	3		1	
1928	402	16,488	51	98	220	1	24	2	6	
1929	385	16,669	53	105	214		12		1	

Note: In 1917-21 a total of 778 belugas (white fish) was also caught.
Source: Dept. of Labour and Commerce, Bureau of Fisheries: Alaska Fisheries and Fur Industries. Washington, 1912 *et seq.*

Table 46. MODERN CATCH IN JAPAN, 1899-1910, AND REVISED FIGURES FOR THE JAPANESE CATCH 1920-1930, BY SPECIES OF WHALE

Year	Total Whales	Year	Total Whales
1899	15	1905	446
1900	42	1906	736
1901	60	1907	1,086
1902	89	1908	1,312
1903	132	1909	835*
1904	428	1910	899*

* plus an unknown number from a couple of smaller companies.

For the total catch of the different species of whales from Japan and Korea for 1910-39 see *International Whaling Statistics*, 1942, table 1, pp. 91-2. For the years 1920-30 there is a great difference between these figures and those from the Whales Research Institute, Tokyo. These revised figures, from the W.R.I., are as follows:

Year	Blue	Fin	Humpback	Sei	Gray	Right	Sperm	Total
1920	37	443	84	389	68	4	251	1,276
1921	53	470	101	474	78	6	301	1,483
1922	36	394	82	390	40	4	567	1,513
1923	35	434	70	492	27	7	370	1,435
1924	28	342	156	642	17	4	247	1,436
1965	31	411	154	491	10	9	354	1,460
1926	29	408	110	563	11	7	495	1,623
1927	10	455	90	551	10	9	443	1,568
1928	16	417	99	309	9	5	650	1,505
1929	16	386	74	364	12	5	606	1,463
1930	56	400	62	411	30	5	753	1,717

Note: The few errors in the 1911-19 and 1931-40 figures in *I.W.S.* are insignificant.

Table 47. THE FIRST SEASON OF ANTARCTIC CATCHING FROM
GRYTVIKEN, 1904-5

Month	Blue	Fin	Humpback	Right	Total
December 1904		1	13		14
January 1905	3	5	17		25
February	4	5	10		19
March	1		24	2	27
April			3	3	6
May		1	1	2	4
June		1			1
July		1			1
August		1			1
September	1	2			3
October	1		16		17
November			32		32
December	1		33		34
January 1906	7	6	40		53
Total for 14 months	18	22	189	7	236
Total for 1904-5	11	16	149	7	183

Table 48. CORRECTED STATISTICS FOR THE WORLD CATCH OF
RIGHT WHALES, 1904-1918

Statistics for the right whale catch are very unreliable. The correct figures are
probably:

	South Shetland	South Georgia	Chile	South Africa	Kerguelen	Northern Seas[1]
1904-5		7				
1905-6		16				6
1906-7	1	34	79			24
1907-8		94	15	14		25
1908-9	4	62	c. 4		1	26
1909-10		40	20	3		17
1910-11	21	89		2		2[2]
1911-12	17	82	11	1		11
1912-13	3	6	170[4]	3		1
1913-14	6[3]	66		3		5
1914-15	2	20	5	1		
1915-16	6	12	2	2		
1916-17		12				
1917-18	13	35	3	1		

[1] The Shetland Isles, Hebrides, Iceland
[2] Iceland, the Faroes
[3] Of these, three at South Orkney
[4] Total 1906-1913

Note: See D.m.h.h., vol. 2, pp. 572-3, notes 14 and 15

Table 49. DIVIDENDS OF THE ANTARCTIC WHALING COMPANIES,
1909-10, 1910-11

The pioneer companies			New companies	
	1909-10	1910-11		1910-11
Compañía de Pesca	40	80	S. Georgia Co.	100
Condor	30	75	Hektor	32
Nor	20	30	Hvalen	0
Sandefj. Hv. selskab	60	120	Laboremus	6½
Sydhavet	15	25	Norge	50
Tønsbergs Hvalfangeri	18	60	Odd	45
Ocean	30	100		

Table 50. REVISED STATISTICS FOR THE CATCH FROM CHILE,
1908-1930

Year	Whales	Oil (barrels)	Year	Whales	Oil (barrels)	Year	Whales	Oil (barrels)
1908	93	—	1916	131	6,000	1924	275	8,600
1909	220	9,372	1917	193	7,700	1925	238	9,450
1910	254	11,000	1918	195	7,000	1926	429	16,405
1911	378	18,000	1919	161	6,000	1927	c. 400	15,540
1912	336	15,306	1920	120	4,600	1928	334	14,019
1913	226	10,200	1921	181	9,900	1929	386	18,234
1914	115	5,600	1922	202	10,200	1930	275	12,364
1915	255	11,500	1923	213	9,340			

Note: Cf. International Whaling Statistics, II, 1931 pp. 34 ff., and XVI, 1942, p. 91.

Table 51. THE PRODUCTION OF THE DIFFERENT QUALITIES OF
WHALE OIL (IN BARRELS) AT LEITH HARBOUR, SOUTH GEORGIA,
1909-1914, AND OLNA, SHETLAND ISLES, 1905-1927

(a) At Leith Harbour

Season	No. 1	No. 2	No. 3	No. 4	Total	% No. 1
1909-10	7,485	3,105	2,882	1,735	15,207	42.0
1910-11	24,226	9,668	11,883	2,359	48,136	50.3
1911-12	17,931	5,134	14,316	2,990	40,371	44.4
1912-13	20,989	6,813	15,601	5,017	48,420	43.3
1913-14	20,620	14,069	2,505	99	37,293	53.3

(b) At Olna

	No. 1	No. 2	No. 3	No. 4	Total	% No. 1
1905	1,813	997	1,358	1,087	5,375	33.7
1913	1,930	767	790	633	4,120	47.0
1922	3,668	96	959	1,970	6,693	55.0
1927	1,545	742	946	306	3,539	43.0

Table 52 THE CATCHING SEASONS ON ALL GROUNDS BETWEEN THE
TWO WORLD WARS

North Atlantic and Arctic

Iceland 1935-9
Faroe Islands 1920-30, 1933-9
Scotland 1920, 1922-9
Norway (west coast) all years
Spitsbergen 1920, 1926-7
Greenland (west coast) 1920, 1922-9
Pelagic 1919-20, 1922-4, 1929-34, 1937
Newfoundland 1919, 1923-30, 1935-7,
   1939
Azores all years (old whaling)
Portugal 1925-7, 1933-9
Spain 1921-7, 1934
Morocco 1939

America, East Coast

West-Indies 1925-6
Brazil all years (?)
Patagonia 1926-9

America, West Coast

Alaska, British Columbia, California
   1919-30, 1932-9
Mexico 1924-9, 1935
Ecuador 1926
Peru 1925-7, 1936-8
Chile all years

Africa and Australia

Mozambique 1923
Natal all years
Cape Province 1918-30, 1936-7
Walvis Bay 1923-30
Angola 1923-8
Congo 1922-6, 1930, 1934-7
Guinea pelagic 1925, 1935, 1937-9
Madagascar pelagic 1937-9
Australia 1922-3, 1925-8, 1936-8
New Zealand all years

East Asia

Japan-Korea all years
Kamchatka-Bering Sea 1925-6, 1933-9

Antarctic

South Georgia all years
South Shetland 1912-31 (shore station)
South Orkney 1920-31
Ross Sea 1923-30
Pelagic all years from 1925

Table 53. CATCH, PRODUCTION AND DIVIDENDS OF THE NORWEGIAN
WHALING COMPANY IN SPAIN, 1921-1927

	Stations	Catchers	Whales	Oil (barrels)	Guano (bags)	Dividend %
1921	1	2	356	10,500	7,800	0
1922	1	2	600	19,784	17,480	12
1923	1	2	1,116	38,472	40,000	24
1924	1	3	913	27,740	30,308	46
1925	2	6[1]	1,151	37,897	41,780	56
1926	2	7	925	36,934	36,519	56
1927	1	4[2]	242	7,058	8,877	0
Total			5,308	168,389	172,764	194

[1] plus 4 for a short while
[2] plus 1 for a short while.

Table 54. THE EXPANSION OF THE PELAGIC WHALING FLEET, 1928-1940

A. Second-hand ships converted to floating factories

	Name	Year	Gross tons	Nationality
1.	Antarctic	1928	9,593	Norway
2.	Frango	1928	6,331	U.S.A.
3.	Ole Wegger	1928	12,201	Norway
4.	Pelagos	1928	12,067	Norway
5.	Southern Empress	1928	12,398	U.K.
6.	Thorshammer	1928	12,215	Norway
7.	Anglo-Norse	1929	7,988	U.K.
8.	Haugar	1929	2,243	Norway
9.	Hectoria	1929	13,797	U.K.
10.	King	1929	641	Norway
11.	Salvestria	1929	9,426	U.K.
12.	Skytteren	1929	12,358	Norway
13.	Solglimt	1929	12,279	Norway
14.	Sourabaya	1929	10,110	U.K.
15.	Southern Princess	1929	12,156	U.K.
16.	Suderøy	1929	7,561	Norway
17.	New Sevilla	1930	13,801	U.K.
18.	Norskehavet	1930	5,133	Norway
19.	Pioner	1930	1,721	Norway
20.	Aleut	1932	5,160	U.S.S.R.
21.	Torodd	1932	8,118	Norway
22.	Jan Wellem	1936	8,829	Germany
23.	Ulysses	1937	10,780	U.S.A.
24.	Tonan Maru	1940	9,866	Japan

B. New floating factories built in Great Britain

	Name	Year	Gross tons	Nationality
25.	Kosmos	1929	17,801	Norway
26.	Vikingen	1929	12,639	U.K.
27.	Sir James Clark Ross	1930	14,362	Norway
28.	Tafelberg	1930	13,640	S. Africa
29.	Kosmos II	1931	16,966	Norway
30.	Svend Foyn	1931	14,596	U.K.
31.	Vestfold	1931	14,547	Panama

C. New floating factories built in Germany

	Name	Year	Gross tons	Nationality
32.	Terje Viken	1936	20,638	U.K.
33.	Walter Rau	1937	14,869	Germany
34.	Unitas	1937	21,845	Germany

continued on next page

THE EXPANSION OF THE PELAGIC WHALING FLEET,
1928-1940 — *continued*

D. *New floating factories built in Japan*

	Name	Year	Gross tons	Nationality
35.	Nisshin Maru	1936	16,801	Japan
36.	Nisshin Maru II	1937	17,553	Japan
37.	Tonan Maru II	1937	19,262	Japan
38.	Tonan Maru III	1938	19,206	Japan
39.	Kyokuyo Maru	1938	17,549	Japan

Notes

Nos. 8, 10, 20 have never operated in the Antarctic.

Nos. 2-5, 11-15, 22-25, 28-32, 35-39 were lost in the Second World War. At that time no. 2 was Japanese and no. 23 Argentinian.

Some of the factories which survived the war afterwards changed name and nationality:

No. 26: 1939-45 *Wikinger,* German; 1945 *Empire Venture,* British; 1946 *Slava,* Soviet.

No. 33: 1945-71 *Kosmos IV,* Norwegian; 1971 *Kyokusei Maru,* Japanese.

No. 34: 1945, *Empire Victory,* British; 1950-7 *Abraham Larsen,* South African; 1957 *Nisshin Maru,* Japanese.

Table 55. THE ANTARCTIC CATCH 1931-2, AND THE CATCH ON THE OTHER GROUNDS 1932

Grounds	Whales	Oil (barrels)	Shore stations	Fl. f.	Catchers
South Georgia	2,205	122,205	2		12
Antarctic pelagic	7,367	686,355		5	33
Natal	1,043	44,112	1		8
U.S.A. (West Coast)	319	14,350	1	1	7
Chile	173	8,760	2		3
Japan-Korea	1,036	20,230	20		20
New Zealand	18	350	1		
Norway	279	8,431	3		9
Arctic pelagic	518	20,159		2	7
Greenland	30		1		1
Total	12,988[1]	925,152	31	8	100[2]

[1] plus 179 sperm whales from the Azores.
[2] plus 2 smaller motor boats in New Zealand.

Table 56. AVERAGE PRICES OF EDIBLE OILS, 1929-1939

	Copra			Palm kernel			Linseed			Soya been			Groundnut			Whale oil				
																World production			Antarctic production		
	£	s	d	£	s	d	£	s	d	£	s	d	£	s	d	£	s	d	£	s	d
1929	34	7	6	35	1	0	35	12	6	30	2	6	35	0	0	26	10	0	29	17	0
1930	29	7	6	29	13	9	35	15	0	25	7	6	31	2	6	25	15	0	25	0	0
1931	21	18	9	22	12	6	17	2	6	16	7	6	25	7	6	22	0	0	21	19	9
1932	23	17	6	23	0	0	16	0	0	18	12	6	32	2	6	13	0	0	11	19	0
1933	18	0	0	18	3	9	19	10	0	17	10	0	23	15	0	11	0	0	13	0	0
1934	13	10	0	14	0	0	21	0	0	14	0	0	20	3	0	8	10	0	10	8	0
1935	20	15	0	20	15	0	24	7	0	21	0	0	32	6	0	15	10	0	12	7	0
1936	24	7	0	24	6	0	25	17	0	23	12	0	32	7	0	19	10	0	17	10	0
1937	25	8	0	26	17	0	28	12	6	24	10	0	31	0	0	21	0	0	20	7	0
1938	16	5	0	17	2	6	33	16	3	17	8	9	21	15	0	13	15	0	13	0	0
1939	16	5	0	17	10	0	24	0	0	18	0	0	21	10	0	15	0	0	14	18	0

Note: Prices are in £ per ton f.o.b. London

Table 57. PRICE AND CONSUMPTION OF MARGARINE AND BUTTER IN GREAT BRITAIN, 1924-1938

	Margarine			Butter			Total consumption per capita (lb.)
	Consumption			Consumption			
	Total tons	Per capita (lb.)	Price per lb.	Total tons	Per capita (lb.)	Price per lb.	
1924	250,000	12.3	6.7	298,000	14.4	22.0	26.7
1929	270,000	13.0	7.5	364,000	17.5	18.5	30.5
1932	205,000	9.4	6.8	452,000	21.5	13.2	30.9
1934	168,000	7.9	5.5	537,000	25.5	10.3	33.2
1936	185,000	8.6	6.0	532,000	24.9	12.8	33.5
1938	217,000	10.0	6.5	519,000	24.0	14.4	34.0

Source: Charles Wilson. *The History of Unilever*, II, p. 331.

Table 58. NATIONALITY OF THE CREWS IN THE ANTARCTIC WHALING FLEETS, 1930-1940

Season	Total	British		German		Japanese		Norwegian		Others	
		Number	%	Number	%	Number	%	Number	%	Number	%
1930-1	10,549							10,594	100		
1934-5	6,664					195	2.93	6,431	96.5	38	0.57
1935-6	7,186					370	5.15	6,731	93.7	85	1.18
1936-7	9,321	454	4.87	255	2.74	837	8.98	7,678	82.3	97	1.04
1937-8	11,227	675	6.01	886	7.89	1,840	16.89	7,615	67.8	221	1.88
1938-9	12,705	866	6.82	1,368	10.91	2,793	21.98	7,517	59.1	143	1.13
1939-40	10,586	978	9.24			2,965	28.01	6,270	59.2	100	0.94

Table 59. FLOATING FACTORIES LOST DURING THE SECOND WORLD WAR
(in chronological order)

	Name	Nationality	When	How lost	Where	En route from	En route to	Laden with	Lives lost
1.	Jan Wellem	Germany	13.4.40	Set on fire	Narvik, Norway	Germany	Norway	War material.	
2.	Salvestria	U.K.	22.7.40	Mined	Scotland	U.S.A.	England	Fuel oil.	10
3.	New Sevilla	U.K.	20.9.40	Torpedoed	Ireland	England	S. Georgia	Catch equipment. 285 whalers.	2
4.	Kosmos	Norway	26.9.40	Captured and sunk	Sao Paulo, Brazil	S. Africa	W. Indies	16,900 tons whale-oil.	
5.	Strombus	Norway	26.10.40	Mined	Swansea	England	S. Georgia	Ballast.	2
6.	Ole Wegger	Norway	14.1.41	Captured	Antarctic	Whaling		9,100 tons whale-oil.	
7.	Solglimt	Norway	14.1.41	Captured	Antarctic	Whaling		3,424 tons whale-oil.	
8.	Pelagos	Norway	15.1.41	Captured	Antarctic	Whaling		10,662 tons whale-oil.	
9.	Terje Viken	U.K.	7.3.41	Torpedoed	N. Atlantic				
10.	Uniwaleco	U.K.	7.3.41	Torpedoed	Trinidad	W. Indies	S. Africa	Fuel oil.	13
11.	Skytteren	Norway	1.4.42	Scuttled	Skagerrak	Sweden	England	Ballast.	
12.	Lancing	Norway	7.4.42	Torpedoed	C. Hatteras	W. Indies	New York	Fuel oil.	1
13.	Hektoria	U.K.	11.9.42	Torpedoed	N. Atlantic	England	New York	Ballast.	1
14.	S. Empress	U.K.	13.10.42	Torpedoed	Newfoundland	New York	England	11,700 tons fuel oil.	42
15.	Sourabaya	U.K.	27.10.42	Torpedoed	N. Atlantic	New York	England	7,880 tons fuel oil, aircraft, vehicles.	79
16.	Kosmos II	Norway	28.10.42	Torpedoed	N. Atlantic	New York	England	24,000 tons fuel oil, war material.	40
17.	Vestfold	Panama	17.1.43	Torpedoed	Iceland	New York	England	Fuel oil, war material.	5
18.	N.T.N. Alonso	Norway	22.2.43	Torpedoed	N. Atlantic	England	New York	Ballast.	3

continued on next page

FLOATING FACTORIES LOST DURING THE SECOND WORLD WAR—continued

	Name	Nationality	When	How lost	Where	En route from	to	Laden with	Lives lost
19.	S. Princess	U.K.	17.3.43	Torpedoed	N. Atlantic	New York	England	10,050 tons fuel oil, locomotives, landing-craft.	4
20.	Svend Foyn	U.K.	19.3.43	Struck iceberg	C. Farvel, Greenland	New York	England	Fuel oil, munitions.	59
21.	Nisshin Maru II	Japan	April 1943	Destroyed	Ryukyu Is.			Military transport.	
22.	Tonan Maru	Japan	28.11.43	Sunk	Off Indo-China			Military transport.	
23.	Frango	Japan	4.1.44	Sunk	Off Saigon			Military transport.	
24.	Tonan Maru III	Japan	20.2.44	Sunk	Caroline Is.			Military transport.	
25.	Nisshin Maru	Japan	May 1944	Sunk	Philippines			Military transport.	
26.	Tonan Maru II	Japan	22.8.44	Sunk	S. China Sea			Military transport.	
27.	Tafelberg	U.K.	8.9.44	Torpedoed	Ireland	New York	England	16,000 tons fuel oil, 60 Sherman tanks.	108
28.	Kyokuyo Maru	Japan	19.9.44	Sunk	Ryukyu Is.			Military transport.	
29.	Ulysses	Argentina	27.9.44	Burnt, explosion	River Plate				
30.	Südmeer	Germany	14.10.44	Sunk in air attack	North Cape, Norway	Finnmark	Germany	Munitions evacuated from Finnmark.	

Notes

1. Raised, broken up 1948.
5. Under Norwegian flag but administered by Chr. Salvesen & Co., Great Britain.
6. Sunk near Rouen, raised, condemned.
7. Later sunk off Cherbourg in air attack.
8. Repaired, operating 1945-62. Broken up.
16. Torpedoed, continued the voyage, torpedoed again 28 October, part of the crew rescued by a British corvette. Torpedoed 30 October.
20. Torpedoed October 1941, rescued and repaired.
21, 22, 23, 24, 25, 26, 28. Exact circumstances and casualties involved unknown.
21. Did not sink, later broken up.
23. At that time bearing the name *Hakko Maru* operating as damaged by a mine on 28 January 1941 and repaired.
24. Salvaged in 1950, repaired and operated in the Antarctic, 1951-66, under the name of *Tonan Maru*.
27. At that time bearing the name *Empire Heritage*. Badly a tanker.
29. At that time bearing the name *Sun Blas* and operating as a tanker. Broken up 1949.

Table 60. WHALING DURING THE SECOND WORLD WAR

	1939-40		1940-1		1941-2		1942-3		1943-4		1944-5	
	Whales	Barrels	Whales	Barrels	Whales	Barrels	Whales	Barrels	Whales	Barrels	Whales	Barrels
Antarctic	32,900	2,544,253	16,363	1,100,008	1,425	77,819[1]	998	50,960[2]	1,799	132,001	2,891	223,540
South Africa	1,035	40,419	759	26,638	498	19,740	724	27,373	819	29,380	729	23,189
Azores[3]	552	10,047	501	9,057	548	13,070	796	13,880	666	8,603	534	10,715
Portugal			61		117		181	917[8]	58	1,470[7]	47	1,123
Norway											192	1,391
Newfoundland, Labrador	78	2,950	72	1,855	71	1,855[7]	152	5,564	147		393	12,730
British Columbia	220	8,700	328	16,630	163	6,150	91	3,230	264	8,963		
California	29	1,607	24	683	26	948	29	760				
North Pacific[4]	673	29,494	579	23,822	3,346	64,500	3,299	72,000				
Peru[5]			1,914	41,359			61	2,111	5	148		
Chile	78	2,234	59	1,626	54	1,546	478	16,723	430	15,880	495	21,066
Japan-Korea	2,035	25,143	2,349	28,684	1,148	10,832	1,491	15,941	2,169	25,182	531	6,082
Kamchatka[6]	109	3,999	543	18,235	554	14,500	90	3,765	88	2,630	107	4,482
New Zealand			86	3,084	71	2,988						
Total	37,709	2,668,756	23,638	1,268,081	8,021	213,948	8,390	213,224	6,445	224,207	5,919	304,318
Of the total, sperm	4,671	167,509	5,641	156,918	4,958	106,693	5,503	123,577	2,614	60,357	1,669	46,682
% sperm	12.4	6.3	23.9	12.4	61.8	49.9	65.7	57.8	40.6	26.9	28.2	15.3

[1] Grytviken 60,807, Leith Harbour 17,012.　[2] Grytviken.　[3] Including Madeira.　[4] Japanese catch.　[5] Pelagic Soviet catch.　[6] Pelagic Norwegian sperm whale catch.　[7] Calculated.　[8] Sperm oil.

Note: The seasons are the Antarctic season plus the following summer season on other grounds, e.g. 1939-40 + 1940.
See International Whaling Statistics, XVII, pp. 1, 34, 48, 59, 71, 83; and revised figures XXIX, pp. 11-13, 20-7; XXXIV, pp. 11-13, 20-7; XXXIII, pp. 12-17; XXXIV, pp. 11, 26. For the Azores see also Discovery Reports, XXVIII, p. 283, Table 30.

Table 61. THE EXPANSION OF THE PELAGIC WHALING FLEET, 1945-1963

Name	Year	Gross tons	Nationality	Whaling seasons
1. Norhval	n. 1945	13,380	Norway	1945-62. Broken up 1966
2. Southern Venturer	n. 1945	14,493	U.K.; 1962 Japan	1945-62. Laid up
3. Balaena	n. 1946	15,303	U.K.; 1960 Japan: Kyokuyo Maru III	1946-76
4. Hashidate Maru	cv. 1946	10,841	Japan	1946-51
5. Kaiko Maru	cv. 1946	2,993	Japan	1948-9. Broken up 1963
6. Nisshin Maru I	cv. 1946	11,051	Japan; 1951 Kinyo Maru	1946-64. Broken up 1965
7. Southern Harvester	n. 1946	15,448	U.K.; 1963 Japan; 1967 U.K.	1946-63. Laid up
8. Transport no. 19	cv. 1946	1,500	Japan	1946-7
9. Willem Barendsz I	cv. 1946	10,509	Netherlands; 1962 Japan: Nitto Maru; 1964 Nitchiei Maru	1946-55, 1962-6 Broken up 1966
10. Kosmos III	n. 1947	18,460	Norway; 1961 Japan: Nisshin Maru III	1947-78
11. Thorshavet	n. 1947	17,081	Norway	1947-67. 1970 cv. floating fish-factory. Lost 1974
12. Transport no. 13, 16	cv. 1947	1,500	Japan	1947
13. Kosmos V	n. 1948	19,000	Norway; 1966 South Africa: Suiderkruis	Operated as tanker. 1966 cv. floating fish-factory oil boring platform
14. Thorshøvdi	n. 1948	18,361	Norway	1948-65. 1967 cv. to
15. Transport no. 9	cv. 1948	1,300	Japan	1948
16. Baikal Maru	cv. 1950	4,801	Japan	1951-4
17. Olympic Challenger	cv. 1950	13,021	Panama; 1956 Japan: Kyokuyo Maru II	1950-70

continued on next page

THE EXPANSION OF THE PELAGIC WHALING FLEET, 1945-1963 — continued

					Operated as tanker
18.	Juan Peron	n. 1951	24,570	Argentina	
19.	Nisshin Maru	n. 1951	16,811	Japan	1951-70
20.	Kyokuyo Maru	cv. 1955	11,448	Japan	1955-65
21.	Willem Barendsz II	n. 1955	26,830	Netherlands; 1966 South Africa	1955-64. 1966 cv. to floating fish-factory
22.	Matsushima Maru	cv. 1956	11,965	Japan; 1957 Tonan Maru II	1956-77
23.	Sovetskaya Ukraina	n. 1959	32,024	Russia	1959-78
24.	Yuri Dolgorukij	cv. 1960	25,376	Russia	1960-75
25.	Sovetskaya Rossiya	n. 1961	32,024	Russia	1961-78
26.	Vladivostok	n. 1962	17,149	Russia	1963-77
27.	Dalnij Vostok	n. 1963	16,974	Russia	1963-76

Notes: The seasons include Antarctic, North Pacific and a few years (1946-54) off Bonin Islands and the coast of Peru.

With some of the floating factories the gross tonnage has been changed by rebuilding.

n. = new (built)
cv. = converted second-hand ship

Table 62. THE AGREEMENTS RELEVANT TO THE WASHINGTON CONFERENCE, 1946

1. The Geneva Convention, 1931 (24 September)
2. The Principal Agreement, 1937 (8 June)
3. The Protocol of 1938 (24 June)
4. The Recommendations of 1939 (20 July)
5. The Protocol of 1944 (7 February)
6. The Supplementary Protocol, 1945 (5 October)
7. The Protocol of November 1945 (26 November)
8. The Supplementary Protocol of March 1946 (15 March)

Notes:
Nos. 2-8 all dated London.

Delegations to the Washington Conference from: Argentina, Australia, Brazil, Canada, Chile, Denmark, France, the Netherlands, New Zealand, Norway, Peru, the U.K., the U.S.A. and the U.S.S.R. Observers from: Ireland, Iceland, Portugal, Sweden and South Africa.

Table 63. THE JAPANESE ANTARCTIC CATCH, 1946-51

Seasons	Catchers	Oil	Meat, blubber	Other products	Total	Whales					
						Blue	Fin	Humpback	Sperm	Total
		(tons)	(tons)	(tons)	(tons)					
1946-7	12	12,260	22,176	61	34,488	690	474		1	1,165
1947-8	12	17,840	26,346	1,225	45,411	710	608		2	1,320
1948-9	14	20,291	34,291	3,143	57,255	631	1,012			1,643
1949-50	16	28,688	38,061	1,399	68,148	817	1,056	67	172	2,112
1950-1	18	28,893	27,860	1,956	54,489	271	2,052	9	409	2,741

Note: These figures (from Japanese Whaling Industry, edited by the Japan Whaling Association, Tokyo, 1954, and from letters from Dr. Hideo Omura of 22 and 29 November 1966) differ from figures in the International Whaling Statistics.

Table 64. THE ANTARCTIC PELAGIC WHALING FLEET, APPLIED CATCHING DAYS, AVERAGE PRODUCTION PER FLOATING FACTORY AND PER CATCHER, 1945-1978

Season	Fl. f.	Catchers	Catchers per fl. f.	Applied catching days	Applied catching days less than the open season	Average production of whale oil (barrels)		per catcher's day/work
						per fl. f.	per catcher	
1945-6	9	77	8.6	121	0	82,197	9,607	
1946-7	15	129	8.6	121	0	115,225	13,398	
1947-8	17	162	9.5	115	7	106,445	11,170	102
1948-9	18	191	10.6	102	6	102,493	9,659	98
1949-50	18	216	12.0	84	23	104,943	8,745	104
1950-1	19	239	12.6	78	29	100,507	7,990	103
1951-2	19	263	13.8	64	33	108,150	7,813	122
1952-3	16	230	14.4	74	22	117,763	8,192	110
1953-4	17	206	12.1	76	20	115,588	9,539	126
1954-5	19	233	12.3	72	19	93,688	7,640	107
1955-6	19	257	13.5	58	34	94,583	6,992	121
1956-7	20	225	11.3	69	22	94,198	8,373	122
1957-8	20	237	11.9	69	22	92,257	7,785	113
1958-9	20	235	11.8	69	22	89,922	7,653	111
1959-60	20	220	11.0	102	0	92,969	8,452	87
1960-1	21	252	12.0	96	5	91,196	7,600	80
1961-2	21	261	12.4	115	2	85,580	6,886	60
1962-3	17	201	11.8	110	7	76,088	6,435	57
1963-4	15	180	12.0	111	7	67,778	5,646	51
1964-5	15	172	11.5	104	13	56,297	4,910	48
1965-6	10	128	12.8	103	14	44,802	3,500	34
1966-7	9	120	13.3	97	20	42,654	3,199	33
1967-8	8	97	12.1	101	17	40,244	3,319	33
1968-9	6	84	14.0	99	18	45,343	3,239	33
1969-70	6	84	14.0	97	20	44,711	3,156	32
1970-1	6	86	14.3	95	22	45,618	3,183	33
1971-2	6	84	14.0	102	16	41,296	2,950	
1972-3	6	78	13.0			28,958	2,228	
1973-4	6	75	12.5			24,967	1,997	
1974-5	6	72	12.0			22,361	1,863	
1975-6	5	56	11.2			12,709	1,135	
1976-7	4	43	10.7			14,803	1,377	
1977-8	3	34	11.3			9,194	811	
1978-9	3	31	10.3					

Note: Since the 1972-3 season the total quota has no longer been set in BWU but separately for each species of whale including the minke whales. There is no scale for converting minke whales to BWU. Minke whales may also be caught before 12 December and after 7 April and consequently it is impossible to give the figures of catching days for BWU. As minke whales are taken primarily for meat, the average production of whale oil is an appropriate statistic for comparison in 1978-9 as only minke whales were taken.

Table 65. ANTARCTIC PELAGIC WHALING, 1945-1978: QUOTAS, SEASONS, CATCH, PRODUCTION

1. The pelagic Antarctic season
2. 1945-59 and 1962-78: the total quota of BWU set by IWC; 1959-62: the total of the single quotas set by each of the five whaling nations
3. The total catch of BWU
4. The difference between the quota and the catch
5. The open (permitted) season for the baleen whaling operations
6. Days of the open season
7. The expeditions' average applied catching days
8. Average production of whale oil per day per floating factory
9. Average catch of BWU per day per catcher

1	2	3	4	5	6	7	8	9
1945-6	16,000	7,381.0	−53.87	24.11-24.3	121	121	737	0.89
1946-7	16,000	15,304.2	− 4.35	8.12- 7.4	121	121	1,037	1.06
1947-8	16,000	16,364.3	+ 2.28	8.12- 7.4	122	115	945	0.92
1948-9	16,000	16,007.4	+ 0.05	15.12- 1.4	108	102	1,015	0.84
1949-50	16,000	16,062.1	+ 0.39	22.12- 7.4	107	84	1,266	0.88
1950-1	16,000	16,416.2	+ 2.60	22.12- 7.4	107	78	1,298	0.86
1951-2	16,000	16,007.7	+ 0.05	2.1 - 7.4	97	64	1,690	0.94
1952-3	16,000	14,866.6	− 7.08	2.1 - 7.4	96	74	1,591	0.86
1953-4	15,500	15,456.4	− 0.28	2.1 - 7.4	96	76	1,521	0.98
1954-5	15,500	15,323.5	− 1.14	7.1 - 7.4	91	72	1,313	0.91
1955-6	15,000	14,874.3	− 0.84	7.1 - 7.4	92	58	1,628	0.99
1956-7	14,500	14,745.2	+ 1.69	7.1 - 7.4	91	69	1,374	0.95
1957-8	14,500	14,850.9	+ 2.42	7.1 - 7.4	91	69	1,336	0.90
1958-9	15,000	15,300.8	+ 2.01	7.1 - 7.4	91	69	1,299	0.94
1947-59	186,000	186,275.4	+ 0.15		99	78	1,356	0.91
1959-60	17,500[1]	15,511.7	+ 3.41[2]	28.12- 7.4	102	102	942	0.73
1960-1	17,780[1]	16,433.5	+ 9.56[2]	28.12- 7.4	101	96	956	0.68
1961-2	17,780[1]	15,252.6	+ 1.68[2]	12.12- 7.4	117	115	744	0.51
1962-3	15,000	11,306.1	−24.62	12.12- 7.4	117	110	689	0.50
1963-4	10,000	8,429.0	−15.71	12.12- 7.4	118	111	611	0.41
1964-5	8,000	6,986.1	−12.67	12.12- 7.4	117	104	543	0.40
1965-6	4,500	4,090.9	− 9.09	12.12- 7.4	117	103	433	0.31
1966-7	3,500	3,511.8	+ 0.34	12.12- 7.4	117	97	439	0.30
1967-8	3,200	2,803.7	−12.39	12.12- 7.4	118	101	399	0.29
1968-9	3,200	2,472.6	−22.73	12.12- 7.4	117	99	460	0.30
1969-70	2,700	2,477.2	− 8.29	12.12- 7.4	117	97	463	0.30
1970-1	2,700	2,470.5	− 8.54	12.12- 7.4	117	95	479	0.30
1971-2	2,300	2,250.8[3]	− 2.14	12.12- 7.4	118	102		
1972-3	1,808	1,524.5[4]	−15.69	12.12- 7.4	117			
1973-4	1,475	1,376.0[5]	− 6.71	12.12- 7.4	117			
1945-6	1.167[6]	1,132.7[6]	− 2.96	12.12- 7.4	117			
1975-6	482[7]	406.5[7]	−15.49	12.12- 7.4	118			
1976-7	310[8]	310.0[8]	0.00	12.12- 7.4	117			
1977-8	128.5[9]	95.0[9]	−26.07	12.12- 7.4	117			
1978-9	—[10]	—[10]	—	—[11]				

Notes: [1] Provided the U.S.S.R. quota was 3,000 BWU; [2] Provided the total quota was 15,000 BWU; [3] Including 3,021 minke whales; [4] Including 5,745 minke whales; [5] Including 7,713 minke whales; [6] Including 7,000 minke whales; [7] Including 6,034 minke whales; [8] Sei whales only (1,858) converted to BWU, plus whales; [10] Only minke whales (5,446) were allowed to be caught; [11] Each factory minke whales; [9] Sei whales only (771) converted to BWU, plus 5,690 minke ships can declare its own continuous season not to exceed six months in any twelve.

Table 66. OPERATIVE SEASONS OF THE SHORE STATIONS IN
SOUTH GEORGIA

Prince Olav Harbour	British	1911-31
Leith Harbour	British	1909-32, 1933-42, 1945-61, 1963-6[1]
Stromness Harbour	Norwegian	1908-31
Husvik Harbour	Norwegian	1907-31, 1945-57, 1958-60, 1960-1[2]
Grytviken	Argentinian	1904-62, 1963-5[1]
Godthul Harbour	Norwegian	1908-29
New Fortuna Bay	Norwegian	1909-20

[1] In the last period operated on hire by a Japanese company
[2] Bought by the British company Albion Star Ltd. and operated these seasons jointly with Grytviken, which had been taken over by the same company

Note: Since 1966 there has been no whaling from South Georgia

Table 67. TOTAL CATCH IN THE ANTARCTIC, 1904-1978

Blue whales	331,042
Fin whales	692,084
Humpback whales	68,307
Sei whales	149,735
Sperm whales[1]	143,020
Others[2]	9,066
Total[3]	1,393,254
Minke whales 1971-8	39,608
Barrels of oil[4]	83,360,382 = 13,893,397 tons

[1] Catch south of 40° S
[2] Mostly baleen whales 1904-15
[3] Including the shore stations
[4] Including oil of minke whales 1971-8

Table 68. THE INTERNATIONAL WHALING COMMISSION

Meetings

1.	London	1949	30 May-9 June	
2.	Oslo	1950	17-21 July	
3.	Cape Town	1951	23-7 July	
4.	London	1952	3-6 June	
5.	London	1953	22-6 June	
6.	Tokyo	1954	19-23 July	
7.	Moscow	1955	18-23 July	
8.	London	1956	16-20 July	
9.	London	1957	24-8 June	
10.	The Hague	1958	23-7 June	
11.	London	1959	22 June-1 July	
12.	London	1960	20-4 June	
13.	London	1961	19-23 June	
14.	London	1962	2-6 July	
15.	London	1963	1-5 July	
16.	Sandefjord	1964	22-6 June	
	London	1965	3-6 May	(extraordinary meeting)
17.	London	1965	28 June-2 July	
18.	London	1966	27 June-1 July	
19.	London	1967	26-30 June	
20.	Tokyo	1968	24-8 June	
21.	London	1969	23-7 June	
22.	London	1970	22-6 June	
23.	Washington	1971	21-5 June	
24.	London	1972	26-30 June	
25.	London	1973	25-9 June	
26.	London	1974	24-8 June	
27.	London	1975	23-7 June	
28.	London	1976	21-5 June	
29.	Canberra	1977	20-4 June	
	Tokyo	1977	6-7 December	(special meeting)
30.	London	1978	26-30 June	
	Tokyo	1978	19-20 December	(special meeting)
31.	London	1979	9-13 July	
32.	Brighton (U.K.)	1980	21-26 July	

Chairmen

S. Bergersen	Norway	1949-51
R. Kellogg	U.S.A.	1952-5
C. J. Lienesch	Netherlands	1956-7
R. G. R. Wall	U.K.	1958
G. R. Clark	Canada	1959-61
W. Sukhoruchenko	U.S.S.R.	1962-6
W. C. Tame	England	1967
I. Fujita	Japan	1968-71
J. L. McHugh	U.S.A.	1972
I. Rindal	Norway	1973-5
A. G. Bollen	Australia	1976-8
T. Asgeirsson	Iceland	1978-

Secretaries (all from U.K.)

A. T. A. Dobson	1949-59
R. S. Wimpenny	1959-66
L. Goldthorpe	1966-7
R. Stacey	1967-76
R. Gambell	1977-

Note: In the absence of the chairman W. C. Tame in 1968, the vice-chairman I. Fujita took the chair. N. A. Mackintosh was secretary to the 1966 meeting.

Table 69. AVERAGE PRICES OF WHALE OIL No. 1, 1874-1977, AND SPERM OIL, 1946-1977

The figures are the middle-prices of highest and lowest annual sale.
Price per long ton = 1,016 kg. = 6 barrels.
From 1920 (*et seq.*): the price is that of the Antarctic production of the previous season.

Whale oil

Year	£	Year	£	Year	£
1874	32	1909	19	1944	44
1875	34	1910	22	1945	45
1876	34	1911	21	1946	57
1877	36	1912	20	1947	84
1878	32	1913	22	1948	100
1879	27	1914	21	1949	90
1880	27	1915	23	1950	99
1881	28	1916	30	1951	141
1882	30	1917	54	1952	93
1883	28	1918	57	1953	73
1884	22	1919	67	1954	77
1885	19	1920	88	1955	83
1886	19	1921	37	1956	89
1887	16	1922	32	1957	85
1888	21	1923	31	1958	73
1889	22	1924	37	1959	76
1890	21	1925	36	1960	73
1891	21	1926	32	1961	67
1892	18	1927	28	1962	46
1893	20	1928	30	1963	62
1894	17	1929	28	1964	82
1895	16	1930	21	1965	85
1896	17	1931	12	1966	71
1897	16	1932	13	1967	51
1898	16	1933	12	1968	46
1899	16	1934	15	1969	73
1900	22	1935	20	1970	103
1901	20	1936	20	1971	88
1902	21	1937	20		$
1903	19	1938	14	1972	168
1904	15	1939	26	1973	380
1905	14	1940	30	1974	537
1906	19	1941	33	1975	348
1907	23	1942	38	1976	345
1908	20	1943	43	1977	460

Sperm oil

Year	£
1946	74
1947	100
1948	84
1949	62
1950	48
1951	90
1952	46
1953	54
1954	62
1955	68
1956	71
1957	83
1858	65
1959	50
1960	66
1961	75
1962	79
1963	86
1964	71
1965	58
1966	56
1967	52
1968	56
1969	74
1970	145
1971	129
1972	107
	$
1973	305
1974	445
1975	375
1976	573
1977	825

Table 70. FIN WHALE CATCH IN WATERS OFF KOREA, 1911-1945
(modified from Kasahara, 1950)

Year	Yellow Sea	Southern Sea of Japan	West-Central Sea of Japan	Total
1911	—	90	93	183
1912	—	?	?	—
1913	—	?	?	—
1914	—	106	62	168
1915	?	?	?	252
1916	156	86	36	278
1917	264	46	20	330
1918	224	35	8	267
1919	154	71	35	260
1920	102	64	21	187
1921	106	22	53	181
1922	93	37	45	175
1923	98	29	40	167
1924	109	12	5	126
1925	97	46	4	147
1926	110	24	15	149
1927	174	74	10	258
1928	182	44	—	226
1929	117	27	—	144
1930	178	45	—	223
1931	115	51	—	166
1932	103	45	—	148
1933	116	45	3	164
1934	82	20	4	106
1935	75	64	—	139
1936	66	66	—	132
1937	128	81	—	209
1938	55	115	—	170
1939	42	92	—	134
1940	—	—	—	—
1941	30	98	—	128
1942	56	106	1	163
1943	38	66	9	113
1944	57	78	30	165
1945	14	—	49	63
Total	3,141	1,785	543	5,721

Table 71. REPUBLIC OF KOREA COASTAL WHALE CATCH BY SPECIES AND YEARS

Year	Minke	Fin	Bryde	Sei	Humpback	Gray	Others
1962	170	82*				0	
1963	291	55*				2	
1964	384	88*				3	
1965	247	17		0	2	4	0
1966	301	14		0	5	5	3
1967	335	20		0	0	0	1
1968	316	25		3	0	0	0
1969	386	35		0	0	0	0
1970	715	25		0	0	0	0
1971	730	25		0	0	0	1
1972	767	1		0	0	0	0
1973	882	4		0	0	0	0
1974	566	52		0	0	0	0
1975	561	13		0	0	0	0
1976	494	0	43	0	0		0
1977	1,033	0	26	0	0		0
1978	1,018	0	34	0	0		0

* Recorded only as large whales.

BIBLIOGRAPHY

This bibliography is strictly limited to literature on the history of the whaling industry, and includes only exceptionally items on whale biology. Nordic titles are translated into English in square brackets.

BIBLIOGRAPHICAL LITERATURE

Aagaard, Bjarne. *Fangst og forskning i Sydishavet* [Hunting and Research in the Antarctic Sea], II, pp. 1033-68. Oslo, 1930

Antarktisk- og hvalfangstlitteratur. Bibliografi [Bibliography of Antarctic and Whaling literature]. Oslo, 1950

Colonial Reports — Falkland Islands, pp. 78-81. 1956 and 1957

Falkland Islands Scientific Bureau. Publications relating to the Falkland Islands Dependencies. 1951

Fjeld-Andersen, Asbjørn. *Oversiktskatalog I over bøker, periodiske skrifter og særtrykk ved Hvalfangstmuseets bibliotek* [Catalogue I of books, periodicals and reprints in the library of the Whaling Museum, Sandefjord]. Sandefjord, 1961

Jenkins James Travis. "Bibliography of Whaling", in *Journal of the Society for the Bibliography of Natural History*, vol. 2, part 4, pp. 71-166. London, 1948

Mackintosh, N. A. *The Stocks of Whales*, pp. 205-20. London, 1965

Pedersen, Th. and Ruud, Johan T. *A Bibliography of Whales and Whaling: Selected Papers from the Norwegian Research Work 1860-1945*. Oslo, 1946

Scott Polar Research Institute, Cambridge (ed.). *Polar Record*. In each issue there is an up-to-date bibliography.

Schubert, Kurt. *Der Walfang der Gegenwart*, pp. 184-206. Stuttgart, 1955

Slijper, E. J. *Whales*, pp. 421-58 (mainly biology). London, 1962. (Translated from Dutch: *Walvissen*. Amsterdam, 1958)

Vartdal, Hroar. *Bøker, fangstjournaler og manuskripter i Hvalfangstmuseet, Sandefjord* [Books, log-books and manuscripts in the Whaling Museum, Sandefjord]. Oslo, 1936

PERIODICALS

Alaska Fisheries and Fur Industries. Department of Commerce and Labor, Bureau of Fisheries, Washington, 1912-24

Annual Reports of the Department of Marine and Fisheries, 1903-23. St. John's, Newfoundland.

Australian Journal of Marine and Freshwater Research, 1948-63

The Canadian Fisherman, 1912-23. Ste Anne de Bellevue, Montreal

Colonial Reports (Annual). Falkland Islands, 1900-65. London

Discovery Reports. Cembridge, 1900-65. London

The Falkland Islands Gazette, 1900-32. Port Stanley

The Falkland Islands Magazine and Church Paper, 1900-14. Port Stanley

Fiskeritidende [Fishing News], 1885-1914. Copenhagen

Hvalrådets skrifter [Reports of the Whaling Board], 1-53. Oslo, 1931-72

International Whaling Commission Reports (Annual). London and Cambridge, 1950-
The Japan Yearbook, 1906-10. Tokyo
New Zealand Marine Department Annual Reports, 1914-16. Wellington
The New Zealand Official Yearbook, 1915-29. Wellington
Norsk Hvalfangst-Tidende [The Norwegian Whaling Gazette], 1912-68. Sandefjord
The Pacific Fisherman, 1904-48
Patents. British, American, Norwegian, relating to the whaling industry, 1842-1967
Progress (Unilever Ltd.), 1926-53. London
Report of the Bureau of Fisheries, 1904, 1905, 1906. Dept. of Commerce and Labor, Washington
Report of the Natal Fisheries Department, 1908-21. Pietermaritzbung
The Scientific Reports of the Whale Research Institute (Annual). Tokyo, 1948-

BOOKS AND ARTICLES

Whaling

Aagaard, Bjarne. *Norwegian Shipping in the Far East,* I-IV. Hongkong, 1905-8
—— *Hvalfangsten. Avisartikler og interviewer* [Whaling. Newspaper articles and Interviews]. Oslo, 1931
—— *Den gamle hvalfangst. Kapitler av dens historie* [Old Whaling. Chapters of its History]. Oslo, 1944 and 1953
—— *Fangst og forskning i Sydishavet* [Whaling and Exploring in the South Polar Seas]: I. *Svunne dager* [Times Past], 1930; II. *Nye tider* [A New Era], 1930; III. 1-2. *Antarktikas historie* [The History of the Antarctic], 1934; IV. See bibliographical literature. Oslo.
Aalton, Fridtjof. *Der Walfischfang Norwegens unter besonderer Berücksichtigung seiner Bedeutung für die norwegische Volkswirtschaft.* Düsseldorf, 1929
Allen, Glover M. "Some Observations on Rorquals of Southern Newfoundland", in *The American Naturalist,* XXXVIII, No. 453, pp. 613-23. Boston, 1904
—— "Whales and whaling in New England", in *The Scientific Monthly,* XXVI, p. 340. New York, 1912
Andrews, Roy Chapman. "A Whaling Expedition in Korea", in *Scientific American Supplement,* vol. 74, p. 376. New York, 1912
—— "The California gray whale", in *Memoirs of the American Museum of Natural History,* new series vol. I, part V. 1914
—— *Whale Hunting with Gun and Camera: A naturalist's account of the modern shore-whaling industry, of whales and their habits, and of hunting experiences in various parts of the world.* New York, 1916
—— *Ends of the Earth.* New York, 1958
Armstrong, Warren. *The True Book about Whaling.* London, 1958
Asplin, Tore. *På hvalfangst med Salvesen* [Whaling with Salvesen]. Tønsberg, 1974
Backer, S. "Walfang im Rossmeer", in *Fischerboote. Norddeutsche Fischerei-Zeitung,* XX, Heft 11. Blankenese, 1928
—— "1st das Aussterben der Wale zu befürchten?", ibid., pp. 114-16
Bakken, Asbjørn and Eriksen, Erling. *Hval og hvalfangst* [Whales and Whaling]. Vestfold-Minne, Tønsberg, 1964
Balle, Johs. "Hvalfangst i Grønlandske Farvande" [Whaling in Greenland Waters], in *Det Grønlandske Selskabs Aarsskrift* [Annual Report of the Greenland Society]. Copenhagen, 1928-9

Barron, William. *Old Whaling Days*. Hull, 1895
Bell, J. J. *The Whalers*. New York and London, 1914
—— *The Whale Hunters and other Stories*. New York and London, 1929
—— "Whaling in Scottish Waters", in *The Scots Magazine*, XIX, pp. 409-18. Edinburgh, 1923
Bell-Marley, H. W. "Hunting the Hump-back Whale", in *The Zoologist*, 4th series, XIII, p. 201. London, 1913
Beltramino, Juan Carlos M. *Mortalidad en Antartide desde fines del siglo XIX*. New York, 1965
Bennet, A. G. *Whaling in the Antarctic*. Edinburgh and London, 1931. See Kemp, Stanley, 1931
Bergersen, Birger. "The International Whaling Convention", in *Norwegian Whaling Gazette*, p. 593. Sandefjord, 1952
—— "Hvalfangst og fangstregulering" [Whaling and whaling regulation], in *Ymer*, pp. 81-7. Stockholm, 1947
Bergland, Sverre. *Southward Bound*. Published privately, n.d.
Bird-lore (organ of the Audubon Society), vol. XXXIV, p. 306. New York, 1932. (Limitation of catch)
Birkeland, K. B. *Paa hvalfangst. Fire aar paa jagt efter verdens største dyr* [Whaling. Four years hunting the biggest animal on Earth]. Minneapolis, 1924
—— *The Whalers of Akutan: an Account of the Modern Whaling in the Aleutian Islands*. New Haven, 1926
Blake, James. "The Threatened Whale", in *The New Statesman and Nation*, vol. 4, new series, pp. 65-6. London, 1937
Blond, Georges. *La grande aventure des baleines*. Paris, 1953. (Translated as *The Great Whale Game*. London, 1954)
Bogen, Hans S. I. *Linjer i den norske hvalfangsts historie* [Outlines of the History of Norwegian Whaling]. Oslo, 1933
—— *Polarårboken* [The Polar Yearbook], 1935, p. 24 (the gunners); 1938, p. 6 (the whalers)
—— *Firma Thor Dahl, Sandefjord, 1887-1937*. Oslo, 1937
—— *Framnæs mek. Værksted 1898-1948*. Oslo, 1948
—— *Aktieselskabet "Ørnen", 10.7.1903-10.1.1953*. Sandefjord, 1953
—— "Compañía Argentina de Pesca S.A., 16.11.1904-16.11.1954", in *Norwegian Whaling Gazette*. Oslo, 1954-5
—— *Lars Christensen og hans samtid I* [L. Chr. and his contemporaries]. Oslo, 1955
Boldt-Christmas, C. E. F. *Loggbok bland valfångare* [Logbook among whalers]. Stockholm, 1950.
Bonnot, Paul. "The Whales of California", in *California Fish and Game*, vol. 15, pp. 203-15. San Francisco, 1939
Bossière, René. "Pour prévenir la disparition des baleines", in *Association Française pour l'Avancement des Sciences, C.R. de la 43e session*, p. 1,008. Paris, 1915
Brennecke, H. J. *Ghost Cruiser H.K. 33*. London, 1954
Brown, James Templeman. "The Whalemen, Vessels and Boats, Apparatus and Methods of the Whale fishery", in *The Fishery and the Fishery Industries of the United States*, sect. V, vol. II. Washington, 1887
Browne, P. W. *Where the Fishers go: The Story of Labrador*. Toronto, 1909. (Also of Newfoundland)
Bruce, William S. "Cruise of the *Balaena* and the *Active* in the Antarctic Seas 1892-3", in *The Geographic Journal*, vol. 7, no. 5. London, 1896. See also Donald, C. W.
Bruun, Daniel. *Det høje Nord* [The Far North]. Copenhagen, 1902

Bruun, Svend Foyn. *Hvalfangerselskapet "Pelagos" A/S 1928 30 juni-1953* [The Whaling Company Pelagos]. Tønsberg, 1953

Bryant, J. "Antarctic Whales in Peril of Extermination", in *Illustrated London News,* vol. 171, no. 4,612, p. 419. London 1927

Budker, Paul. *Baleines et baleiniers.* Paris, 1957. (Translated as *Whales and Whaling,* New York, 1959)

Budker, Paul and Roux, Charles. "The Summer Whaling Season at Cape Lopez", in *Norwegian Whaling Gazette,* pp. 141-5. Oslo, 1968

Bull, H. J. *The Cruise of the* Antarctic *to the South Polar Regions.* London, 1896.

—— "Modern whaling by Norwegians", in *Chamber's Journal,* 7th Series, vol. 2, pp. 183-5. London, 1912

Burfield, S. T. "Belmullet Whaling Station" in The British Association for the Advancement of Science, Report 81, p. 121; 82, p. 143; 84, p. 125. London, 1912, 1913, 1915

Bystrøm, Erling. *Et år på Syd-Georgia* [A Year at South Georgia]. Oslo, 1944

California Fish and Game, vol. 15, p. 337; vol. 16, p. 54. San Francisco, 1929-30

California Sea Products Company. San Francisco, 1914

Catherall, Arthur. *Vanished Whaler.* London, 1939

Chatterton, E. Keble. *Whalers and Whaling: the Story of the Whaling Ships up to the Present Day.* London, 1925

Chicanot, E. L. "Flying with the Sealing Fleet", in *Airways,* III, 2, p. 43. London, 1926

Chrisp, John. *South of Cape Horn: a Story of Antarctic Whaling.* London, 1958

Christensen, Chr. Fred. *The Whaling Factory Ship* Vikingen *with some Notes on Whaling.* North-East Coast Institution of Engineers and Shipbuilders. London, 1931

—— "Notes on whaling and its development", Lloyd's Registered Staff Association session 1938-9, paper no. 1. London, 1938

Church, Albert C. *Whale Ships and Whaling.* New York, 1938. (Splendidly illustrated)

Clark, Franklin S. "Whaling out of Golden Gate", in *Scientific American,* vol. 136, p. 382. New York, 1927

Clarke, Robert. "Open Boat Whaling in the Azores: the History and Present Methods of a Relic Industry", in *Discovery Reports,* XXVI, pp. 281-354. Cambridge, 1954

—— "Whales and Whaling", in *The Advancement of Science,* vol. XI, no. 43, p. 305. London, 1954

—— "A great haul of ambergris", in *Nature,* vol. 174, p. 155. London, 1954

—— "Sperm Whales of the Azores", in *Discovery Reports,* XXVIII. Cambridge, 1956

—— *Sperm Whales of the Southeast Pacific,* I-III. Oslo, 1966-72

Cockrill, W. Ross. *Antarctic Hazard.* London, 1955

Compañía Argentina de Pesca S.A., 1904-1929. Buenos Aires, 1929

Congreve, William. *Treaties on the Congreve Rocket System.* London, 1827

Conolly, James B. "Arctic Whaling of To-day", in *Harper's Monthly Magazine,* vol. CVI, no. DCXXXII, pp. 179-89. New York, 1903

Cook, John A. *Pursuing the Whale.* London, 1926

Cook, John A. and Pedersen, Samson S. *Thar she Blows: Experience of Many Voyages Chasing Whales in the Arctic.* Boston, 1937

Cornwall, Ira E. "Collecting at a Catchalot Whaling Station", in *The Canadian Field-Naturalist,* vol. XLII, no. 1, pp. 9-12. Ottawa, 1928

Crowther, W. L. "Notes on Tasmanian Whaling", in *Papers and Proceedings of the Royal Society of Tasmania for the Year 1919,* pp. 130. Hobart, 1920

Dahl, Johannes. *Aktieselskabet "Ørnen". Fem og tyve års fangst i Sydishavet* [The "Ørnen" Company. Twenty-five Years Whaling in the Antarctic Seas]. Oslo, 1930

Dakin, William John. *Whalemen Adventurers: the Story of Whaling in Australian Waters and other Southern Seas related thereto, from the Days of Sail to Modern Times.* Sydney, 1934

Dautert, Erich. *Big Game in the Antarctic.* Bristol, 1937

Dawbin, W. H. "Whales and Whaling in the Southern Ocean", in *The Antarctic Today,* pp. 151-94. Wellington, 1952

Doen, Willem van der. *Storm, ijs en walvischen.* Amsterdam, 1947. (About a floating factory in the Antarctic 1933-4)

Donald, Charles W. "Cruise of the *Active* in the Antarctic Seas 1892-3", in *The Geographical Journal,* vol. 7, no. 6. London, 1896. See also Bruce, William S.

Dorofev, S. V. and Freiman, S. J. "The marine Mammalia of U.S.S.R. Far East", in *Transactions of the Institute of Fisheries and Oceanography of U.S.S.R.,* III, 21, 32, 128, 153, 202. Moscow, 1936

Dow, George Francis. *Whale Ships and Whaling: a Pictorial History of Whaling during Three Centuries.* Salem, Mass., 1925

Dugan, James. *American Viking: the Chronicle of American Whaling.* London, 1934

Dulles, Foster Rhea. *A Saga of Hans Isbrandtsen.* New York, 1963

Dydymov, A. G. "Russkoe kitobojnoe predprijatic Dal'nem Vostoke" [Russian Whaling in the Far East] in *Russkoe Sudochodstvo* [Russian Shipping], no. 9. St. Petersburg, 1886

Edwards, Everett J. and Rattray, Jeannette Edwards. *Whale off!* New York, 1932

Eliasson, Bror. *Valfångarliv* [Whaling Life]. Stockholm, 1933

Emmerich, Ferdinand. *Der Walfischfänger: Erlebnisse eines deutschen Seemannes in der Polarmeeren.* Dresden, 1924

Engelsen, Harald. *Fra de syv hav* [From the seven Seas]. Oslo, 1929

—— *Villmark* [Wilderness]. Oslo, 1945

Friksen, Erling. See Bakken, Asbjørn

Fairford, Ford. "Whale Hunting in the North Atlantic", in *The Empire Review and Journal of British Trade,* XXX, p. 222. London, 1917

Ferguson, Henry. *Harpoon.* London, 1932

Forretningsliv. Økonomisk Tidsskrift [Business Life: Economic Review], V, no. 40. Oslo, 1930. (Special issue on whaling)

Frank, Wolfgang. *Der wiedererstandne deutsche Walfang. Dargestelt an der Entwickelungsgeschichte der ersten deutschen Walfang-Gesellschaft.* Düsseldorf, 1939

—— *Waljäger. Auf Walfang im südlichen Eis.* Hamburg, 1939

Gardner, Erle Stanley. *Hunting the Desert Whale.* London, 1963

Gilmore, Raymond M. *The Story of the Gray Whale.* San Diego, 1961

Gislason, Magnus. *A hvalveidastödvum* [At a whaling station]. Reykjavik, 1949

Goodall, Thomas B. "With the Whalers at Durban", in *The Zoologist,* 4th series, vol. XVII, pp. 201-11. London, 1913

Grant, Gordon. *Greasy Luck: a Whaling Sketch Book.* London, 1932

Gray, David and Gray, John. *Report on new Whaling Grounds in the Southern Seas,* (with a descriptive Appendix). Aberdeen, 1874. 2nd and 3rd edns. Melbourne, 1887 and 1891

Greaves, Manuel. *Adventures de baleiros.* Horta, Azores, 1950

Grierson, John. "Whaling from the Air", in *The Geographical Journal,* CXI, p. 33. London, 1948

Gruvel, A. "La pêche aux grands cétacées sur la côte occidentale d'Afrique", in *Comptes rendues hebdomadaires des séances de l'Académie des Sciences,* vol. 156, p. 1,705. Paris, 1913

—— "La chasse aux cétacées dans le monde. Son avenir dans les colonies françaises", in *Revue Scientifique, Revue Rose,* LXII, p. 65. Paris, 1925

Grøn, Th. *Blant norske hvalfangere og andre historier* [Among Norwegian Whalers and other stories]. Oslo, 1909

Guldberg, G. A. "Hval- og selfangst" [Whaling and Sealing], in *Norge i det nittende Aarhundrede* [Norway in the Nineteenth Century], II, pp. 179-95. Oslo, 1900

Haffner, Einar. "Norsk hvalfangst i det tyvende aarhundre" [Norwegian whaling in the twentieth century], in *Norge 1814-1914* [Norway 1814-1914]. Oslo, 1914

Hagemann, Sigurd A. A. *Trekk fra hvalfangstlivet* [Details of Whaling Life]. Reprint from *Tønsbergs Blad.* 1932

Haldane, R. C. "Whaling in Shetland", in *Annals of Scottish Natural History,* no. 50, p. 74, Edinburgh, 1904

—— "Notes on Whaling in Shetland", ibid., no. 54, p. 65. 1905

—— "Whaling in Scotland and the Shetlands", ibid. 54, 1905; 59, 1906; 61, 1907; 66, 1908; 70, 1909; 73, 1910; 78, 1911

Haley, C. Nelson. *Whale Hunt.* New York, 1948

Haller, G. *Hvalfangsten med tilknyttede næringer* [Whaling with associated Industries]. Oslo, 1929

Halmond, A. "Electrocuting Whales", in *Popular Mechanics,* XXXI, 504. 1919

Hare, Lloyd. *Salted Tories: the Story of the Whaling Fleet of San Francisco.* Mystic, Conn., 1960

Harmer, Sidney F. *Subantarctic Whales and Whaling,* London, 1919

—— "The Present Position of the Whaling Industry", in *Nature,* CX, p. 827. London, 1922

—— "Scientific Investigations of the Whaling Problem", ibid., CXI, p. 540. 1923

—— *The History of Whaling.* London, 1928

—— "Southern Whaling", in *Proceedings of the Linnean Society,* Session 142, pp. 85-163. London, 1931

Harold, C. G. "Big-Game Hunting in the Bering Sea", in *Country Life,* vol. LXV, no. 1,672, p. 160. London, 1929

Harris, G. H. *The Faroe Islands,* XVI, p. 94. Birmingham, 1927

Hartnell, Crawford. "Whaling on the West Coast of Ireland", in *British Sea Angler's Society Quarterly,* VIII, p. 2. London, 1915

Hauge, Thomas. *Captain Crawfurds Dagbok* [The Diary of Captain Crawfurd]. Oslo, 1953. (The first Norwegian whaling expedition to the Pacific, 1843-6)

Hawley, Frank. *Whales and Whaling in Japan,* I-1. Kyoto, 1958-60. (Part II of *Miscellanea Japonica*)

Hearings before the Committee on Merchant Marine and Fisheries, House of Representatives, 57th Congress, 3rd Session, on H.R. 8595, 8778, 8906, February 23 and 24. Washington, 1938. Concerns the American floating factories *Frango* and *Ulysses*

Hindle, Edward. "The Whaling Industry", in *Journal of the Royal Society of Arts,* vol. C, no. 4864, p. 132. London, 1952

Hinton, Martin A. C. *Report of Papers left by the late Major G. E. H. Barrett-Hamilton relating to the Whales of South Georgia.* London, 1925

Hjertholm, Sverre. *Hvalfangstkonflikten* [The Whaling Conflict]. Oslo, 1936

Hjort, Johan. *Fiskeri og hvafangst i det nordlige Norge* [Fishing and Whaling in North Norway]. Bergen, 1902

—— *Hvaler og hvalfangst* [Whales and Whaling]. Oslo, 1931

—— "The Story of Whaling: a Parable of Sociology", in *The Scientific Monthly,* vol. XLV, p. 19. New York, 1937

Hjort, Johan and Bergersen, Birger; Lie, J., Ruud, Johan T. "[Norwegian] Pelagic Whaling in the Antarctic I-IX, the Seasons 1929-1939", *Reports of the Whale Board,* Norwegian Academy of Science (ed.), Oslo, 1932-41

Hodgson, J. S. See Morley, F. V.

Hohman, Elmo Paul. *The American Whaleman: a study of Life and Labor in the Whaling Industry.* New York, 1928

—— "American and Norwegian Whaling: a comparative study of labor and industrial organisation", in *The Journal of Political Economy of the University of Chicago,* vol. XLIII, pp. 628-52. Chicago, 1935

Honpo no Norway, shiki hogeishi [Whaling after the Norwegian Methods]. Toyo Hogei K.K., Tokyo, 1910. (Norwegian translation, by Masahiko Inadomi, for *Den moderne hvalfangsts historie*)

Hudtwalcker, C. H. *Der Walfang als volkswirtschaftliches Problem.* Forchheim, 1935

—— *Walfang.* Bremerhaven, 1937

Hugo, Otto. *Deutscher Walfang in der Antarktis.* Oldenburg, 1939

Hvalfangernes Assuranceforening Gjensidig [The Whalers' Mutual Insurance Association], *1911-1936.* Sandefjord, 1936

—— *50 years, 1911-1961.* Sandefjord, 1961

Hyde, H. Montgomery. "Unilever and the Law. 2. The Antarctic Whaling Dispute", in *Progress,* no. 3, p. 111. London, 1964

Høva, Ernst. *Efter hval i Sydishavet* [Chasing the Whale in the Southern Seas]. Oslo, 1929

—— *Graven i Leith Harbour* [The Grave in Leith Harbour]. Oslo, 1929

"International action for the protection of whales", in *Bird-lore,* vol. 34, p. 306. July 1932

Isachsen, Gunnar. *Jorden rundt efter blåhvalen* [Round the World in Search of the Blue Whale]. Oslo, 1927

Janssen, Albrecht. *Tausend Jahre deutscher Walfang.* Leipzig, 1937

Japanese Whaling Association (ed.). *Japanese Whaling Industry.* Tokyo, 1954

Jenkins, J. Travis. "Whaling Fisheries of the Faroe Islands", in *Manchester Guardian,* 18 August 1921

—— "Whale-hunt in the Faroes", in *Littell's Living Age,* no. 311, p. 239. Edinburg, October 1921

—— *A History of the Whale Fisheries.* London, 1921

—— *Whales and Modern Whaling.* London 1932

Joesten, Joachim. *Onassis: a biography.* London, 1963

Johnsen, Arne Odd. Spes et Fides: *Dampskipet som innledet den moderne æra i hvalfangsten* [*Spes et Fides:* The steamer that inaugurated the modern era of whaling]. Oslo, 1940

—— "Granatharpunen. En kort utredning om hvordan Svend Foyn løste projektil-problemet" [A short account of the way in which Svend Foyn solved the projectile problem], in *Norwegian Whaling Gazette,* 1940, pp. 222-42

—— *Svend Foyn og hans dagbok* [Svend Foyn and his Diary]. Oslo, 1943

—— *Norwegian Patents relating to Whaling and the Whaling Industry. A statistical and historical Analysis.* Oslo, 1947

—— *Causation Problems of Modern Whaling.* Sandefjord, 1947

—— *En innsats i radioteknikkens tjeneste. Fra gnisttelegrafen til radar og asdic* [On Service of the Radio-technics. From the Spark-telegraph to Radar and Asdic]. Oslo, 1948

—— *Den moderne hvalfangsts historie. Opprinnelse og utvikling.* Vol. 1: *Finnmarks-*

fangstens historie, 1864-1905 [The History of modern Whaling. Genesis and Development. Vol. 1: The History of Finnmark-whaling 1864-1905]. Oslo, 1959. See Tønnessen, Joh. N.

Jonsgård, Åge. "The Stocks of Blue Whales in the Northern Atlantic Ocean and Adjacent Arctic Waters", in *Norwegian Whaling Gazette,* pp. 297-311. Oslo, 1955
—— *Biology of the North Atlantic Fin Whale. Taxonomy, Distribution, Migration and Food.* Oslo, 1966
—— *Biologiske problemer i tilknytning til hvalfangstregulering* [Biological Problems in Connection wth the Regulation of Whaling]. Oslo, 1972

Jónsson, Bjarni. *Fra Islands Næringsliv. Med historisk Oversikt* [Economic Life in Iceland. With an historical Summary]. Oslo, 1914

Jónsson, Jón. *Hvalur og hvalveidar vid Island* [Whales and Whaling near Iceland]. Reykjavik, 1964

Kellogg, Remington. "Whales, Giants of the Sea", in *National Geographic Magazine.* January 1940. Washington

Kejzerling, H. H. *Das Buch der Keyserlinge.* Berlin, 1944

Kircheiss, Carl. *Polarkreis Süd Polarkreis Nord. Als Walfisch- und Seelenfänger rund um die beiden Amerika.* Leipzig, 1933

Klæboe, H. B. *Svend Foyn. Et Mindeskrift* [Svend Foyn. A Commemorative Paper]. Oslo, 1895

Kohl, Ludvig. *Zur grossen Eismauer des Südpols. Eine Fahrt mit norwegischen Walfängen.* Stuttgart, 1926. With the *Sir James Clark Ross,* 1923/4.

Kolkman, Jaap. "Walvis aan Stuurbord. Lotgewallen van de Nederlandse Walviswaartexpeditie". Nijkerk, 1947. (With the *Willem Barendsz,* 1946-7)

Kraul, Otto. *Käpt'n Kraul erzählt.* Berlin, 1939

Kristensen, Leonard. *Antarctic's Reise til Sydishavet eller Nordmændenes Landing paa Syd Victoria Land* [The Voyage of the *Antarctic* to the South Polar Seas or the Landing of the Norwegians in South Victoria Land]. Tønsberg, 1895
—— "Journal of the Right-Whaling Cruise of the Norwegian Steamship *Antarctic* in the South Polar Seas under Command of Captain Leonard Kristensen during the Years 1894-5", in *Transactions of the Royal Geographical Society of Australasia, Victoria Branch,* XII-XIII. Melbourne, 1896. Cf. Bull, H. J., 1898

Langberg, Chr. B. *Die internationalen Abkommen zur Regelung des Walfanges.* Heidelberg, 1940

Larsen, Carl Anton. "Nogle optegnelser af sæl- og hvalfanger *Jasons* reise i Sydishavet 1893 og 1894" [Some notes on the voyage of the sealer and whaler *Jason* in the South Polar Seas] in *The Yearbook of the Norwegian Geographical Society,* Oslo, 1893 and 1894. (2) *Mittheilungen der Geographischen Gesellschaft in Hamburg 1891-2.* Hamburg, 1895. (3) *Scottish Geographical Magazine,* X, p. 4. Edinburgh, 1894. (4) *Geographical Journal,* IV, p. 4. London, 1894

Larsen, Fridtjov Barth. *Hvalbåtliv* [Life in a Whale-catcher]. Oslo, 1933

Larsen, Nico. *Walfang und Walfänger.* Leipzig, 1940

Leach, Henry G. *Antarctic Whaling.* Princeton, 1951

Lennartz, Annemarie. *Señora and the Whalers,* London, 1954. (Translated from *Señora darf nicht an Bord.* Wiesbaden, 1957)

Lillie, Harry D. *The Path through Penguin City.* London, 1955

Lindemann, Moritz. *Die arktische Fischerei der deutschen Seestädte 1620-1868.* Gotha, 1869
—— "Die gegenwärtige Eismeer-Fischerei und der Walfang", in *Abhandlung des deutschen Seefischerei-Vereins,* IV. Berlin, 1899

Lindholm, O. V. "Kitovyj npomysel (otdel'nyj ottisk)" [The Whaling Industry], in *Russkoe Sudochodstvo* [Russian Seafaring]. St. Petersburg, 1888

Liversidge, Douglas. *The Whale Killers.* London, 1963

Lubbock, Basil. *The Arctic Whalers*. Glasgow, 1927
Lucas, F. A. "The Newfoundland Whale Fisheries", in *Science,* new series, vol. XXI, no. 540, p. 113. New York, 1905
—— "The Passing of the Whale". *Zoological Society Bulletin,* no. 30, Suppl. p. 446. New York, 1908
Ludorff, Walter. *Walfang und Ausbeutung für die deutsche Volksernährung und Volkswirtschaft.* Leipzig, 1938
MacDill, Marjorie. "'Thar she blows!' will be shouted from the airplane", in *The Literary Digest,* CIII, 6, p. 52. New York, 1929
Mackenzie, W. C. "The Whaling Industry. Economic Aspects" in *Canadian Geographic Journal,* vol. XXXVIII, no. 3, pp. 140-4. Ottawa, 1949
Mackintosh, N. A. and Wheeler, J. F. C. "Southern Blue and Fin Whales", in *Discovery Reports,* I, pp. 259-540. Cambridge, 1929
Mackintosh, N. A. "The Southern Stocks of Whalebone Whales", ibid., XXII, pp. 197-300. 1942
—— *The Stocks of Whales.* London, 1965
Making New Zealand, vol. I, no. 4. "Pictorial Surveys of a Century. Whalers and Sealers". Wellington, 1939
Marshall, Warner in collaboration with Lars Christensen. *An Outline for Norwegian Post-War Reconstruction.* Washington, 1942
Martin, Robert E. "Hunting Whales with Speedboats", in *Popular Science,* December 1936, pp. 16, 17. New York. (Whaling in New Zealand)
Matthews, Leonard Harrison. *The Whale.* London, 1968. (Richly illustrated)
McCombe, E. A. *Whales and Whalers.* Sydney, 1940
McGrath, P. T. "Wonderful Whale-Hunting by Steam", in *Cosmopolitan,* vol. 37, pp. 49-56. New York, 1904. (Newfoundland)
McLaughlin, W. R. D. *Antarctic Raider.* London, n.d.
—— *Call to the South: a Story of British Whaling in Antarctica.* London, 1962
Melchior, A. *De eerste walviswaart van de* Willem Barendsz. Haarlem, 1947
Mielche, Hakon. *Hval i sikte* [Spotting Whales]. Bergen, 1951
Millais, J. G. *The Mammals of Great Britain and Ireland,* I-III. London, 1904-6. (III, pp. 215-348, on Whales)
—— *Newfoundland and its untrodden Ways.* London, 1907
Mitchell, Edwards. "Les baleines dans le monde", in *Nature Canada,* vol. 2, no. 4. Ottawa, 1973
Möbius, K. "Über den Fang und die Verwertung der Walfische in Japan", in *Sitzungsberichte der Königlichen Preussischen Akademie der Wissenschaften zu Berlin, 1892.* II, pp. 1953-72. Berlin, 1893
Mörch, J. A. "Improvements in Whaling Methods", in *Scientific American,* vol. 99, p. 75. New York, 1908
—— "Manufacture of Whale Products", ibid, Suppl. vol. LXVII, pp. 15, 16. New York, 1909
—— "On the Natural History of Whalebone Whales", in *Proceedings of the General Meeting of the Zoological Society of London,* vol. 2, pp. 661-70, 1911
Mørch-Olsen, Øistein. *Hvalfangst i Sydishavet* [Whaling in the South Polar Sea]. Tønsberg, 1925
Morley, F. V. and Hodgson, J. S. *Whaling North and South.* London, 1927
Murdoch, W. G. Burn. *From Edinburgh to the Antarctic: an artist's notes and Sketches during the Dundee Antarctic Expedition of 1892-93.* London, 1894
—— "Modern Whaling", in *The Nineteenth Century and After,* LXVIII, pp. 351-69. London, 1910
—— *Modern Whaling and Bear Hunting.* London, 1917
Nielsen, Åge Krarup. *En Hvalfangerfærd gjennem Troperne til Sydishavet* [A Whal-

ing Expedition through the Tropics to the South Polar Sea]. Copenhagen, 1921
Næss, Øivind. *Hvalfangerselskabet Globus A/S 1925-1950. Et kapitel av den moderne hvalfangsts historie* [The Whaling Company Globus Ltd. A Chapter in the History of Modern Whaling]. Larvik, 1951
Oesau, Wanda. *Die deutsche Südsee-fischerei auf Wale im 19. Jahrhundert.* Glückstadt, 1937
—— *Schleswig-Holsteins Grönlandfahrt auf Walfischfang und Robbenschlag vom 17-19. Jahrhundert.* Glückstadt, 1937
—— *Hamburgs Grönlandfahrt auf Walfischfang und Robbenschlag.* Glückstadt, 1955
Olsen, Ørjan. "Hvaler og hvalfangst i Syd-Afrika" [Whales and Whaling in South Africa]. *The Yearbook of Bergen Museum,* no. 5, 1914-15
Ommanney, F. D. "Whaling in the Dominion of New Zealand", in *Discovery Reports,* VII, pp. 239-52. Cambridge, 1932
—— *South Latitude.* London, 1938
Ommanney, F. D. and Westwater, F. L. "New Methods in Antarctic Whaling", in *The Geographical Magazine,* vol. XIX, p. 429. London, 1946
Omura, Hideo. "A Review of Pelagic Whaling Operations in the Antarctic based on Effort and Catch Data in 10° Squares of Latitude and Longitude", in *The Scientific Reports of the Whale Research Institute,* no. 25. Tokyo, 1973
—— "Hval i den nordlige delen av det nordlige Stillehav" [Whales in the northern part of the North Pacific], in *Norwegian Whaling Gazette,* 1955, pp. 195-213, 239-248.
Ostler, H. H. "Big Game Hunting Extraordinary", in *Blackwood's Magazine,* CCXL, no. 1454, p. 775. Edinburgh, 1936
Overn, O. M. *Eventyret om den norske hvalfangst i tekst og billeder* [The illustrated story of Norwegian Whaling]. Oslo, 1929
Paturson, Sverre. "Whale Hunting in the Faroe Islands", in *Trident,* vol. 8, no. 9, 90, p. 46. London, 1946
Paulsen, Harald and Risting, Sigurd. "Der norwegische Walfang", in *Handbuch der Seefischerei Nordeuropas,* VII, Heft 1b. Stuttgart, 1938
Paulsen, Johannes. *Neudeutscher Walfang.* 1938
Peele, Miles L. "Whaling in Northeastern Japanese Waters", in *Science,* new series vol. LXXV, no. 1956, p. 666. New York, 1932
Peters, Nicolaus. *Der neue deutsche Walfang.* Hamburg, 1938
Philp, J. E. *Whaling Ways of Hobart Town.* Hobart, 1934
Pike, Gordon C. "Hvalfangsten på kysten av British Columbia" [Whaling on the Coast of British Columbia], in *Norwegian Whaling Gazette,* 1954, p. 69
Pinkerton, Ken. "Whale Spotting", in *Hunting Group Review,* no. 1, p. 20. London, 1963
"Proposed Whaling Station in the County Donegal, Report of Inquiries", in *Department of Agriculture and Technology: Instruction for Ireland, Fisheries.* Dublin, 1908
Rattray, Jeanette E. See Edwards, E. J.
Ree, Ørnulf. *Harpuner og mannfolk* [Harpoons and Men], Moss, 1953
Rempt, Jan D. *Een avontuurlijke onderneming. De Wellem Barendsz vaart ter Waalvisvangst.* 'S-Gravenhage, 1946
Report of the Departmental Committee on Whaling and Whale Curing in the North of Scotland, 1-2. Edinburgh, 1904
Report of the Committee appointed by the Fishery Board for Scotland to enquire into the Scottish Whaling Industry. Edinburgh, 1920
Report of the Interdepartmental Committee on Research and Development in the

Dependencies of the Falkland Islands. London, 1920

Rhoda, Ethel. "Whaling in the Northwest Pacific", in *Overland Monthly*, vol. LXIV, no. 3, pp. 223-32. San Francisco, 1914

Risting, Sigurd. "Hvalfangsten i 1912" [Whaling in 1912]. Appendix to *Norwegian Fisheries Gazette.* Bergen, 1913

—— *Av hvalfangstens historie* [From the History of Whaling]. Oslo, 1922. (The basic work on the history of modern whaling before 1920)

—— "Whaling", in *The Norway Yearbook*, 1924. Oslo, 1932

—— "History and Economic Importance of the Norwegian Whaling Industry", in *Norwegian Trade Review*, February 1926, p. 6. Oslo

—— *Kaptein C. A. Larsen.* Oslo, 1929

—— "Whales and Whaling" in *The History of the Norwegian Mercantile Marine*, vol. III, pp. 328-60. Oslo, 1929

—— In almost every no. of *Norwegian Whaling Gazette*, 1913-35, articles on whales and whaling

—— See also Paulsen, Harald

Robertson, R. B. *Of Whales and Men.* New York, 1954

Rolfsen, Nordahl. *Sjømænd. Norske Sjømænds Oplevelser* [Sailors. Adventures of Norwegian Sailors]. Oslo, 1896

Rudolf, Martin. "Der norwegische Walfang", in *Mitteilung der geographischen Gesellschaft in Hamburg*, XXXVII, 1926

Ruud, Johan T. "Om fangsten av storhval på Norges vestkyst og hvalbestandens størrelse" [The catch of larger whales on the west coast of Norway and the stock of whales] in *Norwegian Whaling Gazette*, 1946, pp. 35-40, 58-64

—— "Internasjonal regulering av hvalfangsten", [International Regulation of the Whaling], ibid., 1956, pp. 374-87

—— "Modern Whaling and its Prospects", in *F.A.O. Fisheries Bulletin*, no. 5, pp. 1-21, 1952. (Cf. *Norwegian Whaling Gazette*, 1954, p. 128)

—— See Hjort, Johan

Ræstad, Arnold. *Hvalfangsten på det frie hav* [Whaling in the open sea]. Oslo, 1928

Salvesen, Harold K. "Modern Whaling in the Antarctic", in *Journal of the Royal Society of Arts*, vol. LXXXI, no. 4191, pp. 408-29. London, 1933

Salvesen, Theodore E. "The Whaling Industry of Today", ibid. LX, pp. 515-23. 1912

—— "The Whale Fisheries of the Falkland Islands and Dependencies", in *Scottish National Antarctic Expedition*, XIX, pp. 479-86. London, 1913

Sambon, Louis. "West India Whaling", in *The Empire Review*, vol. XXXVII, pp. 264-7. London, 1923

Sanderson, Ivan. *Follow the Whale.* Boston, 1956

Sandison, A. "Whale Hunting in the Shetlands", in *Saga-Book of the Viking Club*, vol. I, pp. 42-53. London, 1896

Scammon, C. M. *The Marine Mammals of the North-western Coast of North America.* San Francisco, 1874

Scharff, R. F. "The Irish Whale Fishery", in *The Irish Naturalist*, XIX, p. 229. Dublin, 1910

Scheffer, Victor B. and Slipp, John W. "The Whales and Dolphins of Washington State", incl. in "The History of Whaling in Washington", in *The American Midland Naturalist*, vol. 2, pp. 259-337. Notre Dame, Indiana, 1948

Scheffer, Victor B. *The Year of the Whale.* New York, 1969

Schnakenbeck, W. "Der Walfang", in *Handbuch der Seefischerei Nordeuropas*, V. Heft 3. Stuttgart, 1928

Schubert, Kurt. "Der Walfang der Gegenwart", in *Handbuch der Seefischerei*

Nordeuropas, XI. Stuttgart, 1935

Schultze, Ernst. "Die Entwickelung des Walfanges der Vereinigten Staaten", in *Vierteljahrschrift für Sozial- und Wirtschaftsgeschichte,* XVI, pp. 130-47. Stuttgart, 1922

Schultze, Wilhelm. "Strukturwandel des Walfanges", in *Der deutsche Volkswirt,* no. 15. 1939

Scoresby, William. *An Account of the Arctic Regions, with a History and Description of the Northern Whale Fishery.* Edinburgh, 1820

Serre, Paul. "La dernière saison de la chasse à la baleine dans la mer de Ross", in *La Pêche Maritime,* no. 678. Paris, 1931

Skottun, O. "Hvalfangst og radio" [Whaling and Radio], in *Norwegian Whaling Gazette* 1938, pp. 265-75

Slipp, John W. See Scheffer, Victor B.

Slijper, E. J. *Walvissen.* Amsterdam, 1958. Translated as: *Whales.* London, 1962

—— "A Hundred Years of Modern Whaling", in *Netherlands Commission for International Nature Protection, Meddelingen,* no. 19. Amsterdam, 1965

—— "Walfang und angewandte Walforschung", in *Naturwissenschaftliche Rundschau,* XIX, Heft 2. Stuttgart

Slaattelid, Aasmund. *Med kanon og kamera efter storhvalen* [With Gun and Camera after the Big Whale]. Oslo, 1938

Sørensen, G. *Hvalfangsten. Dens Historie og Mænd* [Whaling: its History and Men]. Oslo, 1912

Sorkness, Asbjørn. *Hvalfangeren* [The Whaler]. Oslo, 1957

South Africa, Union of, Board of Trade and Industries. *The Whaling Industry.* Report no. 337, pp. 15-39. 1950

Southwell, Thomas. "On the Whale Fishery from Scotland, with some Account of the Changes in that Industry and of the Species hunted", in *Annals of Scottish Natural History,* no. 50, pp. 77-90. Edinburgh, 1904

—— "Newfoundland Fin-Whale Fishing in 1905", ibid. no. 60, pp. 193-5. 1906

—— "Some Results of the North-Atlantic Fin-Whale Fishery", in *The Annals and Magazine of Natural History,* XVI, 7th series, pp. 403-21. London, 1905

—— "On the Hunting of Right Whales from Greenland", in *The Zoologist,* XIII, 4th series 26/27. London, 1909

Spengemann, Herbert. *Auf Walfang in der Antarktis.* Bühl-Baden, 1938

Starbuck, Alexander. *History of the American Whale Fishery from its Earliest Inception to the Year 1876.* I-II. New York, 1964

Spears, J. R. *The Story of the New England Whalers.* New York, 1908

Starks, Edwin C. "A History of California Shore Whaling", in *State of California Fish and Game Commission. Fish Bulletin,* no. 6, pp. 1-38. Sacramento, 1927

Steiner, Ragnar. *Med kokeri og hvalbåt* [With Floating Factory and Whale Catcher]. Oslo, 1932

Stevenson, C. H. *Whalebone, its Production and Utilization,* U.S. Dept. of Commerce and Labour, Bureau of Fisheries, Doc. 626. Washington, 1907

Shapiro, Irwin, in consultation with Stackpole, E.A. *The Story of Yankee Whaling.* New York, 1959. (A splendidly illustrated book)

Templeman, Wilfred. *Marine Resources of Newfoundland,* Bulletin 154, pp. 138-44. Ottawa, 1966

Terry, William M. "Japanese Whaling prior to 1946", in *Report 126 of the Natural Resources Section,* G.H.Q., Supreme Commander for Allied Powers. Tokyo, 1950

Thompson, D'Arcy W. "On Whales landed at the Scottish Whaling Stations during the Years 1908-1914 and 1920-1927", in *Fishery Board for Scotland Scientific Investigations,* III. Edinburgh, 1928

Thompson, Harold. *Reports of the Newfoundland Fishery Research Commission*, vol. I. St. John's, 1931

Thorson, Odd. *Aksjeselskapet Kosmos gjennem 25. år. En epoke i Antarktis* [Kosmos Co. Ltd. through 25 Years. An Epoch in the Antarctic]. Oslo, 1953

Tomilin, A. *Hvalfangst i S.S.S.R.* [Whaling in the U.S.S.R.], in *Norwegian Whaling Gazette*, 1936, pp. 54, 66

Tønnessen, Joh. N. *Den moderne hvalfangsts historie. II-IV: Verdensfangsten. Den pelagiske fangst* [The History of modern Whaling, Vols. 2-4. World-wide Whaling. Pelagic Whaling]. Sandefjord, 1967-70. See Johnsen, Arne Odd

—— "Norwegian Antarctic Whaling, 1905-68: an Historical Appraisal", in *Polar Record*, vol. 15, no. 96, pp. 283-90. Cambridge, 1970

Tower, Walter S. "A History of the American Whale Fishery", in Publications of the University of Pennsylvania. Series in Political Economy and Public Law, no. 20. Philadelphia, 1907

Townsend, Charles Haskins. "The distribution of certain whales as shown by logbooks of American whaleships", in *Zoologica*, XIX, no. 1. New York, 1915

—— "Twentieth Century Whaling". *Bulletins of New York Zoological Society*, vol. XXXIII, no. 1. New York, 1930

Vamplew, Wray. *Salvesen of Leith*. Edinburgh, 1975

Vaucaire, Michel. *Histoire de la pêche à la baleine*. Paris, 1914

Verril, A. Hyatt. *The real Story of the Whaler: Whaling past and present*. New York, 1916

Villiers, A. J. *Whaling in the Frozen South: being the Story of the 1923-24 Norwegian Whaling Expedition to the Antarctic*. London, 1925

—— *Sea-Dogs of Today*. London, 1932

—— *Whalers of the Midnight Sun*. London, 1934

Wasberg, Gunnar Christie. *Femti år i konkurranse og fremgang. Aktieselakapet Tønsbergs Hvalfangeri 1907-1957* [Fifty Years of Competition and Progress: Tønsberg Whaling Co. Ltd.]. Tønsberg, 1958

Weberman, Ernest. *Kitobojnyi promysel v. Rossii, c. I. Istoriya promysla Iztvestya Moskovsk. Kommerceskogo Instituta, Kommerceskotechniceskoe otdelnie, kn. 2* [The Whaling Industry in Russia, part I. The History of the Industry. Reports of the Institute of Commerce, Commercial-Technical Department, book 2]. Moscow, 1914. See *Norwegian Whaling Gazette*, 1914, p. 132

Western Australia. Whaling Bill and Debates in the Legislative Council, September and October 1928. Perth

Westwater, F. L. See Ommanney, F. D. 1946

Whaling Conflict 1936, The. Oslo, 1936. (Between Britain and Norway)

Wheeler, J. F. G. "On the stock of whales at South Georgia", in *Discovery Reports*, IX, pp. 353-72. Cambridge, 1934

Wilcox, William A. "The Fisheries of the Pacific Coast", in *U.S. Commission of Fish and Fisheries: Report of the Commission for 1895*, pp. 143-304. Washington, 1895

Willoughby, Verner. "Whaling near Gibraltar", in *Country Life*, vol. L, no. 1286, pp. 249-52. London, 1921

Winterhoff, Edmund. *Walfang in der Antarktis*. Oldenburg/Hamburg, 1974

Wolgast, Ernst. "Walfang und Recht. Eine Studie zur Lage des Walfanges um die Fangsaison 1936/37", in *Zeitschrift für Völkerrecht*, XXI, p. 151. 1937

—— "Der englisch-norwegische Walfangstreit", in *Völkerbund und Völkerrecht*, III, p. 676. 1937

Wood, Walter. "North Sea Whaling", in *Windsor Magazine*, 1922, p. 200 (Whaling in Shetland)

Woollen, William Watson. "Whales and Whale Fisheries of the North Pacific", in

Proceedings of the Indiana Academy of Science, 1919. Bloomington, 1921
"X". "A Whale Hunt", in *Blackwood's Magazine,* CCXI, pp. 91-9. Edinburgh, 1922. (Whaling off Durban)
Zenkowich, B. A. *Jagd auf Meeresriesen.* Lipzia, 1956. (Translated from Russian)
Zoo Life, vol. 10, no. 2. London, 1952. (Special issue on Whaling)

Exploration, Nature, Sovereignty in the Antarctic

Aagaard, Bjarne. "Who discovered Antarctica?", in *Proceedings of the South Pacific Scientific Congress.* San Francisco, 1939
—— *Antarktis 1502-1944. Oppdagelser, naturforhold og suverenitetsforhold* [The Antarctic. Discoveries, Nature and Sovereignty]. Oslo, 1944
—— *Oppdagelser i Sydishavet fra middelalderen til Sydpolens erobring* [Discoveries in the South Polar Seas from the Middle Ages to the Conquest of the South Pole]. Oslo, 1946
Allardyce, William L. *A Short History of the Falkland Islands.* Letchworth, 1909
Bogen, Hans S. I. *Main Events in the History of Antarctic Exploration.* Reprint of the *Norwegian Whaling Gazette,* 1957
Bonner, W. Nigel. "The Introduced Reindeer of South Georgia", in *Falkland Islands Dependencies Survey, Scientific Report,* no. 22. London, 1958
Borchgrevink, Carsten. *Nærmest Sydpolen aaret* 1900 [Nearest to the South Pole in the Year 1900]. Copenhagen, 1905
Boyson, V. F. *The Falkland Islands.* Oxford, 1924
"The British Title to Sovereignty in the Falkland Islands Dependencies", in *Polar Record,* VII. Cambridge, 1958
Brown, R. N. Rudmose. *The Polar Regions.* London, 1912
Brown, R. N. Rudmose; Pirie, J. H. H.; Mossman, R. C. *The Voyage of the Scotia: being the Record of a Voyage of Exploration in the Antarctic Seas.* Edinburg, 1906. (reprint London 1978)
Christensen, Lars. *Such is the Antarctic.* London, 1931
—— *Til Sydishavet* [To the South Polar Seas]. Oslo, 1933
—— *Min siste expedisjon til Antarktis 1936-1937. Med en oversikt over forskningsarbeidene på ferdene 1927-1937* [My Last Expedition to the Antarctic, with a Summary of the Research Work of the Expeditions 1927-1937]. Oslo, 1938
Christie, E. W. Hunter. *The Antarctic Problem: an historical and political Study.* London, 1951
Coleman-Cooke, John. *Discovery II in the Antarctic.* London, 1963
Debenham, Frank. *The Story of a Continent.* London, 1959 and New York, 1961
Delepine, Grace and René. "Les allemands au Kerguelen durant la deuxième guerre mondiale", in *Terres Australes et Antarctiques Françaises,* no. 26, January-March 1964. Paris
Donald, Charles W. "The Late Expedition to the Antarctic", in *Scottish Geographical Magazine,* vol. X, no. 2, Edinburgh, 1894
Ferguson, D. "Geological Observations in South Georgia", in *Transactions of the Royal Society of Edinburgh,* vol. L, part IV, pp. 797-816. Edinburgh, 1915. (With many excellent illustrations)
Gosling, W. G. *Labrador: its Discovery, Exploration and Development.* London, 1910
Harstad, Herlof. *Erobringen av Antarktis* [The Conquest of the Antarctic]. Oslo, 1968
Hayes, J. Gordon. *Antarctica: a Treatise on the Southern Continent.* London, 1928

Hermann, Paul. *Island in Vergangenheit und Gegenwart* [Iceland Past and Present], I-III. Leipzig, 1907-10

I. C. J. Pleadings, Antarctic Cases. *United Kingdom* v. *Argentina; United Kingdom* v. *Chile,* Leiden, 1958

Isachsen, Gunnar. Norvegia *rundt Sydpollandet* [Norvegia around the South Polar Continent]. Oslo, 1934

Kemp, Stanley and Nelson, A. L. "The South Sandwich Islands", in *Discovery Reports,* III. Cambridge, 1931

Leader-Williams, Nigel. "The History of the Introduced Reindeer of South Georgia". Reprint from *Deer,* vol. 4, no. 5. February 1978. (With bibliography)

Lønnberg, Einar. "Contribution to the Fauna of South Georgia", *Kungl. Svenska Vetenskapsakad.'s Handlingar,* XL, no. 5. Stockholm, 1906

Marr, James W. S. "The South Orkney Islands", in *Discovery Reports,* X, pp. 238-382. Cambridge, 1935

Marshall, E. H. "Report on a Visit to the Ross Dependency", in *The Geographical Journal,* LXXV, no. 3, pp. 244-51. London, 1930

Matthews, L. Harrison. *South Georgia: the British Empire's Subantarctic Outpost.* London, 1931

McWhan, Forrest W. *The Falkland Islands Today.* Stirling, 1952

Nicolson, Nigel. *Lord of the Isles.* London, 1960. (Lord Leverhulme and the Hebrides)

Nordenskkjöld, Otto, and Andersen, J. Gunnar, *Antarctica: or Two Years amongst the Ice of the South Pole.* London 1904 (reprint London 1977). (Translated from Swedish edition of 1904)

Petersen, Johannes. *Die Reisen des* Jason *und der* Hertha *in das Antarktische Meer 1893-94, und die wissenschaftlichen Ergebnisse dieser Reisen.* Hamburg, 1895

Potter, W. "Brief Survey of Antarctic Exploration", in *Transactions of the Royal Geographical Society of Australasia, Victoria Branch,* XII-XIII, pp. 117-58. Melbourne, 1896

Quartermain, L. B. *South to the Pole: the Early History of the Ross Sea Sector, Antarctica.* London, 1967

Rankin, Niall. *Antarctic Isle: Wild Life in South Georgia.* London, 1951. (With excellent illustrations)

Saunders, Alfred. *A Camera in the Antarctic.* London, 1950

Scientific Results of the Norwegian Antarctic Expeditions, 1927-1928 et seq., I-III. Oslo, 1935-61

Skattum, C. J. *Sydpol-forskning. En utsikt over dens utvikling gjennom tiderne* [The Exploration of the South Pole. A Survey of its Development through the Ages]. Oslo, 1912

Smedel, Gustav. *Erhvervelse av statshøihet over polarområder* [Acquisition of Sovereignty of Polar Regions]. Oslo, 1930

—— *Suverenitetsspørsmål i polarområder* [Problems of Sovereignty of Polar regions]. Oslo, 1942

Strong, Charles S. *The Real Book about the Antarctic.* New York, 1959

Waldock, C. H. M. "Disputed Sovereignty in the Falkland Islands Dependencies", in *The British Year Book of International Law,* 1948, pp. 311-53. Oxford, 1949

Zabel, Rudolf. "Durch die Mandschurei und Sibirien", in *Reisen und Studien.* Leipzig, 1903. (Whaling from Vladivostok pp. 126-52)

Øynes, Per. "Tamrein i Antarktis" [Domestic Reindeer in the Antarctic], in *Fauna,* p. 148. Oslo, 1960

Oils and Fats Markets

Alsberg, Carl L. and Taylor, Alonso E. "The Fats and Oils: a General View", in *Fats and Oil Studies*, no. 1. Food Research Institute, Stanford University, California, 1928

Barry, T. Hedley. "The Modern Industry", in *The Industrial Chemist*, August 1929, p. 333. London

Brandt, Carl. "The German Fat Plan and its Economic Setting", in *Fats and Oil Studies*, no. 6. Food Research Institute, Stanford University, California, 1938
—— "Whale Oil: an Economic Analysis", ibid. no. 7. 1940
—— "Whaling and Whale Oil during and after World War II", ibid. Pamphlet no. 11. 1948

Brækkan, Olaf R. *Vitamins in Whale Liver*. Oslo, 1948

Falerion, W. *Die Fabrikation der Margarine, des Glyzerins und Stearine*. Berlin, 1920

Faure, H. M. F. "The Outlook of the Oil and Fat Markets" (unpublished MS). London, 1934

Fehr, Frank, & Co. Ltd. *Review of the Oilseed, Oil and Oil Cake Markets* (annually), 1924-66. London

Fette und Seifen, 45. Jahrgang, Heft 1. Berlin, 1938. Special issue on the opening of German pelagic whaling in the Antarctic. *Inter alia:* Wohlthat, H. G. H. "Whaling and the London Agreement for its regulation"; Peters, N. "The biological basis of whaling in the Antarctic"; Sommermeyer, A. "Forty years experience in the construction of machines for whale utilisation"; Fauth, Ph. "Preparation of whales"; Schmalfuss, H. and Werner, H. "The utilisation of whale meat"; Schwieger, A. "The chemistry of whale oil and its standardisation"; Normann, W. "The hydrogenation of whale oil and the application of hydrogenated oil in margarine manufacture"; Lindner, K. "Whale products in soap and sulphonate manufacture"; Pawelzik, H. "The importance of whale oil for paints and varnishes"; Stather, F. "The use of whale oil in leather manufacture"; Fritz, F. "Whale oil in linoleum manufacture"; Bomskov, C. and Unger, F. "Whale products as a source for hormones and vitamins"; Kaufmann, H. P. "Whale products in pharmacy with special reference to whale fat"; Filmer, B. "Spermaceti and cetyl alcohol in cosmetics"; Treff, W. "The aromatic substance Ambra"

Heyerdahl, E. Fred. *Hvalindustrien. En teknisk-kjemisk undersøkelse. I, Råmaterialet* [The Whaling Industry. A technical-chemical investigation. I, the Raw Material]. Oslo, 1937

Holmboe, Carl Fred. *De-No-Fa 1912-1937*. Oslo, 1937. (The first and leading Norwegian factory for hydrogenation of whale oil)

Jorpes, J. Erik. *The Insulin Content of Whale Pancreas*. Oslo, 1950

Lynge, Erik. "Der Walfang. Ein Beitrag zur Weltwirtschaft der Fettstoffe", in *Wandlungen in der Weltwirtschaft*, Heft 7. Leipzig, 1936

Markt, Th. *Die deutsche Fettwirtschaft in und nach dem Kriege*. Hamburg, 1936

Oils and Fats. Production and international Trade, I-II. The International Institute of Agriculture (later F.A.O.). Rome, 1938

Pabst, V. W. *Butter and Oleomargarine: an Analysis of Competing Commodities*. New York, 1937

Pedersen, Torbjørn. *Studies in Whale Oils*. Oslo, 1950

Snodgrass, Katharina. "Margarine as a Butter Substitute", in *Fats and Oil Studies*, no. 4, Food Research Institute, Stanford University, California, 1930

Taylor, Alonso E. See Alsberg, Carl L.

Tveraaen, I. and Klem, Alf. *Contribution to the Study of Whale Oils.* Oslo, 1935
Wilson, Charles. *The History of Unilever: a Study in Economic Growth and Social Change,* I-II. London, 1954

Statistics

Harmer, Sidney. *Modern Whaling Statistics.* London, 1921
Hudtwalker, Carl H. "Über die Walfangstatistik und ihre Probleme", in *Fette und Seifen,* 1938, Heft 1, pp. 108-11. Berlin
International Whaling Statistics. Oslo, 1930-
Journal of the Royal Statistical Society, Series A (General), vol. CXIII, part III. London, 1950. (Special issue on fats and oils)
Norwegian Central Statistical Bureau
Unilever. Annual Reports and Reviews of the Oil and Fat Market

Manuscripts
(* indicates that the item was specially written for the present work)

Bettum, Frithjof. "Hvalfangstens utvikling og dens hovedproblem i dag" [The development of whaling and its main problem today]. 1960
Bock, Peter Gideon. "A Study in International Regulation: the Case of Whaling". 1960
Elliot, G. H. "Whaling at South Georgia, 1904-1959".
—— "Some Economic Aspects of Whaling"
Fagerli, Søren. "The Whale Catchers"*
Foot, Charles Don. "The Old Whaling in the Bering Sea and the North Polar Sea"
Heyerdahl, E. Fred. "Research and Experiments in the Whaling Industry"*
—— "The Economic Development in the Whaling Industry"
Holden, M. "The Development of the Floating Factory"*
—— "The Technical Development of the Whaling Industry"*
Iversen, Thor. "Review of the Development of Whaling in the Southern Oceans"
Johnsen, Arne Odd. "The Radio-technique and Whaling"*
—— "The Development of Boiling Apparatus (Methods for Oil Extraction)"*
Klaveness, Gunnar. "Hvalfangstbegrensningen og dens virkninger" [The Regulation of Whaling and its Effects]
Larsen-Renold, Andrea. "La caccia alla Balena. Caratteri economici delle pesca della Balena e dell' utilizzazione industriale del suo oleo". F.A.O., Rome, 1963
Lea, Einar. "Studies on the Modern Whale Fishery in the Southern Hemisphere". See *Norwegian Whaling Gazette.* 1918, p. 221
Mørck, Finn. "De-No-Fa's historie". See Holmboe, Carl Fred under Oils and Fats Markets
Sommermeyer, August. "Autobiography"
Wegger, Arnt. "Hvalbåtene [the whale catchers]"

Other Unpublished Sources
(apart from those referred to in the Preface)

Heyerdahl, E. Fred. 44 files with catch, research and experiment reports, and diaries from South Sandwich, Bouvet, Kerguelen and the Ross Sea
Unilever Ltd. v. Hvalfangerselskapet Globus A/S, etc. Pleadings and Report of Proceedings, I-IV
Unilever Ltd. v. Bryde & Dahl Hvalfangerselkab A/S, etc. Pleadings and Report

of Proceedings, I-II

The Norwegian Shipping and Trade Mission (Nortraship), London and New York, managers of the Norwegian mercantile marine and whaling fleet during the Second World War

The (Norwegian) Whaling Committee, New York, 1940-5

The British-Norwegian Joint Committee 1943-6. (Planning the reconstruction of the whaling fleet)

Annual Reports of the Norwegian Whaling Control Office, 1932-68

The Norwegian Whale Research Institute, archive

The Norwegian Whale Board, archive

A FINAL NOTE

SUMMARY OF 31st ANNUAL INTERNATIONAL
WHALING COMMISSION, 9–13 JULY 1979

MEMBER NATIONS: Argentina, Australia, Brazil, Canada, *Chile*, Denmark, France, Iceland, Japan, *Republic of Korea*, Mexico, Netherlands, New Zealand, Norway, Panama, Peru, *Seychelles*, South Africa, *Spain*, *Sweden*, United Kingdom, United States, Soviet Union

(Nations joining between July 1978 and July 1979 are italicised)

1. *Moratorium on whaling*
After considerable discussion an amended proposal to the total moratorium was adopted which resulted in a ban on the catching of all whales except minke whales by factory ships.

2. *Whale sanctuaries*
It was agreed to prohibit all whaling within an area designated as the Indian Ocean Sanctuary for ten years, with the provision for a general review after five years.

3. *Bowhead whales*
For the fourth successive meeting the Scientific Committee stated that from a biological viewpoint, the only safe course was to allow no catching from the Bering Sea stock. After a long discussion in which the United States argued that a limited take was essential for the Eskimos and that a zero quota could result in non-compliance with the Commission's decision, a proposal that in 1980 the catch of bowhead whales from the Bering Sea stock would be limited 26 whales struck or 18 landed, gained the required majority.

4. *Catch limits*
The following catch limits were set for the 1979/80 Antarctic season and for the 1980 season elsewhere (1978/9 figures in brackets):

	Southern Hemisphere	North Pacific	North Atlantic	Northern Indian Ocean
Sperm	580 (5,436)	1,350 (3,800)	273 (685)	0 (–)
Fin	0 (0)	0 (0)	604 (470)	– (–)
Sei	0 (0)	0 (0)	100 (84)	– (–)
Bryde's	264 (0)	479 (454)	0 (0)	0 (–)
Minke	8,102 (6,221)	1,361 (400)	2,543 (2,552)	– (–)

The blue, right (including bowhead), humpback, and gray whales remain totally protected from commercial whaling in all areas. The bottlenose whale is protected in the North Atlantic Ocean.

In addition to the aboriginal quota for bowheads described above, quotas of 179 gray whales (Eastern Pacific) and 10 humpbacks (Greenland) were agreed, to be taken by or on behalf of aboriginal peoples.

774

5. *Pirate whaling*
South Africa reported on steps taken to restrict the activities of the *Sierra* which resulted in the closure of the Sierra Fishing Agency, Cape Town.

Member nations undertook:
- (a) to cease importing whale products from non-member countries and exporting whaling vessels and equipment to non-members;
- (b) to consider national legislation prohibiting whaling by non-member nations within their fishery conservation zones.

6. *Review of present management procedure*
It was agreed that the Special Scientific Working Group on Management should meet again to finalise their work in time to allow their report to be adequately considered at the next I.W.C. meeting.

SUMMARY OF 32nd ANNUAL MEETING OF THE INTERNATIONAL WHALING COMMISSION, 21–26 JULY 1980

MEMBER NATIONS: Argentina, Australia, Brazil, Canada, Chile, Denmark, France, Iceland, Japan, Republic of Korea, Mexico, Netherlands, New Zealand, Norway, *Oman*, Peru, Seychelles, South Africa, Spain, Sweden, *Switzerland*, United Kingdom, United States, Soviet Union

(Members joining between July 1979 and July 1980 are italicised. Panama withdrew from the Commission in June 1980).

1. *Moratorium on all commercial whaling and on the taking of sperm whales*
Neither of these proposals obtained the required three quarters majority.

2. *Bowhead whales*
The Scientific Committee reiterated its view that the only safe course was to introduce a zero quota. The United States argued that this was unacceptable as the hunt was necessary on historic, cultural and subsistence grounds. After considerable discussion and a statement from the United States that it would progressively reduce the catch within the I.W.C. quota a catch limit for the three years 1981–3 of 45 whales landed and 65 struck provided that in any one year the number landed does not exceed 17.

3. *Catch limits*
The following catch limits were set for the 1980/1 Antarctic season and for the 1981 season elsewhere (1979/80 figures in brackets):

	Southern Hemisphere		North Pacific		North Atlantic		Northern Indian Ocean	
Sperm	300	(580)	890	(1,350)	130	(273)	0	(0)
Fin	0	(0)	0	(0)	701	(604)	–	(–)
Sei	0	(0)	0	(0)	100	(100)	–	(–)
Bryde's	886*	(264)	529	(479)	0	(0)	0	(0)
Minke	7,072	(8,102)	1,361	(1,361)	2,554	(2,543)	–	(–)
Bottlenose	–	(–)	–	(–)	0	(0)	–	(–)

* This figure includes the "Northern Indian Ocean" and "Peruvian" stocks the boundaries of which extend north of the equator.

The blue, right (including bowhead), humpback and gray whales remain totally protected from commercial whaling in all areas. The bottlenose whale is protected in the North Atlantic Ocean.

4. Humane killing
It was agreed to prohibit the use of the non-explosive harpoon in commercial operations for all whales except minke whales and to hold a Workshop on Humane Killing Methods in the autumn of 1980.

5. Small cetaceans
Although members could not agree on whether the 1946 Convention included responsibilities for small cetaceans, they did agree to provide information on small cetaceans to the Scientific Committee and to consider any advice it may give.

6. Revision of the International Convention for the Regulation of Whaling, 1946
The Commission considered the positions outlined at an informal meeting held prior to the Annual Meeting and agreed that another preparatory meeting of interested parties should be held to improve and update the present Convention.

INDEX

PERSONS

Acheson, Dean, 499, 532, 533
Allardyce, William Lamond, 180, 340
Amlie, Thomas, 76, 77, 80, 81, 85
Amundsen, Roald, 147, 155, 303, 339, 347, 349
Andersen, A., 171, 175
Andersen, Lars, 356, 429, 535, 537, 539, 558, 559
Anderson, F. F., 545
Andersen, Adolf Amandus, 157
Andrews, Roy Chapman, 69
Anvandter, Jorje, 204
Asgeirsson, A., 81

Balcom, Capt. Rube, 114
Balcom, Capt. Sprot, 114
Balcom, Capt. W., 114
Barendsz, William, 95, 523
Barret-Hamilton, Major G. E. H., 345
Bennet, F., 702
Bergersen, Prof. Birger, 447, 450, 452, 453, 462, 64, 489, 491, 512, 514
Bergh, Henry van den, 239
Bernhard, Prince, 521
Binnie, Edward, 289
Birkeland, Kristian, 702
Board, Sir Vivyan, 704
Bogen, P. O., 85, 86, 88, 119, 174, 182, 211
Bottemanne, Capt., 21
Bouvet, J.-B.-C., 147
Brandt, Prof. Karl, 532
Brown, Nathaniel, 196
Bruce, William S., 149, 159
Bryde, Johan, 209–10, 216, 218, 247, 315, 316
Bull, Henrik Johan, 153, 154
Bull, J., 159
Bull, Marcus C., 80, 82, 255
Burn Murdoch, W. G., 91, 92, 149, 159

Carlsson, Henry, 132
Carver, Clifford N., 534
Chamberlain, N., 458, 460
Christensen, Christen, 96, 97, 98, 171, 172, 174, 202, 203, 263, 267, 269, 303, 350, 354, 376

Christensen, Lars, 120, 206, 207, 247, 248, 307, 359, 360, 379, 381, 382, 389, 407–11, 425, 447, 451, 480, 629, 697, 699
Christophersen, Pedro, 160, 166
Clarke, Robert, 323
Congreve, W., 18
Cook, H. F., 220, 269
Cook, James, 147, 165
Corneliussen, Carl, 690
Corneliussen, Erling, 690

Dahl, A. C., 23
Dahl, Thor, 99
Dakin, William John, 221
D'Arcy Cooper, Francis, 383, 389, 392, 394, 395, 397–8, 404, 413, 425, 426, 431, 477, 458
Darnley, C. R., 355, 360–2, 436
Davidsen, Nokard, 106
Didymov, Akim Grigorevitch, 131, 132
Dijk, D. J. van, 501
Dobson, A. T. A., 502, 541
Dormer, Sir Cecil, 440
Dudnik, A. J., 414

Egeland, Jacob J., 211
Eielson, Carl Ben, 277
Ellefsen, Anders, 104
Ellefsen, Hans, 78, 79
Engholm, Basil C., 599
Esmark, H. M. T., 24, 30
Esricht, D. F., 70
Evans, Admiral, 303

Fauth, Philipp, L., 716, 717
Ferguson, Henry, 277
Findley, Sir Mansfeldt de Cardonnel, 295, 297, 304
Fitzsimmons, F. W., 278
Forster, George, 147
Foyn, Svend, 6, 11, 12, 14, 18, 21, 22, 23, 25–36, 41, 43, 47, 50, 55, 56, 59, 60, 65, 68, 70, 71, 75, 76, 80, 115, 131, 132, 148–50, 152, 154, 155, 159, 229, 251, 263, 273, 274, 278, 639, 688
Fujita, I., 609, 638

Gambell, R., 682
Gerlache, Adrien de, 155
Gjelstad, 706
Godber, J. B., 589
Goering, Hermann, 398
Gray, David, 148, 150
Gray, Sir Edward, 180
Gray, John, 148, 150
Grøn, Hans Albert, 84, 85, 86
Gruvel, Prof. A., 217, 319
Gulland, J. A., 635

Hammer, O. C., 20
Hansen, Leganger, 280
Harmer, Sir Sydney F., 342
Hartmann, R. A., 256
Hartog, Jacob, 389, 390
Hawley, Frank, 128
Heard, John J., 181
Henriks, P. D. H., 398
Henriksen, Henrik N., 80, 88
Hirata, M., 692
Hitler, Adolf, 396
Hjort, J., 70, 71, 346, 356, 360, 361
Hoover, Pres. H. C., 532

Ingebrigtsen, Morten Andreas, 264, 275
Irvin, George, 193
Irvin, John H., 193
Irvin, Richard, 193
Isbrandtsen, Hans J., 451
Ishkov, A., 588, 603, 608
Iversen, Ole, 272

Jacobsen, Fridthjof, 163, 539
Jahre Anders, 375–82, 412, 437, 451
Joesten, Joachim, 558, 559
Johnsen, A. O., 16
Johnson, Charles Ocean, 193
Jonsgård, Åge, 100

Kellogg, Remington, 449, 460, 489, 491, 493, 495, 499, 508, 586, 672
Kejzerling, Count Heinrich Hugovitch, 132, 263
Kircheiss, Capt. Karl, 22, 423, 428
Koht, Prof. Halvdan, 440, 448, 449, 450, 452, 455
Korsholm, H. C., 203
Kraul, Capt. Otto, 422, 423, 428, 451
Kristensen, Leonard, 153, 155
Kro, Mons Larsen, 75, 76

Lange, Alex, 98, 172, 181
Larsen, Abraham, E., 211
Larsen, C. A., 96, 150–52, 154–6, 157–68, 171, 199, 224, 258, 268, 282, 287, 303, 346–51, 705
Leverhulme, Lord (William Hesketh Lever), 93, 161, 213, 260, 308, 383, 711
Liebig, Justus von, 724
Leinesch, Prof. G. J., 564
Lillie, H. D., 635, 704, 705
Lilliendahl, G. A., 16, 19, 20, 30, 37, 41, 75, 263
Lindholm, Otto V., 130, 131

MacArthur, General, 529
Mackintosh, N. A., 449, 489, 491, 505, 565, 619, 667
Maltzahn, Baron Jasper von, 423, 428
Manby, G. W., 18
Markham, Sir Clements R., 155
Maurice, Henry G., 436, 460
Mawson, Sir Douglas, 343, 384
Melsom, Hendrik G., 132, 133, 354
Melsom, Magnus E., 354
Melville, Herman, 113
Menke, Dietrich, 424
Millais, J. G., 106
Møller, A. P., 381, 451
Mørch, Jens Andreas, 265, 344, 346, 702
Moyes, William, 197
Mueller, Baron Ferdinand von, 149
Murray, John, 152, 155

Nakabe, Kaneichi, 688
Nansen, Fridtjof, 149, 180
Nielsen, Adolph, 102
Nielsen, Christien, 88
Nobel, Alfred, 229
Nordenskjöld, Otto, 150, 155, 156
Norman, Dr. Wilhelm, 236, 237
Nygaard, Johan O., 412, 716, 717, 719

Oka, Jura, 135–8, 141, 142, 144
Okuhara, H., 592
Omura, Hideo, 530, 621, 692
Onassis, Aristotle, 533–7, 540, 552, 553, 555–61, 570, 633

Pedersen, Morton, 137
Perano, Joseph, 221, 547
Peron, Juan, 538, 540

Philip, Prince, 519
Powell, George, 196

Rasmussen, Johan, 379, 629
Rau, Hans Heinrich, 542, 543
Rechten, P., 22
Reichert, W., 537, 555
Rismüller, Dr. L., 105, 106, 114, 116, 120
Risting, Sigurd, 144, 208, 246, 247, 365, 404
Robertson, R. B., 278
Ross, Sir James Clark, 60, 147, 148, 150, 154, 177
Roys, T. W., 16, 17, 20, 30, 37, 41, 75, 263
Ruud, Johan, T., 406, 449
Ryan, Alfredo L., 538, 539, 540
Rykens, Paul, 411

Sabatier, Paul, 236
Sahlstrom, Carl A., 724
Salvesen, Christian, 80, 82, 85, 88, 91, 159
Salvesen, Capt. H. K., 187, 383, 402, 418, 419, 452, 491, 493, 530
Salvesen, Theodore Emile, 80, 90, 187, 189
Sandberg, H., 43–45
Sars, G. O., 70
Schacht, Hjalmar, 398, 412, 430, 458
Schlieper, H. H., 160
Schmalfuss, H., 724
Schmidt, Capt., 414
Scoresby, William, 18

Scott, Robert Falcon, 147, 155, 303
Sen, B. R., 619
Shackleton, E. H., 155, 303
Sommermeyer, August, 92, 132, 133, 134, 135, 256–9
Sørlle, Peter, 197, 265, 266
Stagholt, Abraham, 17
Sukhoruchenko, M. N., 609
Swinhoe, Ernest, 158, 165, 166

Taft, Pres. William, 120
Takahashi, T., 136
Tornquist, Ernesto, 160
Townsend, Charles H., 344

Vondling, 593

Wall, R. G., 586, 587, 598, 628
Walsøe, J. N., 23
Ward, R., 702
Weddel, James, 148
Welch, G., 22
Werner, H., 724
Wetlesen, Carl, 701
White, R. M., 674
Wilkins, Sir Hubert G., 297
Wilson, J. Innes, 288
Wilson, Pres. Woodrow, 120
Wiseman, Dr., 339
Wohlthat, Helmuth, 411, 412, 430, 450, 453, 458, 460, 469

Yoshida, K., 688
Young, W. Douglas, 340

VESSELS AND COMPANIES

Abraham Larsen, 431, 516, 531, 581
Admiralen, 98–9, 120–1, 159, 172, 174, 181, 188, 263, 268, 687
African Fishing & Trading Co., 193
Akers Shipyard, 269
Alaska Whaling Co., 120, 122
Aleut, 414–15, 583, 665, 667
Alexandra Whaling Co., 88
Alfa Laval, 712
Ambra, 210
American Pacific Whaling Co., 118, 122–3

American Whaling Co., 381, 445, 534
Anglo-Norse, 358, 445–6, 452, 504, 526
Anglo-Norwegian Holding Co., 374, 380
Anglo-Norwegian Whaling Co., 57
Antarctic, 60, 150, 153–6
Antarctic A/S, 376
Antarctic Whaling Investments Co., 377
Archer, Daniels, Midland Co., 652
Arctic Whaling and Fishing Co., 123
Arranmore Whaling Co., 94
Asgeirsson's Company (Icelandic Whaling Co.), 81

780   INDEX

Atlantic Whale Manufacturing Co., 104

Balaena, 428, 518, 570, 592, 598, 602,
    698, 702, 712–13, 722, 725
Baikal Maru, 659
Barrier Whaling Co., 707
Bas II, 348
Beluga Whaling Co., 123
Besstrashnij, 553
Bioproducts Inc., 649
Blacksod Whaling Co., 94–5
Bofors A/B, 273
Bouvet Whaling Co., 379
Bremen   Besigheimer   Oelfabriken
    (B.B.O.), 238, 248–9
British Columbia Packers Ltd., 649
British Marconi Co., 706
British Whaling Co., 375
Bryde and Dahls Hvalfangerselskab,
    191
Brunner, Mond and Co., 236
Bucentaur, 183
Burmeister and Wain, 270
Byron Bay Whaling Co., 547

Cabot, 102
Cabot Steam Whaling Co., 102
California Sea Products Co., 124
Canadian North Pacific Fisheries Ltd.,
    117, 123
Carolyn Frances, 123
Challenger, 148
Choshu-maru, 137
Chuishin Shipyards, 663
H. F. Cook Co., 548
Commander I, 414
Compañia Argentina da Pesca (Pesca),
    158, 162–6, 173, 189, 200, 307, 326,
    363, 393, 422, 535, 538–9
Compañia Ballenera del Norte, 652
Compañia Ballenera Espanola S.A., 321
Compañia de Pesca Norte do Brasil, 206
Consolidated Whaling Corporation, 123
Consorcio Ballenero S.A., 652
Joseph Crosfield and Sons, 235–7
Cruz del Sur, 540

Daiichi Choshu-maru, 136
Dainihon Hogei K. K., 140
Dalnij Vostok, 583, 666–7
Danish   Fisheries   Co.   (Det   Danske
    Fiskeriselskab), 21, 75

Danish   Whaling   and   Fisheries   Co.
    (Dansk Hvalfangst- og Fiskeri Aktie-
    selskab, 80, 86
Deider and Brother, 205
De Laval, 712
Den   Kongelige   Grønlanske   Handel
    (The Royal Greenland Trading Co.),
    269–70
De   Nordiske   Fabriker   (De-No-Fa),
    237–40, 248–9, 294–5, 297, 304, 387,
    392, 458
Discovery, 303, 357
Donkergat Whaling Co., 656

Eirojin Kumiai Co., 135
Electric Whaling Ltd., 704
Elektroacustic GmbH, 696
Empire Heritage, 485
Empire Victory, 431, 515, 525, 698, 713
Enderby, 598
English South Sea Co., 17
Ernesto Tornquist, 326
Erste   Deutsche   Walfgang-Gesellschaft
    mbH, 423, 428, 533
Esperanza, 327

Frank Fehr and Co., 541, 570
Fleurus, 289
Fortuna, 169
Framnæs Mekaniske Verksted, 96
Frango, 381, 445, 452, 534
Frango A/S, 381
Fraternitas, 381, 475
Fraternitas Whaling Co., 451
Fridtjof Nansen, 174–5, 182, 288
Furness Shipbuilding Co., 380, 419–20

General Electric Co., 704
Germania Whaling and Fishing Industry
    Ltd. (Germania Walfgang- und Fisch-
    industrie AG), 81–2
Gibraltar, 263
Gobernador Bories, 157, 175

Hananui II, 269
Hangar, 270
Harland and Wolff, 538
Harris Whaling and Fishing Co., 93
Harris Whaling Co., 383
A. Hartmann AG, 92, 256, 707
Hashidate Maru, 530, 721
Hawthorns of Leith, 269

Hector Whaling Ltd., 195, 374, 426, 428, 457
A/S Hektor, 268, 374, 543
Hektoria, 195–6
Herold, 264
Helsingfors Whaling Co., 130
Hogei Gumi, 136
Horatio, 190–1, 268, 282, 298
Howaldtswerke AG, 667
Hvalfangerselskapet Kosmos A/S, 376–7
Hvalfangerselskapet Hektor A/S, 195
Hvalur H/F, 646
Hydrogenators Ltd., 239–40, 245
Hydrier - Patent - Verwertungs Gesellschaft, 247

Icelandic Whaling Co., 81
International Whaling Co., 375
Richard Irvin and Sons, 92, 193
Irvin and Johnson, 187, 193, 201, 210, 213, 270, 317, 339, 364, 382, 384, 393, 409, 433
Isafold, 76

Jan Wellem, 424, 437–8, 441, 446, 451, 484–5, 515, 717, 725
Jarama, 504, 654
Jason, 150–1, 154
Jinjo Maru, 641
Jotun Fabrikker A/S, 248
Juan Peron, 535–6, 540, 544–5
Anton Judgens, 235, 237–9, 249, 294, 296, 307, 388, 431

Kaiko Maru, 659
A/S Kerguelen, 201
Kinjyo Maru, 571, 602
Kit, 122
Komet, 482
Kooperative Forbundet, 541
Kommandøren, I, 326
Kongsberg of Norway, 274
Kos 55, 622
Kosei Maru, 721
Kosmos, 276, 372, 376–8, 382, 444, 465, 480, 688, 698, 727
Kosmos II, 377–8, 382, 406, 444, 465, 485–6, 706
Kosmos III, 515, 603, 616, 712
Kosmos IV, 428, 518–19, 604, 622, 631, 722
Kosmos V, 518, 544–5

Kosmos Cos., 460, 465, 515, 559–60, 603
Kyokuyo Hogei K.K., 533, 577, 598
Kyokuyo Maru, 421
Kyokuyo Maru II, 533, 566, 577
Kyoritsu Suisan Kogyo K.K., 662
Kvaerner Brug, 707

Lancing 258, 354–5, 358, 377, 486
C. A. Larsen, 351, 354, 385, 443–4, 717, 765
Laura, 34
Lever Bros., 51, 93–4, 187, 194, 213, 248–9, 294, 300, 307, 356, 358, 387, 389
Lizzie S. Sorensson, 118
Lloyds, 105, 556

Margarine-Rohstoff Beschaftungsgesellschaft mbH, 444
Margarine Unie, 235, 387–9
Mary D. Hume, 112
Matsushima Maru, 531, 574, 577
Michail, 133–4, 263

Nagasaki Hogei Goshi K.K., 140
Naigai Suisan K.K., 140
Nebb, 705
Neko, 190
Nestlé, 725
Nederlandsche Maatschappij voor de Valvischavaart NV, 523
Newfoundland Steam Whaling Co., 106
Newfoundland Whaling Co., 102, 109, 182
New Sevilla, 325, 381, 383, 439
New Transvaal Chemical Co., 213
Nielsen-Alonso, 486
Niger Co., 308
Nikon Enyo Gyogyo K.K., 136, 138
Nikkan Hogei Goshi K.K., 140
Nippon Suisan K.K., 138, 531, 577, 661, 721
Nishon Suisan K.K., 661
Nisshin Maru, 419–20, 530–1, 571, 577, 579, 699, 721
Nisshin Maru II, 311, 420, 431, 516, 518
Nisshin Maru III, 515, 603
Nitto Hogei K.K., 660, 694
Norhval, 603, 622, 696, 698–9
North Pacific Sea Products Co., 122–3

North-West Whaling Co., 225
Norwegian Bay Whaling Co., 225–6
Norwegian-Canadian Whaling Co., 108
Norwegian Vestfold Co., 380
Norwest Whaling Co., 546
Norvegia, 359

Ocean Harvest Co., 260
Ole Wegger, 481, 486
Olga, 137–8
Olympic Challenger, 531, 533, 535, 539, 544, 549, 552–3, 556, 559–60, 577–8, 698
Orion, 114–16
Orn, 248
A/S Ornen, 247, 267, 705
Osaka Kasuga Gumi, 140

Pacific Sea Products Inc., 547
Pacific Steam Whaling Co., 114, 116–17
Pacific Tankers Inc., 534
Pacific Whale Fishing Co. 132
Peder Huse, 640
Pelagos, 482, 667
A/S Pelagos, 373, 376
Petfood Ltd., 598, 720, 722
John Pickles and Son, 262
Pinguin ("HK33"), 482
Pioner, 270, 325
Polar Whaling Co., 381, 647
Premier Whaling Co., 240, 315, 383, 655
Procter and Gamble, 237, 308–9, 389, 445, 452
Professor Gruvel, 358
Propesca Peruana, 652

Queen Charlotte Islands Whaling Co., 115, 117
Quelimane Co., 216

Johan Rasmussen and Co., 379, 451
Rau I–VIII, 428
Walter Rau Group, 533
Regina, 137
Rex, 137
Robertsen and Berntsen, 657
Ronald, 268
Rose, Down and Thompson Ltd., 717
A/S Rosshavet, 347, 381, 720
Ross Sea Co., 716
Ross Sea Whaling Co. (Hvalfangerak-

tieselskapet Rosshavet), 348
Run, 657
Run Fishing Co., 716

Saikai-Maru, 136
Saldanha Whaling Ltd., 653, 656
Salvesens (Chr. Salvesen and Co.), 77, 79–80, 108, 187–90, 217, 244, 269–70, 278–80, 314, 317, 338–40, 358–9, 361, 363–4, 378–9, 381, 383, 387, 389–93, 405, 409, 425, 433, 438–9, 441, 445–6, 460, 467, 477, 479–81, 491, 493, 497, 505–6, 515, 518, 525–6, 540, 543, 580–1, 605, 610, 628, 652, 695–6, 699, 706, 712, 719, 722; see also 'Persons' Index.
Salvestria, 363, 480
Sandefjord Whaling Co. (Sandefjords Hvalfangerselskap A/S), 174, 183, 192
Sao Nicolau, 657
Sappho, 166
Sargossa, 707
Scapa, 358
Seeadler, 423
Seki Maru, 688
Sevilla A/S, 380–1
Sierra, 657
Sierra Fishing Agency, 658
Simbra, 699
Skytteren, 374, 383, 385, 443–4, 486
Smiths Dock Co. Ltd., 92, 269–70, 272, 427, 431, 517, 539–40
Sobraon, 106, 182, 203
Sociedad Ballenera Corral S.A., 204
Sociedad Ballenera de Magallanes, 157, 175
Sociedad de Pesca Taiyo, 653
Sociedade Portuguesa de Pesca de Cetaceas Lda. da Lisboa, 322
Società Antardide (Compagnia Generale per la Grande Pesca Oceania), 542
Solglimt, 382, 481, 486
Sopecoba, 504, 526, 654
Sourabaya, 363, 438
South African Whaling Co., 209
Southern Empress, 384, 406, 465, 481, 717
Southern Harvester, 518, 606–7, 695
Southern Princess, 384
Southern Raven, 722
Southern Sealing Co., 193
Southern Sky, 358–9

Southern Star, 431
Southern Venturer, 497, 515, 518–19, 581, 605, 607
Southern Whaling and Sealing Co., 94, 193–4, 210, 213, 260, 270, 306, 391, 479
South Georgia Co., 183, 187, 244, 378
South Georgia Exploration Co., 158, 166, 173–4, 191
Souzmorzverprom Co., 414
Sovetskaya Rossiya, 583, 666
Socetskaya Soyuz, 583
Sovetskaya Ukraina, 583
Spes et Fides, 28–30, 37, 84
Star Whaling Co., 380
St. Abbs Whaling Co., 91–2
St. Ebba, 92
St. Lawrence, 116
Strombus, 481
Suderøy, 570
Südmeer, 450–1, 484
Sumatra Takoshuko K.K. (Sumatra Rubber Co.), 421
Svend Foyn, 434, 481, 486
Sydhavet, 380
Sydis, 450, 720

Tafelberg, 384, 485
Taiyo Gyogyo K.K., 141, 431, 516, 531, 551, 604
Taiyo Hogei K.K., 418, 419, 420
Teikoku Suisan K.K., 140
Telegraf, 98
Terje Viken, 426–8, 431, 712
Thomas Roys, 21
A/S Thor Dahl, 206
Thorshammer, 481, 483–4, 667
Thorshavet, 726
Tierra del Fuego Sheep Farming Co. Ltd., 159
Togo, 138
Tonan Maru, 417, 531, 577
Tonan Maru II, 420–1, 531, 721
Tonan Maru III, 421, 531
Tonsbergs Hvalfangeri, 183, 327, 357, 374, 380, 543, 722
Tornquist Group, 539
"Tosa" Cos., 140
Toyo Gyogyo, 138
Toyo Hogei K.K., 142
Treff I-VIII, 424
Trinacria, 542, 544

Tyee Junior, 117
Tyee Whaling Co., 117, 121

Ulysses, 451–2, 522, 533
Unilever Group, 235, 361, 364, 366, 369–70, 378–9, 383–4, 388–93, 394, 395, 397–8, 400–12, 419, 422, 424–34, 437, 439, 441, 443–4, 449, 456–60 465, 467, 473, 479, 494, 515–16, 522, 529, 533, 552–3, 570, 705, 710, 717, 723
Union Whaling and Fishing Co., 211
Union Whaling Co., 212–13, 315, 382, 393, 431, 515, 518, 525, 581, 655
Unitas, 398, 431, 515, 518, 533, 581, 655, 712, 717, 720, 723
Unitas Deutsche Walfgang GmbH, 431
United Africa Co., 308, 392
United States Whaling Co., 119, 121
United Whalers Ltd., 426, 428, 518, 543, 698, 704–5, 722, 725
Uniwaleco, 476

Van den Bergh Group, 235, 239, 296, 307, 388, 431
Vera Fedtrafineri A/S (Vera Fat Refinery Ltd.), 247
Vesterlide, 202
A/S Vestfold, 380
Vestfold Corporation, 380, 385, 516, 523
Victoria Whaling Co., 117, 122–3
A/S Viking, 210–11, 380, 385
Viking Corporation, 380, 385, 451
Vikingen, 450
Viking Whaling Co., 380
Vladivostok, 666–7

Walter Rau, 428–9, 515, 518, 533, 717, 725
Western Canadian Whaling Co., 649
Western Operating Corporation Ltd., 451, 522, 534
Western Whaling and Trading Co., 123
Western Whaling Corporation, 649
Westley Richards Ltd., 704
Whale Industry Co. of Iceland (Hval Industri Aktieselskabet Island), 81
Whales Products Pty Ltd., 547
White Star Line, 372–3, 383
Wikinger, 450, 515, 522, 583, 717
Willem Barendsz, 594, 598, 602, 607, 622, 698

Willem Barendsz II, 522, 544, 576–7,
  581, 593–4, 598, 722, 726
Württemburg, 424

Yanlung, 666–7
Yuri Dolgorukij, 583

GEOGRAPHICAL

(including whaling stations)

Abrolhos Is., 225
Adelaide I., 357
Admiralty Bay, 172, 356
Admiralty I., 117
Akutan I., 120, 123–4, 665
Alaska, 111–13, 117, 119–20, 123–5,
  130, 477, 649–50, 681
Albany, 224–5, 546
Aleutian Is., 119–20, 124, 126–7, 145,
  658, 665–6
Allardyce Harbour, 168, 189, 543
Alptafjördur, 76
Amsterdam, 349, 524
Amundsen Sea, 157, 359
Amur River, 130
Angola, 209, 210, 213–14, 317–18, 320,
  348, 353, 657
Annobon I., 318
Antarctic, 7, 60, 71, 120, 147–57, 276,
  303, 325
Aquaforte, 104
Arabia, 105
Arakawa, 661
Arctic, 14, 16, 71, 111, 127, 131, 150,
  667
Arran I., 94
Arranmore, 94
Azores, 136, 210, 321, 476–7, 647

Baffin Bay, 111, 324
Baff Peninsula, 168
Bahamas, 658
Balaena, 102
Balleny Is., 347, 351–2, 360, 378
Bamfield, 114
Baranof I., 117–19
Barents Sea, 16, 129
Bay of Corvocado, 202
Bay of Gibraltar, 321
Bay of Tokyo, 145
Bay of Tugar, 130
Beaverton, 108
Bellingshausen Sea, 157, 357

Benzu, 647
Bering Sea, 111, 120, 131, 144, 146,
  384, 414, 416, 658, 666–7
Bering Strait, 119, 127, 129, 326
Biscoe I., 357
Bjørnøya (Bear I.), 41, 49, 59, 60, 98–9,
  264, 523
Blacksod, 94
Bluff, 209–10, 314, 655
Bonin Is., 129, 145, 416, 477, 658–9, 665
Borge Harbour, 196
Bouvet I., 167, 182, 359, 371, 379
Bransfield Strait, 358
British Columbia, 648–9, 670
Bunaveneader, 93, 645

Cabot, 102
C. A. Larsen I., 351
California, 111–12, 123–4, 126, 419, 649
Cambridge, 682
Campbell I., 154
Cape Adare, 155
Capo Blanco, 318
Cape Finisterre, 322
Cape Hangklip, 316
Cape Horn, 112, 349
Cape Leeuwin, 223
Cap Lopez, 214, 654
Cape Province, 316, 320, 655–6
Cape Race, 104
Cape Town, 210, 212, 218, 524
Cartwright, 105
Chile, 111
Chiloë I., 202
Chukchi Peninsula (Chukotka), 128,
  131, 414–15
Coal Harbour, 649
Colla Firth, 91
Colonial Sea, 145
Commander Is., 665
Cook Strait, 221
Corcubion, 647
Coronation I, 196

Corral, 204
Costinha, 653
Coulman I., 351
Cumberland Bay, 158, 163–4, 167–8
Curaçao, 480

Dairen, 663
Danzig, 133
Davis Strait, 111, 324–5
Deception I., 106, 157, 175, 191, 195–6, 277, 288, 302, 356, 371, 427, 543
Denmark Strait, 78
Discovery Inlet, 349, 351–2
Donkergat, 316–7, 656
Dougherty, I., 167
Durban, 209–12, 314, 383, 431, 655
Dutch Harbour, 120
Dutch East Indies, 521

East China Sea, 661, 663, 671
Ellefsen Harbour, 196
Enderby Land, 359

Falkland Is., 82, 177–8, 180, 188–9, 338, 363, 452, 538, 543, 700
Faroe Is., 68, 78, 83–8, 91, 160, 212, 314, 325, 441, 542, 644–6
Fernando Poo Island, 213, 215
Finnmark, 7, 16, 23, 31, 62, 103, 136; see also Finnmark Whaling
Formosa, 135, 145; see also Taiwan
Fredriksen I., 196
French Congo, 209, 213–17, 270, 318–19, 325, 343, 348, 353–5, 504, 526, 545, 654, 657
French West Africa, 503
Fridtjof Nansen Bank, 175
Fukishima, 661

Gabon, see French Congo
Georgia Strait, 115
Getares, 321–2, 647
Gibraltar, 93, 321
Glasgow, 117, 232–3, 238
Godthul Harbour, 191–2, 287, 314
Goto Is., 661
Graham Land, 148–50, 168, 180, 190–1, 357, 555
Gray's Harbour, 118, 123–4, 270
Greenland, 23, 78, 148, 324, 353, 477, 486, 645–6, 700
Grytviken, 148, 158–9, 162–3, 165–6,

169–70, 175, 181–2, 185, 199, 224, 262, 276, 282, 286–9, 347, 388, 393, 422, 476, 481–2, 498, 519, 543, 610, 639
Gulf of Alaska, 669
Gulf of Guinea, 318–19
Gulf of St. Lawrence, 108, 110

Haiyang, 663
Hajdamak, 132
Hamburg, 50, 238
Harris, 93
Haugesund, 56, 75, 81, 212, 382
Hawke's Harbour, 108, 110, 315, 381, 477, 479, 647
Heard I., 167, 181–2
Hebrides, 68, 78, 93–4, 371, 383, 645, 711
Hellisfjordur, 80–1
Hermitage Bay, 102
Herschel I., 112
Hobart, 220
Hokkaido, 145, 660
Honshu, 128, 145, 660–1
Hudson Bay, 648
Huelva, 322
Husvik Harbour, 168, 183, 199, 289, 314, 516, 543, 696, 722
Hvalbukten (Whale Bay), 349
Hvalfjord, 646

Imbituba, 653
Indonesia, 521, 527
Inhambane River, 216
Inishkea Is., 94
Isafjördur, 76, 78, 80–1
Ivory Coast, 658

Jason Harbour, 189
Jervis Bay, 225

Kamchatka, 127, 131, 146, 326, 414–15, 477, 658–9, 665–6, 670
Kerguelen, 148, 153, 201, 482, 614
King Edward Cove, 288–9
King George I, 172
King Haakon VII's Sea, 157
Klondyke, 117
Kobe, 140
Kodiak I., 118
Korean Strait, 128
Kuril Is., 146, 415–16, 658–9, 664, 668

Kuroshio Current, 662
Kyoquot, 116, 123–4
Kyushu, 137, 142, 660–2

Labrador, 105–6, 323, 375, 381, 477, 645, 647–8
Larvik, 25, 84, 88, 192, 222, 358, 606
Laurie I., 179
Leith Harbour, 168, 187–91, 193–4, 199, 278, 280–82, 288, 314–15, 345, 378, 393, 476, 479–82, 516, 543, 610, 628, 639, 689, 726
Liberia, 657
Liverpool, 238, 481
London, 238
Lüderitz Bay, 218

Madagascar, 191, 213, 282–3, 461, 477, 503–4, 526, 545, 654
Madeira, 323, 647
Magallanes, 157
Magdalena Bay, 205, 326
Mahe, 93
Malin Head, 485
Manchuria, 467, 470, 527, 530
Marie Byrd Land, 347
Marlborough, 221
Meleyre, 80
Mjöafjördur, 78
Monterey Bay, 112, 124
Montivideo, 275, 276
Mossamedes, 320
Mosselbaai, 213
Moss Landing, 124
Mozambique, 209, 213, 215–16, 320
Murmansk, 47, 57–8, 63, 129, 485

Naden Harbour, 115, 123–4, 276
Nagasaki, 132, 661
Namibia, see South West Africa
Nanaimo, 115
Nantucket, 101, 111, 323
Narvik, 481, 485
Natal, 212, 314, 655
New Bedford, 70, 102, 111, 220
New England, 25
New Fortuna Bay, 168, 192, 287, 314
Newfoundland, 101–10, 115, 118, 136, 229, 323, 477, 645, 647–8, 675
New Island, 172, 188–9, 191
New Siberian Is., 667
Nikolayevsk, 130

Nordfjördur, 76
Northeastern Sea, 145
Northern Sea, 145
North Pole, 148–9
Northwestern Sea, 145
Notre Dame Bay, 102
Norway Fjord, 196
Norwegian Bay, 224–6
Norwegian Sea, 19, 58, 68–9, 77–8, 89, 100–1, 117–18, 161, 270, 283–4, 324–5, 393, 453, 477
Nova Scotia, 323, 480, 648, 675
Novaya Zemlya, 16

Oceanside, 655
Okhotsk Sea, 130
Okinawa, 660
Olna Firth, 88–9, 91, 280
Onundarfjördur, 78
Oshima, 661
Østerø, 84

Page's Lagoon, 115–16
Paita, 652
Palmer Archipelago, 357
Panama Canal, 117, 125, 349, 414, 419
Patagonia, 354
Persian Gulf, 540
Peter I I., 182, 357
Pisco, 652
Plettenberg, 212–13
Point Cloates, 223–5, 546–7
Polarnoje, 485
Port Hobron, 124
Porto Alexandre, 210
Portuguese East Africa, see Mozambique
Port Stanley, 172, 181, 183, 276, 289, 303
Possession I., 351
Prince Edward Is., 193
Prince Harald Land, 360
Prince Olav Harbour, 193–4, 270, 314, 543, 701, 710–11
Princess Ragnhild Land, 359
Punta Arenas, 157

Queen Charlotte Is., 119, 124, 126, 276
Queen Maud Land, 360
Quintay, 477

Red Sea, 105

Ronas Voe, 88
Rose-au-Rue, 108
Rose Harbour, 115, 123–4, 276
Ross Dependency, 346–7, 482
Ross Ice Shelf, 347–9
Ross Sea, 42, 60, 150, 153, 155, 157, 258, 330, 346–8, 350–3, 359–60, 384, 461, 505, 705
Royal Bay, 168
Ryukuyu Is., 658, 660

Sakhalin, 132, 145, 659
Salamander, 316–17
Saldanha Bay, 210, 276, 314, 317, 320, 656
Salvesen's Cove, 191
Sandefjord, 25, 34, 60, 70, 84, 88, 99, 119, 149–50, 157, 163, 171, 173, 205, 207, 245, 326, 350–1, 354, 364, 559, 621
San Francisco, 112, 114, 117, 124, 706
San Pedro, 202
Sao Tomé, 654
Sea of Japan, 130, 132, 135, 145, 660–1
Seattle, 119
Sechart, 114, 116, 123
Senzaki, 661
Setubal, 322, 507
Seven Is., (Sept Iles), 108
Seychelles, 92
Seydisfjördur, 19
Seymour I., 150
Shetland Is., 68, 78, 84, 88–92, 160, 230, 314, 371
Shikoku, 142, 145
Shumagin I., 119
Siberia, 128, 132, 145, 665, 681
Signy I., 196, 357
Sitka, 118
Sitkalidak I., 124
Somalia, 657
South Georgia, 91, 147–8, 150, 157–9, 165, 168–9, 179, 180–1, 191, 326, 338–9, 345; see also South Georgia Whaling
South Orkneys, 150, 165, 167–8, 179–81, 194–7, 265, 276, 302, 329, 346, 348, 353–7
South Pole, 147
South Sandwich Is., 165, 180, 194, 196, 198–9, 356, 358, 700
South Shetlands, 106, 148, 157, 165,

167–68, 172, 180–1, 190–1, 194, 202, 258, 269, 283, 298, 329, 338, 346, 348, 355–7, 360, 372, 461, 505, 555
South West Africa (Namibia), 82, 213, 218, 320, 422
Southwestern Sea, 145
Spanish Morocco, 323, 647
Spitsbergen, 16, 31, 41, 60, 68, 95–101, 151, 157, 160–1, 186, 209, 229, 324, 523
Spotted Is., 106
Staten I., 198
Stewart I., 349
Straits of Belle Isle, 105, 110
Straits of Magellan, 157, 175, 202
Straits of Tsushima, 129
Stromness Bay, 183, 189, 287–9
Stromness Harbour, 183–4, 192, 194, 250, 314, 380, 543, 706, 709
Strømnaes, 84
Strømo, 84, 86

Taiwan, 659
Tangalooma, 547
Tasmania, 220, 545
Te Awaiti, 221, 547
Theodore I., 191
Tierra del Fuego, 157
Tomie, 661
Tønsberg, 25, 34, 60, 70, 84, 92, 149, 154, 321, 356, 380, 417, 606
Tønsberg Fjord, 196
Tosa Sea, 140
Trinity Peninsula, 150
Tsushima Straits, 661

Unalaska I., 120
Unimak Pass, 120

Vadso, 32, 56, 61
Valdivia, 203
Valparaiso, 203
Vancouver I., 113, 115–16, 119, 126, 649
Varangar Fjord, 23, 31, 55, 61
Vestfold, 14, 25, 70, 75, 81, 188, 192, 279, 336, 728
Vestmanna Is., 78
Victoria, 113–14
Victoria Land, 150, 154–5, 347, 350–1
Vladivostok, 130–1, 134, 414

Waaigat, 316
Walvis Bay, 218, 316, 319–20, 417
Washington State, 118
Weddel Sea, 149–50, 196, 356–7, 424
West Indies, 479
West Tarbert, 94

Whangamumu, 220, 269, 547
Wilkes Land, 378

Yamaguchi, 129, 136
Yellow Sea, 663

SUBJECT INDEX

Aboriginal whaling, 111, 127–8, 646, 650–1, 665, 681
Accidents, 24, 42, 105, 286
Admiralty, 166, 180–1, 695
Adrenocorticoptrin (ACTH), 726–7
African whaling, 176, 208–19, 240, 315–21, 371, 453
Aircraft, 276, 484, 486, 655–6, 697–8
Allied Powers, 292, 294, 296, 398, 481, 484, 486, 498, 515–16, 522–3, 529, 533–4
Ambergris, 112, 223, 322
American whaling, 11, 16, 18–19, 21, 22, 25, 29, 68, 75, 111–29, 148, 220, 228, 263, 314, 371, 381–2, 384, 438, 445–6, 451, 474, 529, 676, 681
Animal feed, 52, 105
Antarctic Exploration Committee, 149, 155
Antarctic sovereignty, 154, 158–9, 165–6, 173, 178–82, 339, 347–8, 379, 452, 538, 554
Antarctic whaling, 9, 41, 91, 96, 99, 101, 106, 146, 157–8, 208, 229, 277, 292, 305, 313–14, 321, 350, 371, 386, 445, 448, 573, 612, 658–9; see also individual countries and species
Antibiotics, 694
Areas, 461, 680, 683
Argentina, 159, 166–7, 178–9, 448, 452, 490, 501, 554, 556
Argentinian whaling, 163–6, 178, 200, 205, 314, 422, 438, 517, 529, 533–4, 538–40, 578
Armaments, 295, 472, 476, 479, 483
Asdic, 251–2, 579, 694–6
Association of Economic Biologists, 342
Association of Norwegian Whaling Companies, 245–6, 282, 447, 463, 479, 557, 559, 569, 585–6, 592
Association of Whaling Companies, 364,

387, 393, 407, 427–8, 433, 446–7, 462–3
Australia, 149, 182, 222, 224, 343, 452, 490, 503–4, 509, 530, 545, 550–1
Australian whaling, 186, 208, 220–26, 240, 371, 445, 453, 542–3, 545–9, 551, 680
Austria, 542
Autolysis, 252–3, 317, 349, 693–4, 700
Avalanches, 168, 189

Bahia oil, 205
Balaenidae, see Right whales
Balaenopteridae, see Rorquals
Baleen, 6, 40, 42, 53, 93, 112–13, 130–1, 150, 218, 242
Baleen whales, 3, 5–6, 364, 386, 453, 504, 549, 575, 667
Balloons, 662
Barrels, 96, 115, 132, 233, 267
Bay whaling, 220–1
Beluga, see White whale
Biologists, 64, 70, 120, 360, 400, 462, 469, 487, 585, 589, 600, 609
Biscayan right whale, see Nordcaper
Biscayan whaling, 101
Blacklisting, 439–40, 442
Blood meal, 428–9
Blubber, 6, 7, 40, 97–8, 120, 128, 130, 134, 175, 250–62, 267, 323, 424, 429, 707, 710
Blue whale (*Balaenoptera musculus*): 3, 4, 118, 241, 453, 488, 586, 600, 612; in Africa, 219, 316–18, 320, 653; in the Antarctic, 96, 150–1, 163–4, 173, 186, 188, 190–1, 194, 197–9, 283, 298, 349–54, 358, 386, 403, 434, 457, 492–3, 506–7, 568, 575, 596, 610, 614–15; in the North Atlantic, 16, 28, 36, 45, 57–9, 63–4, 71, 76–7, 82, 84, 95, 98–100, 102, 106, 110, 322,

645, 647; in the North Pacific, 114–16, 118, 122, 126–7, 141, 415, 649–50, 660, 664–6, 670; protection, 100, 145, 488, 596, 610, 614–16, 626, 650, 660, 667–9, 671, 678, 683; in South America, 202, 327, 627

Blue Whale Unit, 4, 314, 403, 487–8, 493, 511, 607–8, 618

Boiling equipment, 250–63, 267–8, 323, 519, 523, 688

Bolsheviks, 134

Bomb lance, 18–19, 102, 111, 114

Bones, 19, 250–1, 707–8, 710

Bonuses, 14, 46–7, 137, 144, 186, 281, 282, 299, 353, 362–3, 365, 400, 404–5, 414, 435, 465, 473, 546, 728

Bottlenose whale, 14, 75, 95, 118, 126, 150

Bowhead whale (Balaena mysticetus), 28, 50, 68, 112, 114, 120, 126, 523, 650; protection, 345, 650, 665; see also Right whales

Brazil, 551, 580

Brazilian whaling, 205, 653, 680

Britain: 309, 365, 368, 370, 397–8, 419, 431, 433, 448, 459–60, 469, 490–4, 529, 531–2, 657, 702–3, 722; and the Antarctic, 166, 289, 343–4, 355, 360–2; and the I.W.C., 499, 501–3, 505, 508–9, 587, 595, 598, 671–2, 674; and Germany, 295, 345, 398, 450, 454, 468, 472–3, 482; and Norway, 175, 179–82, 294–7, 299–300, 303–5, 355, 360–2, 398–401, 408, 436–42, 450–2, 472, 478, 481–4, 486, 494, 512, 525, 530–2, 539, 598; during the wars, 210, 294–305, 460, 468, 472–5, 478–86, 515

British Antarctic Survey, 168

British-Norwegian Joint Committee, 497

British-Norwegian quota agreements, 399–407

British sovereignty in the Antarctic, 154, 158–9, 165–6, 173, 178–82, 339, 347–8, 379, 452, 538, 554

British whaling: pre-1914, 18–19, 68, 88–95, 101, 118, 129, 187–91, 210–14, 338; between the wars, 280, 314, 371, 373, 379, 393, 405, 408–9, 420, 422, 440–2, 456, 464–5, 699; during the wars, 474–6, 478–81, 484; post-1945, 487, 496–7, 512, 517–20, 522, 525,

529, 541, 567, 571, 573–5, 585, 590, 594, 606, 610, 629, 633, 638, 659, 689, 695, 699–700, 713, 717, 720, 724; see also Companies

British Whaling Association, 580

British whaling regulations, 104, 118, 140, 175, 180–1, 186, 194, 199, 211, 217, 224, 297, 300, 340, 348, 362, 365–6, 408–9, 448

Bryde's whales (Balaenoptera edeni), 3, 5, 219, 511; in Africa, 218–19, 318, 655–7; in the North Pacific, 145, 661; in the Southern Hemisphere, 218

Buoy boats, 696

Bureau of International Whaling Statistics, 400, 495, 682

Butter, 230, 240, 295, 368, 394–6

Buyer's pool, 306–9, 387, 494

Canada, 103–4, 448, 452, 469, 490, 541, 595, 599, 648, 667–8, 670–1, 675

Canadian whaling, 101–10, 123, 125, 314, 323, 647–8, 675

Canning, 428

Cannons, 6

Capelin, 63

Catcher boats: 143, 208, 240–2, 291, 337, 386, 455–7, 517, 573, 639; design, 28–9, 37–9, 76, 92, 117–18, 138, 193–5, 269–76, 332, 420, 579, 622, 688–9, 696; during the wars, 215, 305, 475, 480, 512–13, 516; limiting numbers of, 104, 141, 211, 224, 300, 434, 440, 453–4, 460–2, 495, 561, 569–71, 575–6, 661

Catcher's day work, 329, 332

Catching monopoly, 32–5, 55, 131

Catch reports, 460, 495

Charter catching, 135, 137–40, 431–2, 443–5

Chile, 157, 178, 554

Chilean whaling, 178, 202–4, 314, 422, 627, 651

Chinese whaling, 663

Christianity, 26, 34, 282–3, 286–8

"Churchyard", 183

Clearing arrangements, 411–13, 426, 442, 459–60, 463, 467

Cod fisheries, 61–2

Cold war, 533

Colonial Office, 166–7, 174, 179, 186, 188–9, 193–4, 199, 282, 300, 338–40,

343, 345, 355, 360–3, 543
Combined Food Board, 514, 517
Comité international pour la protection de la baleine, 365, 399
Committee for Whaling Statistics, 365, 400
Compensation, 67, 637
Concessionaires, 348, 361–3
Concessions, 118, 141, 158, 166, 181, 339–40, 342, 346, 348, 355, 360, 364, 372, 517, 543, 645
Conference on the Exploitation and Conservation of the Maritime Species in the South Pacific (Santiago Conference), 554, 652
Congreve's rocket, 18
Conseil International pour l'Exploration de la Mer, 399
Conservation, 9, 109, 120, 141, 319, 492, 494–5, 662
Conservationists, 638, 673
Convoys, 480
Cookers, 40, 80, 96, 163, 224, 251–2, 254–9, 267–8, 523, 707–8, 719
Copra, 527
Cottonseed oil, 10, 161, 309
Cows and calves, 142, 199–200, 220, 224, 226, 317, 365, 400
Crews: British, 88, 188, 437, 441; German, 424, 428–31, 437, 441, 451; Japanese, 417–18, 437, 441–2; Norwegian, 69, 188, 217, 383, 386, 428–31, 437, 441–4, 451, 454, 486, 523–4; others, 125, 133, 217, 224, 524; see also Norwegian crew laws
Crimean war, 130
Customs inspectors, 180–1

Danish whaling, 21, 75, 83–7, 324, 371, 438, 542
Deaths, 42, 77, 105–6, 137, 156, 170–1, 175, 189, 201, 276, 286, 288, 291, 358–9, 485–6, 699–700
Denmark, 85, 324–5, 338, 416, 448, 493, 501, 542, 726
Diesel power, 6, 92, 193, 270, 325, 419–20, 689
Direction finders, 351, 705–6
Discovery Committee, 303–4, 340, 343–4, 346, 355, 360, 362
Discovery Fund, 334
Divisions, 680, 683

Doctors, 170, 174, 205, 288
Dutch whaling: old style, 21, 68, 75, 220, 228; modern, 21, 75, 501, 512, 518–21, 523–5, 550, 565, 573

Ecuador, 202–3, 554
Electricity, 424; see also Harpoons
Employer's Association, 446
Endocrine glands, 726
Eschrichtidae, see Gray whales
Eskimos, 111, 122, 127, 130, 324, 646, 650
Evaporators, 707, 711
Expeditions: purchase of, 536, 539–40, 543, 574, 581; sale/lease of, 442–4, 450–1
Export duty, 289, 301–3, 348, 362
Extinction, risk of, 9, 59, 96, 100, 112, 120, 186, 345, 374, 399, 427, 584, 614, 650

Factory ships; 7, 34, 60, 106–7, 123, 125, 127, 133, 162, 241–2, 290, 332, 359–60, 371–3, 386, 439, 583; ban on, 345, 504, 542, 563, 671; British, 190–1, 379–80; design, 41–2, 96, 118, 258, 263–8, 270, 347, 353–4, 371, 428, 487, 688, 707, 709, 721; during the wars, 215, 297, 299, 305, 473–4, 481, 484–6, 496, 498, 512–13, 515; German, 424, 426–8, 431; Japanese, 135, 373, 417–21, 521–2; laying up of, 381, 391–2, 427, 433–4, 442, 456, 460, 462, 466, 587, 604; Norwegian, 171–5, 182, 195–6, 205, 222–3, 225, 267, 324–7, 348, 351, 376–8, 515; passive, 199–200; see also Expeditions and Vessels and Companies Index
Fat content, 710, 715, 719–20
Fats: 229–30, 295, 367–8, 396, 428, 452, 458, 490, 494, 514, 533; market and demand, 9–10, 51, 161, 227, 229–30, 296, 368, 392, 422, 424, 457, 494, 497, 501, 506, 521, 526–9, 544, 632; price, 51, 161, 230, 367–8, 392, 422, 528, 533
Fatty acids, 7, 709
Fauna Preservation Society, 636
Fauth method, 716, 720
Finance and Administration Committee (I.W.C.), 511
Finnmark whaling, 32–6, 41, 55–71, 75,

77, 85, 96, 103, 130, 157, 160, 209, 227–8, 499

Fin whales (*Balaenoptera physalus*): 3–5, 204, 241, 453, 544; Africa, 219, 316–17, 655–6; Antarctic, 148, 151, 163–5, 190, 197–8, 282, 349, 457, 492, 506–7, 575, 586, 617; North Atlantic, 16, 36, 57–8, 63–4, 78, 84, 95, 102, 106, 321–2, 325, 511, 644–5, 647–8; North Pacific, 114–16, 118, 122, 126–7, 129, 137, 144–5, 415, 649, 660–1, 663, 665–7, 670; protection, 641

Fishermen and whaling, 33, 61–7, 82, 87–90, 94, 103, 120, 304–5

Fishery Board for Scotland, 90

Flagged whales, 694, 696

Flensing, 39–40, 70, 96–8, 174, 252, 262, 349, 353, 662, 707

Floating factory/catcher, 92, 122

Food and Agriculture Organisation (F.A.O.), 499, 502, 506, 508, 528, 619, 673, 682, 715

Football, 289, 727–8

Foreign Office, 166, 296, 340, 345, 438, 454, 470

Forerunners, *see* Whale lines

France: 201, 212, 217, 230, 318, 343, 399, 448, 461, 493; and the I.W.C., 501, 503–4, 510, 551, 654

Freedom of the seas, 8, 361, 555, 585, 671

Free Trade, 490, 541

French Fisheries Congress, 319

French whaling, 101, 318–19, 503–4, 510, 654

Fuses, 24, 274

Geese, 168, 170

Geneva Convention, 1931, 364–5, 399–401, 408–9

German fat plan, 394–9

German markets, 31, 210, 368–70, 393–4, 420, 449–50

German oil reserves, 294, 458, 467–8

German whaling: pre-1918, 31–3, 81–2, 218, 338; between the wars, 22, 329, 371, 373, 380, 395–6, 398–9, 411–13; 422–33, 437–8, 440–4, 450, 454, 456, 463–4, 467, 469, 717, 725; during Second World War, 472, 475, 484–5; post-1945, 515–16, 521, 525, 530, 532–5

Germany: 135, 149, 218, 514–16, 522, 529, 532–5, 537, 558, 725; and Britain, 295, 345, 398, 450, 454, 468, 472–3, 482; and Norway, 294–7, 299, 398, 407, 410–13, 427–8, 437, 442–5, 450, 454, 467, 472–3, 478–9; between the wars, 294–9, 406, 410–13, 425–8, 437, 442–5, 448, 452–7, 460, 462–3, 465, 467–71; during the wars, 294–9, 472–5, 478–86, 514

Gluewater, 40, 52, 254–5, 258–60, 707, 709–13

Glycerine, 200, 229, 294–5

Gold rush, 117

Governors of the Falkland Islands, 158–9, 165–6, 172, 175, 178–80, 186, 282, 289, 297, 696

Gray whales (*Eschrichtius robustus*): 3, 120, 138, 698; catches, 112, 114–15, 118, 123, 126, 129, 145–6, 415, 649; protection, 113, 649–50, 665

Grax, 40, 257–9, 267, 709, 714

Greece, 534

Greenland right whale, *see* Bowhead whale

Gunners: 42, 272–3, 281, 298–9, 359, 362, 383, 535, 656, 688, 689; competition for, 91, 143–4, 242, 285, 363, 418; earnings of, 143–4, 244, 283, 285, 353, 363, 403, 414, 418, 435, 466–7, 524; Japanese, 69, 140, 143, 441, 688; Norwegian, 42, 69–70, 103, 131–3, 136, 143, 225, 283, 414, 418, 424, 429, 439, 441–2, 451, 523–5, 536; others, 42, 414, 441, 451, 536; skill of, 44, 69, 91, 157, 242, 283, 435, 524

Gunner's bridge, 272–3, 332

Harpoon guns, 16–17, 273–4, 688–9

Harpoons: development of, 18–25, 251–2; electric, 687, 700, 702–3; explosive, 6, 11, 18–25, 31, 274, 523, 579, 690–2, 705; hand, 6, 128, 221, 323, 647

Hartmann's apparatus, 92, 257–60, 332, 419, 687

Helicopters, 276, 697–8

Herring, 61, 82, 89–90, 714, 716

Holding Companies, 373–5

Holland, *see* Netherlands and Dutch whaling

Honduras, 534
Horses, 169
House of Lords, 390, 705
Humane killing, 700–5
Humpback whales (*Megaptera nova-
eangliae*): 3–6, 453; Africa, 194, 209,
211, 214–16, 219, 316–19, 344, 354,
504, 526, 549, 653–4, 657; Antarctic
(pre-1939), 148, 150–1, 157, 163–5,
173, 183–4, 186–8, 190, 192, 194,
198–9, 209, 283, 344, 457; Antarctic
(post-1939), 488, 537, 546, 549–52,
575, 615–16, 670–1; Australasia,
220–1, 451, 542, 545–52, 670–1;
North Atlantic, 16, 36, 57–8, 78, 84,
95, 102, 106, 110, 646; North Pacific,
114–16, 118, 121, 123, 125–7, 129,
138, 144–5, 415, 649–50, 660, 665–7;
protection, 186, 461, 469, 471, 478,
488, 505, 526, 545, 549, 551, 618,
626, 639, 649, 654, 667, 669, 671;
South America, 157, 203, 205, 223–4,
226
Hydrogenation, 51, 228, 231–8, 244,
247–9, 295, 304, 308, 367, 389, 541

Ice, 96, 98, 130, 151, 155–7, 187, 190,
196–8, 265, 269, 276, 349–52, 358–9,
486, 507, 698
Ice catching, 158, 197, 267, 288, 324,
351, 356–60, 372–3
Iceland, 20–1, 100, 486, 674
Icelandic whaling: pre-1939, 16, 20–2,
30, 56, 68, 75–85, 93, 161, 176, 212,
229, 314, 422; post-1939, 204, 511,
645–6, 662, 683, 685
Immature whales, 400, 453
Import duty, 309, 393, 395–6
Import of whale products from non-
I.W.C. countries, 502
Import quotas, 395–6
Incidental kills, 676
India, 527
Industrial Revolution, 7
Initial Management Stocks, 684
Inspection of whaling operations: inter-
national, 527, 531, 541, 552, 560, 601,
603, 610; International Observer
Scheme, 579–80, 619–20, 624–7,
677–8, 681; national, 104–5, 200, 365,
507, 552, 557–8, 560, 708
Insurance, 137, 482, 513, 556

Interdepartmental Committee on Research and Development in the
Dependencies of the Falkland
Islands, 301, 303, 342, 344, 355
Interdepartmental Committee on Whaling and the Protection of Whales,
345–6
International Allied Reparations
Agency, 515–16
International control, 9, 216–18, 319,
339, 345, 360–1, 367, 399–400, 440,
442, 487, 489
International Convention for the Regulation of Whaling (1946): 9, 113,
500–1, 503, 508, 510, 551, 649, 658,
660, 665; amendment, 588–9; ratification of, 535, 537, 545, 556–7, 627,
653, 659; revision, 676, 681; violation
of, 527, 554, 557, 578, 589; weakness
of, 566, 585, 608, 632–3; withdrawal
from, 608
International Decade of Cetacean
Research, 675, 681
International Emergency Food Council,
514, 527, 529
International law, 178, 348, 469, 515
International Society for the Protection
of Animals, 657–8
International Whaling Commission, 9,
447, 490, 499–503, 506–12, 526, 532,
542, 544–72, 582, 601, 651, 665,
667–72; meetings: 1949, 504, 542,
550, 654; 1950, 502, 554; 1951, 544;
1954, 100, 554; 1955, 557, 580; 1956,
586; 1957, 563, 580; 1958, 580, 586;
1959, 593, 595; 1960, 598; 1962, 563,
605, 609; 1963, 612; 1964, 621–4, 669;
1965, 626, 636; 1966, 627–31; 1968,
671; 1969, 671; 1971, 674; 1972, 658,
674, 677, 680–1; 1973, 639, 648, 674,
676, 682; 1974, 675; 1976, 675; 1977,
684; 1978, 650; 1979, 508; North
Pacific Committee, 668–9
International Whaling Statistics, 4, 57,
114, 219, 240, 247, 344, 352, 365, 460,
502, 550, 676
Ireland, 13, 438, 446, 448, 452, 469,
485
Irish whaling, 50, 78, 94–5
Italy, 397, 542

Japan: 105, 112, 135–43, 416, 421–2,

443, 522, 529, 533, 633–6; and the I.W.C., 532, 587–97, 600–2, 604–9, 611, 614–15, 618, 621–6, 628, 638, 640, 659, 666, 668–71, 673–80, 682; and whalemeat, 52, 117, 130, 134, 530, 630, 634–5, 638, 653, 657, 659, 661–2, 721–2; and international agreements, 399, 421, 448, 457, 461–2, 469–71; Russo-Japanese war, 134, 138–9, 414; Sino-Japanese war, 134–5

Japanese whaling, 134–46, 240, 398–9, 442, 473–5, 505, 518, 522, 581, 634–5, 642; Antarctic (pre-1945), 329, 371, 373, 407, 415–22, 434, 450, 454, 456–7, 463–4, 470, 479–81; (post-1945), 276, 314, 486–7, 512, 516–17, 519, 529–32, 573–5, 585, 605–6, 610–11, 614–15, 621, 626, 630, 634–5, 639–42, 678, 680, 689, 724; coastal, 137–42, 144–46, 292, 314, 371, 393, 461, 477, 516–17, 658–68; North Pacific (pelagic), 127, 145–6, 415–16, 658–9, 661–9; techniques and equipment, 6, 70, 128–9, 143, 622, 688–92, 720–2; and see Vessels and Companies Index

Japanese Whaling Association, 141–2, 144, 609

Killer whales, 226, 507
Killing techniques, 43–5, 128–9, 646, 688–70, 692, 697, 700–5
Korean war, 569
Korean whaling: 112, 137, 142, 240, 658, 660, 664; regulations, 141–2
Krill, 7, 100

Lactating whales, 400, 404, 421, 506–7
Lances, 6
Land stations, see Shore Stations
Lard, 229, 231
Lawsuits, 391–2, 409–10
League of Nations, 361, 365, 367, 399
Leases, 167, 178, 182, 185, 188–9, 191–4, 338, 362; see also Licenses
Lesser rorqual, see Minke Whale
Levies and taxes: North Atlantic, 85, 90, 104; Korea, 137; Antarctic, 167, 172, 301–2, 344, 365; Australia, 224; see also Licenses
Licensed catching, 302, 319, 346–53,

379
Licenses: 217, 636–7; Antarctic, 118, 167, 180–2, 186, 190–5, 201, 297, 300–3, 324, 338–48, 351, 360–3, 375, 379, 409, 439; North Atlantic, 90, 104–5; Africa, 209–10, 215, 318; North Pacific, 137, 142; Australasia, 222, 224–6; South America, 327, 350
Linseed oil, 10, 160–1, 232
Little piked whale, see Minke Whale
Liver, 657, 723–4
Logbooks, 344, 365, 400–1
Lookouts, 276
London Conferences and Agreements: 464, 467, 532; 1937, 422, 446, 448–57, 462, 471, 490, 492–3, 503–4, 566; 1938, 422, 454, 460–2, 477–8, 490, 504, 566; 1939, 464, 469–71; 1944, 489–90, 493, 695; 1945, 490, 493–6, 501
Lost whales, 61, 83, 214, 332, 337, 357, 507, 650, 694, 703

Magistrates, 168, 282, 289
Maize, 161, 527
Maoris, 220–1
Margarine, 161, 230, 234–6, 294, 306, 392, 406, 466, 542; and whale oil, 51, 228–9, 236, 240, 248, 294–5, 304, 367–70, 388–9, 394, 396–8, 513
Marking, 276, 698
Marshall Aid, 528, 542
Medicine, 726–7
Meiji revolution, 135
Meteorological Office, 149
Mexico, 201–3, 205, 326–7, 499, 673
Migrations: 87, 93, 118, 127, 163, 202–3, 212–14, 218, 221, 344, 357; blue, 71, 78, 84, 95, 100, 110, 126–7, 203, 316, 357–8, 656; Bryde's, 219, 656–7; fin, 78, 84, 95, 100, 127, 145, 203–4, 656; gray, 123–4, 145–6, 650; humpback, 78, 84, 110, 123–4, 126–7, 186, 203, 214, 221, 344, 546, 656–7; right, 78, 95, 203; sei, 84, 87, 110, 127, 656; sperm, 95, 127
Minimum size limits: 144, 457, 469, 505; blue whales, 365, 404, 453, 461, 478; fin whales, 365, 404, 453, 461, 544; humpbacks, 451, 453; sei whales, 505; sperm whales, 461, 478, 483, 505, 617, 626, 668–9, 681

Minke whales: 5, 640; Antarctic, 165, 511, 640–1; N. Atlantic, 640

Ministry of Food, 473, 480–1, 484, 515, 553, 570

Ministry of War and Transport, 481, 485

"Mission to the Heathen", 26–7

Moby Dick, 113

Modern Whaling, 3, 5–7, 9, 50, 96, 101, 111–12, 127–8, 131, 277

Moratorium, 638, 648, 674, 684

Motorboats, 221, 323

Natural History Museum, 218, 342, 344–6

Netherlands: 493, 515, 521, 523–5, 527, 566, 598, 657; and the oil and fat market, 230, 294–6, 309, 368–70, 397, 529, 553; and the I.W.C., 501, 503, 508–9, 550, 564–5, 587–91, 593–6, 602, 621; resignation from, 580, 592–3, 595–6, 601, 605, 609; *see also* Dutch whaling

Netting, 6, 128–9, 141, 221

New Zealand, 348, 353, 363, 448, 469, 490; and the I.W.C., 530, 551, 564–5, 587, 595, 609–10, 669, 675

New Zealand whaling, 220–1, 371, 547–8, 551

Nordcaper (*Eubalaena glacialis*), 3, 5–6, 78, 93, 95, 126; *and see* Right whales

Non I.W.C. catching, 627, 651, 657, 681

Norway: 9–13, 63–7, 155–6, 391, 425, 433–4, 512, 515, 526–7, 529–32, 539–40, 542, 558–9, 632–3; and Britain, 175, 179–82, 294–7, 299–300, 303–5, 355, 360–2, 398–401, 408–9, 436–42, 450–2, 472, 478, 481–4, 486, 494, 512, 525, 530–2, 539, 598; and Germany, 294–7, 299; 382, 398, 407, 410–13, 422, 426–8, 430, 437, 442–5, 450, 454, 459, 467–8, 472–3, 478–9, 481; and international agreements, 448–56, 462, 490–1, 494; and the I.W.C., 499, 501–3, 505, 508–9, 512, 550, 580–1, 600, 606, 618, 623–6, 628, 630, 674, 677; resignation from, 578–80, 585–6, 588–9, 592–3, 595–9, 601–2, 604–5, 608–9, 620–1; during the wars, 294–7, 299–300, 472–82

Norwegian crew laws, 408, 424, 437–8,

445, 500–1, 521–7, 532, 534–6, 538–41, 543, 550, 578

Norwegian Department of Fisheries, 491–2

Norwegian expertise, 67–70, 81, 103, 108, 111, 132, 136, 138–144, 146; *see also* Crews and Gunners

Norwegian Foreign Ministry, 296–347, 448, 454, 541

Norwegian Seamen's Unions, 284, 424, 452

Norwegian Shipping and Trade Mission (Nortraship), 480–3

Norwegian State Institute for Whale Research, 365

Norwegian State Whaling Board, 365, 447, 460

Norwegian whaling: 111, 118–19, 125, 146, 314, 342–3, 370, 392, 394, 398–9, 407, 541, 585, 588, 638, 702–3, 728–9, *see also* Finnmark whaling *and the* Vessels and Companies Index; Africa, 208–18, 319, 320, 343; Antarctic (pre-1918), 150, 158, 162, 171–8, 181, 294, 338, *see also* Concessions and Licenses; Antarctic (1918–39), 314, 329, 371–3, 391, 408, 420, 456, 471; Antarctic (post-1939), 474, 480–1, 486, 512–22, 529–30, 573–5, 610, 631–3, 638, 678, 689, 699, 720, 724; North Atlantic, 91, 95–101, 108, 162, 304, 322–6, 343, 393, 645; Pacific, 326–8, 659; Australia, 222–6; South America, 204–6

Norwegian Whale Gunners' Union, 283

Norwegian Whaling Council, 449, 451, 479, 602, 605, 608, 620

Norwegian Whaling Commission, 478, 480, 484, 486

Norwegian Whaling Gazette, 246, 557–8

Objection period, 509–10

Objections, 510

Observers to I.W.C., 499, 508, 673

Odontoceti, see Toothed Whales

Offal, 694

Of Whales and Men, 278–9

Oil: market (pre-1914), 11, 50–1, 160, 171, 200, 227, 236, 238–40, 243, 245–6; (during the wars), 236, 296;

(between the wars), 236, 306, 309, 364, 367, 388, 390, 394, 396, 404, 410, 418, 421, 425–6, 450, 457; (post-1945), 514, 527–9, 533, 553, 574, 632; price (pre-1914), 10–11, 20, 47–9, 51, 53–4, 58, 78–9, 86, 107, 115, 121–2, 142, 160, 171, 174, 177, 195, 200, 227, 229–33, 243–5, 261; (during the wars), 10–11, 122, 204, 215, 296, 298–302, 364, 470, 473; (between the wars), 10–11, 123–4, 226, 285, 306–9, 317–18, 320–2, 367, 370, 373, 384, 387–96, 404–6, 410–13, 418, 420–2, 424–7, 432, 437, 440–1, 445–7, 449, 457–9, 463, 465–9; (post-1945), 494–5, 498, 513–15, 517, 522, 527–9, 534–6, 539, 544, 552–3, 569–71, 573–4, 576, 582, 604, 630, 632, 652–3, 661, 685; quality, 38, 48, 99, 142–3, 161–2, 173, 253–4, 349, 694, 708–10, 712, 719; sperm oil, 7, 10–11, 128, 146, 228, 476–7, 661, 685–6; whale oil, 7, 10–11, 128, 143, 162, 228–37, 246, 528–9

Oil tanks, 267, 271–2
Oil dealers, 238–9, 296, 506
"Old Peoples Home", 356
Old Style Whaling, 3, 5–6, 8–9, 25, 41, 111–13, 120, 124, 128–9, 135, 144, 205, 220, 228, 263, 323, 476–7
Optimum stocks, 506, 511, 613
Oslo Meeting, 1938, 460
Ottawa Agreement, 1932, 342, 397
Overfishing: 620; Africa, 80, 140, 215, 219, 317, 654; Antarctic, 127, 140, 366, 401, 464, 492, 522, 546, 575, 584, 587; Australia, 140, 546–7; North Atlantic, 35, 48–9, 63, 77–8, 80, 103, 140, 322; North Pacific, 126–7, 140, 570–1; see also Species
Oxygen, pumping into carcass, 252

Panama and Panamanian whaling: 380, 385, 438, 448, 456, 459, 504, 516, 518, 521, 523, 580–1; and the *Olympic Challenger*, 534–5, 537–8, 554–8
Peace Conference, 1951, 531
Pelagic nations, 509, 585–608
"Pelagics", 348, 357, 361, 363
Pelagic whaling: 7, 9, 99, 217, 263, 269, 275, 324, 371; Africa, 318–19, 343,

461; Antarctic (pre-1939), 41, 68, 158, 197, 314, 318–19, 321, 337–8, 342, 346–65, 371–2, 383, 386, 415–22, 424, 453; (post-1939), 486–7, 509, 521, 544, 697–9; North Atlantic, 41, 59, 324–5, 461; North Pacific, 127, 146, 414–15, 658–9, 664–79, *see also* Countries and Vessels *and* Companies Index
Penalties, 505, 708
Penguins, 168, 170
Permanent Commission, 554
Peru and Peruvian whaling, 202–3, 319, 554–5, 627, 651–2
Plankton, 662
Pomor Trade, 65–6
Portugal and Portuguese whaling, 210–11, 213, 318, 323–4, 399, 452, 507, 647
Post Office, 288–9
Potsdam Agreement, 532
Pregnant animals, 403–4
Processing, 39–41, 92, 97, 101, 133–4, 250–63, 687, 689, 707–27; *see also* Boiling Equipment, Cookers and Separators.
Production: Africa, 208, 212–16, 240, 314, 317; Antarctic (pre-1914), 162, 165, 172–3, 176, 185, 188, 190–2, 194, 196–7, 199, 241; (during the wars), 299–300, 476, 483; (between the wars), 306–7, 309, 329–30, 333, 346, 352–3, 358, 378, 382, 385–7, 393, 402–3, 428–9, 433–4, 447, 451, 457, 463–4, 470–1; (post-1945), 488, 506, 518–20, 537, 543, 557–8, 566, 568–9, 572–3, 576, 582, 630, 634–5, 638, 643; Australasia, 221–6, 240, 547; North Atlantic, 20, 87, 89, 94–5, 98–101, 104–5, 108–9, 176, 240, 304, 321–3, 325–6, 644–5; North Pacific, 113, 116, 118–22, 124–5, 130–1, 137, 649, 660, 664, 667; *see also individual countries*
Propellors, 689
Protection stocks, 683
Prussian pursuit, 66
Puritanism, 26
Pygmy blue whale, 614

Quota Agreement, 606–10
Quotas: 402, 406–8, 433–4, 443, 445, 487, 495–7, 499, 508, 511, 541, 545,

584, 586–7, 595, 599–601, 632–3, 639, 641–3, 683–5; barrel, 402–3, 409, 433, 437–8, 490; by areas, 460, 490; by expedition 585; by sex, 680; global, 460, 490, 575, 585, 587, 609–10, 619, 622–5; lowering of, 433, 489, 491, 511, 544, 564–6, 586–7, 625–6, 642, 673–4, 685; national, 490, 496, 499; purchase/transfer of, 402, 405; "16,000", 487–91, 498, 501, 506, 514, 521, 525, 527, 532, 544, 566; special, 589; species, 490, 618, 671, 678; *see also* I.W.C. meetings

Rabbits, 169
Radar, 694–7
Radio, 121, 275–6, 694, 706
Radio buoys, 662, 695
Railways, 210
Rats, 169
Refrigeration plants, 721–2
Refrigeration ships, 325, 418, 629, 657, 721–2
Regulations, national (*and see countries*), 9, 49, 66–7, 82, 85, 90–1, 104, 115, 139, 211, 217, 322, 365, 469, 545
Reichsstelle für Milcherzeugnisse, Öle und Fette, 396
Reindeer, 168, 170
Report on New Whaling Grounds in the Southern Seas, 148–50
Restriction Committee, 401–2
Right Whales: 3, 5, 6, 9, 96; Africa, 318; Antarctic, 91, 148, 150–4, 157, 163, 165, 173, 175, 177, 202–3, 348; North Atlantic, 36, 96, 111; North Pacific, 129–31, 146, 666; protection, 345, 365, 400, 650; *see also* Bowhead *and* Nordcaper
Rorquals, 3, 6, 9–10, 12, 17–19, 28, 70, 145, 151–3, 157, 171, 228
Royal Georgraphical Society, 149, 152, 159
Royal Geographical Society of Australia, 149
Royal Navy, 354, 485
Royal Society of Victoria, 148–9
Rudders, 264–5, 271–2, 689
Rules of Procedure, 673, 679
Russia, *see* Soviet Union
Russian Whaling: 474, 575, 581, 692,

694, 724, 726; aboriginal, 128, 665, 681; North Pacific, 47, 57–8, 129–35, 146, 380, 414–15, 423, 583, 658–9, 664–9; Antarctic, 380, 573–4, 583–5, 621, 634, 678

Safety factors, 492
Sails, 29
Sanctuaries, 224–5, 360, 461, 505, 561–4
Santiago Convention, *see* Conference on the Exploitation and Conservation of the Maritime Species in the South Pacific
Sausages, 93–4
Saws, 262, 707
Schedule (I.W.C.), 500, 503, 505, 508, 512, 560, 588, 676, 680–1, 683
Schlotterhose apparatus, 717
Scientific Committee (I.W.C.), 511, 551, 562–5, 587, 598, 608, 612, 614–18, 620, 623–5, 636, 645, 651, 654
Scientific research, 70, 127, 149, 216, 301, 345, 365, 505–6, 511, 682
Scientific permits, 579, 666
Scrimshaw, 435, 727
Sea elephants, 153, 201
Seals and sealing, 14, 28, 30–1, 50, 65, 75, 96, 108, 147–51, 157, 181, 193, 207, 345, 460, 500, 508, 636, 674
Seasons, 495, North Atlantic, 61, 65, 82; North Pacific, 142, 660, 671; Africa, 211; Antarctic, 300, 639, 402, 405–6, 408–9, 433–4, 439, 443, 453, 457, 460, 487–90, 492, 496, 537, 561, 567, 596; (humpbacks), 461, 469, 471, 478, 568; (blues), 561, 568, 596; (sperms), 639
Secretariat (I.W.C.), 512, 681–2
Sei whales (*Balaenoptera borealis*): 3–5, 511; Africa, 317–18, 653, 655–7; Antarctic, 164, 172–3, 188–9, 283, 616; North Atlantic, 36, 57–8, 78, 84, 87, 95, 102, 110, 322, 646–8; North Pacific, 118, 126–7, 415, 649, 659–61, 666–7, 670–1; South America, 653
Sellers syndicates, 306–7, 364, 387, 389, 404, 406–7, 410, 412, 449, 459, 463, 570
Separators, 52, 251, 259–60, 332, 688, 694, 707, 709–10, 713
Sharks, 89, 210, 226, 724
Sheep, 168–9, 172

Shore stations: 7, 9, 258, 353, 371, 491, 503, 524, 544, 677; North Atlantic, 39–41, 66, 80–81, 97, 371, 714; North Pacific, 371, 658–61, 670–1, 694; Antarctic, 167, 182, 201, 301, 357, 361, 371, 433, 548, 627; Africa, 211, 218, 371; Australasia, 224, 548; see also Geographical including Whaling Stations Index

Sinking of vessels: 42–3, 77, 86, 118, 137, 156, 171, 175, 202, 288, 326, 358–9, 699; during the wars, 191, 205, 215, 484–6

Slipways, 197, 251, 264–6, 325, 351, 354, 359, 372, 437–8, 710

Small cetaceans, 5, 146, 477, 645, 648, 676, 681

Smell, 33, 62, 80, 161, 209

Soap: 229–30, 234–5, 248, 295, 388, 392, 423; use of whale oil in, 7, 10, 161–2, 204, 228, 240, 295–6, 304, 388, 423, 529

South Africa, 79–80, 212, 338, 448, 452, 469, 490, 674

South African whaling, 186, 193, 209–13, 219, 314, 371, 393, 474, 476–7, 543, 655–7, 680

South Georgia whaling: 142, 286–9, 355, 538; up to 1914, 119, 122, 150, 159, 177, 182–94, 300; between the wars, 266, 302, 309, 314, 343, 360, 371–2; during the wars, 282, 284, 516; post-1945, 278–9, 314, 498, 506–7, 516, 519, 543–4, 548, 635; see also "Geographical Including Whaling Stations" Index

Soviet Union: 122, 132, 134, 137, 515, 522, 570, 587–92, 634; and the I.W.C., 501, 503, 508–9, 599–604, 606, 609–11, 621, 623–8, 668–71, 673–4, 676–9, 682, 685; and Norway, 63–6, 130, 326, 588

Spain, 321–2, 375, 542

Spanish whaling, 321–3, 371, 647

Sperm oil, see Oil

Sperm whales (Physeter macrocephalus): 3–6, 129, 146, 228, 323, 548, 635, 680–1; Africa, 210–11, 219, 228, 316, 318, 655–6, 683; Antarctic, 172–3, 283, 616–17, 626, 678–80, 683, 698; Australasia, 225, 228, 548, 683; North Atlantic, 84, 95, 228, 321–3, 325, 476–7, 644–5, 667–8, 681, 683; North Pacific, 111–15, 118, 126–7, 129, 144–6, 228, 415, 649, 661, 664–5, 667–8, 681, 683; South America, 202–5, 445, 476–7, 483, 525–6, 548, 651, 653, 683; females in catches, 617, 626, 681

Sports, 289, 727–8

State run whaling, 509, 525, 574

State subsidised whaling, 509, 524–5, 566, 574, 633

Steam power, 6, 11, 28–9, 70, 92, 96, 111, 214, 262, 688–9

Sterns, 272, 689

Stock exchanges, 373–4, 379

Strainers, 712–13

Strikes, 189, 215, 281–2

Sweden, 338, 496–7, 523, 541, 709

Submarines, 265, 272, 276, 473–4, 486, 695, 702

Super-D-Canters, 709, 713

Sustainable yield, 599, 612–13, 619, 625, 670

Sustained Management Stocks, 683–4

Swimming speed, 6

Tallow, 309

Tanning, 10, 51

Technical Committee (I.W.C.), 511, 612, 630

Telephones, 275, 332, 694, 705–6

Territorial limits, 8, 319, 324, 503–4, 526, 554, 681

Textiles, 10, 51

"Three Wise Men", 600, 609, 612–13, 636

Time to processing, 365, 453, 461, 478

Toothed whales, 3

Torpedoes, 481, 485–6

Tourism, 113, 650

Trade Unions, 215, 225, 281, 284, 410, 435–40, 446, 526, 592

Transfer of matériel to non-I.W.C. countries, 502

Transporters, 386, 391, 412, 481

Try-works, 31

Tuna fishery, 676

Ultrasound, 696

Unemployment, 280, 342, 395, 423, 429, 441, 728

Unesco, 508

United Kingdom, *see* Britain

United Nations, 501–2, 508, 510, 567, 637, 673–4, 705

United States of America: 119, 452, 483, 515–16, 529–30, 556, 659, 697, 726; and international agreements, 401, 448, 469, 490; and the I.W.C., 499–503, 505, 508–9, 532, 556, 578, 580, 598, 623, 625, 668, 671, 674–6, 682; markets, 11–12, 308–9, 368, 393–4, 529

Unlawful catching, 505, 511, 536–7, 549, 551–2, 554–7, 560, 657–8

Unlicensed whaling, 319, 337, 342, 348, 351, 354–5, 362, 379

Uruguay, 535

Utilization: 54, 241, 251–2; Antarctic, 300–1, 314, 435; (pelagic), 351; (shore stations), 169, 187, 190, 195–6, 199–200; Japan, 128, 531, 578, 582; North Atlantic, 41, 51–4, 78–9, 88, 101; North Pacific, 133; regulations, 199–200, 224, 300–1, 365, 400, 404

Vegetable oils, 10, 160, 230–1, 306–8, 392, 425, 450, 467–8, 521

Vitamins, 428, 714, 723–4

Wages, 12–14, 46, 62, 125, 132, 137, 143–4, 192, 211, 244, 281, 283–5, 363, 404, 414, 429, 435–6, 446–7, 454, 465–7, 473, 524, 526, 536, 538, 566, 728

Wall Street Crash, 364, 387

Washington Conference, 1946, 490, 493, 499–500, 532, 585, 700; *see also* International Convention for the Regulation of Whaling, 1946

Wastage: 6, 120, 251; Antarctic, 54, 163, 183–5, 187, 198, 217, 299, 344, 708–13, 715, 718, 720; North Atlantic, 31, 52, 90, 99

Water, 97, 159, 197–8, 218, 224, 263, 320, 324, 707, 719

Weather, 98, 115, 172, 192, 198, 306, 326, 351, 357, 464, 507, 630, 698–9

Whale and Whaling in Japan, 128

Whalebone, *see* Baleen

Whale claw, 354, 356, 403, 687, 706, 710

Whale line, 6, 25, 37, 82, 337, 507, 690, 692–3, 704

Whalemeal, 41, 86, 90, 188, 260–1, 325, 424, 428–9, 484, 543, 598, 646, 654, 713–20

Whalemeat: 85, 112, 219, 250, 260, 304, 423, 493, 566, 598, 608, 640, 642, 645, 707, 710, 719–23; canned, 52–3, 123; extract, 723–6; frozen, 123, 418, 547, 580, 629, 721–2; and Japan, 128–9, 132, 134, 138–9, 142, 464, 477, 505, 509, 529–30, 582, 598, 605, 622, 629, 634–5, 638, 641–2, 649, 653, 657, 659, 662–3, 685, 721–3; price, 132, 138–9, 582, 605, 635, 685, 721

Whale oil — *see* Oil

Whale oil pool, 240, 245, 249

Whale Protection Committee, 66

Whale, value of, 12, 132, 137–9, 142

Whalers' life and conditions, 42–7, 169–71, 205, 215, 275, 277–91, 435, 446, 687, 727–8

Whalers' Mutual Insurance Association, 245

Whales Research Institute, 127

Whaling Employers Association, 284

Whaling fever, 57, 105, 139, 185, 222, 371

Whaling in Japan according to Norwegian Methods, 128

Whaling literature, 277–8

Whaling sickness, 286, 727

White whales, 123, 126, 646

Winch, 37, 40, 354, 693

Winter catching, 102, 115, 142, 163, 192–3, 300

Wireless, 95, 193, 275, 332, 348, 694–5, 705

World Health Organisation, 508

World Opinion, 54, 673, 675–6

World War I, 10, 86, 90, 100, 122, 197, 200, 204, 208, 210, 218, 229, 276, 292–305, 340

World War II, 146, 398, 421, 470, 472–98, 514, 655, 695, 716

Wounded whales, 109–10, 118

Year-round catching, 445–6, 451, 461, 471, 505, 526, 660; *see also* Winter Catching